EUROPEAN STATE AID LAW AND POLICY

THIRD EDITION

European State Aid Law and Policy

Third Edition

Conor Quigley QC

·H A R T·
PUBLISHING
OXFORD AND PORTLAND, OREGON
2015

Published in the United Kingdom by Hart Publishing Ltd
16C Worcester Place, Oxford, OX1 2JW
Telephone: +44 (0)1865 517530
Fax: +44 (0)1865 510710
E-mail: mail@hartpub.co.uk
Website: http://www.hartpub.co.uk

Published in North America (US and Canada) by
Hart Publishing
c/o International Specialized Book Services
920 NE 58th Avenue, Suite 300
Portland, OR 97213-3786
USA
Tel: +1 503 287 3093 or toll-free: (1) 800 944 6190
Fax: +1 503 280 8832
E-mail: orders@isbs.com
Website: http://www.isbs.com

Hart Publishing is an imprint of Bloomsbury Publishing plc.

British Library Cataloguing in Publication Data
Data Available

ISBN: 978-1-84946-627-1

Printed and bound in Great Britain by
CPI Group (UK) Ltd, Croydon CR0 4YY

For Patricia
Antonia, William, Louise

In memory of
Mark Littman Q.C.
(1920-2015)

PREFACE

European State aid law and policy has undergone radical change in recent years. The State Aid Action Plan 2005 introduced a programme of fundamental reform of the EU's substantive and procedural policy instruments for State aid control. A general block exemption dispensed with the requirement of prior notification for many categories of aid, allowing the European Commission to concentrate on assessing aid with a greater impact on competition in trade in the internal market. The financial crisis from 2007 onwards tested the limits of State aid control procedures, with huge notional amounts of aid being made available to support the banking sector. That crisis having largely passed, the Commission once again, in 2012, published a communication on State Aid Modernisation which built on the experience of the Action Plan. New guidelines apply to all the major policy areas for the period 2014-2020, additional categories of aid are covered by the revised block exemption in Regulation (EU) No 651/2014, applying to more than 90% of notified aid, and new procedural rules have been introduced to strengthen the Commission's capacity to operate effectively in its supervisory capacity.

The European Courts have also been highly active over recent years in the area of State aid law, with a series of landmark judgments, particularly concerning the interface between State aid and taxation. Most notably, the EU courts have confirmed that the notion of State aid entails the grant of an economic advantage to the recipient, to be determined by reference to the adoption of the aid measure, which is separate from the determination that the advantage is selective, in that it must favour certain undertakings in relation to other comparable undertakings in order to fall within the scope of Article 107(1) TFEU. The assessment of whether State aid may arise in market transactions by public bodies has been developed. In addition, the recent jurisprudence has sought to strengthen the application of State aid law in national court proceedings to allow for more effective protection of rights of competitors seeking to stop unlawful aid and ensure its suspension or recovery.

Although State aid remains a branch of competition law, the focus of attention has begun to swing towards taxation, in particular, international tax arrangements of multinational groups, as a source of State aid. It has long been accepted that State aid might be granted through the tax system, specifically by way of exemptions and derogations that gave preferential tax advantages to particular undertakings or sectors. In 2014, however, the Commission opened on new frontier with high profile investigations into a number of multinationals in several Member States with a view to assessing whether the system of tax rulings gave rise, in specific circumstances, to State aid. This is set to be the major issue in State aid law over the coming years.

European State aid law and policy is, on the basis of available materials, stated as at 1 September 2015.

CONOR QUIGLEY Q.C.
September 2015

CONTENTS

Part III: SUPERVISION AND ENFORCEMENT

TABLE OF CASES

COURT OF JUSTICE OF THE EUROPEAN UNION

Alphabetical Order

Table of Cases

Numerical Order

GENERAL COURT OF THE EUROPEAN UNION

Alphabetical Order

Numerical Order

TABLE OF EU LEGISLATION

Part I

STATE AID AND ARTICLE 107 TFEU

Chapter One

THE NOTION OF STATE AID IN EU LAW

1.1 CRITERIA FOR STATE AID IN EU LAW

State aid and EU law The control of State aid in EU law is established by Articles 107-108 TFEU. The European Court of Justice has referred to the vital nature of these State aid rules, being the expression of one of the essential tasks with which the EU is entrusted under Article 2 TEU, namely the establishment of an internal market and the promotion of a high degree of competitiveness.[1] Article 107(1) TFEU provides that any aid granted by the State or through State resources in any form whatsoever, which distorts or threatens to distort competition by favouring certain undertakings or the production of certain goods, is, in so far as it affects trade between Member States, incompatible with the internal market. Determining which measures fall within the notion of Article 107(1) TFEU is a matter of EU law to be established on an objective basis, in which the Commission has no discretion.[2] By contrast, the European Commission, pursuant to Article 107(3) TFEU may declare certain aid measures to be compatible with the internal market, which does allow the Commission to exercise its discretion taking account of all the circumstances and the effect of the aid measure on the internal market. Article 108 TFEU establishes a system of supervisory control by which Member States must notify the European Commission in advance of aid measures that they propose to implement, thereby allowing the Commission to determine that a given measure is compatible with the internal market or not, as well as permitting it to exercise a constant review over approved measures once they

---

[1] Case C-369/07, *Commission v Greece* [2009] ECR I-5703, paras 118-119.

[2] Case C-83/98P, *France v Ladbroke Racing Ltd. and Commission* [2000] I-3271, para 25; Case C-487/06P, *British Aggregates Association v Commission* [2008] ECR I-10515, para 111-112; Case C-89/08P, *Commission v Ireland* [2009] ECR I-11245, para 72; Cases C-71/09P, C-73/09P & C-76/09P, *Comitato Venezia vuole vivere v Commission* [2011] ECR I-4727, para 132; Case C-194/09P, *Alcoa Trasformazioni srl v Commission* [2011] ECR I-6311, para 125; Case T-67/94, *Ladbroke Racing v Commission* [1998] ECR II-1, para 52; Case T-613/97, *Ufex v Commission* [2000] ECR I-4055, para 67; Case T-198/01R, *Technische Glaswerke Ilmenau GmbH v Commission* [2002] ECR II-2153, para 76; Case T-152/99, *Hijos de Andrés Molina SA v Commission* [2002] ECR II-3049, para 159; Case T-274/01, *Valmont Nederland NV v Commission* [2004] ECR I-3145, para 37; Case T-266/02, *Deutsche Post AG v Commission* [2008] ECR II-1233, para 71; Cases T-268/08 & T-281/08, *Land Burgenland v Commission* EU:T:2012:90, para 76.

have been put into effect. The Council may also determine, in derogation from Articles 107-108 TFEU, that aid is compatible with the internal market in exceptional circumstances. Aid which is implemented without the requisite approval is deemed illegal and must, normally, be recovered.

State aid criteria in Article 107(1) TFEU There are several criteria that need to be fulfilled for Article 107(1) TFEU to apply, although the proper application of these has not been entirely consistent in the ECJ's case law. The ECJ has repeatedly classified the criteria for the application as comprising four distinct elements, all the conditions of which must be cumulatively fulfilled. First, there must be an intervention by the State or through State resources. Second, the intervention must be liable to affect trade between Member States. Third, it must confer an advantage on the recipient. Fourth, it must distort or threaten to distort competition.[3]

This definition, however, has caused considerable confusion. In particular, by omitting any reference to the notion of aid itself and inserting instead a parallel notion of advantage, without distinguishing between the quite separate concepts of economic advantage, selective advantage and competitive advantage, the EU courts have allowed the criteria for the application of Article 107(1) TFEU to be muddled. For example, both the ECJ and the General Court have frequently stated that measures which, whatever their form, are likely directly or indirectly to favour certain undertakings or are to be regarded as an economic advantage which the recipient undertaking would not have obtained under normal market conditions are regarded as aid,[4] whereas the first of these concerns selective advantage whilst the second is essentially a definition of economic advantage.

---

[3]   Case C-142/87 *Belgium* v *Commission* [1990] ECR I-959, para 25; Cases C-278/92 to C-280/92 *Spain* v *Commission* [1994] ECR I-4103, para 20; Case C-482/99 *France* v *Commission* [2002] ECR I-4397, para 68; Case C-280/00, *Altmark Trans* v *Nahver-kehrsgesellschaft Altmark GmbH* [2003] ECR I-7747, paras 74-75; Case C-206/06, *Essent Netwerk Noord BV* v *Alumimium Delfzijl* BV [2008] ECR I-5497, para 63; Case C-399/08P, *Commission* v *Deutsche Post* AG [2010] ECR I-7831, para 38; Case C-15/14P, *Commission* v *MOL* EU:C:2015:362, para 47; Case C-39/14, *BVVG GmbH* v *Erbs* EU:C:2015:470, para 24; Case T-34/02, *Le Levant 001* v *Commission* [2006] ECR II-267, para 110; Case T-196/04, *Ryanair Ltd* v *Commission* [2008] ECR II-3643, para 36; Case T-442/03, *SIC* v *Commission* [2008] ECR II-1161, para 43; Cases T-309/04, T-317/04, T-329/04 & T-336/04, *TV2/Danmark A/S* v *Commission* [2008] ECR II-2935, para 155.

[4]   Case C-140/09, *Fallimento Traghetti del Mediterraneo SpA* v *Presidenza del Consiglio dei Ministri* [2010] ECR I-5243, para 34; Case C-399/08P, *Commission* v *Deutsche Post* AG [2010] ECR I-7831, para 40; Case C-522/13, *Ministerio de Defensa* v *Concello de Ferrol* EU:C:2014:2262, para 22; Case C-690/13, *Trapeza Eurobank Ergasias* v *ATE* EU:C:2015:235, para 20; Case T-499/10, *MOL* v *Commission* EU:T:2013:592, para 52; Cases T-186/13, T-190/13 & T-193/13, *Netherlands* v *Commission* EU:T:2015:447, para 73.

The notion of competitive advantage has also been conflated with the notions of economic advantage and selective advantage. In *Belgium v Commission*, the Commission was found to have erred in law where it determined that aid arose where the financing of bovine tests in favour of Belgian undertakings conferred an advantage on those undertakings over their competitors in other Member States, since that was an issue which concerned distortion of competition, whereas whether the measure conferred a selective advantage was to be assessed by reference to the treatment of comparable undertakings within the Member State.[5] Nevertheless, whereas the General Court held, in *Netherlands v Commission*, that an economic advantage arises where a measure relieves the recipient of costs that it would otherwise have to bear[6] and, in *Tisza Erőmű kft v Commission*, that the existence of an advantage and distortion of competition are separate criteria,[7] the EU courts have repeatedly held, as regards operating aid, that relieving normal costs in principle distorts competition.[8] It has also recently stated that whether there is an advantage must be examined in the light of the anti-competitive effects caused by the measure in question,[9] and that the application of the market operator principle seeks to determine whether the advantage is, by reason of its effects, such as to distort competition or affect trade between Member States.[10] Moreover, in *OTP Bank v Hungary*, the ECJ, in its analysis of the distortion of competition and effect on trade of a State guarantee which was granted to Hungarian credit institutions to subsidise the granting of loans for housing purposes, noted that the borrowers would usually request additional services from those institutions, such as opening a current account, thereby conferring an advantage on those institutions as it increased the number of their clients and their revenue, as compared with other operators in the market.[11]

State aid entails an economic advantage to the beneficiary A proper understanding of the separate application of these notions of economic, selective and competitive advantage is crucial for a proper appreciation of the application of State aid law. This has, on occasion, been explicitly recognised by the ECJ.[12] In *Air Liquide Industries Belgium v Ville de Seraing*, the ECJ recognised the requirement of establishing the existence of a benefit for an undertaking as an additional separate criterion from that of the selectivity of

---

[5] Case T-538/11, *Belgium v Commission* EU:T:2015:188, para 125

[6] Cases T-231/06 & T-237/06, *Netherlands v Commission* [2010] ECR II-5993, para 136.

[7] Case T-468/08, *Tisza Erőmű kft v Commission* EU:T:2014:235, para 156.

[8] Case C-494/06P, *Commission v Italy* [2009] ECR I-3639, para 53; Case T-369/06, *Holland Malt BV v Commission* [2009] ECR II-3313, para 54.

[9] Case T-500/12 *Ryanair Ltd v Commission* EU:T:2015:73, para 65; Case T-473/12, *Aer Lingus Ltd v Commission* EU:T:2015:78, para 43.

[10] Case T-305/13, *SACE BT SpA v Commission* EU:T:2015:435, para 92.

[11] Case C-672/13, *OTP Bank Nyrt v Hungary* EU:C:2015:185, para 57.

[12] Case C-353/95 P, *Tiercé Ladbroke v Commission* [1997] ECR I-7007, para 26.

the measure.[13]   Similarly, in *Commission v MOL*, following a strong opinion of Advocate General Wahl, it stated that the requirement as to selectivity under Article 107(1) TFEU must be clearly distinguished from the concomitant detection of an economic advantage, so that where the Commission has identified an advantage, as arising directly or indirectly from a particular measure, it is also required to establish that that advantage specifically benefits one or more undertakings.[14] Moreover, the European Commission has recently sought to separate clearly the criteria of economic and selective advantage.[15]

An aid measure gives rise to an economic advantage for a beneficiary where, as a result of the measure in question, the beneficiary gains a financial advantage which it would not have gained but for the adoption of the measure in question. An advantage will be gained where, as a result of the aid, the beneficiary's net financial position is improved or, even if there is no actual improvement in the beneficiary's financial position, where, without the aid, that position would have deteriorated.[16] Thus, the comparison to be drawn in determining the existence of an economic advantage is by reference to the effect of the aid measure itself.[17]

State aid must involve State resources and be imputable to the State In so far as aid must be granted by the State or through State resources, the economic advantage must, on the one hand, be granted directly or indirectly through the use of State resources and, on the other, be imputable or attributable to the State.[18] While this extends to actions by all public authorities, not just central government, the mere fact that the measure at issue was taken by a public undertaking which is under the influence or control of the State is insufficient to impute the actions of the undertaking to the State, so that additional factors must be established.[19] The grant of aid must involve a burden on public financial resources, so that advantages granted by means other than through State resources do not fall within the scope of Article 107(1) TFEU.[20] Private funds may be deemed to be State resources, where they are directed by the State. In these circumstances aid need not necessarily be financed directly by

---

[13] Cases C-393/04 & C-41/05, *Air Liquide Industries Belgium v Ville de Seraing* [2006] ECR I-5293, para 28.

[14] Case C-15/14P, *Commission v MOL* EU:C:2015:362, para 59.

[15] Draft Commission Notice on the notion of State aid pursuant to Article 107(1) TFEU. See also, in the English Court of Appeal, *Professional Contractors Group v IRC* [2001] EWCA Civ 1945, para 28.

[16] Case C-143/99 *Adria-Wien Pipeline and Wietersdorfer & Peggauer Zementwerke* [2001] ECR I-8365, para 41.

[17] Case 173/73, *Italy v Commission* [1974] ECR 709, para 13.

[18] Case C-482/99, *France v Commission* [2002] ECR I-4397, para 24. Case C-262/12, *Association Vent de Colère Fédération nationale v Ministre de l'Écologie* EU:C:2013:851, para 16.

[19] Case C-482/99, *France v Commission* [2002] ECR I-4397, para 51.

[20] Cases C-399/10P & C-401/10P, *Bouygues SA v Commission* EU:C:2013:175, para 99.

the State to be classified as State aid.[21] On the other hand, advantages granted by a State which do not involve a financial burden on the State do not normally constitute State aid within the scope of Article 107(1) TFEU. In particular, legislation that merely has the effect of improving the economic situation of certain undertakings, without imposing a financial burden on the State, is not State aid.[22]

Selective advantage favouring certain undertakings For an economic advantage to be selective within the meaning of Article 107(1) TFEU, it must favour certain undertakings or the production of certain goods. Thus, the notion of selectivity entails a comparison between undertakings, some of which are favoured by the aid measure in question, whereas other comparable undertakings are not so favoured. In relation to generally applicable measures, the accepted principle is that it must be determined that the measure is such as to favour certain undertakings or the production of certain goods compared to others which, in the light of the objective pursued by the system in question, are in a comparable legal and factual situation.[23] The EU courts have, however, recently held that grants of aid to individual beneficiaries of an *ad hoc* measure may, at least in certain cases, be presumed to favour those beneficiaries selectively without there being a need to show a comparator non-beneficiary.[24] In principle, however, it might be preferable to view this as a rebuttable presumption so that, where an undertaking could show exceptionally that there are in fact no comparable undertakings, any economic advantage granted to it should not be deemed to be selective.

The notion of comparable undertakings in regard to selectivity is not the same as that of competing undertakings, which properly applies in the context of distortion of competition. For example, a reduction in corporation tax for shipbuilders will be regarded as a selective benefit as compared to all other undertakings that are subject to the full rate of corporation tax in the Member State concerned. Any benefit as compared to competing shipbuilders in other Member States is a matter concerning distortion of competition, not selectivity.

Distortion of competition and effect on trade Aid must distort or threaten to distort competition by favouring certain undertakings or the production of certain goods for it to come within the scope of Article 107(1) TFEU.

---

[21] Case 78/76, *Steinike und Weinlig v Germany* [1977] ECR 595, paras 21-22; Case 290/83, *Commission v France* [1985] ECR 439, para 14.

[22] Case C-379/98, *Preussen Elektra AG v Schleswag AG* [2001] ECR I-2099, paras 59-61.

[23] Case C-143/99 *Adria-Wien Pipeline and Wietersdorfer & Peggauer Zementwerke* [2001] ECR I-8365, para 41.

[24] Case C-15/14P, *Commission v MOL* EU:C:2015:362, para 60; Case T-150/12, *Greece v Commission* EU:T:2014:191, para 104; Case T-135/12, *France v Commission* EU:T:2015:116, para 44; Case T-385/12, *Orange v Commission* EU:T:2015:117, para 53.

Although this could be interpreted as requiring the distortion of competition to derive from the selective advantage that favours certain undertakings or goods, the ECJ has instead determined that the criteria of distortion of competition and effect on trade are separate from that of selectivity. However, it has set a very low threshold for these criteria to be established, such that any effect on production costs is sufficient to give rise to a distortion of competition. This effectively equates distortion of competition with effect on competition, which is a rather less significant impact. When State aid strengthens the position of an undertaking compared with other undertakings competing in intra-EU trade, the ECJ has held that the latter must be regarded as affected by that aid.[25] Moreover, the Commission merely needs to establish that the aid in question is of such a kind as to affect trade between Member States and to distort or threaten to distort competition, rather than establishing any real effect.[26] *De minimis* aid is generally regarded as not distorting competition or affecting trade between Member States.[27]

Competitors may be established in the same Member State as the recipient of the aid or in other Member States, since the issue is not where those competitors are established but whether the aid distorts competition and has an effect on intra-EU trade.[28] Moreover, the ECJ has consistently held that where undertakings in one Member State are in competition with undertakings in other Member States, the modification of production costs borne by the former necessarily affects trade between Member States.[29] Thus, there is no need to show an actual effect on trade, but merely that the recipient carries on an activity in an economic sector in which the products concerned are subject to trade between Member States.[30]

State aid and taxation The application of the State aid rules to taxation presents specific problems. Taxation can be used to grant aid, normally by way of selective tax exemptions or derogations which lower the tax payable by certain undertakings and thereby grant them an economic advantage. Where such provisions apply to all taxpayers, such as a scheme of general capital allowances, they will not be selective. On the other hand, a deduction for R&D expenditure, whilst nominally applicable to all taxpayers, may, from a certain perspective, be regarded as a State aid to those undertakings which engage in

---

[25] Case 730/79, *Philip Morris v Commission* [1980] ECR 2671, para 11; Case C-53/00, *Ferring SA v ACOSS* [2001] ECR I-9067, para 21; Case C-310/99, *Italy v Commission* [2002] ECR I-2289, para 84; Case C-126/01, *Ministre de l'économie, des finances et de l'industrie v GEMO* [2003] ECR I-13769, para 41.

[26] Case C-301/87, *France v Commission* [1990] ECR I-307, para 33.

[27] Council Regulation (EC) No 994/98, Article 2(1).

[28] Case C-280/00, *Altmark Trans v Nahverkehrsgesellschaft Altmark GmbH* [2003] ECR I-7747, paras 77-78.

[29] Case 173/73, *Italy v Commission* [1974] ECR 709, para 18.

[30] Case C-66/02, *Italy v Commission* [2005] ECR I-10901, para 112.

R&D activities. Applying the notion of selectivity to tax measures also presents problems in relation to identifying comparable undertakings in light of the objective of the measure in question. The relevant reference framework must be ascertained, whether regional or material.[31] Where the tax in question applies to all undertakings, such as with corporation tax, any derogation will be relatively obvious. Where, however, the tax is of limited scope and has a specific purpose, identifying those undertakings that are in a comparable legal and factual situation in light of the objective of the tax provisions in question may raise difficult issues of assessment. Where differential treatment is identified, a further step is necessary to examine whether it is justified by the nature and general scheme of the tax system, in which case it will not be regarded as constituting a selective advantage.[32] Regional tax setting powers that result in a lower tax burden to undertakings established in the region as opposed to the rest of the Member State will not constitute State aid as long as the regional authority has sufficient autonomy.[33]

The ECJ held in *Spain v Commission* that the notion of a selective advantage must be determined by comparison to the general system applicable to undertakings in the same Member State and not to undertakings of other Member States.[34] Since taxation is a national phenomenon imposed within the boundaries of each Member State, distortion of competition arises by virtue of the fact that undertakings in one Member State benefit from a reduction in the levels of national taxation generally applicable within that Member State, whereas competitors in other Member States are subject to the full rate of taxation generally applicable in those other Member States. The fact that the full national rates of taxation differ from State to State is irrelevant in this context. Thus, for example, in *Italy v Commission*, a reduction in the social security charges applicable to undertakings in the textile sector in Italy gave those undertakings a selective advantage compared to other undertakings subject to Italian tax but altered their competitive position in relation to textile manufacturers in other Member States.[35]

Where national legislation allows for discretionary treatment by public authorities, State aid may arise, at least in certain circumstances, if this reduces the tax liability of individual undertakings in comparison to others.[36]

---

[31] Case C-88/03, *Portugal v Commission* [2006] ECR I-7115, para 56.

[32] Case 173/73, *Italy v Commission* [1974] ECR 709, para 15.

[33] Case C-88/03, *Portugal v Commission* [2006] ECR I-7115, para 67; Cases C-428/06 & C-434/06, *Unión General de Trabajadores de la Rioja v Juntas Generales del Territorio Histórico de Vizcaya* [2008] ECR I-6747, para 51.

[34] Case C-73/03, *Spain v Commission* EU:C:2004:711, para 28; Case T-52/12, *Greece v Commission* EU:T:2014:677, para 80; Case T-538/11, *Belgium v Commission* EU:T:2015:188, para 124.

[35] Case 173/73, *Italy v Commission* [1974] ECR 709, para 17; Case C-73/03, *Spain v Commission* EU:C:2004:711, para 28.

[36] Case C-241/94, *France v Commission* [1996] ECR I-4551, paras 23-24.

Misapplication of tax provisions by the tax authority resulting in lower tax liability, by contrast, may raise more complex issues relating to the division of competences between national tax administration and State aid enforcement. In particular, it cannot be right that the Commission can re-evaluate any mistake made in the application of national tax provisions. Mistakes should normally be corrected through the proper application of the tax administration, including review and appeal procedures, and should not be a matter within the scope of application of State aid. Where, however, the exercise of the tax authority's discretion, which results in a selective economic advantage being granted to certain undertakings, including where the discretion is exercised in contravention of the applicable rules, is not corrected through those national procedures, State aid concerns arise. Recent investigations by the Commission into aggressive tax planning by multinational groups of companies are set to test the limits of the application of the State aid rules in this regard.[37]

Market transactions and State aid The State may engage in commercial transactions, such as the acquisition or sale of goods and services, the making of capital investments in commercial companies or the grant of a guarantee to cover future liabilities. The market price is normally the highest price that a private operator acting under normal market competitive conditions is ready to pay for the goods, services or assets in question. In order to determine whether a State measure in the context of commercial relations constitutes aid for the purposes of Article 107(1) TFEU, it is necessary to establish whether the recipient receives an economic advantage which it would not have obtained under normal market conditions.[38] If the measure complies with the market economy operator test, no economic advantage will arise because the beneficiary could theoretically have derived the same benefits from the mere functioning of the market.[39]

The market price is the highest price that a private operator acting under normal market competitive conditions is ready to pay for the goods, services or assets in question, provided that offer is binding and credible. That is so regardless of the reasons, including subjective or strategic reasons, which led that potential buyer to submit that offer.[40] Even where full consideration appears to have been given by the recipient, State aid may be inherent in the transaction if the benefit granted could not have been obtained on the open market, so that, for instance, the provision of capital under normal market

---

[37] For example, Commission Decision SA.38373, *Alleged aid to Apple* (2014).

[38] Case C-39/94, *SFEI v La Poste* [1996] ECR I-3547, para 60.

[39] Case T-244/08, *Konsum Nord ekonomisk förening v Commission* [2011] ECR II-444*, para 62; Cases T-80/06 & T-182/09, *Budapesti Erőmű Zrt v Commission* EU:T:2012:65, para 67; Case T-468/08, *Tisza Erőmű kft v Commission* EU:T:2014:235, para 85; Case T-179/09, *Dunamenti Erőmű zrt v Commission* EU:T:2014:236, para 76.

[40] Cases C-214/12P, C-215/12P & C-223/12P, *Land Burgenland v Commission* EU:C:2013:682, para 99.

conditions but on a scale not normally available in the market may constitute State aid.[41] A distinction must be drawn, in determining the obligations which a private operator might take into account, between the obligations which the State must assume as owner of a company and its additional obligations as a public authority.[42]

Services of general economic interest Services of general economic interest are services provided in the public interest that are paid for or subsidised by the State. Where they are provided by a commercial operator, it must be determined whether the price paid by way of compensation might constitute State aid. The ECJ has determined that State aid does not arise as long as certain requirements are fulfilled. First, the recipient undertaking must actually have clearly defined public service obligations to discharge. Second, the parameters on the basis of which the compensation is calculated must be established in advance in an objective and transparent manner. Third, the compensation cannot exceed what is necessary to cover all or part of the costs incurred in the discharge of public service obligations. Fourth, where the service provider is not chosen pursuant to a public procurement procedure, the level of compensation needed must be determined on the basis of an analysis of the costs which a typical well run and adequately equipped undertaking would incur in providing the services.[43] Otherwise, the compensation will be regarded as State aid and may be compatible with the internal market if the requirements of Article 106(2) TFEU are satisfied.

Subsidiarity and State aid control Article 5(3) TEU provides that, under the principle of subsidiarity, in areas which do not fall within its exclusive competence, the EU shall act only if and so far as the objectives of the proposed action cannot be sufficiently achieved by the Member States, either at central, regional or local level, but can rather, by reason of the scale or effects of the proposed action, be better achieved at EU level. Article 3(1)(b) TFEU provides that the EU has exclusive competence as regards the establishing of competition rules, which include State aid rules, necessary for the functioning of the internal market.

On this basis, in *Mitteldeutsche Flughafen v Commission*, the ECJ rebutted an argument that the Commission, contrary to the principle of subsidiarity, had overstepped its competence in treating capital contributions as State aid. It was

---

[41] Case 84/82, *Germany v Commission* [1984] ECR 1451, *per* Advocate General Slynn, at p. 1501.

[42] Cases C-278-280/92, *Spain v Commission* [1994] ECR I-4103, para 22; Cases C-214/12P, C-215/12P & C-223/12P, *Land Burgenland v Commission* EU:C:2013:682, para 47.

[43] Case C-280/00, *Altmark Trans GmbH v Nahverkehrsgesellschaft Altmark GmbH* [2003] ECR I-7747, paras 89-93.

argued that a decision on transport infrastructure construction constitutes a decision on land use, adopted on the basis of provisions of national public law, and that by making the financing of extensions to infrastructure subject to State aid law, this conferred on the Commission competences which restrict the Member States' prerogatives as regards land use. The ECJ held, given that the Commission had legitimately considered the capital contributions to constitute State aid, it had carried out the review of that measure which it was entrusted to perform under Article 108 TFEU and had therefore not overstepped its competences and thus could not have infringed the principle of subsidiarity.[44] Similar reasoning was adopted by the General Court in *Germany v Commission*, concerning the review by the Commission, on grounds of manifest error of assessment, of a domestic decision classifying certain services as being of general economic interest.[45]

1.2 ECONOMIC ADVANTAGE GRANTED BY THE STATE

Aid granted by the State Pursuant to Article 107(1) TFEU, the notion of State aid applies to any aid granted by a Member State or through State resources in any form whatsoever. Although the notion of aid is not further defined in the EU Treaties,[46] it has come to be regarded, through the case law of the European Union courts, as entailing an intervention by the State or through State resources encompassing a financial burden borne by the State that results in an economic advantage for an undertaking by mitigating the charges which are normally included in its budget.[47] The notion of charges that are normally included in the budget of an undertaking include, in particular, supplementary costs that undertakings must bear as a result of obligations having a legal, regulatory or contractual origin that apply to an economic activity.[48]

State aid is most commonly granted by means of a subsidy from public funds, either by way of direct grant or through a reduction in tax liability. State

---

[44] Case C-288/11P, *Mitteldeutsche Flughafen v Commission* EU:C:2012:821, para 79.
[45] Case T-295/12, *Germany v Commission* EU:T:2014:675, para 176; Case T-309/12, *Zweckverband Tierkörperbeseitigung v Commission* EU:T:2104:676, para 219.
[46] See, C. Quigley, "The notion of a State aid in the EEC" (1988) 13 ELRev 242; J. Winter "Redefining the notion of State aid in Article 87(1) of the Treaty" (2004) CMLRev 475; A. Biondi, "State aid is falling down, falling down: an analysis of the case law on the notion of aid" [2013] CMLRev 1719.
[47] Case 82/77, *Openbaar Ministerie v Van Tiggele* [1978] ECR 25, *per* Advocate General Capotorti, at p. 52; Case C-241/94, *France v Commission* [1996] ECR I-4551, para 34; Case C-280/00, *Altmark Trans v Nahverkehrsgesellschaft Altmark* GmbH [2003] ECR I-7747, para 84; Case C-172/03, *Heiser* [2005] ECR I-1627, para 36; Case T-109/01, *Fleuren Compost BV v Commission* [2004] ECR II-127, para 53.
[48] Case T-538/11, *Belgium v Commission* EU:T:2015:188, para 76.

aid may arise in the context of commercial transactions involving a public authority, in so far as the counterparty is dealt with on terms which are more favourable than the market would normally offer. For example, a loan at a reduced rate of interest granted by a public body, which enables the recipient to avoid having to bear the full costs on the open market, entails a benefit to the recipient of the difference between the reduced rate of interest and the market rate.[49] Whereas direct financial grants self-evidently bestow a gratuitous benefit on the recipient, identifying the criteria for establishing State aid may involve more complex considerations where it arises through the tax system or in the context of commercial transactions. State aid may in this respect be defined as a departure from a benchmark set of rules, or from a normal burden, which confers an economic advantage.[50]

Where there is differential treatment of undertakings in the application of charges, the element which constitutes aid is established by determining the normal application of the system of charges in relation to the nature or general scheme of that system.[51] In order to determine whether a State measure in the context of commercial relations constitutes aid for the purposes of Article 107(1) TFEU, it is necessary to establish whether the recipient receives an economic advantage which it would not have obtained under normal market conditions.[52] In certain circumstances, the notion of normal market conditions may overlap with regulatory matters. The ECJ has held that it is to be interpreted as referring to the conditions regulating the economy when the Member State does not intervene in favour of beneficiaries. In *Greece v Commission*, Greece argued that aid to operators in the cereals sector was necessary due to the exceptional circumstances of the financial crisis in 2008-2009 that caused a serious disturbance in the national economy, so that, since the aid measures in question did not arise in the context of normal market behaviour, they should not be regarded as falling within the scope of Article 107(1) TFEU. This was rejected by the ECJ which held that the existence of exceptional circumstances is not a pertinent criterion that need be taken into account.[53] The notion of market conditions may also extend to legislative measures, such as the alteration of the legislative framework required for the liberalisation of the electricity sector.[54] In this respect, it might also extend to the normal application of tax legislation.

---

[49] Case C-301/87, *France v Commission* [1990] ECR I-307, para 41.

[50] Case C-66/02, *Italy v Commission* [2005] ECR I-10901, *per* Advocate General Stix-Hackl at para 48.

[51] Case C-390/98, *HJ Banks & Co Ltd. v Coal Authority* [2001] ECR I-6117, para 34.

[52] Case C-39/94, *SFEI v La Poste* [1996] ECR I-3547, para 60; Case C-342/96, *Spain v Commission* [1999] ECR I-2459, para 41; Case T-25/07, *Iride SpA v Commission* [2009] ECR II-245, para 46.

[53] Case C-296/14P, *Greece v Commission* EU:C:2015:72, para 34.

[54] Case T-25/07, *Iride SpA v Commission* [2009] ECR II-245, para 51.

Broad interpretation of the notion of State aid   The putting in place and
maintaining of a system of free undistorted competition, within which the
normal competitive conditions are ensured and on which, in particular, the
rules in the field of State aid are based, constitutes one of the essential
objectives of the EU Treaties.[55]   In early cases concerning the ECSC Treaty,
the ECJ declared that the internal market was based on the principle that
conditions of competition between undertakings must result from their natural
and undistorted production conditions, and that the artificial effects of State aid
contravened that principle.[56]   State aid, being a payment by someone other than
the purchaser or consumer, made it possible to fix or maintain selling prices
which were not directly related to production costs and thereby to establish,
maintain and develop economic activity which did not represent the most
rational distribution of production at the highest possible level of
productivity.[57]   In the light of these considerations, Article 107(1) TFEU was
from the outset given a broad interpretation favouring a wide range of
application of the notion of State aid covering much more than that of a
subsidy.[58]   It applies to all economic activities, regardless of whether the
activity in question has been the subject of harmonisation within EU, including
areas which remain within the exclusive competence of the Member States.[59]

Whilst a subsidy is normally a payment in cash or in kind made in support
of an undertaking, the ECJ observed in *Steenkolenmijnen v High Authority* that
the notion of aid places emphasis on its purpose and seems especially devised
for a particular objective which cannot normally be achieved without outside

---

[55]   Case C-308/04P, *SGL Carbon AG v Commission* [2006] ECR I-5977, para 31; Cases C-
75/05P & C-80/05P, *Germany v Kronofrance* [2008] ECR I-6619, para 66; Case C-
369/07, *Commission v Greece* [2009] ECR I-5703, paras 118-119; Case T-25/04,
González y Díez SA v Commission [2007] ECR II-3121, para 55.

[56]   Cases 27-29/58, *Hauts Fourneaux et Fonderies de Givors v High Authority* [1960] ECR
241, p. 254.

[57]   Case 30/59, *De Gezamenlijke Steenkolenmijnen in Limburg v High Authority* [1961]
ECR 1, p. 19.   Article 2 CS provided that one of the aims of the ECSC Treaty was
progressively to bring about conditions which would of themselves ensure the most
rational distribution of production at the highest possible level of productivity, while
safeguarding continuity of employment and taking care not to provoke fundamental and
persistent disturbances in the economies of Member States.

[58]   Case 47/69, *France v Commission* [1970] ECR 487, *per* Advocate General Roemer, at p.
499.   The notion of a subsidy derives from Article XVI of GATT; cf. Council
Regulation (EC) No 3284/94, Article 2.   The fact that a measure would not be
considered a specific subsidy within the meaning of the WTO Agreement on Subsidies
and Countervailing Measures cannot, however, reduce the scope of the definition of aid
under Article 107(1) TFEU: Case C-351/98, *Spain v Commission* [2002] ECR I-8031,
para 44; Case 409/00, *Spain v Commission* [2003] ECR I-1487, para 56.   See also, Case
T-55/99, *CETM v Commission* [2000] ECR II-3207, para 50, where the General Court
stated that the concept of subsidy in the WTO Agreement has no relevance to the
classification of a measure as State aid within Article 107(1) TFEU.

[59]   Case T-538/11, *Belgium v Commission* EU:T:2015:188, paras 65-66.

help. The notion of aid is, therefore, wider than that of a subsidy because it embraces not only positive benefits, such as subsidies themselves, but also interventions which, in various forms, mitigate the charges which are normally included in the budget of an undertaking and which, without being subsidies in the strict meaning of the word, are similar in character and have the same effect.[60] There is, moreover, no hierarchy as between subsidies in the strict sense and other benefits having the same effect. In *Salzgitter v Commission*, it was argued that the Commission should prove that the mitigation of charges which normally might be borne by an undertaking had the same effect as a subsidy in the strict sense. This was rejected by the General Court which held that once it had been proven that a State intervention measure mitigated the charges which should normally be included in the budget of an undertaking, that measure must be classified as State aid and, by virtue of that very classification, had the same effect as a subsidy, so that no additional evidence need be adduced.[61]

State aid in any form whatsoever The notion of State aid encompasses, for the purposes of Article 107(1) TFEU, aid granted in any form whatsoever. Whilst the most common form of awarding State aid is by means of financial grants, now more than 25% of all aid takes the form of exemptions from taxes or social security.[62] In addition, other measures may be less readily identifiable as aid.[63] For example, aid may be granted by the State selling goods or services to an undertaking on preferential terms;[64] through the sale at a negative value of a company that was in need of restructuring;[65] through the provision of a State guarantee on terms better than those available on the

---

[60] Case 30/59, *Steenkolenmijnen v High Authority* [1961] ECR 1, p. 19; Case C-387/92, *Banco Exterior de España SA v Ayuntamiento de Valencia* [1994] ECR I-877, para 13; Case C-200/97, *Ecotrade srl v AFS* [1998] ECR I-7907, para 34; Case C-75/97, *Belgium v Commission* [1999] ECR I-3671, para 23; Case C-256/97, *Déménagements-Manutention Transports SA* [1999] ECR I-3913, para 19; Case C-404/87, *Commission v Portugal* [2000] ECR I-4897, para 44; Case C-156/98, *Germany v Commission* [2000] ECR I-6857, para 25; Case C-390/98, *HJ Banks & Co Ltd. v Coal Authority* [2001] ECR I-6117, para 30; Case C-143/99, *Adria-Wien Pipeline GmbH v Finanzlandesdirektion für Kärnten* [2001] ECR I-8365, para 38; Case C-53/00, *Ferring SA v ACOSS* [2001] ECR I-9067, para 15; Case C-382/99, *Netherlands v Commission* [2002] ECR I-5163, para 60; Case C-5/01, *Belgium v Commission* [2002] ECR I-11991, para 32; Case C-276/02, *Spain v Commission* [2004] ECR I-8091, para 24; Cases C-128/03 & C-129/03, *AEM SpA v Autorità per l'energia elettrica e per il gas* [2005] ECR I-2861, para 38.

[61] Case T-308/00, *Salzgitter AG v Commission* [2004] ECR II-1933, para 84.

[62] State aid scoreboard, 2014.

[63] A list of possible types of aid measures first compiled by the Commission was published at OJ 1963 Spec. Ed. 235.

[64] Case 40/75, *Produits Bertrand v Commission* [1976] ECR 1, para 2; Cases 67, 68 & 70/85, *Van der Kooy v Commission* [1988] ECR 219, para 28; Cases T-268/08 & T-281/08, *Land Burgenland v Commission* EU:T:2012:90, para 47.

[65] Case T-511/09, *Niki Luftfahrt GmbH v Commission* EU:T:2015:284, para 137.

market;[66] through the provision of contractual warranties for no additional consideration;[67] through beneficial payments made on the basis of a State guarantee by a public body;[68] through reimbursement of part of the cost of goods or services;[69] by a loan at a rate of interest below normal commercial rates;[70] through the acquisition of a holding in the capital of a company on non-commercial terms;[71] by writing off a debt[72] or waiver of a debt in exchange for valueless consideration;[73] by the provision of market research and advertising activities or logistical and commercial assistance at reduced rates;[74] by payment satisfying legal or commercial obligations of a company such as outstanding wages or redundancy costs;[75] by exemption from the normal application of insolvency rules allowing companies owing debts to public bodies to continue trading;[76] by measures protecting certain industries from the effect of currency fluctuations;[77] or by an over-allocation of emission trading allowances.[78]

The notion of State resources is very broad, covering all public funds, whatever their source and whatever their destination,[79] and includes financial assistance granted by regional and local authorities[80] and by other public authorities and public bodies, including publicly owned companies.[81]   No distinction is drawn between measures which grant a temporary advantage and those which are permanent in nature,[82] so that aid may be granted through

---

[66]   Case C-275/10, *Residex Capital IV v Gemeente Rotterdam* [2011] ECR I-13043, para 30; Cases T-204/97 & T-270/97, *EPAC v Commission* [2000] ECR II-2267, para 80.
[67]   Case T-452/08, *DHL Aviation SA/NV v Commission* [2010] ECR II-218*, para 36.
[68]   Case C-672/13, *OTP Bank Nyrt v Hungary* EU:C:2015:185, para 43.
[69]   Case C-100/92, *Fonderia A. v Cassa Conguaglio per il Settore Elettrico* [1994] ECR I-561, para 13.
[70]   Cases 62 & 72/87, *Exécutif Régional Wallon v Commission* [1988] ECR 1573, para 4; Case T-16/96, *Cityflyer Express Ltd. v Commission* [1998] ECR II-757, para 53.
[71]   Case 323/82, *Intermills v Commission* [1984] ECR 3809, para 31.
[72]   Case C-246/12P, *Ellinika Nafpigeia AE v Commission* EU:C:2013:133, para 7.
[73]   Case T-217/02, *Ter Lembeek International NV v Commission* [2006] ECR II-4483, para 169.
[74]   Case 78/76, *Steinike und Weinlig v Germany* [1977] ECR 595, para 1; Case C-39/94, *SFEI v La Poste* [1996] ECR I-3547, para 62.
[75]   Case C-241/94, *France v Commission* [1996] ECR I-4551, para 37.
[76]   Case C-200/97, *Ecotrade Srl v AFS* [1998] ECR I-7907, para 45; Case C-295/97, *Piaggio v Ifitalia* [1999] ECR I-3735, para 43; Case C-480/98, *Spain v Commission* [2000] ECR I-8717, para 21.
[77]   Notice on monitoring State aid and reduction of labour costs, para 19.
[78]   Case T-374/04, *Germany v Commission* [2007] ECR II-4431, para 145.
[79]   Case 173/73, *Italy v Commission* [1974] ECR 709, *per* Advocate General Warner, at p. 727.
[80]   Case 248/84, *Germany v Commission* [1987] ECR 4013, para 17; Case C-88/03, *Portugal v Commission* [2006] ECR I-7115, para 55; Cases T-211/04 & T-215/04, *Government of Gibraltar v Commission* [2008] ECR II-3745, para 79; Cases T-267/08 & T-279/08, *Région Nord-Pas-de-Calais v Commission* [2011] ECR II-1999, para 108.
[81]   Case C-482/99, *France v Commission* [2002] ECR I-4397, para 38.
[82]   Case T-67/94, *Ladbroke Racing Ltd. v Commission* [1998] ECR II-1, para 56.

interest-free deferment of the purchase price for goods or services[83] or by extension of the period within which tax or social security contributions must be paid.[84] Indeed, it is not necessary for there to have been an actual or immediate transfer of resources from the State to the beneficiary, since aid may be deferred to a future contingency, such as through the provision of a State guarantee which might only entail an additional burden for the State budget in the event of implementation of the guarantee.[85] At the very least, such guarantees carry a sufficiently real economic risk capable of resulting in costs to the State.[86]

Grant of State aid Aid being granted entails an economic advantage being conferred on the recipient.[87] The relevant criterion for determining that State aid has been granted is the adoption of a legally binding act.[88] Generally, the Commission considers that aid is put into effect not by the action of granting the aid to the recipient but rather by the prior action of instituting or implementing the aid at a legislative level. Aid is, therefore, deemed to have been put into effect as soon as the legislative machinery enabling it to be granted without further formality has been set up.[89] In the absence of legislative measures, determining whether State aid has been granted on an *ad hoc* basis should also normally depend on whether binding measures have been adopted by the State. The General Court has stated that an aid measure may be considered granted even if it has not yet been paid out to the recipient.[90] In *Magdeburger Mühlenwerke v Fza Magdeburg*, however, which concerned an

---

[83] Case C-294/90, *British Aerospace v Commission* [1992] ECR I-493, para 4.

[84] Case C-156/98, *Germany v Commission* [2000] ECR I-6857, para 24; Case C-256/97, *Déménagements-Manutention Transports SA* [1999] ECR I-3913, para 21; Commission Decision 92/35/EEC, *Pari Mutuel Urbain*, OJ 1992 L14/35.

[85] Case C-387/92, *Banco Exterior de España SA v Ayuntamiento de Valencia* [1994] ECR I-877, para 14; Case C-6/97, *Italy v Commission* [1999] ECR I-2981, para 16; Case C-404/97, *Commission v Portugal* [2000] ECR I-4897, para 45; Case C-482/99, *France v Commission* [2002] ECR I-4397, para 36; Cases T-204/97 & T-270/97, *EPAC v Commission* [2000] ECR II-2267, para 80.

[86] Case C-242/13, *Commerz Nederland NV v Havendbedrijf Rotterdam NV* EU:C:2014:2224, para 30.

[87] Case C-353/95 P, *Tiercé Ladbroke v Commission* [1997] ECR I-7007, para 26; Case C-115/12P, *France v Commission* EU:C:2013:596, para 46; Case T-613/97, *Ufex v Commission* [2000] ECR I-4055, para 67; Case T-177/10, *Alcoa Trasformazioni srl v Commission* EU:T:2014:897, para 84.

[88] Case T-109/01, *Fleuren Compost BV v Commission* [2004] ECR II-127, para 74; Cases T-362/05 & T-363/05, *Nuova Agricast srl v Commission* [2008] II-297*, para 80; Case T-11/07, *Frucona Košice as v Commission* [2010] ECR II-5453, para 68; Case T-551/10, *Fri-El Acerra Srl v Commission* EU:T:2013:430, para 39; Case T-397/12, *Diputación Foral de Bizkaia v Commission* EU:T:2015:291, para 33.

[89] Commission letter to the Member States dated 27 April 1989, SG(89) D/5521.

[90] Case T-62/08, *ThyssenKrupp Acciai Speciali Terni SpA v Commission* [2010] ECR II-3229, para 175

application for individual aid pursuant to a German regional aid scheme, the ECJ held that aid must be considered to be granted at the time that the right to receive it is conferred on the beneficiary under the applicable national rules, taking account of all the conditions laid down by national law for obtaining the aid in question.[91] In *Frucona Košice v Commission*, where the Commission had to consider whether aid had been granted by a public authority by applying the private creditor principle in the context of a debt settlement arrangement, the General Court held that the decision of the creditor to approve the proposed arrangement meant, subject to confirmation of that arrangement by the competent court, that the creditor had definitively waived all or part of its claim.[92]

Where the measure is declared to be subject to Commission approval, no aid will be considered as having been granted prior to the approval being given. In *Austria v Commission*, the Commission was held to have erred in holding that a plan by the Austrian authorities constituted a decision to grant aid. Although the Commission argued that an unconditional and legally binding promise had been made to Siemens to grant aid prior to the Commission's approval being sought, the ECJ held that the grant of the aid had in fact been declared in advance to Siemens as being conditional upon approval from the Commission being forthcoming.[93]

Establishing the time at which State aid is granted is also relevant, in that it may be necessary to determine whether the grant of aid is made before the aid is approved by the Commission or before the period within which approved aid may be granted has expired. In *Fleuren Compost v Commission*, the Commission allowed aid for compost manufacturers in the Netherlands for the period 1990 to 1994. Although an application for aid was made in December 1994 and the Netherlands authorities immediately acknowledged receipt, they did not definitively approve the aid until September 1997. The General Court held that the aid was granted only after expiry of the period exempted by the Commission's decision.[94]

Indirect grant of State aid State aid may be granted indirectly through, or may be passed on to, a third party, so that the beneficiaries of a measure do not necessarily correspond to the persons to whom the Member State directly grants a benefit.[95] Where the advantage granted to an undertaking is

---

[91]   Case C-129/12, *Magdeburger Mühlenwerke v Finanzamt Magdeburg* EU:C:2013:200, paras 40-41; Cases T-394/08, T-408/08, T-453/08 & T-454/08, *Regione autonoma della Sardegna v Commission* [2011] ECR II-6255, para 291.

[92]   Case T-11/07, *Frucona Košice as v Commission* [2010] ECR II-5453, paras 70-72.

[93]   Case C-99/98, *Austria v Commission* [2001] ECR I-1101, para 39.

[94]   Case T-109/01, *Fleuren Compost BV v Commission* [2004] ECR II-127, para 77.

[95]   Case C-156/98, *Germany v Commission* [2000] ECR I-6857, para 26; Case C-382/99, *Netherlands v Commission* [2002] ECR I-5163, para 38; Cases T-239/04 & T-323/04, *Italy v Commission* [2007] ECR II-3265, para 123; Case T-93/02, *Confédération*

automatically passed on to a third party, the latter will be regarded as the sole recipient of the aid. Aid within Article 107(1) TFEU may be considered to have been granted to the third party, however, only if it is an undertaking carrying on an economic activity.[96] For example, in *GEMO*, under a French scheme whereby payment was made by the public authorities to private contractors to dispose of animal carcasses and slaughterhouse waste, the beneficiaries of the scheme were the farmers and slaughterhouses that were relieved of the normal financial burden of disposal.[97] A loan granted to an investor on condition that it used the funds to finance restructuring investment in Verlipack was considered as State aid granted to Verlipack.[98] In *KG Holding v Commission*, a subsidy granted to a parent company for the benefit of a wholly-owned subsidary was treated as having been granted to the latter, with the parent being regarded only as an intermediary.[99]

Where aid is granted to a person who is not carrying on any economic activity, but the benefit is passed on to an undertaking, the latter will be regarded as the recipient of aid. Thus, in *Germany v Commission*, tax relief granted to taxpayers investing in East German companies was regarded as indirect State aid for those companies.[100] Similarly, aid granted to employees through a tax exemption on their wages may be passed on to their employers by means of a corresponding reduction in their wages.[101] In *Mediaset v Commission*, aid granted to individual users of digital terrestrial technology, but not for digital satellite decoders, was regarded as indirect aid to digital terrestrial broadcasters.[102] In *Greece v Commission*, aid granted directly to agricultural cooperatives in the form of interest free loans was regarded as being indirectly granted to producers who benefited from price stability in their sales to the cooperatives.[103]

Aid granted by the Netherlands to owners of petrol stations along the German border was considered by the Commission as possibly entailing indirect aid to petrol companies in so far as they controlled resale prices

---

Nationale du Crédit Mutuelle v Commission [2005] ECR II-143, para 95; Case T-424/05, *Italy v Commission* [2009] ECR II-23*, para 108; Case T-445/05, *Associazione Italiana del Risparmio Gestito v Commission* [2009] ECR II-289, para 127; Case T-177/07, *Mediaset SpA v Commission* [2009] ECR II-2341, para 75.

[96] Case T-34/02, *Le Levant 001 v Commission* [2005] ECR II-267, para 120.

[97] Case C-126/01, *Ministre de l'économie, des finances et de l'industrie v GEMO* [2003] ECR I-13769, para 33.

[98] Case C-457/00, *Belgium v Commission* [2003] ECR I-6931, para 60.

[99] Cases T-81/07 to T-83/07, *KG Holding NV v Commission* [2009] ECR II-2411, para 76.

[100] Case C-156/98, *Germany v Commission* [2000] ECR I-6857, para 26.

[101] Case C-319/07P, *3F v Commission* [2009] ECR I-5963, para 75; Case T-30/03, *SID v Commission* [2007] II-34*, para 37.

[102] Case C-403/10P, *Mediaset SpA v Commission* [2011] ECR I-117*, para 81; Case T-177/07, *Mediaset SpA v Commission* [2010] ECR I-2341, para 75.

[103] Case T-150/12, *Greece v Commission* EU:T:2014:191, paras 70-73.

charged at some of the stations.[104] In proceedings against Germany concerning investment aid to be granted in Brandenburg towards a power station fuelled by lignite, the Commission viewed the recipient of the aid as being not the power station but rather the lignite industry in the region. The choice of a power station fuelled by lignite, despite its economic disadvantages and higher costs, would have provided support to the regional industry which would have been able to count on long-term supply contracts.[105] In *Heiser*, however, the ECJ rejected for lack of evidence a contention that aid granted to medical practitioners was systematically passed on by them to sickness insurance bodies in such a way as to cancel out any advantage.[106] Similarly, financial advantages for the promotion of tourist transport to Sicily which were awarded to tour operators and travel agents but which were effectively passed on to tourists were nevertheless considered by the Commission to fall within the scope of Article 107(1) TFEU since it was not able to rule out the existence of aid to the tourist industry as a whole in the region of Sicily.[107]

Link between economic advantage and State resources In order for a measure to be characterised as State aid, it must confer an economic advantage deriving from State resources.[108] For the purposes of establishing the existence of State aid, there must be a sufficiently direct link between, on the one hand, the advantage given to the beneficiary and, on the other, a reduction of the State budget or a sufficiently concrete economic risk of burdens on that budget.[109] In *British Telecommunications v Commission*, an exemption from a levy payable into a pension protection fund on the ground that BT's pensions liability was covered by a State guarantee in the event of insolvency was regarded as an economic advantage to BT. The link between the advantage resulting from the exemption and the use of public resources, characterised by

---

[104] Case C-382/99, *Netherlands v Commission* [2002] ECR I-5163, paras 62-66; Case T-354/99, *Kuwait Petroleum (Nederland) BV v Commission* [2006] ECR II-1475, para 62.

[105] *Twenty-Seventh Report on Competition Policy* (1997), p. 250.

[106] Case C-172/03, *Heiser v Finanzamt Innsbruck* [2005] ECR I-1627, para 47.

[107] *Twenty-Eighth Report on Competition Policy* (1998), p. 249.

[108] Cases C-393/04 & C-41/05, *Air Liquide Industries Belgium SA v Ville de Seraing* [2006] ECR I-5293, para 28; Case C-487/06P, *British Aggregates Association v Commission* [2008] ECR I-10515, paras 62-63; Case C-522/13, *Ministerio de Defensa v Concello de Ferrol* EU:C:2014:2262, para 27; Cases T-425/04, T-444/04, T-450/04 & T-456/04, *France v Commission* [2010] ECR II-2099, para 215; Case T-399/11, *Banco Santander SA v Commission* EU:T:2014:938, para 32; Case T-219/10, *Autogrill España SA v Commission* EU:T:2014:939, para 28.

[109] Cases C-399/10P & C-401/10P, *Bouygues SA v Commission* EU:C:2013:175, para 109; Case C-522/13, *Ministerio de Defensa v Concello de Ferrol* EU:C:2014:2262, para 47; Case C-518/13, *Eventech Ltd. v The Parking Adjudicator* EU:C:2015:9, para 34; Cases T-226/09 & T-230/09, *British Telecommunications plc v Commission* EU:T:2013:466, para 212.

the grant of the guarantee free of charge, was sufficiently direct.[110] BT's arguments that the exemption was justified on grounds of additional pensions liabilities affecting BT in the event of a change in owner, were rejected.[111] Similarly, French legislation relating to pension payments that improved the legal position of France Télécom in comparison to the preceding requirements resulted in an economic advantage being granted.[112] By contrast, in *Enirisorse*, a legislative provision did not constitute an economic advantage within the meaning of Article 107(1) TFEU where it merely prevented the budget of an undertaking from being burdened with a charge which, in a normal situation, would not have existed and which did not seek to reduce a charge which that company would normally have had to bear.[113]

In *Eventech v The Parking Adjudicator*, it was argued that the municipal authority policy whereby London blacks cabs could use bus lanes, whereas other minicabs could not and were subject to a fine if they infringed the prohibition, constituted an economic advantage to black cab operators. The ECJ held that it was inherent in any legal system that conduct defined as lawful does not expose individuals to penalties. Use of the bus lanes by black cabs did not involve any additional burden on the public authorities which might entail a commitment to State resources.[114] As regards the allegation that black cabs had preferential access to State-funded transport infrastructure, the ECJ noted that bus lanes were not operated commercially by the public authorities which did not, therefore, forego revenue by allowing black cabs access. Moreover, the bus lanes were not constructed for the benefit of any specific undertaking or category of undertakings, but formed part of the London road network.[115] The ECJ, accordingly, held that where the State, in order to pursue the realisation of an objective laid down in its legislation, grants a right of privileged access to public infrastructure which is not operated commercially by the public authorities to users of that infrastructure, it does not necessarily confer an economic advantage for the purposes of Article 107(1) TFEU. Furthermore, the identification of the objective pursued is, in principle, a matter within the prerogative of the competent national public authorities alone which have a degree of discretion both as regards whether it is necessary, in

---

[110] Cases T-226/09 & T-230/09, *British Telecommunications plc v Commission* EU:T:2013:466, paras 212-214.

[111] Case C-620/13P, *British Telecommnications plc v Commission* EU:C:2014:2309, paras 27-47; Cases T-226/09 & T-230/09, *British Telecommunications plc v Commission* EU:T:2013:466, paras 46-62.

[112] Case T-135/12, *France v Commission* EU:T:2015:116, para 36; Case T-385/12, *Orange v Commission* EU:T:2015:117, para 37.

[113] Case C-237/04, *Enirisorse SpA v Sotocarbo SpA* [2006] ECR I-2843, para 48; Case T-135/12, *France v Commission* EU:T:2015:116, para 35; Case T-385/12, *Orange v Commission* EU:T:2015:117, para 36.

[114] Case C-518/13, *Eventech Ltd. v The Parking Adjudicator* EU:C:2015:9, para 41.

[115] *Ibid.*, paras 42-44.

order to achieve the regulatory objective pursued, to forgo possible revenue and also as regards how the appropriate criteria for the granting of the right, which must be determined in advance in a transparent and non-discriminatory manner, are to be identified.[116]   The bus lanes policy was based on the regulatory objective of ensuring a safe and efficient transport system, which was linked to the decision to forego possible revenue as it was conceivable that if a charge was imposed on black cabs corresponding to the economic value of their right of access to the bus lanes, that might jeopardise, at least in part, the realisation of that objective, since it might deter some black cabs from using the bus lanes.[117]

Consecutive measures of State intervention In *Bouygues v Commission*, the Commission considered that a loan offer in December 2002, coupled with a statement that France would invest €9 billion in FT, had conferred an economic advantage on FT and potentially committed State resources, even though the loan was not actually implemented.[118]   The General Court held that the Commission had not demonstrated the existence of a separate advantage deriving from the loan offer, given that declarations from July 2002, in particular the announcement in December 2002, had given FT the opportunity to refinance its debts under the conditions prevailing at that time on the bond market.[119]   It took the view that, for each State intervention measure, the Commission was obliged to examine individually whether it conferred a specific advantage through State resources.[120]   On appeal, however, the ECJ determined that several consecutive measures of State intervention might be regarded as a single intervention, in particular where consecutive interventions, especially having regard to their chronology, their purpose and the circumstances of the recipient undertaking at the time, are so closely linked to each other that they are inseparable from one another.[121]   It is not necessary that the reduction in State resources, or even such a risk, should correspond or be equivalent to that advantage, or that the advantage has as its counterpoint such a reduction or such a risk, or that it is of the same nature as the commitment of State resources from which it derives.[122]   Accordingly, the Commission had been correct to consider that the offer of the loan conferred an advantage on FT and that, even if the loan had not been accepted by FT, the appearance given to the market was that FT's financial position was more

---

[116] Case C-518/13, *Eventech Ltd. v The Parking Adjudicator* EU:C:2015:9, paras 48-49.
[117] *Ibid.*, paras 50-51.
[118] Cases C-399/10P & C-401/10P, *Bouygues SA v Commission* EU:C:2013:175, para 28.
[119] Cases T-425/04, T-444/04, T-450/04 & T-456/04, *France v Commission* [2010] ECR II-2099, para 257.
[120] Cases C-399/10P & C-401/10P, *Bouygues SA v Commission* EU:C:2013:175, para 97.
[121] *Ibid.*, paras 103-104; Case C-15/14P, *Commission v MOL* EU:C:2015:362, para 97; Case T-1/12, *France v Commission* EU:T:2015:17, paras 33-34.
[122] Cases C-399/10P & C-401/10P, *Bouygues SA v Commission* EU:C:2013:175, para 110.

secure. In the circumstances, the potential additional burden on State resources resulted in an economic advantage being granted within the meaning of Article 107(1) TFEU.[123] When the case reverted to the General Court, however, it was held that, while an economic advantage had been effected through the declarations in question, no use of State resources had in fact been identified in the Commission's decision.[124] Moreover, by reason of their open, imprecise and conditional character, the declarations could not be interpreted as giving rise to a concrete and firm engagement by, or legal obligation on, France to support FT.[125] By contrast, in *France v Commission*, where several interventions in support of SNCF had been effected, consisting of loans, rescue aid and a capital increase, the General Court upheld the Commission's decision to assess them as a single intervention.[126] The differences in form between a loan and a recapitalisation did not prevent them from being treated as inseparable.[127]

No State aid in the absence of proven advantage The burden of proving an economic advantage lies on the person alleging such advantage. The Commission cannot assume that an undertaking has benefited from an advantage solely on the basis of a negative presumption, based on a lack of information enabling the contrary to be found, if there is no other evidence capable of positively establishing the actual existence of such an advantage.[128] Thus, in the *France Télécom* case, the French Minister for Economic Affairs had made an earlier statement in July 2002 that, if FT were to face financing problems, the French State would take whatever decisions were necessary to overcome them. As a result, Standard & Poors gave FT an investment grade, stating that this was maintained only as a result of the French Government's comments. The Commission stated that this certainly had an effect on the markets and conferred an economic advantage on FT. It took the view, however, that it did not have sufficient information to enable it to demonstrate that the declaration was, at least potentially, of such a character as to commit State resources.[129] Where no advantage is granted, the State aid rules will be inapplicable. Thus, Italian legislation concerning the right of a member to withdraw from a company was not considered to grant any advantage to the company.[130] The conversion by a public body of a shareholder loan into equity

---

[123] *Ibid.*, paras 129-139.

[124] Cases T-425/04 RENV & T-444/04 RENV, *France v Commission* EU:T:2015:450, paras 213-217.

[125] *Ibid.*, paras 244-245.

[126] Case T-1/12, *France v Commission* EU:T:2015:17, paras 40- 45.

[127] *Ibid.*, para 50.

[128] Case C-559/12P, *France v Commission* EU:C:2014:217, para 62; Case T-154/10, *France v Commission* EU:T:2012:452, para 119.

[129] Cases C-399/10P & C-401/10P, *Bouygues SA v Commission* EU:C:2013:175, para 27.

[130] Case C-237/04, *Enirisorse SpA v Sotocarbo SpA* [2006] ECR I-2843, paras 43-49.

in a company which was already so indebted that repayment of the loan was impossible did not confer any economic advantage on the company.[131] A Dutch scheme whereby recycling companies were paid a grant to collect and dispose of car wrecks did not constitute aid, since the companies received no gratuitous advantage but were merely granted a fair remuneration for their activities.[132] In its decision concerning *Kiener Deponie Bachmanning*, the Commission held that the owner of a contaminated site was to be held responsible for decontamination costs. Since the Austrian authorities had financed the cleaning operation, the Commission agreed that no State aid would be involved only if the costs were recovered from the owner of the site.[133] On the other hand, in the case of *Schmidt Schraubenwerke*, the Commission decision that a grant for the decontamination of an industrial site, which had suffered past environmental damage as a result of the operation of a chemical plant, was held not to confer any advantage on the present owner who was not responsible for the pollution and who had not been aware that he would have been responsible for it when he bought the site.[134]

State aid defined in relation to its effects The ECJ has consistently held that Article 107(1) TFEU does not distinguish between measures of State intervention by reference to their causes or aims but defines them in relation to their effects.[135] In *Amministrazione delle Finanze dello Stato v Denkavit Italiana*, the ECJ emphasised that Article 107(1) TFEU refers to decisions whereby Member States, in pursuit of their own economic and social objectives, grant benefits to undertakings in order to encourage the attainment

---

[131] Case T-110/97, *Kneissl Dachstein Sportartikel AG v Commission* [1999] ECR II-2881, paras 119-121; Case T-123/97, *Salomon SA v Commission* [1999] ECR II-2925, paras 63-65.

[132] *Twenty-Eighth Report on Competition Policy* (1998), p. 255. See also, *Thirty-First Report on Competition Policy* (2001), pt. 364.

[133] Commission Decision 1999/272/EC, *Kiener Deponie Bachmanning*, OJ 1999 L109/51.

[134] *Twenty-Eighth Report on Competition Policy* (1998), p. 256.

[135] Case 173/73, *Italy v Commission* [1974] ECR 709, para 13; Case C-241/94, *France v Commission* [1996] ECR I-4551, para 20; Case C-75/97, *Belgium v Commission* [1999] ECR I-3671, para 25; Case C-480/98, *Spain v Commission* [2000] ECR I-8717, para 16; Case C-382/99, *Netherlands v Commission* [2002] ECR I-5163, para 61; Case C-409/00, *Spain v Commission* [2003] ECR I-1487, para 46; Case C-159/01, *Netherlands v Commission* [2004] ECR I-4461, para 51; Case C-172/03, *Heiser v Finanzamt Innsbruck* [2005] ECR I-1627, para 46; Case C-487/06P, *British Aggregates Association v Commission* [2008] ECR I-10515, para 85; Case C-458/09P, *Italy v Commission* [2011] ECR I-179*, para 60; Case C-124/10P, *Commission v EDF* EU:C:2012:318, para 77; Cases C-399/10P & C-401/10P, *Bouygues SA v Commission* EU:C:2013:175, para 102; Case C-522/13, *Ministerio de Defensa v Concello de Ferrol* EU:C:2014:2262, para 28; Case C-39/14, *BVVG GmbH v Erbs* EU:C:2015:470, para 52; Case T-425/11, *Greece v Commission* EU:T:2014:768, para 41.

of those objectives.[136] It follows that the fact that the measure is intended to achieve a particular economic or social aim or to pursue a commercial or industrial policy is not such as to put the measures outside the scope of Article 107(1) TFEU.[137] Indeed, if the aim of a measure is one of economic, social or structural policy, it may be more likely to be classified as aid.[138] Thus, in *Italy v Commission*, a reduction in social security charges in the textile industry was held to constitute State aid regardless of the motives of the Italian Government in seeking to sustain employment in that industry.[139] Similarly, a reduction in social security contributions for undertakings which engaged in the reorganisation of working time with a view to furthering French government policy of job creation was held to constitute aid,[140] and the payment of public funds directly to employees of Cockerill Sambre, a Belgian steel producer, to cover a wage increase amounted to State aid, despite the fact that the intention was to create employment.[141] In *Netherlands v Commission*, the ECJ rejected an argument that a tax exemption for the use of minerals in crop production did not constitute State aid because the system was not intended to generate revenue for the State but was intended to encourage farmers to reduce the use of manure and the burden on the environment to acceptable levels.[142] In *Comitato Venezia vuole vivere v Commission*, the fact that advantages were designed to compensate for the additional costs linked to the particular conditions to which operators in Venice are exposed did not exclude them from classification as aid.[143]

Accordingly, measures that fulfil the criteria of State aid do not fall outside of the scope of Article 107(1) TFEU merely because they might seek to

---

[136] Case 61/79, *Amministrazione delle Finanze dello Stato v Denkavit Italiana* [1980] ECR 1205, para 31.

[137] Case 173/73, *Italy v Commission* [1974] ECR 709, para 13; Case C-241/94, *France v Commission* [1996] ECR I-4551, para 21; Case C-342/96, *Spain v Commission* [1999] ECR I-2459, para 23; Case C-75/97, *Belgium v Commission* [1999] ECR I-3671, para 25; Case C-251/97, *France v Commission* [1999] ECR I-6639, para 37; Case C-73/03, *Spain v Commission*, EU:C:2004:711, para 16; Case C-172/03, *Heiser v Finanzamt Innsbruck* [2005] ECR I-1627, para 46; Cases T-239/04 & T-323/04, *Italy v Commission* [2007] ECR II-3265, para 69; Case T-445/05, *Associazione Italiana del Risparmio Gestito v Commission* [2009] ECR II-289, para 170; Case T-52/12, *Greece v Commission* EU:T:2014:677, para 68.

[138] Case 234/84, *Belgium v Commission* [1986] ECR 2263, *per* Advocate General Lenz, at p. 2271.

[139] Case 173/73, *Italy v Commission* [1974] ECR 709, para 17.

[140] Commission Decision 97/811/EC, *French textile, clothing, leather and footwear industries*, OJ 1997 L334/25.

[141] Case C-5/01 *Belgian v Commission* [2002] ECR I-11991, para 46.

[142] Case C-159/01, *Netherlands v Commission* [2004] ECR I-4461, para 49.

[143] Cases C-71/09P, C-73/09P & C-76/09P, *Comitato Venezia vuole vivere v Commission* [2011] ECR I-4727, paras 93-100.

achieve some other social or economic objective.[144] Equally, Article 107(1) TFEU will not be excluded on the sole ground that the measure in question is intended to act as a lever for attracting investment,[145] forms part of monetary policy[146] or conjunctural policy contributing to general economic development,[147] or that it is aimed at encouraging the listing of new companies on a stock exchange,[148] or that it pursues a public health[149] or environmental[150] or national defence[151] objective. Conversely, where a measure is objectively justified on commercial grounds, the fact that it also furthers a political aim does not necessarily mean that it constitutes State aid. Thus, a commercially justified reduction in the charge set by a publicly owned company in the Netherlands for the supply of gas to nitrate fertiliser producers did not constitute State aid merely because this also reflected a political decision of the Netherlands Government to support those producers.[152]

The ECJ has also relied on the principle that State aid is defined by its effects to ensure a broad application of the notion of State aid. For example, in *Commission v Gibraltar*, it invoked this principle to ensure that measures fall within the scope of application of Article 107(1) TFEU independently of the regulatory techniques used.[153] In *Bouygues v Commission*, the ECJ relied on it to determine that several consecutive measures of State intervention might be regarded as a single intervention, in particular where, having regard to their

---

[144] Case C-487/06P, *British Aggregates Association v Commission* [2008] ECR I-10515, para 84; Cases T-127/99, T-129/99 & T-148/99, *Territorio Histórico de Álava - Diputación Foral de Álava v Commission* [2002] ECR I-1275, para 168; Cases T-269/99, T-271/99 &T-272/99, *Territorio Histórico de Guipúzcoa - Diputación Foral de Guipúzcoa v Commission* [2002] ECR I-4217, para 63; Case T-20/03, *Kahla/Thüringen Porzellan GmbH v Commission* [2008] ECR II-2305, para 197; Cases T-254/00, T-270/00 & T-277/00, *Hotel Cipriani SpA v Commission* [2008] ECR II-3269, para 195; Cases T-226/09 & T-230/09, *British Telecommunications plc v Commission* EU:T:2013:466, para 41.

[145] Cases T-227/01 etc., *Territorio Histórico de Álava – Diputación Foral de Álava v Commission* [2009] ECR II-3029, para 130; Cases T-80/06 & T-182/09, *Budapesti Erőmű Zrt v Commission* EU:T:2012:65, para 83.

[146] Case 57/86, *Greece v Commission* [1988] ECR 2855, para 9.

[147] Case 310/85, *Deufil GmbH v Commission* [1987] ECR 901, paras 7-8.

[148] Case C-458/09P, *Italy v Commission* [2011] ECR I-179*, para 60.

[149] Case C-126/01, *Ministre de l'économie, des finances et de l'industrie v GEMO SA*, [2003] ECR I-13769, *per* Advocate General Jacobs, at para 73; Case T-538/11, *Belgium v Commission* EU:T:2015:188, para 81.

[150] Case T-109/01, *Fleuren Compost BV v Commission* [2004] ECR II-127, para 54.

[151] Case C-522/13, *Ministerio de Defensa v Concello de Ferrol* EU:C:2014:2262, para 28.

[152] Case C-56/93, *Belgium v Commission* [1996] ECR I-723, para 79; Case T-422/07, *Djebel-SGPS SA v Commission* EU:T:2012:11, para 161.

[153] Cases C-106/09P & C-107/09P, *Commission v Government of Gibraltar* [2011] ECR I-11113, para 87; Cases T-226/09 & T-230/09, *British Telecommunications plc v Commission* EU:T:2013:466, para 42.

chronology, their purpose and the circumstances of the recipient undertaking, they are so closely linked to one another as to be inseparable.[154]

Illegality of the aid measure under national law irrelevant The fact that an aid measure is illegal under national law is irrelevant in categorising the measure as State aid. In *DHL Aviation v Commission*, DHL benefited from certain warranties in an agreement related to the use of Leipzig-Halle airport. Insofar as those warranties were provided free of charge, they were considered State aid. Under German law, because the measures had not been notified in advance to the Commission pursuant to Article 108(3) TFEU, they were treated as null and void. Nevertheless, the General Court held that since DHL had been able to use the airport in accordance with the terms laid down in the agreement, they had obtained an economic advantage by virtue of the operation of the agreement.[155] Similarly, in *Diputación Foral de Bizkaia v Commission*, where it was argued that the Spanish civil code rendered null and void transactions which were contrary to regulatory obligations and prohibitions, including Article 107(1) TFEU, the General Court held that the measure in question, constituting a transfer of public land at an undervalue, could not be held not to be illegal under EU law merely because national law was also violated.[156]

1.3 AID MUST BE IMPUTABLE TO THE STATE

Aid must be imputable to the State Article 107(1) TFEU applies to aid granted by the State or through State resources. This requires in all cases that an economic advantage must, on the one hand, be granted directly or indirectly through the use of State resources and, on the other, be imputable or attributable to the State.[157] Aid measures taken by a public authority, for example through the adoption of legislation, will by definition constitute aid granted by the State.[158] As regards measures taken by public undertakings and private undertakings over which the State exercises a dominant influence, any

---

[154] Cases C-399/10P & C-401/10P, *Bouygues SA v Commission* EU:C:2013:175, paras 103-104.

[155] Case T-452/08, *DHL Aviation SA/NV v Commission* [2010] ECR II-218*, para 37.

[156] Case T-397/12, *Diputación Foral de Bizkaia v Commission* EU:T:2015:291, para 36.

[157] Case C-482/99, *France v Commission* [2002] ECR I-4397, para 24. Case C-262/12, *Association Vent de Colère Fédération nationale v Ministre de l'Écologie* EU:C:2013:851, para 16; Case T-243/09, *Fedecom v Commission* EU:T:2012:497, para 46; Case T-52/12, *Greece v Commission* EU:T:2014:677, para 117; Case T-305/13, *SACE BT SpA v Commission* EU:T:2015:435, para 38; Cases T-186/13, T-190/13 & T-193/13, *Netherlands v Commission* EU:T:2015:447, para 63.

[158] Case C-262/12, *Association Vent de Colère Fédération nationale v Ministre de l'Écologie* EU:C:2013:851, para 17.

decision by the undertaking which results in aid being granted will also constitute State aid. Moreover, the State aid rules cannot be circumvented by the creation of autonomous institutions charged with allocating aid.[159] Thus, as the ECJ established in *Steinike und Weinlig v Germany*, Article 107(1) TFEU applies to all State aid without it being necessary to make a distinction whether the aid is granted directly by the State or by public or private bodies established or appointed by it to administer the aid.[160] Nevertheless, for such advantages to be capable of being categorised as aid within the meaning of Article 107(1) TFEU, as well as being granted directly or indirectly through State resources, they must be imputable to the State.[161] Conversely, where a public authority, in relation to an economic activity, acts together with an undertaking over which it exercises control, it is necessary to consider the commercial transaction as a whole in order to determine whether they have acted as a single entity, in which case the market operator test may apply to their actions.[162]

Public undertakings controlled by the State   All benefits granted by a public undertaking do not necessarily amount to State aid.[163] In this respect, the imputability of a measure to the State cannot be inferred from the mere fact that the measure at issue was taken by a public undertaking,[164] so that aid should not be presumed solely because the undertaking is under the influence or control of the State, since even a public undertaking may act with more or less independence, according to the degree of autonomy left to it by the

---

[159] Case C-482/99, *France v Commission* [2002] ECR I-4397, para 23.

[160] Case 78/76, *Steinike und Weinlig v Germany* [1977] ECR 595, para 21; Case 290/83, *Commission v France* [1985] ECR 439, para 14; Case 57/86, *Greece v Commission* [1988] ECR 2855, para 12; Case C-303/88, *Italy v Commission* [1991] ECR I-1433, para 11; Case C-379/98, *Preussen Elektra AG v Schleswag AG* [2001] ECR I-2099, para 58; Case C-126/01, *Ministre de l'économie, des finances et de l'industrie v GEMO* [2003] ECR I-13769, para 23; Case C-345/02, *Pearle BV v Hoofdbedrijfschap Ambachten* [2004] ECR I-7139, para 34; Case T-136/05, *Salvat père & fils v Commission* [2007] ECR II-4063, para 139.

[161] Case C-482/99, *France v Commission* [2002] ECR I-4397, para 24; Case C-126/01, *Ministre de l'économie, des finances et de l'industrie v GEMO* [2003] ECR I-13769, para 24; Case C-345/02, *Pearle BV v Hoofdbedrijfschap Ambachten* [2004] ECR I-7139, para 35; Case T-351/02, *Deutsche Bahn AG v Commission* [2006] ECR II-1047, para 101; Case T-442/03, *SIC v Commission* [2008] ECR II-1161, para 93; Cases T-309/04, T-317/04, T-329/04 & T-336/04, *TV2/Danmark A/S v Commission* [2008] ECR II-2935, para 157.

[162] Case T-196/04, *Ryanair Ltd v Commission* [2008] ECR II-3643, para 59.

[163] Case T-141/03, *Sniace SA v Commission* [2005] ECR II-1197, para 34.

[164] Case C-482/99, *France v Commission* [2002] ECR I-4397, para 51; Case C-242/13, *Commerz Nederland NV v Havendbedrijf Rotterdam NV* EU:C:2014:2224, para 31; Case T-442/03, *SIC v Commission* [2008] ECR II-1161, para 94; Case T-384/08, *Elliniki Nafpigokataskevastiki AE Chartofylakeiou v Commission* [2011] ECR II-380*, para 50.

State.[165]   The ECJ has, however, accepted that, for a measure to be imputable to the State, it cannot be demanded that it be demonstrated, on the basis of a precise enquiry, that in the particular case the public authorities specifically incited the public undertaking to take the measure in question. It recognised that it will, as a general rule, be very difficult for a third party, precisely because of the privileged relations existing between the State and a public undertaking, to demonstrate in a particular case that aid measures taken by such an undertaking were in fact adopted on the instructions of the public authorities.[166]

Accordingly, whether or not a public undertaking is to be considered as acting under the influence of the State, such that the application of its resources may be considered as giving rise to State aid, is to be determined by all the circumstances of the case and the context in which a given measure is taken.[167] In *France v Commission*, concerning financing arrangements granted by a subsidiary of the publicly owned Crédit Lyonnais to Stardust Marine, the ECJ held that the imputability to the State of an aid measure taken by a public undertaking may also be inferred from other indicators.[168] Relevant indicators for establishing State control include the integration of the public undertaking into the structures of the administration of the State, the nature of its activities and the exercise of these on the market in normal conditions of competition with private operators, the legal status of the undertaking, the intensity of the supervision exercised by the public authorities over the management of the undertaking, or any other indicator showing an involvement by the public authorities in the adoption of the measure.[169]

---

[165] Case C-482/99, *France v Commission* [2002] ECR I-4397, para 52; Case C-242/13, *Commerz Nederland NV v Havendbedrijf Rotterdam NV* EU:C:2014:2224, para 31; Case T-442/03, *SIC v Commission* [2008] ECR II-1161, para 95; Case T-384/08, *Elliniki Nafpigokataskevastiki AE Chartofylakeiou v Commission* [2011] ECR II-380*, para 51; Case T-305/13, *SACE BT SpA v Commission* EU:T:2015:435, para 41.

[166] Case C-482/99, *France v Commission* [2002] ECR I-4397, paras 53-54; Case C-242/13, *Commerz Nederland NV v Havendbedrijf Rotterdam NV* EU:C:2014:2224, para 32; Case T-442/03, *SIC v Commission* [2008] ECR II-1161, para 96-97; Case T-384/08, *Elliniki Nafpigokataskevastiki AE Chartofylakeiou v Commission* [2011] ECR II-380*, paras 52-53.

[167] Case C-482/99, *France v Commission* [2002] ECR I-4397, para 55; Case C-242/13, *Commerz Nederland NV v Havendbedrijf Rotterdam NV* EU:C:2014:2224, para 32; Case T-442/03, *SIC v Commission* [2008] ECR II-1161, para 98; Case T-384/08, *Elliniki Nafpigokataskevastiki AE Chartofylakeiou v Commission* [2011] ECR II-380*, para 54; Case T-305/13, *SACE BT SpA v Commission* EU:T:2015:435, para 45.

[168] Case C-482/99, *France v Commission* [2002] ECR I-4397, para 55.

[169] *Ibid.*, para 56; Case C-242/13, *Commerz Nederland NV v Havendbedrijf Rotterdam NV* EU:C:2014:2224, para 33; Case T-442/03, *SIC v Commission* [2008] ECR II-1161, para 99; Case T-468/08, *Tisza Erőmű kft v Commission* EU:T:2014:235, para 170; Case T-305/13, *SACE BT SpA v Commission* EU:T:2015:435, para 47.

Action imputable to the State   Actions of public undertakings may be imputable to the State in a variety of situations.   For example, in *Italy v Commission*, in which the Commission classified capital injections by ENI, a State holding company, into Lanerossi as State aid, the ECJ held that there was considerable evidence that these were the result of action attributable to the Italian authorities.[170]   The case of *Van der Kooy v Commission* involved the fixing of a preferential energy tariff by a company which was 50% owned by the Netherlands State, the other 50% being privately owned.   In holding that this was imputable to the State, the ECJ took account of the fact that the Minister for Economic Affairs was empowered to approve the tariff, with the result that he could block any tariff which did not suit him.   Accordingly, the company did not enjoy full autonomy in the fixing of tariffs but acted under the control of the public authorities and took their requirements into account.[171]   In such circumstances, the company on which the State exerts influence does not apply the tariff as an ordinary economic agent but uses it to confer a pecuniary advantage on energy consumers, in the same way as a grant of aid, forgoing the profit which it would normally realise.[172]   Similarly, in *Netherlands v Commission*, decisions of a 50:50 public private partnership were imputable to the State on the ground that the agreement of the local authority was required.[173]   Grants to French farmers which were financed by the operating surplus of the Caisse nationale de crédit agricole were held by the ECJ to constitute State aid because they were subject to the approval of the public authorities.[174]   Similarly, in *Greece v Commission*, a repayment of interest to exporters was held to be State aid where the Bank of Greece, which administered the refunds, acted under direct State control.[175]

In *Namur-Les Assurances du Crédit v OND*, the board of directors of a public credit insurance establishment was required by law to follow the policy set by the government.   Advocate General Lenz held that since this requirement was binding, it had the effect of an instruction so that where any aid was granted it could be imputed to the State. In addition, if the government failed to intervene to stop the board from granting aid, such aid could be imputed to the State. The involvement of the State in the material decision did not have to go so far as to constitute an instruction since it was sufficient that the board could not take the decision without taking account of the requirements of the public authorities.[176]   Similarly, in *Nitrogénművek*

---

[170]   Case C-303/88, *Italy v Commission* [1991] ECR I-1433, para 11.
[171]   Cases 67, 68 & 70/85, *Van der Kooy v Commission* [1988] ECR 219, para 36.
[172]   *Ibid.*, para 28; Case C-56/93, *Belgium v Commission* [1996] ECR I-723, para 10.
[173]   Cases T-186/13, T-190/13 & T-193/13, *Netherlands v Commission* EU:T:2015:447, para 64.
[174]   Case 290/83, *Commission v France* [1985] ECR 439, para 15.
[175]   Case 57/86, *Greece v Commission* [1988] ECR 2855, para 13.
[176]   Case C-44/93, *Namur-Les Assurances du Crédit v OND* [1994] ECR I-3829, *per* Advocate General Lenz, at p. 3841-2.

Vegyipari Zst v Commission, concerning a Hungarian public development bank, the General Court alluded to the fact that the law which set up the bank provided that it was to pursue certain public policy objectives and that, in particular, its core function was to promote economic development and to contribute effectively to the implementation of the State's economic and development policy. Thus, the bank's activities were not those carried out by a commercial bank in normal market conditions, but those of a public development bank operating at preferential rates and pursuing public policy objectives. As regards its legal status, it was not subject to part of the prudential rules applicable to commercial banks and it had a different legal status from that of any commercial bank. Moreover, it was subject to intense supervision by the public authorities. Those three indicia were sufficient to show that measures adopted by the bank were directly imputable to the Hungarian State.[177]

In *Elliniki Nafpigokataskevastiki AE Chartofylakeiou v Commission*, decisions of a Greek State-owned bank were held to be imputable to the State since not only was the State the majority shareholder which put it in a position to control the bank but the decisions were not taken independently by the banks management but were taken by the government and implemented by the bank.[178] Similarly, in *SACE BT v Commission*, the members of the administrative council of an Italian publicly owned insurance company, were all nominated by the public authorities in agreement with the relevant government ministers. The General Court held that this was likely to constitute an indication that the public authorities were involved in the activities of the company. Moreover, two of those members were officials in the ministries. Nevertheless, these organic indicators, whilst significant in establishing that SACE's margin of independence was limited as regards the State, were not sufficient of themselves to establish imputability of the State in the adoption of the measures in question and had to be considered alongside any other applicable indicators.[179] Imputability was, however, established on the basis of a number of additional indicators, including the objectives assigned by legislation to SACE of promoting the competitiveness of the Italian economy, the support in the form of a State guarantee given to SACE to cover its principal activity, and the control exercised by the public authorities over SACE's actions.[180]

In *Austria v Commission*, the General Court held that a company, which was governed by private law but which was established by legislation to purchase all green electricity in Austria and sell it at prices higher than the

---

[177] Case T-387/11, *Nitrogénművek Vegyipari Zst v Commission* EU:T:2013:98, paras 63-66.
[178] Case T-384/08, *Elliniki Nafpigokataskevastiki AE Chartofylakeiou v Commission* [2011] ECR II-380*, paras 56-59.
[179] Case T-305/13, *SACE BT SpA v Commission* EU:T:2015:435, paras 61-63.
[180] *Ibid.*, para 82.

market price to distributors who were obliged to accept it, was not acting freely on the market with a view to making profit but was circumscribed in its actions by reference to its obligations under the legislation.[181]   Since the aid mechanism was established by law, it was unnecessary to engage in further analysis of the control of the company by the State.[182]   By contrast, in *Commerz Nederland v Havenbedrijf Rotterdam*, the ECJ held that the existence of organisational links between the publicly-owned port and the municipality of Rotterdam tended to demonstrate that the public authorities were involved. However, the fact that the sole director of the port company disregarded that company's statutes, and even deliberately kept secret the granting of a guarantee which the municipality would certainly not have accepted, may have been sufficient to exclude imputability of his actions to the public authorities.[183]

In *Du Pont de Nemours Italiana*, Advocate General Lenz preferred to be rather more cautious in categorising as State aid Italian legislation which required public bodies and companies in which the State held a minimum 30% shareholding to purchase a proportion of their supplies from companies established in the Mezzogiorno. Whilst prices paid for supplies in accordance with the legislation might be higher than prices under an unrestricted tendering procedure, he appeared to accept the view that the bodies were autonomous and, as far as their expenditure was concerned, not dependent on the State. Moreover, it was quite possible that the goods manufactured in the Mezzogiorno were sold at wholly competitive prices, so that there was no additional financial burden imposed on the companies as such.[184]

Measures taken pursuant to an EU obligation   Where a State measure is required to be taken pursuant to an obligation under EU law, the measure will not be regarded as being imputable to the State, since it has no discretion in the matter. Thus, in *Phoenix-Reisen v Commission*, where it was alleged that State aid was granted to undertakings in Germany through public guarantees protecting the salaries of employees of insolvent companies, the Commission dismissed the complaint on the ground that the system of guarantees was required by Council Directive 80/987/EEC concerning the protection of salaried employees in the event of the insolvency of their employer.[185]   In *Deutsche Bahn v Commission*, it was alleged by the German national railway that aid had been granted by Germany on foot of a tax exemption in respect of

---

[181] Case T-251/11, *Austria v Commission* EU:T:2014:1060, paras 70-75.

[182] *Ibid.*, para 87.

[183] Case C-242/13, *Commerz Nederland NV v Havendbedrijf Rotterdam NV* EU:C:2014:2224, paras 35-38.

[184] Case C-21/88, *Du Pont de Nemours Italiana v Unità Sanitaria Locale No 2 di Carrara* [1988] ECR I-889, *per* Advocate General Lenz, at p. 913.

[185] Case T-58/10, *Phoenix-Reisen GmbH v Commission* EU:T:2102:3, para 8.

aviation fuel. It was contended that different tax burdens led to a distortion of competition between undertakings engaged in rail transport, in particular high-speed trains, and undertakings engaged in air transport, in particular low-cost airlines. The Commission's rejection of the complaint was upheld by the General Court on the ground that the taxation of aviation fuel was governed by Council Directive 92/81/EEC on the harmonisation of the structures of excise duties on mineral oils[186] which imposed on Member States a clear and precise obligation not to levy excise duty on fuel used for the purpose of commercial air navigation. In transposing the exemption into national law, Member States were only implementing the directive in accordance with their obligations stemming from the FEU Treaty. Therefore, the national tax exemption was not imputable to the German State but stemmed from an act of the EU legislature.[187] The fact that Germany could have avoided the distortion of competition by extending the exemption to high-speed trains, as permitted by the directive, did not render the actual exemption State aid, since Germany was perfectly entitled to limit itself to transposing the mandatory provisions in the directive and not to use the option extending the exemption.[188]

Similarly, in *Bouygues SA v Commission*, a benefit granted to mobile phone operators in France was not State aid since it was required in order for the French authorities to comply with Council Directive 97/13/EC on the common framework for general authorisations and individual licences in the field of telecommunications services.[189] In order to operate third generation mobile phone services in France, licences had initially been granted to SRL and France Télécom for a particular fee. Subsequently, when a third licence was granted to Bouygues at a much lower fee, the fee payable by SRL and France Télécom was lowered to the same level, which led Bouygues to complain that State aid had been granted through an economic advantage being conferred on the existing licence holders. The General Court held that no State aid was involved since the adjustment to the fee was required in the light of the application of the provisions of the directive governing the award of the licences which required non-discriminatory treatment as between licence holders by the public authorities.[190]

---

[186] OJ 1992 L316/12.

[187] Case T-351/02, *Deutsche Bahn AG v Commission* [2006] ECR II-1047, para 102. See also, Case C-460/07, *Puffer v Unabhängiger Finanzsenat Außenstelle Linz* [2009] ECR I-3251, per Advocate General Sharpston, at para 70.

[188] Case T-351/02, *Deutsche Bahn AG v Commission* [2006] ECR II-1047, para 106. For an example of State aid in the context of exemptions from uniform EU legislation, see Case C-437/97, *Evangelischer Krankenhausverein Wien v Abgabenberufungskommission Wien* [2000] ECR I-1157, *per* Advocate General Saggio, at para 60; Case C-36/99, *Idéal Tourisme SA v Belgium* [2000] ECR I-6049.

[189] OJ 1997 L117/15.

[190] Case T-475/04, *Bouygues SA v Commission* [2007] ECR II-2097, para 111; upheld on appeal, Case C-431/07, *Bouygues SA v Commission*, [2009] ECR I-2665.

1.4 AID MUST BE FINANCED THROUGH STATE RESOURCES

State aid must entail a public financial burden   Article 107(1) TFEU applies to aid granted by the State or through State resources. Thus, the grant of aid must involve a burden on public financial resources. It is now well established that advantages granted by means other than through State resources do not fall within the scope of Article 107(1) TFEU.[191] For example, in *Aiscat v Commission*, a complaint was made by the holder of a concession on one stretch of Italian motorway that the construction of a competing stretch of motorway was financed by an increase in publicly regulated tolls on the former, part of which were used for the construction of the latter. The General Court, however, upheld the Commission's decision which concluded that, under the system of agreements regulating the various motorway concessions, there was no transfer of State resources, since the tolls were raised by one private company and passed onto another, without any public body acquiring, if even transiently, possession or control over the funds.[192] Similarly, the enforcement of obligatory legal requirements concerning the use of own funds do not necessarily result in State aid being granted. Thus, a requirement under the German civil code whereby companies must accumulate financial reserves against future contingent obligations was held by the Commission not to constitute State aid.[193]

Particular issues have arisen in the context of financing electricity production and distribution. The Commission has, for example, declared that a Belgian measure whereby electricity distributors had to buy annually a certain quantity of green certificates did not involve State resources.[194] Similarly, a German requirement that electricity distributors connect green electricity generating plants to their networks and to purchase the electricity at a minimum price that exceeded the market price was held not to be financed by State resources, regardless of the fact that some of the distributors were public undertakings, since all distributors were subject to the same constraints.[195] A statutory charge imposed on Northern Ireland electricity consumers which was paid directly to the electricity provider, without the intermediary of a body collecting the taxes centrally and redistributing them, in order to compensate for the additional costs resulting from long-term delivery contracts at prices

---

[191] Cases C-399/10P & C-401/10P, *Bouygues SA v Commission* EU:C:2013:175, para 99; Case T-487/11, *Banco Privado Português SA v Commission* EU:T:2014:1077, para 50.

[192] Case T-182/10 *Aiscat v Commission* EU:T:2013:9, para 105.

[193] *Thirty-First Report on Competition Policy* (2001), pt. 371.

[194] *Ibid.*, pt. 363.

[195] Case NN 27/2000, *Green certificates*, OJ 2002 C164/5.

actually or potentially higher than market prices, was held by the Commission not to involve State resources.[196]

Aid schemes financed through trade associations Where a private body such as a trade association raises funds from its members and uses these to finance aid schemes for the benefit of its members without any intervention by or direction from the State, the resulting benefit does not constitute State aid since it is not imputable to the State and the funds are not State resources. In *Pearle*, where Dutch legislation provided for trade associations to adopt by-laws imposing levies on their members to meet their operating costs, the ECJ held that the funds from a compulsory levy collected by a public body to finance a collective advertising campaign for opticians' businesses did not constitute State aid since the funds were financed solely from the levies imposed on the undertakings which benefited from the advertising campaign. The public body served merely as a vehicle for the levying and allocating resources collected for a purely commercial purpose previously determined by the opticians' association and had nothing to do with a policy determined by the Netherlands authorities.[197] Similarly, a Belgian scheme for financing certain social actions, such as training workers, according to the needs of the sector, was held not to constitute aid since it was financed solely by contributions from employers on the basis of collective agreements.[198]

In *Doux Élevage v Ministère de l'Agriculture*, a levy was extended by legislation to French turkey producers for the purposes of financing common activities decided by the organisation representing that industry, which was an association that formed no part of the State administration. The mechanism did not involve any direct or indirect transfer of State resources, the sums provided by the payment of those contributions did not go through the State budget and the State did not relinquish any resources which should have been paid into the State budget. The contributions remained private in nature and, in the event of non-payment, were subject to enforcement in the normal civil courts. Only the trade organisation and not the public authorities could use the resources, which were entirely dedicated to pursuing objectives determined by the trade organisation. It followed, held the ECJ, that neither the State's power to recognise a trade organisation nor its power to extend an agreement to all traders in an industry permitted the conclusion that the organisation's activities were imputable to the State.[199]

---

[196] Case N 661/99, *Northern Ireland Electricity*, OJ 2002 C113/3.

[197] Case C-345/02, *Pearle BV v Hoofdbedrijfschap Ambachten* [2004] ECR I-7139, para 36-37; Case C-206/06, *Essent Netwerk Noord BV v Alumimium Delfzijl* BV [2008] ECR I-5497, paras 72-73.

[198] Case NN 136/03, *Belgian sectoral funds*, OJ 2005 C316/3.

[199] Case C-677/11, *Doux Élevage SNC v Ministère de l'Agriculture* EU:C:2013:348, paras 32-41.

State intervention in funds financing aid measures Where, on the other hand, there is a sufficient element of State intervention, private funds may be deemed to be State resources. In these circumstances aid need not necessarily be financed directly by the State to be classified as State aid.[200] In *France v Commission*, concerning co-financing of farmers' organisations, it was held that the State was in a position, through its dominant influence, to guide the use of the resources provided to approved economic agricultural committees to finance specific advantages for certain farmers. The relevant criterion in order to assess whether resources were public, whatever their initial origin, was that of the degree of intervention by the public authority in the definition of the measure and its method of financing.[201] In *TV2/Danmark v Commission*, where TV2, a Danish television company, was financed through a licence fee, the General Court held that the licence fee resources were available to and under the control of the public authorities and were accordingly State resources. The amount of the fee was determined by the Danish authorities, the obligation to pay did not arise from a contractual relationship between TV2 and the person liable to pay, but simply from the ownership of a television or radio receiver, and was enforced in accordance with the rules on the collection of personal taxes, and the Danish authorities determined TV2's share of the income from licence fees.[202]

In *Air France v Commission*, a fund was accumulated from a mixture of public and private sources on the basis of compulsory deposits. These deposits were repayable in certain circumstances so that they could not be said to have been permanently placed at the disposal of the public sector. Nevertheless, since there was a constant balance retained by the fund as a result of continuous deposits and withdrawals, the General Court held that this was sufficient for the fund to be regarded as a public source of finance.[203] The ECJ confirmed this approach in *France v Ladbroke Racing* in relation to unclaimed betting winnings which remained at the disposal of the public authorities in France. The fact that they remained under public control was sufficient to classify them as State resources, irrespective of whether or not they were permanent assets of the public sector.[204] In *Salvat v Commission*, the

---

[200] Case 290/83, *Commission v France* [1985] ECR 439, para 14.

[201] Case T-139/09, *France v Commission* EU:T:2012:496, para 63.

[202] Cases T-309/04, T-317/04, T-329/04 & T-336/04, *TV2/Danmark A/S v Commission* [2008] ECR II-2935, para 158; Case T-8/06, *FAB GmbH v Commission* [2009] ECR II-196*, para 50.

[203] Case T-358/94, *Air France v Commission* [1996] ECR II-2109, para 62.

[204] Case C-83/98 P, *France v Ladbroke Racing Ltd. and Commission* [2000] ECR I-3271, para 50; Case C-482/99, *France v Commission* [2002] ECR I-4397, para 37; Case C-278/00, *Greece v Commission* [2004] ECR 3997, para 52; Case T-67/94, *Ladbroke Racing Ltd. v Commission* [1998] ECR II-1, para 108; Case T-25/07, *Iride SpA v Commission* [2009] ECR II-245, para 25; Cases T-267/08 & T-279/08, *Région Nord-Pas-de-Calais v Commission* [2011] ECR II-1999, para 109; Case T-243/09, *Fedecom v*

legislation establishing a committee in the French wine sector gave a predominant role to the State, in particular by requiring the approval of the committee's decisions by the Minister for Agriculture and conferring on the Minister the power to impose decisions on the committee.[205] Moreover, contrary to the situation in *Pearle*, Salvat, which argued that a levy was imposed on wine producers to finance an aid scheme for their benefit, was unable to show that the beneficiaries of the aid were always those liable to pay the charges.[206]

In a series of cases concerning electricity purchase obligations which were funded by specific levies that were regulated by legislation, the ECJ considered that the funds constituted State resources. In *Essent Netwerk Noord*, the ECJ distinguished the circumstances in that case from those applicable in *Pearle*, emphasising the legislative nature of the fund.[207] In *Association Vent de Colère Fédération nationale*, the sums of money intended to offset the additional costs arising from the obligation to purchase imposed on the undertakings in question were collected from final consumer of electricity in France and entrusted to a national collection agency, the amounts payable by each final consumer being determined by ministerial order and subject to administrative enforcement. The funds were channelled through the collection agency and were centralised in a special account before being paid out to the operators concerned. Since the agency, which acted as an intermediary, was a public body, the sums had to be regarded as remaining under public control and were, accordingly, State resources.[208] A similar system in Spain was also regarded as entailing State resources, the ECJ holding that it was irrelevant that the sums that were intended to compensate the additional costs were not identified as a specific supplement to the electricity tariff or as a fiscal levy.[209] In *Austria v Commission*, an exoneration in favour of large energy users from a general requirement to pay for renewable energy was held to constitute a drain on State resources, since a company under State control was otherwise entitled by legislation to require all undertakings to purchase green electricity at prices higher than the ordinary market price for electricity.[210] Similarly, a Dutch scheme which imposed a charge on electricity customers in order to finance a

---

Commission EU:T:2012:497, para 48; Case T-52/12, *Greece v Commission* EU:T:2014:677, para 119.

[205] Case T-136/05, *Salvat père & fils v Commission* [2007] ECR II-4063, para 154.

[206] *Ibid.*, para 162.

[207] Case C-206/06, *Essent Netwerk Noord v Aluminium Delfzijl BV* [2008] ECR I-5497, para 73.

[208] Case C-262/12, *Association Vent de Colère Fédération nationale v Ministre de l'Écologie* EU:C:2013:851, paras 22-37.

[209] Case C-275/13, *Elcogás SA v Administración del Estado* EU:C:2014:2314, para 31.

[210] Case T-251/11, *Austria v Commission* EU:T:2014:1060, para 76.

fund for the benefit of renewable energy producers did constitute State aid, since the fund was managed by the State.[211]

Mixed public and private resources State aid may also arise where funds which have been accumulated by a private body acting under the influence of the State are subsequently distributed by that body without having actually been appropriated into separate State ownership. In *Steinike und Weinlig v Germany*, a fund was set up under German law to promote the sale and use of products of the German agricultural, forestry and food industrial sector. Although the fund was financed by Government grants as well as by contributions from the undertakings operating in that sector, the ECJ held that the whole of the aid from the fund fell within the scope of Article 107(1) TFEU.[212] Similarly, in *France v Commission*, concerning the financing of agricultural committees by voluntary contributions as well as from public sources, the General Court held that it was not possible to make a distinction according to the method of financing, since the public and private contributions were mixed in an operation fund.[213] On the other hand, in *Doux Élevage SNC v Ministère de l'Agriculture*, it was held that private funds used by trade organisation do not become State resources simply because they are used alongside sums which may originate from the State budget.[214]

Competitive advantages granted by the State The distinction made in Article 107(1) TFEU between aid granted by a Member State and aid granted through State resources does not signify that all advantages granted by a State, whether financed through State resources or not, constitute aid. In support of a wider application of the notion of State aid, it has been argued on several occasions that Article 107(1) TFEU should also apply to competitive advantages granted by the State but which do not involve any financial burden on the State or appropriation of private financial resources. In *Norddeutsches Vieh- und Fleischkontor v BALM*, Advocate General Verloren van Themaat took the view that it was quite possible to argue that the independent grant by Member States of pecuniary advantages which were not paid for by the State were caught by Article 107(1) TFEU, examples of such advantages being reduced rates which the State might require private electricity companies or haulage contractors to grant, without reimbursement, to certain undertakings or in respect of certain products.[215] On this basis, the Commission initially

---

[211] Case N 707/2002, *Dutch Electricity*, OJ 2003 C148/11.

[212] Case 78/76, *Steinike und Weinlig v Germany* [1977] ECR 595, paras 21-22; Case T-52/12, *Greece v Commission* EU:T:2014:677, para 128.

[213] Case T-139/09, *France v Commission* EU:T:2012:496, para 66.

[214] Case C-677/11, *Doux Élevage SNC v Ministère de l'Agriculture* EU:C:2013:348, para 44.

[215] Cases 213-215/81, *Norddeutsches Vieh- und Fleischkontor v BALM* [1982] ECR 3583, *per* Advocate General Verloren van Themaat, at p. 3617.

decided that an obligation imposed on distributors to purchase at minimum prices electricity produced with renewable energy resources constituted State aid even if the State did not make direct use of its budget to assist producers using renewable energy, on the basis that the purchase obligation was tantamount to a compulsory levy on distributors' incomes, the levy being paid directly to producers using renewable forms of energy.[216] Moreover, in its *Georgsmarienhütte* decision, the Commission objected to assistance which was granted to a German steel producer in the form of an exemption from its environmental obligations with regard to the recycling and disposal of industrial dust. In the light of the polluter pays principle, the Commission considered that this constituted the grant of operating aid which relieved the producer from production costs. This appears to have been a separate consideration for the Commission in addition to the fact that the local authorities themselves assumed responsibility for the disposal of the industrial dust, thereby relieving the producer of the costs of disposal.[217]

The ECJ has, however, consistently rejected the notion of a wider approach to defining State aid.[218] In determining whether a measure should fall within the scope of application of Article 107(1) TFEU, the ECJ noted in *Sloman Neptune* that the application of the notification and supervision procedures under Article 108 TFEU should also be considered, so that not all State measures which distort competition are suitable for this type of control.[219] Moreover, in his opinions in *Viscido* and *Preussen Elektra*, Advocate General Jacobs warned against extending too far the boundaries to the scope of application of Article 107(1) TFEU. It was inappropriate to use the State aid provisions of the FEU Treaty to inquire into the entire social and economic life of the Member States, even though particular national policies might have an

---

[216] *Twenty-Seventh Report on Competition Policy* (1997), pt. 24.

[217] Commission Decision 1999/227/ECSC, *Georgsmarienhütte GmbH*, OJ 1999 L83/72. See also Case C-126/01, *Ministre de l'économie, des finances et de l'industrie v GEMO SA*, [2003] ECR I-13769, *per* Advocate General Jacobs, at para 69; Case T-20/03, *Kahla/Thüringen Porzellan GmbH v Commission* [2008] ECR II-2305, para 194.

[218] Cases C-72-73/91, *Sloman Neptun Schiffarts AG v Seebetriebsrat Bodo Ziesemer* [1993] ECR I-887, para 19; Case C-189/91, *Kirsammer-Hack v Sidal* [1993] ECR I-6185, para 16; Cases C-52-54/97, *Viscido v Ente Poste Italiane* [1998] ECR I-2629, para 13; Case C-200/97, *Ecotrade Srl v AFS* [1998] ECR I-7907, para 35; Case C-295/97, *Piaggio v Ifitalia* [1999] ECR I-3735, para 35; Case C-379/98, *Preussen Elektra AG v Schleswag AG* [2001] ECR I-2099, para 58; Case T-95/03, *Asociación de Estaciones de Servicio de Madrid v Commission* [2006] ECR II-4739, para 104; Case C-222/07, *UTECA v Administración General del Estado* [2009] ECR I-1407, para 43; Case T-25/07, *Iride SpA v Commission* [2009] ECR II-245, para 23; Case T-243/09, *Fedecom v Commission* EU:T:2012:497, para 47; Case T-52/12, *Greece v Commission* EU:T:2014:677, para 118.

[219] Cases C-72-73/91, *Sloman Neptun Schiffarts AG v Seebetriebsrat Bodo Ziesemer* [1993] ECR I-887, para 19.

effect on competition.[220]   The notion that Member States would seek to circumvent State aid controls, for example by adopting measures not involving State financing but which would have the same anti-competitive effects, should not, he thought, be exaggerated. In any event, such measures were likely to infringe either some other provision of EU law, such as the principle of equal treatment or the protection of legitimate expectations, or some constitutional or other provision of the relevant national law.[221]

The ECJ's judgment in *Preussen Elektra v Schleswag* concerned German legislation which required electricity distributors to purchase at fixed minimum prices a proportion of their requirements from producers using renewable energy sources and obliged upstream suppliers of electricity from conventional sources partially to compensate the distribution undertakings for the additional costs caused by that purchase obligation. The arguments submitted in favour of the wider approach were, first, that Article 107(1) TFEU referred to aid in any form whatsoever, secondly, that it was intended to ensure the maintenance of equal conditions of competition between traders, thirdly, that all State revenue was ultimately provided from private resources through taxes so that, whatever the nature and number of intermediate entities, the financial burden of an economic advantage conferred by the State on specific undertakings was in any event always borne by private persons and, finally, that if financing through State resources was a necessary element for State aid, Member States would be tempted to find alternative schemes which equally distorted competition but which would circumvent the application of the State aid rules. The ECJ, however, reiterated its objection that there must be a direct or indirect transfer of State resources for Article 107(1) TFEU to apply.[222]

Rejection of a wider approach to State aid Particular support for the wider application of Article 107(1) TFEU came from Advocate General Darmon. In *Sloman Neptune*, he argued that the granting of a dispensation to shipping vessels which had the effect of reducing certain employment-related costs in respect of non-EC seafarers was equivalent to the State-mandated establishment of a fund financed by those employees for the benefit of the

---

[220] Cases C-52-54/97, *Viscido v Ente Poste Italiane* [1998] ECR I-2629, *per* Advocate General Jacobs, at p. 2635; Case C-379/98, *Preussen Elektra AG v Schleswag AG* [2001] ECR I-2099, *per* Advocate General Jacobs, at p. 2138.

[221] Case C-379/98, *Preussen Elektra AG v Schleswag AG* [2001] ECR I-2099, *per* Advocate General Jacobs, at p. 2139.

[222] *Ibid.*, at pp. 2134-2139, comprehensively demolished the arguments which had been suggested to support the wider view. For arguments in favour of a wide approach to the definition of aid, see M. Ross, "State aids: maturing into a constitutional problem" (1995) 13 YEL 79; M. Slotboom, "State aid in Community law: a broad or narrow definition" (1995) 20 ELRev 289; K. Bacon, "State aid and general measures" (1997) 17 YEL 269.

shipowners.[223] The Commission contended that the legislation was enacted to make German shipping more competitive by granting it special advantages and amounted to State aid in that any measure of whatever nature which entails for a particular sector a relief which is not part of a comprehensive system is a State aid even if it is not financed from public funds. The ECJ declined to accept this approach.[224]

A similar argument was rejected in *Kirsammer-Hack v Sidal* which involved German legislation which excluded small businesses from the system of protection of employees against unfair dismissal. Such undertakings, which were not obliged to pay compensation in the event of socially unjustified dismissals or to bear legal expenses incurred in proceedings concerning the dismissal of employees, thereby enjoyed a competitive advantage over other undertakings. The ECJ held, however, that the legislation did not involve any transfer of State resources and that the benefit to small businesses derived solely from the legislature's intention to provide a specific legislative framework for working relationships between employers and employees in such businesses and to avoid imposing on those businesses financial constraints which might hinder their development.[225]

Similarly, in *Viscido v Ente Poste Italiane*, the non-application to Poste Italiane of generally applicable legislation concerning fixed-term employment contracts did not involve any direct or indirect transfer of State resources, even though this might have resulted in it being relieved of certain operating costs.[226] In *Ecotrade Srl v AFS*, Italian legislation established a system of special administration to enable certain large industrial firms to continue trading despite being insolvent. Ecotrade argued that legislatively ordained suspension of private debts pursuant to the system of special administration was a form of aid, even though it did not entail any charge on State resources. The ECJ affirmed, however, that aid necessarily implies advantages granted directly or indirectly through State resources.[227] In *Asociación de Estaciones de Servicio de Madrid v Commission*, it was alleged that legislation amending

---

[223] Cases C-72-73/91, *Sloman Neptun SchiffartsAG v Seebetriebsrat Bodo Ziesemer* [1993] ECR I-887, *per* Advocate General Darmon at p. 912.

[224] Cases C-72-73/91, *Sloman Neptun Schiffarts AG v Seebetriebsrat Bodo Ziesemer* [1993] ECR I-887, para 19.

[225] Case C-189/91, *Kirsammer-Hack v Sidal* [1993] ECR I-6185, para 17.

[226] Cases C-52-54/97, *Viscido v Ente Poste Italiane* [1998] ECR I-2629, para 14.

[227] Case C-200/97, *Ecotrade Srl v AFS* [1998] ECR I-7907, *per* Advocate General Fennelly, at p. 7920. See also Case C-326/95, *Banco de Fomento e Exterior v Martins Pechim* [1996] ECR I-1385, where the ECJ was asked whether the grant of aid arose from Portuguese legislation which conferred on a bank advantages including the power to proceed to recover debts in accordance with the enforcement procedure provided for in fiscal matters and, to that end, to treat as enforceable the certificate of the debt extracted from the bank's books. The ECJ refused to deal with the issue on the ground that the order for reference from the Portuguese court did not contain sufficient information on the factual and legal background to the case.

the rules concerning planning permission for the retail supply of petroleum products by hypermarkets constituted State aid. The General Court upheld the Commission's decision rejecting the complaint on the ground that there was no transfer of State resources involved in the amendment.[228] A Spanish decree requiring television operators to earmark 5% of their operating revenue for the pre-funding of European films and to reserve 60% of that funding for the production of works in Spanish was held, in *UTECA v Administración General del Estado*, not to constitute State aid on favour of the Spanish cinematographic industry.[229] In *Ufex v Commission*, the General Court held that there was no State aid involved where a public company providing express postal services was allowed to advertise, at market rates, on Radio France even supposing that this was in violation of the rules prohibiting commercial advertising on that public radio station.[230] Similarly, an allegation that the company's goods were given favourable customs treatment allowing the goods to be cleared more easily, did not imply any transfer of State resources or an additional charge for the State.[231]

Ancillary measures linked to aid measures In *Trapeza Eurobank Ergasias v ATE*, the ECJ appears to have widened the potential scope of measures that may be taken into account in assessing the applicability of Article 107(1) TFEU to include ancillary measures that are linked to financial subsidies. ATE was a Greek public bank which had the objective of providing credit in the agricultural sector. In order to compensate for the high level of risk involved in the grant of an agricultural credit, Greek legislation conferred special privileges on ATE including: the right to register a mortgage over the property of its debtors, without it being required to conclude a mortgage contract; the right to seek enforcement with an ordinary private document, such as a credit documents, which constituted in itself an enforcement order; and exemption from all fees and duties when registering such a mortgage and seeking enforcement thereof. Pursuant to these powers, ATE registered a mortgage in respect of certain agricultural land which was owned by an undertaking that was also a debtor of Eurobank. When proceedings were brought to enforce the debts in the commercial court, ATE ranked as a preferred creditor. Since the value of the land was less than the debt due to ATE, Eurobank failed to obtain any repayment of its loans. Eurobank claimed that the privileges should be assessed cumulatively in order to determine their compatibility with Article 107(1) TFEU. The ECJ, whilst initially noting that advantages granted from resources other than those of the State do not fall within the scope of Article

---

[228] Case T-95/03, *Asociación de Estaciones de Servicio de Madrid v Commission* [2006] ECR II-4739, para 104.

[229] Case C-222/07, *UTECA v Administración General del Estado* [2009] ECR I-1407, para 47.

[230] Case T-613/97, *Ufex v Commission* [2000] ECR I-4055, paras 108-109.

[231] *Ibid.*, para 110.

107(1) TFEU, stated that the exemption from fees was a selective economic advantage and that that exemption, in connection with the other privileges granted by the legislation, potentially distorted competition and effected trade between Member States. On that basis, it was held that the privileges as a whole were held to be capable of falling within Article 107(1) TFEU.[232]

Incidental reduction in State resources Where an incidental effect of a State measure regulating the conduct of private parties is to reduce the amount of tax or other resources accruing to the State, that measure is not considered as State aid. In *Sloman Neptune*, German legislation provided that contracts of employment concluded by shipping companies with seamen who were nationals of non-member countries and had no permanent residence in Germany could be subjected to working conditions and rates of pay which were not those generally applicable in Germany to German nationals. The effect of this was, *inter alia*, that, since the non-nationals received less pay, the amount of social security contributions paid by their employers was reduced. The Commission's argument that the measure was financed from State resources, since there was a loss of tax revenue as a result of the reduced level of rates of pay, was rejected by the ECJ which held that any advantages to the shipping sector arising under the legislation were not granted through State resources. The system of employment law did not seek, through its object and general structure, to create an advantage which would constitute an additional burden for the State, but only to alter in favour of shipping undertakings the framework within which contractual relations were formed between those undertakings and their employees. The consequences arising from this, in so far as they related to the difference in the basis for the calculation of social security contributions and to the potential loss of tax revenue because of the low rates of pay, were inherent in the system and were not a means of granting a particular advantage to the undertakings concerned.[233]

Similarly, in *Ecotrade Srl v AFS*, the ECJ rejected the Commission's argument that the loss of tax revenue resultant on the extinction of the debts on insolvency constituted a charge on public funds as being an inherent feature of any statutory system laying down a framework for relations between an insolvent undertaking and its creditors.[234] Advocate General Fennelly thought that this was simply too remote a connection with the State's disposal of its

---

[232] Case C-690/13, *Trapeza Eurobank Ergasias v ATE* EU:C:2015:235, paras 27-29.

[233] Cases C-72-73/91, *Sloman Neptune Schiffarts AG v Seebetriebsrat Bodo Ziesemer* [1993] ECR I-887, para 21; Cases C-52-54/97, *Viscido v Ente Poste Italiane* [1998] ECR I-2629, *per* Advocate General Jacobs, at p. 2634.

[234] Case C-200/97, *Ecotrade Srl v AFS* [1998] ECR I-7907, para 36; Case C-480/98, *Spain v Commission* [2000] ECR I-8717, para 18. See also, Case C-379/98, *Preussen Elektra v Schleswag* [2001] ECR I-2099, para 62.

resources to amount to aid.[235] In *Spain v Commission*, however, where a company was allowed to continue trading despite having been declared insolvent and owing large debts to the public authorities, the non-payment of taxes and social security contributions was held to constitute the grant of aid.[236]

Measures having effect equivalent to State aid The notion, propounded by the Commission, that a State measure distorting competition which did not wholly fall within Article 107(1) TFEU could nevertheless be prohibited as having an effect equivalent to State aid has been rejected by the ECJ. In *Commission v France*, the French Government had introduced a package of aid measures which included the payment of grants which were financed from the operating surplus of the Caisse nationale de crédit agricole. This was notified as State aid to the Commission which took the view that, since the payment was not made from State resources, it could not be classified as State aid within the meaning of Article 107(1) TFEU. Nevertheless, the Commission argued that the decision by the Caisse nationale to pay the grants must have been the result of encouragement and pressure from the public authorities. Proceedings were commenced against France alleging infringement of the duty imposed by Article 4(3) TEU to abstain from any measure which could jeopardise the attainment of the objectives of the FEU Treaty. The Commission considered that the grant was a measure having an effect equivalent to State aid which is incompatible with the internal market and was therefore within the scope of Article 4(3) TEU. By its action, the French Government had created a situation equivalent to that resulting from the grant of State aid. This notion was rejected by Advocate General Mancini who held that the wording of Article 107(1) TFEU was sufficiently wide and that it was not necessary to supplement it with a catch-all provision covering any residual measures which are not justifiable on the basis of other provisions of the Treaty and which obstruct trade between Member States.[237] The ECJ agreed, holding that a proper analysis of the scope of the State aid provisions showed that there was no scope for a parallel concept of measures having equivalent effect to aid which were subject to different rules from those which applied to aid properly so-called.[238]

This issue was raised again by the Commission in *Preussen Elektra v Schleswag*. The Commission maintained that if the German legislation which operated to the benefit of producers of renewable electricity was not to be regarded as State aid in the strict sense it constituted a measure intended to

---

[235] Case C-200/97, *Ecotrade Srl v AFS* [1998] ECR I-7907, *per* Advocate General Fennelly, at p. 7920.

[236] Case C-480/98, *Spain v Commission* [2000] ECR I-8717, para 21.

[237] Case 290/83, *Commission v France* [1985] ECR 439, *per* Advocate General Mancini, at p. 442.

[238] Case 290/83, *Commission v France* [1985] ECR 439, para 19.

circumvent the State aid rules, since it had all the harmful effects of State aid in spite of being financed by private resources and, therefore, posed a similar threat to the effectiveness of Articles 107 and 108 TFEU. Advocate General Jacobs interpreted the Commission's argument as amounting to the German legislation being a measure equivalent to State aid which infringed Article 4(3) TEU and which should be sanctioned under Article 108 TFEU by virtue of an extensive interpretation of the concept of aid under Article 107(1) TFEU. He rejected this argument, primarily on the ground that it would enable Article 4(3) TEU to be used to extend the reach of the Treaty so as to provide for Article 107(1) TFEU to encompass measures financed through private resources.[239] The ECJ also rejected this approach, holding that Article 4(3) TEU could not be used to extend the scope of Article 107(1) TFEU to conduct of Member States that did not fall within it.[240]

EU funding and State aid Despite the reference in Article 107(1) TFEU to aid granted in any form whatsoever, only advantages granted directly or indirectly through the financial resources of the State are to be considered as State aid. State aid must entail a burden on State funds, so that European Union funding cannot constitute State aid.[241] In *Norddeutsches Vieh- und Fleischkontor v BALM*, the ECJ held that the financial advantage received by certain traders as a consequence of the misapplication by the national authorities of a tariff quota established by the common organisation of the market in beef and veal could only be dealt with as a breach of the relevant provisions of EU law. It could not be regarded as State aid or as aid granted through State resources since the financial advantage was granted through EU resources because the levy which was waived was part of EU funds.[242] On the other hand, in *Benedetti v Munari*, the Italian intervention board was alleged to have bought wheat at the intervention price and re-sold it at a considerably lower price than permitted by the applicable EU legislation governing the common organisation of the market in cereals. The difference in purchasing and selling prices was considered by Advocate General Reischl to be a financial contribution constituting State aid.[243]

---

[239] Case C-379/98, *Preussen Elektra v Schleswag* [2001] ECR I-2099, *per* Advocate General Jacobs at p. 2146.

[240] Case C-379/98, *Preussen Elektra v Schleswag* [2001] ECR I-2099, para 65.

[241] Where EU funding that is not under the control of the Member State is combined with State aid, only the latter is considered for determining notification thresholds and maximum aid intensities, provided that the total amount of the public funding does not exceed the most favourable funding laid down in the applicable EU rules: Commission Regulation (EU) No 651/2014, Article 8(2).

[242] Cases 213-215/81, *Norddeutsches Vieh- und Fleischkontor v BALM* [1982] ECR 3583, paras 22-23.

[243] Case 52/76, *Benedetti v Munari* [1977] ECR 163, *per* Advocate General Reischl, at p. 190.

1.5 STATE REGULATION AS STATE AID

State regulation and economic activity A distinction must be drawn between
the obligations which the State must assume as an undertaking exercising an
economic activity and its obligations as a public authority.[244] While it is
clearly necessary, when the State acts as an undertaking operating as a private
investor, to analyse its conduct by reference to the private investor principle,
application of that principle must be excluded in the event that the State acts as
a public authority, in which case the conduct of the State cannot be compared
to that of an operator or private investor in a market economy.[245] The exercise
of public authority envisages activities which, by their nature, their purpose or
the rules to which they are subject, are connected with the exercise of powers
which are typically those of a public authority.[246] Nevertheless, in *Ryanair v
Commission*, which concerned the setting of airport charges by regulation of
the Walloon Region, the General Court held that the setting of airport charges
was closely connected with the use and operation of Charleroi airport which
was an economic activity and that it was necessary to differentiate between that
economic activity and activities that fell strictly under public authority
powers.[247] The mere fact that the Walloon Region had regulatory powers in
relation to fixing airport charges did not mean that a scheme reducing those
charges ought not to be examined by reference to the private investor principle,
since such a scheme could have been put in place by a private operator.[248] In
Netherlands v Commission, concerning the Dutch public broadcasting network,
the General Court held that NOS, in performing the task of coordinating and
managing the public broadcasters, could not be regarded as a public authority
exercising public powers. The coordination and management role was, on the
contrary, linked to the economic activity of providing and distributing
television programmes and was no different from the coordination activities
performed by a commercial undertaking for its commercial channels.[249]

State regulation and creation of economic asset value Where the State
acting as a regulator creates an asset owned by an undertaking, it is necessary

---

[244] Cases C-278/92 to C-280/92, *Spain* v *Commission* [1994] ECR I-4103, para 22; Case
         C-334/99, *Germany* v *Commission* [2003] ECR I-1139, para 134; Case T-196/04,
         Ryanair Ltd v Commission [2008] ECR II-3643, para 84.
[245] Case T-196/04, *Ryanair Ltd v Commission* [2008] ECR II-3643, para 85.
[246] Case C-364/92, *SAT Fluggesellschaft v Eurocontrol* [1994] ECR I-43, para 30; Case C-
         113/07P, *SELEX Sistemi Integrati v Commission* [2009] ECR I-2207, para 70; Cases T-
         231/06 & T-237/06, *Netherlands v Commission* [2010] ECR II-5993, para 93.
[247] Case T-196/04, *Ryanair Ltd v Commission* [2008] ECR II-3643, paras 94-98.
[248] *Ibid.*, para 101.
[249] Cases T-231/06 & T-237/06, *Netherlands v Commission* [2010] ECR II-5993, paras 98-
         101.

to determine whether that asset has an economic value and whether that value constitutes a transfer of State resources. In *Bouygues SA v Commission*, the General Court held that the exercise of State functions does not preclude the taking into account of economic facts in connection with the management of a scarce public resource such as the radio frequencies constituting the public airwaves, to which a right of access or a right of usage may be granted. Hence, the Member States simultaneously perform the roles of telecommunications regulator and manager of the public assets that constitute the wireless airwaves. In this regard, the argument to the effect that the assets in question, licences to operate third generation mobile phone services, had no market value since there was no equivalent in the hands of private managers, was not sufficient to preclude such assets from constituting a State resource.[250]

The General Court, however, went on to hold that the waiver by the French authorities of a significant part of the initial licence fee established for SRL and France Télécom did not, in the circumstances, amount to a grant of aid through State resources. The licence fee had not in fact been definitively fixed as binding on SRL and France Télécom who were entitled under the provisions governing the award of the licences to withdraw their applications, in particular in circumstances where they felt that they were not treated equally with other licence holders.[251] Indeed, having regard to the scheme established by Council Directive 97/13/EC on the common framework for general authorizations and individual licences in the field of telecommunications services,[252] which required licences to be granted on a non-discriminatory basis, the General Court held that, although the right to use the wireless space granted to the operators had an economic value, the amount payable as a fee could constitute State aid only if, all other things being equal, there was a difference between the price paid by each of the operators concerned. Moreover, if the national authorities had decided as a general principle that licences would be awarded free of charge, or awarded by means of public auctions or awarded at a standard price, there would be no aid element, provided these terms were applied to all the operators concerned without distinction.[253]

A system in the Netherlands allowing the transfer by undertakings of trading emission allowances was held by the General Court to confer an advantage on the undertakings. Although the measure in question was not based on emission allowances allocated directly by the State, it authorised the undertakings subject to a binding emission standard to trade between themselves the emission allowances which indirectly resulted from that standard, up to the limit of the ceiling applicable to each of them. By making

---

[250] Case T-475/04, *Bouygues SA v Commission* [2007] ECR II-2097, paras 104-105.
[251] *Ibid.*, paras 106-107.
[252] OJ 1997 L117/15.
[253] Case T-475/04, *Bouygues SA v Commission* [2007] ECR II-2097, para 110; upheld on appeal, Case C-431/07, *Bouygues SA v Commission*, [2009] ECR I-2665, para 118.

the allowances tradable, the Netherlands conferred on them the character of intangible assets with a market value. Those assets were put at the disposal of the undertakings concerned free of charge, whereas they could have been sold or put up for auction. Accordingly, the Netherlands had forgone State resources.[254] This was upheld on appeal, the ECJ holding that the tradability of emission allowances was to be regarded as an economic advantage which the recipient could not have obtained under normal market conditions.[255] The granting of this economic advantage could entail an additional burden for the State in the form of an exemption from the obligation to pay fines where undertakings purchased additional allowances on the market. In addition, the ECJ remarked that the Netherlands could have sold the trading rights or put them up for auction, with the result that State resources were foregone.[256]

Fixing of minimum and maximum prices The fixing of minimum prices by the State may involve State aid where the price is fixed at a level which is higher than the market would demand and the purchaser is a public body.[257] Similarly, the fixing of maximum prices by the State in respect of products sold by a public body may entail State aid where the products could in fact have commanded higher prices on the open market. In both cases, the imposition of price levels entails considerations other than those of a commercial operator with the result that the public body purchasing or selling the goods or services foregoes profit. Where, however, the supplier of goods subject to maximum price controls or the purchaser of goods subject to minimum prices is a private operator or consumer, State aid is not involved since there is no transfer of State resources. Thus, in *Van Tiggele*, the ECJ held that the fixing of minimum retail prices with the objective of favouring distributors of a product at the exclusive expense of consumers does not constitute an aid within the meaning of Article 107(1) TFEU. The advantages which such an intervention in the formation of prices entails for the distributors of the product are not granted, directly or indirectly, through State resources.[258]

Compensatory State payments Compensation granted by the State for an expropriation of assets will not normally qualify as State aid, as long as the compensation is proportionate.[259] However, where a Member State intervenes financially in order to reverse adverse economic circumstances of particular undertakings by the adoption of compensatory measures, the award of State aid

---

[254] Case T-233/04, *Netherlands v Commission* [2008] ECR I-591, paras 69-75.

[255] Case C-279/08P, *Commission v Netherlands* [2011] ECR I-7671, paras 88-91.

[256] *Ibid.*, paras 106-108.

[257] *Sixteenth Report on Competition Policy* (1986), p. 151.

[258] Case 82/77, *Openbaar Ministerie v Van Tiggele* [1978] ECR 25, paras 24-25.

[259] Case T-53/08, *Italy v Commission* [2010] ECR II-3187, paras 51-54; Case T-62/08, *ThyssenKrupp Acciai Speciali Terni SpA v Commission* [2010] ECR II-3229, paras 59-62.

cannot be excluded.[260]   Generally, a measure offsetting a structural disadvantage will constitute State aid.[261]   Thus, subsidies granted to undertakings
in the Venice region could not escape the classification of State aid on the
ground that they were intended to compensate for the increased costs arising
out of the structural disadvantages of doing business in that territory.[262]   This
applies regardless of the reasons for the adverse circumstances, including those
incurred by the adoption of legislation that changes the applicable regulatory
framework.   In *Iride v Commission*, where the Italian authorities had
compensated an electricity company in relation to stranded costs arising on the
liberalisation of the electricity sector pursuant to Directive 96/92,[263] it was
argued that the compensation represented merely the restoration of normal
market conditions as compared to competing undertakings which did not have
to bear the stranded costs.   Rejecting this contention, the General Court held
that the alteration to the legislative framework in the electricity sector which
occurred as a result of Directive 96/92 was part of normal market conditions
and that when the investments that gave rise to the stranded costs were made,
the undertaking concerned was taking the normal risks related to possible
future legislative amendments.[264]

In *Steenkolenmijnen v High Authority*, it was argued that a subsidy in
respect of coal miners' wages was cancelled out by the withdrawal of a State-
funded proportion of the employers' contribution to their pension fund so that
production costs remained the same and competition, therefore, was not
distorted.   The ECJ rejected this argument on the ground that the additional
cost to the employers did not in any respect constitute a repayment which was
at all times equivalent to the amount of the aid and that there was only a vague
and unconvincing connection between them.[265]   In *Italy v Commission*, the ECJ
rejected the contention that the loss of revenue due to a reduction in social
security charges in the textile sector was made good through funds accruing
from contributions paid to the unemployment insurance fund.[266]   It also
rejected an argument that a reduction in social security contributions payable
by undertakings in the textile sector was necessary to counteract the fact that
most of the employees in that sector were female who were ineligible for
payment of a family allowance which was restricted to heads of household.
The burden of payment of the allowances was exactly the same for all

---

[260] Case T-52/12, *Greece v Commission* EU:T:2014:677, para 70.
[261] Cases T-226/09 & T-230/09, *British Telecommunications plc v Commission*
EU:T:2013:466, para 67; Case T-135/12, *France v Commission* EU:T:2015:116, para
41; Case T-385/12, *Orange v Commission* EU:T:2015:117, para 42.
[262] Case T-273/00, *Unindustria v Commission* EU:T:2013:37, para 27.
[263] OJ 1997 l27/20.
[264] Case T-25/07, *Iride SpA v Commission* [2009] ECR II-245, para 51.
[265] Case 30/59, *De Gezamenlijke Steenkolenmijnen in Limburg v High Authority* [1961]
ECR 1, p. 31.
[266] Case 173/73, *Italy v Commission* [1974] ECR 709, para 16,

undertakings and the fact that only a small number of employees were entitled to claim the allowance could not constitute either an advantage or a specific disadvantage for the textile undertakings concerned as compared with other undertakings where a higher proportion of employees received the allowances.[267] Equally, in *France and France Télécom v Commission*, an economic advantage granted through the tax system could not be offset by a specific charge that was different from and unconnected to it.[268] In *British Telecommunications v Commission*, the objective of offsetting the structural disadvantage suffered by BT as a result of additional pension liabilities on privatisation could not deprive the advantage conferred by a State guarantee of its character as State aid.[269]

Similarly, in *Greece v Commission*, the ECJ refused to accept that an interest rate rebate in respect of exports did not constitute aid because it merely compensated for the abolition of a previously applicable preferential interest rate system, holding that it was irrelevant that by comparison with the previous export credit system the repayment of interest was economically neutral in its effect on the competitiveness of Greek exports, since the new system, viewed independently from its predecessor, favoured certain undertakings.[270] In *France v Commission*, the ECJ rejected a similar argument that a reduction in social security charges was merely the *quid pro quo* of exceptional additional costs which the relevant undertakings agreed to assume as a result of the negotiation of collective agreements and that, taking account of those additional costs, the reduction was financially neutral. Noting that the additional costs arose from collective agreements concluded between employers and trade unions which the undertakings were bound to observe, the ECJ held that such costs were included by their nature in the budgets of undertakings.[271]

In each case the factual and economic background must be examined in order to determine whether State intervention necessarily constitutes aid. For example, the Irish Government granted financial assistance to a ferry company

---

[267] *Ibid.*, para 14.

[268] Case C-81/10P, *France Télécom SA v Commission* [2011] ECR I-12899, para 43; Cases T-427/04 & T-17/05, *France v Commission* [2009] ECR II-4315, paras 207-213; Cases T-226/09 & T-230/09, *British Telecommunications plc v Commission* EU:T:2013:466, para 72.

[269] Cases T-226/09 & T-230/09, *British Telecommunications plc v Commission* EU:T:2013:466, para 75.

[270] Case 57/86, *Greece v Commission* [1988] ECR 2855, para 10; Case C-143/99, *Adria-Wien Pipeline GmbH v Finanzlandesdirektion für Kärnten* [2001] ECR I-8365, para 41; Case C-148/04, *Unicredito Italiano SpA v Agenzia delle Entrate, Ufficio Genova 1* [2005] ECR I-11137, para 105; Case C-336/04, *Banca Popolare FriulAdria SpA v Agenzia delle Entrate, Ufficio Pordonone* [2006] I-91*, para 36; Cases T-211/04 & T-215/04, *Government of Gibraltar v Commission* [2008] ECR II-3745, para 186.

[271] Case C-251/97, *France v Commission* [1999] ECR I-6639, para 40.

which had commenced operating a ferry service for the transport of live animals from Ireland to the continent. A similar service which was previously provided to exporters by the major commercial ferry companies had been withdrawn in the face of protest from animal rights campaigners. The new company, Gaelic Ferries, charged the exporters the same fees as had previously been applicable, and the aid merely covered their extra costs. Nevertheless, the Commission regarded the support as operating aid which relieved the exporters of a part of the transport costs which they would have had to bear had the State not intervened.[272] A contrasting approach was adopted where, under the German Indemnification and Compensation Act, a scheme was established to purchase land at reduced prices in the former East Germany. The Commission considered that assistance for resettled farmers benefiting from a reduced-price purchase might be deemed compensation for loss suffered in the expropriation of land or deterioration of the farm's assets, whilst other newly settled farmers who had not suffered expropriation or similar damage would be regarded as benefiting from State aid.[273]

Aid to establish comparable position with other Member States A measure does not escape classification as an aid merely because it is intended to place undertakings in the Member State concerned in a comparable position to undertakings in other Member States.[274] In *Commission v France*, the ECJ held that a preferential discount rate for French exports was an aid within the scope of application of Article 107(1) TFEU regardless of the fact that France may have resolved to approximate it to interest rates applicable in the other Member States.[275] In *Italy v Commission*, the ECJ was unimpressed by the argument that the textile industry in Italy was at a disadvantage as compared with the textile industries in other Member States by reason of the fact that the social charges devolving upon employers were appreciably higher in Italy.[276] Similarly, in *Heiser*, the ECJ rejected the argument that an aid was intended to compensate dentists in Austria who had been subject to VAT on the provision

---

[272] Commission Decision 2000/625/EC, *Gaelic Ferries*, OJ 2000 L263/17.

[273] *Twenty-Eighth Report on Competition Policy* (1998), p. 239.

[274] Case C-372/97, *Italy v Commission* [2004] ECR I3679, para 67; Case C-298/00P, *Italy v Commission* [2004] ECR I-4807, para 61; Case C-172/03, *Heiser v Finanzamt Innsbruck* [2005] ECR I-1627, para 54; Cases C-71/09, C-73/09 & C-76/09, *Comitato Venezia vuole vivere v Commission* [2011] ECR I-4727, para 95; Cases T-254/00, T-270/00 & T-277/00, *Hotel Cipriani SpA v Commission* [2008] ECR II-3269, para 182; Case T-172/14R, *Stahlwerk Bous GmbH v Commission* EU:T:2014:558, para 59; Case T-295/12, *Germany v Commission* EU:T:2014:675, para 144.

[275] Cases 6 & 11/69, *Commission v France* [1969] ECR 523, para 21.

[276] Case 173/73, *Italy v Commission* [1974] ECR 709, para 17; Case C-6/97, *Italy v Commission* [1999] ECR I-2981, para 21; Case C-73/03, *Spain v Commission* EU:C:2004:711, para 28; Case T-55/99, *CETM v Commission* [2000] ECR II-3207, para 85; Cases T-298/97 etc., *Alzetta v Commission* [2000] ECR II-2319, para 101.

of their services on the ground that their competitors in other Member States were exempt from VAT.[277]   In *Greece v Commission*, the ECJ rejected an argument that compensation for Greek farmers served to counter the heavier costs of production in Greece which were considerably higher than those in other Member States.[278]

In particular, it is not a legitimate excuse for the grant of aid for a Member State to argue that it is intended to compensate for unlawful aid granted by other Member States. Any breach by a Member State of the prohibition on the grant of State aid contrary to Article 107(1) TFEU cannot be justified by the fact that other Member States are also failing to fulfil this obligation. The effects of more than one distortion of competition on trade between Member States do not cancel one another out but accumulate and the damaging consequences to the internal market are increased.[279]   Thus, the Netherlands was prevented from introducing aid for Dutch shipyards which was purportedly to match illegal aid that had been offered by other Member States.[280]   It should also be clear that a Member State may not adopt measures designed to compensate undertakings which have been ordered to repay previous State aid which was unlawfully granted.[281]

State liability payments   Payment due from the State on foot of a legal obligation does not constitute aid. For example, damages which the State may be ordered to pay to individuals in compensation for damage they have caused to those individuals does not constitute aid.[282]   Similarly, interest due on a late payment of aid, and the detailed arrangements and rates applicable to that interest, does not constitute aid, but falls within the scope of national law.[283]   Equally, where a payment is no longer due, waiver of that payment cannot constitute aid. Thus, in the context of a company restructuring plan which included the waiver of a loan which had been provided by a public body, the Commission regarded the waiver of the loan itself as State aid, which it permitted as being compatible with the internal market, whilst the waiver of a penalty in relation to the earlier failure to repay the loan was treated as not including any aid on the basis that the obligation out of which the penalty arose no longer existed.[284]

---

[277]   Case C-172/03, *Heiser v Finanzamt Innsbruck* [2005] ECR I-1627, paras 52-54.
[278]   Case T-52/12, *Greece v Commission* EU:T:2014:677, para 82.
[279]   Case 78/76, *Steinike und Weinlig v Germany* [1977] ECR 595, para 22; Case T-214/95, *Vlaams Gewest v Commission* [1998] ECR II-717, para 54.
[280]   Commission Decision 2005/122/EC, *Dutch shipyards*, OJ 2005 L39/48.
[281]   Commission Decision 96/434/EEC, *Italian insolvency procedure*, OJ 1996 L180/31.
[282]   Cases 106-120/87, *Asteris v Greece* [1988] ECR 5515, para 24.
[283]   Case C-138/09, *Todaro Nunziatina v Assessorato del Lavoro* [2010] ECR I-4561, para 65.
[284]   *Twenty-Seventh Report on Competition Policy* (1997), p. 247.

Chapter Two

STATE AID WITHIN ARTICLE 107(1) TFEU

2.1 STATE AID AND ARTICLE 107(1) TFEU

Scope of application of Article 107(1) TFEU The scope of application of Article 107(1) TFEU extends to any State aid which distorts or threatens to distort competition by favouring certain undertakings or the production of certain goods in so far as it affects trade between Member States. It follows that, having determined that a measure grants an economic advantage financed through State resources and imputable to the State, there are three further general criteria all of which must be separately and cumulatively fulfilled for the aid to fall within the scope of Article 107(1) TFEU: the measure must favour the recipient such that it grants the advantage selectively; that selective advantage must distort or threaten to distort competition; the measure must be liable to affect trade between Member States.[1] The first of these conditions itself entails two separate matters. First, State aid within Article 107(1) TFEU must be granted, directly or indirectly, to an undertaking carrying on an economic activity. Secondly, that undertaking must receive a selective advantage as a result of the aid in that the aid must favour it as compared to other undertakings.

European Economic Area Agreement The Agreement on the European Economic Area contains provisions on State aid which essentially reproduce Article 107 TFEU and which extend their application throughout the territory of the EEA.[2] The other States party to the EEA Agreement are Iceland, Liechtenstein and Norway.

WTO Agreement on Subsidies and Countervailing Measures European State aid law applies only as respects subsidies granted by Member States that

---

[1] Cases C-227/13P to C-239/13P, *Albergo Quattro Fontane Snc v Commission* EU:C:2014:2177, para 25. Under the ECSC Treaty, Article 4(c) of which prohibited State aid, there was no need to prove a distortion of competition or effect on trade between Member States, although the criterion of selectivity was applicable as the condition that a State measure should relate to a specific undertaking or apply selectively was one of the defining features of State aid: Cases C-280/99 P to C-282/99 P, *Moccia Irme SpA v Commission* [2001] ECR I-4717, paras 32-33; Case T-308/00, *Salzgitter AG v Commission* [2004] ECR II-1933, paras 29 and 91.

[2] Article 61 EEA.

affect trade within the EU or the EEA. For international trade, the rules of the
World Trade Organisation apply. These include an Agreement on Subsidies
and Countervailing Measures which was incorporated into EU law by Council
Regulation (EC) No 3284/94 on protection against subsidised imports from
countries not members of the European Union.[3] A countervailing duty may be
imposed for the purpose of offsetting any subsidy granted, directly or
indirectly, for the manufacture, production, export or transport of any product
whose release for free circulation in the EU causes injury. To be subject to
countervailing measures subsidies must normally be specific. A subsidy is
specific to an enterprise or industry where the grantor, or the legislation under
which it operates, explicitly limits access to a subsidy to certain types of
enterprise or to enterprises located within a designated geographical region. A
subsidy is not specific where the grantor, or the legislation under which it
operates, lays down objective criteria governing eligibility for and the amount
of a subsidy. Countervailing duties only apply where it is established, on the
basis of positive evidence, that there has been either material injury to an EU
industry, a threat of such injury, or material retardation of the establishment of
such an industry.[4]

2.2 UNDERTAKINGS AS RECIPIENTS OF AID

Undertakings carrying on an economic activity For State aid to fall within
the scope of competition law, it must be granted to an undertaking, either
directly or indirectly.[5] For the purposes of EU State aid law, as with
competition law generally, a functional approach has been sanctioned by the
ECJ in determining the notion of an undertaking.[6] An undertaking is any
entity, regardless of its legal status or the way in which it is financed, which
carries on an economic activity, i.e. an activity consisting in offering goods or
services on a given market.[7] Advocate General Jacobs has suggested, as a

---

[3]   OJ 1994 L349/22.

[4]   See, C-D. Ehlermann & M. Goyette, "The interface between EU State aid control and
      the WTO's discipline on subsidies" [2006] EStALQ 695; L. Rubini, The Definition of
      Subsidy and State Aid: WTO and EC Law in Comparative Perspective (OUP, 2009).

[5]   Case T-52/12, *Greece v Commission* EU:T:2014:677, para 41.

[6]   Case C-222/04, *Ministero dell'Economia e delle Finanze v Cassa di Risparmio di
      Firenze SpA* [2006] ECR I-289, *per* Advocate General Jacobs, at para 74; Case T-
      347/09, *Germany v Commission* EU:T:2013:418, para 53.

[7]   Case 118/85, *Commission v Italy* [1987] ECR 2599, para 7; Case C-41/90, *Höfner and
      Elsner v Macrotron* [1991] ECR I-1979, para 21; Case C-35/96 *Commission v Italy*
      [1998] ECR I-3851, para 36; Cases C-180/98 to C-184/98, *Pavlov v Stichting
      Pensioenfinds Medische Specialisten* [2000] ECR I-6451, paras 74-75; Cases C-264/01,
      etc., *AOK Bundesverband v Ichthyol-Gesellschaft Cordes, Hermani & Co* [2004] ECR I-
      2493, para 46; Case C-172/03, *Heiser v Finanzamt Innsbruck* [2005] ECR I-1627, para
      26; Case C-205/03P, *FENIN v Commission* [2006] ECR I-6295, para 25; Case C-222/04,

means of ensuring the full effectiveness of the competition rules, that an entity should also qualify as an undertaking not only where it offers goods and services on a market but also where it carries on other activities which are economic in nature and which could lead to distortions in a market where competition exists.[8] Whilst the beneficiary of State aid must be identifiable, it is not necessary that the actual beneficiaries be identified in advance, since it is common for measures granting aid to confer an option exercisable by a putative beneficiary in order, for example, to induce an undertaking to invest in a particular region.[9] The State aid provisions apply equally to aid granted by a Member State to undertakings in other Member States.[10] Where the undertaking has ceased all economic activity, it may no longer fall within the scope of Article 107(1) TFEU, although appropriate proof must be provided to support this. In *Banco Privado Português SA v Commission*, it was argued that a Portuguese bank that had received rescue aid in the credit crisis was no longer active on the market as a competitor of other financial institutions. However, the General Court rejected this assertion, on the basis that the bank's licence had not been revoked and it continued as an actor present on the market.[11]

Group of companies A group of companies may be regarded as a single undertaking for the purposes of receiving State aid.[12] For these purposes, EU

Ministero dell'Economia e delle Finanze v Cassa di Risparmio di Firenze SpA [2006] ECR I-289, paras 107-108; Case C-237/04, *Enirisorse SpA v Sotocarbo SpA* [2006] ECR I-2843, paras 28-29; Case C-480/09P, *AceaElectrabel Produzione SpA v Commission* [2010] ECR I-13355, para 47; Case C-288/11P, *Mitteldeutsche Flughafen AG v Commission* EU:C:2012:821, para 40; Case T-196/04, *Ryanair Ltd v Commission* [2008] ECR II-3643, para 87; Cases T-443/08 & T-455/08, *Freistaat Sachsen v Commission* [2011] ECR II-1311, para 89; Case T-347/09, *Germany v Commission* EU:T:2013:418, para 26.

[8] Case C-222/04, *Ministero dell'Economia e delle Finanze v Cassa di Risparmio di Firenze SpA* [2006] ECR I-289, *per* Advocate General Jacobs, at para 78.

[9] Cases C-72-73/91, *Sloman Neptune Schiffarts AG v Seebetriebsrat Bodo Ziesemer* [1993] ECR I-887, *per* Advocate General Darmon, at p. 913; Case C-241/94, *France v Commission* [1996] ECR I-4551, *per* Advocate General Jacobs, at p. 4563.

[10] Case C-353/95 P, *Tiercé Ladbroke v Commission* [1997] ECR I-7007, *per* Advocate General Cosmas, at p. 7018.

[11] Case T-487/11, *Banco Privado Português SA v Commission* EU:T:2014:1077, paras 59-63.

[12] Case 323/82, *Intermills v Commission* [1984] ECR 3809, para 11; Case 40/85, *Belgium v Commission* [1986] ECR 2321, para 15; Cases T-371/94 and T-394/94, *British Airways v Commission* [1998] ECR II-2405, para 313; Case T-234/95, *Dradenauer Stahlgesellschaft mbH v Commission* [2000] ECR II-2603, para 124; Case T-137/02, *Polmeier Malchow GmbH v Commission* [2004] ECR II-3541, paras 50-51; Cases T-111/01 & T-133/01, *Saxonia Edelmetalle GmbH v Commission* [2005] ECR II-1579, para 84; Case T-89/09, *Pollmeier Massivholz GmbH v Commission* EU:T:2015:153, paras 122-123.

State aid law may apply different considerations than those applicable in other areas of EU competition law, such as restrictive practices and merger control.[13] If a group of companies is established to be the relevant economic unit, the internal division of functions amongst the various group members should not affect the assessment of any measure as State aid. Thus, in *Italy v Commission*, where payments were made to ENI, a holding company, which owned the Lanerossi group of companies, it was held that the Commission was entitled to regard the funds provided by ENI through Lanerossi to four of its subsidiaries as State aid, without it being necessary to establish that the capital funds received by ENI from the Italian Government were specifically intended to make up the losses of the subsidiaries. It was sufficient to observe that in any event the receipt of the capital funds enabled ENI to release other resources to make up the losses of the subsidiaries.[14]

Usually an economic activity is carried on directly on the market by the relevant undertaking. It may be the case, however, that an operator may be in direct contact with the market while another entity controlling that operator as part of an economic unit which they together form will be regarded as carrying on the economic activity indirectly.[15] In that event, the economic unit must be regarded as a single undertaking. If that were not the case, the simple separation of an undertaking into two different entities, the first of which pursues directly the former economic activity and the second of which controls the first, being fully involved in its management, would be sufficient to deprive the State aid rules of their practical effect. It would enable the second entity to benefit from subsidies or other advantages and to use them in whole or in part for the benefit of the former, in the interest, also, of the economic unit formed by the two entities.[16]

Thus, in *Ministero dell'Economia e delle Finanze v Cassa di Risparmio di Firenze*, the ECJ held that a banking foundation involved in the management of a banking company was an undertaking for the purposes of the State aid rules where it not only held controlling shareholdings in a banking company, but, in addition, actually exercised that control by involving itself directly or indirectly in the management of the latter. Under the Italian regime applicable to the banking sector, a banking foundation controlling the capital of a banking company, while it could not engage directly in the banking activity, had to ensure operational continuity between itself and the controlled bank. Members of the banking foundation's management committee were appointed to the

---

[13] Case C-480/09P, *AceaElectrabel Produzione SpA v Commission* [2010] ECR I-13355, para 66; Case T-303/05, *AceaElectrabel Produzione SpA v Commission* [2009] ECR II-137*, paras 135-138.

[14] Case C-303/88, *Italy v Commission* [1991] ECR I-1433, para 14; Case C-305/89, *Italy v Commission* [1991] ECR I-1603, para 15.

[15] Case C-222/04, *Ministero dell'Economia e delle Finanze v Cassa di Risparmio di Firenze SpA* [2006] ECR I-289, paras 109-110.

[16] *Ibid.*, paras 113-114.

board of directors and members of the controlling body to the supervisory committee of the banking company. The banking foundation had to transfer a defined proportion of the income from its shareholdings in the banking company to a special reserve to be used for subscribing to increases in capital of that banking company, and it could invest the reserve, in particular, in securities of the controlled banking company. Such rules revealed a function of banking foundations going beyond the simple placing of capital by an investor and made possible the exercise of functions relating to control, and also to direction and financial support, illustrating the existence of organic and functional links between the banking foundations and the banking companies, which was confirmed by the maintenance of supervision by the Minister for the Treasury.[17]

Holding companies A holding company which does no more than hold shares in its other companies, even controlling shareholdings, is not regarded as carrying on an activity which can be characterised as economic where its function gives rise only to the exercise of the rights attached to the status of shareholder or member, as well as, if appropriate, the receipt of dividends, which are merely the fruits of the ownership of an asset.[18] On the other hand, an entity which, owning controlling shareholdings in a company, actually exercises that control by involving itself directly or indirectly in the management thereof must be regarded as taking part in the economic activity carried on by the controlled undertaking and must itself, in that respect, be regarded as an undertaking within the meaning of Article 107(1) TFEU.[19] Thus, in *AceaElectrabel v Commission*, a combination of a majority shareholding and control over the board of directors and the executive committee, including the power to block decisions, permitted the Commission to conclude that two companies formed an indivisible whole.[20]

Public undertakings Aid may be granted to public undertakings as well as to private undertakings.[21] In order to make it easier to monitor whether aid has been granted to public undertakings, Commission Directive 2006/111/EC[22] requires transparency in the case of public funds made available by public authorities to public undertakings or through the intermediary of public undertakings or financial institutions, as well as transparency of the use to

---

[17] *Ibid.*, paras 116-118.
[18] *Ibid.*, para 111.
[19] *Ibid.*, paras 112-113; Case C-480/09P, *AceaElectrabel Produzione SpA v Commission* [2010] ECR I-13355, para 49.
[20] Case C-480/09P, *AceaElectrabel Produzione SpA v Commission* [2010] ECR I-13355, paras 52-56.
[21] Case 78/76, *Steinike und Weinlig v Germany* [1977] ECR 595, para 18; Case C-387/92, *Banco Exterior de España v Ayuntamiento de Valencia* [1994] ECR I-877, para 11.
[22] OJ 2006 L318/17.

which public funds are put.[23] This requirement applies in particular to the setting off of operating losses, provision of capital, non-refundable grants, loans on privileged terms, financial advantages by forgoing profits or the recovery of sums due, forgoing of a normal rate of return on public funds used, and compensation for financial burdens imposed by the public authorities.[24]

A public undertaking is any undertaking over which the public authorities may exercise directly or indirectly a dominant influence by virtue of their ownership of it, their financial participation therein, or the rules which govern it.[25] In order to be regarded as a recipient of State aid, a public undertaking does not necessarily have to have a legal identity separate from the State. No distinction is made between the State carrying out its economic activities by way of a distinct body over which it may exercise a dominant influence or directly through a body forming part of the administration of the State.[26] Thus, in *Commission v Italy*, a State entity which carried on the Italian tobacco monopoly without having legal personality separate from the State was held to be capable of receiving State aid. The ECJ held that the fact that a body carrying out economic activities of an industrial or commercial nature was integrated into the State administration and did not have separate legal personality did not prevent the existence of financial relations between the State and that body.[27]

Public bodies exercising public authority Activities which fall within the exercise of public powers are not of an economic nature justifying the application of the FEU Treaty rules of competition.[28] In so far as a public body is engaged in economic activity which may be dissociated from the exercise of public authority, such an entity, as regards this activity, acts as an undertaking. On the other hand, if the economic activity is indissociable from the exercise of public authority, the whole of the body's activities remain linked with the exercise of public authority.[29] Thus, in *Germany v Commission*, which concerned German legislation providing for the transfer of land and forestry to various bodies which had public powers concerning environmental protection, the General Court upheld the Commission's assessment that State aid was involved, given that the secondary activity of these bodies, such as the sale of wood and hunting and fishing licences, entailed an economic activity which

---

[23] Commission Directive 2006/116/EC, Article 1(1).
[24] *Ibid.*, Article 3.
[25] *Ibid.*, Article 2(b).
[26] Case 118/85, *Commission v Italy* [1987] ECR 2599, para 8.
[27] *Ibid.*, para 13.
[28] Case C-364/92, *SAT Fluggesellschaft v Eurocontrol* [1994] ECR I-43, para 30; Case C-49/07, *MOTOE v Greece* [2008] ECR I-4863, para 24; Case T-347/09, *Germany v Commission* EU:T:2103:418, para 27; Case T-309/12, *Zweckverband Tierkörperbeseitigung v Commission* EU:T:2104:676, para 52.
[29] Case T-347/09, *Germany v Commission* EU:T:2103:418, para 29.

was not required by their primary obligations concerning environmental protection.[30]

Non-profit making undertakings The fact that the recipient of the aid may be a non-profit making company is irrelevant as long as it carries on an economic activity in competition with other operators.[31] Thus, the Commission opposed German measures in favour of GAV, a non-profit making company, which operated on the market for the collection and recycling of company waste. Whilst the collection of household waste is traditionally the task of local authorities, the Commission considered that this was not the case with regard to the collection, sorting and marketing of company waste, and that many commercial companies were active in this field in competition with each other.[32] In *Ambulanz Glöckner*, a provider of emergency transport services was held to be an undertaking even though it operated on a non-profit basis, since the activity in question was one that was performed by others for profit. The ECJ recognised that public service obligations may, of course, render the services provided by a given medical aid organisation less competitive than comparable services rendered by other operators not bound by such obligations, but that fact could not prevent the activities in question from being regarded as economic activities.[33] In *Enirisorse v Sotocarbo*, the fact that Sotocarbo was created in order to carry out certain research operations was not conclusive that it was not an undertaking, given that it operated for profit, developing new technologies for the use of coal and providing specialist support services for authorities, public bodies and companies interested in the development of those technologies.[34]

In *MOTOE v Greece*, which concerned the status of ELPA, a non-profit-making association which represents the International Cycling Federation in Greece, the ECJ held that it was necessary to distinguish the participation of a legal person such as ELPA in the decision-making process of the public authorities from the economic activities engaged in by that same legal person, such as the organisation and commercial exploitation of motorcycling events. It followed that the power of such a legal person to give its consent to applications for authorisation to organise those events did not prevent its being considered an undertaking for the purposes of competition

---

[30] Case T-347/09, *Germany v Commission* EU:T:2103:418, paras 40-41.

[31] Case 78/76, *Steinike und Weinlig v Germany* [1977] ECR 595, *per* Advocate General Warner, at p. 584; Cases C-115/97 to C-117/97, *Brentjens Handelsonderneming BV v Stichtng Bedrijfspensioensfonds voor de Handel in Bouwmaterialen* [1999] ECR I-6025, para 85; Case T-347/09, *Germany v Commission* EU:T:2103:418, para 43. See L. Waddington, "The application of the Community State aid rules to voluntary organisations" (1998) 25 LIEI 59.

[32] *Twenty-Fifth Report on Competition Policy* (1995), p. 227.

[33] Case C-475/99, *Ambulanz Glöckner* [2001] ECR I-9098, paras 20-21.

[34] Case C-237/04, *Enirisorse SpA v Sotocarbo SpA* [2006] ECR I-2843, paras 35.

law so far as concerns its economic activities. The fact that MOTOE, a private body whose object was the organisation of motorcycling competitions in Greece whose members included various regional motorcycling clubs, was itself a non-profit-making association had no effect on the classification as an undertaking of a legal person such as ELPA. First, it was not inconceivable that, in Greece, there existed, in addition to the associations whose activities consisted in organising and commercially exploiting motorcycling events without seeking to make a profit, associations which were engaged in that activity and did seek to make a profit and which were thus in competition with ELPA. Secondly, non-profit-making associations which offered goods or services on a given market might find themselves in competition with one another. The success or economic survival of such associations depended ultimately on their being able to impose, on the relevant market, their services to the detriment of those offered by the other operators.[35]

On the other hand, in its decision concerning assistance to Asetra, a non-profit making association grouping together road and urban transport undertakings, to enable it to set up a system providing information and services in the transport field, the Commission found that in so far as Asetra was not an undertaking carrying on economic activities measures supporting it could not be classified as State aid.[36] In a case where a Spanish wine-growing company received aid for the restoration of historic monastery buildings in its possession, the Commission also found that no State aid was involved, since the buildings were not used for the economic activities of the company.[37]

Undertakings having an exclusively social function The mere fact that an undertaking might engage in activity that has a social element does not prevent it from being considered as carrying on an economic activity. Thus, for instance, in *KG Holding v Commission*, a subsidiary company whose principal activity consisted in the provision of services of finding employment for jobseekers, integrating people living with disabilities into the labour market as well as general staff placement services was regarded as being engaged in an economic activity.[38] In sectors such as health, education, scientific research and culture, as Advocate General Tizzano recognised in *Heiser*, it is by no means certain that entities providing particular services should be regarded as undertakings carrying on an economic activity.[39] Thus, in the field of social security, the ECJ held in *Poucet and Pistre* that organisations that fulfil an

---

[35]   Case C-49/07, *MOTOE v Greece* [2008] ECR I-4863, paras 26-28.

[36]   *Thirtieth Report on Competition Policy* (2000), pt. 385.

[37]   *Twenty-Ninth Report on Competition Policy* (1999), pt. 229.

[38]   Cases T-81/07 to T-83/07, *KG Holding NV v Commission* [2009] ECR II-2411, para 179.

[39]   Case C-172/03, *Heiser v Finanzamt Innsbruck* [2005] ECR I-1627, *per* AG Tizzano at para 39.

exclusively social function and are entirely non-profit-making do not fall to be regarded as undertakings.[40] Similarly, in *Freskot*, the Greek organisation for agricultural insurance, which was allocated a function under a compulsory insurance scheme in the context of the essentially social objective pursued by that scheme, was held not to be an undertaking for the purposes of Article 107(1) TFEU.[41] In *Ministero dell'Economia e delle Finanze v Cassa di Rispamio di Firenze*, the ECJ held that a banking foundation carrying on an activity limited to the payment of contributions to non-profit making organisations was not an undertaking. As regards that activity, which was of an exclusively social nature and not carried out on the market in competition with other operators, the banking foundation acted as a voluntary body or charitable organisation and not as an undertaking.[42] Such organisations do not necessarily have to be publicly owned. In a decision concerning Přerov Logistics College, a private third-level college in the Czech Republic, relating to a grant to cover approximately half the cost of acquiring educational equipment, the Commission held that the college was not an undertaking on the ground that it had entered into an agreement with the State to provide a degree course within the national educational curriculum, it did not make any profit and was not conducting any economic activity but was pursuing an educational role of general interest.[43]

On the other hand, for example, in *Enirisorse v Sotocarbo*, where the company acted for profit, it was irrelevant that it had been formed by public institutions and financed by means of resources from the Italian State for the purpose of carrying out certain research activities.[44] In *Ministero dell'Economia e delle Finanze v Cassa di Rispamio di Firenze*, the ECJ also recognised that where a banking foundation, acting itself in the fields of public interest and social assistance, uses the authorisation given it by the national legislature to effect the financial, commercial, real estate and asset operations necessary or opportune in order to achieve the aims prescribed for it, it is capable of offering goods or services on the market in competition with other operators, for example in fields like scientific research, education, art or health. In those circumstances, the banking foundation must be regarded as an undertaking, in that it engages in an economic activity, notwithstanding the fact

---

[40] Case C-159/91 and C-160/91, *Poucet and Pistre v AGF and Concava* [1993] ECR I-637, paras 15-18; Cases C-264/01, C-306/01, C-354/01 & C-355/01, *AOK-Bundesverband* [2004] ECR I-2493, para 47; Cases C-266/04 to C-270/04, C-276/04 & C-321/04 to C-325/04, *Distribution Casino France v Organic* [2005] ECR I-9481, para 54; Case T-319/99, *FENIN v Commission* [2003] ECR II-357, paras 38-39.

[41] Case C-355/00, *Freskot v Greece* [2003] ECR I-5263, para 79; Case T-52/12, *Greece v Commission* EU:T:2014:677, para 43.

[42] Case C-222/04, *Ministero dell'Economia e delle Finanze v Cassa di Risparmio di Firenze SpA* [2006] ECR I-289, paras 120-121.

[43] Case NN 54/2006, *Přerov Logistics College*, OJ 2006 C291/18.

[44] Case C-237/04, *Enirisorse SpA v Sotocarbo SpA* [2006] ECR I-2843, paras 31-32.

that the offer of goods or services is made without profit motive, since that offer will be in competition with that of profit-making operators.[45]

State aid to employees of an undertaking Employees of undertakings that receive aid are not themselves considered to be undertakings for the purposes of Article 107(1) TFEU.[46] In *Danske Busvognmaend v Commission*, a payment was made by the Danish authorities to State employees, who were seconded to Combus, the State-owned bus company, as compensation for them agreeing to opt for employment on a contractual basis directly with Combus with a view to its privatisation. The General Court upheld the Commission's finding that this did not constitute State aid to Combus, since the payment was made to the employees who gave up their right to be employed in the public service.[47] In *Innovative Technology Center v Bundesagentur für Arbeit*, the ECJ was asked whether the provision of vouchers, which released a person seeking employment from his obligation to pay a private employment agency the fee due to it in respect of the job it found for him, conferred an advantage on the employment agency. Advocate General Léger stated that the scheme merely provided for an assignment of the liability to pay the fee due to the employment agency from the employer to the Bundesagentur. By paying that fee directly to the agency, the Bundesagentur was simply paying the consideration for a service rendered, namely the recruitment of a person seeking employment.[48]

However, whilst benefits granted by the State to employees are normally not regarded as State aid since they do not benefit the employer as such, it might be the case that payments out of public funds or tax exemptions for certain employees have the result of reducing or substituting their employment costs and might, therefore, be viewed as being an aid to the employer.[49] For example, an agreement between Cockerill Sambre, a Belgian steel producer, and its employees provided that a wage increase was dependent on the Belgian authorities providing public funding which was to be paid directly to the employees. The ECJ agreed with the Commission's decision finding that the effect of the public financing was to mitigate Cockerill Sambre's normal budgetary burden, in that the wage increase remained a salary cost, regardless

---

[45] Case C-222/04, *Ministero dell'Economia e delle Finanze v Cassa di Risparmio di Firenze SpA* [2006] ECR I-289, paras 122-123.

[46] Case C-22/98, *Becu* [1999] ECR I-5665, para 26; Case C-319/07P, *3F v Commission* [2009] ECR I-5963, para 80; Case T-30/03, *Specialarbejder-forbundet i Danmark v Commission* [2007] ECR II-34*, para 33.

[47] Case T-157/01, *Danske Busvognmaend v Commission* [2004] ECR II-197, paras 56-57.

[48] Case C-208/05, *Innovative Technology Center v Bundesagentur für Arbeit* [2007] ECR I-181, *per* Advocate General Léger at para 34.

[49] Case 30/59, *Steenkolenmijnen v High Authority* [1961] ECR 1, p. 29. See also the Commission notice on monitoring of State aid and reduction of labour costs, OJ 1997 C1/10.

of who actually paid it to the employees.[50] Financial assistance to cover redundancy payments made to employees pursuant to a legal obligation on the employer will generally be regarded as State aid to the employer.[51]

Where redundancy payments are made direct to employees by a public authority and entail no benefit to the employer, such as where the undertaking has been made bankrupt, no State aid will be presumed.[52] Equally, where assistance is granted to an undertaking to cover costs arising from an agreement with a public authority which goes beyond the legal obligations of the undertaking, it might be argued that no State aid is given. In *France v Commission*, a French public authority responsible for employment policy subsidised redundancy payments made by Kimberley Clark to its former employees. Objection to the Commission treating this as State aid was based on the ground that the redundancy payments were greater than those required by law and that this increase was the result solely of the agreement with the public authority. On the available evidence, however, the ECJ confirmed that the Commission was entitled to decide that no payments had been made beyond those for which the undertaking was legally obligated.[53] By contrast, aid to cover redundancy costs for employees of SNCM was regarded by the General Court, overturning a contrary determination by the Commission, as State aid to SNCM.[54]

2.3 SELECTIVE ADVANTAGE FAVOURING CERTAIN UNDERTAKINGS OR THE PRODUCTION OF CERTAIN GOODS

Selective advantage favouring certain undertakings An economic advantage granted by the State or through State resources will only fall to be regarded as State aid within the meaning of Article 107(1) TFEU if it is such as to favour certain undertakings or the production of certain goods.[55] The favouring of certain undertakings or the production of certain goods is an essential prerequisite. In that regard, it is necessary to determine whether or not the measure in question entails advantages accruing exclusively to certain

---

[50] Case C-5/01 *Belgian v Commission* [2002] ECR I-11991, para 42.

[51] Case C-241/94, *France v Commission* [1996] ECR I-4551, para 37.

[52] *Twenty-Fourth Report on Competition Policy* (1994), pt. 501.

[53] Case C-241/94, *France v Commission* [1996] ECR I-4551, para 37.

[54] Cases C-533/12P & C-536/12P, *SNCM SA v Commission* EU:C:2014:2142 , para 71-73; Case T-565/08, *Corsica Ferries France sas v Commission* EU:T:2012:415, paras 138-146.

[55] Case C-279/08P, *Commission v Netherlands* [2011] ECR I-7671, para 61; Case T-538/11, *Belgium v Commission* EU:T:2015:188, para 101.

undertakings or certain sectors of activity.[56]   This may be seen as an application of the general principle of equal treatment.[57]

In relation to State measures that have general application, for Article 107(1) TFEU to be applicable, it must be determined that the measure is such as to favour certain undertakings or the production of certain goods compared to others which, in the light of the objective pursued by the system in question, are in a comparable legal and factual situation.[58] A measure will be considered selective if it is likely to create an advantage for one recipient while not doing so for other undertakings whose situation is comparable to that of the recipient.[59] The fact that aid is not aimed at one or more specific beneficiaries defined in advance, but the beneficiaries are identified pursuant to a number of objective criteria, does not mean that the measure in question does not confer a selective advantage on its beneficiaries.[60]

The condition of selectivity will normally be satisfied where specific undertakings are the sole beneficiaries of an *ad hoc* aid measure.[61] Where the aid is given by way of a direct financial grant to a particular beneficiary, it

---

[56]   Case C-241/94 *France* v *Commission* [1996] ECR I-4551, para 24, Case C-200/97 *Ecotrade* [1998] ECR I-7907, paras 40-41; Case C-75/97, *Belgium* v *Commission* ECR [1999] I-3671, para 26; Case C-15/14P, *Commission* v *MOL* EU:C:2015:362, para 60; Case T-55/99, *CETM* v *Commission* [2000] ECR II-3207, para 40.

[57]   Case C-353/95 P, *Tiercé Ladbroke* v *Commission* [1997] ECR I-7007, *per* Advocate General Cosmas, at p. 7021.

[58]   Case C-143/99 *Adria-Wien Pipeline and Wietersdorfer & Peggauer Zementwerke* [2001] ECR I-8365, para 41; Case C-409/00 *Spain* v *Commission* [2003] ECR I-1487, para 47; Case C-126/01, *Ministre de l'Economie* v *GEMO* [2003] ECR I-13769, para 35; Case C-308/01, *GIL Insurance Ltd. V Commissioners of Customs and Excise* [2004] ECR I-4777, para 68; Case C-172/03, *Heiser* v *Finanzamt Innsbruck* [2005] ECR I-1627, para 40; Case C-182/03 & C-217/03, *Belgium and Forum 187 ASBL* v *Commission* [2006] ECR I-5479, para 119; Case C-88/03, *Portugal* v *Commission* [2006] ECR I-7115, para 54; Cases C-428/06 & C-434/06, *Unión General de Trabajadores de la Rioja* v *Juntas Generales del Territorio Histórico de Vizcaya* [2008] ECR I-6747, para 46; Case C-487/06P, *British Aggregates Association* v *Commission* [2008] ECR I-10515, para 82; Case C-403/10P, *Mediaset SpA* v *Commission* [2011] ECR I-117*, para 36; Case C-279/08P, *Commission* v *Netherlands* [2011] ECR I-7671, para 62; Case C-518/13, *Eventech Ltd.* v *The Parking Adjudicator* EU:C:2015:9, para 55; Case C-672/13, *OTP Bank Nyrt* v *Hungary* EU:C:2015:185, para 45; Case T-233/04, *Netherlands* v *Commission* [2008] ECR I-591, para 86; Cases T-211/04 & T-215/04, *Government of Gibraltar* v *Commission* [2008] ECR II-3745, para 78; Case T-308/00 RENV, *Salzgitter AG* v *Commission* EU:T:2013:30, para 116; Cases T-226/09 & T-230/09, *British Telecommunications plc* v *Commission* EU:T:2013:466, para 86; Case T-399/11, *Banco Santander SA* v *Commission* EU:T:2014:938, para 33; Case T-219/10, *Autogrill España SA* v *Commission* EU:T:2014:939, para 29; Case T-538/11, *Belgium* v *Commission* EU:T:2015:188, para 102.

[59]   Case C-403/10P, *Mediaset SpA* v *Commission* [2011] ECR I-117*, para 62.

[60]   Case T-468/08, *Tisza Erőmű kft* v *Commission* EU:T:2014:235, para 164.

[61]   Case C-15/14P, *Commission* v *MOL* EU:C:2015:362, para 60; Case T-150/12, *Greece* v *Commission* EU:T:2014:191, para 104.

should be relatively obvious that a selective economic advantage has been granted. The General Court has held that there is no requirement to identify a reference framework comparing the beneficiary with other undertakings since that criterion of comparing the beneficiary with other undertakings in a comparable legal and factual situation in light of the objective pursued by the measure in question applies only to general measures. It is not pertinent in relation to determining the selectivity of an *ad hoc* measures relating to a single undertaking which seeks to modify certain competitive constraints that are specific to it.[62] Thus, the General Court held, in relation to legislation reducing pensions payments due specifically from France Télécom, that the measure concerned only that undertaking and was, by that fact alone, selective without it being necessary to determine whether the legislation introduced differential treatment between other telecoms operators finding themselves in a comparable legal and factual situation.[63]

Comparable legal and factual situation In establishing whether undertakings are in a comparable legal and factual situation, it is necessary, first, to identify the policy objective of the measure in question and, secondly, to identify those undertakings that are in a comparable legal and factual situation in the light of that objective. In *Netherlands v Commission*, a measure allowing for the trading of emissions allowances applied to all large industrial facilities, all of which were subject to an emission ceiling. The General Court accepted that the criterion for application of the measure in question was therefore an objective one, without any geographic or sectoral connotation. Only those undertakings covered by the scheme were obliged to comply with the emission standard. Both with regard to the objective pursued and the specific obligations imposed on large industrial facilities by the measure in question, the legal and factual situation of the undertakings subject to that emission ceiling could not be regarded as comparable to that of undertakings to which that ceiling did not apply. Thus, the measure in question, taken as a whole, did not favour certain undertakings or the production of certain goods in the sense of Article 107(1) TFEU.[64] On appeal, the ECJ held that the measure was selective on the basis that all undertakings in the Netherlands were subject in fact to emission restrictions. Large undertakings were in a position to monetise the economic value of the emission reductions that they achieved by converting them into tradable emission allowances, whereas other undertakings had no such possibility.[65] In *Mediaset v Commission*, the ECJ held that aid is

---

[62] Case T-135/12, *France v Commission* EU:T:2015:116, para 44; Case T-385/12, *Orange v Commission* EU:T:2015:117, para 53.

[63] Case T-135/12, *France v Commission* EU:T:2015:116, para 43; Case T-385/12, *Orange v Commission* EU:T:2015:117, para 52.

[64] Case T-233/04, *Netherlands v Commission* [2008] ECR II-591, paras 88-96.

[65] Case C-279/08P, *Commission v Netherlands* [2011] ECR I-7671, paras 63-64.

selectively granted where a measure subsidises the purchase by consumers of a product which is used by an undertaking for the provision of a service while the purchase of the product used by another undertaking for the provision of a similar service is not subsidised.[66] In *OTP Bank v Hungary*, the objective of the aid measure was to subsidise finance granted by Hungarian credit institutions in order to facilitate access to housing for certain categories of household. The ECJ held that this exclusively benefited Hungarian credit institutions, the households not being undertakings, and so was selective as other financial institutions did not benefit from the measure.[67] It was recognised, however, that an amendment to the applicable legislation provided for other economic operators also to benefit from the guarantee, such that the selective nature of the guarantee might be called into question.[68] In *Belgium v Commission*, where obligatory bovine tests were carried out free of charge by the public health authority, the General Court held that there was a selective advantage for the operators in question, since undertakings in other sectors were required to pay for such controls before being permitted to market their products.[69]

By contrast, in *Eventech v The Parking Adjudicator*, which concerned the use of bus lanes by London black cabs, which was prohibited to minicabs, the ECJ found that the two categories of taxi operators were not in a comparable legal and factual situation. It held that the identification of the factual and legal situation of black cabs and minicabs could not be confined to that prevailing in the market sector in which those two categories of conveyors of passengers were in direct competition, namely the pre-booking sector, but had to include all journeys made by these operators. Moreover, black cabs were subject to specific rules that did not apply to minicabs: only black cabs could ply for hire; they were subject to the rule of compellability; they must be recognisable and capable of conveying persons in wheelchairs; and their drivers must set the fares for their services by means of a taxi meter and have a particularly thorough knowledge of London. It followed that black cabs and minicabs were in factual and legal situations which were sufficiently distinct to permit the view that they are not comparable and that the bus lanes policy, therefore, did not confer a selective economic advantage on black cabs.[70]

General measures do not constitute State aid The criterion of selectivity applies to any measure which does not apply generally to all undertakings in a

[66]   Case C-403/10P, *Mediaset SpA v Commission* [2011] ECR I-117*, para 54.
[67]   Case C-672/13, *OTP Bank Nyrt v Hungary* EU:C:2015:185, paras 48-50.
[68]   *Ibid.*, para 59.
[69]   Case T-538/11, *Belgium v Commission* EU:T:2015:188, paras 110-111.
[70]   Case C-518/13, *Eventech Ltd. v The Parking Adjudicator* EU:C:2015:9, paras 59-61. For a further example of selectivity in the English courts, see *JC v The Crown* [2015] EWCA Crim 210.

comparable legal and factual situation.[71] It follows that a State measure that benefits all undertakings within the Member State cannot constitute State aid within Article 107(1) TFEU.[72] In other words, any economic advantage resulting from a general measure applicable without distinction to all economic operators does not constitute State aid.[73] Thus, in relation to a Swedish scheme which promoted employment by granting subsidies to encourage firms to take on long-term unemployed workers, the Commission concluded that there was no State aid within the meaning of Article 107(1) TFEU since the scheme was applicable to all sectors and any firm which met the criteria was automatically entitled to the subsidy.[74] Similarly, a Belgian measure providing for reductions in employers' social security contributions for firms which introduced shorter working hours was deemed to be a general measure.[75]

Since Article 107(1) TFEU does not apply to general measures applicable to all undertakings which meet objective, non-discriminatory and non-discretionary requirements, it is immaterial that only some undertakings choose to benefit from the measure, for that does not render a general measure selective in nature. It was recognised in *MOL v Commission* that this may simply result from an absence of interest of any other operator.[76] In *Hansestadt Lübeck v Commission*, which concerned a regulation setting out airport fees at Lübeck airport, the Commission determined that the fees entailed the selective grant of State aid since they were applicable only to airlines using that airport. However, the General Court disagreed, holding that the measure was general in nature since it applied to any airline using the airport.[77] In *Italy v Commission*, where a measure applied selectively to benefit certain undertakings, the argument that they could, under other procedures and at a later date, be granted the same advantages pursuant to other provisions of Italian law was not relevant, since the measure at issue amounted to a selective extension of those general schemes, granting specific

[71] B. Kurcz and D. Vallindas, "Can general measures be selective? Some thoughts on the interpretation of a State aid definition" [2008] CMLRev 159; A. Bartosch, "Is there a need for a rule of reason in European State aid law? or How to arrive at a coherent concept of material selectivity." [2010] CMLRev 729.

[72] Case C-143/99, *Adria-Wien Pipeline GmbH v Finanzlandesdirektion für Kärnten* [2001] ECR I-8365, para 35; Case T-233/04, *Netherlands v Commission* [2008] ECR I-591, para 85.

[73] Case C-66/02, *Italy v Commission* [2005] ECR I-10901, para 99; Case C-222/04, *Ministero dell'Economia e delle Finanze v Cassa di Risparmio di Firenze SpA* [2006] ECR I-289, para 135; Case T-461/12, *Hansestadt Lübeck v Commission* EU:T:2014:758, para 44.

[74] *Twenty-Eighth Report on Competition Policy* (1998), p. 270.

[75] *Thirty-First Report on Competition Policy* (2001), pt. 369.

[76] Case T-499/10, *MOL v Commission* EU:T:2013:592, para 66, approved on appeal in Case C-15/14P, *Commission v MOL* EU:C:2015:362, para 91.

[77] Case T-461/12, *Hansestadt Lübeck v Commission* EU:T:2014:758, paras 47-55.

advantages to certain undertakings and thereby reinforcing their financial position as compared with that of their competitors.[78]

General measures entailing disguised selectivity Measures potentially open to all undertakings may be deemed to constitute aid within Article 107(1) TFEU if the effect of ostensibly objective requirements is that only certain undertakings may benefit from the measure.[79] For example, an Italian restructuring aid scheme was in fact intended to benefit only one undertaking.[80] A Dutch tariff for the supply of energy which was available only to undertakings in one industrial sector by virtue of the fact that they alone could satisfy certain criteria was held to be sectoral in nature.[81] A proposal for a modification to the Danish Electricity Act with a view to allowing, in principle, all Danish electricity companies to cover past losses on their commercial activities other than production and supply of electricity, constituted State aid as only one company was in fact able to meet the objective requirements.[82]

In *Commission v Italy*, the Commission objected to the taking over by the State of a portion of employers' contributions payable in the case of industrial undertakings and certain undertakings in the services sector to their employees' sickness insurance fund. The contribution taken over by the State was four percent for male employees and ten percent for female employees. Such a system, which entailed a greater reduction in employers' contributions to the sickness insurance scheme for female employees than for male employees, was considered by the Commission to favour certain Italian industries employing large numbers of female employees, such as, in particular, those in the textile, clothing, footwear and leather-goods sector. The system was therefore regarded as constituting State aid to those industries.[83] In *GEMO*, where it was argued that the legislation in question applied generally, the ECJ held that the benefits of the legislation accrued largely to farmers and slaughterhouses.[84]

---

[78]   Cases T-239/04 & T-323/04, *Italy v Commission* [2007] ECR II-3265, para 69.
[79]   *Twenty-Fourth Report on Competition Policy* (1994), pt. 347.
[80]   Cases T-239/04 & T-323/04, *Italy v Commission* [2007] ECR II-3265, para 66.
[81]   Case C-169/84, *Cdf Chimie AZF v Commission* [1990] ECR I-3083, paras 22-23. This conclusion was not affected by the fact that one other undertaking also satisfied the criteria. Similarly, the General Court noted that although aid granted to a particular company may indirectly benefit other undertakings whose affairs depend on its activities, it did not follow that the measure in question was general in nature: Case T-67/94, *Ladbroke Racing Ltd. v Commission* [1998] ECR II-1, para 79.
[82]   *Twenty-Fourth Report on Competition Policy* (1994), p. 513.
[83]   Case 203/82, *Commission v Italy* [1983] ECR 2525, para 4.
[84]   Case C-126/01, *Ministre de l'Economie, des finances et de l'industrie v GEMO* SA [2003] ECR I-13769, para 38; Case C-15/14P, *Commission v MOL* EU:C:2015:362, para 78.

Measures applicable to a whole economic sector Measures may be selective even though they concern a whole economic sector. In *Adria-Wien Pipleline*, a derogation from the normal rate of taxation for the entire manufacturing sector was regarded as entailing State aid.[85] Moreover, a measure which is selective cannot be considered as a general measure even though a Member State may intend ultimately to extend its application to the entire economy.[86] In *Italy v Commission* and *Unicredito Italiano v Agenzia delle Entrate*, certain tax measures applied to the Italian banking sector. The ECJ held that the fact that, in some circumstances, they might also benefit entities which were not undertakings did not call into question that finding, which was sufficient for Article 107(1) TFEU to apply to the aid scheme. In any event, within the banking sector, the measures at issue benefited only the undertakings carrying out the operations covered by the measures. It followed that the measures were selective in relation to other economic sectors and within the banking sector itself.[87] In *Belgium v Commission*, the ECJ held that a measure aimed at promoting the creation of jobs by reducing, for certain undertakings, social security contributions was to be regarded as State aid and that neither the high number of benefiting undertakings nor the diversity and importance of those industrial sectors to which the undertakings belonged warranted the conclusion that the scheme constituted a general measure.[88] Similarly, a Spanish scheme to assist in the purchase of commercial vehicles by natural persons, SMEs, regional public bodies and bodies providing local public services was selective since large undertakings were excluded from the scope of the scheme.[89]

Subsequent alterations to associated general measures Whether State aid has been granted must normally be assessed on the basis of the legal provisions applicable at the time the measure takes effect, regardless of subsequent alterations to associated general measures. In *MOL v Commission*, Hungarian legislation concerning the fees to be charged in relation to oil and gas

---

[85] Case C-143/99, *Adria-Wien Pipeline GmbH v Finanzlandesdirektion für Kärnten* [2001] ECR I-8365, para 55.

[86] Case C-75/97, *Belgium v Commission* [1999] ECR I-3671, para 41; Case C-672/13, *OTP Bank Nyrt v Hungary* EU:C:2015:185, para 49.

[87] Case C-66/02, *Italy v Commission* [2005] ECR I-10901, paras 95-98; Case C-148/04, *Unicredito Italiano SpA v Agenzia delle Entrate, Ufficio Genova 1* [2005] ECR I-11137, paras 45-49; Case T-445/05, *Associazione Italiana del Risparmio Gestito v Commission* [2009] ECR II-289, para 155; Case T-424/05, *Italy v Commission* [2009] ECR II-23*, para 129.

[88] Case C-75/97, *Belgium v Commission* [1999] ECR I-3671, paras 32-34. See also Case C-143/99, *Adria-Wien Pipeline GmbH v Finanzlandesdirektion für Kärnten* [2001] ECR I-8365, para 48; Case C-409/00, *Spain v Commission* [2003] ECR I-1487, para 48; Case C-172/03, *Heiser v Finanzamt Innsbruck* [2005] ECR I-1627, para 42; Case T-55/99, *CETM v Commission* [2000] ECR II-3207, para 52.

[89] Case C-409/00, *Spain v Commission* [2003] ECR I-1487, para 50; Case T-55/99, *CETM v Commission* [2000] ECR II-3207, para 47.

exploration provided, generally, that mining fees were to be fixed at 12% of the quantity mined. In addition, where an extension of the mining licence was requested, a contract was to be agreed with the Mining Authority, whereby the fee would be increased to not more than 1.2 times that rate. In 2005, MOL entered into such an agreement in respect of a licence that was applicable for five years. Subsequently, from 2008, the legislation was altered to provide for a general rate of 30% of the value of the quantity mined. The Commission determined that the 2005 agreement should be assessed in the light not only of the legislation in force at the time it was entered into but also in the light of the 2008 amendment, with the result that, since the 2005 agreement benefited only one company, it selectively favoured MOL. The General Court rejected this analysis, holding that subsequent conditions external to the agreement could not affect the State aid analysis of the agreement in 2005.[90] Nevertheless, the General Court noted that a combination of elements may be categorised as State aid where the State acts in such a way as to protect one or more operators already present on the market, by concluding with them an agreement granting them fee rates guaranteed for the entire duration thereof, whilst having the intention at that time of subsequently exercising its regulatory power, by increasing the fee rate so that other market operators are placed at a disadvantage, be they operators already present on the market on the date on which the agreement was concluded or new operators.[91]

Discretionary general measures   Selectivity may arise where the public authorities can decide on a discretionary basis which and/or to what extent undertakings may benefit from a general measure.[92] Thus, where the body granting financial assistance enjoys a degree of latitude which enables it to choose the beneficiaries or the conditions under which the financial assistance is provided, that assistance cannot be considered to be general in nature.[93] In *Ecotrade Srl v AFS*, Italian legislation establishing a system of special administration to enable certain large industrial firms to continue trading despite being insolvent was held to be capable of constituting State aid. Firms placed under special administration were granted various advantages, in addition to the protection from creditors applicable under normal insolvency rules. The ECJ held that, having regard to the discretion permitted to the authorities to determine which firms would benefit from these provisions, the

---

[90]   Case T-499/10, *MOL v Commission* EU:T:2013:592, para 64.

[91]   *Ibid.*, para 67.

[92]   Case 241/94, *France v Commission* [1996] ECR I-4551, paras 23-24; Case C-256/97, *Déménagements-Manutention Transport SA* [1999] ECR I-3913, para 27; Cases T-127/99, T-129/99 &T-148/99, *Territorio Histórico de Álava - Diputación Foral de Álava v Commission* [2002] ECR II-1275, para 149; Case T-152/99, *Hijos de Andrés Molina SA v Commission* [2002] ECR II-3049, para 157.

[93]   Case C-256/97, *Déménagements-Manutention Transport SA* [1999] ECR I-3913, para 27; Case C-6/12, *P Oy* EU:C:2013:525, para 25.

requirement of selectivity was satisfied.[94] The favoured group need not be specified in the rules of the scheme or be readily identifiable. It is sufficient that the scheme could benefit certain firms particularly, though these are not identifiable in advance.[95] Thus, in *France v Commission*, French legislation whereby redundancy payments could be made at the discretion of a public body was held to be State aid.[96]

Where the margin of discretion is transparent and non-discriminatory, the exercise of discretion should not give rise to State aid. In *Commission v MOL*, the ECJ held that there is a fundamental difference between, on the one hand, the assessment of the selectivity of general schemes for exemption or relief, which, by definition, confer an advantage, and, on the other, the assessment of the selectivity of optional provisions of national law prescribing the imposition of additional charges. In cases in which the national authorities impose such charges in order to maintain equal treatment between operators, the simple fact that those authorities enjoy discretion defined by law, and not unlimited, is not sufficient to establish that the corresponding scheme is selective.[97] In that case, in which Hungarian legislation on fees for the extraction of oil and gas provided for a certain negotiation with the Mining Authority, a margin of discretion in fixing the level of fees was justified by various factors, such as the number of fields involved and their estimated importance in relation to the fields already in production. In the circumstances, the margin of assessment enabled the administration to preserve equal treatment between operators.[98]

Derogations from general measures Advocate General Saggio commented that it does not seem possible to identify with any degree of certainty a criterion of a general nature which provides a clear demarcation line between general and selective measures.[99] Particular difficulty arises in determining whether a measure which derogates from a general measure may itself be regarded as a separate general measure or whether it should be considered as selective.[100] In *Sloman Neptune*, Advocate General Darmon thought that, for a

---

[94] Case C-200/97, *Ecotrade Srl v AFS* [1998] ECR I-7907, para 40; Case C-295/97, *Piaggio SpA v Ifitalia SpA* [1999] ECR I-3735, para 39; Case C-297/01, *Sicilcassa SpA v IRA Construzioni SpA* [2003] ECR I-7849, para 37.

[95] *Twenty-Third Report on Competition Policy* (1993), pt. 390. In his opinion in Case C-379/98, *Preussen Elektra AG v Schleswag AG* [2001] ECR I-2099, at p. 2143, Advocate General Jacobs noted that it was unclear from the judgments in *Ecotrade* and *Piaggio* whether the aid measure in question was the insolvency legislation itself or the individual decision to place an undertaking in special administration.

[96] Case 241/94, *France v Commission* [1996] ECR I-4551, para 24.

[97] Case C-15/14P, *Commission v MOL* EU:C:2015:362, para 64.

[98] *Ibid.*, para 65; Case T-499/10, *MOL v Commission* EU:T:2013:592, para 72.

[99] Cases C-400/97-C402/97, *Administración del Estado v Juntas Generales de Guipúzcoa* [2000] ECR I-1073, *per* Advocate General Saggio at para 33.

[100] See K. Bacon, "State aids and general measures" (1997) 17 YEL 269.

derogating measure to be considered as general in nature, the fundamental precondition was that the measure should constitute a derogation, by virtue of its actual nature, from the scheme of the general system in which it was set.[101] He developed this approach in *Kirsammer-Hack v Sidal*, which concerned an exemption for small businesses from the German legislation on unfair dismissals. In his opinion, the crucial question was to identify the criterion which determines whether a measure is general or normal. It could be argued that the general rule was that workers receive legal protection and that the exemption for small businesses constituted an exception. It was also quite possible to argue that the provision constituted a general measure and that it should be inquired whether exemptions existed within it favouring particular categories of workers or undertakings. However, whichever criterion was taken to establish the general nature of the system, if the justification for the exemption could be established on the basis of the nature of the general system, that exemption would not be regarded as aid. He concluded that, in the context of the law on unfair dismissal, it was wholly justifiable to have special provisions concerning small businesses. These special provisions therefore formed part of the general system and did not amount to selective aid within the meaning of Article 107(1) TFEU.[102]

Derogations justified by the nature of the system　Derogations from general measures will not be regarded as selective where they are justified on the basis of the nature or general scheme of the system.[103]　This principle was first recognised by the ECJ in *Italy v Commission*, concerning a reduction in social security contributions for undertakings in the textiles industry, where it held that the reduction was a measure intended to grant exemption from the charges arising from the normal application of the system without there being any justification for the exemption on the basis of the nature or general scheme of the system.[104]　Accordingly, the Commission approved a Danish scheme aimed at encouraging employers to improve working conditions beyond the requirements of compulsory employment legislation.　Under the scheme, a company active on land, including road transport firms (as opposed to offshore operations and shipping and air transport companies) could receive a grant to

---

[101]　Cases C-72-73/91, *Sloman Neptun SchiffartsAG v Seebetriebsrat Bodo Ziesemer* [1993] ECR I-887, *per* Advocate General Darmon, at p. 915.

[102]　Case C-189/91, *Kirsammer-Hack v Sidal* [1993] ECR I-6185, *per* Advocate General Darmon, at p. 6206.

[103]　Case C-143/99, *Adria-Wien Pipeline GmbH v Finanzlandesdirektion für Kärnten* [2001] ECR I-8365, para 42; Case C-431/07P, *Bouygues SA v Commission* [2009] ECR I-2665, para 42; Case C-279/08P, *Commission v Netherlands* [2011] ECR I-7671, para 63; Case T-442/03, *SIC v Commission* [2008] ECR II-1161, para 64; Case T-52/12, *Greece v Commission* EU:T:2014:677, para 86; Case T-538/11, *Belgium v Commission* EU:T:2015:188, para 103.

[104]　Case 173/73, *Italy v Commission* [1974] ECR 709, para 15.

compensate for a working environment tax. The Commission accepted that the differentiation between land-based firms and others could be justified by the nature and general scheme of the system.[105]

In *SIC v Commission*, the Portuguese public broadcasting operator was transformed from a public undertaking into a public limited company by means of legislation, thereby avoiding registration and notarial charges which would normally occur on the formation of a company. The General Court held that the Commission should have examined whether it was compatible with the logic of the Portuguese legal system for the transformation of public undertakings into public limited companies to occur by legislation, or whether the recourse to legislation for such operations constituted a derogation which was intended to confer an advantage on public undertakings in relation to other undertakings.[106] By contrast, in *Netherlands v Commission*, the General Court, having held that an emissions allowance trading system applicable to large undertakings was not selective because it applied to all comparable undertakings, nevertheless went on to state that even if the view were to be taken that the measure in question differentiated between undertakings and was, therefore, in principle selective, it would have to be held that that differentiation arose from the nature or overall structure of the scheme of which it was part whereby ecological considerations justified distinguishing undertakings which emitted large quantities of nitrous oxides from other undertakings.[107] On appeal, holding that the measures was in fact selective as involving differential treatment between large and smaller undertakings, the ECJ held that a differentiation between undertakings based on a quantitative criterion, in that case being a thermal capacity of more than 20 MWth, could not be regarded as inherent to a scheme having an environmental objective of reducing industrial pollution.[108]

General measures allowing undertakings a choice The mere fact that different undertakings are subjected to different regimes in relation to a particular factor of production does not necessarily mean that this involves any selective advantage. In *Banks v Coal Authority*, operators concerned in the extraction of coal in the United Kingdom subsequent to privatisation of the coal industry had to pay royalties to the Coal Authority in respect of licences and leases. Royalties could be agreed either as a capital sum, a flat-rate rent, or the payment of rent linked to the tonnage of coal extracted. No formula appeared to be more advantageous in principle than another. Instead, the possible advantage of one formula rather than another, all of which were accessible to all the operators without discrimination, depended on a number of

---

[105] *Thirty-First Report on Competition Policy* (2001), pt. 381.
[106] Case T-442/03, *SIC v Commission* [2008] ECR II-1161, paras 66-70.
[107] Case T-233/04, *Netherlands v Commission* [2008] ECR II-591, paras 97-99.
[108] Case C-279/08P, *Commission v Netherlands* [2011] ECR I-7671, paras 76-78.

economic, technical, commercial and financial parameters relying largely upon forecasts which it was for the various operators to assess. Any advantage or disadvantage *vis-à-vis* an operator's competitors resulted directly from the operation of competition and the accuracy of the operators' forecasts.[109]

Financing of infrastructure   Investment in public infrastructure which benefits undertakings generally, rather than one or more specific undertakings, is regarded as a general measure which does not amount to State aid.[110]   Thus, public finance to develop infrastructural works which might be used by firms locating in Isère in France was held not to constitute the provision of aid to Saint Gobain which set up a plant there.[111]   Measures assisting investment in infrastructure in Portugal which benefited a manufacturing joint venture between Volkswagen and Ford was held not to involve State aid, since they would not benefit the joint venture exclusively.[112]   Financing of transport infrastructure, such as roads and canals built and maintained by the public authorities, does not constitute State aid.[113]   On the other hand, the construction, management and provision of infrastructure may constitute an economic activity for the purposes of Article 107(1) TFEU.[114]   In *Mitteldeutsche Flughafen v Commission*, it was held that the construction of a new runway at Leipzig-Halle airport could not be dissociated from the operation of the airport infrastructure, which was an economic activity. In those circumstances, it was unnecessary to determine whether there was a specific market for the activity of airport infrastructure construction. It

---

[109] Case C-390/98, *HJ Banks & Co Ltd. v Coal Authority* [2001] ECR I-6177, paras 48-50. Note, however, the Commission's decision concerning the Italian public broadcaster, where it held that the reduction in concession fees payable by RAI did not constitute aid because it merely reduced the advantage of its private competitors which paid even lower fees: *Twenty-Ninth Report on Competition Policy* (1999), pt. 229.

[110] Moreover, insofar as State aid may arise in the context of financing the construction or upgrade of local infrastructure, other than dedicated infrastructure, that contributes at a local level to improving the business and consumer environment and modernising and developing the industrial base, it is compatible with the internal market and block exempted up to €10 million: Commission Regulation (EU) No 651/2014, Article 56.

[111] Commission Decision 91/390, *Saint Gobain (Eurofloat)*, OJ 1991 L315/11.

[112] Case C-225/91, *Matra SA v Commission* [1993] ECR I-3203, para 29.

[113] Case C-164/02, *Netherlands v Commission* [2004] ECR I-1177, para 7, quoting Commission Decision N 812/2001.

[114] Case C-82/01P, *Aéroports de Paris v Commission* [2002] ECR I-9297, para 78; Case C-288/11P, *Mitteldeutsche Flughafen AG v Commission* EU:C:2012:821, para 43; Case T-128/98, *Aéroports de Paris v Commission* [2001] ECR II-3929, paras 108-118; Cases T-443/08 & T-455/08, *Freistaat Sachsen v Commission* [2011] ECR II-1311, paras 94-100.   See J. Rapp & T. Kleiner, Infrastructure funding: the new frontier in the application of State aid rules." [2013] PPLRev 1.

followed that public financing of the construction of the runway was capable of being classified as State aid.[115]

The grant of capital to a public company in order to fund infrastructure investment does not constitute State aid where the development of the infrastructure is otherwise the responsibility of the public authorities.[116] In its decision on *Infraleuna Infrastruktur*, the Commission allowed grants to be paid to a company set up on the Leuna chemical site whose production facilities had been privatised and sold to one hundred different investors. The objective of Infraleuna, whose shares were mostly owned by the public sector, was to set up and manage all the infrastructure for the site for the benefit of the companies located there. It had also been given the task of clearing the site, which was the responsibility of the public authorities which had sold the plots at the market price for a developed site. The Commission found that, since it was impossible to find a private investor for the infrastructure, setting up Infraleuna was the only alternative available and that the initial capital injection for the company did not constitute State aid.[117] Similarly, the Commission approved a scheme for the provision of infrastructure in Wales which was designed to overcome economic structural difficulties in the market for business premises.[118]

Public financing of costs inherent in the preparation of a building site or an industrial site and in providing connections to various utility services does not fall within Article 107(1) TFEU if the company pays for the use of the infrastructure through direct or indirect charges.[119] In its decision in *Daimler Benz*, the Commission, therefore, decided that no aid was granted in the provision of a site where the company would contribute to the costs through local taxes.[120] However, where preparation of a site for setting up a new production facility benefited the Kimberley Clark company alone, which was the sole owner and user of the installations put in place, the partial public financing provided constituted an aid to that company.[121] Similarly, in its decision on the English Partnerships scheme, the Commission held that State aid was involved where State funding was provided to cover the difference

---

[115] Case C-288/11P, *Mitteldeutsche Flughafen AG v Commission* EU:C:2012:821, paras 46-49; Cases T-443/08 & T-455/08, *Freistaat Sachsen v Commission* [2011] ECR II-1311, paras 111-114.

[116] Case N 478/2004, *Irish Rail*, OJ 2006 C209/8.

[117] Commission Decision 1999/646/EC, *Infraleuna GmbH*, OJ 1999 L260/1.

[118] *Thirtieth Report on Competition Policy* (2000), pt. 317.

[119] *Seventeenth Report of Competition Policy* (1988), p. 220; *Twenty-Fifth Report of Competition Policy* (1995), pt. 158.

[120] Commission Decision 92/465/EEC, *Daimler Benz*, OJ 1992 L263/15.

[121] *Twenty-Fifth Report of Competition Policy* (1995), pt. 158.

between the development costs of certain regeneration sites and their subsequent market value.[122]

In order to help achieve the proper functioning of the internal market and to encourage economic and social cohesion, the EU may contribute to the establishment and development of trans-European networks in the areas of transport, telecommunications and energy infrastructures.[123] Action by the EU to promote the interconnection and interoperability of national networks as well as access to these networks is to take place within the framework of open and competitive markets. Thus, the Commission accepted, for example, that the United Kingdom did not grant State aid in the financing of the construction, maintenance and management of the Channel Tunnel rail link where the private sector partner was chosen through a transparent and non-discriminatory tender procedure.[124]

2.4 DISTORTION OF COMPETITION

Distortion of competition Aid must distort or threaten to distort competition by favouring certain undertakings or the production of certain goods for it to come within the scope of Article 107(1) TFEU. It is not necessary for there to be actual proof of distortion of competition, since it is sufficient to show that the measure threatens to distort competition.[125] Nor is there any need to prove anti-competitive practices on the part of the recipient of the aid.[126] In *Orange v Commission*, the General Court rejected an argument that the aid in question was necessary to allow France Télécom to deal with its competitive handicap on the telecommunications market in France, holding that this clearly affected

---

[122] *Twenty-Ninth Report on Competition Policy* (1999), p. 227. If a public authority purchases land, incurs the costs of development and then sells the developed site at market value, the Commission should not regard any State aid as inherent in the disposal, in line with its practice as set out in the communication on sales of land and buildings by public authorities, OJ 1997 L209/3. See also R. D'Sa, "When is aid not State aid? The implication of the *English Partnerships* decision for European competition law and policy." (2000) 25 ELRev 139. See also, the decision of the Northern Ireland High Court in *Peninsula Securities Limited* [1998] EuLR 699.

[123] Article 170(1) TFEU.

[124] *Twenty-Sixth Report on Competition Policy* (1996), p. 231.

[125] Case C-301/87, *France v Commission* [1990] ECR I-307, para 33; Case C-494/06P, *Commission v Italy* [2009] ECR I-3639, para 49; Case T-214/95, *Vlaams Gewest v Commission* [1998] ECR II-717, para 54; Case T-288/97, *Regione Autonoma Friuli Venezia Giulia v Commission* [2001] ECR II-1169, paras 49-50; Case T-35/99, *Keller SpA v Commission* [2002] ECR II-261, para 85; Cases T-239/04 & T-323/04, *Italy v Commission* [2007] ECR II-3265, para 127; Case T-238/09, *Sniace SA v Commission* [2011] ECR II-430*, para 77.

[126] Cases T-231/06 & T-237/06, *Netherlands v Commission* [2010] ECR II-5993, para 123.

competition on the market.[127] In the case of an aid programme, the Commission may confine itself to examining the characteristics of the programme in question in order to determine whether, by reason of the high amounts or percentages of aid, the nature of the investments for which aid is granted or other terms of the programme, it gives an appreciable advantage to recipients in relation to their competitors and is likely to benefit in particular undertakings engaged in trade between Member States.[128] The fact that competitors of the beneficiary of the aid receive State aid, even illegal aid, is irrelevant in classifying the measure as aid.[129]

In the application of Article 107(1) TFEU, the point of departure is the competitive position existing within the internal market before the adoption of the measure in issue. This pre-existing competitive position of undertakings in the market is the result of numerous factors having varying effects on production costs, such as investment costs, operating costs and taxation, so that the unilateral modification of a particular factor of the cost of production may have the effect of disturbing the existing equilibrium.[130] In principle, aid that releases an undertaking from costs which it would normally have to bear in its day to day management or normal activities distorts the conditions of competition.[131] Competitors may be established in the same Member State as the recipient of the aid or in other Member States, since the issue is not where those competitors are established but whether the aid distorts competition.

In *Heiser*, it was argued that there was no distortion of competition on the ground that the medical practitioners who benefited from the aid measure did not face competition based on prices. The ECJ held that, even if the choice of

---

[127] Case T-385/12, *Orange v Commission* EU:T:2015:117, paras 63-64.

[128] Case 248/84, *Germany v Commission* [1987] ECR 4013, para 18.

[129] Case T-214/95, *Vlaams Gewest v Commission* [1998] ECR II-717, para 54.

[130] Case 173/73, *Italy v Commission* [1974] ECR 709, para 17.

[131] Case C-86/89, *Italy v Commission* [1990] ECR I-3891, para 18; Case C-301/87, *France v Commission* [1990] ECR I-307, para 50; Case C-278/95P, *Seimens v Commission* [1997] ECR I-2507, para 37; Case C-156/98, *Germany v Commission* [2000] ECR I-6857, para 30; Case C-288/96, *Germany v Commission* [2000] ECR I-8237, para 77; Case C-172/03, *Heiser v Finanzamt Innsbruck* [2005] ECR I-1627, para 55; Case C-494/06P, *Commission v Italy* [2009] ECR I-3639, para 53; Cases C-71/09P, C-73/09P & C-76/09P, *Comitato Venezia vuole vivere v Commission* [2011] ECR I-4727, para 136; Case C-458/09P, *Italy v Commission* [2011] ECR I-179*, para 63; Case T-459/93, *Siemens v Commission* [1995] ECR II-1675, para 48; Case T-214/95 *Vlaamse Gewest* v *Commission* [1998] ECR II-717, para 43; Case T-190/00, *Regione Siciliana v Commission* [2003] ECR II-5015, para 130; Case T-217/02, *Ter Lembeek International NV v Commission* [2006] ECR II-4483, para 177; Case T-375/03, *Fachvereinigung Mineralfaserindustrie eV v Commission* [2007] ECR II-121*, para 139; Case T-348/04, *SIDE v Commission* [2008] ECR I-625, para 99; Case T-162/06, *Kronoply GmbH v Commission* [2009] ECR II-1, para 75; Case T-379/09, *Italy v Commission* EU:T:2012:422, para 89; Case T-243/09, *Fedecom v Commission* EU:T:2012:497, para 86; Case T-308/11, *Eurallumina SpA v Commission* EU:T:2014:894, para 85; Case T-177/10, *Alcoa Trasformazioni srl v Commission* EU:T:2014:897, para 92.

a medical practitioner by patients may be influenced by criteria other than the price of the medical treatment, such as its quality and the confidence placed in the medical practitioner, the fact none the less remained that the price was liable to have an influence, or even a substantial influence, on the choice of medical practitioner by the patient, particularly where the patient had to pay most of the cost of the treatment out of his own pocket.[132]

Relevant market Establishing a distortion of competition presupposes, where necessary, the correct identification of the relevant product market and the relevant geographic market, although not in the detailed analytical manner that applies in cases subject to competition law generally. In *Philip Morris v Commission*, where the Commission refused to allow the grant of investment aid to a major tobacco manufacturer in the Netherlands, it was argued that the Commission should, by analogy with Articles 101 and 102 TFEU, have identified the relevant market and the patterns of trade between competitors in order to determine how far the aid in question might affect relations between competitors. The ECJ merely noted that Philip Morris, following the proposed investment, would account for 50% of cigarette production in the Netherlands of which 80% was to be exported and that when financial aid strengthens the position of an undertaking compared with other undertakings competing in intra-EU trade, the latter must be regarded as affected by that aid[133] That implicitly identified the product market as being the market for cigarette production in which Philip Morris competed with other undertakings.[134] Other cases have also recognised the notion that the product market should be properly identified. For instance, in *Exécutif Régional Wallon v Commission*, where the Commission had identified the relevant market as being flat glass production, the ECJ rejected the applicant's contention that the investment in question was intended to promote the production and marketing of a new product constituting a separate product market.[135] In *ACEA v Commission*, it was argued that aid in the form of a tax exemption granted to certain public utility companies did not distort competition since there was no competition as contracts for the services in question were in fact awarded directly to the companies. The General Court held, on the contrary, that the fact that contracts are awarded directly demonstrated the restrictive effects on competition and not the absence of competition on the market.[136]

---

[132] Case C-172/03, *Heiser v Finanzamt Innsbruck* [2005] ECR I-1627, paras 56-57.

[133] Case 730/79, *Philip Morris v Commission* [1980] ECR 2671, paras 10-11.

[134] Case 730/79, *Philip Morris v Commission* [1980] ECR 2671, per Advocate General Capotorti, at p. 2700.

[135] Cases 62 & 72/87, *Exécutif Régional Wallon v Commission* [1988] ECR 1573, para 15.

[136] Case T-297/02, *ACEA SpA v Commission* [2009] ECR II-1683, para 92; Case T-301/02, *AEM SpA v Commission* [2009] ECR II-1757, para 100; Case T-295/12, *Germany v Commission* EU:T:2014:675, para 158; Case T-309/12, *Zweckverband Tierkörperbeseitigung v Commission* EU:T:2104:676, para 204.

Distortion of competition may take place on an adjacent market. In *SIDE v Commission*, the General Court annulled a Commission decision concerning aid for exports of French-language books, on the ground that the Commission should have analysed the distortion of competition in relation to the market for agency services for the export of such books rather than the market for the books themselves.[137] In *Holland Malt v Commission*, the General Court rejected on the facts an argument that the aid was intended for the development of premium malt which was separate from the ordinary malt market and in which the aid recipient had no EU competitors.[138] In *FAB v Commission*, aid for broadcasters was regarded as also capable of distorting competition at the level of the network.[139]

In *Kronofrance v Commission*, the General Court examined the notion of the correct geographic market. In its decision concerning the furniture manufacturing market including wood boards and panels which are heavy and bulky products, the Commission had considered that long-distance transport was too costly and that the transport radius was therefore limited to around 800 km from the producer's place of establishment, it none the less concluded that the relevant geographic market was the EEA. In that regard, the General Court held that if an undertaking competes in its natural supply area with other undertakings whose supply areas overlap with its own, since each of those undertakings has its own radius of supply, competition by an undertaking with those within its radius tends to extend to their natural supply areas and it may therefore be appropriate to consider the EU as a whole, or the EEA, to be the reference geographic market.[140]

Presumption of distortion of competition Although the relevant market must be properly identified, that does not necessarily impose on the Commission an obligation to define the market in detail or to analyse its structure and the ensuing competitive relationships. The Commission merely needs to establish that the aid in question is of such a kind as to affect trade between Member States and distorts or threatens to distort competition, without the need for detailed analysis of the sector in question.[141] Distortion of competition may be

---

[137] Case T-155/98, *SIDE v Commission* [2002] ECR II-1179, para 71.

[138] Case T-369/06, *Holland Malt BV v Commission* [2009] ECR II-3313, para 44.

[139] Case T-8/06, *FAB GmbH v Commission* [2009] ECR II-196*, para 55.

[140] Case T-27/02, *Kronofrance SA v Commission* [2004] ECR II-4177, para 42.

[141] Case 730/79, *Philip Morris v Commission* [1980] ECR 2671, para 12; Cases 62 & 72/87, *Exécutif Régional Wallon v Commission* [1988] ECR 1573, para 18; Case C-494/06P, *Commission v Italy and Wam* [2009] ECR I-3639, para 50; Case C-150/09P, *Iride SpA v Commission* [2010] ECR I-5*, para 72; Case C-480/09P, *AceaElectrabel Produzione SpA v Commission* [2010] ECR I-13355, para 102; Cases T-298/97 etc. *Alzetta v Commission* [2000] ECR II-2319, para 95; Case T-25/07, *Iride SpA v Commission* [2009] ECR II-245, para 68; Case T-369/06, *Holland Malt BV v Commission* [2009] ECR II-3313, para 63; Cases T-226/09 & T-230/09, *British Telecommunications plc v*

easily presumed. In *Philip Morris v Commission*, the ECJ held that, when State aid strengthens the position of an undertaking compared with other undertakings competing in intra-EU trade, the latter must be regarded as affected by that aid.[142] Thus, for example, in *Kahla/Thüringen Porzellan GmbH v Commission*, the General Court merely noted approvingly that the Commission had found that the porcelain market was a highly competitive European product market suffering from overcapacity and that, therefore, financial advantages favouring one undertaking over its competitors threatened to distort competition.[143] In *Italy v Commission*, aid was granted to an undertaking which was part of a group that was the fifth largest in the electrical household appliances industry in Europe, a sector which was marked by a particular degree of exposure to competition.[144]

Distortion of competition and individual aid In *Hotel Cipriani v Commission*, the General Court stated that it was clear from the case law that the requirements concerning the analysis of the Commission of the effect of an aid measure on distortion of competition and trade between Member States varied, very logically, according to the individual or general nature of the measure. In relation to individual aid, the Commission was required to give a specific economic analysis of the market, taking into consideration the size of the recipient, its exports and the amount of the aid, as had been the case in *Philip Morris v Commission*.[145] For example, in *Germany v Commission*, concerning aid for shipbuilding, the ECJ annulled the Commission's decision for providing no information whatsoever as to the situation on the market, the recipient's share of that market or the position of competing undertakings.[146] In *Le Levant v Commission*, the General Court criticised the Commission's decision for not explaining how and on what market competition was affected or likely to be affected by the aid.[147] In *Belgium v Commission*, since the recipient exported about 40% of its output to other Member States and excess production capacity existed in the market in question, the Commission was

---

Commission EU:T:2013:466, para 179; Case T-58/13, *Club Hotel Loutraki AE v Commission* EU:T:2015:1, para 88.

[142] Case 730/79, *Philip Morris v Commission* [1980] ECR 2671, para 11; Case C-53/00, *Ferring SA v ACOSS* [2001] ECR I-9067, para 21; Case C-310/99, *Italy v Commission* [2002] ECR I-2289, para 84; Case C-126/01, *Ministre de l'économie, des finances et de l'industrie v GEMO* [2003] ECR I-13769, para 41.

[143] Case T-20/03, *Kahla/Thüringen Porzellan GmbH v Commission* [2008] ECR II-2305, para 200.

[144] Cases T-239/04 & T-323/04, *Italy v Commission* [2007] ECR II-3265, para 68.

[145] Cases T-254/00, T-270/00 & T-277/00, *Hotel Cipriani SpA v Commission* [2008] ECR I-3269, paras 227-228.

[146] Cases C-329/93, C-62/95 & C-63/95, *Germany v Commission* [1996] ECR I-5151, para 53.

[147] Case T-34/02, *Le Levant 001 v Commission* [2005] ECR II-267, para 123.

entitled to conclude that aid, which had the effect of reducing the recipient's financial costs in comparison with its competitors, distorted or threatened to distort competition in the internal market.[148] In *KG Holding v Commission*, the General Court held, in a case regarding rescue and restructuring aid, that the Commission had set out sufficient facts by indicating the size of the aid involved, the size of the recipient, in terms of employees and capitalisation, and by referring to specified international players on the market on which the recipient was operating.[149] Similarly, in *Budapesti Erőmű Zrt v Commission*, concerning aid granted through long term electricity purchase agreements, the General Court held that the effect of the agreements being to prevent imports from other electricity sources was sufficient to establish a link between the economic advantage granted by the agreements and the impact on competition and trade between Member States.[150]

Distortion of competition and aid schemes In *Hotel Cipriani v Commission*, the General Court held that the Commission could not limit itself to an abstract analysis when considering sectoral aid schemes, but had to establish special factors relating, for example, to the characteristics of the aid scheme or the market concerned, in order to assess the effect of the aid.[151] On the other hand, with regard to multisectoral schemes, the Commission could merely study the characteristics of the programme in order to assess whether, by reason of the large amounts or high percentage of the aid, the characteristics of the investment being supported or other arrangements provided for under the programme, the scheme gave an appreciable advantage to recipients in relation to their competitors and was likely to benefit in particular undertakings engaged in trade between Member States. It followed that, in the case of an aid scheme applicable to all undertakings in a territory, the Commission was not required to show, on the basis of even a summary examination of the situation on the markets, that the scheme would have a foreseeable effect on trade between Member States and competition in all of the sectors concerned.[152]

On appeal, in *Comitato Venezia vuole vivere v Commission*, however, the ECJ emphasised that, although the Commission was not therefore required to carry out an analysis of the aid granted in individual cases, the individual situation of each undertaking would need to be verified at the recovery stage.[153] Consequently, before proceeding to recovery, the national authorities are required to verify, in each individual case, whether the advantage granted is, in

---

[148] Case 234/84, *Belgium v Commission* [1986] ECR 2263, para 22.
[149] Cases T-81/07 to T-83/07, *KG Holding NV v Commission* [2009] ECR II-2411, para 65.
[150] Cases T-80/06 & T-182/09, *Budapesti Erőmű Zrt v Commission* EU:T:2012:65, para 98.
[151] Cases T-254/00, T-270/00 & T-277/00, *Hotel Cipriani SpA v Commission* [2008] ECR I-3269, para 229.
[152] *Ibid.*, paras 230-231.
[153] Cases C-71/09P, C-73/09P & C-76/09P, *Comitato Venezia vuole vivere v Commission* [2011] ECR I-4727, paras 63-64.

the hands of its beneficiary, capable of distorting competition and affecting intra-EU trade.[154]   Nevertheless, that verification must be carried out sufficiently within the framework of the Commission's decision. Thus, the scope of the decision must be clearly identified and must contain, in itself, all the matters essential for its implementation by the national authorities.[155]

Cumulation of small amounts of aid In *Regione Autonoma Friuli Venezia Giulia v Commission*, which concerned aid to the road haulage sector, the General Court held that, because of the structure of the market, a feature of which was the presence of a large number of small-scale undertakings, even relatively modest aid was liable to strengthen the position of the recipient as compared to its competitors.[156] Where the overall amount of aid is small and is divided between a large number of beneficiaries, each of whom receives a negligible sum, the ECJ has held that the relatively small amount of aid or the relatively small size of the undertaking which receives it does not *prima facie* exclude the possibility that intra-EU trade may be affected or competition distorted. Other factors may be decisive, such as whether the aid is cumulative and whether the undertakings that receive it are operating in a sector that is particularly exposed to competition. In several cases, aid to agricultural producers was held to distort competition and affect trade between Member States on the basis that the sector was exposed to fierce competition between the producers whose products were traded in substantial quantities within the EU.[157]

2.5 EFFECT ON TRADE BETWEEN MEMBER STATES

Effect on trade between Member States Article 107(1) TFEU applies to State aid in so far as it affects trade between Member States.   There is

---

[154] *Ibid.*, para 115.

[155] *Ibid.*, para 120. For individual follow-on cases, see Case C-436/12P, *Veolia Acqua Compagnia Generale delle Acque srl v Commission* EU:C:2013:399; Cases C-227/13P to C-239/13P, *Albergo Quattro Fontane Snc v Commission* EU:C:2014:2177; Case C-154/13P, *Ghezzo Giovanni & C. Snc v Commission* EU:C:2014:2182. In Cases C-94/13P, etc., *Cooperativa tra i Lavoratori dell Piccola Pesca di Pellestrina Soc. coop. arl v Commission* EU:C:2014:2183, it was argued, without the point being decided by the ECJ, that this resulted in the burden of proof of aid in individual cases being reversed as regards distortion of competition and effect on trade.

[156] Case T-288/97, *Regione Autonoma Friuli Venezia Giulia v Commission* [2001] ECR II-1169, para 46.

[157] Case C-114/00, *Spain v Commission* [2002] ECR I-7657, para 47; Case C-278/00, *Commission v Greece* [2004] ECR I-3997, paras 69-72; Case C-73/03, *Spain v Commission* EU:C:2004:711, para 29; Case T-379/09, *Italy v Commission* EU:T:2012:422, paras 57-58; Case T-52/12, *Greece v Commission* EU:T:2014:677, paras 104-105.

considerable overlap in the case law of the cumulative conditions of distortion of competition and effect on trade between Member States. In *Philip Morris v Commission*, the ECJ held that, when State aid strengthens the position of an undertaking compared with other undertakings competing in intra-EU trade, that trade must be regarded as affected by the aid.[158] Thus, for instance, in *KG Holding v Commission*, the General Court held that since the aid in question strengthens the recipient's position in relation to other competing undertakings, in particular international undertakings offering comparable services in other Member States, it was necessary to consider that intra-EU trade was affected by the aid.[159] The aim of Article 107(1) TFEU is to prevent trade between Member States from being affected by advantages granted by public authorities which distort competition by favouring certain undertakings or certain products.[160] Accordingly, even if there is no intra-EU trade at the time when the aid is granted, if it is already foreseeable that exports will shortly be directed to other Member States, the Commission is obliged to examine whether there is an effect on trade by virtue of the grant of the aid. In *AITEC*, the General Court therefore annulled a Commission decision concerning aid to a Greek cement producer on the ground that the Commission had failed to examine the effect that the aid was likely to have on future inter-State trade.[161]

Where undertakings in one Member State are in competition with undertakings in other Member States, the modification of production costs borne by the former necessarily affects trade between Member States.[162] In *GEMO*, where the disposal in France of animal carcasses and slaughterhouse waste was subsidised, the ECJ held that this necessarily had a positive impact on meat prices, thus making that product more competitive on the markets of the Member States where such costs are normally paid out of the budgets of competing traders.[163] When State aid strengthens the position of an undertaking compared with other undertakings competing in intra-EU trade, the latter must be regarded as affected by the aid, even if the beneficiary undertaking is itself not involved in exporting. Domestic production may be maintained or increased with the result that undertakings established in other

---

[158] Case 730/79, *Philip Morris v Commission* [1980] ECR 2671, para 11; Case C-494/06P, *Commission v Italy* [2009] ECR I-3639, para 51.

[159] Cases T-81/07 to T-83/07, *KG Holding NV v Commission* [2009] ECR II-2411, para 79.

[160] Case 173/73, *Italy v Commission* [1974] ECR 709, para 13; Case 310/85, *Deufil GmbH v Commission* [1987] ECR 901, para 8, Case C-387/92, *Banco Exterior de España SA v Ayuntamiento de Valencia* [1994] ECR I-877, para 12; Case C-39/94, *SFEI v La Poste* [1996] ECR I-3547, para 58; Cases T-116/01 & T-118/01, *P&O European Ferries (Vizcaya) SA v Commission* [2003] ECR II-2957, para 111.

[161] Cases T-447-449/93, *AITEC v Commission* [1995] ECR II-1971, paras 139-140.

[162] Case 173/73, *Italy v Commission* [1974] ECR 709, para 18.

[163] Case C-126/01, *Ministre de l'économie, des finances et de l'industrie v GEMO* [2003] ECR I-13769, para 42.

Member States have less chance of exporting their products to the markets in the Member State granting the aid.[164]

Effect on trade as a jurisdictional criterion Since there is no threshold or percentage below which trade between Member States can be said not to be affected,[165] the requirement of effect on trade may be regarded as entailing a jurisdictional criterion for the application of Article 107(1) TFEU. Where aid benefits only products which are not subject to any competition or which are not the subject of inter-State trade or where trade in a product is affected only at a purely national level, the measure will not fall within the scope of Article 107(1) TFEU.[166] However, where aid is granted to an undertaking that trades both within a Member State and elsewhere in the internal market, the whole of the aid will be regarded as affecting trade between Member States. In *Italy v Commission*, concerning aid to undertakings in the Italian banking sector, it was argued that the Commission should have investigated whether, if they did not fully affect trade between Member States, the measures at issue affected it only in part. The ECJ rejected this approach, holding that the concept of an effect on trade between Member States must be understood as requiring merely that there be an impact on such trade, or at least the possibility of such an impact.[167]

In *Thermenhotel Stoiser Franz v Commission*, it was argued by the Commission that the applicants, which were hotels in the same Austrian region as the hotel that was the recipient of aid, had no standing to challenge the Commission's decision that the aid was permissible on the ground that there was no effect on trade and thus the dispute did not fall within the scope of Article 107(1) TFEU which extended its field of protection only to competitors not carrying on their business in the Member State which grants the aid. The General Court dismissed this argument as irrelevant in the context of admissibility, but did not go on to examine it as a substantive issue.[168] In

---

[164] Case 102/87, *France v Commission* [1988] ECR 4067, para 19; Cases C-278/92-280/92, *Spain v Commission* [1994] ECR I-4103, para 40; Case C-75/97, *Belgium v Commission* [1999] ECR I-3671, para 47 Case C-156/98, *Germany v Commission* [2000] ECR I-6857, para 33; Case C-310/99, *Italy v Commission* [2002] ECR I-2289, para 84; Case T-288/97, *Regione Autonoma Friuli Venezia Giulia v Commission* [2001] ECR II-1169, para 51; Case T-152/99, *Hijos de Andrés Molina SA v Commission* [2002] ECR II-3049, para 220.

[165] Case T-222/04. *Italy v Commission* [2009] ECR II-1887, para 44.

[166] Case 40/75, *Produits Bertrand v Commission* [1976] ECR 1, *per* Advocate General Reischl, at p. 16; Case 730/79, *Philip Morris v Commission* [1980] ECR 2671, *per* Advocate General Capotorti, at p. 2697; Case C-142/87, *Belgium v Commission* [1990] ECR I-959, *per* Advocate General Tesauro at p. 1001. See, A. Petersen, "State aid and European Union: State aid in the light of trade, competition, industrial and cohesion policies" in I. Harden ed., *State Aid: Community Law and Policy* (Cologne, 1993), p. 22.

[167] Case C-66/02, *Italy v Commission* [2005] ECR I-10901, para 112.

[168] Case T-158/99, *Thermenhotel Stoiser Franz GmbH v Commission* [2004] ECR II-1, para 74.

Fleuren Compost v Commission, however, the General Court emphasised that aid within Article 107(1) TFEU may affect any competing undertaking, whether it is established in the same Member State as the recipient or in another Member State.[169]

Evidence of effect on trade It is not necessary to demonstrate that the aid has an actual effect on trade between Member States, but only to examine whether that aid is liable to affect such trade.[170] It may be that the very circumstances in which the aid is granted are sufficient to show that the aid is capable of affecting trade between Member States.[171] In *Belgium and Forum 187 v Commission*, the ECJ held that a scheme for taxing coordination centres of multinational groups necessarily affected trade between Member States since the coordination centres could only be established by multinational companies that were established in at least four States.[172] In *Administración del Estado v Xunta de Galicia*, the ECJ held that aid to shipbuilding within the scope of Council Directive 90/684/EEC necessarily affected trade between Member States, which was apparent from the recitals in the preamble to that directive which declared that it was intended to ensure, on a world market, fair competition at international level between shipyards by encouraging the production of more technologically advanced ships in order to ensure the survival of an efficient and competitive European shipbuilding industry.[173] In *Nitrogénművek Vegyipari Zst v Commission*, which concerned *ad hoc* aid to an individual undertaking, the Commission established that the recipient was the main fertiliser producer in Hungary and the main supplier on the Hungarian market, while realising 26% of its turnover on exports.[174]

In *Altmark*, the ECJ recognised that public subsidies to an Austrian firm supplying transport services allowed those services to be maintained or increased so that undertakings from other Member States had less chance of providing their transport services in Austria. That finding was not merely hypothetical, since several Member States had since 1995 started to open certain transport markets to competition from undertakings established in other

---

[169] Case T-109/01, *Fleuren Compost BV v Commission* [2004] ECR II-127, para 57.

[170] Case C-301/87, *France* v *Commission* [1990] ECR I-307, para 33; Case C-372/97, *Italy v Commission* [2004] ECR I-3679, para 44; Case C-298/00P, *Italy v Commission* [2004] ECR I-4807, para 49; Cases C-442/03P & C-471/03P *P & O European Ferries (Vizcaya) SA* v *Commission* [2006] ECR I-4845, para 110; Case C-222/04, *Ministero dell'Economia e delle Finanze v Cassa di Risparmio di Firenze SpA* [2006] ECR I-289, para 140; Case C-494/06P, *Commission v Italy* [2009] ECR I-3639, para 49.

[171] Cases 296 & 318/82, *Netherlands and Leeuwarder Papierwarenfabriek v Commission* [1985] ECR 809, para 24.

[172] Case C-182/03 & C-217/03, *Belgium and Forum 187 ASBL v Commission* [2006] ECR I-5479, para 134.

[173] Case C-71/04, *Administración del Estado v Xunta de Galicia* [2005] ECR I-7419, para 35.

[174] Case T-387/11, *Nitrogénművek Vegyipari Zst v Commission* EU:T:2013:98, para 90.

Member States, so that a number of undertakings were already offering their urban, suburban or regional transport services in Member States other than their State of origin.[175] This may be particularly the case where there are relatively low profit margins. Provided that the Commission has evidence of an adequate effect on inter-State trade, it is not relevant that the recipient is endeavouring to direct its products towards new markets and its exports to non-member countries.[176]

Liberalisation of economic activity at EU level The fact that an economic sector has been the subject of liberalisation at EU level may suffice to indicate the real or potential effect of the aid on competition and its effect on trade between Member States.[177] In *Italy v Commission*, concerning aid to undertakings in the Italian banking sector, the ECJ noted that the financial services sector had been the subject of a significant liberalisation process at EU level, which had intensified the competition which may already have resulted from the free of movement of capital.[178] Similarly, in *Essent Netwerk Noord v Aluminium Delfzijl*, where domestic electricity generating undertakings were in competition with electricity producers of other Member States, having regard to the context of the liberalization of the market in electricity and the resulting intense competition, that factor was sufficient to establish that the aid was liable to affect trade.[179] In *Ministerio de Defensa v Concello de Ferrol*, where it was not disputed that the shipbuilding sector was a market open to competition and to trade between Member States, the ECJ held that this was the position not only as regards civil activities, but also as regards the activities of the aid recipient in the military sector.[180]

Even where a market is not fully liberalised, aid may be capable of having an effect on trade between Member States. In *EDF v Commission*, where it was argued that the French internal electricity market was not yet liberalised, the General Court held that the fact that EDF exported electricity to other

---

[175] Case C-280/00, *Altmark Trans v Nahverkehrsgesellschaft Altmark GmbH* [2003] ECR I-7747, paras 78-79.
[176] Case 234/84, *Belgium v Commission* [1986] ECR 2263, para 23.
[177] Case C-409/00, *Spain v Commission* [2003] ECR I-1487, para 75; Case C-66/02, *Italy v Commission* [2005] ECR I-10901, para 116; Case C-148/04, *Unicredito Italiano SpA v Agenzia delle Entrate, Ufficio Genova 1* [2005] ECR I-11137, para 57; Case C-206/06, *Essent Netwerk Noord BV v Alumimium Delfzijl BV* [2008] ECR I-5497, para 77; Case C-494/06P, *Commission v Italy*, [2009] ECR I-3639, para 61; Cases T-80/06 & T-182/09, *Budapesti Erőmű Zrt v Commission* EU:T:2012:65, para 97.
[178] Case C-66/02, *Italy v Commission* [2005] ECR I-10901, para 119; Case C-222/04, *Ministero dell'Economia e delle Finanze v Cassa di Risparmio di Firenze SpA* [2006] ECR I-289, para 145; Case C-667/13, *Portugal v Banco Privado Português SA* EU:C:2015:151, para 51.
[179] Case C-206/06, *Essent Netwerk Noord BV v Alumimium Delfzijl BV* [2008] ECR I-5497, para 77.
[180] Case C-522/13, *Ministerio de Defensa v Concello de Ferrol* EU:C:2014:2262, para 53.

Member States whose electricity markets had already been opened up was sufficient to show an effect on intra-EU trade.[181] In *Fallimento Traghetti del Mediterraneo SpA v Presidenza del Consiglio dei Ministri*, which concerned subsidies paid in respect of maritime services between the Italian islands, it was argued that the cabotage market had not yet been liberalised. Nevertheless, the ECJ held that the fact that the restrictions on the freedom to provide maritime transport services within Member States were abolished after that time did not necessarily exclude the possibility that the subsidies at issue were liable to affect trade between Member States or that they distorted or threatened to distort competition. In particular, it could not be excluded that the recipient was in competition with undertakings on international routes and that, in the absence of any separate accounting for its various activities, there was a risk of cross-subsidisation, that is to say, a risk that the revenue from its cabotage activity which received the subsidies was used for the benefit of activities carried on by it on its international routes.[182]

Local services and effect on trade Aid to firms providing only local services is not likely to affect trade between Member States.[183] That does not mean, however, that only measures relating to exports or imports from Member States are regulated. Matters which are localised within a Member State and which relate to production rather than trade may nevertheless have effects on trade between Member States.[184] It follows that it is not necessary that the beneficiary should itself participate in intra-EU trade.[185] In *Altmark*, the ECJ held that it is not impossible that a public subsidy granted to an undertaking which provides only local or regional transport services and does not provide any transport services outside its State of origin may none the less have an effect on trade between Member States. As a result of the aid the business carried on by the recipient may be maintained or increased with the result that undertakings established in other Member States have less chance of

---

[181] Case T-156/04, *EDF v Commission* [2009] ECR II-4503, para 151.

[182] Case C-140/09, *Fallimento Traghetti del Mediterraneo SpA v Presidenza del Consiglio dei Ministri* [2010] ECR I-5243, para 50.

[183] See, for example SA.37432, *Czech public hospitals*, SA.33149, *Kiel information services*, SA.38035, *Bad Nenndorf rehabilitation clinic*, SA.38208 *UK golf clubs* (2015).

[184] Case 52/76, *Benedetti v Munari* [1977] ECR 163, *per* Advocate General Reischl, at p. 191; Case 730/79, *Philip Morris v Commission* [1980] ECR 2671, *per* Advocate General Capotorti, at p. 2697.

[185] Case C-66/02, *Italy v Commission* [2005] ECR I-10901, para 117; Case C-148/04, *Unicredito Italiano SpA v Agenzia delle Entrate, Ufficio Genova 1* [2005] ECR I-11137, para 58; Cases C-197/11 & C-203/11, *Libert v Flemish Government* EU:C:2013:288, para 78; Case C-518/13, *Eventech Ltd. v The Parking Adjudicator* EU:C:2015:9, para 67; Cases T-239/04 & T-323/04, *Italy v Commission* [2007] ECR II-3265, para 68; Cases T-254/00, T-270/00 & T-277/00, *Hotel Cipriani SpA v Commission* [2008] ECR I-3269, para 248; Case T-303/05, *AceaElectrabel Produzione SpA v Commission* [2009] ECR II-137*, paras 59-68.

penetrating the market of the Member State concerned.[186] The ECJ accepted evidence that showed that several Member States had started to open certain transport services to competition from undertakings established in other Member States, so that a number of undertakings were already offering their urban, suburban or regional transport services in Member States other than their State of origin.[187]

Similarly, in *Heiser*, whereas the ECJ merely held that it was not inconceivable that dentists in Austria would be in competition with their colleagues from other Member States,[188] Advocate General Tizzano accepted that, whilst medical services are predominantly local or regional in character, the market for medical treatment is open to competition and characterised by increasing cross-border trade.[189] In *Administración del Estado v Xunta de Galicia*, the ECJ accepted that it was quite possible that aid granted to undertakings supplying, at a local or regional level, shipbuilding or ship conversion services falling below the tonnage or power thresholds laid down by Directive 90/684/EEC may nevertheless have an effect on trade between Member States. The Galician decree providing for the aid stated that its aim was to permit the Galician shipyards, whose clients were owners of fishing and merchant vessels and of other seagoing vessels, both national and foreign, to offer guarantees and financing conditions similar to those of their competitors. Consequently, inasmuch as it was conceivable that the Galician shipyards which benefited from the aid scheme at issue were in competition with shipyards established in another Member State, the condition regarding effect on trade between Member States had to be considered fulfilled.[190]

In *Libert v Flemish Government*, which concerned subsidies for property developers who provided social housing in Belgium, the ECJ held that it could not be ruled out that the subsidies may have made it more difficult for undertakings other Member States to penetrate the Belgian market or for Belgian undertakings to penetrate other markets.[191] Similarly, a State guarantee to Hungarian credit institutions allowing for subsidised housing loans was regarded as making it more difficult for operators established in other Member States to penetrate the Hungarian market.[192] Equally, in

---

[186] Case C-303/88, *Italy v Commission* [1991] ECR I-1433, para 27; Case C-280/00, *Altmark Trans v Nahverkehrsgesellschaft Altmark GmbH* [2003] ECR I-7747, paras 77-78; Cases T-239/04 & T-323/04, *Italy v Commission* [2007] ECR II-3265, para 128; Case T-579/08, *Eridania Sadam SpA v Commission* [2011] ECR II-366*, para 37.

[187] Case C-280/00, *Altmark Trans v Nahverkehrsgesellschaft Altmark GmbH* [2003] ECR I-7747, para 79.

[188] Case C-172/03, *Heiser v Finanzamt Innsbruck* [2005] ECR I-1627, para 35.

[189] *Ibid.*, per AG Tizzano at para 58.

[190] Case C-71/04, *Administración del Estado v Xunta de Galicia* [2005] ECR I-7419, paras 46-47.

[191] Cases C-197/11 & C-203/11, *Libert v Flemish Government* EU:C:2013:288, para 79.

[192] Case C-672/13, *OTP Bank Nyrt v Hungary* EU:C:2015:185, para 58.

Eventech v The Parking Adjudicator, the ECJ held that it was conceivable that the effect of the London bus lanes policy, whereby only black cabs could use the bus lanes to the exclusion of competing minicabs, was to render less attractive the provision of minicab services in London, with the result that the opportunities for undertakings established in other Member States to penetrate that market were reduced.[193] In a series of cases concerning Italian public utility companies, it was alleged that the aid in question was limited to local public services. However, it was held that the public undertakings competed for the award of public service concessions the market for which was open to competition.[194] Moreover, the public undertakings were not confined to the local public services sector and were also engaged in other economic activities in markets that were open to competition.[195]

Export aid Export aid, granted by a Member State in favour only of national products exported and for the purpose of helping them to compete in other Member States with products originating in the latter, constitutes aid within the meaning of Article 107(1) TFEU.[196] By its nature, such aid has an effect on trade between Member States. Advocate General Roemer thought that the deciding factor is the intention to promote exports and the fact that trade relations would develop differently in the absence of the aid.[197] Article 107(1) TFEU makes no mention, however, of effects on trade with third countries. In *R v Secretary of State for National Heritage, ex parte J Paul Getty Trust*, the English Court of Appeal rejected an argument that Article 107(1) TFEU applied to a grant to a British museum to assist in the purchase of a work of art that would otherwise have been exported to the United States.[198] In *Belgium v Commission*, it was claimed that aid granted for the purpose of export to third countries fell outside of Article 107(1) TFEU and was governed by EU law rules governing the harmonisation of national export aid in the context of the common commercial policy. On the facts, the ECJ rejected the argument that the measures in question could not affect trade between Member States or distort competition in the internal market given that 90% of production was exported outside the EU since evidence produced by the Commission showed that the intention behind the aid was to withdraw from certain overseas

---

[193] Case C-518/13, *Eventech Ltd. v The Parking Adjudicator* EU:C:2015:9, para 70.

[194] Case T-222/04, *Italy v Commission* [2009] ECR II-1877, para 50; Case T-189/03, *ASM Brescia SpA v Commission* [2009] ECR II-1831, para 76.

[195] Case T-297/02, *ACEA SpA v Commission* [2009] ECR II-1683, para 89; Case T-301/02, *AEM SpA v Commission* [2009] ECR I-1757, para 105; Case T-189/03, *ASM Brescia SpA v Commission* [2009] ECR II-1831, para 79.

[196] Cases 6 & 11/69, *Commission v France* [1969] ECR 523, para 20.

[197] Cases 6 & 11/69, *Commission v France* [1969] ECR 523, *per* Advocate General Roemer, at p. 553.

[198] *R v Secretary of State for National Heritage, ex parte J Paul Getty Trust* [1997] EuLR 407.

markets, which were insufficiently profitable, and to target other markets within the EU.[199]

Exports outside of the European Union It has at times been difficult to discern the Commission's approach in regard to aid relating to exports outside of the European Union. For example, in response to a complaint by an EU producer, the Commission investigated aid granted in the island of Réunion for the production of large-diameter steel tubes. Despite substantial overcapacity in the EU steel tubes sector, the Commission allowed the aid on the ground that any impact which the aided production might have on intra-EU trade was marginal, since the production was essentially intended for the market in southern Africa and the Indian Ocean area.[200] In its decision concerning *Carnon Consolidated*, however, the Commission found aid to a tin mining company to be within Article 107(1) TFEU as having an effect on trade between Member States, despite the fact that the company exported all its production outside of the EU. Tin concentrates were extracted in the EU only by Carnon and as a by-product by a company in Portugal. The only intra-EU trade in the product was in respect of a part of the Portuguese production which was exported to Spain.[201] In a decision concerning aid to a Portuguese company in respect of the acquisition and refurbishment of a hotel in Brazil, the Commission held that the relatively small size of the beneficiary of the aid and the fact that this was the first internationalisation experience of the company would result in there being a very limited impact on trade between Member States. The effect on intra-EU trade appears to have arisen in relation to competitors offering tourism services.[202] In *Djebel-SGPS v Commission*, aid to a Portuguese luxury hotel operator aimed at developing its business in Brazil was held to affect trade between Member States, since it favoured the hotel operator compared to its competitors on the international tourism markets.[203]

    In *Italy and Wam v Commission*, where export aid was granted in respect of trade with third countries, the General Court criticised the Commission for failing to specify how trade between Member States was affected.[204] On appeal, the ECJ agreed that the aid in question was not directly connected to the activity of the beneficiary on the EU market, but was intended to finance expenditure for a third country market penetration programme. In those circumstances, the effect of the aid on competition and intra-EU trade was less immediate and was thus required to be identified more clearly.[205]

---

[199] Case C-142/87, *Belgium v Commission* [1990] ECR I-959, para 38.
[200] *Twenty-Sixth Report on Competition Policy* (1996), p. 216.
[201] *Twenty-Fourth Report on Competition Policy* (1994), p. 522.
[202] Commission Decision 2004/168/EC, *Vila Galé*, OJ 2004 L61/76.
[203] Case T-422/07, *Djebel-SGPS SA v Commission* EU:T:2012:11, para 102.
[204] Cases T-304/04 & T-316/04, *Italy v Commission* [2006] ECR II-64*, para 63.
[205] Case C-494/06P, *Commission v Italy and Wam SpA*, [2009] ECR I-3639, para 61.

Subsequently, the Commission adopted a fresh decision in which it clarified that competing undertakings that wished to penetrate third country markets were obliged to finance their own activities in this respect, that the aid in question allowed the recipient to save its resources and thus it could reduce its prices on the export market and consolidate its position on the EU market. This was held to be sufficient to show distortion of competition and effect on intra-EU trade.[206]

2.6 *DE MINIMIS* AID

De minimis aid Given that Article 107(1) TFEU declares State aid incompatible with the internal market only where there is a distortion of competition and there is an effect on trade between Member States, it follows that where these conditions are not fulfilled the aid does not fall within the scope of Article 107(1) TFEU. This raises the question of whether a *de minimis* rule applies to State aid. Under the ECSC Treaty, for aid to be considered to be incompatible with the internal market, it was not necessary for it to distort or threaten to distort competition. The ECJ held that, since all aid was prohibited without restriction, the ECSC Treaty could not contain any *de minimis* rule.[207] Both the EU Courts and the Commission have been less than clear in their approach to this issue to Article 107(1) TFEU, so that an analysis of their policy and practice does not lead to any definitive conclusion, although two possible approaches are discernible.

On the one hand, it can be argued that Article 107(1) TFEU should be interpreted so as to allow aid which is *de minimis* to fall outside of its scope of application where it can be established that such aid has only a very minor effect on competition involving inter-State trade. Moreover, aid which does fall within the scope of application of Article 107(1) TFEU can nevertheless be treated as being of similar effect to aid which is *de minimis* and be exempted from the notification requirements on the ground that it is of minor importance. On the other hand, it can be argued that all State aid which has an effect, no matter how small, on competition involving inter-State trade falls within the scope of application of Article 107(1) TFEU and is only permissible in so far as it is declared compatible with the internal market by the Commission or the Council.

---

[206] Case C-587/12P, *Italy v Commission* EU:C:2013:721, para 25-32; Case C-560/12P, *Wam Industriale SpA v Commission* EU:C:2013:726, paras 22-24; Case T-257/10, *Italy v Commission* EU:T:2012:504, paras 83-87; Case T-303/10, *Wam Industriale SpA v Commission* EU:T:2012:505, paras 31-53.

[207] Case C-111/99P, *Lech Stahlwerke GmbH v Commission* [2001] ECR I-727, para 41; Case C-334/99, *Germany v Commission* [2003] ECR I-1139, para 80.

Effect of *de minimis* aid on competition and trade In *France v Commission*, the ECJ considered that aid to the textile industry in France that did not substantially affect trade between Member States could be acknowledged as permissible.[208] Since this involved aid which had not been notified to the Commission, it may be inferred that the ECJ was sympathetic in principle to the notion that aid which was *de minimis* did not fall within the scope of Article 107(1) TFEU and did not require notification.[209] Equally, the General Court has stated that *de minimis* aid is authorised because it is considered not to distort competition and affect trade between Member States[210] and, more forcefully, that, small amounts of aid being incapable of distorting competition, the Commission should be left to concentrate on cases of genuine interest to the EU.[211] The Commission appeared to adopt this approach in its former guidelines concerning small and medium-sized enterprises[212] and in its early notices on the *de minimis* rule[213] and on cooperation with national courts[214] where it fixed minimum levels below which the *de minimis* rule applied. However, the ECJ has held that whether or not aid is to be regarded as substantially affecting trade is less a matter of quantity than of the circumstances of the case, so that even aid of a relatively small amount is liable to affect trade between Member States where there is strong competition in the sector in question.[215] The agricultural sector, and the fruit and vegetable sector in particular, is exposed to strong competition. Its structure, which is characterised by a large number of small scale operators, is such that the creation of an aid scheme that is available to a large number of operators can have an impact on competition even where the individual grants under the scheme are small.[216] Indeed, in *Alfa Romeo*, it stated that where an undertaking operates in a sector in which there is surplus capacity and

---

[208] Case 47/69, *France v Commission* [1970] ECR 487, para 16.

[209] Case 40/75, *Société des Produits Bertrand v Commission* [1976] ECR 1, *per* Advocate General Reischl at p. 17; Case C-42/93, *Commission v Spain* [1994] ECR I-4175, *per* Advocate General Jacobs at p. 4182.

[210] Case T-52/12R, *Greece v Commission* EU:T:2012:447, para 24.

[211] Cases T-394/08, T-408/08, T-453/08 & T-454/08, *Regione autonoma della Sardegna v Commission* [2011] ECR II-6255, para 304.

[212] OJ 1996, C213/4.

[213] OJ 1996 C68/9.

[214] OJ 1995 C312/8.

[215] Case 259/85, *France v Commission* [1987] ECR 4393, para 24; Case C-303/88, *Italy v Commission* [1990] ECR I-1433, para 27; Cases C-278/92-280/92, *Spain v Commission* [1994] ECR I-4103, paras 41-42; Case C-156/98, *Germany v Commission* [2000] ECR I-6857, para 32; Case C-310/99, *Italy v Commission* [2002] ECR I-2289, para 86; Case C-278/00, *Greece v Commission* [2004] ECR 3997, para 69-70; Cases C-393/04 & C-41/05, *Air Liquide Industries Belgium SA v Ville de Seraing* [2006] ECR I-5293, para 36; Case T-14/96, *BAI v Commission* [1999] ECR II-139, para 77.

[216] Case C-372/97, *Italy v Commission* [2004] ECR I-3679, para 54; Case T-171/02, *Regione autonoma della Sardegna v Commission* [2005] ECR II-2123, para 87.

producers from various Member States compete, any aid which it may receive is liable to affect trade between Member States and impair competition, inasmuch as its continuing presence on the market prevents competitors from increasing their market share and reduces their chances of increasing exports.[217]

In *Philip Morris v Commission*, Advocate General Capotorti took the view that any analogy with the application of the *de minimis* rule applicable to restrictive agreements and Article 101 TFEU[218] was inappropriate.[219] Both the ECJ and the Commission, in *Belgium v Commission*, agreed that a *de minimis* principle did not exist with regard to State aid in that there is no threshold below which intra-EU trade cannot be said to be affected by a grant of aid.[220] Advocate General Lenz explained this approach on the ground that to adopt such a principle in the context of the State aid review procedure would not be appropriate since State aid disrupts the system of undistorted competition which is sought by the FEU Treaty and that there is nothing in the wording of Article 107(1) TFEU to suggest that minor distortions of competition should not be subject to its application. In the light of the extensive derogations from the prohibition on aid which are set out in Article 107(2)-(3) TFEU, it was appropriate to treat all distortions of competition as relevant irrespective of their degree. Given that Member States are under an obligation pursuant to Article 4(3) TEU to facilitate the achievement of the EU's tasks, there were good grounds, in principle, for subjecting their conduct to a stricter standard than the conduct of undertakings.[221]

This latter approach was confirmed by the ECJ in *Altmark* where it held that there is no threshold or percentage below which it may be considered that

---

[217] Case C-305/89, *Italy v Commission* [1991] ECR I-1603, para 26. See also Case T-214//95, *Vlaams Gewest v Commission* [1998] ECR II-717.

[218] In Case 5/69, *Völk v Vervaecke* [1969] ECR 295, paras 5-7, the ECJ held that an agreement may be regarded as not having an appreciable effect on trade for the purposes of Article 101 TFEU when it has only an insignificant effect on the markets, taking into account the weak position which the parties have on the market for the product in question.

[219] Case 730/79, *Philip Morris Holland BV v Commission* [1980] ECR 2671, *per* Advocate General Capotorti, at p. 2699.

[220] Case C-142/87, *Belgium v Commission* [1990] ECR I-959, para 43. See also Cases C-278/92 to 280/92, *Spain v Commission* [1994] ECR I-4103, para 42; Cases C-329/93, C-62/93 & C-63/95, *Germany v Commission* [1996] ECR I-5151, para 52; Case C-156/98, *Germany v Commission* [2000] ECR I-6857, para 39. M. Ross in "A Review of Developments in State Aids 1987-1988" (1989) 26 CMLRev. 167 argued that it would be wrong to recognise any such doctrine of *de minimis* for fear of encouraging Member States not to notify aid on the basis that a particular scheme was insignificant.

[221] Case 234/84, *Belgium v Commission* [1986] ECR 2263, *per* Advocate General Lenz, at p. 2274. See also Case 102/87, *France v Commission* [1988] ECR 4067, at p. 4078; Cases 62 & 72/87, *Exécutif Régional Wallon v Commission* [1988] ECR 1573, at p. 1583.

trade between Member States is not affected and that the relatively small amount of aid or the relatively small size of the undertaking which receives it does not as such exclude the possibility that trade between Member States might be affected.[222] It followed that fulfilment of the criterion of effect on trade in *Altmark* did not depend on the local or regional character of the transport services provided or the scale of the field of activity concerned.[223] This was also the approach of the ECJ in *Heiser* where the aid in question amounted to about €30,000 over an eight year period.[224] In *Fleuren Compost v Commission*, a Dutch recipient of aid argued that it exported barely 2% of its product and that transport costs precluded it from delivering to places more than 200 km from its base. The General Court held that, since a radius of 200 km encompassed parts of Germany and Belgium and the applicant exported substantial amounts, there was a clear effect on trade.[225]

Block exemption for *de minimis* aid The Commission's initial practice of not requiring notification of *de minimis* aid, while easing its administrative burden, would appear to be inconsistent with Article 108(3) TFEU and could have caused difficulties for national courts called upon by competitors to act against unnotified aid, notwithstanding the notice on cooperation between the Commission and national courts. In order to avoid such difficulties and to give greater legal certainty to the Commission's practice, Council Regulation (EC) No 994/98[226] provided the Commission with the power to adopt a regulation to encapsulate the *de minimis* rule.[227] This enabling power, which specifically states that the Commission may decide that certain aid does not meet all the criteria of Article 107(1) TFEU and is therefore exempt from the notification requirements of Article 108(3) TFEU, appears to regard *de minimis* aid as falling outside the scope of Article 107(1) TFEU. Commission Regulation (EC) No 1998/2006,[228] which was adopted pursuant to this enabling power, also reflected the notion that such aid does not meet all the criteria of Article 107(1) TFEU.[229] Regulation (EC) No 1998/2006 was replaced, as of 1 July

---

[222] Case C-280/00, *Altmark Trans v Nahverkehrsgesellschaft Altmark GmbH* [2003] ECR I-7747, para 81.

[223] *Ibid.,* para 82; Case C-372/97, *Italy v Commission* [2004] ECR I-3679, para 60.

[224] Case C-172/03, *Heiser v Finanzamt Innsbruck* [2005] ECR I-1627, para 29-33.

[225] Case T-109/01, *Fleuren Compost BV v Commission* [2004] ECR II-127, para 55.

[226] OJ 1998 L142/1. This was adopted pursuant to Article 109 TFEU which allows the Council to enact rules for the application of Articles 107 and 108 TFEU and to determine the conditions in which Article 108(3) TFEU applies.

[227] Council Regulation (EC) No 994/98, Article 2(1).

[228] OJ 2006 L379/5. This replaced an earlier exemption in Commission Regulation (EC) No 69/2001, OJ 2001 L10/30.

[229] Commission Regulation (EC) No 1998/2006, Article 2(1) stated that such aid measures "shall be deemed not to meet all the criteria" of Article 107(1) TFEU. However, Council Regulation (EC) No 994/98, which states that the Commission may "decide that, having regard to the development and functioning of the internal market, certain

2014, by Commission Regulation (EU) No 1407/2013.[230] Where a Member State seeks to rely on the *de minimis* block exemption, it must present the Commission with requisite proof that the conditions for its application are fulfilled.[231] In *Libert v Flemish Government*, the ECJ commented that such aid was excluded from the concept of State aid.[232] If this approach is correct, it is arguable that other aid which, in the particular circumstances, has no perceptible effect on competition or on trade between Member States therefore falls outside of the scope of Article 107(1) TFEU, even if Regulation (EU) No 1407/2013 is not applicable.

In practice, the Commission has long accepted that minor cases of aid had no perceptible effect on competition. In 1992 it adopted guidelines for small and medium-sized enterprises which exempted from the notification requirement aid to SMEs up to a ceiling of ECU 50,000 over a three-year period.[233] In 1996 these guidelines were amended[234] and the Commission also issued a notice on the *de minimis* rule for State aid,[235] the result of which was to impose for all undertakings[236] a ceiling for aid covered by the *de minimis* rule of ECU 100,000 over a three-year period beginning when the first *de minimis* aid was granted. Commission Regulation (EC) No 69/2001 continued this policy which the Commission had previously followed. Irrespective of the form of aid or of the objective pursued, the total *de minimis* aid granted to any one independent enterprise[237] could not exceed €100,000 over any period of three years. This was increased in Regulation (EC) No 1998/2006 to €200,000

---

aids do not meet all the criteria" of Article 107(1) TFEU, does not on a strict interpretation give the Commission the power to declare aid which is in fact within the scope of Article 107(1) TFEU as being deemed to fall outside its scope. Rather, the Commission's power is limited to declaring that certain aid does not fall within the scope of Article 107(1) TFEU.

[230] OJ 2013 L352/1. Separate regulations apply to *de minimis* aid in the agriculture and fisheries sectors.

[231] Case T-527/13, *Italy v Commission* EU:T:2015:429, para 21.

[232] Cases C-197/11 & C-203/11, *Libert v Flemish Government* EU:C:2013:288, para 81.

[233] OJ 1992 C213/2.

[234] OJ 1996 C213/4.

[235] OJ 1996 C68/9.

[236] This exemption did not apply to industries covered by the ECSC Treaty (see also, Cases T-129/95, T-2/96 & T-97/96, *Neue Maxhütte Stahlwerke GmbH v Commission* [1999] ECR II-17, para 147), shipbuilding, transport, agriculture or fisheries: Notice on the *de minimis* rule for State aid, para 4.

[237] Where aid is granted to several undertakings, it may be considered as having a cumulative affect. Thus, the Commission considered that aid granted by the Netherlands to 633 Dutch petrol stations located near the German border in order to compensate their owners for the losses resulting from an increase in excise duty on diesel constituted aid incompatible with the internal market in so far as many of the stations were ultimately owned by the same undertakings: Commission Decision 1999/705/EC, *Dutch Service Stations*, OJ 1999 L280/87. See Case C-382/99, *Netherlands v Commission* [2002] ECR I-5163; Case T-237/99R, *BP Nederland v Commission* [2000] ECR II-3849.

over three years, and this threshold was maintained in Regulation (EU) No 1407/2013.[238] In any event, it is not possible to separate *de minimis* aid from other aid granted to the same recipient.[239] In view of the risk that even small amounts of aid could fulfil the criteria of Article 107(1) TFEU, the exemption does not apply to certain aid to undertakings in fisheries, aquaculture and agricultural products.[240] Commission Regulation (EC) No 1408/2013[241] governs the rules for *de minimis* aid in the agricultural sector and limits such aid to €15,000 over a three year period. In the fisheries sector, *de minimis* aid is governed by Commission Regulation (EU) No 717/2014[242] which allows for aid up to €30,000 over a three year period. The exemption does not apply in the case of aid to export-related activities towards third countries, namely aid directly linked to the quantities exported, to the establishment and operation of a distribution network or to other current expenditure linked to export activity, or to aid contingent upon the use of domestic over imported goods.[243]

---

[238] Commission Regulation (EU) No 1407/2013, Article 3(2).
[239] Cases T-394/08, T-408/08, T-453/08 & T-454/08, *Regione autonoma della Sardegna v Commission* [2011] ECR II-6255, para 312.
[240] Commission Regulation (EU) No 1407/2013, Article 1(a)-(c).
[241] OJ 2014 L352/9.
[242] OJ 2014 L190/45.
[243] Commission Regulation (EU) No 1407/2013 Article 1(d)-(e).

Chapter Three

TAXATION AND STATE AID

3.1 TAXATION AND STATE AID

Competence of Member States over taxation Application of the EU State aid rules is without prejudice to the power of the Member States to decide on their economic policy and, therefore, on the tax system and the common or normal regime under it which they consider the most appropriate and, in particular, to spread the tax burden as they see fit across the different factors of production and economic sectors.[1] As EU law currently stands, with the exception of value added tax, certain aspects of excise duties and energy taxes, and limited issues in connection with direct taxation, which are the subject of EU directives, taxation, particularly direct taxation, generally falls within the exclusive competence of the Member States which are entitled to devise systems of taxation which they consider best suited to the needs of their economies.[2] Unless otherwise provided for by specific EU legislation, Member States may, accordingly, determine the scope and application of corporation, income, consumption, property, wealth, inheritance and other taxes in the manner that suits their political and economic needs, based on principles such as the ability to pay, wealth redistribution or environmental protection.

Nevertheless, taxation is subject to the full effect of the State aid regime, so that the exercise of Member States' sovereignty in tax matters must be consistent with the State aid provisions of the FEU Treaty.[3] In so far as any tax measures may distort competition in intra-EU trade by giving a selective economic advantage to particular undertakings, Article 107(1) TFEU will prohibit or restrict their full applicability. It has been estimated by the Commission that at times as much as 40% of all State aid is in the form of

---

[1]   Cases T-211/04 & T-215/04, *Government of Gibraltar v Commission* [2008] ECR II-3745, para 146.

[2]   Case C-204/90, *Bachmann v Belgium* [1992] ECR I-249, para 23; Case C-374/04, *Test Claimants in Class IV of the ACT Group Litigation* [2006] ECR I-11673, para 50; Case C-143/99, *Adria-Wien Pipeline GmbH v Finanzlandesdirektion für Kärnten* [2001] ECR I-8365, *per* Advocate General Mischo, at para 51; Case T-67/94, *Ladbroke Racing* v *Commission* [1998] ECR II-1, para 54; Cases T-211/04 & T-215/04, *Government of Gibraltar v Commission* [2008] ECR II-3745, para 146.

[3]   Case T-538/11, *Belgium v Commission* EU:T:2015:188, paras 65-66.

fiscal exemptions,[4] although that proportion is now thought to be about 25%.[5] In accordance with the notion that State aid is defined by its effects, the fiscal aim of a measure cannot suffice to shield it from the application of Article 107(1) TFEU.[6] Even where a measure leads to an overall increase in revenue by reason, for instance, of increased investment activity, if the criteria for State aid are fulfilled, Article 107(1) TFEU will be applicable.[7] State aid may arise on two levels. First, tax legislation itself, by providing for differential treatment favouring certain undertakings, may constitute an aid scheme. Secondly, where the tax is to be assessed annually, such that a lower tax charge is imposed on the undertaking each year, State aid will be granted through each annual tax assessment.[8]

Fiscal State aid has been recognised by the ECJ as long ago as the early 1970s, when, in *Italy v Commission*, it held, dismissing the argument that tax legislation fell within the exclusive sovereignty of the Member States, that Italian legislation reducing the level of social contributions due from undertakings in the textile sector fell within the scope of Article 107(1) TFEU.[9] In 1998 the Commission issued a notice on the application of the State aid rules to measures relating to direct business taxation,[10] which was substantially based on the existing case law of the ECJ and did not entail any change in the criteria for the assessment of tax measures in the light of Article 107(1) TFEU.[11] Since the publication of the notice, however, the principles established in case law and the Commission's practice on fiscal State aid have developed considerably in their complexity. Whilst many of the cases concern issues arising in direct taxation, Article 107(1) TFEU has been applied to all types of taxation, regardless of the nature of the tax or the public authority which is responsible for establishing it. Thus, for example, in *Geurts v Belgium*, Advocate General Kokott considered that an exemption from

---

4 State aid scoreboard, Autumn 2008, p. 49.
5 State aid scoreboard 2014.
6 Case 173/73, *Italy v Commission* [1974] ECR 709, para 13; Case C-159/01, *Netherlands v Commission* [2004] ECR I-4461, para 51; Case T-210/02, *British Aggregates Association v Commission* [2006] ECR II-2789, para 106.
7 Cases C-182/03 & C-217/03, *Belgium and Forum 187 ASBL v Commission* [2006] ECR I-5479, *per* Advocat General Léger at para 308.
8 Case C-81/10P, *France Télécom SA v Commission* [2011] ECR I-12899, para 22.
9 Case 173/73, *Italy v Commission* [1974] ECR 709, paras 12-13.
10 OJ 1998 C384/3. In February, 2004, the Commission produced a report on the implementation of this Notice: COM(2004) 434.
11 Case C-183/02P, *Daewoo Electronics Manufacturing España v Commission* [2004] ECR I-10609, per Advocate General Kokott, at para 51; Cases T-269/99, T-271/99 & T-272/99, *Territorio Histórico de Álava – Diputación Foral de Álava v Commission* [2002] ECR II-4217, para 79; Cases T-346/99, T-347/99 & T-348/99, *Territorio Histórico de Álava – Diputación Foral de Álava v Commission* [2002] ECR II-4259, para 83; Cases T-30/01 etc., *Territorio Histórico de Álava – Diputación Foral de Álava v Commission* [2009] ECR II-2919, para 181.

inheritance tax on controlling interests in family companies constituted State aid, since the exemption was not available in respect of other types of economic operators.[12] A German aid scheme involved temporary exemption from real estate transfer tax in the case of mergers involving property in the former East German länder.[13]

Grant of aid through the tax system State aid may be granted in many differing ways through the tax system, as long as the criteria in Article 107(1) TFEU are fulfilled. Thus, state aid may arise through a measure which grants to certain undertakings a tax reduction or exemption,[14] a tax credit[15] or a tax-free reserve out of profits,[16] or which substitutes a fixed rate levy for the taxes that would otherwise be payable,[17] or which unduly writes off a tax liability.[18] Fiscal State aid generally involves negative expenditure constituting a financial burden borne by the State in that, even though it does not constitute the grant of a subsidy or a positive transfer of State resources as such, it entails an economic advantage in the form of exoneration from the obligation to pay the tax in question and, thus results in a loss of income to the State.[19] That will result in a selective economic advantage where it places the persons to whom it applies in a more favourable financial situation than other taxpayers.[20] Moreover, the fact that undertakings benefiting from an exemption from

---

[12] Case C-464/05, *Geurts v Belgium* [2007] ECR I-9325, *per* Advocate General Kokott at para 48.

[13] *Thirty-Fourth Report on Competition Policy* (2004), pt. 491.

[14] Case C-66/02, *Italy v Commission* [2005] ECR I-10901, para 78; Case C-222/04, *Ministero dell'Economia e delle Finanze v Cassa di Risparmio di Firenze SpA* [2006] ECR I-289, para 132; Case C-304/09, *Commission v Italy* [2010] ECR I-13903, para 6; Case C-522/13, *Ministerio de Defensa v Concello de Ferrol* EU:C:2014:2262, para 29.

[15] Cases T-227/01 etc., *Territorio Histórico de Álava – Diputación Foral de Álava v Commission* [2009] ECR II-3029, para 126.

[16] Case C-354/10, *Commission v Greece* EU:C:2012:109, para 8.

[17] Case C-66/02, *Italy v Commission* [2005] ECR I-10901, para 80.

[18] Case C-507/08, *Commission v Slovakia* [2010] ECR I-13489, paras 6-10.

[19] Case C-169/08, *Presidente del Consiglio dei Ministri v Regione Sardegna* [2009] ECR I-10821, para 58; Case T-425/11, *Greece v Commission* EU:T:2014:768, para 40.

[20] Case C-387/92, *Banco Exterior de España v Ayuntamiento de Valencia* [1994] ECR I-877, para 14; Case C-6/97, *Italy v Commission* [1999] ECR I-2981, para 16; Case C-66/02, *Italy v Commission* [2005] ECR I-10901, para 78; Case C-222/04, *Ministero dell'Economia e delle Finanze v Cassa di Risparmio di Firenze SpA* [2006] ECR I-289, para 132; Cases C-393/04 & C-41/05, *Air Liquide Industries Belgium SA v Ville de Seraing* [2006] ECR I-5293, para 30; Cases C-78/08 – C-80/08, *Ministero dell' Economia e delle Finanze v Paint Graphos* [2011] ECR I-7611, para 46; Cases C-106/09P & C-107/09P, *Commission v Government of Gibraltar* [2011] ECR I-11113, para 72; Case C-5/14, *Kernkraftwerke Lippe-Ems GmbH v Hza Osnabrück* EU:C:2015:354, para 72; Case T-92/02, *Stadtwerke Schwäbisch Hall GmbH v Commission* [2006] ECR II-11*, para 52; Case T-222/04, *Italy v Commission* [2009] ECR II-1877, para 63.

normal taxation enjoy an economic advantage cannot be challenged on the ground that other advantages are available to other undertakings.[21]

State aid may also arise where the payment of tax is merely postponed or where a tax provision grants to certain undertakings a deferral of liability to tax that would otherwise be payable.[22] In *Germany v Commission*, which concerned tax relief granted in relation to investments in companies based in the former East Germany, it was argued that no aid was granted because the relief was merely temporary, in that when the investments were subsequently sold the proceeds would be subject to tax.[23] Rejecting this, the ECJ held that, even though tax still has to be paid at the end of the deferral period, the undertaking concerned has the benefit during that period of a sum equivalent to the difference between the discounted amount of tax at the end of the deferral period, taking interest rates into account, and the amount of tax which would have been owing had the deferral not been granted.[24]

General taxation measures are not State aid Advantages arising from general measures of economic policy which apply without distinction to all economic operators are normally outside of the scope of application of Article 107(1) TFEU and are not considered as measures involving State aid, since the criterion of selectivity is not fulfilled.[25] It follows that measures setting the

---

[21] Case C-182/03 & C-217/03, *Belgium and Forum 187 ASBL v Commission* [2006] ECR I-5479, para 120; Case T-335/08, *BNP Paribas v Commission* [2010] ECR II-3323, para 162.

[22] Case C-66/02, *Italy v Commission* [2005] ECR I-10901, para 78; Case C-222/04, *Ministero dell'Economia e delle Finanze v Cassa di Risparmio di Firenze SpA* [2006] ECR I-289, para 132.

[23] Case C-156/98, *Germany v Commission* [2000] ECR I-6857, para 24. See, however, *R v Secretary of State for Trade and Industry, ex parte BT3G Ltd.* [2001] EuLR 325 (High Court); [2001] 3 CMLR 1588 (Court of Appeal), concerning revenue due from a licence holder for third generation mobile phones, where postponement was held not to constitute State aid on the ground that it was justified by reference to the general system of the statutory licensing provisions.

[24] Case T-308/00, *Salzgitter AG v Commission* [2004] ECR II-1933, para 58.

[25] Case C-156/98, *Germany v Commission* [2000] ECR I-6857, para 22; Cases C-106/09P & C-107/09P, *Commission v Government of Gibraltar* [2011] ECR I-11113, para 73; Case C-6/12, *P Oy* EU:C:2013:525, para 18; Case C-522/13, *Ministerio de Defensa v Concello de Ferrol* EU:C:2014:2262, para 23; Case T-140/13, *Netherlands Maritime Technology Association v Commission* EU:T:2014:1029, para 90. See W. Schön, "Taxation and State aid in the European Union" (1999) 36 CMLRev 911; J. Bourgeois, "State aids, taxation measures and specificity" in *Liber Amicorum M. Waelbroek* (Brussels, 1999); C. Quigley, "General taxation and State aid", in The Law of State Aid in the European Union, ed. Biondi, Eeckhout and Flynn (Oxford, 2003); M. O'Brien, "Company taxation, State aid and fundamental freedoms: is the next step enhanced cooperation?" [2005] ELRev 209; R. Luja, "Group taxation, sectoral tax benefits and *de facto* selectivity in State aid review" [2009] EStALQ 473; G. Matsos, "Systemic misconceptions of State aid law in the area of taxation" [2014] EStALQ 491

general rates of corporate taxation do not constitute State aid, as they are generally applicable throughout the Member State to all undertakings operating within the State. Similarly, any uniform reduction in the general rate will not involve aid being granted within the meaning of Article 107(1) TFEU, since all undertakings are equally affected.[26] A general reform of the tax or social security system in a Member State, with the incidental effect of reducing a particular undertaking's contributions, is outside the scope of Article 107(1) TFEU.[27] It is irrelevant that the situation of the presumed beneficiary of the measure at issue is better or worse in comparison with the situation under the law as it previously stood or, on the other hand, has not altered over time. What matters is whether the tax system at issue, viewed independently from its predecessor, favours certain undertakings within the meaning of Article 107(1) TFEU.[28]

In the absence of harmonisation of particular tax provisions, Member States are not prohibited from granting tax advantages, in the form of exemptions or reduced rates, applicable to certain products or producers. Indeed, tax advantages of this kind may serve legitimate economic or social purposes[29] and differential treatment of economic activities may be justified by reference to their respective statutory and regulatory conditions.[30] As noted by the General Court in *Stadtwerke Schwäbisch Hall GmbH v Commission,* a general tax exemption constitutes an economic advantage granted through State resources in so far as the State renounces the right to levy the tax otherwise chargeable, but does not fall within Article 107(1) TFEU where it is available to all undertakings and is, accordingly, not selective.[31] Thus, tax exemptions which are generally applicable to all persons capable of satisfying the relevant criteria are not regarded, by that fact alone, as fulfilling the criterion of selectivity.[32] Accordingly, the original Maribel scheme in Belgium involving a reduction in social security contributions payable by undertakings employing manual workers was held not to constitute State aid, unlike the Maribel *bis* and *ter* schemes, which were selectively aimed at certain sectors.[33] A Dutch

---

[26]   See, generally, the Commission 1998 Notice on direct taxation and State aid.

[27]   Case 173/73, *Italy v Commission* [1974] ECR 709, *per* Advocate General Warner, at p. 727; Case C-83/98P, *France v Ladbroke Racing Ltd. and Commission* [2000] I-3271, para 29.

[28]   Case 57/86, *Greece v Commission* [1988] ECR 2855, para 10; Case C-143/99, *Adria-Wien Pipeline GmbH v Finanzlandesdirektion für Kärnten* [2001] ECR I-8365, para 41; Cases T-211/04 & T-215/04, *Government of Gibraltar v Commission* [2008] ECR II-3745, para 186.

[29]   Case 148/77, *Hansen v Hauptzollamt Flensburg* [1978] ECR 1787, para 16.

[30]   Case C-353/95P, *Tiercé Ladbroke SA v Commission* [1997] ECR I-7007, para 35.

[31]   Case T-92/02, *Stadtwerke Schwäbisch Hall GmbH v Commission* [2006] II-11*, para 52.

[32]   Case T-399/11, *Banco Santander SA v Commission* EU:T:2014:938, para 49; Case T-219/10, *Autogrill España SA v Commission* EU:T:2014:939, para 45.

[33]   Commission Decision 97/239/EEC, *Maribel*, OJ 1997 L95/25; Case C-75/97, *Belgium v Commission* [1999] ECR I-3671.

legislative measure lowering the tax paid by employers on the salaries of employees working on R&D projects was held by the Commission not to constitute State aid on the ground that it was a general tax measure which was not specific to any region, sector or firm and was granted solely on the basis of objective criteria.[34]

In *Germany v Commission*, a tax concession in favour of taxpayers who sold certain assets and could offset the resulting profit when they acquired other financial assets did not constitute State aid to the taxpayers, in so far as they were undertakings, on the ground that it was a general measure applicable without distinction to all economically active persons.[35] Similarly, in *Banco Santander v Commission* and *Autogrill v Commission*, the General Court held that a tax provision allowing deductibility of the costs of acquisition of shareholdings in non-Spanish companies was in principle available to all Spanish taxpayers.[36] It was noted that the measure did not apply by reference to certain categories of undertakings or production of goods, but was concerned solely with a category of economic operations, of a purely financial nature, which did not require any modification of economic activity by the investing undertakings.[37] In *Stadtwerke Schwäbisch Hall GmbH v Commission*, the General Court held that the treatment of tax reserves for the decommissioning of nuclear power stations and the safe disposal of nuclear waste in Germany did not constitute State aid since it was based on generally applicable provisions allowing for the creation of reserves by all undertakings satisfying the relevant criteria.[38] The Commission also decided that an Italian measure designed to promote the regularisation of firms and workers in the black economy was a general measure. The measure in question, which provided for tax reductions, applied throughout Italy to all firms in all sectors that had not properly declared their employees and did not fully comply with their statutory obligations regarding taxes and social security contributions. Given that there was no discrimination in terms of either the rules themselves or through discretionary powers of the public authorities, the criterion of selectivity was not present.[39] By contrast, a German tax provision allowing an

---

[34]   *Twenty-Seventh Report on Competition Policy* (1997), p. 244. Similar reasoning was followed in *R v Commissioners of Inland Revenue, ex parte Professional Contractors Group* [2001] EuLR 514 (English High Court), [2001] EWCA Civ 1945 (Court of Appeal).

[35]   Case C-156/98, *Germany v Commission* [2000] ECR I-6857, paras 22-23.

[36]   Case T-399/11, *Banco Santander SA v Commission* EU:T:2014:938, para 48; Case T-219/10, *Autogrill España SA v Commission* EU:T:2014:939, para 44.

[37]   Case T-399/11, *Banco Santander SA v Commission* EU:T:2014:938, para 60; Case T-219/10, *Autogrill España SA v Commission* EU:T:2014:939, para 56.

[38]   Case T-92/02, *Stadtwerke Schwäbisch Hall GmbH v Commission* [2006] ECR II-11*, para 93; (judgment set aside on appeal on other grounds in Case C-176/06 P, *Stadtwerke Schwäbisch Hall GmbH v Commission* [2007] ECR I-170*).

[39]   *Thirty-First Report on Competition Policy* (2001), pt. 368.

ailing company to offset losses against profits in future years despite changes in its shareholder structure was held to constitute a system of aid since generally corporate tax law did not allow for a carry forward of losses where there was a significant change in the ownership structure.[40]

Indirect grant of aid through the tax system State aid may be granted indirectly through the tax system. For example, a tax deduction granted in respect of investments made by the taxpayer in firms in particular regions may be classified as the indirect grant of aid to the companies in which the investment is made. Thus, the ECJ held, in *Germany v Commission*, that a tax relief granted to taxpayers who invested in companies situated in Berlin or the former East German *Länder* constituted aid in favour of the target companies. The origin of the advantage indirectly conferred on the companies was the renunciation of tax revenue which would normally have been received by the State, inasmuch as it was this renunciation which enabled the investors to take up holdings in those companies on conditions which were in tax terms more advantageous.[41] Tax incentives granted to banks in order to help fund the formation of consortia to rescue firms in difficulty were considered as constituting aid to those firms.[42] Deductions from private investors' taxable income of the amount invested in a French shipyard were considered by the Commission to amount to aid indirectly granted to the shipyards in so far as the investments allowed the shipyard to obtain orders which it would not otherwise have attracted and enabled the lessee of the vessel to operate it on favourable terms.[43] Similarly in *Confédération Nationale du Crédit Mutuel v Commission,* the General Court thought that favourable tax treatment granted to individuals in France who placed their savings in the *Livrebleu* could be regarded as the indirect grant of aid to Crédit Mutuel which operated the scheme.[44] In *Associazione Italiana del Risparmio Gestito v Commission*, under Italian law specialised investment vehicles were granted an indirect advantage, since the tax reduction on investments in specialised vehicles prompted investors to buy shares in those vehicles, thereby providing them with additional liquidity and extra income in terms of management and entry fees.[45] By contrast, in *Banco Santander v Commission* and *Autogrill v Commission*, the Commission's decision did not seek to determine that aid was passed on

---

[40] SA.29150, *Sanierungsklausel* (2011).

[41] Case C-156/98, *Germany v Commission* [2000] ECR I-6857, para 26; Case C-169/08, *Presidente del Consiglio dei Ministri v Regione Sardegna* [2009] ECR I-10821, para 57.

[42] *Tenth Report on Competition Policy* (1980), pt. 220.

[43] Case T-34/02, *Le Levant 001 v Commission* [2005] ECR II-267, para 23; Commission Decision 2001/882/EC, *Le Levant*, OJ 2001 L327/37.

[44] Case T-93/02, *Confédération Nationale du Crédit Mutuel v Commission* [2005] ECR II-143, para 95.

[45] Case T-445/05, *Associazione Italiana del Risparmio Gestito v Commission* [2009] ECR II-289, para 139; Case T-424/05, *Italy v Commission* [2009] ECR II-23*, para 114.

indirectly to the foreign companies, which did not receive any new investment capital since only their shares were transacted.[46]

Alternative subjective taxpayer choices irrelevant The economic advantage gained by the beneficiary is the difference between the tax due from the beneficiary who has taken advantage of the measure in relation to the transaction in question and the tax that would have been due under the normal tax system in the absence of the preferential scheme. It is not appropriate, in assessing the extent of the economic advantage, to examine any alternative subjective choices that might have been made by the beneficiary of the scheme in the absence of the measure. Thus, in *BNP Paribas v Commission*, where a special regime applied for taxing capital gains on the restructuring of certain bank assets, the General Court rejected the argument that the normal tax regime was not the correct reference framework in that the undertakings concerned would not have disposed of the assets in the absence of the preferential scheme.[47]

Discretionary general measures and individual assessment Where a measure does not apply to all economic operators, it cannot be considered to be a general measure of tax or economic policy.[48] Aid granted through the tax system will normally arise from legislative provisions allowing for differential treatment of taxpayers. In certain circumstances, aid may be granted by the exercise of discretion by the administrative tax authorities.[49] It is not necessary to establish that the conduct of a tax authority is arbitrary. For example, in the Basque tax cases, the tax administration enjoyed a discretion enabling it to vary the amount of, or the conditions for granting, the tax concession in question according to the characteristics of the investment project submitted for its assessment, thereby giving rise to the grant of State aid.[50]

Nevertheless, the mere fact that certain aspects of an individual tax assessment may require the tax authorities to exercise a discretion in determining liability does not necessarily lead to the conclusion that State aid is granted, in particular where the margin of discretion is transparent and non-

---

[46] Case T-399/11, *Banco Santander SA v Commission* EU:T:2014:938, para 59; Case T-219/10, *Autogrill España SA v Commission* EU:T:2014:939, para 55.

[47] Case T-335/08, *BNP Paribas v Commission* [2010] ECR II-3323, paras 167-169.

[48] Case C-66/02, *Italy v Commission* [2005] ECR I-10901, para 99; Case C-148/04, *Unicredito Italiano SpA v Agenzia delle Entrate, Ufficio Genova 1* [2005] ECR I-11137, para 49; Case C-222/04, *Ministero dell'Economia e delle Finanze v Cassa di Risparmio di Firenze SpA* [2006] ECR I-289, para 135.

[49] Case C-241/94, *France v Commission* [1996] ECR I-4551, paras 23-24.

[50] Cases T-127/99, T-129/99 & T-148/99, *Territorio Histórico de Álava - Diputación Foral de Álava v Commission* [2002] ECR I-1275, para 154; Cases T-227/01 etc., *Territorio Histórico de Álava – Diputación Foral de Álava v Commission* [2009] ECR II-3029, para 171.

discriminatory. For example, in *Stadtwerke Schwäbisch Hall GmbH*, concerning the creation of tax reserves for the decommissioning of nuclear power stations and the safe disposal of nuclear waste, the General Court accepted that the rapid development of technical standards entailed a degree of uncertainty as regards future costs.[51] Equally, the requirement of an authorisation from a tax authority does not necessarily engage the State aid rules. In *P Oy*, the ECJ held that the application of an authorisation system which enabled losses to be carried forward was not, in principle, considered to be selective if the competent authorities had, when deciding on an application for authorisation, only a degree of latitude limited by objective criteria which were not unrelated to the tax system, such as the objective of avoiding trade in losses. On the other hand, if the competent authorities had a broad discretion to determine the beneficiaries or the conditions under which financial assistance was provided on the basis of criteria unrelated to the tax system, such as maintaining employment, the exercise of that discretion must be regarded as being capable of favouring certain undertakings.[52]

Tax amnesty favouring certain undertakings Undertakings subject to a particular tax will normally pay the tax assessed within the requisite time limit. In some circumstances where tax has not been paid over a significant period, a Member State may provide for an amnesty as a means of terminating the assessment or collection procedures. The question then arises, from a State aid perspective, whether this is a general measure or whether, on the contrary, it constitutes a selective advantage in favour of those undertakings that benefit from the amnesty. The Commission has set out its policy, according to which State aid will not arise where certain conditions are met.[53] First, the measure should be exceptional in nature, provide a strong incentive for undertakings to comply voluntarily with their tax obligations and enhance tax collection. Secondly, it should be open to any undertaking that has outstanding tax liabilities. Third, it should not entail any *de facto* selectivity. Fourth, the tax administration should have no discretionary power to intervene in the granting or intensity of the amnesty. Finally, the measure should not entail a waiver from verification.

In *3M Italia*, Italian legislation provided that tax disputes arising more than 10 years before its entry into force might be extinguished by payment of an amount equivalent to 5% of the value of the claim. The ECJ held that, even supposing that the application of the amnesty might in a particular situation

---

[51] Case T-92/02, *Stadtwerke Schwäbisch Hall GmbH v Commission* [2006] ECR II-11*, para 101 (judgment set aside on appeal on other grounds in Case C-176/06 P, *Stadtwerke Schwäbisch Hall GmbH v Commission* [2007] ECR I-170*).

[52] Case C-6/12, *P Oy* EU:C:2013:525, paras 26-27; Case T-140/13, *Netherlands Maritime Technology Association v Commission* EU:T:2014:1029, para 30.

[53] SA.33183, *Latvian tax amnesty* (2012).

lead to an economic advantage for a beneficiary of that provision, with respect to the selectiveness of the measure, it applied generally, according to its terms, to all taxpayers who were parties to tax proceedings pending before the Supreme Court, whatever the nature of the tax at issue and where the tax authorities had been unsuccessful at first and second instance. The fact that only taxpayers satisfying those conditions could benefit from the measure could not in itself make it into a selective measure. Moreover, although the measure was of limited temporal application, since in order to benefit from it taxpayers had to submit an application within a period of 90 days from the entry into force of the legislation, that limitation was inherent to measures of this kind, which were necessarily one-off measures, and the period appeared sufficient to allow all taxpayers to whom this general one-off measure applied to seek to benefit from it. It followed that the amnesty could not be classified as State aid.[54]

Misapplication of national fiscal provisions Circumstances may arise where a distortion of competition is caused by a public authority failing properly to apply fiscal measures, such as where a tax authority misapplies national tax provisions resulting in an underassessment of liability of a particular undertaking. If this misapplication is not corrected by the tax authority or the courts under the relevant national law, it must be considered whether the resulting benefit to the undertaking, where this distorts competition in the internal market, is to be regarded as State aid within the scope of Article 107(1) TFEU. In general, remedial action in the sphere of national tax administration should be a matter within the province of national tax law. It would be quite undesirable for the Commission to seek to check whether national tax authorities were always properly applying the relevant provisions. Moreover, this would be consistent with the principle of subsidiarity. Thus, in *ICI*, the misapplication of a discretion by the tax authorities was held, by the English High Court, not to constitute State aid.[55] In *Ufex v Commission*, where it was alleged that certain undertakings were unlawfully subject to stamp duty whereas their publicly-owned competitor was not, the Commission observed that the sole consequence of the tax authorities' error was that the State accrued additional financial revenues. The General Court agreed that it could not be deduced from the possible illegal taxation of one operator that another, correctly taxed, operator received a State aid.[56]

---

[54] Case C-417/10, *Ministero dell'Economia e delle Finanze v 3M Italia SpA* EU:C:2012:184, paras 41-44; Case C-529/10, *Ministero dell'Economia e delle Finanze v Safilo SpA* EU:C:2012:188, paras 27-30.

[55] *R v Attorney General, ex parte ICI* [1985] 1 CMLR 588.

[56] Case T-613/97, *Ufex v Commission* [2000] ECR I-4055, para 122.

However, the English Court of Appeal in *ICI*,[57] whilst agreeing that the inadvertent misapplication of national tax law did not constitute aid, held that persistent misapplication did result in aid being granted. This has been criticised on the ground that the same distortive effects arise from inadvertent and deliberate misapplication of the tax provisions regardless of the intention of the tax authorities.[58] Drawing a distinction between inadvertent and deliberate misapplication does not, moreover, fit easily within the structures established under Article 108 TFEU. Given that Article 108(3) TFEU only requires plans to grant or alter aid to be notified in advance to the Commission prior to being put into effect, the question may be posed as to whether benefits arising from misapplication of national law can be regarded as State aid within the scope of Article 107(1) TFEU where such State action or inaction does not derive from any plan to grant aid. In particular, the notion that only persistent misapplication rather than the initial inadvertent misapplication constitutes aid implies that no aid is granted when the actual financial benefit accrues to the undertaking but that a repeated failure of the authorities to remedy the misapplication results in aid having being granted. Classifying a measure as State aid on the ground of deliberate, but not inadvertent, misapplication is, therefore, incoherent.

Aggressive tax planning In 2014, the Commission instigated a series of investigations into alleged misapplication of national tax provisions concerning advance tax rulings on transfer pricing in the context of aggressive tax avoidance schemes used by multinational groups of companies. Aggressive tax planning takes effect through individual tax rulings where the transfer pricing agreed with the taxpayer results in an economic advantage on the basis that the remuneration received by an entity within the group is not based on remuneration on market terms under normal conditions of competition, thereby leading to a lower taxable profit for the group as a whole. Since this method of reducing the tax burden is available only to taxpayer companies that are members of multinational groups, the advantage is regarded as selective.[59]

In the opening decision in the investigation into Starbuck's tax arrangements involving its Netherlands subsidiary, for example, the Commission held that the Netherlands' tax authorities had accepted the taxpayer's analysis of transfer pricing which was incorrect in that the analysis was inconsistent with normal international rules as established in accordance with the relevant OECD guidelines, thereby granting an economic advantage in each year that the ruling was the basis of a tax assessment. The Commission

---

[57] *R v Attorney General, ex parte ICI* [1987] 1 CMLR 72.

[58] See K.P.E. Lasok, "State aids and remedies under the EEC Treaty" (1986) 7 ECLR 53 and T. Sharpe, "The role of national courts in relation to Community law of State aids" in I. Harden ed., *State Aid: Community Law and Policy* (Cologne, 1993).

[59] *Report on Competition Policy* (2014), p.15.

stated that, while advance pricing agreements that merely contain an interpretation of the relevant tax provisions without deviating from administrative practice do not give rise to a presumption of a selective advantage, rulings that deviated from that practice have the effect of lowering the tax burden of the undertakings concerned as compared to undertakings in a similar legal and factual situation, such that the measure should also be considered selective. The Commission, accordingly, concluded that it appeared that Starbucks had received unlawful State aid by virtue of the misapplication of the national tax provisions by the tax authorities.[60] Even where the OECD Guidelines were not binding measures in national law, the Commission regarded them, as in its opening decision into Apple's operations in Ireland, as being a valid reference document.[61]

The Commission also opened an investigation into a new reform of Gibraltar corporate tax which came into effect in 2011 and which involves the use of tax rulings. The Commission alleged that the Gibraltar tax authorities granted formal tax rulings without performing an adequate evaluation of whether the companies' income has been accrued in or derived from outside Gibraltar. Even if the tax legislation allowed the tax authorities a considerable margin of manoeuvre, a misapplication of its provisions could not be ruled out.[62]

Repayment of unlawfully levied taxes Article 107(1) TFEU does not apply to sums repaid by the State which were unlawfully levied.[63] Since only the amount wrongly charged is repaid, it does not to that extent amount to a distribution of State resources or a charge on public funds.[64] In *Amministrazione delle Finanze dello Stato v Denkavit Italiana*, the Italian authorities sought to invoke the applicability of Article 107(1) TFEU in order to refute liability to repay duties that had been unlawfully levied, arguing that this would result in aid being granted to the recipients. However, the ECJ held that Article 107(1) TFEU did not apply to a duty to repay sums where those sums were not payable by the person who paid them. A national tax system which enables the taxpayer to contest or claim repayment of tax does not constitute an aid. Whether or not it is possible to recover tax depends solely

---

[60] Commission Decision SA,38374, *Alleged State aid to Starbucks*, (2014).

[61] Commission Decision SA.38373, *Alleged aid to Apple* (2014). See also, SA.38375, *Fiat* (2014); SA. 38944, *Amazon* (2014); SA.37667, *Belgian Excess Profits Tax ruling system* (2015).

[62] SA.34914, *Gibraltar tax rulings* (2014).

[63] Case 61/79, *Amministrazione delle Finanze dello Stato v Denkavit Italiana* [1980] ECR 1205, para 31.

[64] Case 61/79, *Amministrazione delle Finanze dello Stato v Denkavit Italiana* [1980] ECR 1205, *per* Advocate General Reischl, at p. 1235.

upon the characteristics of the national legislation on the recovery of sums paid but not owed.[65]

3.2 SELECTIVITY BY DEROGATION FROM NORMAL TAXATION

Selectivity entails derogation from normal taxation Article 107(1) TFEU requires that the economic advantage in question must selectively favour certain undertakings or the production of certain goods. Selectivity applies under a tax system where certain undertakings are taxed in a way that derogates to their benefit from the common or normal regime. The element which constitutes aid is generally established by determining the normal application of the system of charges in relation to the nature or general scheme of that system.[66] In order to determine whether the measure at issue is selective it is appropriate, therefore, to examine whether, within the context of a particular legal regime, that measure constitutes an advantage for certain undertakings in comparison with others which, in the light of the objective pursued by that regime, are in a comparable legal and factual situation.[67] Moreover, having established that a particular measure constitutes *prima facie* a derogation from the normal application of the system, it is necessary to determine whether such derogation is justified by reference to the nature and

---

[65] Case 61/79, *Amministrazione delle Finanze dello Stato v Denkavit Italiana* [1980] ECR 1205, para 31.

[66] Case C-390/98, *HJ Banks & Co Ltd. v Coal Authority* [2001] ECR I-6117, para 34; Case C-88/03, *Portugal v Commission* [2006] ECR I-7115, para 56; Cases C-78/08 – C-80/08, *Ministero dell'Economia e delle Finanze v Paint Graphos* [2011] ECR I-7611, para 49; Case C-6/12, *P Oy* EU:C:2013:525, para 19; Case C-522/13, *Ministerio de Defensa v Concello de Ferrol* EU:C:2014:2262, para 35; Case T-399/11, *Banco Santander SA v Commission* EU:T:2014:938, para 34; Case T-219/10, *Autogrill España SA v Commission* EU:T:2014:939, para 30.

[67] Case C-143/99, *Adria-Wien Pipeline GmbH v Finanzlandesdirektion für Kärnten* [2001] ECR I-8365, para 41; Case C-182/03 & C-217/03, *Belgium and Forum 187 ASBL v Commission* [2006] ECR I-5479, para 119; Case C-88/03, *Portugal v Commission* [2006] ECR I-7115, para 54; Cases C-428/06 & C-434/06, *Unión General de Trabajadores de la Rioja v Juntas Generales del Territorio Histórico de Vizcaya* [2008] ECR I-6747, para 46; Case C-487/06P, *British Aggregates Association v Commission* [2008] ECR I-10515, para 82; Case C-169/08, *Presidente del Consiglio dei Ministri v Regione Sardegna* [2009] ECR I-10821, para 61; Cases C-78/08 – C-80/08, *Ministero dell' Economia e delle Finanze v Paint Graphos* [2011] ECR I-7611, para 49; Cases C-106/09P & C-107/09P, *Commission v Government of Gibraltar* [2011] ECR I-11113, para 75; Case C-5/14, *Kernkraftwerke Lippe-Ems GmbH v Hza Osnabrück* EU:C:2015:354, para 74; Case T-500/12 *Ryanair Ltd v Commission* EU:T:2015:73, para 68; Case T-473/12, *Aer Lingus Ltd v Commission* EU:T:2015:78, para 46.

general scheme of the system, in which case it will be regarded as forming an integral part of the normal application of the system.[68]

In most cases, the parameters of the scheme in question are established by the relevant legislative provisions. However, as the General Court commented in *Banco Santander v Commission* and *Autogrill v Commission*, the selective character of a measure may not necessarily be precisely circumscribed by the measure itself.[69] In *Salzgitter v Commission*, it held that as a general rule, a tax measure which is likely to be found to be State aid differs from a general tax provision in that the number of recipients benefiting from the measure tends to be limited in law or in fact. It does not matter that the selective nature of the measure flows, for example, from a sectoral criterion or from a criterion relating to geographic location in a defined part of the territory of a Member State. What matters for a measure to be found to be State aid, is that the recipient undertakings belong to a specific category determined by the application, in law or in fact, of the criterion established by the measure in question.[70] That requires an examination not only of the contents of the tax provisions in question, but also of their scope on the basis of administrative and judicial practice and the ambit *ratione personae* of the provisions.[71]

Reference framework must be ascertained   Since the existence of an advantage may generally be established only when compared with normal taxation, the relevant reference framework must be determined.[72]   When carrying out this analysis, it is necessary, therefore, first to ascertain the scope of the general system establishing the normal taxation, before determining whether the measure derogates from that system. For example, in *Adria-Wien Pipleline*, the normal taxation in question applied to all production, whether of goods or services, so that a derogation from the normal rate for the manufacturing sector was regarded as entailing State aid.[73] In *Belgium and Forum 187 v Commission*, in order to decide whether a special method of calculating taxable profits for coordination centres of multinational groups constituted an advantage, the ECJ held that it was necessary to compare that

---

[68]   Case 173/73, *Italy v Commission* [1974] ECR 709, para 15; Case C-353/95 P, *Tiercé Ladbroke v Commission* [1997] ECR I-7007, paras 33-35.

[69]   Case T-399/11, *Banco Santander SA v Commission* EU:T:2014:938, para 39; Case T-219/10, *Autogrill España SA v Commission* EU:T:2014:939, para 35.

[70]   Case T-308/00, *Salzgitter AG v Commission* [2004] ECR II-1933, para 38.

[71]   Case C-6/12, *P Oy* EU:C:2013:525, para 20.

[72]   Case C-88/03, *Portugal v Commission* [2006] ECR I-7115, para 56; Cases C-106/09P & C-107/09P, *Commission v Government of Gibraltar* [2011] ECR I-11113, para 90; Cases T-211/04 & T-215/04, *Government of Gibraltar v Commission* [2008] ECR II-3745, para 80; Case T-399/11, *Banco Santander SA v Commission* EU:T:2014:938, para 34; Case T-219/10, *Autogrill España SA v Commission* EU:T:2014:939, para 30.

[73]   Case C-143/99, *Adria-Wien Pipeline GmbH v Finanzlandesdirektion für Kärnten* [2001] ECR I-8365, para 55.

regime to the ordinary system of taxation of company profits.[74] In *Paint Graphos*, which concerned an exemption from corporation tax for producers' and workers' cooperatives, the ECJ observed that for the purpose of calculating corporation tax, the basis of assessment of the cooperative societies concerned was determined in the same way as that of other types of undertaking, namely on the basis of the amount of net profit earned as a result of the undertaking's activities at the end of the tax year. Corporation tax was therefore to be regarded as the legal regime of reference for the purpose of determining whether the measure at issue might be selective.[75] In *Ministerio de Defensa v Concello de Ferrol*, which related to an exemption from Spanish property tax, the relevant reference framework was established by the Spanish legislation which declared that any ownership or use of land entailed, in principle, liability to property tax.[76] In *Ryanair v Commission* and *Aer Lingus v Commission*, which concerned Irish air travel tax that was levied at differential rates of €2 and €10 respectively, the General Court upheld the Commission's finding that the reference system was the taxation of air passengers departing on an aircraft from an airport in Ireland and that the higher rate was the reference rate for determining the existence of State aid, the lower rate applying, as an exception from that reference system, to only some 10-15% of all flights subject to the tax.[77]

In *France and France Télécom v Commission*, French business tax was defined as a local tax payable by reference to the production factors held by a taxable person in each municipality. France Télécom was regarded as being treated selectively, for the period 1994-2003, on the ground that during that period it was assessed to business tax by virtue of a special tax regime, based on a weighted average of all local authorities.[78] However, for the earlier period 1991-1993, it had been subject to a fixed levy in place of the normal business tax. That fixed levy, in the circumstances, was not regarded as State aid as the Commission determined that it was more akin to paying a share of the earnings to the owner of the capital than to taxation. Accordingly, it would seem that the business tax was not, for that period, regarded as a reference framework, although the Commission appears to have accepted this on the basis that the fixed levy in any event offset the total exemption from business tax.[79]

---

[74] Case C-182/03 & C-217/03, *Belgium and Forum 187 ASBL v Commission* [2006] ECR I-5479, para 95.

[75] Cases C-78/08 – C-80/08, *Ministero dell' Economia e delle Finanze v Paint Graphos* [2011] ECR I-7611, para 50.

[76] Case C-522/13, *Ministerio de Defensa v Concello de Ferrol* EU:C:2014:2262, para 36.

[77] Case T-500/12, *Ryanair Ltd v Commission* EU:T:2015:73, para 90; Case T-473/12, *Aer Lingus Ltd v Commission* EU:T:2015:78, para 76.

[78] Case C-81/10P, *France Télécom SA v Commission* [2011] ECR I-12899, para 18; Cases T-427/04 & T-17/05, *France v Commission* [2009] ECR II-4315, para 231.

[79] Cases T-427/04 & T-17/05, *France v Commission* [2009] ECR II-4315, para 68.

Regulatory technique and privileged undertakings The notion that Article 107(1) TFEU does not distinguish between measures of State intervention by reference to their causes or aims but defines them in relation to their effects means that such measures must be defined independently of the techniques used for the adoption of the measure.[80] Thus, the scope of the relevant reference framework may not be reduced by the use of regulatory technique designed to eliminate tax liability for a category of undertakings which would otherwise be subject to the tax, as illustrated by the saga of the Gibraltar corporation tax reforms. Gibraltar had proposed tax reform measures whereby general taxation of company profits would be abolished and replaced by a new general system of corporation tax comprising two bases of assessment, a payroll tax coupled with a business property occupation tax, with a cap on liability of 15% of company profits. Gibraltar maintained that the choice of employment and of occupation of property for business purposes as the bases of taxation was considered essential in the light of the characteristics of Gibraltar's economy, namely limited labour resources, significant dependence on workers commuting daily from Spain, the many small companies and the need to introduce simple taxes given the operational limits of the Gibraltar authorities. It also maintained that the reason underlying the cap limiting liability to payroll tax and the property tax to 15% of profits was the wish to base taxation on the principle of ability to pay and to avoid an overtaxing of companies which could trigger layoffs, serious instability in a small economy such as Gibraltar's and subsequent losses of tax revenue. Moreover, this 15% threshold was aimed at ensuring that taxation was paid from profits and was not transformed into a tax on companies' capital. The Commission's decision, finding that this system constituted material selectivity and thus State aid, was annulled by the General Court on the ground that the Commission had failed to determine whether the various aspects of the tax system introduced by the reform were capable of forming a common or normal tax regime in its own right. Instead, the Commission appeared simply to have found that the requirement to make a profit and the 15% cap constituted derogations from the payroll tax and the business property tax which were, implicitly, considered to form the normal regime introduced by the reform.[81]

On appeal, in *Commission v Government of Gibraltar*, the ECJ agreed that the fact that the payroll tax and the property tax were payable only where the taxable person made a profit and that the amount of tax was capped at 15% of

---

[80] Case C-487/06P, *British Aggregates Association v Commission* [2008] ECR I-10515, para 85; Cases C-106/09P & C-107/09P, *Commission v Government of Gibraltar* [2011] ECR I-11113, para 87; Case C-5/14, *Kernkraftwerke Lippe-Ems GmbH v Hza Osnabrück* EU:C:2015:354, para 75.

[81] Cases T-211/04 & T-215/04, *Government of Gibraltar v Commission* [2008] ECR II-3745, paras 171-173.

profits meant that these were general measures.[82] However, since Article 107(1) TFEU defines measures in relation to their effects, and thus independently of the techniques used, an analysis based solely on the regulatory technique used by the tax system would not allow the effects of the tax measure to be considered, thereby excluding from the outset any possibility that the fact that no tax liability was incurred by offshore companies may be classified as a selective advantage. It followed, the ECJ held, that the requirement to identify a relevant framework by reference to which an advantage may be established does not make the classification of a tax system as selective conditional upon that system being designed in such a way that undertakings which might enjoy a selective advantage are, in general, liable to the same tax burden as other undertakings but benefit from derogating provisions, so that the selective advantage may be identified as being the difference between the normal tax burden and that borne by those former undertakings. The consequence of a contrary approach would be that national tax rules fall from the outset outside the scope of control of State aid merely because they were adopted under a different regulatory technique although they produce the same effects in law and/or in fact as derogating measures. This applies particularly with regard to a tax system which, instead of laying down general rules applying to all undertakings from which a derogation is made for certain undertakings, achieves the same result by adjusting and combining the tax rules in such a way that their very application results in a different tax burden for different undertakings.[83]

Consequently, in the circumstances, the ECJ held that the relevant reference framework was the Gibraltar corporate tax regime which formally applied to all undertakings including offshore companies registered in Gibraltar. The regime favoured offshore companies by choosing bases of assessment which, even though they were founded on criteria that were in themselves of a general nature, in practice discriminated between companies that were in a comparable situation with regard to the objective of the proposed tax reform, namely to introduce a general system of taxation for all companies established in Gibraltar. Combining those bases of assessment not only resulted in taxation according to the number of employees and the size of the business premises occupied, but also, due to the absence of other bases of assessment, excluded from the outset any taxation of offshore companies, since they had no employees and did not occupy business property. Although the general rule is that a different tax burden resulting from the application of a general tax regime is not sufficient on its own to establish selectivity, the criteria forming the basis of assessment which are adopted by a tax system must also, in order to be capable of being recognised as conferring selective advantages, be such

---

[82] Cases C-106/09P & C-107/09P, *Commission v Government of Gibraltar* [2011] ECR I-11113, paras 81-83.

[83] *Ibid.*, paras 88-93.

as to characterise the recipient undertakings, by virtue of the properties which are specific to them, as a privileged category, thus permitting such a regime to be described as favouring certain undertakings or the production of certain goods within the meaning of Article 107(1) TFEU.[84] The ECJ observed that the fact that offshore companies were not taxed was not a random consequence of the regime at issue, but the inevitable consequence of the fact that the bases of assessment were specifically designed so that offshore companies had no tax base under the bases of assessment. Thus, the fact that offshore companies avoided taxation precisely on account of their specific characteristic features gave reason to conclude that those companies enjoyed selective advantages.[85]

Objective pursued by the tax measure In order to determine whether a measure is selective, it is necessary to determine whether it constitutes an advantage for certain undertakings as compared with others which are in a comparable legal and factual situation in light of the objective pursued by that measure.[86] Normally, the objective of a tax measure is simply to raise public finance. Thus, the objective of corporation tax is to tax company profits in the Member State in question.[87] For instance, in *Commission v Gibraltar*, where the Gibraltar authorities intended to provide for no tax liability for offshore companies, the ECJ still regarded them as falling within the scope of Gibraltar corporation tax, the objective of which was to introduce a general system of taxation for all companies established in Gibraltar.[88] In *Ryanair v Commission*, the objective and structure of the Irish air travel tax system was held to be to tax passengers departing from an airport located in Ireland in order to raise money for the State budget.[89] In *France and France Télécom v Commission*, it was held that the objective pursued by French business tax was identified from the fact that it was a local tax payable annually by persons pursuing a self-employed occupation and assessed not on the basis of profits but in accordance with economic criteria related to the value of the production factors, i.e. capital and labour, used in the business in the territory of each local authority in which it had an establishment.[90]

---

[84] *Ibid.*, paras 94-104; Case T-140/13, *Netherlands Maritime Technology Association v Commission* EU:T:2014:1029, para 99.

[85] Cases C-106/09P & C-107/09P, *Commission v Government of Gibraltar* [2011] ECR I-11113, paras 106-107.

[86] Case C-143/99, *Adria-Wien Pipeline GmbH v Finanzlandesdirektion für Kärnten* [2001] ECR I-8365, para 41; Case C-88/03, *Portugal v Commission* [2006] ECR I-7115, para 58.

[87] Cases C-78/08 – C-80/08, *Ministero dell' Economia e delle Finanze v Paint Graphos* [2011] ECR I-7611, para 54.

[88] Cases C-106/09P & C-107/09P, *Commission v Government of Gibraltar* [2011] ECR I-11113, para 101.

[89] Case T-512/11, *Ryanair Ltd v Commission* EU:T:2014:989, para 83.

[90] Cases T-427/04 & T-17/05, *France v Commission* [2009] ECR II-4315, para 231.

A legislature may also have other objectives in mind, such as environmental or social objectives, when formulating tax legislation. In *Ministerio de Defensa v Concello de Ferrol*, the objective of Spanish property tax was to tax the ownership or use of land.[91] In *Presidente del Consiglio dei Ministri v Regione Sardegna*, a regional tax on stopovers of aircraft and pleasure boats in Sardinia was regarded as having an environmental objective, which was to protect and renew environmental resources polluted by tourism, particularly in coastal areas.[92] In *British Aggregates Association v Commission*, the aggregates levy introduced in the United Kingdom had the environmental objective of reducing and rationalising the extraction of minerals commonly used as aggregates by favouring their replacement by recycled products or other products not covered by the levy, thereby helping to protect the environment.[93] In *Kernkraftwerke Lippe-Ems GmbH v Hza Osnabrück*, concerning a German excise duty imposed on nuclear fuel, it was held that the objective of the levy was to raise revenue to contribute, in accordance with the polluter pays principle, to a reduction in the burden entailed for the Federal budget by the rehabilitation required at the mining site where radioactive waste from the use of nuclear fuel was stored.[94] Exceptionally, the policy objective of a tax measure may be quite unrelated to raising revenue for the State. In *3M Italia*, concerning a tax amnesty for taxpayers intended to bring to an end protracted litigation with the Italian tax authorities, the objective was held to be one of ensuring compliance with the principle that final judgment must be given within a reasonable time.[95]

Comparable legal and factual situation It is for the Commission to prove that a measure introduces differential treatment between undertakings that are in a comparable legal and factual situation in light of the objective in question.[96] In general, undertakings subject to income or corporation tax are in a comparable legal and factual situation in light of the objective of that tax, which is to collect revenue on the basis of corporate profits. For example, in *Ministero dell'Economia e delle Finanze v Cassa di Risparmio di Firenze*,

---

[91] Case C-522/13, *Ministerio de Defensa v Concello de Ferrol* EU:C:2014:2262, para 40.

[92] Case C-169/08, *Presidente del Consiglio dei Ministri v Regione Sardegna* [2009] ECR I-10821, per Advocate General Kokott, para 136.

[93] Case T-359/04, *British Aggregates Association v Commission* [2010] ECR II-4227, para 11.

[94] Case C-5/14, *Kernkraftwerke Lippe-Ems GmbH v Hza Osnabrück* EU:C:2015:354, para 78.

[95] Case C-417/10, *Ministero dell'Economia e delle Finanze v 3M Italia SpA* EU:C:2012:184, para 42; Case C-529/10, *Ministero dell'Economia e delle Finanze v Safilo SpA* EU:C:2012:188, para 28.

[96] Case C-279/08P, *Commission v Netherlands* [2011] ECR I-7671, para 62; Case T-399/11, *Banco Santander SA v Commission* EU:T:2014:938, para 50; Case T-219/10, *Autogrill España SA v Commission* EU:T:2014:939, para 46.

Italian tax provisions applicable to certain banking foundations were held to constitute an exception to the general corporation tax scheme such as to give rise to State aid. The undertakings which benefited from them were entitled to tax advantages to which they would have no right under the normal rules of application of that scheme and to which undertakings in other sectors carrying out similar operations or undertakings in the banking sector not carrying out operations such as those to which the rules applied had no right.[97] In *Italy v Commission*, tax relief was given in respect of the costs incurred in listing of new companies on the stock exchange. The Commission found that this constituted selective State aid to companies registered in Italy as opposed to foreign companies doing business in Italy on the ground that the tax relief applied to the world-wide profits of Italian companies but only to the profits generated in Italy of foreign companies. This was upheld by the General Court on the basis that the tax relief applied to a greater extent to Italian companies.[98]

Similar reasoning applies in the context of special tax regimes. For example, in *British Telecommunications plc*, which concerned exemption for BT from a levy payable into a pensions protection fund, on the ground that BT was covered by a public guarantee, BT's argument that its pension scheme was in a different legal and factual situation from other pension schemes coming within the legal framework of the protection of pensions against the employer's insolvency was rejected.[99] In *Ministerio de Defensa v Concello de Ferrol*, where an exemption from property tax was granted to an undertaking operating in the national defence sector, it was held that not only undertakings which owned or used land for purposes partly related to national defence were in a comparable factual and legal situation in the light of the objective of taxing the ownership or use of land, but also those undertakings which owned or used land for exclusively civil purposes.[100] By contrast, in *Kernkraftwerke Lippe-Ems GmbH v Hza Osnabrück*, which concerned an excise duty on nuclear fuel with a consequential impact of the cost of electricity produced from nuclear energy, other methods of producing electricity were not, in light of the objective of that levy, in a comparable legal and factual situation, as only production based on nuclear fuel generated radioactive waste.[101]

---

[97] Case C-66/02, *Italy v Commission* [2005] ECR I-10901, para 100; Case C-148/04, *Unicredito Italiano SpA v Agenzia delle Entrate, Ufficio Genova 1* [2005] ECR I-11137, para 50; Case C-222/04, *Ministero dell'Economia e delle Finanze v Cassa di Risparmio di Firenze SpA* [2006] ECR I-289, para 136.

[98] Case T-211/05, *Italy v Commission* [2009] ECR II-2777, paras 122-123; upheld on appeal in Case C-458/09P, *Italy v Commission* [2011] ECR I-179*, paras 56-60.

[99] Cases T-226/09 & T-230/09, *British Telecommunications plc v Commission* EU:T:2013:466, paras 88-93.

[100] Case C-522/13, *Ministerio de Defensa v Concello de Ferrol* EU:C:2014:2262, para 40.

[101] Case C-5/14, *Kernkraftwerke Lippe-Ems GmbH v Hza Osnabrück* EU:C:2015:354, para 79.

Whether a measure is selective is determined by taking all comparable undertakings into account and not just the undertakings within the same group which enjoy the same advantage.[102]   In *Italy v Commission*, concerning a reduction in excise duty on diesel for agricultural producers using greenhouses, it was held that the duty was normally imposed on all users of diesel, with the objective of raising taxation as well as an environmental objective.   The reduction in question benefited solely greenhouse operators with whom other agricultural producers were in a comparable situation since they also used diesel for their production.   The General Court rejected the argument that the reduction was not selective since it was not addressed to particular categories of producers having particular characteristics but was open to all undertakings which chose to use greenhouses for their production.[103]

Equally, the mere fact that certain undertakings subject to a particular tax must comply with certain conditions in order to qualify for a specific tax relief does not mean that, for those purposes, they are not in a comparable legal and factual situation to other undertakings subject to the same tax.   In *Associazione Italiana del Risparmio Gestito v Commission*, where beneficial tax rules applied to specialised investment vehicles in Italy, the mere fact that the advantage might benefit any investment vehicle fulfilling the conditions in the relevant legislation was not enough to establish that the measure at issue was general in scope rather than selective.[104]   In *Banco Santander v Commission* and *Autogrill v Commission*, the Commission determined that Spanish undertakings that acquired shareholdings in foreign companies, in respect of which tax relief against Spanish tax was available, were in a comparable legal and factual situation to Spanish companies who made investments in other Spanish companies, for which no tax relief was available.   However, the General Court found that, since the tax relief was available to any Spanish undertaking as long as they satisfied the requisite investment criteria and was independent of their economic activity, it was not selective.[105]   In particular, the argument that the measure was selective merely because it required certain pre-conditions to be fulfilled was rejected.[106]

Nevertheless, the circumstances of categories of undertakings falling within the scope of a tax may differ so that they are not treated as being in a comparable legal and factual situation.   For instance, in *Paint Graphos*,

---

[102]   Case T-222/04, *Italy v Commission* [2009] ECR II-1877, para 66; Case T-379/09, *Italy v Commission* EU:T:2012:422, para 47.

[103]   Case T-379/09, *Italy v Commission* EU:T:2012:422, paras 41-48.

[104]   Case T-445/05, *Associazione Italiana del Risparmio Gestito v Commission* [2009] ECR II-289, para 152; Case T-424/05, *Italy v Commission* [2009] ECR II-23*, para 126; Case T-379/09, *Italy v Commission* EU:T:2012:422, para 47.

[105]   Case T-399/11, *Banco Santander SA v Commission* EU:T:2014:938, paras 54-61; Case T-219/10, *Autogrill España SA v Commission* EU:T:2014:939, para 50-57.

[106]   Case T-399/11, *Banco Santander SA v Commission* EU:T:2014:938, para 72; Case T-219/10, *Autogrill España SA v Commission* EU:T:2014:939, para 68.

cooperatives, which were characterised by various factors that distinguished them from other corporate entities, were held not to be in a comparable legal and factual situation to other undertakings for the purposes of Italian corporation tax.[107] A narrow approach will also apply where the parameters for determining those persons who are in a comparable legal and factual situation are set by reference to a more specific feature of the tax measure in question than merely the raising of revenue. For example, in *3M Italia*, persons who did not satisfy the criteria for claiming the benefit of the tax amnesty were not in a comparable legal and factual situation to those taxpayers who could claim the benefit from the point of view of the national legislature's objective of ensuring compliance with the principle that judgment must be given within a reasonable time.[108]

De facto selectivity and general measures General measures may include criteria that, because they may only be fulfilled by a limited category of undertakings, give rise to *de facto* selectivity. On this basis the Commission considered that a certain tax relief provided for in Italian legislation was not a general measure but was intended exclusively for certain undertakings, in particular Montedison in connection with the merger leading to the creation of Enimont.[109] A 10% reduction in corporation tax to captive insurance companies in the Åland islands was also held by the Commission to constitute State aid. The only purpose of companies of this type was to ensure the risk involved by the companies to which they belonged, so that the scheme established *de facto* selectivity between undertakings. Any business, irrespective of its size and the sector in which it operated was legally entitled to set up its own reinsurance company, but only a few large firms were able to achieve economies of scale by using the scheme.[110] In the Basque tax cases, a tax credit applying only to undertakings which made investments in fixed assets exceeding 2,500 million pesetas was held to be selective in that it favoured those undertakings which had at their disposal significant financial resources.[111] By contrast, in *Netherlands Maritime Technology Association v Commission*, where it was alleged that Spanish tax provisions concerning early depreciation of assets acquired through financial leasing arrangement constituted a *de facto* advantage to Spanish shipyards, the General Court

---

[107] Cases C-78/08–C-80/08, *Ministero dell' Economia e delle Finanze v Paint Graphos* [2011] ECR I-7611, para 61.

[108] Case C-417/10, *Ministero dell'Economia e delle Finanze v 3M Italia SpA* EU:C:2012:184, para 42; Case C-529/10, *Ministero dell'Economia e delle Finanze v Safilo SpA* EU:C:2012:188, para 28.

[109] *Twentieth Report on Competition Policy* (1990), pt. 305; Commission Decision 92/389/EEC, OJ 1992 L207/47.

[110] Commission Decision 2002/937/EC, OJ 2002 L329/22.

[111] Cases T-227/01 etc., *Territorio Histórico de Álava – Diputación Foral de Álava v Commission* [2009] ECR II-3029, paras 162-166.

merely held that the tax relief in question, being a general measure applicable to all undertakings in Spain, was not selective.[112]

Differentiation justified by the nature of the general system In *Tiercé Ladbroke v Commission*, the ECJ held that there is no advantage for the purposes of establishing State aid where a difference in treatment is justified by reasons relating to the logic of the system.[113] In its 1998 Notice, the Commission confirmed that the differential nature of tax measures will not be considered as State aid if their economic rationale makes them necessary to the functioning and effectiveness of the tax system, which was for the Member State to justify.[114] In *Netherlands Maritime Technology Association v Commission*, the General Court stated that this approach allowed differentiation with a tax system provided that it was supported by a rational justification.[115] This, however, is clearly wrong, with the principle in question being much more restrictive. In fact, a measure which creates an exception to the application of the general tax system may be justified by the nature and overall structure of the tax system only if the Member State concerned can show that that measure results directly from the basic or guiding principles of its tax system.[116] Tax measures which differentiate between undertakings and which might appear, therefore, to be selective will not constitute State aid where the differentiation arises from the nature or the overall structure of the system of charges of which they are a part.[117]

---

[112] Case T-140/13, *Netherlands Maritime Technology Association v Commission* EU:T:2014:1029, para 91.

[113] Case C-353/95 P, *Tiercé Ladbroke v Commission* [1997] ECR I-7007, paras 33-35; Case C-53/00, *Ferring SA v ACOSS* [2001] ECR I-9067, para 17.

[114] Commission 1998 Notice on State aid and direct taxation, para 23.

[115] Case T-140/13, *Netherlands Maritime Technology Association v Commission* EU:T:2014:1029, para 109.

[116] Case C-6/12, *P Oy* EU:C:2013:525, para 22.

[117] Case 173/73, *Italy v Commission* [1974] ECR 709, para 15; Case C-75/97, *Belgium v Commission* [1999] ECR I-3671, para 33; Case C-143/99, *Adria-Wien Pipeline GmbH v Finanzlandesdirektion für Kärnten* [2001] ECR I-8365, para 42; Case C-351/98, *Spain v Commission* [2002] ECR I-8031, para 42; Case C-409/00, *Spain v Commission* [2003] ECR I-1487, para 52; Case C-355/00, *Freskot v Greece* [2003] ECR I-5263, para 86; Case C-159/01, *Netherlands v Commission* [2004] ECR I-4461, para 42; Cases C-128/03 & C-129/03, *AEM SpA v Autorità per l'energia elettrica e per il gas* [2005] ECR I-2861, para 39; Case C-88/03, *Portugal v Commission* [2006] ECR I-7115, para 52; Case C-487/06P, *British Aggregates Association v Commission* [2008] ECR I-10515, para 56; Case C-522/13, *Ministerio de Defensa v Concello de Ferrol* EU:C:2014:2262, para 42; Case T-210/02, *British Aggregates Association v Commission* [2006] ECR II-2789, para 117; Case T-146/03, *Asociación de Empresarios de Estaciones de Servicio de la Comunidad Autónoma de Madrid v Commission* [2006] ECR II-98*, para 119; Cases T-211/04 & T-215/04, *Government of Gibraltar v Commission* [2008] ECR II-3745, para 144; Case T-445/05, *Associazione Italiana del Risparmio Gestito v Commission* [2009] ECR II-289, para 149; Case T-424/05, *Italy v Commission* [2009] ECR II-23*, para 116;

Thus, in *Italy v Commission*, the Commission determined that a transfer tax exemption for public undertakings that were created by transferring to them certain municipal economic activities was justified by the nature or general scheme of that tax, since it was properly payable on the creation of a new economic entity whereas municipal undertakings and the new public companies were substantially the same economic entities.[118]   On the other hand, concerning a straightforward three year exemption from income tax for these companies, the General Court held that it was manifestly clear that the tax treatment could not be justified by the nature or general scheme of the tax scheme in question.[119]   Similarly, in *BNP Paribas v Commission*, the argument that special tax treatment on bank restructuring was justified on grounds of avoidance of double taxation for the transferring entity was rejected since the provision in question in fact benefited the acquiring entities and could not, therefore, be justified by the inherent logic of the system.[120]

In order for tax exemptions to be justified by the nature or general scheme of the tax system of the Member State concerned, it is also necessary to ensure that those exemptions are consistent with the principle of proportionality and do not go beyond what is necessary, in that the legitimate objective being pursued could not be attained by less far-reaching measures.[121]   Thus, for example, in *France and France Télécom v Commission*, it was held that the tax advantage in question could not be justified since it had not been shown that the same objective could not have been achieved by measures that did not confer an advantage on France Télécom.[122]   In *British Telecommunications v Commission*, it was held that an exemption from a pensions protection levy, on the ground that BT's pensions liability in the event of insolvency was covered by a State guarantee, could not be regarded as inherent in the overall system for pension protection in the United Kingdom which was necessary for the achievement of the objective of that regime.[123]   Similarly, in *Ministerio de Defensa v Concello de Ferrol*, the ECJ held that an exemption for immovable property owned by the State and used for the purposes of national defence did not appear to be directly related to the objectives of the property tax itself.[124]

Case T-500/12 *Ryanair Ltd v Commission* EU:T:2015:73, para 69; Case T-473/12, *Aer Lingus Ltd v Commission* EU:T:2015:78, para 47.

[118] Case T-222/04, *Italy v Commission* [2009] ECR II-1877, para 15.

[119] *Ibid.*, para 65.

[120] Case C-452/10P, *BNP Paribas v Commission* EU:C:2012:366, paras 136-137; Case T-335/08, *BNP Paribas v* Commission [2010] ECR II-3323, paras 199-202.

[121] Cases C-78/08 – C-80/08, *Ministero dell' Economia e delle Finanze v Paint Graphos* [2011] ECR I-7611, para 75.

[122] Cases T-427/04 & T-17/05, *France v Commission* [2009] ECR II-4315, para 236.

[123] Cases T-226/09 & T-230/09, *British Telecommunications plc v Commission* EU:T:2013:466, para 120.

[124] Case C-522/13, *Ministerio de Defensa v Concello de Ferrol* EU:C:2014:2262, para 44.

It is for the Member State concerned to demonstrate that the measure concerned is justified by the nature or overall structure of the tax system.[125] In *Netherlands v Commission*, the Netherlands' claim that a tax exemption on the use of minerals in crop cultivation was justified by the nature and general scheme of the MINAS system which regulated the use of fertilisers failed for lack any relevant scientific evidence in that regard.[126] Similarly, in *Belgium and Forum 187 v Commission*, Forum 187 failed to provide any explanation for its assertion that the differential treatment of coordination centres of multinational groups were justified by the nature of the tax system in force in Belgium.[127] In *Commission v Government of Gibraltar*, it was claimed that the the features of the proposed tax reform were the result of a necessarily small tax administration in Gibraltar and of Gibraltar's small tax base which imposes limitations that are unavoidable and inherent in the functioning and effectiveness of Gibraltar's tax system. Moreover, the use of employment and business property occupation as bases of assessment was the logical choice in the light of Gibraltar's specific circumstances since such a tax regime would create a simple, easily-verified tax which was cheap to collect and which was similar to other taxes which the small Gibraltar tax administration has experience in collecting. However, the ECJ rejected this contention on the basis that the United Kingdom had not adduced any justification to the Commission for the selective advantages in question.[128]

Differentiation must be intrinsic to the system A distinction must be made between, on the one hand, the objectives attributed to a particular tax scheme which are extrinsic to it and, on the other, the mechanisms inherent in the tax system itself which are necessary for the achievement of such objectives.[129] Extrinsic or external matters include objectives of general economic policy.[130] It follows that social or regional objectives fall outside the scope of the

---

[125] Case C-159/01, *Netherlands v Commission* [2004] ECR I-4461, para 43; Case C-88/03, *Portugal v Commission* [2006] ECR I-7115, para 80; Case C-279/08P, *Commission v Netherlands* [2011] ECR I-7671, para 77; Cases C-106/09P & C-107/09P, *Commission v Government of Gibraltar* [2011] ECR I-11113, para 146; Case C-452/10P, *BNP Paribas v Commission* EU:C:2012:366, para 121; Cases T-211/04 & T-215/04, *Government of Gibraltar v Commission* [2008] ECR II-3745, para 144; Cases T-427/04 & T-17/05, *France v Commission* [2009] ECR II-4315, para 232.

[126] Case C-159/01, *Netherlands v Commission* [2004] ECR I-4461, para 46.

[127] Case C-182/03 & C-217/03, *Belgium and Forum 187 ASBL v Commission* [2006] ECR I-5479, paras 124-126.

[128] Cases C-106/09P & C-107/09P, *Commission v Government of Gibraltar* [2011] ECR I-11113, paras 138-152.

[129] Case C-88/03, *Portugal v Commission* [2006] ECR I-7115, para 81; Cases T-211/04 & T-215/04, *Government of Gibraltar v Commission* [2008] ECR II-3745, para 144.

[130] Cases T-227/01 etc., *Territorio Histórico de Álava – Diputación Foral de Álava v Commission* [2009] ECR II-3029, para183.

justification, whereas objectives that are inherent in the tax system itself, such as efficiency in tax collection and progressive taxation, may come within it.[131]

In *Freskot v Greece*, the ECJ held that the scope of a compulsory insurance scheme might be justified in the light of the nature or general scheme of the system of benefits under the scheme, in so far as it was intended to offer a minimum of protection to agricultural holdings against the natural risks to which they were particularly exposed.[132] Where a levy is imposed on the production and importation of certain products in order to discourage use of the products within a Member State, an exemption on exported products may be justified by the nature and general scheme of the system. Thus, in *British Aggregates Association v Commission*, where a levy was imposed on the production of virgin aggregates used as construction materials, an exemption for exports was not considered as a selective advantage constituting State aid.[133] The Commission also permitted an exemption from the UK climate change levy which was granted in respect of energy products that were used as fuel and as raw materials. Since apportionment of the levy between the fuel/non-fuel use of a product was not a viable alternative to the exemption of dual use products, the measure was justified by the logic and nature of the climate change levy.[134] In *Netherlands Maritime Technology Association v Commission*, tax relief allowing early depreciation on certain assets acquired through financial leasing arrangements was subject to a number of conditions that restricted the relief to cases of non-massed produced assets where the lessee was required to pre-finance the asset and therefore bear the financial cost of the asset before it became operational. The General Court accepted the Commission's finding that this differential treatment was justified by factors relating to the period of construction of custom-built assets and the need to meet pre-financing costs during that period.[135]

By contrast, in *Italy v Commission*, tax measures relating to the Italian banking sector were held not to be justified by the nature and general scheme of the Italian tax system. They did not represent an adaptation of the general system to meet particular characteristics of banking undertakings, but were intended as a means of improving the competitiveness of certain banking

---

[131] Case C-88/03, *Portugal v Commission* [2006] ECR I-7115, para 82 and *per* Advocate General Geelhoed, at para 76; Case C-6/12, *P Oy* EU:C:2013:525, para 29

[132] Case C-355/00, *Freskot v Greece* [2003] ECR I-5263, para 86.

[133] Case T-210/02, *British Aggregates Association v Commission* [2006] ECR II-2789, para 153. This was overturned on appeal on the ground that the General Court used different reasoning from that used by the Commission to justify the exemption: Case C-487/06P, *British Aggregates Association v Commission* [2008] ECR I-10515, para 178.

[134] Commission Decision 2002/676/EC, ECSC, *Climate Change Levy*, OJ 2002 L229/15.

[135] Case T-140/13, *Netherlands Maritime Technology Association v Commission* EU:T:2014:1029, paras 107-108.

undertakings at a given time in the development of the sector.[136] In so far as the tax exemption was limited to banking foundations, the ECJ held that it could not be justified by reference to the nature or scheme of the system, since the derogation was not based on the measure's logic or the technique of taxation, but resulted from the objective of financially favouring organisations regarded by the State as socially deserving.[137] Similarly, in *Italy v Commission*, concerning a reduction in excise duty on diesel used by greenhouse agricultural producers, the General Court held that the objective was to safeguard the competitiveness of such producers in the light of varying prices of diesel on the market, a matter that was extrinsic to the Italian fiscal system.[138] Equally, in *P Oy*, the ECJ held that if the tax authorities were to be able to determine the beneficiaries of the deduction of losses on the basis of criteria unrelated to the tax system, such as maintaining employment, such an exercise of power should be regarded as selective and not justified by the nature or general scheme of the system.[139]

Differential treatment of cooperative societies Cooperative societies conform to particular operating principles which clearly distinguish them from other economic operators. Both Council Regulation (EC) No 1435/2003 on the Statute for a European Cooperative Society[140] and the Commission's Communication on the promotion of cooperative societies in Europe,[141] have highlighted those particular characteristics. Those characteristics essentially find expression in the principle of the primacy of the individual, which is reflected in the specific rules on membership, resignation and expulsion. Cooperative societies are not managed in the interests of outside investors and net assets and reserves should be distributed on winding-up to another cooperative entity pursuing similar general interest purposes. Moreover, due to the fact that shares in cooperative societies are not listed on the stock exchange and, therefore, not widely available for purchase, they have no or limited access to equity markets and are therefore dependent for their development on their own capital or credit financing. As a consequence, the profit margin of this particular kind of company is considerably lower than that of capital companies, which are better able to adapt to market requirements. In the light of those special characteristics peculiar to cooperative societies, the ECJ held in *Paint Graphos* that producers' and workers' cooperative societies cannot, in

---

[136] Case C-66/02, *Italy v Commission* [2005] ECR I-10901, para 101; Case C-148/04, *Unicredito Italiano SpA v Agenzia delle Entrate, Ufficio Genova 1* [2005] ECR I-11137, para 51.

[137] Case C-222/04, *Ministero dell'Economia e delle Finanze v Cassa di Risparmio di Firenze SpA* [2006] ECR I-289, para 137.

[138] Case T-379/09, *Italy v Commission* EU:T:2012:422, para 51.

[139] Case C-6/12, *P Oy* EU:C:2013:525, paras 29-30.

[140] OJ 2003 L207/1.

[141] COM(2004) 18 final.

principle, be regarded as being in a comparable factual and legal situation to that of commercial companies provided that they act in the economic interest of their members and their relations with members are not purely commercial but personal and individual, the members being actively involved in the running of the business and entitled to equitable distribution of the results of economic performance.[142]

Producers' and workers' cooperative societies with characteristics other than those normally associated with that type of society would not truly pursue an objective based on mutuality and would therefore have to be distinguished from the model described in the Commission's Communication on the promotion of cooperative societies in Europe. In that event, it would be necessary to determine whether special tax treatment was justified by the nature or general scheme of the system of which they form part.[143] In *Paint Graphos*, the ECJ held that the nature or general scheme of the national tax system may properly be relied on as justification for the fact that cooperative societies which distributed all their profits to their members were not taxed themselves as cooperatives, provided that tax was levied on the individual members. A measure that allowed profits from trade with third parties who are not members of the cooperative society to gain exemption from tax would not, however, be regarded as justified by the nature or general scheme of the system.[144]

Objectives of redistribution and social equality Progressiveness of a tax may be justified by the aim of wealth and income redistribution.[145] In *Portugal v Commission*, concerning reduced tax rates in the Azores, Portugal claimed that the tax reduction across the board for all undertakings in the territory were necessary to satisfy the objectives of redistribution and equality between the Portuguese mainland and the Azores. The ECJ rejected this, holding that such measures, which applied to all economic operators without any distinction as to their financial circumstances, could not be regarded as ensuring that for the purpose of redistribution the criterion of ability to pay was observed. Although it was true that the disadvantages related to the insularity of the Azores might, in principle, be suffered by all economic operators regardless of their financial circumstances, the mere fact that the regional tax system was conceived in such a way as to ensure the correction of such inequalities did not allow the conclusion to be drawn that every tax advantage granted by the authorities of

---

[142] Cases C-78/08 – C-80/08, *Ministero dell' Economia e delle Finanze v Paint Graphos* [2011] ECR I-7611, paras 55-61.

[143] *Ibid.*, paras 62-65.

[144] *Ibid.*, paras 70-74.

[145] Cases T-127/99, T-129/99 & T-148/99, *Territorio Histórico de Álava - Diputación Foral de Álava v Commission* [2002] ECR I-1275, para 164; Cases T-227/01 etc., *Territorio Histórico de Álava – Diputación Foral de Álava v Commission* [2009] ECR II-3029, para179.

the autonomous region concerned was justified by the nature and overall structure of the national tax system. The fact of acting on the basis of a regional development or social cohesion policy was not sufficient in itself to justify a measure adopted within the framework of that policy. Therefore, Portugal had not shown that the adoption by the Azores authorities of the measures at issue was necessary for the functioning and effectiveness of the general tax system.[146] In any event, a measure will not be regarded as justified by the nature and general scheme of the system merely because it is adopted pursuant to the State's objective of financially favouring organisations regarded as socially deserving.[147] The ECJ held, in *Belgium v Commission*, in relation to the Maribel *bis/ter* scheme, that a measure aimed at promoting the creation of jobs by reducing, for certain undertakings, social security contributions must be regarded as State aid if it is not justified by the nature or general scheme of the social welfare system.[148]

Objective of environmental protection In *AEM v Autorità per l'energia elettrica e per il gas*, an Italian measure that imposed an increased charge for a transitional period for access to and use of the national electricity transmission system only on undertakings generating and distributing electricity from hydroelectric or geothermal installations was not considered to entail State aid to other undertakings generating or distributing electricity. The increased charge was intended to offset an advantage relating to the use of renewable energy created, during the transitional period, by the liberalisation of the market in electricity following the implementation of European Parliament and Council Directive 96/92/EC and was held by the ECJ to be attributable to the nature and general scheme of the system of charges in question.[149] Similarly, in *British Aggregates Association v Commission*, the General Court upheld the Commission's decision that the exemption was justified by the nature and general scheme of the levy in the light of the levy's environmental objectives.[150] The tax in question was a special levy in the United Kingdom on virgin aggregates, i.e. rock, gravel or sand, with exemptions for spoils resulting from the extract of certain minerals, including slate, shale, ball clay and china clay. The purpose of the exemption was to encourage the use as construction materials of such products, which generally arose as by-products or waste

---

[146] Case C-88/03, *Portugal v Commission* [2006] ECR I-7115, para 82.

[147] Case C-222/04, *Ministero dell'Economia e delle Finanze v Cassa di Risparmio di Firenze SpA* [2006] ECR I-289, para 137.

[148] Case C-75/97, *Belgium v Commission* [1999] ECR I-3671, paras 32-34. See also Case T-55/99, *CETM v Commission* [2000] ECR II-3207, para 52; Case C-390/98, *HJ Banks & Co Ltd. v Coal Authority* [2001] ECR I-6177, para 33; Case C-143/99, *Adria-Wien Pipeline GmbH v Finanzlandesdirektion für Kärnten* [2001] ECR I-8365, para 48.

[149] Cases C-128/03 & C-129/03, *AEM SpA v Autorità per l'energia elettrica e per il gas* [2005] ECR I-2861, para 43.

[150] Case T-210/02, *British Aggregates Association v Commission* [2006] ECR II-2789, para 134.

products from other processes. On appeal, however, the ECJ held that the need to take account of requirements relating to environmental protection could not justify the exclusion of selective measures from the scope of Article 107(1) TFEU.[151] Subsequently, the Commission, in a fresh decision, held that only the exemption of shale, which was deliberately extracted as to produce aggregates, did not contribute to the environmental objective of the levy.[152]

Where the objective of environmental protection cannot logically be attained by the measure in question, the differential treatment will not be justified by reference to the nature or general system. Thus, in *Adria-Wien Pipeline GmbH v Finanzlandesdirektion für Kärnten*, Austrian legislation provided for an exemption from energy taxes for manufacturing industry where the tax exceeded 0.35% of net production value. The ECJ held that no justification for the grant of advantages to undertakings whose activity consisted primarily in the production of goods could be found in the nature or general scheme of the tax system. Undertakings providing services could, just like undertakings manufacturing goods, be major consumers of energy and incur energy taxes above 0.35% of their net production value. Moreover, the evidence showed that the purpose of the exemption was to preserve the competitiveness of the manufacturing sector. Furthermore, the exemption from energy taxes for manufacturing industry in Austria could not be justified on ecological considerations of the nature or general scheme of the energy tax law. The ecological considerations underlying the legislation did not justify treating the consumption of gas or electricity by undertakings supplying services differently from the consumption of such energy by undertakings manufacturing goods. Energy consumption by each of those sectors was equally damaging to the environment.[153] Subsequently, the Austrian legislation was amended so as to apply also to undertakings providing services, but the Commission decided that this also constituted State aid since there was no justification on environmental grounds for limiting the tax exemption to undertakings whose use of energy exceeded 0.35% of the net value of production on the ground that this had the effect of favouring undertakings which were large energy consumers.[154] Similarly, in *Commission v Netherlands*, concerning trading emissions allowances for large undertakings which were not available to smaller undertakings, the ECJ held that a differentiation between undertakings based on a quantitative criterion, in that

---

[151] Case C-487/06P, *British Aggregates Association v Commission* [2008] ECR I-10515, para 92; Case C-279/08P, *Commission v Netherlands* [2011] ECR I-7671, para 75.

[152] SA.34775, *UK Aggregates Levy* (2015).

[153] Case C-143/99, *Adria-Wien Pipeline GmbH v Finanzlandesdirektion für Kärnten* [2001] ECR I-8365, para 49-54.

[154] Commission Decision 2005/565/EC, OJ 2005 L190/13; Case C-368/04 *Transalpine Ölleitung in Österreich v Finanzlandesdirektion für Tirol* [2006] ECR I-9957, para 18 and *per* Advocate General Jacobs at para 27.

case being a thermal capacity of more than 20 MWth, could not be regarded as inherent to a scheme intended to reduce industrial pollution.[155]

Objective of tax avoidance In *Lunn Poly*, the English Court of Appeal held that differential rates of insurance premium tax, whereby higher rates were applied to insurance sold through travel agents, constituted State aid in favour of direct insurance companies which were liable to account for the tax only at a lower rate. It was accepted that differential rates would not entail State aid if they were justified on grounds of potential tax avoidance by the persons subject to the higher rate, but on the available evidence no such justification was shown.[156] The same issue was referred subsequently to the ECJ in *GIL v Commissioners of Customs and Excise*, where the ECJ observed that IPT was originally introduced as a general taxation measure applicable in principle to all insurance contracts at a single rate. The higher rate of IPT and VAT formed part of an inseparable whole, which was the aim pursued in introducing the higher rate. That rate was introduced to counteract the practice of taking advantage of the difference between the standard rate of IPT and that of VAT by manipulating the prices of rental or sale of appliances and of the associated insurance. Such conduct had given rise to a loss of income in terms of VAT receipts and to shifts in the conditions of competition in the domestic appliance sector. In view of its purpose and effect, the higher rate of IPT had the appearance of a regulatory charge intended specifically as a deterrent to the conclusion of connected insurance contracts. The introduction of a higher rate of IPT on certain contracts was not a tax scheme favouring a specified sector, since it was a system of taxation of insurance premiums intended to compensate for the fact that insurance transactions were not subject to VAT. Thus, even on the assumption that the introduction of the higher rate involved an advantage for operators offering contracts subject to the standard rate, it was justified by the nature and scheme of the tax system of insurance.[157]

3.3 TAXATION AND REGIONAL AUTONOMY

Regional general taxation and State aid Since State aid may be granted by any public authority, whether central, regional or local, it follows that aid may be granted through tax measures adopted by provincial authorities which mitigate the tax burden imposed on undertakings within their jurisdiction.[158] In

---

[155] Case C-279/08P, *Commission v Netherlands* [2011] ECR I-7671, paras 76-78.
[156] *R v Commissioners of Customs and Excise, ex parte Lunn Poly* [1999] EuLR 653.
[157] Case C-308/01, *GIL Insurance Ltd. v Commissioners of Customs and Excise* [2004] ECR I-4777, paras 70-78.
[158] Cases C-400/97-C402/97, *Administración del Estado v Juntas Generales de Guipúzcoa* [2000] ECR I-1073, *per* Advocate General Saggio at para 31.

particular, where an autonomous regional authority has power to apply a Member State's general taxation, any derogation from the general system will, in the same manner as with central tax authorities, constitute State aid.[159] However, where a regional authority has sufficient autonomous power to legislate for general taxation within its territory, the exercise of such autonomy will be regarded as not falling within the scope of application of Article 107(1) TFEU. Despite considerable resistance from the Commission, this principle has been developed by the courts in the course of a series of cases involving regional taxation in the Basque region, the Azores and Gibraltar.

Differential regional taxation In the Commission's 1998 Notice on Direct Taxation, it was stated that only measures whose scope extended to the entire territory of the State escaped the specificity criterion laid down in Article 107(1) TFEU. The normal rate of taxation, therefore, which formed the benchmark, was the prevailing national rate.[160] This approach was supported by Advocate General Saggio who, in the first of the Basque tax cases, *Administración del Estado v Juntas Generales de Guipúzcoa*, delivered an opinion finding that 1993 Basque legislation on urgent fiscal measures to aid investment and stimulate economic activity constituted State aid.[161] This legislation provided for a reduced level of taxation for all companies within the Basque region as compared to that applicable under the common system of taxation elsewhere in Spain. The Basque authorities argued that there was a distinction between fiscal measures adopted by the State, whose scope is limited to a fixed area of the territory, on the one hand, and general measures adopted by a competent authority within the territory, on the other. While in the first case there would be an element of selectivity with regard to taxable persons, since the measure is limited in its scope to some of the taxable persons who could be addressees, in the second case the element of selectivity was lacking, since the measure is addressed to all taxable persons who, under the rules of allocation of competence, are subject to the fiscal legislation of the local authorities. Advocate General Saggio rejected this line of argument, in particular on the ground that the fact that the measure was adopted by the regional authorities, as opposed to central government, was merely a matter of form. If this were not the case, he felt, the State could easily avoid the application, in part of its own territory, of provisions of EU law on State aid

---

[159] Cases T-127/99, T-129/99 &T-148/99, *Territorio Histórico de Álava - Disputación Foral de Álava v Commission* [2002] ECR II-1275, paras 162-170; Cases T-92/00 and T-103/00, *Territorio Histórico de Álava - Disputación Foral de Álava v Commission* [2002] ECR II-1385, paras 49-50.

[160] Commission Notice on Direct Taxation, para 17.

[161] Cases C-400/97-C402/97, *Administración del Estado v Juntas Generales de Guipúzcoa* [2000] ECR I-1073. Following delivery of the Advocate General's Opinion, the Basque authorities cancelled the legislation and the national court withdrew its reference under Article 267 TFEU, so that the case did not proceed to a final judgment.

simply by making changes to the internal allocation of competence on certain matters, thus raising the general nature, for that territory, of the measure in question.[162]

Regional autonomy and general taxation   However, the EU courts have since been more supportive of the notion of regional tax autonomy.   In the *Ramondín* case, which concerned preferential tax treatment for large investments in the Basque region, it was argued that the Commission's decision that this amounted to selective aid infringed the region's legislative competence.   The General Court, dismissing this argument as misconceived since the Commission had not made a finding of regional selectivity in any event, went on to hold that the Commission's decision had no effect on the competence of the Basque authorities to adopt general tax measures applicable to the whole of the region.[163]   The General Court thus appeared implicitly to acknowledge the principle that regional taxation measures could be regarded as general measures for the purposes of State aid.   This approach has been strengthened by the ECJ in its subsequent judgments on the Azores and Basque tax structures, *Portugal v Commission*[164] and *UGT-Rioja v Juntas Generales del Territorio Histórico de Vizcaya*,[165] respectively.

In *Portugal v Commission*, the ECJ confirmed that the very existence of an advantage may be established only when compared with normal taxation, the normal tax rate being the rate in force in the geographical area constituting the reference framework.   It held, however, that the reference framework need not necessarily be defined within the limits of the Member State concerned, so that a measure conferring an advantage in only one part of the national territory is not selective on that ground alone for the purposes of Article 107(1) TFEU.   It is possible that an infra-State body may enjoy a legal and factual status which makes it sufficiently autonomous in relation to the central government of a Member State, with the result that, by the measures it adopts, it is that body and not the central government which plays a fundamental role in the definition of the political and economic environment in which undertakings operate.   In such a case it is the area in which the infra-State body responsible

---

[162]   Cases C-400/97-C402/97, *Administración del Estado v Juntas Generales de Guipúzcoa* [2000] ECR I-1073, *per* Advocate General Saggio at para 37; Case C-88/03, *Portugal v Commission* [2006] ECR I-7115, *per* Advocate General Geelhoed, at para 59.

[163]   Cases T-92/00 & T-103/00, *Territorio Histórico de Álava - Diputación Foral de Álava v Commission* [2002] ECR II-1385, para 27. See also, Cases T-269/99, T-271/99 and T-2728/99, *Territorio Histórico de Álava – Diputación Foral de Álava v Commission* [2002] ECR II-4217, para 56; Cases T-346/99, T-347/99 and T-348/99, *Territorio Histórico de Álava – Diputación Foral de Álava v Commission* [2002] ECR II-4259, para 52.

[164]   Case C-88/03, *Portugal v Commission* [2006] ECR I-7115.

[165]   Cases C-428/06 & C-434/06, *Unión General de Trabajadores de la Rioja v Juntas Generales del Territorio Histórico de Vizcaya* [2008] ECR I-6747.

for the measure exercises its powers, and not the territory of the Member State as a whole, that constitutes the relevant context for the assessment of whether a measure adopted by such a body favours certain undertakings in comparison with others in a comparable legal and factual situation, having regard to the objective pursued by the measure or the legal system concerned.[166]

Following the suggestion of Advocate General Geelhoed,[167] the ECJ, in *Portugal v Commission*, identified three differing situations relating to tax and regional autonomy. In the first situation, which clearly results in State aid, the central government unilaterally decides that the applicable national tax rate should be reduced within a defined geographic area. The second situation corresponds to a model for distribution of tax competences in which all the local authorities at the same level (regions, districts or others) have the autonomous power to decide, within the limit of the powers conferred on them, the tax rate applicable in the territory within their competence. In that case, no aid will arise by virtue of the fact that different tax rates apply in different areas.[168] In the third situation, a regional or local authority adopts, in the exercise of sufficiently autonomous powers in relation to the central power, a tax rate lower than the national rate and which is applicable only to undertakings present in the territory within its competence. In this situation, the legal framework appropriate to determine the selectivity of a tax measure may be limited to the geographical area concerned where the infra-State body, in particular on account of its status and powers, occupies a fundamental role in the definition of the political and economic environment in which the undertakings present on the territory within its competence operate.[169]

Sufficient institutional, procedural and economic autonomy   It follows that political and fiscal independence of central government which is sufficient as regards the application of EU rules on State aid presupposes that the infra-State body not only has powers in the territory within its competence to adopt measures reducing the tax rate, regardless of any considerations related to the conduct of the central State, but that in addition it assumes the political and

---

[166] Case C-88/03, *Portugal v Commission* [2006] ECR I-7115, paras 56-58; Cases C-428/06 & C-434/06, *Unión General de Trabajadores de la Rioja v Juntas Generales del Territorio Histórico de Vizcaya* [2008] ECR I-6747, paras 46-48; Case C-169/08, *Presidente del Consiglio dei Ministri v Regione Sardegna* [2009] ECR I-10821, para 60; Cases T-211/04 & T-215/04, *Government of Gibraltar v Commission* [2008] ECR II-3745, para 80.

[167] Case C-88/03, *Portugal v Commission* [2006] ECR I-7115, *per* Advocate General Geelhoed, at para 50.

[168] Case C-88/03, *Portugal v Commission* [2006] ECR I-7115, paras 63-64.

[169] *Ibid.*, paras 65-66; Cases C-428/06 & C-434/06, *Unión General de Trabajadores de la Rioja v Juntas Generales del Territorio Histórico de Vizcaya* [2008] ECR I-6747, paras 49-50.

financial consequences of such a measure.[170] In *UGT-Rioja v Juntas Generales del Territorio Histórico de Vizcaya*, the Commission argued that this autonomy was subject to a pre-condition that the body played a fundamental role in the definition of the political and economic environment in which undertakings operate. However, the ECJ rejected this contention, holding that this fundamental role was a consequence of, and not a precondition for, such autonomy.[171]

It must, therefore, now be accepted that regional tax measures which apply throughout the particular region will not amount to State aid by virtue of the fact that they result in a lower tax burden that applies in other regions of the Member State concerned, as long as the regional authority has sufficient institutional, procedural and economic autonomy.[172] On this basis, the General Court annulled a Commission decision finding that measures concerning tax reform in Gibraltar constituted State aid by reason of the fact that the proposed tax system differed from that applicable in the United Kingdom. The General Court held, on the contrary, that the applicable reference framework corresponded exclusively to the geographical limits of the territory of Gibraltar, which meant that no comparison could be made between the tax regime applicable to companies established in Gibraltar and that applicable to companies established in the United Kingdom for the purpose of establishing a selective advantage favouring the former.[173] Where, on the other hand, the regional authority exceeds its competence, Article 107(1) TFEU may apply to the measures adopted since the reference framework for assessing whether the law of general application in the infra-State body is selective is no longer necessarily constituted by the regional authority, but could, where appropriate, be extended to the whole territory of the Member State.[174]

Institutional autonomy Institutional autonomy requires that the regional or local authority has, from a constitutional point of view, a political and

---

[170] Case C-88/03, *Portugal v Commission* [2006] ECR I-7115, para 68; Cases C-428/06 & C-434/06, *Unión General de Trabajadores de la Rioja v Juntas Generales del Territorio Histórico de Vizcaya* [2008] ECR I-6747, para 52.

[171] Cases C-428/06 & C-434/06, *Unión General de Trabajadores de la Rioja v Juntas Generales del Territorio Histórico de Vizcaya* [2008] ECR I-6747, para 55; Cases T-211/04 & T-215/04, *Government of Gibraltar v Commission* [2008] ECR II-3745, para 87.

[172] Case C-88/03, *Portugal v Commission* [2006] ECR I-7115, para 67 and *per* Advocate General Geelhoed, at para 54; Cases C-428/06 & C-434/06, *Unión General de Trabajadores de la Rioja v Juntas Generales del Territorio Histórico de Vizcaya* [2008] ECR I-6747, para 51.

[173] Cases T-211/04 & T-215/04, *Government of Gibraltar v Commission* [2008] ECR II-3745, para 115.

[174] Cases C-428/06 & C-434/06, *Unión General de Trabajadores de la Rioja v Juntas Generales del Territorio Histórico de Vizcaya* [2008] ECR I-6747, para 133.

administrative status separate from that of the central government.[175]   In *Portugal v Commission, UGT-Rioja v Juntas Generales del Territorio Histórico de Vizcaya* and *Government of Gibraltar v Commission*, fulfilment of the criterion of institutional autonomy was easily presumed.   Under the Portuguese constitution, the Azores forms an autonomous region with its own political and administrative status and its own self-government institutions.[176] In the Basque region, the combined Basque provincial authorities constituted, for the purposes of establishing institutional autonomy in the region, a single infra-State body with a political and administrative status distinct from that of central government.[177]   In Gibraltar, the Gibraltar authorities were regarded as having, from a constitutional point of view, a political and administrative status separate from that of the central government of the United Kingdom.[178]

Procedural autonomy   Procedural autonomy requires that the measure must have been adopted without the central government being able to directly intervene as regards its content.[179]   The essential criterion for the purpose of determining whether procedural autonomy exists is not the extent of the competence which the infra-State body is recognised as having, but the possibility for that body, as a result of that competence, to adopt a decision independently, in other words, without the central government being able directly to intervene as regards its content.[180]   The mere fact that the measure may be subject to judicial review by national courts is irrelevant in determining whether the body concerned has procedural autonomy.[181]   In *Portugal v Commission*, the criterion of procedural autonomy was deemed to be fulfilled on the ground that the Azores self-government institutions had the power to exercise their own fiscal competence and adapt national fiscal provisions to regional specificities.[182]   In *UGT-Rioja v Juntas Generales del Territorio Histórico de Vizcaya*, where the Basque authorities were required under the Economic Agreement with Spain to notify the State administration of draft tax laws, the Commission argued that the condition of procedural autonomy is not

---

[175] Case C-88/03, *Portugal v Commission* [2006] ECR I-7115, para 67.

[176] *Ibid.*, para 70.

[177] Cases C-428/06 & C-434/06, *Unión General de Trabajadores de la Rioja v Juntas Generales del Territorio Histórico de Vizcaya* [2008] ECR I-6747, paras 75 and 87.

[178] Cases T-211/04 & T-215/04, *Government of Gibraltar v Commission* [2008] ECR II-3745, para 89.

[179] Case C-88/03, *Portugal v Commission* [2006] ECR I-7115, para 67; Cases C-428/06 & C-434/06, *Unión General de Trabajadores de la Rioja v Juntas Generales del Territorio Histórico de Vizcaya* [2008] ECR I-6747, para 95.

[180] Cases C-428/06 & C-434/06, *Unión General de Trabajadores de la Rioja v Juntas Generales del Territorio Histórico de Vizcaya* [2008] ECR I-6747, para 107.

[181] *Ibid.*, para 79.

[182] Case C-88/03, *Portugal v Commission* [2006] ECR I-7115, para 70; Cases T-211/04 & T-215/04, *Government of Gibraltar v Commission* [2008] ECR II-3745, para 93.

satisfied if the infra-State body is subject to the procedural obligation to consult the central government. However, the ECJ rejected this, countering that procedural autonomy does not preclude the establishment of a conciliation procedure in order to avoid conflicts, provided that the final decision taken at the conclusion of that procedure is adopted by the infra-State body and not by the central government.[183] In *Government of Gibraltar v Commission*, the Commission's argument that the United Kingdom retained a residual power of last resort to legislate for Gibraltar was rejected as immaterial on the ground that that power had been exercised only exceptionally and never in the case of taxation, that no United Kingdom law in respect of fiscal matters had ever applied to Gibraltar, and that the residual power was intended solely to allow for the United Kingdom to perform its obligations in respect of Gibraltar under international law.[184]

The Commission also argued in *UGT-Rioja v Juntas Generales del Territorio Histórico de Vizcaya* that the condition of procedural autonomy is not satisfied if the infra-State body is subject to the material obligation to take into account the repercussions of its decisions on the whole territory of the State, for example, for the purpose of complying with the principles of equality, solidarity and equivalence of fiscal pressure. Under the Spanish Constitution, the principle of solidarity required the State to endeavour to establish a fair and adequate economic balance between the different parts of Spanish territory, but the ECJ held that this did not appear to call into question the procedural autonomy of the Basque region. The requirement for an infra-State body to take into account the economic balance between the different parts of the national territory when adopting tax legislation defined the limits of that body's powers, even if the concepts used to define those limits, such as that of economic balance, may be developed in the context of interpretation as part of judicial review. The fact that pre-established limits must be complied with when a decision is adopted does not, however, in principle, call into question the decisional autonomy of the body adopting that decision.[185]

As for the principle in the Economic Agreement between Spain and the Basque region that it was necessary to maintain an overall effective fiscal pressure equivalent to that in force in the rest of Spain and to respect and guarantee freedom of movement and of establishment of persons and free movement of goods, capital and services throughout the territory of Spain, without giving rise to discrimination or a restriction of the possibility of

---

[183] Cases C-428/06 & C-434/06, *Unión General de Trabajadores de la Rioja v Juntas Generales del Territorio Histórico de Vizcaya* [2008] ECR I-6747, para 96.

[184] Cases T-211/04 & T-215/04, *Government of Gibraltar v Commission* [2008] ECR II-3745, paras 95-99.

[185] Cases C-428/06 & C-434/06, *Unión General de Trabajadores de la Rioja v Juntas Generales del Territorio Histórico de Vizcaya* [2008] ECR I-6747, paras 102-104.

commercial competition or distortion in the allocation of resources, the ECJ held that, while it appeared to result from that principle that the Basque authorities did not have very extensive competence in respect of the overall fiscal pressure liable to be established by their regional laws, since that pressure must be equivalent to that which exists in the rest of the Spanish State, overall fiscal pressure was only one of the elements to be taken into consideration when tax laws are being adopted. Provided that they complied with that principle, the Basque authorities thus had the power to adopt tax provisions which differ in many respects from the provisions applicable in the rest of the State.[186]

Economic autonomy   Economic autonomy requires that the financial consequences of a reduction of the national tax rate for undertakings in the region must not be offset by aid or subsidies from other regions or central government.[187]   Such an offset would require a causal link between the tax measure at issue and the financial support from the State.[188]   In *Portugal v Commission*, the Azores authorities were competent under Portuguese law to adapt national taxation rules to regional specificities, and had proceeded to exercise that competence by reducing the corporation tax rates applied to undertakings established in the Azores by 30%.   The ECJ upheld the Commission's decision that the Azores was not economically autonomous. Portugal had failed to demonstrate that the Azores region did not receive any State financing to make good the fall in tax revenue which resulted from reductions in tax rates.   In that regard, the Portuguese constitutional principle of national solidarity required that the State contribute, along with the autonomous regional authorities, to the achievement of economic development and the correction of inequalities deriving from the Azores' insularity and to economic and social convergence with the rest of the national territory.   It was incumbent on both the central and regional authorities to promote the correction of inequalities arising from insularity by reducing the local tax burden and by an obligation to ensure an appropriate level of public services and private activities.   This reduction in tax revenue was offset by a financing mechanism which was centrally managed in the form of budgetary transfers. Accordingly, the ECJ held that the relevant legal framework for determining the selectivity of the tax measures at issue could not be defined exclusively within the geographical limits of the Azores region.   Instead, those measures had to be assessed in relation to the whole of Portuguese territory, in the

---

[186]   *Ibid.*, paras 105-106.
[187]   Case C-88/03, *Portugal v Commission* [2006] ECR I-7115, para 67; Cases C-428/06 & C-434/06, *Unión General de Trabajadores de la Rioja v Juntas Generales del Territorio Histórico de Vizcaya* [2008] ECR I-6747, para 123.
[188]   Cases T-211/04 & T-215/04, *Government of Gibraltar v Commission* [2008] ECR II-4735, para 106.

context of which they appeared to be selective. It followed that the reductions in the tax rates were selective and not general measures.[189] On the other hand, in *Government of Gibraltar v Commission*, the Commission, which had determined that a programme of tax reform in Gibraltar constituted State aid, sought to rely on specific elements of funding from the United Kingdom to support its conclusion that Gibraltar was not economically autonomous from the United Kingdom. However, the General Court held that none of this financing, such as a scheme for assisting SMEs, served to offset any financial consequences that the tax reform would entail for Gibraltar.[190]

In *UGT-Rioja v Juntas Generales del Territorio Histórico de Vizcaya*, where the Basque tax measures entailed *inter alia* a reduction on the corporation tax rates applicable in the rest of Spain, the Commission again sought to invoke the solidarity principle as between central government and the regions in order to show that the Basque region was not economically autonomous, specifically on the ground that a minimum level of services had to be guaranteed throughout the Spanish territory. However, the ECJ, on examination of the Economic Agreement to ascertain whether it might have the effect of compensation by the State for the financial consequences of the Basque tax measures, rejected the Commission's arguments. Compensation in this respect required a causal relationship between the regional tax measure and the amounts assumed by the State.[191] In that regard, the ECJ recognised that, although financial compensation may be declared and specific, it may also be hidden and result only from the actual examination of the financial flows existing between the infra-State body concerned, the Member State which it comes under and the other regions of that Member State. That examination may indicate that a tax reduction decision adopted by the infra-State body results in larger financial transfers in its favour, because of the calculation methods used in order to determine the amounts to be transferred. However, the mere fact that it appears from a general examination of the financial relations between the central State and its infra-State bodies that there are financial transfers between the former and the latter, cannot, in itself, suffice to demonstrate that those bodies do not assume the financial consequences of the tax measures which they adopt and, accordingly, that they do not enjoy financial autonomy, since such transfers may take place for reasons unconnected with the tax measures.[192]

---

[189] Case C-88/03, *Portugal v Commission* [2006] ECR I-7115, paras 71-79; Case T-75/03, *Banco Comercial dos Açores SA v Commission* [2009] ECR II-143*, paras 79-84.

[190] Cases T-211/04 & T-215/04, *Government of Gibraltar v Commission* [2008] ECR II-6747, para 112.

[191] Cases C-428/06 & C-434/06, *Unión General de Trabajadores de la Rioja v Juntas Generales del Territorio Histórico de Vizcaya* [2008] ECR I-6747, para 129.

[192] *Ibid.*, paras 133-135.

Selective advantage within regional autonomy As with material selectivity generally, in order to determine whether a measure is selective where it is adopted by an infra-State body which enjoys autonomy *vis-à-vis* the central government, it is necessary to determine whether, with regard to the objective pursued by that measure, it constitutes an advantage for certain undertakings as compared with others which, within the legal framework in which that body exercises its competences, are in a comparable legal and factual situation.[193] Thus, in *Presidente del Consiglio dei Ministri v Regione Sardegna*, it had to be established whether, having regard to the characteristics of the regional tax on stopovers in Sardinia, the undertakings having their tax domicile outside the territory of the region were, in the light of the nature and objectives of that tax, in a factual and legal situation comparable with that of undertakings which were established in that territory. In that regard, the tax legislation was regarded as having an environmental, rather than a finance raising, objective, which was to protect and renew environmental resources polluted by tourism, particularly in coastal areas. As such, the ECJ held that all persons who received stopover services in Sardinia were in an objectively comparable situation, irrespective of their place of residence or establishment, with regard to that objective. It followed that the tax measure could not be regarded as general, since it did not apply to all operators of aircraft of pleasure boats making a stopover in Sardinia, but instead constitutes State aid in favour of undertakings established in Sardinia.[194] Similarly, in the Basque tax cases, a tax credit applying only to undertakings subject to the Basque tax systems which made investments in fixed assets exceeding 2,500 million pesetas was held to be selective in that it favoured those undertakings which had at their disposal significant financial resources.[195]

3.4 SPECIAL TAXES AND PARAFISCAL LEVIES

Special levies and general taxation Subject to EU rules on harmonisation, Member States retain the power to adopt taxes or levies that apply in respect of particular goods or services. Accordingly, a tax imposed on certain undertakings does not normally constitute State aid to competing undertakings which are not subject to the same tax.[196] It remains unclear, however, to what extent such levies can be regarded as specific measures of general taxation

---

[193] Case C-169/08, *Presidente del Consiglio dei Ministri v Regione Sardegna* [2009] ECR I-10821, para 60.

[194] *Ibid.*, paras 62-64.

[195] Cases T-227/01 etc., *Territorio Histórico de Álava – Diputación Foral de Álava v Commission* [2009] ECR II-3029, paras 162-166.

[196] Case 9/70, *Grad v Finanzamt Traunstein* [1970] ECR 825, *per* Advocate General Roemer, at p. 854.

falling within the tax sovereignty of the Member States so that the State aid rules are inapplicable. In *Ferring v ACOSS*, Advocate General Tizzano noted that the difficulty and subtlety of this question arises from the fact that any new tax imposed on a given category of economic operators may be viewed in theory as an advantage conferred upon all operators who are not subject to that tax but are in more or less close competition with the first category. A broad interpretation of the concept of aid, one that encompasses the levying of a tax on third parties whose competitive relationship with the presumed beneficiaries of the aid is no more than tenuous, entails a risk of unjustified interference in the fiscal policy of Member States. Yet, neither is it possible to consider satisfactory a solution which, by contrast, excludes *a priori* any possibility of identifying a selective advantage in the non-imposition of a new tax on certain economic operators. An interpretation of that sort would in fact provide Member States with a simple mechanism for circumventing EU rules on State aid by means of discriminatory taxation. His view was that it could neither be accepted nor excluded *a priori* that failure to levy a tax on certain parties was tantamount to conferring a selective advantage within the meaning of Article 107(1) TFEU. The solution must be sought on a case by case basis, with regard being had to the particular circumstances of the case and, above all, to the competitive relationship between the operators concerned, the reason for the tax and its effects.[197]

Reference framework for special levies Although A-G Tizzano, in *Ferring v ACOSS*, analysed this issue in terms of competitive relationships, the proper approach,[198] in order to determine whether or not a measure imposing a special levy is selective for the purposes of applying Article 107(1) TFEU, as with general taxation, is to examine whether, within the context of a particular legal system, that measure constitutes an advantage for certain undertakings by comparison with others which are in a comparable legal and factual situation in light of the objective of the measure in question.[199] This requires the determination of the proper reference framework for assessing which undertakings are in such a comparable situation.[200] There is, however, a significant difference in applying this criterion to special levies. In the case of general tax measures, the issue in question usually concerns the determination of whether a specific exemption from the tax, or differential application of the tax, benefits certain undertakings who are identified in the tax measure itself. This may also be the case with a special levy, such as in *British Aggregates*

---

[197] Case C-53/00, *Ferring SA v ACOSS* [2001] ECR I-9067, *per* Advocate General Tizzano, at paras 36-39.

[198] *Ibid.*

[199] Case C-143/99, *Adria-Wien Pipeline GmbH v Finanzlandesdirektion für Kärnten* [2001] ECR I-8365, para 41.

[200] Case C-88/03, *Portugal v Commission* [2006] ECR I-7115, para 56.

Association v Commission, where the United Kingdom legislation on the aggregates levy specifically excluded certain types of aggregates from the scope of the tax.[201] It may, however, also involve examining whether certain undertakings are wholly excluded from the scope of the special levy in question by reason of the fact that the legislation simply makes no reference to their economic activities and, consequently, does not apply to them. Thus, for example, in *Presidente del Consiglio dei Ministri v Regione Sardegna*, a regional tax was levied in Sardinia on stopovers made by aircraft and boats operated by persons having their tax domicile outside the territory of the region. The ECJ observed that the application of that tax made the services concerned more costly for the persons liable for the tax than for operators established in that territory, thus creating a selective economic advantage for some categories of undertaking established in that territory that could distort competition.[202]

Special levies that distort competition As alluded to by A-G Tizzano, this issue is of particular importance where the effect of levying a special tax on certain operators leads to a distortion of competition with other economic operators. In *Ferring v ACOSS*, where there were two directly competing distribution channels for medicinal products in France, wholesale distributors and pharmaceutical laboratories which sold directly to pharmacies, a special tax was imposed solely in respect of direct sales with the objective of restoring the balance of competition between the two medicine distribution channels, which had been distorted by the imposition of public service obligations on wholesale distributors alone. Following the introduction of the direct sales tax, not only did the growth of direct sales recorded in the immediately preceding years cease, but the trend even reversed, with wholesale distributors recovering market share. The ECJ held that not assessing wholesale distributors to the tax on direct sales equated to granting them a tax exemption whereby the French authorities had, in practice, waived their right to receive tax payments from wholesale distributors, thus conferring upon them an economic advantage. Thus, the tax on direct sales could in fact constitute State aid inasmuch as it did not apply to wholesale distributors by overcompensating them in so far as the advantage exceeded the additional costs borne in discharging the public service obligations.[203]

---

[201] Case C-487/06P, *British Aggregates Association v Commission* [2008] ECR I-10515, para 2; Case T-210/02, *British Aggregates Association v Commission* [2006] ECR II-2789, para 3-5.

[202] Case C-169/08, *Presidente del Consiglio dei Ministri v Regione Sardegna* [2009] ECR I-10821, paras 31-32 and 53.

[203] Case C-53/00, *Ferring SA v ACOSS* [2001] ECR I-9067, paras 19-22; Case C-526/04, *Laboratoires Boiron SA v URSSAF* [2006] ECR I-7529, para 36.

In *British Aggregates Association v Commission*, the General Court held that the mere fact that an environmental levy constitutes a specific measure, which extends to certain designated goods or services, and cannot be seen as part of an overall system of taxation which applies to all similar activities which have a comparable impact on the environment, does not mean that similar activities, which are not subject to the levy, benefit from a selective advantage.[204] On appeal, the ECJ disagreed with this conclusion.[205] Advocate General Mengozzi felt that the General Court had excluded *a priori* the possibility that the non-imposition of the environmental levy on some operators might constitute a selective advantage under Article 107(1) TFEU, irrespective of any consideration of the competitive relationship that might exist between those operators and the operators liable to pay the levy, hence independently of an assessment of the effects of the measure in question. In effect, he argued, starting from the premiss that the Member States were free, when defining the scope of an environmental levy, to balance the various interests at stake, the General Court had ultimately accepted that the existence of possible inconsistencies or differences in treatment might be justified even if based on objectives unconnected with the protection of the environment and, consequently, unrelated to the internal logic of the measure in question. Moreover, in terms of the impact on competition, there was no great difference between, on the one hand, the imposition of a general tax with an exemption for certain beneficiaries and, on the other hand, the imposition of a tax on certain taxable persons to the exclusion of others who are in a comparable situation.[206]

In *Kernkraftwerke Lippe-Ems GmbH v Hza Osnabrück*, a special excise duty was imposed on the use of nuclear fuel which increased the costs of producing electricity from nuclear energy. It was argued that the excise duty formed part of a regime for the taxation of energy sources used for the production of electricity, or for the production of electricity which did not contribute to CO_2 emissions, so that the effect of limiting the scope of the excise duty was that energy sources other than nuclear fuel used for the production of electricity were not taxed. The ECJ held, however, that there was no basis for concluding that there was, in fact, a German tax regime which had as its objective the taxation of energy sources used to produce electricity. On the contrary, the tax was a special levy aimed at raising revenue to deal with the costs of storing radioactive waste which, in the context of electricity

---

[204] Case T-210/02, *British Aggregates Association v Commission* [2006] ECR II-2789, para 115.

[205] Case C-487/06P, *British Aggregates Association v Commission* [2008] ECR I-10515, para 86.

[206] Case C-487/06P, *British Aggregates Association v Commission* [2008] ECR I-10515, *per* Advocate General Mengozzi, at paras 98-100.

production, arose only in connection with electricity produced from nuclear energy.[207]

In *Greece v Commission*, the Commission had found that a levy imposed on entry tickets into Greek casinos constituted differential selective taxation where, even though the rate of taxation was 80%, the entry price for both public and private casinos was itself regulated by legislation which established different rates, being €6 for public casinos and €15 for private casinos. The General Court annulled the Commission's decision on the ground that all casinos were subject to the same rate of taxation, so that the fact that a lower actual amount was paid in relation to customers entering public casinos did not constitute an advantage for the casinos.[208] The Commission's argument that the lower ticket price made public casinos more attractive to customers was rejected on the ground that no statistical or economic analysis proving that effect had been included in the Commission's decision.[209] Neither the Commission nor the General Court appears to have considered whether the regulatory technique used of legislating both for the entry price as well as the tax rate could be regarded as allowing public casinos to be considered to be a privileged category that benefited from selective treatment.

Special tax may itself constitute State aid Whereas the ECJ, in *Ferring v ACOSS*, had classified the non-imposition on wholesalers of the tax on direct sales of pharmaceuticals as equating to the grant of a tax exemption,[210] in subsequent proceedings brought by those subject to the tax in which they sought reimbursement of the tax that they had paid, a very different analytical approach was adopted. In *Laboratoires Boiron v URSSAF*, the ECJ stated that the measure constituting the aid was the tax on direct sales itself and not some exemption from that tax. The nature of the aid involved in the tax on direct sales differed from that arising from an exemption from a parafiscal levy of general application. The tax was a charge for which only one of two categories of competing operators was liable. In such a case of unequal liability for a charge, the aid derived from the fact that the wholesalers, with which direct suppliers were in direct competition, were not liable for the charge. It followed that the measure alleged to constitute the aid was the tax on direct sales itself and not some exemption which was separable from the tax.[211] The General Court has subsequently confirmed, however, that the principle in *Laboratoires Boiron v URSSAF* is very much limited to its specific facts, where the absence of tax on the wholesalers was a deliberate objective of the legislation intended

---

[207] Case C-5/14, *Kernkraftwerke Lippe-Ems GmbH v Hza Osnabrück* EU:C:2015:354, paras 76-79.

[208] Case T-425/11, *Greece v Commission* EU:T:2014:768, paras 52-58.

[209] *Ibid.*, para 66.

[210] Case C-53/00, *Ferring SA v ACOSS* [2001] ECR I-9067, para 20

[211] Case C-526/04, *Laboratoires Boiron SA v URSSAF* [2006] ECR I-7529, para 39.

to restore the balance of competition between the two distribution channels, and does not set a general precedent to the effect that an undertaking required to pay a tax may escape liability solely on the ground that the tax is used to finance an aid.[212]

Parafiscal levies that finance State aid   In principle, tax measures which serve to finance an aid do not themselves necessarily fall within the scope of application of the State aid provisions.[213]   In *The Panhellenic Union of Cotton Ginners and Exporters v Commission*, a compulsory levy was imposed on ginning undertakings in favour of the Greek Cotton Board. It was held that this was merely a method of financing the Board and could not be considered an aid in itself.[214] The Commission considered that a Danish scheme imposing a charge on the sale of new batteries containing certain substances considered to be particularly harmful to the environment, the proceeds of which were used to pay companies for the collection and disposal of the products after use, did not constitute State aid because the charge was imposed on all products in a non-discriminatory way and the payment to the collecting firms was based on normal commercial terms.[215]

An aid measure cannot, however, be considered separately from the effects of its method of financing.[216] A measure adopted by a public authority which favours certain undertakings or products does not lose the character of a gratuitous advantage by the fact that it is wholly or partially financed by a levy imposed on the undertakings concerned.[217] It follows that the mere fact that a system of subsidies which benefits certain traders in a specific sector is financed by a parafiscal charge levied on every supply of national goods in that sector is not sufficient to divest that system of its character as aid granted by a Member State.[218] In *Van Calster*, the Belgian authorities, without notifying the Commission in advance, had established a fund with the purpose of combating animal disease in order to promote public health and the economic welfare of livestock farmers.   Initially, the fund was financed by compulsory contributions levied on the slaughter or live export of animals. Subsequently, following a decision of the Commission that this was unlawful,[219] the levy was

---

[212] Case T-533/10; *DTS v Commission* EU:T:2014:629, paras 96-98; Case T-473/12, *Aer Lingus Ltd v Commission* EU:T:2015:78, para 70.

[213] Case T-151/11, *Telefónica de España SA v Commission* EU:T:2014:631, para 99.

[214] Case C-553/03P, *The Panhellenic Union of Cotton Ginners and Exporters v Commission* EU:C:2005:170, para 44; Case T-148/00, *The Panhellenic Union of Cotton Ginners and Exporters v Commission* [2003] ECR II-4415, para 65.

[215] *Twenty-Fifth Report on Competition Policy* (1995), p. 234.

[216] Case 47/69, *France v Commission* [1970] ECR 487, paras 4-8; Cases C-261/01 & C-262/01, *Van Calster v Belgium* [2003] ECR-12249, para 46.

[217] Case 78/76, *Steinike und Weinlig v Germany* [1977] ECR 595, para 22.

[218] Case 259/85, *France v Commission* [1987] ECR 4393, para 23.

[219] Commission Decision 91/538/EEC.

altered to provide that no charge would be levied on animals that had been imported or exported. The ECJ classified such an aid measure as providing for a scheme of charges that forms an integral part of that measure and is intended specifically and exclusively to finance it.[220]

It follows that in such circumstances the aid cannot be considered separately from the effects of its method of financing. On the contrary, consideration of an aid measure by the Commission must necessarily also take into account the method of financing the aid in a case where that method forms an integral part of the measure. Consequently, the method by which an aid is financed may render the entire aid scheme incompatible with the internal market.[221] In such a case, the notification of the aid provided for in Article 108(3) TFEU must also cover the method of financing, so that the Commission may consider it on the basis of all the facts. If this requirement is not satisfied, it is possible that the Commission may declare that an aid measure is compatible, when, if the Commission had been aware of its method of financing, it could not have been so declared. Accordingly, in order to ensure the effectiveness of the obligation to notify and the Commission's full and appropriate consideration of an aid, the Member State is required, in order to comply with that obligation, to notify not only what the ECJ termed aid in the narrow sense, but also the method of financing the aid inasmuch as that method is an integral part of the planned measure.[222]

Hypothecation of levy to aid measure For a tax to be regarded as forming an integral part of an aid measure, it must be hypothecated to the aid measure under the relevant national rules, in the sense that the revenue from the tax is necessarily allocated to the financing of the aid. If there is such hypothecation, the revenue from the tax has a direct impact on the amount of the aid and,

[220] Cases C-261/01 & C-262/01, *Van Calster v Belgium* [2003] ECR-12249, para 44.
[221] *Ibid.*, para 49; Cases C-34/01 to C-38/01, *Enirisorse SpA v Ministero delle Finanze* [2003] ECR I-14243, para 44; Case C-345/02, *Pearle BV v Hoofdbedrijfschap Ambachten* [2004] ECR I-7139, para 29; Case C-174/02, *Streekgeweest Westelijk Noord-Brabant v Staatsecretaris van Financiën* [2005] ECR I-85, para 25; Cases C-128/03 & C-129/03, *AEM SpA v Autorità per l'energia elettrica e per il gas* [2005] ECR I-2861, para 45; Case C-553/03P, *The Panhellenic Union of Cotton Ginners and Exporters v Commission* EU:C:2005:170, para 45; Case C-206/06, *Essent Netwerk Noord BV v Alumimium Delfzijl BV* [2008] ECR I-5497, para 89; Case C-194/09P, *Alcoa Trasformazioni srl v Commission* [2011] ECR I-6311, para 48; Case T-533/10; *DTS v Commission* EU:T:2014:629, para 50; Case T-151/11, *Telefónica de España SA v Commission* EU:T:2014:631, para 100.
[222] Cases C-261/01 & C-262/01, *Van Calster v Belgium* [2003] ECR-12249, paras 50-51; Case C-345/02, *Pearle BV v Hoofdbedrijfschap Ambachten* [2004] ECR I-7139, para 30; Case C-174/02, *Streekgeweest Westelijk Noord-Brabant v Staatsecretaris van Financiën* [2005] ECR I-85, para 26; Case C-206/06, *Essent Netwerk Noord BV v Alumimium Delfzijl* BV [2008] ECR I-5497, para 93; Case C-333/07, *Régie Networks v Direction de Contrôle Fiscal Rhône-Alpes Bourgogne* [2008] ECR I-10807, para 94.

consequently, on the assessment of the compatibility of that aid with the internal market.[223] Thus, in *AEM SpA v Autorità per l'energia elettrica e per il gas*, the ECJ held that, if there was hypothecation of the increased charge for access to and use of the Italian electricity transmission system to a national scheme of aid, in the sense that the revenue from the increase was necessarily allocated for the financing of the aid, that increase would be an integral part of that scheme and must therefore be considered together with the latter.[224] In *Régie Networks v Direction de Contrôle Fiscal Rhône-Alpes Bourgogne*, the ECJ found that a charge imposed on advertising companies was levied specifically to finance aid for local radio stations, so that it was to be regarded as forming an integral part of the aid scheme.[225]

By contrast, in *Streekgeweest Westelijk Noord-Brabant v Staatsecrtaris van Financiën*, aid was granted by means of a temporary exemption from a tax on waste. The ECJ held that, even if the tax advantage was compensated for, as regards the Netherlands budget, by an increase in the amount of the tax on waste, that fact was not sufficient in itself to show that the tax was hypothecated to the tax exemption. The measure did not hypothecate the tax on waste to the financing of the tax exemption, and the tax revenue has no impact on the amount of the aid in that the application of the tax exemption and its extent did not depend on the tax revenue.[226] Similarly, in *Aer Lingus v Commission*, the General Court held, in relation to differential rates of Irish air travel tax, that there was no hypothecation of the revenue, since the tax was not directly allocated to the funding of the aid.[227]

A tax cannot be hypothecated to an exemption from payment of the same tax for a category of businesses.[228] In *Pape v Minister van Landbouw,*

---

[223] Case C-174/02, *Streekgeweest Westelijk Noord-Brabant v Staatsecretaris van Financiën* [2005] ECR I-85, para 26; Case C-175/02, *Pape v Minister van Landbouw, Natuurbeheer en Visserij* [2005] ECR I-127, para 15; Cases C-128/03 & C-129/03, *AEM SpA v Autorità per l'energia elettrica e per il gas* [2005] ECR I-2861, para 46; Cases C-266/04 to C-270/04, C-276/04 & C-321/04 to C-325/04, *Distribution Casino France v Organic* [2005] ECR I-9481, para 40; Cases C-393/04 & C-41/05, *Air Liquide Industries Belgium SA v Ville de Seraing* [2006] ECR I-5293, para 46; Case C-206/06, *Essent Netwerk Noord BV v Alumimium Delfzijl BV* [2008] ECR I-5497, para 90; Case C-333/07, *Régie Networks v Direction de Contrôle Fiscal Rhône-Alpes Bourgogne* [2008] ECR I-10807, para 99; Case T-136/05, *Salvat père & fils v Commission* [2007] ECR II-4063, para 40; Case T-151/11, *Telefónica de España SA v Commission* EU:T:2014:631, para 101.

[224] Cases C-128/03 & C-129/03, *AEM SpA v Autorità per l'energia elettrica e per il gas* [2005] ECR I-2861, para 47.

[225] Case C-333/07, *Régie Networks v Direction de Contrôle Fiscal Rhône-Alpes Bourgogne* [2008] ECR I-10807, paras 100-112.

[226] Case C-174/02, *Streekgeweest Westelijk Noord-Brabant v Staatsecretaris van Financiën* [2005] ECR I-85, paras 27-28.

[227] Case T-473/12, *Aer Lingus Ltd v Commission* EU:T:2015:78, para 69.

[228] Case C-174/02, *Streekgeweest Westelijk Noord-Brabant v Staatsecretaris van Financiën* [2005] ECR I-85, para 28; Cases C-266/04 to C-270/04, C-276/04 & C-321/04 to

Natuurbeheer en Visserij, a levy on manure was considered not to be hypothecated to aid for the transport of manure since the levy could be used for various other non-aid purposes.[229] Similarly, in *Distribution Casino France v Organic*, a levy was imposed on retail stores in France, with the proceeds being used to fund cessation payments for certain traders and craftsmen on their retirement. The surplus revenue from the levy was allocated to the basic old-age insurance scheme for self-employed traders and craftsmen and to two organisations that assisted the trade and craft sectors. In proceedings in the French courts claiming repayment of the levy, it was argued that the various uses to which the revenue was put all constituted State aid which had been granted in breach of Article 108(3) TFEU. The ECJ held that the levy was not hypothecated to the aid measures since the level of the cessation payments were fixed by regulation and was not dependent on the revenue from the levy and the payments to the other funds was also not fixed by reference to the revenue.[230] In *TF1 v Commission*, concerning a tax on advertising that was intended to enable the State to finance an operational subsidy for French public television, the General Court held that the fact that the new tax were introduced to cover these costs was not sufficient, of itself, and without the existence of a regulatory act restricting the use of the tax to this effect, to show that there was a link between the new taxes and the financing of the aid in question.[231] A similar conclusion was reached in *Telefónica de España SA v Commission* concerning financing of Spanish public television.[232]

Imposition of an exceptional tax burden The ECJ has, nevertheless, held that the imposition of an exceptional tax burden on certain undertakings does not constitute State aid in favour of those undertakings that are subject to a lower rate of tax. In *GIL v Commissioners of Customs and Excise*, insurance premium tax (IPT) in the United Kingdom was generally charged at 4%, while a higher rate of 17.5% was applied to certain insurance policies connected with the supply of goods or services. The purpose of the higher rate was to discourage commercial arrangements whereby VAT, also at 17.5%, was being avoided on the ancillary transactions. The ECJ rejected the notion that the imposition of the higher rate constituted State aid in favour of those subject to the lower rate. Standard rate IPT did not constitute a derogation from the general system of taxation of insurance in the United Kingdom. Nor was it a

---

C-325/04, *Distribution Casino France v Organic* [2005] ECR I-9481, para 41; Cases C-393/04 & C-41/05, *Air Liquide Industries Belgium SA v Ville de Seraing* [2006] ECR I-5293, para 46.

[229] Case C-175/02, *Pape v Minister van Landbouw, Natuurbeheer en Visserij* [2005] ECR I-127, para 16.

[230] Cases C-266/04 to C-270/04, C-276/04 & C-321/04 to C-325/04, *Distribution Casino France v Organic* [2005] ECR I-9481, paras 49, 55-56.

[231] Case T-275/11, *TF1 v Commission* EU:T:2013:535, para 58.

[232] Case T-151/11, *Telefónica de España SA v Commission* EU:T:2014:631, para 102.

tax scheme favouring a specified sector, since it was a system of taxation of insurance premiums intended to compensate for the fact that insurance transactions were not subject to VAT.[233]

Advocate General Geelhoed, in *GIL v Commissioners of Customs and Excise*, dismissed the idea that exceptional burdens, in principle, could constitute State aid. Distortions of competition caused by exceptional burdens should, he argued, be dealt with under the provisions of Article 116 TFEU, whereby the Commission could consult the Member States concerned and, if necessary, propose that the Council issue directives to eliminate the distortion. Accordingly, the major difference in legal consequences attaching to distortions stemming from the grant of aid, on the one hand, and exceptional burdens, on the other, called for a careful demarcation between the two. The notion that a distortion created by an exceptional burden may be viewed as the grant of aid in favour of the economic operators who continued to come within the general rule was in principle incorrect. The mere introduction under a general provision not constituting the grant of aid of a higher rate restricted *ratione materiae* or *ratione personae* would have the effect of turning that provision into the grant of aid in favour of the market participants to whom the general rule has continued to apply. First, that would be to extend the substantive scope of the prohibition on State aid far beyond the limits contemplated by the framers of the FEU Treaty. Secondly, it would be to impinge on the scope of Articles 116 and 117 TFEU.[234]

Discriminatory taxation of products Aid cannot be introduced or authorised by a Member State in the form of fiscal discrimination against products originating in other Member States.[235] Fiscal discrimination of this type infringes Article 110 TFEU or, in some cases, Article 30 TFEU. Accordingly, the General Court, in *British Aggregates Association v Commission*, annulled the Commission's decision permitting as compatible with the internal market the specific provision whereby aggregates produced in Northern Ireland were subject to a significant discount from the application of the UK aggregates levy, without having considered whether the imposition of the full rate of levy

---

[233] Case C-308/01, *GIL Insurance Ltd v Commissioners of Customs and Excise* [2004] ECR I-4777, para 76. See also Case C-385/12, *Hervis Sport* EU:C:2014:47, paras 14-15, in which it was argued that being subject to higher rates of taxation on the basis of consolidated group turnover constituted State aid to its competitors who were taxed mainly on the basis of sole turnover.

[234] Case C-308/01, *GIL Insurance Ltd v Commissioners of Customs and Excise* [2004] ECR I-4777, *per* Advocate General Geelhoed at paras 72-74.

[235] Cases 142 & 143/80, *Amministrazione delle Finanze dello Stato v Essevi & Salengo* [1981] ECR 1413, para 28; Case 73/79, *Commission v Italy* [1980] ECR 1533, para 11; Cases C-261/01 and C-262/01, *Van Calster v Belgium* [2003] ECR-12249, para 48; Case T-359/04, *British Aggregates Association v Commission* [2010] ECR II-4227, para 92.

on aggregates imported across the border from Ireland constituted an infringement of either Article 30 TFEU or Article 110 TFEU.[236]

Article 30 TFEU prohibits customs duties on imports and exports and charges having equivalent effect between Member States. This is aimed, in the case of imports, at any charge demanded at the time of or by reason of importation and which is imposed specifically on an imported product to the exclusion of the similar domestic product.[237] Similarly, an internal charge which falls more heavily on exports than on domestic sales has an effect equivalent to a customs duty on export.[238] Article 110 TFEU precludes Member States from imposing, directly or indirectly, on the products of other Member States any internal taxation of any kind in excess of that imposed directly or indirectly on similar domestic products. This provision applies to financial charges within a general system of internal taxation which are charged systematically on domestic and imported products according to the same criteria.[239]

In order to determine whether Article 30 TFEU or Article 110 TFEU might apply, the use to which the financial charge is put must be taken into account. A specific tax, the proceeds of which are added to general taxation revenues, presents no particular State aid problems in this respect. In *Capolongo v Maya*, the ECJ was asked whether a charge imposed on importation into Italy of German packaging, the proceeds of which were used to subsidise the Italian paper processing industry, was compatible with Article 30 TFEU, even though a similar charge was imposed on Italian domestic production. However, when a charge, which is levied equally on domestic products and on imported or exported products, is intended to support activities which specifically profit the domestic products, the general duty levied according to the same criteria on the imported or exported product and the domestic product may constitute for the former a net supplementary tax burden, whilst for the latter it is in reality a set-off against benefits or aid previously received. Consequently, such a charge may constitute discriminatory internal taxation contrary to Article 110 TFEU or, where it is used exclusively to benefit the domestic product, a charge having effect equivalent to a customs duty contrary to Article 30 TFEU.[240] Equally, if a levy is designated to finance activities which serve to make marketing within the country more profitable than exportation or in any other

---

[236] Case T-359/04, *British Aggregates Association v Commission* [2010] ECR II-4227, paras 98-102.

[237] Case 77/72, *Capolongo v Maya* [1973] ECR 611, para 12; Cases C-393/04 & C-41/05, *Air Liquide Industries Belgium SA v Ville de Seraing* [2006] ECR I-5293, para 51.

[238] Case 51/74, *Van der Hulst v Produktschap voor Siergewassen* [1975] ECR 79, para 14.

[239] Case 78/76, *Steinike und Weinlig v Germany* [1997] ECR 595, para 30; Cases C-393/04 & C-41/05, *Air Liquide Industries Belgium SA v Ville de Seraing* [2006] ECR I-5293, para 56; Case C-206/06, *Essent Netwerk Noord BV v Alumimium Delfzijl BV* [2008] ECR I-5497, para 41.

[240] Case 77/72, *Capolongo v Maya* [1973] ECR 611, paras 13-14.

way to give preferential treatment to the product intended for the internal market, to the detriment of that intended for export, it is liable to impede exports and thus to have an effect equivalent to an export duty.[241] Article 30 TFEU operates so as to prohibit the entire charge falling within its scope, whereas Article 110 TFEU applies only to the discriminatory element of the taxation.[242]

The mere fact that a duty imposed by a Member State is utilised for the purpose of financing a system of aid which is recognised as incompatible with the treaty does not give to such duty the character of a charge having equivalent effect to customs duty.[243] A tax within the meaning of Article 110 TFEU may, depending on how the revenue from it is used, constitute State aid.[244] When a measure is financed by discriminatory taxation, which may be considered at the same time as forming part of an aid within the meaning of Article 107(1) TFEU, it may be governed both by the provisions of Article 90 EC and by those applicable to aid granted by Member States. However, while Articles 30 TFEU and 110 TFEU seek to preserve the free movement of goods and competition between domestic products and imported products, Article 107 TFEU has the objective, more generally, of preserving competition between undertakings by prohibiting State aid.[245] Discriminatory tax practices are not exempted from the application of Article 110 TFEU by reason of the fact that they may at the same time be described as a means of financing a State aid.[246] Equally, the ECJ has rejected the assertion that, when an aid is financed out of taxation, the method of financing can only be examined in relation to its compatibility with Article 110 TFEU and that the requirements of Article 107(1) TFEU should be disregarded. Rather, the Commission is required to consider not only whether the method by which it is financed

---

[241] Case 51/74, *Van der Hulst v Produktschap voor Siergewassen* [1975] ECR 79, para 16.

[242] Case 94/74, *IGAV v ENCC* [1975] ECR 699, para 13.

[243] *Ibid.*, para 29.

[244] Cases C-78/90-83/90, *Compagnie Commerciale de l'Ouest v Receveur principal des Douanes de La Pallice-Port* [1992] ECR I-1847, para 35; Case C-17/91, *Lornoy v Belgium* [1992] ECR I-6523, para 28; Case C-266/91, *CELBI v Fazenda Pública* [1993] ECR I-4337, para 21; Case C-72/92, *Herbert Scharbakte GmbH v Germany* [1993] ECR I-5509, para 18; Cases C-34/01 to C-38/01, *Enirisorse SpA v Ministero delle Finanze* [2003] ECR I-14243, para 43; Case C-206/06, *Essent Netwerk Noord BV v Alumimium Delfzijl* BV [2008] ECR I-5497, para 58.

[245] Case C-206/06, *Essent Netwerk Noord BV v Alumimium Delfzijl* BV [2008] ECR I-5497, para 60.

[246] Case 73/79, *Commission v Italy* [1980] ECR 1533, para 9; Case 17/81, *Pabst & Richarz KG v Hauptzollamt Oldenburg* [1982] ECR 1331, para 22; Case 277/83, *Commission v Italy* [1985] ECR 2049, para 16; Case C-234/99, *Nygård v Svineafgiftsfonden* [2002] ECR I-3657, para 55; Case C-206/06, *Essent Netwerk Noord BV v Alumimium Delfzijl* BV [2008] ECR I-5497, para 59.

complies with Article 110 TFEU but also whether in conjunction with the aid which it services it is compatible with Article 107(1) TFEU.[247]

Where a Member State grants a tax advantage in respect of the production of certain goods, Article 110 TFEU requires that this advantage must be extended without discrimination to similar products coming from other Member States. In this respect, Article 110 TFEU does not allow any distinction either according to the reasons, whether social or otherwise, for those special systems, or according to the relative importance of such systems as compared with the ordinary taxation system.[248] Discrimination will not arise in cases where there is a substantial processing of imported products after importation, having the effect of changing the origin of the processed products. Thus, the Commission approved a Dutch scheme of aid for research financed by a levy imposed on processed fruit and vegetables where, in respect of imports, the levy was imposed only on fruit and vegetables that had undergone substantial processing so that the products might be regarded as of Dutch origin. On the other hand, the Commission opposed a French levy which was imposed on table wines marketed in France, including imported wines which were blended with French wines, on the ground that blending was not a substantial process which could alter the origin of the wines from other Member States.[249] The Commission considers that discrimination does not arise where the charge imposed on imported and domestic production is intended to finance marketing controls imposed on the products pursuant to Community directives, since the charge serves to achieve objectives that are in the Community interest.[250]

Reimbursement of taxation on export Article 111 TFEU requires Member States which repay internal taxation on products exported to another Member State not to exceed the internal taxation previously imposed directly or indirectly on those products. Such a tax repayment cannot be regarded as State aid as it does not constitute an advantage within the meaning of Article 107(1) TFEU. In *Commission v Italy*, the ECJ held that the tax imposed directly on products is that imposed on the finished product, whilst that imposed indirectly is that imposed during the various stages of production on the raw materials or semi-finished products used in the manufacture of the products.[251] The Commission appears to consider that a repayment of tax which exceeds the taxation previously imposed is not only contrary to Article 111 TFEU but may

---

[247] Case 47/69, *France v Commission* [1970] ECR 487, para 14; Case 73/79, *Commission v Italy* [1980] ECR 1533, para 6.

[248] Case 148/77, *Hansen v Hauptzollamt Flensburg* [1978] ECR 1787, para 17; Case C-204/97, *Portugal v Commission* [2001] ECR I-3175, para 48.

[249] *Twenty-Third Report on Competition Policy* (1993), pt. 551.

[250] *Twenty-Second Report on Competition Policy* (1992), pt. 507.

[251] Case 45/65, *Commission v Italy* [1965] ECR 857, at p. 866.

also constitute State aid in the hands of the beneficiary.[252] The Commission considers that a Spanish preferential tax regime in favour of outward foreign direct investments was specifically aimed at improving the trading conditions of the beneficiaries taxable in Spain against foreign competitors, including those established in other Member States, with respect to the investments they made abroad being directly or indirectly related to export of products and services from Spain. The Commission accordingly considered that, as far as the aid scheme in question resulted in a remission of internal taxes in respect of exports to other Member States contrary to Article 112 TFEU, it was incompatible with the internal market.[253]

3.5 HARMFUL TAX COMPETITION

National provisions causing distortion of competition   Where national provisions distort the conditions of competition in the internal market, the Council, rather than having to act unanimously, has a specific power, pursuant to Article 116 TFEU, to act by qualified majority. This might be the case, for example, where the tax provisions applicable in a Member State, such as the rates of taxation, are radically different from those applicable in other Member States. Thus, a corporation tax rate of 10% which is generally applicable to all undertakings in a Member State does not constitute State aid within the meaning of Article 107(1) TFEU, but may nevertheless distort the conditions of competition where competing undertakings are subject in other Member States to corporation tax rates of 35% or more. Advocate General Geelhoed, in *GIL v Commissioners of Customs and Excise*, described Articles 107-108 TFEU as *leges speciales* under the aegis of the general rules laid down by Article 116 TFEU.[254]

Article 116 TFEU applies where the Commission finds a difference between national provisions distorts the conditions of competition in the internal market and that the resultant distortion needs to be eliminated. The Commission must first consult the Member States concerned. If such consultation does not result in an agreement eliminating the distortion in question, the Council, acting by a qualified majority on a proposal from the Commission, is empowered to issue the necessary directives.[255]   Pursuant to

---

[252] *Fifteenth Report on Competition Policy* (1985), pt. 227. See also Case T-210/02, *British Aggregates Association v Commission* [2004] ECR II-2789, para 150-151; overturned on appeal, Case C-487/06P, *British Aggregates Association v Commission* [2008] ECR I-10515, para 178.

[253] Case E 22/2004, *Incentives for export related investments*, OJ 2007 C302/3.

[254] Case C-308/01, *GIL Insurance Ltd v Commissioners of Customs and Excise* [2004] ECR I-4777, *per* Advocate General Geelhoed at para 67; Case C-174/02, *Streekgeweest Westelijk Noord-Brabant v Staatsecretaris van Financiën* [2005] ECR I-85, para 24.

[255] Article 116 TFEU.

Article 117 TFEU, a Member State must consult the Commission in advance
where there is reason to fear that the adoption or amendment of a national
provision may cause distortion of the conditions of competition in the internal
market. After consulting the Member States, the Commission is empowered to
recommend to the State concerned such measures as may be appropriate to
avoid the distortion in question.[256] Thus, Article 117 TFEU, which binds the
Member States unambiguously to prior consultation with the Commission in
all those cases where their projected legislation might create a risk, however
slight, of a possible distortion, is designed to prevent the differences between
the legislation of the Member States with regard to the objectives of the FEU
Treaty from becoming more pronounced.[257] If a State does not comply with
such a recommendation, other Member States may not be required, in
pursuance of Article 116 TFEU, to amend their own provisions in order to
eliminate such distortion.[258]

Harmful tax competition: Code of Conduct Although the power under
Article 116 TFEU is readily available to the Council, it has never made use of
it, despite frequent complaints concerning harmful tax competition being
levelled against low rates of taxation applied in countries such as Ireland and
Luxembourg.   This reflects the political sensitivities concerning fiscal
sovereignty and the reluctance of most Member States to have the EU
institutions involved in determining the rates of direct taxation. In 1996, the
Commission produced a report on the development of tax systems in the EU,
which highlighted the economic effects of competition between Member
States,[259] and followed this with a proposal for tackling harmful tax
competition.[260] Accordingly, in December 1997, the Council adopted a Code
of Conduct for Business Taxation which is directed at direct tax measures
which affect, or may affect, in a significant way the location of business
activities in the EU.[261] In particular, the Code of Conduct provides that tax
measures which create a significantly lower effective level of taxation than that

---

[256] Article 117(1) TFEU.

[257] Case 6/64, *Costa v ENEL* [1964] ECR 585, at p. 595. Whilst this is binding on the
Member States as a matter of EU law, Article 117 TFEU is not directly effective and
does not, therefore, create individual rights which national courts must protect.

[258] Article 117(2) TFEU. If the Member State which has ignored the recommendation of
the Commission causes distortion detrimental only to itself, the provisions of Article 116
TFEU do not apply.

[259] COM(96) 546 final.

[260] COM(97) 495 final.

[261] See, C. Pinto, "EU and OECD to fight harmful competition" [1998] Intertax 386; W.W.
Brathan & J.A. McCahery, "Tax coordination and tax competition in the European
Union: evaluating the code of conduct on business taxation" (2001) 38 CMLRev 677;
R.H.C.Luca, "Harmful tax policy: when political objectives interfere with State aid
rules" [2003] Intertax 484; P. Rossi-Maccanico, "Commentary on State aid review of
multinational tax regimes" [2007] EStALQ 25.

which generally applies in the Member State in question are to be regarded as potentially harmful.

When assessing whether such measures are harmful account should be taken *inter alia* of:

- whether advantages are accorded only to non-residents or in respect of transactions carried out with non-residents;
- whether advantages are ring-fenced from the domestic market, so they do not affect the national tax base;
- whether advantages are granted without any real economic activity or substantial economic presence within the Member State offering such tax advantages;
- whether the basis of profit determination in respect of activities within a multinational group of companies departs from internationally accepted principles, notably those agreed within the OECD;
- whether the tax measures lack transparency, including where statutory rules are relaxed at administrative level in a non-transparent way.

Member States committed themselves not to introduce new tax measures which would be considered harmful within the meaning of the Code of Conduct and to examine their existing tax provisions with a view to eliminating any harmful measures as soon as possible.[262]

Commission investigations into harmful tax competition The Commission opened investigations into several favourable tax regimes, particularly those involving alternative tax methods, such as the cost-plus method or the exemption method aimed at cross-border intra-group transactions.[263] It adopted negative decisions on, for example, the tax treatment of Belgian and coordination centres, as well as similar arrangements in France, Luxembourg and Ireland.[264] Luxembourg's legislation on exempt 1929 holding companies provided that holding companies registered in Luxembourg were free from business taxes on dividends, interest, royalties and other earnings, provided they exercised only certain activities including financing, licensing, management and coordination services.[265] A 10% reduction in corporation tax to captive insurance companies in the Åland islands was held to constitute State aid. The aid could not be exempted, but in any case no captive company qualifying for the reduction had actually been set up since the introduction of the scheme in 1993.[266] The United Kingdom accepted the Commission's

---

[262] See Cases T-195/01R & T-207/01R, *Government of Gibraltar v Commission* [2001] ECR II-3915, para 17.

[263] *Thirty-Third Report on Competition Policy* (2003), pts. 479-503.

[264] Commission Decision 2003/755/EC, *Belgian coordination centres*, OJ 2003 L282/25.

[265] Commission Decision 2006/940/EC, *Luxembourg 1929 exempt holding companies*, OJ 2007 L366/47.

[266] Commission Decision 2002/937/EC, *Captive insurance companies*, OJ 2002 L329/22.

proposals to abolish the exempt company tax regime, whereby companies that carried on activities exclusively abroad paid no income tax on profits, but were subject to a fixed annual tax up to £300.[267]

Tax transparency package   In 2015, the Commission presented a tax transparency package of measures as part of its agenda to tackle corporate tax avoidance and harmful competition between Member States. A key element of this is a proposal to introduce EU legislation requiring the automatic exchange of information between Member States on their tax rulings every three months, thereby allowing Member States to be able to ask for more detailed information on a particular ruling. This is not only intended to allow tax authorities to detect abusive tax practices but should encourage healthier tax competition. The Commission also proposed to examine the feasibility of new transparency requirements for companies, such as the public disclosure of certain tax information by multinationals. In addition, the Code of Conduct for Business Taxation will be revamped to take account of more sophisticated corporate tax avoidance schemes that currently do not fall within its scope.[268]

---

[267] Case E 7/2002, *Gibraltar exempt companies*, OJ 2005 C228/9.
[268] See press release IP/15/4610.

Chapter Four

MARKET TRANSACTIONS AND STATE AID

4.1 MARKET TRANSACTIONS AND STATE AID

Market economy operator principle Public authorities and public or private bodies acting under the control of the State may engage in all manner of commercial transactions, such as the acquisition of goods and services or the making of capital investments in commercial companies. Since State resources are used in order to engage in these transactions, it must be considered whether this may result in State aid being granted to the counterparty.[1] However, since Article 345 TFEU recognises that the system of property ownership is not affected by EU law, the principle of equal treatment means that Member States are free to undertake, directly or indirectly, economic activities in the same way as private companies.[2] Advocate General Slynn, in *Germany v Commission*, which concerned investment of capital contributions in an undertaking, considered that aid would arise if the recipient obtained a benefit which it would not have received in the normal course.[3] In *Spain v Commission*, Advocate General Jacobs regarded aid as being granted whenever a State made funds available to an undertaking which in the normal course of events would not be provided by a private investor applying ordinary commercial criteria and disregarding considerations of a social, political or philanthropic nature.[4] This approach, initially referred to as the market economy investor principle or the private investor principle, has been adopted by the ECJ which held in *SFEI v La Poste* that, in order to determine whether a State measure in the context of commercial relations constitutes aid for the purposes of Article 107(1) TFEU, it is necessary to establish whether the recipient receives an economic advantage which it would not have obtained under normal market conditions.[5]

---

[1] For a full analysis, see *The Applicability and Application of the Market Economy Investor Principle*, Małgorzata Agnieszka Cyndecka, University of Bergen (2015).

[2] Case T-565/08, *Corsica Ferries France sas v Commission* EU:T:2012:415, para 77.

[3] Case 84/82, *Germany v Commission* [1984] ECR 1451, *per* Advocate General Slynn, at p. 1501.

[4] Cases C-278/92 to C-280/92, *Spain v Commission* [1994] ECR I-4103, *per* Advocate General Jacobs, at p. 4112.

[5] Case C-39/94, *SFEI v La Poste* [1996] ECR I-3547, para 60; Case C-342/96, *Spain v Commission* [1999] ECR I-2459, para 41; Case C-256/97, *Déménagements-Manutention Transports SA* [1999] ECR I-3913, para 22; Case C-280/00, *Altmark Trans GmbH v*

The principle that, where the State intervenes in the market, its action will constitute the grant of an economic advantage where it does not act in the same way as a private operator under normal market conditions applies to all forms of market transactions including investments, debt collection, the acquisition or provision of goods and services, and the issue of loans or guarantees. It may, therefore, be termed, more generally, the market economy operator principle or the market operator test.[6] Application of the market operator test entails comparing the way in which a public authority acts with the way in which a private operator of a comparable size would have acted in the same circumstances. That test is satisfied where the State in fact merely acts in the same way as any private operator would do acting in normal market conditions. In such circumstances, there is no advantage attributable to intervention by the State, because the beneficiary could theoretically have derived the same benefits from the mere functioning of the market.[7]

The Commission has established its own policy for determining whether a State intervention is in line with market conditions.[8] A transaction should normally be examined on an *ex ante* basis, having regard to the information available at the time the intervention was decided upon, for example on the basis of a business plan in respect of the viability of an investment. For example, since interest rates fluctuate up and down, to an extent that is largely unforeseeable by the lender, a loan must be evaluated from the point of view of the lender at the moment the loan is approved.[9] Compliance with market conditions can be empirically established through specific market data when the transaction is carried out *pari passu* by public and private operators or

---

Nahverkehrsgesellschaft Altmark GmbH [2003] ECR I-7747, para 84; Cases C-34/01 to C-38/01, *Enirisorse SpA v Miinistero delle Finanze* [2003] ECR I-14243, para 30; Case C-451/03, *Servizi Ausiliari Dottori Commercialisti Srl v Calafiori* [2006] ECR I-2941, para 59; Case C-206/06, *Essent Netwerk Noord BV v Alumimium Delfzijl* BV [2008] ECR I-5497, para 79; Case C-124/10P, *Commission v EDF* EU:C:2012:318, para 78; Case C-73/11P, *Frucona Košice as v Commission* EU:C:2013:32, para 71; Cases T-116/01 & T-118/01, *P&O European Ferries (Vizcaya) SA v Commission* [2003] ECR II-2957, para 112; Case T-157/01, *Danske Busvognmaend v Commission* [2004] ECR II-197, para 57; Case T-196/04, *Ryanair Ltd v Commission* [2008] ECR II-3643, para 39; Case T-25/07, *Iride SpA v Commission* [2009] ECR II-245, para 46; Case T-305/13, *SACE BT SpA v Commission* EU:T:2015:435, para 91.

6   Cases T-268/08 & T-281/08, *Land Burgenland v Commission* EU:T:2012:90, para 48; Case T-244/08, *Konsum Nord ekonomisk förening v Commission* [2011] ECR II-444*, para 64; Cases T-80/06 & T-182/09, *Budapesti Erőmű Zrt v Commission* EU:T:2012:65, para 64; Case T-58/13, *Club Hotel Loutraki AE v Commission* EU:T:2015:1, para 53.

7   Case T-244/08, *Konsum Nord ekonomisk förening v Commission* [2011] ECR II-444*, para 62; Cases T-80/06 & T-182/09, *Budapesti Erőmű Zrt v Commission* EU:T:2012:65, para 67; Case T-468/08, *Tisza Erőmű kft v Commission* EU:T:2014:235, para 85; Case T-179/09, *Dunamenti Erőmű zrt v Commission* EU:T:2014:236, para 76.

8   See Commission draft Notice on the notion of State aid.

9   Case T-257/10, *Italy v Commission* EU:T:2012:504, para 151; Case T-303/10, *Wam Industriale SpA v Commission* EU:T:2012:505, para 158.

when the transaction is carried out through an open, transparent and non-discriminatory tender procedure. In other cases, benchmarking might be used in relation to comparable transactions carried out by comparable private operators to establish a reference value or a range of possible values.

Applicability of the market operator test In *Commission v EDF*, the ECJ held that, in situations characterised by all the constituent elements of State aid, the market operator test is among the factors which the Commission is required to take into account for the purposes of establishing the existence of aid.[10] Consequently, where it appears that the market operator test could be applicable, the Commission is under a duty to ask the Member State concerned to provide it with all relevant information enabling it to determine whether the conditions governing that test are met.[11] The Commission is obliged to take account of all the relevant facts, including the nature and subject matter of the measure, its context, the objective pursued and the rules to which the measure is subject.[12] Where the Member State concerned provides the Commission with the necessary evidence, the onus is on the Commission to carry out a global assessment, taking into account all relevant evidence enabling it to determine whether the market operator principle has been satisfied.[13] The Member State, where there is doubt, must establish unequivocally and on the basis of objective and verifiable evidence that the measure implemented falls to be ascribed to the State as shareholder.[14]

Where a public authority acts together with an undertaking that it controls, in applying the market operator test, it is necessary to envisage the commercial transaction as a whole in order to determine whether, taken together, they have acted as rational operators in a market economy, since the examination of a transaction outside its context could lead to purely formal results which do not correspond to economic reality. In assessing the transactions, all the relevant features of the measures and their context must be examined, including those relating to the situation of the authority or authorities responsible for granting

---

[10] Case C-124/10P, *Commission v EDF* EU:C:2012:318, para 103.

[11] *Ibid.*, para 104.

[12] Case C-290/07P, *Commission v Scott SA* [2010] ECR I-7763, para 65; Case C-124/10P, *Commission v EDF* EU:C:2012:318, para 104; Cases T-228/99 & T-233/99, *Westdeutsche Landesbank Girozentrale v Commission* [2003] ECR II-435, para 251; Case T-244/08, *Konsum Nord ekonomisk förening v Commission* [2011] ECR II-444*, para 57; Cases T-80/06 & T-182/09, *Budapesti Erőmű Zrt v Commission* EU:T:2012:65, para 66; Cases T-319/12 & T-321/12, *Spain v Commission* EU:T:2014:604, para 45; Case T-1/12, *France v Commission* EU:T:2015:17, para 33; Case T-305/13, *SACE BT SpA v Commission* EU:T:2015:435, para 96.

[13] Case C-124/10P, *Commission v EDF* EU:C:2012:318, para 86; Cases C-214/12P, C-215/12P & C-223/12P, *Land Burgenland v Commission* EU:C:2013:682, para 60; Case T-305/13, *SACE BT SpA v Commission* EU:T:2015:435, para 96.

[14] Case C-124/10P, *Commission v EDF* EU:C:2012:318, para 82; Cases C-214/12P, C-215/12P & C-223/12P, *Land Burgenland v Commission* EU:C:2013:682, para 61.

the measures.[15] In *Greece v Commission*, which concerned a publicly owned agricultural bank, Greece argued that the bank's importance in the agricultural sector in Greece required it to take account of major sectoral parameters in its lending decisions and to protect its reputation as the principal lender in the sector. The ECJ held, however, that this itself showed that the bank was required to take account of broader interests in its lending decisions than solely its own commercial interest, so that the Commission was entitled to conclude that it did not act as a private investor.[16]

In *Commission v ING Groep*, the Commission argued that it is appropriate to apply the market operator test to the behaviour of public authorities only where they are in a position comparable to that in which private operators may find themselves. In that case, which involved aid to a bank during the credit crisis, a private investor could never have found itself in a situation in which it had provided State aid to ING. The ECJ held, however, that the applicability of the market operator test to a public intervention depends, not on the way in which the advantage was conferred, but on the classification of the intervention as a decision adopted by a shareholder of the undertaking in question. In fact, any holder of securities, in whatever amount and of whatever nature, may wish or agree to renegotiate the conditions of their redemption. It is, consequently, meaningful to compare the behaviour of the State in that regard with that of a hypothetical private investor in a comparable position. What is decisive in the context of that comparison is whether the amendment to the repayment terms of the capital injection satisfied an economic rationality test, so that a private investor might also be in a position to accept such an amendment, in particular by increasing the prospects of obtaining the repayment of that injection.[17]

Where State intervention entails various different consequences for an undertaking, account must be taken of the cumulative effect of these consequences in order to determine whether an advantage has been conferred on the undertaking.[18] In *Poste Italiane SpA v Commission*, the Italian post office operated a banking service. Under Italian law, the deposits held by the post bank had to be lodged with the Italian Treasury which paid an interest rate of 4%. The Commission held that this rate of interest exceeded rates that commercial banks would pay for similar deposits and concluded that the difference between the rate paid and that payable on market terms constituted State aid to Poste Italiane. However, the General Court annulled the decision on the ground that the Commission should have taken into consideration that

---

[15] Case T-196/04, *Ryanair Ltd v Commission* [2008] ECR II-3643, para 59; Case T-244/08, *Konsum Nord ekonomisk förening v Commission* [2011] ECR II-444*, para 57; Case T-58/13, *Club Hotel Loutraki AE v Commission* EU:T:2015:1, para 91.

[16] Case C-278/00, *Greece v Commission* [2004] ECR I-3997, para 44-48.

[17] Case C-224/12P, *Commission v Netherlands and ING Groep NV* EU:C:2014:213, paras 31-36.

[18] Case T-525/08, *Poste Italiane SpA v Commission* EU:T:2013:481, para 61.

the interest rate payable by the Treasury could not be dissociated from the obligation imposed by Italian law that Poste Italiane could lodge its deposits only with the Treasury, thereby depriving it of the possibility, which was in principle open to any other bank, of investing the funds as it sought fit.[19] On the other hand, where the Commission conducts an analysis under the market operator test and concludes that the transaction does not give rise to any advantage for the undertaking concerned, which leads it to find there is no State aid, it cannot be required to examine alternatives to the choice by the notifying Member State.[20]

Market price The market price is the highest price that a private operator acting under normal market competitive conditions is ready to pay for the goods, services or assets in question, provided that offer is binding and credible. That is so regardless of the reasons, including subjective or strategic reasons, which led that potential buyer to submit that offer.[21] In relation to an investment, the market price is the highest price that a private investor acting under normal market conditions is willing to pay for a company in the situation it is in.[22] The reasons which lead a certain bidder to submit an offer of a certain amount are not decisive from the perspective of a private vendor. In particular, it is generally accepted that each element of the conditions relating to the privatisation of a publicly owned company is liable to have distinct advantages and disadvantages for different bidders, including, for example, tax advantages which might accrue to certain bidders from carry-forward of the acquired company's losses. Any such advantages need not be analysed in order to determine the market price, which, in any event, equates to the highest price that a bidder is willing to pay.[23]

The Commission has adopted a communication on the method of setting reference and discount rates which, taking account of the debtor's creditworthiness and available collateral, are used as a proxy for the market rate and to measure the grant equivalent of aid, in particular when it is disbursed in several instalments and to calculate the aid element resulting from interest subsidy schemes.[24] The EU Courts have treated the Commission's

---

[19] *Ibid.*, para 62.

[20] Case C-287/12P, *Ryanair Ltd v Commission* EU:C:2013:395, para 87; Case T-123/09, *Ryanair Ltd v Commission* EU:T:2012:164, para 123.

[21] Cases C-214/12P, C-215/12P & C-223/12P, *Land Burgenland v Commission* EU:C:2013:682, para 99; Cases T-268/08 & T-281/08, *Land Burgenland v Commission* EU:T:2012:90, para 89.

[22] Case C-390/98, *HJ Banks & Co Ltd v Coal Authority* [2001] ECR I-6117, para 77; Case C-277/00, *Germany v Commission* [2004] ECR I-3925, para 80; Cases C-214/12P, C-215/12P & C-223/12P, *Land Burgenland v Commission* EU:C:2013:682, para 92.

[23] Cases C-214/12P, C-215/12P & C-223/12P, *Land Burgenland v Commission* EU:C:2013:682, paras 116-117.

[24] OJ 2008 C14/6.

practice of using the reference rate as an appropriate basis for determining whether aid has been granted through low interest loans as legitimate.[25] In *Italy v Commission*, the General Court rejected an alternative reference rate proposed by the Italian authorities, being maximum rates laid down by Treasury decree for bank loans to local and regional public bodies. Those rates were not fixed in accordance with market conditions, since they were set by reference to other criteria laid down by the public administration.[26]

Although the reference rate communication provides for an increase in the case of debtors without a credit history, the General Court has held that nothing indicates that, in the case of debtors with a credit history, the base rate cannot be increased in the same way.[27] In *Nitrogénművek Vegyipari Zst v Commission*, the Commission was faced with establishing the price that should have been paid for a loan granted by the State-owned public development bank had it been acting as a private operator. The fact that the commercial bank that had previously granted loans to the borrower had ceased to continue to grant it loans was a factor which would have induced other financial institutions to act with circumspection to the borrower.[28] Moreover, the fact that the borrower was in a poor financial shape and that it had ceased production would lead to higher interest rates being applicable, despite high levels of collateral being available.[29]

Establishing the market price in complex transactions Establishing the market price for the sale and purchase of goods or services can involve a complex assessment. In *Budapesti Erőmű Zrt v Commission*, in order to assess whether there was an economic advantage granted by a public undertaking that entered into long term electricity purchasing agreements with privately owned electricity generators in Hungary at a fixed pricing mechanism, the Commission took as its point of reference a market operator who is subject to the same obligations and has the same opportunities as the public undertaking. The Commission identified the main practices of commercial operators on European electricity markets and assessed whether the long term contracts provided the generators with guarantees that a buyer would not find acceptable if it were acting on purely commercial grounds. It compared the agreements with the main features of standard forward and spot contacts, as well other types of contracts prevalent on the electricity markets. That comparison proved that the combination of long term capacity reservation, a minimum

---

[25] Case C-457/00, *Belgium v Commission* [2003] ECR I-6931, paras 71-75; Case C-278/00, *Greece v Commission* [2004] ECR I-3997, paras 61-63; Case T-222/04, *Italy v Commission* [2009] ECR II-1877, para 65

[26] Case T-222/04, *Italy v Commission* [2009] ECR II-1877, para 71.

[27] Case T-387/11, *Nitrogénművek Vegyipari Zst v Commission* EU:T:2013:98, para 84.

[28] *Ibid.*, para 28.

[29] *Ibid.*, para 37.

guaranteed off-take and price setting mechanisms covering variable, fixed and capital costs as laid down in the agreements did not correspond to the usual contracts on the European wholesale electricity markets. The General Court found that this enabled the Commission correctly to conclude that the agreements provided power generators with a better guarantee than that provided under standard commercial contracts and thus gave rise to State aid.[30]

In *Pollmeier Massivholz v Commission*, the market value of land, free of existing unusable buildings, was estimated by an independent expert to be worth €2,490,000, although putting the land into a usable state, which would involve demolition of the buildings, required expenditure of €1.49 million. The General Court, therefore, confirmed the Commission's decision that the market value of the land on its present state was €1 million.[31] Where a sale of property forms part of a broader complex set of transactions, it may not be sufficient to evaluate the value of the property sold in isolation from the other transactions. In *Konsum Nord v Commission*, a supermarket chain owned land in a town centre that had been designated for development by the local authority. As part of a scheme to acquire that land, the local authority transferred to the supermarket a separate plot of land in another location. That plot had previously been the object of a potential purchase by another supermarket chain which had offered a price significantly higher than the sale price agreed with the local authority. Following a complaint, the Commission declared that the sale operated as a grant of aid to the supermarket by reference to the difference between the price paid and that offered by the other supermarket chain. The General Court held, however, that an appraisal of all the circumstances showed that there was a link between the different property transactions, even if this was not in fact formally evidenced in the contract for sale of the plot of land.[32]

Objective commercial justification for transaction In applying the market operator test, it is necessary to ascertain whether a private operator, in possession of the same information as the public authority, would conduct the same commercial transaction.[33] Normally a private operator is not content to obtain a limited return on his investment, but attempts to maximise the return

---

[30] Cases T-80/06 & T-182/09, *Budapesti Erőmű Zrt v Commission* EU:T:2012:65, paras 67-83.

[31] Case T-89/09, *Pollmeier Massivholz GmbH v Commission* EU:T:2015:153, paras 194-195.

[32] Case T-244/08, *Konsum Nord ekonomisk förening v Commission* [2011] ECR II-444*, para 51.

[33] Case C-457/00, *Belgium v Commission* [2003] ECR I-6931, para 47; Case T-16/96, *Cityflyer Express v Commission* [1998] ECR II-757, para 76; Case T-163/05, *Bundesverband Deutscher Banken v Commission* [2010] ECR II-387, para 168.

on his assets in accordance with his circumstances and his interest.[34] It is, however, always necessary to assess properly any commercial reasons underlying the transaction in question. In particular, where the transaction may be objectively commercially justified, the mere fact that the State foregoes a certain amount of income does not necessarily lead to the conclusion that aid has been granted. For example, in *Alcoa Trasformazioni v Commission*, the Commission concluded that the sale of electricity based on the marginal costs of production constituted a market tariff given that the electricity producer had a significant over-capacity.[35] In *Netherlands v Commission*, a renegotiation of a complex contractual arrangement for the redevelopment of a town centre, leading to lower returns for the local authority, did not give rise to State aid where this was justified on the ground that it would lead to earlier completion of the project.[36] Accordingly, it cannot be said that every time a commercial concern in which the State has a shareholding reduces its prices or fails to maximise its profits the loss of income is to be regarded as State aid.[37]

In *Linde v Commission*, the Treuhandanstalt entered into an agreement in 1993 in the context of a privatisation of a chemicals company in the former East Germany in which it agreed to be responsible for the long-term supply of carbon monoxide to the purchaser of the company at a price equivalent to the market price. When it became apparent that the agreed supply price could not cover the costs of production of carbon monoxide, in order to relieve itself of its obligations under the supply contract, the successor to the Treuhandanstalt entered into a new contract with a third party, Linde AG, whereby the latter would produce the required quantities of carbon monoxide. Pursuant to this contract, a very large subsidy was granted to Linde in respect of its initial investment costs. The Commission determined that this subsidy amounted to State aid to Linde and declared incompatible with the common market the amount which exceeded the permissible ceiling under the regional aid guidelines. The General Court, however, analysed the subsidy in the light of the full background to the investment. It held that the comprehensive arrangement represented a normal commercial transaction in the course of which the German authorities acted as rational operators in a market economy, motivated primarily by economic considerations. The Commission's decision was annulled since it had failed to examine whether the value of the investment subsidy reflected in general terms the price which would have been agreed between economic operators in the same situation, although the portion of the

---

[34] Cases T-228/99 & T-233/99, *Westdeutsche Landesbank Girozentrale v Commission* [2003] ECR II-435, para 335.

[35] Case C-194/09P, *Alcoa Trasformazioni srl v Commission* [2011] ECR I-6311, paras 12-13.

[36] Cases T-186/13, T-190/13 & T-193/13, *Netherlands v Commission* EU:T:2015:447, paras 112-114.

[37] Cases 67, 68 & 70/85, *Van der Kooy v Commission* [1988] ECR 219, *per* Advocate General Slynn, at p. 250.

subsidy in excess of that price could have been regarded as State aid. Nor did the Commission establish whether the sum paid to Linde as consideration for its contractual obligations exceeded the cost of those obligations and, if so, the amount by which it did so.[38]

In the context of the establishment of Belgacom as a limited liability company taking over telecoms services from the public authorities, Belgacom was obliged to administer and finance the pension rights of former civil servants. Subsequently, Belgacom negotiated a deal with the Belgian authorities whereby it paid €5 billion to be relieved of this responsibility. The Commission concluded that the transfer was financially neutral in that Belgacom paid an amount corresponding to the net present value of the obligations taken over by the State. It followed that Belgacom did not gain any advantage beyond that which would have been available on normal market conditions and, accordingly, no State aid was involved.[39]

State aid and contractual consideration Contractual consideration involves the furnishing of something in return for agreeing to enter into the contract. In *Amministrazione delle Finanze dello Stato v Denkavit Italiana*, Advocate General Reischl stated that it was essential to the concept of an aid that the grant from the State is made for no consideration.[40] In any event, it is sufficient that the recipient has given less than full consideration, which would be the case, for example, where a public authority agrees to pay more than market value for an investment or for the provision of goods or services. Where a public undertaking enters into a contractual arrangement with a private undertaking under which both parties agree reciprocal supply commitments, the presence of State aid cannot be excluded in principle, so that it is necessary to evaluate the commercial value of the respective obligations entered into by each party.[41] For example, the provision of a loan at a preferential rate of interest constitutes State aid to the extent of the difference between the interest charged and that which would have been paid if the interest rate corresponding to normal market conditions had been applied.[42]

Contractual consideration may be combined with legislative provisions as a source of aid, although this is to be determined on the facts of the case. For

---

[38] Case T-98/00, *Linde v Commission* [2002] ECR II-3961, paras 49-53.

[39] Case N567/2003, *Belgacom*, OJ 2006 C305/11.

[40] Case 61/79, *Amministrazione delle Finanze dello Stato v Denkavit Italiana* [1980] ECR 1205, *per* Advocate General Reischl, at p. 1235.

[41] Case T-14/96, *BAI v Commission* [1999] ECR II-139, para 71; Cases T-116/01 & T-118/01, *P&O European Ferries (Vizcaya) SA v Commission* [2003] ECR II-2957, para 114; Case T-158/99, *Thermenhotel Stoiser Franz GmbH v Commission* [2004] ECR II-1, para 107.

[42] Case T-16/96, *Cityflyer Express v Commission* [1998] ECR II-757, para 53; Cases T-267/08 & T-279/08, *Région Nord-Pas-de-Calais v Commission* [2011] ECR II-1999, para 112.

example, in *Italy v Commission*, concerning the acquisition of private assets on the nationalisation of the Italian electricity sector, compensation was granted to the owner of the assets by way of legislation setting a preferential tariff for 30 years. Subsequently, the Italian authorities extended the tariff and argued that this was based on an ongoing contractual relationship which required equilibrium, so that an extension of the tariff was justified in order to counteract the effect of unforeseen events. The General Court rejected this analysis, holding that the basis for the preferential tariff was solely the legislation.[43]

Consideration granted through tax arrangements Where aid is granted through the tax or social security systems, it would be unusual for any consideration to arise, although it is not impossible in certain circumstances for a tax relief or exemption to constitute a means of payment by the State for goods or services provided. In *Commission v EDF*, however, the ECJ held that an economic advantage must, even where it has been granted through fiscal means, be assessed in the light of the market operator test if, on conclusion of an overall assessment, it appears that, notwithstanding the fact that the means used were instruments of State power, the Member State concerned has conferred that advantage in its capacity as shareholder of the undertaking belonging to it.[44] In *Ferring v ACOSS*, a tax was imposed on direct sales of pharmaceutical products by pharmaceutical laboratories, whereas wholesalers were not subject to the tax in light of the fact that they were required, pursuant to a public service obligation, to carry sufficient stocks so as to be able constantly to supply the needs of the local population. The ECJ held that, provided that the tax on direct sales imposed on the laboratories corresponded to the additional costs actually incurred by the wholesalers in discharging their public service obligation, the tax exemption granted to the wholesale distributors was to be regarded as compensation for the services provided and hence not State aid.[45] It would seem to be the case, therefore, that the amount of the tax exemption should be ascertained on an individual basis in respect of each wholesaler and would be regarded as consideration for the service provided.

Payment facilities on market creditor terms The mere fact that payment facilities are accorded in a discretionary manner by a public creditor is not

---

[43] Case T-53/08, *Italy v Commission* [2010] ECR II-3187, paras 93-96.

[44] Case C-124/10P, *Commission v EDF* EU:C:2012:318, para 86. Subsequently, The Commission found that the amount of tax foregone was in excess of the amounts that a private investor in similar circumstances would have invested: SA.13869 *EDF* (2015).

[45] Case C-53/00, *Ferring SA v ACOSS* [2001] ECR I-9067, para 27; Case C-280/00, *Altmark Trans GmbH v Nahverkehrsgesellschaft Altmark GmbH* [2003] ECR I-7747, para 86.

sufficient to characterise such facilities as State aid. Rather, for credit terms to constitute State aid, the payment facilities accorded must also be clearly more generous than those which would have been accorded by a private creditor in a comparable situation in regard to his debtor, having regard, in particular, to the size of the debt, the legal remedies available to the public creditor, the chances that the debtor's situation will recover if he is allowed to continue to operate and to the risks to the creditor of seeing his losses increase in the latter case.[46] The actions of a public creditor may be compared to those of a private creditor seeking to obtain payment of sums owed to it by a debtor in financial difficulties.[47] An overall assessment must be carried out, taking into account all relevant evidence enabling it to be determined whether the recipient company would manifestly not have obtained comparable facilities from a private creditor.[48] It is not necessary for an assessment to be made on the basis of cautious and pessimistic assumptions.[49] A creditor may be faced with the choice of seeking to put a debtor into liquidation or to commence debt recovery proceedings. That choice may be influenced by a number of factors, which must be properly taken into account in order to determine how a hypothetical private creditor in the same situation of the public creditor would have acted, having evaluated the advantages and disadvantages of the alternative procedures.[50] If the debt is waived on terms which would not be acceptable to a private creditor, the decision of the creditor to approve the arrangement, which involves the creditor definitively waiving all or part of its claim, constitutes the grant of State aid.[51]

In *Salomon v Commission*, following financial difficulties, a company drew up a restructuring plan and on this basis obtained a reduction in its debts to its bankers, some of which were State controlled. The measures taken by the public banks did not contain any element of State aid since their action was

---

[46]   Case C-256/97, *Déménagements-Manutention Transports SA* [1999] ECR I-3913, para 30; Case C-73/11P, *Frucona Košice as v Commission* EU:C:2013:32, para 72; Case C-271/13P, *Rousse Industry AD v Commission* EU:C:2014:175, para 57; Case T-46/97 *SIC v Commission* [2000] ECR II-2125, para 95; Case T-68/03, *Olympiaki Aeroporia Ypiresies AE v Commission* [2007] ECR II-2911, para 283.

[47]   Case C-342/96 *Spain v Commission* [1999] ECR I-2459, para 46; Case C-256/97, *Déménagements-Manutention Transports SA* [1999] ECR I-3913, para 24; Case C-404/04P, *Technische Glaswerke Ilmenau v Commission* [2007] ECR I-1*, para 70; Case C-405/11P, *Commission v Buczek Automotive* EU:C:2013:186, para 47; Case T-152/99, *HAMSA v Commission* [2002] ECR II-3049, para 167; Case T-11/07, *Frucona Košice as v Commission* [2010] ECR II-5453, para 114; Case T-489/11, *Rousse Industry AD v Commission* EU:T:2013:144, para 36.

[48]   Case C-73/11P, *Frucona Košice as v Commission* EU:C:2013:32, para 73.

[49]   Case T-11/07, *Frucona Košice as v Commission* [2010] ECR II-5453, para 165.

[50]   Case C-405/11P, *Commission v Buczek Automotive* EU:C:2013:186, paras 55-56; Case C-271/13P, *Rousse Industry AD v Commission* EU:C:2014:175, para 60; Case T-1/08, *Buczek Automotive v Commission* [2011] ECR II-2107, para 85.

[51]   Case T-11/07, *Frucona Košice as v Commission* [2010] ECR II-5453, paras 70-72.

justified on economic grounds in that their losses would have been considerably higher if the company had been forced into insolvency.[52] In annulling the Commission's decision on alleged State aid to Grupo de Empresas Álvarez, the ECJ criticised the Commission for failing to take into account the fact that the Spanish authorities had produced evidence of various attempts to seize property, bank accounts and debts owed in order to cover outstanding liability for tax and social security payments. The Commission could not properly have concluded that the Spanish authorities had failed to take measures available under Spanish law and had not acted as a private creditor in seeking to recover the amounts owed.[53] By contrast, in *Lenzing v Commission*, the General Court annulled the Commission's decision finding that the Spanish Social Security Fund had not granted any aid to Sniace by virtue of its treatment in the recovery of debts. Certain aspects of the conduct of the Fund had secured a commercial advantage for Sniace by permitting it not to pay its social security debts and concluding a debt restructuring agreement that would not have been acceptable to a private creditor.[54] In *Frucona Košice v Commission*, the ECJ held that, since the duration of bankruptcy proceedings postponed the recovery of sums due and thus might affect their value, this was a factor to be taken into account in assessing the conduct of a prudent and diligent private creditor.[55]

Where a public body agrees to reschedule debts owing to it, the interest charged is intended to make good the loss suffered because of the debtor's delay in performing its obligation to repay the debt, namely default interest. It is therefore incorrect to assess any aid element by reference to the rates of interest in respect of commercial loans where the lender would normally be seeking to make a profit on the loan. In *Spain v Commission*, the Commission had determined that aid was granted to Tubacex, a company declared provisionally insolvent. Tubacex's workers had been paid their wages out of public funds established to protect employees in the event of the insolvency of their employer. Spanish legislation governing the recovery of these amounts from Tubacex required a statutory rate of interest of 9% to be recovered as well. Given that this was below the rate applicable to commercial loans, the Commission found that the reduced rate entailed an element of aid. However, the ECJ held that the payment of employees' wages in these circumstances was not the same as a commercial loan, and that the creditor did not seek to make any special profit on the money which was due to him, but merely wished to

---

[52] Case T-123/97, *Salomon SA v Commission* [1999] ECR I-2925, para 68. See also, *Twenty-Seventh Report on Competition Policy* (1997), p. 237, and *Thirtieth Report on Competition Policy* (2000), pt. 313.

[53] Case C-276/02, *Spain v Commission* [2004] ECR I-8091, para 35.

[54] Case T-36/99, *Lenzing AG v Commission* [2004] ECR II-3597, paras 153-161; upheld on appeal in Case C-525/04P, *Spain v Commission* [2007] ECR I-9947, paras 60-61.

[55] Case C-73/11P, *Frucona Košice as v Commission* EU:C:2013:32, para 81.

recover the sums advanced without suffering any financial loss. The purpose of the interest element was therefore solely to compensate for depreciation of the money. Consequently, in order to determine a comparison with a loan on normal market conditions, the creditor's conduct was to be compared with that of a private creditor acting with a view to recover its debt.[56]

Transactions not obtainable on the open market Even where full consideration appears to have been given by the recipient, State aid may be inherent in the transaction if the benefit granted could not have been obtained on the open market. Thus, the provision of capital under normal market conditions but on a scale not normally available in the market may constitute State aid.[57] The provision of State-backed insurance to cover unmarketable war risks has also been held to constitute State aid, even though a full premium was charged and the scheme was self-financing.[58] In *SACE BT v Commission*, an Italian publicly owned insurance company obtained reinsurance coverage from private reinsurers in respect of 25% of its insurance liability. The rest of its liability was underwritten by its parent company, also State owned, on the same financial terms. It was argued that the reason for failing to attract full coverage on the private market in 2009 was due to the credit crisis and the unavailability of liquidity in the market rather than any increased risk attached to SACE BT's portfolio. The General Court, however, upheld the Commission's decision that a private reinsurer, having regard to the increased risk, would not have provided reinsurance coverage for such a large fraction of SACE BT's liability on the same terms.[59] Similarly, as the ECJ noted in *Déménagements-Manutention Transports*, interest or penalties for late payment of social security contributions which an undertaking experiencing very serious financial difficulties might have to pay in return for payment facilities that are more generous than a market operator would allow could nevertheless still result in State aid being granted since they might not necessarily counteract the advantage gained by the undertaking in not having to effect payment within a reasonable period.[60]

Obligations of a public authority A distinction must be drawn, in determining the obligations which a private operator might take into account, between the obligations which the State must assume as owner of a company

---

[56] Case C-342/96, *Spain v Commission* [1999] ECR I-2459, paras 48-49; Case C-256/97, *Déménagements-Manutention Transport SA* [1999] ECR I-3913, paras 24-25. See A. Criscuolo, "The State in a liberal market economy: a private investor and creditor or a public authority?" (1999) 24 ELRev 531.

[57] Case 84/82, *Germany v Commission* [1984] ECR 1451, *per* Advocate General Slynn, at p. 1501.

[58] *Twenty-Seventh Report on Competition Policy* (1997), p. 227.

[59] Case T-305/13, *SACE BT SpA v Commission* EU:T:2015:435, paras 125-126.

[60] Case C-256/97, *Déménagements-Manutention Transports SA* [1999] ECR I-3913, para 21.

and its additional obligations as a public authority.[61] Interventions by the State which are intended to honour its obligations as a public authority cannot be compared to those of a private market operator.[62] Thus, for example, in *Comitato Venezia vuole vivere v Commission*, which concerned compensation in the form of reductions in social security contributions intended to deal with the competitive disadvantages of undertakings established in Venice, the ECJ dismissed the argument that the private investor test was applicable, since private operators would not pursue such objectives.[63]

In *Hytasa*, the Spanish authorities sought to justify capital injections into companies in the textile and footwear sectors on the ground that it was cheaper to keep the companies in operation rather than to have to suffer the costs of liquidation coupled with ensuing redundancy and employment benefits. The ECJ held that, where the company is constituted with limited liability, the State, as owner of the share capital, is only liable for its debts up to the liquidation value of its assets and is not liable for costs in excess of that amount relating, for instance, to payment of unemployment benefit or aid for the restructuring of industrial infrastructure. Such costs cannot, therefore, be taken into account in determining whether capital injections can be justified since a private investor would not be subjected to them.[64] In a case involving the privatisation of a German steel company for a negative selling price on the ground that this was cheaper than winding up the company, the ECJ upheld the Commission's analysis that certain costs incurred by the authorities were not obligatory and would not have been incurred by a private investor which would instead have chosen the option of winding up.[65]

Similarly, where a public authority is a shareholder in a company that is to be sold, in order to assess whether the same measure would have been adopted in normal market conditions by a private vendor in a situation as close as possible to that of the State, only the benefits and obligations linked to the situation of the State as shareholder, to the exclusion of those linked to its situation as a public authority, are to be taken into account.[66] When carrying

---

[61] Cases C-278-280/92, *Spain v Commission* [1994] ECR I-4103, para 22; Case C-334/99, *Germany v Commission* [2003] ECR I-1139, para 134; Cases C-214/12P, C-215/12P & C-223/12P, *Land Burgenland v Commission* EU:C:2013:682, para 47; Cases T-228/99 & T-233/99, *Westdeutsche Landesbank Girozentrale v Commission* [2003] ECR II-435, para 318; Cases T-268/08 & T-281/08, *Land Burgenland v Commission* EU:T:2012:90, paras 155-156; Case T-282/08, *Grazer Wechselseitige Versicherung AG v Commission* EU:T:2012:91, paras 128-129.

[62] Case T-156/04, *EDF v Commission* [2009] ECR II-4503, para 228.

[63] Cases C-71/09P, C-73/09P & C-76/09P, *Comitato Venezia vuole vivere v Commission* [2011] ECR I-4727, para 101.

[64] Cases C-278-280/92, *Spain v Commission* [1994] ECR I-4103, para 22.

[65] Case C-334/99, *Germany v Commission* [2003] ECR I-1139, paras 138-141.

[66] Case C-124/10P, *Commission v EDF* EU:C:2012:318, para 79; Cases C-214/12P, C-215/12P & C-223/12P, *Land Burgenland v Commission* EU:C:2013:682, para 52.

out that assessment, the manner in which the advantage is provided and the nature by which the State intervenes are irrelevant.[67] If a Member State relies on a test such as the private vendor test, it must, where there is doubt, establish unequivocally on the basis of objective and verifiable evidence that the measure implemented is ascribed to the State as shareholder. That evidence must show clearly that, before or at the time of conferring the economic advantage, the Member State concerned took the decision to make the investment, by means of the measure actually implemented, in the public undertaking. In that regard, it may be necessary to produce evidence showing that the decision is based on economic evaluations comparable to those which, in the circumstances, a rational private vendor in a situation as close as possible to that of the Member State would have carried out, before making the investment, in order to determine its future profitability.[68]

In *Land Burgenland v Commission*, where the liabilities of a publicly owned bank were subject to a statutory State guarantee in the event of the insolvency or liquidation of the bank, an open tender for the sale of the bank resulted in two bids, one substantially lower than the other. The Province of Burgenland chose to award the sale contact to the lower bidder, on the ground that there was a much higher risk that the sale to the higher bidder would result in the guarantee being invoked, regard being had to their respective creditworthiness.[69] The Commission and the EU courts, however, held that the guarantee could not be taken into account when assessing the conduct of the Austrian authorities in the light of the private vendor test.[70] A private vendor would not have entered into such a guarantee and there was no evidence that the introduction or retention of the guarantee was based on economic evaluations carried out by the Austrian authorities for the purposes of establishing its profitability.[71]

---

[67] Case C-124/10P, *Commission v EDF* EU:C:2012:318, paras 91-92; Cases C-214/12P, C-215/12P & C-223/12P, *Land Burgenland v Commission* EU:C:2013:682, para 53.

[68] Case C-124/10P, *Commission v EDF* EU:C:2012:318 paras 82-84; Cases C-214/12P, C-215/12P & C-223/12P, *Land Burgenland v Commission* EU:C:2013:682, paras 57-59.

[69] Cases T-268/08 & T-281/08, *Land Burgenland v Commission* EU:T:2012:90, para 152; Case T-282/08, *Grazer Wechselseitige Versicherung AG v Commission* EU:T:2012:91, para 125.

[70] Cases C-214/12P, C-215/12P & C-223/12P, *Land Burgenland v Commission* EU:C:2013:682, para 50; Cases T-268/08 & T-281/08, *Land Burgenland v Commission* EU:T:2012:90, para 159; Case T-282/08, *Grazer Wechselseitige Versicherung AG v Commission* EU:T:2012:91, para 131.

[71] Cases C-214/12P, C-215/12P & C-223/12P, *Land Burgenland v Commission* EU:C:2013:682, paras 54 & 61.

4.2 PAYMENT FOR GOODS AND SERVICES

Supply of goods and services The sale of goods or services at preferential conditions may give rise to State aid.[72] Loss of revenue through failing to charge a market rate for the provision of goods or services may constitute State aid, being the difference between the market price and the preferential price.[73] A determination of what constitutes normal remuneration for the supply of goods or services presupposes an economic analysis taking into account all the factors which an undertaking acting under normal market conditions should have taken into consideration when fixing the remuneration.[74]

In *Van der Kooy v Commission*, the ECJ held that it might be demonstrated that a preferential tariff fixed by Gasunie for gas provided in the Netherlands to undertakings engaged in hothouse horticulture was objectively justified by economic reasons, such as the need to resist competition from other sources of energy,[75] although fixing tariffs lower than was necessary to take account of the risk of customers converting to other sources would result in the grant of aid.[76] Gasunie subsequently granted discounts for gas sold to Dutch ammonia producers for certain periods when the prices of ammonia were so low that producers throughout Europe were making losses and having to shut down plants.   The Commission found that this price reduction was normal commercial behaviour since, if Gasunie were to ignore the falls in product prices and the resulting financial difficulties of its customers, it would be jeopardising its future markets. There was also a danger that customers would switch to alternative raw materials.[77] On the other hand, in *Cdf Chimie AZF v Commission*, a sectoral tariff for the supply of natural gas, which was less than the generally applicable tariff, was held to be a State aid in so far as the

---

[72] Case C-56/93, *Belgium v Commission* [1996] ECR I-723, para 10; Case C-279/08P, *Commission v Netherlands* [2011] ECR I-7671, para 86; Cases T-116/01 & T-118/01, *P&O European Ferries (Vizcaya) SA v Commission* [2003] ECR II-2957, para 113; Case T-244/08, *Konsum Nord ekonomisk förening v Commission* [2011] ECR II-444*, para 36; Case T-538/11, *Belgium v Commission* EU:T:2015:188, para 71; Case T-511/09, *Niki Luftfahrt GmbH v Commission* EU:T:2015:284, para 123.

[73] Case C-126/01, *Ministre de l'économie, des finances et de l'industrie v GEMO* [2003] ECR I-13769, para 29; Case C-341/06P & C-342/06P, *Chronopost SA v Ufex* [2008] ECR I-4777, para 123; Case T-613/97, *Ufex v Commission* [2006] ECR II-1531, para 159; Case T-308/11, *Eurallumina SpA v Commission* EU:T:2014:894, para 67.

[74] Case C-39/94, *SFEI v La Poste* [1996] ECR I-3547, para 61.

[75] Cases 67, 68 & 70/85, *Van der Kooy v Commission* [1988] ECR 219, para 30.

[76] *Ibid.*, para 55.

[77] *Twenty-Third Report on Competition Policy* (1993), pt. 388. This was also upheld by the ECJ: Case C-56/93, *Belgium v Commission* [1996] ECR I-723, para 10. See also the Commission's decision concerning *Electricité de France* in *Thirtieth Report on Competition Policy* (2000), pt. 306.

reduction was not commercially justified by reference to reduced costs in supplying that sector.[78]

An advantage may stem equally well from a lower price set for a good of equal value as from an identical price set for a good of higher value.[79] In *Bouygues SA v Commission*, where licences for the operation of mobile phone services were issued for the same licence fee first to SRL and France Télécom and subsequently to Bouygues, the latter was, however, unable to show that any temporal advantage had been gained by the former, in particular given that there was a delay in developing the necessary technology until after Bouygues had been awarded its own licence.[80]

Acquisition of goods and services Equally, the State may grant aid by purchasing goods or services for a price in excess of market value. In *BAI v Commission*, where the Spanish provincial authorities undertook to purchase 26,000 travel vouchers from a ferry company to be used on the Bilbao-Portsmouth route by low-income groups, school parties and the elderly, the Commission found that aid had been granted on the ground *inter alia* that the agreed price was higher than the commercial tariff.[81] Where the contract has been the subject of a public tender in accordance with any applicable public procurement rules, it will normally be considered that a proper price has been paid by the public authority so as to rule out the possibility of aid being granted.[82]

Compensation payments for lost or damaged goods under an insurance policy are analogous to the acquisition of goods, such that overcompensation by a public insurance body may be regarded as State aid. For example, in *Greece v Commission*, compensation paid out by the Greek agricultural board was held to be disproportionate to the contributions paid by farmers and higher than would be payable by private insurers for the same risks.[83] Moreover, the fact that the board had to borrow from a bank, with a State guarantee as collateral, showed that the compensation payments could not have been effected on the same basis by private insurance companies.[84]

---

[78] Case C-169/84, *Cdf Chimie AZF v Commission* [1990] ECR I-3083, para 51.

[79] Case T-475/04, *Bouygues SA v Commission* [2007] ECR II-2097, para 111.

[80] *Ibid.*, para 116; upheld on appeal, Case C-431/07P, *Bouygues SA v Commission* [2008] ECR I-2665, para 120.

[81] The Commission's finding that a replacement scheme was commercially justifiable was itself annulled by the General Court : Case T-14/96, *BAI v Commission* [1999] ECR II-139, para 80.

[82] Cases T-116/01 & T-118/01, *P&O European Ferries (Vizcaya) SA v Commission* [2003] ECR II-2957, para 118; Case T-8/06, *FAB GmbH v Commission* [2009] ECR II-196*, para 53.

[83] Case T-52/12, *Greece v Commission* EU:T:2014:677, para 54.

[84] *Ibid.*, para 61.

Acquisition in excess of actual needs The mere fact that a Member State purchases goods and services on market conditions is not sufficient for that transaction to constitute a commercial transaction concluded under conditions which a private operator would have accepted, or in other words a normal commercial transaction, if it turns out that the State did not have an actual need for those goods and services.[85] In *BAI v Commission*, the Commission's decision, to the effect that an agreement by a Spanish provincial authority to purchase tickets on a ferry service operating on the Bilbao-Portsmouth route for the benefit of low-income groups, school parties and the elderly did not entail State aid where the tickets were purchased at market value, was, however, annulled by the General Court on the ground that it was not in fact apparent that the agreement was objectively commercially justifiable.[86]

Supplies linked to reserved sectors In *Ufex v Commission*, the General Court reviewed the Commission's decision concerning logistical and commercial support provided by La Poste to its subsidiary, SFMI/Chronopost, which carried on express delivery services. The Commission had considered that the internal prices at which products and services are provided between companies belonging to the same group did not involve any financial advantage whatsoever if they were full-cost prices, i.e. total costs plus a mark-up to remunerate equity capital investment. However, the General Court held that this did not necessarily entail a calculation by reference to normal market conditions. Given that La Poste might, by virtue of its position as the sole public undertaking in a reserved sector, have been able to provide some of the logistical and commercial assistance at lower cost than a private undertaking not enjoying the same rights, an analysis taking account solely of La Poste's costs could not, in the absence of other evidence, preclude classification of the measures in question as State aid. Hence, the Commission should at least have checked that the payment received in return by La Poste was comparable to that demanded by a private holding company or a private group of undertakings not operating in a reserved sector, pursuing a structural policy and guided by long term prospects.[87]

On appeal, in *Chronopost v Ufex*, the ECJ overruled the General Court on the ground that it had failed to take account of the fact that an undertaking such as La Poste was in a situation which is very different from that of a private undertaking acting under normal market conditions. La Poste was entrusted with a service of general economic interest, essentially consisting in the

---

[85]   Cases T-116/01 & T-118/01, *P&O European Ferries (Vizcaya) SA v Commission* [2003] ECR II-2957, para 117.

[86]   Case T-14/96, *BAI v Commission* [1999] ECR II-139, para 80; Cases T-116/01 & T-118/01, *P&O European Ferries (Vizcaya) SA v Commission* [2003] ECR II-2957, para 122-132.

[87]   Case T-613/97, *Ufex v Commission* [2000] ECR I-4055, paras 74-75.

obligation to collect, carry and deliver mail for the benefit of all users throughout France, at uniform tariffs and on similar conditions as to quality. To that end, La Poste had to acquire, or was afforded, substantial infrastructures and resources (the postal network), enabling it to provide the basic postal service to all users, even in sparsely populated areas where the tariffs did not cover the cost of providing the service in question. Because of the characteristics of the service which the La Poste network must be able to ensure, the creation and maintenance of that network were not in line with a purely commercial approach and was, therefore, not a market network. That network would never have been created by a private undertaking. Moreover, the provision of logistical and commercial assistance was inseparably linked to the La Poste network, since it consisted precisely in making available that network which had no equivalent on the market. Accordingly, in the absence of any possibility of comparing the situation of La Poste with that of a private group of undertakings not operating in a reserved sector, normal market conditions, which were necessarily hypothetical, had to be assessed by reference to the objective and verifiable elements which were available. The costs borne by La Poste in respect of the provision to its subsidiary of logistical and commercial assistance could constitute such objective and verifiable elements. On that basis, there was no question of State aid to SFMI-Chronopost if, first, it was established that the price charged properly covered all the additional, variable costs incurred in providing the logistical and commercial assistance, an appropriate contribution to the fixed costs arising from use of the postal network and an adequate return on the capital investment in so far as it was used for SFMI-Chronopost's competitive activity and, second, there was nothing to suggest that those elements had been underestimated or fixed in an arbitrary fashion.[88]

4.3 INVESTMENTS ON MARKET TERMS

Acquisition of capital in a company The FEU Treaty itself is neutral as to public or private ownership of property, given that Article 345 TFEU recognises that the Treaty shall in no way prejudice the rules in the Member States governing the system of property ownership.[89] The principle of equal treatment between the public and private sectors implies that Member States which invest in companies on market conditions are not considered as granting

---

[88] Cases C-83/01P, C-93/01P & C-94/01P, *Chronopost SA v Ufex and Commission* [2003] ECR 6993, paras 33-40; Case C-341/06P & C-342/06P, *Chronopost SA v Ufex* [2008] ECR I-4777, para 148.

[89] Case 323/82, *Intermills v Commission* [1984] ECR 3809, *per* Advocate General Verloren van Themaat, at p. 3842; C-261/89, *Italy v Commission* [1991] ECR I-4437, para 8; Case T-613/97, *Ufex v Commission* [2000] ECR I-4055, para 77.

State aid.[90] Article 345 TFEU cannot, however, be considered to restrict the scope of the concept of State aid for the purposes of Article 107(1) TFEU.[91] Thus, the acquisition of a holding in the capital of a company may constitute State aid, even where the capital is intended for productive investment.[92] In *Netherlands and Leeuwarder Papierwarenfabriek v Commission*, Advocate General Slynn concluded that the question was whether the purchase of shares by the State can be regarded as an investment for the purposes of obtaining income or capital appreciation, the aim of the ordinary investor, or whether it is merely a vehicle for providing financial support for a particular company.[93] In his view, the essence of a State aid is that it is non-commercial in the sense that the State steps in where the market would not go.[94]

Commission guidelines on capital injections The Commission published guidelines in 1984 setting out its approach to public acquisitions of capital. It identified four situations in which public authorities may have occasion to acquire a capital shareholding in a company: the setting up of a company; partial or total transfer of ownership from the private to the public sector; in an existing public enterprise, injection of fresh capital or conversion of endowment funds into capital; in an existing private sector company, participation in an increase in share capital.[95] Straightforward acquisition of a holding in the capital of an existing company without any injection of fresh capital does not constitute aid to the company. Nor is State aid involved where fresh capital is contributed in circumstances that would be acceptable to a private investor operating under normal market economy conditions. For example, no State aid will be involved in a fresh capital injection into a company corresponding to new investment needs where the company's financial position is sound. On the other hand, there is State aid where the contribution would not be acceptable to a private investor operating under normal market economy conditions. State aid will arise, for example, where a

---

[90]   Case C-142/87, *Belgium v Commission* [1990] ECR I-959, para 29; Case C-303/88, *Italy v Commission* [1991] ECR I-1433, para 20; Cases C-533/12P & C-536/12P, *SNCM v Commission* EU:C:2014:2142, para 30; Case T-358/94, *Air France v Commission* [1996] ECR II-2109, para 70; Case T-565/08, *Corsica Ferries France sas v Commission* EU:T:2012:415, para 77.

[91]   Cases T-116/01 & T-118/01, *P&O European Ferries (Vizcaya) SA v Commission* [2003] ECR II-2957, para 152.

[92]   Case 323/82, *Intermills v Commission* [1984] ECR 3809, para 31; Case T-20/03, *Kahla/Thüringen Porzellan GmbH v Commission* [2008] ECR II-2305, para 236. See C. Koenig & A. Bartosch, "EC State aid law reviewing equity injections and loan grants by the public sector: a comparative analysis" (2000) 21 ECLR 377.

[93]   Cases 296 & 318/82, *Netherlands and Leeuwarder Papierwarenfabriek v Commission* [1985] ECR 809, *per* Advocate General Slynn, at p. 811.

[94]   Cases 67, 68 & 70/85, *Van der Kooy v Commission* [1988] ECR 219, *per* Advocate General Slynn, at p. 251.

[95]   Bulletin EC 9-1984.

capital investment is made into a company whose financial position, particularly the structure and volume of debt, is such that a normal return cannot be expected within a reasonable time. Moreover, State aid may be involved where the acquisition of a holding is simultaneously combined with other forms of State aid or in any case where the holding is taken in an industry suffering from structural overcapacity.

Market economy investor principle The ECJ examined this issue in detail in *Belgium v Commission* which involved a subscription of capital by a Belgian regional investment agency in a company manufacturing equipment for the food industry. Substantial State aid having already been granted to this company, the Commission decided that the further aid was incompatible with the internal market since the company's financial situation constituted such a handicap as to make it very unlikely that it could have raised on the private capital markets the sums necessary for its survival. Belgium argued that, by prohibiting the increase in public capital subscription, the Commission was discriminating against the public authorities by comparison with a private shareholder. In its view, it was normal and legitimate for a shareholder to support, by subscribing additional capital, an undertaking which that shareholder controlled and which was experiencing temporary difficulties. Upholding the Commission's decision, the ECJ agreed that an appropriate way of establishing whether a measure is State aid is to apply the criterion of determining to what extent the undertakings would be able to obtain the sums in question on the private capital markets. A private shareholder may reasonably subscribe the capital necessary to secure the survival of an undertaking which is experiencing temporary difficulties but is capable of becoming profitable again. However, such funding would probably be unavailable on the private capital markets where the undertaking had been making substantial losses for several years.[96] It may be noted, however, that the mere fact that previous capital injections made into a company were classified as aid does not mean that a subsequent injection cannot be classed as an investment which satisfies the private investor test.[97] Where there is a series of separate investments in the same beneficiary, they may be separately assessed by reference to the market investor principle where they are sufficiently dissociable or jointly assessed where they are so closely linked as to be inseparable from one another.[98]

In approving an investment by the municipality of Amsterdam in a glass fibre telecommunications project, the Commission noted that the investment

---

[96] Case 234/84, *Belgium v Commission* [1986] ECR 2263, paras 14-17. See also, in the English High Court, *Sky Blues Sports & Leisure Ltd. v Coventry City Council* (2014).

[97] Case T-11/95, *BP Chemicals Ltd. v Commission* [1998] ECR II-3235, para 170.

[98] *Ibid.*, para 171; Cases T-319/12 & T-321/12, *Spain v Commission* EU:T:2014:604, para 146-147; Case T-1/12, *France v Commission* EU:T:2015:17, paras 41-50.

was on equal terms with two private investors active in the sector, both of which took significant stakes in the investment. All investors were to bear any losses in the event of the business underperforming. The Commission emphasised that it is not sufficient for public authorities to become involved in projects merely by claiming that they are acting like a normal market investor. It needs to be comprehensively demonstrated, for instance by means of a sound business plan and a significant investment by private investors, that the public investment conforms to the conditions of the market.[99] By contrast, in *SNCM v Commission*, the mere fact that a capital contribution was made jointly and concurrently with private investors was held not to exclude it automatically from being classified as State aid, when other factors were to be taken into account. In particular, a sale cancellation clause was regarded as removing any uncertainty for the private purchasers in the event of one of the triggering events and thus was liable to alter the risk profiles of the capital contributions of the public and private investments.[100]

The exercise of ascertaining whether the transaction took place under normal market conditions is not necessarily to be made by reference solely to the undertaking benefiting from the transaction, since it is the interaction between the various economic operators which is precisely the feature of a market economy. Nor does that exercise require the constraints connected with the nature of the asset transferred to be disregarded altogether. Rather, it is necessary to make a complete analysis of all factors that are relevant to the transaction at issue and its context, including the situation of the beneficiary undertaking and of the relevant market. In particular, an examination should be carried out, in the case of an investment, of whether the undertaking would have been able to procure funds entailing the same advantages, under similar conditions, from other investors.[101]

In *Club Hotel Loutraki v Commission*, Greece granted an exclusive licence for the operation of video lottery terminals to OPAP, a State-owned organisation, in exchange for a fee of €560 million for a period of ten years and simultaneously extended OPAP's exclusive rights for the operation of certain games of chance for a further period of ten years in return for a payment of €375 million and 5% of gross gaming revenues during that period. These arrangements were put in place in order to increase OPAP's market value with a view to it being privatised. A complaint was made to the Commission by operators of other games of chance that the payment of €560 million was too

---

[99] Commission Decision 2008/729/EC, *Citynet Amsterdam*, OJ 2008 L247/27.

[100] Cases C-533/12P & C-536/12P, *SNCM v Commission* EU:C:2014:2142, paras 54-55; Case T-565/08, *Corsica Ferries France sas v Commission* EU:T:2012:415, para 117-130.

[101] Cases T-228/99 & T-233/99, *Westdeutsche Landesbank Girozentrale v Commission* [2003] ECR II-435, para 327; Case T-163/05, *Bundesverband Deutscher Banken v Commission* [2010] ECR II-387, paras 36-37; Cases T-186/13, T-190/13 & T-193/13, *Netherlands v Commission* EU:T:2015:447, paras 87-88.

low. The Commission stated that the existence of an advantage could be excluded if, when granting exclusive rights to OPAP, Greece had left it with only the minimum return which an average company would have needed to cover its operational and capital costs. Although the Commission assessed the agreements jointly, it determined the net present value of each agreement separately, using the discounted cash flow method on the basis of forecasted revenues and expenses and taking into account the reasonable market return that could be left to OPAP, and then compared that value with the consideration paid by OPAP for the grant of the exclusive rights. When the Commission initially found that the payment for the extension of exclusive rights for the games of chance was higher than the net present value of that agreement, whereas €560 million was significantly lower than the net present value of the VLT agreement, the Greek authorities agreed to introduce an additional levy applicable to revenues from VLTs which reduced the net present value of the VLT agreement. On that basis, the Commission accepted that the combined consideration did not entail an economic advantage to OPAP as it had agreed to pay an amount that was higher than the cumulated value of all of the exclusive rights conferred on it. The applicants' argument that the two agreements should be assessed separately since they operated on different markets, was rejected by the General Court which accepted that they entailed similar activities. Moreover, since the two arrangements were entered into with a view to the subsequent privatisation of OPAP, the Commission was correct to view them as taking place within the same economic context.[102]

Comparison with private investor Advocate General Lenz, in *Belgium v Commission*, explored some related issues. In the case of a financial transaction between a Member State and a public undertaking, special criteria must be used in order to try to differentiate between entrepreneurial conduct and State conduct. Advantages which the State confers on a public undertaking by way of grant could equally be entrepreneurial investment. The same consideration might apply to the foregoing of profits or the offsetting of losses, since a private businessman may also be in a situation where he has to take such steps. Consequently, the test for State aid might be whether, in comparable circumstances, a private businessman acting on the basis of relevant economic considerations would not support the undertaking concerned in such a manner. This allows the State as the proprietor of an undertaking a substantial measure of freedom of action.[103] The ECJ agreed and held that the test is, in particular, whether in similar circumstances a private shareholder, having regard to the foreseeability of obtaining a return and leaving aside all social, regional-policy and sectoral considerations, would have subscribed the

---

[102] Case T-58/13, *Club Hotel Loutraki AE v Commission* EU:T:2015:1, paras 87-92.

[103] Case 234/84, *Belgium v Commission, per* Advocate General Lenz, at p. 2271.

capital in question.[104]   Moreover, as pointed out by the General Court in *Westdeutsche Landesbank Girozentrale v Commission*, the requirement that the behaviour of an informed private investor be taken into account in order to assess the behaviour of a public investor, when the behaviour of a private investor is not subject to such a constraint, cannot be regarded as discriminating against the public investor. The private investor can count only on his own resources in order to finance his investments whereas the public investor has access to resources flowing from the exercise of public power, in particular from taxation.[105]

The question as to what alternative investment opportunities might have been of interest to the public investor is irrelevant. It is not a question of determining whether it could have obtained a better return on its funds by investing them differently or in another undertaking, but whether, by investing the funds in the investment under the agreed conditions, it conferred an advantage on the recipient which it could not have obtained in any other way.[106] The evidence must show clearly that, before or at the same time as conferring the economic advantage, the Member State concerned took the decision to make an investment, by means of the measure actually implemented, in the public undertaking. In that regard, it may be necessary to produce evidence showing that the decision is based on economic evaluations comparable to those which, in the circumstances, a rational private investor in a situation as close as possible to that of the Member State would have had carried out, before making the investment, in order to determine its future profitability. By contrast, for the purposes of showing that, before or at the same time as conferring the advantage, the Member State took that decision as a shareholder, it is not enough to rely on economic evaluations made after the advantage was conferred, on a retrospective finding that the investment made by the Member State concerned was actually profitable, or on subsequent justifications of the course of action actually chosen.[107]

---

[104] Case 234/84, *Belgium v Commission* [1986] ECR 2263, para 14; Cases C-278-280/92, *Spain v Commission* [1994] ECR I-4103, para 21; Case C-482/99, *France v Commission* [2002] ECR I-4397, para 70; Case C-334/99, *Germany v Commission* [2003] ECR I-1139, para 133; Cases T-129/95, T-2/96 & T-97/96, *Neue Maxhütte Stahlwerke GmbH v Commission* [1999] ECR II-17, para 120; Case T-296/97, *Alitalia v Commission* [2000] ECR II-3871, para 81; Case T-20/03, *Kahla/Thüringen Porzellan GmbH v Commission* [2008] ECR II-2305, para 242; Case T-156/04, *EDF v Commission* [2009] ECR II-4503, para 230; Case T-565/08, *Corsica Ferries France sas v Commission* EU:T:2012:415, para 78.

[105] Cases T-228/99 & T-233/99, *Westdeutsche Landesbank Girozentrale v Commission* [2003] ECR II-435, paras 271-272; Case T-156/04, *EDF v Commission* [2009] ECR II-4503, para 231.

[106] Case T-163/05, *Bundesverband Deutscher Banken v Commission* [2010] ECR II-387, para 58.

[107] Case C-124/10P, *Commission v EDF* EU:C:2012:318, paras 83-85.

The comparison between the conduct of public and private investors must be made by reference to the attitude which a private investor would have had at the time of the transaction in question, having regard to the available information and foreseeable developments at that time.[108] Moreover, although no State aid is involved where an intervention by public authorities takes place at the same time as a significant intervention by private operators and under comparable conditions,[109] where private investments in the same undertaking occur only after the allocation of public funds, the presence of aid cannot be ruled out.[110] In *Kahla/Thüringen Porzellan GmbH v Commission*, the General Court upheld the Commission's finding that the State had not acted like a private investor on the ground that the risks were high and future revenue had not been analysed.[111] On the other hand, in *INMA v Commission*, the General Court recognised that aid might not be involved where a public company acted as a private investor in preferring to cover a subsidiary's losses in order to minimise the costs which it might incur as guarantor and sole shareholder.[112]

Public investment through fiscal measures In *Commission v EDF*, the Commission objected to an investment made by France in a State-owned electricity company by means of converting a tax debt into a capital injection and refused to consider applying the private investor on the basis that the test was inapplicable to the adoption of tax legislation which constituted a means that was only open to the State and not to private investors. This decision was annulled by the General Court which held that the fact that the intervention by the State takes the form of fiscal legislation is not, in itself, sufficient to rule out the possibility that the intervention by the State in the capital of an undertaking pursues an economic objective which could also be pursued by a private investor.[113] On appeal, the ECJ confirmed that the financial situation of the recipient public undertaking depended not on the means used to place it at an advantage, however that may have been effected, but on the amount that it ultimately received. Consequently, when considering whether the private investor test was applicable, the General Court had not erred in law by focusing its analysis, not on the fiscal nature of the means employed by the French State, but on the improvement in EDF's financial situation. Accordingly, in view of the objectives underlying Article 107(1) TFEU and the

---

[108] Cases T-228/99 & T-233/99, *Westdeutsche Landesbank Girozentrale v Commission* [2003] ECR II-435, paras 244-246; Case T-20/03, *Kahla/Thüringen Porzellan GmbH v Commission* [2008] ECR II-2305, para 238.

[109] Case T-358/94, *Air France v Commission* [1996] ECR II-2109, paras 148-149.

[110] Case C-301/87, *France v Commission* [1990] ECR I-307 para 40; Case T-20/03, *Kahla/Thüringen Porzellan GmbH v Commission* [2008] ECR II-2305, para 254.

[111] Case T-20/03, *Kahla/Thüringen Porzellan GmbH v Commission* [2008] ECR II-2305, paras 216-217.

[112] Case T-323/99, *INMA v Commission* [2002] ECR II-545, para 100.

[113] Case T-156/04, *EDF v Commission* [2009] ECR II-4503, para 237.

private investor test, an economic advantage must, even where it has been granted through fiscal means, be assessed in the light of the private investor test, if it appears that the Member State concerned conferred that advantage in its capacity as shareholder of the undertaking.[114]

Social and regional considerations In *Italy v Commission*, concerning aid to ENI-Lanerossi, it was argued that a distinction should be drawn between private investors, whose sole motive is profit, and private entrepreneurs, such as an industrial holding company, whose decisions may be governed not merely by short-term profitability but also by social and regional considerations.[115] The ECJ accepted that a parent company may, for a limited period, bear the losses of one of its subsidiaries in order to enable the latter to close down its operations under the best possible conditions. Such decisions may be motivated not solely by the likelihood of indirect material profit but also by other considerations, such as a desire to protect the group's image or to redirect its activities. However, when injections of capital by a public investor disregard any prospect of profitability, even in the long term, such provision of capital must be regarded as aid within the meaning of Article 107(1) TFEU.[116]

Advocate General Van Gerven saw no fundamental distinction in the way that public and private investors might operate. He argued that a private investor would not be wholly uninfluenced by considerations of a social nature or of regional or sectoral policy. In a mixed economy in which the interests of the private and public sector are closely interwoven and the interests of workers are strongly represented, even a large private holding company could not remain totally insensitive to employment and economic development in the area in which it operated and might be prepared to transfer funds from one subsidiary to another in order to help cover temporary losses. It would, however, be in breach of its obligations towards its shareholders, creditors and employees if it covered substantial losses of undertakings operating in a sector characterised by over-capacity without drawing up a serious restructuring plan.[117] The reasonable investor would require such a plan in order to be persuaded that there was a real chance of recovery and that a fresh injection of capital would be effective.[118]

The ECJ broadly agreed with this approach and, in the *Alfa Romeo* case, held that although the conduct of a private investor with which the intervention of the public investor pursuing economic policy aims must be compared need

---

[114] Case C-124/10P, *Commission v EDF* EU:C:2012:318, paras 91-92.
[115] Case C-303/88, *Italy v Commission* [1991] ECR 1433, para 18.
[116] *Ibid.*, paras 21-22; Cases C-278-280/92, *Spain v Commission* [1994] ECR I-4103, para 26.
[117] Case C-303/88, *Italy v Commission* [1991] ECR I-1433, *per* Advocate General Van Gerven, at p. 1459.
[118] Case C-305/89, *Italy v Commission* [1991] ECR I-1603, *per* Advocate General Van Gerven, at p. 1626.

not be the conduct of an ordinary investor laying out capital with a view to realising profit in the relatively short term, it must at least be the conduct of a private holding company or a private group of undertakings pursuing a structural policy, whether general or sectoral, and guided by the prospects of profitability in the longer term.[119]   Accordingly, investment by the Italian authorities in Seleco, a company which was in serious financial difficulties and in respect of which a credible and realistic restructuring plan had not been put in place, was regarded as State aid.[120] Moreover, in *Alitalia v Commission*, the General Court held that it would not be correct to compare the action of employees of the company who might have invested in the company in a desire to ensure its survival in order to keep their jobs.[121]

In *Corsica Ferries France v Commission*, the General Court held that both the content of national social legislation and the practice of social relations within large groups of undertakings develop over time and differ within the EU. It was necessary that the monitoring of State aid should reflect such developments, as regards both the investments made by private companies and those made by the State. In a social market economy, a reasonable private investor would not disregard either its responsibility towards all the stakeholders in the company or the development of the social, economic and environmental context. Challenges relating to social responsibility and entrepreneurial context are capable of having a major impact on the specific decisions and strategic planning of a reasonable private investor. It followed that the long term economic rationale of a reasonable private operator's conduct could not be assessed without taking account of such concerns.[122] For that purpose, the payment by a private investor of additional redundancy payments might be a legitimate and appropriate practice, with a view to fostering a calm social dialogue and maintaining the brand image of a company, and in contradistinction to social protection costs which are a matter for the State.[123] The assumption by a public company of such costs, however, in the absence of any economic rationale, will be regarded as State aid.[124]

Protecting the brand image of a Member State Whilst the protection of the brand image of a company is a relevant consideration, the protection of the brand image of a Member State as a global investor in the market economy can constitute, under specific circumstances and with a particularly cogent reason, sufficient justification to demonstrate the long term economic rationale of the

---

[119] Case C-305/89, *Italy v Commission* [1991] ECR I-1603, para 20; Case T-198/01, *Technische Glaswerke Ilmenau GmbH v Commission* [2004] ECR II-2717, para 99; Case T-565/08, *Corsica Ferries France sas v Commission* EU:T:2012:415, para 80.

[120] Cases C-328/99 & C-399/00, *Italy v Commission* [2003] ECR I-4135, paras 44-46.

[121] Case T-296/97, *Alitalia SpA v Commission* [2000] ECR II-3871, para 84.

[122] Case T-565/08, *Corsica Ferries France sas v Commission* EU:T:2012:415, paras 81-82.

[123] *Ibid.*, para 83.

[124] *Ibid.*, para 84.

assumption of additional costs such as additional redundancy payments. On the other hand, summary reference to the brand image of a Member State, as a global player, is not enough to support a finding that there is no aid.[125] Otherwise, there would be a distortion of competition in favour of undertakings operating in Member States in which the public economic sector was relatively more developed or in which social dialogue has been adversely affected to a particular degree.[126]

Public private partnerships Public private partnerships are used normally in order to finance the construction, maintenance and management of infrastructure or the provision of related services.[127] They are usually high-value, complex transactions involving detailed negotiation between the public and private partners. There are four recognised phases in establishing PPPs: the tendering of a contract, the creation of the partnership, the financing of the PPP, and the operation of the PPP. State aid is capable of arising at each of these stages.[128] It is advisable for the partner to be chosen and for the terms of the contract to be settled following an open tendering procedure. In practice, however, the negotiated procedure or a competitive dialogue is used for complex projects. Where these are sufficiently transparent, it is likely that no State aid issue will arise. In the London Underground case, where the contract was awarded using a negotiated procedure, the Commission considered that the price payable to the infrastructure companies was a fair market price despite the fact that changes had occurred after the final selection of the bidders and during the negotiations. The changes were not so substantial as to be likely to have attracted prospective tenderers which did not consider tendering following the publication in the *Official Journal of the European Union* of the original tender notice and the preferred bidders remained the best value for money in the light of the changes made after selection of the bidders.[129] On the other hand, where the PPP project competes with other undertakings, such as in the provision of broadband infrastructure, the financing of a PPP may give rise to State aid.[130] Where the PPP project concerns the provision of a service of

---

[125] Cases C-533/12P, & C-536/12P, *SNCM v Commission* EU:C:2014:2142, paras 40-41; Case T-565/08, *Corsica Ferries France sas v Commission* EU:T:2012:415, para 85.

[126] Case T-565/08, *Corsica Ferries France sas v Commission* EU:T:2012:415, para 85.

[127] For detailed analysis of the interaction of State aid and PPPs, see J. Battista & J.J. Piernas Lopez, "The respect of State aid rules in PPPs", in W. Mederer, N. Pesaresi & M. van Hoof (ed.), *EU Competition Law*, Volume IV, Book Two, Chapter 11 (Claeys & Casteels, 2008).

[128] Commission communication on the application of EU law on public procurement and concessions to public-private partnerships, COM(2007) 6661.

[129] Case N 264/2002, *London Underground*, OJ 2002 C309/15.

[130] See, for example, Case N 284/2005, *Irish metropolitan area network*, OJ 2006 C207/3.

general economic interest and does involve State aid, Article 106(2) TFEU may apply.[131]

4.4 SALE OF PUBLIC ASSETS

Sale of public land and buildings by public authorities In 1990, the Commission investigated the sale of land by Derbyshire Council in the United Kingdom to Toyota for the building of a new car production plant. The site was independently valued at ECU 32.6 million, whereas it had been sold at ECU 26.5 million. Accordingly, the Commission took the view that the difference in price constituted State aid.[132] On the basis of this and other experiences, the Commission issued a communication on State aid elements in sales of land and buildings by public authorities.[133] This communication concerns only sales of publicly owned lands and buildings. It does not concern the public acquisition of land and buildings or the letting and leasing of land by public authorities, which might also contain State aid elements.

Open and unconditional bidding procedure A sale of land and buildings following a sufficiently well-publicised, open and unconditional bidding procedure, comparable to an auction, accepting the best or only bid is by definition at market value and consequently does not contain State aid. An offer is unconditional when any buyer is generally free to acquire the land or buildings and use it for his own purposes. Restrictions may be imposed for the prevention of public nuisance or for reasons of environmental protection or to avoid purely speculative bids. Urban and regional planning restrictions do not affect the unconditional nature of an offer. If it is a condition of the sale that the future owner is to assume special obligations for the benefit of the public authorities or in the general public interest, the offer is to be regarded as unconditional only if all potential buyers would have to, and be able to, meet that obligation.[134]

The fact that a different valuation existed prior to the bidding procedure, e.g. for accounting purposes or to provide a proposed initial minimum bid, is irrelevant. For this purpose, an offer is sufficiently well publicised when it is repeatedly advertised over a reasonably long period in the press and through estate agents addressing a broad range of potential buyers. If this open bidding procedure is not used, an independent evaluation must be carried out by one or

---

[131] See, for example, Case N 321/01, *Fréjus tunnel*, OJ 2001, C211/47; Case N 420/2005, *Mont Blanc tunnel*, OJ 2007 C90/4; Case N 149/2006, *Irish roads*, OJ 2006 C209/7.

[132] *Twenty-First Report on Competition Policy* (1991), pt. 239.

[133] OJ 1997 L209/3.

[134] Commission Notice on State aid elements in sales of land and buildings by public authorities, para 2.1.

more independent asset valuers[135] prior to the sale negotiations in order to establish the market value on the basis of generally accepted market indicators and valuation standards.[136]   The economic disadvantage of any special obligations that relate to the land and buildings and which are imposed on the sale in the public interest should be evaluated by the independent valuers and set off against the purchase price.[137]   The market price thus established is the minimum purchase price that can be agreed without granting State aid.[138]   The cost to a public authority of previously acquiring the property is an indicator of the market value unless a significant period of time has elapsed since the acquisition.   In principle, the market value should not be set below this primary cost during a period of at least three years after acquisition unless the independent valuer specifically identifies a general decline in property prices in the relevant market.[139]

Alternative methods of valuation   While it is clear that the best bid or an expert report are likely to provide prices corresponding to actual market values, it is not inconceivable that other methods may also achieve the same result.[140] For example, where land has not been independently valued prior to sale, it may be necessary at a later stage to determine whether or not State aid was involved in the sale.   The General Court has recognised that such a determination, which is by nature retrospective, is surrounded by uncertainty.[141]   In *Scott v Commission*, it annulled a Commission decision which calculated the value of land sold in 1987 on the basis of the cost to the public authority of the land 12 years earlier plus the costs of improvements. The General Court held that even though the costs incurred in purchasing and

---

[135] Whilst the valuer must be independent in the carrying out of his tasks, State valuation officers and public employees are to be regarded as independent provided that undue influence over their findings is effectively excluded.

[136] See, for example, Commission Decision 2001/803/EC, *Ojala-Yhtymä Oy*, OJ 2001 L304/20.

[137] The economic burden related to obligations imposed on all landowners under the ordinary law is not to be discounted.

[138] If, after a reasonable effort to sell the land and buildings at the market value, it is clear that the value set cannot be obtained, a divergence of up to 5% from that value can be deemed to be in line with market conditions. If this value also cannot be obtained, a new valuation may be carried out which is to take account of the experience gained and of the offers received.

[139] Commission Notice on State aid elements in sales of land and buildings by public authorities, para 2.2.

[140] Case C-239/09 *Seydaland Vereinigte Agrarbetriebe* [2010] ECR I-13083, para 39; Case C-39/14, *BVVG GmbH v Erbs* EU:C:2015:470, para 31; Case T-488/11, *Sarc BV v Commission* EU:T:2014:497, para 98.

[141] Cases T-127/99, T-129/99 & T-148/99, *Diputación Foral de Álava v Commission* [2002] ECR II-1275, para 73; Case T-274/01, *Valmont Nederland BV v Commission* [2004] ECR II-3145, para 45; Case T-366/00, *Scott SA v Commission* [2007] ECR II-797, para 93.

improving land may be a secondary or indirect indication of the value of the property, those factors were not the best proof of that value. Instead, the private investor principle required the Commission to assess the open market sale value of the property in question in 1987. That price was not necessarily determined by the costs incurred by the vendor because it was influenced by various factors, including supply and demand on the market at the time of the sale.[142] On appeal, however, the ECJ held that key information relied on by the Commission was clearly identifiable and it had no compelling reason to doubt the reliability of the cost-based analysis.[143]

In *Seydaland v BVVG*, the ECJ considered German legislation which allowed for the valuation of agricultural land on the basis of regional reference rates. It held that Article 107(1) TFEU did not preclude provisions of national law laying down calculation methods for determining the value of agricultural land offered for sale by public authorities to the extent that those methods provide for the updating of prices, where prices for such land are rising sharply, so that the price actually paid by the purchaser reflects, in so far as possible, the market value of the land.[144]

Privatisation and State aid Privatisation of the assets or shares in a public company will not involve State aid where the sale is on the open market.[145] For example, the United Kingdom Government's plan, with a view to transferring management costs to the private sector, to sell claims held by the Student Loans Company Limited, a public company which gave loans to students for higher education, was approved by the Commission after having established that it was being carried out according to market rules, involving an open procedure with the sale going to the highest bidder.[146]

Where a privatisation is effected by the sale of shares on the stock exchange, it is generally assumed to be on market conditions and not to involve aid. Before flotation, debt may be written off or reduced without this giving rise to a presumption of aid as long as the proceeds of the flotation exceed the reduction in debt. If the company is privatised by a trade sale, i.e. by sale of the company as a whole or in parts, the following conditions must be observed if it is to be assumed, without further examination, that no aid is involved: a competitive tender must be held that is open to all comers, transparent and not conditional on the performance of other acts such as the acquisition of other assets other than those bid for or the continued operation of certain businesses; the company must be sold to the highest bidder; and bidders must be given

---

[142] Case T-366/00, *Scott SA v Commission* [2007] ECR II-797, para 106.
[143] Case C-290/07P, *Commission v Scott SA* [2010] ECR I-7763, paras 71-75.
[144] Case C-239/09 *Seydaland Vereinigte Agrarbetriebe GmbH v BVVB GmbH* [2010] ECR I-13083, paras 43-48.
[145] See Evans, "Privatisation and State aid control in EC law" (1997) 18 ECLR 259.
[146] *Twenty-Seventh Report of Competition Policy* (1997), p. 226.

enough time and information to carry out a proper valuation of the assets as the basis for their bid. In other cases, aid may be involved, in particular where the sale takes place after negotiation with a single prospective purchaser or a number of selected bidders, or where debt is written off or converted into equity, or where the sale is on conditions that are not customary in comparable transactions between private parties.[147]

For the purposes of checking the market price, account may be taken of, in particular, the form of the transfer of a company, for example public tendering, deemed to ensure that a sale takes place under market conditions or any expert's report prepared at the time of the transfer. It follows that, where a public authority proceeds to sell an undertaking belonging to it by way of an open, transparent and unconditional tender procedure, it can be presumed that the market price corresponds to the highest offer, provided that it is established, first, that the offer is binding and credible and, secondly, that the consideration of economic factors other than price is not justified.[148] In such circumstances, there is no need to resort to other methods in order to check the market price, such as independent studies.[149] Reliance on such studies for the purposes of determining market price would only make sense if no tender procedure was carried out or if the tender procedure was not open, transparent and unconditional.[150] Moreover, any deficiency in the bidding process can be ignored where this has not affected the amount of the highest bid.[151] Nevertheless, in the case of *Kali und Salz GmbH*, the Commission decided that no State aid was involved in a sale of a public shareholding which was not made by way of an open tender procedure since it was satisfied that the final price was obtained following a procedure in which no potential investor was arbitrarily excluded.[152]

Approval from regulatory authorities In certain cases, particularly where a company is being sold, a regulatory authority may have to approve the sale on, for example, competition or financial supervision grounds, which might lead to delay or uncertainty where a particular purchaser has been selected by the vendor. In *Land Burgenland v Commission*, the issue arose as to whether such

---

[147] *Twenty-Third Report on Competition Policy* (1993), pt. 403.

[148] Cases C-214/12P, C-215/12P & C-223/12P, *Land Burgenland v Commission* EU:C:2013:682, para 94.

[149] *Ibid.* para 95.

[150] Cases T-268/08 & T-281/08, *Land Burgenland v Commission* EU:T:2012:90, para 72; Case T-282/08, *Grazer Wechselseitige Versicherung AG v Commission* EU:T:2012:91, para 79.

[151] Cases C-214/12P, C-215/12P & C-223/12P, *Land Burgenland v Commission* EU:C:2013:682, para 96; Cases T-268/08 & T-281/08, *Land Burgenland v Commission* EU:T:2012:90, para 90; Case T-282/08, *Grazer Wechselseitige Versicherung AG v Commission* EU:T:2012:91, para 81.

[152] *Thirtieth Report on Competition Policy* (2000), pt. 318.

a consideration might be taken into account by a public authority in selecting the purchaser. It was claimed that the uncertain outcome and the length of the authorisation procedure in the event of a sale of an Austrian bank to a consortium which included a Ukrainian undertaking justified selecting an alternative Austrian bid which was, however, for a lower amount. The Commission accepted that a private vendor could accept a lower bid if it was obvious that the sale to the higher bidder was unrealisable and, more specifically, that it would not have chosen a buyer who in all probability would not have obtained the necessary permission from the competent authorities. Nevertheless, it held that, in the circumstances of the case, the probably longer duration of the regulatory procedure was not such as to constitute an obstacle to a sale of the bank to the consortium. The General Court agreed, holding that, although the public authorities had some latitude for prognosis in determining whether the regulatory authorities would deny authorisation, no particular urgency had been established on the basis of hard evidence which justified refusing to delay the sale to the consortium.[153]

Regulation of speculative land prices The State may seek to regulate the sale of land at speculative prices by prohibiting sales at prices in excess of normal market value. In *BVVG v Erbs*, German legislation allowed the public authorities to prohibit the sale of agricultural land where the sale price, even where it was agreed as a result of an open procedure, was considered as disproportionate, which was so where the price exceeded 50% of the agricultural value of the land. Whilst the intention was to retain agricultural land at affordable prices for farmers, the effect was that the inability to accept higher offers resulted, in the case of sale of publicly owned land, in a loss of potential State resources and, accordingly, an economic advantage for the buyer. The ECJ held that this might result in State aid since the higher price reflected the actual market value of the land. It also held, however, that factors other than price might be taken into consideration in determining market price. That would be the case, in particular, where the highest bid is distinctly higher than any other price offered and the estimated market price, so that it may be considered manifestly speculative in nature. Consequently, a rule of national law enabling a public authority to reject a bid for agricultural land which was disproportionate could not be considered as State aid, provided the application of the rule resulted in a price which was as close as possible to the market value of the land.[154]

Monitoring trustee In exceptional circumstances, the Commission may require additional safeguards in order to ensure that assets are sold at market

---

[153] Cases T-268/08 & T-281/08, *Land Burgenland v Commission* EU:T:2012:90, paras 132-135.
[154] Case C-39/14, *BVVG GmbH v Erbs* EU:C:2015:470, paras 37-42.

value. In *Ryanair v Commission*, the Italian authorities put in place a monitoring trustee to ensure that the assets of its airline, Alitalia, were sold at market value. This involved the appointment of an independent expert who had to send the Commission detailed periodic reports concerning compliance with the notified sale process and compliance with certain undertakings by the Italian authorities together with a subsequent exhaustive report from an independent financial adviser as to the conformity of the sale with the market price.[155]

4.5 STATE GUARANTEES

State guarantees State guarantees capable of both placing the undertakings to which they apply in a more favourable position than others and creating a sufficiently concrete risk of imposing an additional burden on the State in the future may place a burden on the resources of the State where they are given on terms that are less stringent than those available on the open market.[156] It may be noted, however, that guarantees by the State in respect of loans by public undertakings that are imputable to the State are treated as transparent and irrelevant. Thus, in *Nitrogénművek Vegyipari Zst v Commission*, where a loan on preferential terms was granted, on the basis of a State guarantee, by a Hungarian public development bank whose decisions in this respect were imputable to the State, the issue to be determined was whether a private investor would have granted loans in the situation of the Hungarian public authorities, rather than whether a private investor would have granted loans in the situation of the public undertaking as a result of the State guarantees.[157]

The Commission has issued a notice on the application of the Article 107 TFEU to State aid in the form of guarantees.[158] Usually the aid beneficiary is the borrower who, by virtue of a guarantee given by the State or other public body, can obtain lower interest rates and/or offer less security. The benefit of a State guarantee is that the risk associated with the guarantee is carried by the State. Where a premium is not paid by the borrower on normal market terms, a benefit is granted to the borrower at the moment the guarantee is given,

---

[155] Case T-123/09, *Ryanair Ltd v Commission* EU:T:2012:164, para 150.

[156] Cases C-399/10P & C-401/10P, *Bouygues SA v Commission* EU:C:2013:175, paras 106-107; Case T-487/11, *Banco Privado Português SA v Commission* EU:T:2014:1077, para 52.

[157] Case T-387/11, *Nitrogénművek Vegyipari Zst v Commission* EU:T:2013:98, para 74.

[158] OJ 2008 C155/10. This replaces the previous Commission notice of 2000. See also, "Application of the European Community Rules on State Aid to State Guarantees", a special supplement to Butterworths Journal of International Banking and Financial Law, January 2002.

regardless of whether any payments are ever made under the guarantee.[159] The Commission also regards as aid in the form of a guarantee the more favourable funding terms obtained by enterprises whose legal form rules out bankruptcy or other insolvency procedures or provides for coverage of losses by the State. The same applies to the acquisition by the State of a holding in an undertaking if unlimited liability is accepted. Where a borrower is unable to find a credit institution prepared to lend on any terms, the entire amount of the secured loan which it obtains must be regarded as aid.[160] Thus, State guarantees given to firms in difficulty must be regarded as aid equal to the amount of the loan guaranteed.[161] For example, in *Commission v Italy*, repayment of rescue aid granted through a guarantee to an Italian company that was in difficulty for the sum of €15 million was required in the full amount guaranteed, plus interest.[162] Similarly, a Netherlands scheme for reinsuring non-marketable risks (e.g. civil war, expropriation or nationalisation) relating to investments by Dutch companies was considered State aid, even though the scheme was self-financing with the State body charging risk premiums which were to be calculated as a percentage of the amount of the investment and in terms of the political risks involved in each particular country.[163]

In its notice on State aid in the form of guarantees, the Commission establishes conditions ruling out the existence of aid for both individual guarantees and guarantee schemes, although where all of these conditions are not fulfilled, that does not necessarily connote the presence of aid. Where an aid element is found to exist, the Commission identifies the criteria, which are largely based on the conditions for establishing the non-existence of aid, that it will apply to identify the extent of the aid.[164]

Characteristics of guarantees In their most common form, guarantees are associated with a loan or other financial obligation to be contracted by a borrower with a lender; they may be granted as individual guarantees or within guarantee schemes. Various forms of guarantee may exist, depending on their legal basis, the type of transaction covered, their duration, whether they are limited or unlimited, etc. These include general guarantees and guarantees provided by a specific instrument. Guarantees may be provided directly or as counter guarantees provided to a first level guarantor. The Commission also regards as aid in the form of a guarantee the more favourable funding terms

[159] Case C-200/97, *Ecotrade v AFS* [1998] ECR I-7907, para 43; Case C-559/12P, *France v Commission* EU:C:2014:217, paras 102-104; Cases T-204/97 & T-270/97, *EPAC v Commission* [2000] ECR II-2267, para 80; Case T-384/08, *Elliniki Nafpigokatas-kevastiki AE Chartofylakeiou v Commission* [2011] ECR II-380*, para 92.

[160] Case C-288/96, *Germany v Commission* [2000] ECR I-8237, para 31.

[161] Case C-334/99, *Germany v Commission* [2003] ECR I-1139, para 138.

[162] Case C-353/12, *Commission v Italy* EU:C:2013:651, para 15.

[163] *Twenty-Seventh Report on Competition Policy* (1997), p. 227.

[164] Commission notice on guarantees, para 4.1-4.5.

obtained by enterprises whose legal form rules out bankruptcy or other insolvency procedures or provides an explicit State guarantee or coverage of losses by the State. The same applies to the acquisition by a State of a holding in an enterprise if unlimited liability is accepted instead of the usual limited liability. Guarantees may clearly originate from a contractual source, such as formal contracts, letters of comfort, or another legal source as opposed to guarantees whose form is less visible, such as side letters, oral commitments, possibly with various levels of comfort that can be provided by this guarantee. Especially in the latter case, the lack of appropriate legal or accounting records often leads to very poor traceability. This is true both for the beneficiary and for the State or public body providing it and, as a result, for the information available to third parties.[165]

Advantage provided by State guarantee The benefit of a State guarantee is that the risk associated with the guarantee is carried by the State. Such risk-carrying by the State should normally be remunerated by an appropriate premium. Where the State forgoes all or part of such a premium, there is both a benefit for the undertaking and a drain on the resources of the State. Thus, even if it turns out that no payments are ever made by the State under a guarantee, there may nevertheless be State aid within the meaning of Article 107(1) TFEU. The aid is granted at the moment when the guarantee is given, not when the guarantee is invoked nor when payments are made under the terms of the guarantee. Whether or not a guarantee constitutes State aid, and, if so, what the amount of that State aid may be, must be assessed at the moment when the guarantee is given.[166] In order to determine whether an advantage is being granted through a guarantee or a guarantee scheme, account should be taken of the effective possibilities for a beneficiary undertaking to obtain equivalent financial resources by having recourse to the capital market. State aid is not involved where a new funding source is made available on conditions which would be acceptable for a private operator under the normal conditions of a market economy.[167]

Aid to the borrower Usually, the aid beneficiary is the borrower who obtains a financial advantage inasmuch as the financial cost that it bears is less than that which it would have borne if it had had to obtain the same financing and the same guarantee at market prices.[168] For example, in *Banco Privado Português v Commission*, a Portuguese bank which was in financial difficulty during the credit crisis was granted a State guarantee to cover a loan at a rate of

---

[165] *Ibid.*, para 1.2.
[166] *Ibid.*, para 2.1.
[167] *Ibid.*, para 3.1.
[168] Case C-275/10, *Residex Capital IV CV v Gemeente Rotterdam* [2011] ECR I-13043, para 39.

return that was clearly less than the level generally considered appropriate in the market.[169] When the borrower does not need to pay a premium, or pays a low premium, it obtains an advantage. Compared to a situation without guarantee, the State guarantee enables the borrower to obtain better financial terms for a loan than those normally available on the financial markets. Typically, with the benefit of the State guarantee, the borrower can obtain lower rates and/or offer less security. In some cases, the borrower would not, without a State guarantee, find a financial institution prepared to lend on any terms. State guarantees may thus facilitate the creation of new business and enable certain undertakings to raise money in order to pursue new activities. Likewise, a State guarantee may help a failing firm remain active instead of being eliminated or restructured, thereby possibly creating distortions of competition.[170]

Aid to the lender In certain circumstances, the beneficiary of aid granted through a guarantee may be the lender, rather than the borrower, or both the borrower and the lender.[171] Even if usually the aid beneficiary is the borrower, it cannot be ruled out that under certain circumstances the lender will directly benefit from the aid. In particular, for example, if a State guarantee is given *ex post* in respect of a loan or other financial obligation already entered into without the terms of this loan or financial obligation being adjusted, or if one guaranteed loan is used to pay back another, non-guaranteed loan to the same credit institution, then there may also be aid to the lender, in so far as the security of the loans is increased.[172] In *Residex Capital IV v Gemeente Rotterdam*, a loan was guaranteed by a public authority in circumstances where the financial situation of the borrower was such that it would not have been able to obtain a loan on the capital markets. As a result, it was only by means of the guarantee that the lender granted the loan, although no payment for establishing the guarantee was made by the lender to the public authority. In those circumstances, the ECJ held that it could not be excluded that the guarantee was granted for the benefit of the lender, so that it would have obtained its own economic advantage, since the security of its claim increased as a result of the guarantee.[173] In *OTP Bank v Hungary*, a State guarantee, which was intended to facilitate access to housing by reimbursing credit

---

[169] Case T-487/11, *Banco Privado Português SA v Commission* EU:T:2014:1077, para 56.

[170] Commission notice on guarantees, para 2.2.

[171] Case C-457/00, *Belgium v Commission* [2003] ECR I-6931, para 57; Case C-275/10, *Residex Capital IV CV v Gemeente Rotterdam* [2011] ECR I-13043, para 37; Case C-672/13, *OTP Bank Nyrt v Hungary* EU:C:2015:185, para 47; Case T-150/12, *Greece v Commission* EU:T:2014:191, para 48.

[172] Commission notice on guarantees, para 2.3.

[173] Case C-275/10, *Residex Capital IV CV v Gemeente Rotterdam* [2011] ECR I-13043, paras 40-42.

institutions 80% of the amount of loans granted to individual beneficiaries, was held to be exclusively for the benefit of the credit institutions.[174]

Individual guarantees and State aid   Regarding an individual State guarantee, the Commission considers that the fulfilment of all the following conditions will be sufficient to rule out the presence of State aid, although failure to comply with any of the conditions will not mean that the guarantee is automatically regarded as State aid.   First, the borrower must not be in financial difficulty, within the meaning of the Commission's guidelines on rescue and restructuring aid.   Second, the extent of the guarantee must be capable of being properly measured when it is granted, such that the guarantee must be linked to a specific financial transaction, for a fixed maximum amount and limited in time.   Third, except in the case of guarantees covering debt securities, the guarantee must not cover more than 80% of the outstanding loan or other financial obligation.[175]   Finally, a market-oriented price must be paid for the guarantee.[176]

When the price paid for the guarantee is at least as high as the corresponding guarantee premium benchmark that can be found on the financial markets, the guarantee does not contain aid.   If no corresponding guarantee premium benchmark can be found on the financial markets, the total financial cost of the guaranteed loan, including the interest rate of the loan and the guarantee premium, has to be compared to the market price of a similar non-guaranteed loan.   In both cases, in order to determine the corresponding market price, the characteristics of the guarantee and of the underlying loan should be taken into consideration.   This includes: the amount and duration of the transaction; the security given by the borrower and other experience affecting the recovery rate evaluation; the probability of default of the borrower due to its financial position, its sector of activity and prospects; as well as other economic conditions.   This analysis should notably allow the borrower to be classified by means of a risk rating.[177]

Valuation of individual guarantees for SMEs   If the borrower is an SME, the Commission will accept a simpler evaluation of whether or not a loan guarantee involves aid.   In that case, a guarantee would be deemed as not constituting aid if a minimum annual premium, constituting a safe-harbour premium, is charged on the amount effectively guaranteed by the State, based

---

[174] Case C-672/13, *OTP Bank Nyrt v Hungary* EU:C:2015:185, para 48.
[175] This limitation of 80% does not apply to a public guarantee granted to finance a company whose activity is solely constituted by a properly entrusted service of general economic interest and when this guarantee has been provided by the public authority having put in place this entrustment.
[176] Commission notice on guarantees, para 3.2.
[177] *Ibid.*, para 3.2(d).

on the rating of the borrower. These safe-harbour premiums are established in line with the margins determined for loans to similarly rated undertakings in the Commission's communication on reference and discount rates.[178] For SMEs which do not have a credit history or a rating based on a balance sheet approach, such as certain special purpose companies or start-up companies, the minimum annual premium is set at 3.8% but this can never be lower than the premium which would be applicable to the parent company or companies.[179]

Guarantee schemes and State aid For a State guarantee scheme, the Commission considers that the fulfilment of all the following conditions will rule out the presence of State aid, although failure to comply with any of the conditions will not mean that the guarantee scheme is automatically regarded as State aid. First, the scheme must be closed to borrowers in financial difficulty. Second, the extent of the guarantees must be capable of being properly measured when they are granted, such that the guarantees must be linked to specific financial transactions, for a fixed maximum amount and limited in time. Third, under the same conditions as apply for individual guarantees, the guarantees must not cover more than 80% of each outstanding loan or other financial obligation. Fourth, the terms of the scheme must be based on a realistic assessment of the risk, taking account of the quality of the borrower, securities, duration of the guarantee, etc, so that the premiums paid by the beneficiaries make it, in all probability, self-financing. Risk classes have to be defined, the guarantee has to be classified in one of these risk classes and the corresponding guarantee premium has to be charged on the guaranteed or counter-guaranteed amount. Fifth, the adequacy of the level of the premiums has to be reviewed at least once a year on the basis of the effective loss rate of the scheme over an economically reasonable time horizon, and premiums adjusted accordingly if there is a risk that the scheme may no longer be self-financing.[180] Sixth, in order to be viewed as being in line with market prices, the premiums charged have to cover the normal risks associated with granting the guarantee, the administrative costs of the scheme, and a yearly remuneration of an adequate capital, even if the latter is not at all or only partially constituted. Finally, in order to ensure transparency, the scheme must provide for the terms on which future guarantees will be granted, such as eligible companies in terms of rating and, when applicable, sector and size, maximum amount and duration of the guarantees.[181]

Valuation of guarantee schemes for SMEs In order to facilitate the access to finance for SMEs, especially through the use of guarantee schemes, they may

---

[178] OJ 2008 C14/6.
[179] Commission notice on guarantees, para 3.3.
[180] This adjustment may concern all issued and future guarantees or only the latter.
[181] Commission notice on guarantees, para 3.4.

make use of safe-harbour premiums as defined for individual guarantees to SMEs. Guarantee schemes in favour of SMEs can, in principle, be deemed self-financing and not constitute State aid if the minimum safe-harbour premiums based on the ratings of undertakings are applied.

Alternatively, guarantee schemes may allow for the application of a single premium and avoid the need for individual ratings of beneficiary SMEs. The Commission recognises that carrying out an individual risk assessment of each borrower is a costly process, which may not be appropriate where a scheme covers a large number of small loans for which it represents a risk pooling tool. Consequently, where a scheme only relates to guarantees for SMEs and the guaranteed amount does not exceed a threshold of €2.5 million per company in that scheme, the Commission may accept a single yearly guarantee premium for all borrowers. In order for the guarantees granted under such a scheme to be regarded as not constituting State aid, however, the scheme has to remain self-financing and all the other conditions set out above have to be fulfilled.[182]

---

[182] *Ibid.*, para 3.5.

Chapter Five

COMPATIBILITY OF STATE AID WITH THE INTERNAL MARKET

5.1 COMPATIBILITY OF STATE AID WITH THE INTERNAL MARKET

Compatibility of State aid with the internal market In principle, State aid is, pursuant to Article 107(1) TFEU, incompatible with the internal market. Effectively, this means that State aid is prohibited unless it has been notified to and approved, or been deemed to have been approved, by the Commission or the Council.[1] Member States have thus implicitly undertaken not to create any more aid, save as otherwise provided in the FEU Treaty.[2] However, although State aid is recognised as being incompatible with the internal market because it constitutes an obstacle to its essential aim of rational distribution of production,[3] the prohibition in Article 107(1) TFEU is neither absolute nor unconditional and Article 107(1) TFEU itself contains the proviso that aid is incompatible with the internal market save as provided in the FEU Treaty.[4] It follows that there is no question of an unrestricted prohibition since aid is only incompatible to the extent that nothing is provided to the contrary.[5]

State aid may be compatible with the internal market, and therefore permissible, in a number of cases. First, certain aid is declared by Article 107(2) TFEU to be compatible with the internal market. Secondly, the Commission has a discretion under Article 107(3) TFEU enabling it to determine that certain aid is compatible with the internal market. Thirdly, the Council, pursuant to Article 107(3)(e) TFEU may decide that other categories of aid may be permissible and it may also, by virtue of Article 108(2) TFEU in derogation from the rules which normally apply, decide that aid which a Member State is granting or intends to grant shall be considered to be compatible with the internal market if such a decision is justified by

---

[1]   Case T-348/04, *SIDE v Commission* [2008] ECR I-625, para 58.
[2]   Case 6/64, *Costa v ENEL* [1964] ECR 565, p. 596.
[3]   Case 30/59, *De Gezamenlijke Steenkolenmijnen in Limburg v High Authority* [1961] ECR 1, p. 20.
[4]   Case 78/76, *Steinike und Weinlig v Germany* [1977] ECR 595, para 8; Case C-301/87, *Commission v France* [1990] ECR I-307, para 15; Case C-39/94, *SFEI v La Poste* [1996] ECR I-3547, para 36.
[5]   Case 9/70, *Grad v Finanzamt Traunstein* [1970] ECR 825, *per* Advocate General Roemer, at p. 853.

exceptional circumstances.[6] It should be noted that these powers are limited to determining whether aid is to be regarded as compatible with the internal market. They do not empower the Commission or the Council to determine the interpretation of the notion of aid falling with Article 107(1) TFEU.[7]

The grant of aid cannot, therefore, be regarded as automatically contrary to the FEU Treaty.[8] However, exceptions to the general rule that State aid is incompatible with the internal market must be interpreted strictly.[9] It has been suggested that State aid which on its face comes within the scope of Article 107(1) TFEU is subject to a rebuttable presumption of incompatibility with the internal market.[10] Whilst the ECJ has adopted a more neutral approach by holding that when a measure falls within Article 107(1) TFEU it must be determined to what extent any exception applies,[11] the burden of proving that the conditions for the application of one of the derogations are satisfied falls upon the Member State concerned.[12] On the other hand, where aid falls within the scope of derogating rules, the aid is, as a matter of principle, at the outset incompatible with the internal market and is considered to be compatible with the internal market only on condition that it complies with the criteria for derogation contained in the decision approving those rules.[13]

---

[6] Specific provisions of the FEU Treaty provide for aid for agriculture (Articles 38-44 TFEU), transport (Article 93 TFEU) and security (Article 346 TFEU).

[7] Case C-110/03, *Belgium v Commission* [2005] ECR I-2801, para 58; Case C-71/04, *Administración del Estado v Xunta de Galicia* [2005] ECR I-7419, para 37.

[8] Case 323/82, *Intermills v Commission* [1984] ECR 3809, para 32.

[9] Cases C-280/99P to C-282/99P, *Moccia Irme and Others* v *Commission* [2001] ECR I-4717, para 40; Case C-277/00, *Germany v Commission* [2004] ECR I-3925, para 20; Case T-150/95, *UK Steel Association* v *Commission* [1997] ECR II-1433, para 114; Case T-109/01, *Fleuren Compost BV v Commission* [2004] ECR II-127, para 75; Case T-318/00, *Freistaat Thüringen v Commission* [2005] ECR II-4179, para 176; Case T-348/04, *SIDE v Commission* [2008] ECR I-625, para 62; Cases T-362/05 & T-363/05, *Nuova Agricast srl v Commission* [2011] ECR II-297*, para 80; Case T-551/10, *Fri-El Acerra Srl v Commission* EU:T:2013:430, para 24; Case T-150/12, *Greece v Commission* EU:T:2014:191, para 156; Case T-135/12, *France v Commission* EU:T:2015:116, para 61; Case T-385/12, *Orange v Commission* EU:T:2015:117, para 81.

[10] Case 248/84, *Germany v Commission* [1987] ECR 4013, *per* Advocate General Darmon, at p. 4028. See also A. Evans and S. Martin, "Socially acceptable distortion of competition: Community policy on State aid" (1991) 16 ELRev 79.

[11] Case 730/79, *Philip Morris v Commission* [1980] ECR I-2671, para 18; Case 248/84, *Germany v Commission* [1987] ECR 4013, para 19.

[12] Case 730/79, *Philip Morris v Commission* [1980] ECR 2671, *per* Advocate General Capotorti, at p. 2702; Case 248/84, *Germany v Commission* [1987] ECR 4013, *per* Advocate General Darmon, at p. 4032; Case T-68/03, *Olympiaki Aeroporia Ypiresies AE v Commission* [2007] ECR II-2911, para 34.

[13] Cases C-356/90 & C-180/91 *Belgium v Commission* [1993] ECR I-2323, paras 30 and 33; Case C-400/92 *Germany v Commission* [1994] ECR I-4701, para 15; Case C-36/00 *Spain v Commission* [2002] ECR I-3243, para 47; Case C-71/04, *Administración del Estado v Xunta de Galicia* [2005] ECR I-7419, para 34.

State aid and other Treaty provisions The Commission is required to ensure that Articles 107 and 108 TFEU are applied consistently with other provisions of the EU Treaties.[14] Accordingly, State aid cannot be declared by the Commission to be compatible with the internal market if any of its conditions contravene other provisions of the Treaties.[15] Similarly, State aid cannot be declared by the Commission to be compatible with the internal market if any of its conditions contravene the general principles of EU law, such as the principle of equal treatment.[16] In assessing aid as being compatible with the internal market, the Commission may not be required to give effect to an unlawful act committed in the assessment of other amounts of aid.[17] Equally, measures adopted on the basis of other provisions of the Treaties cannot restrict the scope and effectiveness of the State aid rules.[18] Moreover, the mere fact that a measure may be consistent with, for example, the objectives of the common agricultural policy is not sufficient to preclude the application of the State aid rules.[19]

Economic and monetary union In the context of economic and monetary union, it is no longer possible for those Member States which have adopted the euro as their single currency to set individual exchange rates or interest rates, so that these tools of economic management are foregone. As regards Denmark, Sweden and the United Kingdom, which have each retained their own national currency, the setting of exchange rates and interest rates are normally regarded as measures of general economic policy so that the lowering of interest rates or devaluation of a currency do not constitute State aid in favour of undertakings who benefit financially. Member States must,

---

[14] Case C-225/91 *Matra* v *Commission* [1993] ECR I-3203, para 42; Case 110/03, *Belgium v Commission* [2005] ECR I-2801, para 64.

[15] Cases C-134/91 & C-135/91, *Kerafina and Vioktimatiki* [1992] ECR I-5699, para 20; Case C-156/98, *Germany v Commission* [2000] ECR I-6857, para 78; Case C-204/97 *Portugal* v *Commission* [2001] ECR I-3175, para 41; Case C-113/00 *Spain* v *Commission* [2002] ECR I-7601, para 78; Case C-456/00, *France* v *Commission* [2002] ECR I-11949, para 30; Case C-390/06, *Nuova Agricast Srl v Ministero delle Attività Produttive* [2008] ECR I-2577, para 50; Case C-504/07, *Antrop v Conselho de Ministros* [2009] ECR I-3867, para 28; Case T-184/97, *BP Chemicals Ltd. v Commission* [2000] ECR II-3145, para 55; Case T-289/03, *BUPA Ltd v Commission* [2008] ECR II-81, para 314; Case T-359/04, *British Aggregates Association v Commission* [2010] ECR II-4227, para 92; Case T-511/09, *Niki Luftfahrt GmbH v Commission* EU:T:2015:284, para 215.

[16] Case C-390/06, *Nuova Agricast Srl v Ministero delle Attività Produttive* [2008] ECR I-2577, para 51; Case C-67/09P *Nuova Agricast srl v Commission* [2010] ECR I-9811, para 65.

[17] Case T-25/04, *González y Díez SA v Commission* [2007] ECR II-3121, para 183.

[18] Case T-387/04, *Energie Baden-Württemberg AG v Commission* [2007] ECR II-1195, para 134.

[19] Case T-379/09, *Italy v Commission* EU:T:2012:422, para 70.

nevertheless, regard their economic policies as a matter of common concern and coordinate them within the Council.[20] The grant of State aid must be balanced against constraints on national public finances and must, in particular, be consistent with the framework of economic and monetary union and the Stability and Growth Pact. As regards economic policy, Article 126 TFEU requires Member States to avoid excessive government deficits.[21] Budgetary discipline requires that Member States do not normally exceed a ratio of 3% of government deficit to GDP and a ratio of 60% of government debt to GDP.[22] Direct lending to public undertakings and State guarantees of external borrowing is part of the government deficit which is subject to control through the excessive deficit procedure, whereas borrowing for commercial operations is not taken into account.[23] In so far as Member States retain reserved powers in the monetary field, the exercise of these powers cannot be used in order to effect the unilateral adoption of measures which would be contrary to the State aid provisions of the Treaty, such as subsidies on interest payable on export credits.[24]

5.2 AID WHICH IS COMPATIBLE WITH THE INTERNAL MARKET

Aid which is compatible with the internal market The following categories of State aid are, pursuant to Article 107(2) TFEU, to be considered compatible with the internal market:
(a) aid having a social character, granted to individual consumers, provided that such aid is granted without discrimination related to the origin of the products concerned;
(b) aid to make good the damage caused by natural disasters or exceptional occurrences;
(c) aid granted to the economy of certain areas of the Federal Republic of Germany affected by the division of Germany, in so far as such aid is required in order to compensate for the economic disadvantages caused by that division.

Since Article 107(2) TFEU is an exception to the general principle that aid is incompatible with the internal market, its provisions must be interpreted

---

[20] Article 121(1) TFEU.
[21] This does not apply to the United Kingdom: Protocol 15, annexed to the FEU Treaty, on certain provisions relating to the United Kingdom, Article 5.
[22] Article 126(2) TFEU; Protocol 12, annexed to the FEU Treaty, on the excessive deficit procedure, Article 1.
[23] Protocol 12, Article 2.
[24] Cases 6 & 11/69, *Commission v France* [1969] ECR 523, para 17; Case 95/81, *Commission v Italy* [1982] ECR 2187, para 16; Case 57/86, *Greece v Commission* [1988] ECR 2855, para 9.

narrowly.[25] Although the Commission has no discretion as to the compatibility of these categories of aid with the internal market, they must nevertheless be notified in advance pursuant to Article 108(3) TFEU prior to being put into effect, so as to allow the Commission the opportunity to verify that the conditions for the derogation are fulfilled.[26] Once it is established that the aid comes within the scope of one of these provisions, the Commission cannot withhold its authorisation and must regard it as compatible with the internal market.[27] Thus, whereas the Commission is entitled to adopt guidelines or notices establishing the criteria for aid to be compatible with the internal market, in *Olympic Airways v Commission*, the General Court held that it was not entitled to limit aid which complied with Article 107(2)(b) TFEU on the ground that those criteria were not satisfied.[28]

Aid having a social character Article 107(2)(a) TFEU provides that aid having a social character, granted to individual consumers, is permissible. The ultimate beneficiary of the aid must be the individual consumer, rather than an undertaking. Thus, the provision of cheap bread for the benefit of lower income groups would come within the scope of Article 107(2)(a) TFEU, whereas aid granted directly to the mill in the form of subsidised wheat would not.[29] The Commission opened an investigation into a French tax scheme for insurance companies that offer complementary health insurance contracts with strong solidarity components in order to ascertain that the criteria for the application of Article 107(2)(a) TFEU applied.[30]

---

[25] Case C-156/98, *Germany v Commission* [2000] ECR I-6857,para 49; Case C-301/96, *Germany v Commission* [2003] ECR I-9919, para 66; Case C-278/00, *Greece v Commission* [2004] ECR 3997, para 81; Case C-73/03, *Spain v Commission* EU:C:2004:711, para 36; Cases C-346/03 & C-529/03, *Atzeni v Regione aotonoma della Sardegna* [2006] ECR I-1875, para 79; Joined Cases T-132/96 & T-143/96, *Freistaat Sachsen v Commission* [1999] ECR II-3663, para 132; Case T-171/02, *Regione autonoma della Sardegna v Commission* [2005] ECR II-2123, para 165; Case T-200/04, *Regione autonoma della Sardegna v Commission* [2005] ECR II-34*, para 43; Case T-268/06, *Olympiaki Aeroporia Ypiresies AE v Commission* [2008] ECR II-1091, para 52; Case T-70/07, *Cantieri Navali Termoli SpA v Commission* [2008] ECR II-250*, para 56; Case T-445/05, *Associazione Italiana del Risparmio Gestito v Commission* [2009] ECR II-289, para 179.

[26] Case T-308/00, *Salzgitter AG v Commission* [2004] ECR II-1933, para 74.

[27] Case 730/79, *Philip Morris Holland BV v Commission* [1980] ECR 2671, para 17; Case T-268/06, *Olympiaki Aeroporia Ypiresies AE v Commission* [2008] ECR II-1091, para 51.

[28] Case T-268/06, *Olympiaki Aeroporia Ypiresies AE v Commission* [2008] ECR II-1091, para 53.

[29] Case 52/76, *Benedetti v Munari* [1977] ECR 163, *per* Advocate General Reischl, at p. 190.

[30] Case C 50/2007, *Health insurance contracts*, OJ 2008 C38/10.

The aid must be granted without discrimination related to the origin of the products concerned.[31] The notion of discrimination in this provision must be taken to refer to the origin or the supplier of the product concerned, not to measures distinguishing between that product and competing products. For instance, aid to elderly people to help with their heating bills if they used electricity must be granted without discrimination regarding the origin of the electricity (i.e. whether it is domestically produced or imported from other Member States), but that does not mean that aid must also be granted for coal or gas heating.[32]

Since the aid must be granted to individuals, it will not be regarded as entailing a social character where it is available generally.[33] Equally, aid should not normally be available to the entire population of a given region. When Article 107(2)(a) TFEU was invoked as the basis for allowing an aid scheme in the free zone of Gorizia in Italy, the Commission objected initially on the ground that the entire population of Gorizia could not be regarded as being in need of social aid. However, approval was forthcoming when the Italian authorities made certain changes to the scheme, in particular by introducing a limitation on the quotas of tax-free products reserved for the population.[34] Article 107(2)(a) TFEU may be of certain relevance in the case of direct operational subsidisation of air routes provided the aid is effectively for the benefit of final consumers. The aid must have a social character, i.e. it must, in principle, only cover specific categories of passengers travelling on a route, such as children, handicapped persons or low income people. Exceptionally, where the route concerned links a remote region, mainly islands, the aid could cover the entire population of the region.[35] A block exemption for social aid for transport for residents of remote regions was introduced by Commission Regulation (EU) No 651/2014.[36]

Damage caused by natural disasters and exceptional occurrences Article 107(2)(b) TFEU provides that aid to make good the damage caused by natural disasters or exceptional occurrences is compatible with the internal market. Aid was accordingly authorised for the region of Valle d'Aosta to offset the damage caused by floods and torrential rain that hit the region in October

---

[31] Cases C-442/03P & C-471/03P, *P&O European Ferries (Vizcaya) SA v Commission* [2006] ECR I-4845, para 123; Cases T-116/01 & T-118/01, *P&O European Ferries (Vizcaya) SA v Commission* [2003] ECR II-2957, para 163; Commission Decision 2001/247/EC, *Ferries Golfo de Vizcaya*, OJ 2001 L89/28.

[32] *Twenty-Fourth Report on Competition Policy* (1994), pt. 354.

[33] Case T-445/05, *Associazione Italiana del Risparmio Gestito v Commission* [2009] ECR II-289, para 182.

[34] *Twenty-Second Report on Competition Policy* (1992), pt. 495.

[35] Guidelines on aid for airports and airlines 2014, para 156. See, for example, *Thirtieth Report on Competition Policy* (2000), pt. 378.

[36] Commission Regulation (EU) No 651/2014, Article 51.

2001.[37]   Natural disasters also include droughts, tornadoes, forest fires, earthquakes, volcanic eruptions, and diseases of plants and animals of catastrophic proportions.[38]   Exceptional occurrences would include war, serious civil disturbance, nuclear explosions and other cases of *force majeure*. The attacks in the United States on September 11, 2001, were recognised as constituting exceptional occurrences.[39]   In response, the Commission issued a communication authorising aid on the basis of Article 107(2)(b) TFEU for airlines in respect of losses related to the attacks.

There must be a direct link between the aid and the damage caused by the exceptional occurrence and the aid must be limited to that which is necessary to make good the damage.[40]   Thus, a reduction in social security contributions, which was proportionate to the wage bill on the beneficiary undertakings, could not be regarded as designed to remedy the damage caused by the natural catastrophe of the situation of Venice.[41]   As regards aid for airlines following September 11, 2001, the Commission allowed costs caused by the closure of US airspace and the extra costs of insurance.   By contrast, a reduction in VAT on the sale of agricultural land was held not to be sufficiently directly related to losses to farmers flowing from an increase in Spanish petrol prices.[42]   A direct connection between the exceptional occurrence and the damage does not necessarily presuppose that they occur at the same time.[43]   If the Commission considers that the aid will lead to over-compensation, it will not be authorised. For instance, whilst authorising aid granted for the reconstruction of La Valtellina in Italy following flooding, the Commission challenged other aid providing general support for business activity in the region and going beyond the mere restoration of firms damaged by natural disasters.[44]   Where the object

---

[37]   *Thirty-First Report on Competition Policy* (2001), pt. 474.

[38]   *Eighth Report on Competition Policy* (1978), p. 164.

[39]   Case T-70/07, *Cantieri Navali Termoli SpA v Commission* [2008] ECR II-250*, para 59.

[40]   Case C-73/03, *Spain v Commission* EU:C:2004:711, para 37; Cases C-346/03 and C-529/03, *Atzeni v Regione aotonoma della Sardegna* [2006] ECR I-1875, para 79; Case C-303/09, *Commission v Italy* [2011] I-102*, para 7; Case T-268/06, *Olympiaki Aeroporia Ypiresies AE v Commission* [2008] ECR II-1091, para 52.

[41]   Cases C-71/09P, C-73/09P & C-76/09P, *Comitato Venezia vuole vivere v Commission* [2011] ECR I-4727, para 175.

[42]   Case C-73/03, *Spain v Commission* EC:C:2004:711, para 38; Commission Decision 2003/293/EC (OJ 2003 L111/24).

[43]   Case T-268/06, *Olympiaki Aeroporia Ypiresies AE v Commission* [2008] ECR II-1091, para 68.

[44]   *Twenty-Second Report on Competition Policy* (1992), pt. 497.   See also, for example, Commission Decision 1999/100/EC, *Aid to lentil producers in Greece*, OJ 1999 L32/25; Commission Decision 2005/315/EC, *Tremonti bis*, OJ 2005 L100/46.

of the aid is development, rather than reconstruction, it would fall to be examined under Article 107(3)(a) or (c) TFEU.[45]

Aid may cover both the costs of repairing damage as well as compensation for economic loss. The notion of exceptional occurrences does not extend, however, to purely financial loss caused by commercial decisions of economic operators, whatever the motive. Equally, aid to cover costs which can be classified as part of normal entrepreneurial risk does not fall within Article 107(2)(b) TFEU.[46] If a diligent operator is required to take precautions against the consequences of an event, that event cannot, by definition, be regarded as an exceptional occurrence.[47] Thus, aid to cover the costs of preventative action in anticipation of natural disasters would not be allowed where such action would normally be taken as part of a commercial operation, such as the use of insecticide to protect crops against disease. The Commission refused, therefore, to authorise aid to exporters of live animals who were obliged to use more expensive ferry services when the commercial operators withdrew their facilities in the light of pressure from animal rights activists.[48] On the other hand, aid to help prepare against excessive weather conditions might be acceptable.

Aid to compensate for losses due to the BSE crisis in the mid-1990s came within Article 107(2)(b) TFEU. This included aid for slaughterers designed to prevent widespread company failures in the short term and allowing the slaughtering sector to adjust in an orderly fashion to changed market circumstances, temporary aid to renderers ensuring that animal waste and by-products would continue to be collected from abattoirs and safely disposed of, and aid for a publicity campaign seeking to restore consumer confidence in British beef.[49] Aid was also permitted for damage suffered in the beef and veal sector in Belgium and Italy, even though the embargo had been imposed on the United Kingdom.[50] The Commission authorised aid granted by Germany to deep-sea fishing operators to compensate for substantial losses of income due to bad weather off the coast of Greenland where they carried out a large proportion of their activities.[51] On the other hand, damage to agricultural

---

[45] Case C-364/90, *Italy v Commission* [1993] ECR I-2097, *per* Advocate General Jacobs, at p. 2113.

[46] Case T-70/07, *Cantieri Navali Termoli SpA v Commission* [2008] ECR II-250*, para 81.

[47] Case T-268/06, *Olympiaki Aeroporia Ypiresies AE v Commission* [2008] ECR II-1091, para 66.

[48] Commission Decision 2000/625/EC, *Gaelic Ferries*, OJ 2000 L263/17.

[49] *Twenty-Sixth Report on Competition Policy* (1996), p. 234.

[50] *Twenty-Eighth Report on Competition Policy* (1998), p. 237. See also, *Thirty-First Report on Competition Policy* (2001), pts. 463-464.

[51] *Sixteenth Report on Competition Policy* (1986), p. 291.

production caused by field mice was not accepted as an exceptional occurrence justifying aid.[52]

Following the floods in summer 2005 in Germany and Austria that caused disasters of unprecedented proportions, the Commission approved aid subject to strict surveillance mechanisms to ensure that there was no over-compensation. A centralised mechanism was required to be put in place to determine to what extent the damage might have been covered by insurance and to guarantee that the maximum possible support was not exceeded. Losses associated with temporary interruptions in the production process and with the loss of orders, customers or markets were not considered as eligible for aid.[53]

A block exemption for certain aid schemes for damage caused by natural disasters was introduced in 2014 by Commission Regulation (EU) No 651/2014. Aid schemes to make good the damage caused by earthquakes, avalanches, landslides, floods, tornadoes, hurricanes, volcanic eruptions and wild fires of natural origin may be compatible with the internal market where there is a direct causal link between the natural disaster and the damages suffered by the affected undertaking. Eligible costs are the costs arising from the damage incurred as a direct consequence of the natural disaster, as assessed by an independent expert recognised by the competent national authority or by an insurance undertaking.[54]

Division of Germany Aid granted to the economy of certain areas of the Federal Republic of Germany affected by the division of Germany is deemed compatible with the internal market pursuant to Article 107(2)(c) TFEU in so far as such aid is required in order to compensate for the economic disadvantages caused by that division. Prior to German reunification in 1990, this was intended as the basis for the grant of aid to places such as West Berlin and the border regions with the former German Democratic Republic. For example, aid was approved to cover part of the cost of an industrial site for Daimler-Benz AG in West Berlin to compensate for the additional costs arising from urban planning requirements implicitly imposed by the local authorities as a result of the division of the city.[55] Aid was also approved for the restoration of a rail service in Bavaria which had been disrupted in 1952 as a result of the division of Germany.[56]

Following German reunification, the State aid rules were stated by the Commission to be applicable to the new *Länder* from the outset in order to maintain a balance between the needs of the former East Germany as it underwent the necessary economic changes and the avoidance of distortions of

---

[52] *Twenty-Eighth Report on Competition Policy* (1998), p. 237.
[53] *Thirty-Fifth Report on Competition Policy* (2005), pt. 576.
[54] Commission Regulation (EU) No 651/2014, Article 50.
[55] Commission Decision 92/465/EEC, *Daimler-Benz AG*, OJ 1992 L263/15.
[56] *Twenty-Fourth Report on Competition Policy* (1994), p. 495.

competition.[57] Aid was channelled through the Treuhandanstalt to restructure
State-owned companies through privatization. Whilst the writing off of debts
incurred under the imposition of the centralised economic and political system
in the former East Germany and exemption from liability for environmental
damage caused before 1 July 1990 were not to be considered as aid since they
did not confer any advantage on the beneficiary,[58] in other respects the
Commission sought to apply the State aid rules in the normal way. It preferred
to deal with regional or sectoral aid in accordance with Article 107(3)(a)-(c)
TFEU, whilst recognising that some decisions approving aid may exceptionally
be taken on the basis of Article 107(2)(c) TFEU.[59] In any event, the
Commission took the view that there is no longer any economic justification
for continuing to subsidise West Berlin and the area along the former border
with East Germany.[60]

In the light of German reunification, a proposal was made at the time of the
negotiations for the Maastricht Treaty to delete this provision, but no such
action was taken due to resistance by the German Government. Nor was it
repealed by the Treaty of Amsterdam. Nevertheless, Article 107(2)(c) TFEU,
whilst remaining in force, must be interpreted narrowly.[61] It is limited to
compensation for the economic disadvantages caused by the isolation which
the establishment or maintenance of the frontier entailed, such as the breaking
of communications links or the loss of markets as a result of the breaking off of
commercial relations between the two parts of German territory. However, the
economic disadvantages suffered by the new *Länder* as a whole have not been
directly caused by the geographical division of Germany. It follows that the
differences in development between the original and the new *Länder* are
explained by other causes, such as the different politico-economic systems
established in each State on either side of the frontier.[62] Moreover, general
references to the economic consequences of the division of Germany cannot
serve to justify increased levels of aid intensity under Article 107(3) TFEU.[63]

---

[57] *Twentieth Report on Competition Policy* (1990), pt. 173. See also the Commission
     communication on German unification, COM (90) 400 final.
[58] *Twenty-First Report on Competition Policy* (1991), pt. 249.
[59] *Twenty-Fourth Report on Competition Policy* (1994), pt. 354.
[60] *Twentieth Report on Competition Policy* (1990), pt 178.
[61] Case C-156/98, *Germany v Commission* [2000] ECR I-6857, para 49; Case C-334/99,
     Germany v Commission [2003] ECR I-1139, para 117; Case C-301/96, *Germany v
     Commission* [2003] ECR I-9919, para 66.
[62] Case C-156/98, *Germany v Commission* [2000] ECR I-6857, paras 52-55; Case C-
     334/99, *Germany v Commission* [2003] ECR I-1139, para 120; Case C-301/96,
     Germany v Commission [2003] ECR I-9919, para 67; Cases, C-57/00P & C-61/00P,
     Freistaat Sachsen v Commission [2003] ECR I-9975, para 25; Case C-277/00,
     Germany v Commission [2004] ECR I-3925, para 53; Cases T-132/96 & T-143/96,
     Freistaat Sachsen v Commission [1999] ECR II-3663, paras 134-137.
[63] Case T-357/02 RENV, *Freistaat Sachsen v Commission* [2011] ECR II-5415, para 79.

5.3 AID WHICH MAY BE COMPATIBLE WITH
THE INTERNAL MARKET

Aid which may be compatible with the internal market The following categories of State aid may, pursuant to Article 107(3) TFEU, be considered to be compatible with the internal market:

(a) aid to promote the economic development of areas where the standard of living is abnormally low or where there is serious underemployment;

(b) aid to promote the execution of an important project of common European interest or to remedy a serious disturbance in the economy of a Member State;

(c) aid to facilitate the development of certain economic activities or of certain economic areas, where such aid does not adversely affect trading conditions to an extent contrary to the common interest;

(d) aid to promote culture and heritage conservation where such aid does not affect trading conditions and competition in the EU to an extent that is contrary to the common interest;

(e) such other categories of aid as may be specified by decision of the Council acting by a qualified majority on a proposal from the Commission.

Seriously underdeveloped areas Article 107(3)(a) TFEU provides that aid may be granted to promote the economic development of areas where the standard of living is abnormally low or where there is serious underemployment. This exemption concerns only those regions where the economic situation is extremely unfavourable in relation to the EU as a whole,[64] so that the assessment of these factors must be made not with reference to the national average in the Member State concerned but in relation to the EU level.[65] The Commission must, therefore, take into account the EU interest and may not refrain from assessing the impact of the measures on the relevant market or markets in the EU as a whole, including the impact of the aid on trade between Member States and any sectoral repercussions at EU level.[66] When considering proposed aid, the Commission may take account of factors such as the geographical remoteness of the region from the principal markets, the relative economic backwardness of the region, and other factors which increase the cost of transport, storage, non-local employees and infrastructure.[67] Under the guidelines on regional aid, the Commission's

---

[64] Case 248/84, *Germany v Commission* [1987] ECR 4013, para 19; Case C-310/99, *Italy v Commission* [2002] ECR I-2289, para 77.

[65] Case 730/79, *Philip Morris v Commission* [1980] ECR 2671, para 25.

[66] Case C-113/00, *Spain v Commission* [2002] ECR I-7601, para 67; Case T-304/08, *Smurfit Kappa Group plc v Commission* EU:T:2012:351, para 82.

[67] Case C-225/91, *Matra SA v Commission* [1993] ECR I-3203, para 27.

policy is that Article 107(3)(a) TFEU applies to regions having a per capita GDP of less than 75% of the Community average.[68]

In order to satisfy the criterion of promoting economic development, it must be possible to foresee that the aid will bring to the area a lasting increase in income or reduction in unemployment.[69] *Ad hoc* restructuring aid for a single company is not generally within the scope of Article 107(3)(a) TFEU since it is not regional aid as such, although aid which is not primarily intended to promote the development of certain economic regions but which is granted in the form of aid for specific undertakings in difficulty may fall within Article 107(3)(a) TFEU where the Member State concerned establishes that the aid in question actually fulfils the regional specificity criterion.[70] Sectoral repercussions of aid may also need to be taken into consideration. In sectors suffering from overcapacity, aid cannot normally be approved by the sole fact that it falls within the scope of a general regional aid scheme which has been authorised pursuant to Article 107(3)(a) TFEU. Rather, the Commission must take the EU interest into account and consider the impact of the aid on trade between Member States and the sectoral repercussions to which it might give rise at EU level.[71] In order to be compatible with the internal market, the planned aid must be necessary for the development of less favoured areas. To that end, it must be shown that, without the planned aid, the investment intended to support the development of the region in question would not take place. If, on the other hand, it appears that that investment would take place even without the planned aid, the conclusion must be that the aid serves merely to improve the situation of the recipient undertakings, without however meeting the requirement that it be necessary for the development of less favoured areas.[72]

Projects of common European interest Aid to promote the execution of an important project of common European interest is permissible pursuant to Article 107(3)(b) TFEU. The ECJ endorsed the Commission's view that a project may not be described as being of common European interest for these purposes unless it forms part of a transnational European programme supported jointly by a number of Member States or arises from concerted action by them to combat a common threat such as environmental pollution.[73] Thus, for

---

[68] Regional aid guidelines 2014-2020, para 150.
[69] Case 310/85, *Deufil GmbH v Commission* [1987] ECR 901, para 17.
[70] Cases C-278-280/92, *Spain v Commission* [1994] ECR I-4103, para 49. The ECJ also stated that the Commission was under an obligation to specify the criteria according to which it considered *ad hoc* aid, exceptionally, to be regional in character.
[71] Case C-169/95, *Spain v Commission* [1997] ECR I-135, paras 17-20; Cases T-126 &T-127/96, *Breda Fucine Meridionale SpA v Commission* [1998] ECR II-3437, para 101.
[72] Cases C-630/11P to C-633/11P, *HGA srl v Commission* EU:C:2013:387, para 105.
[73] Cases 62 & 72/87, *Exécutif Régional Wallon v Commission* [1988] ECR 1573, paras 22-23. See also, Case 730/79, *Philip Morris v Commission* [1980] ECR 2671, para 25.

example, the Commission approved aid for investments centred in a business park which straddled the Belgian, French and Luxembourg borders. The Commission accepted that the industrial development of the zone presented particular problems which were better dealt with by a coordinated inter-State approach.[74] On the other hand, an aid measure benefiting mostly economic operators in a single Member State cannot benefit from Article 107(3)(b) TFEU.[75] For example, aid granted through selective tax measures benefiting the Italian banking sector could not be justified as a project of common European interest. The benefits were aimed only at operators established in Italy in order to strengthen their competitive position on the internal market. Moreover, the argument that this was part of a privatisation process was also rejected, on the ground that a privatisation process undertaken by a Member State could not, by itself, be considered as constituting a project of common European interest.[76]

In 2014, the Commission issued a communication setting out the criteria for the analysis of the compatibility with the internal market of State aid to promote the execution of important projects of common European interest.[77] This communication applies to all economic sectors, but does not apply to undertakings in difficulty within the meaning of the guidelines on rescue and restructuring aid.[78] The project must contribute in a concrete, clear and identifiable manner to one or more EU objectives and must have a significant impact on competitiveness, sustainable growth, addressing societal challenges or value creation across the EU. It must represent an important contribution to the EU's objectives, for instance by being of major importance for the Europe 2020 strategy, the European Research Area, the European strategy for key enabling technologies (KETs), the Energy Strategy for Europe, the 2030 framework for climate and energy policies, the European Energy Security Strategy, the Electronics Strategy for Europe, the Trans-European Transport and Energy networks, the Union's flagship initiatives such as the Innovation Union, Digital Agenda for Europe, the Resource Efficient Europe, or the Integrated Industrial Policy for the Globalisation Era. The project must normally involve more than one Member State and its benefits must not be confined to the financing Member States, but extend to a wide part of the EU. The benefits of the project must be clearly defined in a concrete and identifiable manner and must not be limited to the undertakings or to the sector

---

[74] *Sixteenth Report on Competition Policy* (1986), p. 180.

[75] Cases C-71/09P, C-73/09P & C-76/09P, *Comitato Venezia vuole vivere v Commission* [2011] ECR I-4727, para 176; Cases T-254/00, T-270/00 & T-277/00, *Hotel Cipriani SpA v Commission* [2008] ECR II-3269, para 337.

[76] Case C-66/02, *Italy v Commission* [2005] ECR I-10901, paras 139-142; Case C-148/04, *Unicredito Italiano SpA v Agenzia delle Entrate, Ufficio Genova 1* [2005] ECR I-11137, paras 74-77.

[77] OJ 2014 C188/4.

[78] Communication on aid for IPCEI, paras 9-10.

concerned but must be of wider relevance and application to the European economy or society through positive spillover effects which are clearly defined in a concrete and identifiable manner.[79] The Commission concluded that a Sweden-Denmark rail-road infrastructure project was a project of common European interest.[80]

Aid pursuant to Article 107(3)(b) TFEU is commonly used to support research and development projects. R&D&I projects must be of a major innovative nature or constitute an important added value in terms of R & D&I in the light of the state of the art in the sector concerned.[81] For example, the Commission approved the Jessi programme, the purpose of which was to strengthen European electronic industry by creating know-how and research networks throughout Europe in which scientists, producers of components and systems-users worked together in order to ensure an independent European position on basis microelectronics technology.[82] The Commission has also applied this provision in the case of projects, such as high definition television, related to the formulation of industrial standards that could enable the Community's industries to secure the full benefit of the single market. Approval was granted to aid for research and development concerning microelectronic technology falling within the scope of the MEDEA+ programme.[83] Environmental, energy or transport projects must either be of great importance for the environmental, energy, including security of energy supply, or transport strategy of the Union or contribute significantly to the internal market, including, but not limited to those specific sectors.[84]

The aid amount must not exceed the minimum necessary for the aided project to be sufficiently profitable. The maximum aid level will be determined with regard to the identified funding gap in relation to the eligible costs. If justified by the funding gap analysis, the aid intensity could reach up to 100% of the eligible costs.[85]

Serious disturbance in the economy Aid to remedy a serious disturbance in the economy of a Member State is permissible pursuant to Article 107(3)(b) TFEU. The derogation in Article 107(3)(b) TFEU is to be interpreted strictly.[86] It follows from the context and general scheme of Article 107(3)(b)

---

[79] *Ibid.*, paras 14-17
[80] SA.38371, *Oresund fixed link* (2014).
[81] Communication on aid for IPCEI, para 21.
[82] *Twenty-Second Report on Competition Policy* (1992), pt. 356; *Twenty-Fifth Report on Competition Policy* (1995), p. 238.
[83] Cases 62 & 72/87, *Exécutif Régional Wallon v Commission* [1988] ECR 1573, para 25.
[84] Communication on aid for IPCEI, para 22.
[85] *Ibid.*, paras 30-31.
[86] Case T-150/12, *Greece v Commission* EU:T:2014:191, para 146; Case T-52/12, *Greece v Commission* EU:T:2014:677, para 160; Case T-457/09, *Westfälisch-Lippischer*

TFEU that the disturbance must affect the economy of the Member State as a whole rather than to any particular region.[87] Furthermore, the disturbance must be serious compared to the situation prevailing in the European Union generally.[88] The Commission has a large margin of appreciation in determining if the measures proposed by Member States in this regard may be permitted.[89] This hitherto rarely-used provision was the basis for allowing, for example, aid granted by several Member States to protect employment during the recession in the mid-1970s[90] and aid in the context of privatisation of hundreds of Greek firms and public-sector banks as part of a national economic recovery plan, account being taken of the particularly serious economic situation in Greece at the time.[91] When the severity of the credit crisis in 2007-2009 became obvious, the Commission used Article 107(3)(b) TFEU as the basis for allowing Member States considerable latitude in their fiscal responses to safeguarding financial institutions and the flow of money into the economy.[92] However, even then, Article 107(3)(b) TFEU could not be used to justify individual aid for a sole public development bank that was in financial difficulty.[93] Aid will not be permitted pursuant to Article 107(3)(b) TFEU where it would permit the transfer to the Member State in question of an investment which could be effected in other Member States in a less favourable economic position.[94] Moreover, since the aid must be limited to remedying the disturbance in the economy, it should not result in the beneficiaries being placed in a stronger position than they would have been in the absence of the disturbance.[95]

Where balance of payments difficulties have arisen, the Commission preferred to authorise remedial action pursuant to Article 143 TFEU rather than Article 107(3)(b) TFEU. Article 143 TFEU applies where a Member State is in difficulties or is seriously threatened with difficulties as regards its balance of payments either as a result of an overall disequilibrium in its balance of payments, or as a result of the type of currency at its disposal, and where such

---

Sparkassen- und Giroverband v Commission EU:T:2014:683, para 200; Case T-487/11, *Banco Privado Português SA v Commission* EU:T:2014:1077, para 83.

[87] Case C-301/96, *Germany v Commission* [2003] ECR I-9919, para 106; Cases T-132/96 & T-143/96, *Freistaat Sachsen v Commission* [1999] ECR II-3663, para 167, confirmed on appeal in Cases C-57/00P & C-61/00P, *Freistaat Sachsen v Commission* [2003] ECR I-9975, para 97.

[88] Commission Decision 84/508/EEC, *Belgian polypropylene fibre and yarn*, OJ 1984 L283/42.

[89] Case T-150/12, *Greece v Commission* EU:T:2014:191, para 147.

[90] *Fifth Report on Competition Policy* (1975), p. 93; *Seventh Report on Competition Policy* (1977), p. 167.

[91] *Twenty-First Report on Competition Policy* (1991), pt. 251.

[92] See Chapter 15 on State aid and the credit crisis.

[93] Case T-387/11, *Nitrogénművek Vegyipari Zst v Commission* EU:T:2013:98, para 127.

[94] Case 730/79, *Philip Morris v Commission* [1980] ECR 2671, para 25.

[95] Commission Decision 88/167/EEC, *Greek industry*, OJ 1988 L76/18.

difficulties are liable to jeopardise the functioning of the internal market or the common commercial policy. On this basis, the Commission allowed France to adopt preferential rediscount rates entailing export aid which could not be permitted under Article 107(3)(b) TFEU.[96]

Development of certain economic activities or areas   Article 107(3)(c) TFEU allows for the approval of aid to facilitate the development of certain economic activities or of certain economic areas. In relation to regional aid, this exemption is wider in scope than that available under Article 107(3)(a) TFEU inasmuch as it permits the development of certain areas without being restricted by the economic conditions necessary for the application of that exemption, thereby allowing the Commission to authorise regional aid intended to further the economic development of areas of a Member State which are disadvantaged in relation to the national average.[97]   The Commission's guidelines on regional aid set out the Commission's policy in determining these eligible regions.

In addition, Article 107(3)(c) TFEU allows for the adoption of horizontal aid measures, i.e. aid that applies across all sectors, such as aid for SMEs, research, development and innovation and aid for environmental protection. Equally, the fact that an aid measure pursues a policy objective, such as a high level of public health protection which is recognised by Article 168 TFEU, may be ground for assessing the aid as compatible with the internal market. On this basis, the Commission approved a Swedish scheme intended to reduce the presence of allergenic substances or other materials that constitute health hazards in buildings.[98]   However, aid which does not facilitate the development of certain economic activities or certain economic areas does not fall within Article 107(3)(c) TFEU, even if it has a specific objective, such as tax relief for costs of listing on a stock exchange which was intended to increase the number of listed companies.[99]

Article 107(3)(c) TFEU also permits the authorisation of sectoral aid and, in particular, of restructuring aid for firms in difficulty. However, it must be remembered that Article 107(3)(c) TFEU allows aid for the development of economic areas or activities, not for the development of individual undertakings. Aid granted to individual undertakings must therefore have as its purpose the development of the particular sector or region. In consequence, it is the overall position in a given sector which should be taken into consideration in assessing compatibility with the internal market, not the

---

[96]   Cases 6 & 11/69, *Commission v France* [1969] ECR 523, para 28.
[97]   Case 248/84, *Germany v Commission* [1987] ECR 4013, para 19.
[98]   *Thirtieth Report on Competition Policy* (2000), pt. 411.
[99]   Case T-211/05, *Italy v Commission* [2009] ECR II-2777, para 183.

position of a few undertakings operating in that sector.[100] Moreover, the mere
fact that the aid might contribute to improving the quality of life of the
recipients is not such as to show that it facilitates the development of the
economic activity in which they are engaged.[101] The Commission takes a
generally favourable attitude to aid to promote tourism and craft activities as
they contribute to diversifying and maintaining economic activity and create
jobs in SMEs and in less favoured areas.[102] Thus, for example, the
Commission permitted a French scheme involving employment aid for the
hotels, cafes and restaurants sector, which covered the additional costs for
employers in providing improved working conditions.[103] Equally, it takes a
favourable view of schemes to aid development of cooperative and mutual
societies. By assisting investment, training and technical assistance, these
measures can focus primarily on job creation, particularly for young people
and the long-term unemployed.[104] A number of individual aid measures have
been approved that aim to develop aspects of the financial services sector that
were subject to market failure. In the United Kingdom, for example, the
Commission approved the establishment of an occupational pensions scheme
aimed at low to moderate income earners who were not served by the existing
market,[105] funding for creating the Green Investment Bank, which is to invest
only in projects that cannot obtain financing on the markets,[106] and the creation
of Flood Re, a reinsurance scheme aimed at ensuring the availability of
domestic insurance at affordable prices for flood-related damage.[107]

Where market conditions seem apt to ensure normal development, State aid
cannot be regarded as facilitating the development of the activity or area in
question.[108]   Thus, in *FAB v Commission*, aid in the Berlin-Brandenburg
region for switching television broadcasting from analogue to digital
transmission could not be declared compatible with the internal market, since
the principal broadcasters in the region had already confirmed that they were
prepared to make the switch before the aid had been announced and
broadcasters in other regions had already switched without any public
subsidy.[109] The ECJ has also endorsed the Commission's view that, in sectors

---

[100] Case 84/82, *Germany v Commission* [1984] ECR 1451, *per* Advocate General Slynn,
at p. 1504. See also, Case C-459/10P, *Freistaat Sachsen v Commission* [2011] I-109*,
para 51; Case T-396/08, *Freistaat Sachsen v Commission* [2010] ECR II-141*, para
112.

[101] Case T-379/09, *Italy v Commission* EU:T:2012:422, para 84.

[102] *Twenty-Second Report on Competition Policy* (1992), pt. 446.

[103] Case N 330/2004, *Employment aid for the restaurant sector*, OJ 2005 C97/3.

[104] *Twenty-First Report on Competition Policy* (1991), pt. 272.

[105] Case N/158/2009, *NEST* (2010).

[106] SA.33984, *Green Investment Bank* (2012).

[107] SA.38535, *Flood Re* (2015).

[108] Case 730/79, *Philip Morris v Commission* [1980] ECR 2671, para 26.

[109] Case T-8/06, *FAB GmbH v Commission* [2009] ECR II-196*, para 81.

characterised by intensive international competition, aid the purpose of which is to strengthen the position of the beneficiaries in relation to those competitors which do not benefit from it, implies that the aid is not aimed at developing the sector in general.[110]

Aid must ensure that there is an improvement in the way in which the economic activity is carried out. Consequently, State aid granted to a firm in difficulty which is used to offset losses and does not form part of a satisfactory restructuring programme such that the positive effects of the aid can be of a lasting nature is not permissible under Article 107(3)(c) TFEU.[111] In *Boussac*, the Commission refused to allow aid to a textile producer on the ground that it was not such as to enable the recipient to restore its competitiveness in a sector marked by overproduction and increased competition from third countries. The ECJ upheld this decision, noting that it could not be expected that the producer would be in a position to survive on its own in the future without further aid.[112] Equally, merely keeping alive an ailing company in a period of recession does not amount to facilitating development.[113] Operating aid is not perceived as developing an activity or an area and is therefore not permissible pursuant to Article 107(3)(c) TFEU.[114] In *Exécutif Régional Wallon v Commission*, the ECJ agreed with the Commission that, since it was perfectly normal and in the interests of the producer that it should use the most modern and economic techniques and materials in order to reduce its running costs, aid for renovation of plant could not be regarded as investment aid satisfying the requirement of facilitating development laid down in Article 107(3)(c) TFEU and should instead be considered as operating aid.[115]

The aid must itself be intended to develop an area or activity for undertakings situated in the EU, although their activity may be aimed at third countries. For example, the Commission authorised the granting of tax concessions to firms setting up in the Trieste centre for financial services and

---

[110] Case C-66/02, *Italy v Commission* [2005] ECR I-10901, para 148; Case C-148/04, *Unicredito Italiano SpA v Agenzia delle Entrate, Ufficio Genova 1* [2005] ECR I-11137, para 82.

[111] Case C-42/93, *Spain v Commission* [1994] ECR I-4175, paras 26-28; Case C-278-280/92, *Spain v Commission* [1994] ECR I-4103, para 67; Case C-17/99, *France v Commission* [2001] ECR I-2481, para 45; Cases T-126 & T-127/96, *Breda Fucine Meridionale SpA v Commission* [1998] ECR II-3437, para 98; Case T-17/03, *Schmitz-Gotha Fahrzeugwerke GmbH v Commission* [2006] ECR II-1139, para 43; Cases T-102/07 & T-120/07, *Freistaat Sachsen v Commission* [2010] ECR II-585, para 73.

[112] Case C-301/87, *France v Commission* [1990] ECR I-307, para 54.

[113] Case 84/82, *Germany v Commission* [1984] ECR 1451, *per* Advocate General Slynn, at p. 1502.

[114] Case C-288/96, *Germany v Commission* [2000] ECR I-8237, para 90; Case T-459/93, *Siemens v Commission* [1995] ECR II-1675, para 48; Case T-379/09, *Italy v Commission* EU:T:2012:422, para 89.

[115] Cases 62 & 72/87, *Exécutif Régional Wallon v Commission* [1988] ECR 1573, para 29; Case T-55/99, *CETM v Commission* [2000] ECR II-3207, para 84.

insurance, which was designed to develop financial relations between the EU and central and east European countries by collecting funds on international markets for use in financial transactions with those countries. The reason for the Commission's approval lay in the importance to the EU of a developed private capital market for Central and Eastern Europe.[116] The Commission also has authorised aid under Article 107(3)(c) TFEU for SMEs to develop their markets or to invest abroad.[117]

In 2014, the Commission announced the creation of the European Fund for Strategic Investment, with the objective of generating investment of €315 billion in the EU. To maximise such investments, the Commission formulated a set of principles, for the purposes of State-aid assessment which a project will have to meet to be eligible for support under the EFSI. Projects, which should be open to all users including competing operators, should address unmet needs rather than duplicate existing infrastructure, crowd in private financing to the maximum extent possible and avoid crowding out privately financed projects.[118]

Extent contrary to the common interest Aid under Article 107(3)(c) TFEU is permissible only to the extent that it does not adversely affect trading conditions contrary to the common interest. In this respect, it is appropriate to take account of the regime applicable to competing undertakings.[119] It is for the Member State concerned to adduce proof that the aid is not contrary to the common interest.[120] The Commission takes the view that the beneficial effects of the aid must be balanced against the adverse effects on trading conditions and the maintenance of undistorted competition.[121] Accordingly, aid should be limited to the minimum necessary.[122] Account is taken, in particular, of the effects of the aid in relation to competing products or undertakings.[123] Thus,

---

[116] *Twenty-Fifth Report on Competition Policy* (1995), p. 197. The Commission subsequently required the repeal of this measure on the ground that it constituted operating aid: *Thirty-Second Report on Competition Policy* (2002), pt. 405.

[117] *Twenty-Sixth Report on Competition Policy* (1996), pt. 224.

[118] *Report on Competition Policy* (2014), pp. 12-13.

[119] Case T-135/12, *France v Commission* EU:T:2015:116, para 65; Case T-385/12, *Orange v Commission* EU:T:2015:117, para 85.

[120] Case T-379/09, *Italy v Commission* EU:T:2012:422, para 87.

[121] *Fourteenth Report on Competition Policy* (1984), pt. 202. Advocate General Slynn seemed to disagree with this conclusion in Case C-84/82, *Germany v Commission* [1984] ECR 1451, at p. 1506, where he stated that in Case 47/67, *France v Commission* [1970] ECR 487, the ECJ appeared to have taken the view that there should only be an inquiry as to whether trading conditions are affected to an extent contrary to the common interest but did not require that to be balanced against the beneficial effects of the aid.

[122] Case T-349/03, *Corsica Ferries France sas v Commission* [2005] ECR II-2197, para 317.

[123] Cases 62 & 72/87, *Exécutif Régional Wallon v Commission* [1988] ECR 1573, paras 30-32; Case C-403/10P, *Mediaset SpA v Commission* [2011] ECR I-117*, paras 101-105.

the Commission decided to prohibit aid that Spain intended to grant to Babcock Wilcox España for future investments in the equity of joint ventures through which it would contract future orders on the ground that this was very close to the market, formed part of the commercial policy of the company and, consequently, could seriously distort competition to an extent contrary to the common interest.[124]   Similarly, in *Mediaset v Commission*, the fact that aid granted in respect of the use of digital terrestrial technology caused a distortion in relation to competing digital satellite technology was held to be sufficient ground for holding that the measure affected trading conditions and was incompatible with the internal market.[125]   However, consideration may also need to be given to wider economic interests than those of competitors. Thus, in *Thermenhotel Stoiser Franz v Commission*, the General Court agreed with the Commission's assessment that aid to a new 5-star hotel should be considered in the context of a regional need to develop quality tourism infrastructure at a standard higher than that of the existing 4-star hotels and that this would boost the regional employment market by leading to the direct creation of 150 jobs as well as further jobs for manual workers in the wider tourism sector.[126]

In determining whether an aid is contrary to the common interest, the issue should be considered qualitatively, rather than solely in quantitative terms.[127] Thus, in *France v Commission*, aid to textile producers in France was financed by a quasi-fiscal charge on all textile products, both domestically produced and imported, sold in France. The result of this method of financing the aid was that the more undertakings from other Member States succeeded in increasing sales in France by their marketing efforts, the more they contributed to an aid which was essentially intended for their competitors who had not made such efforts. The ECJ held that the Commission was correct in determining that the aid, because of the method by which it was financed, had the effect of adversely affecting trade to an extent contrary to the common interest within the meaning of Article 107(3)(c) TFEU.[128]   In *Falck v Commission*, the ECJ considered the application of this requirement in the context of the ECSC Treaty, given that Article 4(b) CS prohibited discrimination between producers, purchasers or consumers. It held that although any aid measure is likely to favour one undertaking in relation to another, the Commission cannot approve aid the grant of which may result in manifest discrimination between

---

[124]   *Thirty-First Report on Competition Policy* (2001), pt. 392.

[125]   Case C-403/10P, *Mediaset SpA v Commission* [2011] ECR I-117*, para 104.

[126]   Case T-158/99, *Thermenhotel Stoiser Franz GmbH v Commission* [2004] ECR II-1, paras 137-138.

[127]   Case 47/69, *France v Commission* [1970] ECR 487, *per* Advocate General Roemer, at pp. 501-502.

[128]   Case 47/69, *France v Commission* [1970] ECR 487, para 23; Cases C-261/01 and C-262/01, *Van Calster v Belgium* [2003] ECR-12249, para 47.

the public and private sectors. In such a case, the grant of aid would involve distortion of competition to an extent contrary to the common interest.[129]

When aid is granted in a market with overcapacity, it is regarded as such as to affect trading conditions to an extent contrary to the common interest.[130] In *Philip Morris v Commission*, the Commission refused to permit certain proposed aid to a tobacco manufacturer in the Netherlands on the ground that most of the increased production would be exported to other Member States. Growth in consumption had slackened such that it was not possible to conclude that trading conditions would remain unaffected by the aid to an extent contrary to the common interest.[131] Similarly, in *Deufil v Commission*, the ECJ upheld the decision of the Commission to refuse to allow financial assistance to a textiles manufacturing company in respect of the acquisition of new machinery. Having regard to the existing surplus of capacity in the industry, any artificial lowering of investment costs would weaken the competitive position of other producers and would have the effect of reducing capacity utilisation and depressing prices contrary to the common interest.[132] Moreover, in *Holland Malt v Commission*, the ECJ held that aid in a market suffering from overcapacity adversely affected intra-EU trade to an extent contrary to the common interest, irrespective of the beneficial effects for the region of the activity concerned.[133]

Where competitors of a recipient of aid had financed from their own resources restructuring and improvements in productivity and quality, the Commission is entitled to disallow the aid on the ground that their competitiveness would be reduced.[134] Other factors to be taken into account include stagnant demand and decline in employment in the sector concerned.[135] In a sector characterised by narrow profit margins, even relatively little aid intended to improve productivity may adversely affect trading conditions contrary to the common interest when it helps the recipient to compete more effectively by reducing its investment costs and strengthening its position against other producers.[136]

Where relevant, the particular circumstances of the recipient should always be taken into account. In *Intermills v Commission*, the Commission's decision to refuse to allow aid to be granted in the form of the acquisition of a capital holding in a Belgian paper manufacturer was annulled by the ECJ. The Commission regarded the capital holding as rescue aid which threatened to do serious damage to the conditions of competition, as the free interplay of market

---

[129] Case 304/85, *Falck v Commission* [1987] ECR 871, para 27.
[130] Case C-464/09P, *Holland Malt BV v Commission* [2010] ECR I-12443, para 48.
[131] Case 730/79, *Philip Morris v Commission* [1980] ECR 2671, para 26.
[132] Case 310/85, *Deufil GmbH v Commission* [1987] ECR 901, para 16.
[133] Case C-464/09P, *Holland Malt BV v Commission* [2010] ECR I-12443, para 53.
[134] Case C-301/87, *France v Commission* [1990] ECR I-307, para 50.
[135] Cases 62 & 72/87, *Exécutif Régional Wallon v Commission* [1988] ECR 1573, para 17.
[136] Case 259/85, *France v Commission* [1987] ECR 4393, para 24.

forces would normally call for the closure of the company, thereby allowing more competitive firms to develop. However, the ECJ held that the settlement of an undertaking's debts in order to ensure its survival does not necessarily affect trading conditions to an extent contrary to the common interest. The Commission had not shown why the company's activities on the market, following the assistance of the aid, were likely to have such an adverse effect on trading conditions that the company's disappearance would have been preferable to its rescue.[137]   Similarly, in *Leeuwarder Papierwarenfabriek*, the Commission's decision refusing to permit certain aid was criticised for failing to consider the essential fact, which might have caused it to make a different assessment, that the aid in question was accompanied by a restructuring of the undertaking which, by diverting its production to high-quality products, led to a reduction in its production capacity and market share.[138]

Culture and heritage conservation   Aid to promote culture and heritage conservation is permitted pursuant to Article 107(3)(d) TFEU.   Moreover, Article 167 TFEU also recognises that the EU is to contribute to the flowering of the cultures of the Member States, while respecting their national and regional diversity and at the same time bringing the common cultural heritage to the fore.   Action by the EU is to be aimed at encouraging cooperation between Member States and supporting their action in relation to cultural heritage and artistic and literary creation.   In its action under other provisions of the FEU Treaty, including competition and State aid policy, the EU must take cultural aspects into account, in particular in order to respect and to promote the diversity of its cultures.[139]   Article 107(3)(d) TFEU was inserted by the Maastricht Treaty in 1992, although aid for culture and heritage conservation had been authorised prior to that amendment pursuant to Article 107(3)(c) TFEU.   Nevertheless, the Maastricht Treaty did not lay down any transitional or retroactive provisions for the application of Article 107(3)(d) TFEU and there is nothing in that provision from which it could be concluded that it is intended to govern situations which arose prior to the date when it entered into force.[140]

The notion of culture within the meaning of Article 107(3)(d) TFEU must be interpreted restrictively.[141]   Moreover, there must be a sufficiently close link between the aid measure and the preservation of cultural heritage.[142]   In *FAB v Commission*, concerning the switchover to digital television broadcasting, the

---

[137] Case 323/82, *Intermills v Commission* [1984] ECR 3809, para 39.

[138] Cases 296 & 318/82, *Netherlands and Leeuwarder Papierwarenfabriek v Commission* [1985] ECR 809, para 26.

[139] Article 167 TFEU.

[140] Case T-348/04, *SIDE v Commission* [2008] ECR I-625, para 56.

[141] Case T-8/06, *FAB GmbH v Commission* [2009] ECR II-196*, para 87.

[142] Cases C-71/09P, C-73/09P & C-76/09P, *Comitato Venezia vuole vivere v Commission* [2011] ECR I-4727, para 170.

General Court held that Article 107(3)(d) TFEU could not be invoked to support the grant of State aid to the broadcasters since there was nothing to suggest that the switchover would lead to a greater variety and diversity in programmes and, consequently, an increase in cultural offering.[143] Nevertheless, it may cover a wide range of activity, including those specific to particular Member States. A Spanish scheme for dubbing and subtitling films in Catalan was approved in line with the objective of promoting multilingualism and cultural diversity.[144] In Poland, aid was authorised for protection and security works in the heritage salt mines of Wieleczka and Bochnia, which are major tourist attractions.[145] The Commission also approved a French tax credit in favour of the creation of video games, whereby video games producers could deduct 20% of the costs of production.[146] A block exemption declaring aid for culture and heritage conservation compatible with the internal market is available for aid that fulfils the conditions of Commission Regulation (EC) No 651/2014, Article 53.

Aid is permissible under Article 107(3)(d) TFEU only where it does not adversely affect trading conditions and competition in the EU to an extent that is contrary to the common interest. In the case of aid for a Dutch aviation museum which was connected to certain commercial activities, given the poor economic viability of the museum activities alone, the Commission had no doubt that aid was necessary for the project to be carried out.[147] Article 107(3)(d) TFEU was also the basis for permitting the grant of aid to Coopérative d'Exportation du Livre Français to enable it to handle small orders placed by foreign bookshops, thereby allowing readers in non-French-speaking countries to obtain works in French at reasonable prices. Book publishing and distribution in Europe was, in principle, not dependent on public support. The Commission concluded that the aid, which was intended to offset the extra cost involved in handling small orders, only pursued a cultural objective and did not support the other, commercial, activities of CELF.[148] However, where the cultural content of an activity becomes subordinate to commercial interest, it is

---

[143] Case T-8/06, *FAB GmbH v Commission* [2009] ECR II-196*, para 88.
[144] Case N33/10, *Dubbing and subtitling in Catalan* (2010).
[145] Cases NN66/2010 and NN/67/2010, *Polish salt mines* (2010).
[146] Commission Decision 2008/354/EC, *Video games*, OJ 2008 L118/16. See also, SA.36139, *Tax relief for UK video games* (2014).
[147] Case N 221/2003, *Dutch aviation museum*, OJ 2003 C301/7.
[148] Commission Decision 1999/133/EC, *CELF*, OJ 1999 L 44/37, annulled in Case T-155/98, *SIDE v Commission* [2002] ECR I-1179. See also, Case C-332/98, *France v Commission* [2000] ECR I-4833; Case T-49/93, *SIDE v Commission* [1995] ECR II-2501, where a previous decision of the Commission authorising the aid to CELF had been annulled on the ground that the Commission had not properly analysed the impact of the aid on the internal market.

less likely that the Commission will rely on Article 107(3)(d) TFEU to permit any aid.[149]

Other categories of aid specified by the Council   Pursuant to Article 107(3)(e) TFEU, the Commission may authorise aid in respect of such categories as may be specified by the Council. It is for the Council to state the category of aid and for the Commission to exercise its discretion as to whether aid should be authorised in any given case, although the criteria established by the Council may leave little or no room for the exercise of any real discretion by the Commission. Thus, the Council authorised State aid to shipbuilding pursuant to Article 107(3)(e) TFEU and established criteria for determining that such aid would be deemed compatible with the internal market. It followed that the Commission's role in this context was limited to checking that the conditions were observed.[150] However, the Council also provided that the Commission may authorise aid in respect of shipbuilding for use in a developing country. This gave a discretion to the Commission, not only to verify that the aid complied with the criteria, but also to decide whether it should be permitted.[151] In the absence of a Council decision, the Commission has no independent power under Article 107(3)(e) TFEU to approve aid.[152]

Article 107(3)(e) TFEU only allows the Council to declare that certain categories of aid may be considered compatible with the internal market. It does not provide for the Council to exempt such categories from the notification procedure under Article 108 TFEU. On the other hand, in *Administración del Estado v Xunta de Galicia*, the ECJ did not take issue with the fact that Council Directive 90/684/EEC on state aid to shipbuilding, adopted pursuant to Article 107(3)(e) TFEU, provided for more stringent notification requirements in addition to those in Article 108 TFEU.[153] Additional notification requirements are also specified in Council Decision 2010/787/EU on aid to facilitate the close of uncompetitive coal mines, which was adopted on the basis of Article 107(3)(e) TFEU.[154]

---

[149] E. Psychogiopoulou, "State aids to the publishing industry and cultural policies in Europe" [2013] EStALQ 69.

[150] Cases C-356/90 & C-180/91 *Belgium v Commission* [1993] ECR I-2323, para 33; Case C-400/92 *Germany* v *Commission* [1994] ECR I-4701, para 15; Case C-36/00 *Spain* v *Commission* [2002] ECR I-3243, para 47; Case C-71/04, *Administración del Estado v Xunta de Galicia* [2005] ECR I-7419, para 34.

[151] Case C-400/92, *Commission v Germany* [1994] ECR I-4701, para 20.

[152] Cases T-254/00, T-270/00 &T-277/00, *Hotel Cipriani SpA v Commission* [2008] ECR II-3269, para 332; Cases T-278/00 etc. *Albergo Quattro Fontane Snc v Commission* EU:T:2013:77, para 60.

[153] Case C-71/04, *Administración del Estado v Xunta de Galicia* [2005] ECR I-7419, para 26.

[154] Council Decision 2010/787/EU, Article 7.

5.4 AID WHICH THE COUNCIL DETERMINES TO BE COMPATIBLE WITH THE INTERNAL MARKET

Additional categories of aid   Pursuant to Article 107(3)(e) TFEU, the Council, acting on a qualified majority on a proposal from the Commission, may, taking account of economic and social requirements, extend the range of aids which may be considered to be compatible with the internal market in addition to those set out at Article 107(3)(a)-(d) TFEU.[155]   Whereas the Council may extend the range of aid which may be declared compatible with the internal market, by fixing an abstract and general framework, the Commission undertakes a specific examination to determine whether or not the aid falls within the category as defined.   The Council does not, therefore, substitute itself for the Commission in making a specific assessment of the compatibility of aid in a given case.[156]   In any event, Article 107(3)(e) TFEU does not give an automatic right to the Council to permit other categories of aid as it sees fit.   Since the Council can only take such a decision by acting on a proposal from the Commission, the latter retains the initiative in determining whether there is a need or desire for any further categories to be declared.   The Council has in the past availed itself of this power in the case of shipbuilding, where the various measures adopted have included operating aid, which does not fall within Article 107(3)(c) TFEU.[157]   Provisions on State aid for the coal industry after the expiry of the ECSC Treaty have also been based on Article 107(3)(e) TFEU.[158]

Exceptional circumstances   Article 108(2) TFEU provides that, on application by a Member State, the Council may decide that aid which that State is granting or intends to grant shall be considered to be compatible with the internal market, in derogation from the provisions of Article 107 TFEU, if such a decision is justified by exceptional circumstances.   This applies both to new aid which the Commission may consider is not compatible with the internal market and to existing aid which the Commission may consider is no longer compatible with the internal market.   The Council is, therefore, the

---

[155] Joined Cases C-356/90 & C-180/91 *Belgium v Commission* [1993] ECR I-2323, paras 27-32; Case T-266/94 *Foreningen af Jernskibs- og Maskibbyggerier i Danmark, Skibsværftsforeningen v Commission* [1996] ECR II-1399, para. 93.

[156] Case C-400/92, *Commission v Germany* [1994] ECR I-4701, *per* Advocate General Darmon, at p. 4708. See also, Case C-311/94, *Ijssel-Vliet v Minister van Economische Zaken* [1996] ECR I-5063, paras 26-28; Case T-584/08, *Cantiere Navale De Poli SpA v Commission* [2011] ECR II-63, paras 60-61.

[157] Council Regulation (EC) No 1540/98; Council Regulation (EC) No 1177/2002. Aid to shipbuilding is no longer governed by special provisions..

[158] Council Regulation (EC) No 1407/2002; Council Decision 2010/787/EU.

institution of last resort in deciding whether exceptional circumstances exist,[159] subject to review by the General Court and the ECJ.[160] The notion of exceptional circumstances involves the idea of something extraordinary, unforeseen and not permanent. It might apply to facts or situations which may relate to one sector in particular or to the economy in general but which, assessed in the context of a specific Member State or a specific sector, show that there has been a change on such a scale as compared to what was previously considered normal or at least not extraordinary, that corrective measures are needed for which there is no provision in the existing rules governing the sector in question.[161] Given that the Council is called upon to carry out an assessment of a complex economic situation, it is entitled to a broad measure of discretion as to the nature and scope of the measures to be taken.[162] For example, in a series of cases concerning aid for the purchase of agricultural land in Hungary, Latvia, Lithuania and Poland, in light of the unusual and unforeseeable character and the extent of the effects of the credit crisis on agriculture in those Member States, the Council was entitled to consider that those effects constituted exceptional circumstances.[163] Nevertheless, the Council may not rely on Article 108(2) TFEU to authorise aid which is contrary to other provisions of EU law.[164]

5.5 STATE AID, COMPETITION POLICY AND THE INTERNAL MARKET

Internal market and competition policies   The internal market and competition policies of the Treaty are central to the establishment and proper functioning of the internal market. Free movement of goods, persons, services

---

[159] Case C-122/94, *Commission v Council* [1996] ECR I-881, *per* Advocate General Cosmas, at p. 903.

[160] For example, in Case 253/84, *GAEC v Council and Commission* [1987] ECR 123, Advocate General Slynn advised that Council Decision 84/361/EEC was *ultra vires* because it had not been shown that exceptional circumstances existed.

[161] Case C-122/94, *Commission v Council* [1996] ECR I-881, *per* Advocate General Cosmas, at p. 909.

[162] Case C-122/94, *Commission v Council* [1996] ECR I-881, para 19. In the face of Commission opposition, the Council adopted Decisions 2002/361-363/EC on 3 May 2002 authorising the grant of aid by the Netherlands, Italy and France in favour of road transport undertakings, OJ 2002 L131/12-14.

[163] Case C-111/10, *Commission v Council* EU:C:2013:785, para 98; Case C-117/10, *Commission v Council* EU:C:2013:786, para 114; Case C-118/10, *Commission v Council* EU:C:2013:787, para 105; Case C-121/10, *Commission v Council* EU:C:2013:784, para 99.

[164] Case 253/84, *GAEC v Council and Commission* [1987] ECR 123, *per* Advocate General Slynn, at p. 146; Case C-438/92, *Rustica Semences SA v Finanzamt Kehl* [1994] ECR I-3519, *per* Advocate General Jacobs at p. 3527.

and capital in an area without internal frontiers in conjunction with the institution of a system ensuring that competition is not distorted is intended to result in the optimal use of the economic factors of production and distribution. Given that the prohibitions on restrictions contained in the free movement provisions of the Treaty are definitive, and subject to few exceptions, it is clear that there is a potential conflict where State aid is permitted, particularly where such aid has a significant effect on competitive structures within the internal market. Nevertheless, the ECJ has held that the fact that a system of State aid may, simply because it benefits certain undertakings or products, hinder, at least indirectly, the importation of similar or competing products coming from other Member States is not in itself sufficient to put an aid on the same footing as a restriction within the meaning of Article 34 TFEU. A contrary approach would alter the scope of Article 107(1) TFEU and interfere in the system adopted in the FEU Treaty for the division of powers for keeping aid under review. Moreover, those aspects of aid which contravene a provision of the Treaty, such as Article 34 TFEU, may be so indissolubly linked to the object of the aid that it is impossible to evaluate them separately so that their effect on the compatibility of the aid viewed as a whole must of necessity be determined in the light of the procedure prescribed in Article 108 TFEU.[165] This applies equally to aspects of aid which contravene the competition law rules but which may be so indissolubly linked to the object of the aid that it is impossible to evaluate them separately.[166]

In the case of the public procurement rules, which require public authorities to award contracts to the lowest bidder, it has been argued that tenderers which have received State aid should be excluded from the tendering process since they enjoy a substantial competitive advantage compared to other tenderers such that the contracting authority is unable to ascertain reliably whether the price offered is reasonable or corresponds to the market situation. In response, the ECJ has held that the fact that contracting authorities allow bodies, which have received subsidies enabling them to submit tenders at prices appreciably lower than those of other, unsubsidised, tenderers, to take part in a procedure for the award of a public procurement contract does not amount to a breach of the principle of equal treatment.[167] It may, however, be permissible for contracting authorities, in certain circumstances, to take into account the existence of subsidies, and in particular of incompatible aid, in order, where

---

[165] Case 74/76, *Iannelli v Meroni* [1977] ECR 557, paras 9-14; Case T-57/11, *Castelnou Energía v Commission* EU:T:2014:1021, paras 181-183; Case T-511/09, *Niki Luftfahrt GmbH v Commission* EU:T:2015:284, para 216.

[166] Case C-225/91, *Matra SA v Commission* [1993] ECR I-3203, para 41; Cases T-197/97 & T-198/97, *Weyl Beef Products BV v Commission* [2001] ECR II-303, para 76.

[167] Case C-94/99, *ARGE Gewässerschutz v Bundesministerium für Land und Forstwirtschaft* [2000] ECR I-11037, para 25; Case C-568/13, *Azienda Ospedaliero-Universitaria di Careggi-Firenzi v Data Medical Service SrL* EU:C:2014:2466, para 43.

appropriate, to exclude tenderers in receipt of such aid.[168] In that regard, the fact that the public entity concerned has separate accounts for its activities on the market and for its other activities may make it possible to establish whether a tender is abnormally low as a result of the effect of an element of State aid. However, the contracting authority may not conclude from the absence of such separate accounts that such a tender was made possible by the grant of State aid which is incompatible with the FEU Treaty.[169]

Nevertheless, the mere fact that a measure constitutes State aid is not necessarily sufficient to preclude the application of the rules relating to free movement or competition law. On the contrary, the Commission is required to ensure as far as possible that the State aid provisions are applied consistently with other provisions of the FEU Treaty. In particular, those factors which may be regarded as not being necessary for the attainment of the objective of the aid or for its proper functioning may be separated from the aid scheme. Thus, discriminatory aspects of aid, particularly discrimination on grounds of nationality which are generally contrary to the free movement provisions, are prohibited where they can be separated from the rest of the aid scheme.[170]

Free movement of goods: Articles 34-35 TFEU Articles 34 and 35 TFEU prohibit quantitative restrictions on the import and export, respectively, of goods in trade between Member States. In the case of restrictions on imports, the ECJ has held that Article 34 TFEU applies to all trading rules enacted by Member States which are capable of hindering, directly or indirectly, actually or potentially, intra-EU trade,[171] although this does not extend to national rules restricting or prohibiting certain selling arrangements which apply to all traders operating within the Member State and provided that they affect in the same manner, in law and in fact, the marketing of domestic and imported products.[172] However, the effect of an interpretation of Article 34 TFEU which is so wide as to treat a State aid as being similar to a quantitative restriction would be to alter the scope of Article 107(1) TFEU and to interfere in the system adopted in the Treaty for the division of powers by means of the procedure for keeping aids under review. It follows that, however wide the application of Articles 34 and 35 TFEU may be, they do not normally include

---

[168] Case C-94/99, *ARGE Gewässerschutz v Bundesministerium für Land und Forstwirtschaft* [2000] ECR I-11037, para 29; Case C-305/08, *Conisma v Regione Marche* [2009] ECR I-12129, para 33; Case C-568/13, *Azienda Ospedaliero-Universitaria di Careggi-Firenzi v Data Medical Service SrL* EU:C:2014:2466, para 44.

[169] Case C-568/13, *Azienda Ospedaliero-Universitaria di Careggi-Firenzi v Data Medical Service SrL* EU:C:2014:2466, para 45.

[170] Case 18/84, *Commission v France* [1985] ECR 1339, para 13; Case C-156/98, *Germany v Commission* [2000] ECR I-6857, para 85.

[171] Case 8/74, *Procureur du Roi v Dassonville* [1974] ECR 837, para 5.

[172] Cases C-267-268/91, *Keck* [1993] ECR I-6097, para 16.

obstacles to trade covered by Article 107(1) TFEU. The fact that a system of aids provided by the State or by means of State resources may, simply because it benefits certain national undertakings or products, hinder, at least indirectly, the importation of similar or competing products coming from other Member States is not in itself sufficient to put an aid on the same footing as a measure having an effect equivalent to a quantitative restriction within the meaning of Article 34 TFEU. Moreover, those aspects of aid which contravene a provision of the FEU Treaty, such as Article 34 TFEU, may be so indissolubly linked to the object of the aid that it is impossible to evaluate them separately so that their effect on the compatibility of the aid viewed as a whole must of necessity be determined in the light of the procedure prescribed in Article 108 TFEU.[173]

Nevertheless, Article 107 TFEU may not be used to frustrate the rules on the free movement of goods. The mere fact that a measure might be regarded as aid within the meaning of Article 107(1) TFEU is not a sufficient reason to exempt it from the prohibition contained in Article 34 TFEU.[174] It is not acceptable for aid to include arrangements whose restrictive effects exceed what is necessary to enable the aid to attain the objectives permitted by Article 107(3) TFEU.[175] The fact that the inevitable consequence of aid is some restriction on trade does not mean that all restrictive effects which the aid produces must be regarded as permissible. Instead, it may be possible, when a system of aid is being analysed, to separate those conditions or factors which, even though they form part of this system, may be regarded as not being necessary for the attainment of its object or for its proper functioning.[176] Some elements of aid may, accordingly, be impermissible on account of their incompatibility with Article 34 TFEU where the aim pursued is attainable by other means which are less restrictive of the free of movement of goods.[177] In *Iannelli v Meroni*, an aid was granted to newspaper publishers in Italy through subsidies to the cost of newsprint, but this was limited to newsprint produced in Italy or imported by the Italian State agency and did not extend to newsprint imported directly by the publishers. The ECJ held that this limitation would be regarded as incompatible with Article 34 TFEU unless it could be shown that it was necessary for the attainment of the object of the aid or for its proper functioning.[178] In *Commission v France*, the ECJ was more forthright and rejected completely a similar argument concerning discriminatory tax

---

[173] Case 74/76, *Iannelli v Meroni* [1977] ECR 557, paras 9-14; Case T-57/11, *Castelnou Energía v Commission* EU:T:2014:1021, para 196.

[174] Case 18/84, *Commission v France* [1985] ECR 1339, para 13; Case 103/84, *Commission v Italy* [1986] ECR 1759, para 19; Case C-21/88, *Du Pont de Nemours Italiana v Unità Sanitaria Locale No 2 di Carrara* [1990] ECR I-889, para 20.

[175] Case T-162/06, *Kronoply GmbH v Commission* [2009] ECR II-1*, para 66.

[176] Case 74/76, *Iannelli v Meroni* [1977] ECR 557, para 14.

[177] Case C-21/88, *Du Pont de Nemours Italiana v Unità Sanitaria Locale No 2 di Carrara* [1990] ECR I-889, *per* Advocate General Lenz, at p. 913.

[178] Case 74/76, *Iannelli v Meroni* [1977] ECR 557, para 15.

treatment whereby newspaper publishers in France enjoyed certain tax advantages in respect of their publications printed in France but not in respect of publications printed in other Member States. This was held to be a discriminatory restriction on the importation of printed matter from other Member States.[179] Similarly, the Commission took exception to an Irish aid scheme for mushroom growers whereby aid was available only to producers who bought their compost from Irish composting companies.[180]

It follows that the mere fact that the measure may possibly be defined as aid is not an adequate reason for exempting it from the application of Article 34 TFEU.[181]   Article 107 TFEU, therefore, could not be relied on to justify a requirement imposed on municipal transport authorities in Italy to purchase vehicles manufactured in Italy in order to qualify for public subsidies for the cost of their transport fleet, since this was an unlawful restriction on trade.[182] Nor was it permissible for Italian legislation to oblige all public bodies and authorities, as well as companies in which the State had a shareholding, to obtain at least 30% of their requirements from suppliers established in the Mezzogiorno. Although this was intended to form part of a package of regional aid to southern Italy, it nevertheless was contrary to Article 34 TFEU.[183]   In *Commission v Ireland*, the Irish Government subsidised an advertising campaign exhorting consumers in Ireland to buy Irish manufactured goods. Although it was conceded that the effect of the campaign might be to discourage imports from other Member States, it was argued that the legality of the measure should be judged on the basis of Article 107 TFEU. Advocate General Capotorti thought that there was no contravention of Article 34 TFEU and accepted that the campaign was governed by Article 107 TFEU on the ground that it took the place of advertising initiatives which individual Irish manufacturers could lawfully have undertaken and that the State financing reduced the costs of those manufacturers, thereby distorting competition in the internal market.[184]   The ECJ, however, rejected this approach on the ground that, whilst Article 107 TFEU might be applicable to the financing of such a campaign, the campaign itself did not necessarily escape the prohibitions laid down in Article 34 TFEU.[185]

---

[179] Case 18/84, *Commission v France* [1985] ECR 1339, para 13.

[180] *Twenty-Third Report on Competition Policy* (1993), pt. 548.

[181] Case 18/84, *Commission v France* [1985] ECR 1339, para 13.

[182] Case 103/84, *Commission v Italy* [1986] ECR 1759, para 19. See also Case C-263/85, *Commission v Italy* [1991] ECR I-2457.

[183] Case C-21/88, *Du Pont de Nemours Italiana v Unità Sanitaria Locale No 2 di Carrara* [1988] ECR I-889, para 21; Case C-351/88, *Laboratori Bruneau v Unità Sanitaria Locale RM/24 di Monterotondo* [1991] ECR I-3641, para 7.

[184] Case 249/81, *Commission v Ireland* [1982] ECR 4005, *per* Advocate General Capotorti, at p. 4032.

[185] Case 249/81, *Commission v Ireland* [1982] ECR 4005, para 18.

State monopolies: Article 37 TFEU   Article 37 TFEU sets out rules governing the operation of State monopolies of a commercial character. Member States are required to adjust any State monopolies of a commercial character so as to ensure that no discrimination regarding the conditions under which goods are procured and marketed exists between EU nationals. Member States must also refrain from introducing any new measure which is contrary to these principles or which restricts the scope of the provisions dealing with the prohibition of customs duties and quantitative restrictions between Member States. These requirements apply to any body through which a Member State, in law or in fact, either directly or indirectly supervises, determines or appreciably influences imports or exports between Member States.[186]

Both Article 37 TFEU and Article 107(1) TFEU pursue the same objective, which is to ensure that intervention by the Member States does not distort the conditions of competition within the internal market or create discrimination against the products of other Member States. However, the application of those provisions presupposes distinct conditions peculiar to the State measure which they are intended to govern. Accordingly, unlike Articles 107 and 108 TFEU, pursuant to which the actual economic effect of an aid granted by a State may be assessed, Article 37 TFEU is intended to render the sales policy of a State monopoly subject to the requirements of the free movement of goods and of the equal opportunities which must be accorded to products imported from other Member States. Furthermore, Article 37 TFEU and Articles 107 and 108 TFEU differ as to their legal consequences, above all in that the intervention of the Commission plays a large part in the implementation of the latter. A measure effected through the intermediary of a public monopoly which may also be considered as an aid is consequently governed by both provisions. It follows that the operations of a State monopoly are not exempted from the application of Article 37 TFEU by reason of the fact that they may at the same time be classified as an aid. It is, therefore, clear that, in all cases where the arrangements for marketing a product entail the intervention of a public monopoly acting pursuant to its exclusive right, the specific provisions of Article 37 TFEU are applicable even if the relationship between the monopoly and the producers may be in the nature of an aid.[187]

Free movement of persons and services: Articles 45, 49 and 56 TFEU   The mere fact that aid is granted to an undertaking cannot be construed as discrimination on grounds of nationality against other undertakings within the

---

[186] Article 37 TFEU. These provisions apply equally to monopolies delegated by the State to others bodies.
[187] Case 91/78, *Hansen v Hauptzollamt Flensburg* [1979] ECR 935, paras 9 and 13. See also, Case 253/83, *Kupferberg v Hauptzollamt Mainz* [1985] ECR 157, paras 15-16.

scope of Article 18 TFEU.[188] Articles 45, 49 and 56 TFEU, concerning free movement of persons and services, whilst generally prohibiting restrictions on freedom of movement, constitute specific applications of the general prohibition on discrimination on grounds of nationality in Article 18 TFEU.[189] The Commission has objected to several aid schemes which have included provisions which breached the prohibition on discrimination on grounds of nationality. For instance, it refused to sanction State aid for shipbuilding under a Greek scheme whereby aid was available only to Greek nationals for the construction of vessels in Greek yards.[190] State aid for film production was disapproved of by the Commission where the schemes provided that aid would be awarded only where the director of the film was a national of the Member State in question.[191] In *FEDICINE v Spain*, a complaint was made concerning Spanish legislation which provided that film distributors in Spain were entitled to a licence to dub films from third countries only if they undertook to distribute Spanish films. It was argued that this induced them to favour the distribution of Spanish films to the detriment of the distribution of films from other countries. Whilst this was held to restrict freedom to provide services contrary to Article 56 TFEU, the Commission rejected the argument that it fell within the scope of Article 107(1) TFEU on the ground that there was no transfer of State resources and no financial favouring of certain undertakings.[192] Even where State resources have been involved, however, the Commission has relied on Article 56 TFEU alone, and not Article 107 TFEU, where there is a clear infringement of the freedom to provide services. For instance, it required the German authorities to withdraw a circular which had been issued to civil servants requiring them to fly with Lufthansa on the ground that this was an infringement of Article 106(1) TFEU in conjunction with Article 56 TFEU.[193] On the other hand, in *Presidente del Consiglio dei Ministri v Regione Sardegna*, concerning a regional tax in Sardinia on stopovers of aircraft and pleasure boats, the ECJ held that both the provisions of freedom to provide services and State aid were infringed.[194] By contrast, in *Ryanair v Commission* and *Aer Lingus v Commission*, a challenge to the higher rate of Irish air travel tax as being contrary to Article 56 TFEU and consequently unenforceable, so that it could not be used as a valid reference

---

[188] Case T-158/99, *Thermenhotel Stoiser Franz GmbH v Commission* [2004] ECR II-1, para 147.

[189] Case 36/74, *Walrave and Koch v Association Union Cycliste Internationale* [1974] ECR 1405, para 6; Case 13/76, *Donà v Mantero* [1976] ECR 1333, para 6; Case C-10/90, *Masgio v Bundesknappschaft* [1991] ECR I-1119, para 13.

[190] *Nineteenth Report on Competition Policy* (1989), pt. 152.

[191] *Ibid.*, pts. 191-193.

[192] Case C-17/92, *FEDICINE v Spain* [1993] ECR I-2239, at p. 2248.

[193] *Twentieth Report on Competition Policy* (1990), pt. 357.

[194] Case C-169/08, *Presidente del Consiglio dei Ministri v Regione Sardegna* [2009] ECR I-10821.

rate for determining the amount of State aid inherent in the lower rate of the tax, was dismissed on the ground that Article 56 TFEU merely prohibited differential tax rates, but did not result in the higher rate in itself constituting a prohibited restriction on freedom to provide services.[195]

Discrimination on grounds of nationality may also arise indirectly by reference to residence or some other criterion which has a similar effect.[196] Thus, the Commission rejected a German film production aid scheme which required the director to be from a German cultural background.[197] Aid under the German Indemnification and Compensation Act which was limited to farmers who had been resident in the former East Germany was regarded by the Commission as discriminatory contrary to Articles 18, 45 and 49 TFEU.[198] Similarly, the Commission refused to approve an aid scheme eligibility for which was restricted to firms whose registered office was in the Land of Saxony-Anhalt.[199] The ECJ has, on several occasions, held that granting tax benefits only to residents of a Member State or taxing non-residents at a higher rate of tax may constitute indirect discrimination by reason of nationality.[200] Aid effected through tax exemptions will not be approved by thc Commission if the benefit is restricted on grounds of nationality. Thus, the ECJ approved the Commission'' refusal to authorise a scheme of aid by way of tax relief granted for the reinvestment of profits in equity stakes in companies established in West Berlin or the former East Germany.[201] It also rejected a system of tax aid for investment in the Basque country which involved discrimination.[202]

---

[195] Case T-500/12, *Ryanair Ltd v Commission* EU:T:2015:73, para 83; Case T-473/12, *Aer Lingus Ltd v Commission* EU:T:2015:78, para 58.

[196] Case 152/73, *Sotgiu v Deutsche Bundespost* [1974] ECR 153, paras 10-11; Case C-221/89, *R v Secretary of State for Transport, ex parte Factortame Ltd.* [1991] ECR I-3905, para 32.

[197] *Twenty-Second Report on Competition Policy* (1992), pt. 442.

[198] Commission Decision 1999/268/EC, *German Compensation Act*, OJ 1990 L107/21. See also, Case T-114/00, *Aktionsgemeinschaft Recht und Eigentum eV v Commission* [2002] ECR II-5121; Case C-78/03P, *Commission v Aktionsgemeinschaft Recht und Eigentum eV* [2005] ECR I-10737.

[199] *Twenty-Sixth Report on Competition Policy* (1996), p. 208.

[200] Case C-175/88, *Biehl v Administration des contributions du Grand-Duché de Luxembourg* [1990] ECR 1779, para 16; Case C-330/91, *The Queen v IRC, ex parte Commerzbank AG* [1993] ECR I-4017, para 20; Case C-279/93, *Finanzamt Köln-Altstadt v Schumacker* [1995] ECR I-225, para 29; Case C-80/94, *Wielockx v Inspecteur der Directe Belastingen* [1995] ECR I-2493, para 22; Case C-107/94, *Asscher v Staatssecretaris van Financiën* [1996] ECR I-3089, para 56; Case C-118/96, *Safir v Skattemyndigheten i Dalarnas Län* [1998] ECR I-1897, para 34.

[201] Case C-156/98, *Germany v Commission* [2000] ECR I-6857, para 85; Commission Decision 98/476/EC, *s58(2) of the German Income Tax Act*, OJ 1998 L212/50.

[202] Commission Decision 93/337/EEC, *Basque tax concessions*, OJ 1993 L134/25. See also, Cases C-400/97-C402/97, *Administración del Estado v Juntas Generales de Guipúzcoa* [2000] ECR I-1073, *per* Advocate General Saggio at para 37.

Free movement of capital: Article 63 TFEU   All restrictions on the movement of capital and on payments between Member States and between Member States and third countries is prohibited by Article 63 TFEU.[203] Pursuant to Article 65(1)(a) TFEU, this prohibition is without prejudice to the right of Member States to apply the relevant provisions of their tax law which distinguish between taxpayers who are not in the same situation with regard to their place of residence or with regard to the place where their capital is invested.[204]   Article 65(1)(a) TFEU applies, however, only in respect of the relevant provisions of national tax law which existed at the end of 1993 so that no new discriminatory provisions could be introduced after that date.[205]   In so far as discriminatory treatment might arise as between taxpayers by reference to their place of residence, this might in any event be incompatible with the taxpayer's rights of freedom of movement under Articles 45 or 49 TFEU.   On the other hand, where such treatment constitutes a restriction on the right of establishment which is compatible with the FEU Treaty, that restriction is not affected by the provisions concerning free movement of capital.[206]   Thus, differential tax treatment which is permissible on grounds, for example, of the coherence of the tax system would not be prohibited by Article 63 TFEU.[207] However, conflicts between Article 107 TFEU and Article 63 TFEU may arise in the case of differential tax treatment relating to the place where capital is invested.   Tax relief granted to individuals for investing in a company can amount to State aid to the company.[208]   In *Verkooijen*, the ECJ held that where a Member State introduces a tax relief in relation to a shareholding held in companies established within its territory, it must equally apply that relief to shares held in companies established in other Member States in order to comply with EU law concerning free movement of capital.[209]   Since Article 63

---

[203] This provision was introduced by the Maastricht Treaty and came into effect on 1 January 1994, although free movement of capital had previously been achieved for most Member States as of 1 January 1990 pursuant to Council Directive 88/361/EEC.

[204] Article 65(3) TFEU provides that the measures permitted by Article 65(1)(a) TFEU must not constitute a means of arbitrary discrimination or a disguised restriction on the free movement of capital and payments.

[205] Declaration on payments and capital movements between Member States, OJ 1992 C191/99.

[206] Article 65(2) TFEU states that the provisions concerning free movement of capital and payments shall be without prejudice to the applicability of restrictions on the right of establishment which are compatible with the Treaty.

[207] Case C-204/90, *Bachmann v Belgium* [1992] ECR I-249, para 27; Case C-300/90, *Commission v Belgium* [1992] ECR I-305, para 20; cf. Case C-80/94, *Wielockx v Inspecteur der Directe Belastingen* [1995] ECR I-2493, para 22.   See also, Case C-336/96, *Gilly v Directeur des Services Fiscaux du Bas-Rhin* [1998] I-2793; Case C-391/97, *Gschwind v FZA Aachen-Aussenstadt* [1999] ECR I-5451.

[208] See Case C-156/98, *Germany v Commission* [2000] ECR I-6857, para 28.

[209] Case C-35/98, *Staatssecretaris van Financiën v Verkooijen* [2000] ECR I-4071, para 36.

TFEU precludes restrictions on the basis of where capital is invested, it could be argued that where tax relief is granted for any type of investment within the territory of the State, relief must equally be granted in relation to an equivalent investment made in the territory of any other Member State. This would, however, negate the advantages in granting tax based regional development incentives. By analogy with the approach adopted by the ECJ in relation to the free movement of goods, it might be preferable not to apply Article 63 TFEU where this would alter the scope of Article 107 TFEU and interfere in the system established for keeping aid schemes under review.[210]

Restrictive agreements and abuse of dominance: Articles 101-102 TFEU
Article 3(1) TFEU grants the EU exclusive competence to establish competition rules necessary for the functioning of the internal market. Pursuant to this principle, Article 101(1) TFEU prohibits as incompatible with the internal market all agreements between undertakings, decisions by associations of undertakings and concerted practices which may affect trade between Member States and which have as their object or effect the prevention, restriction or distortion of competition within the internal market. Article 102 TFEU prohibits as incompatible with the internal market any abuse by one or more undertakings of a dominant position within the internal market or in a substantial part of it in so far as that abuse may affect trade between Member States. Since these provisions concern the competition rules applicable to undertakings, they are distinct from Articles 107 and 108 TFEU and do not directly involve State aid. Thus, for example, the imposition of a levy by a public body in accordance with its statutory powers in order to finance the activities of domestic producers, in the absence of any allegation of the levy being set at an excessive level, does not fall within the scope of Article 102 TFEU as being a possible abuse of dominance.[211] However, aspects of aid which contravene the competition law rules may be so indissolubly linked to the object of the aid that it is impossible to evaluate them separately.[212] Where that is so, the effects of those aspects on the compatibility or incompatibility of the aid as a whole must be assessed under Article 108 TFEU, unless it is possible to separate from the system of aid those conditions or factors which entail restrictive effects which go beyond what is necessary for the aid is to attain the objectives permissible under the FEU Treaty.[213]

---

[210] Case 74/76, *Iannelli v Meroni* [1977] ECR 557, para 12.
[211] Case 2/73, *Geddo v Ente Nazionale Risi* [1973] ECR 865, para 9 and *per* Advocate General Trabucchi at p. 892.
[212] Case C-225/91, *Matra SA v Commission* [1993] ECR I-3203, para 41; Cases T-197/97 & T-198/97, *Weyl Beef Products BV v Commission* [2001] ECR II-303, para 76.
[213] Cases T-197/97 & T-198/97, *Weyl Beef Products BV v Commission* [2001] ECR II-303, paras 77-78.

Nevertheless, the obligation on the part of the Commission to ensure that the State aid provisions are applied consistently with other provisions of the FEU Treaty is all the more necessary where those other provisions also pursue the objective of undistorted competition in the internal market. When adopting a decision on the compatibility of aid with the internal market, the Commission must be aware of the risk of individual traders undermining competition[214] and the Commission must not authorise State aid without verifying that the recipient is not in a position which contravenes Articles 101 and 102 TFEU.[215] Equally, the grant of State aid may have to be taken into account in any assessment for the purposes of exempting a restrictive agreement from the application of Article 101(3) TFEU in so far as such aid makes it possible, by lowering the recipient's costs, to distort competition and has the effect of reinforcing the anticompetitive nature of the agreement.[216] However, the provisions under the FEU Treaty concerning restrictive agreements and abuses of dominant positions involve independent procedures governed by specific rules. Consequently, when taking a decision on the compatibility of aid, the Commission is not obliged to await the outcome of a parallel procedure commenced under Council Regulation (EC) No 1/2003 once it has reached the conclusion, based on an economic analysis of the situation and without any manifest error in the assessment of the facts, that the recipient of the aid is not in breach of Articles 101 and 102 TFEU.[217] As regards, Article 101 TFEU, if the Commission subsequently decides on full examination of the facts that an exemption is not warranted under Article 101(3) TFEU, the General Court thought that the result would be that any aid granted on the basis of the authorisation decision would have to be repaid.[218] That conclusion must, however, be questionable, since the aid cannot be regarded as unlawful where it has been authorised by the Commission. It would only be where the Member State has provided incorrect information which was a determining factor that the Commission has power to revoke a previous decision authorising aid and require repayment.[219]

Merger control: Council Regulation (EC) No 139/2004 Pursuant to Council Regulation (EC) No 139/2004 on the control of concentrations between undertakings, the Commission has to appraise proposed mergers with a view to

---

[214] Case C-225/91, *Matra SA v Commission* [1993] ECR I-3203, paras 42-43; Case T-156/98, *RJB Mining plc v Commission* [2001] ECR II-337, paras 112-113; Cases T-197/97 & T-198/97, *Weyl Beef Products BV v Commission* [2001] ECR II-303, para 75.

[215] Case C-164/98 P, *DIP International Film srl v Commission* [2000] ECR I-447, para 29; Case T-49/93, *SIDE v Commission* [1995] ECR II-2501, para 75.

[216] Case T-17/93, *Matra Hachette SA v Commission* [1994] ECR II-595, para 48.

[217] Case C-225/91, *Matra SA v Commission* [1993] ECR I-3203, paras 44-45.

[218] Case T-17/93, *Matra Hachette SA v Commission* [1994] ECR II-595, para 47.

[219] Council Regulation (EC) No 659/1999, Articles 9, 11(1) and 14.

establishing whether or not they are compatible with the internal market. In making this appraisal, the Commission has to take account of the need to maintain and develop effective competition within the internal market and the market position of the undertakings concerned and their economic and financial power.[220] In *RJB Mining plc v Commission*, the General Court held that, in adopting a decision on the compatibility of a concentration with the internal market, the Commission could not ignore the consequences which the grant of State aid to the undertakings concerned would have on the maintenance of effective competition in the relevant market. This did not mean that the Commission, in adopting a decision on the merger in accordance with the applicable procedure, must necessarily await the outcome of the investigation into the compatibility of the State aid with the internal market.[221] However, where it was apparent that the Commission had not taken certain aid into consideration at all before authorising the merger, it could not be said to have assessed the financial and commercial strength of the recipient in the context of the merger.[222]

Approximation of laws: Articles 113-115 TFEU General measures, in particular generally applicable fiscal and social measures, do not normally result in the grant of State aid within the meaning of Article 107(1) TFEU. Such measures are, therefore, not subject to control by the Commission in accordance with Article 108 TFEU, but instead may be dealt with in the context of harmonisation or approximation of national legislative or administrative provisions in order to eliminate distortions of competition as between Member States.[223] In addition to specific legislative bases in the Treaty for the adoption of EU measures, such as Article 113 TFEU relating to harmonisation of indirect taxation, the Council has a general power under Article 114 TFEU to issue directives for the approximation of laws, regulations and administrative provisions of the Member States as directly affect the establishment and functioning of the internal market.[224] Whilst, in relation to

---

[220] Council Regulation (EC) No 139/2004, Article 2(1). Similarly, for mergers within the scope of the ECSC Treaty, Article 66(2) CS provided for the Commission to authorise a merger if it found that this would not give the relevant undertakings the power to hinder effective competition in a substantial part of the market or to evade the rules on competition in the ECSC Treaty. The examination procedures under the Merger Regulation cannot, however, be equated with those under Article 108 TFEU: Case T-158/00, *ARD v Commission* [2003] ECR II-3825, para 365.

[221] Case T-156/98, *RJB Mining plc v Commission* [2001] ECR II-337, paras 114-115.

[222] *Ibid.*, para 125.

[223] Case T-151/11, *Telefónica de España SA v Commission* EU:T:2014:631, para 98. See also, *Seventeenth Report on Competition Policy* (1987), pt. 172; Cases C-72-73/91, *Sloman Neptun Schiffarts AG v Seebetriebsrat Bodo Ziesemer* [1993] ECR I-887, *per* Advocate General Darmon, at p. 917.

[224] Article 115 TFEU.

most matters affecting the establishment of the internal market, the Council may act on a qualified majority,[225] fiscal provisions and laws not concerned with the establishment of the internal market may only be harmonised by the Council acting unanimously.[226]   It should be noted that whereas the compatibility with the internal market of a measure which constitutes State aid under Article 107(1) TFEU is solely for the Commission to determine, if a measure is subject only to harmonisation pursuant to Articles 113-115 TFEU, it is the Council, albeit acting on a proposal from the Commission, which has the power to issue the necessary directives.   Moreover, the discretion given to the Council as to whether or not to exercise its legislative power must necessarily be much wider than that of the Commission under Articles 107-108 TFEU.   In *Deutsche Bahn v Commission*, a complaint was made that the exemption granted by Council Directive 92/81/EEC in respect of excise duty on aviation fuel distorted competition between high-speed rail services and low-cost airlines.   The General Court held that, even if this distortion of competition was the result of a new competitive relationship since the adoption of the Directive, it was for the EU's legislature to evaluate the situation and decide on any amendments to the provisions currently in force.[227]   In *Commission v Ireland*, which also concerned an exemption granted by that directive, the General Court's finding that the concept of distortion of competition was the same in regard to harmonisation of fiscal and the State aid rules was overturned on appeal by the ECJ.   Council decisions on the basis of that directive authorising a Member State to introduce an exemption from excise duty could not have the effect of preventing the Commission from exercising its powers under Article 108 TFEU.[228]

Where the Council has adopted harmonising legislation pursuant to Articles 113-115 TFEU, it may not be possible for it to rely on Article 108(2) TFEU to authorise aid which entails a derogation from the provisions of that legislation. For example, in the case of VAT, the Council must adopt a directive or a decision pursuant to its powers under the Sixth Directive 77/388/EEC if it wishes to authorise aid which entails a derogation from the rates of VAT which are to be charged.[229]   When such derogations are implemented, the competition provisions must still be respected.

---

[225] Article 114 TFEU.

[226] Articles 114(2) and 115 TFEU.

[227] Case T-351/02, *Deutsche Bahn AG v Commission* [2006] ECR II-1047, para 112.

[228] Case C-212/12P, *Commission v Ireland* EU:C:2013:812, paras 45-54; Cases T-50/06 RENV, T-56/06 RENV, T-60/06 RENV, T-62/06 RENV & T-69/06 RENV, *Ireland v Commission* EU:T:2012:134, paras 63-72.

[229] Case 253/84, *GAEC v Council and Commission* [1987] ECR 123, *per* Advocate General Slynn, at p. 146; Case C-438/92, *Rustica Semences SA v Finanzamt Kehl* [1994] ECR I-3519, *per* Advocate General Jacobs, at p. 3527.

Chapter Six

SERVICES OF GENERAL ECONOMIC INTEREST

6.1 PAYMENT FOR SERVICES
OF GENERAL ECONOMIC INTEREST

Early cases on payment for public services Article 14 TFEU requires the European Union, without prejudice *inter alia* to the State aid provisions in the FEU Treaty, to use its powers in such a way as to make sure that services of general economic interest operate on the basis of principles and conditions which enable them to fulfil their missions. Given, however, that services in the general interest are financed out of State resources, there is a constant tension between the need to determine the correct payment for such services and the application of the State aid rules. In early decisions of the European Court of Justice and the Commission where a public authority made a payment to an undertaking which was required to perform a service in the public interest, the primary concern, in order to avoid any distortion of competition, was to ensure that the payment did not over-compensate the service provider. In *Procureur de la République v ADBHU*, which concerned indemnities granted to certain undertakings for services performed in collecting and disposing of waste oils, the ECJ held that the indemnities did not constitute State aid but rather were consideration for services rendered.[1] Advocate General Lenz took the view that as long as the amounts paid out did not exceed actual costs plus a reasonable profit they could be regarded as a *quid pro quo* for the obligations imposed on the undertakings in the public interest.[2] Where this condition was not complied with, the Commission concluded that State aid was involved. For example, the method adopted by the Portuguese authorities to compensate for the losses incurred by TAP in fulfilling public service obligations on the airline routes to Madeira and the Azores gave rise to State aid concerns.[3]

Thus, the Commission's practice was to regard payment to undertakings which fulfilled public service obligations as not entailing State aid as long as the financing merely offset the identifiable additional costs incurred. This

---

[1] Case 240/83, *Procureur de la République v ADBHU* [1985] ECR 531, para 18; Case C-280/00, *Altmark Trans GmbH v Nahverkehrsgesellschaft Altmark GmbH* [2003] ECR I-7747, para 85.

[2] Case 240/83, *Procureur de la République v ADBHU* [1985] ECR 531, *per* Advocate General Lenz, at p. 536.

[3] Commission Decision 94/666/EC, *TAP*, OJ 1994 L260/27.

approach appeared to find favour with Advocate General Fennelly in *France v Commission* where he argued that, depending on the precise circumstances in which the public authorities paid for benefits at market prices, it was possible to argue that there was no aid element at all.[4] Particularly where the contract at issue for the performance of the public service obligation in question had been the subject of a public tender in accordance with any applicable public procurement rules, the Commission was content to accept that a proper price would be paid by the public authority so as to rebut any presumption of aid being granted.[5]

State aid approach to payment for SGEIs   On this compensation-based approach for the payment of SGEIs, the system of State financing for the Portuguese public television channels operated by RTP was initially held by the Commission not to constitute State aid. The public television channels had to meet obligations imposed by the public authorities, which the private channels were not required to perform, to include coverage of the entire national territory and of the autonomous regions of Madeira and the Azores, to keep audiovisual archives, to cooperate with countries whose official language is Portuguese, to make available broadcasting time for religious programmes, and to provide an international channel. The Commission decided, having regard to the system of analytical accounting established by the Portuguese authorities, that the State financing merely offset the additional costs associated with the public obligations.[6]

However, in *FFSA v Commission*, a tax exemption granted to La Poste, which was applicable to its total profits, regardless of whether its income derived from commercial services or from services entailing a public obligation, was classified by the Commission as State aid, although since the value to La Poste of the overall exemption was less than the total cost of complying with the public service obligations, the aid was permitted pursuant to Article 106(2) TFEU as being necessary for the performance of the tasks entrusted to La Poste. This approach was upheld by the General Court.[7] Following this, in *SIC v Commission*, the General Court annulled the Commission decision concerning Portuguese television, holding that the payments had indeed by their nature granted a financial advantage to RTP and that the fact that the grants were merely intended to offset the additional costs of the public service tasks could not prevent them from being classified as

4   Case C-251/97, *France v Commission* [1999] ECR I-6639, *per* Advocate General Fennelly at p. 6648.
5   Cases T-116/01 & T-118/01, *P&O European Ferries (Vizcaya) SA v Commission* [2003] ECR II-2957, para 118; Guidelines on State aid to maritime transport, para 9.
6   *Twenty-Sixth Report on Competition Policy* (1996), p. 242.
7   Case T-106/95, *FFSA v Commission* [1997] ECR II-229, para 178; upheld on appeal at Case C-174/97P, *FFSA v Commission* [1998] ECR I-1303.

State aid.[8] The Commission, in its subsequent communication[9] on services of general economic interest relied on these judgments as authority for the proposition that compensation granted by a State to an undertaking for the performance of general interest obligations constituted State aid within the meaning of Article 107(1) TFEU.[10]

***Ferring* and a return to the compensation approach** When the issue was next considered by the ECJ, rather than adopt the General Court's State aid based approach, it appeared to reflect the previous compensation-based analysis. In *Ferring v ACOSS*, a tax was imposed on direct sales of pharmaceutical products by pharmaceutical laboratories, whereas wholesalers were not subject to the tax as compensation for the fact that they were required, pursuant to a public service obligation, to carry sufficient stocks so as to be able constantly to supply the needs of the local population. The ECJ held that, provided that the tax on direct sales imposed on the laboratories corresponded to the additional costs actually incurred by the wholesalers in discharging their public service obligation, the exemption of the distributors from the scope of the tax was to be regarded as compensation for the services provided and hence not State aid.[11]

On the basis of the principle recognised in *Ferring v ACOSS*, it would be possible to establish that State aid is not involved where separate accounts are properly kept by undertakings in respect of their operation of services of general economic interest. Moreover, in July 2000, an amendment was introduced into Commission Directive 80/723/EEC on the transparency of financial relations between Member States and public undertakings requiring undertakings operating services of general economic interest and carrying on ordinary commercial activities to keep separate accounts for those different activities.[12] Similarly, where a contract for the provision of such services is awarded following an open public tender procedure, it should be clear that the remuneration awarded is intended as a *quid pro quo* for the provision of the services without any element of aid.[13] By contrast, where it was not clear from

---

[8] Case T-46/97, *SIC v Commission* [2000] ECR II-2125, para 82. See also the Commission's communication on the application of State aid rules to public service broadcasting, OJ 2001 C320/5.

[9] OJ 2001 C17/4. See also the Commission's Report to the European Council on services of general interest, COM (2001) 598 final.

[10] Communication on services of general interest in Europe, para 26.

[11] Case C-53/00, *Ferring SA v ACOSS* [2001] ECR I-9067, para 27; Case C-280/00, *Altmark Trans GmbH v Nahverkehrsgesellschaft Altmark GmbH* [2003] ECR I-7747, para 86.

[12] Commission Directive 2000/52/EC. See now, Commission Directive 2006/111/EC, OJ 2006 L318/17.

[13] Case C-126/01, *Ministre de l'économie, des finances et de l'industrie v GEMO SA*, [2003] ECR 13769, *per* Advocate General Jacobs, at para 119.

the outset that the State funding satisfies this criterion, Advocate General Jacobs, in *GEMO*, thought that the measure in question could be classified as State aid and require justification pursuant to Article 106(2) TFEU. An example of this latter approach was a Spanish law exempting public banks from the payment of corporate taxes, where it was unclear precisely how the exemption related to any specific general interest obligation.[14]

***Altmark* criteria for establishing State aid**   The *Ferring* judgment was perceived as being unsatisfactory on the ground that it left rather too much uncertainty as to when State aid may or may not be involved. Accordingly, when the issue came before the ECJ again, in the *Altmark Trans* case, a certain reappraisal was called for. Advocate General Léger, considering that Article 106(2) TFEU would be deprived of any substantial effect, felt that a return was needed to the State aid-based approach, whereby the presumption was that State aid was inherent in the payment by the public authorities for public services.[15]   However, the ECJ held that where a State measure must be regarded as compensation for the services provided by the recipient undertakings in order to discharge public service obligations, so that those undertakings do not enjoy a real financial advantage and the measure thus does not have the effect of putting them in a more favourable competitive position than the undertakings competing with them, such a measure is not caught by Article 107(1) TFEU.[16]   In an attempt to satisfy both the State aid and the compensation approaches to Article 106(2), the ECJ set out a number of conditions that must be satisfied for a measure establishing compensation for fulfilling services imposed in the general economic interest not to be regarded as entailing State aid.[17]

---

[14]   *Ibid.*, para 120.   This example was drawn from Case C-387/92, *Banco Exterior de España v Ayuntamiento de Valencia* [1994] ECR I-877.   See also, Cases C-34/01 to C-38/01, *Enirisorse SpA v Ministero delle Finanze* [2003] ECR I-14243, *per* Advocate General Stix-Hackl, at paras 153-160.

[15]   Case C-280/00, *Altmark Trans GmbH v Nahverkehrsgesellschaft Altmark GmbH* [2003] ECR I-7747, *per* Advocate General Léger, first opinion, at paras 73-98, second opinion, at paras 28-52.

[16]   Case C-280/00, *Altmark Trans GmbH v Nahverkehrsgesellschaft Altmark GmbH* [2003] ECR I-7747, para 87; Cases C-34/01 to C-38/01, *Enirisorse SpA v Ministero delle Finanze* [2003] ECR I-14243, para 31; Case C-140/09, *Fallimento Traghetti del Mediterraneo SpA v Presidenza del Consiglio dei Ministri* [2010] ECR I-5243, para 35; Case C-399/08P, *Commission v Deutsche Post AG* [2010] ECR I-7831, para 41; Case T-266/02, *Deutsche Post AG v Commission* [2008] ECR II-1233, para 72; Case T-354/05, *TF1 v Commission* [2009] ECR II-471, para 127.

[17]   Case C-280/00, *Altmark Trans GmbH v Nahverkehrsgesellschaft Altmark GmbH* [2003] ECR I-7747, para 88; Cases C-34/01 to C-38/01, *Enirisorse SpA v Ministero delle Finanze* [2003] ECR I-14243, para 31; Case C-451/03, *Servizi Ausiliari Dottori Commercialisti Srl v Calafioi* [2006] ECR I-2941, para 61; Case C-399/08P,

First, the recipient undertaking must actually have public service obligations to discharge, and the obligations must be clearly defined. Second, the parameters on the basis of which the compensation is calculated must be established in advance in an objective and transparent manner, to avoid it conferring an economic advantage which may favour the recipient undertaking over competing undertakings. Third, the compensation cannot exceed what is necessary to cover all or part of the costs incurred in the discharge of public service obligations, taking into account the relevant receipts and a reasonable profit for discharging those obligations. Fourth, where the undertaking which is to discharge public service obligations, in a specific case, is not chosen pursuant to a public procurement procedure, the level of compensation needed must be determined on the basis of an analysis of the costs which a typical undertaking, well run and adequately equipped so as to be able to meet the necessary public service requirements, would have incurred in discharging those obligations, taking into account the relevant receipts and a reasonable profit for discharging the obligations.[18] Where these conditions are fulfilled, the compensation does not constitute State aid and does not have to be notified to the Commission. Conversely, a State measure which does not comply with one or more of those conditions must be regarded as State aid within the meaning of that provision.[19]

The Commission has adopted a communication on the application of the State aid rules to compensation granted for the provision of services of general economic interest in line with the principles established by the EU courts' case law.[20] The principles in *Altmark* apply equally to factual and legal situations arising before the judgment was delivered.[21] It is quite possible, however, that prior decisions of the Member States to grant compensation for public service obligations, and Commission decisions in relation to such payments, do not

---

Commission v Deutsche Post AG [2010] ECR I-7831, para 42; Case T-157/01, *Danske Busvognmaend v Commission* [2004] ECR II-197, para 98.

[18] Case C-280/00, *Altmark Trans GmbH v Nahverkehrsgesellschaft Altmark GmbH* [2003] ECR I-7747, paras 89-93; Case C-140/09, *Fallimento Traghetti del Mediterraneo SpA v Presidenza del Consiglio dei Ministri* [2010] ECR I-5243, para 36; Case C-690/13, *Trapeza Eurobank Ergasias v ATE* EU:C:2015:235, para 32; Case T-266/02, *Deutsche Post AG v Commission* [2008] ECR II-1233, para 73; Cases T-309/04, T-317/04, T-329/04 & T-336/04, *TV2/Danmark A/S v Commission* [2008] ECR II-2935, para 189; Case T-79/10, *Colt Télécommunications France v Commission* EU:T:2013:463, para 88; Case T-258/10, *Orange v Commission* EU:T:2013:471, para 107; Case T-325/10, *Iliad v Commission* EU:T:2013:472, para 113; Case T-275/11, *TFI v Commission* EU:T:2013:535, para 127.

[19] Case C-280/00, *Altmark Trans GmbH v Nahverkehrsgesellschaft Altmark GmbH* [2003] ECR I-7747, para 94; Commission Decision 2005/842/EC, recital 5.

[20] OJ 2012 C8/4.

[21] Case T-289/03, *BUPA Ltd v Commission* [2008] ECR II-81, para 158; Case T-189/03, *ASM Brescia SpA v Commission* [2009] ECR II-1831, para 125; Case T-222/04, *Italy v Commission* [2009] ECR II-1877, para 110.

comply precisely within the criteria established by the ECJ.[22] Nevertheless, the General Court, while holding that those principles are fully applicable in such cases, has also stated that it is appropriate to apply the *Altmark* criteria, in accordance with the spirit and the purpose which prevailed when they were laid down, in a manner adapted to the particular facts of the case rather than to make a literal application of those criteria.[23]

Public service obligations must be clearly defined The first of the *Altmark* criteria is that the recipient undertaking must actually have public service obligations to discharge, and the obligations must be clearly defined.[24] This concept of public service obligation corresponds to that of a service of general economic interest in Article 106(2) TFEU.[25] Thus, the service in question must actually be a service of general economic interest, as opposed to a service provided to the public.[26] Services of general economic interest must also be distinguished from regulated services. The mere fact that the Member State, acting in the general interest in the broad sense, imposes certain rules of authorisation, functioning or control on all the operators in a particular sector does not in principle mean that there is a service of general economic interest.[27]

In EU law and for the purposes of applying the State aid rules, there is no clear and precise regulatory definition of the concept of an SGEI mission and no established legal concept definitively fixing the conditions that must be

---

[22] Case T-93/02, *Confédération Nationale du Crédit Mutuel v Commission* [2005] ECR II-143, para 120.

[23] Case T-289/03, *BUPA Ltd v Commission* [2008] ECR II-81, paras 159-160; Cases T-254/00, T-270/00 & T-277/00, *Hotel Cipriani SpA v Commission* [2008] ECR II-3269, para 218; Case T-388/03, *Deutsche Post AG v Commission* [2009] ECR II-199, para 112; Case T-222/04. *Italy v Commission* [2009] ECR II-1887, para 110; Case T-347/09, *Germany v Commission* EU:T:2103:418, para 81.

[24] Case C-280/00, *Altmark Trans GmbH v Nahverkehrsgesellschaft Altmark GmbH* [2003] ECR I-7747, para 89; Cases C-34/01 to C-38/01, *Enirisorse SpA v Ministero delle Finanze* [2003] ECR I-14243, para 32; Case C-451/03, *Servizi Ausiliari Dottori Commercialisti Srl v Calafiori* [2006] ECR I-2941, para 62; Case C-140/09, *Fallimento Traghetti del Mediterraneo SpA v Presidenza del Consiglio dei Ministri* [2010] ECR I-5243, para 37; Cases C-197/11 & C-203/11, *Libert v Flemish Government* EU:C:2013:288, para 87; Case T-289/03, *BUPA Ltd v Commission* [2008] ECR II-81, para 161; Case T-189/03, *ASM Brescia SpA v Commission* [2009] ECR II-1831, para 126; Case T-222/04. *Italy v Commission* [2009] ECR II-1887, para 111; Cases T-80/06 & T-182/09, *Budapesti Erőmű Zrt v Commission* EU:T:2012:65, para 90; Case T-325/10, *Iliad v Commission* EU:T:2013:472, para 192; Case T-295/12, *Germany v Commission* EU:T:2014:675, para 70; Case T-309/12, *Zweckverband Tierkörper-beseitigung v Commission EU*:T:2104:676, para 130.

[25] Case T-289/03, *BUPA Ltd v Commission* [2008] ECR II-81, para 162; Case T-295/12, *Germany v Commission* EU:T:2014:675, para 72..

[26] Cases T-116/01 & T-118/01, *P&O European Ferries (Vizcaya) SA v Commission* [2003] ECR II-2957, para 136.

[27] Case T-289/03, *BUPA Ltd v Commission* [2008] ECR II-81, para 178.

satisfied before a Member State can properly invoke the existence and protection of an SGEI mission, either within the meaning of the first *Altmark* condition or within the meaning of Article 106(2) TFEU.[28] Protocol No 26 attached to the EU Treaties recognises the wide discretion of Member States in identifying services of general economic interest depending on their geographical, social and cultural situations.[29] In defining services of general economic interest, Member States have a wide discretion which can be queried only in the case of manifest error.[30] Moreover, the Commission's guidelines on services of general economic interest, not having the character of EU legislation, cannot restrict the right of Member States to denote services as being of general economic interest.[31] In *Altmark*, the ECJ held that it was for the national court to examine whether the public service obligations in question were clear from the national legislation or the licences at issue in the national court proceedings.[32]

Nevertheless, the Member States' competence in this regard is not unlimited and may not be exercised in an arbitrary manner.[33] In *BUPA v Commission*, the General Court confirmed that there were certain minimum criteria common to every mission establishing a service of general economic interest. These are the presence of an act of public authority entrusting the operators in question with such a mission and the universal and compulsory nature of that mission. Furthermore, the Member State must indicate the reasons why it considers that the service on question, because of its specific nature, deserves to be characterised as a service of general economic interest and to be distinguished from other economic activities.[34] In *Fallimento Traghetti del Mediterraneo SpA v Presidenza del Consiglio dei Ministri*, the ECJ accepted that agreements for the provision of maritime services between

---

[28] Case T-289/03, *BUPA Ltd v Commission* [2008] ECR II-81, para 165; Case T-325/10, *Iliad v Commission* EU:T:2013:472, para 119.

[29] Case T-57/11, *Castelnou Energía v Commission* EU:T:2014:1021, para 132.

[30] Case T-106/95, *FFSA v Commission* [1997] ECR II-229, para 99; Case T-17/02, *Fred Olsen SA v Commission* [2005] ECR II-2031, para 216; Case T-289/03, *BUPA Ltd v Commission* [2008] ECR II-81, para 166; Case T-442/03, *SIC v Commission* [2008] ECR II-1161, para 195; Cases T-309/04, T-317/04, T-329/04 & T-336/04, *TV2/Danmark A/S v Commission* [2008] ECR II-2935, para 101; Cases T-231/06 & T-237/06, *Netherlands v Commission* [2010] ECR II-5993, para 223; Case T-137/10, *CBI v Commission* EU:T:2102:584, para 99; Case T-325/10, *Iliad v Commission* EU:T:2013:472, para 119; Case T-295/12, *Germany v Commission* EU:T:2014:675, para 44.

[31] Case T-295/12, *Germany v Commission* EU:T:2014:675, para 50.

[32] Case C-280/00, *Altmark Trans GmbH v Nahverkehrsgesellschaft Altmark GmbH* [2003] ECR I-7747, para 89.

[33] Case T-565/08, *Corsica Ferries France sas v Commission* EU:T:2012:415, para 56; Case T-295/12, *Germany v Commission* EU:T:2014:675, para 46; Case T-57/11, *Castelnou Energía v Commission* EU:T:2014:1021, para 133.

[34] Case T-289/03, *BUPA Ltd v Commission* [2008] ECR II-81, para 172.

the Italian islands, which had to satisfy requirements relating to the economic and social developments of the regions concerned, specifying the routes to be served, the frequency of those services and the types of vessels allocated to each route, established public service obligations that were to be discharged.[35] Similarly, maritime services to Corsica were deemed to satisfy the requirements of meeting a real need for public service.[36] In *Servizi Ausiliari Dottori Commercialisti Srl v Calafiori*, the ECJ held that a Member State could, conceivably, characterise as a public service the tax assistance services intended to help taxpayers to fulfil their tax obligations and to facilitate the accomplishment of the tasks for which the tax authorities were responsible.[37] However, in *Enirisorse v Ministero delle Finanze*, it did not appear, from the documents before the ECJ, that Italian port operators who provided services of loading and unloading goods had been entrusted with public service obligations, and still less that such duties had been clearly defined.[38] In *Germany v Commission*, the General Court upheld the Commission's decision finding that the public authorities had manifestly erred in classifying certain provisions dealing with the disposal of animal carcasses as services of general economic interest in light of the polluter pays principle.[39]

Entrusted by act of public authority Services of general economic interest must be entrusted by an act of public authority.[40] This may be by means of legislative, regulatory or administrative action, and may be accepted by the operator concerned entering into contractual relations with the authority. The mandate conferring the public service mission may be defined by more than one act, possibly involving a general sectoral regulation in combination with individual acts addressed to specific establishments.[41] In *BUPA v Commission*, Irish legislation was characterised by the General Court as creating and defining a specific mission consisting in the provision of private medical insurance services in compliance with certain obligations which restricted the commercial freedom of the insurers to an extent going considerably beyond ordinary conditions of authorisation to exercise an activity in a specific

---

[35] Case C-140/09, *Fallimento Traghetti del Mediterraneo SpA v Presidenza del Consiglio dei Ministri* [2010] ECR I-5243, para 41.

[36] Case T-565/08, *Corsica Ferries France sas v Commission* EU:T:2012:415, para 59.

[37] Case C-451/03, *Servizi Ausiliari Dottori Commercialisti Srl v Calafiori* [2006] ECR I-2941, para 63.

[38] Cases C-34/01 to C-38/01, *Enirisorse SpA v Ministero delle Finanze* [2003] ECR I-14243, para 34.

[39] Case T-295/12, *Germany v Commission* EU:T:2014:675, paras 54-65.

[40] Case C-320/05P, *Fred Olsen SA v Commission* [2007] ECR II-131*, para 135; Case T-17/02, *Fred Olsen SA v Commission* [2005] ECR II-2031, para 186; Case T-289/03, *BUPA Ltd v Commission* [2008] ECR II-81, para 181.

[41] Case T-137/10, *CBI v Commission* EU:T:2012:584, para 108.

sector.[42] By contrast, in *Danske Busvognmaend v Commission*, the General Court, in rejecting the contention that Combus had been entrusted with public service obligations, held that contractual obligations to operate bus services, carry passengers and collect tariffs had not been imposed unilaterally.[43]

The entrustment of a service of general economic interest to an operator does not necessarily require the grant of an exclusive or special right to carry it out, although that may be the chosen instrument where necessary. Thus, in *BUPA v Commission*, the General Court rejected an argument that the existence of a mission entrusting a service of general economic interest was precluded because all private medical insurers were in principle subject to certain obligations.[44] In *Valmont Nederland v Commission*, where a public authority substantially contributed to the costs of constructing a privately owned car park which was then also made available for use by other undertakings under an agreement in the public interest concluded with the public authority, the Commission's decision declaring the car park semi-public and thereby concluding that State aid had been provided by the public authority in respect of 50% of the public financing was annulled on the ground that it failed to assess properly the extent to which that financing could be regarded as compensation to the owner of the car park in respect of a public service obligation to allow others to use the car park free of charge.[45]

Universal and compulsory nature of the services   The universal and compulsory nature of a service of general economic interest does not require that the service be universal in the strict sense, such as the public social security system. It does not mean that the service in question must respond to a need common to the whole population or be supplied throughout a territory.[46] Rather, it is sufficient that the operator entrusted with a particular mission is under an obligation to provide that service to any user requesting it. In other words, the compulsory nature of the service is established if the service provider is obliged to contract, on consistent conditions, without being able to reject the other contracting party. That element makes it possible to distinguish a service of general economic interest from any other service provided on the market and, accordingly, from any other activity carried out in complete freedom. Accordingly, the fact that the obligations in question have only a limited territorial or material application or that the services concerned are enjoyed by only a relatively limited group of users does not necessarily call in

---

[42]   Case T-289/03, *BUPA Ltd v Commission* [2008] ECR II-81, para 182.
[43]   Case T-157/01, *Danske Busvognmaend v Commission* [2004] ECR II-197, paras 80 and 98.
[44]   Case T-289/03, *BUPA Ltd v Commission* [2008] ECR II-81, paras 179-180.
[45]   Case T-274/01, *Valmont Nederland BV v Commission* [2004] ECR II-3145, para 133.
[46]   Case T-289/03, *BUPA Ltd v Commission* [2008] ECR II-81, para 186.

question the universal nature of the mission.[47] Thus, in *BUPA v Commission*, the open enrolment obligation entailing the obligation for every private medical insurer to offer an insurance contract to every person who requested it, independently of age, sex or health, was sufficient for the compulsory nature of the services in question to be recognised by the General Court. That compulsory nature was reinforced by the fact that the obligation to contract was associated with other constraints that restricted the commercial freedom of the insurers to determine the terms of contracts, namely the community rating, lifetime cover and minimum benefit obligations.[48]

The universality criterion does not require that the service in question be free of charge or that it be offered without consideration of economic profitability. The fact that certain potential users do not have the necessary financial resources to take advantage of the service does not undermine its universal nature provided that the service in question is offered at uniform and non-discriminatory rates and on similar quality conditions for all.[49]

Objective and transparent parameters for compensation   The second *Altmark* criterion is that the parameters on the basis of which the compensation is calculated must be established in advance in an objective and transparent manner, to avoid it conferring an economic advantage which may favour the recipient undertaking over competing undertakings.[50] Member States are free to determine how to comply with this criterion, having a broad discretion in determining the complex economic assessment of the requisite compensation.[51] Payment by a Member State of compensation for the loss incurred by an undertaking without the parameters of such compensation having been established beforehand, where it turns out after the event that the operation of certain services in connection with the discharge of public service obligations was not economically viable, therefore constitutes a financial measure which

---

[47]   *Ibid.*, para 190.
[48]   *Ibid.*, para 192.
[49]   *Ibid.*, para 203.
[50]   Case C-280/00, *Altmark Trans GmbH v Nahverkehrsgesellschaft Altmark GmbH* [2003] ECR I-7747, para 90; Cases C-34/01 to C-38/01, *Enirisorse SpA v Ministero delle Finanze* [2003] ECR I-14243, para 35; Case C-451/03, *Servizi Ausiliari Dottori Commercialisti Srl v Calafiori* [2006] ECR I-2941, para 64; Case C-140/09, *Fallimento Traghetti del Mediterraneo SpA v Presidenza del Consiglio dei Ministri* [2010] ECR I-5243, para 38; Case T-289/03, *BUPA Ltd v Commission* [2008] ECR II-81, para 209; Case T-325/10, *Iliad v Commission* EU:T:2013:472, para 205; Case T-295/12, *Germany v Commission* EU:T:2014:675, para 84; Case T-309/12, *Zweckverband Tierkörper-beseitigung v Commission* EU:T:2104:676, para 145.
[51]   Cases T-309/04, T-317/04, T-329/04 & T-336/04, *TV2/Danmark A/S v Commission* [2008] ECR II-2935, para 227; Case T-295/12, *Germany v Commission* EU:T:2014:675, para 87.

falls within the concept of State aid.[52]   In *BUPA v Commission*, the General
Court confirmed that the requirement of objective and transparent parameters
does not prevent the national legislature from leaving to the national authorities
a certain discretion to determine the compensation for the costs incurred in
discharging the obligations to provide the service.[53]   However, in *Enirisorse v
Ministero delle Finanze*, this criterion was not satisfied.   Italy argued that the
allocation of a major part of the port charges to the port operators, together
with the rates charged by the latter, was essential in order to maintain those
rates at a level which the traders could bear and that such allocation made it
possible for the ports concerned to continue to operate.   The ECJ held,
however, this did not show what exactly the supposed public service consisted
of, or whether it concerned only loading and unloading in the ports in question,
or whether services such as docking safety were also covered.[54]   In *Libert v
Flemish Government*, the ECJ held that subsidies for property developers
linked to the provision of social housing were not such as to identify the
parameters on the basis of which the compensation was calculated.[55]

Compensation necessary to discharge the obligation   In *Ferring v ACOSS*,
the ECJ held that if it were the case that the advantage for wholesale
distributors in not being assessed to the tax on direct sales of medicines
exceeded the additional costs that they bore in discharging the public service
obligations imposed on them, that advantage, to the extent that it exceeded the
additional costs mentioned, could not, in any event, be regarded as necessary to
enable them to carry out the particular tasks assigned to them.[56]   Thus, the third
Altmark criterion is that the compensation cannot exceed what is necessary to
cover all or part of the costs incurred in the discharge of public service
obligations, taking into account the relevant receipts and a reasonable profit for
discharging those obligations.   Compliance with such a condition is essential to
ensure that the recipient undertaking is not given any advantage which distorts
or threatens to distort competition by strengthening that undertaking's
competitive position.[57]

---

[52]   Case C-280/00, *Altmark Trans GmbH v Nahverkehrsgesellschaft Altmark GmbH* [2003]
ECR I-7747, para 91.

[53]   Case T-289/03, *BUPA Ltd v Commission* [2008] ECR II-81, para 214.

[54]   Cases C-34/01 to C-38/01, *Enirisorse SpA v Ministero delle Finanze* [2003] ECR I-
14243, para 37.

[55]   Cases C-197/11 & C-203/11, *Libert v Flemish Government* EU:C:2013:288, para 90.

[56]   Case C-53/00, *Ferring SA v ACOSS* [2001] ECR I-9067, para 32.

[57]   Case C-280/00, *Altmark Trans GmbH v Nahverkehrsgesellschaft Altmark GmbH* [2003]
ECR I-7747, para 92; Cases C-34/01 to C-38/01, *Enirisorse SpA v Ministero delle
Finanze* [2003] ECR I-14243, para 39; Case C-451/03, *Servizi Ausiliari Dottori
Commercialisti Srl v Calafioi* [2006] ECR I-2941, para 66; Case C-140/09, *Fallimento
Traghetti del Mediterraneo SpA v Presidenza del Consiglio dei Ministri* [2010] ECR I-
5243, para 39; Case C-399/08P, *Commission v Deutsche Post AG* [2010] ECR I-7831,

Compensation must be proportionate to the costs of providing the service.[58] In *Enirisorse v Ministero delle Finanze*, the ECJ, although it had not been given details of the cost of the services or of the assessment of the compensation which it was claimed was necessary, held that it was clear that the amount of the proceeds of the port charges paid to the port operators did not reflect the costs actually incurred by them for the purposes of supplying their loading and unloading services, since that amount was linked to the volume of goods transported by all users and shipped to the ports in question so that the amount paid varied with the level of activity in the port concerned.[59] In *Deutsche Post v Commission*, the General Court annulled the Commission's decision that State aid had been granted to Deutsche Post, since the Commission had failed to examine whether the total amounts of resources transferred to Deutsche Post exceeded the total amount of the additional costs associated with the service of general economic interest.[60] In *Iliad v Commission*, concerning the financing of broadband network infrastructure, the applicant argued that infrastructure would also be used in commercially viable areas. However, the General Court held that, even though the compensation was to cover only the costs of deployment of the infrastructure in non-profitable areas, the receipts generated by the use of the infrastructure in commercial areas could be used for the financing of the service of general economic interest in the non-profitable areas.[61]

Proportionality of costs will be presumed where the selection has been effected on the basis of an adequate public procurement process. In *Iliad v Commission*, concerning a concession for the financing of broadband infrastructure in which only three candidates had submitted costs proposals, the General Court upheld the Commission's assessment that, in the circumstances, an adequate procurement process had been carried out permitting a substantial degree of effective competition between the three tenders.[62] In assessing the costs that are to be covered by the relevant compensation, difficulties may arise in relation to the appropriate assessment of economic data. Advocate General Jaaskinen noted in *Commission v Deutsche Post* that where the Member State concerned cannot provide precise information concerning, for example, the internal allocation of general costs or the appropriate rate of return on capital

---

para 43; Case T-325/10, *Iliad v Commission* EU:T:2013:472, para 220; Case T-295/12, *Germany v Commission* EU:T:2014:675, para 92; Case T-309/12, *Zweckverband Tierkörperbeseitigung v Commission* EU:T:2104:676, para 170.

[58] Case T-289/03, *BUPA Ltd v Commission* [2008] ECR II-81, para 224.

[59] Cases C-34/01 to C-38/01, *Enirisorse SpA v Ministero delle Finanze* [2003] ECR I-14243, para 38.

[60] Case C-399/08P, *Commission v Deutsche Post AG* [2010] ECR I-7831, para 46; Case T-266/02, *Deutsche Post AG v Commission* [2008] ECR II-1233, para 91-94.

[61] Case T-325/10, *Iliad v Commission* EU:T:2013:472, para 192; Case T-258/10, *Orange v Commission* EU:T:2013:471, para 202.

[62] Case T-325/10, *Iliad v Commission* EU:T:2013:472, paras 241-246.

investment where capital is allocated to various different activities, a presumption based on experience or common sense is permissible.[63] Transparency may be enhanced by *ex post* monitoring. For example, in the case of multi-annual budgetary public contributions made to France Télévisions, the Commission considered that the fact that the amount of the subsidy was subject to appropriate *ex post* controls followed by, if necessary, recovery of the excess, prevented any over-compensation.[64]

Compensation without public procurement procedure Contracts awarded in breach of the applicable public procurement rules may entail State aid even where reasonable payment is made for the services. In the *Transmed* decision, the Commission held that aid had been granted where a contract for a public service obligation had been awarded in breach of the tendering rules set out in the Commission's guidelines on aid for maritime transport. Although the Commission also found that the compensation for providing the service was no greater than the additional costs involved, it ordered that the contract had to be terminated and replaced by a new contract which would be advertised in accordance with the applicable rules.[65]

Operators may, however, in certain circumstances, be entrusted with services of general economic interest without being subjected to a public procurement procedure.[66] The fourth *Altmark* criterion is that, where the undertaking which is to discharge public service obligations, in a specific case, is not chosen pursuant to a public procurement procedure which would allow for the selection of the tenderer capable of providing those services at the least cost to the community, the level of compensation needed must be determined on the basis of an analysis of the costs which a typical undertaking, well run and adequately provided with assets so as to be able to meet the necessary public service requirements, would have incurred in discharging those obligations, taking into account the relevant receipts and a reasonable profit for discharging the obligations.[67] It follows that it is no longer sufficient merely to

---

[63] Case C-399/08P, *Commission v Deutsche Post AG* [2010] ECR I-7831, per AG Jaaskinen, para 70.

[64] Case T-275/11, *TFI v Commission* EU:T:2013:535, paras 19 and 106.

[65] Commission Decision 2001/156/EC, *Transmed*, OJ 2001 L57/32.

[66] Case T-17/02, *Fred Olsen SA v Commission* [2005] ECR II-2031, para 239; Case T-442/03, *SIC v Commission* [2008] ECR II-1161, para 145.

[67] Case C-280/00, *Altmark Trans GmbH v Nahverkehrsgesellschaft Altmark GmbH* [2003] ECR I-7747, para 93; Case C-451/03, *Servizi Ausiliari Dottori Commercialisti Srl v Calafiori* [2006] ECR I-2941, para 67; Case C-140/09, *Fallimento Traghetti del Mediterraneo SpA v Presidenza del Consiglio dei Ministri* [2010] ECR I-5243, para 40; Case T-289/03, *BUPA Ltd v Commission* [2008] ECR II-81, para 245; Case T-388/03, *Deutsche Post AG v Commission* [2009] ECR II-199, para 114; Case T-325/10, *Iliad v Commission* EU:T:2013:472, para 242; Case T-295/12, *Germany v Commission* EU:T:2014:675, para 127; Case T-309/12, *Zweckverband Tierkörperbeseitigung v Commission* EU:T:2104:676, para 186.

ascertain that the compensation is less than the costs to the undertaking concerned in providing the service.[68] Instead, as the General Court held in *BUPA v Commission*, in light of the purpose of this criterion, the Commission is required to satisfy itself that the compensation does not entail the possibility of offsetting any costs that might result from inefficiency on the part of the insurers.[69] Thus, in *Germany v Commission*, which concerned the transfer of land and forestry to various environmental protection bodies, the General Court upheld the Commission's decision holding that the fourth *Altmark* criterion had not been complied with, given that no analysis of the comparative costs had been carried out by the German authorities.[70]

Payment on account for public service obligations   In *Fallimento Traghetti del Mediterraneo SpA v Presidenza del Consiglio dei Ministri*, which related to maritime services connecting the Italian islands, the relevant Italian legislation required that the subsidies were to provide for operation of the services under conditions of economic equilibrium, and that the subsidies were to be determined on a prospective basis by reference to net income, the amortisation of investments, operating costs, organisational costs and financial burdens. However, the necessary operating agreements pursuant to that legislation did not come into effect for some years after the commencement of the maritime services, payment for which was made on account pending approval of the agreements.   The ECJ held that it followed that, in the absence of those agreements, the *Altmark* criteria were not fulfilled.   The subsidies were paid during the entire period without the public service obligations imposed on the recipient undertakings being clearly defined, without the parameters on the basis of which the compensation for those obligations was calculated being established in advance in an objective and transparent manner, and without ensuring that that compensation did not exceed what was necessary to cover the costs arising from the discharge of those obligations.   The fact that the subsidies were paid on account did not eliminate the advantage conferred on the recipient undertaking or the effects which an advantage of that kind may have on competition.[71]

---

[68]   Case T-388/03, *Deutsche Post AG v Commission* [2009] ECR II-199, para 116.

[69]   Case T-289/03, *BUPA Ltd v Commission* [2008] ECR II-81, para 249; Case T-347/09, *Germany v Commission* EU:T:2103:418, para 81; Case T-295/12, *Germany v Commission* EU:T:2014:675, para 132.

[70]   Case T-347/09, *Germany v Commission* EU:T:2103:418, para 82.

[71]   Case C-140/09, *Fallimento Traghetti del Mediterraneo SpA v Presidenza del Consiglio dei Ministri* [2010] ECR I-5243, para 44-45.

6.2 COMPATIBILITY OF STATE AID UNDER ARTICLE 106(2) TFEU

Public undertakings and Article 106 TFEU Article 106(1) TFEU confirms that the obligations imposed by EU competition law apply equally to public undertakings.[72] Member States must comply with their obligations as regards public undertakings and undertakings which have been granted special or exclusive rights. In this respect, the Commission is empowered, pursuant to Article 106(3) TFEU to issue directives or take decisions determining that a given State measure is incompatible with the rules of the FEU Treaty, including the State aid rules, and to indicate what measures the Member State concerned must adopt in order to comply with its obligations under EU law.[73] The purpose of Article 106(3) TFEU is to ensure freedom to compete and to protect economic operators against measures whereby a Member State might frustrate the fundamental economic freedoms enshrined in the Treaty.[74] The Commission's power may be exercised by adopting a directive addressed to all Member States, as in the case of Commission Directive 2006/111/EC, which requires transparency in the financial relations between public authorities and public undertakings.[75] In addition, however, the Commission may take a decision under Article 106(3) TFEU directed at a single Member State with a view to identifying State aid inherent in a State measure and requiring its alteration.[76]

Services of general economic interest and Article 106(2) TFEU Given the place occupied by services of general interest in the shared values of the EU as well as their role in promoting social and territorial cohesion, the FEU Treaty requires that such services be allowed to operate on the basis of principles and conditions which enable them to fulfil their missions.[77] This entails some modification of the generally applicable rules of competition law. Under Article 106(2) TFEU, undertakings entrusted with the operation of services of general economic interest or having the character of a revenue-producing

---

[72] Cases T-204/97 and T-270/97, *EPAC v Commission* [2000] ECR II-2267, para 122; Cases T-228/99 & T-233/99, *Westdeutsche Landesbank Girozentrale v Commission* [2003] ECR II-435, para 193.

[73] In relation to the status of complaints requesting the Commission to act, see Case T-567/10, *Vivendi v Commission* [2011] ECR II-317* and Case T-568/10, *Vivendi v Commission* [2011] ECR II-319*.

[74] Case T-17/96, *TF1 v Commission* [1999] ECR II-1757, para 50.

[75] OJ 2006 L318/17. Cf. Cases 188-190/80, *France, Italy and the United Kingdom v Commission* [1982] ECR 2545; Case C-325/91, *France v Commission* [1993] ECR I-3283.

[76] Cases C-48/90 & C-66/90, *Netherlands v Commission* [1992] ECR I-565, paras 22-30.

[77] Article 14 TFEU. See M. Ross, "Article 16 EC and services of general interest: from derogation to obligation?" (2000) 25 ELRev 22.

monopoly are subject to the EU rules on competition, including those relating to State aid, in so far as the application of such rules does not obstruct the performance, in law or in fact, of the particular tasks assigned to them.[78] This permits Member States to confer on undertakings to which they entrust the operation of services of general economic interest exclusive rights which may hinder the application of the competition rules in so far as restrictions on competition, or even the exclusion of all competition, by other economic operators are necessary to ensure the performance of the particular tasks assigned to the undertakings possessed of the exclusive rights.[79]

As Article 106(2) TFEU permits a derogation from the competition rules of the FEU Treaty, it must be strictly defined.[80] It seeks to reconcile the Member States' interest in using certain undertakings, in particular in the public sector, as an instrument of economic or fiscal policy with the EU's interest in ensuring compliance with the rules on competition and preservation of the unity of the internal market.[81] In determining the extent of the exemption from the competition rules which may be allowed in order to enable the undertaking entrusted with the task of general interest to perform it, it is necessary to take into consideration the economic conditions in which the undertaking operates, in particular the costs which it has to bear, and the legislation to which it is subject.[82] State aid may be granted in relation to services of general economic interest only where there is a market failure in the provision of the services in question.[83] It is not necessary that the financial balance or economic viability of the undertaking entrusted with the operation of the service of general economic interest should be threatened. It is sufficient that, in the absence of the rights at issue, it would not be possible for the undertaking to perform the particular tasks entrusted to it.[84]

Article 106(2) TFEU further provides that the derogation which it allows from the application of the rules on competition must not affect the development of trade to such an extent as would be contrary to the common interests of the EU. The General Court has held that, in order for an aid

[78] Article 106(2) TFEU. Cf. Case 78/76, *Steinike und Weinlig v Germany* [1997] ECR 585, para 18; Case C-387/92, *Banco de Crédito Industrial SA v Ayuntamiento de Valencia* [1994] ECR I-877, para 11.

[79] Case C-320/91, *Corbeau* [1993] ECR I-2533, para 14; Case C-393/92, *Municipality of Almelo v Energiebedrijf Ijsselmij NV* [1994] ECR I-1477, para 46.

[80] Case 127/73, *Belgische Radio en Televisie v SABAM (No 2)* [1974] ECR 313, para 19; Case C-157/94, *Commission v Netherlands* [1997] ECR I-5699, para 37; Case T-520/09, *TF1 v Commission* EU:T:2012:352, para 104.

[81] Cases T-568/08 & T-573/08, *Metropole Television* (M6) v Commission [2010] ECR II-3397, para 137; Case T-275/11, *TF1 v Commission* EU:T:2013:535, para 131.

[82] Case C-393/92, *Municipality of Almelo v Energiebedrijf Ijsselmij NV* [1994] ECR I-1477, para 49; Case C-53/00, *Ferring v ACOSS* [2001] ECR I-9067, para 32.

[83] Case T-325/10, *Iliad v Commission* EU:T:2013:472, para 164.

[84] Cases T-568/08 & T-573/08, *Metropole Television* (M6) v Commission [2010] ECR II-3397, para 138; Case T-275/11, *TF1 v Commission* EU:T:2013:535, para 132.

scheme to infringe this provision, it must alter trade and competition in a substantial manner and in a manifestly disproportionate measure in relation to the objective sought to be achieved by the Member States.[85]

In the absence of EU rules governing the matter, the Commission is not entitled to rule on the basis of the public service tasks assigned to the public operator, such as the level of costs linked to that service, or the expediency of the political choices made in this regard by the national authorities. It follows that the question of whether an undertaking may fulfil its public service obligations at lower cost is irrelevant for assessing compatibility of the State funding of that service. Instead, Article 106(2) TFEU seeks to prevent, through an assessment of the proportionality of the aid, an operator from benefiting from funding that exceeds the net costs of the public service.[86]

Examples of services of general economic interest Article 106(2) TFEU has been held to apply to public postal services consisting in the obligation to collect, carry and distribute mail on behalf of all users throughout the territory of the Member State concerned, at uniform tariffs and on similar quality conditions, irrespective of the specific situations or the degree of economic profitability of each individual operation.[87] Electricity supply services are also included where the undertaking concerned must ensure that throughout the relevant territory all consumers receive uninterrupted supplies of electricity in sufficient quantities to meet demand at any given time, at uniform rates and on terms which may not vary save in accordance with objective criteria applicable to all customers.[88] State aid has been permitted, therefore, in respect of the laying of an electricity cable between Sweden and the Åland Islands in Finland, as has aid for the construction of a natural gas network and the distribution of natural gas in Denmark.[89] On the other hand, Article 106(2) TFEU was held not to be applicable to the financing of a cableway installation in Bolzano since the purpose of the service was tourism and as such was clearly commercial and competitive.[90]

The General Court has held that, whereas the transport services at issue in the *Altmark* case concerned an economic activity that is unquestionably subject to competition, the criteria developed by the ECJ in that case cannot be applied

[85] Case T-533/10; *DTS v Commission* EU:T:2014:629, para 155.
[86] Cases T-568/08 & T-573/08, *Metropole Television (M6) v Commission* [2010] ECR II-3397, paras 139-140.
[87] Case C-320/91, *Corbeau* [1993] ECR I-2533, para 15; *Twenty-Fifth Report on Competition Policy* (1995), p. 226; Notice from the Commission on the application of the competition rules to the postal sector and on the assessment of certain State measures relating to postal services, OJ 1998 C39/2.
[88] Case C-393/92, *Municipality of Almelo v Energiebedrijf Ijsselmij NV* [1994] ECR I-1477, para 48.
[89] *Twenty-Eighth Report on Competition Policy* (1998), pp. 247-248.
[90] *Thirtieth Report on Competition Policy* (2000), pt. 319.

with the same rigour to the hospital sector which is not necessarily subject to the same degree of competition and market forces. Instead, consideration must be given to the principle of solidarity in the method of financing hospital services through social charges or public contributions and in the fact that services may be provided free of charge. Moreover, Article 106(2) TFEU must be applied taking account of the freedom of Member States to determine their own public health policies as recognised by Article 168(5) TFEU.[91]

Framework for State aid in the form of public service compensation If public service compensation does not meet the *Altmark* conditions and if the general criteria for the applicability of Article 107(1) TFEU are satisfied, such compensation constitutes State aid that must be notified to the Commission in accordance with Article 108(3) TFEU.[92] The Commission has adopted a framework, the purpose of which is to spell out the conditions under which such State aid can be found compatible with the internal market pursuant to Article 106(2) TFEU.[93] State aid in the form of public service compensation that does not meet the *Altmark* criteria may be declared compatible with the internal market if it is necessary to the operation of the services of general economic interest and does not affect the development of trade to such an extent as would be contrary to the interests of the EU.[94] However, the Commission has also set out a number of conditions that should be met in order to achieve an appropriate balance.

The framework is applicable to public service compensation granted to undertakings in connection with all economic activities, with the exception of the land transport sector, and the public service broadcasting sector which is covered by the communication from the Commission on the application of State aid rules to public service broadcasting. The provisions of the framework apply without prejudice to any stricter specific provisions relating to public service obligations contained in sectoral EU legislation and measures.[95]

Block exemption under Commission Decision 2012/21/EU In order to reduce the number of notifications under Article 108(3) TFEU requiring individual assessment, the Commission adopted Decision 2012/21/EU on the application of Article 106(2) TFEU to State aid in the form of public service compensation granted to certain undertakings entrusted with the operation of

---

[91]   Case T-137/10, *CBI v Commission* EU:T:2012:584, para 89.
[92]   Case T-520/09, *TF1 v Commission* EU:T:2012:352, para 93; Case T-137/10, *CBI v Commission* EU:T:2012:584, para 81; Case T-275/11, *TF1 v Commission* EU:T:2013:535, para 129.
[93]   OJ 2012 C8/15, replacing an earlier framework in OJ 2005 C297/04
[94]   See, for example, Case 451/10P, *Television Francaise 1 SA v Commission* [2011] I-85*; Cases T-568/08 & T-573/08, *M6 and TF1 v Commission* [2010] II-3397.
[95]   Framework for State aid in the form of public service compensation, para 8.

services of general economic interest.[96]   This lays down the conditions under which, without prejudice to the application of stricter provisions relating to public service obligations contained in sectoral EU legislation, certain types of public service compensation constitute State aid compatible with Article 106(2) TFEU and exempts compensation satisfying those conditions from the prior notification requirement.[97]

Decision 2012/21/EU applies to State aid in the form of public service compensation granted to undertakings entrusted with services of general economic interest which falls within one of the following categories:[98]

(a) compensation not exceeding an annual amount of €15 million for the provision of SGEIs in areas other than transport and transport infrastructure;

(b) compensation for the provision of SFGEIs by hospitals providing medical care, including, where applicable, emergency services;[99]

(c) compensation for the provision of SGEIs meeting social needs as regards health and long term care, child care, access to and reintegration into the labour market, social housing and the care and social inclusion of vulnerable groups;

(d) compensation for SGEIs as regards air or maritime links to islands on which average annual traffic during the two financial years preceding that in which the SGEI was assigned does not exceed 300,000 passengers;

(e) compensation for SGEIs as regards airports and ports for which average annual traffic during the two financial years preceding that in which the SGEI was assigned does not exceed 200,000 passengers, in the case of airports, and 300,000 passengers, in the case of ports.

Genuine service of general economic interest   Member States have a wide margin of discretion regarding the nature of services that could be classified as being services of general economic interest.   The aid must be granted for a genuine and correctly defined SGEI.   Member States cannot attach specific public service obligations that are already provided or can be provided satisfactorily and under conditions such as price, objective quality characteristics, continuity and access to the services, consistent with the public interest by undertakings operating under normal market conditions.[100] Responsibility for operation of the SGEI must be entrusted to the undertaking concerned by way of one or more official acts, the form of which may be

---

[96]   OJ 2012 L7/3. This replaced Commission Decision 2005/842/EC.

[97]   Commission Decision 2012/21/EU, Articles 1 and 3.

[98]   *Ibid.*, Article 2.

[99]   The pursuit of ancillary activities directly related to the main activities, notably in the field of research, does not prevent application of this provision.

[100]   Cases T-80/06 & T-182/09, *Budapesti Erőmű Zrt v Commission* EU:T:2012:65, para 92; Framework for State aid in the form of public service compensation, paras 12-13.

determined by each Member State. The act or acts must specify, in particular, the content and duration of the public service obligations, the undertakings and territory concerned, the nature of any exclusive or special rights assigned to the undertaking, the parameters for calculating, controlling and reviewing the compensation, and the arrangements for avoiding and repaying any over-compensation.[101]

Amount of compensation   Member States have a wide discretion in determining the amount of compensation payable for services of general economic interest.[102]   It is important to recognise, however, that the fourth *Altmark* criterion is not applicable in determining the compensation payable in accordance with Article 106(2) TFEU.[103]   It follows that it is irrelevant that the service might be provided at a lower cost.[104]   Nevertheless, the amount of compensation may not exceed what is necessary to cover the net costs incurred in discharging the public service obligations, including a reasonable profit. The amount of compensation can be established on the basis of either the expected costs and revenues or the costs and revenues actually incurred, or a combination of the two.   Where it is based on the expected costs and revenues, they must be specified in the entrustment act and be based on plausible and observable parameters concerning the economic environment in which the SGEI is provided.   Under the framework, the cost estimation must reflect the expectation of efficiency gains achieved by the SGEI provider over the lifetime of the entrustment.[105]

Costs to be taken into consideration   Under the block exemption, the costs to be taken into consideration include all the costs incurred in the operation of the SGEI.   Where the activities of the undertaking in question are confined to the SGEI, all its costs may be taken into consideration.   Where the undertaking also carries out activities falling outside the scope of the SGEI, only the costs associated with the service of general economic interest may be taken into consideration.   The costs allocated to the SGEI may cover all the variable costs incurred in providing the SGEI, an appropriate contribution to fixed costs common to both the service of general economic interest and other activities and an adequate return on the own capital assigned to the SGEI.   The costs linked with investments, notably concerning infrastructure, may be taken into

---

[101] Framework for State aid in the form of public service compensation, paras 15-16; Commission Decision 2012/21/EU, Article 4.

[102] Case T-289/03, *BUPA v Commission* [2008] CR II-81, para 220; Case T-151/11, *Telefónica de España SA v Commission* EU:T:2014:631, para 159.

[103] Case T-137/10, *CBI v Commission* EU:T:2012:584, paras 292; Case T-275/11, *TFI v Commission* EU:T:2013:535, para 130.

[104] Case T-137/10, *CBI v Commission* EU:T:2012:584, para 293.

[105] Framework for State aid in the form of public service compensation, paras 21-23; Commission Decision 2012/21/EU, Article 5(1)-(2).

account when necessary for the functioning of the service of general economic interest. The costs linked to any activities outside the scope of the SGEI must cover all the direct costs, an appropriate contribution to fixed common costs and an adequate return on capital.[106] The framework sets out a methodology for establishing net avoided costs, which should normally be the basis for determining costs, where net costs are those which are necessary to discharge the public service obligations. Otherwise, a methodology based on cost allocation may be used.[107]

Revenue to be taken into consideration The revenue to be taken into account must include at least the entire revenue earned from the SGEI. If the undertaking in question holds special or exclusive rights linked to an SGEI that generates profit in excess of the reasonable profit, or benefits from other advantages granted by the State, these must be taken into consideration, irrespective of their classification for the purposes of Article 107(1) TFEU, and are added to its revenue. The Member State may also decide that the profits accruing from other activities outside the scope of the SGEI must be allocated in whole or in part to the financing of the SGEI.[108]

Reasonable profit Reasonable profit should be taken to mean a rate of return on own capital that would be required by a typical company considering whether or not to provide the SGEI for the whole period of the entrustment act, taking into account the level of risk. The level of risk depends on the sector concerned, the type of service and the characteristics of the compensation mechanism. In determining what amounts to a reasonable profit, the Member State may introduce incentive criteria relating, among other things, to the quality of service provided and gains in productive efficiency.[109]

Over-compensation Member States must check regularly, or arrange for checks to be made, to ensure that there has been no over-compensation. Since over-compensation is not necessary for the operation of the service of general economic interest, it constitutes incompatible State aid that must be repaid to the State, and for the future, the parameters for the calculation of the compensation must be updated. Under the block exemption, where the amount of over-compensation does not exceed 10% of the amount of annual

---

[106] Commission Decision 2012/21/EU, Article 5(3)

[107] Framework for State aid in the form of public service compensation, para 24-31.

[108] Framework for State aid in the form of public service compensation, para 32; Commission Decision 2012/21/EU, Article 5(4).

[109] Framework for State aid in the form of public service compensation, para 33; Commission Decision 2012/21/EU, Article 5(5)-(6).

compensation, such over-compensation may be carried forward to the next year.[110]

Cross-subsidisation When a company carries out activities falling both inside and outside the scope of the service of general economic interest, the internal accounts must show separately the costs and receipts associated with the service of general economic interest and those associated with other services, as well as the parameters for allocating costs and revenues. Where an undertaking is entrusted with the operation of several services of general economic interest either because the authority assigning the service of general economic interest is different or because the nature of the service of general economic interest is different, the undertaking's internal accounts must make it possible to ensure that there is no over-compensation at the level of each service of general economic interest.[111]

Under the framework, any over-compensation may be used to finance another service of general economic interest operated by the same undertaking, but such a transfer must be shown in the undertaking's accounts and be carried out in accordance with the rules and principles set out in the framework, notably as regards prior notification. The Member States must ensure that such transfers are subjected to proper control. The transparency rules laid down in Commission Directive 2006/111/EC apply.[112]

***De minimis* aid for SGEI providers** In accordance with Council Regulation (EC) No 994/98, the Commission adopted Commission Regulation (EU) No 360/2012 providing for that aid for SGEI providers below certain thresholds is deemed not to meet all the criteria of Article 107(1) TFEU and is therefore exempt from notification under Article 108(3) TFEU. The total amount of *de minimis* aid granted to any one undertaking may not exceed €500,000 over a three year period as long as certain conditions are fulfilled. In particular, it must be possible to calculate precisely the gross grant equivalent of the aid without the need to undertake a risk assessment.[113]

---

[110] Framework for State aid in the form of public service compensation, paras 47-50; Commission Decision 2012/21/EU, Article 6.

[111] Framework for State aid in the form of public service compensation, para 44; Commission Decision 2012/21/EU, Article 5(9).

[112] Framework for State aid in the form of public service compensation, para 18.

[113] Commission Regulation (EU) No 360/2012, Article 2.

Part II

EU STATE AID POLICY

Chapter Seven

STRUCTURE OF EU STATE AID POLICY

7.1 STATE AID IN THE EUROPEAN UNION

State aid and distortion of competition Despite the fact that Article 107(1) TFEU provides that State aid is *prima facie* incompatible with the internal market, all Member States of the European Union continue to provide for varying degrees of financial support for industries operating within their territory. Aid may be awarded in order, for example, to encourage productive investments in particular regions or sectors of the economy, or to allow industry to adapt to new technologies or environmental requirements, or to facilitate investment in research and development. This may be considered, at least within certain limits, to be beneficial to the economy generally by providing for a stronger productive base.[1] By contrast, under the ECSC Treaty, State aid to the coal and steel industries was *prima facie* prohibited.[2] This tougher approach to State aid may be explained by the nature of the ECSC Treaty which focused specifically on creating a single market in coal and steel, whereby production was pooled and where the industry was characterised by overcapacity and the need for modernization and rationalization in the face of international competition.[3]

The Commission distinguishes between what is sometimes described as good aid, which is well-designed, targeted at identified market failures and objectives of common interest, and bad aid, which does not provide real incentives for companies, crowds out private investment and keeps inefficient and non-viable companies on life support.[4] In particular, State aid for inefficient firms can frustrate free competition and the operation of the internal market by preventing the most efficient allocation of resources. It may result in the export of unemployment where products which benefited from State aid are exported to another Member State and sold there at a cheaper price than domestic produce of that State, thereby endangering and threatening the unity

---

[1] *Eleventh Report on Competition Policy* (1981), pt. 179.

[2] Article 4(c) CS. Cf. Cases T-12/99 & T-63/99, *UK Coal plc v Commission* [2001] ECR II-2153, paras 54-55.

[3] State aid which was compatible with the objectives of the ECSC Treaty was, nevertheless, permitted in accordance with Article 95 CS. The ECSC Treaty expired on 23 July 2002.

[4] *Report on Competition Policy* (2012), accompanying document, p.1.

of the internal market.[5] With the development of the single market and the advent of economic and monetary union, preventing the distortion of competition in favour of domestic industry has become more important as the Member States, being progressively less able to use other measures of economic policy to benefit their own producers, may become more strongly tempted to grant State aid. At the same time, distortion of competition is felt all the more keenly as progress is made towards market integration.[6] State aid granted within the European Union may also encourage the adoption of retaliatory measures by third countries in international trade.[7]

National State aid policies It should be noted at the outset that no EU legislation has been adopted aiming to harmonize national rules governing the award of State aid. Aid is granted by the Member States in accordance with relevant national law and policy. EU law does not itself directly determine the content of national State aid provisions, so that it remains for each Member State to determine the circumstances in which it wishes to grant aid and the persons to whom such aid is to be paid.[8] The Commission cannot force a Member State to pay State aid, and the Member State retains the right to withdraw a notification of aid or an aid scheme and not to implement an aid scheme that has been approved.[9] Rather, EU intervention in the field of State aid is largely negative in nature, the role of the Commission, and occasionally the Council, being to supervise the award of State aid in order to ensure that competition in the internal market is not unduly distorted. On the other hand, the adoption of increasingly detailed regulatory provisions at EU level with respect to certain types of aid that are regarded as compatible with the internal market leaves a reduced margin of discretion to the Member States. By specifying the type of aid that is compatible with the internal market in accordance with block exemption regulations, guidelines, frameworks and communications, Member States are encouraged to adopt common measures, even if, in principle, they remain entitled to notify other measures for approval by the Commission on the basis of Article 107(3) TFEU.[10]

State aid in the European Union up to 2004 EU State aid policy has had to reflect the fact that the Member States have consistently used substantial

---

[5] *Twelfth Report on Competition Policy* (1982), pt. 158.

[6] Case C-303/88, *Italy v Commission* [1991] ECR I-1433, *per* Advocate General Van Gerven, at pp. 1462-3.

[7] Ninth Survey on State Aid in the European Union, para 2.

[8] Case 282/85, *DEFI v Commission* [1986] ECR 2469, *per* Advocate General Mancini, at p. 2474.

[9] Case C-390/06, *Nuova Agricast Srl v Ministero delle Attività Produttive* [2008] ECR I-2577, *per* Advocate General Mazák at para 62; Case C-138/09, *Todaro Nunziatina v Assessorato del Lavoro* [2010] ECR I-4561, paras 52-53.

[10] Commission Regulation (EU) No 651/2014, preamble, para 7.

amounts of aid as a tool of economic and industrial policy. Several surveys of State aid up to the 1990s were carried out by the European Commission in order to analyse the scope of aid actually granted by the Member States.[11] Sustained high levels of State aid throughout the 1980s belied the widespread understanding that the rise in State intervention in the early years of that decade was a temporary phenomenon due to restructuring in various industries following the second oil-price crisis.[12] Total aid granted annually by the Member States in the 1980s exceeded 3% of GDP and rose to 4% in the early 1900s.[13] During the 1990s, the Commission's policy of reducing State aid began to bear fruit. By this stage, the Commission had issued several communications setting out a restrictive policy in relation to most types of aid. After peaking in 1993-94, State aid volumes began to show a downward trend.[14] For the period 1996 to 1998, the Member States spent an average of €93 billion annually on aid.[15] Total annual aid fell to some €79 billion by 1999, representing an aid level of 1% of GDP.[16] By 2000, total aid was assessed at €82 billion, representing 0.99% of GDP.[17]

With levels of State aid remaining sufficiently high so as to continue to create distortions of competition, in 2000, the Council called for a shift in emphasis from supporting individual companies or sectors towards tackling horizontal objectives of EU interest, such as employment and training, regional development, environment and research. In its 2001 broad economic policy guidelines, the Commission repeated this need to reduce overall State aid levels and to increase transparency with a view to reducing the overall level of aid in relation to GDP by 2003. The Commission's view was that State aid was essentially justified to rectify market failures and that, if there was a need for intervention, State aid was only one of a number of possible instruments that might be used. Member States were, therefore, encouraged to consider other forms of intervention, such as regulation, taxation or direct public provision of certain goods or services.[18] Particular attention was given to ensuring that the beneficial effects of liberalisation were not undermined by State aid measures.[19]

---

[11] Nine surveys on State aid were adopted by the Commission covering the periods 1981-1999.

[12] *Twentieth Report on Competition Policy* (1990), pt. 190.

[13] *Eighteenth Report on Competition Policy* (1988), pt. 163; *Twenty-Seventh Report on Competition Policy* (1997), pt. 196; *Twenty-Eighth Report on Competition Policy* (1998), pt. 181.

[14] Cf. the Sixth and Seventh Surveys on State Aid in the European Union.

[15] For a summary of the Eighth Survey on State Aid, see *Thirtieth Report on Competition Policy* (2000), pt. 290-292.

[16] Ninth Survey on State Aid; State aid scoreboard, December 2001.

[17] State aid scoreboard, Spring 2002, pp. 5-6.

[18] State aid scoreboard, December 2001, para 1.

[19] *Thirty-Second Report on Competition Policy* (2002), pt. 329.

State Aid Action Plan 2005-2009 Following the accession of the countries from Central and Eastern Europe in 2004, the Commission re-examined EU State aid policy with a view to effecting a fundamental reform of the substantive and procedural policy instruments governing the compatibility of State aid with the internal market during the period 2005-2009. The aim was to base the reform package on ensuring less and better targeted aid, a refined economic approach and more effective procedures. This was to entail a shared responsibility between the Commission and the Member States, in particular with the Member States being fully committed to comply with their obligations to notify proposed aid and to enforce the rules properly. The Commission focused on the notion of market failure as being essential for justifying State aid. However, it re-emphasised its previous policy that it was not enough for State aid to target market failure. Before resorting to State aid, it should be verified whether other less distortive measures could remedy the market failure. State aid should be the appropriate policy instrument and should be designed so that it effectively solves the market failure, by creating an incentive effect and being proportionate.

As regards procedures, the Commission sought to create a hierarchy whereby aid measures that clearly were compatible with the internal market would be permitted, leaving the Commission free to concentrate its analysis on the most distortive aid measures. To this end, it developed a system of block exemptions covering a large number of individual categories of aid and ultimately combined most of these in a single general block exemption in Commission Regulation (EC) No 800/2008. Aid that did not comply with all the conditions of the block exemptions was to be notified to the Commission for individual assessment. However, in respect of those measures that did not present a significant problem in determining their compatibility with the internal market, the Commission set out in frameworks and guidelines the criteria that it would apply. Where, on the other hand, the aid measure was for a very large amount or might otherwise cause significant distort of competition, the Commission carried out a detailed assessment in which it balanced the positive effects of the aid with the negative effects of distortion of competition, using in-depth economic analysis.

By 2007, the overall level of State aid had fallen to €65 billion, representing 0.5-0.6% of GDP. The Commission noted that this could be attributed to three factors. First, in line with expectations during a period of economic growth, Member States granted considerably less rescue and restructuring aid, which had decreased from an average of €6.8 billion per year in 2002-2004 to €1.8 billion per year in 2005-2007. Second, State aid to the coal sector had halved to less the €4 billion per year. Third, the downward trend was even more accentuated in the EU-12.[20] Moreover, the average share of horizontal

---

[20]   State aid scoreboard, Autumn 2008, pp. 4-5.

objectives in total aid increased from 67% in 2002-2004 to 81% in 2005-2007, compared with only 50% in the 1990s. Much of this trend was due to an increase in environmental tax exemptions, in particular for energy intensive industries. The share of R&D&I aid also rose significantly.[21]

State aid in the European Union 2009-2014 Following the credit crisis that triggered turmoil in the financial markets in 2008, massive intervention was made by the Member States to curb the adverse effects of the shock. Between 1 October 2008 and 1 October 2012, the Commission approved aid to the financial sector totalling a nominal €5,058 billion representing 40.3% of EU GDP. Non-crisis aid, however, remained at low levels. Aid in 2009-2011 amounted to €60 billion or 0.51% of EU GDP and continued to fall slightly thereafter. In 2014, it stood at 0.49% of GDP. Roughly 90% of aid is granted for horizontal objectives, including regional aid, R&D&I aid and aid for environmental protection and energy, the other 10% being sectoral aid.[22]

State aid modernisation 2014-2020 In 2012, the Commission published a communication on State aid modernisation[23] based on the Europe 2020 growth strategy which seeks to make the EU a smart, sustainable and inclusive economy, helping deliver high levels of employment, productivity and social cohesion. Stronger and better targeted State aid control can encourage the design of more effective growth-enhancing policies. A more focused State aid framework will allow Member States to better contribute both to the implementation of the Europe 2020 strategy as well as to budgetary consolidation. The modernisation of State aid control is needed to strengthen the quality of the Commission's scrutiny and to shape that instrument into a tool promoting a sound use of public resources for growth-oriented policies and limiting competition distortions that would undermine a level playing field in the internal market. Accordingly, the Commission outlined an integrated strategy for reform with the following objectives: (i) to foster sustainable, smart and inclusive growth in a competitive internal market; (ii) to focus Commission *ex ante* scrutiny on cases with the biggest impact on internal market whilst strengthening the Member States cooperation in State aid enforcement; (iii) to streamline the rules and provide for faster decisions.

In place of previously different rules in some of the guidelines, common principles were established for to the assessment of compatibility of all aid measures, dealing with assessment of market failure, incentive effect, proportionality and negative effects on competition. Many of the guidelines and frameworks were subsequently revised, leading to a more coherent set of principles applicable to horizontal aid for the period 2014-2020. This also led

---

[21] *Ibid.*, p. 7.
[22] State aid scoreboard, 2014.
[23] COM(2012) 209 final.

to a revision of the block exemption regulation to reflect these same principles. In addition, the scope of the block exemption regulation was considerably broadened by Council Regulation (EU) No 733/2013[24] to include a number of new categories in Commission Regulation (EU) No 651/2014. With more measures exempt from the notification requirement under Article 108(3) TFEU, the onus was increased on Member States to ensure *ex ante* compliance with the State aid rules of *de minimis* measures and block-exempted schemes and cases. Moreover, *ex post* control by the Commission will also be increased.

7.2 STRUCTURE OF EU STATE AID POLICY

Structure of EU State aid policy In formulating EU policy on State aid, the Commission, rather than seeking to define permissible aid solely within the confines of each of the separate categories set out in Article 107(2)-(3) TFEU, has instead approached the subject matter from a different perspective which reflects the purpose of the aid. The main areas of policy deal with regional investment, investment by small and medium-sized enterprises (SMEs), risk capital for SMEs, employment and training, research and development and innovation, environmental protection and energy, restructuring of undertakings in serious difficulty, aviation, broadband infrastructure, cinematography and services of general economic interest. Specific additional or alternative rules apply for certain sectors, such as shipbuilding, coal and steel which suffer from overcapacity and for agriculture, transport and production for military purposes which have additional legal bases in the FEU Treaty. Special measures were temporarily put in place to deal with the effects of the credit crisis in 2008. Whilst these policy areas cover the vast bulk of aid awarded by the Member States, occasionally aid is proposed which does not fall within these classifications. The Commission, in these cases, is obliged to examine the proposal on its own merits in accordance with Article 107(3) TFEU.[25] In such a case, where there are guidelines covering the relevant sector or subject matter, but which do not apply to the particular decision, the Commission, in accordance with the principle of equal treatment, may apply the principles established in the guidelines in making its assessment.[26]

Aid covered by each of these policy areas must be justified by reference to one or more of the legal categories set out in Article 107(3) TFEU or some other specific provision. For example, the compatibility with the internal market of aid for research and development for SMEs in assisted areas, which

---

[24] OJ 2013 L204/11.
[25] Case T-375/03, *Fachvereinigung Mineralfaserindustrie eV v Commission* [2007] ECR II-121*, para 141.
[26] *Ibid.*, para 148.

is regulated pursuant to the Commission's framework on research and development aid, might be considered from a legal perspective simultaneously by reference to Article 107(3)(a) TFEU as regional aid, Article 107(3)(b) TFEU as being a research project of common European interest and Article 107(3)(c) TFEU as aid for the development of the economic activity of SMEs. Investment aid for large enterprises is now generally permitted only within Article 107(3)(a) TFEU or Article 107(3)(c) TFEU areas. Aid in respect of SMEs, employment and training, and restructuring of firms in difficulty are generally considered as facilitating the development of certain economic activities and are, accordingly, permitted throughout the internal market by Article 107(3)(c) TFEU. Similarly, aid for research and development and innovation or for environmental protection is also primarily within the scope of Article 107(3)(c) TFEU as facilitating the development of certain economic activities, although it may also fall within Article 107(3)(b) TFEU if the project is of common European interest. Cultural aid is permitted pursuant to Article 107(3)(d) TFEU, although it may also engage with Article 107(3)(c) TFEU where certain economic activities are developed. As to the intensity of aid, Article 107(3)(c) TFEU allows relatively limited levels of aid, whereas higher levels are generally permitted where Article 107(3)(a), (b) or (d) TFEU apply. Services of general economic interest are governed by reference to Article 106(2) TFEU.

State aid must contribute to EU objectives The Commission has a wide discretion as to whether or not to permit aid on the basis of Article 107(3) TFEU.[27] Generally, State aid may be permissible only where there has been a market failure, so that the Commission is entitled to refuse to authorise aid when it is satisfied that market forces alone without State intervention would ensure a normal development of production.[28] Nevertheless, the Commission must consider all relevant factors in making its assessment.[29] This assessment may involve the examination and appraisal of economic facts and conditions which may be both complex and liable to change rapidly.[30]

---

[27] Case 730/79, *Philip Morris v Commission* [1980] ECR 2671, para 17; Cases 62 & 72/87, *Exécutif Régional Wallon v Commission* [1988] ECR 1573, para 21; Case C-372/97, *Italy v Commission* [2004] ECR I-3679, para 83; Case C-464/09P, *Holland Malt BV v Commission* [2010] ECR I-12443, para 46; Case T-152/99, *Hijos de Andrés Molina SA v Commission* [2002] ECR II-3049, para 48; Case T-348/04, *SIDE v Commission* [2008] ECR I-625, para 60; Cases T-267/08 & T-279/08, *Région Nord-Pas-de-Calais v Commission* [2011] ECR II-1999, para 1129.

[28] Case 730/79, *Philip Morris v Commission* [1980] ECR 2671, paras 23-25; Cases C-630/11P to C-633/11P, *HGA srl v Commission* EU:C:2013:387, para 104.

[29] Cases 296 & 318/82, *Netherlands and Leeuwarder Papierwarenfabriek v Commission* [1985] ECR 809, para 26.

[30] Case C-301/87, *France v Commission* [1990] ECR I-307, para 15; Case T-348/04, *SIDE v Commission* [2008] ECR I-625, para 60.

The Commission's discretionary power should only be exercised when the aid proposed by the Member States takes the form of a contribution by the beneficiary over and above the effects of normal play of market forces to the achievement of one or more of the EU objectives set out in Article 107(3) TFEU.[31] Its economic and social assessments must be made in an EU context,[32] so that, for instance, it is entitled to refuse to allow proposed aid which would result in the transfer to the Member State concerned of an investment which could be effected in another Member State in a less favourable economic situation.[33] The national interest of a Member State or the benefits obtained by the recipient of the aid in contributing to the national interest do not by themselves justify the positive exercise of the Commission's discretionary powers where this is not necessary for the attainment of the objectives specified in Article 107(3) TFEU.[34] Moreover, the Commission cannot be influenced, for example, by supposed legitimate expectations of recipients triggered by national authorities as to the possibility of an extension of certain effects of an expired State aid scheme, and this cannot constitute a basis for an obligation of the Commission to lay down a transitional provision.[35]

Commission notices, communications, guidelines and frameworks The Commission needs to use its resources efficiently in assessing State aid. With this in mind, it has adopted a programme of codification of its practice with regard to the most common types of aid. Such codification increases the transparency and predictability of policy and is intended to boost confidence in the consistent enforcement of the rules. This facilitates the evaluation of the compatibility of many individual awards of aid of a relatively straightforward

---

[31] *Tenth Report on Competition Policy* (1980), pt. 213. See K. Mortelsman, "The compensatory justification criterion in the practice of the Commission in decisions on State aids" (1984) 21 CMLR 405.

[32] Case 730/79, *Philip Morris v Commission* [1980] ECR 2671, para 24; Case C-301/87, *France v Commission* [1990] ECR I-307, para 49; Case C-303/88, *Italy v Commission* [1991] ECR I-1433, para 34; Case C-355/95P, *TWD v Commission* [1997] ECR I-2549, para 26; Case C-278/95P, *Siemens SA v Commission* [1997] ECR I-2597, para 35; Case C-156/98, *Germany v Commission* [2000] ECR I-6857, para 67; Case C-310/99, *Italy v Commission* [2002] ECR I-2289, para 45; Case T-162/06, *Kronoply GmbH v Commission* [2009] ECR II-1, para 97.

[33] Case 730/79, *Philip Morris v Commission* [1980] ECR 2671, para 25.

[34] Case 730/79 *Philip Morris* v *Commission* [1980] ECR 2671, para 17; Case 310/85 *Deufil* v *Commission* [1987] ECR 901, para 18; Case C-400/92 *Germany* v *Commission* [1994] ECR I-4701, para 21; Case C-390/06, *Nuova Agricast Srl v Ministero delle Attività Produttive* [2008] ECR I-2577, para 68; Case T-348/04, *SIDE v Commission* [2008] ECR I-625, para 98; Case T-162/06, *Kronoply GmbH v Commission* [2009] ECR II-1, para 65.

[35] Case C-390/06, *Nuova Agricast Srl v Ministero delle Attività Produttive* [2008] ECR I-2577, *per* Advocate General Mazák at para 79.

kind,[36] although codification has long been criticised as introducing unnecessary rigidity into the system.[37] The ECJ has confirmed that the Commission may adopt a policy as to how it will exercise its discretion and issue guidelines accordingly, provided that they do not depart from the rules in the EU Treaties.[38] Moreover, the Commission's policy instruments must be interpreted not just on the basis of their wording but also in the light of Article 107 TFEU and its objective of undistorted competition in the internal market.[39] In accordance with the principles of equal treatment and the protection of legitimate expectations, the Commission is then bound by these policy statements where they have been accepted by the Member States[40] and the

---

[36] *Twenty-Third Report on Competition Policy* (1993), pt. 380.

[37] See G. Della Cananea, "Administration by Guidelines: The Policy Guidelines of the Commission in the Field of State Aid" in Harden (ed.), *State Aid: Community Law and Policy* (Cologne, 1993).

[38] Case 310/85, *Deufil v Commission* [1987] ECR 901, para 22; Case C-313/90, *CIRFS v Commission* [1993] ECR I-1125, para 35; Case C-288/96, *Germany v Commission* [2000] ECR I-8237, para 62; Case C-310/99, *Italy v Commission* [2002] ECR I-2289, para 52; Case C-382/99, *Netherlands v Commission* [2002] ECR I-5163, para 24; Case C-351/98, *Spain v Commission* [2002] ECR I-8031, para 53; Case C-91/01, *Italy v Commission* [2004] ECR I-4355, para 45; Cases C-182/03 & C-217/03 *Belgium and Forum 187 v Commission* [2006] ECR I-5479, para 72; Cases C-75/05P & C-80/05P, *Germany v Kronofrance* [2008] ECR I-6619, para 60; Case C-464/09P, *Holland Malt BV v Commission* [2010] ECR I-12443, para 47; Case T-380/94, *AIUFFASS v Commission* [1996] ECR II-2169, para 57; Case T-214/95, *Vlaamse Gewest v Commission* [1998] ECR II-717, para 79; Case T-187/99, *Agrana Zucker und Stärke AG v Commission* [2001] ECR II-1587, para 56; Case T-35/99, *Keller SpA v Commission* [2002] ECR II-261, para 77; Case T-27/02, *Kronofrance SA v Commission* [2004] ECR II-4177, para 79; Case T-171/02, *Regione autonoma della Sardegna v Commission* [2005] ECR II-2123, para 29; Case T-17/03, *Schimtz-Gotha Fahrzeugwerke GmbH v Commission* [2006] ECR II-1139, para 42; Case T-301/01, *Alitalia SpA v Commission* [2008] ECR II-1753, para 405; Cases T-443/08 & T-455/08, *Freistaat Sachsen v Commission* [2011] ECR II-1311, para 104; Cases T-115/09 & T-116/09, *Electrolux AB v Commission* EU:T:2012:76, para 38; Case T-304/08, *Smurfit Kappa Group plc v Commission* EU:T:2012:351, para 84.

[39] Case T-27/02, *Kronofrance v Commission* [2004] ECR II-4177, para 89; Case T-369/06, *Holland Malt BV v Commission* [2009] ECR II-3313, para 132.

[40] Case C-313/90, *CIRFS v Commission* [1993] ECR I-1125, para 36; Case C-351/98, *Spain v Commission* [2002] ECR I-8031, para 53; Case C-409/00, *Spain v Commission* [2003] ECR I-1487, para 95; Case C-91/01, *Italy v Commission* [2004] ECR I-4355, para 45; Cases C-75/05P & C-80/05P, *Germany v Kronofrance* [2008] ECR I-6619, para 61; Case C-464/09P, *Holland Malt BV v Commission* [2010] ECR I-12443, para 46; Case C-667/13, *Portugal v Banco Privado Português SA* EU:C:2015:151, para 69; Case T-137/02, *Pollmeier Malchow GmbH v Commission* [2004] ECR II-3541, para 54; Case T-176/01 *Ferriere Nord SpA v Commission* [2004] ECR II-3931, para 134; Case T-349/03, *Corsica Ferries France SAS v Commission* [2005] ECR II-2197, para 139; Case T-198/01, *Technische Glaswerke Ilmenau GmbH v Commission* [2004] ECR II-2717, para 149; Case T-268/06, *Olympiaki Aeroporia Ypiresies AE v Commission* [2008] ECR II-1091, para 50; Cases T-267/08 & T-279/08, *Région Nord-Pas-de-Calais v*

parties concerned are therefore entitled to rely on them and to enforce their application in the courts.[41] It follows that guidelines, whilst not qualifying as legal rules, may, in certain circumstances, produce legal effects.[42]

By assessing specific aid in the light of its guidelines, the Commission cannot be considered to exceed the limits of its discretion or to waive that discretion. On the one hand, policy statements concern a defined sector or activity and are based on the desire to follow a policy established in relation to it.[43] Criteria for permitting aid must be formulated, interpreted and applied in as uniform a way as possible in order to maintain consistency and ensure equality of treatment as regards State aid.[44] On the other hand, the Commission retains the power to repeal or amend any guidelines if the circumstances so require. In particular, where its policy statements are superseded by developments in the case law of the EU courts, the Commission is required to take those developments into account.[45] It follows that, since the Commission is entitled to change its policy, Member States, recipients and other economic operators may not invoke any legitimate expectation that an existing situation which is capable of being altered by the Commission in the exercise of its discretionary power will be maintained.[46]

Aid not covered by the Commission's policy statements may none the less be approved if it satisfies the conditions in Article 107(3) TFEU.[47] Thus, the

---

Commission [2011] ECR II-1999, para 130; Case T-551/10, *Fri-El Acerra Srl v Commission* EU:T:2013:430, para 28.

[41] Case T-149/95 *Ducros* v *Commission* [1997] ECR II-2031, para 62; Case T-35/99, *Keller SpA v Commission* [2002] ECR II-261, para 77; Case T-349/03, *Corsica Ferries France SAS v Commission* [2005] ECR II-2197, para 141; Cases T-115/09 & T-116/09, *Electrolux AB v Commission* EU:T:2012:76, para 41.

[42] Cases C-189/02P, etc., *Dansk Rørindustri A/S v Commission* [2005] ECR I-5425, paras 209-211; Cases C-465/09P – C-470/09P, *Territorio Histórico de Álava – Diputación Foral de Álava v Commission* [2011] ECR I-83*, para 120.

[43] Case T-214/95, *Vlaamse Gewest v Commission* [1998] ECR II-717, para 89; Case T-349/03, *Corsica Ferries France SAS v Commission* [2005] ECR II-2197, para 140.

[44] Cases C-278-280/92, *Spain v Commission* [1994] ECR I-4103, para 51; Case C-310/99, *Italy v Commission* [2002] ECR I-2289, para 58. See also Cases T-227/99 & T-134/00, *Kvaerner Warnow Werft GmbH v Commission* [2002] ECR II-1205, para 92.

[45] Case C-288/11P, *Mitteldeutsche Flughafen AG v Commission* EU:C:2012:821, para 64; Cases T-443/08 & T-455/08, *Freistaat Sachsen v Commission* [2011] ECR II-1311, para 106.

[46] Case T-376/07, *Germany v Commission* [2009] ECR II-4293, para 42; Case T-551/10, *Fri-El Acerra Srl v Commission* EU:T:2013:430, para 45.

[47] Case T-288/97, *Regione Autonoma Friuli Venezia Giulia v Commission* [2001] ECR II-1169, para 72; Case T-137/02, *Pollmeier Malchow GmbH v Commission* [2004] ECR II-3541, para 63; Case T-375/03, *Fachvereinigung Mineralfaserindustrie v Commission* [2007] ECR II-121*, para 143; Cases T-254/00, T-270/00 & T-277/00, *Hotel Cipriani SpA v Commission* [2008] ECR II-3269, para 294; Case T-357/02 RENV, *Freistaat Sachsen v Commission* [2011] ECR II-5415, para 44; Case T-304/08, *Smurfit Kappa Group plc v Commission* EU:T:2012:351, para 90.

General Court has stated that, while the Commission can establish general implementing measures which structure the way in which it exercises the discretion conferred upon it by Article 107(3) TFEU, it cannot wholly deprive itself of that discretion where it assesses a specific case. That is particularly so in relation to cases which it has not expressly referred to, or indeed has not regulated, in those general implementing rules. That discretion is, therefore, not exhausted by the adoption of such general rules and there is in principle no obstacle to an individual assessment outside the context of those rules.[48] Thus, for example, in *Smurfit Kappa v Commission*, the Commission was required to assess the compatibility of regional investment aid which was not specifically regulated by the regional aid guidelines in accordance with its wide discretion under Article 107(3) TFEU in order to ascertain whether the expected benefits in terms of regional development outweighed distortions of competition and the impact of the subsidised project on trade between Member States.[49]

The adoption of guidelines or frameworks must be solely for the purposes of making transparent the State aid rules and cannot be used for other purposes, in particular the promotion of industrial policy. Thus, when the Commission was formulating its first framework for the motor vehicle industry, it refused to use the framework as a means of furthering industrial policy, stating that the sole aim of the framework was to impose strict discipline in the granting of aid to ensure that competition was not distorted. Nevertheless, the German Government initially objected to the framework, considering that it contained undesirable industrial policy objectives whilst the Spanish authorities, on the contrary, stated that they would agree to the framework only if it formed part of a European industrial policy which extended to the whole of the sector concerned. The Commission insisted, however, that acceptance of the framework could not be subject to any preconditions whatsoever.[50] Moreover, guidelines cannot operate to restrict the scope of EU legislation covering the same subject matter. Thus, Directive 2008/4/EC on the promotion of energy cogeneration was not to be regarded as limited in scope to high efficiency cogeneration, in respect of which State aid might be granted pursuant to the environmental guidelines, just because the preamble to that directive stated that public support should be consistent with those guidelines.[51]

Block exemption regulations   Council Regulation (EC) No 994/98[52] empowered the Commission to adopt regulations declaring that certain general

---

[48]   Case T-357/02 RENV, *Freistaat Sachsen v Commission* [2011] ECR II-5415, para 44.
[49]   Case T-304/08, *Smurfit Kappa Group plc v Commission* EU:T:2012:351, para 91.
[50]   *Nineteenth Report on Competition Policy* (1989), pt. 127.
[51]   Case C-195/12, *IBV v Région Wallonne* EU:C:2103:598, para 39.
[52]   OJ 1998 L142/1.

categories of aid are compatible with the internal market.[53]   The categories originally listed were SMEs, research and development, environmental protection, employment and training and regional aid.[54]   Additional categories were added by Council Regulation (EU) No 733/2013 as follows: cultural and heritage conservation; making good the damage caused by natural disasters; making good the damage caused by certain adverse weather conditions in fisheries; forestry; promotion of food sector products; conservation of marine and freshwater biological resources; sports; residents of remote regions for transport; basic broadband infrastructure; infrastructure in support of objectives of common interest.[55]   Initially, the Commission exercised its powers only in relation to training and SMEs with the adoption of Regulations (EC) Nos 68/2001 and 70/2001 respectively.[56]   Subsequently, the Commission adopted Regulation (EC) No 2204/2002 on employment aid[57] and Regulation (EC) No 1628/2006 on national regional investment aid.[58]   These were replaced, initially by Commission Regulation (EC) No 800/2008 and, subsequently, by Commission Regulation (EU) No 651/2014 which provides for a general block exemption covering several different categories of State aid.[59]

Belgium challenged the adoption of Regulation 2204/2002, alleging that it was inconsistent with the power granted by the Council in Regulation (EC) No 994/98. The ECJ rejected Belgium's argument that the Commission had not respected either the terms or the purpose of Regulation (EC) No 994/98, which require, so far as the criteria for the compatibility of aid with the internal market are concerned, simple codification by the Commission of its pre-existing practice and consequently exclude the adoption of new, stricter criteria. There was no basis for stating that the Commission was required to lay down criteria for compatibility that were in total conformity with its pre-existing practice and not to use its experience to lay down new criteria, including even stricter criteria than the existing ones.[60]

Ratione temporis **of substantive State aid policy**   The principles of legal certainty and the protection of legitimate expectations, by virtue of which the effects of EU legislation must be clear and predictable for those who are subject to it, require the application of substantive provisions to the facts which

---

[53]   See A. Sinnaeve, "Block exemptions for State aid: More scope for State aid control by Member States and competitors" (2001) 38 CMLRev 1479.

[54]   Council Regulation (EC) No 994/98, Article 1.

[55]   Council Regulation (EU) No 733/2013, Article 1(2).

[56]   OJ 2001 L10/20; OJ 2001 L10/33.

[57]   OJ 2002 L337/3.

[58]   OJ 2006 L302/29.

[59]   OJ 2008 L214/3.

[60]   Case C-110/03, *Belgium v Commission* [2005] ECR I-2801, paras 51-53.

fall within their scope of application *ratione materiae* and *ratione temporis*.[61] Since the Commission adapts and changes its policy instruments on a regular basis, it is not uncommon that the substantive policy rules might change between the time of notification of a proposed aid and the date of the Commission's decision concerning the compatibility of the aid with the internal market. In those circumstances, it is necessary to determine which set of rules should be applied, in particular in order to ensure respect for the principle of legitimate expectations.

Generally, the rules that apply to determine the compatibility of aid with the internal market which has been notified but not yet put into effect are those in force at the time that the Commission takes its decision.[62] A new rule applies immediately to the future effects of a situation which came about under an old rule, where the situation remains current and has not been definitively established under the old rule.[63] In *Commission v Freistaat Sachsen*, the ECJ analysed the position with regard to an aid scheme for SMEs that had been notified by Germany at a time when the SME guidelines were in force, but which had been assessed by the Commission in accordance with the provisions of Commission Regulation (EC) No 70/2001 which came into effect shortly after the notification, and concluded that the new rules were properly applicable.[64] It reasoned that the prohibition in Article 108(3) TFEU on putting the measure into effect prior to acquiring Commission approval was designed to ensure that the system of aid could not become operational before the Commission had a reasonable opportunity to study the proposal in detail. Moreover, the criteria of assessment of the compatibility of State aid in force on the date when the Commission took its decision were, as a rule, better adapted to the context of competition at that time.[65] Similarly, in *Budapesti Erőmű Zrt v Commission*, which concerned a measure which was treated as new aid on the date of accession by Hungary to the EU, the General Court held that only the environmental guidelines applicable at that time could be considered and not earlier guidelines that had been in force at the time the

---

[61] Case T-25/04, *González y Díez SA v Commission* [2007] ECR II-3121, para 59; Case T-348/04, *SIDE v Commission* [2008] ECR I-625, para 66.

[62] Case C-167/11P, *Cantiere Navale De Poli SpA v Commission* EU:C:2012:164, para 51; Case C-200/11P, *Italy v Commission* EU:C:2012:165, para 37; Case T-92/11, *Andersen v Commission* EU:T:2013:143, para 39; Case T-551/10, *Fri-El Acerra Srl v Commission* EU:T:2013:430, para 56.

[63] Case C-162/00, *Land Nordrhein-Westfalen v Pokrzeptowiz-Meyer* [2002] ECR I-1049, para 50; Case C-334/07P, *Commission v Freistaat Sachsen* [2008] ECR I-9465, para 43; Case T-25/04, *González y Díez SA v Commission* [2007] ECR II-3121, para 70; Case T-348/04, *SIDE v Commission* [2008] ECR I-625, para 55; Case T-584/08, *Cantiere Navale De Poli SpA v Commission* [2011] ECR II-63, para 35; Case T-3/09, *Italy v Commission* [2011] ECR II-95, para 59.

[64] Case C-334/07P, *Commission v Freistaat Sachsen* [2008] ECR I-9465, para 53.

[65] *Ibid.*, paras 46-52.

measure initially entered into force prior to accession.[66] Exceptionally, Commission guidelines may specifically state that decisions on notified aid will be assessed on the basis of earlier guidelines in force at the time of notification. In that event, those earlier guidelines will apply, without the Commission breaching the principles of legal certainty or legitimate expectation.[67] By contrast, the legality of a decision cannot be called into question by reference to guidelines adopted after the decision has been adopted.[68] In *Pollmeier Massivholz v Commission*, the General Court held that a Commission decision concerning aid which had been granted in December 2006 was governed by Regulation (EC) No 69/2001 on *de minimis* aid, which was applicable at the date of the grant of the aid and which specifically provided that it applied to aid granted until June 2007, rather than Regulation (EC) No 1998/2006 which was in force at the time the decision was taken.[69]

The analysis as to whether a measure is compatible with the internal market normally requires an assessment of whether, during the period in which the aid in question was paid, that aid was likely to distort competition.[70] Once it has produced its effects, aid becomes definitively compatible or incompatible with the internal market.[71] Thus, as regards unlawful aid that has been paid without being notified, the applicable substantive rules are normally those in force at the time the aid was paid.[72] Substantive rules of State aid policy must be interpreted as applying to situations existing before their entry into force only in so far as it clearly follows from their wording, objectives or general scheme that such an effect must be given to them.[73] For example, the 1998 regional aid guidelines provided that the Commission would assess compatibility on the basis of those guidelines in all cases as soon as they were applicable.[74] This

---

[66] Cases T-80/06 & T-182/09, *Budapesti Erőmű Zrt v Commission* EU:T:2012:65, para 102.

[67] Cases C-465/09P–C-470/09P, *Diputación Foral de Vizcaya v Commission* [2011] ECR I-83*, paras 127-128; Case T-92/11, *Andersen v Commission* EU:T:2013:143, para 55.

[68] Case C-621/13P, *Orange SA v Commission* EU:C:2015:114, para 49; Case T-258/10, *Orange SA v Commission* EU:T:2013:471, para 96.

[69] Case T-89/09, *Pollmeier Massivholz GmbH v Commission* EU:T:2015:153, paras 75-77.

[70] Case T-348/04, *SIDE v Commission* [2008] ECR I-625, para 59.

[71] *Ibid.*, para 58.

[72] Case T-584/08, *Cantiere Navale De Poli SpA v Commission* [2011] ECR II-63, para 37; Case T-3/09, *Italy v Commission* [2011] ECR II-95, para 61; Case T-92/11, *Andersen v Commission* EU:T:2013:143, para 40.

[73] Cases 212/80-218/80, *Meridionale Industria Salumi* [1981] ECR 2735, para 9; Case C-162/00, *Land Nordrhein-Westfalen v Pokrzeptowicz-Meyer* [2002] ECR I-1049, para 49; Cases C-74/00P & C-75/00P, *Falck SpA v Commission* [2002] ECR I-7869, para 119; Case C-369/09P, *ISD Polska v Commission* [2011] ECR I-2011, para 98; Case T-25/04, *González y Díez SA v Commission* [2007] ECR II-3121, para 58.

[74] Cases T-30/01 etc., *Territorio Histórico de Álava – Diputación Foral de Álava v Commission* [2009] ECR II-2919, para 215.

applies irrespective of whether such rules might produce favourable or unfavourable effects for the person concerned.[75]

The strict incentive requirement also entails that a derogation concerning State aid must be limited in its application to the period after it became effective, at least where the aid in question has already been disbursed.[76] Thus, in *SIDE v Commission*, the Commission was found to have erred in law by applying Article 107(3)(d) TFEU to the period before it came into effect on 1 November 1993 instead of applying the substantive rules in force during the period in question.[77] To consider that aid which has not been notified can be declared compatible with the internal market by virtue of a derogation which was not in force when that aid was paid would result in conferring an advantage on the Member State which granted it in relation to any other Member State which might have intended to grant similar aid but refrained from doing so since there was no derogation authorising this. Similarly, an advantage would be conferred on the Member State in question in relation to any other Member State which, since it intended to grant aid for the same period, notified the aid before the derogation in question came into effect and, as a consequence, obtained a decision from the Commission stating that the aid was incompatible with the internal market. That would serve to encourage Member States not to notify aid which they considered incompatible with the internal market, in the absence of an applicable derogation, in the hope that such a derogation might be adopted subsequently.[78]

In *Falck v Commission*, the ECJ held that, under the ECSC Treaty, the compatibility of aid with the internal market could be assessed only in light of the rules in force under the applicable steel aid code on the date on which it was actually paid.[79] The Commission was wrong to have assessed the aid under the provisions of the code applicable at the time that the decision was taken, which had replaced the rules applicable at the time when the aid was granted. It was clear from the general scheme and the objectives of successive steel aid codes that those codes had been adopted according to the needs existing at any given period. Accordingly, the application of rules adopted at a particular period, according to the then prevailing situation, to aid paid in the course of an earlier period did not correspond to the general scheme and

---

[75] Case T-348/04, *SIDE v Commission* [2008] ECR I-625, para 54.

[76] Case T-348/04, *SIDE v Commission* [2008] ECR II-625, para 62; Case T-150/12, *Greece v Commission* EU:T:2014:191, para 156; Case T-52/12, *Greece v Commission* EU:T:2014:677, para 169.

[77] Case T-348/04, *SIDE v Commission* [2008] ECR II-625, para 61.

[78] Case T-348/04, *SIDE v Commission* [2008] ECR II-625, para 67; Case T-150/12, *Greece v Commission* EU:T:2014:191, para 158; Case T-52/12, *Greece v Commission* EU:T:2014:677, para 171.

[79] Cases C-74/00P & C-75/00P, *Falck SpA v Commission* [2002] ECR I-7869, para 117; Case C-408/04P, *Commission v Salzgitter* AG [2008] ECR I-2767, para 92; Case T-308/00 RENV, *Salzgitter AG v Commission* EU:T:2013:30, para 105.

objectives of that type of rules.[80] Similarly, in *González y Díez SA v Commission*, where a decision concerning the coal sector was adopted after the expiry of the ECSC Treaty, it was held that, since it applied to a legal situation which was definitively established prior to the expiry of that Treaty, the fact that the regulatory framework had since been subsumed under Article 108(2) TFEU did not alter the requirement to apply the substantive provisions applicable at the time the aid was granted.[81]

7.3 PRINCIPLES OF EU STATE AID POLICY

Principles of EU State aid policy In exercising its discretion, the Commission has to ensure that the aims of free competition and EU solidarity are reconciled, whilst complying with the principle of proportionality.[82] For aid to be compatible with the internal market, it must not only further a recognised EU objective but it must also be necessary and proportionate to that end.[83] The Commission's communication on State aid modernisation established certain common principles that are applicable to the assessment of compatibility of all aid measures. In particular, aid must aim at an objective of common interest in accordance with Article 107(3) TFEU, it must be targeted towards a situation where aid can bring about a material improvement that the market cannot deliver and the proposed aid measure must be an appropriate policy instrument to address the objective of common interest. An incentive test is applicable such that the aid must change the behaviour of the recipient in such a way that it engages in additional activity. Moreover, the principle of proportionality requires that the amount and intensity of the aid must be limited to the minimum needed to induce the additional investment or activity by the recipient. Negative effects on competition and trade must be sufficiently limited, so that the overall balance is positive. Aid should be transparent in order to enable its intensity to be measured and to determine whether it is accumulated with any other aid.

Aid should normally be given only for investment purposes. Operating aid is generally prohibited, on the basis that it does not lead to the development of a region or activity, although it is permitted in certain circumstances. Aid for exports to other Member States is normally expressly prohibited, since this

---

[80] Cases C-74/00P & C-75/00P, *Falck SpA v Commission* [2002] ECR I-7869, para 120.

[81] Case T-25/04, *González y Díez SA v Commission* [2007] ECR II-3121, para 59.

[82] Case T-380/94, *AIUFFASS v Commission* [1996] ECR II-2169, para 54; Case T-348/04, *SIDE v Commission* [2008] ECR I-625, para 98.

[83] Case 730/79, *Philip Morris v Commission* [1980] ECR 2671, para 18; Case T-55/99, *CETM v Commission* [2000] ECR II-3207, para 163; Case T-9/98, *Mitteldeutsche Erdoel-Raffinerie GmbH v Commission* [2002] ECR II-3367, para 115.

would have the effect of distorting competition that is not in the common interest.

Incentive effect In order for aid to benefit from one of the derogations contained in Article 107(3) TFEU, it must not only comply with one of the objectives set out in that provision, but it must also be necessary for the attainment of those objectives.[84] Aid which improves the financial situation of the recipient undertaking without being necessary for the attainment of the objectives specified in Article 107(3) TFEU cannot be considered compatible with the internal market.[85] Accordingly, the incentive effect of an aid measure falls within the examination of its compatibility with the internal market.[86] A finding that an aid measure is not necessary can arise in particular from the fact that the aid project has already been started, or even completed, by the undertaking concerned prior to the application for aid being submitted to the competent authorities. In such a case, the aid concerned cannot operate as an incentive.[87] The EU courts have held that such a requirement is a simple, relevant and suitable criterion enabling the Commission to presume that the planned aid is necessary.[88] Thus, in *Kronoply v Commission*, aid to cover the costs of an investment that had already been undertaken could not be regarded as necessary for that investment.[89] Similarly, the Commission adopted a negative decision in relation to a two-year extension of an 8% investment premium granted to enterprises located in the east German *länder* in so far as the date by which qualifying investments had to be completed was put back from 1996 to 1998 without any alteration to the date for the start of the

---

[84] Case 730/79, *Philip Morris* v *Commission* [1980] ECR 2671, para 17; Case T-187/99, *Agrana Zucker und Stärke AG v Commission* [2001] ECR II-1587, para 74; Case T-551/10, *Fri-El Acerra Srl v Commission* EU:T:2013:430, para 49.

[85] Case C-390/06, *Nuova Agricast Srl v Ministero delle Attività Produttive* [2008] ECR I-2577, para 68; Case C-459/10P, *Freistaat Sachsen v Commission* [2011] I-109*, para 36; Case C-544/09P, *Germany v Commission* [2011] ECR I-128*, para 44; Cases C-630/11P to C-633/11P, *HGA srl v Commission* EU:C:2013:387, para 104; Case T-21/06, *Germany v Commission* [2009] ECR II-197*, para 64.

[86] Case C-129/12, *Magdeburger Mühlenwerke v Finanzamt Magdeburg* EU:C:2013:200, para 45; Case T-551/10, *Fri-El Acerra Srl v Commission* EU:T:2013:430, para 49.

[87] Case C-390/06, *Nuova Agricast Srl v Ministero delle Attività Produttive* [2008] ECR I-2577, para 69; Case T-422/07, *Djebel-SGPS SA v Commission* EU:T:2012:11, para 124.

[88] Cases C-630/11P to C-633/11P, *HGA srl v Commission* EU:C:2013:387, para 106; Cases T-394/08, T-408/08, T-453/08 & T-454/08, *Regione autonoma della Sardegna v Commission* [2011] ECR II-6255, para 215.

[89] Case C-117/09P, *Kronoply GmbH v Commission* [2010 ECR I-85*, para 38; Case T-162/06, *Kronoply GmbH v Commission* [2009] ECR II-1, para 98

investment. This was considered additional operating aid to the same projects and would not encourage new projects.[90]

For aid falling within the scope of the block exemption in Commission Regulation (EU) No 651/2014, the incentive effect is considered to be present if, before work on the project or activity has started, the beneficiary has submitted an application for the aid to the Member State concerned. Before granting *ad hoc* regional investment aid to large undertakings, it must also be verified that the project would not have been carried out in the area concerned or would not have been sufficiently profitable for the beneficiary in the area concerned in the absence of the aid. In other cases of *ad hoc* aid, it must be shown that the aid leads to a material increase in the scope of the project or in the amount spent by the beneficiary on the project or that there is a material increase in the speed of completion of the project. These conditions do not apply to fiscal aid if the fiscal measure establishes a legal right to aid in accordance with objective criteria and without further exercise of discretion by the Member State concerned, where the measure was adopted before work on the aided project or activity started. An incentive effect is deemed to be present in the case of regional operating aid, aid for access to finance for SMEs, aid for the recruitment of disadvantaged or disabled workers, aid in the form of reductions in environmental taxes, aid to make good damage caused by certain natural disasters, social aid for transport for residents of remote regions and aid for culture and heritage conservation.[91] The Commission's guidelines and frameworks also include specific provisions concerning the establishment of an incentive effect.

Intensity of aid The Commission's early practice was to measure the intensity of aid as net grant equivalent calculated by reference to the benefit accruing to the recipient after payment of taxes on its profits. For example, where a grant was tax free and was entered in the accounts as income, the benefit received was deemed to be equal to the full value of the grant. If the grant was fully taxable in the first year, the net grant equivalent was calculated by taking the net grant after tax as a proportion of the investment. Thus, if the investment was 100, the grant 20 and the tax rate 40%, the net grant equivalent was 12%. This approach was condemned by the General Court in *Alzetta v Commission* which held that the Commission was not empowered to take into consideration the incidence of tax on the amount of financial aid allocated when it assessed the compatibility of the aid with the internal market. Such charges were not levied specifically on the aid itself but were levied downstream and applied to

---

[90]   Commission Decision 98/194/EC, *Investment projects in the new Länder*, OJ 1998 L73/38; Case T-9/98, *Mitteldeutsche Erdoel-Raffinerie GmbH v Commission* [2001] ECR II-3367, para 123.

[91]   Commission Regulation (EU) No 651/2014, Article 6(1)-(5).

the aid in the same way as income received.[92] Accordingly, the Commission now calculates aid on the basis of gross grant equivalent.[93]

Aid payable in several instalments is discounted to its value at the moment it is granted. The eligible costs are discounted to their value at the moment the aid is granted. The interest rate to be used for discounting purposes is the discount rate applicable at the moment the aid is granted. Where aid is granted by means of tax advantages, discounting of aid tranches is on the basis of the discount rates applicable at the various times the tax advantage takes effect. Where aid is granted in the form of repayable advances which, in the absence of an accepted methodology to calculate their gross grant equivalent, are expressed as a percentage of the eligible costs and the measure provides that in case of a successful outcome of the project, as defined on the basis of a reasonable and prudent hypothesis, the advances will be repaid with an interest rate at least equal to the discount rate applicable at the moment the aid is granted, the maximum aid intensities may be increased by 10 percentage points.[94]

Cumulation of aid Aid may be granted to an undertaking in relation to several different matters. For example, a firm in an assisted region may benefit simultaneously from regional investment aid, training aid and aid for research and development purposes. Cumulation of aid poses difficulties for the Commission in determining whether there may be a distortion of competition contrary to the common interest. Accordingly, the Commission considers the cumulative effect of aid granted under different schemes and from different sources.[95] In determining whether notification thresholds and maximum aid intensities are respected, the total amount of State aid for the aided activity or project or undertaking is taken into account. Where EU funding that is not under the control of the Member State is combined with State aid, only the latter is considered for determining whether these limits are respected, provided that the total amount of public funding granted in relation to the same eligible costs does not exceed the most favourable funding rate laid down in the applicable EU rules.[96]

Aid with identifiable eligible costs exempted by the block exemption regulation may be cumulated with any other State aid, as long as those measures concern different identifiable eligible costs. Aid may be accumulated with other aid in respect of the same eligible costs, partly or fully overlapping, only if such cumulation does not result in exceeding the highest aid intensity or aid amount applicable to the aid under the block exemption. Aid without

---

[92] Cases T-298/97, etc., *Alzetta v Commission* [2000] ECR II-2319, para 89.
[93] Commission Regulation (EU) No 651/2014, Article 7(2).
[94] *Ibid.*, Article 7(3)-(5).
[95] *Twentieth Report on Competition Law* (1990), pt. 306.
[96] Commission Regulation (EU) No 651/2014, Article 8(1)-(2).

identifiable eligible costs may be cumulated with any other State aid without identifiable eligible costs, up to the highest relevant total financing threshold fixed in the specific circumstances of each case by the block exemption regulation or individual Commission decision.[97]

State aid exempted under the block exemption regulation may not be cumulated with any *de minimis* aid in respect of the same eligible costs if such cumulation would result in an aid intensity exceeding those laid down in the block exemption regulation.[98]

General investment aid Much of EU State aid policy is aimed at encouraging specific investment aid on the basis of regional, sectoral, environmental or other criteria. General investment aid schemes, being schemes not aimed at a specific industry or region and which do not pursue a specific EU objective, do not qualify for exemption under either Article 107(3)(a) TFEU or Article 107(3)(c) TFEU. Such schemes had been used as a general investment incentive available on a wide scale, or, when they were used more selectively, were simply a means of helping individual firms on an *ad hoc* basis. Such assistance had repercussions contrary to economic and social cohesion and to regional development. Not only did it reduce the cost of investment by the recipient firms by comparison with their competitors in other Member States, it also attracted to the States concerned mobile investment which might have located elsewhere in the EU. In addition, a general aid scheme in one Member State could neutralise the attraction of regional aid available in other Member States and in the Member State's own development areas.[99] While the Commission had long had a negative attitude to general investment aid schemes,[100] in 1990, it launched a policy aimed at eliminating them altogether. By 1993, this policy had been largely achieved.[101] Thus, for example, the 1959 Belgian law on economic expansion was repealed in 1992 and replaced by new provisions which were consistent with the Commission's policies.[102] In the United Kingdom, the Industrial Development Act 1982, section 8, provided the Government with the power to award aid to individual companies anywhere in the United Kingdom. The Commission agreed not to require the abolition of this provision only after receiving satisfactory assurances that advance notification would be given to the Commission of all plans to grant aid to individual companies outside of approved schemes. The Commission made it clear, however, that it would take an unfavourable view of any proposal to

---

[97]   *Ibid.*, Article 8(3)-(4).
[98]   *Ibid.*, Article 8(5).
[99]   *Twentieth Report on Competition Policy* (1990), pt. 171.
[100] *Ninth Report on Competition Policy* (1979), pt. 184; *Nineteenth Report on Competition Policy* (1989), pt. 121.
[101] *Twenty-Third Report on Competition Policy* (1993), pt. 417.
[102] *Twenty-Second Report on Competition Policy* (1992), pt. 417 and 457.

provide financial assistance for general investment purposes outside of assisted areas.[103] General sectoral aid schemes are equally prohibited, so that the Commission refused to allow, for instance, an Italian aid scheme intended to facilitate the restructuring of the consumer electronics industry through the acquisition of minority and temporary holdings in the capital of firms in the industry.[104]

Operating aid In principle, operating aid distorts the conditions of competition in that it releases an undertaking from costs which it would normally have to bear in its day to day management or normal activities.[105] It may be granted only in exceptional circumstances.[106] As well as aid towards overheads, operating aid includes any financial assistance granted without any specific conditions attached.[107] Thus, aid to cover the costs of an investment that has already been undertaken is regarded as operating aid.[108] Operating aid includes aid granted indirectly in the form of tax relief granted to individuals in respect of investment in companies, where the companies are free to use the funds for any purpose.[109] Thus, a Spanish measure allowing for complete exemption from corporation tax for ten years on condition that the taxpayer invested a certain amount in fixed assets and created at least 10 jobs was held to be operating aid, as the tax relief was not specifically linked to either investment or job creation but depended on achieving taxable profits, subject to

---

[103] *Twenty-First Report on Competition Policy* (1991), pt. 242.

[104] *Ibid.*, pt. 253.

[105] Case C-86/89, *Italy v Commission* [1990] ECR I-3891, para 18; Case C-301/87, *France v Commission* [1990] ECR I-307, para 50; Case C-278/95P, *Seimens v Commission* [1997] ECR I-2507, para 37; Case C-156/98, *Germany v Commission* [2000] ECR I-6857, para 30; Case C-288/96, *Germany v Commission* [2000] ECR I-8237, para 77; Case C-172/03, *Heiser v Finanzamt Innsbruck* [2005] ECR I-1627, para 55; Case C-494/06P, *Commission v Italy* [2009] ECR I-3639, para 53; Cases C-71/09P, C-73/09P & C-76/09P, *Comitato Venezia vuole vivere v Commission* [2011] ECR I-4727, para 136; Case C-458/09P, *Italy v Commission* [2011] ECR I-179*, para 63; Case T-459/93, *Siemens v Commission* [1995] ECR II-1675, para 48; Case T-214/95 *Vlaamse Gewest* v *Commission* [1998] ECR II-717, para 43; Case T-190/00, *Regione Siciliana v Commission* [2003] ECR II-5015, para 130; Case T-217/02, *Ter Lembeek International NV v Commission* [2006] ECR II-4483, para 177; Case T-375/03, *Fachvereinigung Mineralfaserindustrie eV v Commission* [2007] ECR II-121*, para 139; Case T-348/04, *SIDE v Commission* [2008] ECR I-625, para 99; Case T-162/06, *Kronoply GmbH v Commission* [2009] ECR II-1, para 75; Case T-379/09, *Italy v Commission* EU:T:2012:422, para 89; Case T-243/09, *Fedecom v Commission* EU:T:2012:497, para 86; Case T-308/11, *Eurallumina SpA v Commission* EU:T:2014:894, para 85; Case T-177/10, *Alcoa Trasformazioni srl v Commission* EU:T:2014:897, para 92.

[106] Cases C-71/09P, C-73/09P & C-76/09P, *Comitato Venezia vuole vivere v Commission* [2011] ECR I-4727, para 168.

[107] Case C-86/89, *Italy v Commission* [1990] ECR I-3891, para 18.

[108] Case T-162/06, *Kronoply GmbH v Commission* [2009] ECR II-1, para 74.

[109] Case C-156/98, *Germany v Commission* [2000] ECR I-6857, para 30.

compliance with the relevant conditions.[110] Tax relief for costs of listing on a stock exchange was considered as operating aid since it was not concerned with a specific investment, but was an operation by which companies pursued financial objectives with a view to obtaining access to capital.[111] In its decision on aid to Olympic Airways, the Commission categorised the following as operating aid: the toleration by the Greek State of the non-payment, or deferment of the payment dates, of social security contributions for October to December 2001, value added tax on fuel and spare parts, rent payable to airports for the period 1998 to 2001, airport charges and a tax imposed on passengers on departure from Greek airports.[112] In *Germany v Commission*, it was argued that a security granted to Jadekost to enable it to take out a loan should not have been classified as operating aid since the loan could have been used to finance investments, leaving Jadekost's own funds to be employed to cover its liquidity requirements. However, this was rejected by the ECJ which agreed with the Commission's view that aid which is intended to improve the recipient's liquidity, without any obligations being attached, must be regarded as operating aid.[113] In *Freistaat Sachsen v Commission*, aid to cover the costs of overseas marketing offices constituted operating aid on the ground that winning new markets and efforts to remain on the market were part of the normal strategy of each undertaking wishing to maintain a lasting presence on the market and that associated costs must be regarded as part of the normal operating costs of those undertakings.[114]

Operating aid is rarely permitted by the Commission since, in particular as regards aid justified by Article 107(3)(a) TFEU and Article 107(3)(c) TFEU, it does not satisfy the criterion of development of the area or economic activity concerned. In *Regione Siciliana v Commission*, aid to help reschedule part of past debts was operating aid, which was not excused merely by the fact that interest rates were higher in Sicily than in the rest of Italy.[115] Exceptionally, operating aid may be allowed in Article 107(3)(a) TFEU regions provided that it is awarded to tackle specific or permanent handicaps faced by undertakings in disadvantaged regions.[116] Operating aid has also been permitted for specific types of industry or service, such as certain transport services, shipbuilding and film production, and for environmental protection.

---

[110] Cases T-30/01 etc., *Territorio Histórico de Álava – Diputación Foral de Álava v Commission* [2009] ECR II-2919, para 227.

[111] Case C-458/09P, *Italy v Commission* [2011] ECR I-179*, para 64; Case T-211/05, *Italy v Commission* [2009] ECR II-2777, para 182.

[112] Case C-415/03, *Commission v Greece* [2005] ECR I-3875, para 5; Commission Decision 2003/372/EC *Olympic Airways* OJ 2003 L132/1.

[113] Case C-288/96, *Germany v Commission* [2000] ECR I-8237, para 48.

[114] Case T-357/02 RENV, *Freistaat Sachsen v Commission* [2011] ECR II-5415, para 102.

[115] Case T-190/00, *Regione Siciliana v Commission* [2003] ECR II-5015, para 131.

[116] Guidelines on national regional aid 2014-2020, para 16.

Aid for exports In *Commission v France*, the ECJ held that a preferential discount rate for exports from France was an aid within Article 107(1) TFEU despite the fact that it was applicable to all national products exported.[117] Standard Commission policy is that aid for exports within the EU is incompatible with the functioning of the internal market and will not benefit from an exemption, whatever the intensity, form, grounds or purpose.[118] Commission Regulation (EU) No 651/2014 specifically excludes exemption for export-related activities, i.e. aid directly linked to the quantities exported, to the establishment and operation of a distribution network or to current expenditure linked to the export activity.[119] Similar provisions apply in various guidelines and frameworks.

Aid for exports outside of the European Union, which is not necessarily prohibited, falls within the scope of application of the EU's external trade policy. In this respect, Member States should progressively harmonise the systems whereby they grant aid for exports to third countries to the extent necessary to ensure that competition between EU undertakings is not distorted. Nevertheless, as State aid in the EU evolves, account has to be taken of the international context and, in particular, the multilateral obligations imposed by WTO rules. In any event, this should not be used as a means of circumventing the Commission's prohibition on export aid within the EU.[120]

Member States maintain an active policy of supporting their export industry, principally through the grant of favourable terms for export credits and export-credit insurance. In the light of this, the Commission, in 1997, issued a communication on the application of the State aid provisions to short-term export credit insurance, the purpose of which is to remove distortions of competition caused by State aid in that sector of the export-credit insurance business in which there is competition between public or publicly-supported insurers and private insurers.[121] Medium and long-term export-credit risks are regarded as largely non-marketable at present. Marketable risks are defined as being commercial risks on non-public debtors established in the EU and in the majority of OECD countries, whilst all other risks, i.e. political and catastrophe risks and commercial risks on public buyers and on non-OECD countries, are considered as not yet marketable. From 2002, the definition of marketable risks includes commercial and political risks on public and non-public debtors in the EU and in the OECD countries. For marketable risks, the maximum risk

---

[117] Cases 6 & 11/69, *Commission v France* [1969] ECR 523, paras 20-21.

[118] *Seventh Report on Competition Policy* (1977), pt. 166; *Eleventh Report on Competition Policy* (1981), pt. 247.

[119] Commission Regulation (EU) No 651/2014, Article 1(2)(c).

[120] *Sixteenth Report on Competition Policy* (1986), pt. 257.

[121] OJ 1997 C281/4, amended by OJ 2001 C217/2, OJ 2004 C307/12 and OJ 2005 C325/22. See J. Battista & K. Van de Casteele, "Export credit insurance", in W. Mederer, N. Pesaresi & M. van Hoof (ed.), *EU Competition Law*, Volume IV, Book Two, Chapter 10 (Claeys & Casteels, 2008).

period is less than two years.[122]   Where cover for marketable risks is temporarily unavailable from private insurers or from public insurers operating for their own account, such risks are to be considered as non-marketable. In those cases, the public or publicly supported export-credit insurers may take on the risk for the account or with the guarantee of the State, although the premium rates for such risks should be aligned with the rates charged by private insurers for the type of risk in question.[123]

Transparency of aid An essential condition for ensuring the coordination and assessment of general systems of aid is that aid be transparent. Transparency requires that opaque aid must not be introduced and that all aid must be capable of being measured as a percentage of the investment or expenditure incurred by the recipient.[124] In order to benefit from the block exemption in Commission Regulation (EU) No 651/2014, aid is considered as transparent where it is possible to calculate precisely the gross grant equivalent of the aid *ex ante* without any need to undertake a risk assessment.[125] Aid is transparent where it is comprised in grants and interest rate subsidies or, in the case of loans, where the gross grant equivalent has been calculated on the basis of the reference rate prevailing at the time of the grant.[126] Aid comprised in guarantees will be regarded as transparent where the gross grant equivalent has been calculated on the basis of safe harbour premiums laid down in a Commission notice or it is calculated in accordance with an approved methodology.[127] As regards aid comprised in fiscal measures, transparency will be established where the measure provides for a cap ensuring that the applicable threshold is not exceeded.[128] Aid in the form of repayable loans is considered transparent only if the total amount of the repayable advance does not exceed the applicable threshold.[129]

The Commission publishes the names of beneficiaries of notified individual aid and the amount of aid in its decisions. Under common rules applicable under the horizontal aid guidelines, Member States are required, as a condition for granting aid, to establish comprehensive State aid websites, at regional or national level, for the publication of information on aid measures and their beneficiaries. A standard format is used which allows the information to be easily published on the internet, searched and downloaded. The transparency

---

[122] Communication on short-term export-credit insurance, para 2.5. The OECD countries covered by this arrangement are Australia, Canada, Iceland, Japan, New Zealand, Norway, Switzerland and the United States of America.

[123] *Ibid.*, para 4.4.

[124] Council Resolution of 20 October 1971, para 4.

[125] Commission Regulation (EU) No 651/2014, Article 5(1).

[126] *Ibid.*, Article 5(2)(a)-(b).

[127] *Ibid.*, Article 5(2)(c).

[128] *Ibid.*, Article 5(2)(d).

[129] *Ibid.*, Article 5(2)(j).

requirement applies in general to all State aid, except for smaller aid awards of less than €500,000.[130]

Effects of previously granted aid The cumulative effects of previously granted aid, particularly unlawful aid, may legitimately be taken into account by the Commission in determining whether further aid is compatible with the internal market. In *TWD v Commission*, the Commission was held to be entitled to require the recovery of previous aid which had been granted without authorization as a condition for permitting further aid.[131] That applies regardless of whether the earlier aid as granted as individual aid or aid granted under a scheme.[132] The Commission now applies this principle as a matter of course.[133] It is for the Member State and the potential beneficiary of new aid to provide the Commission with sufficient evidence showing that the new aid and the earlier unlawful aid do not have a cumulative effect[134]

---

[130] Commission communication on State aid and transparency, OJ 2014 C198/30.

[131] Case C-355/95P, *TWD v Commission* [1997] ECR I-2549, paras 25-27; Case C-150/09P, *Iride SpA v Commission* [2010] ECR I-5*, para 70; Case C-480/09P, *AceaElectrabel Produzione SpA v Commission* [2010] ECR I-13355, para 97; Cases T-244/93 & T-486/93, *TWD v Commission* [1995] ECR II-2265, para 56; Case T-348/04, *SIDE v Commission* [2008] ECR I-625, para 60; Case T-25/07, *Iride SpA v Commission* [2009] ECR II-245, para 83.

[132] Case C-150/09P, *Iride SpA v Commission* [2010] ECR I-5*, para 50; Case C-480/09P, *AceaElectrabel Produzione SpA v Commission* [2010] ECR I-13355, para 96; Case T-25/07, *Iride SpA v Commission* [2009] ECR II-245, para 88.

[133] Commission notice on the recovery of unlawful and incompatible aid, paras 75-78, OJ 2007 C272/4.

[134] Case C-480/09P, *AceaElectrabel Produzione SpA v Commission* [2010] ECR I-13355, paras 99-101; Case T-303/05, *AceaElectrabel Produzione SpA v Commission* [2009] ECR I-137*, para 187.

Chapter Eight

REGIONAL AID

8.1 COMMISSION POLICY ON REGIONAL AID

Objectives of regional aid policy   Article 3(3) TEU requires the European Union *inter alia* to work for the sustainable development of Europe based on balanced economic growth and the promotion of economic, social and territorial cohesion. The primary objective of State aid control in the field of regional aid is to allow aid for regional development while ensuring a level playing field between Member States, in particular by preventing subsidy races that may occur when they try to attract or retain businesses in disadvantaged areas of the EU, and to limit the effects of regional aid on trade and competition to the minimum necessary.[1]   Moreover, Article 174 TFEU provides that the European Union, in the context of the strengthening of economic and social cohesion, should aim at reducing disparities between the levels of development of the various regions and the backwardness of the less-favoured regions. EU policies and actions are to take these objectives into account and contribute to their achievement.[2]   Nevertheless, regional aid control comes under the competition rules of the FEU Treaty which is distinct from the provisions governing the strengthening of economic and social cohesion, such that, while they are complementary, there is no hierarchy as between the objectives pursued by the two policies. Accordingly, it is not the case that the State aid control of national regional aid is to be treated in a flexible manner in the light of the objectives of economic and social cohesion.[3]

The identification of regions that may benefit from regional aid in accordance with Article 107(3)(a) TFEU and Article 107(3)(c) TFEU is fundamental to the application of much of EU State aid policy. Most importantly, this determines the areas within which regional aid may be granted. These disadvantaged regions are generally referred to as assisted regions or assisted areas. Whereas the geographical development objective distinguishes regional aid from other categories of State aid, classification as an assisted area also has a significant impact on the award of horizontal aid such as aid for research, development and innovation, for energy or

---

[1]   Regional aid guidelines 2014-20, para 3.
[2]   Article 175 TFEU.
[3]   Cases T-254/00, T-270/00 & T-277/00, *Hotel Cipriani SpA v Commission* [2008] ECR II-3269, para 299.

environmental purposes or for employment and training, since the intensity of such aid awarded to undertakings in assisted areas may be higher than elsewhere, although regional top-ups for aid granted for such purposes is not regarded as regional aid.[4]

Early development of European Union policy on regional aid First steps towards an EU policy on regional aid were taken in 1968 when the Commission proposed to the Member States that it be given advance notice of all significant cases of general regional aid. In 1971, following a communication from the Commission setting out the principles it intended to apply to regional aid,[5] the Council adopted a resolution[6] recognising that regional aid, when judiciously applied, formed one of the essential instruments of regional policy and enabled Member States to follow regional policies aimed at a more balanced growth between the various regions of the same country and of the European Community. However, given the risks of outbidding for mobile investments, State aid to the central regions was henceforth to be subject to a maximum level of 20% of the investment. The main principles agreed by the Council were that regional aid should be transparent and should be regionally specific. Where problems of varying nature, intensity and urgency occurred, the intensity of aid was to be varied accordingly.[7] Peripheral areas were omitted from regional aid policy at that time, since the problems associated with them were not regarded as of such immediate importance.[8]

Following the accession of Denmark, Ireland and the United Kingdom, the Commission in 1975 extended its regional aid policy to all regions of the Member States and a fresh communication was issued in 1978.[9] In the 1980s, the accession of Greece, Portugal and Spain made it necessary for the Commission to refine its methods and criteria for assessing regional aid in the EU's peripheral regions. The economic and social problems of these areas, which were predominantly agricultural, industrially underdeveloped and had widespread underemployment, called for a rethinking of the Commission's policy towards regional aid.[10] In addition, the Single European Act, which was in force from 1987, required the strengthening of economic and social cohesion and, in particular, the aim of reducing disparities between the various regions and the backwardness of the less-favoured regions.[11] Moreover, the

---

[4] *Ibid.*, para 4.
[5] OJ 1971 C111/7.
[6] OJ 1971 C111/1
[7] Council Resolution of 20 October 1971, para 5.
[8] *Ibid.*, para 1.
[9] OJ 1979 C3/9.
[10] *Sixteenth Report on Competition Policy* (1986), p. 262.
[11] Article 158 EC (now Article 174 TFEU).

formulation and implementation of the EU's policies and actions had to take this objective into account.[12]

The 1988 communication on regional aid A further communication on regional aid was issued in 1988.[13] In the light of the principle that regional aid should be the exception rather than the norm, the Commission considered *prima facie* that the total extent of assisted regions should be smaller than that of unassisted regions. In practice, this meant that the total coverage of assisted areas in the EU must be less than 50% of the EU population, with Article 107(3)(a) areas accounting for 22.7% of the EU population and Article 107(3(c) areas accounting for 24%.[14] In permitting regional investment aid, the Commission pursued the objective of increasing economic and social cohesion between the more developed and the less developed regions. Just as cohesion required the authorisation of higher levels of State aid in the more disadvantaged regions, in the more prosperous regions investment aid was to be concentrated on the areas genuinely needing it, leading to a gradual reduction in the assisted area coverage.[15] With regard to co-financing by the EU of certain investments with a view to strengthening economic and social cohesion, Council Regulation (EEC) No 2052/88[16] entrusted the structural funds with the tasks, *inter alia*, of promoting the development and structural adjustment of the regions whose development is lagging behind (Objective 1), revitalising regions affected by serious industrial decline (Objective 2), speeding up the adjustment of agricultural structures (Objective 5(a)), promoting the development of rural areas (Objective 5(b)) and promoting the development and structural adjustment of regions with an extremely low population density (Objective 6).[17] Nevertheless, there was no attempt to harmonise regions under the structural funds with the regions designated under Article 107(3)(a) and Article 107(3)(c).

The 1998 guidelines on regional aid The criteria applied by the Commission when examining the compatibility of regional aid with the internal market were reviewed and simplified by the Commission in 1998 with the publication of new guidelines on national regional aid.[18] These guidelines, which applied to

---

[12] Article 159 EC (now Article 175 TFEU).
[13] OJ 1988 C212/2.
[14] Regional aid guidelines 1998, footnote 11.
[15] *Twenty-Third Report on Competition Policy* (1993), pt. 465.
[16] OJ 1988 L185/9, amended by Council Regulation (EC) No 2081/93, OJ 1993 L193/5, and Council Decision 95/1/EC, OJ 1995 L1/1.
[17] See F. Wishlade, "Competition policy, cohesion and the coordination of State aids" (1993) 14 ECLR 143.
[18] OJ 1998 C74/9, amended by OJ 2000 C258/5. See also, the Commission's communication on the links between regional and competition policy, OJ 1998 L90/3; F. Wishlade,

all regional aid systems in the EU from 2000 until 2006, remained consistent with the criteria in the 1971 Council Resolution. The Commission considered that regional aid could play the role that is assigned to it effectively and hence justify the consequent distortions of competition, provided that it was used sparingly and was concentrated on the most disadvantaged regions.[19] The 1998 guidelines applied to regional aid granted in every sector of the economy, subject to certain limited exceptions.[20] Regional aid was required to be designed to develop the less-favoured regions by supporting investment and job creation in a sustainable context and by promoting the expansion, modernisation and diversification of the activities of establishments located in those regions and encouraging new firms to settle there. Except in the case of poles of development, regional aid could not be granted in a pinpoint manner, i.e. to isolated geographical points having practically no influence on the development of a region.[21] For the period 2000-2006, the combined coverage of assisted areas was a total of 42.7% of the EU population, comprising 19.8% for Article 107(3)(a) areas and 22.9% for Article 107(3)(c) areas.[22]

Article 107(3)(a) areas were designated by reference to the criterion that the region had a *per capita* gross domestic product (GDP), measured in purchasing power standards (PPS), of less than 75% of the EU average.[23] On this basis, for the period 2000-2006, all of Greece qualified, as did the Burgenland region in Austria, the French overseas departments, the five new länder in Germany, the Border Midlands West region of Ireland, substantial parts of Italy, Portugal and Spain, and Cornwall and the Scilly Isles, Merseyside, South Yorkshire, West Wales and the Valleys in the United Kingdom.

Article 107(3)(c) areas were selected according to a formula that allowed a certain degree of discretion to the Member States. So as to afford national authorities sufficient latitude when it came to choosing eligible regions without jeopardising the effectiveness of the system at EU level, the determination of eligible regions consisted of, first, the fixing by the Commission, for each country, of a ceiling on the coverage of such aid and, secondly, the selection of eligible regions.[24] The allocation of these areas was distributed among the different Member States in the light of the relative socio-economic situation of the regions within each Member State, assessed in an EU context, by using a distribution key which took account of regional disparities.[25]

"Competition policy or cohesion policy by the back door? The Commission guidelines on national regional aid" (1998) 19 ECLR 343.

[19] Regional aid guidelines 1998, para 1.
[20] *Ibid*, para 2.
[21] 1971 Council Resolution, para 4.
[22] Commission notice on national regional aid ceilings, OJ 1999 C16/5.
[23] Regional aid guidelines 1998, para 3.5.
[24] *Ibid.*, para 3.8.
[25] *Ibid.*, para 3.9. An adjustment was made in order to guarantee to each Member State that the population assisted in Article 107(3)(c) areas was at least equal to 15% and did

Regional aid guidelines 2007-2013 The enlargement of the European Union in 2004 to include the countries of central and eastern Europe presented a challenge to the EU's regional aid policy, with the scope of assisted areas climbing under the 1998 guidelines to 52.2% of the EU-25 population. Following a comprehensive review, the Commission adopted new guidelines for the period 2007-2013.[26] In particular, the fact that most of the territory of the new Member States was significantly less developed than the EU-15 led to a transformation of those regions that could be classified as Article 107(3)(a) areas, given that the criterion remained the same as before, i.e. that the region had a *per capita* GDP, measured in PPS, of less than 75% of the EU average. Nevertheless, the Commission stuck to the principle that regional aid must be the exception rather than the norm, so that the total population coverage of assisted regions must be substantially less than that of unassisted areas.[27]

Having regard to the need for a reduction in overall levels of State aid and in view of the widely shared concerns about the distortive effects of investment aid for large companies, the Commission decided that the overall population coverage of the regional aid guidelines for 2007-2013 should be limited to that which was necessary to allow coverage of the most disadvantaged regions, as well as a limited number of regions which were disadvantaged in relation to the national average in the Member State concerned. Accordingly, it fixed the limit for the overall population coverage to 42% of the EU-25 population, rising to 45.5% of the population of EU-27 on the accession of Bulgaria and Romania in 2007.[28]

Regional aid guidelines 2014-2020 The present guidelines are the regional aid guidelines 2014-2020 which came into effect on 1 July 2014.[29] The Commission continues to emphasise that regional aid can only play an effective role if it is used sparingly and proportionately and is concentrated on the most disadvantaged regions of the European Union. In particular, the permissible aid ceilings should reflect the relative seriousness of the problems affecting the development of the regions concerned. Furthermore, the advantages of the aid in terms of the development of less-favoured regions must outweigh the resulting distortions of competition. Regional aid can be effective in promoting the economic development of disadvantaged areas only if it is awarded to induce additional investment or economic activity in those

---

not exceed 50% of its population not designated as Article 107(3)(a) areas: Annex III, para 8.

[26] OJ 2006 C54/13.

[27] See, J. Battista, "Latest developments in regional and horizontal State aid" [2005] EStALQ 407.

[28] Regional aid guidelines 2007-13, paras 12-14. Application of the safety net resulted in a total population coverage of about 46.6% on an EU-27 basis. For a summary of the designated assisted areas, see Annex V of the guidelines.

[29] OJ 2013 C209/1.

areas.[30] In certain very limited, well-identified cases, the obstacles that these particular areas may encounter in attracting or maintaining economic activity may be so severe or permanent that investment aid alone may not be sufficient to allow the development of that area, in which case regional investment aid may be supplemented by regional operating aid not linked to an investment.[31] The overall ceiling is set at 46.5% of EU-28, reflecting the current difficult economic situation of many Member States.[32]

The Commission will apply the principles set out in the regional aid guidelines to regional aid in all sectors of economic activity, apart from fisheries and aquaculture, agriculture, the transport sector, airports and the energy sector which are subject, wholly or partly, to separate regulations or guidelines. Regional aid to the steel and synthetic fibres sectors will not be considered to be compatible with the internal market.[33] Regional aid may not be awarded to firms in difficulty, as defined by the Commission's guidelines on State aid for rescuing and restructuring firms in difficulty.[34] Regional investment aid may be granted to broadband networks provided there is no network in the area of the same category, access to the network is on a non-discriminatory basis and aid is allocated on the basis of a competitive election process.[35] Similarly, regional investment aid to research infrastructures may be granted on a transparent and non-discriminatory basis.[36]

Regional aid maps The areas that a Member State wishes to designate as Article 107(3)(a) or Article 107(3)(c) areas must be identified in a regional aid map which must be notified to the Commission and approved by the Commission before regional aid can be awarded to undertakings located in the designated areas. The maps must also specify the maximum aid intensities applicable in these areas. These approved regional aid maps, which are published in the *Official Journal of the European Union*, form the basis of the areas within which regional aid measures may be regarded as compatible with the internal market.[37] Areas not on the map are not eligible for regional aid.[38]

Block exemption for regional aid A block exemption from the obligation of notification under Article 108(3) TFEU was first introduced by Commission Regulation (EC) No 800/2008 in respect of regional investment and

---

[30] See, F. Wishlade, "To what effect? The overhaul of the Regional Aid Guidelines – the demise of competition effects and rise of incentive effect? [2013] EStALQ 659.

[31] Regional aid guidelines 2014-2020, paras 5-6.

[32] *Ibid.*, para 148.

[33] *Ibid.*, paras 9-11.

[34] *Ibid.,* para 18.

[35] *Ibid.*, para 12.

[36] *Ibid.*, para 13.

[37] *Ibid.*, paras 145 & 178-179.

[38] Case C-154/13P, *Ghezzo Giovanni & C. Snc v Commission* EU:C:2014:2182, para 34.

employment aid schemes. This was replaced from 1 July 2014 by Commission Regulation (EU) No 651/2014, Articles 13-16 of which provide for a block exemption for regional investment aid measures, regional operating aid schemes and regional urban development aid.

Notifiable aid under the regional aid guidelines 2014-2020 In principle, Member States must notify regional aid pursuant to Article 108(3) TFEU with the exception of measures that fulfil the conditions laid down in the block exemption. The Commission applies the regional aid guidelines to notified regional aid schemes and individual aid. Individual aid granted under a notified scheme must be separately notified under Article 108(3) TFEU if the aid from all sources exceeds the notification threshold under the guidelines.[39] Thus, where the aid intensity is 10%, 15%, 25%, 35% or 50%, the notification threshold is €7.5 million, €11.25 million, €18.75 million, €26.25 million or €37.5 million, respectively.[40]

    Individual aid is also notifiable if it is granted to a beneficiary that has closed down the same or similar activity in the EEA two years preceding the date of applying for aid or at the moment of aid application has the intention to close down such an activity within a period of two years after the investment to be subsidised is completed.[41] Investment aid granted to a large undertaking to diversify an existing establishment in an Article 107(3)(c) area into new products is also notifiable.[42]

Notifiable aid excluded from the block exemption The block exemption in Regulation (EU) No 651/2014, Articles 13-15 applies generally to regional investment aid measures and regional operating aid schemes. It does not apply, specifically, to aid which favours activities in the steel sector, the coal sector, the shipbuilding sector, the synthetic fibres sector, the transport sector as well as the related infrastructure, energy generation, distribution and infrastructure.[43] Equally, it does not apply to regional aid schemes covering transport costs of goods produced in the outermost regions or in sparsely populated areas granted in favour of agricultural products and certain other listed products, or transport of goods by pipeline.[44] Individual aid is also excluded if it is granted to a beneficiary that has closed down the same or similar activity in the EEA two years preceding the date of applying for aid or at the moment of aid application has the intention to close down such an activity within a period of two years after the investment is completed.[45]

---

[39] Regional aid guidelines 2014-2020, para 23.
[40] *Ibid.*, para 20(n).
[41] *Ibid.*, para 23.
[42] *Ibid.*, para 24.
[43] Commission Regulation (EU) No 651/2014, Article 13(1)(a).
[44] *Ibid.*, Article 13(1)(c).
[45] *Ibid.*, Article 13(1)(d).

As a general rule, regional aid should be granted under a multi-sectoral aid scheme which forms an integral part of a regional development strategy with clearly defined objectives. Regional aid schemes which are targeted at a limited number of specific sectors of economic activity require individual notification.[46] Regional operating aid granted to undertakings whose principal activities concern financial and insurance activities or to undertakings that perform intra-group activities are also excluded from the scope of the block exemption.[47]

8.2 DESIGNATION OF ASSISTED AREAS

Article 107(3)(a) TFEU areas Under the regional aid guidelines 2014-2020, designation as an assisted area under Article 107(3)(a) TFEU applies to regions where the standard of living is abnormally low or where there is serious underemployment. This concerns only areas where the economic situation is extremely unfavourable in relation to the EU as a whole. The Commission considers that these conditions are fulfilled if the region, being a NUTS II geographical unit, has a *per capita* gross domestic product (GDP), measured in purchasing power standards (PPS), of less than 75% of the EU average.[48] This applies to the whole territory of Bulgaria, Croatia, Estonia, Latvia, Lithuania, parts of the Czech Republic, Greece, Hungary, Italy, Malta, Poland, Portugal, Romania, Slovakia, Slovenia and Spain, as well as Cornwall and the Scilly Isles and West Wales and the Valleys in the United Kingdom.[49]

In recognition of the special handicaps which they face by reason of their remoteness and specific constraints in integrating into the internal market, the Commission considers that regional aid for the EU's outermost regions also falls within the scope of the derogation in Article 107(3)(a) TFEU, whether or not the regions concerned have a GDP *per capita* of less than 75% of the EU average.[50] The outermost regions are specified in Article 349 TFEU as the Azores, Madeira, the Canary Islands, Guadeloupe, Martinique, Réunion, French Guyana, Saint Bartélemy and Saint Martin.

Article 107(3)(c) TFEU areas Article 107(3)(c) TFEU gives the Commission power to authorise aid intended to further the economic development of areas of a Member State which are disadvantaged in relation to the national

---

[46] *Ibid.*, Article 13(1)(b). Schemes aimed at tourism activities, broadband infrastructures or processing and marketing of agricultural products are not considered to be targeted at specific sectors of economic activity.

[47] Commission Regulation (EU) No 651/2014, Article 13(1)(e).

[48] Regional aid guidelines 2014-2020, paras 149-151(a).

[49] *Ibid.*, Annex I.

[50] *Ibid.*, para 151(b).

average.[51]   Under the regional aid guidelines 2014-20, the Commission identifies two separate categories of Article 107(3)(c) areas, those that fulfil certain pre-established conditions and those that a Member State may, at its own discretion, designate provided that it demonstrates that such areas fulfil certain socio-economic criteria.

There are two categories of predefined Article 107(3)(c) areas: former Article 107(3)(a) areas and sparsely populated areas. The former are NUTS II regions that were designated as (a) areas during the period 2011-2013 but which no longer fall within that category. The latter are NUTS II regions with less than 8 inhabitants per km^2 or NUTS III regions with less than 12.5 inhabitants per km^2.[52]

The total coverage ceiling for non-predefined Article 107(3)(c) areas in the EU is obtained by subtracting the population of the eligible Article 107(3)(a) areas and of the predefined Article 107(3)(c) areas from the overall coverage ceiling set by the Commission and allocating this among the Member States by applying a formula set out in the regional aid guidelines that uses a number of criteria.   First, to address the difficulties of Member States that have been particularly affected by the economic crisis, the total coverage of those Member States benefitting from financial assistance under specific EU facilities, such as the European Financial Stabilisation Mechanism, should not be reduced compared to the period 2007-2013.   Second, the total coverage of each Member State's Article 107(3)(a) and Article 107(3)(c) regions should not be reduced by more than 50% compared to the period 2007-2013.   Third, each Member State should have a population coverage of at least 7.5% of its national population.[53]

Selection of eligible Article 107(3)(c) regions In selecting eligible regions, the criteria used by Member States for designating Article 107(3)(c) areas should reflect the diversity of situations in which the award of regional aid may be justified.   The criteria should therefore address certain socio-economic, geographical or structural problems likely to be encountered in such areas and should provide sufficient safeguards that the award of regional aid will not adversely affect trading conditions to an extent contrary to the common interest.   Accordingly, a Member State may designate non-predefined Article 107(3)(c) areas on the basis of a number of criteria:[54]

(a)   regions which form contiguous zones with a minimum population of at least 100,000 and which are located within either NUTS-II or NUTS-III

---

[51]   *Ibid.*, para 153.

[52]   *Ibid.*, paras 156-161 and Annex I. Parts of NUTS III regions with less than 12.5 inhabitants per km^2 or other contiguous areas adjacent to those NUTS III regions may also be designated, provided that the areas designated have less than 12.5 inhabitants per km^2

[53]   *Ibid.*, paras 163-166.

[54]   *Ibid.*, para 168.

regions which have either a GDP per capita of less than the EU-27 average, or which have an unemployment rate which is higher than 115% of the national average;

(b) NUTS-III regions with less than 100,000 population which have either a GDP per capita of less than the EU-27 average or which have an unemployment rate which is higher than 115% of the national average;

(c) islands and other regions categorised by similar geographical isolation which have either a GDP per capita of less than the EU-27 average, or which have an unemployment rate which is higher than 115% of the national average, or have fewer than 5,000 inhabitants;

(d) NUTS-III regions or parts thereof adjacent to an Article 107(3)(a) region as well as NUTS-III regions or parts thereof which share a land border with a country which is not a Member State of the EEA or EFTA;

(e) other regions which form contiguous zones with a minimum population of at least 50,000 which are undergoing major structural change, or are in serious relative decline.

Amendment to regional aid map On its own initiative, a Member State may decide to establish a reserve of national population coverage consisting of the difference between the population coverage ceiling for that Member State, as allocated by the Commission, and the coverage used for the assisted areas designated in its regional aid map. If a Member State has decided to establish such a reserve, it may, at any time, use the reserve to add new Article 107(3)(c) areas in its map until its national coverage ceiling is reached. The Member State must notify the Commission each time it intends to use its population reserve to add new assisted areas prior to putting into effect such amendments.[55] For example, France notified an extension to its regional aid map in 2009 adding 10 areas that had suffered significant job losses over the previous 12 months.[56] The Commission will establish a mid-term review of the designated assisted areas in 2016.[57]

8.3 BLOCK EXEMPTION FOR REGIONAL INVESTMENT AID

Block exemption for regional investment aid measures Whereas the block exemption in Regulation (EC) No 800/2008 applied only to investment aid schemes,[58] Commission Regulation (EU) No 651/2014 states that all regional investment aid measures are compatible with the internal market and are

---

[55] Regional aid guidelines 2014-2020, paras 180-18.
[56] Case N 2/2009, *French regional aid map* OJ 2009 C95/3.
[57] Regional aid guidelines 2014-2020, paras 183-185.
[58] Commission Regulation (EC) No 800/2008, Article 13(1).

exempt from the notification requirement of Article 108(3) TFEU, provided that the conditions laid down in the block exemption regulation are fulfilled.[59]

In Article 107(3)(a) areas, aid may be granted for an initial investment regardless of the size of the beneficiary. In Article 107(3)(c) areas, aid may be granted to SMEs for any form of initial investment.[60] Initial investment is defined as an investment in tangible and intangible assets related to the setting-up of a new establishment, extension of the capacity of an existing establishment, diversification of the output of an establishment into products not previously produced in the establishment or a fundamental change in the overall production process of an existing establishment. The acquisition of assets belonging to an establishment that has closed or would have closed had it not been purchased, and is bought by an investor unrelated to the seller and excludes sole acquisition of the shares of an undertaking, may also be considered as an initial investment.[61]

Aid to large enterprises in Article 107(3)(c) areas may only be granted for an initial investment in favour of new economic activity in the area concerned.[62] Initial investment for new activity is limited to investment in assets related to the setting up of a new establishment or to the diversification of the activity of an establishment under the condition that the new activity is not the same or a similar activity to the activity previously performed in the establishment. The acquisition of assets belonging to an establishment that has closed or would have closed had it not been purchased, and is bought by an investor unrelated to the seller under the condition that the new activity is not the same or a similar activity to the activity performed in the establishment prior to the acquisition, may also be considered as an initial investment.[63]

In addition to the general provisions concerning incentive effect, as regards any *ad hoc* aid granted to a large enterprise, the Member State should ensure that the beneficiary has analysed, in an internal document, the viability of the aided project or activity with aid and without aid. The Member State should verify that this internal document confirms a material increase in the scope of the project/activity, a material increase in the total amount spent by the beneficiary on the subsidised project or activity or a material increase in the speed of completion of the project/activity concerned. Regional aid should be considered to have an incentive effect if the investment project would not have been carried out in the assisted region concerned in the absence of the aid.[64]

---

[59]   Commission Regulation (EU) No 651/2014, Article 14(1)-(2).
[60]   *Ibid.*, Article 14(3).
[61]   *Ibid.*, Article 2(49).
[62]   *Ibid.*, Article 14(3).
[63]   *Ibid.*, Article 2(51)
[64]   *Ibid.*, Article 6(3)(a).

Eligible costs The eligible costs are investment costs in tangible and intangible assets or the estimated wage costs arising from job creation as a result of an initial investment, calculated over a period of two years.[65] The investment shall be maintained in the recipient area for at least five years, or at least three years in the case of SMEs, after completion of the investment. This shall not prevent the replacement of plant or equipment that has become outdated or broken within this period, provided that the economic activity is retained in the area concerned for the relevant minimum period.[66]

Assets acquired The assets acquired must be new except for SMEs and for the acquisition of an establishment. Costs related to the lease of tangible assets may be taken into account under the following conditions:
-    for land and buildings, the lease must continue for at least five years after the expected date of completion of the investment project for large undertakings or three years in the case of SMEs;
-    for plant or machinery, the lease must take the form of financial leasing and must contain an obligation for the beneficiary of the aid to purchase the asset upon expiry of the term of the lease.

In the case of acquisition of the assets of an establishment belonging to an establishment that has closed or would have closed had it not been purchased, and is bought by an investor unrelated to the seller and excludes sole acquisition of the shares of an undertaking, only the costs of buying the assets from third parties unrelated to the buyer may be taken into consideration. The transaction must take place under market conditions. If aid has already been granted for the acquisition of assets prior to their purchase, the costs of those assets is deducted from the eligible costs related to the acquisition of an establishment. Where a member of the family of the original owner, or an employee, takes over a small enterprise, the condition that the assets be bought from third parties unrelated to the buyer is waived. The acquisition of shares does not constitute initial investment.[67]

Fundamental change in production process For aid granted for a fundamental change in the production process, the eligible costs must exceed the depreciation of the assets linked to the activity to be modernised in the course of the preceding three fiscal years. For aid granted for a diversification of an existing establishment, the eligible costs must exceed by at least 200% the book value of the assets that are reused, as registered in the fiscal year preceding the start of works.[68]

---

[65]   *Ibid.*, Article 14(4).
[66]   *Ibid.*, Article 14(5).
[67]   *Ibid.*, Article 14(6).
[68]   *Ibid.*, Article 14(7).

Intangible assets   Intangible assets are eligible for the calculation of investment costs if they fulfil the following conditions:
- they must be used exclusively in the establishment receiving the aid;
- they must be amortisable;
- they must be purchased under market conditions from third parties unrelated to the buyer; and
- they must be included in the assets of the undertaking receiving the aid and must remain associated with the project for which the aid is granted for at least five years or three years in the case of SMEs.

For large undertakings, costs of intangible assets are eligible only up to a limit of 50% of the total eligible investment costs for the initial investment.[69]

Estimated wage costs   Where eligible costs are calculated by reference to the estimated wage costs, the following conditions shall be fulfilled:
- the investment project must lead to a net increase in the number of employees in the establishment concerned, compared with the average over the previous 12 months, meaning that any job lost shall be deducted from the apparent created number of jobs during that period;
- each post must be filled within three years of completion of works; and
- each job created through the investment must be maintained in the area concerned for a period of at least five years from the date the post was first filled, or three years in the case of SMEs.[70]

Broadband network development   Regional aid for broadband network development must fulfil the following conditions:
- aid may be granted only in areas where there is no network of the same category (either basic broadband or NGA) and where no such network is likely to be developed on commercial terms within three years from the decision to grant the aid; and
- the subsidised network operator must offer active and passive wholesale access under fair and non-discriminatory conditions including physical unbundling in the case of NGA networks; and
- aid must be allocated on the basis of a competitive selection process.[71]

Research infrastructures   Regional aid for research infrastructures may be granted only if the aid is made conditional on giving transparent and non-discriminatory access to the aided infrastructure.[72]

---

[69]   *Ibid.*, Article 14(8).
[70]   *Ibid.*, Article 14(9).
[71]   *Ibid.*, Article 14(10).
[72]   *Ibid.*, Article 14(11).

Aid intensity The aid intensity may not exceed the maximum aid intensity established in the regional aid map which is in force at the time the aid is granted in the area concerned. Where the aid intensity is calculated on a combination of investment costs and wage costs, the maximum aid intensity may not exceed the most favourable amount resulting from the application of that intensity on the basis of investment costs or wage costs.[73]

For large investment projects the aid amount may not exceed the adjusted aid amount calculated in accordance with the formula $R \times (A + 0{,}50 \times B + 0 \times C)$, where: R is the maximum aid intensity applicable in the area concerned established in an approved regional map and which is in force on the date of granting the aid, excluding the increased aid intensity for SMEs; A is the initial €50 million of eligible costs, B is the part of eligible costs between €50 million and €100 million and C is the part of eligible costs above €100 million.[74]

Single investments Any initial investment started by the same beneficiary at group level within a period of three years from the date of start of works on another aided investment in the same NUTS III will be considered to be part of a single investment project. Where such single investment project is a large investment project, the total aid amount for the single investment project may not exceed the adjusted aid amount for large investment projects.[75]

Financial contribution by the beneficiary The aid beneficiary must provide a financial contribution of at least 25% of the eligible costs, either through its own resources or by external financing, in a form, which is free of any public support. In the outermost regions an investment made by an SME may receive an aid with a maximum aid intensity above 75%, in which case the remainder must be provided by way of a financial contribution from the aid beneficiary.[76]

European Territorial Cooperation projects For an initial investment linked to European territorial cooperation projects covered by Regulation (EU) No 1299/2013, the aid intensity of the area in which the initial investment is located will apply to all beneficiaries participating in the project. If the initial investment is located in two or more assisted areas, the maximum aid intensity will be the one applicable in the assisted area where the highest amount of eligible costs is incurred. In Article 107(3)(c) areas, this provision will apply to large undertakings only if the initial investment concerns a new economic activity.[77]

---

[73] *Ibid.*, Article 14(12).
[74] *Ibid.*, Article 14(12) and 2(20).
[75] *Ibid.*, Article 14(13).
[76] *Ibid.*, Article 14(14).
[77] *Ibid.*, Article 14(15).

8.4 COMPATIBILITY CRITERIA IN THE REGIONAL AID GUIDELINES

Common assessment principles To assess whether a notified aid measure can be considered compatible with the internal market pursuant to the regional aid guidelines 2014-2020, the Commission analyses whether the design of the aid measure ensures that the positive impact of the aid towards an objective of common interest exceeds its potential negative effects on trade and competition. In accordance with the Communication on State aid modernisation, the Commission will consider an aid measure compatible with the internal market only if it satisfies each of the following criteria: contribution to a well-defined objective of common interest; need for State intervention; appropriateness of the measure; incentive effect; proportionality of the aid; avoidance of undue negative effects on competition and trade between Member States; and transparency of the aid. The overall balance of certain categories of schemes may further be made subject to a requirement of *ex post* evaluation. In such cases, the Commission may limit the duration of those schemes, normally to four years or less, with a possibility to re-notify their prolongation afterwards.[78] The guidelines consider the application of these criteria generally and to investment aid schemes, individual investment aid and operating aid schemes, respectively.

Contribution to a common objective The primary objective of regional aid is to reduce the development gap between the different regions in the European Union. Through its equity or cohesion objective regional aid may contribute to the achievement of the Europe 2020 strategy delivering an inclusive and sustainable growth.[79]

Need for State intervention As regards aid granted for the development of areas included in the regional aid map, the Commission considers that the market is not delivering the expected cohesion objectives set out in the EU Treaties without State intervention. Therefore, aid granted in those areas should be considered compatible with the internal market pursuant to Article 107(3)(a) and (c) TFEU.[80]

Appropriateness of regional aid The regional aid measure must be an appropriate policy instrument to address the policy objective concerned. An aid measure will not be considered compatible if other less distortive policy instruments or other less distortive types of aid instrument make it possible to

---

[78]   Regional aid guidelines 2014-2020, paras 25-27.
[79]   *Ibid.*, paras 30.
[80]   *Ibid.*, para 49.

achieve the same positive contribution to regional development.[81] Member States should ensure that the aid is awarded in the form that is likely to generate the least distortions of trade and competition. In this respect, if the aid is awarded in forms that provide a direct pecuniary advantage (for example, direct grants, exemptions or reductions in taxes, social security or other compulsory charges, or the supply of land, goods or services at favourable prices, etc.), the Member State must demonstrate why other potentially less distortive forms of aid such as repayable advances or forms of aid that are based on debt or equity instruments (for example, low-interest loans or interest rebates, state guarantees, the purchase of a share-holding or an alternative provision of capital on favourable terms) are not appropriate.[82]

Incentive effect Regional aid can only be found compatible with the internal market if it has an incentive effect. An incentive effect is present when the aid changes the behaviour of an undertaking in a way it engages in additional activity contributing to the development of an area which it would not have engaged in without the aid or would only have engaged in such activity in a restricted or different manner or in another location. The aid must not subsidise the costs of an activity that an undertaking would have incurred in any event and must not compensate for the normal business risk of an economic activity.[83]

The existence of an incentive effect can be established in two possible scenarios, termed, respectively, an investment decision and a location decision. In scenario 1, the aid gives an incentive to adopt a positive investment decision because an investment that would otherwise not be sufficiently profitable for the beneficiary can take place in the area concerned. In scenario 2, the aid gives an incentive to opt to locate a planned investment in the relevant area rather than elsewhere because it compensates for the net disadvantages and costs linked to a location in the area concerned. If the aid does not change the behaviour of the beneficiary by stimulating additional investment in the area concerned, it can be considered that the same investment would take place in the region even without the aid. Such aid lacks incentive effect to achieve the regional objective and cannot be approved as compatible with the internal market. However, for regional aid awarded through cohesion policy funds in Article 107(3)(a) regions to investments necessary to achieve standards set by EU law, the aid may be considered to have an incentive effect if, in absence of the aid, it would not have been sufficiently profitable for the beneficiary to

---

[81] *Ibid.*, para 50.

[82] *Ibid.*, paras 57-58. For aid schemes implementing the objectives and priorities of operational programmes, the financing instrument chosen in the programme is considered to be an appropriate instrument.

[83] Regional aid guidelines 2014-2020, para 60.

make the investment in the area concerned, thereby leading to the closure of an existing establishment in that area.[84]

Proportionality of the aid amount In principle, the amount of the regional aid must be limited to the minimum needed to induce additional investment or activity in the area concerned. As a general rule, notified individual aid will be considered to be limited to the minimum, if the aid amount corresponds to the net extra costs of implementing the investment in the area concerned, compared to the counterfactual in the absence of aid. Likewise, in the case of investment aid granted to large undertakings under notified schemes, Member States must ensure that the aid amount is limited to the minimum on the basis of a 'net-extra cost approach'. For scenario 1 situations concerning investment decisions, the aid amount should therefore not exceed the minimum necessary to render the project sufficiently profitable, for example to increase its IRR beyond the normal rates of return applied by the undertaking concerned in other investment projects of a similar kind or, when available, to increase its IRR beyond the cost of capital of the company as a whole or beyond the rates of return commonly observed in the industry concerned. In scenario 2 situations concerning location incentives, the aid amount should not exceed the difference between the net present value of the investment in the target area with the net present value in the alternative location. All relevant costs and benefits must be taken into account, including, for example, administrative costs, transport costs, training costs not covered by training aid, and wage differences. Where the alternative location is in the EEA, subsidies granted in that other location are not to be taken into account.[85]

To ensure predictability and a level playing field, the Commission further applies maximum aid intensities for investment aid. For notified schemes, these maximum aid intensities serve as safe harbours for SMEs, in that as long as the aid intensity remains below the maximum permissible, the criterion of aid being limited to the minimum is deemed to be fulfilled. For all other cases, the maximum aid intensities are used as a cap to the net-extra costs approach. The maximum aid intensities are modulated in function of three criteria: the socio-economic situation of the area concerned, as a proxy for the extent to which the area is in need of further development and, potentially, the extent to which it suffers from a handicap in attracting and maintaining economic activity; the size of the beneficiary as proxy for the specific difficulties to finance or implement a project in the area; and the size of the investment project, as indicator for the expected level of distortion of competition and trade. Accordingly, higher aid intensities are allowed the less developed the target region is, and if the aid beneficiary is an SME. In view of the expected

---

[84] *Ibid.*, paras 61-63.
[85] *Ibid.*, paras 77-80.

higher distortions of competition and trade, the maximum aid intensity for large investment projects must be scaled down.[86]

Assessment of negative effects on competition and trade For regional aid to be compatible with the internal market, the negative effects of the aid measure in terms of distortions of competition and impact on trade between Member States must be limited and outweighed by the positive effects in terms of contribution to the objective of regional development. Two main potential distortions of competition and trade may be caused by regional aid: product market distortions and location effects, both of which may lead to allocative inefficiencies, whereby the economic performance of the internal market may be undermined, and to concerns about the distribution of economic activity across regions.[87]

Product market distortions arise in that State aid prevents the market mechanism from delivering efficient outcomes by rewarding the most efficient producers and putting pressure on the least inefficient to improve, restructure or exit the market. A substantial capacity expansion induced by State aid in an underperforming market could lead to a squeeze on profit margins, a reduction of competitors' investments or even the exit of competitors from the market, with competitors that would otherwise be able to stay on the market being forced out. It may also prevent undertakings from entering or expanding in the market and it may weaken incentives for competitors to innovate. This results in inefficient market structures which are also harmful to consumers in the long run. Further, the availability of aid may induce complacent or unduly risky behaviour on the part of potential beneficiaries.[88] Aid may also have distortive effects in terms of increasing or maintaining substantial market power on the part of the beneficiary. Even where aid does not strengthen substantial market power directly, it may do so indirectly, by discouraging the expansion of existing competitors or inducing their exit or discouraging the entry of new competitors.[89]

Apart from distortions on the product markets, regional aid by nature also affects the location of economic activity. Where one area attracts an investment due to the aid, another area loses out on that opportunity. These negative effects in the areas adversely affected by aid may be felt through lost economic activity and lost jobs including those at the level of subcontractors. It may also be felt in a loss of positive externalities such as clustering effect, knowledge spillovers, education and training.[90] The geographical specificity of regional aid distinguishes it from other forms of horizontal aid in that it is

---

[86] *Ibid.*, paras 81-86.
[87] *Ibid.*, paras 112-113.
[88] *Ibid.*, para 114.
[89] *Ibid.*, para 115.
[90] *Ibid.*, para 116.

intended to influence the choice made by investors about where to locate investment projects. When regional aid off-sets the additional costs stemming from the regional handicaps and supports additional investment in assisted areas without attracting it away from other assisted areas, it contributes not only to the development of the region, but also to cohesion and ultimately benefits the EU as a whole. With regard to the potential negative location effects of regional aid, these are already limited to a certain degree by regional aid maps, which define exhaustively the areas where regional aid may be granted, taking account of the equity and cohesion policy objectives and the maximum permissible aid intensities. However, an understanding of what would have happened in the absence of the aid remains important to appraise the actual impact of the aid in the cohesion objective.[91]

The Commission has identified a number of situations where the negative effects of the aid manifestly outweigh any positive effects, so that the aid cannot be declared compatible with the internal market. In particular, maximum aid intensities established by the Commission constitute a basic requirement for compatibility. In general, the greater the positive effects to which the aided project is likely to give rise and the higher the likely need for aid, the higher the cap on aid intensity will be.[92] For investment decisions, where the creation of capacity by the project takes place in a market which is structurally in absolute decline, the Commission considers it to be a negative effect, which is unlikely to be compensated by any positive effect. In location decisions, where without aid the investment would have been located in a region with a regional aid intensity which is higher or the same as the target region, this will constitute a negative effect that is unlikely to be compensated by any positive effect.[93] Where the beneficiary closes down the same or a similar activity in another area in the EEA and relocates that activity to the target area, if there is a causal link between the aid and the relocation, this will constitute a negative effect that is unlikely to be compensated by any positive elements. Also, when appraising notified measures, the Commission will request all necessary information to consider whether the State aid would result in a substantial loss of jobs in existing locations within the EEA.[94]

Maximum aid intensities The intensity of regional investment aid in Article 107(3)(a) areas must not exceed:
- 50% GGE in NUTS II regions whose GDP per capita is below or equal to 45% of the EU-27 average;
- 35% GGE in NUTS II regions whose GDP per capita is between or equal to 45% and 60% of the EU-27 average;

---

[91]   *Ibid.*, para 117.
[92]   *Ibid.*, paras 118-119.
[93]   *Ibid.*, paras 120-121.
[94]   *Ibid.*, paras 122-123.

- 25% GGE in NUTS II regions with a GDP per capita above 60% of the EU-27 average.

These maximum aid intensities may be increased by up to 20 percentage points in outermost regions that have a GDP per capita below or equal to 75% of the EU-27 average or by up to 10% in other outermost regions.[95]

The intensity of regional investment aid in Article 107(3)(c) areas must not exceed:

- 50% GGE in sparsely populated areas and in NUTS III regions that border a country outside the EEA and EFTA;
- 10% GGE in non-pre-defined Article 107(3)(c) areas.

In the former Article 107(3)(a) areas, the aid intensity of 10% may be increased by up to 5 percentage points until31 December 2017. If the Article 107(3)(c) area is adjacent to an Article 107(3)(a) area, the maximum intensity in NUTS 3 regions within that area which are adjacent to an Article 107(3)(a) area may be increased so that the difference in aid intensity between the two areas does not exceed 15 percentage points.[96]

For SMEs, these maximum aid intensities may be increased by up to 20 percentage points for small enterprises and by up to 10 percentage points for medium-sized enterprises.[97]

8.5 NOTIFIED REGIONAL INVESTMENT AID SCHEMES

Contribution to EU objective of regional development Regional aid schemes should form an integral part of a regional development strategy with clearly defined objectives and should be consistent with and contribute towards these objectives. This is the case in particular for measures implemented in accordance with regional development strategies defined in the context of the European Regional Development Fund, the European Social Fund, the Cohesion Fund, the European Agricultural Fund for Rural Development or the European Maritime and Fisheries Fund with a view to contributing towards the objectives of the Europe 2020 strategy. For aid schemes outside an operational programme financed from the cohesion policy funds, Member States should demonstrate that the measure is consistent with and contributes to the development strategy of the area concerned.[98]

Aid for initial investment Under both the regional aid guidelines and the block exemption, regional aid schemes may be put in place in Article 107(3)(a) areas to support initial investments of SMEs or of large undertakings. In

---

[95] *Ibid.*, paras 172-173.
[96] *Ibid.*, paras 174-176.
[97] *Ibid.*, para 177.
[98] Regional aid guidelines 2014-2020, paras 32-33.

Article 107(3)(c) areas, schemes may be put in place to support initial investments of SMEs and initial investment in favour of new activity of large undertakings.[99] Aid for investments by large undertakings in Article 107(3)(c) areas that does not create new economic activities may not be regarded as compatible with the internal market.[100] An initial investment means an investment in tangible and intangible assets related to the setting-up of a new establishment, the extension of the capacity of an existing establishment, the diversification of the output of an establishment into products not previously produced in the establishment, or a fundamental change in the overall production process of an existing establishment. It also covers an acquisition of assets directly linked to an establishment provided the establishment has closed or would have closed if it had not been purchased, and is bought by an investor unrelated to the seller, although the sole acquisition of the shares of an undertaking does not qualify as initial investment.[101]

To ensure that the investment makes a real and sustained contribution to the development of the area concerned, the investment must be maintained in the area concerned for at least five years, or three years for SMEs, after its completion. This obligation to maintain the investment in the area concerned for a minimum period should not prevent the replacement of plant or equipment that has become outdated or broken within this period, provided that the economic activity is retained in the area concerned for the minimum period. However, regional aid may not be awarded to replace that plant or equipment.[102] If the aid is calculated on the basis of wage costs, the posts must be filled within three years of the completion of works. Each job created through the investment must be maintained within the area concerned for a period of five years from the date the post was first filled. For investments carried out by SMEs, Member States may reduce this five-year period for the maintenance of an investment or jobs to a minimum of three years.[103] To ensure that the investment is viable, the Member State must ensure that the beneficiary provides a financial contribution of at least 25% of the eligible costs from its own resources.[104]

Appropriateness of regional aid Regional investment aid is not the only policy instrument available to Member States to support investment and job creation in disadvantaged regions. Member States can use other measures such as infrastructure development, enhancing the quality of education and training, or improvements in the business environment. In the case of notifiable aid,

---

[99] *Ibid.*, para 34

[100] *Ibid.*, para 15.

[101] *Ibid.*, para 20(h).

[102] *Ibid.*, para 36.

[103] *Ibid.*, para 37.

[104] *Ibid.*, para 38. Higher aid intensities may apply in the outermost regions.

Member States must indicate why regional aid is an appropriate instrument to tackle the common objective of equity or cohesion when introducing a scheme outside an operational programme financed from the cohesion policy funds. If a Member State decides to put in place a sectoral aid scheme outside an operational programme, it must demonstrate the advantages of such an instrument compared to a multi-sectoral scheme or other policy options. In addition to impact assessments, the Commission may take into account the results of *ex post* evaluations to assess the appropriateness of the proposed scheme.[105]

Incentive effect Works on an individual investment can start only after submitting the application form for aid. If works begin before submitting the application form for aid, any aid awarded in respect of that individual investment will not be considered compatible with the internal market. Annex V to the guidelines provides a standard application form for regional aid, in which SMEs and large companies must explain counterfactually what would have happened had they not received the aid indicating whether the aid concerns an investment decision or a location decision. In addition, large companies must submit documentary evidence in support of the counterfactual described in the application form. The granting authority must carry out a credibility check of the counterfactual and confirm that regional aid has the required incentive effect.[106]

Proportionality of the aid amount For aid to SMEs, increased maximum aid intensities may be used. However, SMEs may not benefit from these increased intensities where the investment relates to a large investment project, i,e, a project having an initial investment of over €50 million.[107] For aid to large undertakings, the Member State must ensure that the aid amount corresponds to the net extra costs of implementing the investment in the area concerned, compared to the counterfactual in the absence of aid, subject to maximum aid intensities as a cap.[108] For aid to large investment projects, it must be ensured that the aid does not exceed the scaled down intensity. Where aid is awarded to a beneficiary for an investment that is considered to be part of a single investment project, the aid must be scaled down for the eligible costs exceeding €50 million.[109]

---

[105] Regional aid guidelines 2014-2020, paras 51-54.
[106] *Ibid.*, paras 64-68.
[107] *Ibid.*, para 87.
[108] *Ibid.*, para 88.
[109] *Ibid.*, para 89.

Eligible costs   Eligible costs means, for the purposes of investment aid, costs of tangible or intangible assets.[110]   The assets acquired should be new, except for SMEs or in the case of acquisition of an establishment.[111]   Under the guidelines, for SMEs, up to 50% of the costs of preparatory studies or consultancy costs linked to the investment may also be considered as eligible costs.[112]   For aid awarded for a fundamental change in the production process, the eligible costs must exceed the depreciation of the assets linked to the activity to be modernised in the course of the preceding three fiscal years.[113]   For aid awarded for a diversification of an existing establishment, the eligible costs must exceed by at least 200% the book value of the assets that are reused, as registered in the fiscal year preceding the start of works.[114]

Costs related to the lease of tangible assets may be taken into account under the following conditions: for land and buildings, the lease must continue for at least five years after the expected date of completion of the investment for large companies, and three years for SMEs; for plant or machinery, the lease must take the form of financial leasing and must contain an obligation for the beneficiary of the aid to purchase the asset at the expiry of the term of the lease.[115]   In the case of acquisition of an establishment only the costs of buying the assets from third parties unrelated to the buyer should be taken into consideration.   The transaction must take place under market conditions. Where aid has already been granted for the acquisition of assets prior to their purchase, the costs of those assets should be deducted from the eligible costs related to the acquisition of an establishment.   If the acquisition of an establishment is accompanied by an additional investment eligible for aid, the eligible costs of this latter investment should be added to the costs of purchase of the assets of the establishment.[116]

For large undertakings, costs of intangible assets are eligible only up to a limit of 50% of the total eligible investment costs for the project.   For SMEs, the full costs related to intangible assets may be taken into consideration. Intangible assets which are eligible for the calculation of the investments costs must remain associated with the assisted area concerned and must not be transferred to other regions.   To this end, the intangible assets must fulfil the following conditions: they must be used exclusively in the establishment receiving the aid; they must be amortisable; they must be purchased under market conditions from third parties unrelated to the buyer.   The intangible assets must be included in the assets of the undertaking receiving the aid and

---

[110]   *Ibid.*, para 20(e).
[111]   *Ibid.*, para 94.
[112]   *Ibid.*, para 95.
[113]   *Ibid.*, para 96.
[114]   *Ibid.*, para 97.
[115]   *Ibid.*, para 98.
[116]   *Ibid.*, para 99

must remain associated with the project for which the aid is awarded for at least five years (three years for SMEs).[117]

Regional aid may also be calculated by reference to the expected wage costs arising from job creation as a result of an initial investment. Aid can compensate only the wage costs of the person hired calculated over a period of two years and the resulting intensity cannot exceed the applicable aid intensity in the area concerned.[118]

Assessment of negative effects In an assessment of notified aid under the regional aid guidelines, investment aid schemes must not lead to significant distortions of competition and trade. In particular, even where distortions may be considered limited at an individual level, on a cumulative basis schemes might still lead to high levels of distortions. Such distortions might concern the output markets by creating or aggravating a situation of overcapacity or creating, increasing or maintaining the substantial market power of some recipients in a way that will negatively affect dynamic incentives. Aid available under schemes might also lead to a significant loss of economic activity in other areas of the EEA. In case of a scheme focussing on certain sectors, the risk of such distortions is even more pronounced. Therefore, the Member State has to demonstrate that these negative effects will be limited to the minimum taking into account, for example, the size of the projects concerned, the individual and cumulative aid amounts, the expected beneficiaries as well as the characteristics of the targeted sectors. In order to enable the Commission to assess the likely negative effects, the Member State could submit any impact assessment at its disposal as well as *ex-post* evaluations carried out for similar predecessor schemes. When awarding aid under a scheme to individual projects, the granting authority must verify and confirm that the aid does not result in manifest negative effects.[119]

8.6 NOTIFIED INDIVIDUAL REGIONAL INVESTMENT AID

Individual regional investment aid The purpose of regional aid must be to develop a particular region and not just a specific undertaking located within the region. However, aid may, exceptionally, be granted on an *ad hoc* basis. In those circumstances, it is for the Member State concerned to establish that the aid in question actually fulfils the regional specificity criterion.[120] The Commission has long held to the policy that the positive impact on

---

[117] *Ibid.*, paras 100-102.

[118] *Ibid.*, para 103. See Case C-415/07, *Lodato Gennaro & C. SpA v Instituto Nazionale della Previdenza Sociale* [2009] ECR I-2599, paras 28-32.

[119] Regional aid guidelines 2014-2020, paras 124-126.

[120] Cases C-278/92-C-280/92, *Spain v Commission* [1994] ECR I-4103, para 49.

development must demonstrably outweigh the distortion of competition caused by the aid.[121] For instance, the Commission approved *ad hoc* investment aid for a chemical producer in the Netherlands on the ground that the region involved had traditionally been closely connected with the chemical industry. The fact that the investment concerned headquarters, rather than production capacity, did not alter this assessment.[122] In authorising individual aid granted by the Czech authorities to cover investment for operating new lignite deposits, the Commission noted that this would safeguard 350 direct jobs in a primarily agricultural region suffering from high unemployment and structural difficulties and that the distortive effects on competition would be fairly limited.[123] By contrast, the Commission blocked *ad hoc* aid in Slovakia which would have created significant distortions of competition in the market for graphic arts pre-press processing equipment in which the proposed beneficiary had an important share.[124]

Contribution to a common objective The regional aid guidelines 2014-2020 require that, to demonstrate the regional contribution of individual investment aid notified to the Commission, Member States may use a variety of indicators that can be both direct and indirect. The number of direct jobs created, the quality of those jobs and the skills required may be taken into account, together with any commitment to training activities, both general and specific, to improve the skills of the workforce, including traineeships and apprenticeships. In addition, the number of jobs created indirectly in the local supplier network may be considered as helping to integrate the investment in the region concerned, ensuring more widespread spillover effects. Proven clustering effect, allowing undertakings in the same industry to specialise more efficiently will also be considered positively, as will significant knowledge spillovers in the region through technology transfers. The projects' contribution to the region's ability to create new technology through local innovation can also be considered, as will cooperation of the new production facility with local higher education institutions. Moreover, the duration of the investment and possible future follow-on investments are an indication of a durable engagement of a company in the region concerned.[125] For *ad hoc* aid, the Member State must demonstrate, in addition to the requirements laid down for individual investments under investment aid schemes, that the project is coherent with and contributes towards the development strategy of the area concerned.[126] The Commission refused to permit Slovakian aid for a firm engaged in the

---

[121] *Thirty-Fifth Report on Competition Policy* (2005), pt. 500.

[122] Case N 492/2004, *SABIC*, OJ 2005 C176/11.

[123] Case N 597/2004, *Lignit Hodonín*, OJ 2005 C250/11.

[124] Commission Decision 2008/551/EC, *Glunz & Jensen*, OJ 2008 L178/38.

[125] Regional aid guidelines 2014-2020, para 40.

[126] *Ibid.*, para 42.

extraction and processing of gravel and stone, on the basis that the location of sites was determined by the availability of natural resources, so that the investment should take place even in the absence of the aid and the aid would not, therefore, contribute to regional development.[127]

Appropriateness of regional aid For *ad hoc* aid, the Member State must demonstrate how the development of the area concerned is better ensured by such aid than by aid under a scheme or other types of measures.[128]

Incentive effect In addition to the requirements applicable to individual investments under investment aid schemes, for notified individual aid, the Member State must provide clear evidence that the aid effectively has an impact on the investment decision or the location decision, specifying which of these applies. To allow a comprehensive assessment, the Member State must provide not only information concerning the aided project but also a comprehensive description of the counterfactual scenario, in which no aid is awarded to the beneficiary by any public authority in the EEA. In the case of investment decisions, the Member State may prove the existence of the incentive effect of the aid by providing company documents that show that the investment would not be sufficiently profitable without the aid. In the case of location decisions, the Member State may prove, subject to verification by the Commission, the incentive effect of the aid by providing company documents showing that a comparison has been made between the costs and benefits of locating in the area concerned and those in alternative areas.[129] If the aid does not change the behaviour of the beneficiary by stimulating additional investment in the area concerned, there is no positive effect for the region. Therefore, aid will not be considered compatible with the internal market in cases where it appears that the same investment would take place in the region even without the aid having been granted.[130]

Proportionality of the aid amount For investment decisions, the Commission will verify whether the aid amount exceeds the minimum necessary to render the project sufficiently profitable. For location decisions, the Commission will compare the net present value of the investment for the target area with the net present value of the investment in the alternative location. Calculations used for the analysis of the incentive effect can also be used to assess if the aid is proportionate. The aid intensity must not exceed the permissible adjusted aid intensity.[131] Where regional aid is granted in the form

---

[127] Commission Decision 2008/734/EC, *Alas Slovakia*, OJ 2008 L248/19.
[128] Regional aid guidelines 2014-2020, para 55.
[129] *Ibid.*, paras 69-71.
[130] *Ibid.*, para 74. See, for example, Decision 2012/466/EU, *Petrogal*, OJ 2012 L220/1.
[131] Regional aid guidelines 2014-2020, paras 104-107.

of repayable advances, the maximum aid intensities established in a regional aid map in force at the moment the aid is granted may not be increased.[132]

Assessment of negative effects   In assessing investment decisions, the Commission places particular emphasis on the negative effects linked with the build-up of overcapacity in declining industries, the prevention of exit, and the notion of substantial market power.   These negative effects must be counterbalanced with the positive effects of the aid.   However, if it is established that the aid would result in the manifest negative effects, the aid cannot be found compatible with the internal market because it is unlikely to be compensated by any positive element.[133]   In order to identify and assess the potential distortions of competition and trade, Member States should provide evidence permitting the Commission to identify the product markets concerned (that is to say, products affected by the change in behaviour of the aid beneficiary) and to identify the competitors and customers/consumers affected. The Commission will use various criteria to assess these potential distortions, such as market structure of the product concerned, performance of the market (declining or growing market), process for selection of the aid beneficiary, entry and exit barriers and product differentiation.   A systematic reliance on State aid by an undertaking might indicate that the undertaking is not able to withstand competition on its own or that it enjoys undue advantages compared to its competitors.[134]

The Commission distinguishes two main sources of potential negative effects on product markets: cases of significant capacity expansion which leads to or deteriorates an existing situation of overcapacity, especially in a declining market; and cases where the aid beneficiary holds substantial market power. In order to evaluate whether the aid may serve to create or maintain inefficient market structures, the Commission will take into account the additional production capacity created by the project and whether the market is underperforming. Where the market in question is growing, there is normally less reason to be concerned that the aid will negatively affect dynamic incentives or will unduly impede exit or entry. More concern is warranted when markets are in decline. In this respect the Commission distinguishes between cases for which, from a long-term perspective, the relevant market is structurally in decline (that is to say, shows a negative growth rate), and cases for which the relevant market is in relative decline (that is to say, shows a positive growth rate, but does not exceed a benchmark growth rate).[135]

Underperformance of the market will normally be measured compared to the EEA GDP over the last three years before the start of the project

---

[132]   Commission Regulation (EU) No 651/2014, Article 7(6).
[133]   Regional aid guidelines 2014-2020, para 128.
[134]   *Ibid.*, para 129-131.
[135]   *Ibid.*, para 132-135.

(benchmark rate); it can also be established on the basis of projected growth rates in the coming three to five years. Indicators may include the foreseeable future growth of the market concerned and the resulting expected capacity utilisation rates, as well as the likely impact of the capacity increase on competitors through its effects on prices and profit margins. In certain cases, assessing the growth of the product market in the EEA may not be appropriate to entirely assess the effects of aid, in particular if the geographic market is worldwide. In such cases, the Commission will consider the effect of the aid on the market structures concerned, in particular, its potential to crowd out producers in the EEA.[136]

In order to evaluate the existence of substantial market power, the Commission will take into account the position of the beneficiary over a period of time before receiving the aid and the expected market position after finalising the investment. The Commission will take account of market shares of the beneficiary, as well as of market shares of its competitors and other relevant factors, including, for example the market structure by looking at the concentration in the market, possible barriers to entry, buyer power and barriers to expansion or exit.[137]

8.7 REGIONAL AID FOR LARGE INVESTMENT PROJECTS

1998 framework for large investment projects Since the regional ceilings are in general designed to provide an incentive for the type of investment facing the biggest problems and are usually in excess of the average regional handicaps, the Commission in 1998 adopted a framework on regional aid for large investment projects, the purpose of which was to limit this net incentive for large projects to a level which avoids as much as possible adverse sectoral effects caused by the project.[138]   Under this framework, the Commission decided on a case by case basis a maximum allowable intensity for large investment projects which might lead to authorised aid intensities being limited to below the applicable regional ceiling. The Commission emphasised that its intention was strictly to limit the scope of the additional rules to large-scale projects, often capital-intensive in nature, which could have a serious impact on unaided competitors. The intention was also to examine more critically the planned levels of aid for those projects which do not have, directly or indirectly, a significant impact on employment in the region concerned, which is an important objective of regional policy.

The applicable intensity level was calculated by multiplying the authorised maximum aid intensity for large firms in the region concerned by three factors

---

[136] *Ibid.*, paras 137-138.
[137] *Ibid.*, para 139.
[138] OJ 1998 C107/7.

representing competition, capital-labour and regional impact, respectively. The competition factor took account, in particular, of any structural overcapacity in the sector concerned and/or whether there was a declining market.[139] The capital-labour factor was invoked only for highly capital-intensive projects which might make little contribution to the creation of new jobs or the reduction of unemployment. This criterion would also take account of the possible distorting effect of aid on the price of the final product. The higher the capital intensity of the investment project, the more distortive the effects of capital grants on competition were likely to be.[140] The regional impact factor took account of the beneficial effects on the economies of the assisted region. For example, job creation could be used as an indicator of the project's contribution to the development of a region. Even though a capital intensive investment might only create a few jobs directly, it might nevertheless create a significant number of jobs indirectly in the region.[141]

One of the largest individual investment projects ever assessed by the Commission involved a semiconductor investment in Sicily, where the Commission approved aid amounting to €542.3 million out of a total of €2,066 million eligible costs. The intensity of 26.25% net grant equivalent, which was the maximum allowable under the framework, was justified by the fact that the project created 1,150 direct jobs and up to 800 indirect jobs.[142] Similarly, aid of €250 million was approved for the construction of a new €800 million pulp mill in Saxony-Anhalt, where 580 direct jobs and 1,000 indirect jobs would be created. Given the positive impact on employment as well as the fact that the sector concerned was not characterised by structural overcapacity, the intensity of 31% was acceptable.[143] By contrast, the Commission challenged plans to subsidise the construction of a new plant in Brandenburg for the production of corrugated base paper. The initial proposal was for an intensity of 35%, but the Commission was willing to approve a subsidy for only 26.25% of the investment costs since the sector was in relative decline.[144] Similarly, it reduced the amount of aid proposed for the construction of a caprolactum complex in Brandenburg on the ground that the product market was in relative decline, and also required that the last instalment of the aid could be paid out only after verification that all 528 proposed jobs had in fact been created.[145]

---

[139] 1998 framework on regional aid for large investment projects, paras 3.2, 3.4, 3.10. See also, Cases C-75/05P & C-80/05P, *Germany v Kronofrance* [2008] ECR I-6619, paras 67-73; Case T-27/02, *Kronofrance v Commission* [2004] ERCR II-4177.

[140] 1998 framework on regional aid for large investment projects, paras 3.7-3.8.

[141] *Ibid.*, para 3.9 When applying this factor, the Commission gave a higher rating to the creation of jobs in an Article 107(3)(a) region than in an Article 107(3)(c) region in recognition of the more severe economic problems faced by the former.

[142] Case N 844/2001, *ST Microelectronics*, OJ 2002 C146/10.

[143] Case 240/2002, *Saxony-Anhalt*, OJ 2002 C232/2.

[144] Commission Decision 2002/824/EC, OJ 2002 L296/50.

[145] *Thirty-Second Report on Competition Policy* (2002), pt. 442.

2002 multi-sectoral framework A new framework was announced in 2002, which came effect as of 1 January 2004.[146] Compared to the previous rules, the new framework was a simpler instrument. Projects up to €50 million could attract aid up to 100% of the applicable regional ceiling. For the part between €50 million and €100 million, the aid intensity was up to 50% of the regional ceiling and, for the part exceeding €100 million, the maximum intensity was 34% of the regional ceiling.[147] Member States were required to notify every case of regional investment aid if the aid proposed was more than the maximum allowable aid that an investment of €100 million could obtain under the framework. Individually notified projects were not eligible for aid if either the aid beneficiary accounted for more than 25% of the product market or the capacity created by the project was more than 5% of the market unless the average annual growth rate of consumption of the product concerned over the past five years is above the average annual growth rate of GDP in the EEA.[148] The Commission intended to draw up a list of specific thresholds for sectors with serious structural difficulties, but it subsequently abandoned this idea on the ground that it was not technically feasible.[149]

Large investment projects under the regional aid guidelines 2007-2013 The rules in the 2002 multi-sectoral framework were incorporated into the regional aid guidelines 2007-13.[150] Subsequently, the Commission issued a communication on large investment projects.[151] A number of indicative criteria were set out which might be used to demonstrate the regional contribution of the aid insofar as it might attract individual investment and activity to the region, including: the number of direct jobs created, the quality and the skills level; indirect job creation; the commitment of the beneficiary to general and specific workforce training; external economies of scale and other benefits arising from clustering effects; the technological intensity of the activity and the scope for knowledge spill-over; the contribution of the project to the region's ability to create new technology through local innovation, e.g. through cooperation with higher education; the duration of the investment and scope for follow-on investment. In *Dell Poland*, the Commission concluded that an investment of €54.5 million would significantly contribute to the regional development of the Lodz region, based on a finding that the aid

---

[146] The new rules applied to the steel sector as of 24 July 2002, and to the motor vehicle and synthetic fibres sectors as of 1 January 2003. U. Soltesz, "The new multi-sectoral framework on regional aid – overkill or an 'appropriate measure'?" (2005) 26 ECLR 112.

[147] 2002 framework on regional aid for large investment projects, para 21.

[148] *Ibid.*, para 24.

[149] Regional aid guidelines 2007-13, fn 59.

[150] F. Wishlade, "The control of regional aid to large investment projects: workable comptromise or arbitrary constraint?" [2008] EStALQ 495.

[151] OJ 2009 L223/3.

provided an incentive effect for Dell to locate in Lodz by compensating for less favourable investment conditions in comparison with another envisaged location in eastern Europe. Regarding the negative effects of the aid, the Commission found that the aid would not cause the crowding out of competitors or the creation of significant production capacity in an underperforming market since it had been demonstrated that the plant would have been built in any event, regardless of the aid, albeit in a different location. On balance, the Commission concluded that the positive effects of the aid outweighed the negative effects on trade.[152]

The guidelines provided that a large investment project is an initial investment with an eligible expenditure above €50 million. In order to prevent a large investment project from being artificially divided into sub-projects in order to escape the provisions of the guidelines, a large investment project was considered to be a single investment project when the initial investment was undertaken in a period of three years by one or more companies and consisted of fixed assets combined in an economically indivisible way. To assess whether an initial investment was economically indivisible, the Commission took into account the technical, functional and strategic links and the immediate geographical proximity. The economic indivisibility was assessed independently from ownership. This implied that to establish whether a large investment project constituted a single investment project, the assessment should be the same irrespective of whether the project is carried out by one undertaking, by more than one undertakings sharing the investment costs or by more undertakings bearing the costs of separate investments within the same investment project (for example in the case of a joint venture).[153] For example, the Commission decided that a cluster of nine investments in Poland concerning the production of flat screen televisions modules by LG Philips did not constitute a single investment project.[154] In the case of *Deutsche Solar*, Germany initially notified regional investment aid in excess of €50 million in respect of two facilities, which prompted the Commission to open a formal investigation procedure, following which the proposed aid was reduced to €45 million and withdrawn in respect of one facility, allowing the Commission to approve it as a single investment project on the basis that the positive impact of the investment on regional development outweighed the potential distortions of competition.[155]

Regional investment aid for large investment projects was subject to an adjusted regional aid ceiling, whereby the part of the investment between €50 million and €100 million was limited to 50% of the regional ceiling and the

---

[152] Case C 46/2008, *Dell Poland*, OJ 2010 L29/8.
[153] Regional aid guidelines 2007-13, para 60; Commission Regulation (EC) No 800/2008, Article 13(10).
[154] Case N 245/2006, *LG Philips LCD Poland*, OJ 2007 C278/1.
[155] Case C 34/2008, *Deutsche Solar AG*, OJ 2011 L7/40.

part exceeding €100 million was limited to 34% of the regional ceiling.[156] Where the total amount of the aid exceeded 75% of the maximum amount of aid that an investment with eligible expenditure of €100 million could receive, under certain conditions concerning market share threshold the Commission could approve the aid.[157] The General Court, however, held that aid falling under that threshold still had to be assessed in a formal investigation if the Commission was not able to satisfy itself that the aid presented no serious difficulties for assessment.[158] Thus, in *Smurfit Kappa v Commission*, which concerned regional investment aid to Propapier for the construction of a paper mill, a sector suffering from structural overcapacity, the Commission's decision, at the end of the preliminary assessment, declaring the aid compatible with the internal market on the ground that the relevant market share had not been exceeded was annulled on the ground that the Commission had failed to assess whether the advantages in terms of regional development would outweigh the distortions of competition in the sector in question.[159] Subsequently, the Commission re-affirmed its conclusion that the aid to Propapier was compatible with the internal market.[160]

Large investment projects under the regional aid guidelines 2014-2020
The Commission has modified its policy regarding regional aid to large investment projects under the regional aid guidelines 2014-2020, in particular by abandoning the market share filter mechanism. Although the Commission considered abolishing the right of Member States to award aid at all to large undertakings in Article 107(3)(c) areas, in the end the 2014-2020 guidelines retained this possibility, although the prevailing view is that the assessment criteria will be difficult to overcome for large investment projects.[161] A large investment project is an initial investment with eligible costs exceeding €50 million, calculated at prices and exchange rates on the date of the award of the aid.[162] For aid to large investment projects, it must be ensured that the aid does not exceed the scaled down intensity, using the same criteria as before. Where

---

[156] To calculate whether the eligible expenditure for large investment projects reaches the various thresholds in the guidelines, the eligible expenditure to be taken into account is either the traditional investment costs or the wage costs, whichever is the higher: Regional aid guidelines 2007-13, para 61.

[157] Regional aid guidelines 2007-13, para 68.

[158] See, H.W. Friederiszick and N. Tosini, "The relevance of market screens in the regional aid guidelines" [2013] EStALQ 46; J.P. Otter and B. Balasingham, "Regional State aid: market definintion in large investment projects of the automotive industry", [2013] EStALQ 516.

[159] Case T-304/08, *Smurfit Kappa Group plc v Commission* EU:T:2012:351, para 94.

[160] Case SA.23827, *Propapier*. OJ 2015 L179/54.

[161] See, M. Todino and A. Zanazzo, "New guidelines on regional aid – is the party over for large investment projects?", [2013] EStALQ 676.

[162] Regional aid guidelines 2014-2020, para 20(l); Commission Regulation (EU) No 651/2014, Article 2(52).

aid is awarded to a beneficiary for an investment that is considered to be part of a single investment project, the aid must be scaled down for the eligible costs exceeding €50 million.[163]

8.8 REGIONAL OPERATING AID SCHEMES

Regional operating aid Regional aid aimed at reducing the current expenses of an undertaking constitutes operating aid and will not be regarded as compatible with the internal market, unless it is awarded to tackle specific or permanent handicaps faced by undertakings in disadvantaged regions. Operating aid may be considered compatible if it aims to reduce certain specific difficulties faced by SMEs in particularly disadvantaged areas falling within the scope of Article 107(3)(a) TFEU, or to compensate for additional costs to pursue an economic activity in an outermost regions or to prevent or reduce depopulation in very sparsely populated areas.[164]

Contribution to a common objective The Commission takes the view in the regional aid guidelines 2014-2020 that operating aid schemes will promote the development of disadvantaged areas only if the challenges facing these areas are clearly identified in advance. The obstacles to attracting or maintaining economic activity may be so severe or permanent that investment aid alone is not sufficient to allow the development of those areas. As regards aid to reduce certain specific difficulties faced by SMEs in Article 107(3)(a) areas, the Member States concerned must demonstrate the existence and importance of those specific difficulties and must demonstrate that an operating aid scheme is needed as those specific difficulties cannot be overcome with investment aid. As regards operating aid to compensate certain additional costs in the outermost regions, the permanent handicaps which severely restrain the development of the outermost regions include remoteness, insularity, small size, difficult topography and climate, and economic dependence on a few products. The Member State concerned must identify the specific additional costs related to these permanent handicaps that the operating aid scheme is intended to compensate. As regards operating aid to prevent or reduce depopulation in very sparsely populated areas, the Member State concerned must demonstrate the risk of depopulation of the relevant area in the absence of the operating aid.[165] For example, the Commission approved the application of a reduced rate of excise duty on traditional rum produced in the French

---

[163] Regional aid guidelines 2014-2020, para 89.
[164] *Ibid.*, para 16.
[165] *Ibid.*, paras 43-46.

overseas departments, taking into account the economic dependence of those regions on the sugar cane/rum sector.[166]

Appropriateness of regional aid The Member State must demonstrate that the aid is appropriate to achieve the objective of the scheme for the problems that the aid is intended to address. To demonstrate that the aid is appropriate, the Member State may calculate the aid amount *ex ante* as a fixed sum covering the expected additional costs over a given period, to incentivise undertakings to contain costs and develop their business in a more efficient manner over time. However, where future costs and revenue developments are surrounded by a high degree of uncertainty and there is a strong asymmetry of information, the Member State may also wish to adopt compensation models that are not entirely *ex ante*, but rather a mix of *ex ante* and *ex post*, for example, using claw backs such as to allow sharing of unanticipated gains.[167]

Incentive effect The incentive effect of aid granted under operating aid schemes will be considered to be present if it is likely that, in the absence of aid, the level of economic activity in the area or region concerned would be significantly reduced due to the problems that the aid is intended to address. The Commission will therefore consider that the aid induces additional economic activity in the areas or regions concerned, if the Member State has demonstrated the existence and substantial nature of those problems in the area concerned.[168]

Proportionality of the aid amount The Member State must demonstrate that the level of the aid is proportionate to the problems that the aid is intended to address. In particular, the following conditions must be fulfilled: the aid must be determined in relation to a predefined set of eligible costs that are fully attributable to the problems that the aid is intended to address, as demonstrated by the Member State; the aid must be limited to a certain proportion of those predefined set of eligible costs and must not exceed those costs; the aid amount per beneficiary must be proportional to the level of the problems actually experienced by each beneficiary.[169] As regards aid to compensate for certain additional costs in the outermost regions, the eligible costs must be fully attributable to one or several of the permanent handicaps referred to in Article 349 TFEU. Those additional costs must exclude transport costs and any additional costs that may be attributable to other factors and must be quantified in relation to the level of costs incurred by similar undertakings established in

---

[166] Case N 179/2002, *Rum from French overseas departments*, OJ 2002 C252/17.
[167] Regional aid guidelines 2014-2020, para 56.
[168] *Ibid.*, paras 75-76.
[169] *Ibid.*, paras 108-109.

other regions of the Member State concerned.[170]   As regards aid to reduce certain specific difficulties faced by SMEs in 'a' areas, the level of the aid must be progressively reduced over the duration of the scheme.[171]   A scheme intended to encourage job-creating economic activities in the Madeira free zone was approved on the basis that the tax concessions involved were proportionate to the impact of the activities on local development which suffered from structural handicaps as a result of the distance of Madeira from Portuguese mainland economic centres, while excluding from its scope businesses carrying on activities that had no real impact on regional development.[172]

Assessment of negative effects   If the aid is necessary and proportional to achieve the relevant common objective, the negative effects of the aid are likely to be compensated by positive effects.   However, in some cases, the aid may result in changes to the structure of the market or to the characteristics of a sector or industry which could significantly distort competition through barriers to market entry or exit, substitution effects, or displacement of trade flows.   In those cases, the identified negative effects are unlikely to be compensated by any positive effects.[173]

Block exemption for regional operating aid schemes   Regional operating aid schemes in outermost regions and sparsely populated areas are covered by the block exemption in Commission Regulation (EU) No 651/2014, Article 15, up to 100% of certain eligible costs.   First, such schemes may compensate for the additional transport costs of goods which have been produced in areas eligible for operating aid, as well as additional transport costs of goods that are further processed in these areas, in cases where the beneficiaries have their production activity in those areas, the aid is objectively quantifiable in advance and these additional transport costs are calculated on the basis of the lowest possible costs of transporting the goods.   Only for outermost regions, additional transport costs of goods that are further processed in these areas may include the costs of transporting goods from any place of their production to these areas.   Second, compensation may be granted for the additional operating costs other than transport costs, incurred in outermost regions as a direct effect of their permanent handicaps in cases where the beneficiaries have their economic activity in an outermost region and the annual aid amount per beneficiary under all operating aid schemes does not in the outermost region concerned exceed 15% of the gross value added annually created by the beneficiary; or

---

[170]   *Ibid.*, para 110.
[171]   *Ibid.*, para 111.
[172]   Case N 222/A/2002, *Madeira Free Zone*, OJ 2002 C65/23.
[173]   Regional aid guidelines 2014-2020, para 140.

25% of the annual labour costs incurred by the beneficiary; or 10% of the annual turnover of the beneficiary.[174]

Operating aid for financial and intra-group activities   Because of the specific nature of financial and intra-group activities, operating aid granted for these activities has only a very limited likelihood of promoting regional development but a very high risk of distorting competition. Regional operating aid of this type is excluded from the block exemption.[175]   The Commission will generally not approve any operating aid to the financial services sector or for intra-group activities.[176]   For example, while approving aid in the form of tax reductions in the Azores region under Article 107(3)(a) TFEU, it specifically excluded the application of the reductions to firms operating in the financial sector or providing intra-group services.[177]

8.9 REGIONAL URBAN DEVELOPMENT AID

Development of urban development aid policy   In 1997, the Commission introduced guidelines on aid for small enterprises in deprived urban areas[178] in recognition of the fact that market forces were inadequate to achieve the objective of renovating the most disadvantaged urban areas in the EU.   In order to be eligible for aid, the enterprise had to carry on its principal economic activity and invest in the designated area and had to reserve at least 20% of the new jobs created for persons having their domicile in a deprived urban area. Aid was conditional on job creation, with the maximum level of aid being fixed at 26% net grant equivalent of the investment or €10,000 per job created. Although the guidelines were based on a decision of the Commission concerning the French Urban Regeneration Pact,[179] they were never otherwise used by the Member States, and the Commission withdrew them in 2002.[180]

Under the regional aid guidelines 2007-13, the Commission introduced a separate category of eligible area, which might cover deprived urban areas as

---

[174] Commission Regulation (EU) No 651/2014, Article 15.   See, for example, Case N 203/2004, *Volvo Lastvagnar*, OJ 2005 C92/10; Case N 152/2007, *Swedish regional transport*, OJ 2007 C284/3.

[175] Commission Regulation (EU) No 651/2014, Article 13(1)(e).

[176] Regional aid guidelines 2014-2020, para 17.

[177] Commission Decision 2003/442/EC, *Azores regional aid*, OJ 2003 L150/52, confirmed in Case C-88/03, *Portugal v Commission* [2006] ECR I-7115, paras 99-107. See also, Case N 421/2006, *Zona Franca Madeira*, OJ 2007 C240/1; Case N 376/2006, *Zona Especial Canaria*, OJ 2007 C30/4.

[178] OJ 1997 C146/6.

[179] *Twenty-Sixth Report on Competition Policy* (1996), p. 210.

[180] OJ 2002 C119/21.   The Commission proceeded to compile a vademecum on State aid control and regeneration of deprived urban areas to highlight the available State aid instruments that could be relied on as a substitute.

well as other areas with particular local difficulties. In order to allow Member States greater flexibility to target very localised regional disparities, below the NUTS-III level, Member States could designate other smaller areas which do not meet the conditions described above for eligible Article 107(3)(c) regions provided they have a minimum population of 20,000 and are relatively more in need of economic development than other areas in that region, on the basis of recognised economic indicators such as GDP *per capita*, employment or unemployment levels, local productivity or skills indicators. Regional aid might be approved by the Commission in these areas for SMEs.[181] No equivalent appears in the regional aid guidelines 2014-2020. Instead, in Commission Regulation (EU) No 651/2014, a new category of regional urban development aid has been created for which a block exemption is available.

Regional urban development aid Urban development projects must be implemented via urban development funds in assisted areas, be co-financed by the European Structural and Investment Funds and support the implementation of an integrated sustainable urban development strategy. The total investment in an urban development project under any urban development aid measure may not exceed €20 million. The urban development aid must leverage additional investment from private investors at the level of the urban development funds or the urban development projects, so as to achieve an aggregate amount reaching a minimum 30% of the total financing provided to an urban development project. Private and public investors may provide cash or an in-kind contribution or a combination of those for the implementation of an urban development project.[182]

The urban development measures fulfil certain conditions. Urban development fund managers must be selected through an open, transparent and non-discriminatory call and may be required to fulfil predefined criteria objectively justified by the nature of the investments. The independent private investors must be selected through an open, transparent and non-discriminatory call aimed at establishing the appropriate risk-reward sharing arrangements whereby, for investments other than guarantees, asymmetric profit-sharing is to be given preference over downside protection. If the private investors are not selected by such a call, the fair rate of return to the private investors must be established by an independent expert selected via an open, transparent and non-discriminatory call. In the case of asymmetric loss-sharing between public and private investors, the first loss assumed by the public investor must be capped at 25% of the total investment. In the case of guarantees to private investors in urban development projects, the guarantee rate must be limited to 80% and total losses assumed by a Member State must be capped at 25% of the

---

[181] Regional aid guidelines 2007-13, para 31. Belgium, Denmark, Finland, France, Germany, Ireland and Italy designated certain areas as falling within this category.

[182] Commission Regulation (EU) No 651/2014, Article 16(1)-(7).

underlying guaranteed portfolio. The investors must be allowed to be represented in the governance bodies of the urban development fund, such as the supervisory board or the advisory committee. There must be provision a due diligence process in order to ensure a commercially sound investment strategy for the purpose of implementing the urban development aid measure.[183]

Urban development funds must be managed on a commercial basis and ensure profit-driven financing decisions. This is considered to be the case when the managers of the urban development fund fulfil the following conditions. The managers must be obliged by law or contract to act with the diligence of a professional manager in good faith and avoiding conflicts of interest; best practices and regulatory supervision shall apply. The remuneration of the managers must conform to market practices. This requirement is considered to be met where a manager is selected through an open, transparent and non-discriminatory call, based on objective criteria linked to experience, expertise and operational and financial capacity. The managers must receive a remuneration linked to performance, or share part of the investment risks by co-investing own resources so as to ensure that their interests are permanently aligned with the interests of the public investors. They must set out an investment strategy, criteria and the proposed timing of investments in urban development projects, establishing the *ex ante* financial viability and their expected impact on urban development. A clear and realistic exit strategy must exist for each equity and quasi-equity investment.[184]

---

[183] *Ibid.*, Article 16(8).
[184] *Ibid.*, Article 16(9).

Chapter Nine

STATE AID FOR
SMALL AND MEDIUM-SIZED ENTERPRISES

9.1 COMMISSION POLICY ON STATE AID FOR SMEs

Commission policy on State aid for SMEs Whilst investment aid for large enterprises outside of assisted regions is normally not allowed by the Commission, a different approach is taken in the case of aid for small and medium-sized enterprises (SMEs) which are regarded as performing better as regards job creation and innovation as compared with larger enterprises. SMEs are also regarded as the main motor of structural change and regeneration since they facilitate shifts of economic resources from declining to expanding sectors. The ECJ has also recognised that the particular interests of SMEs entitle the Commission to afford them special consideration, whilst noting that the Commission need not approve systematically all schemes giving preferential treatment to such enterprises.[1] SMEs are also afforded preferential consideration under many other EU State aid policies, such as regional aid, employment aid, training aid, and aid for research and development and for environmental protection.

On the basis of its experience in assessing aid to SMEs, the Commission issued guidelines on the compatibility with the internal market of investment and start-up aid in 1992,[2] which were revised and extended in 1996.[3] Council Regulation (EC) No 994/98[4] now provides for the Commission to adopt regulations declaring certain aid for SMEs to be compatible with the internal market and not to be subject to the notification requirements of Article 108(3) TFEU.[5] Pursuant to this power, the Commission adopted Regulation (EC) No 70/2001 on aid to SMEs,[6] which was superseded by the general block exemption in Commission Regulation (EC) No 800/2008. The block exemption rules are now set out in Commission Regulation (EU) No 651/201, which contains specific provisions concerning SMEs in relation to investment

---

[1] Case C-364/90, *Italy v Commission* [1993] ECR I-2097, para 24.
[2] OJ 1992 C213/2.
[3] OJ 1996 C213/4.
[4] OJ 1998 L142/1.
[5] Council Regulation (EC) No 994/98, Article 1(a)(i).
[6] OJ 2001 L10/33, amended by Commission Regulation (EC) No 364/2004 (OJ 2004 L63/28) and Commission Regulation (EC) No 1976/2006 (OJ 2006 L368/85).

aid, aid for consultancy and for participation in fairs, aid for cooperation costs incurred by SMEs participating in European Territorial Cohesion projects and aid for access to finance in the form of risk finance aid, aid for start-ups and aid for scouting costs.[7] In addition, the Commission has adopted guidelines for assessing State aid to promote risk capital investments where the block exemption is inapplicable.[8] The Commission may also assess aid measures directly on the basis of Article 107(3) TFEU.[9]

Definition of SMEs by the European Commission Since the advantages afforded to SMEs are in most cases exceptions to the general rules, such as in the area of State aid, the definition of an SME must be interpreted strictly.[10] Small and medium-sized enterprises were defined in Commission Recommendation 96/280/EC[11] as independent enterprises which had fewer than 250 employees (50 for small enterprises) and had either an annual turnover of €40 million (€7 million for small enterprises) or an annual balance sheet total not exceeding €27 million (€5 million for small enterprises). In determining whether these thresholds applied, it was necessary to cumulate the relevant figures for the beneficiary enterprise and for all enterprises that it directly or indirectly controlled through possession of 25% or more of the capital or voting rights.[12] Eligible enterprises needed to conform to the criterion of independence for SMEs; i.e., with certain exceptions, they must not have been owned as to 25% or more of the capital or the voting rights by one enterprise, or jointly by several enterprises, falling outside the definition of an SME or a small enterprise, whichever may apply.[13] This definition was incorporated into Regulation (EC) No 70/2001.[14]

Following the General Court's decision in *Pollmeier Malchow v Commission*,[15] a new definition of SMEs, first set out in Commission Recommendation 2003/361/EC, was applied as of 1 January 2005.[16] This definition of SMEs is now also set out in Annex I to Regulation (EU) No 651/2014. Certain improvements were incorporated into the definition in order to ensure, in particular, that SMEs are properly autonomous.

---

[7] Commission Regulation (EU) No 651/2014, Articles 17-24. The provisions in Commission Regulation (EC) No 800/2008 concerning aid for small enterprises created by female entrepreneurs have not been retained.

[8] OJ 2009 C19/4.

[9] Case T-357/02 RENV, *Freistaat Sachsen v Commission* [2011] ECR II-5415, para 42.

[10] Case C-110/13, *HaTeFo GmbH v Fza Haldensleben* EU:C:2014:114, para 32.

[11] OJ 1996 L107/4.

[12] Commission Recommendation 96/280/EC, Article 1(4).

[13] *Ibid.*, Annex, Article 1(3).

[14] Commission Regulation (EC) No 70/2001, Annex I.

[15] Case T-137/02, *Pollmeier Malchow GmbH v Commission* [2004] ECR II-3541, paras 61-62.

[16] OJ 2003 L124/36. This was incorporated into Commission Regulation (EC) No 70/2001, Annex I.

Micro, small and medium-sized enterprises Enterprises are specified as including any entity engaged in an economic activity, irrespective of its legal form, including self-employed persons and family businesses engaged in craft or other activities, and partnerships or associations regularly engaged in an economic activity.[17] The category of SME is sub-divided in three classifications. The category of micro, small and medium-sized enterprises is made up of enterprises which employ fewer than 250 persons and which have an annual turnover not exceeding €50 million and/or an annual balance sheet total not exceeding €43 million. Within the SME category, a small enterprise is defined as an enterprise which employs fewer than 50 persons and whose annual turnover and/or annual balance sheet total does not exceed €10 million, and a micro-enterprise is defined as an enterprise which employs fewer than 10 persons and whose annual turnover and/or annual balance sheet total does not exceed €2 million.[18]

SMEs must be autonomous An autonomous SME is any enterprise which is not classified as a partner enterprise or as a linked enterprise.[19] The purpose of the independence criterion is to ensure that the measures intended for SMEs genuinely benefited the enterprises for which size represented a handicap and not enterprises belonging to a large group which had access to funds and assistance not available to competitors of equal size. In order to ensure that only genuinely independent SMEs are included, legal arrangements must not be allowed in which SMEs form an economic group much stronger than an independent SME. It must also be ensured that the definition is not circumvented on formal grounds.[20] Partner enterprises are enterprises which are not classified as linked enterprises and where one holds, either solely or jointly with one or more linked enterprises, 25% or more of the capital or voting rights of another enterprise. However, an enterprise may be ranked as autonomous where the investment is held by the following independent investors:[21]

(a) public investment corporations, venture capital companies, individuals or groups of individuals with a regular venture capital investment activity who invest equity capital in unquoted businesses (business angels),

---

[17] *Ibid.*, Article 1.

[18] *Ibid.*, Article 2. Staff includes employees, owner-managers and partner; apprentices or students engaged in vocational training are not included as staff: Article 5.

[19] Commission Regulation (EU) No 651/2014, Annex I, Article 3(1).

[20] Case C-91/01, *Italy v Commission* [2004] ECR I-4355, para 50; Case C-110/13, *HaTeFo GmbH v Fza Haldensleben* EU:C:2014:114, para 33.

[21] Commission Regulation (EU) No 651/2014, Annex I, Article 3(2). Except in these cases, an enterprise cannot be considered an SME if 25% or more of the capital or voting rights are directly or indirectly controlled, jointly or individually, by one or more public bodies: Article 3(4).

provided the total investment of those business angels in the same enterprise is less than €1,250,000;

(b) universities or non-profit research centres;
(c) institutional investors, including regional development funds;
(d) autonomous local authorities with an annual budget of less than €10 million and less than 5,000 inhabitants.

Linked enterprises Linked enterprises are enterprises which have any of the following relationships with each other: [22]

(a) an enterprise has a majority of the shareholders' or members' voting rights in another enterprise;
(b) an enterprise has the right to appoint or remove a majority of the members of the administrative, management or supervisory body of another enterprise;
(c) an enterprise has the right to exercise a dominant influence over another enterprise pursuant to a contract entered into with that enterprise or to a provision in its memorandum or articles of association;[23]
(d) an enterprise, which is a shareholder in or member of another enterprise, controls alone, pursuant to an agreement with other shareholders in or members of that enterprise, a majority of shareholders' or members' voting rights in that enterprise.

Enterprises having any of these relationships through one or more other enterprises, or any one of the independent investors, are also considered to be linked. Enterprises which have one or other of such relationships through a natural person or group of natural persons acting jointly are also considered linked enterprises if they engage in their activity or in part of their activity in the same relevant market or in adjacent markets, i.e. the market for a product or service situated directly upstream or downstream of the relevant market.

In *HaTeFo*, a company was owned by three shareholders, one of which, holding 24.8% of the shares, also held 50% of the shares in another company. Two of the shareholders were also managing directors of both companies. Considered in isolation, HaTeFo was an SME. However, the ECJ held that enterprises which do not formally have one or other of the relationships set out above, but which, because of the role played by a natural person or group of natural persons acting jointly, nevertheless constitute a single economic unit, must also be regarded as linked enterprises for the purposes of that provision, since they engage in their activities or in part of their activities in the same relevant market or in adjacent markets. Moreover, the condition that natural persons are acting jointly is satisfied where those persons work together in

---

[22] Commission Regulation (EU) No 651/2014, Annex I, Article 3(3).
[23] There is a presumption that the independent investors listed above do not exercise a dominant influence if they are not involving themselves directly or indirectly in the management of the enterprise, without prejudice to their rights as shareholders.

order to exercise an influence over the commercial decisions of the enterprises concerned which precludes those enterprises from being regarded as economically independent of one another. Whether that condition is satisfied depends on the circumstances of the case, and that is not necessarily conditional on the existence of contractual relations between those persons or even a finding that they intended to circumvent the definition of an SME. In the circumstances, the two companies could be regarded as constituting, through a group of natural persons acting jointly, a single economic unit, so that they should be regarded as linked enterprises.[24]

9.2 SME INVESTMENT AID

SME investment aid SME investment aid falling within the block exemption provided by Regulation (EU) No 651/2014 may be granted for investment by SMEs operating inside or outside the EU.[25] An investment must consist of an investment in tangible and/or intangible assets relating to the setting-up of a new establishment, the extension of an existing establishment, diversification of the output of an establishment into new additional products or a fundamental change in the overall production process of an existing establishment. Alternatively, an investment may involve the acquisition of the assets belonging to an establishment, where the establishment has closed or would have closed had it not been purchased, the assets are purchased from third parties unrelated to the buyer and the transaction takes place under market conditions. Where a member of the family of the original owner, or an employee, takes over a small enterprise, the condition that the assets must be bought from third parties unrelated to the buyer is waived. The sole acquisition of the shares of an undertaking does not constitute investment.[26]

Individual aid, whether granted *ad hoc* or on the basis of a scheme, must be notified to the Commission in advance pursuant to Article 108(3) TFEU where the aid exceeds €7.5 million per undertaking per project.[27]

Intensity of investment aid for SMEs For SME aid to benefit from the block exemption under Commission Regulation (EU) No 651/2014, the gross intensity of the aid must not exceed 20% of the eligible costs in the case of small enterprises and 10% in the case of medium-sized enterprises.[28] The eligible costs are either or both of the investment's eligible tangible and intangible costs or the estimated wage costs of employment directly created by

---

[24]   Case C-110/13, *HaTeFo GmbH v Fza Haldensleben* EU:C:2014:114, paras 34-38.
[25]   Commission Regulation (EU) No 651/2014, Article 17(1).
[26]   *Ibid.*, Article 17(3).
[27]   *Ibid.*, Article 4(1)(c).
[28]   *Ibid.*, Article 17(6).

the investment project, calculated over a period of two years.[29] Where the aid is calculated on the basis of the investment's costs, the eligible costs of tangible investment are the costs relating to investment in land, buildings, machinery and equipment. Eligible costs of intangible investment are the costs of acquisition of the technology, including patents, licences, know-how or other intellectual property.[30] Intangible assets must be regarded as amortizable assets, be purchased from third parties under market conditions and remain included in the assets of the undertaking for at least three years. They must be used exclusively in the undertaking receiving the aid.[31]

Where the aid is calculated on the basis of jobs created, the following conditions are applicable: the jobs must be created within three years of the completion of the investment; the aid must lead to a net increase in the number of employees in the particular establishment, compared with the average over the previous twelve months; and the employment created must be maintained during a minimum period of three years.[32]

9.3 AID FOR DIRECT FOREIGN INVESTMENT

Aid for direct foreign investment Although aid for direct foreign investment by SMEs is not included in the block exemption regulation and therefore remains subject to prior notification to the Commission pursuant to Article 108(3) TFEU, it has in the past been generally favourably viewed by the Commission. Such investments result from a firm's desire to develop new business outlets by investing and selling on foreign markets rather than by exporting. Investment generally takes the form of setting up a joint venture or a subsidiary abroad, either by acquiring shares or purchasing a local firm. The Commission's approach is that whilst such aid is certainly State aid, it may in certain cases, apart from its effects on the competitiveness of EU industry and the development of cooperation with third countries, promote other EU objectives such as the development of SMEs. It is possible, on the other hand, that such aid could run counter to the objective of economic and social cohesion inasmuch as it could encourage the siting of subsidiaries or production plants in third countries, to the detriment of investment within the EU.[33]

The Commission approved a programme for the Land of Brandenburg whereby aid was granted for investment projects in pre-accession Poland

---

[29] *Ibid.*, Article 17(2). This ensures that the capital factor of an investment is not treated more favourably than the labour factor.
[30] *Ibid.*, Article 2(28)-(29).
[31] *Ibid.*, Article 17(4).
[32] *Ibid.*, Article 17(5).
[33] *Twenty-Sixth Report on Competition Policy* (1996), pt. 224.

involving company start-ups and the formation of joint ventures.[34] It also approved a Dutch scheme involving State-backed soft loans to encourage Netherlands-based SMEs to invest in emerging markets and thus contribute to lasting economic cooperation with local enterprises.[35] The Commission is less likely to favour State aid for large enterprises in relation to their direct investments abroad. For example, whilst it permitted an Austrian scheme aimed at supporting investments in third countries if the aid was granted to SMEs, it required advance individual notice of any such aid being granted to large companies.[36] Moreover, the Commission refused to approve aid which Austria wished to grant to Lift GmbH for an investment project in China, concluding that the aid was incompatible with the internal market since it was to be granted to a large company whose competitors were all European and which was already firmly established in China. The aid failed to meet the necessity criterion, i.e., that without it the company would not make the investment, particularly since the intended beneficiary had already commenced production using rented facilities. The Commission considered that, given the strategic nature of the Chinese market, the aid was liable to distort competition between Member States to an extent contrary to the common interest.[37]

9.4 SME AID FOR ANCILLARY PURPOSES

Aid to improve the general business environment Following its crackdown on general investment schemes, the Commission was able to note in 1990 the positive trend that Member States were tending to allocate budgets to schemes that were more likely to strengthen the general efficiency and competitiveness of the economy. In the forefront of such aid schemes were programmes to improve the general business environment, particularly for SMEs. Such programmes aided the use of specialised consultants, training, the dissemination of advanced technology and the improvement of production and management methods.[38] Thus, for instance, the Commission took a favourable view of schemes proposed by the Spanish Government that offered aid to improve the quality standards achieved by Spanish industry. Firms carrying out projects in the areas of dissemination, training, diagnosis and technical assistance and improvement of quality control systems were eligible for grants of up to 50% gross of the cost of the projects.[39] This policy was reflected in Commission Regulation (EC) No 70/2001 and Regulation (EC) No 800/2008

---

[34] *Ibid.*, p. 250.
[35] *Twenty-Eighth Report on Competition Policy* (1998), p. 272.
[36] *Twenty-Sixth Report on Competition Policy* (1996), p. 251.
[37] Commission Decision 1999/365/EC, *Lift GmbH*, OJ 1999 L142/32.
[38] *Twentieth Report on Competition Policy* (1990), pt. 294.
[39] *Ibid.*, pt. 296.

and is continued in the block exemption in Regulation (EU) No 651/2014 which provides for aid for consultancy or aid for participation in fairs to fall within the scope of the block exemption

Aid for consultancy   Aid to SMEs for services provided by outside consultants is permissible under the block exemption where the gross aid does not exceed 50% of the costs of such services. The services concerned must not be a continuous or periodic activity nor may they relate to the SME's usual operating expenditure, such as routine tax consultancy services, regular legal services, or advertising.[40] Individual aid, whether granted *ad hoc* or on the basis of a scheme, must be notified to the Commission in advance pursuant to Article 108(3) TFEU where the aid exceeds €2 million per undertaking per project.[41]

Aid for SME participation in fairs Aid may also be granted for participation of SMEs in fairs and exhibitions up to 50% of the costs of renting, setting up and running the stand, although this exemption only applies to the first participation of the enterprise in any particular fair or exhibition.[42] Individual aid, whether granted *ad hoc* or on the basis of a scheme, must be notified to the Commission in advance pursuant to Article 108(3) TFEU where the aid exceeds €2 million per undertaking per project.[43]

Aid for costs of European Territorial Cooperation projects   Aid for cooperation costs incurred by SMEs participating in the European Territorial Cooperation projects covered by European Parliament and Council Regulation (EC) No 1299/2013 is compatible with the internal market where the aid intensity does not exceed 50% of the eligible costs. The eligible are costs for organisational cooperation including the cost of staff and offices to the extent that it is linked to the cooperation project, costs of advisory and support services linked to cooperation and delivered by external consultants and service providers, and travel expenses, costs of equipment and investment expenditure directly related to the project and depreciation of tools and equipment used directly for the project. The advisory and support services may not be a continuous or periodic activity nor relate to the undertaking's usual operating costs, such as routine tax consultancy services, regular legal services or routine advertising.[44] Individual aid, whether granted *ad hoc* or on the basis of a scheme, must be notified to the Commission in advance pursuant

---

[40]   Commission Regulation (EU) No 651/2014 , Article 18.
[41]   *Ibid.*, Article 4(1)(d).
[42]   *Ibid.*, Article 19.
[43]   *Ibid.*, Article 4(1)(e).
[44]   *Ibid.*, Article 20.

to Article 108(3) TFEU where the aid exceeds €2 million per undertaking per project.[45]

9.5 AID FOR RISK FINANCE INVESTMENTS IN SMEs

Commission policy regarding risk finance aid schemes The Commission takes the view that the development of the risk finance market and the improvement of access to risk finance for SMEs, small mid-caps and innovative mid-caps is of great importance to the EU economy. Encouraging the development and expansion of new businesses, especially innovative and high-growth businesses, can have a great potential to create jobs. Therefore, an efficient risk finance market for SMEs is crucial for entrepreneurial companies to be able to access the necessary funding at each stage of their development. SMEs may face difficulties in gaining access to finance, particularly in the early stages of their development. SMEs, especially when they are young, are often unable to demonstrate their creditworthiness or the soundness of their business plans to investors. SMEs are likely not to be able to access the necessary finance as long as they lack a proven track record and sufficient collateral. As a result, business finance markets may fail to provide the necessary equity or debt finance to newly created and potentially high-growth SMEs resulting in a persistent capital market failure. Small mid-caps and innovative mid-caps may, in certain circumstances, face the same market failure. The existence of this financing gap may justify the grant of State aid in certain specific circumstances. If properly targeted, State aid to support the provision of risk finance to those companies can be an effective means to alleviate the identified market failures and to leverage private capital.[46]

The Commission issued a communication on its approach to State aid and risk capital in 2001.[47] This was replaced in 2006 by the Commission's guidelines on State aid to promote risk capital investments in SMEs, which introduced greater flexibility in the application of the rules and a more refined economic approach.[48] In particular, the guidelines contained elements to ensure that profit-driven and professional investment decisions were strengthened in order to encourage private investors to co-invest with the State. In light of the State aid modernisation programme, the Commission deemed it appropriate to substantially review its policy instruments so as to promote a more efficient and effective provision of various forms of risk finance to a larger category of eligible undertakings.[49] The present guidelines on risk

---

[45] *Ibid.*, Article 4(1)(f).
[46] Risk finance guidelines, paras 1-5.
[47] OJ 2001 C235/3.
[48] OJ 2006 C194/2.
[49] Risk finance guidelines, para 14.

finance came into effect on 1 July 2014.[50] Commission Regulation (EU) No 651/2014, Article 21 provides a block exemption for risk finance aid. The guidelines, which apply where a measure is not covered by the block exemption, will be applied by the Commission only in respect of aid schemes. They will not be applied in respect of *ad hoc* measures providing risk finance aid to individual undertakings, except in the case of measures aiming at supporting a specific alternative trading platform.[51] Exceptionally, the Commission may assess risk finance aid on the basis of Article 107(3)(c) TFEU directly.[52]

The Commission does not consider that there is a general market failure related to access to finance by large undertakings.[53] Moreover, companies listed on the official list of a stock exchange or a regulated market cannot be supported through risk finance aid, since the fact that they are listed demonstrates their ability to attract private financing.[54] Risk finance aid measures have to be deployed through financial intermediaries or alternative trade platforms, except for fiscal incentives on direct investments in eligible undertakings. It follows that a measure whereby the Member State or a public entity makes direct investments in companies without the involvement of such intermediary vehicles does not fall under the scope of the risk finance guidelines.[55]

Risk finance measures excluded from the guidelines Risk finance aid measures in the total absence of private investors will not be declared compatible under the risk finance guidelines.[56] Equally, risk finance aid measures where no appreciable risk is undertaken by the private investors, and/or where the benefits flow entirely to the private investors, will not be declared compatible under the guidelines, since sharing the risks and rewards is a necessary condition to limit the financial exposure of, and to ensure a fair return to, the State.[57] Without prejudice to risk finance aid in the form of replacement capital, risk finance aid may not be used to support buyouts.[58] Risk finance aid will not be considered compatible with the internal market if awarded to undertakings in difficulty. However, for the purposes of the guidelines, SMEs within seven years from their first commercial sale that

---

[50] OJ 2014 C19/4.

[51] Risk finance guidelines, para 19.

[52] Examples are Cases SA.32835, *Northwest Urban Investment Fund* and SA.32147, *JESSICA Holding Fund Andalucia* (2011).

[53] Risk finance guidelines, para 21.

[54] *Ibid.*, para 22.

[55] *Ibid.*, para 20.

[56] *Ibid.*, para 23. In such cases, the Member State may consider alternative options, such as regional investment aid or start-up aid.

[57] Risk finance guidelines, para 24.

[58] *Ibid.*, para 25.

qualify for risk finance investments following due diligence by the selected financial intermediary will not be considered as undertakings in difficulty, unless they are subject to insolvency proceedings or fulfil the criteria under their domestic law for being placed in collective insolvency proceedings at the request of their creditors.[59]

The Commission will not apply the guidelines to aid to export-related activities towards third countries or Member States, namely aid directly linked to the quantities exported, the establishment and operation of a distribution network or to other current costs linked to the export activity, as well as aid contingent upon the use of domestic over imported goods.[60] Risk finance aid will not be considered compatible with the internal market if awarded to undertakings that have received illegal State aid which has not been fully recovered.[61] Equally, the Commission will not apply the guidelines to measures which entail an infringement of EU law, in particular, the provisions concerning free movement of goods, services or capital or freedom of establishment, such as where the aid is subject to the obligation for financial intermediaries, their managers or final beneficiaries to have their headquarters in the territory of the Member State concerned.[62]

Pari passu **investments**   In general, the Commission will consider an investment to be in line with the market economy operator test, and thus not to constitute State aid, if it is effected *pari passu* between public and private investors. An investment is considered *pari passu* when it is made under the same terms and conditions by public and private investors, where both categories of operators intervene simultaneously and where the intervention of the private investor is of real economic significance.[63] A transaction is presumed to be made under the same terms and conditions if public and private investors share the same risks and rewards and hold the same level of subordination in relation to the same risk class. If the public investor is in a better position than the private investor, for instance because it receives a priority return in time compared to the private investors, the measure may also be considered to be in line with normal market conditions, as long as the private investors do not receive any advantage.[64] Where a measure allows private investors to carry out risk finance investments into a company on terms more favourable than public investors, those private investors may receive an advantage.[65] Such an advantage may take different forms, such as preferential

---

[59]   *Ibid.*, para 26(a).

[60]   *Ibid.*, para 27.

[61]   *Ibid.*, para 26(b).

[62]   *Ibid.*, para 28.

[63]   Case N 172/2000, *Irish Seed and Venture Capital Fund Scheme*, OJ 2001 C37/48.

[64]   Risk finance guidelines, paras 31-32.

[65]   For example, Case N 7051999, *UK High Technology Fund*, OJ 2000 C315/21.

returns or reduced exposure to losses in the event of underperformance of the underlying transaction compared to the public investors.[66]

An additional condition is that the funding provided by private investors must be economically significant in the light of the overall volume of the investment. The Commission considers that, in the case of risk finance measures, 30% independent private investment can be considered economically significant.[67] For instance, in the *Citynet Amsterdam* decision,[68] the Commission considered that two private operators taking up one third of the total equity investments in a company (considering also the overall shareholding structure and that their shares were sufficient to form a blocking minority regarding any strategic decision of the company) could be considered economically significant. By contrast, in *Agricultural Bank of Greece*,[69] the private participation only reached 10% of the investment, as opposed to 90% by the State, so that the Commission concluded that *pari passu* conditions were not met, since the capital injected by the State was neither accompanied by a comparable participation of a private shareholder nor was it proportionate to the number of shares held by the State. In a case where the public authorities already owned investment instruments that were convertible into shares, the Commission was satisfied that the conversion into shares was *pari passu* with private investors who were investing in new shares.[70]

Aid to financial intermediaries In general, the Commission considers that a financial intermediary is a vehicle for the transfer of aid to investors and/or enterprises in which the investment is made, rather than a beneficiary of aid in its own right, irrespective of whether the financial intermediary has legal personality or is merely a bundle of assets managed by an independent management company. However, measures involving direct transfers to, or co-investment by, a financial intermediary may constitute aid unless such transfers or co-investments are made on terms which would be acceptable to a normal market operator.[71] Where the risk finance measure is managed by an entrusted entity, without that entity co-investing with the Member State, the entrusted entity is considered as a vehicle to channel the financing and not a beneficiary of aid, as long as it is not overcompensated. Where the manager of the financial intermediary or the management company are chosen through an open, transparent, non-discriminatory and objective selection procedure or the manager's remuneration fully reflects the current market levels in comparable situations, it will be presumed that the manager does not receive State aid.[72] In

---

[66] Risk finance guidelines, para 36.
[67] *Ibid.*, para 34.
[68] Case C 53/2006, *Citynet Amsterdam*, OJ 2008 L 247/27.
[69] Case N 429/10, *ATE*, OJ 2011 C 317/5.
[70] Case C 33/2007, *IBG Risk Capital Fund Sachsen-Anhalt*, OJ 2007 C246/20.
[71] Risk finance guidelines, paras 37-38.
[72] *Ibid.*, paras 39-40.

its decision on the *Wales Early Stage Fund*, the Commission considered that aid might have been given to the management which was chosen without a tender procedure.[73]

Block exemption for risk finance aid schemes Under the block exemption in Commission Regulation (EU) No 651/2014, Article 21, risk finance aid up to €15 million may take the form of equity or quasi-equity investments, loans or guarantees, as well as tax incentives for private investors who are natural persons.[74] Eligible undertakings are unlisted SMEs that (a) have not been operating in any market or (b) have been operating for less than 7 years following their first commercial sale or (c) require an initial risk finance investment which, based on a business plan prepared with a view to entering a new product or geographic market, is higher than 50% of their average annual turnover in the preceding 5 years.[75] The risk finance aid may also cover follow-on investments, as long as this was foreseen in the original business plan and the rules on linked enterprises are not breached.[76] Support for replacement capital may be provided only if this is combined with new capital representing at least 50% of each investment round.[77] No more than 30% of investments may be used for liquidity management purposes.[78] The risk finance aid must leverage additional finance from independent financial investors at the level of the financial intermediaries or the eligible undertakings so as to achieve an aggregate private participation rate of 10%, 40% or 60% for initial investment, investment within 7 years or other investments, respectively.[79]

Other than in the case of tax incentives in respect of direct investments, risk finance measures must be implemented via one or more financial intermediaries who are to be chosen on the basis of an open, transparent and non-discriminatory selection aimed at establishing appropriate risk-reward sharing arrangements, with asymmetric profit sharing being given preference over downside protection. In the case of asymmetric loss-sharing between public and private investors, the first loss assumed by the private investor must be capped at 25% of the total investment. In the case of guarantees, the guarantee rate must be limited to 80% and total losses assumed by a Member

---

[73] Case N 562/2006, *Wales Early Stage Fund*, OJ 2007 C67/10.
[74] Commission Regulation (EU) No 651/2014, Article 21(2)-(4) and (9).
[75] *Ibid.*, Article 21(5). Risk finance aid for SMEs that do not fulfil these conditions may also be compatible with the internal market provided the conditions in Article 21(18) are fulfilled.
[76] Commission Regulation (EU) No 651/2014, Article 21(6).
[77] *Ibid.*, Article 21(7).
[78] *Ibid.*, Article 21(8).
[79] *Ibid.*, Article 21(10)-(11).

State must be capped at a maximum of 25% of the underlying guaranteed portfolio.[80]

Risk finance measures must ensure profit-driven financing decisions. In particular, risk finance must be based on a viable business plan, with a clear and realistic exit strategy for each equity and quasi-equity investment.[81] Measures providing guarantees, which may not exceed 80% of the underlying loan, or loans to eligible undertakings must be such that the financial intermediary undertakes investments that would not have been carried out or would have been carried out in a restrictive or different manner.[82]

A risk finance measure may not discriminate between financial intermediaries on the basis of their place of establishment or incorporation in any Member State.[83] Financial intermediaries must be managed on a commercial basis, acting in good faith and avoiding conflicts of interest. Their remuneration, which should be linked to performance or risk-sharing, must conform to market practices, which is presumed to be the case where the manager is selected through an open, transparent and non-discriminatory selection call, based on objective criteria linked to experience, expertise and operational and financial capacity.[84] A Member State may assign the implementation of a risk finance measure to an entrusted entity.[85]

Block exemption for additional aid measures for access to finance Under the block exemption in Commission Regulation (EU) No 651/2014, Articles 22-24, aid for access to finance for SMEs may also take the form of aid for start-ups, aid in favour of alternative trading platforms specialised in SMEs and aid for scouting costs. In the case of start-up aid schemes, eligible undertakings are unlisted small enterprises up to five years following their registration which have not yet distributed profits. Start-up aid may take the form for up to 10 years duration of loans at preferential interest rates and up to a maximum nominal amount of €1 million or guarantees at preferential rates up to a maximum of €1.5 million of the amount guaranteed. Grants up to €0.4 million may also be made, with increased grants of $0.6 million for undertakings established in Article 107(3)(c) areas and €0.8 in Article 107(3)(a) areas. These amounts may be doubled for small and innovative enterprises.[86]

Aid may be granted in favour of alternative trading platforms specialised in SMEs. The aid measure may take the form of tax incentives to independent

---

[80] Commission Regulation (EU) No 651/2014, Article 21(13).
[81] *Ibid.*, Article 21(14).
[82] *Ibid.*, Article 21(16)
[83] *Ibid.*, Article 21(12).
[84] *Ibid.*, Article 21(15).
[85] *Ibid.*, Article 21(17).
[86] *Ibid.*, Article 22(1)-(5).

private investors that are natural persons in respect of their risk finance investments made through an alternative trading platform.[87]

Aid for scouting costs is allowable in respect of up to 50% of the costs for initial screening and formal due diligence undertaken by managers of financial intermediaries or investors to identify eligible target undertakings.[88]

Notifiable risk finance aid Risk finance aid that does not fall within the block exemption or which is not *de minimis* must be notified to the Commission in accordance with Article 108(3) TFEU for assessment pursuant to Article 107(3)(c) TFEU. In the risk finance aid guidelines, the Commission identifies three separate categories of measure that may arise in this context. For risk finance measures which target undertakings that do not fulfil all the eligibility requirements under the block exemption, the Commission will require the Member State to conduct an in-depth *ex ante* assessment, since the market failure affecting the eligible undertakings covered by the block exemption regulation can no longer be presumed. In the case of those measures whose design parameters differ from those set out in the block exemption, while targeting the same eligible undertakings, the existence of a market failure needs to be proven only to the extent necessary to justify the use of parameters going beyond the limits set out in the block exemption. In respect of large schemes which fall outside of the block exemption by virtue of their large budget, when carrying out this assessment, the Commission will verify whether the conditions laid down in the block exemption are satisfied and, should this be the case, will evaluate whether the design of the measure is appropriate in the light of the *ex ante* assessment underpinning the notification. If a large scheme does not fulfil all these eligibility and compatibility conditions, the Commission will duly consider the evidence provided in the context of the *ex ante* assessment both as regards the existence of a market failure and the appropriateness of the design of the measure. In addition, it will carry out an in-depth assessment of the potential negative effects that such schemes could have on the affected markets. In general, the Commission will apply the compatibility conditions in the block exemption to its assessment of these risk finance measures.[89]

In accordance with the State aid modernisation programme, in assessing whether the aid measure ensures that the positive impact of the aid towards an objective of common interest exceeds its potential negative effects on trade between Member States and competition, the Commission will consider an aid scheme compatible with the internal market only where it satisfies each of the following criteria: contribution to a well-defined objective of common interest; need for State intervention; appropriateness of the aid measure; incentive

---

[87] *Ibid.*, Article 23.
[88] *Ibid.*, Article 24.
[89] Risk finance guidelines, paras 46-51.

effect; proportionality of the aid; avoidance of undue negative effects on competition and trade between Member States; and transparency of aid. The overall balance may also be made subject to ex post evaluation, in which case the Commission may limit the duration of the scheme, with the possibility of notifying its prolongation.[90]

Contribution to a common objective For risk finance aid, the general policy objective is to improve the provision of finance to viable SMEs from their early-development up to their growth stages and, in certain circumstances, to small mid-caps and innovative mid-caps, so as to develop in the longer run a competitive business finance market in the EU, which should contribute to overall economic growth. The Member State must carry out an *ex ante* assessment in order to identify the policy targets and define the relevant performance indicators. The size and duration of the measure should be adequate for the policy targets. In principle, the performance indicators may include:

(a) the required or envisaged private sector investment;
(b) the expected number of final beneficiaries invested in, including the number of start-up SMEs;
(c) the estimated number of new undertakings created during the implementation of the risk finance measure and as a result of the risk finance investments;
(d) the number of jobs created in the final beneficiary undertakings between the date of the first risk finance investment under the risk finance measure and the exit;
(e) where appropriate, the proportion of investments made in conformity with the market economy operator test;
(f) milestones and deadlines within which certain predefined amounts or percentage of the budget are to be invested;
(g) returns/yield expected to be generated from the investments;
(h) where appropriate, patent applications made by the final beneficiaries, during the implementation of the risk finance measure.

These indicators are relevant both for the purpose of evaluating the effectiveness of the measure and for assessing the validity of the investment strategies drawn up by the financial intermediary in the context of the selection process.[91]

To ensure that financial intermediaries involved in the risk finance measure deliver the relevant policy objectives, they must demonstrate how their proposed investment strategy may contribute to the achievement of the policy objectives and targets. The Member State must ensure that the investment strategy of the intermediaries remains at all times aligned with the agreed

---

[90] *Ibid.*, paras 53-56.
[91] *Ibid.*, paras 57-59.

policy targets, for instance via appropriate monitoring and reporting mechanisms and the participation of representatives of the public investors in the representation bodies of the financial intermediary, although the Member State may not participate directly in individual investment and divestment decisions.[92]

Need for State intervention The Commission considers that there is no general market failure as regards access to finance for SMEs, but only a failure related to certain groups of SMEs, depending on the specific economic context of the Member State and the sector concerned. Therefore, the risk finance measure must be established on the basis of an *ex ante* assessment demonstrating the existence of a funding gap affecting eligible undertakings in the targeted development stage, geographic area and, if applicable, economic sector. Both the structural and cyclical (that is to say, crisis-related) problems leading to suboptimal levels of private funding must be analysed. To ensure that the financial intermediaries involved in the measure target the identified market failures, a due diligence process shall take place to ensure a commercially sound investment strategy focusing on the identified policy objective and respecting the defined eligibility requirements and funding restrictions. The guidelines provide specific additional criteria to be applied to measures falling outside the block exemption and measures with design parameters not complying with the block exemption.[93]

Appropriateness of the aid measure The choice of the specific form of the risk finance measure must be duly justified by the *ex ante* assessment which must analyse national and EU policy actions targeting the same identified market failures, taking into account the effectiveness and efficiency of other policy tools and must demonstrate that the identified market failures cannot be adequately addressed by other policy tools that do not entail State aid. Moreover, the proposed risk finance measure must be consistent with the overall policy of the Member State concerned regarding SME access to finance and be complementary to other policy instruments addressing the same market needs. The Commission will also assess whether the design of the measure provides for an efficient funding structure, taking into account the investment strategy of the fund, so as to ensure sustainable operations. In this respect, the Commission will look positively at measures which involve sufficiently large funds in terms of portfolio size, geographic coverage, in particular if they operate across several Member States, and diversification of the portfolio, as such funds may be more efficient and therefore more attractive for private investors, compared to smaller funds. The guidelines set out detailed specific

---

[92] *Ibid.*, paras 60-62.
[93] *Ibid.*, paras 63-88.

conditions in respect of financial instruments, fiscal instruments and alternative trading platforms.[94]

For example, in the case of Invest Northern Ireland Venture 2003, in which the risk capital tranches were significantly higher that those applicable under the 2001 risk capital communication, the UK provided a market study showing that this was justified by reference to the equity gap caused due to Northern Ireland's political legacy and its relative geographical position.[95] In the case of the NESTA IIP fund, which provided seed capital to very early-stage micro and small enterprises, the UK provided evidence that there was a serious market failure at that stage due to high transaction costs, higher perceived risk for investing in early stage companies and shortage of exit options.[96] In order to justify a grant of £3 million in order to set up a regional equity market place for SMEs in the West Midlands, the UK submitted detailed information showing declining equity investments in the region for small enterprises and the need for public intervention to boost the market.[97]

Incentive effect of the aid At the level of the eligible undertakings, an incentive effect is present when the final beneficiary can raise finance that would not be available otherwise in terms of form, amount or timing. Risk finance measures must incentivise market investors to provide funding to potentially viable eligible undertakings above the current levels and/or to assume extra risk. A risk finance measure is considered to have an incentive effect if it mobilises investments from market sources so that the total financing provided to the eligible undertakings exceeds the budget of the measure.[98] Hence, a key element in selecting the financial intermediaries and fund managers should be their ability to mobilise additional private investment. The assessment of the incentive effect is closely linked to the assessment of the market failure. Further, the suitability of the measure to achieve the leverage effect ultimately depends on the design of the measure as regards the balance of risks and rewards between public and private finance-providers, which is also closely related to the question whether the design of the risk finance State aid measure is appropriate. Therefore, once the market failure has been properly identified and the measure has an appropriate design, it can be assumed that an incentive effect is present.[99]

Proportionality of the aid As a general rule, at the level of the final beneficiaries, risk finance aid is considered to be proportionate if the total

---

[94] *Ibid.*, paras 89-129.
[95] Commission Decision 2005/644/EC, *Invest Northern Ireland 2003*, OJ 2005 L236/14.
[96] Case NN 81/2005, *NESTA IIP*, OJ 2006 C85/3.
[97] Commission Decision 2008/126/EC, *Investbx*, OJ 2008 L 45/1.
[98] See, for example, Case N 263/2007, *Saxon Early Stage Fund*, OJ 2008 C93/1.
[99] Risk finance guidelines, paras 130-132.

amount of syndicated funding (public and private) provided under the risk finance measure is limited to the size of the funding gap identified in the *ex ante* assessment. At the level of the investors, aid must be limited to the minimum necessary to attract private capital in order to achieve the minimum leverage effect and bridge the funding gap. The measure must ensure a balance between the preferential conditions offered by a financial instrument in order to maximise the leverage effect while addressing the identified market failure and the need for the instrument to generate sufficient financial returns to remain operationally viable. The exact nature and value of the incentives must be determined through an open and non-discriminatory selection process in the context of which financial intermediaries, as well as fund managers or investors are called to present competing bids. Where private investors are not selected through such a process, for instance because the selection procedure has proven to be ineffective or inconclusive, a fair rate of return must be established by an independent expert on the basis of an analysis of market benchmarks and market risk. The guidelines set out detailed specific conditions in respect of financial instruments, fiscal instruments and alternative trading platforms.[100]

Avoidance of undue negative effects on competition and trade In the case of risk finance measures, the potential negative effects have to be assessed at each level where aid may be present: the investors, the financial intermediaries and their managers, and the final beneficiaries. To enable the Commission to assess the likely negative effects, the Member State may submit, as part of the *ex ante* assessment, any study at its disposal, as well as *ex post* evaluations carried out for similar schemes, in terms of the eligible undertakings, funding structures, design parameters and geographic area.[101]

At the level of the market for the provision of risk finance, State aid may result in crowding out private investors. This might reduce the incentives for private investors to provide funding to eligible undertakings and encourage them to wait until the State provides aid for such investments. This risk becomes more relevant, the higher the amount of the total financing into the final beneficiaries, the larger the size of those beneficiary undertakings and the more advanced their development stage, as private financing becomes progressively available in those circumstances. Moreover, State aid should not replace the normal business risk of investments that the investors would have undertaken even in the absence of State aid. However, to the extent that the market failure has been properly defined, it is less likely that the risk finance measure will result in such crowding out.[102]

---

[100] Risk finance guidelines, paras 133-154.
[101] *Ibid.*, paras 155-156.
[102] *Ibid.*, para 157.

At the level of financial intermediaries, aid may have distortive effects in terms of increasing or maintaining an intermediary's market power, for example in the market of a particular region. Even where aid does not strengthen the financial intermediary's market power directly, it may do so indirectly, by discouraging the expansion of existing competitors, inducing their exit or discouraging the entry of new competitors. The conditions on commercial management and profit-oriented decision-making set out in the risk finance provisions of the block exemption are essential to ensure that the selection of the final beneficiary undertakings is based on a commercial logic, those conditions cannot be derogated from under the guidelines, including where the measure involves public financial intermediaries.[103]

Investment funds of a small scale, with limited regional focus and without adequate governance arrangements will be analysed with a view to avoiding the risk of maintaining inefficient market structures. Regional risk finance schemes may not have sufficient scale and scope due to a lack of diversification linked to the absence of a sufficient number of eligible undertakings as investment targets. Those investments could distort competition and provide undue advantages to certain undertakings. Moreover, such funds may be less attractive to private investors, in particular institutional investors, as they may be seen more as a vehicle to serve regional policy objectives, rather than a viable business opportunity offering acceptable returns on investment.[104]

At the level of the final beneficiaries, the Commission will assess whether the measure has distortive effects on the product markets where those undertakings compete. For instance, the measure may distort competition if it targets companies in underperforming sectors. A substantial capacity expansion induced by State aid in an underperforming market might, in particular, unduly distort competition, as the creation or maintenance of overcapacity could lead to a squeeze on profit margins, a reduction of competitors' investments or even their exit from the market. It may also prevent companies from entering the market. This results in inefficient market structures which are also harmful to consumers in the long run. Where the market in the targeted sectors is growing, there is normally less reason to fear that the aid will negatively affect dynamic incentives or will unduly impede exit or entry. Therefore, the Commission will analyse the level of production capacities in the given sector, in the light of the potential demand. In order to enable the Commission to carry out such an assessment, the Member State must indicate whether the risk finance measure is sector specific, or gives preference to certain sectors over others.[105]

---

[103] *Ibid.*, para 158-160.

[104] *Ibid.*, para 161.

[105] *Ibid.*, para 162.

Where the measure has negative effects, the Member State must identify the means to minimise such distortions. For instance, the Member State may demonstrate that the negative effects will be limited to the minimum, taking into account, for example, the overall investment amount, the type and number of beneficiaries and the characteristics of the targeted sectors. In balancing positive and negative effects, the Commission will also take into account the magnitude of such effects.[106]

Evaluation To ensure that distortions of competition and trade are limited, the Commission may require that certain schemes be subject to a limited duration and to an evaluation, which must address the effectiveness of the aid measure in the light of its predefined general and specific objectives and indicators and the impact of the measure on markets and competition. This may apply in the case of large schemes, schemes with a regional focus, schemes which are modified, schemes containing novel characteristics and schemes where the Commission so requests in its approval decision. The evaluation must be carried out by an expert independent from the State aid granting authority on the basis of a common methodology.[107]

---

[106] *Ibid.*, para 165.
[107] *Ibid.*, paras 170-172.

Chapter Ten

TRAINING AND EMPLOYMENT AID

10.1 COMMISSION POLICY ON TRAINING AND EMPLOYMENT AID

EU objectives on training and employment The Member States and the European Union are required, pursuant to Article 145 TFEU, to work towards developing a coordinated strategy for employment and particularly for promoting a skilled, trained and adaptable workforce and labour markets responsive to economic change with a view to achieving *inter alia* the development of economic activities and a high level of employment. Article 147 TFEU requires the EU to contribute to a high level of employment by encouraging cooperation between Member States and by supporting and complementing their action. This employment objective is also to be taken into consideration in the formulation and implementation of EU policies and activities. It follows that the Commission is required to ensure the necessary consistency between its State aid policy and EU action relating to employment. Nevertheless, in the sphere of State aid, the Commission enjoys a wide discretion, the exercise of which involves assessments of an economic and social nature which must be made within an EU context. That will in particular be the case when the Commission wishes to reconcile the objective of ensuring undistorted competition in the internal market with other EU objectives such as the promotion of employment.[1]

In 1993, the White Paper on growth, competitiveness and employment stressed the important part played by training in enhancing competitiveness and in creating and maintaining jobs. Five priority areas were subsequently identified by the European Council as being central to tackling unemployment in the EU: boosting investment in education and training; improving internal and external flexibility mechanisms in order to enhance the employment-content of growth; reducing indirect labour costs, in particular by reducing direct taxation of labour; improving the effectiveness of active policies, notably by redirecting public expenditure on passive income support for the unemployed; and stepping up measures to promote the employment of underprivileged groups in the labour market, such as the long-term unemployed, young people and older workers.

The Lisbon European Council in March 2000 set a strategic goal for the European Union to become the most competitive and dynamic knowledge-

---

[1] Case 110/03, *Belgium v Commission* [2005] ECR I-2801, paras 66-67.

based economy in the world. The Lisbon conclusions stressed the central role of education and training as the main instruments to increase human capital and its impact on growth, productivity and employment. Training usually has positive external effects for society as a whole since it increases the pool of skilled workers from which undertakings can draw and it improves the competitiveness of the economy and promotes a knowledge society capable of embracing a more innovative development path.[2]

Development of Commission policy on training and employment aid   On the basis of its experience, the Commission adopted guidelines on aid to employment in 1995[3] and a framework on training aid in 1998.[4]   It was recognised that, by granting employment aid to certain enterprises or to the production of certain goods, Member States take over part of their labour costs, which are part of the general cost of production, and thereby distort competition. Without rigorous controls and strict limits, employment aid could thus have harmful macroeconomic effects which cancel out its immediate effects on job creation, such as protecting inefficient enterprises, diluting the effect of regional aid and shifting unemployment to other Member States. Nevertheless, recognising that unemployment at unacceptably high levels was a serious economic and social problem that would not be sufficiently addressed by an upturn in economic activity, the Commission's 1995 guidelines on State aid to employment made explicit its intention to give sympathetic consideration to State aid designed to improve the employment situation.[5]

In the 1998 framework on training aid, the Commission recognised that training costs were increasingly forming part of the costs that have to be borne by firms if they were to remain competitive. As such, training aid intended to reduce the costs that certain firms would normally have to bear, in their own interests, conferred on them an advantage within the scope of Article 107(1) TFEU.[6]   There were several reasons for considering training aid as being compatible with the internal market, particularly since it helped to correct certain imperfections in the market.   Generally, the Commission was favourable to State aid for training purposes going beyond improving initial training, vocational training and the training of the unemployed. It called for policies to be developed by the Member States to encourage workers to improve their skills and adaptability and to induce firms to invest in training their workforce.[7] Training usually has positive external benefits for society as a whole, by increasing the pool of skilled workers and increasing the

---

[2]   Commission communication on training aid, para 1.
[3]   OJ 1995 C334/4. See also the Commission's Notice on monitoring of State aid and reduction of labour costs, OJ 1997 C1/10.
[4]   OJ 1998 C343/10.
[5]   1995 guidelines on aid to employment, para 3.
[6]   1998 framework on training aid, para 7.
[7]   Ibid., para 5.

competitiveness of EU industry. Given that smaller firms, in particular, were less likely to invest in training since there was a considerable risk that the trained worker would leave for employment in another firm, training aid should not necessarily be regarded as operating aid but rather as encouraging investment that would not otherwise be made. Training also plays an essential part in introducing new technologies and stimulating innovation and investment and may also help to create and maintain jobs. As such, it could be considered compatible with the internal market as facilitating the development of certain economic activities, provided that it had an incentive effect and was proportionate.[8] The Commission also recognised that the existence of a skilled workforce is a major factor in a firm's location decision. Training is important not only to the worker, who becomes more employable and less likely to be made redundant, and to the firm, for which it is a performance-enhancing factor, but also to the economy of the regions, a highly skilled workforce being an undeniable asset when it comes to attracting new investment. Such aid could, therefore, be compatible with the internal market on regional aid grounds.[9]

Block exemptions for employment and training aid Council Regulation (EC) No 994/98[10] provides for the Commission to adopt regulations declaring certain aid for employment and training to be compatible with the internal market and not to be subject to the notification requirements of Article 108(3) TFEU.[11] On the basis of this power, the Commission adopted two block exemptions:[12] Commission Regulation (EC) No 68/2001 on training aid,[13] and Commission Regulation (EC) No 2204/2002 on aid for employment.[14] In 2007, more than 80% of all training aid and around one third of all employment aid was awarded under these block exemption regulations.[15] They were repealed by Commission Regulation (EC) No 800/2008.[16] Whereas the criteria for compatibility of training aid with the internal market are generally retained in the block exemption, currently in Commission Regulation (EU) No 651/2014, employment aid was subsumed into the rules on regional aid and aid for SMEs, leaving only specific provisions concerning aid for employment of

---

[8] *Ibid.*, paras 9, 23-24, 27-29.
[9] *Ibid.*, paras 3, 29.
[10] OJ 1998 L142/1.
[11] Council Regulation (EC) No 994/98, Article 1(a)(iv).
[12] Special focus on State aid for employment and training, State aid Scoreboard, Spring 2004, pp. 22-35.
[13] OJ 2001 L10/20, as subsequently amended by Commission Regulation (EC) No 363/2004 (OJ 2004 L63/20).
[14] OJ 2004 L337/3.
[15] State aid scoreboard, Autumn 2008, pp. 40-41.
[16] OJ 2008 L214/3.

disadvantaged and disabled workers.[17]   The Commission has also issued
communications on its approach to assessing training aid[18] and aid for
disadvantaged and disabled workers[19] that does not fall within the scope of the
block exemption.

10.2 TRAINING AID

Training measures and State aid Many training measures are not caught by
Article 107(1) TFEU, but constitute general measures because they are open to
all enterprises in all sectors without discrimination and without discretionary
power for the authorities applying the measure, e.g. general tax incentive
schemes, such as automatic tax credits, open to all firms investing in employee
training. Other training measures do not fall within the scope of Article 107(1)
TFEU because they directly benefit people everywhere and do not grant an
advantage to certain enterprises or sectors. Examples are: schooling and initial
training (such as apprenticeships and day-release schemes); the training or retraining of unemployed people, including traineeships in enterprises; and
measures directly targeted at workers or even at certain categories of workers,
affording them the opportunity of receiving training unconnected with the firm
or industry in which they work.

Training institutions Aid to public training or educational institutes for the
provision of training in the context of national educational programmes will
generally not fall within Article 107(1) TFEU where they are not regarded as
carrying on an economic activity. In its consideration of a reform of the Italian
vocational training institutions, the Commission noted that the activity carried
out by the training institutes concerned was twofold. On the one hand, they
ensured institutional, social targeted vocational training, addressed to
individuals, delivered in the framework of the public education system and
paid for by the State on the basis of the reimbursement of certain eligible costs.
On the other hand, in several cases, they exploited market training activities,
addressed both to undertakings and their employees and individuals who paid a
market price. Indeed, an obligation to separate the accounts, related to these
two fields of activity, had been imposed by Italy on the training institutions.
Thus, whilst the former could be considered not to involve any economic
activity, as regards the latter, the Commission could not exclude that some
activities carried out by the training institutions, even in the case of vocational

---

[17]   Commission Regulation (EU) No 651/2014, Articles 31-35.
[18]   OJ 2009 C188/1.
[19]   OJ 2009 C188/6.

training given in the framework of the public education system, were to be qualified as economic activities.[20]

Commission policy on training aid The Commission's reasons, as set out in Regulation (EU) No 651/2014, for maintaining a liberal approach to training aid are that training usually has positive external effects for society as a whole since it increases the pool of skilled workers from which other firms may draw, improves the competitiveness of EU industry and plays an important role in the EU's employment strategy. SMEs are recognised as being confronted with handicaps and higher relative costs that they have to bear when they invest in the training of their workers. Furthermore, the intensity of aid may be increased when training is given to disadvantaged or disabled workers. The characteristics of training in the maritime sector justify a specific approach for that sector.[21]

The Commission previously distinguished between specific training and general training. Specific training is training involving tuition directly and principally applicable to an employee's present or future position in an assisted firm and providing qualifications which are not or are only to a limited extent transferable to other firms or fields of work. Such training mainly benefits the enterprise itself, and involves a certain risk of distortion of competition.[22] By contrast, general training is training involving tuition which is not applicable only or principally to an employee's present or future position in an assisted firm, but which provides qualifications that are largely transferable to other firms or fields of work and thereby substantially improve the employability of the employee. Training is considered general if, for example, it is jointly organised by different independent enterprises or if employees of different enterprises may avail themselves of the training, or if it recognised, certified or validated by public authorities or other recognised institutions.[23] Thus, for example, the Commission raised no objections to training aid for the employees of two French aero-engineering companies which were converting from military to civil activities, the result of which would be redundancies among the employees. The aid would principally benefit the employees, offering them additional qualifications which could be used in other companies.[24] Similarly, when Opel Austria developed a new small-size petrol engine and sought training aid for their employees in order to manufacture it, the Commission approved the aid on the basis that it was not company specific, taking account of the innovative nature of the project and that this would lead

---

[20] Commission Decision 2006/225/EC, *Italian vocational training institutes*, OJ 2006 L81/25.

[21] Commission Regulation (EU) No 651/2014, preamble, para 53.

[22] Commission Regulation (EC) No 800/2008, Article 38(a) and preamble, para 63.

[23] *Ibid.*, Article 38(b) and preamble, para 63.

[24] *Twenty-Eighth Report on Competition Policy* (1998), p. 269.

to genuinely qualitative changes in the required skills of the workforce.[25]
However, whereas the block exemption in Regulation (EC) No 800/2008
allowed for considerably higher intensities of aid for general training, no such
distinction is drawn in Regulation (EU) No 651/2014.

Eligible costs for training aid   The eligible costs of a training project are
limited to the following:[26]

(a) trainers' personnel costs, for the hours during which trainer participate in
    the training;
(b) trainers' and trainees' operating costs directly relating to the training
    project, such as travel expenses, materials and supplies, depreciation of
    tools and equipment;[27]
(c) costs of advisory services linked to the training project;
(f) trainees' personnel costs and general indirect costs (administrative costs,
    rent, overheads) for the hours during which trainees participate in the
    training.

Intensity of training aid   Aid may not be granted for training which
undertakings carry out to comply with national mandatory standards on
training.[28]   Otherwise, the aid intensity must not exceed 50% of the eligible
costs.[29]   The aid intensity may be increased, up to a maximum aid intensity of
70%, as follows:[30]

(a) by 10% if the training is given to disabled or disadvantaged workers;
(b) by 10% if the aid is awarded to medium-sized enterprises and by 20% if
    the aid is awarded to small enterprises.

Where training aid is granted in the maritime transport sector, the
Commission allows an intensity of 100%, provided that the trainees are not
active members of the crew but are supernumerary on board and that the
training is carried out on board ships entered on EU registers.[31]

Individual notification and assessment of training aid   Large amounts of aid
remain subject to an individual assessment in order to determine their
compatibility with the internal market.   Accordingly, the exemption from
notification under Article 108(3) TFEU does not apply in the case of training
aid where the amount of aid per training project exceeds €2,000,000.[32]   In the

---

[25]   *Twenty-Fifth Report on Competition Policy* (1995), pp. 209-210.
[26]   Commission Regulation (EU) No 651/2014, Article 31(3).
[27]   Accommodation costs are excluded except for the minimum necessary accommodation
       costs for trainees' who are workers with disabilities.
[28]   Commission Regulation (EU) No 651/2014, Article 31(2).
[29]   *Ibid.*, Article 31(4).
[30]   *Ibid.*
[31]   *Ibid.*, Article 31(5).
[32]   *Ibid.*, Article 4(1)(n).

past, the Commission has generally been favourable to aid that complies with the substantive rules of the block exemption regulation. For example, it permitted a total of €44 million in training aid in the context of an €84 million training programme aimed at improving the skills and employability of workers in the Fiat Group in Italy.[33] Aid was also permitted for a training programme for Webasto in Portugal, which supplies motor vehicle component parts, on the grounds that the training was predominantly general training for newly recruited employees in a brand new plant in a economically weak region.[34]

Assessment of notified training aid In its 2009 communication on compatibility of State aid for training subject to individual notification, the Commission set out the principles that it applies when assessing aid under Article 107(3)(c) TFEU directly. The Commission emphasised that the criteria set out in this guidance will not be applied mechanically. The level of the Commission's assessment and the kind of information it may require will be proportional to the risk of distortion of competition and the scope of the analysis will depend on the nature of the case.[35] Member States should demonstrate that there is a market failure justifying the aid. In its analysis, the Commission will, among other things, consider whether it is specific or general, with general training producing more positive externalities. The more transferable the skills the higher the likelihood of positive externalities. Training will be considered to provide transferable skills if, for example, training is jointly organised by several independent undertakings or if employees of different undertakings may benefit from the training or if training is certified by a diploma or is transferable to other undertakings.[36]

Necessity and proportionality of training aid State aid for training must result in the aid beneficiary changing its behaviour so that it provides more and/or better training than would have been the case without the aid. Member States should demonstrate to the Commission the existence of the incentive effect and the necessity of the aid.[37] Aid will not be permitted where, for example, it is intended to finance training activity that the recipient would have engaged in anyway, even without the aid. On that basis, the Commission refused to allow part of the aid that the Belgian authorities intended to award to Ford in respect of its motor vehicle manufacturing plant at Genk. In particular, aid for training related to the launch of new models, being part of the operating

---

[33] *Thirty-Third Report on Competition Policy* (2003), pt. 472. See also, Case N 502/2005, *Germany – N3 Engine Overhaul Services GmbH*, OJ 2006 C214/2.
[34] Case N 653/2005, *Webasto*, OJ 2006 C306/14.
[35] Communication on training aid, para 4.
[36] *Ibid.*, para 9.
[37] *Ibid.*, paras 12-15.

expenses that are incurred by car manufacturers on the basis of the market forces alone, and was regarded as operating aid.[38] By contrast, aid to Fiat Auto,[39] Club Med Guadeloupe[40] and Vauxhall Motors[41] was found by the Commission to be necessary and compatible. The amount of aid must be kept to the minimum in order to achieve the objective of the aid. The Commission will not accept intensities of aid higher than those applicable under the block exemption.[42]

Negative effects If the aid is proportionate to achieve the objective of the aid, the negative effects of the aid are likely to be limited and an analysis of the negative effects may not be necessary. However, in some cases, even where aid is necessary and proportionate for a specific undertaking to increase the amount of training provided, the aid may result in a change in the behaviour of the beneficiary which significantly distorts competition. In those cases, the Commission will conduct a thorough analysis of the distortion of competition. The extent of the distortion of competition caused by the aid can vary depending on the characteristics of the aid and of the markets affected. Factors to be taken into account will be selectivity, size of the aid, repetition and duration of the aid and the effect of the aid on the undertaking's costs. The Commission will also assess the structure of the market and the characteristics of the sector or industry. When examining the characteristics of the sector, the Commission will look among other things at the importance of the trained workforce for the business, the existence of overcapacity, whether the markets in the industry are growing, mature or declining, and the financing strategies of competitors for training. Training aid may, in particular cases, lead to distortions of competition in respect of market entry and exit, effect on trade flows and crowding out of training investment.[43]

10.3 EMPLOYMENT AID

Employment policy measures and State aid The Commission has recognised that many employment policy measures do not constitute State aid within the meaning of Article 107(1) TFEU because they constitute aid to

---

[38] Commission Decision 2006/939/EC, OJ 2006 L366/32. See also, Commission Decision 2007/612/EC, *General Motors Antwerp*, OJ 2007 L243/71; Commission Decision 2008/878/EC, *DHL Leipzig*, OJ 2008 L312/31. Andres Garcia Bermudez and Christophe Galand, "Recent training aid cases in the car industry", Competition Policy Newsletter, Spring 2007, page 104.

[39] Case N 541/2006, *Fiat Auto*, OJ 2007 C220/2.

[40] Case N 206/2007, *Club Med Guadaloupe*, OJ 2007 C284/5.

[41] Case C 23/2007 , *Vauxhall Motors*.

[42] Communication on training aid, para 16.

[43] *Ibid.*, paras 17-27. See, for example, Case N 344/2010, *De Tomaso Automobili* (2011).

individuals that does not favour certain undertakings or the production of certain goods, or because they do not affect trade between Member States or because they are general measures to promote employment which do not distort or threaten to distort competition by favouring certain undertakings or the production of certain goods. Such measures, which may include general reduction of the taxation of labour and social costs, boosting investment in general education and training, measures to provide guidance and counselling, general assistance and training for the unemployed and improvements in labour law do not constitute State aid.[44]

An example of an employment scheme that was regarded by the Commission as a general measure not falling within the scope of Article 107(1) TFEU was the New Deal scheme in the United Kingdom which was aimed at helping the unemployed, in particular young people who had been unemployed for six months or more, to find work and improve their prospects of remaining in sustained employment. The job subsidy was aimed specifically at young people whom it had not been possible to place in unsubsidised employment and was intended to provide an incentive to employers to consider employing those young people which they might otherwise overlook. The subsidy was available for employers in all sectors and lasted for a minimum of six months but ceased if the employee left the employment. As the scheme applied to all economic sectors, all regions and all enterprises taking on young or long-term unemployed, the Commission concluded that it contained no specificity and thus did not constitute State aid.[45] Similarly, a Danish job rotation scheme was regarded as a general measure which provided for grants where an unemployed person took over the job of an employee who was temporarily absent on training. When the training was over, the trained person would return to his job and the newly hired person would stay on.[46] Another Danish scheme allowing for the writing off of student debt owed by socially vulnerable groups in order to enable them to enter the labour market was not regarded as falling within Article 107(1) TFEU on the ground that the aid was granted to individuals not engaged in an economic activity.[47] By contrast, a scheme which was concerned with integrating into the labour market people suffering from severe physical or mental problems and which provided for subsidies corresponding to up to two-thirds of the employment costs, depending on the degree of disability, did fall within Article 107(1) TFEU. Although the measures applied to all companies in all economic sectors, the authorities had a certain discretionary power with regard to the selection of the companies,

---

[44] Commission Regulation (EC) No 2204/2002, preamble, para 6.
[45] Case N 374/98, *New Deal*.
[46] *Thirty-First Report on Competition Policy* (2001), pt. 380.
[47] Case N 314/2006, *Danish student loan scheme*, OJ 2007 C29/4.

persons concerned and the amount of aid. Accordingly, the Commission concluded that the measure was selective and constituted State aid.[48]

Employment aid usually takes the form of grants and exemptions for certain enterprises from employers' social security contributions or from certain taxes. Examples include a scheme under which employers who recruited a person who had been out of work for at least two years were granted a partial exemption from social security contributions for a four year period;[49] a scheme under which an employer taking on a long-term unemployed person on a permanent contract was entitled to a monthly indemnity equal to between 40% and 80% of the employee's wage for a period of one year;[50] and a scheme allowing for annual reductions in the tax base for each newly created job.[51]

Employment aid under the block exemption regulations Under Commission Regulation (EC) No 2204/2002, which was designed to facilitate Member States' job creation schemes, certain aid for the creation of employment was compatible with the internal market and exempt from notification to the Commission under Article 108(3) TFEU. In respect of aid schemes for the creation of employment and aid that could be awarded under such schemes, the gross aid intensity was limited to 15% in the case of small enterprises and 7.5% in the case of medium-sized enterprises, with higher rates applicable in assisted areas.[52]

A new approach was adopted under the general block exemption in Commission Regulation (EC) No 800/2008 and is continued in Commission Regulation (EU) No 651/2014, whereby employment aid is assessed as investment aid in the context of regional aid and aid for SMEs. As regards the criteria for employment costs, in order to be considered an eligible cost investment aid, employment directly created by an investment project must fulfil the following conditions:[53]

(a) employment must be created within three years of completion of the investment, and

(b) the investment project must lead to a net increase in the number of employees in the establishment concerned, compared with the average over the previous twelve months, and

(c) the employment created must be maintained during a minimum period of five years in case of large enterprise and a minimum period of three years in case of SMEs.

---

[48] Case NN 10/02, *Danish social measures*, OJ 2002 C146/11.

[49] *Nineteenth Report on Competition Policy* (1999), pt. 197.

[50] *Twentieth Report on Competition Policy* (2000), pt. 281-282.

[51] *Thirty-Fifth Report on Competition Policy* (2005), pt. 550-553.

[52] Commission Regulation (EC) No 2204/2002, Article 4(1)-(2). Employment aid to large undertakings was not covered by this exemption: Cases T-239/04 & T-323/04, *Italy v Commission* [2007] ECR II-3265, para 93.

[53] Commission Regulation (EU) No 651/2014, Articles 14(9) and 17(5).

Aid to maintain jobs, namely financial support given to an undertaking to retain workers who would otherwise be laid off, is regarded as similar to operating aid and is not covered by the block exemption.

10.4 AID FOR EMPLOYMENT OF DISADVANTAGED AND DISABLED WORKERS

Disadvantaged and disabled workers A disabled worker is any person recognised as disabled under national law, or having a recognised limitation which results from physical, mental, intellectual or sensory impairment which, in interaction with various barriers, may hinder their full and effective participation in a work environment on an equal basis with other workers.[54] A disadvantaged worker is any person who:[55]

(a) has not been in regular paid employment for the previous 6 months;
(b) is between 15 and 24 years of age;
(c) has not attained an upper secondary educational or vocational qualification (ISCED 3) or is within two years after completing full-time education and who has not previously obtained his or her first regular paid employment;
(d) is over the age of 50 years;
(e) lives as a single adult with one or more dependents;
(f) works in a sector or profession where the gender imbalance in the sector or profession concerned is at least 25% higher than the average gender imbalance across all economic sectors in the Member State and belongs to that underrepresented group;
(g) is a member of an ethnic minority within a Member State and who requires development of his or her linguistic, vocational training or work experience profile to enhance prospects of gaining access to stable employment.

Aid for the employment of disadvantaged or disabled workers The Commission has long been sympathetic to aid schemes aimed at disadvantaged or disabled workers. The block exemption in Regulation (EU) No 651/2014 provides that aid schemes for the recruitment of disadvantaged or disabled workers are compatible with the internal market and exempt from the requirement of prior notification to the Commission under Article 108(3) TFEU.[56]

In the case of the recruitment of disadvantaged workers, the aid intensity must not exceed 50% of the eligible costs.[57] Eligible costs are the wage costs

---

[54] Commission Regulation (EU) No 651/2014, Article 2(3).
[55] *Ibid.*, Article 2(4).
[56] *Ibid.*, Articles 32-34.
[57] *Ibid.*, Article 32(6).

over a maximum period of 12 months following recruitment, or 24 months following recruitment where the worker concerned is a severely disadvantaged worker.[58] Where the period of employment is shorter than 12 months, or 24 months in the case of severely disadvantaged workers, the aid shall be reduced *pro rata* accordingly.[59]

In the case of employment of disabled workers, the aid intensity must not exceed 75% of the eligible costs.[60] Eligible costs are the wage costs over any given duration during which the disabled worker is being employed.[61]

Where the recruitment does not represent a net increase, compared with the average over the previous twelve months, in the number of employees in the undertaking concerned, the post or posts must have fallen vacant following voluntary departure, disability, retirement on grounds of age, voluntary reduction of working time or lawful dismissal for misconduct and not as a result of redundancy.[62] Except in the case of lawful dismissal for misconduct, the disadvantaged worker must be entitled to continuous employment for a minimum period consistent with national legislation or collective agreements governing employment contracts.[63]

Aid for compensating additional costs of workers with disabilities Aid for compensating the additional costs of employing disabled workers is compatible with the internal market and exempt from the notification requirement of Article 108(3) TFEU. The aid intensity must not exceed 100% of the eligible costs.[64] Eligible costs are costs other than wage costs which the employer has to bear and which are additional to those which the undertaking would have incurred if employing workers who are not disabled, over the duration during which the worker concerned is being employed, including:[65]

(a) costs of adapting premises;
(b) costs of employing staff for time spent solely on the assistance of the disabled workers and training such staff to assist workers with disabilities;
(c) costs of adapting or acquiring equipment, or acquiring and validating software for their use by disabled workers, including adapted or assistive technology facilities, which are additional to those which the beneficiary would have incurred if employing workers who are not workers with disabilities;
(d) costs directly linked to transport of workers with disabilities to the working place and for work related activities;

---

[58] *Ibid.*, Article 32(2).
[59] *Ibid.*, Article 32(5).
[60] *Ibid.*, Article 33(5).
[61] *Ibid.*, Article 33(2).
[62] *Ibid.*, Article 32(3) and 33(3).
[63] *Ibid.*, Article 32(4) and 33(4).
[64] *Ibid.*, Article 34(1) and (5).
[65] *Ibid.*, Article 34(2).

(e) wage costs for the hours spent by a worker with disabilities on rehabilitation;

(f) where the beneficiary provides sheltered employment, the costs of constructing, installing or modernising production units of the establishment concerned, and any costs of administration and transport which result directly from the employment of workers with disabilities.

Aid for compensating costs of assistance to disadvantaged workers Aid for compensating the costs of assistance provided to disadvantaged workers is compatible with the internal market and exempt from the notification requirement of Article 108(3) TFEU. The aid intensity may not exceed 50% of the eligible costs.[66]

Eligible costs are the costs of employing staff solely for time spent on the assistance of the disadvantaged workers over a maximum period of 12 months following recruitment of a disadvantaged worker or over a maximum period of 24 months following recruitment of a severely disadvantaged worker, together with the costs of training such staff to assist disadvantaged workers.[67] The assistance provided must consist of measures to support the disadvantaged worker's autonomy and adaptation to the work environment, in accompanying the worker in social and administrative procedures, facilitation of communication with the entrepreneur and managing conflicts.[68]

Individual notification of large grants of aid The block exemption does not apply to any individual aid, whether granted *ad hoc* or on the basis of a scheme, where the grant equivalent exceeds the following threshold:

(a) aid for the recruitment of disadvantaged workers: €5 million per undertaking per year;[69]

(b) aid for the employment of disabled workers: €10 million per undertaking per year;[70]

(c) aid compensating for additional expenses of employing disabled workers: €10 million per undertaking per year;[71]

(d) aid compensating for the costs of assistance provided to disadvantaged workers: 4 million per undertaking per year.[72]

Assessment of notified aid for disadvantaged and disabled workers In its 2009 communication on compatibility of State aid for employment of disadvantaged and disabled workers subject to individual notification, the

---

[66] *Ibid.*, Article 35(1) and (4).
[67] *Ibid.*, Article 35(2).
[68] *Ibid.*, Article 35(3).
[69] *Ibid.*, Article 4(1)(o).
[70] *Ibid.*, Article 4(1)(p).
[71] *Ibid.*, Article 6(1)(q).
[72] *Ibid.*, Article 6(1)(r).

Commission set out the principles which it applies when assessing aid under Article 107(3)(c) TFEU directly. The Commission emphasised that criteria set out in this guidance will not be applied mechanically. The level of the Commission's assessment and the kind of information it may require will be proportional to the risk of distortion of competition and the scope of the analysis will depend on the nature of the case.[73]

Necessity and proportionality of the aid State aid for the employment of disadvantaged and disabled workers must result in the aid beneficiary changing its behaviour so that the aid results in a net increase in the number of disadvantaged or disabled employees in the undertaking concerned. Newly recruited disadvantaged or disabled employees should only fill newly created posts or posts that have fallen vacant following voluntary departure, disability, retirement on grounds of age, voluntary reduction of working time or lawful dismissal for misconduct. Posts resulting from redundancy are not to be filled with subsidised disadvantaged or disabled workers. Thus State aid cannot be used to replace workers in respect of whom the undertaking no longer receives a subsidy and who have consequently been dismissed. The Member State must demonstrate that the aid is paid in respect of a disadvantaged or disabled worker in an undertaking, where the recruitment would have not occurred without the aid. It must also demonstrate that the aid is necessary and that the amount is kept to the minimum in order to achieve the objective of the aid. It should provide evidence that the aid amount does not exceed the net additional costs of employing the categories of workers concerned compared to the costs of employing workers who are not disadvantaged or disabled.[74]

Negative effects If the aid is proportionate to achieve the objective of the aid, the negative effects of the aid are likely to be limited and an analysis of the negative effects may not be necessary. However, in some cases, even where the aid is necessary and proportionate for a specific undertaking to increase the employment of categories of workers concerned by the measure, the aid may result in a change in the behaviour of the beneficiary which significantly distorts competition. The extent of the distortion of competition caused by the aid can vary depending on the characteristics of the aid and of the markets affected. Factors to be taken into account will be selectivity, size of the aid, repetition and duration of the aid and the effect of the aid on the undertaking's costs. The Commission will also assess the structure of the market, the characteristics of the sector or industry and the situation on the national or regional labour market. When examining the characteristics of the sector, the Commission will look among other things at the importance of the trained workforce for the business, the existence of overcapacity, and whether the

---

[73] Communication on aid for employment of disadvantaged and disabled worker, para 4.
[74] *Ibid.*, paras 10-12.

markets in the industry are growing, mature or declining. Aid may, in particular cases, lead to distortions of competition in respect of substitution and displacement effects, market entry and exit, investment incentives and effect on trade flows. In particular, as regards substitution and displacement effects, the Commission recognises that jobs given to a certain category of workers may simply replace jobs for other categories. A wage subsidy which targets a specific subgroup of workers splits the labour force into subsidised workers and unsubsidised workers, and may induce undertakings to replace unsubsidised workers with subsidised workers. Since undertakings which employ subsidised workers compete in the same markets for goods or services as those which do not employ subsidised workers, wage subsidies can contribute to the reduction of jobs elsewhere in the economy. [75]

---

[75] *Ibid.*, paras 14-27.

Chapter Eleven

STATE AID FOR RESEARCH AND DEVELOPMENT AND INNOVATION

11.1 COMMISSION POLICY ON AID FOR R&D&I

Commission policy on aid for R&D&I Article 3(3) TEU lists the promotion of research and technological development as an objective of the EU. This is expanded in Article 179 TFEU which formulates the EU objective of strengthening the scientific and technological bases of EU industry and encouraging it to become more competitive at international level and requires the EU to encourage research and technological development between firms, research centres and universities. With a view to strengthening the technological base of EU industry and developing its international competitiveness, in 1985 the Commission called for a major drive in relation to technology.[1] This strategy lay behind programmes such as Esprit, RACE and Brite, which were designed to exploit the potential of the European market and the synergetic effects of joint efforts by the EU, the Member States and the undertakings and research centres concerned. The Commission also took a favourable view of State aid for research and development, justifying its approach by reference to the aims pursued by such aid, the considerable amount of finance often required for research and development projects and the risks attached to them.[2]

The first framework for State aid for research and development was adopted in 1986.[3] In 1996, the Commission adopted a second framework in which it reiterated its traditionally favourable view of State aid for research and development.[4] The third framework, adopted in 2006, extended its remit to cover aid for innovation to the extent that it relates to precise activities which clearly address the market failures that are hampering innovation.[5] Moreover, Commission Regulation (EC) No 800/2008 contained provisions allowing for the block exemption of several categories of State aid for R&D&I.[6] A new

---

[1]   Memorandum "Towards a European Technology Community", COM (85) 350 final.
[2]   *Sixteenth Report on Competition Policy* (1986), point 247.
[3]   OJ 1986 C83/2.
[4]   OJ 1996 C45/5.
[5]   OJ 2006 C323/1.
[6]   OJ 2008 L214/3.

framework for State aid for R&D&I was adopted for the period 2014-2020[7] and revised block exemption criteria were established by Commission Regulation (EU) No 651/2014, Articles 25-30.

Scope of the R&D&I framework 2014-2020   The principles set out in the R&D&I framework 2014-2020 apply to State aid for R&D&I in all sectors governed by the FEU Treaty, including those sectors which are subject to specific EU rules on State aid, unless those rules provide otherwise.   EU funding that is centrally managed by EU institutions and bodies and which is not directly or indirectly under the control of Member States does not constitute State aid.   Where EU funding is combined with State aid, only the latter will be considered in determining whether notification thresholds and maximum aid intensities are respected or, in the context of the framework, are subject to a compatibility assessment.   Aid for R&D&I for firms in difficulty is excluded from the scope of the framework.[8]

Categories of permissible R&D&I aid   Several categories of R&D&I aid measures have been identified by the Commission as being capable of being considered compatible with the internal market under Article 107(3)(c) TFEU. Aid may be granted in accordance with the R&D&I framework and the block exemption in Commission Regulation (EU) No 651/2014 for the following: R&D projects, feasibility studies, construction and upgrade of research infrastructures, innovation activities and innovation clusters.   Aid that satisfies the relevant conditions for the application of the block exemption is compatible with the internal market and exempt from the notification requirement of Article 108(3) TFEU.[9]

Notifiable R&D&I aid   Commission Regulation (EU) No 651/2014 requires that aid exceeding specified thresholds is not covered by the block exemption and must, accordingly, be individually notified to the Commission.   These thresholds for R&D&I are as follows:[10]

(a)   for R&D where the project is predominantly fundamental research, €40 million per undertaking per project;

(b)   for R&D where the project is predominantly industrial research, €20 million per undertaking per project;

---

[7]   OJ 2014 C198/1.

[8]   Framework on State aid for R&D&I 2014-2020, paras 8-10.

[9]   Commission Regulation (EU) No 651/2014, Articles 25-30.

[10]   *Ibid.*, Article 4(1)(i)-(m). The threshold amounts in (a)-(c) are doubled for R&D in a Eureka project or where the project is implemented by a joint undertaking established on the basis of Article 185 TFEU or Article 187 TFEU. If the aid for R&D projects is granted in the form of repayable advances, subject to certain conditions, each of these amounts may be increased by 50%.

(c) for R&D where the project is predominantly experimental development, €15 million per undertaking per project;

(d) aid for feasibility studies in preparation for research activities, €7.5 million per study;

(e) for investment aid for research infrastructures, €20 million per infrastructure;

(f) for aid for innovation clusters, €7.5 million per cluster;

(g) for innovation aid for SMEs, €5 million per undertaking per project;

(h) for aid for process and organisational innovation, €7.5 million per undertaking per project.

Resort to the framework will be necessary where the aid is not transparent. For example, the Commission authorised the Flemish Region to participate in the capital increase of OCAS, a research and development unit of Arcelor which planned to transform itself into a more autonomous and profitable company in the market for R&D. Belgium argued that the company was profitable enough to attract investment from private sources and that Arcelor was itself participating in the capital increase in the same amount. The Commission, after a detailed analysis of the case, concluded that the profit forecasts were not precise and high enough to consider the return expected sufficient to compensate for the high risk of the project. Accordingly, the investment was considered as State aid but was nevertheless authorised on the ground that it incited Arcelor to undertake additional research.[11]

Publicly funded research organisations Research organisations and research infrastructures are recipients of State aid if their public funding fulfils all conditions of Article 107(1) TFEU. The beneficiary must qualify as an undertaking, the decisive criterion for that qualification being that it carries out an economic activity consisting of offering products or services on a given market. Where the same entity carries out activities of both economic and non-economic nature, the public funding of the non-economic activities will not fall under Article 107(1) TFEU if the two kinds of activities and their costs, funding and revenues can be clearly separated so that cross-subsidisation of the economic activity is effectively avoided. Primary activities of research bodies are regarded as non-economic, in particular, education for more and better skilled human resources, independent R&D for more knowledge and better understanding, including collaborative R&D, and wide dissemination of research results on a non-exclusive and non-discriminatory basis, for example through teaching, open-access databases, open publications or open software. Knowledge transfer activities are also generally of a non-economic nature where they are conducted either by the research body or jointly with, or on behalf of other such entities, and where all profits from those activities are reinvested in its primary activities. Where the research body is used almost

---

[11] Case N315/2004, *OCAS*, OJ 2005 C159/24.

exclusively for a non-economic activity, its funding may fall outside State aid rules in its entirety, provided that the economic use remains purely ancillary. On the other hand, where they are used to perform economic activities, such as renting out equipment or laboratories, supplying services to undertakings or performing contract research, public funding of those economic activities will generally be considered State aid. If the public financing is passed on to final beneficiaries in its entirety, the research body will be regarded merely as an intermediary that does not benefit from any aid.[12]

Indirect State aid through research organisations Where a research organisation or research infrastructure is used to perform contract research or provide a research service to an undertaking, which typically specifies the terms and conditions of the contract, owns the results of the research activities and carries the risk of failure, no State aid will usually be passed to the undertaking if the research body receives payment of an adequate remuneration for its services, in particular at market price. If there is no market price, the remuneration should be based either on the full cost of the service provided plus a profit margin or on the result of arm's length negotiations.[13]

A project is considered to be carried out through effective collaboration where at least two independent parties pursue a common objective based on the division of labour and jointly define its scope, participate in its design, contribute to its implementation and share its financial, technological, scientific and other risks, as well as its results. Where collaboration projects are carried out jointly by undertakings and research organisations or research infrastructures, no indirect State aid is awarded to the participating undertakings through those entities due to favourable conditions of the collaboration if: the participating undertakings bear the full cost of the project; or the results of the collaboration which do not give rise to intellectual property rights may be widely disseminated and any IPR resulting from the activities of research bodies are fully allocated to them; or any IPR resulting from the project, as well as related access rights are allocated to the different collaboration partners in a manner which adequately reflects their work packages, contributions and respective interests; or the research body receives compensation equivalent to the market price for the IPR which result from its activities and are assigned to the participating undertakings, or to which participating undertakings are allocated access rights. If these conditions are not fulfilled, the full value of the contribution of the research organisations or research infrastructures to the project will be considered as an advantage for the collaborating undertakings.[14]

---

[12] Framework on State aid for R&D&I 2014-2020, paras 17-23.
[13] *Ibid.*, para 25.
[14] *Ibid.*, paras 27-30.

Public procurement of R&D services Public purchasers may procure research and development services from undertakings, through both exclusive development and pre-commercial procurement procedures. No State aid will be granted where an open tender procedure for the public procurement is carried out in accordance with the applicable EU directives. In all other cases, including pre-commercial procurement, the Commission will consider that no State aid is awarded to undertakings where the price paid for the relevant services fully reflects the market value of the benefits received by the public purchaser and the risks taken by the participating providers. This will be the case where the following conditions are all fulfilled: the selection procedure is open, transparent and non-discriminatory; the envisaged contractual arrangements describing all rights and obligations of the parties, including with regard to IPR, are made available to all interested bidders in advance of the bidding procedure; the procurement does not give any of the participant providers any preferential treatment in the supply of commercial volumes of the final products or services to a public purchaser in the Member State concerned; and all results which do not give rise to IPR may be widely disseminated and any IPR are fully allocated to the public purchaser or any service provider to which results giving rise to IPR are allocated is required to grant the public purchaser unlimited access to those results free of charge, and to grant access to third parties, for example by way of non-exclusive licenses, under market conditions.[15]

11.2 COMPATIBILITY CRITERIA UNDER THE R&D&I FRAMEWORK

Common assessment principles To assess whether a notified aid measure can be considered compatible with the internal market pursuant to the framework on R&D&I aid 2014-2020, the Commission analyses whether the design of the aid measure ensures that the positive impact of the aid towards an objective of common interest exceeds its potential negative effects on trade and competition.   In accordance with the Communication on State aid modernisation, the Commission will consider an aid measure compatible with the internal market only if it satisfies each of the following criteria: contribution to a well-defined objective of common interest; need for State intervention; appropriateness of the measure; incentive effect; proportionality of the aid; avoidance of undue negative effects on competition and trade between Member States; and transparency of the aid. The overall balance of certain categories of schemes may further be made subject to a requirement of *ex post* evaluation. In such cases, the Commission may limit the duration of

---

[15]   *Ibid.*, paras 31-33.

those schemes, normally to four years or less, with a possibility to re-notify their prolongation afterwards.[16]

Contribution to an objective of common interest In 2002, the European Council adopted a clear goal for the future development of research spending, to the effect that overall spending on R&D&I in the EU should be increased with the aim of approaching 3% of gross domestic product by 2010, with two-thirds of this new investment coming from the private sector. To reach this objective, research investment should have grown at an average rate of 8% every year, shared between a 6% growth rate for public expenditure and a 9% yearly growth rate for private investment. By 2007, however, the overall R&D investment in the EU of €7.2 billion was only 1.8% of GDP, with only Sweden and Finland reaching the EU target of 3%.[17] An estimated total of €62.4 billion was awarded during the period 2008-2013, representing a little over 2% of GDP, compared to around 3% in the United States and Japan.[18] The Europe 2020 strategy identifies R&D as a key driver for achieving the EU's objectives of smart, sustainable and inclusive growth. To that extent, the Commission again set out a headline target of 3% of EU GDP to be invested in R&D&I by 2020, aiming, in particular, at improving framework conditions and access to finance for research and innovation in order to ensure that innovative ideas can be turned into products and services that create growth and jobs.[19]

The general objective of R&D&I aid is the promotion of R&D&I in the EU. In doing so, R&D&I aid should contribute to the achievement of the Europe 2020 strategy of delivering smart, sustainable and inclusive growth. Member States considering awarding aid for R&D&I must precisely define the objective pursued and, in particular, explain how the measure intends to promote R&D&I. For measures co-financed by the European Structural and Investments Funds, Member States may rely on the reasoning in the relevant operational programmes. With respect to notifiable aid schemes, the Commission takes a favourable view of aid measures which are an integral part of a comprehensive programme or action plan to stimulate R&D&I activities or smart specialisation strategies, and are supported by rigorous evaluations of similar past aid measures demonstrating their effectiveness. With respect to aid which is awarded for projects or activities that are also financed by the EU, either directly or indirectly, the Commission will consider that the contribution to a well-defined objective of common interest has been established. To demonstrate that individual aid contributes to an increased level of R&D&I activities, Member States may rely on an increase in project size, scope, speed

---

[16] *Ibid.*, paras 35-37.
[17] State aid scoreboard, Autumn 2008, p. 34.
[18] *Report on Competition Policy* (2014), accompanying document, p.7.
[19] Commission communication on a European 2020 flagship initiative – Innovation Union, COM(2010) 546 final.

or total amount spent.   In order to conclude that the aid contributes to increasing the level of R&D&I in the EU, the Commission will consider not only the net increase of R&D&I carried out by the undertaking, but also the contribution of the aid to the overall increase of R&D&I spending in the sector concerned, as well as to the improvement of the EU situation with regard to R&D&I in the international context.[20]

Need for State intervention   Member States should explain how the aid measure can effectively mitigate the market failure associated with reaching the objective of promoting R&D&I without that aid.   R&D&I takes place through a series of activities, which are usually upstream to a number of product markets and exploit available capabilities to develop new or improved products, services and processes in those product markets or completely new ones, thereby fostering growth in the economy, contributing to territorial and social cohesion or furthering the general consumer interest.   However, given the available R&D&I capabilities, market failures may be an obstacle to reaching the optimal output and may lead to an inefficient outcome.   Although R&D&I may have significant positive externalities, such as knowledge spillovers or enhanced opportunities for other economic actors to develop complementary products and services, a number of projects might have an unattractive rate of return from a private perspective.   State aid may therefore contribute to the implementation of projects which result in an overall societal or economic benefit.   R&D&I activities are characterised by a high degree of uncertainty. Under certain circumstances, due to imperfect and asymmetric information, private investors may be reluctant to finance valuable projects and highly-qualified personnel may be unaware of recruitment possibilities in innovative undertakings.   As a result, the allocation of human and financial resources may not be adequate and projects which may be valuable for society or the economy may not be carried out.   Furthermore, the ability of undertakings to coordinate with each other or to interact in order to deliver R&D&I may be impaired for various reasons, including difficulties in coordinating among a large number of collaboration partners where some of them have diverging interests, problems in designing contracts, and difficulties in coordinating collaboration due for example to sensitive information being shared.[21]

Appropriateness of State aid   The Commission will assess whether and to what extent aid for R&D&I can be considered an appropriate instrument to increase R&D&I activities, given that other less distortive instruments may achieve the same results, having regard to any impact assessment of the

---

[20]   Framework on R&D&I aid 2014-2020, paras 42-47.   See, for example, Case N 435/2007, *Minimage*, OJ 2008, C137/1; Case N 674/2006, *Neoval*, OJ 2007 C120/2.

[21]   Framework on R&D&I aid 2014-2020, paras 48-49.

proposed measure that has been carried out. The choice of the aid instrument should be made in view of the market failure which it seeks to address. For instance, where the underlying market failure is a problem of access to external debt finance due to asymmetric information, Member States should normally resort to aid in the form of liquidity support, such as a loan or guarantee, rather than a grant. Where it is also necessary to provide the firm with a certain degree of risk sharing, a repayable advance should normally be the aid instrument of choice. In particular, where aid is awarded in a form other than liquidity support or a repayable advance for activities that are close to the market, Member States must justify the appropriateness of the chosen instrument for tackling the specific market failure in question.[22]

Incentive effect R&D&I aid can only be found compatible with the internal market if it has an incentive effect. An incentive effect occurs where the aid changes the behaviour of an undertaking in such a way that it engages in additional activities, which it would not carry out or it would carry out in a restricted or different manner without the aid. The aid must not subsidise the costs of an activity that an undertaking would anyhow incur and must not compensate for the normal business risk of an economic activity. The Commission considers that aid does not present an incentive for the beneficiary wherever work on the relevant R&D&I activity has already started prior to the aid application by the beneficiary to the national authorities. Where start of works takes place before the aid application is submitted by the beneficiary to the national authorities, the project will not be eligible for aid.[23] For notifiable individual aid, there must be provide clear evidence that the aid has a positive impact on the decision of the undertaking to pursue R&D&I activities which would otherwise not have been pursued, including a comprehensive description of the counterfactual scenario that would have happened or could reasonably have been expected to happen without aid. The counterfactual scenario may consist in the absence of an alternative project or in a clearly defined and sufficiently predictable alternative project considered by the beneficiary in its internal decision making, and may relate to an alternative project that is wholly or partly carried out outside the EU.[24]

For example, in approving Portuguese aid for BIAL in support of an R&D project for the development of drugs in the central nervous system area, the Commission accepted that the aid had a clear incentive effect especially in view of the large risks inherent in the ambitious programme.[25] Aid to Océ, a

---

[22] *Ibid.*, paras 56-61. See, for example, Case N 887/2006, *Bernin*, OJ 2007 C200/2; Case N 89/2007, *HOMES*, OJ 2007 C275/3; Case N 185/2007, *Nanosmart*, OJ 2007 C284/3.

[23] Framework on R&D&I aid 2014-2020, paras 62-63.

[24] *Ibid.*, paras 66-71. See Decision 2009/179/EC, *Industria de Turbo Propulsores*, OJ 2009 L66/3.

[25] Case N 126/2005, *BIAL*, OJ 2005 C275/3.

company producing copiers and printers, for an R&D project concerning inkjet printing technology was approved. The Commission assessed the nature of the R&D in the light of Océ's earlier R&D in the field, the cost structure of the project and the state of the art technologies in relation to market developments. It concluded that the aid would have an incentive effect as Océ's R&D spending and R&D personnel had increased considerably, the project bore high technical risks and Océ's efforts went well beyond what was considered normal in the sector.[26]

Proportionality of the aid The amount of R&D&I aid must be limited to the minimum needed for carrying out the aided activity. In order to ensure that the level of aid is proportionate to the market failures which it is intended to address, the framework on R&D&I aid and the block exemption regulation establish eligible costs and maximum intensities for each category of aid. These are established on the basis of three criteria: (i) the closeness of the aid to the market, as a proxy for its expected negative effects and the need for it, taking into account the potential higher revenues that can be expected from the aided activities; (ii) the size of the beneficiary as a proxy for the more acute difficulties generally faced by smaller undertakings to finance a risky project; and (iii) the acuteness of the market failure, such as the expected externalities in terms of dissemination of knowledge. Aid intensities should generally be lower for activities linked to development and innovation than for research activities.[27] For notifiable individual aid, mere compliance with a set of predefined maximum aid intensities is not sufficient to ensure proportionality. In order to establish whether the aid is proportional, the Commission will verify that its amount does not exceed the minimum necessary for the aided project to be sufficiently profitable, for example by making possible to achieve an internal rate of return corresponding to the sector or firm specific benchmark or hurdle rate. Where it is shown that the aid beneficiary faces a clear choice between carrying out either an aided project or an alternative one without aid, the aid will be considered to be limited to the minimum only if its amount does not exceed the net extra costs of implementing the activities concerned compared to the counterfactual project. Where there are multiple potential candidates for carrying out the aided activity, the proportionality requirement is more likely to be met if the aid is awarded on the basis of transparent, objective and non-discriminatory criteria. [28]

If a Member State awards aid on the basis of a valid methodology by way of a repayable advance, the aid may be awarded on the basis of the gross grant equivalent of the repayable advance, up to the aid intensities set out in the

---

[26] Commission Decision 2001/637/EC, *Océ*, OJ 2001 L223/10.

[27] Framework on R&D&I aid 2014-2020, paras 72-77.

[28] *Ibid.*, paras 86-91. See, for example, Case N 674/2006, *Neoval*, OJ 2007 C120/2; Case N 349/2007, *OSIRIS*, OJ 2007 C304/5.

framework. In all other cases, the repayable advance is to be expressed as a percentage of the eligible costs and may exceed the applicable maximum aid intensities by 10 percentage points, subject to the following conditions:

(a) in case of a successful outcome, the measure must provide that the advance is to be repaid with interest;

(b) in case of a success exceeding the outcome defined as successful, the Member State should request payments beyond repayment of the advance amount including interest according to the applicable discount rate;

(c) in case the project fails, the advance does not have to be fully repaid. In case of partial success, the repayment should be proportional to the degree of success achieved.[29]

The aid intensity of a fiscal measure can be calculated either on the basis of individual projects or, at the level of an undertaking, as the ratio between the overall tax relief and the sum of all eligible R&D&I costs incurred in a period not exceeding three consecutive fiscal years. In the latter case, the fiscal measure may apply without distinction to all eligible activities, but must not exceed the applicable aid intensity for experimental development.[30]

Negative effects on competition and trade The Commission identifies two main potential distortions of competition and trade between Member States caused by R&D&I aid, namely product market distortions and location effects. Both types may lead to allocative inefficiencies, undermining the economic performance of the internal market, and distributional concerns, in that the aid affects the distribution of economic activity across regions. Moreover, even where distortions may be considered limited at individual level, on a cumulative basis aid schemes might lead to high levels of distortions.[31]

As far as distortions on the product markets are concerned, aid for R&D&I may have an impact on competition in innovation processes and in the product markets where the results of the R&D&I activities are exploited. Aid can hamper competition in innovation processes and product markets in three ways, namely by distorting the competitive entry and exit process, by distorting dynamic investment incentives and by creating or maintaining market power. In assessing the negative effects of individual aid, the Commission will focus its analysis on the foreseeable impact of the R&D&I aid on competition between undertakings in the product markets concerned, giving more weight to risks for competition and trade that arise in the near future and with particular likelihood. To the extent that a specific innovative activity will be associated with multiple future product markets, the impact of the aid will be looked upon on the set of markets concerned. In certain cases the results of R&D&I

---

[29] *Ibid.*, paras 78-80. See, for example, Cases N654/2008, *Bombardier* (2009) and N204/2010, *Volvo Aero* (2011).

[30] Framework on R&D&I aid 2014-2020, para 82.

[31] *Ibid.*, paras 94-95.

activities, for example in the form of intellectual property rights, are themselves traded in technology markets, for instance through patent licensing or trading. In those cases, the Commission may also consider the effect of the aid on competition in technology markets. In its analysis of the potential distortion of dynamic incentives, the Commission will consider the following elements: market growth, aid amount, closeness to the market, open selection process, exit barriers, incentives to compete for a future market, product differentiation and intensity of competition. In its assessment of market power, the Commission will consider market structure, levels of entry barriers, buyer power and selection process. As regards market structures, the Commission will consider whether the aid is awarded in markets featuring overcapacity or in declining industries. Situations where the market is growing or where aid for R&D&I is likely to change the overall growth dynamics of the sector, notably by introducing new technologies, are less likely to give rise to concerns.[32]

Distortions of competition influencing the choice of a location can arise across Member States, either when firms compete across borders or consider different locations. Aid aimed at relocating an activity in another region within the internal market may not lead directly to a distortion in the product market, but it displaces activities or investments from one region into another. In particular where R&D&I aid is close to the market, it may result in some territories benefiting from more favourable conditions in respect of subsequent production, particularly because of comparatively lower production costs as a result of the aid or due to higher levels of R&D&I activities pursued through the aid. This may lead undertakings to re-locate to those territories. Location effects may also be relevant to research infrastructures. If aid is mainly used to attract an infrastructure to a particular region at the expense of another, it will not contribute to promoting further R&D&I activities in the EU. In its analysis of notifiable individual aid, the Commission will accordingly take into account any evidence that the aid beneficiary has considered alternative locations.[33]

Thus, for example, the Commission approved a major French programme covering R&D into personalised medicines for infectious diseases, cancer and genetic diseases. In weighing up the positive and negative aspects of the aid, the Commission took account of the fact that it would make a significant contribution to improving the entire health chain associated with cancer and orphan diseases.[34] Approval was also given in respect of a telecommunications scheme contributing to the development of a significant common architecture incorporating mobile communication, microelectronics and distance management of cards and services. The Commission considered that benefits would accrue to the EU as a whole, with little distortion of competition since

---

[32]   *Ibid.*, paras 96-101, 106-115.
[33]   *Ibid.*, paras 102 and 116-118.
[34]   Case N 709/2007, *ADNA*, OJ 2009 C35/3.

the results of the programme would be made widely available.[35] In its decision on aid to *Turbomeca*, the Commission noted the fact that the aided project was aimed at developing a product in a market that would otherwise be dominated by one market player.[36]

11.3 AID FOR R&D PROJECTS

Aid for research and development projects Aid may be granted in respect of research and development projects.[37] The aided part of the research project must fall within the categories of fundamental research and applied research, which is subdivided into industrial research or experimental development. Such aid is mainly targeted at the market failure related to positive externalities (knowledge spillovers), but may also address a market failure caused by imperfect and asymmetric information or, mainly in collaboration projects, a coordination failure.

Fundamental research means experimental or theoretical work undertaken primarily to acquire new knowledge of the underlying foundations of phenomena and observable facts, without any direct practical application or use in view.[38] Industrial research means the planned research or critical investigation aimed at the acquisition of new knowledge and skills for developing new products, processes or services or for bringing about a significant improvement in existing products, processes or services.[39] For example, in the *IFS* decision, the Commission accepted that aid for a project carried out by a pharmaceutical company involving pre-clinical tests could be classified as industrial research, having regard to the high rate of unsuccessful tests during the drug development phase.[40] Experimental development means the acquiring, combining, shaping and using of existing scientific, technological, business and other relevant knowledge and skills for the purpose of producing plans and arrangements or designs for new, altered or improved products, processes or services. It may comprise prototyping, demonstrating, piloting, testing and validation of new or improved products, processes or services in environments representative of real life operating conditions where the primary objective is to make further technical improvements on products, processes or services that are not substantially set. This may include the

---

[35] Case N 602/2007, *MaXSSIM*, OJ 2008 C 177/3.

[36] Case N 447/07, *Turbomeca*, OJ 2008 C94/10.

[37] Framework on R&D&I aid 2014-2020, para 12(a); Commission Regulation (EU) No 651/2014, Article 25(1).

[38] Framework on R&D&I aid 2014-2020, para 15(m); Commission Regulation (EU) No 651/2014, Article 2(84).

[39] Framework on R&D&I aid 2014-2020, para 15(q); Commission Regulation (EU) No 651/2014, Article 2(85).

[40] *Thirty-third Report on Competition Policy* (2003), pt 467.

development of a commercially usable prototype or pilot which is necessarily the final commercial product and which is too expensive to produce for it to be used only for demonstration and validation purposes.[41] The Commission has, however, refused to approve aid where the activity is too close to the market.[42]

Intensity of aid for R&D projects The aid intensity for R&D projects may not exceed 100% for fundamental research, 50% for industrial research and 25% for experimental development.[43] Projects involving collaboration between research organisations and undertakings are encouraged.[44] The aid intensities for industrial research and experimental development may be increased, where the aid is given to SMEs, by 10 percentage points for medium-sized enterprises and by 20 percentage points for small enterprises. A bonus of 15 percentage points may be added, up to a maximum aid intensity of 80%: (i) if the project involves effective collaboration between at least two undertakings which are independent of each other on condition that no single undertaking bears more than 70% of the eligible costs of the collaboration project and the project involves collaboration with at least one SME or is carried out in at least two different Member States; or (ii) if the project involves effective collaboration between an undertaking and a research organisation on condition that the research organisation bears at least 10% of the eligible project costs and it has the right to publish the results of the research projects insofar as they stem from research carried out by that organisation; or (iii) in the case of industrial research, if the results of the project are widely disseminated through technical and scientific conferences or through publication in scientific or technical journals or in open access repositories, or through free or open source software.[45]

Eligible costs Eligible costs, which must be allocated to a specific category of research and development, are the following:[46]
(a) personnel costs, i.e. costs of researchers, technicians and other supporting staff to the extent employed on the research project;

---

[41] Framework on R&D&I aid 2014-2020, para 15(j); Commission Regulation (EU) No 651/2014, Article 2(86).
[42] See, for example, Commission Decision 2004/286/EC, *Gamesa*, OJ 2004 L91/49.
[43] Framework on R&D&I aid 2014-2020, Annex II; Commission Regulation (EU) No 651/2014, Article 25(5).
[44] See, for example, Case N 473/2000, *LINK*, OJ 2001 C199/11; Case N 636/200, *Irish research, technology and innovation initiative*, OJ 2001 C94/3; Case N214/2004, *Bell Laboratories*, OJ 2006 C72/2.
[45] Framework on R&D&I aid 2014-2020, Annex II; Commission Regulation (EU) No 651/2014, Article 25(6).
[46] Framework on R&D&I aid 2014-2020, Annex I; Commission Regulation (EU) No 651/2014, Article 25(3).

(b) costs of instruments and equipment to the extent and for the period used for the research project. If such instruments and equipment are not used for their full life for the research project, only the depreciation costs corresponding to the life of the research project, as calculated on the basis of good accounting practice, are considered as eligible;

(c) costs for buildings and land, to the extent and for the duration used for the research project. With regard to buildings, only the depreciation costs corresponding to the life of the research project, as calculated on the basis of good accounting practice are considered as eligible. For land, costs of commercial transfer or actually incurred capital costs are eligible;

(d) cost of contractual research, technical knowledge and patents bought or licensed from outside sources at market prices, where the transaction has been carried out at arm's length and there is no element of collusion involved, as well as costs of consultancy and equivalent services used exclusively for the research activity;

(e) additional overheads incurred directly as a result of the project;

(f) other operating expenses, including costs of materials, supplies and similar products incurred directly as a result of the project.

11.4 AID FOR OTHER CATEGORIES OF R&D&I ACTIVITIES

Aid for technical feasibility studies Aid may be granted for technical feasibility studies preparatory to industrial research or experimental development activities, which aim at overcoming the market failure related to imperfect and asymmetric information.[47] For example, Spain granted aid designed to foster studies with a view to launching technologies to improve traffic safety.[48] The aid intensity must not exceed 50% for large enterprises, 60% for medium-sized enterprises and 70% for small enterprises.[49] The eligible costs are the costs of the study.[50]

Investment aid for research infrastructures Aid for the construction or upgrade of research infrastructures that perform economic activities, which mainly addresses the market failure stemming from coordination difficulties, may be compatible with the internal market. High-quality research infrastructures are increasingly necessary for ground-breaking research, as they attract global talent and are essential for example for information and

---

[47] Framework on R&D&I aid 2014-2020, para 12(b); Commission Regulation (EU) No 651/2014, Article 25(3)

[48] Case N 676/99, *PTF*, OJ 2000 C272/44. See also, SA.33193, *Flanders scheme* (2011).

[49] Framework on R&D&I aid 2014-2020, Annex II; Commission Regulation (EU) No 651/2014, Article 25(5) and (7).

[50] Framework on R&D&I aid 2014-2020, Annex I; Commission Regulation (EU) No 651/2014, Article 25(4).

communication technologies and key enabling technologies. Under the block exemption regulation, the price charged for the operation or use of the infrastructure must correspond to a market price. Access to the infrastructure must be open to several users and be granted on a transparent and non-discriminatory basis. Undertakings which have financed at least 10% of the investment costs of the infrastructure may be granted preferential access under more favourable conditions. In order to avoid overcompensation, such access must be proportional to the undertaking's contribution to the investment costs. The aid intensity may not exceed 50% of the eligible costs, being the investment costs in intangible and tangible assets. Where a research infrastructure receives public funding for both economic and non-economic activities, Member States must put in place a monitoring and claw-back mechanism in order to ensure that the applicable aid intensity is not exceeded as a result of an increase in the share of economic activities compared to the situation envisaged at the time of awarding the aid.[51]

Aid for innovation activities Aid for innovation activities is mainly targeted at market failures related to positive externalities (knowledge spill-overs), coordination difficulties and, to a lesser extent, asymmetric information. With respect to SMEs, such innovation aid may be awarded for obtaining, validating and defending patents and other intangible assets, for the secondment of highly qualified personnel, and for acquiring innovation advisory and support services. Moreover, in order to encourage large enterprises to collaborate with SMEs in process and organisational innovation activities, the costs incurred by both SMEs and large enterprises for such activities may also be supported.[52]

Innovation aid with a maximum intensity of 50% of eligible costs may be granted to SMEs in respect of: obtaining, validating and defending patents and other intangible assets; secondment of highly qualified personnel from a research and knowledge-dissemination organisation or a large enterprise, working on R&D&I activities in a newly created function within the beneficiary and not replacing other personnel; and innovation advisory and support services. In the particular case of aid for innovation advisory and support services, the aid intensity can be increased up to 100% of the eligible costs provided that the total amount of aid for such services does not exceed €200,000 per undertaking within any three year period.[53]

Aid for process and organisational innovation is compatible with the internal market. Under the block exemption regulation, aid to large

---

[51] Framework on R&D&I aid 2014-2020, Article 12(c) and Annexes I and II; Commission Regulation (EU) No 651/2014, Article 26.

[52] Framework on R&D&I aid 2014-2020, Article 12(d). See, for example, Case X173/2010, *BMWi-Innovationsgutscheine*.

[53] Framework on R&D&I aid 2014-2020, Annexes I and II; Commission Regulation (EU) No 651/2014, Article 28. See, for example, Case N301/2010, *Green Labs DK* (2011).

undertakings will only be compatible if they effectively collaborate with SMEs in the aided activity and the collaborating SMEs incur at least 30% of the total eligible costs. The eligible costs are: personnel costs; costs of instruments, equipment, buildings and land to the extent and for the period used for the project; costs of contractual research, knowledge and patents bought or licensed from outside sources at arm's length conditions; and additional overheads and other operating costs, including costs of materials, supplies and similar products, incurred directly as a result of the project. The aid intensity may not exceed 15% of the eligible costs for large undertakings and 50% of the eligible costs for SMEs.[54]

Aid for innovation clusters Aid for innovation clusters aims at tackling market failures linked with coordination problems hampering the development of clusters, or limiting the interactions and knowledge flows within and between clusters. Under the block exemption, the aid must be granted exclusively to the legal entity operating the innovation cluster. Access to the cluster's premises, facilities and activities must be open to several users and be granted on a transparent and non-discriminatory basis. Undertakings which have financed at least 10% of the investment costs of the innovation cluster may be granted preferential access under more favourable conditions. In order to avoid overcompensation, such access must be proportional to the undertaking's contribution to the investment costs and these conditions shall be made publicly available. Fees charged for using the cluster's facilities and for participating in the cluster's activities must correspond to the market price or reflect their costs.[55]

Investment aid may be granted for the construction or upgrade of innovation clusters. The aid intensity may not exceed 50% of the eligible costs, which are the investment costs in intangible and tangible assets. The aid intensity may be increased by 15 percentage points for innovation clusters located in Article 107(3)(a) areas and by 5 percentage points for innovation clusters located Article 107(3)(c) areas.[56]

Operating aid may be granted for the operation of innovation clusters. It shall not exceed 10 years. The eligible costs of operating aid are the personnel and administrative costs, including overhead costs, relating to: animation of the cluster to facilitate collaboration, information sharing and the provision or channelling of specialised and customised business support services; marketing of the cluster to increase participation of new undertakings or organisations and

---

[54] Framework on R&D&I aid 2014-2020, Annexes I and II; Commission Regulation (EU) No 651/2014, Article 29.

[55] Framework on R&D&I aid 2014-2020, Article 12(e), Commission Regulation (EU) No 651/2014, Article 27(1)-(4).. See, for example, Case N336/2007, *Innovation clusters in Trento* (2007); N507/2009, *Inoklaster LT* (2009).

[56] Framework on R&D&I aid 2014-2020, Annexes I and II; Commission Regulation (EU) No 651/2014, Article 27(5)-(6).

to increase visibility; and management of the cluster's facilities; organisation of training programmes, workshops and conferences to support knowledge sharing and networking and transnational cooperation. The aid intensity of operating aid may not exceed 50% of the total eligible costs during the period over which the aid is granted.[57]

---

[57] Framework on R&D&I aid 2014-2020, Annexes I and II; Commission Regulation (EU) No 651/2014, Article 27(7)-(8).

Chapter Twelve

STATE AID FOR ENVIRONMENTAL PROTECTION

12.1 COMMISSION POLICY ON STATE AID FOR
ENVIRONMENTAL PROTECTION

Commission policy on State aid for environmental protection As early as 1973, in the field of environmental protection, the Council and the Member States had accepted the polluter pays principle under which economic agents should bear the full cost of the pollution caused by their activities.[1] In 1974 the Commission adopted a memorandum on State aid in environmental matters which envisaged that environmental policies both at national and EU level were to be implemented, not by the grant of State aid, which simply passed the cost on to the public, but by imposing obligations on polluters in order to make them pay the cost of protecting the environment.[2] Article 3(3) TEU now stipulates that sustainable development is one of the objectives of the European Union, based on economic prosperity, social cohesion and a high level of protection of the environment. In addition, Article 11 TFEU provides that environmental protection requirements must be integrated into all EU policies and activities, in particular with a view to promoting sustainable development and Article 191(2) TFEU states that environment policy is to be based on the precautionary principle and on the principles that preventive action should be taken, that environmental damage should as a priority be rectified at source and that the polluter should pay. National support mechanisms are capable of contributing toward these objectives.[3] The General Court has, therefore, held that the Commission, when faced with an aid measure that is intended to protect the environment, must take these principles into account. It may be noted, however, that, where a measure does not have an environmental objective, the Commission is not required to take account of environmental

---

[1] Declaration of the Council of the European Communities and of the representatives of the Governments of the Member States of 22 November 1973, Part I, Title II, para 5.

[2] Commission Memorandum of 6 November 1974 on State aid in environmental matters; *Fourth Report on Competition Policy* (1974), pt. 175-182. Amendments were made in 1980 and 1986: see, respectively, *Tenth Report on Competition Policy* (1980), pts 222-226, and *Sixteenth Report on Competition Policy* (1986), pt 259.

[3] Case C-195/12, *Industrie do Bois de Vielsalm SA v Région Wallonne* EU:2013:598, para 59; Cases C-204/12 to C-208/12, *Essent Belgium NV v Vlaamse Reguleringsinstantie voor de Elektriciteits en Gasmarkt* EU:C:2013:2192, para 94.

regulation, since an aid which might have harmful effects on the environment is not necessarily contrary to the establishment of the internal market.[4]

Guidelines on aid for environmental protection were first adopted by the Commission in 1994.[5] On the basis of the experience gained and in the light of developments at national and international level during the 1990s particularly as regards energy taxes, the Commission adopted revised guidelines in 2001[6] and in 2008,[7] introducing provisions that in particular sought to ensure better targeted aid, improved economic analysis and more effective procedures, and taking into account developments in environmental policy and environmental technologies. Moreover, Commission Regulation (EC) No 800/2008 introduced provisions allowing for the block exemption of several categories of State aid for environmental protection.[8] Total expenditure for environmental purposes increased from €7 billion in 2001 to over €12 billion in 2011.[9] The present environmental and energy aid guidelines came into force on 1 July 2014[10] together with the revised block exemption provisions in Commission Regulation (EU) No 651/2014, Articles 36-49.

The EU's Europe 2020 strategy focuses on creating the conditions for smart, sustainable and inclusive growth. To that end, a number of headline targets have been set, including targets for climate change and energy sustainability: (i) a 20% reduction in EU greenhouse gas emissions when compared to 1990 levels; (ii) raising the share of EU energy consumption produced from renewable resources to 20%; and (iii) a 20% improvement in the EU's energy-efficiency compared to 1990 levels. In January 2014, the Commission proposed more ambitious energy and climate objectives to be met by 2030:[11] (i) a reduction in greenhouse gas emissions by 40% relative to the 1990 level; (ii) an EU-wide binding target for renewable energy of at least 27%; (iii) renewed ambitions for energy efficiency policies; and (iv) a new governance system and a set of new indicators to ensure a competitive and secure energy system.[12] The headline targets in the Europe 2020 strategy are particularly important for the 2014-2020 environmental and energy aid guidelines. In order to support achieving those targets, that strategy put forward the notion of a resource efficient Europe as a flagship initiative that

---

[4] Case T-57/11, *Castelnou Energía v Commission* EU:T:2014:1021, para 189.

[5] OJ 1994 C72/39.

[6] OJ 2001 C37/3.

[7] OJ 2008 C82/1.

[8] Commission Regulation (EC) No 800/2008, Articles 17-25.

[9] State aid scoreboard, Autumn 2012.

[10] OJ 2014 C200/1.

[11] Communication from the Commission to the European Parliament, the Council, the European Economic and Social Committee and the Committee of the Regions — A policy framework for climate and energy in the period from 2020 to 2030 (COM(2014) 15 final) of 22.1.2014.

[12] Environmental and energy aid guidelines 2014-2020, paras 3-4.

aims to create a framework for policies to support the shift towards a resource-efficient and low-carbon economy which helps to: boost economic performance while reducing use of resources; identify and create new opportunities for economic growth and greater innovation and boost the EU's competitiveness; ensure security of supply of essential resources; and fight against climate change and limit the environmental impacts of the use resources.[13] The Commission has also stated that the objectives of a secure, affordable and sustainable energy market will be undermined unless electricity grids are upgraded, obsolete plants are replaced by competitive and cleaner alternatives and energy is used more efficiently throughout the whole energy chain.[14] Delivery of the objective of reducing greenhouse gas emissions should follow a cost-efficient approach, providing flexibility to Member States to define a low-carbon transition appropriate to their specific circumstances and encourage research and innovation policy to support the post-2020 climate and energy framework. The guidelines respect those principles and prepare the ground for the 2030 Framework.[15]

Scope of the environmental and energy guidelines 2014-2020　The environmental and energy aid guidelines 2014-2020 apply to State aid granted for environmental protection or energy objectives in all sectors governed by the FEU Treaty. They apply equally to transport, coal, agriculture, forestry, and fisheries and aquaculture, unless specific rules provide otherwise.[16] For agriculture and fisheries and aquaculture, the guidelines apply to aid for environmental protection in favour of undertakings active in the processing and marketing of products and, under certain conditions, to undertakings active in primary production.[17]

The guidelines do not apply to:[18]

(a) the design and manufacture of environmentally friendly products, machines or means of transport with a view to operating with fewer natural resources and action taken within plants or other production units with a view to improving safety or hygiene;

(b) the financing of environmental protection measures relating to air, road, railway, inland waterway and maritime transport infrastructure;

(c) stranded costs as defined in the Commission Communication relating to the methodology for analysing State aid linked to stranded costs;

---

[13] *Ibid.*, paras 5-6.

[14] *Ibid.*, para 8; Commission communication: Energy 2020 – A strategy for competitive, sustainable and secure energy.

[15] Environmental and energy aid guidelines 2014-2020, para 9.

[16] The environmental and energy aid guidelines are without prejudice to the guidelines on State aid for railways.

[17] Environmental and energy aid guidelines 2014-2020, para 14.

[18] *Ibid.*, para 15.

(d)   State aid for research, development and innovation which is subject to the rules set out in the Community framework for State aid for research and development and innovation;

(e)   State aid to biodiversity measures.

Environmental and energy aid may not be awarded to firms in difficulty as defined by the guidelines on State aid for rescuing and restructuring firms in difficulty.[19]

Categories of permissible environmental and energy aid Several categories of environmental and energy aid measures have been identified by the Commission as being capable of being considered compatible with the internal market under Article 107(3)(c) TFEU. Aid may be granted in accordance with the conditions in the block exemption in Commission Regulation (EU) No 651/2014 for the following: investments enabling undertakings to go beyond EU standards or to increase the level of environmental protection in the absence of EU standards or for early adaptation to future EU standards; investments for energy efficiency measures, energy efficient projects in buildings and high-efficiency cogeneration; the promotion of energy from renewable energy sources; investments in remediation of contaminated sites, energy efficient district heating and cooling, waste recycling and re-utilisation and energy infrastructure; and environmental studies. Aid may also take the form of reductions in or exemptions from environmental taxes. Aid that satisfies the relevant conditions for the application of the block exemption is compatible with the internal market and exempt from the notification requirement of Article 108(3) TFEU.[20] More detailed provisions concerning these categories of aid are set out in the environmental and energy aid guidelines 2014-2020. In addition, the guidelines also allow aid relating to carbon and capture storage, generation adequacy, aid in the form of tradable permit schemes and aid for the relocation of undertakings.[21]

Notifiable environmental and energy aid Commission Regulation (EU) No 651/2014 requires that aid exceeding specified thresholds is not covered by the block exemption and must, accordingly, be individually notified to the Commission. The thresholds for environmental and energy aid are as follows:[22]

(a)   for investment aid for environmental protection, excluding investment aid for the remediation of contaminated sites and aid for the distribution network part of the energy efficient district heating and cooling installation: €15 million per undertaking per investment project;

---

[19]   *Ibid.*, para 16.
[20]   Commission Regulation (EU) No 651/2014, Articles 36-49.
[21]   Guidelines on environmental and energy aid 2014-2020, chapter 3.
[22]   Commission Regulation (EU) No 651/2014, Article 4(1)(s)-(x).

(b) for investment aid for energy efficiency projects: €10 million;

(c) for investment aid for remediation of contaminated sites: €20 million per undertaking per investment project;

(d) for operating aid for the production of electricity from renewable sources and operating aid for the promotion of energy from renewable sources in small scale installations: €15 million per undertaking per project. When the aid is granted on the basis of a competitive bidding process: €150 million per year taking into account all relevant schemes;

(e) for investment aid for the district heating or cooling distribution network: €20 million per undertaking per investment project;

(f) for investment aid for energy infrastructure: €50 million per undertaking, per investment project.

Under the guidelines, individual aid granted on the basis of an aid scheme must be notified where the specified thresholds are exceeded:[23]

(a) investment aid: where the aid amount exceeds EUR 15 million for one undertaking;

(b) operating aid for the production of renewable electricity and/or combined production of renewable heat: where the aid is granted to renewable electricity installations at sites where the resulting renewable electricity generation capacity per site exceeds 250 MW;

(c) operating aid for the production of biofuel: where the aid is granted to a biofuel production installation at sites where the resulting production exceeds 150 000 tonnes per year;

(d) operating aid for cogeneration: where aid is granted to cogeneration installation with the resulting cogeneration electricity capacity exceeding 300 MW;

(e) aid for energy infrastructure: where the aid amount exceeds €50 million for one undertaking, per investment project;

(f) aid for Carbon Capture and Storage: where the aid amount exceeds €50 million per investment project;

(g) aid in the form of a generation adequacy measure: where the aid amount exceeds €15 million per project per undertaking.

Aid in the form of tax exemptions and reductions from environmental taxes and exemptions from the financing of energy from renewable sources will not be subject to the conditions for individually notified aid. However, aid granted in the form of fiscal aid not covered by the provisions governing that aid in the guidelines will be subject to an individual assessment if the thresholds in those provisions are exceeded.[24]

Environment aid measures not covered by the guidelines Where a matter is not dealt with in the guidelines, the Commission may consider the

---

[23] Guidelines on environmental and energy aid 2014-2020, para 20.

[24] *Ibid.*, para 21.

compatibility of the aid directly on the basis of Article 107(3)(c) TFEU.[25] For example, the United Kingdom notified the waste and resources action programme (WRAP) which comprised a grant funding scheme and a guarantee scheme. The logic behind all projects funded by WRAP was to create a demand for waste products by subsidising investments in recycling facilities with the aim of encouraging local authorities to collect them. The 2001 environmental aid guidelines were inapplicable because they normally applied to investments that aimed at reducing the pollution caused by the aid beneficiary, whereas WRAP was meant to apply to situations where the whole economic activity of the beneficiary was environmentally beneficial. In approving the measures, the Commission noted that they supported waste recycling which was a priority EU environmental objective and that the aid was necessary to overcome the extra costs linked to the recycling of certain waste products that are hardly reprocessed at all or to the development of new recycling technologies that were not market tested. The aid measures, which were in line with the eligible costs and aid intensities in the guidelines, were therefore proportionate to the objectives pursued.[26]

12.2 COMPATIBILITY CRITERIA IN THE EEAG GUIDELINES

Common assessment principles To assess whether a notified aid measure can be considered compatible with the internal market pursuant to the environmental and energy aid guidelines 2014-2020, the Commission analyses whether the design of the aid measure ensures that the positive impact of the aid towards an objective of common interest exceeds its potential negative effects on trade and competition. In accordance with the Communication on State aid modernisation, the Commission will consider an aid measure compatible with the internal market only if it satisfies each of the following criteria: contribution to a well-defined objective of common interest; need for State intervention; appropriateness of the measure; incentive effect; proportionality of the aid; avoidance of undue negative effects on competition and trade between Member States; and transparency of the aid. The overall balance of certain categories of schemes may further be made subject to a requirement of *ex post* evaluation. In such cases, the Commission may limit the duration of those schemes, normally to four years or less, with a possibility to re-notify their prolongation afterwards.[27]

State aid with environmental protection and energy objectives will be considered compatible with the internal market within the meaning of Article

---

[25] Case T-375/03, *Fachvereinigung Mineralfaserindustrie eV Deutsche Gruppe der Eurima v Commission* [2007] II-121*, para 143.

[26] *Thirty-Third Report on Competition Policy* (2003), pts. 452-454.

[27] Environmental and energy aid guidelines 2014-2020, paras 26-28.

107(3)(c) TFEU if it leads to an increased contribution to the EU environmental or energy objectives without adversely affecting trading conditions to an extent contrary to the common interest. The specific handicaps of assisted areas will be taken into account.[28]

Contribution to an objective of common interest The general objective of environmental aid is to increase the level of environmental protection compared to the level that would be achieved in the absence of the aid. The Europe 2020 strategy in particular set targets and objectives for sustainable growth to support the shift towards a resource-efficient, competitive low carbon economy. A low carbon economy with a significant share of variable energy from renewable sources requires an adjustment of the energy system and in particular considerable investments in energy networks. The primary objective of aid in the energy sector is to ensure a competitive, sustainable and secure energy system in a well-functioning EU energy market. Member States intending to grant environmental or energy aid will have to define precisely the objective pursued and explain the expected contribution of the measure towards this objective. When introducing a measure co-financed by the European Structural and Investments Funds, Member States may rely on the reasoning in the relevant operational programmes in indicating the environmental or energy objectives pursued.[29]

To demonstrate the contribution of an individually notifiable aid towards an increased level of environmental protection, Member States may use a variety of indicators. For abatement technologies, the amount of greenhouse gases or pollutants that are permanently not emitted in the atmosphere, resulting in reduced input from fossil fuels, should be assessed. In the case of aid for going beyond existing EU standards, the absolute amount and relative size of the increase in the level of environmental protection over and above the EU standard should be shown, indicating the reduction of pollution that would not be achieved by the standard in the absence of the aid. In the case of aid for early implementation of EU standards, details should be given of the increase in the rate at which future standards are to be implemented.[30]

Need for State intervention Member States should identify the market failures hampering an increased level of environmental protection or a well-functioning secure, affordable and sustainable internal energy market. Negative externalities are most common for environmental aid measures and arise when the firm in question does not face the full cost of pollution. In this case, undertakings acting in their own interest may have insufficient incentives to take the negative externalities arising from production into account. In other

---

[28] *Ibid.*, para 23.
[29] *Ibid.*, paras 30-31.
[30] *Ibid.*, para 33.

words, the production costs that are borne by the undertaking are lower than the costs borne by society. Positive externalities, i.e. the fact that part of the benefit from an investment will accrue to market participants other than the investor, may occur for instance in case of investments in eco-innovation, system stability, new and innovative renewable technologies and innovative demand-response measures or in case of energy infrastructures or generation adequacy measures that benefit many Member States or a wider number of consumers. This may lead undertakings to underinvest.[31]

The mere existence of market failures in a certain context is not sufficient to justify State intervention. In particular, other policies and measures may already be in place, including sectoral regulation, mandatory pollution standards, pricing mechanisms such as the EU Emissions Trading System and carbon taxes. Additional measures including State aid may only be directed at the market failure that remains unaddressed by such other policies and measures. It is also important to show how State aid reinforces other policies and measures in place that aim at remedying the same market failure.[32]

For notifiable individual aid, the Commission will assess the specific need for aid in the case at hand. Depending on the specific market failure addressed, the Commission will take into account the following factors: whether other policy measures already sufficiently address the market failure, in particular the existence of environmental or other EU standards, the EU ETS or environmental taxes; whether State intervention is needed, taking into account, the cost of implementation of national standards for the aid beneficiary in the absence of aid compared to the costs, or absence thereof, of implementation of those standards for the main competitors of the aid beneficiary; in the case of coordination failures, the number of undertakings required to collaborate, diverging interests between collaborating parties and practical problems to coordinate collaboration, such as linguistic issues, sensitivity of information and non-harmonised standards.[33]

Appropriateness of the aid   The aid measure must be an appropriate instrument to address the policy objective concerned. State aid is not the only policy instrument available to Member States to promote increased levels of environmental protection or to achieve a well-functioning secure, affordable and sustainable EU energy market. There may be other, better placed instruments to achieve those objectives, such as regulation and market-based instruments. Soft instruments, such as voluntary eco-labels, and the diffusion of environmentally friendly technologies may also play an important role in achieving a higher level of environmental protection.[34]

---

[31]   *Ibid.*, para 35.
[32]   *Ibid.*, paras 36-37.
[33]   *Ibid.*, paras 38-39.
[34]   *Ibid.*, paras 40-41.

Respect for the polluter pays principle through environmental legislation ensures in principle that the market failure linked to negative externalities will be rectified. Therefore, State aid is not an appropriate instrument and cannot be granted insofar as the beneficiary of the aid could be held liable for the pollution under existing EU or national law. Moreover, where an efficient, market-based mechanism has been put in place to deal specifically with the problem of externalities, an additional support measure to address the same market failure may undermine the efficiency of that market-based mechanism. Different measures to remedy different market failures may also counteract each other. For example, a measure addressing a generation adequacy problem needs to be balanced with the environmental objective of phasing out environmentally or economically harmful subsidies. Similarly, a measure to reduce greenhouse gas emissions can increase the supply of variable power which might negatively affect generation adequacy concerns.[35]

Member States should ensure that aid is awarded in the form that is likely to generate the least distortions of trade and competition. The choice of the aid instrument should be coherent with the market failure that the aid measure aims at addressing. In particular where the actual revenues are uncertain, for instance in case of energy saving measures, a repayable advance may constitute the appropriate instrument. For aid schemes implementing the objectives and priorities of operational programmes, the financing instrument chosen in this programme is in principle presumed to be an appropriate instrument. For operating aid, the Member State must demonstrate that the aid is appropriate to achieve the objective of the scheme to which the aid is targeted, for example by calculating the aid amount *ex ante* as a fixed sum covering the expected additional costs over a given period so as to incentivise undertakings to minimise their costs and develop their business in a more efficient manner over time.[36]

Incentive effect Environmental and energy aid can only be found compatible with the internal market if it has an incentive effect. An incentive effect occurs when the aid induces the beneficiary to change its behaviour to increase the level of environmental protection or to improve the functioning of a secure, affordable and sustainable energy market, a change in behaviour which it would not undertake without the aid.[37] For example, under the Energy Efficiency Directive 2012/27/EU, large enterprises have to carry out energy audits every four years, so that aid for energy audits for large enterprises can have an incentive effect only to the extent that the aid does not compensate an energy audit required by the directive, whereas, since the same obligation is not imposed on SMEs, State aid granted to SMEs for carrying out the energy

---

[35] *Ibid.*, paras 42-44.

[36] *Ibid.*, paras 45-47.

[37] *Ibid.*, para 50.

audit can have an incentive effect.[38]   For measures subject to individual notification, the Member State must fully demonstrate the incentive effect of the aid by providing clear evidence that the aid has an effective impact on the investment decision, including, where possible, a comprehensive description of the counterfactual scenario, in which no aid is awarded to the beneficiary.[39]

Proportionality of the aid   Environmental and energy aid is considered to be proportionate if the aid amount per beneficiary is limited to the minimum needed to achieve the environmental protection or energy objective aimed for. As a general principle, aid will be considered to be limited to the minimum necessary if the aid corresponds to the net extra costs necessary to meet the objective, compared to the counterfactual scenario in the absence of aid. For measures which are not subject to an individual assessment, a simplified method that would focus on calculating the extra investment costs may be used. Measures which are not subject to an individual assessment will be deemed proportionate if the aid amount does not exceed the maximum aid intensity. Those maximum aid intensities also serve as a cap to the aid given for notifiable measures.[40]

For individual aid, however, compliance with the maximum intensity is not sufficient to ensure proportionality. As a general rule, individually notifiable aid will be considered to be limited to the minimum if the aid amount corresponds to the net extra costs of the investment, compared to the counterfactual scenario in the absence of aid, taking into account all relevant costs and benefits over the lifetime of the project. If no specific alternative project can be identified as a counterfactual scenario, the Commission will verify whether the aid amount exceeds the minimum necessary to make the project sufficiently profitable, for instance whether it increases its internal rate of return beyond the normal rates of return applied by the undertaking concerned in other investment projects of a similar kind.   When that benchmark is not available, the cost of capital of the company as a whole or rates of return commonly observed in the industry concerned may be used for that purpose.[41]   For operating aid granted by way of a competitive bidding process, the proportionality of individual aid is presumed to be met if the general conditions are fulfilled.[42]

Eligible costs   The eligible costs for environmental aid are the extra investment costs in tangible and/or in intangible assets which are directly linked to the achievement of the common objective.   Where the costs of

---

[38]   *Ibid.*, paras 56-57.
[39]   *Ibid.*, para 58.
[40]   *Ibid.*, paras 69-71.
[41]   *Ibid.*, paras 83-85.
[42]   *Ibid.*, para 87.

achieving the common interest objective can be identified in the total investment costs as a separate investment, for instance, because the green element is a readily identifiable add-on component to a pre-existing facility, the costs of the separate investment constitute the eligible costs. For measures related to remediation of contaminated sites, the eligible costs are equal to the cost of the remediation work less the increase in the value of the land. In all other cases, the eligible costs are the extra investment costs established by comparing the aided investment with the counterfactual situation in the absence of State aid.[43]

Maximum aid intensities In order to ensure predictability and a level playing field, the Commission applies maximum aid intensities for each category of aid.[44] The aid intensity may be increased by 15 percentage points for energy and environmental investments located in Article 107(3)(a) areas and by 5 percentage points for energy and environmental investments located in Article 107(3)(c) areas. It can also be increased by 10 percentage points for medium sized enterprises and 20 percentage points for small enterprises. With regard to SMEs which may be faced, on the one hand, with relatively higher costs to achieve environmental or energy objectives compared to the size of their activity and, on the other hand, with capital market imperfections which force them to bear such costs, higher aid intensities may also be warranted. In the case of eco-innovation, in particular with resource efficiency measures, the aid intensity may be increased by 10 percentage points, provided that following cumulative conditions are fulfilled: the eco-innovation asset or project must be new or substantially improved; the expected environmental benefit must be significantly higher than the improvement resulting from the general evolution of the state of the art in comparable activities; and the innovative character of the assets or projects involves a clear increased degree of risk, in technological, market or financial terms.[45] Where aid to the beneficiary is granted in a competitive bidding process on the basis of clear, transparent and non-discriminatory criteria, the aid amount may reach 100% of the eligible costs.[46]

Negative effects on competition and trade For environment and energy aid to be compatible with the internal market, the negative effects of the aid measure in terms of distortions of competition and impact on trade between Member States must be limited and outweighed by the positive effects in terms

---

[43] *Ibid.*, paras 72-74. Annex 2 to the guidelines contains a list of the relevant counterfactual scenarios or eligible cost calculations.

[44] Environmental and energy aid guidelines 2014-2020, para 77 and Annex I.

[45] *Ibid.*, para 78. The aid intensity must never exceed 100% of eligible costs.

[46] Environmental and energy aid guidelines 2014-2020, para 80. The aid must be granted on the basis of the initial bid submitted by the bidder, therefore excluding subsequent negotiations.

of contribution to the objective of environmental protection. Aid for environmental purposes will by its very nature tend to favour environmentally friendly products and technologies at the expense of other, more polluting ones and that effect of the aid will, in principle, not be viewed as an undue distortion of competition, since it is inherently linked to the very objective of the aid. When assessing the potential negative effects of environmental aid, the Commission will take into account the overall environmental effect of the measure in relation to its negative impact on the market position and profits, of non-aided firms, particularly those that operate on an environmentally friendly basis without aid.[47] One potentially harmful effect of environmental and energy aid is that it prevents the market mechanism from delivering efficient outcomes by rewarding the most efficient and innovative producers and putting pressure on the least inefficient to improve, restructure or exit the market. Aid may also have distortive effects by strengthening or maintaining substantial market power of the beneficiary. It may also give rise to effects on trade and location choice. For example, aid aimed at preserving economic activity in one region or attracting it away from other regions may displace activities or investments from one region into another without any net environmental impact.[48]

There are situations where the negative effects of the aid manifestly outweigh any positive effects, such that the aid cannot be found compatible with the internal market. The maximum aid intensities set by the Commission constitute a basic requirement for compatibility. Likewise, environmental and energy aid that merely leads to a change in location of the economic activity without improving the existing level of environmental protection in the Member States will not be considered compatible with the internal market.[49] By contrast, if aid measures are proportionate and well targeted to the market failure they aim to address, the risk that the aid will unduly distort competition is more limited. In order to keep the distortions of competition and trade to a minimum, the Commission will place great emphasis on the selection process. Where possible, the selection process should be conducted in a non-discriminatory, transparent and open manner, without unnecessarily excluding companies that may compete with projects to address the same environmental or energy objective. The selection process should lead to the selection of beneficiaries that can address the environmental or energy objectives using the least amount of aid or in the most cost-effective way.[50] The Commission will in particular assess the negative effects of the aid by considering any reduction in or compensation for production unit costs. If the new equipment will lead to reduced costs per unit produced compared to the situation without the aid or if

---

47 Environmental and energy aid guidelines 2014-2020, paras 88-90.
48 *Ibid.*, paras 91-93.
49 *Ibid.*, paras 94-96.
50 *Ibid.*, paras 97-99.

the aid compensates a part of the operating cost, it is likely that the beneficiaries will increase sales. The more price elastic the product, the greater the potential of the aid for distorting competition. Similarly, in the case of new products, if the beneficiaries obtain a new or a higher quality product, it is likely that they will increase their sales and possibly gain a first mover advantage.[51]

In the case of individually notified aid, the Commission will also take into account whether the aid leads to: supporting inefficient production, thereby impeding productivity growth in the sector; distorting dynamic incentives; creating or enhancing market power or exclusionary practices; or artificially altering trade flows or the location of production. The Commission may consider the planned introduction of energy and environmental support schemes, other than the one notified, which directly or indirectly benefit the beneficiary with a view to assessing the cumulative impact of the aid. The Commission will also assess whether the aid results in some territories benefiting from more favourable production conditions, notably because of comparatively lower production costs as a result of the aid or because of higher production standards achieved through the aid. This may result in companies staying in or re-locating to the aided territories, or to displacement of trade flows towards the aided area. In its analysis of notifiable individual aid, the Commission will accordingly take into account any evidence that the aid beneficiary has considered alternative locations.[52]

12.3 CATEGORIES OF AID FOR ENVIRONMENTAL PROTECTION

Aid for exceeding EU standards Investment aid enabling undertakings to go beyond EU standards for environmental protection or increase the level of environmental protection in the absence of EU standards is permissible under the guidelines and the block exemption. Normally, an undertaking does not have an incentive to go beyond mandatory standards if the cost of doing so exceeds the benefit for the undertaking. In such cases, aid may be granted to give an incentive to undertakings to improve environmental protection. The investment must enable the beneficiary to increase the level of environmental protection resulting from its activities by going beyond the applicable EU standards, irrespective of the presence of mandatory national standards that are more stringent than the EU standard. Alternatively, the investment must enable the beneficiary to increase the level of environmental protection resulting from its activities in the absence of EU standards. Aid may not be

---

[51] *Ibid.*, para 100.
[52] *Ibid.*, paras 101-103.

granted where improvements bring companies into line with EU standards already adopted and not yet in force.[53]

In the case of individual notifiable aid, where an undertaking is adapting to a national standard going beyond EU standards or adopted in the absence of EU standards, the Commission will verify that the aid beneficiary would have been affected substantially in terms of increased costs and would not have been able to bear the costs associated with the immediate implementation of national standards. For investments that bring undertakings above the minimum levels required by EU standards, the Commission can still find no incentive effect, in particular if such investments correspond to the minimum technical standards available in the market. If the aid does not change the behaviour of the beneficiary by stimulating additional activities, that aid does not have incentive effect in terms of promoting environmental behaviour in the EU or strengthening the functioning of the EU energy market.[54] For example, aid was granted by Italy in respect of interventions in the production process of plastic additives aimed at reducing the environmental impact of the factory by tackling the amount of chlorine acids and liquid waste. The Italian authorities provided evidence that the project went beyond the best available techniques according to EU standards.[55] The Commission has also authorised aid in favour of investments for carbon capture and sequestration to reduce CO_2 emissions[56] and for noise reduction.[57]

Aid for the acquisition of new transport vehicles for road, railway, inland waterway and maritime transport complying with adopted EU standards is permissible, when such acquisition occurs before these EU standards enter into force and where, once mandatory, they do not apply retroactively to already purchased vehicles. Aid for retrofitting of transport vehicles with an environmental protection objective may also be permitted.[58] For example, in the *Volvo Truck* case, the Commission approved aid for investments that reduced the noise level from producing trucks during night time and the level of volatile organic compounds from painting the trucks, which resulted in emission levels better than required by the EU standards.[59]

The eligible costs shall be the extra investment costs necessary to go beyond the applicable EU standards or to increase the level of environmental protection in the absence of EU standards. Costs not directly linked to the

[53]   *Ibid.*, para 55; Commission Regulation (EU) No 651/2014, Article 36(1)-(3).
[54]   Environmental and energy aid guidelines 2014-2020, paras 66-68.
[55]   Case N 506/2005, *CIBA Speciality Chemicals SpA*, OJ 2006 C276/16. See also, Case N 346/2004, *Altair*, OJ 2005 C131/10; Case N528/2006, *Solvay*, OJ 2008 C80/1.
[56]   Case N 861/2006, *Clean fossil energy*, OJ 2007 C141/1.
[57]   Case N 266/2006, *Nijmeegsche IJzergieterij*, OJ 2006 C306/12.
[58]   Environmental and energy aid guidelines 2014-2020, para 54; Commission Regulation (EU) No 651/2014, Article 36(4).
[59]   Case N 75/2005, *Volvo Trucks*, OJ 2005 C230/6.

achievement of a higher level of environmental protection are not eligible.[60] The aid intensity must not exceed 40% of the eligible costs. The guidelines provide that the aid intensity may be up to 50% in the case of investment in eco-innovation. The relevant aid intensity may be increased by 20 percentage points for aid awarded to small enterprises and by 10 percentage points for aid awarded to medium-sized enterprises. The aid intensity may be increased by 15 percentage points for investments located in Article 107(3)(a) areas and by 5 percentage points for investments located in Article 107(3)(c) areas.[61] Where the investment aid is granted in a genuinely competitive bidding process, the guidelines provide that the aid intensity may amount to up to 100% of the investment cost.[62]

Aid for early adaptation to EU standards Aid encouraging undertakings to comply with new EU standards which increase the level of environmental protection and are not yet in force is permissible under the guidelines and the block exemption, provided that the EU standards have been adopted, and the investment has been implemented and finalised at least one year before the entry into force of the standard concerned. The eligible costs are the extra investment costs necessary to go beyond the applicable EU standard. Costs not directly linked to the achievement of a higher level of environmental protection are not eligible.[63]

The aid intensity must not exceed 20% of the eligible costs for small enterprises, 15% for medium-sized enterprises and 10% for large undertakings, if the implementation and finalisation of the investment take place more than three years before entry into force of the new EU standard, and 15% for small enterprises, 10% for medium-sized enterprises and 5% for large undertakings if the implementation and finalisation take place between one and three years before the entry into force of the new standard. The aid intensity may be increased by 15 percentage points for investments located in Article 107(3)(a) areas and by 5 percentage points for investments located in Article 107(3)(c) areas.[64]

Investment aid to energy from renewable sources The EU set ambitious climate change and energy sustainability targets in particular as part of its EU 2020 strategy. It is expected that in the period between 2020 and 2030 established renewable energy sources will become grid-competitive, implying

---

[60] Commission Regulation (EU) No 651/2014, Article 36(5).
[61] Environmental and energy aid guidelines 2014-2020, Annex I; Commission Regulation (EU) No 651/2014, Article 36(6)-(8).
[62] Environmental and energy aid guidelines 2014-2020, Annex I.
[63] *Ibid.*, para 53; Commission Regulation (EU) No 651/2014, Article 37(1)-(3).
[64] Environmental and energy aid guidelines 2014-2020, Annex I; Commission Regulation (EU) No 651/2014, Article 37(4)-(5).

that subsidies and exemptions from balancing responsibilities should be phased out.[65] Market instruments, such as auctioning or competitive bidding process open to all generators producing electricity from renewable energy sources, should normally ensure that subsidies are reduced to a minimum. However, given the different stage of technological development of renewable energy technologies, the guidelines allow technology specific tenders to be carried out by Member States, on the basis of the longer term potential of a given new and innovative technology, the need to achieve diversification; network constraints and grid stability and system integration costs.[66]

The environmental and energy guidelines and the block exemption approve certain types of investment aid for the promotion of energy from renewable sources, subject to various conditions. Investment aid in new and existing capacity for food-based biofuel is not permitted, other than aid to cover the costs of converting food-based biofuel plants into advanced biofuel plants. Aid may not be granted for biofuels which are subject to a supply or blending obligation.[67] While the EU ETS and CO_2 taxes help to internalise the costs of greenhouse gas emissions, aid can contribute to the achievement of the related, but distinct, EU objectives for renewable energy.[68] Aid for the production of hydropower, which has a positive impact on greenhouse gas emissions, may be granted provided it complies with Directive 2000/60/EC on EU water policy.[69] Aid for energy from renewable sources using waste, including waste heat, as input fuel can make a positive contribution to environmental protection, provided that it does not circumvent that principle.[70] The Commission will authorise aid schemes for a maximum period of 10 years.[71]

For investment aid, the aid intensity must not exceed 45%, with increases permitted up to 20 percentage points for aid awarded to small enterprises and 10 percentage points for aid awarded to medium-sized enterprises. The aid intensity may be increased by 15 percentage points for investments located in Article 107(3)(a) areas and by 5 percentage points for investments located in Article 107(3)(c) areas. Where the investment aid is granted in a genuinely competitive bidding process, the aid intensity may amount to up to 100% of the investment cost.[72] The eligible costs are the extra costs necessary to promote

---

[65] Environmental and energy aid guidelines 2014-2020, paras 107-108.

[66] *Ibid.*, paras 109-111.

[67] *Ibid.*, paras 112-114; Commission Regulation (EU) No 651/2014, Article 41(2)-(3).

[68] Environmental and energy aid guidelines 2014-2020, paras 115-116.

[69] *Ibid.*, para 117; Commission Regulation (EU) No 651/2014, Article 41(4).

[70] Environmental and energy aid guidelines 2014-2020, para 118.

[71] *Ibid.*, para 121. Existing and newly notified schemes concerning food-based biofuel should be limited to 2020.

[72] Environmental and energy aid guidelines, Annex I; Commission Regulation (EU) No 651/2014, Article 41(7)-(10).

the production of energy from renewable sources, excluding costs not directly linked to the achievement of a higher level of environmental protection.[73]

Operating aid for energy from renewable sources Operating aid may be granted for the promotion of electricity from renewable sources. In order to incentivise the market integration of electricity from renewable sources, the environmental and energy guidelines provide that, from 2016, all new operating aid schemes and measures must comply with the following conditions: aid must be granted as a premium in addition to the market price whereby the generators sell their electricity directly in the market; beneficiaries must be subject to standard balancing responsibilities, unless no liquid intra-day markets exist; and measures must be put in place to ensure that generators have no incentive to generate electricity under negative prices.[74] In a transitional phase covering 2015 and 2016, aid for at least 5% of the planned new electricity capacity from renewable energy sources should be granted in a competitive bidding process on the basis of clear, transparent and non-discriminatory criteria. From 1 January 2017, aid must be granted in a competitive bidding process, unless the Member State demonstrates that only one or a very limited number of projects or sites could be eligible, or a competitive bidding process would lead to higher support levels or low project realisation rates. The bidding process may be limited to specific technologies where a process open to all generators would lead to a sub-optimal result which cannot be addressed in the process design in view of, in particular, the longer-term potential of a given new and innovative technology, the need to achieve diversification, network constraints and grid stability, system integration costs or the need to avoid distortions on the raw material markets from biomass support.[75] The aid may only be granted until the plant has been fully depreciated according to normal accounting rules and any investment aid previously received must be deducted from the operating aid.[76] The block exemption also provides for operating aid to be considered compatible with the internal market where the aid is granted in a competitive bidding process, with specific provisions applicable to small scale installations.[77]

---

[73] Commission Regulation (EU) No 651/2014, Article 41(6).

[74] Environmental and energy aid guidelines 2014-2020, paras 124-125. These conditions do not apply to installations with an installed electricity capacity of less than 500 kW or demonstration projects, except for electricity from wind energy where an installed electricity capacity of 3 MW or 3 generation units applies.

[75] Environmental and energy aid guidelines 2014-2020, paras 126-127. Aid may be granted without a competitive bidding process to installations with an installed electricity capacity of less than 1 MW, or demonstration projects, except for electricity from wind energy, for installations with an installed electricity capacity of up to 6 MW or 6 generation units.

[76] Environmental and energy aid guidelines 2014-2020, para 129.

[77] Commission Regulation (EU) No 651/2014, Articles 42-43.

As regards aid for energy from renewable sources other than electricity, operating aid will be considered compatible with the internal market if the following cumulative conditions are met: the aid per unit of energy does not exceed the difference between the total levelised costs of producing energy (LCOE) from the particular technology in question and the market price of the form of energy concerned; the LCOE may include a normal return on capital, with investment aid being deducted from the total investment amount in calculating the LCOE; the production costs are updated regularly, at least every year; and aid is only granted until the plant has been fully depreciated according to normal accounting rules in order to avoid that operating aid based on LCOE exceeds the depreciation of the investment.[78] In the case of biomass, which requires relatively low investment costs but higher operating costs which may prevent a biomass plant from operating even after depreciation of the installation, operating aid, subject to certain conditions, may be permitted where the aid is granted on the basis of the energy produced from renewable sources and compensates the difference in operating costs borne by the beneficiary and the market price or the costs of fossil fuels.[79]

Member States may grant support for renewable energy sources by using market mechanisms such as green certificates that allow all renewable energy producers to benefit indirectly from guaranteed demand for their energy, at a price above the market price for conventional power. The price of these green certificates is not fixed in advance, but depends on market supply and demand. The Commission will consider this aid to be compatible with the internal market if Member States can provide sufficient evidence that such support: is essential to ensure the viability of the renewable energy sources concerned; does not, for the scheme in the aggregate, result in overcompensation over time and across technologies, or in overcompensation for individual less deployed technologies in so far as differentiated levels of certificates per unit of output are introduced; and does not dissuade renewable energy producers from becoming more competitive. Any investment aid previously received must be deducted from the operating aid.[80]

An example of aid for renewable energy sources is a German measure with a budget of €180 million providing aid for solar collector installations, biomass installations for heating or CHP, electric heat pump installations for water or room heating, geothermic installations, photovoltaic installations and small hydroelectric plants.[81]

Aid for energy efficiency measures   The Energy Efficiency Directive 2012/27/EU establishes a common framework to promote energy efficiency

---

[78]   Environmental and energy aid guidelines 2014-2020, para 131.
[79]   *Ibid.*, para 133.
[80]   *Ibid.*, paras 135-137.
[81]   Case N 458/2006, *German renewable energy measures*, OJ 2007 C9/1.

pursuing the overall objective of achieving the EU's 2020 headline target of saving 20% of the its primary energy consumption. This puts an obligation on Member States to achieve specified targets but does not impose energy efficient targets on undertakings.[82] Investment aid enabling undertakings to achieve energy savings is permissible under the guidelines and the block exemption. The guidelines also permit operating aid to be awarded.[83]

Eligible costs are the extra investment costs necessary to achieve the higher levels of energy efficiency. Costs not directly linked to the achievement of a higher level of environmental protection are not eligible.[84] For investment aid, the aid intensity must not exceed 30% of the eligible costs, with increases permitted up to 20 percentage points for aid awarded to small enterprises and 10 percentage points for aid awarded to medium-sized enterprises. The aid intensity may be increased by 15 percentage points for investments located in Article 107(3)(a) areas and by 5 percentage points for investments located in Article 107(3)(c) areas. In addition, where the investment aid is granted in a genuinely competitive bidding process, the guidelines provide that the aid intensity may amount to up to 100% of the investment cost.[85]

Operating aid may be granted under the guidelines where the aid is limited to compensating for net extra production costs resulting from the investment, taking account of benefits resulting from energy saving and the aid is subject to a limited duration of five years. In determining the amount of operating aid, any investment aid granted to the undertaking in question in respect of the new plant must be deducted from production costs.[86]

Aid for energy efficiency projects in buildings Investment aid may be granted for energy efficiency projects in buildings pursuant to the block exemption. Eligible costs are the overall costs of the energy efficiency project. The aid must be granted in the form of an endowment, equity, guarantee or loan to an energy efficiency fund or other financial intermediary, which shall fully pass it on to the final beneficiaries being the building owners or tenants. The aid granted by the energy efficiency fund or other financial intermediary to the eligible energy efficiency projects may take the form of loans or guarantees. The nominal value of the loan or the amount guaranteed must not exceed €10 million per project at the level of the final beneficiaries and the guarantee should not exceed 80% of the underlying loan. The repayment by the building owners to the energy efficiency fund or other financial intermediary must not be less than the nominal value of the loan. The energy

---

[82] Environmental and energy aid guidelines 2014-2020, paras 138-144.
[83] *Ibid.*, paras 149-150; Commission Regulation (EU) No 651/2014, Article 38(1).
[84] Commission Regulation (EU) No 651/2014, Article 38(3).
[85] Environmental and energy aid guidelines 2014-2020, Annex I; Commission Regulation (EU) No 651/2014, Article 38(4)-(6).
[86] Environmental and energy aid guidelines 2014-2020, para 150.

efficiency aid must leverage additional investment from private investors reaching at minimum 30% of the total financing provided to an energy efficiency project. When the aid is provided by an energy efficiency fund, the leverage of private investment can be done at the level of the energy efficiency fund and/or at the level of the energy efficiency projects, so as to achieve an aggregate minimum 30% of the total financing provided to an energy efficiency project.[87]

In order to provide energy efficiency aid, Member States can set up energy efficiency funds and/or can use financial intermediaries, which must be managed on a commercial basis and ensure profit-driven financing decisions, on the following conditions:[88]

(a) financial intermediary managers, as well as energy efficiency fund managers, must be selected through an open, transparent and non-discriminatory process;

(b) independent private investors shall be selected through an open, transparent and non-discriminatory call aimed at establishing the appropriate risk-reward sharing arrangements whereby, for investments other than guarantees, asymmetric profit-sharing shall be given preference over downside protection. If the private investors are not selected by such a call, the fair rate of return to the private investors shall be established by an independent expert selected via an open, transparent and non-discriminatory call;

(c) in the case of asymmetric loss-sharing between public and private investors, the first loss assumed by the public investor shall be capped at 25% of the total investment;

(d) in the case of guarantees, the guarantee rate shall be limited to 80% and total losses assumed by a Member State shall be capped at 25% of the underlying guaranteed portfolio;

(e) investors shall be allowed to be represented in the governance bodies of the energy efficiency fund or financial intermediary, such as the supervisory board or the advisory committee;

(f) the energy efficiency fund or financial intermediary shall be established according to the applicable laws and the Member State must provide for a due diligence process in order to ensure a commercially sound investment strategy for the purpose of implementing the energy efficiency aid measure.

Aid for high efficiency co-generation Investment aid for high-efficiency co-generation is permissible under the guidelines and the block exemption. The

---

[87]   Commission Regulation (EU) No 651/2014, Article 39(1)-(7).
[88]   *Ibid.*, Article 39(8)-(9).

guidelines also permit operating aid to be granted.[89] Cogeneration of heat and electricity (CHP) is the most efficient way of producing electricity and heat simultaneously. By producing both electricity and heat together, less energy is wasted in production. The guidelines state that, in order to ensure that aid contributes to a higher level of environmental protection, aid for district heating and district cooling and CHP will only be considered compatible with the internal market if granted for investment, including upgrades, to high-efficient CHP and energy-efficient district heating and district cooling.[90] For investment aid to fall within the block exemption, which applies only in the case of newly installed or refurbished capacities, the new cogeneration unit must provide overall primary energy savings compared to separate production of heat and electricity as provided for by the Energy Efficiency Directive 2012/27/EU. The improvement of an existing cogeneration unit or conversion of an existing power generation unit into a cogeneration unit must result in primary energy savings compared to the original situation.[91]

For investment aid, eligible costs are the extra investment costs for the equipment needed for the installation to operate as a high-efficiency cogeneration installation, compared to conventional electricity or heating installations of the same capacity or the extra investment cost to upgrade to a higher efficiency when an existing installation already meets the high-efficiency threshold.[92] The aid intensity must not exceed 45%, although this may be increased by 20 percentage points for aid awarded to small enterprises and by 10 percentage points for aid awarded to medium-sized enterprises. The aid intensity may be increased by 15 percentage points for investments located in Article 107(3)(a) areas and by 5 percentage points for investments located in Article 107(3)(c) areas. In addition, where the investment aid is granted in a genuinely competitive bidding process, the guidelines provide that the aid intensity may amount to up to 100% of the investment cost.[93]

Operating aid for high energy efficient cogeneration plants may be granted under the guidelines on the basis of the conditions applying to operating aid for electricity from renewable energy sources either to undertakings generating electric power and heat to the public where the costs of producing such electric power or heat exceed its market price or for the industrial use of the combined production of electric power and heat where it can be shown that the production cost of one unit of energy using that technique exceeds the market price of one unit of conventional energy.[94]

---

[89] Environmental and energy aid guidelines 2014-2020, paras 149-151; Commission Regulation (EU) No 651/2014, Article 40(1).

[90] Environmental and energy aid guidelines 2014-2020, para 139.

[91] Commission Regulation (EU) No 651/2014, Article 40(2)-(3).

[92] *Ibid.*, Article 40(4).

[93] Environmental and energy aid guidelines 2014-2020, Annex I; Commission Regulation (EU) No 651/2014, Article 40(4)-(6).

[94] Environmental and energy aid guidelines 2014-2020, para 151.

Aid for energy efficient district heating and cooling Investment aid for the installation of energy efficient district heating and cooling systems is compatible with the internal market in accordance with the block exemption. The eligible costs for the production plant are the extra costs needed for the construction, expansion and refurbishment of one or more generation units to operate as an energy efficient district heating and cooling system compared to a conventional production plant. The aid intensity must not exceed 45%, although this may be increased by 20 percentage points for aid awarded to small enterprises and by 10 percentage points for aid awarded to medium-sized enterprises. The aid intensity may be increased by 15 percentage points for investments located in Article 107(3)(a) areas and by 5 percentage points for investments located in Article 107(3)(c) areas. In addition, where the investment aid is granted in a genuinely competitive bidding process, the guidelines provide that the aid intensity may amount to up to 100% of the investment cost.[95] The eligible costs for the distribution network shall be the investment costs. The aid amount for the distribution network may not exceed the difference between the eligible costs and the operating profit. The operating profit shall be deducted from the eligible costs *ex ante* or through a claw-back mechanism.[96]

Aid for resource efficiency and waste management The Commission considers that market failures are particularly relevant for resource efficiency and that State aid may in such cases be necessary. For individual measures, Member States need to demonstrate quantifiable benefits in this policy area, particularly the amount of resources saved or the resource efficiency gains.[97] State aid for the management of waste, in particular for activities aimed at the prevention, re-use and recycling of waste, can make a positive contribution to environmental protection. This includes the re-use or recycling of water or minerals that would otherwise be unused as waste. In particular, in light of the polluter pays principle, undertakings generating waste should not be relieved of the costs of its treatment. Moreover, the normal functioning of the secondary materials market should not be negatively impacted. Under the guidelines, the Commission will consider aid for waste management to serve an objective of common interest in accordance with the principles of waste management if the investment is aimed at reducing waste generated by other undertakings and does not extend to waste generated by the beneficiary of the aid, it does not indirectly relieve the polluters from a burden that should be borne by them, the investment goes beyond the state of the art, the materials treated would otherwise be disposed of, or be treated in a less environmentally friendly

---

[95] Environmental and energy aid guidelines 2014-2020, Annex I; Commission Regulation (EU) No 651/2014, Article 46(1)-(4).

[96] Commission Regulation (EU) No 651/2014, Article 46(5)-(6)

[97] Environmental and energy aid guidelines 2014-2020, paras 152-154.

manner, and the investment does not merely increase demand for the materials to be recycled without increasing collection of those materials. Investment aid for waste management and re-utilisation is also permissible under the block exemption.[98]

Eligible costs are the extra investment costs necessary to realise an investment leading to better or more efficient recycling or re-use activities compared to a conventional process of re-use and recycling activities with the same capacity that would be constructed in the absence the aid. The aid intensity must not exceed 35% of the eligible costs. This may be increased by 10 percentage points for medium-sized enterprises and by 20 percentage points for small enterprises. The aid intensity may be increased by 15 percentage points for investments located in Article 107(3)(a) areas and by 5 percentage points for investments located in Article 107(3)(c) areas. In addition, where the investment aid is granted in a genuinely competitive bidding process, the guidelines provide that the aid intensity may amount to up to 100% of the investment cost.[99]

An example of a waste management scheme approved by the Commission is a French scheme for the elimination of dangerous waste for water. The objective of the scheme was to preserve water resources by promoting the elimination of waste that could pollute the subsurface and surface of water or disturb the functioning of purification plants. Grants were calculated on the basis of the difference between the cost to treat waste in the dedicated procedure and the cost of disposal of the same water.[100] The United Kingdom notified aid under the WRAP programme in favour of Shotton, a newsprint producer located in north Wales, which was intended to adapt Shotton's facilities to produce newsprint from waste paper rather than virgin pulp. Although the Commission recognised the environmental benefits of reusing waste paper instead of putting it into landfill, it held that the environmental guidelines only provided for aid for investments that improve a company's individual environmental record, whereas in this case the aid was intended to improve the United Kingdom's environmental record in general. The approved aid was limited, therefore, to that part which was related to the building of a sludge combustor which was meant to reduce Shotton's own pollution.[101]

The Commission has also authorised operating aid for hazardous waste disposal as a service of general economic interest under Article 106(2) TFEU. Aid in the Netherlands granted to companies specialising in the collection and

---

[98] Environmental and energy aid guidelines 2014-2020, paras 158; Commission Regulation (EU) No 651/2014, Article 47.

[99] Environmental and energy aid guidelines 2014-2020, Annex I; Commission Regulation (EU) No 651/2014, Article 47(7)-(9).

[100] Case N 496/2002, *French waste water treatment scheme*, OJ 2003 C108/5. See also, Commission Decision 2005/164/EC, *Stora Enso Langerbrugge NV*, OJ 2005 L53/66.

[101] Commission Decision 2003/814/EC, *Shotton*, OJ 2003 L314/26.

destruction of halon and CFCs was approved.[102]   In the *AVR* decision, the
Commission accepted that there was an obvious public interest in appropriate
treatment for the disposal of hazardous waste and that the measure was
consistent with the polluter pays principle.[103]

Aid to Carbon Capture and Storage   Carbon capture and storage (CCS) is a
technology that can contribute to mitigating climate change.   In the transition
to a fully low-carbon economy, CCS technology can reconcile the demand for
fossil fuels, with the need to reduce greenhouse gas emissions.   In some
industrial sectors, CCS may currently represent the only technology option able
to reduce process-related emissions at the scale needed in the long term.   Given
that the cost of capture, transport and storage is an important barrier to the
uptake of CCS, State aid can contribute to fostering the development of this
technology.   The Commission, in the guidelines, recognises that such aid may
be compatible with the internal market.   Aid may be provided to support fossil
fuel and, or biomass power plants (including co-fired power plants with fossil
fuels and biomass) or other industrial installations equipped with CO_2 capture,
transport and storage facilities, or individual elements of the CCS chain.   The
aid, which may be either investment aid or operating aid, must be limited to the
additional costs for capture, transport and storage of the CO_2 emitted.   The
counterfactual scenario would consist in a situation where the project is not
carried out as CCS is similar to additional infrastructure which is not needed to
operate an installation. In view of this counterfactual scenario, the eligible
costs are defined as the funding gap. Aid for CCS may be 100% of the eligible
costs.[104]   For example, the Commission authorised aid for a CCS
demonstration project in Rotterdam covering the whole cycle where the CO_2
from power generation is captured and stored in a depleted gas field.[105]

Aid in the form of reductions in environmental taxes   Environmental taxes
are imposed in order to increase the costs of environmentally harmful
behaviour, thereby discouraging such behaviour. In principle, environmental
taxes should reflect the overall costs to society, and correspondingly, the
amount of tax paid per unit of emission should be the same for all emitting
firms.   While reductions in or exemptions from environmental taxes may
adversely impact that objective, such an approach may nonetheless be needed
where the beneficiaries would otherwise be placed at such a competitive
disadvantage that it would not be feasible to introduce the environmental tax in
the first place.   Indeed, granting a more favourable tax treatment to some
undertakings may facilitate a higher general level of environmental taxes.   The

---

[102]   Case N 638/2002, *Collection and destruction of halon and CFCs*, OJ 2003 C82/19.
[103]   Commission Decision 2006/237/EC, *AVR*, OJ 2006 L84/37.
[104]   Environmental and energy aid guidelines 2014-2020, paras 160-166 and Annex I.
[105]   Case N381/2010, *Rotterdam harbour area* (2010).

tax reductions should be necessary and based on objective, transparent and non-discriminatory criteria, and the undertakings concerned should make a contribution towards increasing environmental protection. The Commission will consider that tax reductions do not undermine the general objective pursued and contribute at least indirectly to an increased level of environmental protection, if a Member State demonstrates that the reductions are well targeted to undertakings being mostly affected by a higher tax and that a higher tax rate is generally applicable than would be the case without the exemption.[106]

Aid schemes in the form of reductions in environmental taxes fulfilling the conditions of Directive 2003/96/EC[107] are permissible under the block exemption. The beneficiaries of the reduction must at least pay the minimum tax level set by the directive. Aid schemes in the form of tax reductions shall be based on a reduction of the applicable environmental tax rate or on the payment of a fixed compensation amount or on a combination of these mechanisms.[108] The guidelines extend this possibility to all environmental taxes that are harmonised by EU directives.[109]

Reductions in or exemptions from other non-harmonised environmental taxes are permissible under the guidelines, subject to an assessment by the Commission of the necessity and proportionality of the aid and its effects on the economic sectors concerned. The Commission will consider the aid to be necessary if the following cumulative conditions are met: the choice of beneficiaries must be based on objective and transparent criteria, and the aid must be granted in principle in the same way for all competitors in the same sector if they are in a similar factual situation; the environmental tax without reduction must lead to a substantial increase in production costs for each sector or category of individual beneficiaries; the substantial increase in production costs cannot be passed on to customers without leading to important sales reductions. The Commission will consider the aid to be proportionate if one of the following conditions is met: aid beneficiaries pay at least 20% of the tax; the reduction is conditional on the conclusion of agreements committing the undertakings to achieve environmental protection objectives which have the same effect as if beneficiaries were to pay at least 20% of the tax.[110]

In case of a carbon tax levied on energy products used for electricity production, the electricity supplier is liable to pay the tax. Such carbon tax can be designed in a way that supports and is directly linked to the EU ETS allowance price by taxing carbon. However, the electricity price increases if those costs are passed on to the electricity consumer. In that case, the effect of

---

[106] Environmental and energy aid guidelines 2014-2020, paras 167-170.
[107] Council Directive 2003/96/EC restructuring the Community framework for the taxation of energy products and electricity, OJ 2003 L283/51.
[108] Commission Regulation (EU) No 651/2014, Article 44.
[109] Environmental and energy aid guidelines 2014-2020, paras 173-175.
[110] *Ibid.*, paras 176-178.

the carbon tax is similar to the effect of ETS allowance costs being passed on and included in the electricity price as indirect emissions costs. If the tax is designed in a way that it is directly linked to the EU ETS allowance price and aims to increase the allowance price, compensation for those higher indirect costs may be considered. The Commission will consider the measure compatible with the internal market only if the following cumulative conditions are met: aid is only granted to sectors and subsectors listed in the ETS State aid guidelines[111] to compensate for additional indirect cost resulting from the tax; the aid intensity and maximum aid intensities are calculated as defined in those guidelines; and aid is granted as a lump sum that can be paid to the beneficiary in the year in which the costs are incurred or in the following year.[112]

Thus, the Commission approved tax reductions to the Danish cement industry which complied with the guidelines,[113] but refused a similar scheme concerning the Dutch ceramic industry on the ground that the tax exemption was not proportional or necessary.[114] A reduction in the UK Climate Change Levy was approved for aluminium and steel recycling processes.[115]

Aid by reductions in funding of support for renewable energy Funding of support to energy from renewable sources through charges has no direct environmental effect. The increase in electricity costs may be explicit through a specific charge which is levied from electricity consumers on top of the electricity price or indirect through additional costs faced by electricity suppliers due to obligations to buy renewable energy which are subsequently passed on to electricity consumers. A typical example would be the mandatory purchase by electricity suppliers of a certain percentage of renewable energy through green certificates for which the supplier is not compensated. In principle and to the extent that the costs of financing renewable energy support are recovered from energy consumers, they should be recovered in a way that does not discriminate between consumers of energy. However, some targeted reductions in these costs may be needed to secure a sufficient financing base for support to energy from renewable sources and hence help reaching the renewable energy targets set at EU level.[116]

Aid to compensate for the financing of support to energy from renewable sources is permitted by the guidelines. Member States must demonstrate that the additional costs reflected in higher electricity prices faced by the beneficiaries only result from the support to energy from renewable sources.

---

[111] OJ 2012 C158/4, Annex II.

[112] Environmental and energy aid guidelines 2014-2020, paras 179-180.

[113] Case N327/08, *Tax reduction for large polluters* (2009).

[114] Case C5/09, *Netherlands ceramics* (2009).

[115] SA.31349, *Climate Change Levy reduction* (2011).

[116] Environmental and energy aid guidelines 2014-2020, paras 181-182.

The additional costs cannot exceed the funding of support to energy from renewable sources. The aid should be limited to sectors that are exposed to a risk to their competitive position due to the costs resulting from the funding of support to energy from renewable sources as a function of their electro-intensity and their exposure to international trade.[117] The Commission will consider the aid to be proportionate if the aid beneficiaries pay at least 15% of the additional costs without reduction. This may be reduced to 4% of gross added value of the undertaking concerned, or 0.5% in the case of undertakings having an electro-intensity of at least 20%. The aid may be granted in the form of a reduction from charges, or as a fixed annual compensation amount, or as a combination of the two.[118] Transitional rules allowing for the progressive introduction of these measures may apply until the end of 2018.[119]

Aid for energy infrastructure   The Commission has estimated total investment needs in energy infrastructures of European significance until 2020 at about €200 billion, based on an evaluation of the infrastructure needed to allow the EU to meet the overarching policy objectives of completing the internal energy market, ensuring security of supply and enabling the integration of renewable sources of energy. Where market operators cannot deliver the infrastructure needed, State aid may be necessary in order to overcome market failures, particularly as regards infrastructure projects having a cross-border impact or contributing to regional cohesion. Aid to energy infrastructure should in principle be investment aid, including its modernisation and upgrade.[120]   Aid is permitted under both the guidelines and the block exemption.[121]

Under the block exemption, investment aid for the construction or upgrade of energy infrastructure in assisted areas may be granted. The energy infrastructure must be subject to full tariff and access regulation according to internal energy market legislation. Eligible costs are the investment costs. The aid amount must not exceed the difference between the eligible costs and the operating profit of the investment.[122] Aid for investments in electricity and gas storage projects and oil infrastructure must be individually notified pursuant to Article 108(3) TFEU and assessed under the guidelines.[123]

---

[117] These sectors are listed in Annex III to the guidelines. A Member State can include an undertaking in its national scheme granting reductions from costs resulting from renewable support if the undertaking has an electro-intensity of at least 20 % and belongs to a sector with a trade intensity of at least 4 % at EU level, even if it does not belong to a sector listed in Annex III.

[118] Environmental and energy aid guidelines 2014-2020, paras 183-192.

[119] *Ibid.*, paras 193-200.

[120] *Ibid.*, para 201.

[121] *Ibid.*, para 202; Commission Regulation (EU) No 651/2014, Article 48(1).

[122] Commission Regulation (EU) No 651/2014, Article 48(2)-(5).

[123] *Ibid.*, Article 48(6).

Under the guidelines, the Commission takes the view that tariffs are the appropriate means to fund energy infrastructure. It recognises, however, that, for projects of common interest as defined in Regulation (EU) No 347/2013, smart grids, and infrastructure investments in assisted areas, market failures in terms of positive externalities and coordination problems are such that financing by means of tariffs may not be sufficient, so that State aid may be viewed as compatible with the internal market. For oil infrastructure project, State aid is generally not permitted, other than in exceptional circumstances. The aid amount must be limited to the minimum needed to achieve the infrastructure objectives sought. For aid to infrastructure, the counterfactual scenario is presumed to be the situation in which the project would not take place. The eligible cost is therefore the funding gap. Aid intensity of 100 % of the eligible costs may be granted.[124]

Aid for generation adequacy With the increasing share of renewable energy sources, electricity generation is in many Member States shifting from a system of relatively stable and continuous supply towards a system with more numerous and small-scale supply of variable sources. Market and regulatory failures may cause insufficient investment in generation capacity, for example, in a situation where wholesale prices are capped and electricity markets fail to generate sufficient investment incentives. As a result, some Member States consider the introduction of measures to ensure generation adequacy, typically by granting support to generators for the mere availability of generation capacity. Measures for generation adequacy can be designed in a variety of ways, in the form of investment and operating aid, and can pursue different objectives. They may, for example, aim at addressing short-term concerns brought about by the lack of flexible generation capacity to meet sudden swings in variable wind and solar production, or they may define a target for generation adequacy, which Member States may wish to ensure regardless of short-term considerations. In its assessment, the Commission will take account, among others, the impact of variable generation and of demand-side participation, the actual or potential existence of interconnectors, and any other element which might cause or exacerbate the generation adequacy problem, such as regulatory or market failures, including for example caps on wholesale prices.[125]

Under the guidelines, aid for generation adequacy may be considered compatible with the internal market. The aid should remunerate solely the service of pure availability provided by the generation operator and should not include any remuneration for the sale of electricity. The measure should be open and provide adequate incentives to both existing and future generators and to operators using substitutable technologies, such as demand-side

---

[124] Environmental and energy aid guidelines 2014-2020, paras 203-215 and Annex I.
[125] *Ibid.*, paras 216-224.

response or storage solutions. The aid should, therefore, be delivered through a mechanism which allows for potentially different lead times, corresponding to the time needed to realise new investments by new generators using different technologies. The measure should also take into account to what extent interconnection capacity could remedy any possible problem of generation adequacy. The calculation of the overall amount of aid should result in beneficiaries earning a rate of return, which can be considered reasonable. A competitive bidding process on the basis of clear, transparent and non-discriminatory criteria, effectively targeting the defined objective, will be considered as leading to reasonable rates of return under normal circumstances. The measure should have built-in mechanisms to ensure that windfall profits cannot arise and should be constructed so as to ensure that the price paid for availability automatically tends to zero when the level of capacity supplied is expected to be adequate to meet the level of capacity demanded.[126]

In assessing the negative effects on competition and trade, the Commission will consider: the participation of generators using different technologies and of operators offering measures with equivalent technical performance, for example, demand side management, interconnectors and storage; the participation of operators from other Member States where such participation is physically possible in particular in the regional context; participation of a sufficient number of generators to establish a competitive price for the capacity; and avoidance of negative effects on the internal market, for example due to export restrictions, wholesale price caps, bidding restrictions or other measures undermining the operation of market coupling, including intra-day and balancing markets. The measure should: not reduce incentives to invest in interconnection capacity; not undermine market coupling, including balancing markets; not undermine investment decisions on generation which preceded the measure or decisions by operators regarding the balancing or ancillary services market; not unduly strengthen market dominance; give preference to low-carbon generators in case of equivalent technical and economic parameters.[127]

Aid for the remediation of contaminated sites Investment aid to undertakings repairing environmental damage by remediating contaminated sites is permissible under the block exemption and the guidelines. This builds on previous Commission practice following the English Partnerships decision where the Commission approved a UK aid measure aimed at remediating contaminated land, brownfield land and derelict land. That measure was intended to bring such land back into productive use by addressing detrimental effects of previous usage and making it suitable for new use, thereby reducing

---

[126] *Ibid.*, paras 225-231.
[127] *Ibid.*, paras 232-233..

pressure on greenfield land and limiting urban sprawl.[128]   Under the block
exemption, the investment must lead to the repair of the environmental damage
concerned, including damage to the quality of the soil or of surface water or
groundwater. Where the polluter is clearly identified, that person must finance
the remediation in accordance with the polluter pays principle, and no State aid
may be granted. Where the polluter is not identified or cannot be made to bear
the costs, the person responsible for the remediation or decontamination work
may receive aid. The eligible costs are equal to the cost of the remediation
work less the increase in the value of the land. All expenditure incurred by an
undertaking in remediating its site, whether or not such expenditure can be
shown as a fixed asset on its balance sheet, may be considered as eligible
investment.   Aid intensity for the remediation of contaminated sites may
amount to up to 100% of the eligible costs.[129]

Aid involved in tradable permit schemes   Aid involved in tradable permit
schemes is permissible under the guidelines.   Tradable permit schemes may
involve State aid in various ways, for example, when Member States grant
permits and allowances below their market value. This type of aid may be
used to target negative externalities by allowing market-based instruments
targeting environmental objectives to be introduced. If the global amount of
permits granted by the Member State is lower than the global expected needs
of undertakings, the overall effect on the level of environmental protection will
be positive.[130]   The first cases concerned a Danish CO_2 trading scheme.[131]
Further schemes were introduced by the Netherlands[132] and the United
Kingdom.[133]

Under the guidelines, the following conditions must be met: the tradable
permit schemes must be set up in such a way as to achieve environmental
objectives beyond those intended to be achieved on the basis of EU standards
that are mandatory for the undertakings concerned; the allocation must be
carried out in a transparent way, based on objective criteria and on data sources
of the highest quality available, and the total amount of tradable permits or
allowances granted to each undertaking for a price below their market value
must not be higher than its expected needs as estimated for the situation in
absence of the trading scheme; the allocation methodology must not favour
certain undertakings or certain sectors, unless this is justified by the

---

[128]   Case N 385/2002, *Support for land remediation*, OJ 2003 C195/16. See also, Case N
     812/2001, *Treatment of dredging sludge*, OJ 2002 C248/23; Case N 85/2005,
     Netherlands Soil Protection Agreement, OJ 2005 C229/9.
[129]   Commission Regulation (EU) No 651/2014, Article 45.
[130]   Environmental and energy aid guidelines 2014-2020, para 234.
[131]   Case N 653/1999, *Danish emission trading scheme*, OJ 2002 C322/9.
[132]   Case N 35/2003, *NOₓ emission trading scheme*, OJ 2003 C277/7.
[133]   Case N 416/2001, *UK emission trading scheme*, OJ 2002 C88/16; Case N 47/2006,
     Dispersed oil trading system, OJ 2006 C232/2.

environmental logic of the scheme itself or where such rules are necessary for consistency with other environmental policies; and, in particular, new entrants must not in principle receive permits or allowances on more favourable conditions than existing undertakings operating on the same markets. Granting higher allocations to existing installations compared to new entrants should not result in creating undue barriers to entry.[134]

The Commission will assess the necessity and proportionality of State aid using the following criteria: the choice of beneficiaries must be based on objective and transparent criteria, and the aid must be granted in principle in the same way for all competitors in the same sector or relevant market if they are in a similar factual situation; full auctioning must lead to a substantial increase in production costs for each sector or category of individual beneficiaries; the substantial increase in production costs cannot be passed on to customers without leading to important sales reductions; and it must not be possible for individual undertakings in the sector to reduce emission levels in order to make the price of the certificates bearable.[135] The intensity of the aid may be up to 100%.[136]

Aid for relocation of undertakings Investment aid for relocation of undertakings to new sites for environmental protection reasons is permissible under the guidelines. The change of location must be dictated by environmental protection or prevention grounds and must have been ordered by the administrative or judicial decision of a competent public authority or agreed between the undertaking and the competent public authority. Moreover, the undertaking must comply with the strictest environmental standards applicable in the new region where it is located. The beneficiary can be an undertaking established in an urban area or in a special area of conservation designated under the Habitats Directive 92/43/EEC,[137] which lawfully carries out an activity that creates major pollution and must, on account of that location, move from its place of establishment to a more suitable area. Alternatively, the beneficiary may be an establishment or installation falling within the scope of the Seveso III Directive 2012/18/EU.[138] For example, the Commission approved aid to Akzo Nobel in connection with the relocation of two plants producing chlorine and mono-chloro acetic acid on the basis that the relocation would significantly reduce the need for chlorine transport.[139]

---

[134] Environmental and energy aid guidelines 2014-2020, para 235.
[135] *Ibid.*, para 236.
[136] *Ibid.*, Annex I.
[137] OJ 1992 L206/7, as amended.
[138] Environmental and energy aid guidelines 2014-2020, paras 237-239.
[139] Case N 304/03, *Akzo Nobel*, OJ 2005 C81/4. See also, Case N 385/2002, *Support for land remediation*, OJ 2003 C195/16.

In order to determine the amount of eligible costs in the case of relocation aid, the Commission will take into account related costs and benefits. Costs include those connected with the purchase of land or the construction or purchase of new plant of the same capacity as the plant abandoned and any penalties imposed on the undertaking for having terminated the contract for the renting of land or buildings. Benefits include the yield from the sale or renting of the plant or land abandoned, any compensation paid in the event of expropriation, any other gains connected with the transfer of the plant, notably gains resulting from an improvement in the technology used and accounting gains associated with better use of the plant, together with investments relating to any capacity increase. The aid intensity must not exceed 50% of the eligible investment costs. This may be increased by 10 percentage points for medium-sized enterprises and by 20 percentage points for small enterprises. The aid intensity may be increased by 15 percentage points for investments located in Article 107(3)(a) areas and by 5 percentage points for investments located in Article 107(3)(c) areas.[140]

Aid for environmental studies Aid to undertakings for studies directly linked to investments for the purposes of achieving increased standards or energy saving or of producing renewable energy is permissible under the guidelines and the block exemption. This is intended to address the market failure linked to asymmetric information, whereby undertakings often underestimate the possibilities and benefits related to energy saving and renewable energy, which leads to under-investment. The eligible costs shall be the costs of the study. The aid intensity must not exceed 50%, which may be increased by 20 percentage points for studies undertaken on behalf of small enterprises and by 10 percentage points for studies undertaken on behalf of medium-sized enterprises. The aid intensity may be increased by 15 percentage points for investments located in Article 107(3)(a) areas and by 5 percentage points for investments located in Article 107(3)(c) areas.[141]

---

[140] Environmental and energy aid guidelines 2014-2020, paras 240-241 and Annex I.
[141] *Ibid.*, Annex I; Commission Regulation (EU) No 651/2014, Article 49.

Chapter Thirteen

RESCUE AND RESTRUCTURING AID

13.1 COMMISSION POLICY ON
RESCUE AND RESTRUCTURING AID

Commission guidelines on rescue and restructuring aid The Commission first adopted guidelines on State aid for rescuing and restructuring firms in difficulty in 1994[1] and again in 1999.[2] In 2004 revised guidelines[3] introduced somewhat stricter rules than previously applied, aiming at a closer scrutiny of State aid for rescue and restructuring.[4] The present guidelines[5] were adopted in 2014 with a view to compliance with the reformed principles set out in the State aid modernisation programme and taking into account the EU's Europe 2020 strategy.[6]

Rescue and restructuring aid are among the most distortive types of State aid. Exit of less efficient undertakings allows their more efficient competitors to grow and returns assets to the market, where they can be applied to more productive uses. By interfering with this process, rescue and restructuring aid may significantly slow economic growth in the sectors concerned. A further concern is the moral hazard problem created by State aid whereby undertakings anticipating that they are likely to be rescued when they run into difficulty may embark upon excessively risky and unsustainable business strategies. State aid for rescuing and restructuring undertakings in difficulty may also undermine the internal market by shifting an unfair share of the burden of structural adjustment and the attendant social and economic problems to other Member States. This may also lead to the creation of entry barriers and the undermining of incentives for cross-border activities, contrary to the objectives of the internal market.[7] Many decisions on rescue and restructuring aid involve very

---

[1] OJ 1994 C368/12

[2] OJ 1999 C288/2.

[3] OJ 2004 C244/2.

[4] *Thirty-Fourth Report on Competition Policy* (2004), pt. 357. E. Valle & K. Van de Casteele, "Revision of the rescue and restructuring guidelines: a crackdown?" (2004) EStALQ 9.

[5] OJ 2014 C249/1.

[6] Rescue and restructuring aid guidelines 2014-2020, para 5. H.A. Petzold, "Rescue and restructuring guidelines – thoughts and comments on the Commission's draft" [2014] EStALQ 289.

[7] Rescue and restructuring aid guidelines 2014-2020, paras 6-10.

large amounts of aid in complex economic circumstances. Even before the advent of the 2007 credit crisis, in the period 2000-2005 rescue and restructuring aid amounted to €24 billion.[8]

Scope of the rescue and restructuring aid guidelines   The rescue and restructuring aid guidelines 2014-2020 apply to firms in all sectors, except to those operating in the coal and steel sectors and those covered by specific rules for financial institutions, without prejudice to any specific sectoral rules.[9]

Aid measures in favour of large undertakings must be notified individually to the Commission pursuant to Article 108(3) TFEU. Under certain conditions, the Commission may authorise schemes for smaller amounts of aid to SMEs and smaller State-owned undertakings.[10] Rescue and restructuring aid is not covered by the general block exemption regulation, with the exception of aid schemes to make good the damage caused by certain natural disasters.[11] Given that its very existence is in danger, a firm in difficulty cannot be considered an appropriate vehicle for promoting other public policy objectives, until such time as its viability is assured. Consequently, the Commission considers that aid to firms in difficulty may contribute to the development of economic activities without adversely affecting trade to an extent contrary to the common interest only if the conditions set out in the guidelines are met.[12]

Where restructuring aid is examined under the guidelines, the grant of any other aid during the restructuring period, even in accordance with a scheme that has already been authorised, is liable to influence the Commission's assessment of the extent of the compensatory measures required. Notifications of aid for restructuring must indicate all other aid of any kind which is planned to be granted to the recipient firm during the restructuring period, unless it is covered by the *de minimis* rule or by exemption regulations. The Commission will take such aid into account when assessing the restructuring aid. Any aid actually granted to a large or medium-sized enterprise during the restructuring period, including aid granted in accordance with an approved scheme, must be notified individually to the Commission to the extent that the latter was not informed thereof at the time of its decision on the restructuring aid. The

---

[8]   See the special focus on rescue and restructuring aid in State Aid Scoreboard, Autumn 2006, pp. 28-34. In one decision alone, the aid amounted to €3 billion: Commission Decision 2005/418/EC, *Alstom*, OJ 2005 L150/24. Most restructuring aid is awarded by the big Member States: France, Germany, Italy, Spain and the United Kingdom.

[9]   Rescue and restructuring aid guidelines 2014-2020, para 18.

[10] *Ibid.*, para 37.

[11] Commission Regulation (EU) No 651/2014, Article 1(4)(c). See, for example, Commission Decision 2004/32/EC, *Porcelanas del Principado*, OJ 2004 L11/1.

[12] Rescue and restructuring aid guidelines 2014-2020, para 23.

Commission must ensure that the grant of aid under approved schemes is not liable to circumvent the requirements of the guidelines on restructuring aid.[13]

Notion of a firm in difficulty The rescue and restructuring guidelines apply to aid granted to firms in difficulty. There is no EU law definition of what constitutes a firm in difficulty,[14] although the General Court has held that the level of losses and of financial indebtedness are criteria capable by themselves of establishing that a firm is in difficulty.[15] For the purposes of the guidelines, an undertaking is considered to be in difficulty when, without intervention by the State, it will almost certainly be condemned to going out of business in the short or medium term. An undertaking is considered to be in difficulty if at least one of the following circumstances occurs:[16]

(a) in the case of a limited liability company, where more than half of its subscribed share capital has disappeared as a result of accumulated losses;

(b) in the case of a company where at least some members have unlimited liability for the debt of the company, where more than half of its capital as shown in the company accounts has disappeared as a result of accumulated losses;

(c) where the undertaking is subject to collective insolvency proceedings or fulfils the criteria under its domestic law for being placed in collective insolvency proceedings at the request of its creditors;

(d) in the case of an undertaking that is not an SME, where, for the past two years, the undertaking's book debt to equity ratio has been greater than 7.5 and its EBITDA interest coverage ratio has been below 1.0.

In *Freistaat Sachsen v Commission*, concerning aid to the Biria Group under a regional development programme, the General Court rejected the argument that a different definition of the concept of firm in difficulty might exist alongside that contained in the restructuring guidelines,[17] although it has also held that there is nothing to prevent a firm from establishing that it is in

---

[13] *Ibid.*, paras 127-130. See, for example, Commission Decision 2007/492/EC, *Biria Group*, OJ 2007 L183/27.

[14] Case T-349/03, *Corsica Ferries France SAS v Commission* [2005] ECR II-2197, para 183; Cases T-267/08 & T-279/08, *Région Nord-Pas-de-Calais v Commission* [2011] ECR II-1999, para 109.

[15] Case T-349/03, *Corsica Ferries France sas v Commission* [2005] ECR II-2197, para 191; Cases T-102/07 & T-120/07, *Freistaat Sachsen v Commission* [2010] CR II-585, para 135; Cases T-267/08 & T-279/08, *Région Nord-Pas-de-Calais v Commission* [2011] ECR II-1999, para 146; Case T-209/11, *MB System GmbH v Commission* EU:T:2013:338, para 43.

[16] Rescue and restructuring aid guidelines 2014-2020, para 20.

[17] Cases T-102/07 & T-120/07, *Freistaat Sachsen v Commission* [2010] ECR II-585, para 76.

financial difficulty by the use of other evidence.[18] In order to assess whether the capital has disappeared, it must also be ascertained whether the reserves of the company are capable of absorbing the losses.[19] Even where a company has managed to escape insolvency, it may still be in difficulty if it remains in a fragile state.[20]

One time, last time principle The Commission applies a one-time last-time rule to rescue and restructuring aid, whereby aid maybe awarded to an undertaking only once within ten year.[21] The General Court has confirmed that this principle is of particular importance in assessing the compatibility of restructuring aid.[22] In order to reduce moral hazard, excessive risk-taking incentives and potential competitive distortions, aid should be granted to undertakings in difficulty in respect of only one restructuring operation. The need for an undertaking that has already received rescue and restructuring aid to obtain further such aid demonstrates that the undertaking's difficulties are either of a recurrent nature or were not dealt with adequately when the earlier aid was granted. Repeated State interventions are likely to lead to problems of moral hazard and distortions of competition that are contrary to the common interest.[23]

When planned rescue or restructuring aid is notified to the Commission, the Member State must specify whether the undertaking concerned has already received rescue aid, restructuring aid or temporary restructuring support in the past, including any non-notified aid. If so, and where less than 10 years, or five years in the case of the primary agricultural production sector, have elapsed since the aid was granted or the restructuring period came to an end or implementation of the restructuring plan was halted, the Commission will not allow further aid pursuant to the guidelines.[24] Exceptions to that rule are permitted as follows: where restructuring aid follows the granting of rescue aid as part of a single restructuring operation; where rescue aid or temporary restructuring support has been granted but was not followed by restructuring aid if the firm could reasonably be believed to be viable in the long-term

---

[18] Case T-349/03, *Corsica Ferries France SAS v Commission* [2005] ECR II-2197, para 185; Cases T-102/07 & T-120/07, *Freistaat Sachsen v Commission* [2010] ECR II-585, paras 104-105.

[19] Commission Decision 2008/696/EC, *Cuppa Chups*, OJ 2008 L235/10.

[20] Case T-209/11, *MB System GmbH v Commission* EU:T:2013:338, para 47.

[21] Rescue and restructuring aid guidelines 2014-2020, para 8. The application of this principle to rescue aid was introduced in the 2004 guidelines, although previous Commission practice did not allow for repeated rescue aid: cf. Commission Decision 98/664/EC, *Thüringer Motorenwerke*, OJ 1998 L316/20; Commission Decision 2002/935/EC, *Grupo de Empresas Alvarez*, OJ 2002 L329/1.

[22] Case T-511/09, *Niki Luftfahrt GmbH v Commission* EU:T:2015:284, para 115.

[23] Rescue and restructuring aid guidelines 2014-2020, para 70.

[24] *Ibid.*, para 71.

following the granting of rescue aid and new rescue or restructuring aid becomes necessary after at least five years due to unforeseeable circumstances for which the company is not responsible; or in exceptional and unforeseeable circumstances for which the company is not responsible.[25] For example, the Commission derogated from a strict application of the one-time last-time rule in its decision on restructuring aid for Bull where there was an exceptional downturn in the communications technology sector.[26]

Group of companies A firm belonging to or being taken over by a larger business group is not normally eligible for rescue and restructuring aid, except where it can be demonstrated that the firm's difficulties are intrinsic and are not the result of an arbitrary allocation of costs within the group and that the difficulties are too serious to be dealt with by the group itself.[27] This might be the case where the rest of the group is only a managing company[28] or where the group has been unable financially to save the firm.[29] Exceptionally, where the firm in difficulty can be clearly separated from the group, the Commission may consider aid for that firm on its own merits.[30] Where a business group has received rescue aid, restructuring aid or temporary restructuring support, the Commission will normally not allow further rescue or restructuring aid to the group itself or any of the entities belonging to the group unless 10 years have elapsed since the aid was granted or the restructuring period came to an end or implementation of the restructuring plan was halted, whichever occurred the latest. Where an entity belonging to a business group has received rescue aid, restructuring aid or temporary restructuring support, the group as a whole as well as the other entities of the group remain eligible for rescue or restructuring aid with the exception of the earlier beneficiary of the aid.[31]

Newly created firms A newly created firm is not eligible for rescue or restructuring aid even if its initial financial position is insecure. This is the case, for instance, where a new firm emerges from the liquidation of a previous firm or merely takes over such firm's assets. A firm will in principle be considered as newly created for the first three years following the start of operations in the relevant field of activity. Only after that period will it become eligible for rescue or restructuring aid, provided that it qualifies as a firm in difficulty under the guidelines, and it does not form part of a larger

---

25 Rescue and restructuring aid guidelines 2014-2020, para 72.
26 Commission Decision 2005/941/EC, *Bull*, OJ 2005 L342/81. See also, Commission Decision 2000/732/EC, *Korn Farzeuge und Technik*, OJ 2000 L295/21.
27 Rescue and restructuring aid guidelines 2014-2020, para 22. See, for example, Commission Decision 2007/674/EC, *Ernault*, OJ 2007 L277/25.
28 Case N584/2004, *AB Vingriai*, OJ 2005 C187/15.
29 Case NN 39/2006, *De Poortere*, OJ 2007 C259/16.
30 See, for example, Case N 386/2004, *SNCF Freight*, OJ 2005 C172/3.
31 Rescue and restructuring aid guidelines 2014-2020, para 74.

business group.[32]   Accordingly, the Commission determined that aid to two newly created French ship repair companies was ineligible for approval.[33]

Where a firm in difficulty creates a subsidiary, the subsidiary, together with the firm in difficulty controlling it, will be regarded as a group and may receive aid in accordance with the guidelines.[34]   Such a shell company is not a newly created company for the purposes of the guidelines, but will be regarded as an instrument for effecting the restructuring of the firm.[35]

Transfer of ownership or assets   The application of the one time, last time rule is not affected by any changes in ownership of the firm following the grant of aid or by any judicial or administrative procedure which has the effect of putting its balance sheet on a sounder footing, reducing its liabilities or wiping out its previous debts where it is the same firm that is continuing in business.[36] Where a firm takes over assets of another firm, and in particular one that has been the subject of one of these procedures or of collective insolvency proceedings and has already received rescue or restructuring aid, the purchaser is not subject to the one time, last time requirement, provided that there is no economic continuity between the old undertaking and the purchaser.[37]

Aid to cover the social costs of restructuring   Restructuring normally entails reductions in or abandonment of the affected activities.   Such retrenchments are often necessary in the interests of rationalisation and efficiency, quite apart from any capacity reductions that may be required as a condition for granting aid. Regardless of the underlying reasons, such measures will generally lead to reductions in the beneficiary's workforce. The obligations an undertaking itself bears under employment legislation or collective agreements with trade unions to provide certain benefits to redundant workers, such as redundancy payments or measures to increase their employability, are part of the normal costs of business which an undertaking must meet from its own resources. That being so, any contribution by the State to those costs must be counted as aid. The Commission has no *a priori* objection to such aid when it is granted to an undertaking in difficulty, for it brings economic benefits above and beyond the interests of the undertaking concerned, facilitating structural change and reducing hardship. Besides providing direct financial support, such aid is commonly provided in connection with a particular restructuring scheme for training, counselling and practical help with finding alternative employment,

---

[32]   *Ibid.*, para 21.

[33]   Commission Decision 2005/90/EC, *SORENI*, OJ 2005 L31/44; Commission Decision 2005/314/EC, *CMR*, OJ 2005 L100/26.

[34]   Rescue and restructuring aid guidelines 2014-2020, para 22.

[35]   See, for example, Commission Decision 2002/200/EC, *Babcock Wilcox España*, OJ 2002 L67/50.

[36]   Rescue and restructuring aid guidelines 2014-2020, para 73.

[37]   *Ibid.*, para 75.

assistance with relocation, and professional training and assistance for employees wishing to start new businesses. Given that such measures, which increase the employability of redundant workers, further the objective of reducing social hardship, the Commission consistently takes a favourable view of such aid when it is granted to undertakings in difficulty.[38]

13.2 COMPATIBILITY CRITERIA IN THE R&R AID GUIDELINES

Common assessment principles State aid to undertakings in difficulty may be approved as compatible with the internal market, normally under Article 107(3)(c) TFEU, where such aid does not adversely affect trading conditions to an extent contrary to the common interest.[39] In particular, this could be the case where the aid is necessary to correct disparities caused by market failures or to ensure economic and social cohesion. In accordance with the communication on State aid modernisation, the Commission will consider an aid measure compatible with the internal market only if it satisfies each of the following criteria: contribution to a well-defined objective of common interest; need for State intervention; appropriateness of the measure; incentive effect; proportionality of the aid; avoidance of undue negative effects on competition and trade between Member States; and transparency of the aid. If any of these criteria is not met, the aid will not be considered to be compatible with the internal market. The overall balance of certain categories of schemes may further be made subject to a requirement of *ex post* evaluation. In such cases, the Commission may limit the duration of those schemes, normally to four years or less, with a possibility to re-notify their prolongation afterwards.[40]

Contribution to an objective of common interest Given the importance of market exit to the process of productivity growth, merely preventing an undertaking from exiting the market does not constitute a sufficient justification for aid. Clear evidence should be provided that aid pursues an objective of common interest, in that it aims to prevent social hardship or address market failure by restoring the long-term viability of the undertaking, in particular by showing one or more of the following circumstances:[41]

(a) the unemployment rate in the region concerned is either higher than the EU or national average, persistent and accompanied by difficulty in creating new employment in the region or regions concerned;

---

[38] *Ibid.*, paras 30-35.
[39] *Ibid.*, para 36.
[40] *Ibid.*, paras 38-40.
[41] *Ibid.*, paras 43-44.

(b)   there is a risk of disruption to an important service which is hard to replicate and where it would be difficult for any competitor simply to step in;

(c)   the exit of an undertaking with an important systemic role in a particular region or sector would have potential negative consequences;

(d)   there is a risk of interruption to the continuity of provision of an SGEI;

(e)   the failure or adverse incentives of credit markets would push an otherwise viable undertaking into bankruptcy;

(f)   the exit of the undertaking concerned from the market would lead to an irremediable loss of important technical knowledge or expertise;

(g)   or similar situations of severe hardship would arise.

The grant of State aid may be justified by one of those circumstances only if the general conditions for the authorisation of rescue or restructuring aid, as laid down in the guidelines, are satisfied, so that the existence of one of those circumstances does not suffice, in itself.[42]   The fact that high levels of unemployment might result from the firm going out of business, or that suppliers of the firm would be seriously affected, may justify aid.[43]   It may be necessary to support a firm which is a strategically important supplier of services of general economic interest, such as in the case of British Energy.[44] In its decision approving aid in Lithuania for AB Vingriai, the Commission took account of the fact that the heavy debt burden, the loss of markets and the excessive workforce were all inherited from a period when the Lithuanian economy was still in transition to a market basis.[45]

Need for State intervention   Member States that intend to grant restructuring aid must provide a comparison with a credible alternative scenario not involving State aid, demonstrating how the relevant objectives would not be attained, or would be attained to a lesser degree, in the case of that alternative scenario.   Such scenarios may, for example, include debt reorganisation, asset disposal, private capital raising, sale to a competitor or break-up, in each case either through entry into an insolvency or reorganisation procedure or otherwise.[46]

Appropriateness of aid   Member States should ensure that aid is awarded in the form that allows the objective to be achieved in the least distortive way.   In the case of undertakings in difficulty, aid must be in the appropriate form to

---

[42]   Case T-198/01, *Technische Glaswerke Ilmenau GmbH v Commission* [2004] ECR II-2717, para 170.

[43]   See, for example, Commission Decision 2005/418/EC, *Alstom*, OJ 2005 L150/24; Commission Decision 2005/878/EC, *Herlitz*, OJ 2005 L324/64.

[44]   Commission Decision 2005/407/EC, *British Energy*, OJ 2005 L142/26.

[45]   Case N584/2004, *AB Vingriai*, OJ 2005 C187/15.

[46]   Rescue and restructuring aid guidelines 2014-2020, para 53.

address the beneficiary's difficulties and be properly remunerated.[47] Member States are free to choose the form that restructuring aid takes, although, in doing so, they should ensure that the instrument chosen is appropriate to the issue that it is intended to address. In particular, Member States should assess whether beneficiaries' problems relate to liquidity or solvency and select appropriate instruments to address the problems identified. For instance, in the case of solvency problems, increasing assets through recapitalisation might be appropriate, whereas in a situation where the problems mainly relate to liquidity, assistance through loans or loan guarantees might be sufficient.[48]

Incentive effect   Member States that intend to grant restructuring aid must demonstrate that in the absence of the aid, the beneficiary would have been restructured, sold or wound up in a way that would not have achieved the objective of common interest of preventing social hardship or addressing market failure.[49]

Proportionality of the aid   Rescue aid must be restricted to the amount needed to keep the beneficiary in business for six months.[50]   Equally, the amount and intensity of restructuring aid must be limited to the strict minimum necessary to enable restructuring to be undertaken, in the light of the existing financial resources of the beneficiary, its shareholders or the business group to which it belongs.   In particular, a sufficient level of own contribution to the costs of the restructuring and burden sharing must be ensured, taking account of any rescue aid granted beforehand.[51]

Negative effects   In addition to the one time last time rule whereby rescue and restructuring aid may normally be awarded only once within ten years,[52] when restructuring aid is granted, measures must be taken to limit distortions of competition, so that adverse effects on trading conditions are minimised as much as possible and positive effects outweigh any adverse ones.   The Commission will assess the appropriate form and scope of such measures, which will normally consist of structural measures requiring divestments and reductions of business activities.   In addition, the Commission may accept behavioural measures or market opening measures in place of some or all of the structural measures that would otherwise be required.[53]

---

[47]   *Ibid.*, para 54.

[48]   *Ibid.*, para 58.

[49]   *Ibid.*, para 59.

[50]   *Ibid.*, para 60.

[51]   *Ibid.*, para 61. See, for example, Commission Decision 2003/194/EC, *Schmitz-Gotha*, OJ 2003 L77/41.

[52]   Rescue and restructuring aid guidelines 2014-2020, paras 70-75.

[53]   *Ibid.*, paras 76-77.

13.3 RESCUE AID

Rescue aid Rescue aid is by nature temporary and reversible assistance. Its primary objective is to make it possible to keep an ailing firm afloat for the time needed to work out a restructuring or liquidation plan. The general principle is that rescue aid makes it possible temporarily to support a company confronted with an important deterioration of its financial situation reflected by an acute liquidity crisis or technical insolvency. Such temporary support should allow time to analyse the circumstances which gave rise to the difficulties and to develop an appropriate plan to remedy those difficulties.[54] Normally, rescue aid should be limited to 6 months.[55] Rescue aid may also be granted to undertakings that are not in difficulty but that are facing acute liquidity needs due to exceptional and unforeseen circumstances.[56]

The Member State must, not later than six months after the rescue aid measure has been authorised or, in the case of unlawful aid, not later than six months after disbursement of the first instalment to the beneficiary, communicate to the Commission a restructuring plan or a liquidation plan or proof that the loan has been reimbursed in full and/or that the guarantee has been terminated. Where a restructuring plan has been submitted, the authorisation of the rescue aid will automatically be extended until the Commission reaches its final decision on the restructuring aid, unless the Commission decides that an extension is not justified or should be limited in time or scope.[57] In the *Compagnia Italiano Turismo* case, where the Commission initially approved rescue aid for a period of six months, that approval was revoked where a restructuring plan was submitted but was judged inadequate to ensure the firm's return to viability.[58] Similarly, in the *Ernault* case, the restructuring plan was submitted, but was subsequently withdrawn, leading the Commission to require the rescue aid to be immediately withdrawn.[59]

Rescue aid may not be used to finance structural measures, such as acquisition of significant businesses or assets, unless they are required during the rescue period for the survival of the beneficiary.[60] When the French

---

[54] *Ibid.*, para 26.

[55] *Ibid.*, para 55(c). See, Commission Decision 2002/783/EC, *Neue Erba Lautex*, OJ 2002 L282/48; Case C 31/08, *Volailles de Périgord*, OJ 2008 C317/13; Case NN 15/2006, *New Interline*, OJ 2007 C120/12.

[56] Rescue and restructuring aid guidelines 2014-2020, para 29.

[57] *Ibid.*, para 55(d). Once a restructuring plan has been put in place and is being implemented, all further aid will be considered as restructuring aid.

[58] Case NN 16/06, *Compagnia Italiano Turismo*, OJ 2006 C244/14. See, M. Lienemeyer, "Terminating rescue aid", *Competition Policy Newsletter*, Spring 2007, p. 127.

[59] Commission Decision 2007/674/EC, *Ernault*, OJ 2007 L277/25.

[60] Rescue and restructuring aid guidelines 2014-2020, para 55(e).

authorities granted a rescue loan of €450 million to Bull, the Commission was concerned that the aid appeared to be part of a long-term restructuring process, rather than rescue aid, and that the loan might be used to cover restructuring costs. The French authorities, however, were able to convince the Commission that the restructuring costs had been financed by the sale of assets, not by the rescue loan.[61] A rescue aid package in respect of Alstom included public participation in Alstom's capital increase and the payment of a subordinated loan. Under pressure from the Commission, the French authorities agreed to modify the package, replacing the direct capital stake by debt instruments which would not have irreversible effects on the market.[62]

Notification of rescue aid Although the conditions giving rise to rescue aid frequently occur at short notice, any aid should still be notified in advance to the Commission in accordance with Article 108(3) TFEU. The Commission will normally try to take a decision within one month where the aid is limited to €10 million.[63] Member States may not invoke urgency as an excuse for disregarding the obligation not to implement aid without notifying the Commission and awaiting its approval.[64] It must be said, however, that this appears to be a rule that is frequently not observed in practice.

Rescue aid must consist of loans or loan guarantees Rescue aid must consist of temporary liquidity support in the form of loan guarantees or loans.[65] The level of remuneration that a beneficiary is required to pay for rescue aid should reflect the underlying creditworthiness of the beneficiary, discounting the temporary effects of both liquidity difficulties and State support, and should provide incentives for the beneficiary to repay the aid as soon as possible. The Commission requires remuneration to be set at a rate not less than the reference rate set out in its Reference Rate Communication[66] for weak undertakings offering normal levels of collateralisation, which is currently 1-year IBOR plus 400 basis points, and to be increased by at least 50 basis points for rescue aid the authorisation of which is extended. Where there is evidence that this rate does not represent an appropriate benchmark, for example where it differs substantially from the market pricing of similar instruments recently issued by the beneficiary, the Commission may adapt the required level of remuneration accordingly.[67] Where the interest rate does not satisfy this condition, the loan will not be regarded as permissible rescue aid.[68]

---

[61] Commission Decision 2003/599/EC, *Bull*, OJ 2003 L209/1.
[62] Case C 58/2003, *Alstom*, OJ 2003 C269/15.
[63] Rescue and restructuring aid guidelines 2014-2020, para 121.
[64] Cases T-239/04 & T-323/04, *Italy v Commission* [2007] ECR II-3265, para 89.
[65] Rescue and restructuring aid guidelines 2014-2020, para 55(a).
[66] OJ 2008 C14/6.
[67] Rescue and restructuring aid guidelines 2014-2020, paras 56-57.
[68] Commission Decision 1999/484/EC, *HAMSA*, OJ 1999 L193/1.

Rescue aid must be limited to the minimum necessary Rescue aid must be restricted to the amount needed to keep the firm in business for the period during which the aid is authorised.[69] In the case of rescue aid to the British Energy group of companies, the Commission found that the aid was limited to the amount necessary to keep the group afloat. In this respect, the UK Government had put in place a rigorous mechanism aimed at ensuring that money could be drawn only when, and to the amount, strictly necessary. The need for each payment requested was to be established in advance by independent auditing experts. Furthermore, the UK Government undertook to report monthly to the Commission on the payments made to British Energy and to inform the Commission of any substantial change in the situation of the group.[70]

13.4 RESTRUCTURING AID

Restructuring aid Restructuring must be based on a feasible, coherent and far-reaching plan to restore a firm's long-term viability, while at the same time allowing for adequate own contribution and burden sharing and limiting the potential distortions of competition.[71] Restructuring aid cannot be limited to financial aid designed to make good past losses without tackling the reasons for those losses. Accordingly, restructuring usually involves one or more of the following elements: the reorganisation and rationalisation of the firm's activities on to a more efficient basis, typically involving the withdrawal from loss-making activities, the restructuring of those existing activities that can be made competitive again and, possibly, diversification towards new and viable activities. It typically also involves financial restructuring, such as capital injections by new or existing shareholders or debt reduction by existing creditors.[72]

Member States are free to choose the form that restructuring aid takes. However, in doing so, they should ensure that the instrument chosen is appropriate to the issue that it is intended to address. In particular, Member States should assess whether beneficiaries' problems relate to liquidity or solvency and select appropriate instruments to address the problems identified.

---

[69] Rescue and restructuring aid guidelines 2014-2020, para 60. A formula is set out in Annex I to the guidelines. Any aid exceeding the result of that calculation will only be authorised if it is duly justified by the provision of a liquidity plan setting out the beneficiary's liquidity needs for the coming six months.

[70] Case NN 101/2002, *British Energy*; Commission Decision 2005/407/EC, *British Energy*, OJ 2005 L142/26.

[71] Rescue and restructuring guidelines aid 2014-2020, para 27; Cases C-278/92-C-280/92, *Spain v Commission* [1994] ECR I-4103, para 67; Case C-17/99, *France v Commission* [2001] ECR I-2481, para 45.

[72] Rescue and restructuring aid guidelines 2014-2020, para 45.

For instance, in the case of solvency problems, increasing assets through recapitalisation might be appropriate, whereas in a situation where the problems mainly relate to liquidity, assistance through loans or loan guarantees might be sufficient.[73]

When restructuring aid is granted, measures must be taken to limit distortions of competition, so that adverse effects on trading conditions are minimised as much as possible and positive effects outweigh any adverse ones. Measures to limit distortions of competition will usually take the form of structural measures. Where appropriate to address the distortions of competition in particular cases, the Commission may accept behavioural measures or market opening measures in place of some or all of the structural measures that would otherwise be required.[74] The Commission will consider possible commitments from the Member State concerning the adoption of measures, either by the Member State itself or by the beneficiary, that are aimed at promoting more open, sound and competitive markets, for instance by favouring entry and exit. This could in particular include measures to open up certain markets directly or indirectly linked to the beneficiary's activities to other EU operators.[75] The Commission may impose any conditions and obligations it considers necessary to ensure that the aid does not distort competition to an extent contrary to the common interest, in the event that the Member State concerned has not given a commitment that it will adopt such provisions. For example, it may require the Member State to take certain measures itself, to impose certain obligations on the beneficiary or to refrain from granting other types of aid to the beneficiary during the restructuring period.[76]

Restructuring plan restoring long-term viability The grant of the aid must be conditional on implementation of the restructuring plan which must be endorsed by the Commission in all cases of *ad hoc* aid.[77] Failure to present a restructuring plan will result in the aid being declared incompatible with the common market.[78] For example, the Commission refused to approve aid granted by Spain to a textiles and clothing producer which had been in financial difficulties for some years. The aid, which was granted in the form of a failure to collect tax and social security debts in excess of €100 million, could not be approved in the light of the guidelines *inter alia* because there were insufficient guarantees for the restoration of the company's viability. The aid

---

[73] *Ibid.*, para 58.
[74] *Ibid.*, para 76-77.
[75] *Ibid.*, para 86.
[76] *Ibid.*, para 95.
[77] *Ibid.*. para 46.
[78] See, for example, Commission Decision 1999/395/EC, *Sniace*, OJ 1999 L149/40; Commission Decision 2005/786/EC, *Chemische Werke Piesteritz*, OJ 2005 L296/19.

had instead allowed the company to continue production despite mounting debts without taking restructuring measures.[79]

The restructuring plan, the duration of which must be as short as possible, must restore the long-term viability of the firm within a reasonable timescale and on the basis of realistic assumptions as to future operating conditions. The plan must be submitted in all relevant detail to the Commission. The restructuring plan must identify the causes of the beneficiary's difficulties and the beneficiary's own weaknesses, and outline how the proposed restructuring measures will remedy the beneficiary's underlying problems. Information must be provided on the business model of the beneficiary, demonstrating how the plan will foster its long-term viability, including, in particular, information on the beneficiary's organisational structure, funding, corporate governance and all other relevant aspects. The plan should assess whether the beneficiary's difficulties could have been avoided through appropriate and timely management action and, where that is the case, should demonstrate that appropriate management changes have been made. Where the beneficiary's difficulties stem from flaws in its business model or corporate governance system, appropriate changes will be required. The expected results of the planned restructuring should be demonstrated in a baseline scenario as well as in a pessimistic or worst-case scenario. Assumptions should be compared with appropriate sector-wide benchmarks, accompanied by a market survey and a sensitivity analysis identifying the driving parameters of the beneficiary's performance and the main risk factors to be faced. The beneficiary's return to viability should derive mainly from internal measures, entailing in particular withdrawal from activities which would remain structurally loss-making in the medium term. Long-term viability is achieved when an undertaking is able to provide an appropriate projected return on capital after having covered all its costs including depreciation and financial charges, showing that it should be able to compete in the marketplace on its own merits.[80]

Where the Commission considers that the restructuring plan will not lead to the restoration of the beneficiary's viability within a reasonable time, based on realistic assumptions, it will oppose the aid.[81] Thus, it prohibited aid to Euromoteurs as the aid would not restore the company's long-term viability. Moreover, the Commission discovered that incompatible aid had previously been paid and ordered its recover, which had a further negative effect on the chances of the restoration of the company's viability.[82] Similarly, where the restructuring plan does not provide sufficient information for the Commission

---

[79] Commission Decision 2003/876/EC, *Puigneró*, OJ 2003 l337/14.
[80] Rescue and restructuring aid guidelines 2014-2020, paras 47-52.
[81] See, for example, Commission Decision 2002/779/EC, *Zeuro*, OJ 2002 L282/1; Commission Decision 2002/783/EC, *Neue Erba Lautex*, OJ 2002 L282/48.
[82] Commission Decision 2006/747/EC, *Euromoteurs*, OJ 2006 L307/213.

to be able to conclude that it will result in the beneficiary returning to viability, it must reject the plan.[83]

Significant own contribution In order to ensure that the aid is limited to the minimum necessary, a significant contribution to the restructuring costs is required from the own resources of the aid beneficiary, its shareholders or creditors or the business group to which it belongs, or from new investors. Such own contribution should normally be comparable to the aid granted in terms of effects on the solvency or liquidity position of the beneficiary. For example, where the aid to be granted enhances the beneficiary's equity position, the own contribution should similarly include measures that are equity-enhancing, such as raising fresh equity from incumbent shareholders, the write-down of existing debt and capital notes or the conversion of existing debt to equity, or the raising of new external equity on market terms. The Commission will take account of the extent to which own contribution has a comparable effect to the aid granted when assessing the necessary extent of the measures to limit distortions of competition.[84]

Contributions must be real, that is to say actual, excluding future expected profits such as cash flow, and must be as high as possible. Own contribution will normally be considered to be adequate if it amounts to at least 50% of the restructuring costs. In exceptional circumstances and in cases of particular hardship, the Commission may accept a contribution that does not reach 50% of the restructuring costs, provided that the amount of that contribution remains significant.[85] For example, in its *CBW Chemie* decision, the Commission accepted a contribution of 19% because the undertaking was subject to a management buy-out.[86] In the *ABX Logistics* case, the Commission accepted a contribution of 43.4% in the case of a large undertaking where the restructuring involved large capacity cuts.[87] The beneficiary may be expected to sell assets that are not essential to the core business in order to fund its contribution. Where the contribution from private shareholders is inadequate, the Commission will not be prepared to authorise the aid.[88]

Adequate burden sharing Where State support is given in a form that enhances the beneficiary's equity position, for example where the State provides grants, injects capital or writes off debt, this can have the effect of protecting shareholders and subordinated creditors from the consequences of

---

[83] See, for example, Commission Decision 2000/732/EC, *Korn Fahrzeuge und Technik*, OJ 2000 L295/21.

[84] Rescue and restructuring aid guidelines 2014-2020, para 62.

[85] *Ibid.*, paras 63-64.

[86] Commission Decision 2000/393/EC, *CBW Chemie*, OJ 2000 L150/32.

[87] Commission Decision 2006/947/EC, *ABX Logistics*, OJ 2006 L383/21.

[88] See, for example, Commission Decision 1999/647/EC, *Addinol Mineralöl*, OJ 1999 L260/19.

their choice to invest in the beneficiary, creating moral hazard and
undermining market discipline. Consequently, aid to cover losses should only
be granted on terms which involve adequate burden sharing by existing
investors. Adequate burden sharing will normally mean that incumbent
shareholders and, where necessary, subordinated creditors must absorb losses
in full. Subordinated creditors should contribute to the absorption of losses
either via conversion into equity or write-down of the principal of the relevant
instruments. In any case, cash outflows from the beneficiary to holders of
equity or subordinated debt should be prevented during the restructuring period
to the extent legally possible, unless that would disproportionately affect those
that have injected fresh equity. Adequate burden sharing will also mean that
any State aid that enhances the beneficiary's equity position should be granted
on terms that afford the State a reasonable share of future gains in value of the
beneficiary, in view of the amount of State equity injected in comparison with
the remaining equity of the company after losses have been accounted for.[89]

The Commission may allow exceptions from full implementation of the
burden sharing measures where they would otherwise lead to disproportionate
results. Such situations could include cases where the aid amount is small in
comparison with the own contribution, or where subordinated creditors would
receive less in economic terms than under normal insolvency proceedings and
if no State aid were granted. The Commission will not systematically require a
contribution by senior debt holders to restoring a beneficiary's equity position.
However, it may treat any such contribution as grounds for a reduction in the
necessary extent of measures to limit distortions of competition.[90]

Structural measures entailing reduction of business activity Undertakings
benefiting from restructuring aid may be required to divest assets or reduce
capacity or market presence. Such measures should take place in particular in
the market or markets where the undertaking will have a significant market
position after restructuring, in particular those where there is significant excess
capacity.[91] Divestments to limit distortions of competition should take place
without undue delay, taking into account the type of asset being divested and
any obstacles to its disposal, and in any case within the duration of the
restructuring plan. Divestments, write-offs and closure of loss-making
activities which would at any rate be necessary to restore long-term viability
will generally not be considered sufficient to address distortions of
competition.[92] The guidelines provide no definition of significant market
position, although it would seem that a market share that is not negligible will

---

[89] Rescue and restructuring aid guidelines 2014-2020, paras 65-67.
[90] *Ibid.*, paras 68-69.
[91] Decision 2010/175/EC, *Gdansk Shipyard*, OJ 2010 L181/19.
[92] Rescue and restructuring aid guidelines 2014-2020, para 78; Case SA.30908, *Czech Airlines* (2012).

suffice.[93] By contrast, where there is no evidence of over-capacity on the market, the Commission might not require any capacity reduction.[94] In *Electrolux v Commission*, the Commission approved aid to the French household appliances producer FagorBrandt, on the basis that the restructuring plan involved the sale of certain activities, plant closures and a workforce reduction. However, the General Court held that the compensatory measures were inadequate in that they had no real effect on reducing the adverse effects resulting from the aid on the household appliances market.[95]

In order for such measures to strengthen competition and contribute to the internal market, they should favour the entry of new competitors, the expansion of existing small competitors or cross-border activity. Retrenchment within national borders and fragmentation of the internal market should be avoided. Measures to limit distortions of competition should not lead to a deterioration in the structure of the market. Structural measures should therefore normally take the form of divestments on a going concern basis of viable stand-alone businesses that, if operated by a suitable purchaser, can compete effectively in the long term. In the event that such an entity is not available, the beneficiary could carve out and subsequently divest an existing and appropriately funded activity, creating a new and viable entity that should be able to compete in the market. Structural measures that take the form of divestment of assets alone and do not involve the creation of a viable entity able to compete in the market are less effective in preserving competition and will therefore only be accepted in exceptional cases where the Member State concerned demonstrates that no other form of structural measures would be feasible or that other structural measures would seriously jeopardise the economic viability of the undertaking.[96]

The beneficiary should facilitate divestitures, for example through ring-fencing of activities and by agreeing not to solicit clients of the divested business. Where it appears that it may be difficult to find a buyer for the assets which a beneficiary proposes to divest, it will be required, as soon as it becomes aware of such difficulties, to identify alternative divestments or measures to be taken in relation to the market or markets concerned if the primary divestment fails.[97]

In the services sector, particularly financial services, capacity cuts will often involve branch closures.[98] In the *MobilCom* decision, the Commission,

---

[93]   Case N 584/2004, *AB Vingriai*, OJ 2005 C187/15; Commission Decision 2007/509/EC, *Fabryka Samochodow Osobowych*, OJ 2007 L187/30.

[94]   See, for example, Commission 2005/940/EC, *Jahnke Stahlbau*, OJ 2005 L342/72.

[95]   Cases T-115/09 & T-116/09, *Electrolux AB v Commission* EU:T:2012:76, para 58.

[96]   Rescue and restructuring aid guidelines 2014-2020, paras 79-80.

[97]   *Ibid.*, paras 81-82.

[98]   Commission Decision 98/490/EC, *Crédit Lyonnais*, OJ 1999 L221/28; Commission Decision 1999/288/EC, *Banco di Napoli*, OJ 1999 L116/36; Commission Decision 1999/508/EC, *Société Marseillaise de Crédit*, OJ 1999 L198/1.

having accepted that there was a considerable potential distortion of competition, imposed specific conditions concerning the internet marketing of certain services.[99] Special considerations apply where the firm has a very strong market share or monopoly. Restructuring aid was granted by the French authorities to Imprimerie Nationale, a State-owned company operating in the printing industry. While enjoying a legal monopoly for certain official fiduciary documents, it was also active on various competitive printing markets. The aid was authorised by the Commission in exchange for significant compensatory measures to limit any adverse effects on IN's competitors. In particular, in order to prevent any aggravation of restrictions of competition resulting from IN's legal monopoly activities, steps were taken to rule out any risk of cross-subsidisation.[100]

Behavioural measures Behavioural measures aim at ensuring that aid is used only to finance the restoration of long-term viability and that it is not abused to prolong serious and persistent market structure distortions or to shield the beneficiary from healthy competition. The Commission requires that beneficiaries refrain from acquiring shares in any company during the restructuring period, except where indispensable to ensure the long-term viability of the beneficiary, and from publicising State support as a competitive advantage when marketing their products and services. These behavioural measures must be applied in all cases, to avoid undermining the effects of structural measures, and should in principle be imposed for the duration of the restructuring plan. In addition, in exceptional circumstances, it may be necessary to require beneficiaries to refrain from engaging in commercial behaviour aimed at a rapid expansion of their market share relating to specific products or geographic markets by offering terms, such as regards prices and other commercial conditions, which cannot be matched by competitors that are not in receipt of State aid. Such restrictions will only be applied where no other remedy, structural or behavioural, can adequately address the competition distortions identified, and where such a measure will not itself restrict competition in the market concerned.[101]

Market opening measures The Commission may also consider possible commitments from the Member State concerning the adoption of measures, either by the Member State itself or by the beneficiary, that are aimed at promoting more open, sound and competitive markets, for instance by favouring entry and exit. This could in particular include measures to open up certain markets directly or indirectly linked to the beneficiary's activities to other EU operators. Such initiatives may replace other measures to limit

---

[99]   Commission Decision 2005/346/EC, *MobilCom*, OJ 2005 L116/55.

[100] Case N 370/2004, *Imprimerie Nationale*, OJ 2008 C54/1.

[101] Rescue and restructuring aid guidelines 2014-2020, paras 83-85.

distortions of competition that would normally be required of the beneficiary.[102]

Assessment of measures to limit distortions of competition Measures to limit distortions of competition should address both moral hazard concerns and possible distortions in the markets where the beneficiary operates. The extent of such measures will depend on several factors, such as, in particular: the size and nature of the aid and the conditions and circumstances under which it was granted; the size and the relative importance of the beneficiary in the market and the characteristics of the market concerned; and the extent to which moral hazard concerns remain following the application of own contribution and burden-sharing measures. In particular, the Commission will consider the size, where appropriate by means of approximations, and nature of the aid both in absolute terms and in relation to the beneficiary's assets and the size of the market as a whole. As regards the size and the relative importance of the beneficiary on its market or markets both before and after the restructuring, the Commission will evaluate the likely effects of the aid on those markets as compared to the likely outcome in the absence of State aid. The measures will be tailored to market characteristics to make sure that effective competition is preserved. With regard to moral hazard concerns, the Commission will also assess the degree of own contribution and burden sharing. Greater degrees of own contribution and burden sharing than those required under the guidelines, by limiting the amount of aid and moral hazard, may reduce the necessary extent of measures to limit distortions of competition.[103]

Since restructuring activities may threaten to undermine the internal market, measures to limit distortions of competition that help to ensure that national markets remain open and contestable will be considered positively. Measures limiting distortions of competition should not compromise the prospects of the beneficiary's return to viability, which might be the case if a measure is very costly to execute or, in exceptional cases duly substantiated by the Member State concerned, would reduce the activity of the beneficiary to such an extent that its return to viability would be compromised, nor should they come at the expense of consumers and competition. Aid to cover the social costs of restructuring must be clearly identified in the restructuring plan, since aid for social measures exclusively for the benefit of redundant employees will be disregarded for the purposes of determining the extent of measures to limit distortions of competition. In the common interest the Commission will ensure, in the context of the restructuring plan, that the social effects of the restructuring in Member States other than the one granting aid are kept to the minimum.[104]

---

[102] *Ibid.*, para 86.
[103] *Ibid.*, paras 87-90.
[104] *Ibid.*, paras 91-93.

Implementation of restructuring plan The company must fully implement the restructuring plan and must discharge any other obligations laid down in the Commission decision authorising the aid. The Commission will regard any failure to implement the plan or to fulfil the other obligations as misuse of the aid.[105]   Where restructuring operations cover several years and involve substantial amounts of aid, the Commission may require payment of the restructuring aid to be split into instalments and may make payment of each instalment subject to the satisfactory implementation of each stage in the restructuring plan.[106]

In its *Alstom* decision, the Commission required that an independent trustee be appointed to perform a detailed review of the sales process of assets of the company.[107] In its decision on *Imprimerie Nationale*, the Commission also required that an independent expert examine IN's accounts and cost-allocation arrangements to confirm the absence of any cross-subsidisation.[108] Similarly, in the *British Energy* decision, the Commission sought to ensure that the restructuring aid could not be used for purposes other than meeting its historical nuclear liabilities. In particular, BE was required to separate its nuclear generation, non-nuclear generation and trade businesses, with cross-subsidisation being prohibited. In addition, for a period of six years, BE was prohibited from increasing its generation capacity and from setting its prices at less than the wholesale market prices of its direct competitors.[109]

Amendment of the restructuring plan Where restructuring aid has been approved, the Member State concerned may, during the restructuring period, ask the Commission to agree to changes to the restructuring plan and the amount of the aid. For instance, in the case of *Italstrada*, the Commission accepted that a serious crisis required additional restructuring measures.[110] Where restructuring aid has been approved, the Member State concerned may, during the restructuring period, ask the Commission to agree to changes to the restructuring plan and the amount of the aid. The Commission may allow such changes where they meet the following conditions: the revised plan must still show a return to viability within a reasonable time scale; if the restructuring costs are increased, the own contribution must increase correspondingly; if the amount of the aid is increased, measures to limit distortions of competition must be more extensive than those initially imposed; if the proposed measures to limit distortions of competition are more limited than those initially imposed, the amount of the aid must be correspondingly reduced; the new

---

[105] *Ibid.*, para 122.
[106] *Ibid.*, para 123.
[107] Commission Decision 2005/418/EC, *Alstom*, OJ 2005 L150/24.
[108] Case N 370/2004, *Imprimerie Nationale*, OJ 2008 C54/1.
[109] Commission Decision 2005/407/EC, *British Energy*, OJ 2005 L142/26.
[110] Commission Decision 1999/269/EC, *Italstrada*, OJ 1999 L109/1.

timetable for implementation of the measures to limit distortions of competition may be delayed with respect to the timetable initially adopted only for reasons outside the beneficiary's or the Member State's control. If that is not the case, the amount of the aid must be correspondingly reduced.[111] Constant requests to amend the restructuring plan may, however, lead the Commission to conclude that successful restructuring of the undertaking concerned is impossible.[112]

Restructuring aid in assisted areas Economic and social cohesion being a priority objective of the EU under Article 174 TFEU, the Commission must take the needs of regional development into account when assessing restructuring aid in assisted areas. However, the Commission's view is that the fact that an ailing firm is located in an assisted area does not justify a permissive approach to aid for restructuring. In the medium to long term it does not help a region to prop up companies artificially. Furthermore, in order to promote regional development, it is in the region's own best interest to apply its resources to develop as soon as possible activities that are viable and sustainable. Finally, distortions of competition must be minimised even in the case of aid to firms in assisted areas. In this context, regard must also be had to possible harmful spill-over effects which could take place in the area concerned and other assisted areas.[113]

Thus, the conditions for allowing restructuring aid are equally applicable to assisted areas, even when the needs of regional development are considered.[114] In assisted areas, however, and unless otherwise stipulated in rules on State aid in a particular sector, the conditions for authorising aid may be less stringent in terms of reduction capacity or market presence.[115] In those cases, a distinction will be drawn between areas eligible for regional aid under Article 107(3)(a) TFEU and those eligible under Article 107(3)(c) TFEU so as to take account of the greater severity of the regional problems in the former areas. Where the specific circumstances of assisted areas so require, for example where a beneficiary faces particular difficulties in raising new market financing as a result of its location in an assisted area, the Commission may accept a contribution which is less than 50% of the restructuring costs for the purposes of own contribution.[116]

Aid to SGEI providers in difficulty In assessing State aid to providers of services of general economic interest in difficulty, the Commission will take

[111] Rescue and restructuring aid guidelines 2014-2020, paras 124-125.
[112] Commission Decision 2000/129/EC, *Lautex*, OJ 2000 L42/19.
[113] Rescue and restructuring aid guidelines 2014-2020, para 97.
[114] Case C-169/95, *Spain v Commission* [1997] ECR I-135, paras 17-20.
[115] See, for example, Decision 2011/414/EU, *Varvaressos*, OJ 2011 L184/9.
[116] Rescue and restructuring aid guidelines 2014-2020, para 98.

account of the specific nature of SGEI and, in particular, of the need to ensure continuity of service provision in accordance with Article 106(2) TFEU. SGEI providers may require State aid in order to continue to provide SGEI on terms that are compatible with their long-term viability. The restoration of long-term viability may, therefore, be based on the assumption, in particular, that any State aid that meets the compatibility requirements the EU State aid rules for SGEIs will continue to be available for the duration of any entrustment entered into before or during the restructuring period. Where the Commission assesses aid to SGEI providers in difficulty under the rescue and restructuring guidelines, it will take into account all State aid received by the provider in question, including any compensation for public service obligations. However, since SGEI providers can derive a large proportion of their normal revenues from public service compensation, the total amount of aid determined in this manner may be very large in comparison with the size of the beneficiary and may overstate the burden on the State in relation to the beneficiary's restructuring. When determining the own contribution, therefore, the Commission will disregard any public service compensation that meets the compatibility requirements under EU State aid rules. To the extent that assets are necessary for the provision of SGEI, it may not be practicable to require the divestment of such assets by way of measures to limit distortions of competition. In such cases, the Commission may require alternative measures to be taken to ensure that competition is not distorted to an extent contrary to the common interest, in particular by introducing fair competition in respect of the SGEI in question as soon as possible. Where an SGEI provider is not able to comply with the conditions of the guidelines, the aid in question cannot be found compatible. In such cases, however, the Commission may authorise the payment of such aid as is necessary to ensure continuity of the SGEI until a new provider is entrusted with the service. The Commission will only authorise aid where the Member State concerned demonstrates on objective grounds that the aid is strictly limited to the amount and duration indispensable to entrust a new provider with the service.[117]

13.5 RESCUE AND RESTRUCTURING AID SCHEMES FOR SMES

Rescue and restructuring aid schemes for SMEs Aid schemes applying to large undertakings cannot benefit from the rescue and restructuring aid guidelines.[118] The Commission considers, however, that aid for rescue and restructuring aid to small or medium-sized enterprises or smaller State-owned undertakings should be provided pursuant to aid schemes.[119] The use of

---

[117] *Ibid.*, paras 99-103.
[118] Cases T-239/04 & T-323/04, *Italy v Commission* [2007] ECR II-3265, para 24.
[119] Rescue and restructuring aid guidelines 2014-2020, para 104.

schemes helps to limit distortions of competition linked to moral hazard, by allowing a Member State to make a clear statement *ex ante* concerning the terms on which it may decide to grant aid to undertakings in difficulty. Schemes must specify the maximum amount of aid that can be awarded to any one undertaking as part of an operation to provide rescue aid, restructuring aid or temporary restructuring support. The maximum total amount of aid granted to any one undertaking may not be more than €10 million, including any aid obtained from other sources or under other schemes. Whilst the compatibility of such schemes will be assessed in the light of the general conditions set out in the guidelines, simplified conditions apply in certain respects, to enable Member States to apply those conditions without further reference to the Commission and to reduce the burden on SMEs and smaller State-owned undertakings of providing the information required. In view of the small size of the aid amounts and the beneficiaries at stake, the Commission considers that the potential for significant distortions of competitions is more limited in such cases.[120]

Whilst the failure of an individual SME is unlikely to involve a significant degree of social hardship or market failure, there is a greater concern in relation to SMEs that value may be destroyed when SMEs that have the potential to restructure so as to restore their long-term viability are denied the chance to do so by liquidity problems. As regards the grant of aid under schemes, therefore, it is sufficient for a Member State to determine that the failure of the beneficiary would likely involve social hardship or a market failure, in particular that: the exit of an innovative SME or an SME with high growth potential would have potential negative consequences; the exit of an undertaking with extensive links to other local or regional undertakings, particularly other SMEs, would have potential negative consequences; the failure or adverse incentives of credit markets would push an otherwise viable undertaking into bankruptcy; or similar situations of hardship duly substantiated by the beneficiary would arise. By way of derogation from the normal requirement, beneficiaries under schemes are not required to submit a market survey.[121] Simplified provisions apply concerning the rescue aid.[122] Member States may consider an own contribution to be adequate if it amounts to at least 40% of the restructuring costs in the case of medium-sized enterprises or 25% of the restructuring costs in the case of small enterprises.[123]

Assessment of negative effects of aid A Member State that intends to grant rescue aid, restructuring aid or temporary restructuring support must verify whether the one time last time principle is complied with. For that purpose, the

---

[120] *Ibid.*, paras 104-106.
[121] *Ibid.*, paras 107-108.
[122] *Ibid.*, paras 107-108
[123] *Ibid.*, para 111.

Member State must determine whether the undertaking concerned has already received rescue aid, restructuring aid or temporary restructuring support in the past, including any non-notified aid. If so, and where less than 10 years, or five years in the case of the primary agricultural production sector, have elapsed since the rescue aid or temporary restructuring support was granted or the restructuring period came to an end or implementation of the restructuring plan was halted, further aid must not be granted, except:[124]

(a)   where temporary restructuring support follows the granting of rescue aid as part of a single restructuring operation;

(b)   where restructuring aid follows the granting of rescue aid or temporary restructuring support as part of a single restructuring operation;

(c)   where rescue aid or temporary restructuring support has been granted in accordance with these guidelines and that aid was not followed by restructuring aid, if it could reasonably have been believed that the beneficiary would be viable in the long term when the aid was granted, and new rescue or restructuring aid or temporary restructuring support becomes necessary after at least five years due to unforeseeable circumstances for which the beneficiary is not responsible; or

(d)   in exceptional and unforeseeable circumstances for which the beneficiary is not responsible.

Measures limiting distortions of competition are likely to have a disproportionate impact on small enterprises, particularly given the burden of carrying out such measures. By way of derogation from the normal practice, therefore, Member States are not obliged to require such measures from small enterprises, except where otherwise provided by rules on State aid in a particular sector. However, small enterprises should not normally increase their capacity during a restructuring period.[125]

Temporary restructuring support   Temporary restructuring support is liquidity assistance designed to support the restructuring of an undertaking by providing the conditions needed for the beneficiary to design and implement appropriate action to restore its long-term viability. Temporary restructuring support may only be granted to SMEs and smaller State-owned undertakings.[126] It may also be granted to undertakings that are not in difficulty but that are facing acute liquidity needs due to exceptional and unforeseen circumstances.[127] Temporary restructuring support schemes may allow for liquidity aid for periods longer than six months provided certain the following are met. The support must consist of aid in the form of loan guarantees or loans. Temporary restructuring support must comply with the

---

[124]   *Ibid.*, para 112.

[125]   *Ibid.*, para 113.

[126]   *Ibid.*, para 28.

[127]   *Ibid.*, para 29.

general provisions of the guidelines, as modified. It may be granted for a period not exceeding 18 months, less any immediately preceding period of rescue aid. Before the end of that period the Member State must approve a restructuring plan or liquidation plan, or the loan must be reimbursed or the guarantee terminated. Not later than six months after disbursement of the first instalment to the beneficiary, less any immediately preceding period of rescue aid, the Member State must approve a simplified restructuring plan. That plan must, as a minimum, identify the actions that the beneficiary must take to restore its long-term viability without State support.[128]

Remuneration for temporary restructuring support should be set at a rate not less than the reference rate set out in the Communication from the Commission on the revision of the method for setting the reference and discount rates for weak undertakings offering normal levels of collateralisation. To provide incentives for exit, the rate should increase by not less than 50 basis points once 12 months have elapsed from the time of disbursement of the first instalment to the beneficiary. Temporary restructuring support must be restricted to the amount needed to keep the beneficiary in business for 18 months.[129]

Duration and evaluation of aid schemes The Commission may require Member States to limit the duration of certain schemes normally to four years or less and to conduct an evaluation of those schemes. Evaluations will be required for schemes where the potential distortions are particularly high, that is to say schemes where there is a risk of significant restrictions of competition if their implementation is not reviewed in due time. Given the objectives and in order not to impose disproportionate burdens on Member States in respect of smaller aid projects, this only applies to aid schemes with large budgets or containing novel characteristics, or when significant market, technology or regulatory changes are anticipated.[130]

---

[128] *Ibid.*, paras 114-115.
[129] *Ibid.*, paras 116-117.
[130] *Ibid.*, paras 118-120.

Chapter Fourteen

SECTORAL AID

14.1 SECTORAL AID

Commission policy on sectoral aid   Pursuant to Article 107(3)(c) TFEU, State aid may be compatible with the internal market in so far as it is intended to facilitate the development of certain economic activities. Thus, aid that is determined according to sectoral criteria may be permissible where this leads to the development of that sector. While many aid schemes are sectoral in nature, the Commission has not sought to develop a sectoral approach in the development of its State aid policy. Indeed, on the contrary, in the context of, for example, regional aid, it prefers aid schemes to be multisectoral. In general, also, the main policy instruments governing horizontal aid, such as the framework on R&D&I and the guidelines on environmental protection, draw no distinction between different sectors, other than to restrict their application in certain circumstances. Nevertheless, certain sectors have been subjected to different treatment under the State aid rules. In particular, sectors that suffered from over-capacity, such as motor vehicles, synthetic fibres and textiles were subject to individual treatment by the Commission. Initially, separate frameworks were established for State aid in these sectors. These were replaced by the multi-sectoral framework on regional aid for large investments in 2002 and, insofar as separate treatment for large undertakings has survived, have now been subsumed into the regional aid guidelines.

Sectors subject to additional State aid rules   Articles 107(1) TFEU applies generally to all economic sectors, save as otherwise provided. There are a number of provisions in the FEU Treaty that provide for specific treatment of State aid in relation to particular sectors. First, agricultural and fisheries policy is governed by Articles 38-44 TFEU. Article 42 TFEU provides that the rules on competition, including State aid, apply to the production of and trade in agricultural products only to the extent determined by the Council and the European Parliament. Second, Article 93 TFEU provides that State aid for transport is permissible if it meets the needs of coordination of transport or if it represents reimbursement for the discharge of certain obligations inherent in the concept of public service. Third, Article 346(1)(b) TFEU precludes the application of the State aid rules to the production of and trade in arms, munitions and war material that are necessary for the protection of Member States' essential interests of their security. In addition, pursuant to Article

107(3)(e) TFEU, which allows the Council to adopt additional substantive State aid rules, particular provisions have been adopted concerning State aid for coal and shipbuilding. Following the expiry of the ECSC Treaty which prohibited State aid for the steel sector, the Commission has maintained a general prohibition on investment aid for the steel sector. In a number of specific sectors, the Commission has issued communications and guidelines setting out its specific State aid policy.

14.2 AGRICULTURE, FORESTRY AND FISHERIES

Agriculture and competition policy Agricultural products are the products of the soil, of stockfarming and products of first-stage processing directly related to these products.[1] These include live animals, meat, fish and dairy produce, trees and plants, fruit and vegetables, coffee, tea and cocoa, sugar and spices, cereals, malt and starches, oil seeds, wines and other fermented beverages, unmanufactured tobacco, cork, flax and hemp.[2] Pursuant to Article 42 TFEU, the provisions of the FEU Treaty relating to rules on competition, including the provisions concerning State aid, apply to the production of and trade in agricultural products only to the extent determined by the European Parliament and the Council within the framework of the common agricultural policy, in particular by the establishment of common organisations of the market.[3] This acknowledges that the common agricultural policy takes precedence over the objectives of the FEU Treaty in the field of competition.[4] However, the mere fact that a measure may be consistent with the objectives of the common agricultural policy is not sufficient to preclude the application of the State aid rules.[5]

In determining the extent to which the competition rules are to be applied, the following objectives must be taken into account: increasing agricultural productivity, ensuring a fair standard of living for the agricultural community, stabilising markets, assuring the availability of supplies, and ensuring that supplies reach consumers at reasonable prices.[6] In working out the common

---

[1] Article 38 TFEU.

[2] A full list is in Annex I TFEU.

[3] Article 42 TFEU.

[4] Case C-280/93, *Germany v Commission* [1994] ECR I-4973, para 61; Case C-311/94, *IJssel-Vliet Combinatie BV v Minister van Economische Zaken* [1996] ECR I-5023, para 31; Case C-456/00, *France v Commission* [2002] ECR I-11949, para 33; Case T-379/09, *Italy v Commission* EU:T:2012:422, para 70.

[5] Case T-379/09, *Italy v Commission* EU:T:2012:422, para 70.

[6] Article 39(1) TFEU. The EU institutions have a permanent duty to reconcile any conflict between these individual aims. For the purposes of that duty, they may allow one of them temporary priority: Cases 279-280/84 & 285-286/84, *Rau v Commission*

agricultural policy and the special methods for its application, account must be
taken of the particular nature of agricultural activity, which results from the
social structure of agriculture and from structural and natural disparities
between the various agricultural regions, the need to effect the appropriate
adjustment by degrees, and the fact that agriculture constitutes a sector closely
linked with the economy as a whole.[7] The Council, on a proposal from the
Commission, may, in particular, authorise the granting of aid for the protection
of enterprises handicapped by structural or natural conditions or within the
framework of economic development programmes.[8]

Application of State aid rules to agriculture Agricultural now accounts for
about a sixth of all State aid, with some €8 billion awarded to the agricultural
sector in 2013, down from €11.8 billion of aid granted in 2007.[9] Specific
provisions governing the application of State aid rules to the agricultural sector
have been adopted by the Council in the context of the establishment of rules
governing common organisations of the market. The regulations establishing
common organisations of the market invariably provide that Articles 107-108
TFEU apply to that particular product. Nevertheless, the application of the
State aid rules remains subordinate to the provisions governing the common
organisation of the market established by those regulations.[10] For example, in
Pigs and Bacon Commission v McCarron, a bonus payable on the export of
bacon from Ireland was held to be contrary to the provisions of the common
organisation of the market in pigmeat by distorting the conditions of
competition on the market and was therefore prohibited. It followed that the
legality of the bonus could not be evaluated by reference to the State aid
provisions of the FEU Treaty.[11] Similarly, national subsidies to the sugar
industry which were incompatible with the common organisation of the market
in sugar could not be declared lawful on the basis of Article 107 TFEU.[12]

Once a common organisation of the market has been established, Member
States must refrain from taking any unilateral measure even if that measure is
likely to support the common agricultural policy.[13] Thus, in *Italy v*

[1987] ECR 1069, para 21; Case T-82/96, *ARAP v Commission* [1999] ECR II-1889,
    para 87.
[7] Article 39(2) TFEU.
[8] Article 42 TFEU.
[9] State aid scoreboard, 2014.
[10] Case 177/78, *Pigs and Bacon Commission v McCarren* [1979] ECR 2161, para 11; Case
    C-456/00, *France v Commission* [2002] ECR I-11949, para 32; Case C-283/03 *Kuipers
    v Productschap Zuivel* [2005] ECR I-4255, para 34.
[11] Case 177/78, *Pigs and Bacon Commission v McCarren* [1979] ECR 2161, para 21.
[12] Case 72/79, *Commission v Italy* [1980] ECR 1411, para 12.
[13] Case 216/84, *Commission v France* [1988] ECR 793, para 18; Case C-86/89, *Italy v
    Commission* [1990] ECR I-3891, para 19; Case C-173/02, *Spain v Commission* [2004]
    ECR I-9735, para 19.

Commission, where Italy sought to grant aid to wine producers in addition to that allowed under the regulations governing the common organisation of the market in wine on the ground that the latter was insufficient, the ECJ held that it was for the EU to seek solutions to such problems, not the Member States.[14] In *Spain v Commission*, it was emphasised that the lawfulness of aid did not depend on the possible effects that the aid might have on the functioning of the market even if it was not such as to distort the functioning of the market.[15] For products not subject to a common organisation of the market, the rules on competition are only partially applicable so that the Commission is unable to prevent the grant of trade-distorting State aid, even when applied to intra-EU trade.[16] Regulation (EC) No 1184/2006[17] on the application of the competition rules to agriculture provides that the provisions of Article 108(1) TFEU and the first sentence of Article 108(3) TFEU do apply to these products,[18] with the result that Member States are required to inform the Commission of the aid. The Commission may submit its comments to the Member State concerned, but it is unable to oppose the aid.[19]

Where the Council provides that the provisions of Articles 107-108 TFEU are to apply in a common organisation of the market, this includes granting the Council itself the power pursuant to Article 108(2) TFEU to declare certain aid compatible with the internal market if such a decision is justified by exceptional circumstances.[20] It follows that Article 108(2) TFEU is available to the Council as a basis for a measure derogating from the provisions on the common organisation of the market.[21] Consequently, any allegation that aid approved under Article 108(2) TFEU undermines the common organisation of the market may be examined only to the extent that it can be demonstrated that the Council has exceeded the limits of its discretionary power under that provision.[22]

State aid for agriculture In 2006, the Commission adopted guidelines setting out its policy on State aid for agriculture and forestry.[23] These guidelines have

---

[14] Case C-86/89, *Italy v Commission* [1990] ECR I-3891, para 19. See also, Case 90/86 *Zoni* [1988] ECR 4285, para 26; Case C-113/00, *Spain v Commission* [2002] ECR I-7601, para 74; Case C-114/00, *Spain v Commission* [2002] ECR I-7657, para 90.

[15] Case C-173/02, *Spain v Commission* [2004] ECR I-9735, para 31.

[16] *Twentieth Report on Competition Policy* (1990), pt. 337.

[17] OJ 2006 L214/7.

[18] Council Regulation (EEC) No 26/62, Article 3.

[19] Case 114/83, *Société d'Initiatives et de Coopération Agricoles v Commission* [1984] ECR 2589, para 27.

[20] Case C-122/94, *Commission v Council* [1996] ECR I-881, para 13.

[21] Case 253/84, *GAEC v Council and Commission* [1987] ECR 123, *per* Advocate General Slynn, at p. 146.

[22] Case C-122/94, *Commission v Council* [1996] ECR I-881, para 15.

[23] OJ 2006 C319/1.

been replaced by new expanded guidelines issued in 2014 which are applicable for the period 2014-2020.[24] In addition, Commission Regulation (EU) No 702/2014 provides for a block exemption for certain categories of aid in the agricultural and forestry sectors and in rural areas.[25] The categories of aid that may be awarded in accordance with the guidelines are divided into rural development measures, risk and crisis management measures and other types of aid.

Rural development measures may provide for the following categories of aid: aid for investment in agricultural holdings linked to primary agricultural production; investment aid in favour of the conservation of cultural and natural heritage; relocation of farm buildings; aid for investments in connection with the processing and marketing of agricultural products; environmental and animal welfare aid; start-up aid for young farmers and the development of small farms; aid for the transfer of agricultural holdings; start-up aid for producer groups and organisations; aid for agri-environment-climate commitments and animal welfare commitments; aid for disadvantages related to Natura 2000 areas and to the Water Framework Directive; aid to areas facing natural or other specific constraints; aid for organic farming; aid for the participation of producer of agricultural products in quality schemes; aid for provision of technical support in the agricultural sector; and aid for cooperation in the agricultural sector. Risk crisis management measures include: aid to compensate for damage to agricultural production or the means of agricultural production caused by natural disasters, adverse weather conditions or animal and plant diseases, or for fallen stock; aid to compensate for damage caused by protected animals; aid for payment of insurance premiums and financial contributions to mutual funds; aid for closing production capacity. Other types of aid include aid to the livestock sector; aid for promotion measures in favour of agricultural products; aid for the outermost regions; aid for agricultural land consolidation; aid for rescuing and restructuring undertakings in difficulty; and aid for research and development.

Aid for the forestry sector Forestry is not a product listed in Annex I of the FEU Treaty, so that aid to forestry holdings is subject in its entirety to the full applicability of Articles 107-108 TFEU.[26] Under the agricultural and forestry aid guidelines, the Commission has a generally favourable policy on State aid for forestry. The measures may concern the following investment aid: aid for afforestation and creation of woodland; aid for the establishment of agro-forestry systems; aid for the prevention and restoration of damage to forests,

---

[24] OJ 2014 C204/1.
[25] OJ 2014 L193/1. This replaced the block exemption in Commission Regulation (EC) No 1857/2006, OJ 2006 L358/3.
[26] Cases C-346/03 & C-529/03, *Atzeni v Regione Autonoma della Sardegna* [2006] ECR I-1875, para 43.

aid for improving the reliance and environmental value of forest eco-systems, aid for forestry technologies and processing, mobilising and marketing forest products, aid for infrastructure related to the development, modernisation or adaptation of forestry. Aid may also be granted for the following: disadvantages related to Natura 2000 forest areas; forest environment and climate services and forest conservation; knowledge transfer, advisory services and cooperation the forestry sector; start-up aid for producer groups and organisations in the forestry sector; other aid to the forestry sector with ecological, protective and recreational objectives; aid for research and development in the forestry sector and aid for forest land consolidation.

Aid in rural areas The guidelines also provide for aid in rural areas which are co-financed by the EAFRD or granted as additional national financing to such co-financed measures. Aid may be granted in the following categories: investments concerning the processing of agricultural products into non-agricultural products, the production of cotton or investments in the creation and development of non-agricultural products; basic services and village renewal in rural areas; business start-up aid for non-agricultural activities in rural areas; agri-environment-climate commitments to other land managers and undertakings in rural areas not active in the agricultural sector; disadvantages related to Natura 2000 to other land managers; knowledge transfer, information actions and advisory services in rural areas; new participation of active farmers in quality schemes for cotton and foodstuffs; information and promotion activities concerning cotton and foodstuffs covered by a quality scheme; cooperation in rural areas; and setting up of mutual funds.

Block exemption for aid to agriculture, forestry and rural areas Commission Regulation (EU) No 702/2014 provides that certain categories of aid for the agricultural and forestry sectors and in rural areas may benefit from a block exemption. The categories of aid are as follows: aid in favour of SMEs active in primary agricultural production, the processing of agricultural products and the marketing of agricultural products; aid for investments in favour of conservation of cultural and natural heritage located on agri-cultural holdings; aid to make good damage caused by natural disaster in the agricultural sector; aid for research and development in the agricultural and forestry sectors; aid in favour of forestry; and aid in favour of SMEs in rural areas co-financed by the EAFRD or granted as addition national finance to such co-financed measures.

Aid for fisheries Council Regulation (EU) No 1379/2013[27] governs the common organisation of the market in fishery and aquaculture products. The

---

[27] OJ 2013 L354/1..

Commission has adopted guidelines for the examination of State aid to fisheries and aquaculture[28] as well as a block exemption for aid to SMEs in Regulation (EU) No 1388/2014.[29]   The block exemption applies to a very broad range of aid measures aimed at sustainable development of fisheries and aquaculture and marketing and processing related measures.   As well as aid covered in the block exemption and the horizontal aid guidelines, the following categories of aid are permissible under the guidelines: aid for damage caused by natural disasters and exceptional occurrences; aid to make good the damage caused by adverse climatic events; aid to support costs relating to the prevention, control and eradication of animal diseases in aquaculture; aid schemes financed by special charges imposed on certain fishery or aquaculture products; operating aid in the outermost regions. In addition, Commission Regulation (EU) No 651/2014 provides specific block exemption rules permitting aid for research and development in the fishery and aquaculture sector.[30]

De *minimis* aid   Due to the large number of small holdings, the normal limits on *de minimis* aid in Commission Regulation (EU) No 1407/2013 allowing €200,000 are inapplicable.   Instead, Commission Regulation (EU) No 1408/2013[31] governs the rules for *de minimis* aid in the agricultural sector and limits such aid to €15,000 over a three year period. In the fisheries sector, *de minimis* aid is governed by Commission Regulation (EU) No 717/2014[32] which allows for aid up to €30,000 over a three year period. The total amount of *de minimis* aid in each Member State is subject to a set national cap of its annual output in agriculture and fisheries.[33]

14.3 BROADCASTING, MEDIA AND COMMUNICATIONS

Public broadcasting   The broadcast media play a central role in the functioning of modern democratic societies, in particular in the development and transmission of social values. Therefore, the broadcasting sector is subject to specific regulation in the general interest reflecting common values, such as freedom of expression and the right of reply, pluralism, protection of copyright, promotion of cultural and linguistic diversity, protection of minors

---

[28]   OJ 2015 C217/1..
[29]   OJ 2014 L369/37.
[30]   Commission Regulation (EU) No 651/2014, Article 30.
[31]   OJ 2014 L352/9.
[32]   OJ 2014 L190/45.
[33]   Commission Regulation (EC) No 1408/2013, Article 3(3) and Annex; Commission Regulation (EU) No 717/2014, Article 3(3) and Annex.

and of human dignity, and consumer protection.[34] In addition to the fact that public services in the general interest are specifically recognised in Article 14 TFEU and Article 106(2) TFEU, a protocol was appended to the FEU Treaty which states that the provisions of the Treaty are without prejudice to the competence of Member States to provide for the funding of public service broadcasting insofar as such funding is granted to broadcasting organisations for the fulfilment of the public service remit as conferred, defined and organised by each Member State.[35] In view of the complexity of the State aid rules in the context of public service broadcasting,[36] the Commission adopted a communication setting out the approach it intended to apply.[37]

The existence of State aid has to be assessed on a case by case basis and depends also on the specific nature of the funding.[38] Licence fees collected from television owners are classified as State funds.[39] Aid may be authorised by the Commission pursuant to Article 107(3)(d) TFEU as aid to promote culture or under Article 106(2) TFEU concerning services of general economic interest. However, the notion of culture within the meaning of Article 107(3)(d) TFEU is to be construed restrictively, and is distinct from the educational and democratic needs of a Member State. Consequently, aid can only be assessed under Article 107(3)(d) TFEU where separate funding has been set aside to promote culture alone.[40] As regards Article 106(2) TFEU, State aid will be permitted where the public remit is clearly defined and the aid is proportionate to the task entrusted to the broadcasting organisation.[41] The choice of financing, whether solely from public funds or combined with advertising revenues, falls within the competence of the Member States as long as competition in the relevant markets, such as sale of programmes or advertising, is not affected in a disproportionate manner.[42] Thus, the Commission required the Spanish authorities to remove the unlimited State guarantee benefiting the public service broadcaster.[43]

---

[34] Commission communication on services of general interest in Europe, COM (2000) 580 final, p. 35.

[35] Protocol 29, on the system of public broadcasting in the Member States.

[36] Cf. Case T-46/97, *SIC v Commission* [2000] ECR II-2125.

[37] OJ 2009 C257/1. This replaced an earlier communication: OJ 2001 C320/5. See A. Bartosch, "The financing of public broadcasting and EC State aid law" (1999) ECLR 197; R. Crauford Smith, "State support for public service broadcasting" (2001) 28 LIEI 3; A. Held & A. Kliemann, "The 2009 broadcasting communication and the Commission's decisional practice two years after its entry into force" 2012 EStALQ 37.

[38] Case NN 70/98, *Kinderkanal and Phoenix*, OJ 1999 C238/3; Case NN 88/98, *BBC News 24*, OJ 2000 C78/6. See also, Case N 279/2008, *France Télévisions*.

[39] *Twenty-Ninth Report on Competition Policy* (1999), pt. 226.

[40] Communication on State aid and public service broadcasting, para 34.

[41] See, for example, Case E 3/2005, *ARD and ZDF*, OJ 2007 C185/1.

[42] Communication on State aid and public service broadcasting, para 59.

[43] Case E 8/2005, *RTVE*, OJ 2006 C239/17.

In carrying out the proportionality test, the Commission starts from the consideration that the State funding is normally necessary for the undertaking to carry out its public service tasks. However, the funding should not exceed the net costs of the public service mission, taking into account other direct and indirect revenues derived from the public service mission.[44] It may be justifiable for the public service broadcaster to keep a surplus as a buffer against possible fluctuations in costs and revenues.[45] The Commission will also consider whether any distortion of competition is justified. For example, a broadcaster, insofar as lower revenues are covered by State aid, might be tempted to depress the prices of advertising or other non-public service activities on the market, resulting in a reduction of revenue for competitors. Such conduct could not be considered as intrinsic to the public service mission attributed to the broadcaster.[46]

Digital broadcasting The transition from analogue to digital broadcasting has great advantages in terms of more efficient spectrum usage and increased transmission possibilities. A number of Member States have initiated support programmes for the rollout of digital broadcasting. In its first decision on the matter, the Commission required the Austrian authorities to modify substantially its proposed scheme so as to comply with requirements of the principle of technological neutrality to ensure that the aid would not unjustifiably favour digital transmission over other competing television platforms. The scheme consisted of financial support for pilot projects and research activities regarding digital TV transmission, incentives for consumers to purchase digital recorders, grants to develop innovative digital services and subsidies to broadcasters to compensate for additional transmission costs when broadcasting analogue and digital TV in parallel.[47] By contrast, the Commission blocked a number of schemes where the aid was not based on specific switchover costs and was decided after the switchover had been agreed. The subsidies indirectly benefited the digital broadcasting network over competing platforms, such as cable and satellite and thus infringed the principle of technological neutrality.[48] Similarly, Spanish aid for the transition to digital terrestrial television in remote areas and for the operation and maintenance of the digital terrestrial infrastructure was regarded as unduly

---

44 Communication on State aid and public service broadcasting, paras 70-71. See, fore example, Case N 54/2005, *French international news channel*, OJ 2005 C256/25.

45 Commission Decision 2008/136/EC, *Dutch public service broadcasters*, OJ 2008 L49/1.

46 Communication on State aid and public service broadcasting, paras 92-94.

47 Case N 622/2003, *Digitalisierungsfonds*, OJ 2005 C228/12.

48 Commission Decision 2006/513/EC, *DVB-T Berlin-Brandenburg*, OJ 2006 L200/14; Commission Decision 2007/374/EC, *Italian digital decoders*, OJ 2007 L147/1; Case C 34/2006, *DVB-T North Rhine Westphalia*.

distorting competition, since it went exclusively to terrestrial operators whereas alternative digital transmission platforms were effectively excluded.[49]

Films and audiovisual works The Commission recognises that the European film and television industry makes an important contribution to diversified European culture and it has authorised several aid schemes accordingly.[50] Every Member State in which films are made provides some level of aid to the film industry. Taking account of the strong competitive pressures from third country productions, which are dominant in the industry, the Commission assesses the compatibility of aid with the internal market with a view to avoiding distortions of competition in the EU film industry. It also seeks to promote cross-border financial, cultural and economic cooperation in order to give national cultural works a broader financial basis for their production and distribution. In 2001, the Commission adopted a communication on cinematographic and other audiovisual works.[51] This was replaced in 2013 by a communication on State aid for films and other audiovisual works.[52] A block exemption for aid schemes to support audiovisual works was also introduced in 2014 by Commission Regulation (EU) No 651/2014.[53]

It is generally accepted by the Commission that aid is important to sustain European audiovisual production, on the basis that it is difficult for film producers to obtain a sufficient level of upfront commercial backing to put together a financial package so that production projects can proceed. In addition to the production of films, the communication explores issues related to cultural criteria, territorial spending obligations, competition to attract major foreign products, cross-border productions and film heritage.[54] Film production support schemes may require that up to 160% of the aid amount awarded to the production of a given audiovisual work is spent in the territory granting the aid. Alternatively, the aid amount awarded to the production of a given audiovisual work may be calculated as a percentage of the expenditure on film production activities in the granting Member State, typically in case of support schemes in the form of tax incentives. In both cases, Member States may require a minimum level of production activity in their territory, not exceeding 50% of the overall production budget.[55] In the case of schemes designed to support the scriptwriting, development, production, distribution and promotion of audiovisual works, the aid intensity must in principle also be limited to 50% of the production budget, although in the case of cross-border

---

[49] SA.28599, *DTT – Spain* (2013).
[50] *Twenty-Fifth Report on Competition Policy* (1995), pt. 199.
[51] *Eighteenth Report on Competition Policy* (1988), pt. 244.
[52] OJ 2013 C332/1.
[53] Commission Regulation (EU) No 651/2014, Article 54.
[54] E. Pyscogiopoulou, "The cultural criterion in the European Commission's assessment of State aids to the audiovisual sector" [2010] LIEI 273.
[55] Communication on films and audiovisual works 2013, para 50.

productions funded by more than one Member State and involving producers from more than one Member State may be up to 60% of the production budget.[56] The modernisation of cinemas, including their digitisation, may be aided where the Member States can justify the necessity, proportionality and adequacy of such aid.[57]

Thus, for example, the Commission approved a UK film tax incentive scheme aimed at encouraging film-makers to produce culturally British films.[58] The Commission approved a German film support scheme aimed at promoting the quality and diversity of German film production. The scheme also supports script writing and distribution and exhibition of films in Germany. The beneficiaries of the scheme would be primarily cinemas with low revenues which could otherwise face closure.[59] A Latvian scheme was designed to support and promote the development of Latvian film culture, particularly in rural areas given the fact that most cinemas were concentrated in Riga.[60]

Media pluralism Media pluralism is supported by the Commission and State aid, where appropriate, may be granted. For example, the Commission authorised amendments to a Finnish press support scheme. The subsidies were granted to newspapers and the corresponding electronic media published in Finnish minority languages and in Swedish, as well as for the production of Swedish language news services. The targeted beneficiaries were small circulation newspapers with a maximum circulation of 15,000 copies and the subsidies could not exceed 40% of the newspaper's operating costs. In the absence of specific guidelines for dealing with State aid to the press, the Commission authorised the measure directly on the basis of Article 107(3)(c) TFEU. While acknowledging that the beneficiaries may compete to some extent with other companies involved in the production of newspapers, the Commission came to the conclusion that the very limited impact on competition was largely compensated by the positive effects of the scheme on the promotion of media pluralism and multilingualism in Finland.[61]

Postal services Postal services, since they are an essential vehicle of communication and trade, are vital for all economic social activities. In 1998, the Commission issued a notice setting out the approach it would take when applying the competition rules to the behaviour of postal operators.[62] Following the adoption of the third Postal Directive 2008/06/EC in 2008,

---

[56] Communication on films and audiovisual works 2013, para 52.

[57] *Ibid.*, para 53.

[58] Case N 461/05, *UK film tax incentive*, OJ 2007 C9/1.

[59] Case N 477/2008, *German film support scheme*.

[60] Case N 233/2008, *Latvian film support scheme*, OJ 2008 C229/4.

[61] Case N 537/2007, *Aid for Finnish newspapers*, OJ 2008 C168/2.

[62] Commission notice on the application of the competition rules to the postal sector and on the assessment of certain State measures relating to postal services, OJ 1998 C39/2.

which provided for the abolition of the reserved area in all Member States, the role of State aid control increased in importance.[63] France was required to remove the aid arising from the State guarantee to La Poste, which was achieved by La Poste being converted into a public limited company.[64]

In particular, public postal operators generally are subject to a universal service obligation, the costs of which were frequently subsidised. The Commission confirmed that the State aid rules applied equally to postal services, but recognised that they might be classified by Member States as services of general economic interest, with aid being subject to the rules governing aid under Article 106(2) TFEU. For instance, it found that the level of compensation previously granted to the Belgian postal operator had exceeded the compensation necessary for the provision of the SGEIs, whilst approving revised compensation based on new net avoided costs methodology and strict efficiency requirements.[65] By contrast, it approved United Kingdom aid to Post Office Limited which was not only limited to the necessary level of compensation but was linked to a strategic plan to modernise and improve the provisions of its services over the following years.[66]

Broadband and telecommunications connectivity Connecting rural communities with broadband services may not be commercially attractive for private operators because the low population density does not allow them to attract enough subscribers to justify their investment. Schemes designed to counter this problem were approved under Article 107(3)(c) TFEU as facilitating the development of certain economic activities or areas. On the other hand, the Commission blocked aid to fund networks where the area is already adequately served by broadband networks at prices similar to other regions.[67] Thus, the Commission approved a scheme to help bring broadband to rural areas of Germany that currently did not have access, given that DSL coverage in urban areas of Germany was 99%, whereas in rural areas the figure was only 58.5%.[68] Similarly, a joint UK-Irish scheme to provide telecommunications connectivity in North-West Ireland was approved. There was no direct international connectivity to that part of Ireland, all existing submarine cables being located on the east and south coast. That made the cost of international backhaul services to the region much higher than in other parts of the UK or Ireland. The Commission approved the aid on the basis of Article 107(3)(c) TFEU on the ground that the project would contribute to offsetting

---

[63] Commission Report on Competition Policy 2008, para 106.
[64] Case C56/2007, *La Poste*, OJ 2010 L274/1.
[65] N1/2013, *bpost* (2013)
[66] SA.33054, *Post Office Ltd.* (2012) and SA.38788, *Post Office Ltd.* (2015).
[67] Commission Decision 2007/175/EC, *Broadband development Appingedam*, OJ 2007 L86/1.
[68] Case N 115/2008, *Broadband in rural areas of Germany*, OJ 2008 C194/3.

regional imbalances in Ireland and facilitate the provision of electronic communications networks and services.[69]

On the basis of its experience, the Commission adopted broadband guidelines in 2009.[70] These were replaced in 2013 by new guidelines for the application of State aid rules in relation to the rapid deployment of broadband networks.[71] The EU 2020 plan and the EU's Digital Agenda for Europe seek to bring basic broadband to all Europeans by 2013 and to ensure that, by 2020, all Europeans have access to much higher internet speeds of above 30 Mbps and 50% or more of European households subscribe to internet connections above 100 Mbps. It is estimated that up to €270 billion investments are needed in order to achieve the latter target. In some cases, Member States may consider that the provision of a broadband network should be regarded as a service of a general economic interest within the meaning of Article 106(2) TFEU. Applying this principle to the broadband sector, the Commission considers that in areas where private investors have already invested in a broadband network infrastructure or are further expanding the network and are already providing competitive broadband services with an adequate broadband coverage, setting up a parallel competitive and publicly funded broadband infrastructure cannot be considered as an SGEI. However, where it can be demonstrated that private investors are not in a position to provide in the near future adequate broadband coverage to all citizens or users, thus leaving a significant part of the population unconnected, compensation may be granted to an undertaking entrusted with the operation of an SGEI provided the conditions of the SGEI communication are fulfilled. Moreover, the deployment and the operation of a broadband infrastructure can qualify as an SGEI only if such infrastructure provides all users in a given area with universal connectivity, residential and business users alike. Support for connecting businesses only would not be sufficient.[72]

Broadband investment aid in assisted areas falls within the scope of regional aid. Otherwise, State aid to support broadband deployment will generally be assessed by the Commission under Article 107(3)(c) TFEU as sectoral aid. In order to assess market failure and equity objectives in relation to basic broadband networks, a distinction is made between the types of areas that may be targeted, classifying them as white, grey and black areas. White areas are those in which there is no broadband infrastructure and it is unlikely to be developed in the near future. A policy to provide broadband in these

---

[69]   Case N 248/2008, *Communications link in North West Ireland*, OJ 2008 C323/4.

[70]   OJ 2009 C235/7.

[71]   OJ 2013 C25/1. See, A. Kliemenn and O. Stehmann, "EU State aid control in the broadband sector – the 2013 guidelines and recent case practice" [2013] EStALQ 493; F. Chirico and N. Gaal, "A decade of State aid control in the field of broadband" [2014] EStALQ 28.

[72]   Broadband guidelines 2013, paras 18-25.

areas has genuine cohesion and economic development objectives. Grey areas are those in which one network operator is present and another network is unlikely to be developed in the near future. The mere existence of one network operator does not necessarily imply that no market failure or cohesion problem exists. If that operator has market power, however, it may provide citizens with a suboptimal combination of service quality and prices, so that certain categories of users may not be adequately served or, in the absence of regulated wholesale access tariffs, retail prices may be higher than those charged for the same services offered in more competitive but otherwise comparable areas. State aid may be granted in grey areas if it is proved that no affordable or adequate services are offered to satisfy the needs of citizens or business users. A black area is one where there are or there will be in the near future at least two basic broadband networks of different operators and broadband services are provided under competitive conditions. It can be assumed that there is no market failure. Accordingly, there is very little scope for State aid unless there is a clearly demonstrated market failure.[73] Where aid is granted, it will generally be kept to a minimum by selection of network providers through a competitive selection process ensuring transparent and non-discriminatory treatment of all bidders.[74]

More stringent requirements must be satisfied in relation to State aid supporting the rapid deployment of NGA networks[75] and for aid to ultra-fast broadband networks.[76] The Commission approved aid by the United Kingdom for ultra-fast broadband network in two districts of Birmingham where private operators had little or no investment plans. The network was designed in a pro-competitive manner, exceeding in several respects the requirements of the guidelines. In particular, open access was to be granted for 25 years for alternative operators, whereas the guidelines required only seven years, and the network was to be operated on a wholesale basis so as to ensure more competition at the retail level.[77] A German €3 billion scheme providing NGA roll-out throughout the country, including rural areas, was approved, subject to no aid being provided in respect of vectoring technology which bundles a large number of customers together to be served by only one provider.[78]

A block exemption for broadband infrastructures was introduced in 2014 by Commission Regulation (EU) No 651/2014. Investment aid may be granted for broadband network development up to a maximum of €10 million. The investment may be located in areas where there is no infrastructure of the same category, in either basic broadband or NGA network, and where no such

---

[73] *Ibid.*, paras 66-72.
[74] *Ibid.*, para 78.
[75] *Ibid.*, paras 79-81.
[76] *Ibid.*, paras 82-85
[77] SA.33540, *Birmingham ultra-fast broadband* (2012).
[78] SA.38348, *German high speed internet roll-out* (2015).

infrastructure is likely to be developed on commercial terms within three years. The network operator must offer the widest possible active and passive wholesale access, under fair and non-discriminatory conditions, including physical unbundling in the case of NGA networks. Such wholesale access must be granted for at least seven years and the right of access to ducts or poles must not be limited in time. In the case of aid for the construction of ducts, the ducts shall be large enough to cater for several cable networks and different network topologies. The wholesale access price must be based on the pricing principles set by the national regulatory authority and on benchmarks that prevail in other comparable, more competitive areas of the Member State or the EU taking into account the aid received by the network operator.[79]

14.4 COAL AND STEEL

ECSC Treaty The ECSC Treaty governed the common market in coal and steel until July 2002, when it expired.[80] Competition law concerning the coal and steel sectors was, therefore, to be applied pursuant to the ECSC Treaty,[81] although the provisions of the EC Treaty applied to the coal and steel sectors in so far as the ECSC Treaty did not apply to them.[82] In any event, although the ECSC Treaty established its own rules for the products within its scope of application, the concepts relating to the control of State aid which correspond to those in the FEU Treaty are to be interpreted in a similar manner to the extent that this is not incompatible with the ECSC Treaty.[83]

Article 2 CS declared that one of the aims of the European Coal and Steel EU was the establishment of conditions which ensured the most rational distribution of production at the highest possible level of productivity. The common market under the ECSC Treaty was based on the principle that conditions of competition between coal and steel producing undertakings must result from their natural and undistorted production conditions. State aid contravened that principle in that its effect was artificially to alter production

---

[79] Commission Regulation (EU) No 651/2014, Article 52.

[80] Cf. Communication from the Commission concerning certain aspects of the treatment of competition cases resulting from the expiry of the ECSC Treaty, OJ 2002 C152/5.

[81] Case C-128/92, *H.J. Banks & Co Ltd. v British Coal Corporation* [1994] ECR I-1209, para 10.

[82] Case 328/85, *Deutsche Babcock Handel GmbH v Hza Lübeck-Ost* [1987] ECR 5119, para 10. See, for instance, the framework for certain steel sectors not covered by the ECSC Treaty, OJ 1988 C320/3.

[83] Case C-323/00P, *Dradenauer Stahlgesellschaft mbH v Commission* [2002] ECR I-3919, para 42; Case T-234/95, *Dradenauer Stahlgesellschaft mbH v Commission* [2000] ECR II-2603, para 115.

conditions.[84] Subsidies or aids granted by Member States, or special charges imposed by States, in any form whatsoever, were recognised as incompatible with the common market for coal and steel and were accordingly prohibited by Article 4(c) CS.[85] However, that prohibition did not mean that all State aid within the purview of the ECSC was regarded as incompatible with the objectives of that Treaty. Rather, the Commission was empowered by Article 95 CS to authorise such State aid as it might consider necessary.[86] The criterion of need was satisfied in particular where the sector concerned was in a state of exceptional crisis.[87] Intervention by the Commission pursuant to Article 95 CS was to be limited and proportionate.[88] Aid which was likely to distort competition on the common market in coal and steel could, therefore, not be authorised.[89]

Coal The Commission recognised that structural changes on the international and EU energy markets since the early 1960s has forced the coal industry in the EU to make major modernisation, rationalisation and restructuring efforts. Since 1965, pursuant to Article 95 CS, the Commission had established a series of framework decisions temporarily providing for State aid to be granted to the coal industry. Decision No 3632/93/ECSC contained the rules which applied to State aid to the coal industry for the period from 1994 until the expiry of the ECSC Treaty in July 2002.[90] After the expiry of the ECSC Treaty, Council Regulation (EC) No 1407/2002[91] determined the categories of aid to the coal industry that may be considered compatible with the proper functioning of the internal market. Thus was replaced, as of 1 January 2012, by Council Decision 2010/787/EU on State aid to facilitate the closure of uncompetitive coal mines, adopted on the basis of Article 107(3)(e) TFEU.[92] Aid may cover only costs in connection with coal for the production of electricity, the combined production of heat and electricity, the production of coke and the fuelling of blast furnaces in the steel industry, where such use takes place in the EU.[93] The rationale of Council Decision 2010/787/EU is substantially different from that of

---

[84] Cases 27-29/58, *Hauts Fourneaux et Fonderies de Givors v High Authority* [1960] ECR 241, p. 254.

[85] Article 4(c) CS; Case 30/59, *De Gezamenlijke Steenkolenmijnen in Limburg v High Authority* [1961] ECR 1, p. 20.

[86] Case T-239/94, *EISA v Commission* [1997] ECR II-1839, paras 61-64.

[87] Case T-106/96, *Wirtschaftsvereinigung Stahl v Commission* [1999] ECR II-2155, para 62.

[88] Case 31/59, *Acciaieria e Tubificiio di Brescia v High Authority* [1960] ECR 71, *per* Advocate General Roemer, at p. 88; Case T-106/96, *Wirtschaftsvereinigung Stahl v Commission* [1999] ECR II-2155, para 141.

[89] Case 214/83, *Germany v Commission* [1985] ECR 3053, para 30; Case C-441/97P, *Wirtschaftsvereinigung Stahl v Commission* [2000] ECR I-10293, para 53.

[90] OJ 1994 L49/1.

[91] OJ 2002 L205/1.

[92] OJ 2010 L336/24.

[93] Council Decision 2010/787/EU, Article 2(3).

Regulation (EC) No 1407/2002.[94] The operation of coal production units, which must have been active at the end of 2009, must be definitively closed by the end of 2018, with aid being progressively decreased during the intervening years. The amount of aid, which must not exceed the difference between costs and revenue, must not cause the prices for EU coal at utilisation point to be lower than those for coal for a similar quantity from third countries.[95] Coal is excluded for the scope of the 2014 rescue and restructuring aid guidelines for undertakings in difficulty.[96] In approving aid for the closure of uncompetitive coal mines, the Commission has required a mitigation plan addressing the environmental and climate impact of the measure.[97]

Steel In order to meet the needs of restructuring the steel sector, the Commission relied on Article 95 CS in order to establish, from the beginning of the 1980s, a EU scheme contained in a series of codes under which the grant of aid to the steel industry could be authorised in certain specific cases. Commission Decision No 2496/96/ECSC set out the rules which applied until the expiry of the ECSC Treaty in July 2002.[98] Moreover, aid not falling within the categories exempted by the provisions of the code could qualify for an individual derogation if the Commission, with the Council's assent, considered, in the exercise of its discretion under Article 95 CS, that such aid was necessary to attain the objectives of the ECSC Treaty.[99] On the expiry of the ECSC Treaty, the Commission's framework for large investments applied to the steel sector.[100] In addition, the Commission issued a communication for rescue and restructuring aid and closure aid for the steel sector.[101]

Under the regional aid guidelines 2014-2020, the Commission has continued its policy that regional investment aid to the steel industry is not compatible with the internal market.[102] Aid to cover payments to workers of steel undertakings made redundant or accepting early retirement may be deemed compatible with the internal market provided that the payments arise from the partial or total closure of steel plants, that they do not exceed those which are customary and that they are limited to 50% of the portion which is

---

[94] Case T-176/11R, *Carbunión v Council* [2011] ECR II-434*, para 32.

[95] Council Decision 2010/787/EU, Article 3.

[96] Rescue and restructuring aid guidelines 2014, para 18.

[97] SA.24642, *German closure plan 2008-2018* (2011); SA.33033, *Aid to Petroşan* (2011).

[98] OJ 1996 L338/42.

[99] Case C-210/98, *Salzgitter AG v Commission* [2000] ECR I-5843, para 53; Case C-441/97P, *Wirtschaftsvereinigung Stahl v Commission* [2000] ECR I-10293, para 40; Case C-1/98P, *British Steel plc v Commission* [2000] ECR I-10349, para 34.

[100] 2002 framework on regional aid for large investment projects, para 41.

[101] OJ 2002 C70/21.

[102] Regional aid guidelines 2014-2020, para 9.

payable by the undertaking concerned.[103] In addition, aid to steel undertakings which permanently cease production of steel products may be deemed compatible with the internal market provided, in particular, that they regularly produced steel products[104] and they close and destroy the installation used for such production within six months.[105] Restructuring aid was not provided for in Commission Decision No 2496/96/ECSC, although, pursuant to Article 95 CS, restructuring aid to a number of individual steel producers had been allowed.[106] Following the expiry of the ECSC Treaty, the Commission's declared policy is that rescue and restructuring aid for the steel industry is not compatible with the internal market.[107] Steel is excluded for the scope of the 2014 rescue and restructuring aid guidelines for undertakings in difficulty.[108]

14.5 ENERGY

Energy conservation State aid rules in relation to energy conservation are now developed in great detail in the environmental and energy guidelines 2014-2020, in particular concerning renewable energy. Aid outside the scope of those guidelines will generally not be permitted where energy conservation is not achieved. For example, the Commission ordered Italy and Austria not to implement aid ear-marked for energy intensive businesses.[109] By contrast, it approved a United Kingdom measure to ensure adequacy of electricity generation by means of a market-wide capacity mechanism.[110]

Nuclear energy The State aid rules apply to electricity produced from nuclear power plants. Member States are free to determine the energy mix that goes into electricity production. In relation to construction of a nuclear power plant at Hinkley point, the United Kingdom proposed to establish a price support mechanism ensuring that the operator of the plant would receive stable revenues for 35 years and would benefit from a State guarantee covering any debt that it would obtain on the financial markets to fund the construction of

---

[103] Communication on rescue and restructuring aid and closure aid for the steel sector, para 2.1.

[104] Regular production presupposes production for 8 hours a day, 5 days a week: *Twenty-Sixth Report on Competition Policy* (1996), p. 213.

[105] Communication on rescue and restructuring aid and closure aid for the steel sector, para 2.2-2.3; cf. Commission Decision No 2496/96/ECSC, Article 4(2)-(4).

[106] *Twenty-Third Report on Competition Policy* (1993), pt. 481-182; Commission Decision 96/315/ECSC, *Irish Steel*, OJ 1996 L121/16.

[107] Communication on rescue and restructuring aid and closure aid for the steel sector, para 1.

[108] Rescue and restructuring aid guidelines 2014, para 18.

[109] Case C38/B/2008, *Preferential electricity tariffs in Sardinia* (2011); Case C24/2009, *Austrian Green Electricity Act* (2011).

[110] SA.35980, *UK capacity market* (2014)

the plant. The Commission accepted that there was a genuine market failure, as the promoters of the project would be unable, due to its unprecedented nature and scale, to raise the necessary financing on the markets without State support. It approved the aid, subject to raising the guarantee fee and ensuring that the gains generated by the project would be better shared with electricity consumers. The Commission took into account the fact that Hinkley Point would use EPR technology which was not yet operational anywhere in the world, with three other similar projects currently under construction in France, Finland and China, respectively.[111]

Security of energy supplies The EU energy sector is characterised by a high dependency on imports, as the EU produces only 48% of its energy needs, with dependency anticipated to increase to more than 80% in the case of oil and gas by 2035. The Commission's Green Paper in 2000 on a European strategy for the security of energy supply stated that the diversification of energy sources, particularly external supplies of primary energy sources, makes it possible to create the conditions for greater security of supply.[112] That strategy included the development of indigenous sources of primary energy, more especially sources of energy used in the production of electricity, including renewable energy. For example, the Commission approved Irish aid to the Electricity Supply Board in compensation for an obligation to use peat, a domestic primary energy source. The compensation was based on the difference between the generation cost for electricity out of peat and the average electricity market price.[113] Similarly, aid was authorised to compensate Spanish electricity generators for using indigenous coal for some of their production as a public service obligation.[114]

Latvian aid for the construction of a thermal power plant was approved on the basis of a number of special factors including the isolation of the Latvian energy market, Latvia's increasing dependence on gas and the closure of the Lithuanian nuclear power plant.[115] Aid for the construction of LNG terminals in Poland[116] and Lithuania[117] and an interconnection and cross-border power line between Poland and Lithuania was also approved.[118]

Electricity industry Electricity is treated as a product with specific characteristics, based on the fact that it is a homogenous product produced from heterogeneous sources. Historically, this allowed the electricity sector to

---

[111] SA.34947, *Hinlkey Point* (2014).
[112] COM (2000) 769 final,
[113] Competition policy newsletter, February 2002, p.95.
[114] Case N178/2010, *Indigenous coal plants* (2010).
[115] Case N675/2009, *Latvian generation capacity* (2010).
[116] SA.31953, *Swinoujsciu LNG terminal* (2011).
[117] SA.35165, *Revithoussa LNG terminal* (2013).
[118] SA.30980, *Poland/Lithuania cross-border power line* (2011).

establish a privileged status, often combined with intense and complex intervention by the State. The Commission has been particularly concerned by aid granted in the form of regulated electricity tariffs which may result in undue price advantages for electricity end-users. By 2010, in the majority of Member States, regulated tariffs in favour of large and medium-sized undertakings had been abolished or were being phased out.[119]

Following the introduction of EU legislation liberalising the electricity markets, certain electricity companies were faced with long-term commitments and guarantees that they could no longer maintain. The Commission, which was sympathetic to this problem, issued a communication on State aid linked to stranded costs arising in this way. Commitments or guarantees of this nature may, in practice, take a variety of forms, including long-term purchase contracts, investments undertaken with an implicit or explicit guarantee of sale or investments undertaken outside the scope of normal activity. In order to qualify as stranded costs, they must have become uneconomical as a result of liberalisation and must significantly affect the competitiveness of the undertaking. Since the aid is designed to facilitate the transition to a liberalised electricity market, the Commission may be favourable towards it to the extent that any distortion of competition is counterbalanced by the contribution made to the achievement of an EU objective which market forces could not achieve. Aid granted for stranded costs enables electricity undertakings to reduce the risks relating to their historic commitments or investments and, thus, encourages them to maintain their investments in the long term. Moreover, if there were no compensation for stranded costs, there would be a greater risk that costs might be passed on to captive customers.[120] Thus, for example, the Commission approved a scheme in Hungary aimed at compensating power generators for certain costs resulting from the termination of long-term power purchase agreements.[121]

Emissions trading schemes A scheme for greenhouse gas emission allowance trading within the EU was established by Directive 2003/87/EC as part of the package of measures to fight climate change and promote renewable and low-carbon energy.[122] This provides that temporary state aid measures might be adopted for certain categories of undertakings fulfilling specified conditions. Commission guidelines on these State aid measures were adopted in 2012 for the period 2012-2020.[123] The sectors eligible for aid include producers of

---

[119] Report on Competition Policy (2010), para 92.

[120] Commission communication on State aid linked to stranded costs (2001).

[121] N691/2009, *Hungarian stranded costs compensation* (2010).

[122] As amended by Directive 2009/29/EC which improved and amended the EU ETS with effect from 1 January 2013. See G. Catti de Gasperi, "Making State aid control greener: The EU Emissions Trading System and its compatibility with Article 107 TFEU" [2010] EStALQ 785.

[123] OJ 2012 C158/4.

aluminium, copper, fertilisers, steel, paper, cotton, chemicals and some plastics. The rules enable Member States to prevent production shifts from the EU to third countries with less environmental regulation, which could undermine the objective of global reduction of greenhouse gas emissions. A request by Germany to apply support in the case of non-ferrous metal production was refused.[124]

Aid may be granted to undertakings in sectors deemed to be exposed to a significant risk of carbon leakage due to ETS allowance costs relating to greenhouse gas emissions passed on in electricity prices. The maximum aid amount that may be granted must be calculated according to a formula that takes into account the installation's baseline production levels or the installation's baseline electricity consumption levels, as well as the CO_2 emission factor for electricity supplied by combustion plants in different geographic areas. In case of electricity supply contracts that do not include any CO_2 costs, no State aid may be granted. The aid intensity must not exceed 85% of the eligible costs in 2013-2105, 80% in 2016-2018 and 75% in 2019-2020.[125]

Investment aid may be granted to highly efficient power plants, including new power plants that are CCS-ready. The aid must result in lower CO_2 emissions compared to the state of the art technology. For new plants that are ready and start implementation of the full CCS chain before 2020, aid may be 15% of the eligible investment costs. For new plants that are CCS-ready but do not start full implementation by 2020, the maximum aid intensity is 10%. For plants not fulfilling these conditions, the maximum aid intensity is 5%.[126]

Member States fulfilling certain conditions relating to the interconnectivity of their national electricity network or their share of fossil fuels in electricity production and the level of GDP per capita in comparison to the EU's average, have the option to temporarily deviate from the principle of full auctioning and grant free allowances to electricity generators in operation by 31 December 2008 or to electricity generators for which the modernisation investment process was physically initiated by 31 December 2008. In exchange for granting free allowances to power generators, eligible Member States have to present a national investment plan setting out the investments undertaken by the recipients of the free allowances or by other operators in retrofitting and upgrading the infrastructure, in clean technologies and in diversifying their energy mix and sources of supply. State aid may be granted for up to 100% of the eligible investment costs.[127]

Member States may exclude small installations and hospitals from the EU ETS, as long as they are subject to measures that achieve equivalent reduction

---

[124] SA.30068, *Non-ferrous metal producers* (2013).
[125] ETS aid guidelines 2012-2020, paras 11 and 26.
[126] *Ibid.*, paras 15 and 36-38.
[127] *Ibid.*, paras 16 and 42.

of greenhouse gas emissions. Any aid involved is compatible with the internal market as long as such equivalent measures are applicable.[128]

14.6 SECURITY

Products intended for military purposes Security of the State raises specific problems in relation to trade and competition. Article 346(1)(b) TFEU states that the provisions of the FEU Treaty shall not prevent any Member State from taking such measures as it considers necessary for the protection of the essential interests of its security which are connected with the production of or trade in arms, munitions and war materials. This is intended to preserve the freedom of action of the Member States in certain matters affecting national defence and security and confers on them a wide discretion in assessing the needs receiving the protection of the essential interests of their security.[129] The arms, munitions and war materials covered by that regime are set out in the list drawn up by the Council on 15 April 1958.[130] Where a Member State adopts an aid measure in favour of the production of or trade in products appearing on that list on the basis of considerations linked to the need to protect the essential interests of its internal security, the competition rules do not apply to the aid so that, in particular, the Member State is not required to notify the Commission of the aid at the draft stage and the Commission cannot use the examination procedure laid down in Article 108 TFEU.[131]

The derogation allowed pursuant to Article 346(1)(b) TFEU is to be interpreted restrictively.[132] Where it is contended that the Commission should have had regard to the derogation in Article 346(1)(b) TFEU, the burden is on the Member State to show that the products in question falls within its scope. In *BFM v Commission*, BFM, which was active in the defence sector, challenged the Commission's decision classifying restructuring aid which it had been granted as unlawful, arguing that the aid fell within the scope of Article 346(1) TFEU and was therefore exempt from the application of Article 107(1) TFEU. However, the General Court found that none of the aid in question was specifically linked with military projects forming part of the national defence policy. Whilst BFM alleged that some of the aid was connected with imbalances arising from its activities in the defence sector, it conceded that it was impossible to establish a causal link between the contribution of fresh capital and its destination. It followed that, even if BFM

---

[128] *Ibid.*, para 43.
[129] Case T-26/01, *Fiocchi Munizioni SpA v Commission* [2003] ECR II-3951, para 58.
[130] Article 346(2) TFEU.
[131] Case T-26/01, *Fiocchi Munizioni SpA v Commission* [2003] ECR II-3951, para 59.
[132] Case C-246/12P, *Ellinika Nafpigeia AE v Commission* EU:C:2013:133, para 17.

were active in the defence sector, the aid could not be considered as falling within the derogation.[133]

The Commission investigated a number of state measures in favour of the Greek producer of military products ELVO, including a waiver on tax debts accumulated between 1988 and 1998. According to Greece, the aid favoured only the military production of ELVO and therefore fell under Article 346 TFEU. However, the Commission found that the effects of the aid were not limited to military production but also favoured ELVO's civilian activities and distorted competition in the civilian vehicle market, and it ordered that part of the aid to be recovered.[134] Similarly, in *Ellinika Nafpigeia AE v Commission*, aid to a Greek shipyard was partially disallowed in so far as it was not for military purposes.[135]

Examination of effects on competition Measures falling within the scope of Article 346(1)(b) TFEU must not adversely affect the conditions of competition in the internal market regarding products which are not intended for specifically military purposes.[136] Article 346(1)(b) TFEU thereby draws a strict distinction between the production and trade in arms, munitions and war material, on the one hand, and all other economic activity, on the other. This distinction applies equally when the same undertaking engages in activities that are both military and civil.[137] For example, where products intended for military purposes are mixed use products that are also capable of being put to civilian use or are intended for export, there may be a risk that competition will be distorted.[138] However, even if it is alleged that there is a distortion of competition as a result of the aid, the procedure in Article 108 TFEU for examining State aid does not apply where Article 346(1) TFEU is invoked by a Member State and such invocation appears to be *prima facie* credible. In *Fiocchi Munizioni SpA v Commission*, a complaint was made to the Commission by an Italian undertaking operating in the arms and munitions manufacturing and marketing sector alleging that unlawful aid had been granted by Spain to a Spanish arms producer. The Spanish authorities replied to the Commission's inquiry to the effect that the Spanish company was a public undertaking devoted entirely to the production of arms, tanks and munitions and that, therefore, its activities were covered by Article 346(1)(b) TFEU. The General Court agreed with the Commission that it was accordingly

---

[133] Cases T-126-127/96, *Breda Fucine Meridionale SpA v Commission* [1998] ECR II-3437, para 89.

[134] Case C 47/2005, *ELVO*.

[135] Case C-246/12P, *Ellinika Nafpigeia AE v Commission* EU:C:2013:133, para 27; Case T-391/08, *Ellinika Nafpigeia AE v Commission* EU:T:2012:12, para 74.

[136] Article 346(1)(b) TFEU.

[137] Case C-246/12P, *Ellinika Nafpigeia AE v Commission* EU:C:2013:133, para 19.

[138] Case T-26/01, *Fiocchi Munizioni SpA v Commission* [2003] ECR II-3951, para 63.

required to take the view that Article 108 TFEU did not apply to its investigation into the alleged aid.[139]

In place of the investigation procedure under Article 108 TFEU, Article 348 TFEU provides that if measures taken pursuant to Article 346(1)(b) TFEU have the effect of distorting the conditions of competition in the internal market, the Commission, together with the Member State concerned, must examine how the measures may be adjusted to the rules laid down in the FEU Treaty. In those circumstances, however, the Commission is neither required to take a decision concerning the measures at issue, nor, as opposed to its powers under Article 106(3) TFEU, empowered to address a decision or directive indicating to the Member State concerned what steps should be taken to render the aid compatible with the internal market.[140] Thus, when the Commission examined allegedly unlawful aid granted in Germany in favour of Lürssen Maritime Beteiligungen GmbH, it accepted the German Government's defence that part of the aid fell within Article 346(1)(b) TFEU and declined to decide on the compatibility with the internal market in respect of that element of the aid, whilst finding that the rest of the aid was incompatible with the internal market.[141] Article 348 TFEU is to be strictly interpreted and only allows for measures concerning military activities to be subject to the derogating procedure.[142] Although the examination procedure provided for by Article 348 TFEU principally relies on cooperation from the Member State concerned, if the Commission or any Member State considers that another Member State is making improper use of the powers under Article 346(1)(b) TFEU, it may, by derogation from the procedure laid down in Article 258 TFEU and 259 TFEU, bring the matter directly before the European Court of Justice.[143]

14.7 SHIPBUILDING

State aid for shipbuilding State aid for shipbuilding has in the past been subject to a series of measures adopted under Article 107(3)(e) TFEU, under which aid granted, whether directly or indirectly, for shipbuilding, ship repair and ship conversion might have been considered compatible with the internal market only if it complied with the provisions of the framework on State aid for shipbuilding.[144] Regional aid to shipbuilding, ship repair or ship

---

[139] *Ibid.*, para 72.

[140] Case T-26/01, *Fiocchi Munizioni SpA v Commission* [2003] ECR II-3951, para 74.

[141] Commission Decision 1999/763/EC, *Lürssen Maritime Beteiligungen GmbH*, OJ 1999 L301/8.

[142] Case C-246/12P, *Ellinika Nafpigeia AE v Commission* EU:C:2013:133, para 42; Case T-391/08, *Ellinika Nafpigeia AE v Commission* EU:T:2012:12, para 44.

[143] Article 348 TFEU.

[144] OJ 2003 C317/11; OJ 2008 C173/3; OJ 2011 C364/9.

conversion was deemed compatible with the internal market only if it was for investment in upgrading or modernising existing yards and did not exceed an intensity of 22.5% in Article 107(3)(a) TFEU regions or 12.5% in Article 107(3)(c) TFEU regions or the applicable regional aid ceiling, which ever was the lower. Otherwise, the general rule under the frameworks was that aid to shipbuilding might be granted in accordance with the normal horizontal rules governing SMEs, employment and training aid, R&D&I, environmental protection and rescue and restructuring. Specific provisions governed State aid for innovation aid to shipbuilding.[145] The framework on State aid to shipbuilding expired at the end of 2013. Regional aid to shipbuilding is now covered by the regional aid guidelines 2014-2020[146] and aid for innovation is subject to the normal rules of the R&D&I guidelines 2014-2020.[147]

14.8 SPORT

Sport and State aid In the field of sport, in particular in the field of amateur sport, public financing of certain facilities and events may need to be considered in the light of the rules on State aid. It should generally be the case that financing of facilities such as a sports stadium will not normally be considered as State aid where no undertaking benefits from the finance or where there is no perceptive effect on trade between Member States. Financing of sports or leisure facilities will only potentially constitute State aid within Article 107(1) TFEU where the facilities are either operated or used by undertakings. If they are operated by a public authority and used only for the benefit of the public, State aid should not arise as an issue. Equally, where undertakings using or operating the facilities do so on market terms, no State aid will be regarded as having been granted. Thus, for example the Commission concluded that no State aid was involved in the financing of the infrastructure necessary for the operation of the Terra Mitica theme park in Alicante, since Terra Mitica covered the costs of connection to the general infrastructure, which was available to the community as a whole.[148] In two decisions on cableway installations in Italy and Austria, the Commission distinguished between installations addressing general transport needs and installations for the practice of sports.[149] Support for a Dutch aviation heritage project was directed at the development of an aviation theme park, the purpose of which was to conserve aviation heritage in a museum. In order to guarantee a viable and independent future for the museum, several commercial activities

---

[145] Framework on State aid for shipbuilding 2011, section 3.
[146] Regional aid guidelines 2014-2020, para 10, footnote 9.
[147] Framework on aid for shipbuilding 2011, para 10.
[148] Commission Decision 2003/227/EC, *Terra Mitica*, OJ 2003 L91/23.
[149] *Thirty-Second Report on Competition Policy* (2002), pt. 453.

were being developed with a view to supporting the museum's activities in the future. An example of those commercial activities was an international conference centre right in the middle of the theme park. The museum activities and the commercial activities came under separate headings in the budget of the investment project, with the aid being aimed solely at the museum activities. However, the Commission decided that it was not able to exclude a spillover effect into the commercial activities, with the result that the measure constituted State aid.[150]

To the extent that measures in the field of sports do constitute State aid, they must be notified to and assessed by the Commission which may treat them as compatible with the internal market on the basis of Article 107(3)(c) TFEU when an economic activity is being developed or Article 107(3)(d) TFEU if the emphasis of the activity in question is more specifically of a cultural nature, recognising that Article 165 TFEU requires the EU to contribute to the promotion of sporting issues, while taking account of the specific nature of sport, its structures based on voluntary activity and its social and educational function. Thus, the Commission approved aid under Article 107(3)(c) TFEU for a German climbing wall which was considered an economic activity.[151]

Sport and multifunctional recreational infrastructures   Commission Regulation (EU) No 651/2014 provides for a block exemption for sport and multifunctional recreational infrastructures. The block exemption applies only where the sport infrastructure is not used exclusively by a single professional sport user but is sued by other professional or non-professional sport users for at least 20% of the time each year. Access to the sport or multifunctional recreational infrastructures must be open to several users and be granted on a transparent and non-discriminatory basis. Undertakings which have financed at least 30% of the investment costs of the infrastructure may be granted preferential access under more favourable conditions, provided those conditions are made publicly available. If sport infrastructure is used by professional sport clubs, Member States shall ensure that the pricing conditions for its use are made publicly available. Any concession or other entrustment to a third party to construct, upgrade and/or operate the infrastructure must be assigned on an open, transparent and non-discriminatory basis. Investment aid may be granted for both sport and multifunctional recreational infrastructure, whereas operating is permitted only for sports infrastructure.[152]

---

[150] Case N 221/2003, *Aviation heritage project*, OJ 2003 C301/7.
[151] SA.33952, *Deutscher Alpenverein* (2011).
[152] Commission Regulation (EU) No 651/2014, Article 55.

14.9 TRANSPORT

Transport and State aid Articles 90-100 TFEU establish the rules concerning the EU's transport policy in so far as they apply to rail, road and inland waterways. Article 107 TFEU applies equally to State aid to this sector.[153] In addition, special provision for State aid is made in Article 93 TFEU pursuant to which aid is compatible with the FEU Treaty if it meets the needs of coordination of transport or if it represents reimbursement for the discharge of certain obligations inherent in the concept of a public service. It follows that the effect of Article 93 TFEU is not to exempt aid to transport from the general system of the FEU Treaty concerning State aid but, on the contrary, to provide an additional basis for permitting State aid, whilst Articles 107-108 TFEU apply generally to control other types of aid.[154] The Commission may also apply Article 106(2) TFEU which relieves, where necessary, services of general economic interest from compliance with the competition rules. Since the provisions of the common transport policy apply only to transport by rail, road and inland waterway,[155] it follows that the FEU Treaty, including the competition and State aid provisions, applies generally to air transport and maritime transport.[156]

Rail, road and inland waterway transport The Commission has for some years pursued a policy of shifting the balance between modes of transport and promoting modes that are less damaging to the environment in order to achieve a sustainable transport system. Rail transport is the strategic sector on which the success of the efforts to shift this balance depends. The Commission, therefore, takes a favourable approach to aid to the rail sector, both with regard to rail services and, in particular, to investments in rail infrastructure which, due to heavy investment costs, are not viable without public co-financing.[157] For instance, it approved aid for the high speed rail link between London and the Channel Tunnel[158] and aid for multimodal transport in Belgium that was intended to shift freight from road to rail.[159] Similarly, aid for inland waterway

---

[153] Commission Decision 65/271/EEC, Article 9(2); Council Regulation (EC) No 1370/2007, Article 3(3).

[154] Case 156/77, *Commission v Belgium* [1978] ECR 1881, para 10.

[155] Article 100(1) TFEU.

[156] Case 167/73, *Commission v France* [1974] ECR 359, paras 29-32; Joined Cases 209-213/84, *Ministère Public v Asjes* [1986] ECR 1425, paras 39-42. See also Case C-49/89, *Corsica Ferries France v Direction Générale des Douanes Françaises* [1989] ECR 4441.

[157] *Thirty-First Report on Competition Policy* (2001), pt. 428.

[158] Case N 420/08, *UK high speed rail link* (2009).

[159] SA.38611, *Belgian multimodal aid* (2014).

transport, which is safe, clean and efficient in terms of energy consumption, is regarded as being in the common interest.[160]

Regulation (EC) No 1370/2007[161] governs compensation for fulfilling obligations inherent in the concept of a public service by rail and by road. This must be narrowly interpreted so as to be limited to aid that is directly and exclusively necessary for the performance of the public transport service *per se*, and does not include subsidies intended to cover deficits incurred by a transport undertaking as a result of circumstances other than its task of providing transport, such as the consequences of unsound financial management which is not an inherent factor in the transport sector.[162] Public service compensation for the operation of public passenger transport services or for complying with tariff obligations established through general rules paid in accordance with this Regulation are compatible with the internal market.[163] This Regulation contains an exhaustive list of the circumstances in which aid under Article 93 TFEU may be granted, so that the Member States may no longer rely directly on Article 93 TFEU itself in situations not covered by the Regulation.[164] Moreover, where the requirements of the regulation are not fulfilled, any compensation payments are not compatible with EU law and may not be separately considered in the light of the provisions on state aid, in particular Article 107 TFEU.[165] The Commission takes a favourable view of aid which facilitates the development of combined transport or which is intended for investment in combined transport infrastructure.[166] Guidelines were adopted by the Commission in relation to Regulation (EC) No 1370/2007 in 2014 clarifying the rules on compensation for public service obligations.[167]

Railway undertakings may be obliged under national law to bear certain costs which would not normally be borne by operators carrying on other economic activities, including other forms of transport activity. Council Regulation (EEC) No 1192/69[168] provides for a system of compensation for such costs by determining the financial burdens borne by railway undertakings by comparison with their position if they operated under the same conditions as

---

[160] Council Regulation (EC) No 718/1999 (OJ 1999 L90/1) on a EU fleet capacity to promote inland waterway transport encourages Member States to take measures to promote this form of transport.

[161] OJ 2007 L315/1. This repealed Council Regulations (EC) Nos 1191/69 and 1107/70, effective as of 3 December 2009.

[162] Case T-157/01, *Danske Busvognmaend v Commission* [2004] ECR II-197, paras 85-86.

[163] Regulation (EC) No 1370/2007, Article 9(1).

[164] Case C-280/00, *Altmark Trans GmbH v Nahverkehrgesellschaft Altmark GmbH* [2003] ECR I-7747, paras 107-108; Case T-157/01, *Danske Busvognmaend v Commission* [2004] ECR II-197, para 100.

[165] Case C-504/07, *Antrop v Conselho de Ministros* [2009] ECR I-3867, para 28.

[166] *Thirtieth Report on Competition Policy* (2000), pt. 387.

[167] OJ 2014 C92/1.

[168] OJ 1969 L156/8.

other transport undertakings.[169] Since this compensation is provided for by EU legislation, the Commission does not require it to be notified and assessed in advance, as is the case normally with State aid.[170]

Council Directive 91/440/EEC on the development of the EU's railways seeks to improve the efficiency of the railway system. Member States are obliged to develop their national railway infrastructure. Financing may be made available by the Member States, having due regard to Articles 93 and 107 TFEU, in order to cover new investments.[171] Aid may also be granted to reduce the indebtedness of railway undertakings to a level which does not impede sound financial management and to improve their financial situation.[172] The Commission's guidelines on State aid for railway undertakings set out the criteria that will be applied in assessing the compatibility of aid.[173]

Council Regulation (EEC) No 1101/89[174] on structural improvements in inland waterway transport established a scrapping scheme coordinated at EU level to bring about a substantial reduction in structural overcapacity in the fleets operating on the linked inland waterway networks of Belgium, France, Germany, Luxembourg and the Netherlands. Each Member State whose inland waterways are linked to those of another Member State and the tonnage of whose fleet is above 100,000 tonnes was to establish a scrapping fund.[175] The contributions to be paid to the scrapping fund and the scrapping premiums were set at uniform rates in order to avoid distortion of competition.[176]

Maritime transport The aim of EU maritime policy is to ensure freedom of access to shipping markets across the world for safe and environmentally friendly ships, preferably registered in EU Member States with EU nationals employed on board. In 1986, the Council adopted a liberalisation package which provides that there should generally be no further requirement other than establishment in the EU to confer the right to provide shipping services between the EU and third countries or between Member States. Council Regulation (EEC) No 4055/86 established freedom to provide services for all EU established carriers, irrespective of whether they operate vessels under EU or third country flags. Whilst EU markets have been opened up, the proportion of ships entered in Member States' registers and the number of EU seafarers employed has declined significantly, although the accession of Cyprus in 2004 brought the largest ship management industry in the world into the EU. The

---

[169] For the various classes of financial burden envisaged, see Council Regulation (EEC) No 1192/69, Article 4.

[170] Council Regulation (EEC) No 1192/69, Article 13(2).

[171] Council Directive 91/440/EEC, Article 7.

[172] *Ibid.*, Article 9.

[173] OJ 2008 C184/13.

[174] OJ 1989 L116/25.

[175] Council Regulation (EEC) No 1101/89, Article 3(1).

[176] *Ibid.*, Article 6.

Commission identified the problem as emanating in particular from the fiscal and social arrangements in some Member States which result in higher expenses for EU-registered ships as compared to those of third countries, including those flying flags of convenience. Given that shipping is such an internationally oriented activity, the Commission, therefore, adapted its general policy on State aid in order to counter some of the effects of lower costs in third countries. The present guidelines on State aid to maritime transport, which were first issued by the Commission in 1989 and revised in 1997, were adopted in 2004.[177] These guidelines apply also to the towing at sea of other vessels, oil platforms, etc. Towage is covered if more than 50% of the towage activity effectively carried out by a tug during a given year constitutes maritime transport. Similarly, dredgers are included where more than 50% of their operational time consists in maritime transport. In addition, the Commission issued guidance in 2008 on State aid complementary to EU funding for the launching of the motorways of the sea, a project to improve the environmental performance of the freight transport system.[178]

Many Member States have taken special measures to improve the fiscal climate for shipowning companies, including, for instance, accelerated depreciation on investment in ships or the right to reserve profits made on the sale of ships for a number of years on a tax-free basis, provided that these profits are reinvested in ships. These tax relief measures which apply in a special way to shipping are considered to be State aid. Equally, the system of replacing the normal corporate tax system by a tonnage tax, where the shipowner pays an amount of tax linked directly to the tonnage operated, is regarded by the Commission as a State aid. In view of the importance of such activities to the economy of the EU and in support of the objectives stated earlier, these types of fiscal incentive can generally be endorsed by the Commission. However, they may also, exceptionally, be approved where they apply to the entire fleet operated by a shipowner established within a Member State's territory liable to corporate tax, provided that it is demonstrated that the strategic and commercial management of all ships concerned is actually carried out from within the territory and that this activity contributes substantially to economic activity and employment in the EU.[179] By contrast, the Commission will oppose measures that may distort competition in the case of overcapacity on the market. For example, it required amendments to two schemes, one of which offered compensation to shipowners laying up their vessels during periods of overcapacity and the other required the exchange of recommendations on vessel charter rates.[180]

---

[177] OJ 2004 C13/3.
[178] OJ 2006 C317/10.
[179] Guidelines on State aid for maritime transport, section 3.1.
[180] *Report on Competition Policy* (2013), accompanying document, p.58.

Aid for shipping companies can be related to employment costs by reducing the rates of social protection and income tax for EU seafarers.[181] Aid for crew relief may be granted in the form of payment of the costs of repatriation of EU seafarers. Investment aid for fleet renewal may be permitted where this is compatible with the framework on State aid for shipbuilding.[182] Other investment aid may be permitted to improve equipment on board or to promote the use of safe and clean ships. Regional investment aid may be permitted under the regional aid guidelines. Training aid on board ships registered in Member States is treated favourably by the Commission. Training aid may apply to supernumerary trainees, enhancing officers' skills and retraining high-sea fishermen to work as seafarers. Aid may also be granted for public service obligations.[183] A block exemption for social aid for maritime transport for residents of remote regions was introduced by Commission Regulation (EU) No 651/2014.[184] The Commission has also applied the maritime guidelines by analogy to aid for cable-laying and other vessels.[185]

Start-up aid is permitted for new or improved short sea shipping services with a maximum duration of three years and a maximum intensity of 30% of operational cost and 10% of investments costs.[186] Regulation (EC) No 1692/2006 establishing the second Marco Polo programme for the granting of EU financial assistance to improve the environmental performance of the freight transport system is an EU funding instrument directly and explicitly supporting the motorways of the sea in order to shift freight traffic away from roads. Complementary to this EU funding, the Commission permits State aid having a maximum intensity of 35% of operational costs and a maximum duration of five years. Start-up aid cannot be cumulated with public service compensation.[187]

Additional specific rules were adopted in 2009[188] in relation to ship management companies, which are companies that provide a variety of out-sourced services to shipowners, such as technical survey, crew recruiting and training, crew management and vessel operation. In order to qualify for aid, ship management companies must present a clear link to the EU and its economy and eligible activities must be entirely carried out from the territory of the EU. That economic link will be proven by the fact that the ship

---

[181] Guidelines on State aid for maritime transport, section 3.2.

[182] The framework on State aid for shipbuilding expired at the end of 2013.

[183] Guidelines on State aid for maritime transport, sections 4-9.

[184] Commission Regulation (EU) No 651/2014, Article 51.

[185] Case C22/07, _Danish cable laying vessels_, OJ 2009 L119/23; Case N714/2009, _Dutch cable layers, pipeline layers, research vessels and crane vessels_ (2010).

[186] Guidelines on State aid for maritime transport, section 10.

[187] Commission communication on State aid complementary to EU funding for the launching of the motorways of the sea, paras 8-9.

[188] Commission communication providing guidance on State aid to ship management companies, OJ 2009 C132/6.

management is carried out in the EU and that mainly EU nationals are employed in land-based activities or on ships. The economic link between the managed ships and the EU will be deemed fulfilled if at least two thirds of the tonnage of the managed ships is managed from the EU. Ship management companies must comply with EU and international standards, in particular those relating to security, safety, training and certification of seafarers, environmental performance and on-board working conditions. The tax base to be applied to the ship management companies should be approximately 25%, in terms of tonnage or notional profit, of that applied to the ship owner for the same ship or tonnage.[189]

Maritime ports The motorways of the sea project concerns flows of freight on sea-based logistical routes in such a way as to improve existing maritime links or to establish new viable regular and frequent maritime links for the transport of goods between Member States so as to reduce road congestion and/or to improve access to peripheral and islands regions, consisting of facilities and infrastructure concerning at least two ports in two different Member States. The Commission's guidelines for the development of the trans-European transport network[190] allow EU support for the development of infrastructure to the extent necessary for the financial viability of the project, with start-up support limited to two years with a maximum intensity of 30%. This applies also in the context of the motorways of the seas project.[191] Thus, the Commission approved aid for a project linking the French port of Nantes-Saint Nazaire with the Spanish port of Gijón aimed at capturing 3-5% of the road traffic currently passing through the west Pyrenees.[192]

In 2010, the Commission launched a study to better understand the functioning of ports and the public financing of their infrastructure, which resulted in a number of decisions.[193]

Air transport In the past, EU air transport was characterised by a high level of State intervention and bilateralism, with considerable distorting effects on competition caused by control of fares, market access and capacity sharing. With the liberalisation of the air transport sector in the EU which introduced a much greater degree of competition, there was a clear need for a stricter application of the State aid rules. The Commission, therefore, issued guidelines in 1994 on State aid in the air transport sector.[194] These were

---

[189] *Ibid.*, sections 3-5.

[190] OJ 1996 C228/1.

[191] Commission communication on State aid complementary to EU funding for the launching of the motorways of the sea, paras 11-17.

[192] Cases N573/2009 and N647/2009, *Nantes-Gijón maritime link* (2010).

[193] *Report on Competition Policy* (2014), accompanying document, p.67.

[194] OJ 1994 C350/5.

repealed by the 2014 guidelines on State aid to airports and airlines which allow, in respect of airlines, only start-up aid and aid of a social character under Article 107(2)(a) TFEU.[195]

Operating aid may be granted in limited circumstances, in particular to cover public service obligations pursuant to Regulation (EC) No 1008/2008 which have been imposed on scheduled air services on specific routes to regional airports provided that such route is considered vital for the economic development of the region concerned.[196] Aid in the form of public service compensation is not required to be notified to the Commission where it satisfies the terms of Decision 2012/21/EU,[197] which covers airports where the average annual traffic does not exceed 200,000 passenger and airlines as regards air links to islands to islands where the average annual traffic does not exceed 300,000 passengers.[198] Operating aid for air transport services may also be allowed where it is falls within the scope of under Article 107(2)(a) TFEU. The aid must effectively be for the benefit of final consumers and, except where it is for routes to remote regions, the aid must have a social character, benefiting certain categories of passenger, such as children, persons with disabilities, people on low income, students, the elderly, etc.[199] A block exemption for social aid for air transport for residents of remote regions was introduced by Commission Regulation (EU) No 651/2014.[200] In the light of the events on September 11, 2001, the Commission approved certain operating aid for airlines pursuant to Article 107(2)(b) TFEU. Aid was allowed to cover extra insurance and security costs and losses suffered by the closure of air space.[201]

Start-up aid may be granted to airlines for launching a new route with the aim of increasing the connectivity of a region, as long as this route is not already served by high-speed rail or from another airport in the same catchment area under comparable conditions. This will only be considered compatible for routes linking an airport with less than 3 million passengers per annum to another airport within the Common European Aviation Area. Start-up aid for routes linking an airport located in a remote region to another airport will be compatible irrespective of the size of the airports concerned. Aid for routes linking an airport with more than 3 million passengers and less than 5 million passengers per annum not located in remote regions can be considered compatible with the internal market only in duly substantiated exceptional cases, whereas aid for routes linking an airport with more than 5 million

---

[195] OJ 2014 C99/3.
[196] Council Regulation (EC) No 1008/2008, Articles 16-17.
[197] OJ 2012 L7/3.
[198] Commission Decision 2012/21/EU, Article 2(1).
[199] Guidelines on State aid to airports and airlines 2014, para 156.
[200] Commission Regulation (EU) No 651/2014, Article 51.
[201] *Thirty-First Report on Competition Policy* (2001), pt. 446.

passengers not located in remote regions cannot be considered compatible with the internal market. Start-up aid may cover up to 50% of airport charges in respect of a route for a maximum period of three years. The eligible costs are the airport charges in respect of the route.[202]

Restructuring aid has been granted on a significant scale by certain Member States to their flagship airlines. Although specific considerations, similar to those which apply generally under the guidelines on rescue and restructuring aid, were set out in the 1994 guidelines,[203] the rescue and restructuring aid guidelines 2014 now apply fully to aid to airlines.

The Commission has investigated several alleged aid schemes involving discounts on airport charges given to low cost airlines, often in combination with marketing agreements of doubtful value to the airports. In 2014, it adopted a series of negative decisions regarding aid received by Ryanair, Germanwings, Transavia, TuiFly and Meridiana through their arrangements with a number of airports in France, Germany and Italy, ordering recovery of €12.3 million.[204]

State aid for airports The operation and construction of airports can be regarded as economic activities in which undertakings are engaged in competition.[205] Only 8% of airports in the EU are privately owned, while 77% are publicly owned and 14% are in mixed ownership.[206] Due to the growth in the number of airports and the prevalence of schemes to induce airlines to operate from them, the Commission issued guidelines on State aid and the financing of airports in 2005.[207] It defined the following categories: large EU airports, with more than 10 million passengers a year; national airports, with over 5 million passengers; large regional airports with over 1 million passengers; and small regional airports with an annual passenger volume of fewer than 1 million. New guidelines on State aid to airports and airlines came into effect in 2014.[208] These categorise airports as those with more than 5 million, 3 million and 1 million passengers per annum and those with fewer than 1 million passengers per annum.

Investment aid to airports will be permitted where it increases the mobility of EU citizens and the connectivity of regions, combats air traffic congestion at major hub airports or facilitates regional development, as long as it does not duplicate unprofitable airports or create additional unused capacity. The maximum permissible aid intensity is up to 75% for airports with fewer than 1

---

[202] Guidelines on State aid to airports and airlines 2014, paras 138-155.
[203] Guidelines on State aid in the aviation sector 1994, section V.2.
[204] *Report on Competition Policy* (2014), accompanying document, p.66.
[205] Case C-82/01P, *Aéroports de Paris v Commission* [2002] ECR I-9297, para 78.
[206] *Report on Competition Policy* (2011), p.21.
[207] OJ 2005 C312/1.
[208] OJ 2014 C99/3.

million passengers, up to 50% for those with between 1 million and 3 million passengers, 25% for those with between 3 million and 5 million passengers, with no aid being allowed or larger airports. Aid to airports in remote regions may be increased by up to 20%.[209] Operating aid, which must be kept to the minimum necessary, may also be granted, either as individual aid or under a scheme, for a transitional period of 10 years from 2014, although airports with in excess of 700,000 passenger per annum should generally be able to cover their operating costs.[210] The Commission blocked aid to Gydnia-Kosakowo airport in Poland and Zweibrücken airport in Germany, because it was not possible to justify major public investments in airports located only around 30 km from an existing uncongested airport.[211]

---

[209] Guidelines on State aid to airports and airlines 2014, paras 83-105.
[210] *Ibid.*, paras 112-130.
[211] *Report on Competition Policy* (2014), accompanying document, p.66.

Chapter Fifteen

STATE AID AND THE FINANCIAL CRISIS

15.1 STATE AID AND THE FINANCIAL CRISIS

Response to the 2008 financial crisis Unprecedented economic turmoil hit the European and global economy in 2008. This was initially triggered in mid-2007 by problems with sub-prime mortgage lending in the United States that impacted heavily on other financial markets, leading to a loss of confidence between financial institutions and a systemic crisis for the entire banking sector. When European financial markets were first affected, some European banks encountered severe difficulties due to their exposure to collateralised debt obligations (CDOs) and because of their inherently unsustainable business model. European central banks addressed the liquidity crisis by injecting high amounts of liquidity into the financial markets. As the crisis of confidence among banks dramatically worsened in mid-September 2008 with the bankruptcy of Lehman Brothers, the financial crisis entered a phase marked by very serious problems of prominent US and European banks and the efforts of governments to rescue distressed financial institutions. Knock-on effects resulted in a collapse of confidence that created a systemic risk of collapse. Stock markets fell rapidly, liquidity seized up, and recession hit the eurozone and several Member States as businesses in the real economy found it increasingly difficult to access finance and to sustain turnover. In particular, the total amount of long-term debt securities with a maturity of over one year issued by financial institutions in the eurozone decreased by 40% in the third quarter of 2008. This led to increased fears that other major systemic institutions could collapse and lead to severe difficulties for the entire financial system.

Action was taken at several levels in order to deal with the effects of the crisis. In order to prevent insolvency of several banks, and potential contamination or negative spillover effects, Member States intervened with aid measures in favour of individual banks in accordance with the EU rules on rescue aid for firms in difficulty. On the supply side, national financial rescue policies focused on restoring liquidity and capital of banks and the provision of guarantees. The European Central Bank and national central banks outside the eurozone adjusted the provision of liquidity to the banking system and cut interest rates to unprecedented low levels. Policy action on the demand side was based on the European Economic Recovery Plan,[1] a discretionary fiscal stimulus of some €200 billion, entailing a budgetary expansion by Member States of €170 billion and EU funding of €30 billion, aimed at boosting demand and stimulating confidence over 2009-2010. In addition, a European Financial Stabilisation Mechanism was established allowing for up to €500 billion to be provided to Member States that found themselves in exceptional difficulty.

Commission communications on State aid to the financial sector As the Commission gained experience based on its discussions with the Member States and their various proposals for tackling the crisis, a coherent framework of temporary State aid measures was quickly put in place.[2] First, in October 2008, the Commission issued a communication (the Banking Communication) setting out its initial approach to the application of the State aid rules to measures, in particular the provision of State guarantees, taken in relation to financial institutions in the context of the global financial crisis.[3] This was followed in December 2008 with a communication on measures for the recapitalisation of financial institutions (the Recapitalisation Communication).[4] In February 2009, a third communication dealt with the treatment of impaired assets in the banking sector (the Impaired Assets Communication).[5] Finally, on 22 July 2009, the Commission adopted the Restructuring Communication[6] setting out detailed restructuring conditions for those banks that received large amounts of aid and that had unsustainable business models. In October 2011, the European Commission published a Working Paper giving a detailed evaluation of its decisions adopted within the framework of the application of the temporary State aid measures in response to the financial and economic crisis.[7]

Temporary framework on access to finance Whilst these communications were all aimed at the banking sector, the Commission also adopted in December 2008 a framework allowing, on a temporary basis until 31

---

[1]   Commission Communication: A European Economic Recovery Plan COM(2008)800, 26.11.2008.
[2]   "State aid interventions in the current financial and economic crisis", State aid scoreboard, special edition, Spring 2009.
[3]   OJ 2008 C270/8.
[4]   OJ 2009 C10/2.
[5]   OJ 2009 C72/1.
[6]   OJ 2009 C195/9.
[7]   Commission Staff Working Paper: The effects of temporary State aid rules adopted in the context of the financial and economic crisis, SEC(2011) 1126. For a summary, see C. Quigley, "Review of the temporary State aid rules adopted in the context of the financial and economic crisis" Journal of European Competition Law & Practice (2012), Issue 3.

December 2010, subsequently extended to 31 December 2011, Member States to inject more State aid into the general economy by loosening some of the rules that apply under the various horizontal State aid policy instruments.[8] The temporary additional measures provided for in the framework pursued two objectives. First, in the light of the exceptional and transitory financing problems linked to the banking crisis, it aimed to unblock bank lending to companies and thereby guarantee continuity in their access to finance. Second, the intention was to encourage companies to continue investing in the future, in particular in a sustainable growth economy.

Whereas *de minimis* aid was limited to €200,000 over three years, the temporary framework allowed Member States to put in place aid schemes awarding cash grants up to €500,000 per undertaking. Member States committed in total some €81 billion to these schemes, as approved by the Commission, but in fact only about a quarter of that was actually taken up. Other specific measures concerned aid in the form of guarantees and subsidised interest rates, aid for the production of green products and a relaxation of the controls on State aid and risk capital.

Rescue aid under Article 107(3)(c) TFEU Initially, the financial institutions affected by the crisis were directly exposed to a significant amount of CDOs and/or had funded this through short term wholesale financing which had dried up after the summer of 2007. In the case of the German banks, IKB and Sachsen LB, Germany essentially granted a liquidity facility to Sachsen LB and a risk shield to IKB without which both banks would not have been able to continue their business. The Commission concluded that the aid had been limited to the minimum necessary and was accompanied by a significant own contribution by the beneficiary and was, accordingly, permissible under Article 107(3)(c) TFEU. Additionally, compensatory measures were put in place to minimise potential distortions of competition created by the aid.[9] UK mortgage lender Northern Rock became a victim of the crisis in September 2007, due to its dependence on wholesale funding, including issuing mortgage-backed securities, covered bonds and medium and short term unsecured funding,. The Commission considered that the guarantees granted by the UK authorities could be authorised as rescue aid until a restructuring plan was drawn up.[10] WestLB was also faced with the downgrades of the structured portfolio in its balance sheet and established with the help of its owners a risk shield of €5 billion for its most impaired assets, thereby freeing it from the

---

[8]   OJ 2009 C83/1.
[9]   Case C 9/2008, *Sachsen LB*; Case C 10/2008, *IKB*.
[10]   Case NN 70/2008, *Northern Rock*. See, Sir Jeremy Lever QC, "Northern Rock's rescue State aid" [2008] JIBFL 227.

obligation to provide the required capital. The Commission authorised the risk shield for six months or until approval of a restructuring plan.[11]

By September 2008, Bradford and Bingley, the UK mortgage bank, had fallen into difficulties and the UK authorities designed a package of measures to ensure financial stability, protect retail depositors and support the orderly winding down of the company, while its retail deposit book was sold to Abbey National after a competitive process. At the same time, deposits of individual customers remained fully protected. In this case, the Commission went to the limit of what could be approved as rescue aid under the guidelines as the winding down of the company and the sale of the deposit book to a competitor constituted a structural measure which could exceptionally be justified in view of the tensions in the financial market and the need to protect Bradford and Bingley's creditors.[12] Hypo Real Estate also faced a liquidity crisis due to its short-term refinancing strategy. A number of German banks together with the German Federal government provided loan guarantees which the Commission authorised as rescue aid.[13]

Systemic crisis aid pursuant to Article 107(3)(b) TFEU It quickly became apparent that Article 107(3)(c) TFEU would not be an adequate basis for the measures needed to tackle the wider systemic crisis. In particular, banks and financial institutions that were otherwise fundamentally sound had become unable to access credit on the financial markets. The Commission, therefore, decided to invoke Article 107(3)(b) EC, which allows State aid to remedy a serious disturbance in the economy of a Member State, to permit Member States to take the necessary action. It followed that State aid might be approved on conditions that were less strict than those applying under the rescue and restructuring guidelines.[14] In the case of both schemes and *ad hoc* interventions, the Commission emphasised that while the assessment of the aid should follow the general principles laid down in the rescue and restructuring guidelines adopted pursuant to Article 107(3)(c) TFEU, the prevailing circumstances might allow the approval of exceptional measures such as structural emergency interventions, protection of rights of third parties such as creditors, and rescue measures potentially going beyond six months. Recourse to Article 107(3)(b) TFEU would be possible not on an open-ended basis but only as long as the crisis situation justified its application. This entailed the need for all general schemes set up on this basis to be reviewed on a regular basis and terminated as soon as the economic situation of the Member State in question so permitted. While acknowledging that it was impossible to predict

---

[11]   Case NN 25/2008, *WestLB*, OJ 2008 C189/3.

[12]   Case NN 41/2008, *Bradford & Bingley*, OJ 2008 C290/2.

[13]   Case NN 44/2008, *Hypo Real Estate*, OJ 2008 C293/1.

[14]   Case T-457/09, *Westfälisch-Lippischer Sparkassen- und Giroverband v Commission* EU:T:2014:683, para 213.

the duration of the current extraordinary problems in the financial markets and that it may be indispensable in order to restore confidence to signal that a measure would be extended as long as the crisis continued, the Commission considered it a necessary element for the compatibility of any general scheme that the Member State must carry out a review at least every six months and report back to the Commission on the result of such review.[15]

Crisis aid decisions Between 1 October 2008 and 1 October 2014, the Commission took more than 450 decisions authorising State aid measures to the financial sector with a total value in excess of €5,000 billion, the bulk of which was authorised in 2008, mainly comprising guarantees on banks' bonds and deposits. These guarantees and other forms of liquidity support peaked in 2009. After that, the aid focused more on recapitalisation of banks and impaired assets, with new guarantees being approved in those Member States, such as Italy and Spain, which experienced an increase in their sovereign spreads. In fact, however, the actual burden on State finances was only a fraction of the amount of aid approved by the Commission. In return for their financial support, Member States received a total of €147.8 billion in revenues related to recapitalisation and asset relief measures, together with fees for bank guarantees.[16] In accordance with its established practice, the Commission reviewed each proposed State aid measure for its appropriateness, necessity and proportionality. State aid should be appropriate to achieve the objective of remedying the serious disturbance in the economy, in accordance with Article 107(3)(b) TFEU, by being targeted to restoring financial stability. The criterion of necessity required that aid be limited both in time and in scope, thus ensuring that all measures were temporary and had a pre-defined and reasonable budget. Proportionality required that the positive effects of aid should be properly balanced against the resulting distortions of competition in order for the latter to be limited to a minimum. The Commission practice focused on three points: (i) ensuring that aid provided by Member States was adequately remunerated and where possible incentivised exit from State support; (ii) ensuring that sufficient safeguard conditions were attached to the aid to limit distortions of competition; and (iii) ensuring that remuneration and safeguard conditions were stricter for distressed banks than for safe banks, with in-depth restructuring where appropriate.

Recourse to State aid support for the banking sector was widespread throughout most of the Member States of the European Union, with some 95% of the EU banking sector being eligible to access aid schemes. The amount of aid pledged varied from more than €500 billion (United Kingdom, Germany) to less than €3 billion (Cyprus, Latvia). As a percentage of the financial sector in the national economy, aid pledged varied between more than 30% in Ireland

---

[15] Banking Communication, para 10.
[16] State aid scoreboard, 2014.

to less than 1% in Italy. In fact, five Member States (Bulgaria, Czech Republic, Estonia, Malta and Romania) did not adopt any specific measures, three (Poland, Slovakia and Lithuania) did not actually use any of the measures that they adopted, and use by Finland of its adopted measures was marginal. The majority of Member States adopted both guarantee and recapitalisation measures, whereas impaired asset relief measures were adopted in only nine Member States.

The aid used was concentrated in the Member States where the banking sectors are the largest. The top three banking markets, the United Kingdom, France and Germany, accounting for 60% of the EU banking sector, received 60% of the total amount of aid granted. However, those Member States were not where the aid was highest in relative terms, i.e. as a share of the total banking sector size. Whereas Member States granted on average the equivalent of 2.9% of the total assets of their national financial institutions, France, Germany and the United Kingdom were close to that average at 2.0%, 3.8% and 3.1% respectively. By contrast, Greece (11.8%), Ireland (8.9%), Latvia (8.0%), Slovenia (5.6%) and the Netherlands (4.3%) were substantially higher than the EU average. A total of 215 financial institutions received some form of aid. Of the 114 that received asset support relief, with the singular exception of Denmark which supported a very large number of beneficiaries (47), in general aid was concentrated on a small number of critical banks. In twelve Member States, the three major beneficiaries of aid received more than 80% of the total aid granted. The United Kingdom gave asset support aid only to four banks, France to eight and Germany to nine. The ten largest beneficiaries of asset support aid received two-thirds of the total asset support in the EU, whilst the ten largest beneficiaries of liability support received about half of all liability support. Nevertheless, it is clear that many of the largest banks in the EU did not require support. Out of the top 25 banks in the EU, ten did not receive any direct State aid.[17]

Phasing out of crisis aid measures   The Commission was able to begin phasing out its special crisis related measures from 2010 onwards. In order to encourage exit from State aid schemes, the Commission instigated a process of tightening up on the approval conditions in its Communications. From 1 July 2010, the conditions of access to guarantees were made more stringent and fees for guarantees were increased.[18] In addition, banks issuing new or renewed guaranteed debt which took or maintained their overall reliance on State guarantees beyond 5% of their total outstanding liabilities or a total amount of €500 million would have to undergo a viability review by the Commission.

---

[17]   See the Commission's Working Paper on the effects of temporary State aid rules adopted in the context of the financial and economic crisis.

[18]   European Commission Working Paper on the application of State aid rules to government guarantee schemes covering bank debt to be issued after 30 June 2010.

In December 2010, the crisis regime was extended by the Prolongation Communication, which recognised the continuing need to approve aid pursuant to Article 107(3)(b) TFEU until 31 December 2011.[19] Henceforth, however, every beneficiary of a recapitalisation or impaired asset measure was obliged to submit a restructuring plan for approval by the Commission. This effectively did away with the distinction between sound and distressed banks that had been recognised since the beginning of the crisis. Instead, since the banking sector faced fewer difficulties in raising capital on the markets or through retained earnings, most banks could meet their capital needs without recourse to State aid, with the result that those banks that continued to need State support were required to undertake the necessary restructuring efforts and return to viability without undue delay. The Prolongation Communication was intended to signal that banks had to prepare for a return to normal market mechanisms without State support when market conditions permitted and financial sector gradually emerged from crisis conditions.[20] Nevertheless, in December 2011, the Commission once again prolonged the application of its Communications, with amendments applicable from 1 January 2012.[21] In particular, this second Prolongation Communication supplemented the Recapitalisation Communication, by providing more detailed guidance on remuneration for capital instruments that do not bear a fixed return and for fees payable in return for guarantees on bank liabilities, as well as explaining how the Commission undertakes the proportionality assessment of the long-tern viability of banks.

A revised Banking Communication was issued by the Commission, setting out its policy from 1 August 2013.[22] This replaced the 2008 Banking Communication and amended the Impaired Assets, Recapitalisation and Restructuring Communications. Given the continuing stress in financial markets and the risk of wider negative spill-over effects, the Commission remains of the view that Article 107(3)(b) TFEU is appropriate as a basis for assessing the compatibility of aid to the financial sector as long as the crisis persists.[23] However, it took the view that, in the light of improved market conditions, there was less need for structural rescue measures solely on the basis of a preliminary assessment based on the notion that all banks needed rescuing. Recapitalisation and impaired asset measures would henceforth be

---

[19] Commission Communication on the application, from 1 January 2011, of State aid rules to support measures in favour of banks in the context of the financial crisis (OJ 2010 C329/7).

[20] M. Lienemeyer and L. Le Mouël, "The European Commission's phasing-out process for exceptional crisis-related measures" [2011] EStALQ 41.

[21] Commission Communication on the application, from 1 January 2012, of State aid rules to support measures in favour of banks in the context of the financial crisis, COM(2011) 8744.

[22] OJ 2013 C216/1.

[23] Banking Communication 2013, para 6.

approved only once the bank's restructuring plan is approved. Guarantee schemes will continue to be available in order to provide liquidity only to banks without a capital shortfall.[24] Nevertheless, the changes wrought by the 2013 Banking Communication shift the burden-sharing balance significantly, with a marked emphasis on bail-in by equity and subordinated debt holders.[25] As of 1 January 2015, the State aid rules apply alongside the provisions of the Bank Recovery and Resolution Directive 2014/59/EU which provides common rules for resolving banks in difficulties and aims to protect taxpayers from having to bail-out troubled banks.[26]

15.2 STATE GUARANTEES FOR FINANCIAL INSTITUTIONS

The Banking Communications   Given the scale of the crisis, which also endangering fundamentally sound banks, the high degree of integration and interdependence of European financial markets, and the drastic repercussions of the potential failure of a systemically relevant financial institution further exacerbating the crisis, the Commission recognised in the 2008 Banking Communication that Member States might consider it necessary to adopt appropriate measures to safeguard the stability of the financial system. Due to the particular nature of the problems in the financial sector such measures might have extended beyond the stabilisation of individual financial institutions and included general schemes. The Commission set out rules governing the treatment of State guarantees for banks, dealing with the material and temporal scope of the guarantees and requirements concerning private sector contribution and avoidance of distortions of competition. These conditions were tightened up as of 1 July 2010 and revised as of 1 August 2013 by the Banking Communication 2103.

By early April 2009, the Commission had approved guarantee measures adopted in 16 Member States covering an approximate maximum amount of €2,300 billion.[27] By October 2014, this total had increased to €3,892.6 billion, representing 29.8% of GDP. In 2013, outstanding guarantees, which had peaked at €835.8 billion in 2009, amounted to €352.3 billion. In fact, however, only €3.13 billion of the total guarantees provided were called on and Member States received €38.2 billion in fees for giving the guarantees.[28]

---

[24]   *Ibid.*, para 23.
[25]   M. Lienemeyer, C. Kerle and H. Malikova, "The new State aid Banking Communication: the beginning of the bail-in era will ensure a level playing field of enhanced burden sharing", [2014] EStALQ 277.
[26]   OJ 2014 L173/190.
[27]   State aid scoreboard, Spring 2009, p. 16.
[28]   State aid scoreboard, 2014.

Discrimination on grounds of nationality   A significant distortion of competition may arise where some market players are excluded from the benefit of the guarantee. The eligibility criteria of financial institutions for coverage by such a guarantee had to be objective, taking due account of their role in the relevant banking system and the overall economy, and non-discriminatory so as to avoid undue distortive effects on neighbouring markets and the internal market as a whole. In application of the principle of non-discrimination on grounds of nationality, all institutions incorporated in the Member State concerned, including subsidiaries, and with significant activities in that Member State had to be covered by the scheme.[29]   Thus, the Commission required amendments to initial proposals of the Irish Government to afford guarantees in respect only of the six main Irish banks, in order to ensure that there would be no discrimination against other banks with substantial activity in Ireland.[30]

Guarantees covering the liabilities of financial institutions   In some cases, it was necessary to reassure depositors that they would not suffer losses, so as to limit the possibility of bank runs and undue negative spillover effects on healthy banks. In principle, therefore, in the context of a systemic crisis, general guarantees protecting retail deposits (and debt held by retail clients) could be a legitimate component of the public policy response. As regards guarantees going beyond retail deposits, the selection of the types of debt and liabilities covered had to be targeted, to the extent practicable, to the specific source of difficulties and restricted to what could be considered necessary to confront the relevant aspects of the financial crisis, as they could otherwise delay the necessary adjustment process and generate harmful moral hazard. In the application of this principle, the drying-up of interbank lending due to an erosion of confidence between financial institutions might also have justified guaranteeing certain types of wholesale deposits and even short and medium-term debt instruments, to the extent such liabilities were not already adequately protected by existing investor arrangements or other means. The extension of the coverage of any guarantee to further types of debt beyond this relatively broad scope required a closer scrutiny as to its justification. Such guarantees could not, in principle, include subordinated debt or an indiscriminate coverage of all liabilities, as that would merely have tended to safeguard the interests of shareholders and other risk capital investors. If such debt were covered, thereby allowing expansion of capital and thus of lending activity, specific restrictions were necessary.[31]   In fact, most guarantee schemes put in place by the Member States showed a clear preference for guaranteeing instruments

---

[29]   Banking Communication 2008, para 18.
[30]   Case NN 48/2008, *Irish Banks*, OJ 2008 C312/2.
[31]   Banking Communication 2008, paras 19-23.

representing senior (as opposed to subordinated) liabilities, in the hope that, in case of default, the State would be entitled to a degree of compensation.

Duration of guarantee schemes The duration and scope of any guarantee scheme going beyond retail deposit guarantee schemes had to be limited to the minimum necessary. Taking into account the unpredictable duration of the fundamental shortcomings in the functioning of financial markets, the Commission considered it a necessary element for the compatibility of any general scheme for the Member State to carry out a review every six months, covering the justification for the continued application of the scheme and the potential for adjustments to deal with evolution in the situation of financial markets. Provided that such regular review was ensured, the approval of the scheme might have covered a period longer than six months and up to two years in principle, with further extension, upon Commission approval, as long as the crisis in the financial markets so required. If the scheme permitted guarantees to continue to cover the relevant debt until a maturity date later than the expiry of the issuance period under the scheme, additional safeguards were necessary in order to prevent excessive distortion of competition, such as a shorter issuance period, deterrent pricing conditions and appropriate quantitative limits on the debt covered.[32]

Private sector contribution required In application of the general State aid principle that the amount and intensity of the aid must be limited to the strict minimum, Member States were to take appropriate steps to ensure a significant contribution from the beneficiaries and/or the financial sector to the cost of the guarantee and, where the need arose, the cost of State intervention if the guarantee has to be drawn upon. The exact calculation and composition of such contribution would depend on the particular circumstances.   The Commission considered that an adequate combination of some or all of the following elements would satisfy the requirement of aid being kept to the minimum. First, the guarantee scheme had to be based on an adequate remuneration by the beneficiary financial institutions individually and/or the financial sector at large. Bearing in mind the difficulty of determining a market rate for guarantees of this nature and dimension in the absence of a comparable benchmark, and taking into account the potential difficulties in the circumstances of the credit crisis for beneficiaries to bear the amounts that might properly be charged, the fees charged for the provision of the scheme should come as close as possible to what could be considered a market price. Second, if the guarantee had to be activated, a further significant private sector contribution could consist in the coverage of at least a considerable part of the outstanding liabilities incurred by the beneficiary undertaking or by the sector,

---

[32] *Ibid.*, para 24.

the Member State's intervention being limited to amounts exceeding this contribution. Third, where beneficiaries might not immediately be able to pay an appropriate remuneration in its entirety, a clawback/better fortunes clause would require beneficiaries to pay either an additional remuneration for the provision of the guarantee as such (in case it does not have to be activated) or to reimburse at least a part of any amounts paid by the Member State under the guarantee (in case it needs to be drawn upon) as soon as they are in a position to do so.[33]

The Commission adopted a pricing formula based on a recommendation of October 2008 from the European Central Bank. This provided that the price of State guarantees on bank debt with maturities exceeding one year should be based on the risk profile of the beneficiary plus an add-on fee. The risk profile was measured through the median 5-year senior debt CDS spread in the reference period 1 January 2007 through 31 August 2008. The CDS spread is a widely available and liquid measure of the perceived market assessment of the credit risk associated with individual banks. The add-on fee was valued at 50 basis points and was imposed to cover the operational costs incurred by the Member State for guaranteeing the beneficiary's debt as well as to represent a premium on State support. The add-on could be lower where the guarantee was collateralised since the risk taken by the Member State in that event was lower. The price of State guarantees on bank debt with maturities of less than or equal to one year was to be equal to an overall flat fee of 50 basis points. A flat fee for short term debt was considered appropriate since CDS spreads might not provide an adequate measure of credit risk for such debt. In 2010, the price of State guarantees was increased in order to induce banks to seek private sector solutions by bringing the pricing of State support closer to current market conditions and to better reflect individual banks' creditworthiness.[34] From January 2012, the reference in the pricing formula to CDS spreads was replaced with median CDS spreads over a three year period in order to isolate the risk from changes in CDS spreads.

Member States largely implemented the ECB recommendations. Small modifications to the pricing mechanism for short-term debt were introduced in the Cypriot and Irish schemes, which reduced the fee to 25 basis points, and the French and Slovenian schemes reduced the fee when liabilities were collateralised. For long-term debt only Sweden introduced a reduced add-on of 25 basis points on top of the five year historic CDS median.

Avoidance of undue distortions of competition Given the inherent risks that any guarantee scheme would entail negative effects on non-beneficiary banks, including those in other Member States, the system had to include appropriate

---

[33] *Ibid.*, paras 25-26.

[34] The increase was required to be at least 20 basis points for banks with a rating of A+ or A, 30 basis points for Banks rated A- and 40 basis points for banks rated below A-.

mechanisms to minimise such distortions and the potential abuse of the preferential situations of beneficiaries brought about by a State guarantee. Such safeguards, which are also important to avoid moral hazard, were to include adequate behavioural constraints ensuring that beneficiary financial institutions did not engage in aggressive expansion against the background of the guarantee to the detriment of competitors not covered by such protection. This could be done, for example, by restrictions on commercial conduct, such as advertising invoking the guaranteed status of the beneficiary bank, pricing or on business expansion, e.g. through the introduction of a market share ceiling; limitations to the size of the balance-sheet of the beneficiary institutions in relation to an appropriate benchmark (e.g. gross domestic product or money market growth). Member States could also prohibit conduct that would be irreconcilable with the purpose of the guarantee such as, for example, share repurchases by beneficiary financial institutions or the issuance of new stock options for management.[35] In order to phase out the guarantee regime after 30 June 2010, schemes had to include thresholds of 5% of total outstanding guaranteed liabilities to total liabilities and of €500 million for the absolute amount of guaranteed liability. If those thresholds were exceeded, the Member State concerned had to submit a review demonstrating the bank's long-term viability to the Commission within three months, unless the bank was the subject of restructuring proceedings.

Most adopted schemes featured a limitation of balance sheet expansion or a ban on aggressive commercial policies. Several countries, such as France, Ireland and the Netherlands, introduced limitations in the remuneration payable to the management of financial institutions. Others included commitments as regards the use of the new funding for the real economy (e.g. Austria, Cyprus) or a dividend ban (e.g. Denmark, Poland). Some Member States provided for exit incentives in the remunerations mechanism as an incentive aimed at limiting guarantees for only short- and medium-term debt. For example, Italy provided for a step-up clause in the remuneration for maturities longer than two years and Portugal reserved the right to revise the fee if the market situation were to improve.[36]

The 2013 Banking Communication The Banking Communication 2013 repealed the 2008 Banking Communication as of 1 August 2013. Henceforth, guarantees and liquidity support have to be limited to banks which have no capital shortfall and which meet certain requirements. Guarantees may only be granted for new issues of senior debt, so that subordinated debt is excluded. Guarantees may be granted on debt instruments with maturities from three months to five years. The remuneration levels remain as under the

---

[35] Banking Communication 2008, para 27.
[36] Commission Paper on the effects of temporary State aid rules adopted in the context of the financial and economic crisis.

Prolongation Communication. A restructuring plan must be submitted to the Commission within two months where the total guaranteed liabilities exceed both a ratio of 5% of total liabilities and a total amount of €500 million. For any credit institution which causes the guarantee to be called upon, an individual restructuring or wind-down plan must be submitted within two months after the guarantee has been activated. The recipients of guarantees and liquidity support must refrain from advertising referring to State support and from employing any aggressive commercial strategies which would not take place without that support.[37]

Provision of liquidity by central banks The ordinary activities of central banks do not fall within the scope of State aid rules. Dedicated support to individual credit institutions, however, may constitute aid unless certain conditions are cumulatively fulfilled. First, the credit institution must be temporarily illiquid but solvent at the moment of the liquidity provision which occurs in exceptional circumstances and is not part of a larger aid package. Second, the facility must be secured by collateral to which appropriate haircuts are applied, in relation to its quality and market value. Third, the central bank must charge a penal interest rate to the beneficiary. Finally, the measure must be taken at the central bank's own initiative and, in particular, must not be backed by any counter-guarantee by the State.[38]

15.3 RECAPITALISATION OF FINANCIAL INSTITUTIONS

The Recapitalisation Communication In the 2008 Banking Communication, the Commission included its initial thoughts concerning possible State aid involved in recapitalising banks.[39] By December 2008, the Commission had approved a number of recapitalisation schemes as well as individual recapitalisation measures in line with these principles. Recapitalisation, notably in the form of ordinary and preferred shares, had been authorised, subject in particular to the introduction of market-oriented remuneration rates, appropriate behavioural safeguards and regular review. However, as the nature, scope and conditions of other proposed recapitalisation schemes varied considerably, both Member States and potential beneficiary institutions had called for more detailed guidance as to whether specific forms of recapitalisation would be acceptable under State aid rules. In particular, some Member States envisaged the recapitalisation of banks, not primarily to rescue them but rather to ensure lending to the real economy. This prompted the Commission to issue the Recapitalisation Communication. This was amended,

---

[37] Banking Communication 2013, para 59.

[38] *Ibid.*, para 62.

[39] *Ibid.*, paras 34-42.

as regards pricing and recapitalisation, as of 1 January 2012, by the Prolongation Communication and, as of 1 August 2013, by the 2013 Banking Communication.

Recapitalisation was the second most used instrument to support the financial sector, after the guarantees on liabilities. By early April 2009, the Commission had approved recapitalisation schemes in 11 Member States amounting to a total volume of €275 billion and a number of *ad hoc* interventions worth more than €40 billion,[40] including Nord LB[41] and Bayern LB[42] in Germany, Fortis[43] and KBC[44] in Belgium, ING[45] in the Netherlands and Anglo-Irish Bank[46] and Bank of Ireland.[47] An overall total amount of €821.1 billion was approved by October 2014, representing some 6.3% of GDP, with €448 billion being granted by the Member States. The four Member States that supported their banks the most were the United Kingdom (€100 billion), Germany (€64 billion), Ireland (€63 billion) and Spain (€62 billion), the top receiving banks being RBS (€50 billion), Anglo Irish Bank (€32 billion and Bankia (22 billion).[48]

Objectives of recapitalisation Recapitalisation of banks can serve a number of objectives. First, recapitalisations contribute to the restoration of financial stability and help restore the confidence needed for the recovery of inter-bank lending. Moreover, additional capital provides a cushion in recessionary times to absorb losses and limits the risk of banks becoming insolvent. During the credit crisis, some fundamentally sound banks required capital injections to respond to a widespread perception that higher capital ratios were necessary in view of the past underestimation of risk and the increased cost of funding. Second, recapitalisations can have as objective to ensure lending to the real economy. Fundamentally sound banks may prefer to restrict lending in order to avoid risk and maintain higher capital ratios. State capital injection may prevent credit supply restrictions and limit the pass-on of the financial markets' difficulties to other businesses. Third, State recapitalisation may also be an appropriate response to the problems of financial institutions facing insolvency as a result of their particular business model or investment strategy. A capital injection from public sources providing emergency support to an individual bank may also help to avoid short term systemic effects of its possible insolvency. In the longer term, recapitalisation could support efforts to prepare

---

[40] State aid scoreboard, Spring 2009, pp. 19-20.
[41] Case N 655/2008, *Nord LB*, 2009 C63/16.
[42] Case N 615/2008, *Bayern LB*, OJ 2009 C80/4.
[43] Case NN 42/2008, *Fortis*, OJ 2009 C80/7.
[44] Case N 602/2008, *KBC*.
[45] Case N 528/2008, *ING*, OJ 2008 C328/10.
[46] Case N 9/2009, *Anglo-Irish Bank*.
[47] Case N 149/2009, *Bank of Ireland*.
[48] State aid scoreboard, 2014.

the return of the bank in question to long term viability or its orderly winding-up.[49]

Possible competition concerns With these common objectives in mind, the assessment of any recapitalisation scheme or measure had to take into account possible distortions of competition at three different levels. First, recapitalisation by one Member State of its own banks should not give those banks an undue competitive advantage over banks in other Member States. A coherent and coordinated approach to the remuneration of public capital injections, and to the other conditions attached to recapitalisation, was indispensable to the preservation of a level playing field. Unilateral and uncoordinated action in this area could also undermine efforts to restore financial stability. Second, recapitalisation schemes which were open to all banks within a Member State without an appropriate degree of differentiation between beneficiary banks according to their risk profiles could give an undue advantage to distressed or less-performing banks compared to banks which were fundamentally sound and better-performing. Third, public recapitalisation, in particular its remuneration, should not have the effect of putting banks that did not have recourse to public funding, but sought additional capital on the market, in a significantly less competitive position. A public scheme which crowded out market-based operations would have frustrated the return to normal market functioning.[50]

Recapitalisation of fundamentally sound banks Where State capital injections were on equal terms with significant participation (30% or more) of private investors, the Commission stated that it would accept the remuneration set in the deal.[51] The Commission placed considerable weight on the distinction between fundamentally sound and other banks. An overall remuneration needed to adequately factor in the following elements: current risk profile of each beneficiary; characteristics of the instrument chosen, including its level of subordination; risk and all modalities of payment; built-in incentives for exit (such as step-up and redemption clauses); and an appropriate benchmark risk-free rate of interest. The Commission was prepared to accept the price for recapitalisations of fundamentally sound banks at rates below current market rates, in order to facilitate banks to avail themselves of such instruments and thereby to favour the restoration of financial stability and ensuring lending to the real economy. At the same time, the total expected return on recapitalisation to the State was not to be too distant from current market prices because (i) it should avoid the pre-crisis under-pricing of risk, (ii) it needed to reflect the uncertainty about the timing and level of a new price

---

[49] Recapitalisation Communication, paras 4-6.
[50] *Ibid.*, paras 7-10.
[51] *Ibid.*, para 21.

equilibrium, (iii) it needed to provide incentives for exiting the scheme and (iv) it needed to minimise the risk of competition distortions between Member States, as well as between those banks which raise capital on the market today without any State aid. A remuneration rate not too distant from current market prices was also essential to avoid crowding out recapitalisation via the private sector and facilitating the return to normal market conditions.[52]

Entry level price for recapitalisations The Commission considered that an adequate method to determine the price of recapitalisations was provided by the recommendations of the European Central Bank on 20 November 2008. The remunerations calculated using this methodology represented an appropriate starting basis (entry level) for the required nominal rate of return for the recapitalisation of fundamentally sound banks. The required rate of return by the government on recapitalisation instruments for fundamentally sound banks — preferred shares and other hybrid instruments — could be determined on the basis of a price corridor defined by the required rate of return on subordinated debt, representing a lower boundary, and the required rate of return on ordinary shares, representing an upper boundary. The Commission would accept a minimum remuneration based on the above methodology for fundamentally sound banks on the basis of the type of capital chosen, an appropriate benchmark risk-free interest rate, and the individual risk profile at national level of all eligible financial institutions (including both financially sound and distressed banks). Member States could choose a pricing formula that in addition included step-up or payback clauses. Such features should be appropriately chosen so that, while encouraging an early end to the State's capital support of banks, they should not result in an excessive increase in the cost of capital. The Commission would also accept alternative pricing methodologies, provided they would lead to remunerations that were higher than this methodology.[53] Amended provisions applied as of 1 January 2012. In particular, recapitalisation measures were to contain appropriate incentives for banks to exit from State support as soon as possible. In relation to shares with variable remuneration, for example by issuing warrants to the incumbent shareholders to allow them to buy back the newly issued shares from the State at a price that implies a reasonable annual return for the State, a higher discount was required to reflect the capped upside potential for the Member State.

The primary aim of the schemes was to restore financial stability and to ensure lending to the economy by providing Tier 1 capital injections so as to allow beneficiaries to continue their lending activity. The ECB recommendation provided a price corridor for Tier 1 capital, with lower and upper bounds depending on criteria such as seniority in profit and loss, voting

---

[52] *Ibid.*, paras 22-25.
[53] *Ibid.*, paras 26-30.

conditions, etc. The lower bound was defined by the required rate of return on preferred shares and other hybrid instruments having economic features similar to subordinated debt (i.e. not redeemable by the issuer before a fixed period and redeemable at par value). This was calculated as the sum of the relevant government bond yield, the issuing bank's five year historic CDS spread on subordinated debt and an add-on fee of 300 basis points per annum to cover operational costs. The upper bound was defined by the required rate of return on preferred shares and other hybrid instruments having features similar to those of ordinary shares (i.e. non-cumulative, without the responsibility of pay back, or perpetual instruments with convertibility to ordinary shares). This was the sum of the relevant government bond yield, an equity risk premium of 500 basis points per annum and an add-on fee of 100 basis points per annum. As a result, the average price corridor in mid-November 2008 for the average eurozone bank for Tier 1 capital instruments was 7% to 9.3%

Incentives for State capital redemption Recapitalisation measures needed to contain appropriate incentives for State capital to be redeemed when the market so allowed. The simplest way to provide an incentive for banks to look for alternative capital was for Member States to require an adequately high remuneration for the State recapitalisation. For that reason, the Commission considered it useful that an add-on be generally added to the entry price determined to incentivise exit. A pricing structure including increase over time and step-up clauses would reinforce this mechanism to incentivise exit. If a Member State preferred not to increase the nominal rate of remuneration, it could consider increasing the global remuneration through call options or other redemption clauses, or mechanisms that encouraged private capital raising, for instance by linking the payment of dividends to an obligatory remuneration of the State which increased over time. Member States could also consider using a restrictive dividend policy to ensure the temporary character of State intervention. A restrictive dividend policy would be coherent with the objective of safeguarding lending to the real economy and strengthening the capital basis of beneficiary banks. At the same time, it would be important to allow for dividend payment where this represented an incentive to provide new private equity to fundamentally sound banks.[54]

The Commission assessed proposed exit mechanisms on a case-by-case basis. In general, the higher the size of the recapitalisation and the higher the risk profile of the beneficiary bank, the more necessary it was to set out a clear exit mechanism. The combination of the level and type of remuneration and, where and to the extent appropriate, a restrictive dividend policy, needed to represent, in its entirety, a sufficient exit incentive for the beneficiary banks. In particular, restrictions on payment of dividends were not needed where the

---

[54] Recapitalisation Communication paras 31-33.

level of pricing correctly reflected the banks' risk profile, and step-up clauses or comparable elements provide sufficient incentives for exit and the recapitalisation is limited in size.[55]

Prevention of undue distortions of competition The Commission stressed the need for safeguards against possible abuses and distortions of competition in recapitalisation schemes and required capital injections to be limited to the minimum necessary and not to allow the beneficiary to engage in aggressive commercial strategies which would be incompatible with the underlying objectives of recapitalisation. As a general principle, the higher the remuneration the less there was a need for safeguards, as the level of price would limit distortions of competition. Banks receiving State recapitalisation should also avoid advertising it for commercial purposes.[56]

Safeguards might be necessary to prevent aggressive commercial expansion financed by State aid. In principle, mergers and acquisitions could constitute a valuable contribution to the consolidation of the banking industry with a view to achieving the objectives of stabilising financial markets and ensuring a steady flow of credit to the real economy. In order not to privilege those institutions with public support to the detriment of competitors without such support, mergers and acquisitions should generally be organised on the basis of a competitive tendering process. The extent of behavioural safeguards would be based on a proportionality assessment, taking into account all relevant factors and, in particular, the risk profile of the beneficiary bank. While banks with a very low risk profile might require only very limited behavioural safeguards, the need for such safeguards increased with a higher risk profile. The proportionality assessment would be further influenced by the relative size of the capital injection by the State and the level of capital endowment. When Member States used recapitalisation with the objective of financing the real economy, they had to ensure that the aid effectively contributed to this. To that end, in accordance with national regulation, they were to attach effective and enforceable national safeguards to recapitalisation which ensured that the injected capital was used to sustain lending to the real economy.[57]

In the first schemes approved by the Commission, in the United Kingdom, Germany and Greece, a cap was imposed on the growth rate of the beneficiaries' balance sheets in order to limit potential aggressive expansion. However, these limits were dropped for fundamentally sound banks following the adoption of the Recapitalisation Communication since they could impede the lending activities of beneficiaries. Some schemes imposed structural limitations on beneficiaries in the form of maintaining an increased capital adequacy ratio or included a ban or a limitation on the payment of dividends.

---

[55] *Ibid.*, para 34.
[56] *Ibid.*, paras 35-36.
[57] *Ibid.*, paras 37-39.

All schemes included potential changes in the governance of the beneficiary and its executive compensation policy, including constraints of remuneration of top management. Some Member States imposed the appointment of new board members or their direct participation in the board, in some cases with veto powers on key decisions.

Rescue recapitalisations of other banks The recapitalisation of banks which were not fundamentally sound had to be subject to stricter requirements. As far as remuneration was concerned, it should in principle reflect the risk profile of the beneficiary and be higher than for fundamentally sound banks. This was without prejudice to the possibility for supervisory authorities to take urgent action where necessary in cases of restructuring. Where the price could not be set to levels that corresponded to the risk profile of the bank, it would nevertheless need to be close to that required for a similar bank under normal market conditions. Notwithstanding the need to ensure financial stability, the use of State capital for these banks could only be accepted on the condition of either a bank's winding-up or a thorough and far-reaching restructuring, including a change in management and corporate governance where appropriate. Therefore, either a comprehensive restructuring plan or a liquidation plan would have to be presented for these banks within six months of recapitalisation. Such a plan would be assessed according to the principles of the rescue and restructuring guidelines for firms in difficulties, and would have to include compensatory measures. Until redemption of the State, behavioural safeguards for distressed banks in the rescue and restructuring phases should, in principle, include a restrictive policy on dividends (including a ban on dividends at least during the restructuring period), limitation of executive remuneration or the distribution of bonuses, an obligation to restore and maintain an increased level of the solvency ratio compatible with the objective of financial stability, and a timetable for redemption of State participation.[58]

Burden sharing measures under the Banking Communication 2013 In accordance with the 2013 Banking Communication, new provisions were added to the requirements in order for recapitalisation measures to be approved. Recapitalisation aid can only arise where the bank does not have any capital shortfall. The bank must, therefore, produce a capital raising plan in which it sets out all capital raising measures that it may be able to implement. These include, in particular, rights issues, voluntary conversion of subordinated debt instruments into equity, liability management exercises, capital-generating sales of assets and portfolios, securitisation of portfolios in order to generate capital from non-core activities, earnings retention and other

---

[58] *Ibid.*, paras 43-45.

measures reducing capital needs. In addition, there should be incentives for bank managements to undertake far-reaching restructuring in good times so as to minimise the need for State support. Moreover, banks should apply strict executive remuneration policies, including a cap on remuneration combined with incentives ensuring that the bank is implementing its restructuring plan towards sustainable, long term objectives.

Burden sharing will normally entail, after losses are first absorbed by equity, contributions by capital holders and subordinated debt holders. They must contribute to reducing the capital shortfall to the maximum extent, either by a conversion into Tier 1 equity or a write down of principal. The Commission does not require contribution from senior bondholders, in particular from insured or uninsured deposits or bonds, as a mandatory component of burden sharing. Except where such measures would endanger financial stability or lead to disproportionate results, where the bank no longer meets the minimum regulatory capital requirements, subordinated debt must be converted or written down and State aid must not be granted before equity, hybrid capital and subordinated debt have fully contributed to offset any losses.[59] These changes had already been partly envisaged in the case of the recapitalisation of two banks in Cyprus, Bank of Cyprus and Laiki Bank, where subordinated bond holders had been bailed in, although in those cases uninsured depositors also lost their funds.[60]

Outflows of funds must be prevented at the earliest stage possible. From the time that the bank knows it has capital needs, it must not pay dividends or shares or coupons on hybrid capital instruments, repurchase its own shares or call in or buy back hybrid capital instruments, perform capital management transactions without prior Commission approval, engage in aggressive commercial practices, or acquire a stake in any undertakings, whether by asset or share transfer. It must also refrain from advertising referring to State support.[61]

15.4 IMPAIRED ASSETS RELIEF

The Impaired Assets Communication   Several Member States announced their intention to provide some form of relief for impaired bank assets. Those announcements, in parallel with a similar initiative in the United States, triggered a wider debate within the EU on the merits of asset relief as a government support measure for banks. In the context of that debate, the Commission produced the Impaired Assets Communication in consultation

---

[59]   Banking Communication 2013, paras 40-46.
[60]   *Report on Competition Policy* (2013), p. 46. In those cases, the bail-in of uninsured deposits meant that no recapitalisation based on State funds was required.
[61]   Banking Communication 2013, para 47.

with the European Central Bank, building on the following guiding principles: voluntary participation, with possible priority for institutions with large concentrations of impaired assets; relatively broad definition of assets eligible for support; transparent valuation of assets based on independent third-party expert opinions, an adequate degree of risk sharing; sufficiently long duration of the asset-support schemes, possibly matching the maturity structure of the eligible assets; governance of institutions which should continue to be run according to business principles and favouring of schemes that envisage well defined exit strategies; and conditionality of public support schemes to some measurable yardsticks, such as commitments to continue providing credit to appropriately meet demand according to commercial criteria.[62]

In the end, only a small number of Member States availed of impaired asset relief measures, mostly on an *ad hoc* basis, the only effective scheme being applied in Ireland through the National Assets Management Agency, NAMA. Austria adopted a support mechanism in the form of an asset guarantee, only to be drawn in the case of insolvency of the beneficiary. This amounted to a capital injection of the value of the guaranteed asset and was treated similarly to recapitalisation. The German scheme allowed financial institutions to transfer structured securities to a special purpose vehicle for a period of 20 years, while ultimately bearing the full risks of losses related to the assets. The Lithuanian scheme consisted of an asset purchase with a minimum haircut of 20% off the real economic value. Although the Commission approved asset relief measures totaling €669.1 billion, measures actually implemented involved €188.2 billion.[63]

State aid and asset relief measures It is the normal duty of banks to assess the risk of the assets they acquire and to make sure they can cover any associated losses. Public asset relief measures are State aid inasmuch as they free the beneficiary bank from or compensate for the need to register either a loss or a reserve for a possible loss on its impaired assets and/or free regulatory capital for other uses. Any aid for asset relief measures should, however, comply with the general principles of necessity, proportionality and minimisation of distortions of competition. Any asset relief measure had to be based on a clear identification of the magnitude of the bank's asset related problems, its intrinsic solvency prior to the support and its prospects for return to viability, taking into due consideration all possible alternatives, in order to facilitate the necessary restructuring process, prevent distortion in the incentives of all players and avoid waste of State resources without contributing to resumption in the normal flow of credit to the real economy.[64]

---

[62] Impaired Assets Communication, Annex I.

[63] State aid scoreboard, 2014. Y. Boudghene and S. Maes, "Empirical review of EU asset relief measures in the period 2008-2012" [2012] EStALQ 777.

[64] Impaired Assets Communication, paras 15-19.

Burden sharing of costs As a general principle, banks ought to bear the losses associated with impaired assets to the maximum extent. Once assets have been properly evaluated and losses are correctly identified, and if this would lead to a situation of technical insolvency without State intervention, the bank ought either be put into administration or be wound up. In such a situation, with a view to preserving financial stability and confidence, protection or guarantees to bondholders might have been be appropriate. Where putting a bank into administration or its orderly winding up appeared unadvisable for reasons of financial stability, aid in the form of guarantee or asset purchase, limited to the strict minimum, could be awarded to banks so that they could continue to operate for the period necessary to allow to devise a plan for either restructuring or orderly winding-up. In such cases, shareholders were also expected to bear losses at least until the regulatory limits of capital adequacy are reached. Nationalisation options could also be considered.[65]

Where it was not possible to achieve full burden-sharing *ex ante*, the bank had to be requested to contribute to the loss or risk coverage at a later stage, for example in the form of claw-back clauses or, in the case of an insurance scheme, by a clause of first loss, to be borne by the bank (typically with a minimum of 10%) and a clause of residual loss sharing, through which the bank participates to a percentage (typically with a minimum of 10%) of any additional losses. As a general rule, the lower the contribution upfront, the higher the need for a shareholder contribution at a later stage, either in the form of a conversion of State losses into bank shares and/or in the form of addition compensatory measures.[66]

From 1 August 2013, the Banking Communication 2013 applies the same additional requirements concerning burden sharing and contributions as apply in respect of recapitalisation.[67]

Incentives to participate in asset relief programmes As a general feature, impaired asset relief programmes were to have an enrolment window limited to six months from the launch of the scheme by the government. This limited incentives for banks to delay necessary disclosures in the hope of higher levels of relief at a later date, and was intended to facilitate a rapid resolution of the banking problems before the economic downturn further aggravates the situation. During the six-month window, the banks were to be able to present eligible assets baskets to be covered by the asset relief measures, with the possibility of rollover. Appropriate mechanisms had to be devised so as to ensure that the banks most in need of asset relief participated in the government measure. Such mechanisms could include mandatory participation in the programme, and were to include at least mandatory disclosure to the

---

[65] *Ibid.*, paras 21-23.
[66] *Ibid.*, paras 24-25.
[67] Banking Communication 2013, paras 32-49.

supervisory authorities. The obligation for all banks to reveal the magnitude of their asset-related problems was intended to contribute to the clear identification of the need and necessary scope for an asset relief scheme at the Member State level.

Where participation was not mandatory, the scheme could include appropriate incentives (such as the provision of warrants or rights to existing shareholders so that they may participate in future private capital-raising at preferential terms) to facilitate take-up by the banks without derogating from the principles of transparency and disclosure, fair valuation and burden sharing. Participation after the expiration of the six month enrolment window was to be possible only in exceptional and unforeseeable circumstances for which the bank was not responsible, and subject to stricter conditions, such as higher remuneration to the State and/or higher compensatory measures. Access to asset relief was always to be conditional on a number of appropriate behavioural constraints. In particular, beneficiary banks had to be subject to safeguards which ensured that the capital effects of relief were used for providing credit to meet demand appropriately according to commercial criteria and without discrimination and not for financing a growth strategy, in particular acquisitions of sound banks, to the detriment of competitors. Restrictions on dividend policy and caps on executive remuneration had also to be considered. The specific design of behavioural constraints was to be determined on the basis of a proportionality assessment taking account of the various factors that may imply the necessity of restructuring.[68]

Eligibility of assets When determining the range of eligible assets for relief, a balance needed to be found between meeting the objective of immediate financial stability and the need to ensure the return to normal market functioning over the medium turn. Assets commonly referred to as toxic assets, for example, US mortgage-backed securities and associated hedges and derivatives, which triggered the financial crisis and had largely become illiquid or subject to severe downward value adjustments, appeared to account for the bulk of uncertainty and scepticism concerning the viability of banks. Restricting the range of eligible assets to such assets limited the State's exposure to possible losses and contribute to the prevention of competition distortions. However, an overly narrow relief measure would risk falling short of restoring confidence in the banking sector, given the differences between the specific problems encountered in different Member States and banks and the extent to which the problem of impairment had spread to other assets. This pleaded in favour of a pragmatic approach including elements of flexibility, which ensured that other assets also benefited from relief measures to an appropriate extent and where duly justified. However, assets that could not be

---

[68] Impaired Assets Communication, paras 26-31.

considered impaired were not to be covered by a relief programme. Asset relief was not to provide an open-ended insurance against future consequences of recession.[69]

Valuation of assets   A correct and consistent approach to the valuation of assets is of key importance to prevent undue distortions of competition and to avoid subsidy races between Member States. As a first stage, assets were to be valued on the basis of their current market value, whenever possible. In general, any transfer of assets covered by a scheme at a valuation in excess of the market price constituted State aid. The then market value may, however, have been quite distant from the book value of those assets, or non-existent in the absence of a market. As a second stage, the value attributed to impaired assets in the context of an asset relief program (the transfer value) were inevitably above current market prices in order to achieve the relief effect. To ensure consistency in the assessment of the compatibility of aid, the Commission considered a transfer value reflecting the underlying long-term economic value (the real economic value) of the assets, on the basis of underlying cash flows and broader time horizons, an acceptable benchmark indicating the compatibility of the aid amount as the minimum necessary. Uniform hair-cuts applicable to certain asset categories had to be considered to approximate the real economic value of assets that were so complex that a reliable forecast of developments in the foreseeable future would appear impracticable.[70]

15.5 RESTRUCTURING OF FINANCIAL INSTITUTIONS

The Restructuring Communication   Restructuring measures formed a major element in the State aid response to the credit crisis. The Restructuring Communication set out the Commission's approach to restructuring aid for financial institutions, which applied instead of the normal restructuring aid guidelines. The general principle was that where a financial institution received aid, a viability plan or a more fundamental restructuring plan was required in order to establish individual banks' long term viability without reliance on State support. The notification of the plan had to include a comparison with alternative options, including a break up of the bank or absorption by another bank, in order to allow for an assessment of whether more market oriented, less costly or less distortive solutions were available. The restructuring plan had to identify the causes of the bank's difficulties and weaknesses and outline how the restructuring measures would remedy them. Long term viability would be achieved when a bank was able to cover all its

---

[69]   *Ibid.*, paras 32-36.
[70]   *Ibid.*, 37-40.

costs and provide an appropriate return on equity and compete on the marketplace for capital on its own merits. This required that any State aid received would be either redeemed over time or be remunerated on market conditions. In light of the crisis conditions, structural measures were allowed to be in place for a longer time than normal, but were envisaged as being for a maximum of five years.[71]

Approximately 85% of banks that received recapitalisation aid and all banks that received impaired asset relief support were subject to restructuring. The 15 largest beneficiaries were from a small number of Member States: the United Kingdom (RBS and Lloyds Banking Group); Ireland (Anglo Irish Bank and Allied Irish Bank); Belgium (Fortis, supported also by the Netherlands and Luxembourg, and Dexia, supported also by France and Luxembourg); Germany (Bayern LB, Commerzbank, HSH Nordbank, IKB, LBBW and West LB); and the Netherlands (ING and ABN Amro). By the end of 2010, of the 26 banks in respect of which a decision had been taken by the Commission, all but four were restructured, with the remainder being liquidated (Fiona in Denmark, Kaupthing Luxembourg in Luxembourg and Dunfermline and Bradford & Bingley in the United Kingdom). Subsequently, Portugal's BPP was liquidated and Ireland's Anglo Irish Bank (which had been instrumental in leading the property development boom) was renamed the Irish Bank Resolution Corporation and stripped of its trading capacity. By 2014, the Commission had analysed the restructuring of 111 banks, of which 52 were restructured and 33 were liquidated.[72]

Sale or winding-up of a bank The sale of an ailing bank to another financial institution could contribute to long term viability, as long as the purchaser is viable and capable of absorbing the transfer. However, where this might have led to consolidation of the financial sector, appropriate remedies were required to be put in place so as to avoid undue distortions of competition. A negative sale price could exceptionally be accepted as not involving State aid to the buyer if the seller would have had to face higher costs on liquidation.[73]

Under the Banking Communication 2008, controlled liquidation might have been applied to an individual financial institution when it had become clear that the latter could not be restructured successfully. Controlled winding-up might also have constituted an element of a general guarantee scheme, e.g. where a Member State undertook to initiate liquidation of the financial institutions for which the guarantee needs to be activated. In the context of liquidation, particular care had to be taken to minimise moral hazard, notably by excluding shareholders and possibly certain types of creditors from

---

[71] Restructuring Communication, paras 9-16.
[72] Commission Paper on the effects of temporary State aid rules adopted in the context of the financial and economic crisis.
[73] Restructuring Communication, paras 17-20.

receiving the benefit of any aid in the context of the controlled winding-up procedure. As long as the beneficiary financial institution continued to operate it was not to pursue any new activities, but merely continue the ongoing ones. The Restructuring Communication explicitly recognised that the acquisition of good assets and liabilities of a bank in difficulty may also be an option for a healthy bank as it could be a cost effective way to expand deposits and ensure viability.[74] For example, the Commission approved a plan to wind down Anglo-Irish Bank and the Irish Nationwide Building Society over a period of ten years.[75] Similarly, the German Landsbank WestLB was split up with a small part of its activities being transferred to Helaba, the remaining assets and liabilities being transferred to a bad bank to be wound down.[76]

Under the Banking Communication 2013, additional provisions govern liquidation aid as of 1 August 2013. Member States are urged to encourage the exit of non-viable banks in an orderly manner. It should be demonstrated that liquidation aid enables the credit institution to be effectively wound up in an orderly fashion, while limiting the amount of aid to the minimum necessary keep it afloat during the liquidation. The wind-up phase should be limited to the period necessary to ensure orderly liquidation. The bank's pricing policy must be designed to encourage customers to find more attractive alternatives. The bank's licence should be limited to the activities that are strictly necessary for the winding up.[77]

Own contribution by the financial institution In order to limit distortions of competition and address moral hazard, aid had to be limited to the minimum necessary and an appropriate own contribution to restructuring costs was required of the aid beneficiary. In order to limit the aid amount, banks were required first to use their own resources to finance restructuring. This might have involved a necessity to sell certain assets. Any derogation from an adequate burden sharing which might have been granted at the rescue stage for reasons of financial stability had to be compensated by additional measures at the restructuring stage. Banks could not use any State aid that they had received to remunerate their own funds where those activities did not generate sufficient profits. For example, the discretionary offset of losses, such as releasing reserves or reducing equity, in order to guarantee the payment of dividends and coupons on outstanding subordinated debt, was in principle not compatible with the objective of burden sharing.[78] The degree of dilution depended on the type of capital injected, with injections through ordinary

---

[74] Banking Communication 2008, paras 43-50; Restructuring Communication, para 21. See, for example, Case NN 36/2008, *Roskilde*, OJ 2008 C238/5.

[75] SA.32504, *Anglo Irish Bank* (2011).

[76] SA.29590, *WestLB* (2011).

[77] Banking Communication 2013, paras 72-76.

[78] Restructuring Communication, paras 24-26. Case N615/2008, *Bayern LB*.

shares being more effective in that regard than the issue of preferred shares. Some 45% of capital injected by the Member States in restructured banks was in the form of ordinary shares, while 47% was Tier 1 capital mostly in the form of preferred shares.

Prevention of undue distortions of competition Measures to limit distortions of competition must be tailor-made to address distortions on the markets where the beneficiary bank operates following its return to viability. Depending on the nature of the distortion, it might be addressed through measures in respect of liabilities or assets. Generally, where there was a greater burden sharing and the own contribution was higher, fewer negative consequences result from moral hazard, such that the need for further measures is reduced. In relation to the markets on which the beneficiary continued to operate, if divestment was not considered desirable, limitation on organic growth might be preferred. Where divestment was required, this involved selling subsidiaries or branches, portfolios of customers or business units or other measures, including on the retail market. A limit might also be imposed on the bank's expansion in certain business or geographical areas, for instance via market-oriented remedies such as specific capital requirements.[79] Dexia, for example, had to sell its US subsidiary FSA as well as some non-core businesses. In the United Kingdom, Lloyds Banking Group and RBS were each required to divest a 5% market share to a new entrant or small existing competitor on the market.[80]

Banks were not entitled to use State aid to acquire competing businesses. In exceptional cases, acquisitions could be approved by the Commission where they were part of a consolidation process necessary to restore financial stability. Where the imposition or divestments or the prohibition on acquisitions was not appropriate, a claw back mechanism, for example in the form of a levy, was acceptable. State aid could not be used to offer terms, for example as regards rates or collateral, which could not be matched by non-aided competitors. Where limitation on pricing behaviour was not appropriate, alternative remedies might be considered. In some cases, such as ING, where the Commission received evidence that aggressive pricing and commercial practices had contributed to structural difficulties, a price leadership ban was imposed. The Commission was also favorable to looking at measures aimed at developing more sound competitive markets, for instance by facilitating entry and exit.[81] For instance, Ireland was ordered to facilitate the entry into the market of competitors through enhanced electronic banking, so as to counter the high cost of maintaining a network branch.

---

[79] Restructuring Communication, paras 30-32. Case C10/2008, *IKB*; Case N244/2009, *Commerzbank*.

[80] In fact, neither bank found a willing buyer, so that the divestment requirement had to be amended: SA.29834, *Lloyds Banking Group* (2014); SA.38304, *RBS* (2014).

[81] Restructuring Communication, paras 39-45.

Part III

SUPERVISION AND ENFORCEMENT

Chapter Sixteen

ASSESSMENT OF STATE AID BY THE EUROPEAN COMMISSION

16.1 SUPERVISORY CONTROL OF STATE AID

Article 108 TFEU and Council Regulation (EC) No 659/1999 Centralised supervisory control by the European Commission is considered essential to the effective enforcement of the FEU Treaty rules on State aid. Pursuant to Article 108 TFEU, the Commission has the power to supervise any plans of the Member States to grant or alter aid and to keep under constant review all systems of aid existing in those States. Until 1999, the exercise of this power was developed by the Commission, subject to judicial review by the European Court of Justice and the General Court.[1] Council Regulation (EC) No 659/1999 laying down detailed rules for the application of Article 108(1) TFEU codified and reinforced the Commission's practice.[2] Regulation (EC) No 659/1999 entered into force on 16 April 1999 so that, in accordance with the principle that procedural rules generally apply to all disputes pending at the time that they enter into force unless otherwise provided, it applies to any administrative procedure before the Commission from that date.[3] Substantial amendments to the procedural regime were effected by Council Regulation (EU) No 734/2013 as of August 2013.[4]

Article 108 TFEU and Regulation (EC) No 659/1999 should be read together and the previous case law obviously remains relevant. Even where innovations were introduced into the pre-existing procedural framework, that

---

[1] See J. Winter, "Supervision of State aid: Article 93 in the Court of Justice" (1993) 30 CMLRev 311; J. Temple Lang, "EU State aid rules – the need for substantive reform" [2014] EStALQ 440.

[2] Council Regulation (EC) No 659/1999, Preamble, recital 2; Case C-400/99, *Italy v Commission* [2005] ECR I-3657, para 23. For a summary of the background to the adoption of Regulation (EC) No 659/1999 see A. Sinnaeve and P. Slot, "The new regulation on State aid procedures" (1999) 36 CMLRev 1153.

[3] Case C-368/04 *Transalpine Ölleitung in Österreich v Finanzlandesdirektion für Tirol* [2006] ECR I-9957, para 34; Case T-369/00, *Départment du Loiret v Commission* [2003] ECR II-1795, paras 50-51; Case T-274/01, *Valmont Nederland BV v Commission* [2004] ECR II-3145, para 56; Case T-171/02, *Regione autonoma della Sardegna v Commission* [2005] ECR II-2123, para 56; Case T-25/04, *González y Díez SA v Commission* [2007] ECR II-3121, para 58; Cases T-254/00, T-270/00 & T-277/00, *Hotel Cipriani SpA v Commission* [2008] ECR II-3269, para 357.

[4] OJ 2014 L204/15.

case law may legitimately be referred to, precisely because the innovation must be interpreted in the context into which it has been inserted.[5] Nevertheless, since Regulation (EC) No 659/1999 was adopted pursuant to Article 109 TFEU which allows the Council to make regulations for the application of Article 108(1) TFEU, the Council was not necessarily obliged to follow the pre-existing case law in all respects and some divergences or developments may be apparent. In so far as there are differences between the previous case law concerning the application of Article 108 TFEU and the provisions of the Regulation, the latter should generally prevail, unless there is a conflict with the substantive interpretation of Article 108 TFEU itself or with the application of some superior rule of EU law.[6] It may also be noted that, as Regulation (EC) No 659/1999 constitutes a measure of secondary legislation adopted for the purposes of Articles 107 and 108 TFEU, it cannot restrict the scope of those provisions, particularly as the Commission derives its powers directly from them, so that those provisions may be the basis for the exercise of power by the Commission that is not specifically provided for in the regulation.[7] On the other hand, the provisions of Regulation (EC) No 659/1999 were intended to provide legal certainty in procedural matters, in particular concerning existing aid and unlawful aid, so that the Commission may not circumvent those procedures.[8]

Council Regulation (EC) No 659/1999 is directly applicable throughout the territory of the European Union, so that, in general, no further measures are required for it to take effect.[9] It provides authority, however, for the Commission to adopt implementing provisions concerning notifications, annual reports, time limits and interest rates payable on unlawful aid.[10] This power has been exercised in Commission Regulation (EC) No 794/2004.[11] The Advisory Committee on State aid, which comprises representatives of the Member States chaired by a representative of the Commission,[12] must be

---

[5] Case C-276/03P, *Scott SA v Commission* [2005] ECR I-8437, *per* Advocate General Jacobs at para 64.

[6] Case C-99/98, *Austria v Commission* [2001] ECR I-1101, Case C-480/98, *Spain v Commission* [2000] ECR I-8717 and Cases T-298/97 etc., *Alzetta v Commission* [2000] ECR II-2319 illustrate some possible conflicts between Article 108 TFEU and Regulation (EC) No 659/1999.

[7] Cases C-182/03 & C-217/03, *Belgium and Forum 187 ASBL v Commission* [2006] ECR I-5479, para 71; Case T-527/13, *Italy v Commission* EU:T:2015:429, para 68.

[8] Case T-527/13, *Italy v Commission* EU:T:2015:429, para 91.

[9] Article 288 TFEU.

[10] Council Regulation (EC) No 659/1999, Article 27.

[11] OJ 2004 L140/1; as amended by Commission Regulation (EC) No 1627/2006 (OJ 2006 L302/10), Commission Regulation (EC) No 1935/2006 (OJ 2006 L407/1), Commission Regulation (EC) No 271/2008 (OJ 2008 L82/1), Commission Regulation (EC) No 1147/2008 (OJ 2008 L313/1) and Commission Regulation (EU) No 372/2014 (OJ 2009 C109/14)

[12] Council Regulation (EC) No 659/1999, Article 28.

consulted prior to the adoption by the Commission of implementing provisions. In addition, the Committee discusses Commission proposals for State aid policy instruments, such as frameworks, guidelines and notices. The Committee is not, however, consulted by the Commission prior to the adoption of individual decisions. At various stages in the control procedure the Commission is required to take decisions pursuant to the provisions of Regulation (EC) No 659/1999. Commission decisions should normally be taken by the whole Commission acting collegiately and not solely by the Commissioner with responsibility for competition policy.[13]

Code of best practice and simplified procedures The Commission has also adopted a code of best practice for the conduct of State aid control procedures.[14] This should be read in conjunction with and as a supplement to the regulatory rules governing State aid procedures and is intended to contribute to speedier, more transparent and more predictable procedures at each step of the investigation. In addition, the Commission issued a notice on a simplified procedure for certain types of State aid.[15] This applies in the case of measures that fall within the standard assessment or safe harbour sections of the Commission's guidelines and frameworks, measures corresponding to well-established Commission decision-making practice, or measures prolonging or extending existing schemes. The simplified procedure applies only to notified aid.

Commission decisions on new and existing aid The supervisory system established by Article 108 TFEU and Regulation (EC) No 659/1999 distinguishes between new aid and existing aid, and also between lawful aid and unlawful aid or misuse of aid. Different procedures and consequences apply depending on whether the aid is classifiable as new aid or as existing aid. In particular, new aid must not be implemented prior to the Commission taking a decision on its compatibility with the internal market, and any aid implemented in breach of this requirement will be regarded as unlawful and subject to recovery. On the other hand, existing aid may continue to be implemented by the Member State but is the subject of a constant review allowing the Commission to recommend its abolition or amendment as no longer being compatible with the internal market. Existing aid which has been used for an improper purpose, however, will be treated as a misuse of aid, and may also be subject to recovery. In the case of new aid, there are two separate

---

[13] Case T-435/93, *ASPEC v Commission* [1995] ECR II-1281, para 125; Case T-442/93, *AAC v Commission* [1995] ECR II-1329, para 106; Cases T-371 & 394/94, *British Airways v Commission* [1998] ECR II-2405, paras 116-117; Cases T-427/04 & T-17/05, *France v Commission* [2009] ECR II-4315, para 118.

[14] OJ 2009 C136/13.

[15] OJ 2009 C136/3.

stages in the Commission's investigation procedures: first, a preliminary investigation and, secondly, in cases where the Commission has serious difficulty in concluding that the aid is compatible with the internal market, a formal investigation. Similarly, where the Commission, in the course of its constant review of existing aid, wishes to determine that aid is no longer compatible with the internal market and the Member State does not agree to the Commission's recommendation, a formal investigation procedure must be commenced.

As regards new aid, Article 108(3) TFEU provides that plans to grant or alter aid must be notified to the Commission prior to being put into effect.[16] Following its preliminary examination of the notified measure, the Commission must take a decision on its compatibility with the internal market pursuant to Regulation (EC) No 659/1999, Article 4. In this respect, the Commission may decide that the plan does not in fact amount to aid within the meaning of Article 107(1) TFEU[17] or that it does constitute aid but is compatible with the internal market,[18] in which case the Member State may proceed to put the measure into effect. If, on the other hand, the Commission has serious doubts that any such plan is compatible with the internal market, it must proceed to a full review of the proposed measure by means of a formal investigation procedure leading to a decision pursuant to Regulation (EC) No 659/199, Article 7.[19] If that procedure results in a decision that the aid is not compatible with the internal market, the aid must not be put into effect.[20] In fact, most notified measures are approved and only a small proportion are subject to a formal investigation.[21] If new aid is not notified to the Commission or if the aid is notified but is implemented prior to a decision being made or being deemed to be made declaring it compatible with the internal market, the aid will be regarded as unlawful. In that event, the Commission is still required to assess the compatibility of the aid with the internal market, although unlawful aid that is found to be incompatible must normally be the subject of a recovery order imposed on the Member State.[22]

Existing aid is, pursuant to Article 108(1) TFEU and Regulation (EC) No 659/1999, Articles 17-19, subject to constant review by the Commission. As part of this review, the Commission may propose to the Member States any appropriate measures required for the progressive development or by the functioning of the internal market.[23] If the Member States accept these

---

[16]   Article 108(3) TFEU; Council Regulation (EC) No 659/1999, Article 2(1).
[17]   Council Regulation (EC) No 659/1999, Article 4(2).
[18]   *Ibid.*, Article 4(3).
[19]   Article 108(3) TFEU; Council Regulation (EC) No 659/1999, Article 4(4).
[20]   Council Regulation (EC) No 659/1999, Article 7(5).
[21]   *Thirty-Second Report on Competition Policy* (2002), pt. 339.
[22]   Council Regulation (EC) No 659/1999, Article 14(1).
[23]   Article 108(1) TFEU; Council Regulation (EC) No 659/1999, Article 18.

proposals, they become bound by them.[24] Where the Commission's proposals are not accepted, the Commission should institute the formal investigation procedure into the operation of the aid.[25] If, as a result of that procedure, the Commission finds that the aid is not compatible with the internal market, it must order that the aid be altered or abolished, unless the Council decides otherwise.[26] The Commission's decision concerning the abolition or amendment of existing aid only takes effect as to the future.[27] Existing aid which has been granted prior to the Commission taking a decision that it is no longer compatible may not be the subject of a recovery order. Exceptionally, where aid has been authorised but is subsequently used for purposes for which it has not been approved, the Commission may decide, following a formal investigation procedure, that the aid has been misused and may order its recovery.[28]

Sector inquiries by the Commission Where the information available to the Commission substantiates a reasonable suspicion that State aid measures in a particular sector or based on a particular aid instrument may materially restrict or distort competition within the internal market in several Member States, or that existing aid measures in a particular sector in several Member States are not, or no longer, compatible with the internal market, the Commission may conduct an inquiry across various Member States into the sector of the economy of the aid instrument concerned. In the course of that inquiry, the Commission may request the Member States and/or the undertakings or associations of undertakings concerned to supply the necessary information. The Commission must publish a report on the results of the inquiry and invite the Member States and undertakings concerned to submit comments. Information obtained from sector inquiries may be used in the framework of investigation procedures under Regulation (EC) No 659/1999.[29]

Council decisions approving aid in exceptional circumstances On application by a Member State pursuant to Article 108(2), the Council may, acting unanimously, decide that aid which that State is granting or intends to grant shall be considered to be compatible with the internal market, in derogation from the provisions of Article 107 TFEU or from regulations adopted under Article 109 TFEU, if such a decision is justified by exceptional

---

[24] Council Regulation (EC) No 659/1999, Article 19(1).

[25] *Ibid.*, Article 19(2).

[26] Article 108(2) TFEU; Council Regulation (EC) No 659/1999, Article 7(5).

[27] Case T-354/05, *TF1 v Commission* [2009] ECR II-471, para 166.

[28] Article 108(2) TFEU; Council Regulation (EC) No 659/1999, Article 16.

[29] Council Regulation (EC) No 659/1999, Article 20a (inserted by Council Regulation (EU) No 734/2013). The first exercise of this power was in April 2015 when the Commission launched a sector inquiry into electricity capacity mechanisms.

circumstances.[30] If, as regards the aid in question, the Commission has already initiated the formal investigation procedure, the fact that the Member State concerned has made its application to the Council has the effect of suspending that procedure until the Council has made its attitude known. If, however, the Council has not made its attitude known within three months of the application being made, the Commission must give its decision on the case.[31]

The Council's power in Article 108(2) TFEU must be interpreted strictly.[32] Where the Commission has already taken a decision declaring aid incompatible with the internal market, the Council has no power to declare to the contrary. In *Commission v Germany*, Advocate General Mayras took the view that, since the effect of applying to the Council is to suspend the procedure before the Commission, it is not open to the Member State to apply to the Council after the Commission has taken a decision which has brought that procedure to an end.[33] This conclusion was subsequently confirmed by the ECJ in *Commission v Council*, on the ground that, since the Council's power under Article 108(2) TFEU was clearly exceptional, where the Commission had already taken a decision that aid was incompatible with the internal market, the Council was no longer authorised to adopt a decision in relation to the same aid measure.[34] The Commission decision at issue in that case had declared certain unlawful aid that had been paid to Portuguese pig farmers to be incompatible with the internal market and had ordered its recovery. The Council's decision was in fact concerned with aid that was intended to compensate the farmers for having to repay the unlawful aid. The ECJ held, however, that to allow a Member State to grant new aid, in an amount equivalent to that of the unlawful aid and which was intended to neutralise the impact of the repayments which the beneficiaries were obliged to make pursuant to the Commission's recovery decision, would clearly amount to undermining the effectiveness of the Commission's decision.[35]

In a series of cases involving aid in Hungary, Latvia, Lithuania and Poland, those Member States had accepted Commission guidelines aimed at

---

[30] Article 108(2) TFEU. The Council may publish the decision in the *Official Journal of the European Union*: Council Regulation (EC) No 659/1999, Article 26(5).

[31] Article 108(2) TFEU.

[32] Case C-110/02, *Commission v Council* [2004] ECR I-6333, paras 29-31; Case C-212/12P, *Commission v Ireland* EU:C:2013:812, para 48; Case C-111/10, *Commission v Council* EU:C:2013:785, para 39; Case C-117/10, *Commission v Council* EU:C:2013:786, para 51; Case C-118/10, *Commission v Council* EU:C:2013:787, para 43; Case C-121/10, *Commission v Council* EU:C:2013:784, para 40; Case T-527/13, *Italy v Commission* EU:T:2015:429, para 54.

[33] Case 70/72, *Commission v Germany* [1973] ECR 813, *per* Advocate General Mayras, at p. 835.

[34] Case C-110/02, *Commission v Council* [2004] ECR I-6333, paras 31-33; Case C-399/03, *Commission v Council* [2006] ECR I-5629, para 24.

[35] Case C-110/02, *Commission v Council* [2004] ECR I-6333, paras 43-45; Case C-399/03, *Commission v Council* [2006] ECR I-5629, paras 27-28.

terminating aid for the acquisition of agricultural land by 2009. Following the credit crisis, however, they asked the Council to approve new measures extending the aid until 2013. The Commission's applications to challenge the Council's decisions approving the aid were rejected by the ECJ, on the ground that the decisions concerned new aid and, due to the changed circumstances brought on by the credit crisis, were not indissolubly linked to the pre-existing aid schemes, so that the Commission could not be regarded as having definitively ruled on the compatibility of the new measures.[36]

Subsequent revocation of Commission decisions approving aid A decision adopted on the basis of false or incomplete information may be revoked.[37] Council Regulation (EC) No 659/1999, Article 9 provides that the Commission, after having given the Member State concerned the opportunity to submit its comments, may subsequently revoke a decision which finds that a measure does not constitute aid or that aid is compatible with the internal market where the decision was based on incorrect information provided during the investigation procedure which was a determining factor for the decision.[38] Before revoking a decision and taking a new decision, however, the Commission must open the formal investigation procedure. Aid which has been granted may be treated in much the same way as unlawful aid and may be required to be suspended pending the Commission's examination. Aid which is subsequently declared incompatible with the internal market must be repaid.[39] The Commission may also revoke a decision on the basis that it is tainted with procedural or substantive illegality. In *González y Díez SA v Commission*, for example, the Commission withdrew a decision on the ground that it had doubts that it had complied with the applicable procedural rules. Such a retrospective withdrawal of an unlawful administrative act which has created subjective rights is permissible, provided that the institution which adopted the decision acts within a reasonable time and complies with the legitimate expectations of beneficiaries of the act who have been entitled to rely on its lawfulness.[40]

The mechanism of Regulation (EC) No 659/1999, Article 9 is not, however, to be used as a means to reopen the Commission's investigation in the absence of an allegation that the decision was taken on the basis of incorrect

---

[36] Case C-111/10, *Commission v Council* EU:C:2013:785, para 66; Case C-117/10, *Commission v Council* EU:C:2013:786, para 82; Case C-118/10, *Commission v Council* EU:C:2013:787, para 73; Case C-121/10, *Commission v Council* EU:C:2013:784, para 67.

[37] Cases 42/59 & 49/59, *SNUPAT v High Authority* [1961] ECR 53, at p.87; Case T-527/13, *Italy v Commission* EU:T:2015:429, para 90.

[38] See, for example, Commission Decision 2001/856/EC, *Verlipack*, OJ 2001 L320/28, which was upheld in Case C-457/00, *Belgium v Commission* [2003] ECR I-6931.

[39] Council Regulation (EC) No 659/1999, Article 9; cf. Articles 11(1) and 14.

[40] Case T-25/04, *González y Díez SA v Commission* [2007] ECR II-3121, paras 97-98.

information. Thus, in *Otto Wöhr v Commission*, a request by an interested party to the Commission to open the formal investigation procedure could not be treated as falling within the scope of this provision, since it did not in fact allege that the decision was based on incorrect information.[41] Similarly, in *Kronoply v Commission*, the notion that it could be used to approve an alteration of aid already authorised and granted was rejected.[42]

Supervision under the EEA Agreement The application of the State aid rules in the EFTA Member States participating in the EEA Agreement is supervised by the EFTA Surveillance Authority, while the Commission supervises the application of the State aid rules contained in the EEA Agreement in the Member States of the European Community.[43] The EFTA Surveillance Authority was established by an Agreement between the EFTA Member States participating in the EEA.[44] Amongst its duties is to give effect to the provisions of the EEA Agreement concerning State aid and to ensure that those provisions are applied by the EFTA Member States participating in the EEA Agreement. Protocol 3 on the functions and powers of the EFTA Surveillance Authority in the field of State aid concerning the enforcement of the State aid rules contained in the EEA Agreement contains provisions akin to those found in Article 108. The EFTA Surveillance Authority has adopted acts corresponding to those applicable in EU law in the field of State aid.[45]

Protocol 27 to the EEA Agreement also makes provision for co-operation between the Commission and the EFTA Surveillance Authority. The EFTA Surveillance Authority is represented at the Commission's multilateral meetings and vice-versa. Exchanges of views take place on draft Commission notices or recommendations on general policy issues in the State aid field. Meetings take place between the Commission and the EFTA Surveillance Authority both periodically and to discuss specific cases at the request of one party. The opening of proceedings either by the Commission under Article 108(2) EC or by the EFTA Surveillance Authority under Article 1(2) of Protocol 3 of the EEA Agreement are brought to the notice of the other body by direct communication and to interested parties by way of notices in the *Official Journal of the European Union* and the EEA supplement. Final decisions, injunctions and proposals of appropriate measures are communicated in a similar manner. The Commission and the EFTA Surveillance Authority must also refer to the competent authority any complaints about State aid which are alleged to have occurred within the

---

[41]   Case T-222/00, *Otto Wöhr GmbH v Commission* [2001] ECR II-3463, paras 43-46.

[42]   Case T-162/06, *Kronoply GmbH v Commission* [2009] ECR II-1, para 41.

[43]   Article 62 of the EEA Agreement.

[44]   Agreement between the EFTA States on the establishment of a Surveillance Authority and a Court of Justice, OJ 1994 L344/1.

[45]   These are published in one volume entitled the Procedural and Substantive Rules in the Field of State Aid and are also available at www.efta.int/structure/SURV/efta-srv.cfm.

other's jurisdiction. The competent authority replies to the complainant and informs the other of the outcome of the investigation.

16.2 NEW AND EXISTING AID

New aid New aid means all aid which is not existing aid and comprises:[46]
(i)   a new aid scheme;
(ii) a new individual award of aid which does not come within a previously notified aid scheme;
(iii) an individual award of aid which does fall within a previously notified scheme, but which is required by the Commission to be individually approved prior to being put into effect;
(iv) any alteration to an existing aid or aid scheme.

Existing aid Existing aid comprises:[47]
(i)   aid existing at the time of the entry into force of the FEU Treaty[48] in the Member State concerned;[49]
(ii) aid schemes and individual aid which has been authorised by the Commission or the Council;
(iii) aid which has been notified to the Commission where, after a period of two months, the Commission has not made a decision regarding its compatibility with the internal market;
(iv) aid which was unlawful aid but which falls outside the limitation period of ten years in which the Commission can order recovery;
(v)   aid which is deemed to be an existing aid because it can be established that at the time it was put into effect it did not constitute an aid within the meaning of Article 107(1) TFEU, and subsequently became an aid due to

---

[46]   Council Regulation (EC) No 659/1999, Article 1(c).

[47]   *Ibid.*, Article 1(b).

[48]   The ECSC Treaty, which generally prohibited State aid pursuant to Article 4(c) CS, made no provision for existing aid. Thus, a Spanish scheme providing for tax reductions for firms exporting or operating abroad, including firms in the steel industry, which had existed before Spain's accession to the European Union was regarded as incompatible with the ECSC Treaty, whilst appropriate measures had to be adopted pursuant to Article 108(1) TFEU in relation to the aid generally: Commission communication, *Spanish tax law*, OJ 1997 C329/4.

[49]   For the original six Member States of Belgium, France, Germany, Luxembourg, Italy and the Netherlands, this was 1 January 1958. Denmark, Ireland and the United Kingdom acceded in 1973, Greece in 1981 and Portugal and Spain in 1986. Austria, Finland and Sweden joined on 1 January 1995. On 1 May 2004, the European Union was enlarged by 10 new Member States: Cyprus, Czech Republic, Estonia, Hungary, Latvia, Lithuania, Malta, Poland, Slovakia and Slovenia. Bulgaria and Romania joined in 2007, and Croatia in 2013, bringing the total to 28 Member States.

the evolution of the internal market without having been altered by the Member State.

Existing aid and accession agreements Normally, on accession to the European Union, aid existing on the date of accession is classified as existing aid. In relation to Austria, Finland and Sweden, which had been members of the European Economic Area from 1 January 1994, only those aid measures applied prior to accession on 1 January 1995 which were communicated to the Commission by 30 June 1995 were deemed to be existing aid. Existing aid and plans to grant or alter aid, communicated to the Commission prior to accession, were deemed to have been notified on 1 January 1995.[50] More complicated arrangements applied to the accessions from 2004 onwards, given the fact that the central and east European countries historically had a strong State involvement in individual undertakings, which had been the focus of attention under the Europe Agreements that preceded accession.

Under the 2004 Accession Agreement concerning Cyprus, Czech Republic, Estonia, Hungary, Latvia, Lithuania, Malta, Poland, Slovakia and Slovenia, aid measures which were put into effect prior to 10 December 1994 are deemed to be existing aid. In addition, measures that had been approved as being compatible with the internal market prior to November 2002 were included on a list of existing aid. Measures not included on that list and other measures which were submitted for approval prior to accession were subject to an interim procedure under which the measures could be assessed as compatible with the internal market and treated as existing aid. Where such measures were not approved, they were subject to a formal investigation procedure upon accession. All other aid measures which continue in effect after accession are treated as new aid.[51] In the Accession Agreement for Bulgaria and Romania, similar provisions are contained as regards Bulgaria whereas more restrictive arrangements apply to Romania.[52] Specific provisions also applied when Croatia acceded in 2013.[53]

---

[50] Act of Accession of Austria, Finland and Sweden, Article 144. Article 172(5) provides that aid granted during 1994 which, in contravention of the EEA Agreement, was not notified to the EFTA Surveillance Authority or was implemented prior to approval by the Authority, is not existing aid. All decisions taken by the EFTA Surveillance Authority before 1 January 1995 remain valid with respect to Article 107 TFEU unless the Commission decides otherwise. For a case involving special provisions under the Act of Accession, see Case T-187/99, *Agrana Zucker und Stärke AG v Commission* [2001] ECR II-1587.

[51] Act of Accession of Cyprus, Czech Republic, Estonia, Hungary, Latvia, Lithuania, Malta, Poland, Slovakia and Slovenia, Annex IV, Chapter 3; Case T-468/08, *Tisza Erőmű kft v Commission* EU:T:2014:235, para 72; Case T-179/09, *Dunamenti Erőmű zrt v Commission* EU:T:2014:236, para 57.

[52] Act of Accession of Bulgaria and Romania, Annex V, Chapter 2.

[53] Act of Accession of Croatia, Annex IV.

In *Kremikovtzi AD v Ministar na Ikonomikata*, the ECJ held that aid granted prior to accession but which no longer gave rise to expenditure by the acceding Member State after the date of accession is not considered as either new aid or existing aid.[54] By contrast, in *Budapesti Erőmű Zrt v Commission*, where aid was granted to electricity generators through the medium of long term purchasing agreements, which had been negotiated in 1996 prior to accession but not included in the list of approved aid, the General Court held that, provided the agreements were still applicable after the date of accession, they could only be regarded as new aid on the date of accession.[55]

Aid schemes and individual aid Aid schemes are defined as comprising two categories of measures.[56] First, an aid scheme is an act on the basis of which, without further implementing measures being required, individual aid awards may be made to undertakings defined within the act in a general and abstract manner. The acts in question are not limited to legislative acts, but include any measures allowing for the grant of aid in certain circumstances.[57] Secondly, aid schemes include any act on the basis of which aid which is not linked to a specific project may be awarded to one or several undertakings for an indefinite period of time or for an indefinite amount. This latter definition is intended to ensure that such measures are not classified as individual aid, so that, if necessary, the Commission will be in a position to propose appropriate measures in relation to them pursuant to Article 108(1) TFEU. New aid schemes must be notified and approved in advance of being put into effect. Aid schemes and grants of individual aid which have been authorised by the Commission or by the Council and which are then implemented become existing aid.[58] This applies in the case of all new aid which has been authorised as well as any existing aid which has been altered by agreement pursuant to Article 108(1) TFEU or following a decision of the Commission or the Council pursuant to Article 108(2) TFEU.

Individual aid requires notification where it is not awarded on the basis of an aid scheme or where it is awarded on the basis of an aid scheme but is stated under the terms of the scheme to be a notifiable award.[59] A specific grant of aid made in pursuance of a previously authorised scheme which satisfies the conditions laid down in the approval decision must be regarded as authorised aid and, thus, as existing aid. Conversely, where it is not covered by the

---

[54] Case C-262/11, *Kremikovtzi AD v Ministar na Ikonomikata* EU:C:2012:760, paras 55-62.

[55] Cases T-80/06 & T-182/09, *Budapesti Erőmű Zrt v Commission* EU:T:2012:65, para 52.

[56] Council Regulation (EC) No 659/1999, Article 1(d).

[57] Case T-203/10 RENV, *Stichting Woonpunt v Commission* EU:T:2015:286, para 50; Case T-202/10 RENV, *Stichting Woonlinie v Commission* EU:T:2015:287, para 50.

[58] Commission Regulation (EC) No 659/1999, Article 1(b)(ii); Case 84/82, *Germany v Commission* [1984] ECR 1451, para 12.

[59] Council Regulation (EC) No 659/1999, Article 1(e).

approval decision concerning the general aid, the individual aid must be regarded as new aid.[60] It follows that a decision whereby the Commission authorises a general State aid scheme on condition that individual significant cases be notified with a view to an assessment of their impact on intra-EU trade cannot constitute blanket approval of all aid granted pursuant to that scheme, since the obligation to notify significant cases must be interpreted as a reservation on the approval contained in the decision itself.[61]

Reservations of this type may arise from Commission frameworks or guidelines which have been accepted by the Member States in the context of the application of the Commission's powers of review under Article 108(1) TFEU. For example, in *CIRFS v Commission*, the Commission, in a decision authorising a regional aid scheme in France as compatible with the internal market, had specified that approval was without prejudice to compliance with any present or future special rules on aid to particular industries. The Commission's stated policy at that time in relation to synthetic fibres for textile or industrial applications, which suffered from over-capacity, was that no new regional or sectoral aid which would increase production capacity was to be approved. When the Commission subsequently examined a plan from the French Government to grant regional aid for a new textile plant, it decided that the proposed aid was not subject to prior notification on the ground that it fell within the scope of its previous approval of the regional aid scheme. This decision was annulled by the ECJ which held that the proposed aid was impliedly excluded from the scope of the authorisation and therefore constituted new aid which was subject to the obligation of prior notification.[62]

Alterations to and extensions of existing aid Any alteration to or extension of an existing aid or aid scheme is treated as new aid.[63] A Member State cannot, by amending an aid scheme after its approval by the Commission, unilaterally extend the scope of that approval.[64] Only where the alteration

---

[60] Case C-47/91, *Italy v Commission* [1994] ECR I-4635, paras 25-26; Case C-321/99P, *ARAP v Commission* [2002] ECR I-4287, para 60.

[61] Cases T-447-449/93, *AITEC v Commission* [1995] ECR II-1971, para 129; Case T-422/07, *Djebel-SGPS SA v Commission* EU:T:2012:11, para 144.

[62] Case C-313/90, *CIRFS v Commission* [1993] ECR I-1125, para 51.

[63] Council Regulation (EC) No 659/1999, Article 1(c)(iv); Case C-295/97, *Piaggio v Ifitalia* [1999] ECR I-3735, para 48; Cases C-346/03 and C-529/03, *Atzeni v Regione autonoma della Sardegna* [2006] ECR I-1875, para 51; Case C-138/09, *Todaro Nunziatina v Assessorato del Lavoro* [2010] ECR I-4561, para 46; Case C-111/10, *Commission v Council* EU:C:2013:785, para 58; Case T-162/06, *Kronoply GmbH v Commission* [2009] ECR II-1, para 85; Case T-542/11, *Alouminion AE v Commission* EU:T:2014:859, para 53; Case T-291/11, *Portovesme srl v Commission* EU:T:2014:896, paras 113-115.

[64] Cases C-630/11P to C-633/11P, *HGA srl v Commission* EU:C:2013:387, para 91; Case T-109/01, *Fleuren Compost BV v Commission* [2004] ECR II-127, para 80; Cases T-

affects the actual substance of the original scheme is the latter transformed into a new aid scheme. It follows that where the alteration is severable from the existing aid, only the new provisions need be notified.[65] Thus, in *Italy v Commission*, the Commission's decision which treated an amendment to an approved scheme as involving new aid and ordered recovery of the entire aid was annulled, the General Court holding that the Commission had failed to assess whether the modification was severable.[66] Where only the alteration is to be classified as new aid, not the altered aid measure in full, the pre-existing aid will continue to be regarded as approved existing aid.[67] Transitional rules, which maintain the effects of a new State aid scheme which has not been notified to the Commission and has been declared incompatible with the internal market, constitutes a new State aid scheme.[68]

In order to constitute a new aid, the modification of existing aid must be substantial.[69] Commission Regulation (EC) No 794/2004 provides that an alteration to existing aid means any change, other than modifications of a purely formal or administrative nature which cannot affect the evaluation of the compatibility of the aid measure with the internal market.[70] An alteration to an existing scheme will arise where new provisions change any of the basic features of the previous system of aid such as, for example, the aims pursued, the persons and bodies affected or the source of its finances[71] or an extension to the period of application of the aid scheme beyond that originally notified.[72] On the other hand, mere administrative improvements to a system which do not

---

394/08, T-408/08, T-453/08 & T-454/08, *Regione autonoma della Sardegna v Commission* [2011] ECR II-6255, para 179.

[65] Cases 91 & 127/83, *Heiniken Brouwerijen v Inspecteurs der Vennootschaapsbelasting* [1984] ECR 3435, para 21; Cases T-195/01 & T-207/01, *Government of Gibraltar v Commission* [2002] ECR II-2309, paras 109-111; Cases T-116/01 & T-118/01, *P&O European Ferries (Vizcaya) SA v Commission* [2003] ECR II-2957, para 60; Cases T-231/06 & T-237/06, *Netherlands v Commission* [2010] ECR II-5993, para 177; Case T-151/11, *Telefónica de España SA v Commission* EU:T:2014:631, para 63; Case T-527/13, *Italy v Commission* EU:T:2015:429, para 75.

[66] Case T-527/13, *Italy v Commission* EU:T:2015:429, paras 78-80.

[67] *Ibid.*, para 74.

[68] Case C-297/01, *Sicilcassa SpA v IRA Construzioni SpA* [2003] ECR I-7849, para 45.

[69] Case T-151/11, *Telefónica de España SA v Commission* EU:T:2014:631, para 62.

[70] Commission Regulation (EC) No 794/2004, Article 4(1).

[71] Case 51/74, *Van der Hulst v Produktschap voor Siergewassen* [1975] ECR 79, *per* Advocate General Trabucchi, at p. 105.

[72] Case 70/72, *Commission v Germany* [1973] ECR 813, para 14; Case C-138/09, *Todaro Nunziatina v Assessorato del Lavoro* [2010] ECR I-4561, para 47; Cases C-630/11P to C-633/11P, *HGA srl v Commission* EU:C:2013:387, para 94; Case T-190/00, *Regione Siciliana v Commission* [2003] ECR II-5015, para 73; Cases T-254/00, T-270/00 & T-277/00, *Hotel Cipriani SpA v Commission* [2008] ECR II-3269, para 362; Cases T-394/08, T-408/08, T-453/08 & T-454/08, *Regione autonoma della Sardegna v Commission* [2011] ECR II-6255, para 178.

accentuate the intensity of aid need not be notified.[73] Moreover, adjustments
of minor importance that can properly be described as negligible will not be
regarded as resulting in new aid. Minor adjustment to take account of inflation
would be regarded as negligible. In the case of aid granted in accordance with
a formula, automatic increases in amounts resulting from the operation of the
formula in inflationary conditions, as distinct from increases resulting from a
change in the formula, would not be alterations in the aid.[74] The Commission
does not require notification of increases in the authorised budget of an
existing aid scheme up to 20% of the budget originally notified.[75] A simplified
notification procedure applies in the case of increases in the budget of an
authorised aid scheme exceeding 20% or prolongation of an existing authorised
scheme by up to six years. Simplified procedures also apply in the case of the
tightening of the criteria for the application of an authorised scheme, a
reduction in aid intensity or a reduction of eligible expenses.[76]

Increase in scope of an existing aid Whether alterations to existing aid
amount to new aid is to be determined by reference to the scope of the
provisions governing the aid, and not to its scale or amount. In *Namur-Les
Assurances du Crédit SA v Office Nationale du Ducroire*, the ECJ analysed the
extension of the field of activity of OND, a public body responsible for
guaranteeing certain risks relating to foreign trade transactions which was
accorded a number of advantages, including a State guarantee and exemption
from taxes. Although the legislation setting up OND contained no restriction,
in terms of subject matter or geographical area, on OND's field of activity in
export credit insurance, a cooperation agreement between OND and COBAC, a
private insurer, provided that only in exceptional circumstances was OND to
insure commercial risks relating to the export of goods and services to western
Europe, which were normally to be assumed by COBAC. That cooperation
agreement was terminated by OND on the ground that it was contrary to EU
competition rules and OND, with ministerial approval, then entered the market
for credit risk insurance in western Europe. It was alleged that, in view of the
advantages accorded to OND, the enlargement of its field of activity
constituted new State aid which enabled OND to become a competitor of
private export credit insurance companies whilst maintaining the advantages
which it already enjoyed.

The ECJ held that whether aid may be classified as new aid or as alteration
of existing aid must be determined by reference to the provisions providing for

---

[73] Cases 166 & 220/86, *Irish Cement Limited v Commission* [1988] ECR 6473, *per*
Advocate General Darmon, at p. 6495.

[74] Case 177/78, *Pigs and Bacon Commission v McCarren* [1979] ECR 2161, *per* Advocate
General Warner, at p. 2204; Case 222/82, *Apple and Pear Development Council v Lewis*
[1983] ECR 4083, *per* Advocate General Rozès, at p. 4134.

[75] Commission Regulation (EC) No 794/2004, Article 4(1).

[76] *Ibid.*, Article 4(2).

the aid. Having noted that OND's field of activity was not limited by law but by the effects of the cooperation agreement between it and COBAC, it held that the emergence of new aid or the alteration of existing aid was not to be assessed according to the scale of the aid or its amount in financial terms at any moment in the life of the undertaking if the aid was provided under earlier statutory provisions which remain unchanged. To take the contrary view would be tantamount to requiring the notification of all measures affecting the activity of an undertaking in receipt of existing aid and would give rise to legal uncertainty for undertakings and Member States.[77]

In a group of cases concerning the Italian electricity system, the General Court held that an extension beyond the period allowed by the Commission in a previous decision of a preferential tariff constituted new aid. The Italian authorities had nationalised the Italian electricity sector in 1962, but had largely excluded electricity production for self-consumption with some exceptions including Terni, an owner of a hydroelectric plant. As compensation, a special tariff for the sale of electricity to that undertaking was established for the period 1963 to 2005 which the Commission accepted, in so far as the preferential tariff constituted aid, was compatible with the internal market. When the preferential tariff was extended by the Italian authorities, however, the Commission held that this constituted new aid for which there was no longer any justification. The General Court held that the Terni tariff had been granted by way of compensation for a very specific period and the extension could not be regarded as an integral part of the compensation for nationalisation of the assets.[78] Similarly, in relation to an exemption from income tax for certain Italian public sector companies, even though the undertakings in question assumed the existing rights and obligations of municipal undertakings, the legislation which defined their substantive sphere of activity and the geographical area in which they could operate changed substantially.[79] In *Netherlands v Commission*, concerning funding for the

---

[77] Case C-44/93, *Namur-Les Assurances du Crédit SA v Office Nationale du Ducroire*, [1994] ECR I-3829, paras 28-32; Cases C-15/98 & C-105/99, *Italy v Commission* [2000] ECR I-8855, *per* Advocate General Fennelly, at paras 62-63; Cases T-195/01R & T-207/01R, *Government of Gibraltar v Commission* [2001] ECR II-3915, paras 64-69; Case T-35/99, *Keller SpA v Commission* [2002] ECR II-261, para 62; Cases T-265/04, T-292/04 & T-504/04, *Tirrenia di Navigazione SpA v Commission* [2009] ECR II-21*, para 124; Case T-584/08, *Cantiere Navale De Poli SpA v Commission* [2011] ECR II-63, para 64; Cases T-231/06 & T-237/06, *Netherlands v Commission* [2010] ECR II-5993, para 180.

[78] Case T-53/08, *Italy v Commission* [2010] ECR II-3187, para 65; Case T-62/08, *ThyssenKrupp Acciai Speciali Terni SpA v Commission* [2010] ECR II-3229, para 140; Case T-63/08, *Cementir Italia srl v Commission* [2010] ECR II-123*, para 140; Case T-64/08, *Nuova Terni Industrie Chimiche SpA v Commission* [2010] ECR II-125*, para 140.

[79] Case T-297/02, *ACEA SpA v Commission* [2009] ECR II-1683, paras 123-124; Case T-301/02, *AEM SpA v Commission* [2009] ECR II-1757, paras 126-127; Case T-189/03,

Dutch public broadcasting network, *ad hoc* grants of aid were held to be separate from an existing general system of aid, and were therefore new aid, even though there were characteristics of the ad hoc payments that were similar in some respects to the general system.[80] By contrast, in *Alouminion AE v Commission*, aid was granted through a contract which was subsequently repudiated by the Greek authorities. When that repudiation was rescinded by court order and the original contract resumed its effects, the resurrected aid was held by the General Court to be existing aid on the basis that the aid measure should never have been regarded as ineffective.[81]

Aid deemed to be authorised In *Lorenz v Germany*, the ECJ held that where aid has been notified but the Commission has not taken a decision based on its preliminary assessment within two months following notification, the aid is deemed to have been authorised by the Commission and such aid is deemed to be existing aid.[82] A subsequent attempt by the Commission to establish that the two-month limit was no more than a guideline which could be varied depending on the circumstances was rejected by the ECJ.[83] The rule is now encapsulated in Regulation (EC) No 659/1999, Article 4(6). Before implementing the aid, the Member State must, for reasons of legal certainty, give prior notice to the Commission[84] which then publishes a short notice to that effect in the *Official Journal of the European Union*.[85] Compliance with that obligation is designed to establish, in the interest of the parties concerned, the date from which the aid falls under the scheme for existing aid. If no such notice is given to the Commission, the aid cannot be regarded as existing aid,[86] no authorisation is deemed to have been made and the Commission is not precluded from initiating a formal investigation procedure after the expiry of the two-month period.[87] Moreover, the aid will be classified as non-notified

---

ASM Brescia SpA v Commission [2009] ECR II-1831, paras 106-107; Case T-222/04, *Italy v Commission* [2009] ECR II-1877, paras 99-100.

[80] Cases T-231/06 & T-237/06, *Netherlands v Commission* [2010] ECR II-5993, para 182.

[81] Case T-542/11, *Alouminion AE v Commission* EU:T:2014:859, paras 55-57.

[82] Council Regulation (EC) No 659/1999, Article 1(b)(iii); Case 120/73, *Lorenz v Germany* [1973] ECR 1471, para 4; Case C-312/90, *Spain v Commission* [1992] ECR I-4117, para 18; Case C-39/94, *SFEI v Commission* [1996] ECR I-3547, para 38; Case C-367/95P, *Commission v Sytraval* [1998] ECR I-1719, para 37; Case C-99/98, *Austria v Commission* [2001] ECR I-1101, para 32; Case C-334/99, *Germany v Commission* [2003] ECR I-1139, para 49.

[83] Case C-99/98, *Austria v Commission* [2001] ECR I-1101, para 74.

[84] Council Regulation (EC) No 659/1999, Article 4(6); Case 120/73, *Lorenz v Germany* [1973] ECR 1471, para 4.

[85] Council Regulation (EC) No 659/1999, Article 26(4).

[86] Case T-187/99, *Agrana Zucker und Stärke AG v Commission* [2001] ECR II-1587, para 39.

[87] Case T-176/01, *Ferriere Nord SpA v Commission* [2004] ECR II-3931, paras 63-64; Case T-171/02, *Regione autonoma della Sardegna v Commission* [2005] ECR II-2123, para 49.

new aid,[88] which may result in the Commission issuing a suspension injunction[89] or bringing proceedings at the ECJ for interim measures[90] to suspend implementation of the aid measure.[91]

Pursuant to Regulation (EC) No 659/1999, Article 4(6), the Member State concerned may implement the aid unless the Commission takes a decision, within a period of 15 working days following receipt of the notice, to initiate the formal investigation procedure. In *Austria v Commission*, however, the ECJ held, concerning the application of Article 108(3) TFEU prior to the adoption of Regulation (EC) No 659/1999, that the Commission had no additional right of objection once the two-month period had expired.[92] The Commission has expressed the view that the provisions of Article 4(6) now override the previous law.[93] In *Spain v Commission*, whilst no challenge was made to the legality of the 15-day provision in Article 4(6), the Commission's decision to open a formal investigation procedure in that case was annulled since the decision, although taken within 15 days of notification by the Spanish authorities of their intention to implement the aid, was not actually notified until after the expiry of that period.[94]

Regulation (EC) No 659/1999, Article 15(1) introduced a new provision concerning limitation periods for the recovery of unlawful aid. Where aid has been unlawfully implemented, the Commission now has ten years in which to order its recovery. Any aid with regard to which this limitation period has expired is deemed to be existing aid.[95] Otherwise, a scheme which has not been notified cannot be deemed to be authorised even where the Commission has been aware of its existence. In *Piaggio v Ifitalia*, the Commission classified as existing aid an Italian insolvency law which potentially offered assistance to certain undertakings, but which had not been notified pursuant to Article 108(3) TFEU. Its position was based *inter alia* on its doubts as to whether the scheme constituted aid within the meaning of Article 107(1) TFEU and the infrequent application of the scheme. The ECJ held that this approach was wrong and that the determination of whether a measure was new or existing aid could not depend on a subjective assessment of the Commission.[96]

---

[88] Case C-278/00, *Greece v Commission* [2004] ECR 3997, para 33
[89] Council Regulation (EC) No 659/1999, Article 11(1).
[90] Article 279 TFEU.
[91] Case 171/83R, *Commission v France* [1983] ECR 2621, para 16.
[92] Case C-99/98, *Austria v Commission* [2001] ECR I-1101, para 85.
[93] *Thirty-First Report on Competition Policy* (2001), pt. 479.
[94] Case C-398/00, *Spain v Commission* [2002] ECR I-5643, para 34. Article 297(3) TFEU provides that decisions must be notified to those to whom they are addressed and take effect upon such notification.
[95] Council Regulation (EC) No 659/1999, Articles 1(b)(iv), 15(3).
[96] Case C-295/97, *Piaggio SpA v Ifitalia* [1999] ECR I-3735, para 47; Cases T-195/01R & T-207/01R, *Government of Gibraltar v Commission* [2001] ECR II-3915, para 72; Cases T-195/01 & T-207/01, *Government of Gibraltar v Commission* [2002] ECR II-2309, para 121.

Deemed authorisation under Regulation (EC) No 659/1999, Article 4(6) only arises in the case of notified aid. The notion that aid is deemed to be approved despite the Commission remaining silent on the matter does not apply in the case of aid that is not notified to the Commission. Mere silence on the part of the Commission cannot produce binding legal effects capable of affecting the interests of the applicant other than where that result is expressly contemplated by a provision of EU law. Thus, in the Basque tax cases, it was held that the mere fact that the Commission did not, for a very long time, open a formal investigation following a complaint from a competitor of a beneficiary of the tax exemptions in question could not in itself confer on the measure the objective nature of existing aid.[97]

Evolution of the internal market The State aid criteria are of a dynamic nature, such that a measure that was not State aid when it came into effect may become so subsequently.[98] Aid will be deemed to be existing aid if it can be established that at the time it was put into effect it did not constitute an aid within the meaning of Article 107(1) TFEU, and subsequently became an aid due to the evolution of the internal market and without having been altered by the Member State.[99] This may be understood as referring to a change in the economic and legal framework of the sector concerned.[100] It applies both to individual aid measures and aid schemes.[101] It would cover aid which has been granted by a Member State but which did not at the time fulfil all the conditions of Article 107(1) TFEU. For example, at the time an aid scheme was established, there may not have been any trade between Member States or there may have been no competition involving the goods or services or undertakings in question.[102] With the development of the internal market, trade or competition in the goods or services concerned could have the effect that the aid satisfies the criteria of Article 107(1) TFEU. By deeming this to be existing aid, the Member State is not confronted with problems of determining the point at which the aid becomes notifiable as new aid, whereas the Commission remains competent to propose appropriate measures pursuant to

---

[97] Cases C-465/09P – C-470/09P, *Territorio Histórico de Álava – Diputación Foral de Álava v Commission* [2011] ECR I-83*, paras 100-102; Cases T-30/01 etc., *Territorio Histórico de Álava – Diputación Foral de Álava v Commission* [2009] ECR II-2919, paras 150-153.

[98] Case T-468/08, *Tisza Erőmű kft v Commission* EU:T:2014:235, para 79; Case T-179/09, *Dunamenti Erőmű zrt v Commission* EU:T:2014:236, para 63.

[99] Council Regulation (EC) No 659/1999, Article 1(b)(v).

[100] Cases C-182/03 & C-217/03, *Belgium and Forum 187 ASBL v Commission* [2006] ECR I-5479, para 70; Case C-89/08P, *Commission v Ireland* [2009] ECR I-11245, para 71; Cases T-30/01 etc., *Territorio Histórico de Álava – Diputación Foral de Álava v Commission* [2009] ECR II-2919, para 173.

[101] Cases T-80/06 & T-182/09, *Budapesti Erőmű Zrt v Commission* EU:T:2012:65, para 61.

[102] See, for example, the arguments in Cases T-195/01R & T-207/01R, *Government of Gibraltar v Commission* [2001] ECR II-3915, para 81.

Article 108(1) TFEU and to ensure that the aid is not applied in the future in a way which is incompatible with the internal market.[103] For example, the Commission had originally viewed the low rate of corporation tax applicable in Ireland to manufacturing industry to be a general measure which did not constitute State aid. With the development of the services sector, and in particular of competition in services which had previously not been open to intra-Community trade, the Commission decided that the preferential tax treatment of manufacturing over services companies not only constituted State aid but also ranked as operating aid and therefore had to be eliminated, although a transitional period was agreed during which the lower rate remained in effect.[104] In its decision on Aer Rianta, the operator of certain Irish airports, in determining that an exemption from corporation tax in Ireland was existing aid, the Commission took into account that in the past the Commission had not perceived tax exemptions to airports as affecting trade between Member States and distorting competition, since the provision and operation of airport facilities was not previously clearly identified as a competitive activity.[105]

The concept of evolution of the internal market does not apply in a situation where the Commission alters its appraisal on the basis of a more rigorous application of the rules on State aid. In *Ireland, France and Italy v Commission*, exemptions from excise duty on mineral oils used for the production of alumina had previously been approved by the Commission, which had stated in its decisions that the exemptions did not give rise to distortions of competition or interfere with the working of the internal market. When the Commission subsequently refused to continue the exemptions, the General Court annulled its decision on the ground that it had failed to consider whether Article 1(b)(v) of Regulation (EC) No 659/1999 applied.[106] This was annulled on appeal *inter alia* on the ground that whether the measure constituted aid could not depend on the previous conduct of the Commission.[107] More generally, the ECJ has confirmed that the concept of State aid, whether existing or new, corresponds to an objective situation and cannot depend on previous conduct or statements of the institutions.[108] Thus, an argument in the Basque tax cases that the Commission's development of its

---

[103] Such aid cannot, therefore, be considered as illegal aid, so that it cannot be the subject of a recovery order even if the Commission ultimately decides that the aid is incompatible with the internal market.

[104] *Twenty-Eighth Report on Competition Policy* (1998), p. 272.

[105] *Thirty-First Report on Competition Policy* (2001), pt. 455.

[106] Cases T-50/06 etc., *Ireland v Commission* [2007] ECR II-172*, para 59. See also, by contrast, Case T-332/06, *Alcoa Trasformazioni Srl v Commission* [2009] ECR II-29*, para 135.

[107] Case C-89/08, *Commission v Ireland* [2009] ECR I-11245, paras 75-76.

[108] Cases C-182/03 & C-217/03, *Belgium and Forum 187 ASBL v Commission* [2006] ECR I-5479, para 71; Case C-89/08P, *Commission v Ireland* [2009] ECR I-11245, para 72; Cases T-268/08 & T-281/08, *Land Burgenland v Commission* EU:T:2012:90, para 76.

policy regarding tax and State aid amounted to evolution of the internal market so as to exempt the tax regimes from assessment as new aid was rejected by the General Court, which held that the notion of aid was to be determined objectively and could not depend on a subjective assessment by the Commission.[109] Equally, in *Adiamix* , the ECJ rejected an argument that the adoption by the Commission of its 1998 communication on direct tax and State aid somehow allowed fiscal aid regimes to be classified as existing aid.[110] Similarly, in *Mitteldeutsche Flughafen v Commission*, developments in the case law concerning the financing of airport infrastructure construction were unable to support an argument that aid for the construction of a runway at Leipzig-Halle airport only came within the scope of Article 107(1) TFEU later as a result of the evolution of the internal market.[111]

Measures becoming aid following liberalisation by EU law Where certain measures become aid following the liberalisation by EU law of an activity which was previously closed to competition, Regulation (EC) No 659/1999, Article 1(b)(v) provides that they will not be considered as existing aid after the date fixed for liberalisation. Liberalisation results in a change in the economic and legal framework of the sector in question.[112] For example, the cabotage sector was closed to intra-EU competition before it was liberalised by Regulation (EC) No 4059/89.[113] Similarly, EU legislation concerning the electricity internal market substantially altered the legal framework under which power generators conducted their business.[114] Such measures would presumably be considered as new aid which should be notified sufficiently in advance of the date fixed for liberalisation to enable the Commission to have made its decision concerning the compatibility of the aid with the internal market by that date. Otherwise the aid might have to be suspended pending the Commission's decision.

---

[109] Cases T-269/99, T-271/99 & T-272/99, *Territorio Histórico de Álava – Diputación Foral de Álava v Commission* [2002] ECR II-4217, para 80; Cases T-346/99, T-347/99 & T-348/99, *Territorio Histórico de Álava – Diputación Foral de Álava v Commission* [2002] ECR II-4259, para 84.

[110] Case C-202/14, *Adiamix SAS v Direction départmentale des finances publique de l'Orne* EU:C:2014:2420, para 28.

[111] Case C-288/11P, *Mitteldeutsche Flughafen AG v Commission* EU:C:2012:821, paras 72-73; Cases T-443/08 & T-455/08, *Freistaat Sachsen v Commission* [2011] ECR II-1311, paras 191-193.

[112] Case T-288/97, *Regione autonoma Friuli-Venezia Giulia v Commission* [2001] ECR II-1169, para 89; Cases T-30/01 etc., *Territorio Histórico de Álava – Diputación Foral de Álava v Commission* [2009] ECR II-2919, para 173.

[113] Cases T-298/97 etc., *Alzetta v Commission* [2000] ECR II-2319, para 146; Case T-288/97, *Regione autonoma Friuli-Venezia Giulia v Commission* [2001] ECR II-1169, para 89.

[114] Cases T-80/06 & T-182/09, *Budapesti Erőmű Zrt v Commission* EU:T:2012:65, para 58.

16.3 NOTIFICATION OF NEW AID

Obligatory prior notification of aid measures Pursuant to Article 108(3) TFEU, the Commission must be informed, in sufficient time to enable it to submit its comments, of any plans to grant or alter aid. Accordingly, Regulation (EC) No 659/1999, Article 2(1) requires that any plans to grant new aid must be notified in advance to the Commission by the Member State concerned. When a Member State notifies a plan to grant new aid, the Commission must, without delay, acknowledge receipt of the notification.[115] The obligation to notify rests with the Member State and cannot be regarded as satisfied by notification of the aid measure to the Commission from the recipient.[116] Moreover, the Commission cannot on any account permit a derogation from the notification procedure laid down by Article 108(3) TFEU.[117] No obligation exists on the Member States or the Commission to notify any other interested party.[118] Given that aid is defined as meaning any measure fulfilling all the criteria laid down by Article 107(1) TFEU,[119] it follows that all plans to grant new aid must be notified, even where the Member State takes the view that the aid is compatible with the internal market having regard to Article 107(2)-(3) TFEU.[120] Equally, the fact that a Member State may not appreciate, due to the complexity of a particular measure, that an advantage has been granted does not affect the duty of the Member State to notify and does not give rise to any legitimate expectation on the part of the recipient.[121]

The obligation to notify strictly extends only to those measures that fulfil the criteria of State aid within Article 107(1) TFEU.[122] Although, there is no obligation to notify measures which do not constitute State aid, in the past the Commission has been of the view that the obligation to notify applies even

---

[115] Council Regulation (EC) No 659/1999, Article 2(1).
[116] Cases C-442/03P & C-471/03P, *P&O European Ferries (Vizcaya) SA v Commission* [2006] ECR I-4845, para 103; Cases T-116/01 & T-118/01, *P&O European Ferries (Vizcaya) SA v Commission* [2003] ECR II-2957, para 64.
[117] Cases T-116/01 & T-118/01, *P&O European Ferries (Vizcaya) SA v Commission* [2003] ECR II-2957, para 70.
[118] Case 84/82, *Germany v Commission* [1984] ECR 1451, para 13; Cases 91 & 127/83, *Heiniken Brouwerijen v Inspecteurs der Vennootschaapsbelasting* [1984] ECR 3435, para 15. See also Case C-367/95P, *Commission v Sytraval* [1998] ECR I-1719, para 58.
[119] Council Regulation (EC) No 659/1999, Article 1(a).
[120] Cases 31/77R & 53/77R, *Commission v United Kingdom* [1977] ECR 921, para 18; Case 171/83R, *Commission v France* [1983] ECR 2621, para 12.
[121] Case C-81/10P, *France Télécom SA v Commission* [2011] ECR I-12899, para 62.
[122] Cases 91 & 127/83, *Heiniken Brouwerijen v Inspecteurs der Vennootschaapsbelasting* [1984] ECR 3435, para 11; Case C-71/04, *Administración del Estado v Xunta de Galicia* [2005] ECR I-7419, para 32; Cases T-254/00, T-270/00 & T-277/00, *Hotel Cipriani SpA v Commission* [2008] ECR II-3269, para 107.

though the Member State concerned may consider that the plan does not have all the characteristics necessary to come within the scope of Article 107(1) TFEU.[123] This approach may still apply, pursuant to the Member States' duty of cooperation under Article 4(3) TEU, at least where there is some reason to suspect that aid may be involved. For instance, whilst privatisations by flotation or competitive tender need not be notified to the Commission, although Member States may notify if they desire the added legal security of a formal clearance, privatisations in the sensitive sectors must all be notified to the Commission in advance.[124] Moreover, Regulation (EC) No 659/1999, while not specifically providing for non-aid measures to be notified, does provide for the Commission to take decisions that certain measures do not constitute aid. It follows that a Member State would not be prejudiced by notifying a measure which it contends does not in any event constitute a plan to grant aid.[125]

Pre-notification contacts The Commission encourages pre-notification contacts, even in seemingly standard cases. These provide the Commission services and the Member States with the possibility to discuss the legal and economic aspects of a proposed project informally and in confidence prior to notification, and thereby enhance the quality and completeness of notifications. This paves the way for a more speedy treatment of notifications once they are formally submitted. Pre-notification contacts are strongly recommended for cases where there are particular novelties or special features. Member States should provide the necessary information in a draft notification form, leading within two weeks to an initial pre-notification contact with the Commission. As a general rule, pre-notification contacts should not last longer than two months and should be followed by a complete notification. Should pre-notification contacts not bring the desired results, the Commission may declare the pre-notification closed. The beneficiary should be involved, particularly in cases with major technical, financial and project-related implications. Contacts are held in strict confidence and discussions take place on a voluntary basis.[126]

Aid must not be put into effect pending authorisation Aid which is notifiable must not be put into effect until the Commission or the Council has taken, or is deemed to have taken, a decision authorising the aid.[127] In this respect, for aid to be regarded as authorised requires an explicit decision to have been taken by the Commission or the Council declaring the aid

---

[123] Commission communication on illegally granted aid, OJ 1983 C318/3.
[124] *Twenty-Third Report on Competition Policy* (1993), pt. 403.
[125] Council Regulation (EC) No 659/1999, Articles 4(2) and 7(2).
[126] Code of Best Practice, paras 10-18.
[127] Article 108(3) TFEU; Council Regulation (EC) No 659/1999, Article 3.

compatible with the internal market.[128] The prohibition of implementation is effective during the whole of the assessment period and thus includes both the period for a preliminary assessment and, if applicable, the period of the formal investigation procedure.[129] The Commission considers that a Member State fails to fulfil its obligation to notify where the process of putting aid into effect is initiated. Member States will fall foul of the notification requirement by notifying aid legislation which already confers the unreserved power to give aid, albeit not yet exercised. To avoid such technical and often unintended breaches, the Commission recommends Member States' authorities to write a reserve clause into legislation whereby the aid granting body can make payments only after the Commission has cleared the aid.[130] If a measure is intended to take effect as soon as it is adopted, it must be notified in draft form to the Commission.[131] Member States may not invoke urgency as an excuse for infringing this obligation.[132]

Aid may not be retroactive In *Van Calster*, an aid scheme introduced in 1988, which was not notified to the Commission, imposed a levy on the slaughter of animals in Belgium. The Commission subsequently declared the scheme incompatible with the internal market on the ground that it imposed a levy equally on imported animals. A replacement scheme imposing the levy solely on domestic animals was notified to the Commission and approval was granted in 1996, on the basis of which the Belgian authorities then sought to apply the levy retroactively to animals slaughtered in Belgium since 1988. Although this levy was the same as that which had been authorised by the Commission in 1996, the ECJ held that the scheme could not be applied retroactively since this would not be compatible with the requirement to notify an aid scheme in advance. It felt that a contrary approach would allow the Member States to put a plan for State aid into effect without notifying it to the Commission with the consequences of a failure to notify being avoided by abolishing the measure and reintroducing it simultaneously with retroactive effect. The illegality of the scheme, owing to infringement of the obligation to notify prior to its implementation, was not affected by the fact that the measure was held to be compatible with the internal market by a final decision of the Commission.[133] Even though it could determine compatibility of the measure,

---

[128] Cases T-30/01 etc., *Territorio Histórico de Álava – Diputación Foral de Álava v Commission* [2009] ECR II-2919, para 196.

[129] Case 120/73, *Lorenz v Germany* [1973] ECR 1471, para 4.

[130] *Twenty-Third Report on Competition Policy* (1993), pt. 397.

[131] Case T-188/95, *Waterleiding Maatschappij v Commission* [1998] ECR II-3713, para 118; Case T-62/08, *ThyssenKrupp Acciai Speciali Terni SpA v Commission* [2010] ECR II-3229, para 235.

[132] Cases T-239/04 & T-323/04, *Italy v Commission* [2007] ECR II-3265, para 89.

[133] Cases C-261/01 & C-262/01, *Van Calster v Belgium* [2003] ECR-12249, paras 60-62.

the Commission had no competence to decide that an aid scheme put into effect contrary to Article 108(3) TFEU was legal.[134]

Exemption from notification The Council is entitled, pursuant to Article 109 TFEU, to make regulations determining the categories of aid which are exempt from the notification procedure. Use of this power was exercised in Council Regulation (EC) No 994/98[135] on the basis of which the Commission may declare that certain regional aid and aid in favour of small and medium-sized enterprises (SMEs), research and development, environmental protection, and employment and training is compatible with the internal market and is not subject to the notification requirement.[136] Regulation (EU) No 733/2013[137] extended this list to aid in favour of other categories of horizontal aid, including culture and heritage conservation, making good the damage caused by natural disasters, forestry, sports, transport in remote regions, broadband infrastructure and other infrastructure in support of these matters.[138] Pursuant to this power, the Commission adopted various exemptions which are now contained in one general block exemption in Commission Regulation (EU) No 651/2014.[139] In order to benefit from any of these exemptions, any aid or aid scheme must comply with all the applicable provisions of the regulation.[140]

Council Regulation (EC) No 994/98 also provides that the Commission may declare that certain aid is *de minimis*, provided that aid granted to the same undertaking over a given period of time does not exceed a certain fixed amount.[141] Accordingly, *de minimis* aid falling within the scope of Commission Regulation (EU) No 1407/2013[142] need not be notified to the Commission pursuant to Article 108(3) TFEU.[143] Member States must establish the necessary machinery in order to ensure that the total amount of aid, granted to the same beneficiary under the *de minimis* rule, does not exceed the ceiling of €200,000 over a period of three years. To that end, whenever a Member State grants such aid, it must inform the recipient about the *de minimis* character of the aid and obtain from the recipient full information about other *de minimis* aid received during the previous three years. The

---

[134] *Ibid.*, paras 73.
[135] OJ 1998 L142/1. See also, as regards certain aid for combined transport infrastructure, Council Regulation (EEC) No 1191/69, Article 17(2) and Council Regulation (EEC) No 1107/70, Article 5(2), as amended, and Council Regulation (EC) 1370/2007.
[136] Council Regulation (EC) No 994/98, Article 1(1).
[137] OJ 2013 L204/11.
[138] Council Regulation (EU) No 733/2013, Article 2(a).
[139] OJ 2014 L187/1.
[140] Commission Regulation (EU) No 651/2014, Article 3.
[141] Council Regulation (EC) No 994/98, Article 2(1).
[142] OJ 2013 L352/1. This repealed and replaced Commission Regulation (EC) No 1998/2006, OJ 2006 L379/5.
[143] Commission Regulation (EU) No 1407/2013, Article 3(1).

Member State may only grant the new aid after having checked that this will not raise the total amount of *de minimis* aid received during the three year period to a level exceeding €200,000.[144]

Notification and Article 106(2) TFEU Even though State aid to undertakings entrusted with the operation of services of general economic interest may be exempt from the application of Article 107(1) TFEU pursuant to Article 106(2) TFEU, the supervisory power of the Commission under Article 108 TFEU nevertheless covers aid granted to such undertakings.[145] Aid must be notified, even where the Member State takes the view that the aid is compatible with the internal market having regard to Article 106(2) TFEU.[146] In *France v Commission*, concerning aid to assist the overseas distribution of French language books, France argued that, where an undertaking operated a service of general economic interest which was covered by Article 106(2) TFEU, while the aid should be notified to the Commission pursuant to Article 108 TFEU, it was unnecessary to wait for the Commission's final decision before implementing the aid on the ground that the competition rules did not apply to such activities. The ECJ rejected this argument, holding the obligation to notify could not be separated from the obligation to suspend temporarily the implementation of the aid.[147]

A block exemption, setting out the conditions under which State aid in the form of public service compensation granted to certain undertakings entrusted with the operation of services of general economic interest is to be regarded as compatible with the internal market, is established by Commission Decision 2012/12/EU.[148] State aid that meets the conditions on compatibility laid down in this decision is exempt from the obligation of prior notification in Article 108(3) TFEU.[149]

Notification must contain all necessary information The Commission is empowered to adopt provisions concerning the form, content and other details of notifications.[150] A general format for standardised notification is set out in Annex IV to Commission Regulation (EC) No 794/2004.[151] The notification, in order to be regarded as complete, must contain all necessary information to

---

[144] Commission Regulation (EU) No 1407/2013, Article 3(2).

[145] Case C-387/92, *Banco Exterior de España v Ayuntamiento de Valencia* [1994] ECR I-877, para 17.

[146] Case C-332/98, *France v Commission* [2000] ECR I-4833, para 31; Cases C-261/01 & C-262/01, *Van Calster v Belgium* [2003] ECR-12249, para 61; Case C-172/03, *Heiser v Finanzamt Innsbruck* [2005] ECR I-1627, para 51.

[147] Case C-332/98, *France v Commission* [2000] ECR I-4833, para 32.

[148] OJ 2012 L7/3.

[149] Commission Decision 2012/12/EU, Article 3.

[150] Council Regulation (EC) No 659/1999, Article 27.

[151] As inserted by Commission Regulation (EU) No 372/2014.

enable the Commission to take a preliminary decision on the compatibility or incompatibility of the proposed aid with the internal market.[152] In order to ensure that the correct information is notified, the Commission encourages Member States to engage in pre-notification contact. Regulation (EC) No 659/1999 states that the information provided must constitute a complete notification for the purposes both of a preliminary examination pursuant to Article 108(3) TFEU and, if the Commission decides to institute it, of the formal investigation pursuant to Article 108(2) TFEU.[153]

Nevertheless, the ECJ has taken the view that the scheme of Article 108(3) TFEU does not require such extensive information at the outset. It has consistently held that the preliminary stage of the procedure for reviewing aid, which is intended merely to enable the Commission to form a *prima facie* opinion on the partial or complete compatibility of the aid in question, must be distinguished from the examination under the formal investigation procedure, which is designed to enable the Commission to be fully informed of all the facts of the case.[154] In *Austria v Commission*, it held that it was sufficient if the Commission had at its disposal, during the preliminary phase, all such information as would enable it to conclude, without any extensive review being called for, whether a given State measure was compatible with the internal market or raised doubts as to its compatibility. Consequently, for the purposes of the preliminary investigation, in order for a notification to be regarded as complete, it was sufficient for it to contain such information as would enable it to form a *prima facie* opinion of the compatibility of the aid with the internal market.[155]

Requests for further information from the Member State The ECJ also held in *Austria v Commission* that Article 108(3) TFEU does not require the Member States to reply swiftly to any requests for further information made by the Commission, so that a Member State was not precluded from relying on the two month time limit where it had failed to answer such requests promptly.[156] Regulation (EC) No 659/1999, Article 5(1) now provides that where the

---

[152] Council Regulation (EC) No 659/1999, Article 2(2); Case C-364/90, *Italy v Commission* [1993] ECR I-2097, para 20; Case T-17/03, *Schmitz-Gotha Fahrzeugwerke v Commission* [2006] ECR II-1139, para 48; Cases T-102/07 & T-120/07, *Freistaat Sachsen v Commission* [2010] ECR II-585, para 114; Case T-57/11, *Castelnou Energía v Commission* EU:T:2014:1021, para 61.

[153] Council Regulation (EC) No 659/1999, Articles 4(5) and 5(1)-(3).

[154] Case C-198/91, *William Cook plc v Commission* [1993] ECR I-2487, para 22; Case C-225/91, *Matra SA v Commissiom* [1993] ECR I-3203, para 16; Case C-367/95P, *Commission v Sytraval* [1998] ECR I-1719, para 38; Case C-204/97, *Portugal v Commission* [2001] ECR I-3175, para 32.

[155] Case C-99/98, *Austria v Commission* [2001] ECR I-1101, paras 53-56; Case C-204/97, *Portugal v Commission* [2001] ECR I-3175, para 34; Case T-171/02, *Regione autonoma della Sardegna v Commission* [2005] ECR II-2123, para 40.

[156] Case C-99/98, *Austria v Commission* [2001] ECR I-1101, para 77.

Commission considers that the information provided is incomplete, it must request all necessary additional information.[157] The reply by the Member State to the Commission's request for further information is considered to be an integral part of the notified aid scheme.[158] The notification will then be regarded as complete on receipt by the Commission of the additional information.[159] If the Member State concerned does not provide the information requested within the period stipulated by the Commission, or if it provides incomplete information, the Commission must send a reminder allowing an appropriate additional period within which the information is to be provided.[160] A notification will be considered as complete if, within two months from its receipt, or from the receipt of additional information requested, the Commission does not request any further information.[161] If the initial plan to grant aid is altered during the period of the preliminary assessment, it is not necessary to notify separately the alterations by means of a new procedure. Information concerning the alterations may be supplied to the Commission in the course of the consultations which take place with the Member State following the initial notification.[162]

The Commission is also entitled to use other means in order to obtain the necessary information to enable it take a decision. It is entitled to engage outside consultants, although it has no obligation to do so.[163] Thus, in *Scott v Commission*, the General Court held that it was within the Commission's power to obtain an expert report on the value of properties in the locality in question at the time of the sale. Such an expert report would have been particularly useful because of the inherent uncertainty involved in the Commission's determination of the market value of property, which was necessarily a retrospective process.[164]

---

[157] The Commission endeavours to group requests for information, so that only one comprehensive information request is sent, normally within 4-6 weeks after the date of notification: Code of Best Practice, para 25.

[158] Case C-537/08P, *Kahla Thuringen Porzellan GmbH v Commission* [2010] I-12917, para 45.

[159] Case T-520/09, *TF1 v Commission* EU:T:2012:352, para 62; Case T-57/11, *Castelnou Energía v Commission* EU:T:2014:1021, para 61.

[160] Council Regulation (EC) No 659/1999, Article 5(2).

[161] *Ibid.*, Article 4(5).

[162] Case 84/82, *Germany v Commission* [1984] ECR 1451, para 13; Cases 91 & 127/83, *Heiniken Brouwerijen v Inspecteurs der Vennootschaapsbelasting* [1984] ECR 3435, para 17. See also, Case 214/83, *Germany v Commission* [1985] ECR 3053.

[163] Case T-106/95, *FFSA & Others v Commission* [1997] ECR II-229, para 102; Joined Cases T-371/94 & T-394/94, *British Airways and Others v Commission* [1998] ECR II-2405, para 72; Case T-366/00, *Scott SA v Commission* [2007] ECR II-797, para 137.

[164] Case T-366/00, *Scott SA v Commission* [2007] ECR II-797, para 137.

Withdrawal of notification   A notification may be withdrawn at any time before the Commission has made a decision.[165]   Where the Commission has requested supplementary information pursuant to Regulation (EC) No 659/1999, Article 5(2),[166] the notification will be deemed to be withdrawn, pursuant to Article 5(3), if the information is not provided within the period stipulated by the Commission.[167]   The notification will not be deemed to be withdrawn if, before the expiry of the period stipulated by the Commission, the period has been extended with the consent of both the Commission and the Member State concerned.   Nor will the notification be deemed to be withdrawn if the Member State concerned, in a duly reasoned statement, informs the Commission that it considers the notification to be complete because the additional information requested is not available or has already been provided.[168]

Professional secrecy   Extensive information may be obtained through the application of Council Regulation (EC) No 659/1999 for the purposes of determining whether a given measure is compatible with the rules on State aid.[169]   Any person submitting information to the Commission must clearly indicate which information it considers to be confidential.[170]   The Commission and the Members States, their officials and other servants, including independent experts appointed by the Commission, must not disclose information which they have acquired through the application of these provisions which is covered by the obligation of professional secrecy.[171] Where the Commission takes a decision, the Commission must notify the Member State concerned prior to publication, giving it the opportunity to indicate to the Commission which information it considers to be covered by the obligation of professional secrecy.[172]   The Commission has adopted a communication setting out how it intends to deal with requests by Member States to consider that parts of State aid decisions not be disclosed when the decision is published.   This involves the identification of the information which might be covered by the obligation of professional secrecy and the procedure to be followed when dealing with such requests.[173]

---

[165]   Council Regulation (EC) No 659/1999, Article 8(1).
[166]   Case C-624/13P, *Iliad SA v Commission* EU:C:2015:112, para 64.
[167]   The Commission must inform the Member State concerned that the notification has been deemed to be withdrawn.
[168]   Council Regulation (EC) No 659/1999, Article 5(3).
[169]   *Ibid.*, Articles 2(2), 5, 6(2), 10, 16, 17(1), 20 and 22.
[170]   *Ibid.*, Article 11b.
[171]   *Ibid.*, Article 24. See also, Article 7(9)-(10), inserted by Regulation (EU) No 734/2013.
[172]   *Ibid.*, Article 25.
[173]   OJ 2004 C297/6.

Professional secrecy applies both to business secrets and other confidential information.[174]   Business secrets can only concern information relating to a business which has actual or potential economic value, the disclosure or use of which could result in economic benefits for other companies.   Typical examples include methods of assessing manufacturing or distribution costs, production secrets and processes, supply sources, quantities produced and sold, market shares, customer and distributor lists, marketing plans, cost price structure, sales policy, and information on the internal organisation of the undertaking.   Confidential information might include certain types of information that is communicated to the Commission on condition that confidentiality is observed.[175]   In *Idromacchine v Commission*, the Commission was held to have infringed the requirement of professional secrecy by including in a decision confidential information that was regarded as harmful to Idromaccine's business.[176]

16.4 PRELIMINARY ASSESSMENT OF NEW AID

Preliminary assessment of new aid   Member States must notify plans to grant or alter aid sufficiently in advance of their intended implementation to allow for adequate consideration and investigation by the Commission.[177]   The Commission is under a duty to examine a case diligently and impartially.[178]   It must examine the notification of new aid as soon as it is received[179] and form a *prima facie* opinion on the partial or complete compatibility with the internal market of the plans which have been notified to it.[180]   In addition, the Commission must examine all the facts and points brought to its notice by persons whose interests may be affected by the granting of the aid.[181]   It is therefore in the light of both the information notified by the State concerned and that provided by any complainants that the institution must make its assessment in the context of the preliminary examination.[182]   In addition, the

---

[174]   Case T-353/94, *Postbank v Commission* [1996] ECR II-921, para 86; Case T-88/09, *Idromacchine srl v Commission* [2011] ECR II-7833, para 45.

[175]   Communication on professional secrecy in State aid cases, section 3.

[176]   Case T-88/09, *Idromacchine srl v Commission* [2011] ECR II-7833, para 47.

[177]   Article 108(3) TFEU; Council Regulation (EC) No 659/1999, Article 2(1).

[178]   Cases T-228/99 & T-233/99, *Westdeutsche Landesbank Girozentrale v Commission* [2003] ECR II-435, para 167.

[179]   Council Regulation (EC) No 659/1999, Article 4(1).

[180]   Case 120/73, *Lorenz v Germany* [1973] ECR 1471, para 3.

[181]   Case C-367/95P, *Commission v Sytraval* [1998] ECR I-1719, para 51.

[182]   Case C-204/97, *Portugal v Commission* [2001] ECR I-3175, para 35.

Commission may commission independent consultants,[183] although it must properly assess the evidential value of any reports thus provided.[184]

Consultation with Member States and interested parties In the context of the procedure for reviewing State aid, the preliminary stage of the procedure for reviewing aid under Article 108(3) TFEU must be distinguished from the formal examination under Article 108(2) TFEU which follows a decision by the Commission that it has serious difficulties in determining that the aid is compatible with the internal market. It is only in connection with the latter examination, which is designed to enable the Commission to be fully informed of all the facts of the case, that the Commission is obliged to give the parties concerned notice to submit their comments.[185]

In accordance with the objective of Article 108(3) TFEU and its duty of sound administration, the Commission may, however, amongst other things, engage in talks with the notifying State or with third parties, including complainants, in an endeavour to overcome, during the preliminary procedure, any difficulties encountered.[186] That power presupposes that the Commission may adjust its position according to the results of the dialogue engaged in, without that adjustment having to be interpreted, *a priori*, as establishing the existence of serious difficulties within the meaning of Article 108(2) TFEU.[187] In certain circumstances, the Commission must give the Member State concerned an opportunity to comment before taking a decision to initiate the formal investigation procedure. For example, in *Italy v Commission*, the ECJ held that in view of the legal consequences of such a decision, which implies a classification of the measures concerned as new aid even where the Member State concerned is unlikely to subscribe to that classification, the Commission

---

[183] Case T-106/95, *FFSA v Commission* [1997] ECR II-229, para 102; Case T-72/98, *Astilleros Zamacona v Commission* [2000] ECR I-1683, para 55.

[184] Case T-274/01, *Valmont Nederland BV v Commission* [2004] ECR II-3145, para 72.

[185] Cases C-75/05P & C-80/05P *Germany v Kronofrance* [2008] ECR I-6619, para 36; Case T-304/08, *Smurfit Kappa Group v Commission* EU:T:2012:351, para 45; Case T-512/11, *Ryanair Ltd. v Commission* EU:T:2014:989, para 57.

[186] Case T-73/98, *Prayon-Rupel v Commission* [2001] ECR II-867, para 45; Case T-36/06, *Bundesverband deutscher Banken v Commission* [2010] ECR II-537, para 126; Case T-30/03 RENV, *3F v Commission* [2011] ECR II-6651, para 54; Case T-325/10, *Iliad v Commission* EU:T:2013:472, para 75; Case T-57/11, *Castelnou Energía v Commission* EU:T:2014:1021, para 75.

[187] Case C-287/12P, *Ryanair Ltd v Commission* EU:C:2013:395, para 71; Case T-73/98, *Société Chimique Prayon-Rupel SA v Commission* [2001] ECR II-867, para 45; Case T-426/04, *Tramarin Snc di Tramarin Anrea e Sergio v Commission* [2005] ECR II-4765, para 29; Case T-95/03, *Asociación de Estaciones de Servicio de Madrid v Commission* [2006] ECR II-4739, para 139; Case T-375/04, *Scheucher-Fleisch GmbH v Commission* [2009] ECR II-4155, para 73; Case T-123/09, *Ryanair Ltd v Commission* EU:T:2012:164, para 78; Case T-58/13, *Club Hotel Loutraki AE v Commission* EU:T:2015:1, para 43.

must first broach the subject of the measures in question with the Member State so that the latter has an opportunity, if appropriate, to inform the Commission that, in its view, those measures do not constitute aid or else constitute existing aid.[188]

Nevertheless, there is no obligation on the Commission at the preliminary stage to consult the other Member States or any interested parties, including complainants.[189] Since it is not under any obligation at this stage to consult interested parties, failure to consult cannot be construed as an infringement of the right to be heard.[190] It is irrelevant that the Commission might have come to a different view had it consulted any interested party.[191] Moreover, in *Commission v Sytraval*, the ECJ held that there is no obligation on the Commission to examine of its own motion objections which the complainant would certainly have raised had it been given the opportunity of taking cognisance of the information obtained by the Commission in the course of its investigation. This did not mean, however, that the Commission was not obliged, where necessary, to extend its investigation of a complaint beyond a mere examination of the matters raised by the complainant. Since the Commission is required to conduct a diligent and impartial examination of the complaint, this may make it necessary for it to examine matters not expressly raised by the complainant.[192]

Duration of the preliminary assessment Whilst the duration of the period required for the preliminary examination must allow for sufficient time, the Commission must act diligently and take account of the interest of Member States of being informed of the position quickly, particularly in spheres where the necessity to intervene may be of an urgent nature. In this respect, the Commission could not be regarded as acting with proper diligence if it failed to define its attitude within a reasonable period. Accordingly, in *Lorenz v Germany*, the Court of Justice held that, in the absence of any regulation

---

[188] Case C-400/99, *Italy v Commission* [2005] ECR I-3657, para 29; Case T-211/05, *Italy v Commission* [2009] ECR II-2777, para 37.

[189] Case 84/82, *Germany v Commission* [1984] ECR 1451, para 13; Cases 91 & 127/83, *Heiniken Brouwerijen v Inspecteurs der Vennootschaapsbelasting* [1984] ECR 3435, para 15; Case C-198/91, *William Cook plc v Commission* [1993] ECR I-2487, para 22; Case C-367/95P, *Commission v Sytraval* [1998] ECR I-1719, para 58; Cases T-195/01 & T-207/01, *Government of Gibraltar v Commission* [2002] ECR II-2309, para 144; Case T-158/99, *Thermenhotel Stoiser Franz GmbH v Commission* [2004] ECR II-1, para 90.

[190] Case C-225/91, *Matra v Commission* [1993] ECR I-3203, para 54; Case T-88/09, *Idromacchine srl v Commission* [2011] ECR II-7833, para 36.

[191] Case C-34/12P, *Idromacchine srl v Commission* EU:C:2013:552, para 47; Case T-88/09, *Idromacchine srl v Commission* [2011] ECR II-7833, para 38.

[192] Case C-367/95P, *Commission v Sytraval* [1998] ECR I-1719, paras 60-62; Case T-266/02, *Deutsche Post AG v Commission* [2008] ECR II-1233, para 92.

specifying this period, two months was appropriate.[193] This has been confirmed by Regulation (EC) No 659/1999, Article 4(5), which provides that the decision must be taken within two months from the day following receipt of a complete notification, although the period can be extended with the consent of both the Commission and the Member State concerned.[194] Where appropriate, the Commission may fix shorter time limits.[195] It follows that the length of the Commission's preliminary assessment should normally be no more than two months following receipt of a complete notification.[196] If a Member State modifies its notification during the course of the preliminary assessment, the two month period starts from the date on which the modified notification is completed.[197] Under the simplified procedure, where there are no special circumstances, the Commission aims to take a decision within twenty working days finding that there is no aid or that the aid is compatible with the internal market.[198]

Decision following preliminary assessment Article 108(3) TFEU itself does not require the Commission to take a decision where it has found that there is no aid within Article 107(1) TFEU or where the aid is compatible with the internal market, although the ECJ stated in *Lorenz v Germany* that, in the interests of sound administration, the Commission should inform the Member State concerned.[199] Regulation (EC) No 659/1999, Article 4(1) provides, however, that, as long as a notification has not been withdrawn, the Commission must take a decision regarding the compatibility of the proposed aid.[200] It may decide either that the measure is not an aid within the meaning of Article 107(1) TFEU[201] or that it is an aid within the scope of Article 107(1) TFEU but is compatible with the internal market.[202] The Commission may also take a decision finding that the measure constitutes aid but is exempted by

---

[193] Case 120/73, *Lorenz v Germany* [1973] ECR 1471, para 4; Case 84/82, *Germany v Commission* [1984] ECR 1451, paras 11-12; Case C-99/98, *Austria v Commission* [2001] ECR I-1101, paras 32 & 74.

[194] Council Regulation (EC) No 659/1999, Article 4(5); Case C-99/98, *Austria v Commission* [2001] ECR I-1101, para 76; Case T-520/09, *TF1 v Commission* EU:T:2012:352, para 58; Case T-375/03, *Fachvereinigung Mineralfaserindustrie v Commission* [2007 ECR II-121*, para 119; Case T-325/10, *Iliad v Commission* EU:T:2013:472, para 46.

[195] Council Regulation (EC) No 659/1999, Article 4(5).

[196] Case T-388/03, *Deutsche Post AG v Commission* [2009] ECR II-199, para 97; Case T-520/09, *TF1 v Commission* EU:T:2012:352, para 58.

[197] Case T-520/09, *TF1 v Commission* EU:T:2012:352, para 63.

[198] Notice on a simplified procedure, para 22.

[199] Case 120/73, *Lorenz v Germany* [1973] ECR 1471, para 5.

[200] Council Regulation (EC) No 659/1999, Article 4(1); Case T-60/05, *Ufex v Commission* [2007] ECR II-3397, para 106.

[201] Council Regulation (EC) No 659/1999, Article 4(2).

[202] *Ibid.*, Article 4(3).

virtue of Article 106(2) TFEU. On the other hand, the Commission cannot take a negative decision at the end of the preliminary assessment finding that the aid is incompatible with the internal market. Instead, if the Commission has doubts as to whether the measure is compatible, it must take a decision to open the formal investigation procedure.[203]

Decision allowing the measure Where the Commission finds that the notified measure does not constitute an aid within the meaning of Article 107(1) TFEU, it must record that finding by way of a decision.[204] Similarly, where the Commission finds that no doubts are raised as to the compatibility with the internal market of the notified measure, in so far as it falls within the scope of Article 107(1) TFEU, it must take a decision not to raise objections and that the measure is compatible with the internal market. The Commission's decision must specify which exception under the FEU Treaty is applicable.[205] Summary notices of decisions that a measure does not fall within Article 107(1) TFEU or that it is compatible with the internal market are published in the *Official Journal of the European Union*.[206] Such publication of an authorisation notice is regarded as an adequate means of informing all the parties concerned that State aid has been authorised by the Commission on the basis of Article 108(3) TFEU.[207] In any event, the scope of a decision by which the Commission raises no objections to an aid scheme must be determined not only by reference to the actual wording of that summary decision but also by taking account of the actual notification by the Member State concerned.[208]

The Commission may take such a decision only if the preliminary assessment does not reveal serious difficulties.[209] Moreover, this is the exclusive criterion for the Commission in coming to this decision, so that it may not decide to approve the aid in reliance on any other circumstances, such as third party interests, considerations of economy of procedure or any other ground of administrative or political convenience.[210] It is not open to the

---

[203] *Ibid.*, Article 4(4).

[204] *Ibid.*, Article 4(2).

[205] *Ibid.*, Article 4(3).

[206] *Ibid.*, Article 26(1). A copy of the full decision may be obtained from the Commission in the authentic language version.

[207] Cases T-197/97 & T-198/97, *Weyl Beef Products BV v Commission* [2001] ECR II-303, para 49.

[208] Case C-138/09 *Todaro Nunziatina v Assessorato del Lavoro* [2010] ECR I-4561, para 31; Case C-67/09P *Nuova Agricast v Commission* [2010] ECR I-9811, para 64; Case C-537/08P, *Kahla Thuringen GmbH v Commission* [2010] ECR I-12917, para 44; Case C-200/11P, *Italy v Commission* EU:C:2012:165, para 27.

[209] Case 84/82, *Germany v Commission* [1984] ECR 1451, para 13; Case T-475/04, *Bouygues SA v Commission* [2007] ECR II-2097, para 92.

[210] Case T-73/98, *Société Chimique Prayon-Rupel SA v Commission* [2001] ECR II-867, para 44; Case T-388/03, *Deutsche Post AG v Commission* [2009] ECR II-199, para 90;

Commission to impose conditions at this stage, although, in the course of its correspondence with the Member State, the latter may agree to alter its original plan or to give certain commitments so as to defuse any concerns raised by the Commission. Nevertheless, it is not permissible for the Commission, within the confines of the preliminary assessment, to enter into lengthy negotiations with the Member State concerned in order to secure amendments to the proposed measure with a view to making it compatible with the internal market.[211]

The Commission is entitled, however, at the preliminary assessment stage, to accept commitments offered by the Member State concerned.[212] In *Ryanair v Commission*, Italy agreed in the course of negotiations to accept certain commitments, which led the Commission to adopt a decision pursuant to Article 4(2) of Regulation (EC) No 659/1999 that the measure in question did not constitute aid. Ryanair argued that the Commission could not adopt a conditional decision, since there was no equivalent to Article 7(4) of the regulation available to the Commission at the end of the preliminary assessment stage. It was held, however, that the commitments formed an integral part of the notification and that the Commission was entitled to adopt a definitive decision on that basis finding that there was no aid.[213]

Decision classifying measure as new aid Under Article 108(3) TFEU, the Commission must act, without delay, if it considers that any plan to grant or alter aid is not compatible with the internal market.[214] Exercise of this power presupposes that the measure in question constitutes new aid. In view of the legal consequences of initiating the formal investigation procedure with regard to measures treated as new aid, where the Member State concerned contends that those measures do not constitute aid within the meaning of Article 107(1) TFEU or constitute existing aid, the Commission must first broach the subject of the measures in question with the Member State concerned so that the latter has an opportunity, if appropriate, to inform the Commission that, in its view, those measures do not constitute aid or constitute existing aid.[215]

In any event, the Commission must undertake a sufficient examination of the question on the basis of the information notified to it at that stage by that Member State, even if the outcome of that examination is not definitive. By

---

Case T-375/04, *Scheucher-Fleisch GmbH v Commission* [2009] ECR II-4155, para 72; Case T-304/08, *Smurfit Kappa Group plc v Commission* EU:T:2012:351, para 78.

[211] Case 84/82, *Germany v Commission* [1984] ECR 1451, paras 14-15.

[212] Case C-287/12P, *Ryanair Ltd v Commission* EU:C:2013:395, para 69; Case T-58/13, *Club Hotel Loutraki AE v Commission* EU:T:2015:1, para 42.

[213] Case C-287/12P, *Ryanair Ltd v Commission* EU:C:2013:395, paras 67-69; Case T-123/09, *Ryanair Ltd v Commission* EU:T:2012:164, paras 94-95.

[214] Article 108(3) TFEU.

[215] Case C-400/99, *Italy v Commission* [2005] ECR I-3657, para 29; Case T-211/05, *Italy v Commission* [2009] ECR II-2777, para 37.

virtue of the principle in Article 4(3) TEU of sincere cooperation between Member States and institutions, and in order not to delay the procedure, it is the responsibility of a Member State which considers that the measures in question do not constitute new aid to provide the Commission, at the earliest moment possible after the Commission has drawn its attention to those measures, with the information on which its position is based. If that information is such as to remove any doubts as to the absence of any element of new aid in the measures examined, the Commission cannot initiate the formal investigation procedure. Conversely, if that information is not such as to overturn the doubts as to the existence of elements of new aid and if doubts also exist as to the compatibility thereof with the internal market, the Commission must then initiate that procedure.[216]

Decision to open formal investigation Where the Commission finds that doubts are raised as to the compatibility with the internal market of a notified measure, it must decide to initiate the formal investigation procedure in Article 108(2) TFEU and Regulation (EC) No 659/1999, Article 6 in order to gather all necessary views from the Member State concerned and from other interested parties.[217] This is the exclusive criterion for opening a formal investigation.[218] A notice is published in the *Official Journal of the European Union* containing a summary of the decision along with the full decision in its authentic language version.[219]

The Commission must initiate the formal investigation procedure if the preliminary examination does not enable it to overcome all the difficulties involved in determining whether the measure constitutes State aid, unless, in the course of that initial investigation, the Commission is able to satisfy itself that the measure is in any event compatible with the internal market.[220]

---

[216] Case C-400/99, *Italy v Commission* [2005] ECR I-3657, para 48.

[217] Council Regulation (EC) No 659/1999, Article 4(4); Case 84/82, *Germany v Commission* [1984] ECR 1482, para 13; Case C-198/91, *William Cook plc v Commission* [1993] ECR I-2487, para 29; Case C-225/91, *Matra SA v Commission* [1993] ECR I-3203, para 33; Case C-487/06P, *British Aggregates Association v Commission* [2008] ECR I-10515, para 113; Case T-73/98, *Société Chimique Prayon-Rupel SA v Commission* [2001] ECR II-867, para 43; Case T-388/02, *Kronoply GmbH v Commission* [2008] ECR II-305*, para 59; Case T-210/02, *British Aggregates Association v Commission* [2006] ECR II-2789, para 166; Case T-289/03, *BUPA Ltd v Commission* [2008] ECR II-18, para 328; Case T-388/03, *Deutsche Post v Commission* [2009] ECR II-199, para 88; Case T-325/10, *Iliad v Commission* EU:T:2013:472, para 36.

[218] Case T-388/03, *Deutsche Post AG v Commission* [2009] ECR II-199, para 90; Case T-512/11, *Ryanair Ltd. v Commission* EU:T:2014:989, para 60.

[219] Council Regulation (EC) No 659/1999, Article 26(2).

[220] Case 84/82, *Germany v Commission* [1984] ECR 1451, para 13; Case C-198/91, *William Cook plc v Commission* [1993] ECR I-2487, para 29; Case C-225/91, *Matra SA v Commissiom* [1993] ECR I-3203, para 33; Case C-367/95P, *Commission v Sytraval*

Moreover, where it encounters serious difficulties, the Commission must initiate the formal procedure, having no discretion in this regard.[221]

Factors giving rise to serious doubts Whether or not the measure gives rise to serious difficulties in assessing its compatibility is to be determined objectively.[222] It is for the Commission to decide, on the basis of the factual and legal circumstances of the case, whether the difficulties involved in assessing a State measure either as to its classification as State aid or, if it is classified in this way, as to its compatibility require the initiation of the formal investigation procedure.[223] In this respect, the Commission enjoys a certain margin of discretion in identifying and evaluating the circumstances of the case in order to determine whether or not they present serious difficulties.[224]

Nevertheless, if the examination carried out by the Commission during the preliminary examination procedure is insufficient or incomplete, this will constitute evidence of the existence of serious difficulties.[225] For example, in *Ryanair v Commission*, the General Court held that the Commission's preliminary assessment of the exemption of transit passengers from Irish air

[1998] ECR I-1719, para 39; Case C-204/97, *Portugal v Commission* [2001] ECR I-1101, para 33; C-148/09 P, *Belgium* v *Deutsche Post* [2011] ECR I-8573, para 77; Case T-11/95, *BP Chemicals Limited v Commission* [1998] ECR II-3235, para 166; Case T-46/97, *SIC v Commission* [2000] ECR II-2125, para 72; Case T-512/11, *Ryanair Ltd. v Commission* EU:T:2014:989, para 58.

221 Case T-388/03, *Deutsche Post AG v Commission* [2009] ECR II-199, para 91; Case T-512/11, *Ryanair Ltd. v Commission* EU:T:2014:989, para 61.

222 Case C-431/07P, *Bouygues SA v Commission* [2009] ECR I-2665, para 63; Case C-148/09P, *Belgium v Deutsche Post* [2011] ECR I-8573, para 79; Case C-47/10P, *Austria v Commission* [2011] ECR I-10707, para 71; Case T-73/98, *Société Chimique Prayon-Rupel SA v Commission*, para 47; Cases T-195/01R & T-207/01R, *Government of Gibraltar v Commission* [2001] ECR II-3915, para 78; Case T-388/03, *Deutsche Post AG v Commission* [2009] ECR II-199, para 92; Case T-375/04, *Scheucher-Fleisch GmbH v Commission* [2009] ECR II-4155, para 74; Case T-359/04, *British Aggregates v Commission* [2010] ECR II-4227, para 56; Case T-512/11, *Ryanair Ltd. v Commission* EU:T:2014:989, para 62; Case T-57/11, *Castelnou Energía v Commission* EU:T:2014:1021, para 81.

223 Case C-198/91, *William Cook plc v Commission* [1993] ECR I-2487, para 30; Case T-388/03, *Deutsche Post AG v Commission* [2009] ECR II-199, para 89; Case T-512/11, *Ryanair Ltd. v Commission* EU:T:2014:989, para 59.

224 Case T-73/98, *Société Chimique Prayon-Rupel SA v Commission* [2001] ECR II-867, para 45; Case T-375/04, *Scheucher-Fleisch GmbH v Commission* [2009] ECR II-4155, para 73.

225 Case T-388/03, *Deutsche Post AG v Commission* [2009] ECR II-199, para 95; Case T-36/06, *Bundesverband deutscher Banken v Commission* [2010] ECR II-537, para 49; Case T-359/04, *British Aggregates v Commission* [2010] ECR II-4227, para 57; Case T-304/08, *Smurfit Kappa Group plc v Commission* EU:T:2012:351, para 81; Case T-137/10, *CBI v Commission* EU:T:2012:584, para 75; Case T-325/10, *Iliad v Commission* EU:T:2013:472, para 81.

travel tax was incomplete and insufficient.[226] In *Pollmeier Massivholz v Commission*, the General Court held that the Commission should have examined the legality of using a particular interest rate in relation to a guarantee and that, had it done so, it would have encountered serious difficulties requiring the opening of a formal investigation.[227]

Even though complaints submitted by third parties may constitute indications of serious difficulties, their relevance very much depends on the evidence contained in the complaints and not on the mere fact that observations have been submitted.[228] The number and extent of any complaints lodged against the measure in question cannot, therefore, be taken into account in determining that the Commission should have serious doubts.[229]

The mere fact that the case involves an analysis of economically complex facts does not of itself show that the Commission may be faced with serious doubts as to the appraisal of the existence of aid or of its compatibility with the internal market.[230] Requests for supplementary information from the Commission to the notifying Member State during the preliminary examination are evidence, though not proof, of the existence of serious difficulties.[231] Equally, the mere fact that discussions took place between the Commission and the Member State concerned during the preliminary examination stage, and that, in that context, the Commission asked for additional information about the measures submitted for its review, is not of itself conclusive that the Commission was confronted with serious difficulties of assessment. That does not, however, exclude the possibility that the content of the discussions between the Commission and the Member State concerned during that stage of the procedure may, in certain circumstances, be capable of revealing the existence of such difficulties.[232] For example, in *Deutsche Post v Commission*,

---

[226] Case T-512/11, *Ryanair Ltd. v Commission* EU:T:2014:989, para 101.

[227] Case T-89/09, *Pollmeier Massivholz GmbH v Commission* EU:T:2015:153, paras 185-186.

[228] Case T-140/13, *Netherlands Maritime Technology Association v Commission* EU:T:2014:1029, para 58.

[229] Case T-79/10, *Colt Télécommunications France v Commission* EU:T:2013:463, para 73; Case T-57/11, *Castelnou Energía v Commission* EU:T:2014:1021, para 82; Case T-140/13, *Netherlands Maritime Technology Association v Commission* EU:T:2014:1029, para 60.

[230] Case T-289/03, *BUPA Ltd v Commission* [2008] ECR II-81, para 333.

[231] Case C-646/11P, *3F v Commission* EU:C:2013:36, para 32; Case T-73/98, *Société Chimique Prayon-Rupel SA v Commission* [2001] ECR II-867, para 98; Case T-388/03, *Deutsche Post AG v Commission* [2009] ECR II-199, para 99; Case T-30/03 RENV, *3F v Commission* [2011] ECR II-6651, para 70; Case T-140/13, *Netherlands Maritime Technology Association v Commission* EU:T:2014:1029, para 74.

[232] Case 84/82, *Germany v Commission* [1984] ECR 1451, para 14; Case C-225/91, *Matra SA v Commissiom* [1993] ECR I-3203, para 38; Case T-46/97, *SIC v Commission* [2000] ECR II-2125, para 89; Case T-95/03, *Asociación de Estaciones de Servicio de Madrid v Commission* [2006] ECR II-4739, para 139; Case T-375/03, *Fachvereinigung Mineralfaserindustrie eV v Commission* [2007] ECR II-121*, para 124; Case T-30/03

the fact that the Commission issued three requests for information which led to the period of the preliminary assessment being prolonged constituted evidence of the existence of serious difficulties.[233] By contrast, in *Club Hotel Loutraki v Commission*, several rounds of contact between the Commission and the Greek authorities over a period of many months were excused as being necessary due to the technical nature of assessing the market value of agreements conferring exclusive rights rather than as evidence of any serious difficulties.[234]

Mere inertia on the part of the Member State in the course of the preliminary assessment is not an indication of serious difficulties.[235] On the other hand, persistent refusal to provide the information requested which results in the prolongation of the preliminary assessment may indicate, by its very nature, the existence of such difficulties. The Commission cannot rely, in deciding whether to initiate the formal investigation procedure, on the fact that it is the notifying Member State that is responsible for that situation, since to do so would deprive interested third parties of the procedural guarantees conferred on them by Article 108(2) TFEU and allow Member States to evade their duty of genuine cooperation.[236]

Where the time spent on the preliminary examination considerably exceeds two months in the case of notified aid or a reasonable period in the case of non-notified aid, this may, as long as it is supported by other factors, lead to the conclusion that the Commission has encountered serious difficulties of assessment necessitating initiation of the formal investigation procedure.[237] This assessment of the excessiveness of the length of the examination requires an individual case by case analysis having regard to the nature of the measure,

---

RENV, *3F v Commission* [2011] ECR II-6651, para 71; Case T-520/09, *TF1 v Commission* EU:T:2012:352, paras 76-77; Case T-57/11, *Castelnou Energía v Commission* EU:T:2014:1021, para 70; Case T-140/13, *Netherlands Maritime Technology Association v Commission* EU:T:2014:1029, para 74; Case T-58/13, *Club Hotel Loutraki AE v Commission* EU:T:2015:1, para 47.

[233] Case T-388/03, *Deutsche Post AG v Commission* [2009] ECR II-199, para 106.

[234] Case T-58/13, *Club Hotel Loutraki AE v Commission* EU:T:2015:1, para 50.

[235] Case T-520/09, *TF1 v Commission* EU:T:2012:352, para 81.

[236] Case T-73/98, *Société Chimique Prayon-Rupel SA v Commission* [2001] ECR II-867, para 100.

[237] Case 84/82, *Germany v Commission* [1984] ECR 1451, paras 15-17; Case C-148/09P, *Belgium v Deutsche Post AG* [2011] ECR I-8573, para 81; Case C-624/13P, *Iliad SA v Commission* EU:C:2015:112, para 56; Case T-46/97, *SIC v Commission* [2000] ECR II-2125, para 102; Case T-73/98, *Société Chimique Prayon-Rupel SA v Commission* [2001] ECR II-867, para 93; Case T-95/03, *Asociación de Estaciones de Servicio de Madrid v Commission* [2006] ECR II-4739, para 135; Case T-375/03, *Fachvereinigung Mineralfaserindustrie eV v Commission* [2007] ECR II-121*, para 117; Case T-388/03, *Deutsche Post AG v Commission* [2009] ECR II-199, para 88; Case T-520/09, *TF1 v Commision* EU:T:2012:352, para 54; Case T-201/10, *IVBN v Commission* EU:T:2012:385, para 54; Case T-325/10, *Iliad v Commission* EU:T:2013:472, para 43; Case T-512/11, *Ryanair Ltd. v Commission* EU:T:2014:989, para 64; Case T-140/13, *Netherlands Maritime Technology Association v Commission* EU:T:2014:1029, para 66.

in particular where it involves complex factors.[238] For example, in *Club Hotel Loutraki v Commission*, a period of ten months was not regarded as giving rise to serious difficulties where the Commission was engaged with the Greek authorities in gathering and assessing information of a technical nature.[239]

When considering the amount of aid, the decisive factor is not the actual amount so much as its impact on competition and intra-EU trade. Accordingly, the size of an investment or aid cannot in itself constitute a serious difficulty, as otherwise the Commission would be obliged to initiate the formal investigation procedure whenever the aid exceeded a certain level.[240] Where an aid measure does not comply with Commission guidelines, this should raise doubts as to the compatibility of the measure with the internal market. For example, in *Austria v Commission*, it was held that aid for agricultural products that was limited to national products contrary to the agricultural aid guidelines, should have raised doubts for the Commission in its preliminary assessment.[241]

Assessment of aid schemes In the case of an aid scheme, the Commission may confine itself to examining the general characteristics of the scheme without being required to examine each particular case in which it applies, in order to determine whether, by reason of the high amounts or percentages of aid, the nature of the investments for which aid is granted or other terms of the programme, it gives an appreciable advantage to recipients in relation to their competitors and is likely to benefit particular undertakings engaged in trade between Member States.[242] The Commission should not approve a scheme for aid which is compatible with the internal market if it is framed in such a way that it is also capable of providing for aid which is not compatible with the internal market. The opportunity which is given to the Member State

---

[238] Case T-520/09, *TF1 v Commission* EU:T:2012:352, para 68; Case T-512/11, *Ryanair Ltd. v Commission* EU:T:2014:989, para 69; cf. Case C-148/09P, *Belgium v Deutsche Post* [2011] I-8573, per AG Jääskinen at pars 90-91.

[239] Case T-58/13, *Club Hotel Loutraki AE v Commission* EU:T:2015:1, para 62.

[240] Case C-225/91, *Matra v Commission* [1993] ECR I-3203, para 36; Case T-520/09, *TF1 v Commission* EU:T:2012:352, para 88.

[241] Case C-47/10P, *Austria v Commission* [2011] ECR I-10707, para 85; Case T-375/04, *Scheucher-Fleisch GmbH v Commission* [2009] ECR II-4155, para 86.

[242] Case 248/84, *Germany v Commission* [1987] ECR 4013, para 18; Case C-75/97, *Belgium v Commission* [1999] ECR I-3671, para 48; Cases C-15/98 & C-105/99, *Italy v Commission* [2000] ECR I-8855, para 51; Case C-310/99, *Italy v Commission* [2002] ECR I-2289, para 89; Case C-351/98, *Spain v Commission* [2002] ECR I-8031, para 67; Case C-278/00, *Greece v Commission* [2004] ECR I-3997, para 24; Cases T-239/04 & T-323/04, *Italy v Commission* [2007] ECR II-3265, para 142; Case T-445/05, *Associazione Italiana del Risparmio Gestito v Commission* [2009] ECR II-289, para 68; Case T-222/04. *Italy v Commission* [2009] ECR II-1887, para 123; Case T-357/02 RENV, *Freistaat Sachsen v Commission* [2011] ECR II-5415, para 31; Cases T-394/08, T-408/08, T-453/08 & T-454/08, *Regione autonoma della Sardegna v Commission* [2011] ECR II-6255, para 91.

concerned to give notice of a planned aid scheme and, once the Commission has approved it after examining its general characteristics, to dispense with notification of individual aid measures granted pursuant to that scheme, subject, where appropriate, to conditions and obligations imposed in that respect, cannot justify the grant of individual aid measures which would have been declared incompatible if they had been the subject of an individual notification. In particular, it cannot lead to individual aid measures being granted which, although consistent with one of the objectives of Article 107(3) TFEU, would none the less not be necessary in order for that objective to be met.[243]

The Commission must therefore check that planned aid schemes submitted for its examination are set up in such a way as to ensure that the individual aid measures to be granted according to their provisions will be limited to firms which are actually eligible for them.[244] For instance, it refused to approve a Finnish regional aid scheme which provided for permissible accelerated depreciation on investments in assisted areas, but which did not exclude those sectors subject to specific EU rules. Since the scheme was based on a law which was automatically applicable and did not allow for administrative discretion in individual cases, the tax authorities' commitment to ensuring compliance with the State aid rules was not sufficient for the Commission to conclude that the scheme was compatible with the internal market in sensitive sectors. Rather, it required the law to be amended to effectively prevent it from being applied to such sectors.[245]

Assessment of individual aid under an authorised scheme In cases where the Commission has previously approved a general aid scheme, individual implementing measures do not need to be notified, subject to any reservation to that effect by the Commission in the approval decision, since the factors to be taken into consideration by the Commission in assessing the individual aid would be the same as those which it applied on examining the general scheme.[246] Where the Commission examines a specific grant of an aid alleged to be made in pursuance of a previously authorised scheme, it must first examine whether the aid is covered by the general scheme and satisfies the conditions laid down in the approval decision and may not simply proceed to examine the aid in the context of Article 107 TFEU. Failure to follow this

[243] Case 730/79, *Philip Morris* v *Commission* [1980] ECR 2671, para 17; Case T-187/99, *Agrana Zucker und Stärke AG* v *Commission* [2001] ECR II-1587, para 74; Case T-126/99, *Graphischer Maschinenbau* v *Commission* [2002] ECR II-2427, para 34.
[244] Case T-171/02, *Regione autonoma della Sardegna* v *Commission* [2005] ECR II-2123, para 104.
[245] OJ 1998 C377/5.
[246] Case C-47/91, *Italy* v *Commission* [1994] ECR I-4635, para 21; Case C-321/99P, *ARAP* v *Commission* [2002] ECR I-4287, para 60; Case T-20/03, *Kahla/Thüringen Porzellan GmbH* v *Commission* [2008] ECR II-2305, para 92.

procedure would mean that the Commission could, whenever it examined an individual aid, go back on its decision approving the aid scheme, thereby jeopardising the principles of the protection of legitimate expectations and legal certainty from the point of view of both the Member States and recipients. Aid which constitutes the strict and foreseeable application of the conditions laid down in the decision approving the aid scheme is thus considered to be existing aid, which does not need to be notified to the Commission or examined in the light of Article 107 TFEU.[247] By contrast, if the measures are not covered by the schemes relied on they constitute new aid measures whose compatibility with the internal market has to be examined by the Commission.[248]

The mere fact that the Commission has doubts as to the conformity of an individual aid with its decision approving a scheme does not suffice to allow it to invoke Article 108(3) TFEU. Prior to initiating that procedure, the Commission must order the Member State concerned to supply to it, within such period as it may specify, all such documentation, information and data as are necessary in order that it may examine the compatibility of the aid in question with its decision approving the aid scheme. If the Member State fails to provide that information, the Commission may directly assess compatibility of the individual aid as if it were new aid.[249] In those circumstances, the Commission may also order the suspension of the individual aid as if it were new aid.[250]

If a Member State notifies an aid measure as new aid, it cannot subsequently complain that a refusal by the Commission to treat it as having been authorised by a previous approval infringes the principles of the protection of legitimate expectations or legal certainty. In *Regione Siciliana v Commission*, where aid was notified to the Commission as new aid but the Italian authorities subsequently argued that it was covered by a previous approval only when the Commission opened the formal investigation procedure, the General Court held that the Commission had acted lawfully in

---

[247] Case C-47/91, *Italy v Commission* [1994] ECR I-4635, para 24; Case C-278/95P, *Siemens v Commission* [1997] ECR I-2507, para 31; Case C-321/99P, *ARAP v Commission* [2002] ECR I-4287, para 83; Case T-435/93, *ASPEC v Commission* [1995] ECR II-1281, para 105; Case T-442/93, *AAC v Commission* [1995] ECR II-1329, para 86; Case T-176/01, *Ferriere Nord SpA v Commission* [2004] ECR II-3931, para 51; Case T-20/03, *Kahla/Thüringen Porzellan GmbH v Commission* [2008] ECR II-2305, para 93; Cases T-30/01 etc., *Territorio Histórico de Álava – Diputación Foral de Álava v Commission* [2009] ECR II-2919, para 197; Cases T-102/07 & T-120/07, *Freistaat Sachsen v Commission* [2010] ECR II-585, paras 59-60.

[248] Case T-20/03, *Kahla/Thüringen Porzellan GmbH v Commission* [2008] ECR II-2305, para 94.

[249] Case C-47/91, *Italy v Commission* [1994] ECR I-4635, paras 33-35.

[250] *Ibid.*, para 35.

proceeding to take a final decision on the basis that the measure constituted a new aid.[251]

Assessment in the light of previous decisions Since State aid is a legal concept that must be interpreted on the basis of objective factors, the classification of a measure as State aid must be determined regardless of any previous administrative practice by the Commission.[252] Accordingly, it is not an infringement of the principle of equal treatment for the Commission to carry out an individual appraisal of the circumstances specific to the case, and it is not bound by previous decisions.[253] On the contrary, the Commission must base each of its decisions only in light of the objectives rules in the FEU Treaty.[254]

Nevertheless, when the Commission considers the compatibility of State aid with the internal market it must take all relevant factors into account, including, where appropriate, the circumstances already considered in any applicable previous decision and the obligations which that decision may have imposed on a Member State.[255] The Commission must appraise any new fact capable of altering its assessment, regard being had to the purpose of the new aid and all relevant economic circumstances at the time when it is granted. If, however, the Commission is not informed by the Member State concerned of any new fact allowing it to assess whether the aid in question might benefit from one of the derogations provided for by Article 107 TFEU, it is justified in basing its decision on the assessment it had already made in its previous decision.[256]

An examination of the cumulative effect of the aid with any earlier unlawful aid is justified on account of the fact that the advantages conferred by the grant of earlier incompatible aid which has not yet been recovered continue to produce effects on competition.[257] For example, in a case involving the

---

[251] Case T-190/00, *Regione Siciliana v Commission* [2003] ECR II-5015, paras 76-80. See also, Case T-176/01, *Ferriere Nord SpA v Commission* [2004] ECR II-3931, para 54.

[252] Cases C-57/00P & C-61/00P, *Freistaat Sachsen v Commission* [2003] ECR I-9975, paras 52-53; Cases C-182/03 & C-217/03, *Belgium and Forum 187 ASBL v Commission* [2006] ECR I-5479, para 71; Case C-89/08P, *Commission v Ireland* [2009] ECR I-11245, para 72; Case T-171/02, *Regione autonoma dells Sardegna v Commission* [2005] ECR II-2123, para 177.

[253] Cases T-268/08 & T-281/08, *Land Burgenland v Commission* EU:T:2012:90, paras 76-77.

[254] Case C-138/09, *Todaro Nunziatina v Assessorato del Lavoro* [2010] ECR I-4561, para 21; Cases T-319/12 & T-321/12, *Spain v Commission* EU:T:2014:604, para 158; Case T-308/11, *Eurallumina SpA v Commission* EU:T:2014:894, para 80.

[255] Case C-261/89, *Italy v Commission* [1991] ECR 4437, para 20; Case C-355/95P, *TWD v Commission* [1997] ECR I-2549, para 26; Case C-110/02, *Commission v Council* [2004] ECR I-6333, para 39; Case T-527/13, *Italy v Commission* EU:T:2015:429, para 61

[256] Case C-261/89, *Italy v Commission* [1991] ECR 4437, paras 21-23.

[257] Cases T-115/09 & T-116/09, *Electrolux AB v Commission* EU:T:2012:76, para 66.

restructuring of two Italian companies, aid had been granted over and above that which had been previously permitted by the Commission. When further aid was proposed, the Commission took the view that its compatibility with the internal market could only be assessed in the context of an overall examination of all aid granted and therefore a re-assessment of the compatibility of the aid previously authorised was required.[258] In *TWD v Commission*, the Commission required the recovery of previous aid which had been granted without authorisation as a condition for approving further aid as being compatible with the internal market.[259]

Where one of the conditions set out in a previous decision cannot be fulfilled, the Commission must re-examine the aid in order to establish that it remains compatible with the internal market. In *Ryanair v Commission*, the General Court considered that the effect of failure to comply with a condition imposed in a conditional decision is to raise the presumption that further grants of the aid are incompatible with the internal market. If the Commission's review leads to only a relatively minor deviation from the initial condition which leaves it in no doubt as to the compatibility of further aid with the internal market, it may allow the derogation from its original decision without re-opening the formal investigation procedure. If, however, the Commission concludes that further aid would not be compatible with the internal market or if it has doubts as to such compatibility, it must re-open the formal investigation procedure. Moreover, the Commission is not entitled to depart from the scope of its initial decision without re-opening the formal investigation procedure.[260] By analogy with Article 108(3) TFEU, payment of any further aid must be suspended until the Commission adopts its final decision.[261]

If the Commission has information which shows that a Member State, in implementing aid, has not complied with the conditions laid down in a previous decision, the proper procedure is for the Commission to institute proceedings at the ECJ pursuant to Article 108(2) TFEU alleging a breach of that previous decision. On the other hand, if the Commission considers that the implementing measure constitutes new aid which has not been notified, it must examine the new aid in accordance with the procedures of Article 108(3) TFEU and Regulation (EC) No 659/1999. In any event, it is not permissible for the Commission to adopt a further decision finding that the aid is

---

[258] *Twenty-Eighth Report on Competition Policy* (1998), p. 251. See, however, the Commission's approach in Case T-110/97, *Kneissl Dachstein Sportartikel AG v Commission* [1999] ECR II-2881, paras 106-112, and Case T-123/97, *Salomon SA v Commission* [1999] ECR II-2925, paras 51-61.

[259] Cases T-244/93 & T-486/93, *TWD v Commission* [1995] ECR II-2265, para 56. See also, Case T-184/97, *BP Chemicals Ltd v Commission* [2000] ECR II-3145, para 14.

[260] Case T-140/95, *Ryanair Limited v Commission* [1998] ECR II-3327, para 88; Case T-68/03, *Olympiaki Aeroporia Ypiresies AE v Commission* [2007] ECR II-2911, para 92.

[261] Case T-140/95, *Ryanair Limited v Commission* [1998] ECR II-3327, para 87.

incompatible with the internal market merely by reference to its previous decision without instigating the proper procedures.[262]

16.5 REVIEW OF EXISTING AID

Constant review of existing aid In cooperation with the Member States, the Commission, pursuant to Article 108(1) TFEU and Regulation (EC) No 659/1999, Article 17, keeps under constant review all systems of aid existing in those States. This applies equally to all systems of aid, whether approved by the Commission or the Council.[263] Systems of aid within the meaning of Article 108(1) TFEU include both decisions in individual cases and aid schemes, although constant review will usually be necessary, or even appropriate, only in the latter case.[264] Constant review assumes regular, periodic cooperation between the Member States and the Commission. This obligation is binding so that neither a Member State nor the Commission may unilaterally release itself from it.[265] Where an aid scheme has been approved, the Commission may examine the compatibility of any individual application of that scheme.[266] Equally, where the Commission alters its appraisal of a measure that it previously did not consider to constitute aid, it may treat the measure as existing aid and review it in accordance with Article 108(1) TFEU.[267]

Existing aid may be implemented as long as the Commission has not found it to be incompatible with the internal market.[268] Even where the Commission decides to review the compatibility of the aid and opens a formal investigation procedure, there is no obligation on the Member State concerned to suspend the operation of the aid scheme pending the Commission's final decision.[269] Equally, in the case of undertakings covered by Article 106(2) TFEU benefiting from existing aid, as long as the Commission has not found such aid to be incompatible with the internal market, it is not necessary to examine

---

[262] Case C-294/90, *British Aerospace v Commission* [1992] ECR I-493, paras 11-14.

[263] Case T-527/13, *Italy v Commission* EU:T:2015:429, para 54.

[264] Case C-44/93, *Namur-Les Assurances du Crédit SA v Office Nationale du Ducroire*, [1994] ECR I-3829, *per* Advocate General Lenz, at p. 3852.

[265] Case 173/73, *Italy v Commission* [1974] ECR 709, para 7; Case C-135/93, *Spain v Commission* [1995] ECR I-1651, para 24.

[266] Case C-321/99P, *ARAP v Commission* [2002] ECR I-4287, para 76.

[267] Cases C-182/03 & C-217/03, *Belgium and Forum 187 ASBL v Commission* [2006] ECR I-5479, para 75.

[268] Case C-387/92, *Banco Exterior de España v Ayuntamiento de Valencia* [1994] ECR I-877, para 20; Case C-262/11, *Kremikovtzi AD v Ministar na Ikonomikata* EU:C:2012:760, para 49; Case C-6/12, *P Oy* EU:C:2013:525, para 36.

[269] Case C-312/90, *Spain v Commission* [1992] ECR I-4117, para 17; Case C-47/91, *Italy v Commission* [1992] ECR I-4145, para 25; Case C-400/99, *Italy v Commission* [2001] ECR I-7303, para 48.

whether and to what extent that aid is capable of falling outside the scope of the prohibition in Article 107(1) TFEU by virtue of Article 106(2) TFEU.[270]

All the necessary information to carry out the review must be obtained by the Commission from the Member State concerned.[271] Where the Commission considers that an existing aid scheme is not, or is no longer, compatible with the internal market, it must inform the Member State concerned of its preliminary view and give it the opportunity to submit its comments. The normal period for the receipt of such comments is one month, although, in duly justified cases, the Commission may extend this period.[272] Although interested parties may submit information to the Commission concerning existing aid, they have no right to be involved in the review procedure at this stage.[273]

Recommendation of appropriate measures Following this review, the Commission is required to propose to the Member States any appropriate measures required by the progressive development or by the functioning of the internal market.[274] These proposals are merely recommendations.[275] Where the Commission, in the light of the information submitted by the Member State, concludes that the existing aid is not, or is no longer, compatible with the internal market, it must issue a recommendation to the Member State concerned. The recommendation may propose, in particular, substantive amendment of the aid scheme or the introduction of procedural requirements or the abolition of the aid scheme.[276] Again, at this stage, interested parties have no right to be consulted.[277]

Where the Member State concerned accepts the proposed measure, it becomes bound by its acceptance to implement it and to abide by its terms.[278]

---

[270] Case C-387/92, *Banco Exterior de España v Ayuntamiento de Valencia* [1994] ECR I-877, para 21.

[271] Council Regulation (EC) No 659/1999, Article 17(1).

[272] *Ibid.*, Article 17(2).

[273] Case T-354/05, *TF1 v Commission* [2009] ECR II-471, para 101; Case T-206/10, *Vesteda Groep BV v Commission* EU:T:2012:283, para 48.

[274] Article 108(1) TFEU.

[275] Case T-330/94, *Salt Union Ltd v Commission* [1996] ECR II-1475, para 35; Case T-203/10 RENV, *Stichting Woonpunt v Commission* EU:T:2015:286, para 63; Case T-202/10 RENV, *Stichting Woonlinie v Commission* EU:T:2015:287, para 63;

[276] Council Regulation (EC) No 659/1999, Article 18.

[277] Case T-354/05, *TF1 v Commission* [2009] ECR II-471, paras 102-103; Case T-201/10, *IVBN v Commission* EU:T:2012:385, para 50.

[278] Council Regulation (EC) No 659/1999, Article 19(1); Case C-313/90, *CIRFS v Commission* [1993] ECR I-1125, para 35; Case C-311/94, *IJssel-Vliet v Minister van Economische Zaken* [1996] ECR I-5023, para 44; Case C-288/96, *Germany v Commission* [2000] ECR I-8237, para 65; Case C-242/00, *Germany v Commission* [2002] ECR I-5603, para 28; Case C-69/05, *Commission v Luxembourg* [2006] ECR I-7*, para 9; Case C-121/10, *Commission v Council* EU:C:2013:784, para 52; Case T-203/10 RENV, *Stichting Woonpunt v Commission* EU:T:2015:286, para 65; Case T-202/10 RENV, *Stichting Woonlinie v Commission* EU:T:2015:287, para 65.

The Member State must inform the Commission of its acceptance, and the Commission then records that finding and informs the Member State accordingly. A notice is published in the *Official Journal of the European Union*.[279] This may be regarded as reflecting the duty on Member States, pursuant to Article 4(3) TEU, to take all appropriate measures to ensure the fulfilment of their obligations arising out of the EU Treaties.[280] Any subsequent aid which is inconsistent with the agreed measure would be regarded as new aid and would be required to be notified to the Commission for prior approval pursuant to Article 108(3) TFEU.[281] Acceptance of the recommendation also binds the Commission, so that, where such a measure has been agreed by the Member States until a certain date, the Commission may not unilaterally extend the period of its application beyond that date.[282]

Commission recommendations are not, however, binding on Member States as a matter of general EU law.[283] Accordingly, if the Member State concerned does not accept the Commission's proposals, the Commission, where it still considers, having taken into account the arguments of the Member State, that those measures are necessary, cannot immediately enforce the recommendation but must initiate the formal investigation procedure under Article 108(2) TFEU.[284] It may be noted, however, that if the Member State accepts the recommendation, Regulation (EC) No 659/1999 does not provide any possibility for opening a formal investigation.[285] Thus, in *IVBN v Commission*, where a complaint had been made concerning existing aid, the subsequent acceptance by the Netherlands of the Commission's recommendations meant that there was no basis for opening a formal investigation.[286]

Acceptance of guidelines and frameworks The Commission has formulated a number of guidelines or frameworks concerning different types of State aid in order to establish their compatibility with the internal market. Such measures reflect the Commission's desire to publish directions on the approach it intends to follow.[287] In the context of the constant review of State aid

---

[279] Council Regulation (EC) No 659/1999, Article 26(1).

[280] See the submissions of the Commission as summarized by Advocate General Lenz in Case C-311/94, *IJssel-Vliet v Minister van Economische Zaken* [1996] ECR I-5023, at p. 5039.

[281] Case C-313/90, *CIRFS v Commission* [1993] ECR I-1125, para 51.

[282] Case C-292/95, *Spain v Commission* [1997] ECR I-1931, para 30.

[283] Article 288 TFEU; Case 70/72, *Germany v Commission* [1973] ECR 813, *per* Advocate General Mayras at p. 834; Case C-313/90, *CIRFS v Commission* [1993] ECR I-1125, *per* Advocate General Lenz at p. 1154; Case C-135/93, *Spain v Commission* [1995] ECR I-1651, *per* Advocate General Lenz, at p. 1161; Cases T-132/96 & 143/96, *Freistaat Sachsen v Commission* [1999] ECR II-3663, para 209.

[284] Council Regulation (EC) No 659/1999, Article 19(2).

[285] Case T-201/10, *IVBN v Commission* EU:T:2012:385, para 47.

[286] *Ibid.*, para 49.

[287] Case T-214/95, *Vlaams Gewest v Commission* [1998] ECR II-717, para 79; Case T-187/99, *Agrana Zucker und Stärke AG v Commission* [2001] ECR II-1587, para 56.

pursuant to the Commission's obligations under Article 108(1) TFEU, these guidelines and frameworks may be stated to constitute appropriate measures which the Commission proposes to the Member States. Once a set of guidelines have been accepted by the Member States, it remains applicable until it ends or is replaced by a further agreement with the Member States in accordance with Article 108(1) TFEU. In *CIRFS v Commission*, it was argued by the Commission that a discipline agreed with all the Member States providing that no new State aid was to be granted to undertakings in the synthetic fibres industry had been impliedly amended by virtue of a subsequent individual decision by which it authorised the grant of certain aid by Germany to a manufacturer of synthetic fibres. According to the Commission, the principle of equal treatment required that it take this decision into account in applying the discipline to aid intended for other undertakings. This was rejected by the ECJ which held simply that a measure of general application could not be impliedly amended by an individual decision. Neither the principle of equal treatment nor the protection of legitimate expectations could be relied on to justify a repetition of an incorrect interpretation of a measure.[288]

Refusal to accept guidelines or frameworks If a Member State refuses to accept guidelines or a framework, the Commission will commence the formal investigation procedure in relation to all relevant existing aid schemes in that Member State in order to evaluate them in the light of the guidelines or framework. This will normally have the effect of forcing the Member State concerned to accept the Commission's policy. The application of guidelines and frameworks is best illustrated by the problems encountered by the Commission in respect of its frameworks on State aid to the motor vehicle industry. The Commission proposed a framework for the motor vehicle sector which was to enter into force on 1 January 1989, valid for two years at the end of which the Commission would review its utility and scope. In December 1990, the Commission decided to extend the framework and to review it again after a further two years. In December 1992, the Commission, following a further meeting with the Member States at which most of them expressed their satisfaction with the framework, took the view that the 1990 decision had extended the framework for an indefinite period and decided not to modify the framework and that it should remain valid until the next review organised by the Commission.

The ECJ held that the Commission was wrong in its view that the 1990 decision had extended the framework for an indefinite period, since this would be incompatible with the obligation of regular, periodic cooperation imposed by Article 108(1) TFEU. The 1990 decision, therefore, had extended the framework only until the end of 1992, and the 1992 decision had itself to be interpreted as having extended the framework only until its next review, which

---

[288] Case C-313/90, *CIRFS v Commission* [1993] ECR I-1125, paras 42-45.

had to take place within a further period of two years.[289] In breach of this requirement, the Commission failed to review the framework in December 1994 and in July 1995 it again unilaterally prolonged its validity. Again, the ECJ held that the Commission was wrong. Without any prolongation, the framework ceased to exist in December 1994. Any decision to prolong it could only be adopted according to the same procedure as that required for the adoption of the decision which established the original framework, i.e. in consultation with, and by agreement of, the Member States.[290] In July 1997, the Commission adopted a new framework for state aid to the motor vehicle industry which was accepted by all Member States with the exception of Sweden. Formal investigations proceedings were initiated by the Commission pursuant to Article 108(2) TFEU in October 1997 against all existing Swedish schemes which could be the basis for state aid in the motor vehicle sector as from 1 January 1998. During the proceedings, the Swedish authorities accepted the Commission's position and the proceedings were, therefore, closed.[291]

16.6 PRELIMINARY ASSESSMENT OF UNLAWFUL AID AND MISUSE OF AID

Unlawful aid Unlawful aid means any new aid put into effect by a Member State in contravention of Article 108(3) TFEU and includes aid which is unnotified, aid which is notified to the Commission but is put into effect before the Commission or the Council has come to a decision on its compatibility with the FEU Treaty and aid which exceeds the provisions which have been authorised.[292] In *Italy v Commission*, Advocate General Warner argued that where aid was unlawfully introduced, the only recourse open to the Commission should be to bring an action for failure of the Member State to comply with its obligations under the FEU Treaty pursuant to Article 258 TFEU, and that the Commission should not proceed to examine the aid to determine its compatibility with the internal market. This was based on the view that, if the Commission were to proceed to an examination of the aid, the Member State concerned would be in a more advantageous position than one which complied with its lawful obligations. To insist, on the other hand, upon

---

[289] Case C-135/93, *Spain v Commission* [1995] ECR I-1651, paras 27-29.

[290] Case C-292/95, *Spain v Commission* [1997] ECR I-1931, para 30.

[291] *Twenty-Eighth Report on Competition Policy* (1998), p. 227.

[292] Council Regulation (EC) No 659/1999, Article 1(f); Case 120/73, *Lorenz v Germany* [1973] ECR 1471, para 8; Case C-301/87, *France v Commission* [1990] ECR I-307, para 20. Any State aid which was granted by Austria, Finland or Sweden during 1994 and which was not notified to the EFTA Surveillance Authority or which was granted before the Authority took a decision in relation to it pursuant to the EEA Agreement is regarded as unlawful aid: Act of Accession of Austria, Finland or Sweden, Article 172(5).

the procedure under Article 258 TFEU being adopted in such a case would mean that the infringing Member State could be required to abolish the new aid on the simple ground that it was invalidly introduced and compelled, if it wished to introduce it, to comply with Article 108(3) TFEU.[293] This view was not, however, endorsed by the ECJ which held, in *France v Commission*, that, even where a Member State has unlawfully introduced aid, the Commission is obliged to proceed to examine the compatibility of the aid with the internal market.[294]

Misuse of aid Misuse of aid applies only in respect of existing aid.[295] It arises where aid is used by the beneficiary in contravention of a decision of the Commission declaring aid to be compatible with the internal market.[296] Aid is misused where, for example, the Commission authorises investment aid but the beneficiary deflects the aid to cover operating costs.[297] In the *Leuna* case, the Commission took action against aid which had been granted as regional investment aid but was used to finance the production of a synthetic fibres product which was already in oversupply.[298] In its decision concerning *Sophia Jacoba GmbH and Preussag Anthrazit GmbH*, the Commission declared aid to certain undertakings as having been misused where it was applied in a manner which led to discrimination between products contrary to Article 4 CS.[299] Misuse of aid may arise also where aid which is authorised for a particular subsidiary in a company group is used to benefit a different subsidiary in the same group as, for example, where aid granted to the German Bremer Vulkan shipyard was diverted from its intended beneficiary.[300] In the *Irish Mushrooms* case, the Commission objected to the misuse of a scheme which had been authorised with the intention of avoiding redundancies in SMEs whose earnings had dropped sharply due to currency depreciation. The aid was granted to exporters of mushrooms contrary to an understanding of the

---

[293] Case 173/73, *Italy v Commission* [1974] ECR 709, at p. 725.

[294] Case C-301/87, *France v Commission* [1990] ECR I-307, para 21.

[295] Council Regulation (EC) No 659/1999, recital 15; Case T-527/13, *Italy v Commission* EU:T:2015:429, para 68.

[296] Council Regulation (EC) No 659/1999, Article 1(g); Cases T-111/01 and T-133/01, *Saxonia Edelmetalle GmbH v Commission* [2005] ECR II-1579, para 96.

[297] Commission Decision 1999/580/ECSC, *ESF Elbestahlwerk Feralpi GmbH*, OJ 1999 L220/28.

[298] *Twenty-Third Report on Competition Policy* (1993), pt. 410.

[299] Commission Decision 1999/184/ECSC, *Sophia Jacoba GmbH and Preussag Anthrazit GmbH*, OJ 1999 L60/74.

[300] Commission Decision 1999/274/EC, *Bremer Vulkan*, OJ 1999 L108/34. See also, Commission Decision 2000/796/EC, *Compact Discs Albrechts GmbH*, OJ 2000 L318/62.

Commission that products such as mushrooms which were subject to a common market organisation would be excluded.[301]

Where the beneficiary breaches a condition set by the Commission in its authorisation, this may result in a declaration of misuse of aid. For example, the Commission found there to have been a misuse of aid where shipbuilding aid was allowed as development aid for Indonesia but the vessel was used outside of Indonesia.[302] In order to demonstrate that aid granted under an authorised aid scheme has been misused, it must be established that the aid was used in a manner contrary to that scheme as approved by the Commission, that is, in breach of the national rules governing that scheme or supplementary conditions which have been accepted by the Member State as part of approval of the scheme by the Commission.[303] In *Freistaat Thüringen v Commission*, where a guarantee scheme was approved for covering loans intended to finance investment, the Commission assessed that the aid had been misused when funds secured on the guarantee were subsequently used for purposes other than investment.[304] By contrast, breach of a mere supplementary condition imposed unilaterally by the public authority granting the aid, without that condition having been explicitly provided for by the relevant national rules, as approved by the Commission, cannot be considered sufficient evidence to show that the aid has been misused within the meaning of Article 108(2) TFEU. Otherwise, the foreseeability of control carried out by the Commission on the basis of that provision would be undermined.[305]

On the question of whether Member States may misuse aid, the General Court has given two quite contradictory answers. In *Regione autonoma della Sardegna v Commission*, it held that an infringement of an approval decision which is attributable to the Member State rather than the beneficiary cannot be regarded as misuse of aid.[306] By contrast, in *Ellinika Nafpigeia v Commission*, however, the General Court held that, whereas Article 1(g) of Regulation (EC) No 659/1999 restricted the definition of misuse of aid to misuse by the beneficiary, a wider notion of misuse of aid should be applicable in relation to Article 108(2) TFEU, allowing this to apply also where a Member State has failed to respect the conditions imposed on the approval of aid.[307]

---

[301] *Twenty-Second Report on Competition Policy* (1992), pt. 470; *Twenty-Third Report on Competition Policy* (1993), pt. 548.

[302] Commission Decision 1999/142/EC, *Indonesian shipping aid*, OJ 1999 L46/52.

[303] Case T-318/00, *Freistaat Thüringen v Commission* [2005] ECR II-4179, para 114.

[304] *Ibid.*, para 115.

[305] *Ibid.*, para 149-150.

[306] Cases T-394/08, T-408/08, T-453/08 & T-454/08, *Regione autonoma della Sardegna v Commission* [2011] ECR II-6255, para 181.

[307] Case T-391/08, *Ellinika Nafpigeia v Commission* EU:T:2012:126, para 165; Case T-527/13, *Italy v Commission* EU:T:2015:429, para 68.

Information on unlawful aid or misuse of aid   Any interested party may submit a complaint to the Commission concerning any alleged unlawful aid or misuse of aid.[308]   Where the Commission has in its possession information submitted in a complaint by an interested party regarding alleged unlawful aid or misuse of aid, it must examine that information without undue delay.   The Commission may also on its own initiative examine information from whatever source regarding unlawful aid.[309]   The complainant must demonstrate that it is an interested party.[310]   Whereas until 2013 there were no formal requirements that had to be fulfilled for sending this information,[311] Regulation (EU) No 734/2013 introduced a requirement that the complainant must complete a form as required by the Commission providing mandatory information.[312]   The standard format is now set out in Commission Regulation (EU) No 372/2014, Annex IV.[313]   Regardless of whether the complaint is well-founded or not, upon receiving the complaint the Commission is deemed to be in possession of information within the meaning of Article 10(1) of Regulation (EC) No 659/1999 and must examine that information without delay.[314]   The examination of such information gives rise to the initiation of the preliminary assessment stage under Article 108(3) TFEU.[315]   If the Commission considers that the complaint is not in the required form or that the facts and points of law put forward by the complainant do not provide sufficient grounds to show, on the basis of a *prima facie* examination, the existence of unlawful aid or misuse of aid, it must inform the complainant and call upon it to submit comments within one month.   If the complainant fails to make its views known, the complaint is deemed to be withdrawn.[316]

If necessary, the Commission must request information from the Member State concerned.[317]   As with notified new aid, the Member State must provide a complete notification of the measure, giving all necessary information in order to enable the Commission to determine whether the measure is an aid within

---

[308]   Council Regulation (EC) No 659/1999, Article 20(2).

[309]   *Ibid.*, Article 10(1); cf. Article 16; Case T-351/02, *Deutsche Bahn AG v Commission* [2006] ECR II-1047, para 41.   Article 10(1) was amended by Regulation (EU) No 734/2013, prior to which the Commission was required to examine information from whatever source alleging unlawful aid.

[310]   Commission Regulation (EC) No 794/2004, Article 11a, inserted by Commission Regulation (EU) No 372/2014.

[311]   Case C-615/11P, *Commission v Ryanair Ltd* EU:C:2013:310, para 33; Case T-442/07, *Ryanair Ltd v Commission* [2011] ECR II-333*, para 33.

[312]   Council Regulation (EC) No 659/1999, Article 20(2) as amended.

[313]   OJ 2014 L109/14.

[314]   Case T-351/02, *Deutsche Bahn AG v Commission* [2006] ECR II-1047, para 41.

[315]   Case C-521/06P, *Athinaïki Techniki v Commission* [2008] ECR I-5829, para 37; Case C-322/09P, *NDSHT v Commission* [2010] ECR I-11911, para 49; Case C-615/11P, *Commission v Ryanair Ltd* EU:C:2013:310, para 28.

[316]   Council Regulation (EC) No 659/1999, Article 20(2) as amended.

[317]   *Ibid.*, Article 10(2).

the meaning of Article 107(1) TFEU and, if so, whether the aid is compatible with the internal market.[318] Where the Commission considers that the information provided by the Member State is incomplete, it must request all necessary additional information.[319] If the Member State does not provide the information requested within the period prescribed by the Commission or provides incomplete information, the Commission must send a reminder, allowing an appropriate additional period within which the information is to be provided.[320]

Information injunctions   Where, despite a reminder, the Member State concerned does not provide the information requested within the period prescribed by the Commission, or where it provides incomplete information, the Commission must issue an information injunction pursuant to Article 10(3) of Regulation (EC) No 659/1999 in the form of a decision requiring the information to be provided. Such an injunction, being a decision within the meaning of Article 288 TFEU, is binding on the Member State concerned.[321] At its request, any interested party may obtain a copy of this decision.[322] If the Commission does not issue an information injunction in this way, it is not entitled to terminate the investigation and take its decision on the basis of the available evidence. In order to avail of that option, the Commission must first have used all its powers to cause the Member State to provide it with all the necessary information.[323] Thus, in *Greece v Commission*, the Commission's decision was annulled on the ground that it had failed to serve on Greece an order to provide additional information concerning the level of rents for aircraft in order to determine whether the rents contained an element of aid.[324]

The injunction must specify what information is required and prescribe an appropriate period within which it is to be supplied.[325]   The information

---

[318] *Ibid.*, Article 2(2).

[319] *Ibid.*, Article 5(1).

[320] *Ibid.*, Article 5(2).

[321] Cases C-463/10P & C-475/10P, *Deutsche Post AG v Commission* [2011] ECR I-9639, paras 43-44.

[322] Council Regulation (EC) No 659/1999, Article 20(3).

[323] Cases C-324/90 & C-342/90, *Germany and Pleuger Worthington v Commission* [1994] ECR I-1173, paras 26-29; Case T-323/99, *INMA v Commission* [2002] ECR II-545, para 91; Cases T-116/01 & T-118/01, *P&O European Ferries (Vizcaya) SA v Commission* [2003] ECR II-2957, para 177; Case T-274/01, *Valmont Nederland BV v Commission* [2004] ECR II-3145, para 60; Case T-318/00, *Freistaat Thüringen   v Commission* [2005] ECR II-4179, para 73; Case T-366/00 *Scott SA v Commission* [2007] ECR II-797, para 144; Case T-266/02, *Deutsche Post AG v Commission* [2008] ECR II-1233, para 75.

[324] Cases T-415/05, T-416/05 & T-423/05, *Greece v Commission* [2010] ECR II-4749, paras 246-249.

[325] Council Regulation (EC) No 659/1999, Article 10(3); Case C-301/87, *France v Commission* [1990] ECR I-307, para 19.

requested must be sufficiently precise, failing which the Commission will not be regarded as having taken sufficient steps to cause the Member State to provide the information. In *Scott v Commission*, the General Court held that an order to produce all documents, information and useful data in order to allow the Commission to examine the compatibility with Article 107 TFEU of the measures was too general for the purposes of Article 10(3).[326] On the other hand, the Commission is not required to refer to all the information in its possession regarding the investigation, or to set out a rigorous legal analysis of the allegations, although it must indicate clearly any presumptions that it seeks to verify.[327] Moreover, the information sought must have a correlation with the alleged infringement of the State aid rules, in the sense that the Commission can reasonably conclude that the requested documents will help determine the existence of the alleged infringement.[328] Once the Commission has the necessary information at its disposal, it must take a decision as to the compatibility of the aid with the internal market, and it is not appropriate for it to take an interim decision requiring the Member State to produce further information.[329]

Article 10(3) of Regulation (EC) No 659/1999 does not specify any time limit within which the information must be produced, thereby leaving it to the Commission to fix the relevant period in the injunction decision.[330] Nevertheless, the appropriate period must be such as to allow the person to whom the decision is addressed to give an exact and full response, having regard to the degree of difficulty in collecting the relevant information.[331]

Decision on basis of available information If the Member State fails to comply with the information injunction, the Commission is required, pursuant to Article 13(1) of Regulation (EC) No 659/1999, to proceed to examine the aid on the basis of the available information.[332] In *Saxonia Edelmetalle v Commission*, the beneficiary of aid argued that, since the German authorities had failed to respond to an information injunction, the Commission should have questioned the beneficiary directly before adopting its decision ordering recovery. The General Court held that the Commission was not under any duty to consult the parties concerned on the ground that it followed from Regulation

---

[326] Case T-366/00, *Scott SA v Commission* [2007] ECR II-797, paras 154-155.
[327] Case T-570/08 RENV, *Deutsche Post AG v Commission* EU:T:2013:589, para 99.
[328] *Ibid.*, para 119.
[329] Case C-17/99, *France v Commission* [2001] ECR I-2481, para 28.
[330] Case T-570/08 RENV, *Deutsche Post AG v Commission* EU:T:2013:589, para 65.
[331] *Ibid.*, para 85.
[332] Council Regulation (EC) No 659/1999, Article 13(1); Case C-301/87, *France v Commission* [1990] ECR I-307, para 22; Case C-520/07P, *Commission v MTU Friedrichshafen GmbH* [2009] ECR I-8555, para 54; Case T-196/02, *MTU Friedrichshafen GmbH v Commission* [2007] ECR II-2889, para 45; Case T-25/07, *Iride SpA v Commission* [2009] ECR II-245, para 89.

No 659/1999, Article 13(1) that, in such a situation, the Commission was empowered to end the formal investigation procedure and to adopt a decision on the basis of the information available.[333] The right to take a decision on the basis of the available information cannot, however, be interpreted as releasing the Commission entirely from the obligation to base its decisions on reliable and coherent evidence to support its conclusions. The Commission is, at the very least, required to ensure that the information at its disposal, even if incomplete and fragmented, constitutes a sufficient basis on which to conclude that an undertaking has benefited from an advantage amounting to State aid, particularly where it imposes a recovery order on the beneficiary. It follows that the Commission cannot assume that an undertaking has benefited from an advantage constituting State aid solely on the basis of a negative presumption, based on a lack of information enabling the contrary to be found, if there is no other evidence capable of positively establishing the actual existence of such an advantage.[334]

In *Scott v Commission*, the General Court held that, in view of the fact that a recovery order can have repercussions for third parties, the Commission must also use all of the powers available to it to avoid the possibility that the failure of a Member State to cooperate could have negative and unwarranted consequences for those third parties.[335] Accordingly, it held that the Commission was not entitled to adopt a decision on the basis of the information made available by the Member State because the parties had furnished conflicting information to it which it had effectively refused to take into consideration.[336] This was overturned on appeal, the ECJ holding that the additional information was too vague.[337]

Preliminary assessment of unlawful aid Council Regulation (EC) No 659/1999, Article 13(1) provides that the preliminary examination of possible unlawful aid must result in a decision pursuant to Article 4 of the Regulation finding that the measure does not constitute aid within the meaning of Article 107(1) TFEU, or that it is aid but that the Commission has no doubts as to its compatibility with the internal market, or that there are doubts as to its compatibility with the internal market requiring initiation of the formal investigation procedure.[338] As with notified aid, the Commission may, and sometimes must, discuss the measure at issue with the Member State which granted the aid and interested parties before it takes a decision following its

---

[333] Cases T-111/01 & T-133/01, *Saxonia Edelmetalle GmbH v Commission* [2005] ECR II-1579, para 58.

[334] Case C-520/07P, *Commission v MTU Friedrichshafen GmbH* [2009] ECR I-8555, paras 55-58.

[335] Case T-366/00 *Scott SA v Commission* [2007] ECR II-797, para 149.

[336] *Ibid.*, para 150.

[337] Case C-290/07P, *Commission v Scott SA* [2010] ECR I-7763, para 95.

[338] Council Regulation (EC) No 659/1999, Article 13(1); cf. Article 4(2)-(4).

preliminary assessment.[339] Decisions, or summary notices, must be published in the *Official Journal of the European Union* under the same conditions as apply generally to notified measures.[340] At its request, any interested party may obtain a copy of the decision.[341] Where the Commission has acted on a complaint, it must send a copy of the decision to the complainant.[342]

Preliminary assessment of misuse of aid Given that misuse of aid can only arise in the context of existing aid, the Commission's preliminary assessment is confined to determining whether to open the formal investigation procedure. Neither Article 108(2) TFEU nor Council Regulation (EC) No 659/1999, Article 16 provides for a formal decision to be taken where the Commission determines, following a preliminary assessment of the evidence, that there has not been a misuse of aid.

Commission priorities in relation to complaints The General Court has recognised that the Commission is entitled to set priorities in relation to complaints on State aid matters. In *Ufex v Commission*, it distinguished the requirements under State aid investigations from those applying in the case of competition law. Contrasting the position in relation to a complaint alleging an abuse of dominant position, where the Commission has a discretionary power to determine priorities and is not obliged to rule on whether or not there has been an infringement, the General Court noted that in State aid matters, the Commission, which has exclusive jurisdiction to determine whether aid is incompatible with the internal market, has, at the end of the preliminary stage of the investigation, a duty to take a decision.[343] Although the Commission is bound to take a decision on each complaint where there is evidence of unlawful aid, it is nevertheless entitled to give differing degrees of priority to the complaints brought before it.[344]

In *Bouygues SA v Commission*, the complaint, extending to almost ninety pages not including the annexes, related to a total of eleven measures. Accordingly, the General Court considered that the Commission, which initiated the formal investigation procedure three and a half months after the lodging of the complaint for some of the measures to which it related and thus dealt with part of the complaint, and in so doing gave priority to the very measures that raised serious difficulties, was entitled, in the light of its workload and its right to set the priorities for investigations, to postpone

---

[339] Case C-400/99, *Italy v Commission* [2005] ECR I-3657, para 29; Case T-351/02, *Deutsche Bahn AG v Commission* [2006] ECR II-1047, para 41.

[340] Council Regulation (EC) No 659/1999, Article 26(1)-(3).

[341] *Ibid.*, Article 20(3).

[342] *Ibid.*, Article 20(2).

[343] Case T-60/05, *Ufex v Commission* [2007] ECR II-3397, para 106-107.

[344] Case C-119/97P *Ufex v Commission* [1999] ECR I-1341, para 88; Case T-475/04, *Bouygues SA v Commission* [2007] ECR II-2097, para 158.

dealing with the measure, which in the Commission's opinion did not raise serious difficulties, without it being open to an accusation of lack of diligence in that regard. In that context, the period of almost two years between the lodging of the complaint and the decision did not reveal a lack of diligence on the part of the Commission.[345]

In its Code of Best Practice, the Commission states that it will use its best endeavours to investigate a complaint within an indicative time frame of twelve months. Since it is entitled to give priority to cases brought before it, it can postpone dealing with a measure which is not a priority. Within twelve months, therefore, the Commission will come to a preliminary assessment in priority cases or send an initial letter to the complainant setting out its preliminary views in non-priority cases.[346]

Insufficient grounds for taking a view Where the Commission, following a complaint by an interested party, considers that on the basis of the available evidence there are insufficient grounds for taking a view on the case, it must inform the interested party in accordance with Regulation (EC) No 659/1999, Article 20(2).[347] The letter informing the complainant of that initial view is merely a preliminary act, which would not be subject to judicial review.[348] As the ECJ held in *Athinaïki Techniki v Commission*, the Commission is required in that event to allow the interested parties, given their right to be associated with the formal investigation procedure, to submit additional comments within a reasonable period.[349] Following receipt of any additional comments or, in the absence of any such comments, at the end of that reasonable period, the Commission may then close the file. In conflicting decisions of the General Court and the ECJ, there was some difference of opinion as to whether the Commission was able to close the file without being considered to have taken a decision bringing the preliminary assessment to an end within the meaning of Article 4(2)-(3) of Regulation (EC) No 659/1999. Whereas the General Court had taken the view that closing a file would not constitute a decision unless the Commission had in fact taken a clear and explicit position on the matter, the ECJ decided that the Commission is always required to take a decision when it closes the file.

In *Athinaïki Techniki v Commission*, the General Court held that generally, where the Commission closed the file without defining its position, it did not thereby take a decision which had legal effects, so that an addressee of a letter from the Commission stating that the file had been closed was not able to bring

---

[345] Case T-475/04, *Bouygues SA v Commission* [2007] ECR II-2097, paras 159-160.
[346] Code of Best Practice, paras 47-48.
[347] Case T-351/02, *Deutsche Bahn AG v Commission* [2006] ECR II-1047, para 43.
[348] Case C-521/06P, *Athinaïki Techniki v Commission* [2008] ECR I-5829, para 50.
[349] *Ibid.*, para 39.

annulment proceedings against the Commission.[350] By contrast, in *Deutsche Bahn v Commission*, a letter from the Commission informing the complainant that its complaint was rejected on the basis that the measure did not constitute aid was held by the General Court to be a decision within the meaning of Article 4(2) in which the Commission had taken a clear and explicit position, rather than merely a statement informing the applicant within the meaning of Article 20(2) that there were insufficient grounds for taking a view on the case.[351] On appeal in *Athinaïki Techniki v Commission*, the ECJ held that, since Article 10(1) of Regulation (EC) No 659/1999 required the Commission to examine alleged unlawful aid, including allegations made by complainants pursuant to Article 20(2), and Article 13(1) stated that the examination of possible unlawful aid must result in a decision pursuant to Article 4(2), (3) or (4), it followed that the Commission was bound, once its preliminary assessment was completed, either to adopt a definitive decision rejecting the complaint or to open the formal investigation procedure. Failure to do so would constitute a failure to act.[352]

Moreover, a decision rejecting the complaint could not be considered as preliminary or preparatory since it could not be followed, in the context of that administrative procedure, by any other decision amenable to judicial review.[353] Thus, where the Commission refuses to open the formal investigation procedure, it has adopted a measure which is definitive and which cannot be characterised as a mere provisional measure.[354] Subsequently, in *NDSHT v Commission*, the General Court held that a letter rejecting a complaint, which the Commission treated as dealing with existing aid, was not a decision subject to judicial review, but was merely an informal communication pursuant to Article 20(2).[355] On appeal, the ECJ rejected this analysis, holding that the Commission's letter constituted a refusal to open the formal investigation procedure.[356] In *Aiscat v Commission*, the General Court rejected the Commission's argument that this imposed an obligation of excessive examination in cases where the information supplied in the complaint was vague or concerned a very broad field.[357]

In rejecting the Commission's contention that the letter to the complainant could not be a decision since it had not been addressed or communicated to the Member State in question but was a response to the complainant, the General

---

[350] Case T-94/05, *Athinaïki Techniki v Commission* [2006] ECR II-73*, para 30.
[351] Case T-361/02, *Deutsche Bahn AG v Commission* [2005] (unreported), para 20; Case T-351/02, *Deutsche Bahn AG v Commission* [2006] ECR II-1047, para 47.
[352] Case C-521/06P, *Athinaïki Techniki AE v Commission* [2008] ECR I-5829, para 40.
[353] *Ibid.*, para 54.
[354] Case C-322/09, *NDSHT v Commission* [2010] ECR I-11911, para 53; Case T-182/10 *Aiscat v Commission* EU:T:2013:9, para 105.
[355] Case T-152/06, *NDSHT v Commission* [2009] ECR II-1517, para 44.
[356] Case C-322/09, *NDSHT v Commission* [2010] ECR I-11911, para 58.
[357] Case T-182/10 *Aiscat v Commission* EU:T:2013:9, para 31.

Court, in *Deutsche Bahn v Commission*, held, first, that it was concerned with the substance rather than the form of the measure and, secondly, that the Commission could not exclude such a decision from review by the courts by declaring that it did not take a decision, by trying to withdraw it or by deciding not to address it to the Member State, which in any event amounted to an infringement of the obligation in Article 25 of Regulation (EC) No 659/1999.[358] Similar reasoning was adopted by the ECJ in *Athinaïki Techniki v Commission*, holding, in particular, that the procedural rules governing judicial review had to be implemented in such a way as to contribute to the attainment of the objective of ensuring effective judicial protection of individual rights under EU law.[359]

Duration of preliminary investigation of unlawful aid   As regards the duration of the Commission's preliminary assessment, Advocate General Slynn, in *RSV v Commission*, thought that, where unlawful aid had been subsequently notified, the Commission should come to a preliminary conclusion on the compatibility of the aid with the internal market with due diligence, which he found to be within a period of two months.[360]   Council Regulation (EC) No 659/1999, Article 11(2), now provides that, where unlawful aid has been effectively recovered, the Commission must take a decision within the time limits applicable to notified aid.[361]   Otherwise, the Commission is not bound by the two month time limit applicable to preliminary assessments.[362]   It follows that the rule in Council Regulation (EC) No 659/1999, Article 4(6), whereby notified aid may be deemed compatible with the internal market if the Commission does not take a decision within two months, is not applicable where the Commission initiates a procedure in relation to unnotified aid.[363]

No specific time limits apply in relation to complaints made to the Commission concerning aid which has not been notified. Nevertheless, the Commission cannot prolong indefinitely its preliminary investigation into alleged unlawful aid. Whether or not the duration of an initial investigation procedure is reasonable must be determined in relation to the particular

---

[358] Case T-351/02, *Deutsche Bahn AG v Commission* [2006] ECR II-1047, para 52; Case T-182/10 *Aiscat v Commission* EU:T:2013:9, para 29.

[359] Case C-521/06P, *Athinaïki Techniki AE v Commission* [2008] ECR I-5829, paras 41-45.

[360] Case 223/85, *RSV v Commission* [1987] ECR 4617, *per* Advocate General Slynn at p. 4646.

[361] Council Regulation (EC) No 659/1999, Article 11(2).

[362] *Ibid.*, Articles 13(2); cf. Article 4(5); Case C-301/87, *France v Commission* [1990] ECR I-307, para 27; Case T-95/96, *Gestevisión Telecinco SA v Commission*, [1998] ECR II-3407, para 79.

[363] Cases C-630/11P to C-633/11P, *HGA srl v Commission* EU:C:2013:387, para 75; Cases T-116/01 & T-118/01, *P&O European Ferries (Vizcaya) SA v Commission* [2003] ECR II-2957, para 217.Cases T-394/08, T-408/08, T-453/08 & T-454/08, *Regione autonoma della Sardegna v Commission* [2011] ECR II-6255, para 96.

circumstances of each case and, especially, its context, the various procedural stages to be followed by the Commission, the complexity of the case and its importance for the various parties involved.[364]   In *Gestevisión Telecinco v Commission*, two complaints were made to the Commission concerning aid which had been awarded to public television companies in Spain. After 47 months and 26 months respectively, the Commission had still not taken any decisions in the context of its preliminary investigation, on the ground that it was still collecting information and opinions from the Member States. The General Court held that this period was so long that it should have been sufficient to enable the Commission to close the preliminary stage of its investigation into the aid and thus be in a position to adopt a decision unless it could show exceptional circumstances justifying such lengthy periods.[365] Similarly, in *TF1 v Commission*, a period of 31 months was regarded as too long.[366]   In *Asociación de Estaciones de Servicio de Madrid v Commission*, whilst acknowledging that the complainant had submitted various arguments with supporting documentation to the Commission which the latter was obliged to investigate, the General Court held that those circumstances did not justify the duration of the initial investigation being almost 28 months. In particular, in so far as the Commission's conclusion that the contested measure did not constitute a transfer of State resources was based on an analysis of the applicable legislation, it did not appear that the Commission was required to enquire extensively into the facts or take other measures requiring a significant amount of time. Moreover, the relatively short length of the Commission's actual decision seemed to rebut the Commission's argument that the case was particularly complex.[367]

   In its decision in *Air One v Commission*, on the other hand, the General Court held that a period of less than six months between lodging of the complaint and the applicant's formal notice under Article 265 TFEU calling on the Commission to define its position was not unreasonable, given the complexity of the case and the fact that the Commission had not been inactive but had sought information from the Italian authorities.[368]   Similarly, in *Asklepios Kliniken v Commission*, where the period between the complaint and the letter calling on the Commission to act was twelve months, the General Court held that the period was not unreasonably long in the circumstances. That case involved the issue of whether compensation for public services

---

[364] Case T-95/96, *Gestevisión Telecinco SA v Commission*, [1998] ECR II-3407, para 74-75; Case T-17/96, *TF1 v Commission* [1999] ECR II-1757, para 74-75; Case T-95/03, *Asociación de Estaciones de Servicio de Madrid v Commission* [2006] ECR II-4739, paras 121-122.

[365] Case T-95/96, *Gestevisión Telecinco SA v Commission*, [1998] ECR II-3407, para 81.

[366] Case T-17/96, *TF1 v Commission* [1999] ECR II-1757, para 77.

[367] Case T-95/03, *Asociación de Estaciones de Servicio de Madrid v Commission* [2006] ECR II-4739, paras 123-129.

[368] Case T-395/04, *Air One SpA v Commission* [2006] ECR II-1343, paras 62-67.

constituted State aid and was undeniably complicated. In addition, the Commission was entitled to wait until delivery of the important judgment in *Altmark*,[369] which was pending at the time.[370] In the Basque tax cases, the period of 79 months taken for the Commission to take its decision at the end of the preliminary assessment was excused on the ground that the Spanish authorities consistently delayed in providing responses to the Commission's requests for information.[371] Similarly, in *3F v Commission*, the General Court held that a period of four years was justified by the particular circumstances of the case, in particular the fact that discussions had taken place with the Member State and that the applicant had made repeated additional submissions that had to be taken into account.[372]

A Member State which has unlawfully granted aid and which subsequently fails to provide the Commission with appropriate information concerning the aid cannot rely on the prolonged length of the examination procedure as a ground for a legitimate expectation regarding the compatibility of the aid in question with the internal market. Otherwise, it would be able to rely on its own unlawful act to deprive the provisions of Article 108(3) TFEU of their effectiveness.[373] Thus, in *Départment du Loiret v Commission*, the General Court held that the reluctance by the French authorities to provide the information requested by the Commission meant that the latter could not be criticised for excessive delay or lack of diligence in the conduct of the administrative procedure.[374]

16.7 FORMAL INVESTIGATION PROCEDURE

Formal investigation procedure The Commission must initiate the formal investigation procedure under Article 108(2) TFEU where the Commission is notified of plans to grant or alter aid and doubts are raised as to the compatibility of the plan with the internal market,[375] or where the Commission considers that existing aid is not compatible with the internal market and the Member State concerned does not accept the Commission's proposals to alter

---

[369] Case C-280/00, *Altmark Trans GmbH v Regierungspräsidium Magdeburg* [2003] ECR I-7747.

[370] Case T-167/04, *Asklepios Kliniken GmbH v Commission* [2007] ECR II-2379, paras 87-89.

[371] Cases C-465/09P – C-470/09P, *Territorio Histórico de Álava – Diputación Foral de Álava v Commission* [2011] ECR I-83*, para 149; Cases T-30/01 etc., *Territorio Histórico de Álava – Diputación Foral de Álava v Commission* [2009] ECR II-2919, para 264.

[372] Case C-646/11P, *3F v Commission* EU:C:2013:36, para 34; Case T-30/03 RENV, *3F v Commission* [2011] ECR II-6651, para 68.

[373] Case C-303/88, *Italy v Commission* [1991] ECR I-1433, para 43.

[374] Case T-369/00, *Départment du Loiret v Commission* [2003] ECR II-1789, para 56.

[375] Article 108(3) TFEU; Council Regulation (EC) No 659/1999, Article 4(4).

or abolish the aid.[376] Equally, a formal investigation may be opened in respect of unlawful aid or misuse of aid. The decision to initiate the formal investigation procedure under Article 108(2) TFEU must, pursuant to Council Regulation (EC) No 659/1999, Article 6(1), summarise the relevant issues of fact and law, include a preliminary assessment as to the aid character of the measure, and set out the Commission's doubts as to the compatibility of the aid with the internal market.[377] A notice is published in the *Official Journal of the European Union* containing a summary of the decision along with the full decision in its authentic language version[378] and calling upon the Member State concerned and other interested parties to submit comments.[379]

Comments from interested parties   Any interested party may submit comments to the Commission following a decision to open a formal investigation.[380] The notion of interested party covers an indeterminate group of persons.[381] Interested parties are the Member States and any person, undertaking or association of undertakings whose interests might be affected by the granting of the aid, in particular the beneficiary of the aid, competing undertakings and trade associations.[382] This may also extend to undertakings which are not direct competitors of the beneficiary of the aid, but which require the same raw material for their production process, provided that they demonstrate that their interests could be adversely affected by the grant of the aid.[383] For that purpose, it is necessary for them to establish that the aid is likely to have a specific effect on their situation.[384] Customers, suppliers and employees, including representatives of the employees of the recipient, may

---

[376] Article 108(2) TFEU; Council Regulation (EC) No 659/1999, Article 19(2).

[377] *Ibid.*, Article 6(1); Case C-194/09P, *Alcoa Trasformazioni srl v Commission* [2011] ECR I-6311, para 102; Case T-397/12, *Diputación Foral de Bizkaia v Commission* EU:T:2015:291, para 58.

[378] Council Regulation (EC) No 659/1999, Article 26(2).

[379] Article 108(2) TFEU; Council Regulation (EC) No 659/1999, Article 6(1).

[380] Council Regulation (EC) No 659/1999, Article 20(1).

[381] Case 323/82, *Intermills v Commission* [1984] ECR 3809, para 16; Case C-83/09P, *Commission v Kronoply GmbH* [2011] ECR I-4441, para 63; Case C-47/10P, *Austria v Commission* [2011] ECR I-10707, para 132.

[382] Council Regulation (EC) No 659/1999, Article 1(h); Case 323/82, *Intermills v Commission* [1984] ECR 3809, para 17; Case C-78/03P, *Commission v Aktionsgemeinschaft Recht und Eigentum* [2005] ECR I-10737, para 36; Cases C-75/05P & C-80/05P, *Germany v Kronofrance* [2008] ECR I-6619, para 39; Case C-487/06P, *British Aggregates Association v Commission* [2008] ECR I-10515, para 29; Cases T-197/97 & T-198/97, *Weyl Beef Products BV v Commission* [2001] ECR II-303, para 49; Case T-388/02, *Kronoply GmbH v Commission* [2008] ECR II-305*, para 61.

[383] Case C-83/09P, *Commission v Kronoply GmbH* [2011] ECR I-4441, para 64; Case T-388/02, *Kronoply GmbH v Commission* [2008] II-305*, paras 73-74.

[384] Case C-319/07P, *3F v Commission* [2009] ECR I-5963, para 33; Case C-83/09P, *Commission v Kronoply GmbH* [2011] ECR I-4441, para 65; Case C-47/10P, *Austria v Commission* [2011] ECR I-10707, para 132.

also be considered as interested parties.[385]   Since this results in an indeterminate number of persons to whom notice must be given, it follows that publication of the notice in the *Official Journal of the European Union* is sufficient and the Commission is not obliged to give individual notice to particular persons.[386]   The Commission may also send a copy of the opening decision to identified third parties in order to seek to improve the factual basis of the investigation.[387]   In the formal investigation procedure, the principle of sound administration requires the Commission to comply with the principle of equal treatment as between the parties concerned.[388]   It should always be borne in mind, nevertheless, that the procedure under Article 108(2) TFEU is an administrative procedure, with no quasi-judicial aspects.[389]

Comments from interested parties must, in accordance with Article 6(1) of Council Regulation (EC) No 659/1999, be made within a period set by the Commission which should normally not exceed one month, although, in duly justified cases, the Commission may extend the period.[390]   In *Le Levant v Commission*, the General Court held that a refusal by the Commission to extend the period may be challenged, in particular where the consequence would be that a person against whom an adverse decision may be taken has not been given the opportunity to make his views known effectively regarding the facts held against him by the Commission.[391]   Moreover, there is nothing in Regulation (EC) No 659/1999 that might prevent the Commission from accepting late submissions.[392]   In *Scott v Commission*, the existence of an advantageous sale price constituting State aid on the transfer of a property was vigorously contested during the administrative procedure and was the subject of a detailed exchange of correspondence between the French authorities, the alleged recipient and the Commission.   In those circumstances, the General

---

[385] Case 323/82, *Intermills v Commission* [1984] ECR 3809, *per* Advocate General Verloren van Themaat, at p. 3837; Case T-189/97, *Comité d'Entreprise de la Société Française de Production v Commission* [1998] ECR II-335, para 41.

[386] Case 323/82, *Intermills v Commission* [1984] ECR 3809, para 17; Cases C-74/00P and C-75/00P, *Falck v Commission* [2002] ECR I-7869, para 80; Cases T-129/95, T-2/96 & T-97/96 *Neue Maxhütte Stahlwerke* v *Commission* [1999] ECR II-17, para 232; Cases T-111/01 and T-133/01, *Saxonia Edelmetalle GmbH v Commission* [2005] ECR II-1579, para 48; Case T-150/12, *Greece v Commission* EU:T:2014:191, para 58.

[387] Cases C-74/00P & C-75/00P, *Falck Spa v Commission* [2002] ECR I-7869, para 83; Case T-198/01, *Technische Glaswerke Ilmenaua GmbH v Commission* [2004] ECR II-2717, para 195; Code of Best Practice, para 34.

[388] Case T-198/01R, *Technische Glaswerke Ilmenaua GmbH v Commission* [2002] ECR II-2153, para 85; Cases T-254/00, T-270/00 & T-277/00, *Hotel Cipriani SpA v Commission* [2008] ECR II-3269, para 210.

[389] Case C-83/09P, *Commission v Kronoply GmbH* [2011] ECR I-4441, *per* Advocate General Jaaskinen, at para 40.

[390] Council Regulation (EC) No 659/1999, Article 6(1).

[391] Case T-34/02, *Le Levant 001 v Commission* [2005] ECR II-267, para 97.

[392] Case T-366/00, *Scott SA v Commission* [2007] ECR II-797, para 57.

Court held that the Commission could not shelter itself behind a formalistic interpretation of its State aid obligations and refuse the recipient an opportunity to submit its further comments on a controversial aspect of the inquiry by unreasonably rejecting additional information.[393] On appeal, the ECJ held that the additional information was not in fact of such quality as to require the Commission to take it into consideration or to reopen the formal investigation procedure.[394] Advocate General Mengozzi, considered that the question of whether the Commission should accept late information should be governed by the principle of good administration. This would preclude the Commission from systematically refusing any information provided by the recipient after the deadline for submission of comments from interested parties and allow the Commission to accept such information where it was of real use for the investigation, provided that it did not lead to delay in the adoption of the final decision. It would be for the party providing the information to prove that it should be taken into consideration.[395]

Notice to interested parties must be adequate The decision to open the formal investigation procedure must give the interested parties the opportunity effectively to participate in that procedure and to respond as fully as possible.[396] The aim of the notice is to obtain from interested parties all information required for the guidance of the Commission with regard to its future action,[397] thereby guaranteeing the other Member States and the sectors concerned an opportunity to make their views known and allowing the Commission to be informed of all the facts of the case.[398] The Commission's assessment in the opening decision is necessarily preliminary in nature, such that the Commission cannot be required to present a complete analysis of the aid in question at that stage. The Commission must, however, define sufficiently the framework of its investigation so as not to render meaningless the right of interested parties to submit their comments.[399] Thus, for example,

---

[393] *Ibid.*, paras 58-62.

[394] Case C-290/07P, *Commission v Scott SA* [2010] ECR I-7763, para 95.

[395] *Ibid.*, *per* AG Mengozzi, at paras 63-66.

[396] Case C-49/05P, *Ferriere Nord SpA v Commission* [2008] ECR I-68*, para 92; Cases C-106/09P & C-107/09P, *Commission v Government of Gibraltar* [2011] ECR I-11113, para 168; Cases T-195/01 & T-207/01, *Government of Gibraltar v Commission* [2002] ECR II-2309, para 138; Cases T-81/07 to T-83/07, *KG Holding NV v Commission* [2009] ECR II-2411, para 117; Case T-500/12 *Ryanair Ltd v Commission* EU:T:2015:73, para 45.

[397] Case 70/72, *Commission v Germany* [1973] ECR 813, para 19; Case 323/82, *Intermills v Commission* [1984] ECR 3809, para 17; Case T-266/94, *Skibsværftsforeningen v Commission* [1996] ECR II-1399, para 256.

[398] Case 84/82, *Germany v Commission* [1984] ECR 1451, para 13.

[399] Case T-354/99, *Kuwait Petroleum (Nederland) BV v Commission* [2006] ECR II-1475, para 85; Cases T-273/06 & T-297/06, *ISD Polska v Commission* [2009] ECR II-2185,

in *Greece v Commission*, concerning aid to Olympic Airways that had been transferred to a successor company through a sub-lease of aircraft that was allegedly less than the rents under the head lease, the Commission's decision was annulled on the ground that the decision to open the formal investigation contained no preliminary assessment of the rents paid with a view to determining whether they contained any element of aid.[400] Publication serves only to indicate to interested parties that the procedure has been initiated. It is not intended to give the impression that the Commission has already made a finding as to the classification of the measure as aid or the compatibility of the aid with the internal market, whilst the obligation on the Commission to make known its reservations is intended to permit the parties concerned to ensure that their interests are defended.[401]

The Commission, whilst not being required specifically to solicit comments from any individual,[402] is obliged duly to place the interested parties in a position to put forward their comments in the course of the formal investigation procedure.[403] The General Court has recognised that the mere fact of being informed of the opening of a formal investigation procedure does not suffice to enable an interested party to effectively make known its observations, so that the decision to open that procedure must be sufficiently precise to enable the parties concerned to participate in an effective manner.[404] For example, the alleged beneficiary of the aid should be identified, since it is the beneficiary who will be required to repay any aid that is found to have been unlawfully granted. In the absence of an indication that a party is a beneficiary of the aid in dispute, that type of interested party cannot be regarded as having been duly called on to submit his comments, because he may legitimately believe that such comments are not necessary, since he is not named as the

---

para 126; Cases T-427/04 & T-17/05, *France v Commission* [2009] ECR II-4315, para 137.

[400] Cases T-415/05, T-416/05 & T-423/05, *Greece v Commission* [2010] ECR II-4749, para 240.

[401] Case 323/82, *Intermills v Commission* [1984] ECR 3809, para 21; Cases T-269/99, T-271/99 & T-272/99, *Territorio Histórico de Álava – Diputación Foral de Álava v Commission* [2002] ECR II-4217, para 84; Cases T-346/99, T-347/99 & T-348/99, *Territorio Histórico de Álava – Diputación Foral de Álava v Commission* [2002] ECR II-4259, para 77.

[402] Case T-354/99, *Kuwait Petroleum (Nederland) BV v Commission* [2006] ECR II-1475, para 82; Cases T-267/08 & T-279/08, *Région Nord-Pas-de-Calais v Commission* [2011] ECR II-1999, para 75.

[403] Cases C-74/00P & C-75/00P, *Falck v Commission* [2002] ECR I-7869, para 170; Case T-109/01, *Fleuren Compost BV v Commission* [2004] ECR II-127, paras 45-46; Case T-354/99, *Kuwait Petroleum (Nederland) BV v Commission* [2006] ECR II-1475, para 83; Cases T-309/04, T-317/04, T-329/04 & T-336/04, *TV2/Danmark A/S v Commission* [2008] ECR II-2935, para 139.

[404] Cases T-111/01 & T-133/01, *Saxonia Edelmetalle GmbH v Commission* [2005] ECR II-1579, para 50; Case T-332/06, *Alcoa Trasformazioni Srl v Commission* [2009] ECR II-29*, para 80.

beneficiary of the aid to be recovered.[405] Thus, in *Le Levant v Commission*, where private investors took advantage of tax breaks to invest in the building of a ship and the Commission's decision to open the formal investigation gave the firm impression that the beneficiary of the aid was the owner of the ship who had indirectly benefited from the tax breaks, the General Court held that the investors were legitimately able to believe that they were not targeted by the decision. Accordingly, as they were not identified as beneficiaries of the aid in the decision to open the procedure, the private investors had not been, at that stage, called upon to submit their comments within the meaning of Regulation No 659/1999, Article 6(1) or Article 108(2) TFEU.[406]

Similarly, in *KG Holding v Commission*, a decision was partially annulled to the extent that the subject matter of the recovery order was not alluded to in the decision initiating the formal investigation.[407] By contrast, in *Kuwait Petroleum v Commission*, which concerned aid granted to numerous service stations near the Netherlands border with Germany, the applicant failed in its argument that the notice of intention to initiate the formal investigation procedure was too vague for it to consider itself as an interested party as an oil company. The General Court held that the Commission had stated in its decision to initiate the formal investigation procedure that it could not rule out the possibility that the oil companies would be considered the recipients of aid, and had effectively set out its queries at to the actual recipients of the aid, in particular with respect to the control which the oil companies exercised through exclusive supply agreements. Furthermore, the applicant had understood this sufficiently well to provide the Commission with relevant information.[408] In *Commission v Government of Gibraltar*, the fact that the Commission had not specifically referred to offshore companies in its opening decision did not give rise to any legitimate expectation that that sector might be excluded, given that the Commission had clearly intimated that its investigation would cover sectors that would escape taxation under the reform plans.[409] In *Ryanair v Commission*, concerning State aid through differential rates of Irish air travel tax, Ryanair claimed that it had been denied the opportunity to comment on recovery of the aid since the sum to be recovered from each beneficiary and the identification of each beneficiary had not been mentioned in precise terms in the opening decision. The General Court rejected this, holding that interested parties could reasonably expect, since the

---

[405] Case T-34/02, *Le Levant 001 v Commission* [2005] ECR II-267, para 83.

[406] *Ibid.*, para 91.

[407] Cases T-81/07 to T-83/07, *KG Holding NV v Commission* [2009] ECR II-2411, para 134.

[408] Case T-354/99, *Kuwait Petroleum (Nederland) BV v Commission* [2006] ECR II-1475, paras 84-89.

[409] Cases C-106/09P & C-107/09P, *Commission v Government of Gibraltar* [2011] ECR I-11113, paras 169-171.

lower rate of tax was characterised as State aid, that the Commission would order the recovery of the aid from its beneficiaries.[410]

Request for information made to other sources   Additional information collection powers were granted to the Commission by Council Regulation (EU) No 734/2013 which introduced Articles 6a and 6b into Regulation (EC) No 659/1999.   Article 6b provides that, after the initiation of the formal investigation procedure, in particular as regards technically complex cases subject to substantive assessment, the Commission may, if the information provided by a Member State during the course of the preliminary investigation is not sufficient, request any other Member State or undertaking or association of undertakings to provide all relevant market information necessary to enable the Commission to complete its assessment of the measure, taking due account of the principle of proportionality inn particular for SMEs.   The Commission may request such information only if the investigation has been ineffective to date and, in so far as beneficiaries are concerned, if the Member State concerned agrees to the request.[411]   Member States must reply within one month.   Undertakings should reply within the time limit set by the Commission in the information request.   The Commission may also issue a formal decision requesting information from undertakings or associations of undertakings.[412] The Commission must give the Member State which has allegedly granted the aid the opportunity of making known its views on the information received pursuant to these requests.[413]

Penalties may be imposed, up to 1% of total turnover and having regard to the nature, gravity and duration of the infringement, on undertakings or associations of undertakings which supply incorrect, incomplete or misleading information in response to a decision or which do not supply the information within the prescribed time limit.   Periodic penalty payments may also be imposed up to 5% of average daily turnover.[414]

Evidence to contradict Commission's preliminary assessment   Since the decision to initiate the formal investigation procedure must contain an adequate preliminary analysis by the Commission setting out the reasons for its doubts regarding the compatibility of the aid with the internal market, it is for the Member State concerned and, where appropriate, the recipient of the aid to

---

[410]   Case T-500/12 *Ryanair Ltd v Commission* EU:T:2015:73, para 50.
[411]   Commission Regulation (EC) No 659/1999, Article 6a(1)-(2).
[412]   *Ibid.*, Article 6a(5)-(7).
[413]   *Ibid.*, Article 7(8).
[414]   *Ibid.*, Article 6b. The power to impose penalties is subject to a limitation period of three years (Article 15a) and the power to enforce penalties is subject to a limitation period of five years (Article 15b).

adduce evidence to show that the aid is compatible with the internal market.[415] Where no comments are received from any interested parties, the Commission is entitled to proceed to determine the aid as being incompatible with the internal market.[416] The Commission cannot be criticised for failing to take account of matters of fact or of law which could have been submitted to it during the administrative procedure but which were not, since it is under no obligation to consider, of its own motion or on the basis of prediction, what information might have been submitted to it.[417]

It follows that, if an interested party believes that some of the facts contained in the decision to initiate the formal investigation procedure are incorrect, it must inform the Commission during the administrative procedure or risk not being able to challenge those facts in subsequent litigation.[418] Moreover, there is nothing to prevent interested parties from raising concerns about the measure under investigation other than those that the Commission has raised in the opening decision.[419]

In the case of unlawful aid, the Commission must not take account of factors subsequent to the grant of the aid, as this would confer an advantage on Member States which failed in their obligation to give notice at the planning stage of aid which they intend to grant. Thus, in *Freistaat Sachsen v Commission*, concerning aid granted in 2001, no reliance could be placed on the 2002 financial accounts of the recipient to show that it was not a firm in difficulty when it received the aid.[420]

Right of the defendant Member State to be heard Respect for the right to be heard is, in all proceedings initiated against a person which are liable to culminate in a measure adversely affecting that person, a fundamental principle of EU law which must be guaranteed even in the absence of specific rules. That principle requires that the defendant be afforded the opportunity during the

---

[415] Case C-49/05P, *Ferriere Nord SpA v Commission* [2008] ECR I-68*, para 92; Case T-109/01, *Fleuren Compost BV v Commission* [2004] ECR II-127, para 45; Case T-176/01, *Ferriere Nord SpA v Commission* [2004] ECR II-3931, paras 93-94; Case T-200/04, *Regione autonoma della Sardegna v Commission*, [2005] II-34* para 51; Cases T-254/00, T-270/00 & T-277/00, *Hotel Cipriani SpA v Commission* [2008] ECR II-3269, para 208; Case T-379/09, *Italy v Commission* EU:T:2012:422, para 82.

[416] Case C-113/00, *Spain v Commission* [2002] ECR I-7601, para 39; Case T-109/01, *Fleuren Compost BV v Commission* [2004] ECR II-127, para 48.

[417] Case C-367/95P, *Commission v Sytraval* [1998] ECR I-1719, para 60; Case T-109/01, *Fleuren Compost BV v Commission* [2004] ECR II-127, para 49; Case T-25/07, *Iride SpA v Commission* [2009] ECR II-245, para 101; Case T-11/07, *Frucona Košice as v Commission* [2010] ECR II-5453, para 51.

[418] Cases C-278/92 to C-280/92, *Spain v Commission* [1994] ECR I-4103, para 31; Case T-318/00, *Freistaat Thüringen v Commission* [2005] ECR II-4179, para 88.

[419] Case T-151/11, *Telefónica de España SA v Commission* EU:T:2014:631, para 45.

[420] Cases T-102/07 & T-120/07, *Freistaat Sachsen v Commission* [2010] ECR II-585, para 120.

administrative procedure to make known in an effective manner its views on the truth and relevance of the facts, charges and circumstances relied on by the Commission.[421]   Since the administrative procedure regarding State aid is opened against the Member State concerned, it is clear that Member States have the right to be heard.   Comments received from any interested parties must be submitted to the Member State which has granted or intends to grant the aid in order to ensure that the right to be heard is effected.   The Member State may reply to the comments submitted within a prescribed period. Normally, this period should not exceed one month, although, in duly justified cases, the Commission may extend the period.   If an interested party so requests, on grounds of potential damage, its identity must be withheld from the Member State concerned.[422]

The Commission is not itself required to take a position during the formal investigation on comments received from interested parties, but it is required to submit to the Member State concerned the comments received so as to afford it an opportunity to comment further.[423]   In so far as the Member State has not been afforded the opportunity to comment on those observations on which the Commission proposes to base its decision, the Commission may not use them in its decision against the Member State.[424]   Where the Member State has been given notice to submit its comments, it has no subsequent right to be informed by the Commission of its position before adopting its decision, and it has no right to a hearing in this respect.[425]

The mere fact that, in the final decision, the Commission alters its analysis cannot entail infringement of the rights of the defence unless the information contained in the opening decision or, subsequently, provided during the administrative procedure, has not enabled the Member State to discuss properly all the matters contained in the final decision.   On the other hand, differences

---

[421]   Case C-301/87, *France* v *Commission* [1990] ECR I-307, para 29, Cases C-48/90 & C-66/90, *Netherlands* v *Commission* [1992] ECR I-565, para 44; Cases T-228/99 & T-233/99, *Westdeutsche Landesbank Girozentrale v Commission* [2003] ECR II-435, para 121; Case T-68/03, *Olympiaki Aeroporia Ypiresies AE v Commission* [2007] ECR II-2911, para 37; Case T-301/01, *Alitalia SpA v Commission* [2008] ECR II-1753, para 169; Cases T-309/04, T-317/04, T-329/04 & T-336/04, *TV2/Danmark A/S v Commission* [2008] ECR II-2935, para 136.

[422]   Council Regulation (EC) No 659/1999, Article 6(2).

[423]   Cases C-106/09P & C-107/09P, *Commission v Government of Gibraltar* [2011] ECR I-11113, para 178.

[424]   Case 234/84, *Belgium v Commission* [1986] ECR 2263, paras 27-29; Case 40/85, *Belgium v Commission* [1986] ECR 2321, paras 28-30; Case 259/85, *France v Commission* [1987] ECR 4393, para 12; Cases C-74/00P & C-75/00P, *Falck v Commission* [2002] ECR I-7869, para 81.   See also Case C-301/87, *France v Commission* [1990] ECR I-307, *per* Advocate General Jacobs, at p. 334.

[425]   Cases T-129/95, T-2/96 & T-97/96 *Neue Maxhütte Stahlwerke* v *Commission* [1999] ECR II-17, para 231; Case T-198/01, *Technische Glaswerke Ilmenau GmbH v Commission* [2004] ECR II-2717, para 156.

between the opening decision and the final decision, arising as a result of the Commission's review of the arguments put forward by the Member State, cannot give rise to infringement of the rights of the defence.[426]   Since the formal investigation may well have brought new facts to light, it follows that the final decision may contain findings that differ from those in the decision to open the formal investigation procedure.[427]   For example, in *Netherlands v Commission*, concerning funding for the public television network, differences between the facts relied on in the opening and final decisions resulted from data provided to the Commission after the opening decision.[428]   In *Diputación Foral de Bizkaia v Commission*, the mere fact that the Commission had not declared aid illegal in the opening decision but did make such a finding in the final decision was held by the General Court not to be a ground for annulment of the latter decision.[429]

Right of recipients and other interested parties to be heard   In the procedure for reviewing State aid, interested parties other than the Member State responsible for granting the aid cannot claim a right to debate the issues with the Commission in the same way as that Member State.[430]   Instead, they have, effectively, the role of a source of information for the Commission.[431]   It follows that undertakings that receive aid and local authorities within that State which grant the aid are considered, in the same way as competitors of the recipients of the aid, only to be interested parties in this procedure.[432]   Since

---

[426]   Cases T-427/04 & T-17/05, *France v Commission* [2009] ECR II-4315, para 138.

[427]   Case T-424/05, *Italy v Commission* [2009] ECR II-23*, para 69; Case T-387/11, *Nitrogénművek Vegyipari Zst v Commission* EU:T:2013:98, para 77; Case T-397/12, *Diputación Foral de Bizkaia v Commission* EU:T:2015:291, para 59.

[428]   Cases T-231/06 & T-237/06, *Netherlands v Commission* [2010] ECR II-5993, para 50.

[429]   Case T-397/12, *Diputación Foral de Bizkaia v Commission* EU:T:2015:291, para 65.

[430]   Cases C-74/00P & C-75/00P, *Falck v Commission* [2002] ECR I-7869, para 82; Cases C-106/09P & C-107/09P, *Commission v Government of Gibraltar* [2011] ECR I-11113, para 181; Case T-198/01, *Technische Glaswerke Ilmenau GmbH v Commission* [2004] ECR II-2717, paras 61 and 192; Case T-68/03, *Olympiaki Aeroporia Ypiresies AE v Commission* [2007] ECR II-2911, para 43; Cases T-427/04 & T-17/05, *France v Commission* [2009] ECR II-4315, para 149; Case T-62/08, *ThyssenKrupp Acciai Speciali Terni SpA v Commission* [2010] ECR II-3229, para 162; Case T-362/10, *Vtesse Networks Ltd v Commission* EU:T:2014:928, para 95; Case T-57/11, *Castelnou Energía v Commission* EU:T:2014:1021, para 115.

[431]   Cases T-371/94 & T-394/94, *British Airways v Commission* [1998] ECR II-2405, para 59; Cases T-228/99 & T-233/99, *Westdeutsche Landesbank Girozentrale v Commission* [2003] ECR II-435, para 125; Case T-198/01, *Technische Glaswerke Ilmenau GmbH v Commission* [2004] ECR II-2717, para 192; Case T-366/00, *Scott SA v Commission* [2007] ECR II-797, para 53; Case T-301/01, *Alitalia SpA v Commission* [2008] ECR II-1753, para 172; Case T-442/03, *SIC v Commission* [2008] ECR II-1161, para 222; Cases T-425/04 RENV & T-444/04 RENV, *France v Commission* EU:T:2015:450, para 161.

[432]   Case T-158/96, *Acciaierie di Bolzano SpA v Commission* [1999] ECR II-3927, para 42; Cases T-228/99 & T-233/99, *Westdeutsche Landesbank Girozentrale v Commission*

the procedure is not initiated against the recipient of the aid, it does not have a special role in the procedure and cannot rely on rights as extensive as the rights of the defendant Member State.[433] Where, for instance, the Commission published a notice in the *Official Journal of the European Union* inviting the beneficiaries of aid initially authorised by a previous decision to submit their observations on possible violation of the decision in question due to use of that aid in a manner contrary to that decision and those beneficiaries did not take advantage of that opportunity, the Commission did not violate any of their rights.[434] Moreover, the General Court has explicitly ruled that procedural rights in State aid matters cannot be extended on the basis of general principles of EU law, such as the right to be heard or sound administration.[435]

Nevertheless, beneficiaries, in particular, are entitled to rely on the principle that any person against whom an adverse decision may be taken must be given the opportunity to make his views known effectively regarding the facts held against him by the Commission as a basis for the disputed decision.[436] That principle will be infringed where the beneficiaries of aid to be recovered have not, in practice, been able to submit their observations in the course of the formal investigation because they had not been identified by the Commission in the initiating decision or at a later stage and where it cannot be excluded that had it not been for such an irregularity, the outcome of the procedure might have been different.[437] Furthermore, when requesting the production of and evaluating evidence, the Commission cannot assume that there is an identity of interest between the Member State and the recipient of aid. In particular with

---

[2003] ECR II-435, para 122; Case T-176/01, *Ferriere Nord SpA v Commission* [2004] ECR II-3931, para 74; Case T-354/99, *Kuwait Petroleum (Nederland) BV v Commission* [2006] ECR II-1475, para 80; Case T-301/01, *Alitalia SpA v Commission* [2008] ECR II-1753, para 155; Cases T-309/04, T-317/04, T-329/04 & T-336/04, *TV2/Danmark A/S v Commission* [2008] ECR II-2935, para 137; Cases T-267/08 & T-279/08, *Région Nord-Pas-de-Calais v Commission* [2011] ECR II-1999, para 71; Cases T-231/06 & T-237/06, *Netherlands v Commission* [2010] ECR II-5993, para 36.

[433] Cases C-74/00P & C-75/00P, *Falck v Commission* [2002] ECR I-7869, para 83; Case T-109/01, *Fleuren Compost BV v Commission* [2004] ECR II-127, para 44; Case T-354/99, *Kuwait Petroleum (Nederland) BV v Commission* [2006] ECR II-1475, para 80; Case T-366/00, *Scott SA v Commission* [2007] ECR II-797, para 54; Case T-198/01, *Technische Glaswerke Ilmenau GmbH v Commission* [2004] ECR II-2717, para 193.

[434] Cases C-74/00P & C-75/00P, *Falck v Commission* [2002] ECR I-7869, para 84; Case T-109/01, *Fleuren Compost BV v Commission* [2004] ECR II-127, para 47; Cases T-111/01 & T-133/01, *Saxonia Edelmetalle GmbH v Commission* [2005] ECR II-1579, para 53.

[435] Case T-62/08, *ThyssenKrupp Acciai Speciali Terni SpA v Commission* [2010] ECR II-3229, para 167; Case T-362/10, *Vtesse Networks Ltd v Commission* EU:T:2014:928, para 96.

[436] Cases C-48/90 & C-66/90, *Netherlands v Commission* [1992] ECR I-565, paras 50-51.

[437] Case T-34/02 *Le Levant 001 and Others v Commission* [2006] ECR II-267, para 97; Case T-68/03, *Olympiaki Aeroporia Ypiresies AE v Commission* [2007] ECR II-2911, para 42.

regard to the calculation of the value of the aid, and in light of the fact that the aid is reimbursed to the Member State in question and not to the European Union, the Commission cannot assume that a Member State has an interest in minimising the amount to be recovered in order to ensure that the recipient of the aid is treated in an equitable manner.[438]

The Commission must take account of the legitimate expectations which the parties concerned may entertain as a result of what was said in the decision to open the formal investigation procedure and must not base its final decision on the absence of elements which, in the light of those indications, the parties concerned were unable to consider that they must provide to it.[439] In *Ferriere Nord v Commission*, the General Court held that where there is a change in the relevant circumstances, such as where the Commission adopts fresh policy guidelines relating to the exercise of its discretion to permit aid, the parties concerned must have a further opportunity to submit their comments,[440] unless the Commission does not derive from the new guidelines any principles or criteria for assessment which would have altered its analysis of the aid.[441] This approach was approved by the ECJ on appeal.[442]

Right of interested parties to the extent appropriate Interested parties only have the right to be involved in the administrative procedure to the extent appropriate in the light of the circumstances of the case.[443] Thus, the Commission is not obliged to gather supplementary information from interested parties if it does not think it is useful.[444] In *British Airways v Commission*, the General Court observed that the Commission had been notified by France of aid which it intended to grant to Air France, together with

---

[438] Case T-366/00, *Scott SA v Commission* [2007] ECR II-797, para 59.

[439] Case T-6/99, *ESF v Commission* [2001] ECR II-1523, para 126; Case T-176/01, *Ferriere Nord SpA v Commission* [2004] ECR II-3931, para 88; Case T-25/04, *González y Díez SA v Commission* [2007] ECR II-3121, para 125.

[440] Case T-176/01, *Ferriere Nord SpA v Commission* [2004] ECR II-3931, para 75.

[441] *Ibid.*, para 80.

[442] Case C-49/05P, *Ferriere Nord SpA v Commission* [2008] ECR I-68*, para 71; Case C-334/07P, *Commission v Freistaat Sachsen* [2008] ECR I-9465, para 56.

[443] Cases C-74/00P & C-75/00P, *Falck v Commission* [2002] ECR I-7869, para 83; Case C-49/05P, *Ferriere Nord SpA v Commission* [2008] ECR I-68*, para 69; Case C-521/06P, *Athinaïki Techniki v Commission* [2008] ECR I-5829, para 38; Cases T-371/94 & T-394/94, *British Airways v Commission* [1998] ECR II-2405, para 60; Case T-613/97, *Ufex v Commission* [2000] ECR II-4055, para 89; Case T-198/01R, *Technische Glaswerke Ilmenau GmbH v Commission* [2002] ECR II-2153, para 81; Cases T-228/99 & T-233/99, *Westdeutsche Landesbank Girozentrale v Commission* [2003] ECR II-435, para 125; Cases T-309/04, T-317/04, T-329/04 & T-336/04, *TV2/Danmark A/S v Commission* [2008] ECR II-2935, para 137; Cases T-267/08 & T-279/08, *Région Nord-Pas-de-Calais v Commission* [2011] ECR II-1999, para 78; Case T-488/11, *Sarc BV v Commission* EU:T:2014:497, para 79; Case T-362/10, *Vtesse Networks Ltd v Commission* EU:T:2014:928, para 95.

[444] Case T-387/11, *Nitrogénművek Vegyipari Zst v Commission* EU:T:2013:98, para 118.

supporting documentation, and the relevant Commission departments had held a series of meetings with French officials. The amount of information in the Commission's possession was, therefore, already relatively extensive, leaving outstanding only a small number of doubts which information supplied by interested parties might have dispelled. While providing such parties with general information on the essentials of the planned aid, therefore, the Commission was entitled to confine itself to concentrating its communication in the *Official Journal of the European Union* on those aspects of the plan concerning which it still harboured doubts.[445]

Similarly, in *Westdeutsche Landesbank Girozentrale v Commission* the General Court, in rejecting an allegation of infringement of the right to be heard, considered the fact that the applicants had been able, in meetings with the Commission, to discuss various aspects of the case and to present supporting documents to the Commission. [446] In the *Olympic Airways* case, where the applicant argued that it was the sole possible source of the evidence which the Commission considered necessary, the General Court held that this did not justify the Commission having to ask it for information since it was in principle for the Member State concerned to provide the Commission with all the necessary information. Under those circumstances, the applicant's procedural rights could be affected neither by the Commission's alleged failure to identify the essential evidence necessary to still its doubts nor by the absence of requests for additional information. Moreover, the applicant was able to take part indirectly in the administrative procedure, through the intermediary of Greece, which was its sole shareholder. In addition, the Olympic Airways' management had taken part in the meetings between the Commission's staff and the Greek authorities throughout the administrative procedure.[447]

Another reason for restricting the extent of the rights of interested parties to participate in the administrative procedure results from the requirements of professional secrecy imposed on the Commission.[448] It follows that interested parties are not entitled to receive documents containing business secrets.[449] Nor is the Commission obliged to grant access to the non-confidential part of the file.[450] In view of the limited nature of their rights to participation and to information, the Commission is not obliged to forward to interested parties the observations or information it has received from the Member State

---

[445] Cases T-371/94 & T-394/94, *British Airways v Commission* [1998] ECR II-2405, para 62.
[446] Cases T-228/99 & T-233/99, *Westdeutsche Landesbank Girozentrale v Commission* [2003] ECR II-435, paras 127-129.
[447] Case T-68/03, *Olympiaki Aeroporia Ypiresies AE v Commission* [2007] ECR II-2911, paras 44-45.
[448] Article 339 TFEU; Council Regulation (EC) No 659/1999, Article 24.
[449] Cases T-371/94 & T-394/94, *British Airways v Commission* [1998] ECR II-2405, para 63.
[450] Case T-198/01, *Technische Glaswerke Ilmenau GmbH v Commission* [2004] ECR II-2717, para 198; Cases T-494/08 to T-500/08 & T-509/08, *Ryanair Ltd v Commission* [2010] ECR II-5723, paras 70.

concerned.[451] Nevertheless, the General Court has held, drawing on the European Charter of Fundamental Rights, that the Commission must carry out its investigations in a manner which is impartial as between all the relevant interested parties.[452] In *Technische Glaswerke Ilmenau GmbH v Commission*, it held that, notwithstanding the restrictive character of the recipient's rights to information and participation, the Commission could be required to forward to it on request the observations which a competitor had made on the recipient's own submissions which had been made to the Commission in the course of its investigation.[453]

Right of access to documents Article 15(3) TFEU confers on any citizen of the European Union, and any natural or legal person residing or having its registered office in a Member State, a right of access to European Parliament, Council and Commission documents, subject to the principles and the conditions laid down by the Council for reasons of public or private interest. European Parliament and Council Regulation (EC) No 1049/2001, which grants access to documents held by the European Parliament, Council and Commission, applies to State aid control.[454] Article 4(2), however, provides that access shall be refused where disclosure would undermine the protection of court proceedings and legal advice or the purpose of inspections and investigations, unless there is an overriding public interest in disclosure.

In *Technische Glaswerke Ilmenau v Commission*, the Commission had opened a formal investigation into aid granted by Germany, during which the recipient requested the Commission to give it access on a non-confidential basis to its file, which request was rejected. The General Court held that the right of access applied in State aid cases, and that the Commission was entitled to rely on Article 4(2) only if it had previously assessed, firstly, whether access to the document would specifically and actually undermine the protected interest and, secondly, whether there was no overriding public interest in disclosure.[455] On appeal, however, the ECJ held that it is, in principle, open to the Commission to base its decisions in that regard on general presumptions which apply to certain categories of documents, as considerations of a generally similar kind are likely to apply to requests for disclosure relating to documents of the same nature. As regards procedures for reviewing State aid,

---

[451] Case T-613/97, *Ufex v Commission* [2000] ECR II-4055, para 90; Cases T-267/08 & T-279/08, *Région Nord-Pas-de-Calais v Commission* [2011] ECR II-1999, para 75.

[452] Article 41(1) of the European Charter of Fundamental Rights provides that everyone has the right to have his affairs treated impartially and without discrimination by the European Union institutions.

[453] Case T-198/01R, *Technische Glaswerke Ilmenau GmbH v Commission* [2002] ECR II-2153, para 85.

[454] See, for example, Case T-76/02, *Messina v Commission* [2003] ECR II-3203.

[455] Case T-237/02, *Technische Glaswerke Ilmenau v Commission* [2006] ECR II-5131, para 76.

such general presumptions may arise from Regulation (EC) No 659/1999, Article 20 of which did not lay down any right of access to documents for interested parties in the context of the formal investigation procedure. It follows that there is a general presumption that disclosure of documents in the administrative file in principle would undermine protection of the objectives of investigation activities, although this does not exclude the right of interested parties to demonstrate that a given document is not covered by that presumption, or that there is a higher public interest justifying the disclosure of the document concerned by virtue of Article 4(2) of Regulation (EC) No 1049/2001.[456]

These principles apply equally where the Commission has taken a decision which has closed the investigation, at least where legal proceedings are pending.[457]

Duration of formal investigation procedure It is a general principle of EU law that the fundamental requirement of legal certainty has the effect of preventing the Commission from indefinitely delaying the exercise of its powers, so that the conduct of an administrative procedure should be of reasonable duration.[458] The decision bringing the formal investigation procedure to an end must, therefore, be taken by the Commission within a reasonable period and, in any event, as soon as the Commission's doubts as to the compatibility of the measure with the internal market have been removed,[459] so that the Commission is not entitled to open the formal investigation procedure and then leave it in abeyance or postpone a decision indefinitely.[460] In the case of existing aid or unnotified aid, where the aid scheme is already operational, the Commission cannot be required to extend the formal investigation to consider any subsequent modifications made by the Member State, as this would enable the Member State to draw out the procedure for as long as it pleased and thereby postpone the adoption of a final

---

[456] Case C-139/07P, *Technische Glaswerke Ilmenau v Commission* [2010] ECR I-5885, paras 54-62; Cases C-514/11P & C-605/11P, *LPN v Commission* EU:C:2013:738, para 56; Case C-365/12P, *Commission v Energie Baden-Württemberg AG* EU:C:2014:112, para 80; Cases T-494/08 to T-500/08 & T-509/08, *Ryanair Ltd v Commission* [2010] ECR II-5723, paras 70-72; Cases T-109/05 & T-444/05, *Navigazione Libera del Golfo srl v Commission* [2011] ECR II-2479, paras 131-133; Case T-456/13, *Sea Handling SpA v Commission* EU:T:2015:185, paras 50-68.

[457] Case T-456/13, *Sea Handling SpA v Commission* EU:T:2015:185, paras 70-72.

[458] Case C-74/00P & C-75/00P, *Falck and Acciaierie di Bolzano v Commission* [2002] ECR I-7869, para 140; Cases C-346/03 & C-529/03, *Atzeni v Regione aotonoma della Sardegna* [2006] ECR I-1875, para 61; Case T-190/00, *Regione Siciliana v Commission* [2003] ECR II-5015, para 136; Case T-171/02, *Regione autonoma della Sardegna v Commission* [2005] ECR II-2123, para 53.

[459] Case 59/79, *Fédération Nationale des Producteurs de Vins de Table et Vins de Pays v Commission* [1979] ECR 2425, para 2.

[460] Case 223/85, *RSV v Commission* [1987] ECR 4617, *per* Advocate General Slynn, at p. 4644.

decision.[461]   In accordance with the Code of Best Practice, however, the Commission, in exceptional circumstances and by common agreement with the Member State concerned, may suspend the formal investigation. Suspension might occur if, for example, the Member State formally request a suspension in order to bring its project into line with State aid rules, or if there is pending litigation in the EU courts regarding similar issues.[462]

Reasonableness of the duration of the procedure is to be determined in relation to the particular circumstances of the case and, in particular, its context, the complexity of the case and its importance to the parties involved.[463]   Council Regulation (EC) No 659/1999, Article 7(6) provides, in the case of notified aid and review of existing aid, that the Commission must as far as possible endeavour to adopt a decision within a period of 18 months from the opening of the procedure, although this time limit may be extended by internal agreement between the Commission and the Member State concerned.[464]   This time limit is not applicable in the case of unlawful aid or misuse of aid,[465] although once unlawful aid has been recovered, the Commission is to take a decision within the time limits applicable to notified aid.[466]

In any event, the period of 18 months is merely indicative, so that taking a final decision within 18 months is merely an objective and not mandatory.[467] Even a period of over 33 months was not excessive, where the length could be attributed to the delay in the Member State providing information.[468]   Once the 18 months time limit has expired, and should the Member State concerned so request, the Commission must, within two months, take a decision on the basis of the information available to it.   If appropriate, where the information provided is not sufficient to establish compatibility with the internal market,

---

[461]   Cases C-15/98 & C-105/98, *Italy v Commission* [2000] ECR I-8855, para 43.

[462]   Code of Best Practice, para 41.

[463]   Case T-95/96, *Gestevisión Telecinco SA v Commission*, [1998] ECR II-3407, para 75; Case T-190/00, *Regione Siciliana v Commission* [2003] ECR II-5015, para 136.

[464]   Council Regulation (EC) No 659/1999, Article 7(6); cf. Article 19(2). The Commission has stated that it endeavours to come to a decision within four months after the submission of the last information from the Member State: Code of Best Practice, para 44,

[465]   *Ibid.*, Article 13(2); cf. Article 16. Cases C-630/11P to C-633/11P, *HGA srl v Commission* EU:C:2013:387, para 74; Cases T-394/08, T-408/08, T-453/08 & T-454/08, *Regione autonoma della Sardegna v Commission* [2011] ECR II-6255, para 101.

[466]   Council Regulation (EC) No 659/1999, Article 11(2).

[467]   Case C-49/05P, *Ferriere Nord SpA v Commission* [2008] ECR I-68*, para 51; Case T-190/00, *Regione Siciliana v Commission* [2003] ECR II-5015, para 139; Case T-176/01, *Ferriere Nord SpA v Commission* [2004] ECR II-3931, para 69; Case T-171/02, *Regione autonoma della Sardegna v Commission* [2005] ECR II-2123, para 56; Case T-301/01, *Alitalia SpA v Commission* [2008] ECR II-1753, para 160.

[468]   Cases C-346/03 & C-529/03, *Atzeni v Regione aotonoma della Sardegna* [2006] ECR I-1875, para 62; Case T-171/02, *Regione autonoma della Sardegna v Commission* [2005] ECR II-2123, para 60.

the Commission must take a negative decision finding the aid incompatible with the internal market.[469]

Decision terminating the formal investigation procedure In the case of new aid, if a notification is withdrawn, the Commission closes the formal investigation procedure[470] and publishes a short notice to that effect in the *Official Journal of the European Union*.[471] Otherwise, the formal investigation procedure must be closed by means of a decision pursuant to Regulation (EC) No 659/1999, Article 7.[472] The Commission may decide that the measure does not constitute aid[473] or, where appropriate following modification by the Member State concerned, it may take a positive or conditional decision that the measure is aid but that the doubts as to its compatibility with the internal market have been removed.[474] Alternatively, the Commission may take a negative decision finding that the aid is not compatible with the internal market.[475]

Since the Commission must actually take a decision, mere silence after a certain period of time cannot be construed as implied approval.[476] The decision must be published in the *Official Journal of the European Union*.[477] Any interested party which has submitted comments to the Commission in respect of the measure and any beneficiary of individual aid are sent copies of the decision.[478]

If a conditional or negative decision is taken in relation to unlawful aid or misused aid, the Member State concerned may be ordered to alter or abolish the aid immediately without the Commission, as in the case of existing aid, having to fix a period of time for this purpose.[479] At its request, any interested party may obtain a copy of the decision.[480] Where the Commission has acted on a complaint, it must send a copy of the decision to the complainant.[481]

Corrective decision during administrative procedure Regulation (EC) No 659/1999 does not expressly provide for any mechanism for corrective decisions to be taken by the Commission during the course of the assessment

---

[469] Council Regulation (EC) No 659/1999, Article 7(7).
[470] Council Regulation (EC) No 659/1999, Article 8(1)-(2).
[471] *Ibid.*, Article 26(4).
[472] *Ibid.*, Article 7(1).
[473] *Ibid.*, Article 7(2).
[474] *Ibid.*, Article 7(3)-(4).
[475] *Ibid.*, Article 7(5).
[476] Case T-171/02, *Regione autonoma della Sardegna v Commission* [2005] ECR II-2123, para 69.
[477] Council Regulation (EC) No 659/1999, Article 26(3).
[478] *Ibid.*, Article 20(1).
[479] Case 173/73, *Italy v Commission* [1974] ECR 709, para 9.
[480] Council Regulation (EC) No 659/1999, Article 20(3).
[481] *Ibid.*, Article 20(2).

procedures.[482] Nevertheless, there may be cases, exceptionally, where a preliminary decision opening a formal investigation procedure may need to be revisited. In *HGA v Commission*, the Italian authorities, which had notified a scheme of aid for hotels in Sardinia, adopted an additional measure which provided for an extension of the approved aid scheme to an earlier date. Following a complaint against alleged misuse of aid through the initial aid scheme, the Commission opened a formal investigation into the application of the aid scheme for projects commenced prior to the date specified in the approval decision. Subsequently, the Commission became aware of the additional Italian measure that had not been notified. It adopted a fresh opening decision correcting and extending the formal investigation in order specifically to refer to that additional measure as an allegation of new aid rather than misuse of aid. The ECJ held that the Commission was entitled to correct or, where necessary, extend the formal investigation procedure, if it discovers that the initial decision to open that procedure was based on an incomplete set of facts or on an incorrect legal characterisation of those facts. As long as the procedural rights of the parties were not undermined, considerations of procedural economy and the principle of sound administration highlighted the preferability of the adoption of a corrective decision over the closure of the procedure and the subsequent opening of a fresh procedure, which would have led, in essence, to the adoption of a decision having the same content as the corrective decision.[483]

Where the Commission has at any stage acted unlawfully in the procedure for taking a decision, it may withdraw the decision and replace it with a fresh decision. In this regard, the requirements of good administration and legal certainty and the principle of effective legal protection require that the procedure for replacing the illegal measure should be resumed at the point at which the illegality occurred and the Commission is precluded from recommencing the procedure by going back further than that precise point.[484] In *Athinaiki Techniki v Commission*, the Commission, which had been deemed to have taken a decision that closed the preliminary assessment, sought to reopen the preliminary assessment procedure by requiring further evidence from the complainant. The ECJ held that it was not open to the Commission to do so and that, since the preliminary assessment was in fact completed, it could

---

[482] Cases C-630/11P to C-633/11P, *HGA srl v Commission* EU:C:2013:387, para 50.

[483] *Ibid.*, paras 51-52; Cases T-394/08, T-408/08, T-453/08 & T-454/08, *Regione autonoma della Sardegna v Commission* [2011] ECR II-6255, para 72; Cases T-425/04 RENV & T-444/04 RENV, *France v Commission* EU:T:2015:450, para.

[484] Case C-362/09P, *Athinaiki Teckniki AE v Commission* [2010] ECR I-13275, para 70; Case C-389/11P, *Région Nord-Pas-de-Calais v Commission* EU:C:2012:408, para 112; Case T-301/01, *Alitalia SpA v Commission* [2008] ECR I-1753, paras 99 and 142; Cases T-267/08 & T-279/08, *Région Nord-Pas-de-Calais v Commission* [2011] ECR II-1999, para 83.

only continue the procedure by taking a fresh decision to close the preliminary assessment procedure.[485]

Decision approving the measure   Where the Commission finds that the measure does not constitute aid within the meaning of Article 107(1) TFEU, it must record that finding by way of a decision.[486]   For an aid to come within the scope of Article 107(1), it must fulfil all the criteria laid down in that provision.[487]   Thus where a measure otherwise constitutes an aid, it will not fall within the scope of Article 107(1) TFEU if it is not granted by a Member State or through State resources, or if it does not distort or threaten to distort competition, or if it does not favour certain undertakings or the production of certain goods, or if it does not affect trade between Member States.

Where the Commission finds that a measure constitutes aid but that the doubts as to its compatibility with the internal market have been removed, it must take a positive decision that the aid is compatible with the internal market. That decision must specify which exception under the FEU Treaty has been applied.[488]

Conditional decision   The Commission may attach to a positive decision conditions subject to which an aid may be considered compatible with the internal market and may lay down obligations to enable compliance with the decision to be monitored.[489]   Conditions may be specified directly by the decision itself or by reference to other, more general, measures. For instance, in *TWD v Commission*, the Commission was entitled to authorise payment of aid to Textilwerke Deggendorf on condition that previous illegally paid aid was first repaid.[490]   In *CIRFS v Commission*, a decision permitting a scheme of regional State aid in France was conditional in that it was specified to be without prejudice to compliance with present or future special rules on aid to particular industries. The subsequent grant by the French authorities within the relevant region of individual aid which was incompatible with established rules controlling aid to the textile industry because of over-capacity was held not to fall within the scope of the approval decision. The ECJ rejected an argument that the rules, which were contained in a discipline agreed between the Commission and the Member States, constituted no more than guidelines which merely set out the conduct which the Commission intended to follow.

---

[485] Case C-362/09P, *Athinaiki Teckniki AE v Commission* [2010] ECR I-13275, paras 68-74.
[486] Council Regulation (EC) No 659/1999, Article 7(2).
[487] *Ibid.*, Article 1(a).
[488] *Ibid.*, Article 7(3).
[489] *Ibid.*, Article 7(4).
[490] Case C-355/95P, *TWD v Commission* [1997] ECR I-2549, para 27.

Rather, the rules constituted a measure of general application, the terms of which had objective significance and were of binding effect.[491]

Negative final decision Where the Commission finds that new aid is not compatible with the internal market, it must take a negative final decision that the aid may not be put into effect.[492] In the case of existing aid, the decision must order the State concerned to alter or abolish the aid.[493] Such a decision can only take effect on condition that the Commission indicates to the Member State concerned those aspects of the aid which are regarded as incompatible with the FEU Treaty and therefore subject to abolition or alteration.[494] Where the Commission orders the abolition of aid without stipulating how this is to be achieved, the fact that the Member State has a discretion in choosing how to achieve that objective does not invalidate the decision, since it merely leaves to the Member State itself the method of implementing the decision.[495] On the other hand, in *Commission v Germany*, Germany was held not to be bound by a Commission decision, which ordered the termination of non-selective aid whilst implicitly approving the continuing grant of selective aid, on the ground that the Commission had not indicated the grounds of selectivity to be applied.[496] Where the Commission requires in its decision that the legislative provisions giving rise to aid be abolished, the Member State concerned is under an obligation to ensure their formal repeal.[497] A Member State is entitled to take the view that it has complied with a decision to abolish aid where it has taken *bona fide* steps to abolish the provisions giving rise to the aid. If it replaces those provisions with other financial measures, the Commission always has the power to consider that new aid has been granted and to act accordingly.[498]

Period of time to alter or abolish existing aid Because the procedure in Article 108(2) TFEU is based on the idea of cooperation, the Commission, in the case of existing aids, must allow the Member State concerned a period of time within which to comply with the decision taken.[499] Where the Commission does not fix the period within which the aid must be discontinued but sets a date by which it must be informed of the action taken in that regard,

---

[491] Case C-313/90, *CIRFS v Commission* [1993] ECR I-1125, paras 32-36, 44.

[492] Council Regulation (EC) No 659/1999, Article 7(5).

[493] Article 108(2) TFEU.

[494] Case 70/72, *Commission v Germany* [1973] ECR 813, para 20; Case 52/84, *Commission v Belgium* [1986] ECR 89, para 9.

[495] Cases 67, 68 & 70/85, *Van der Kooy v Commission* [1988] ECR 219, para 66.

[496] Case 70/72, *Commission v Germany* [1973] ECR 813, para 23.

[497] Case 130/83, *Commission v Italy* [1984] ECR 2849, para 7.

[498] Case 213/85, *Commission v Netherlands* [1988] ECR 281, para 31, and *per* Advocate General Slynn, at p. 294.

[499] Case 173/73, *Italy v Commission* [1974] ECR 709, para 7.

that date constitutes the time limit within which the decision must be implemented.[500] The length of time given to the Member State to comply with the decision is a matter within the discretion of the Commission, taking into account, in particular, the domestic procedures necessary for the implementation of its decision. On the other hand, if the implementation of the decision can be effected by simple administrative measures, capable of being taken immediately, there seems to be no reason why the Commission should not insist that those measures are taken as quickly as possible, or that they are at least taken without unjustifiable delay.[501] Thus, if aid takes the forms of financial payments being made directly by the Member State, no more monies should be paid out. If the aid takes the form of a tariff laid down establishing the price of goods or services, then that tariff must be abolished and replaced. Such a process may not be able to be effected immediately, but the necessary action must nevertheless be taken with the requisite speed.[502]

Transitional measures when altering or abolishing existing aid   Since a decision to allow aid under Article 107(3) TFEU constitutes a derogation from the general rule that State aid is incompatible with the internal market, the duration of its validity must be limited.[503]   Given that such decisions must be interpreted restrictively, it follows that an operator cannot reasonably expect that the decision would authorise aid after the expiry of the period covered by the decision. Nor could it legitimately expect that the Commission will grant a fresh authorisation of the aid after the expiry of that period.[504]   Similarly, a refusal of the Commission to permit aid to operators making applications after the end of that period does not infringe the principle of equal treatment as, by definition, any authorisation of limited duration gives rise to unequal treatment according to whether a given situation does or does not come within the temporal scope of that decision and is, accordingly, objectively justifiable.[505] Equally, where the Commission opens a formal investigation into an existing aid scheme, a diligent economic operator can no longer have a legitimate expectation that the aid regime will remain in force.[506]

The Commission must, nevertheless, take account of the legitimate interests of aid recipients when ordering the alteration or abolition of existing aid.

---

[500]   Case 213/85, *Commission v Netherlands* [1988] ECR 281, para 19.

[501]   Case 70/72, *Commission v Germany* [1973] ECR 813, *per* Advocate General Mayras, at p. 842.

[502]   Case 213/85, *Commission v Netherlands* [1988] ECR 281, *per* Advocate General Slynn, at p. 290.

[503]   Case C-67/09P, *Nuova Agricast srl v Commission* [2010] ECR I-9811, para 80.

[504]   *Ibid.*, para 74.

[505]   *Ibid.*, para 80; Case C-167/11P, *Cantiere Navale De Poli SpA v Commission* EU:C:2012:164, para 76.

[506]   Case C-129/12, *Magdeburger Mühlenwerke v Finanzamt Magdeburg* EU:C:2013:200, para 47.

Failure to do so will infringe the principle of legal certainty and the protection of legitimate expectations, unless there is some overriding public interest.[507] In *Belgium and Forum 187 v Commission*, the Commission had initially determined that the tax treatment of coordination centres for multinationals under Belgian legislation did not constitute State aid. On a subsequent reappraisal, it decided that the measures in Belgium and the Netherlands did constitute State aid which distorted competition and ordered their abolition. The limited transitional provisions in the Commission's decisions were challenged as infringing the legitimate expectations of certain of those companies that had expected their authorisation to be renewed. It was held that the centres were entitled to expect that a Commission decision reversing its previous approach would give them the time necessary to address that change in approach. It followed that the centres with an application for renewal pending on the date when the Commission's decision was notified were entitled to have a legitimate expectation that a reasonable transitional period would be granted in order for them to adjust to the consequences of that decision.[508] Moreover, the fact that transitional provisions were adopted in respect of some coordination centres meant that the failure to provide similar arrangements for other centres amounted to an infringement of the principle of equal treatment.[509]

By contrast, the ECJ, overturning the General Court, held that certain Netherlands centres were unable to rely on the principle of legitimate expectation where they had merely submitted a request for authorisation, as opposed to renewal, prior to the Commission's decision. Those centres that had requested a first authorisation were not in the same position as those that were already beneficiaries under the scheme.[510] Similarly, the argument that the Commission had infringed the principle of equal treatment was dismissed on the basis that the difference in treatment was justified.[511] In *Magdeburger Mühlenwerke v Finanzamt Magdeburg*, a German regional aid scheme operated on the basis of granting aid after the investment was complete, so that an operator would take the decision to invest on the basis that payment of the aid would be made on completion of the investment operation. Following a

---

[507] Case 74/74, *CNTA v Commission* [1975] ECR 533, para 44; Cases C-182/03 & C-217/03, *Belgium and Forum 187 ASBL v Commission* [2006] ECR I-5479, para 148-149; Case C-519/07P, *Commission v Koninklijke Friesland Campina NV* [2009] ECR I-8495, para 85; Case C-67/09P *Nuova Agricast srl v Commission* [2010] ECR I-9811, para 69; Case T-348/03, *Koninklijke Friesland Foods NV v Commission* [2007] ECR II-101*, para 127.

[508] Cases C-182/03 & C-217/03, *Belgium and Forum 187 ASBL v Commission* [2006] ECR I-5479, para 163.

[509] *Ibid.*, para 173.

[510] Case C-519/07P, *Commission v Koninklijke Friesland Campina NV* [2009] ECR I-8495, paras 88-94.

[511] *Ibid.*, para 102.

decision by the Commission ruling that the aid was incompatible with the
internal market in respect of certain types of investment operations, the
scheme, which constituted existing aid, was amended, without any transitional
provisions covering operators who had taken an investment decision but had
not yet completed the investment operation. The ECJ merely noted that no
transitional provisions were in place and held that the operators could not, once
the formal investigation procedure had been commenced, rely on any
legitimate expectation that the aid scheme would continue.[512]

16.8 *EX POST* CONTROLS

Reporting requirements imposed on Member States Member States must
submit to the Commission annual reports on all existing aid schemes. Where,
despite a reminder, the Member State concerned fails to submit an annual
report in respect of any specific scheme, the Commission may proceed to
propose any appropriate measures.[513]   Commission Regulation (EU) No
651/2014 requires the Member States to provide annual reports in respect of
the application of aid covered by the block exemption.[514] Similar requirements
apply pursuant to the various guidelines and frameworks pursuant to which
notified aid may be declared compatible with the internal market.

Ex post **State aid monitoring**   Monitoring and follow-up of State aid
expenditure have long been essential components of EU State aid control
policy. The Commission has launched regular *ex post* monitoring exercises
since 2006 in order to ensure effective enforcement of the State aid rules, in
particular since an increasing number of aid measures are covered by the block
exemption regulation. Monitoring implies a check at two levels: first, at the
level of the general legislation in order to determine that it is compatible with
the approved scheme or the block exemption; secondly, a few significant
individual applications of the national aid measure are examined in detail to
ensure compliance with, for example, eligible costs and maximum aid
intensities.

Where the Commission has serious doubts as to whether its decisions not to
raise objections, or positive decisions or conditional decisions with regard to
individual aid, are being complied with, the Member State concerned, after
having been given the opportunity to submit its comments, must allow the

---

[512] Case C-129/12, *Magdeburger Mühlenwerke v Finanzamt Magdeburg* EU:C:2013:200,
para 47. It may be noted that this case involved a reference from a German court in
which the applicant sought payment of the aid and that no challenge had been made to
the Commission decision itself for failing to provide for transitional measures.

[513] Council Regulation (EC) No 659/1999, Article 21.

[514] Council Regulation (EU) No 651/2014, Article 11.

Commission to undertake on-site monitoring visits pursuant to Council Regulation (EC) No 659/1999, Article 22. The officials authorised by the Commission are empowered, in order to verify compliance with the decisions concerned, to enter premises and land of the undertaking concerned, to ask for oral explanations on the spot and to examine books and other business records and take, or demand, copies.[515] The Commission must inform the Member State concerned in good time and in writing of the intended visit. If the Member State has any duly justified objection to the Commission's choice of experts, the experts are to be appointed in internal agreement with the Member State. Officials authorised by the Member State may be present at the monitoring visit.[516]

Where an undertaking opposes a monitoring visit, the Member State must afford the necessary assistance to the Commission officials and experts to enable them to carry out the visit.[517] The Commission must provide the Member State with a copy of any report produced as a result of the visit.[518] The Commission is not obliged to instigate an on-site monitoring visit, particularly where it already has sufficient information to enable it to take a decision.[519] Although on-site monitoring visits are recognised as being particularly appropriate in cases of alleged misuse of aid, the Commission is not obliged to order such a visit prior to taking its decision where it has no serious doubts that the beneficiary has not complied with the approval decision.[520]

***Ex post* State aid evaluation** The Commission has also introduced a system of *ex post* evaluation of State aid measures. Typically, the assessment of aid schemes *ex ante* is performed without sufficient evaluation of their actual impact on markets over time. The overall objective of *ex post* State aid evaluation is to assess the relative positive and negative effects of aid schemes that have been put into effect. Based on this assessment, the evaluation can confirm whether the assumptions underlying the *ex ante* approval of the scheme remain valid and can help improve the design of future aid schemes and rules governing State aid.

A common methodology for State aid evaluation was established by the Commission in 2014 in the context of the State aid modernisation programme. This is intended to ensure that schemes financed by State aid are more effective and create less distortion on the market, as well as to improve the efficiency of

---

[515] Council Regulation (EC) No 659/1999, Article 22(1)-(2).

[516] *Ibid.*, Article 22(3)-(4).

[517] *Ibid.*, Article 22(6).

[518] *Ibid.*, Article 22(5).

[519] Cases T-111/01 & T-133/01, *Saxonia Edelmetalle GmbH v Commission* [2005] ECR II-1579, para 98.

[520] Council Regulation (EC) No 659/1999, Article 22(1) and Recital 20; Cases T-111/01 & T-133/01, *Saxonia Edelmetalle GmbH v Commission* [2005] ECR II-1579, para 100.

future schemes. Evaluation should also allow the direct incentive effect of aid on the beneficiary to be assessed and examine the proportionality and appropriateness of the scheme. The exercise should normally allow for ongoing evaluations, to be conducted while the scheme is in operation rather than purely *ex post*. [521]

---

[521] SWD(2014) 179 final.

Chapter Seventeen

RECOVERY OF UNLAWFUL AID

17.1 RECOVERY OF UNLAWFUL OR MISUSED AID

Suspension and recovery of unlawful or misused aid In line with the principle of effectiveness, the Commission's powers under Article 108(3) TFEU are to be given a broad interpretation in view of the essential importance of those provisions for ensuring the proper functioning of the internal market.[1] In *Commission v Germany*, the ECJ held that to be of practical effect, an order for the abolition of unlawful aid may include an order for recovery.[2] Following the decisions in *France v Commission*[3] and in *Belgium v Commission*[4] and in accordance with Regulation (EC) No 659/1999, Article 14(1), it is now settled law that the recovery of unlawful aid is the logical consequence of a finding that it is unlawful and incompatible with the internal market, so that the Commission must order recovery.[5] It is only in exceptional circumstances that it would be inappropriate to order repayment of aid.[6] In similar vein, misused aid is also subject to recovery.[7] The Commission, however, has no power to make a recovery order in the case of unnotified aid which is subsequently determined to be compatible with the internal market.

---

[1] Case C-301/87, *France v Commission* [1990] ECR I-307, *per* Advocate General Jacobs, at p. 340.

[2] Case 70/72, *Commission v Germany* [1973] ECR 813, para 13; Cases C-328/99 and C-399/00 *Italy* v *Commission* [2003] ECR I-4035, para 65; Case C-277/00 *Germany* v *Commission* [2004] ECR I-3925, para 73.

[3] Case C-301/87, *France v Commission* [1990] ECR I-307, para 22.

[4] Case 142/87, *Belgium v Commission* [1990] ECR I-959, para 18.

[5] Case C-183/91, *Commission v Greece* [1993] ECR I-3131, para 16; Case C-404/87, *Commission v Portugal* [2000] ECR I-4897, para 38; Case C-261/99, *Commission v France* [2001] ECR I-2537, para 22; Case C-390/98, *HJ Banks & Co Ltd. v Coal Authority* [2001] ECR I-6117, para 74; Case C-99/02, *Commission v Italy* [2004] ECR I-3353, para 15; Case C-277/00, *Germany* v *Commission* [2004] ECR I-3925, para 74; Case C-529/09, *Commission v Spain* EU:C:2013:31, para 90; Case C-674/13, *Commission v Germany* EU:C:2015:302, para 37.

[6] Case C-5/89, *Commission v Germany* [1990] ECR I-3925, para 16; Case C-39/94, *SFEI v La Poste* [1996] ECR I-3547, para 70; Case C-199/06, *CELF v SIDE* [2008] ECR I-469, para 42; Case C-275/10, *Residex Capital IV CV v Gemeente Rotterdam* [2011] ECR I-13043, para 35.

[7] Council Regulation (EC) No 659/1999, Article 16, cf. Article 14(1); Cases T-111/01 & T-133/01, *Saxonia Edelmetalle GmbH v Commission* [2005] ECR II-1579, para 115.

Recovery of aid granted prior to Commission approval may, however, be enforced through national court proceedings.[8]

In *France v Commission*, the ECJ instituted a system of protective interim measures which it regarded as necessary in cases where the practices engaged in by the Member States of implementing aid without notifying the Commission rendered nugatory the system established by Article 108 TFEU. The power to issue injunctions suspending unlawful aid is now encapsulated in Council Regulation (EC) No 659/1999, Article 11(1). Once it has been established that aid has been granted or altered without notification or that aid has been misused, the Commission may issue an injunction requiring the Member State to suspend the aid until the Commission has taken a decision on the compatibility of the aid with the internal market.[9] Furthermore, in the case of unlawful aid, although not in the case of misuse of aid, Regulation (EC) No 659/1999, Article 11(2) provides that the Commission may also issue an injunction requiring the Member State provisionally to recover the aid until the Commission has taken a final decision on the compatibility of the aid.[10] A provisional recovery order may be issued only if the following criteria are all fulfilled: according to established practice, there must be no doubts about the aid character of the measure; there must be an urgency to act; and there must be a serious risk of substantial and irreparable damage to a competitor.[11] Before issuing a suspension injunction or a recovery injunction, the Commission must give the Member State concerned the opportunity to submit its comments.[12] At its request, any interested party may obtain a copy of these decisions.[13]

Significant numbers of recovery orders have been adopted by the Commission in recent years. In the years 2012-2014, the amounts each year recovered by the Member States have been €2.4 billion, €726 million and €301 million, respectively.

---

[8] Case C-354/90, *FNCEPA v France* [1991] ECR I-5505, para 13-14; Cases C-261/01 & C-262/01, *Van Calster v Belgium* [2003] ECR-12249, para 76.

[9] Council Regulation (EC) No 659/1999, Article 11(1); Case C-301/87, *France v Commission* [1990] ECR I-307, para 19; Case C-400/99, *Italy v Commission* [2001] ECR I-7303, para 47.

[10] Cf. Commission communication on recovery of unlawful aid, OJ 1995 C156/5. Previously, it was not entirely clear that the Commission had power to order interim recovery: Case T-107/96, *Pantochim SA v Commission* [1998] ECR II-311, para 51. Accordingly, Council Regulation (EC) No 659/1999, Article 11(2) is stated to apply only to unlawful aid implemented after the entry into force of that Regulation.

[11] Council Regulation (EC) No 659/1999, Article 11(2). Where a provisional recovery order is made, the Commission may authorise the Member State concerned to couple the refunding of the aid with the payment of rescue aid to the firm concerned.

[12] Council Regulation (EC) No 659/1999, Article 11(1)-(2); Case C-301/87, *France v Commission* [1990] ECR I-307, para 19.

[13] Council Regulation (EC) No 659/1999, Article 20(3).

Implementation of recovery decisions The Member States are obliged, by virtue of Article 4(3) TEU, to facilitate the achievement of the Commission's tasks, which includes ensuring that its decisions are implemented.[14] A Member State to whom a decision is addressed obliging it to recover aid is obliged, pursuant to Article 288 TFEU, to take all the necessary measures to ensure the implementation of the decision. This must result in the actual recovery of the sums owed in order to eliminate the distortion of competition caused by the competitive advantage procured by the unlawful aid.[15] The Commission has issued a notice in which it sets out the requirements imposed on the Member States in relation to the recovery of unlawful aid.[16] Recovery of unlawful aid, which is the responsibility of the authorities of the Member State which granted the aid, must be effected without delay and in accordance with the procedures under the national law of the Member State concerned, provided, in accordance with the principle of effectiveness, that they allow the immediate and effective execution of the Commission's decision.[17] Recovery must be achieved within the period specified in the recovery decision.[18]

A recovery decision is addressed to the Member State, not the recipient, and the decision itself imposes no direct obligation requiring payment on the recipient as such.[19] It follows that the decision cannot be considered in itself as requiring the recipient to repay the aid, so that the amount to be repaid by virtue of the decision alone does not constitute a debt due from the recipient.[20] Consequently, a Member State which is obliged to recover unlawful aid is free to choose the means of fulfilling the recovery obligation, provided that the

---

[14] Case 96/81 *Commission* v *Netherlands* [1982] ECR 1791, para 6; Case C-382/99, *Netherlands* v *Commission* [2002] ECR I-5163, para 91.

[15] Case C-331/09, *Commission* v *Poland* [2011] ECR I-2933, para 55; Case C-529/09, *Commission* v *Spain* EU:C:2013:31, para 91; Case C-674/13, *Commission* v *Germany* EU:C:2015:302, para 38.

[16] OJ 2007 C272/4.

[17] Council Regulation (EC) No 659/1999, Article 14(3); Case 94/87, *Commission* v *Germany* [1989] ECR I-175, para 12; Case C-24/95, *Land Rheinland-Pfalz* v *Alcan Deutschland* [1997] ECR I-1591, para 24; Case C-404/87, *Commission* v *Portugal* [2000] ECR I-4897, para 55; Case C-378/98, *Commission* v *Belgium* [2001] ECR I-5107, para 51; Case C-382/99, *Netherlands* v *Commission* [2002] ECR I-5163, para 90; Case C-209/00, *Commission* v *Germany* [2002] ECR I-11695, para 32; Case C-232/05, *Commission* v *France* [2006] ECR I-10071, para 49; Case C-419/06, *Commission* v *Greece* [2008] ECR I-27*, para 59; Case C-369/07, *Commission* v *Greece* [2009] ECR I-5703, para 66; Case C-210/09, *Scott SA* v *Ville d'Orleans* [2010] ECR I-4613, para 21; Case C-529/09, *Commission* v *Spain* EU:C:2013:31, para 92; Case C-674/13, *Commission* v *Germany* EU:C:2015:302, para 39.

[18] Case C-304/09, *Commission* v *Italy* [2010] ECR I-13903, para 32; Case C-305/09, *Commission* v *Italy* [2011] ECR I-3225, para 27.

[19] Case C-574/13P(R), *France* v *Commission* EU:C:2014:36, para 22.

[20] Case T-360/04, *FG Marine* v *Commission* [2007] II-92*, paras 57-58; Case T-27/13R, *Elan* v *Commission* EU:T:2013:122, para 18; Case T-366/13R, *France* v *Commission* EU:T:2013:396, para 29.

measures chosen do not adversely affect the scope and effectiveness of EU law.[21] According to the Commission, this implies that the authorities responsible should carefully consider the full range of recovery instruments available under national law and select the procedure most likely to secure the immediate execution of the decision.[22] If national procedural rules do not enable the enforcement of recovery, the Member State must take steps to put the necessary mechanisms in place.[23]

The obligation to recover unlawful aid is not dependent on the form in which the aid was granted.[24] Thus, for example, the fact that the aid was granted under a private law contract cannot prevent a recovery order from being made.[25] The recovery obligation is, however, subject to the qualification that recovery of aid may not be ordered by the Commission if this would be contrary to a general principle of EU law.[26] Moreover, measures which are themselves inconsistent with EU law do not constitute proper implementation of a decision requiring the recovery of illegal aid.[27]

Re-establishing the previously existing position The obligation on a Member State to abolish unlawful aid has as its main purpose the re-establishment of the previously existing situation by eliminating the distortion of competition caused by the competitive advantage afforded by the aid.[28] That objective is obtained once the aid is repaid by the recipient who thereby forfeits the advantage which it enjoyed over its competitors on the market, and

---

[21] Case C-209/00, *Commission v Germany* [2002] ECR I-11659, para 34; Case C-369/07, *Commission v Greece* [2009] ECR I-5703, para 67; Case C-210/09, *Scott SA v Ville d'Orleans* [2010] ECR I-4613, para 20; Case C-527/12, *Commission v Germany* EU:C:2014:2193, para 40.

[22] Notice on the recovery of unlawful aid, para 52.

[23] Case C-214/07, *Commission v France* [2008] ECR I-8357, *per* Advocate General Sharpston, at para 76.

[24] Case C-183/91, *Commission v Greece* [1993] ECR I-3131, para 16; Case C-404/87, *Commission v Portugal* [2000] ECR I-4897, para 38; Case C-404/00, *Commission v Spain* [2003] ECR I-6695, para 44; Case T-198/01, *Technische Glaswerke Ilmenau GmbH v Commission* [2004] ECR II-2717, para 132.

[25] Case C-278/00, *Greece v Commission* [2004] ECR I-3997, para 113.

[26] Council Regulation (EC) No 659/1999, Article 14(1).

[27] Case C-209/00, *Commission v Germany* [2002] ECR I-11695, para 36.

[28] Case C-348/93, *Commission v Italy* [1995] ECR I-673, para 26; Case C-24/95, *Land Rheinland Pfalz v Alcan Deutschland* [1997] ECR I-1591, para 23; Case C-277/00 *Germany v Commission* [2004] ECR I-3925, para 76; Case C-369/07, *Commission v Greece* [2009] ECR I-5703, para 120; Case C-520/07P, *Commission v MTU Friedrichshafen GmbH* [2009] ECR I-8555, para 57; Case C-275/10, *Residex Capital IV CV v Gemeente Rotterdam* [2011] ECR I-13043, para 34; Case T-318/00, *Freistaat Thüringen v Commission* [2005] ECR II-4179, para 310; Case T-324/00, *CDA Datenträger Albrechts GmbH v Commission* [2004] ECR II-4309, para 79; Case T-366/00 *Scott SA v Commission* [2007] ECR II-797, para 94.

the situation prior to payment is restored.[29] This must result in the actual recovery of the sums owed.[30] Misused aid must also, in principle, be recovered from the undertaking which has had the actual use thereof, in order to eliminate the distortion of competition caused by the competitive advantage afforded by that aid.[31] Exceptionally, where the aid takes the form of a tax that is imposed only on certain undertakings, reimbursement of the sums paid by way of the tax could be an effective way of re-establishing the *status quo ante*, thereby eliminating the distortions of competition arising from asymmetrical imposition of the tax.[32]

By requiring reimbursement of the aid, the recipient is supposed to find itself in a position similar to that in which it would have been if the aid had not been granted, even though this might lead to the liquidation of the recipient. In that event, the relevant national rules must not preclude enforcement of the recovery decision.[33] Since the legal requirement is that unlawful aid must be recovered, it is irrelevant that recovery can no longer restore stability to the market.[34]

Protection of legitimate expectations A recipient of aid which is granted unlawfully is not precluded, in opposing recovery, from relying on exceptional circumstances on the basis of which it legitimately assumed the aid to be lawful.[35] The right to rely on the principle of the protection of legitimate expectations, which constitutes one of the fundamental principles of the EU

---

[29] Case C-348/93, *Commission v Italy* [1995] ECR I-673, para 27; Case C-350/93, *Commission v Italy* [1995] ECR I-699, para 22; Case C-209/00, *Commission v Germany* [2002] ECR I-11695, para 35; Case C-457/00 *Belgium* v *Commission* [2003] ECR I-6931, para 55; Case C-372/97, *Italy v Commission* [2004] ECR I-3679, para 103-104; Case C-277/00 *Germany v Commission* [2004] ECR I-3925, para 75; Case C-419/06, *Commission v Greece* [2008] ECR I-27*, para 54; Case C-369/07, *Commission v Greece* [2009] ECR I-5703, para 120; Case C-275/10, *Residex Capital IV CV v Gemeente Rotterdam* [2011] ECR I-13043, para 34; Case T-198/01, *Technische Glaswerke Ilmenau GmbH v Commission* [2004] ECR II-2717, para 132; Case T-452/08, *DHL Aviation SA/NV v Commission* [2010] ECR II-218*, para 32.

[30] Case C-415/03, *Commission* v *Greece* [2005] ECR I-3875, para 44; C-207/05, *Commission* v *Italy* [2006] ECR I-70*, para 36-37; Case C-232/05, *Commission* v *France* [2006] ECR I-10071, para 42.

[31] Cases T-111/01 and T-133/01, *Saxonia Edelmetalle GmbH v Commission* [2005] ECR II-1579, para 115.

[32] Case C-53/00, *Ferring SA v ACOSS* [2001] ECR I-9067, *per* Advocate General Tizzano, at para 23.

[33] Case 52/84, *Commission v Belgium* [1986] ECR 89, para 14; Case T-198/01, *Technische Glaswerke Ilmenau GmbH v Commission* [2004] ECR II-2717, para 139.

[34] Case C-305/89, *Commission v Italy* [1991] ECR I-1605, para 41.

[35] Cases T-116/01 & T-118/01 *P & O European Ferries (Vizcaya) and Diputación Foral de Vizcaya v Commission* [2003] ECR II-2957, paras 201-204; Cases T-427/04 & T-17/05, *France v Commission* [2009] ECR II-4315, para 263; Case T-328/09, *Producteurs de légumes de France v Commission* EU:T:2012:498, para 22.

law, extends to any individual who is in a situation in which it is clear that the EU authorities have, by giving him precise assurances, led him to entertain legitimate expectations.[36] Regardless of the form in which it is communicated, information that is precise, unconditional and consistent and comes from an authorised and reliable source constitutes such assurance. It must be borne in mind, however, that the risk attaching to illegality is the consequence of the practical effect of the obligation to notify in Article 108(3) TFEU. Thus, even though the Commission had stated in its 1983 communication on illegal State aid that it would publish a notice warning aid recipients of the risks involved, a failure to publish such a notice did not constitute an exceptional circumstance giving rise to a legitimate expectation that the aid was somehow lawful.[37]

A person may not plead infringement of the principle of the protection of legitimate expectations unless he has been given precise assurances by the authorities.[38] The mere fact that the aid scheme has been referred to in press articles of which the Commission might have been aware cannot give rise to any legitimate expectation that the measure in question did not constitute unlawful aid.[39] In *Regione autonoma della Sardegna v Commission*, it was argued that the Commission's silence over a period of seven months from receipt of the last information requested in the course of the formal investigation procedure gave rise to a legitimate expectation that the aid was compatible with the internal market. The General Court rejected this on the ground that no legitimate expectation could arise until a decision approving the aid had actually been taken by the Commission and the period for bringing an annulment action against it had expired.[40] Even where the Commission has taken a decision not to raise any objection to a measure or declaring aid to be compatible with the internal market, a recipient cannot be deemed to have a legitimate expectation that the measure is lawful until the expiry of the period during which an annulment action against the decision may be taken.[41] The

---

[36] A. Giraud, "A study of the notion of legitimate expectations in State aid recovery proceedings: 'Abandon all hope, ye who enter here'?" [2008] CMLRev 1399.

[37] Cases C-471/09P etc., *Territorio Histórico de Vizcaya – Diputación Foral de Vizcaya a v Commission* [2011] ECR I-111*, para 64; Cases T-30/01 etc., *Territorio Histórico de Álava – Diputación Foral de Álava v Commission* [2009] ECR II-2919, paras 304-308.

[38] Case C-537/08P, *Kahla Thuringen GmbH v Commission* [2010] ECR I-12917, para 63; Cases T-66/96 & T-221/97, *Mellett v Court of Justice* [1998] ECR-SC II-1305, paras 104 & 107; Case T-20/03, *Kahla/Thüringen Porzellan GmbH v Commission* [2008] ECR II-2305, para 146; Case T-332/06, *Alcoa Trasformazioni Srl v Commission* [2009] ECR I-29*, para 102.

[39] Case T-328/09, *Producteurs de légumes de France v Commission* EU:T:2012:498, para 27; Case T-243/09, *Fedecom v Commission* EU:T:2012:497, para 96.

[40] Case T-171/02, *Regione autonoma della Sardegna v Commission* [2005] ECR II-2123, para 65.

[41] Case C-169/95 *Spain v Commission* [1997] ECR I-135, para 53; Case C-91/01, *Italy v Commission* [2004] ECR I-4355, para 66; Case C-199/06, *CELF v SIDE* [2008] ECR I-469, para 67; Case T-126/99, *Graphischer Maschinenbau v Commission* [2002] ECR II-

ECJ confirmed in *CELF v SIDE* that, where an action for annulment has been brought under Article 263 TFEU, the recipient is not entitled to harbour such assurance so long as the court has not delivered a definitive ruling.[42]

Legitimate expectation arising from prior Commission action Legitimate expectation concerning the legality of State aid may arise from prior action by the Commission. For example, the Commission cannot require recovery of aid to the detriment of a recipient who has complied with the aid conditions laid down by the Commission in an authorising decision.[43] Thus, in *ESF v Commission*, the Commission, having previously authorised certain State guarantees covering operating loans to a steel producer, was held to have infringed the principle of the protection of legitimate expectations in ordering recovery of the aid several years later when it re-examined the guarantees on the basis of further information and found them to be incompatible with the internal market.[44] In *RSV v Commission*, where the Commission had been aware of the award of unnotified aid and had unduly delayed in taking steps to seek to recover it, thereby giving the impression that it would not object to the aid, the ECJ held that the recipient may be entitled to rely on the principle of the protection of legitimate expectations to prevent the Commission from subsequently ordering recovery of the aid.[45] This was subsequently regarded by the ECJ as an exceptional case on the ground that it concerned a sector which had for some years been receiving State aid approved by the Commission and its object was to meet the additional costs of an operation which had already received authorised aid.[46] In *Fleuren Compost v Commission*, a period of more than five years between the Commission first contacting the Netherlands authorities and the adoption of the decision ordering recovery of the aid was not, in the circumstances, deemed unreasonable.[47]

Legitimate expectations deriving from court decisions In certain cases, it is possible that legitimate expectations may arise from reliance on decisions of

---

2427, para 42; Case T-171/02, *Regione autonoma della Sardegna v Commission* [2005] ECR II-2123, para 65.

[42] Case C-199/06, *CELF v SIDE* [2008] ECR I-469, para 68; Case C-1/09, *CELF v SIDE* [2010] ECR I-2099, para 45.

[43] Cases T-227/99 & T-134/00, *Kvaerner Warnow Werft GmbH v Commission* [2002] ECR II-1205, para 92; Case T-20/03, *Kahla/Thüringen Porzellan GmbH v Commission* [2008] ECR II-2305, para 148.

[44] Case T-6/99, *ESF v Commission* [2001] ECR II-1523, para 189.

[45] Case 223/85, *RSV v Commission* [1987] ECR 4617, para 17.

[46] Case C-334/99, *Germany v Commission* [2003] ECR I-1139, para 44; Case C-372/97, *Italy v Commission* [2004] ECR I-3679, para 117; Case C-278/00, *Greece v Commission* [2004] ECR I-3997, para 106.

[47] Case T-109/01, *Fleuren Compost BV v Commission* [2004] ECR II-127, paras 147-148.

the courts. In *Adria-Wien Pipeline GmbH v Finanzlandesdirektion für Kärnten*, the ECJ held that Austrian legislation limiting an energy tax rebate to undertakings which manufactured goods was State aid insofar as the tax exceeded 0.35% of net production value on the ground that undertakings providing services were excluded from the scope of the exemption.[48] Subsequently, the Austrian legislation was amended so as to apply also to undertakings providing services, but the Commission decided that this also constituted State aid since there was no justification on environmental grounds for limiting the tax exemption to undertakings whose use of energy exceeded 0.35% of the net value of production on the ground that this had the effect of favouring undertakings which were large energy consumers. Taking into consideration the possibility the beneficiaries may have believed in good faith, on the basis of the ECJ's judgment in *Adria Wien Pipeline*, that the measure had ceased to be selective when it was extended to service providers, the Commission concluded that recovery of the aid would, in those circumstances, be contrary to the principle of the protection of legitimate expectations.[49]

In *Ladbroke Racing*, the Commission found that an exemption from a levy constituted State aid to the French betting organisation PMU, but nevertheless refrained from ordering recovery of the aid granted prior to the opening of its investigations on the ground that the PMU entertained legitimate expectations as to the legality of the exemption by reason of a judgment of the French Conseil d'Etat according to which operations of racecourse undertakings were agricultural and therefore qualified for exemption from the levy. This decision was annulled on the ground that the Commission merely referred to the decision of the Conseil d'Etat without in any way indicating why it amounted to an exceptional circumstance giving rise to legitimate expectations on the part of the recipient of the aid.[50]

Legitimate expectation and the diligent businessman In view of the mandatory nature of the supervision of State aid by the Commission, undertakings to which an aid has been granted may not, in principle, entertain a legitimate expectation that the aid is lawful unless it has been granted in compliance with the procedure in Article 108(3) TFEU.[51] A diligent

---

[48] Case C-143/99, *Adria-Wien Pipeline GmbH v Finanzlandesdirektion für Kärnten* [2001] ECR I-8365, para 53.

[49] Commission Decision 2005/565/EC, OJ 2005 l190/13; Case C-368/04 *Transalpine Ölleitung in Österreich v Finanzlandesdirektion für Tirol* [2006] ECR I-9957, para 19.

[50] Case C-83/98P, *France v Ladbroke Racing Ltd. and Commission* [2000] I-3271, paras 60-61.

[51] Case C-5/89, *Commission v Germany* [1990] ECR I-3437, para 14; Case C-334/99, *Germany v Commission* [2003] ECR I-1139, para 41; Case C-91/01, *Italy v Commission* [2004] ECR I-4355, para 65; Cases C-183/02P & C-187/02P, *Daewoo Electronics Manufacturing España SA v Commission* [2004] ECR I-10609, para 44; Case C-148/04, *Unicredito Italiano SpA v Agenzia delle Entrate, Ufficio Genova 1* [2005] ECR I-11137,

businessman should normally be able to determine whether that procedure has been followed.[52] This applies equally to small businesses.[53] The fact that aid is granted through a general measure, the application of which does not depend on any demonstration of acceptance by the recipient, does not affect the requirement to repay the aid on grounds of legitimate expectation or legal security.[54] It is not sufficient for the recipient merely to seek assurances from the Member State. Even if the Member State has mistakenly indicated that the aid is covered by a Commission approval, this will not give rise to a legitimate expectation on the part of the recipient or affect the right of the Commission to order recovery.[55]

If the measure was one which was not obviously aid, it may be argued that a diligent businessman could not have known that the measure constituted aid. In *SFEI v La Poste*, the measures alleged to constitute aid consisted of certain types of logistical and commercial assistance by a public parent company to its subsidiaries. Whether or not these measures constituted aid depended on whether the parent received adequate remuneration for its services, a matter on which the Commission took several years to reach a decision. In such circumstances, Advocate General Jacobs thought that, even if the measures constituted aid, it might be inappropriate to order repayment.[56] On the other hand, even where the aid is granted through the medium of private banks without any direct involvement on the part of the public authorities, the recipient may be taken as knowing that aid has been granted if the circumstances permit. For instance, in *CETM v Commission*, a Spanish scheme to grant aid for the replacement of commercial motor vehicles through subsidised bank loans had been well publicised in the press, so that a borrower

---

para 104; Case C-408/04P, *Commission v Salzgitter AG* [2008] ECR I-2767, para 104; Case C-672/13, *OTP Bank Nyrt v Hungary* EU:C:2015:185, para 77; Case T-288/97, *Regione Autonoma Friuli Venezia Giulia v Commission* [2001] ECR II-1169, para 107; Cases T-127/99, T-129/99 &T-148/99, *Territorio Histórico de Álava - Diputación Foral de Álava v Commission* [2002] ECR II-1275, para 236; Case T-34/02R, *B. v Commission* [2002] ECR II-2803, para 75; Cases T-239/04 & T-323/04, *Italy v Commission* [2007] ECR II-3265, para 154; Cases T-254/00, T-270/00 & T-277/00, *Hotel Cipriani SpA v Commission* [2008] ECR II-3269, para 392; Case T-328/09, *Producteurs de légumes de France v Commission* EU:T:2012:498, para 21; Case T-308/11, *Eurallumina SpA v Commission* EU:T:2014:894, para 60; Case T-177/10, *Alcoa Trasformazioni srl v Commission* EU:T:2014:897, para 61.

[52] Case C-169/95, *Spain v Commission* [1997] ECR I-135, para 51; Case C-24/95, *Land Rheinland-Pfalz v Alcan Deutschland* [1997] ECR I-1591, para 25; Case C-334/99, *Germany v Commission* [2003] ECR I-1139, para 42; Cases C-346/03 and C-529/03, *Atzeni v Regione autonoma della Sardegna* [2006] ECR I-1875, para 64.

[53] Case T-109/01, *Fleuren Compost BV v Commission* [2004] ECR II-127, para 140.

[54] Case T-75/03, *Banco Comercial dos Açores SA v Commission* [2009] ECR II-143*, para 126.

[55] Case T-109/01, *Fleuren Compost BV v Commission* [2004] ECR II-127, paras 143-144.

[56] Case C-39/94, *SFEI v La Poste* [1996] ECR I-3547, *per* Advocate General Jacobs, at p. 3573.

could not rely on the principle of legitimate expectation to argue that he did not realise that the cheap loans were State financed.[57]

Recovery of aid is not disproportionate   It was argued in *Belgium v Commission*, where the recipient was the subject of composition proceedings, that the obligation to recover the aid was disproportionate to the objectives laid down in Articles 107 and 108 TFEU, inasmuch as the declaration of debt by the Member State in the composition procedure would cause serious damage to the other creditors. This argument was dismissed, on the ground that, since it is the logical consequence of a finding that aid is unlawful, recovery of State aid which has been unlawfully granted, for the purpose of restoring the previously existing situation, cannot in principle be regarded as disproportionate.[58]   The same applies to the charging of interest in respect of the period between the payment of the aid and its actual repayment.[59]   In *Italy v Commission*, concerning aid for the Italian banking sector, it was argued that the fact that the aid only partially affected trade between Member States should be taken into account, particularly as regards the extent to which the aid was recoverable, by virtue of the principle of proportionality. The ECJ rejected this approach, holding that the requirement of recovery extended to the aid as a whole.[60]   Nevertheless, recovery must be limited to the financial advantages actually arising from placing the aid at the disposal of the beneficiary, and be proportionate to those advantages.[61]

Recovery of aid does not constitute a penalty   Despite the comment of Advocate General Mazák, in *CELF v SIDE*, that recovery is needed in order to

[57]   Case T-55/99, *CETM v Commission* [2000] ECR II-3207, paras 124-127.
[58]   Case C-142/87, *Belgium v Commission* [1990] ECR I-959, para 66; Cases C-278-280/92, *Spain v Commission* [1994] ECR I-4103, para 75; Case C-75/97, *Belgium v Commission* [1999] ECR I-3671, para 68; Case C-404/87, *Commission v Portugal* [2000] ECR I-4897, para 54; Case C-372/97, *Italy v Commission* [2004] ECR I-3679, para 103; Case C-66/02, *Italy v Commission* [2005] ECR 10901, para 113; Case C-148/04, *Unicredito Italiano SpA v Agenzia delle Entrate, Ufficio Genova 1* [2005] ECR I-11137, para 113; Case C-419/06, *Commission v Greece* [2008] ECR I-27*, para 55; Case C-1/09, *CELF v SIDE* [2010] ECR I-2099, para 54; Case T-288/97, *Regione Autonoma Friuli Venezia Giulia v Commission* [2001] ECR II-1169, para 105; Case T-198/01, *Technische Glaswerke Ilmenau GmbH v Commission* [2004] ECR II-2717, para 133; Cases T-254/00, T-270/00 & T-277/00, *Hotel Cipriani SpA v Commission* [2008] ECR II-3269, para 389; Case T-445/05, *Associazione Italiana del Risparmio Gestito v Commission* [2009] ECR II-289, para 193.
[59]   Case C-169/95, *Spain v Commission* [1997] ECR I-135, para 47.
[60]   Case C-66/02, *Italy v Commission* [2005] ECR I-10901, paras 112-113.
[61]   Case T-308/00 RENV, *Salzgitter AG v Commission* EU:T:2013:30, para 138; Case T-500/12, *Ryanair Ltd v Commission* EU:T:2015:73, para 135; Case T-473/12, *Aer Lingus Ltd v Commission* EU:T:2015:78, para 104.

penalise the recipient in respect of unlawful aid,[62] it is clear that recovery of unlawful State aid is not to be equated with a penalty.[63] It follows that the Commission cannot impose on a beneficiary of unlawful aid a sanction requiring the recovery of an amount greater than that corresponding to the aid that it actually received.[64] In *CETM v Commission*, the General Court declared that a decision ordering the recovery of unlawful aid cannot constitute a penalty, even if it is implemented long after the aid in question was granted.[65] Similarly, in *Commission v Greece*, the ECJ rejected an argument, where unlawful aid had been granted in the form of a tax exemption, that recovery of the aid must necessarily take the form of a retroactive tax, contrary to principles of EU law. Rather, recovery could be achieved merely by ordering the undertakings which had received the aid to pay sums corresponding to the amount of the tax exemption unlawfully granted to them.[66]

Recovery of unlawful aid and bankruptcy proceedings The fact that a beneficiary of unlawful aid is insolvent or subject to bankruptcy proceedings has no effect on its obligation to repay unlawful aid.[67] In relation to bankrupt undertakings that have received aid, the restoration of the previous situation and the elimination of the distortion of competition resulting from the unlawfully paid aid may, in principle, be achieved by registration of the liability relating to the repayment of the aid in question in the schedule of liabilities.[68] This must result in the insolvency of the undertaking and the permanent cessation of its activity.[69] In its notice on recovery of unlawful aid, the Commission emphasises that, even though recovery is made according to national bankruptcy rules, national authorities must ensure that due account is

---

[62] Case C-199/06, *CELF v SIDE* [2008] ECR I-469, per Advocate General Mazák at para 33.

[63] Cases C-74/00 & C-75/00, *Falck SpA v Commission* [2002] ECR I-7869, para 178; Case T-487/11, *Banco Privado Português SA v Commission* EU:T:2014:1077, para 132.

[64] Case T-308/00 RENV, *Salzgitter AG v Commission* EU:T:2013:30, para 117.

[65] Case T-55/99, *CETM v Commission* [2000] ECR II-3207, para 164; Case T-369/00, *Département du Loiret v Commission* [2003] ECR II-1789, para 57; Case T-366/00 *Scott SA v Commission* [2007] ECR II-797, para 94.

[66] Case C-183/91, *Commission v Greece* [1993] ECR I-3131, para 17.

[67] Case C-610/10, *Commission v Spain* EU:C:2012:781, para 71; Case C-353/12, *Commission v Italy* EU:C:2013:651, para 33; Case C-37/14, *Commission v France* EU:C:2015:90, para 84.

[68] Case 52/84, *Commission v Belgium* [1986] ECR 89, para 14; Case C-142/87 *Belgium v Commission* [1990] ECR I-959, paras 60-62; Case C-277/00 *Commission v Germany* [2004] ECR I-3925, para 85; Case C-331/09, *Commission v Poland* [2011] ECR I-2933, para 60; Case C-454/09, *Commission v Italy* [2011] ECR I-150*, para 35; Case C-613/11, *Commission v Italy* EU:C:2013:192, para 42. Cases T-81/07 to T-83/07, *KG Holding NV v Commission* [2009] ECR II-2411, para 192.

[69] Case C-331/09, *Commission v Poland* [2011] ECR I-2933, para 63-64; Case C-454/09, *Commission v Italy* [2011] ECR I-150*, para 36; Case C-610/10, *Commission v Spain* EU:C:2012:781, para 104.

taken throughout insolvency proceedings of the EU interest. The Member State should immediately register its claims in the bankruptcy proceedings and, where the insolvency administrator refuses to register a recovery claim, should dispute such refusal and lodge an appeal. To ensure the immediate and effective implementation of the recovery decision, the national authorities responsible for the execution of the recovery decision should also appeal any decision of the insolvency administrator or the insolvency court to allow a continuation of the insolvent beneficiary's activity beyond the time limits set in the recovery decision. In the case of liquidation, and as long as the aid has not been fully recovered, the Member State should oppose any transfer of assets that is not carried out on market terms or that is organised so as to circumvent the recovery decision.[70]

Accordingly, the ECJ has held that, where a new undertaking has in fact been created to carry on the activities of the insolvent recipient of aid, the pursuit of those activities may, where the aid concerned has not been recovered in its entirety, prolong the distortion of competition brought about by the competitive advantage which that undertaking enjoyed in the market as compared with its competitors. Such a newly created company may, if it retains that advantage, be required to repay the aid in question. That is the case where it is established that the new company continues genuinely to derive a competitive advantage because of the receipt of the aid, especially where it acquires the assets without paying the market price or where it is established that the effect of the company's creation is circumvention of the obligation to repay the aid. That applies, in particular, if the payment of a market price is not sufficient to cancel out the competitive advantage linked to receipt of the unlawful aid.[71] In those circumstances, the registration in the schedule of liabilities of the liability to repay the unlawful aid is not sufficient, on its own, to make the distortion of competition disappear.[72]

Illegality of aid measure under national law The fact that an aid measure is unlawful under national law has no effect on the obligation to repay aid that was actually put at the disposal of the recipient. In particular, attainment of the objective of recovery, which is to ensure that the recipient forfeits any advantage on the market that it has enjoyed over its competitors, cannot depend on the consequences under national law of failure to comply with Article 108(3) TFEU. Thus, in *DHL Aviation v Commission*, the fact that failure to notify in advance an aid measure consisting of contractual warranties provided free of charge by the public authorities rendered those warranties null and void

---

[70]   Notice on the recovery of unlawful aid, paras 60-68.

[71]   Case C-610/10, *Commission v Spain* EU:C:2012:781, para 106; Case C-529/09, *Commission v Spain* EU:C:2013:31, para 109.

[72]   Case C-610/10, *Commission v Spain* EU:C:2012:781, para 107; Case C-529/09, *Commission v Spain* EU:C:2013:31, para 106.

in German law had no effect on the obligation to recover the advantage that had actually been received.[73]

Compatibility of recovery with other provisions of EU law Other attempts to invoke principles of EU law to invalidate recovery orders have been even less successful. In *Commission v Belgium*, it was argued that an order for recovery of unlawful capital investment was contrary to the Second Company Law Directive, Article 15 of which prohibits distributions to shareholders if net assets would thereby fall below the amount of the subscribed capital, and Article 32 of which provides that no payment may be made to shareholders until the creditors have obtained satisfaction for their claims.[74] Advocate General Lenz, whilst recognising that these provisions were undoubtedly based on the principle that the share capital of a public limited company has to serve as security for the creditors of the company and may not be reduced to their detriment, dismissed both arguments. First, since distributions to shareholders only concerned payments out of company profits and since the undertaking concerned did not actually make a profit, there was no possibility of repaying the illegal capital holding by way of a distribution. Secondly, the provisions on the reduction of capital could only refer to lawfully subscribed capital. Since the recovery order applied in respect of unlawfully subscribed capital, those provisions could not apply in favour of the creditors of the company, because they were not entitled to demand the retention of unlawfully subscribed share capital as a security for their claims on the company.[75]

17.2 DECISIONS ORDERING RECOVERY OF UNLAWFUL AID

Full amount of unlawful aid must be recovered Recovery of aid extends to the whole amount of the unlawful aid granted, regardless of subsequent events. The Commission is not required to show that the recipient still retains an advantage from the aid at the date of the recovery order.[76] Where aid is granted in the form of a price reduction, the amount to be recovered is the amount of that reduction, and it is not open to the recipient to argue that some lesser amount should be recovered.[77] Thus, in *Technische Glaswerke Ilmenau GmbH v Commission*, the General Court rejected the argument that the public authority that granted the aid would have lost the value of the transferred assets

---

[73] Case T-452/08, *DHL Aviation SA/NV v Commission* [2010] ECR II-218*, paras 40-41.

[74] Council Directive 77/91/EEC, OJ 1997 L26/1.

[75] Case 52/84, *Commission v Belgium* [1986] ECR 89, *per* Advocate General Lenz, at pp. 98-99.

[76] Case C-295/07P, *Commission v Départment du Loiret* [2008] ECR I-9363, para 63.

[77] Case T-198/01, *Technische Glaswerke Ilmenau GmbH v Commission* [2004] ECR II-2717, para 135.

to creditors under the liquidation that would otherwise have taken place.[78] In *Unicredito Italiano*, concerning aid granted through tax reductions to undertakings in the Italian banking sector, the ECJ held that it would not be right to determine the amounts to be repaid in the light of various operations which could have been implemented by the undertakings if they had not opted for the type of operation which was coupled with the aid. Re-establishing the *status quo ante* means returning, as far as possible, to the situation which would have prevailed if the operations at issue had been carried out without the tax reduction. That does not imply reconstructing past events differently on the basis of hypothetical elements such as the choices, often numerous, which could have been made by the operators concerned, since the choices actually made with the aid might prove to be irreversible. Re-establishing the *status quo ante* merely enables account to be taken, at the stage of recovery of the aid by the national authorities, of tax treatment which may be more favourable than the ordinary treatment which, in the absence of unlawful aid and in accordance with domestic rules which are compatible with EU law, would have been granted on the basis of the operation actually carried out.[79]

Calculation of the amount to be recovered If the Commission, pursuant to its obligation to conduct a diligent and impartial examination of the case under Article 108 TFEU, decides to order the recovery of a specific amount, it must assess as accurately as the circumstances of the case will allow the actual value of the benefit received from the aid by the beneficiary. In restoring the situation existing prior to the payment of the aid, the Commission is obliged to ensure that the real advantage resulting from the aid is eliminated and it must thus order recovery of the aid in full. The Commission may not, out of sympathy with the beneficiary, order recovery of an amount which is less than the value of the aid received by the latter, nor is it entitled to mark its disapproval of the serious character of the illegality by ordering recovery of an amount in excess of the value of the benefit received by the recipient of the aid. It is to be noted in this regard that the Commission may not be faulted because its assessment is approximate. In the case of a non-notified aid, it may be that the circumstances of the case are such that the Commission has difficulty in

---

[78] Case T-198/01, *Technische Glaswerke Ilmenau GmbH v Commission* [2004] ECR II-2717, para 138, upheld on appeal in Case C-404/04P, *Technische Glaswerke Ilmenau GmbH v Commission* [2007] ECR I-1*, paras 93-98.

[79] Case C-148/04, *Unicredito Italiano SpA v Agenzia delle Entrate, Ufficio Genova 1* [2005] ECR I-11137, paras 114-119; Case T-445/05, *Associazione Italiana del Risparmio Gestito v Commission* [2009] ECR II-289, para 203; Case T-468/08, *Tisza Erőmű kft v Commission* EU:T:2014:235, para 296; Case T-179/09, *Dunamenti Erőmű zrt v Commission* EU:T:2014:236, para 191.

determining the precise value of the aid, particularly where a significant period of time has elapsed since the grant of aid.[80]

The amount to be recovered may be gauged by reference to the statement of reasons contained in the decision.[81] Thus, in its decision finding that the tax treatment of France Télécom amounted to State aid, the Commission declared that the actual amount of the aid was between €798 million and €1,140 million.[82] The ECJ held that this was sufficient for the aid to be recovered as being a minimum of €798 million. The fact that the exact amount of aid to be recovered had not been laid down definitively did not prevent the authorities from implementing the recovery procedure for the minimum amount of aid or from cooperating effectively in determining the final amount of the aid to be recovered.[83] In *Commission v Greece*, concerning recovery of aid from Olympic Airways, the ECJ held that the decision contained sufficient indications, including detailed tables, allowing verification of the parameters used by the Commission in its calculations.[84]

In *Aer Lingus v Commission* and *Ryanair v Commission*, the General Court annulled a Commission decision ordering recovery of aid to airlines arising from differential rates of air travel tax. Since the rates in question were €2 and €10 per passenger, although this was to be collected by the airlines, the Commission had ordered recovery of €8 per passenger. However, the General Court held that it was necessary to make a distinction between the formal or legal passing on of the tax to the passengers and the economic passing on, which consisted in determining to what extent the airline bore the economic cost of the tax by possibly adjusting the ticket price exclusive of the tax. In the circumstances, the Commission was wrong to assume that the advantage actually obtained and retained by the airlines amounted, in all cases, to €8 per passenger.[85]

Recovery must include interest Council Regulation (EC) No 659/1999, Article 14(2) provides that the amount to be recovered pursuant to a recovery

---

[80] Case T-366/00 *Scott SA v Commission* [2007] ECR II-797, paras 95-96; Case T-500/12, *Ryanair Ltd v Commission* EU:T:2015:73, paras 114-115; Case T-473/12, *Aer Lingus Ltd v Commission* EU:T:2015:78, paras 85-86; Case T-305/13, *SACE BT SpA v Commission* EU:T:2015:435, paras 149 and 160.

[81] Case C-355/95 P, *TWD v Commission* [1997] ECR I-2549, para 21; Case C-415/03, *Commission v Greece* [2005] ECR I-3875, para 41; Case C-441/06, *Commission v France* [2007] ECR I-8887, para 33; Case C-419/06, *Commission v Greece* [2008] ECR I-27*, para 48.

[82] Commission Decision 2005/709/EC *France Télécom*, OJ 2005 L269/30.

[83] Case C-441/06, *Commission v France* [2007] ECR I-8887, para 28; Cases T-427/04 & T-17/05, *France v Commission* [2009] ECR II-4315, para 301.

[84] Case C-419/06, *Commission v Greece* [2008] ECR I-27*, para 45.

[85] Case T-500/12, *Ryanair Ltd v Commission* EU:T:2015:73, paras 119-130; Case T-473/12, *Aer Lingus Ltd v Commission* EU:T:2015:78, paras 90-99.

order must include interest payable from the date on which the aid was at the disposal of the beneficiary until the date of its recovery, since otherwise the aid would result in the grant of an interest free loan for the period prior to recovery.[86] This applies equally to injunctions for the provisional recovery of unlawful aid.[87] Previously, interest was calculated according to national law, which might allow for either simple or compound interest.[88] Now, pursuant to Commission Regulation (EC) No 794/2002, Article 11(2), given the objective of restoring the situation existing before the aid was unlawfully granted, interest is calculated on a compound basis until the date of recovery of the aid.[89] With regard to the determination of the applicable rates, the General Court has approved reliance on the Commission's published reference rates as representing the average level of interest rates in force in each of the Member States and, therefore, as giving a valid indication of the market rates for loans for industrial investments.[90]

In *Spain v Commission*, part of the aid which was ordered to be recovered was due from companies which had been declared insolvent. Spanish insolvency legislation provided that the debts of undertakings which had been declared insolvent ceased to produce interest with effect from the date of the relevant declaration. This rule, justified by the common interest of all the creditors in not burdening the insolvent undertaking's assets with new debts likely to worsen the situation, applied to all creditors alike, whether public or private. The ECJ held that this legislation could not be regarded as rendering the recovery of the aid required by EU law virtually impossible. It, therefore, annulled the Commission's decision in so far as it required recovery of interest without taking this limitation into account.[91] It may be noted that neither Regulation (EC) No 659/1999, Article 14(2) nor Regulation (EC) No 794/2002, Article 11(2) make any reference to special provisions concerning interest laid down by national law. Given that these provisions are directly applicable, they may be presumed to supersede any conflicting national provisions.

Calculation by national authorities of amounts to be recovered   The Commission is not obliged to determine the precise amount of aid to be

---

[86]   Case C-348/93, *Commission v Italy* [1995] ECR I-673, para 27; Case C-480/98, *Spain v Commission* [2000] ECR I-8717, para 35; Case T-459/93, *Siemens SA v Commission* [1995] ECR II-1675, para 98; Case T-158/96, *Acciaierie di Bolzano SpA v Commission* [1999] ECR II- 3927, para 98; Case T-35/99, *Keller SpA v Commission* [2002] ECR II-261, para 107.

[87]   Council Regulation (EC) No 659/1999, Article 11(2).

[88]   Commission's letter to Member States SG(91) D/4577 of 4 March 1991.

[89]   Commission Regulation (EC) No 794/2002, preamble, recital 14, and Article 11(2). This change of policy was formally announced in May 2003, OJ 2003 C110/21.

[90]   Case T-308/00 RENV, *Salzgitter AG v Commission* EU:T:2013:30, para 141.

[91]   Case C-480/98, *Spain v Commission* [2000] ECR I-8717, para 38.

recovered where its calculation requires factors laid down by national regulation to be taken into account. It is sufficient that its decision leaves no room for doubt as to the measures which constituted the aid in question or as to the period in which those measures were taken. In those circumstances, the Commission may legitimately confine itself to declaring that there is an obligation to repay and leave it to the national authorities to calculate the exact amount of the aid to be repaid.[92]

The national authorities may be best placed to obtain the information as regards the undertakings that have benefited from the aid.[93] In particular, when it is faced with an aid scheme, the Commission is generally not in a position, nor is it required, to identify exactly the amount of aid received by individual recipients. Accordingly, the specific circumstances of one of the recipients of aid can be assessed only at the recovery stage.[94] The Commission is not obliged to determine the incidence of tax on the amount of aid to be recovered, since that calculation falls within the scope of national law. That does not prevent the national authorities, when recovering the sums in question, from deducting certain sums, where appropriate, from the amount to be recovered pursuant to their internal rules, provided that the application of those rules does not make such recovery impossible in practice or discriminate in relation to comparable cases governed by national law.[95]

Where aid results from a public authority failing to recover debts in the same way as a private market operator, the Commission is not required to determine, for each new aid, the time at which a private creditor would have ceased to tolerate delays in payment, the precise steps that he would have taken and their consequences so as to permit the Member State concerned to quantify

---

[92]   Case 102/87, *France v Commission* [1988] ECR 4067, para 33; Case C-480/98, *Spain v Commission* [2000] ECR I-8717, paras 25-26; Case C-415/03, *Commission v Greece* [2005] ECR I-3875, para 39-40; Case C-441/06, *Commission v France* [2007] I-8887, para 29; Case C-419/06, *Commission v Greece* [2008] ECR I-27*, para 44-46; Case C-39/06, *Commission v Germany* [2008] ECR I-93*, para 37; Case C-369/07, *Commission v Greece* [2009] ECR I-5703, para 48-49; Case C-403/10P, *Mediaset SpA v Commission* [2011] ECR I-117*, paras 126-127; Case C-81/10 P *France Télécom* v *Commission* [2011] ECR I-12899, para 102; Case C-69/13, *Mediaset SpA v Commission* EU:C:2014:71, para 21; Case C-271/13P, *Rousse Industry AD v Commission* EU:C:2014:175, para 77; Case C-674/13, *Commission v Germany* EU:C:2015:302, para 40; Case T-68/03, *Olympiaki Aeroporia Ypiresies AE v Commission* [2007] ECR II-2911, para 291; Case T-288/06, *Regionalny Fundusz Gospodarczy SA v Commission* [2009] ECR II-2247, para 57; Case T-177/10, *Alcoa Trasformazioni srl v Commission* EU:T:2014:897, para 88.

[93]   Case T-25/07, *Iride SpA v Commission* [2009] ECR II-245, para 89.

[94]   Case C-310/99, *Italy v Commission* [2002] ECR I-2289, para 91; Case T-354/99, *Kuwait Petroleum (Nederland) BV v Commission* [2006] ECR II-1475, para 67; Case T-297/02, *ACEA SpA v Commission* [2009] ECR II-1683, para 158; Case T-301/02, *AEM SpA v Commission* [2009] ECR II-1757, para 164.

[95]   Case T-459/93, *Siemens SA v Commission* [1995] ECR II-1675, para 83; Case T-67/94, *Ladbroke Racing Ltd. v Commission* [1998] ECR II-1, para 188.

in each case the advantage obtained by the debtor. The General Court held, in the *Olympic Airways* case, that the advantage to the debtor of tolerance of non-payment or delayed payment of his debt is constituted precisely by the exemption from, or delay in, payment of the debt from the time at which it fell due. That advantage does not necessarily coincide with the amount which the creditor could have recovered if he had ceased to tolerate the default or delay in payment. Thus, in order to establish whether the debtor has enjoyed an advantage, the Commission merely has to verify whether, at the latest, at the time that its decision was adopted, a private creditor in the same situation would clearly not have continued to tolerate the default or delay in payment. That consideration does not require it to determine the precise moment at which a private creditor would have ceased to tolerate the default or delay in payment and would have taken steps to obtain payment of the debt.[96]

In *Budapesti Erőmű Zrt v Commission*, where the Commission found that long term electricity purchasing agreements concluded by a publicly owned undertaking entailed aid for the electricity generators, it ordered recovery of an amount that was to be calculated by the Hungarian authorities on the basis of an appropriate simulation of the market as it would have been had the agreements not been in force. The General Court held that the Commission was entitled to insist that the counterfactual scenario was one in which all electricity was deemed to have been traded through spot contracts. It rejected criticisms that this approach did not allow for the fact that the power generators would have received different revenues and borne different costs, as this would have subjected the calculation of the recoverable amounts to speculative assumptions.[97]

Recovery by means other than payment Aid may be recovered by means other than transfer of funds, so long as the means chosen have the same effect and are provided for under the national legal system as a mechanism for extinguishing debts.[98] Thus, for example, a set-off operation may constitute an appropriate means by which State aid may be recovered.[99] Any such measure must be a suitable instrument for re-establishing the conditions of competition which have been distorted by the grant of the illegal aid, be capable of being identified as such by the Commission and other interested parties and be unconditional and immediately applicable.[100]

---

[96] Case T-68/03, *Olympiaki Aeroporia Ypiresies AE v Commission* [2007] ECR II-2911, paras 292-294

[97] Cases T-80/06 & T-182/09, *Budapesti Erőmű Zrt v Commission* EU:T:2012:65, para 115.

[98] Case C-209/00, *Commission v Germany* [2002] ECR I-11695, paras 57; Case C-369/07, *Commission v Greece* [2009] ECR I-5703, para 81.

[99] Case C-369/07, *Commission v Greece* [2009] ECR I-5703, para 68.

[100] Case C-209/00, *Commission v Germany* [2002] ECR I-11695, paras 58; Case C-369/07, *Commission v Greece* [2009] ECR I-5703, para 81.

As regards the implementation of a decision requiring the recovery of unlawful aid, where a Member State recovers that aid by means other than a cash payment, it must provide the Commission with all the information enabling it to establish that the means chosen constitute an adapted implementation of the decision. In contrast to recovery by way of a cash payment, which by its nature lends itself to supervision by the Commission, alternative measures proposed by a Member State for the fulfilment of its obligation to ensure recovery of unlawful aid may make it necessary to assess complex matters. In order for the Commission to be able to make such an assessment, however, it requires information which it cannot obtain without close cooperation on the part of the Member State concerned. It follows that, although a State may recover illegal aid by means other than a cash payment, it must ensure that the measures it chooses are sufficiently transparent to enable the Commission to satisfy itself that they are suitable for the purpose of eliminating the distortion of competition caused by that aid. Where a Member State decides not to recover aid by way of a cash payment but chooses to take alternative measures, it is obliged to provide the Commission with the evidence enabling it to establish that such measures are suitable for achieving the result required by the decision.[101] Thus, the ECJ upheld the Commission's refusal, in its decision concerning unlawful aid in the restructuring of WestLB, to accept the German Government's proposal for recovery on the ground that the proposed right to receive an additional share of the company's surpluses in the event of its liquidation or of a change in the shareholders' holdings in the capital related to an uncertain future event.[102]

Recovery of aid may even involve the return of money to the aided company. In the Seleco decision, the Commission found that aid had been granted when an Italian company was allowed to repurchase 65.2 billion lira of debt owed to a public authority for 20 billion lira. The ECJ upheld the Commission's decision that repayment of the aid required the 20 billion lira to be repaid to Seleco, with the public authority being left with the option of registering the outstanding 65.2 billion lira debt as an unsecured creditor.[103]

Identification of persons from whom aid is to be recovered Although the decision ordering unlawful aid to be recovered is addressed to the Member State concerned, it is quite proper for the Commission to state as accurately as possible from whom the aid is to be recovered.[104] The identification of the person from whom recovery should be made may be inherent in the recovery

---

[101] Case C-209/00, *Commission v Germany* [2002] ECR I-11695, paras 40-43; Case C-369/07, *Commission v Greece* [2009] ECR I-5703, paras 79-80.

[102] Case C-209/00, *Commission v Germany* [2002] ECR I-11695, para 60.

[103] Cases C-328/99 & C-399/00, *Italy v Commission* [2003] ECR I-4135, paras 54-55.

[104] Case C-303/88, *Italy v Commission* [1991] ECR I-1433, *per* Advocate General Van Gerven, at p. 1466.

decision. For example, where a Member State invests capital in a company and the Commission orders the recovery of the investment as unlawful aid, such a decision is itself sufficiently precise so as to require the return to the investor of the capital unlawfully invested.[105] The decision would be complied with by the implementation of a decision of the other shareholders in the company agreeing to buy back the State participation in the company's capital.[106] If the Member State has any serious doubts as to the identity of the persons from whom it should claim recovery, it should consult the Commission for clarification.[107]

Recovery may only be claimed from a beneficiary The Commission is not entitled to order recovery from persons who have not benefited from the unlawful aid. In order to determine the beneficiary of State aid from whom recovery may be ordered, it is necessary to identify the undertaking which has actually benefited from it.[108] Recovery may equally be ordered regardless of whether the beneficiary was a direct or indirect recipient of the aid.[109] Thus, in *KG Holding v Commission*, aid granted to a parent company for the benefit of a wholly-owned subsidiary was to be recovered from either company or both.[110] In *Le Levant v Commission*, the General Court annulled the Commission's decision ordering recovery from private investors who had obtained tax relief in relation to their investment in the building of a shipping vessel. The Commission had found that the shipyard did not benefit directly from the aid and that the operator of the vessel no longer obtained any competitive advantage from the aid, but it did not explain how the private investors were placed in an advantageous position by the aid in question.[111] Similarly, in *CDA Datenträger Albrechts v Commission*, the Commission's decision ordering recovery of aid from a company that was a member of a group that had received the aid was quashed on the ground that the company had not itself benefited from the aid.[112]

---

[105] Case 52/84, *Commission v Belgium* [1986] ECR 89, para 14, and *per* Advocate General Lenz, at p. 97.

[106] Case 5/86, *Commission v Belgium* [1987] ECR 1773, para 10.

[107] Case C-303/88, *Italy v Commission* [1991] ECR I-1433, para 58.

[108] Case C-457/00, *Belgium v Commission* [2003] ECR -6931, para 55; Case C-277/00, *Germany v Commission* [2004] ECR I-3925, para 75; Cases T-81/07 to T-83/07, *KG Holding NV v Commission* [2009] ECR II-2411, para 175.

[109] Case T-445/05, *Associazione Italiana del Risparmio Gestito v Commission* [2009] ECR II-245, para 198.

[110] Cases T-81/07 to T-83/07, *KG Holding NV v Commission* [2009] ECR II-2411, paras 176-177.

[111] Case T-34/02, *Le Levant 001 v Commission* [2005] ECR II-267, paras 119-120.

[112] Case T-324/00, *CDA Datenträger Albrechts GmbH v Commission* [2004] ECR II-4309, para 94; Case T-318/00, *Freistaat Thüringen v Commission* [2005] ECR II-4179, para 325.

This principle applies equally in the case of misuse of aid. For instance, in *Saxonia Edelmetalle*, restructuring aid had been approved in respect of the Lintra group of companies including a holding company and several subsidiaries. Subsequently, after the applicant, which was one of the subsidiaries, had been individually privatised, it was found that part of the aid which had remained in the accounts of the holding company had been misused. The Commission ordered recovery of that part of the aid from each of the subsidiaries using a formula which was based on the amount of restructuring aid that each subsidiary had initially received. The General Court overturned this decision on the ground that the Commission had no information identifying the actual amounts of aid that had been misused by the individual companies. Whilst the Commission could order recovery of the misused aid, it was for the German authorities to determine the individual amounts payable.[113]

Recovery from hypothetical beneficiary The Commission may not impose on a particular undertaking an obligation to repay, even jointly and severally, a fixed part of the amount of the aid declared to be incompatible, where the transfer of State resources from which that undertaking benefited is hypothetical. In *MTU Friedrichshafen GmbH v Commission*, the Commission had merely found that on the basis of the information available, it could not be ruled out that MTU had indirectly benefited from State aid when know-how was acquired on conditions deemed to be favourable from a company that had directly received State aid. It followed that the obligation to repay jointly and severally was based on assumptions that the information available to the Commission allowed it neither to confirm nor rebut. The General Court, annulling the decision, held that recovery could only be required from the actual beneficiary.[114]

Recovery following transfer of assets or shares Recovery of aid granted illegally is a civil law liability arising out of the unlawful and thus undue payment of aid and as such may be transferred to an undertaking other than the original recipient. Aid may, therefore, be recovered either from the original beneficiary or, if the circumstances permit, from the party which has taken over liability for repayment from the beneficiary.[115] The latter would arise, in particular, where the party taking over the assets continues to benefit from a

---

[113] Cases T-111/01 and T-133/01, *Saxonia Edelmetalle GmbH v Commission* [2005] ECR II-1579, paras 118-126.

[114] Case T-196/02, *MTU Friedrichshafen GmbH v Commission* [2007] ECR II-2889, paras 46-51.

[115] Case C-305/89, *Commission v Italy* [1991] ECR I-1605, *per* Advocate General Van Gerven, at pp. 1633-4; Case T-291/06, *Operator ARP v Commission* [2009] ECR II-2275, para 64.

competitive advantage resulting from the grant of the aid.[116] For the purposes of checking the financial conditions of the transfer, consideration may be had, in particular, to the form of the transfer, for example, public tendering, deemed to ensure that a sale takes place under market conditions, and to any expert's report prepared at the time of the transfer. Other factors that might be taken into consideration include the time of the transfer, the purpose of the transfer, the transfer price, the identity of the shareholders or owners of the firms, the moment at which the transfer was carried out in relation to the Commission's investigation, and the economic logic of the transaction.[117] Where the assets have been acquired by a number of different buyers, there is nothing in principle to prevent the financial conditions of each of the transactions from being checked for their compliance with market conditions.[118] In *ISD Polska v Commission*, the General Court confirmed that the Commission had been entitled, following a transfer of assets which left the aid recipient an empty shell, to impose joint and several liability on the acquiring companies.[119]

In the case of *System Microelectronic Innovation GmbH*, where the main business of a company that received aid was hived off into a subsidiary that was subsequently sold at market value, the ECJ, while overturning the Commission's decision on the facts, noted that it is certainly possible that, in the event that hive-off companies are created in order to continue some of the activities of the undertaking that received the aid, where that undertaking has gone bankrupt, those companies may also, if necessary, be required to repay the aid in question, where it is established that they actually continue to benefit from the competitive advantage linked with the receipt of the aid. This could be the case, *inter alia*, where those hive-off companies acquire the assets of the company in liquidation without paying the market price in return or where it is established that the creation of such companies evades the obligation to repay that aid.[120] In *Commission v Spain*, where a decision had been adopted finding that aid to Indosa was to be recovered, Indosa's activities were transferred to CMD, a wholly-owned subsidiary of Indosa, which had been created by Indosa's insolvency administrator and to which all of Indosa's assets and staff had been transferred. Given that the assets had not been transferred in accordance with an open and transparent procedure, the Commission concluded that CMD was continuing the subsidised activity and that, in

---

[116] Case C-277/00, *Germany v Commission* [2004] ECR I-3925, para 86; Case C-214/07, *Commission v France* [2008] ECR I-8357, para 58. C. Koenig, "Determining the addressee of a decision ordering the recovery of State aid after the sale of substantial assets of the undertaking in receipt of aid" (2001) 22 ECLR 238.

[117] Cases C-328/99 & C-399/00, *Italy v Commission* [2000] ECR I8855, paras 78-85; Cases T-415/05, T-416/05 & T-423/05, *Greece v Commission* [2010] ECR II-4749, para 135.

[118] Case C-214/07, *Commission v France* [2008] ECR I-8357, paras 59-61.

[119] Cases T-273/06 & T-297/06, *ISD Polska v Commission* [2009] ECR II-2185, para 112.

[120] Case C-277/00, *Germany v Commission* [2004] ECR I-3925, para 86; Case C-610/10, *Commission v Spain* EU:C:2012:781, para 106.

consequence, the aid had to be recovered from CMD.[121] Similarly, in *Commission v Greece*, which concerned the transfer of assets from Olympic Airways to a new company in such a way as to create an obstacle to the effective recovery from Olympic Airways, the obligation to repay the aid was transferred to the new company.[122]

In *CDA Datenträger Albrechts v Commission*, the Commission's decision ordering recovery from an undertaking to whom the initial recipient had sold its business was annulled on the ground that the Commission was not entitled on the facts to conclude that there was an intention to evade the consequences of the recovery decision.[123] In *Operator ARP v Commission*, where the applicant claimed that the value of public law obligations which it assumed exceeded considerably the market value of assets transferred to it, the General Court annulled the Commission's recovery decision on the ground that the Commission could not assert, without further explanation, that there was a risk of circumvention or that the applicant had enjoyed the actual benefit of a competitive advantage connected with the receipt of the aid in question.[124]

Where aid has been granted through a parent company for the benefit of a subsidiary which is subsequently transferred to a third party, the decision ordering recovery of the aid may specify that recovery is to be claimed from the parent company, as being the holding company to which the subsidiary belonged at the relevant time.[125] It would not be correct, however, to order recovery of the aid payments from the new owner where the price paid for the transferred undertaking was the appropriate market value for the specific assets which were acquired.[126] In those circumstances, the purchaser cannot be considered as having benefited from an economic advantage.[127] In *Banks v Coal Authority*, aid was granted to certain publicly owned companies which were subsequently privatised at full open market value, with the aid element being assessed at the market price and included in the purchase price. The ECJ held, therefore, that the new owners could not be regarded as having benefited from the aid. Rather, it was the seller, in those circumstances, which kept the benefit of the aid, so that recovery of the aid was to be effected through repayment by the seller.[128] Nevertheless, given that the seller was, from an

---

[121] Case C-529/09, *Commission v Spain* EU:C:2013:31, para 31.

[122] Case C-415/03, *Commission v Greece* [2005] ECR I-3875, paras 33-34; Cases T-415/05, T-416/05 & T-423/05, *Greece v Commission* [2010] ECR II-4749, paras 139-142.

[123] Case T-324/00, *CDA Datenträger Albrechts GmbH v Commission* [2004] ECR II-4309, para 105; Case T-318/00, *Freistaat Thüringen v Commission* [2005] ECR II-4179, para 336.

[124] Case T-291/06, *Operator ARP v Commission* [2009] ECR II-2275, para 69.

[125] Case C-305/89, *Commission v Italy* [1991] ECR I-1605, para 40.

[126] *Ibid., per* Advocate General Van Gerven, at p. 1633.

[127] Case T-511/09, *Niki Luftfahrt GmbH v Commission* EU:T:2015:284, para 133.

[128] Case C-390/98, *HJ Banks & Co Ltd v Coal Authority* [2001] ECR I-6117, paras 77-78; Cases C-74/00 and C-75/00, *Falck SpA v Commission* [2002] ECR I-7869, para 180; Case C-277/00, *Germany v Commission* [2004] ECR I-3925, para 80.

economic standpoint, identifiable with the provider of the aid, in that both seller and aid provider were subsumed within the State, repayment by the seller would serve no purpose. In that event, the distortion of competition caused during the period when the aid was effective could only be remedied by compensation for damage caused to competitors by the competitive advantage enjoyed by the aid recipients.[129]

Period for the recovery of unlawful aid In the past, the Commission's recovery decisions specified a period of two months within which the Member State concerned was required to communicate to the Commission the measures it had taken to recover the aid. The Commission now recognises, however, that this period is usually too short. In its notice on the recovery of unlawful aid, it states that it will specify two time limits in its decisions. Within two months following the entry into force of the decision, the Member State must inform the Commission of the measures planned or taken. Within four months following the entry into force of the decision, the Member State must have actually executed the decision.[130]

A Member State is deemed to comply with the recovery decision when the aid has been fully reimbursed within the prescribed time limit or, in the case of an insolvent beneficiary, when the company is liquidated under market conditions. The Commission may also accept, in duly justified cases, a provisional implementation of the decision when it is subject to litigation before the national court or the EU courts. This must result in the beneficiary being deprived of the advantage linked to the unlawful aid, for example, by the amount to be recovered being placed into a blocked account.[131]

Limitation period for recovery of unlawful aid Prior to the adoption of Council Regulation (EC) No 659/1999, the Commission had on occasion decided against ordering recovery of unlawful aid in view of the time that had elapsed since the aid had been granted. For instance, in 1990, the Commission held that aid that had been granted in 1986 by Italy without being notified in advance was incompatible with the internal market, but nevertheless decided not to require its recovery in view of the time that had elapsed since the Commission had been informed about the aid.[132] There was, however, no legislative provision for a limitation period as regards action by the Commission in respect of non-notified aid, so that the Commission could not be required to refrain from ordering recovery on the sole ground of the length of period since the aid had been granted. In *BFM v Commission*, where the Commission acted in 1995 against unlawful aid which had been granted in

---

[129] Case C-390/98, *HJ Banks & Co Ltd v Coal Authority* [2001] ECR I-6117, paras 79-80.
[130] Notice on the recovery of unlawful aid, para 42.
[131] *Ibid.*, paras 69-70.
[132] *Twentieth Report on Competition Policy* (1990), pt. 267.

1985, the General Court rejected arguments that a recovery order would be in breach of the principles of legal certainty and the protection of legitimate expectations or, alternatively, that a limitation period of 5 years should apply by analogy to that laid down by legislation in other areas of EU law.[133]

It may be, however, that whereas a recipient of aid cannot have a legitimate expectation that aid was properly granted unless the provisions of Article 108(3) TFEU have been respected, there are circumstances where the Commission's ability to investigate alleged unlawful aid would be compromised due to the passage of time, allowing the Member State or a recipient to contend that its right to a fair determination of its obligations would be infringed. For instance, where aid is alleged to have been granted in breach of the market investor principle, it may be impossible for the Member State or the recipient to gather appropriate evidence establishing the prevailing market conditions several years after the event. In *Salzgitter v Commission*, the CFI, found that the Commission, having known of the aid in 1988 but not having acted until 1998 to order recovery, had breached the principle of legal certainty.[134] Reversing this decision on appeal, and stressing that this case involved the ECSC Treaty which contained a particularly strict State aid regime, the ECJ held that a delay by the Commission in exercising its supervisory powers and ordering recovery does not render its decision unlawful except in exceptional cases which show that the Commission manifestly failed to act and clearly breached its duty of diligence.[135]

Now, for reasons of legal certainty,[136] Article 15 of Council Regulation (EC) No 659/1999 provides that the powers of the Commission to order recovery in cases of unlawful aid or misuse of aid is subject to a limitation period of ten years, beginning on the day on which the aid is awarded to the beneficiary either as individual aid or as aid under an aid scheme.[137] In the case of multi-annual schemes, entailing payment on a periodic basis, for the purpose of calculating the limitation period, the aid must be regarded as not having been awarded until the date on which it was in fact received by the beneficiary.[138] It follows that, even in the case of a scheme which has been in place for more than ten years, the Commission may order recovery where the actual grant of aid was within the last ten years.[139] Given that Article 14(1) of Regulation (EC) No 659/1999 requires the Commission to order the recovery

---

[133] Cases T-126-127/96, *Breda Fucine Meridionale SpA v Commission* [1998] ECR II-3437, paras 67-69.

[134] Case T-308/00, *Salzgitter AG v Commission* [2004] ECR II-1933, para 182.

[135] Case C-408/04P, *Commission v Salzgitter AG* [2008] ECR I-2767, para 105-106.

[136] Council Regulation (EC) No 659/1999, Preamble, recital 14; Case C-408/04P, *Commission v Salzgitter AG* [2008] ECR I-2767, para 102.

[137] Council Regulation (EC) No 659/1999, Article 15(1)-(2).

[138] Case C-81/10P, *France Télécom SA v Commission* [2011] ECR I-12899, para 82.

[139] Cases T-254/00, T-270/00 & T-277/00, *Hotel Cipriani SpA v Commission* [2008] ECR II-3269, para 364.

of unlawful aid unless this would be contrary to a general principle of EU law, it would appear that the Commission no longer has any wider discretion to refrain from issuing such an order in respect of aid which falls within the ten year limitation period. This limitation period applies to all unlawful aid and is independent of any question of whether the recipient had any legitimate expectation in the legality of the aid when it was granted.[140]

It is unclear, however, to what extent this limitation period should apply to circumstances where the aid was granted prior to the coming into force of Regulation (EC) No 659/1999 on 16 April 1999. The CFI in *Scott v Commission* and *Départment du Loiret v Commission* held that Regulation (EC) No 659/1999 contained procedural rules, including those concerning the limitation period in Article 15, relating to the application of Article 108 TFEU and as such were applicable to any decision taken by the Commission after it came into force.[141] Even though Regulation (EC) No 659/1999 was not applicable in August 1987, so that the grant on that date of the aid in issue did not then have the effect of causing a limitation period of 10 years to begin to run, that date must none the less be taken as the starting date of that period when Article 15 is applied to the facts in July 2000.[142] On appeal, Advocate General Jacobs cast doubt on this approach on the ground that there were serious conceptual and practical difficulties in assessing past events on the basis of rules that were not in existence when they occurred, in particular where questions of legal certainty arose.[143] Nevertheless, the General Court and Advocate General Jacobs agreed that any legal certainty deriving from the limitation period arose only on 16 April 1999, when the Regulation entered into force.[144]

Interruption to the limitation period Article 15(2) of Regulation (EC) No 659/1999 provides that any action taken by the Commission, or by a Member State acting at the request of the Commission, with regard to the unlawful aid interrupts the limitation period. Each interruption starts time running afresh.[145] In the twin cases of *Scott v Commission* and *Départment du Loiret v*

---

[140] Case C-276/03P, *Scott SA v Commission* [2005] ECR I-8437, para 37 and *per* Advocate General Jacobs at paras 99-101, overturning the CFI in Case T-366/00, *Scott SA v Commission* [2003] ECR II-1763, para 61.

[141] Case T-366/00, *Scott SA v Commission* [2003] ECR II-1763, paras 52-53; Case T-369/00, *Départment du Loiret v Commission* [2003] ECR II-1789, paras 50-51.

[142] Case T-366/00, *Scott SA v Commission* [2003] ECR II-1763, para 56.

[143] Case C-276/03P, *Scott SA v Commission* [2005] ECR I-8437, *per* Advocate General Jacobs at para 48. Since the point was not taken on appeal, the ECJ did not deal with it.

[144] Case T-366/00, *Scott SA v Commission* [2003] ECR II-1763, para 62; Case C-276/03P, *Scott SA v Commission* [2005] ECR I-8437, *per* Advocate General Jacobs at paras 107-108.

[145] Council Regulation (EC) No 659/1999, Article 15(2). The limitation period is suspended for as long as the decision of the Commission is the subject of proceedings before the ECJ.

Commission, aid was allegedly granted to Scott in August 1987 in order to encourage it to establish a factory in Le Loiret in France. Following a complaint to the Commission in December 1996, it requested the French authorities, in January 1997, to provide further information and proceeded to take a decision ordering recovery in July 2000 some twelve years after the aid had been granted. As to whether a mere request for information by the Commission could amount to action such as to interrupt the limitation period, in the wider context of the Commission's powers to gather information, the General Court held that such a request imposed an immediate obligation on the French authorities to provide all the necessary information and thus had the requisite legal effect.[146] Scott argued that the limitation period could not be interrupted as regards the recipient of the aid unless it had been informed at that stage of the Commission's investigation. On appeal, this was rejected by the ECJ,[147] with Advocate General Jacobs stating that the aim of creating legal certainty in having a limitation period was neutral and objective, rather than partial and subjective.[148]

17.3 INFRINGEMENT PROCEEDINGS AGAINST MEMBER STATES

Infringement proceedings against Member States A Member State to which a decision requiring recovery of illegal aid is addressed is obliged under Article 288 TFEU to take all measures necessary to ensure implementation of that decision.[149] Proceedings may be brought by the European Commission or by any Member State in the European Court of Justice against a Member State for introducing unlawful State aid or for maintaining in force State aid which is incompatible with the internal market and which the Commission has required to be abolished. Under Article 258 TFEU, which is applicable where a Member State is accused of having failed to fulfil an obligation under the Treaty, the Commission must first deliver a reasoned opinion on the matter after giving the Member State concerned the opportunity to submit its observations. If the Member State does not comply with the Commission's opinion, the matter may proceed to the ECJ. Infringement proceedings against a Member State may similarly be brought by other Member States pursuant to Article 259 TFEU. Derogating from this general approach, where a Member

---

[146] Case T-369/00, *Départment du Loiret v Commission* [2003] ECR II-1789, paras 81-82.

[147] Case C-276/03P, *Scott SA v Commission* [2005] ECR I-8437, paras 30-35.

[148] Case C-276/03P, *Scott SA v Commission* [2005] ECR I-8437, *per* Advocate General Jacobs at para 79.

[149] Case C-209/00, *Commission v Germany* [2002] ECR I-11695, para 31; Case C-404/00, *Commission v Spain* [2003] ECR I-6695, para 21; Case C-232/05, *Commission v France* [2006] ECR I-10071, para 42; Case C-331/09, *Commission v Poland* [2011] ECR I-2933, para 55; Case C-529/09, *Commission v Spain* EU:C:2013:31, para 91; Case C-674/13, *Commission v Germany* EU:C:2015:302, para 38.

State refuses to comply with a Commission decision finding that aid is incompatible with the internal market, Article 108(2) TFEU dispenses with the need for a reasoned opinion and permits the Commission to refer the matter immediately to the ECJ. This is justified by the fact that the Commission has already by its formal notice enabled the Member State, as well as the other parties concerned, to submit its comments.[150]

Infringement proceedings should normally relate to an actual, present infringement, rather than to record a failure which existed in the past.[151] Thus, in *Germany v Commission*, where the Bavarian authorities had allegedly failed to take the proper steps to recover aid which had been granted unlawfully, the ECJ held that the Commission was wrong to bring infringement proceedings against Germany since, by the time the infringement proceedings were commenced, the recipient of the aid had been placed in liquidation with the effect, in accordance with German law, of suspending all pending proceedings against it.[152] Furthermore, the Commission had not pointed to an imminent risk that Germany might repeat the infringement, or to other specific reasons for which the recording of an infringement might, exceptionally, be necessary.[153]

Infringement proceedings pursuant to Article 108(2) TFEU　Article 108(2) TFEU sets up a special procedure for the Commission to establish the incompatibility of State aid with the internal market. Pursuant to Article 108(2) TFEU, the Commission may bring an action against the Member State concerned only if that State does not comply with a decision whereby the Commission orders it to abolish or alter the aid in question. Prior to that decision, the Commission must give notice to the parties concerned to submit their observations, thereby guaranteeing the other Member States and the sectors concerned an opportunity to make their views known and allowing the Commission to be fully informed of all the facts of the case before making its decision.[154] This procedure may also be applicable in cases where conditions

---

[150] Case 70/72, *Commission v Germany* [1973] ECR 813, *per* Advocate General Mayras, at p. 835.

[151] Case C-362/90, *Commission v Italy* [1992] ECR I-2353, paras 9-13; Case C-276/99, *Germany v Commission* [2001] ECR I-8055, para 24.

[152] Case C-276/99, *Germany v Commission* [2001] ECR I-8055, para 29.

[153] *Ibid.*, para 32.

[154] The Commission must use the procedure under Article 108(2) TFEU if it wishes to establish that aid is incompatible with the internal market and cannot act for this purpose under Article 258 TFEU. This special procedure, therefore, provides all the parties concerned with guarantees which are specifically adapted to the special problems created by State aid with regard to competition in the internal market and which go much further than those provided for in the preliminary procedure laid down in Article 258 TFEU in which only the Commission and the Member State concerned participate: Case 290/83, *Commission v France* [1985] ECR 439, para 17; Cases C-356/90 & C-180/91, *Belgium v Commission* [1993] ECR I-2323, para 18.

in a decision of the Council approving aid pursuant to Article 108(2) TFEU have been infringed.[155]

If the Member State concerned does not comply with a conditional or negative decision, including a decision requiring recovery of unlawful aid, the Commission may refer the matter directly to the ECJ.[156] Equally, if the Commission has commenced examination of the aid and has issued a suspension injunction or a recovery injunction which the Member State fails to comply with, it may, while carrying out its examination on the substance of the matter on the basis of the information available, refer the matter to the ECJ.[157] Since Article 108(2) TFEU does not provide for a pre-litigation phase and therefore no reasoned opinion is issued to the Member State allowing a certain period within which to comply with the decision, the period for allowing compliance with the decision is the period laid down in the decision itself or, where appropriate, that subsequently fixed by the Commission.[158] Thus, the Commission is fully entitled to commence infringement proceedings within a short period.[159] The mere fact that the Commission might have a subsequent meeting with the Member State concerned in order to discuss the situation does not imply that the Commission has agreed an extension of the time limit for the adoption of the recovery measures in the absence of other elements demonstrating the Commission's intention to grant such an extension.[160] Where the Member State claims that it has in fact taken appropriate steps to comply with the recovery decision, the burden of proof lies with the Member State. Thus, in *Commission v Spain*, where Spain contended that it had established an appropriate procedure to implement the decisions properly, the ECJ found that it had produced no supporting evidence, in particular, of the identity of the beneficiaries of the aid, of the amounts of aid granted and of the procedures that were in fact under way for the purposes of recovery.[161]

---

[155] Case T-527/13, *Italy v Commission* EU:T:2015:429, para 58.

[156] Council Regulation (EC) No 659/1999, Article 23(1). See also Case 173/73, *Italy v Commission* [1974] ECR 709, para 9; Case 156/77, *Commission v Belgium* [1978] ECR 1881, para 23; Case 213/85, *Commission v Netherlands* [1988] ECR 281, para 7.

[157] Council Regulation (EC) No 659/1999, Article 12; Case C-301/87, *France v Commission* [1990] ECR I-307, para 23.

[158] Article 108(2) TFEU; Case C-378/98, *Commission v Belgium* [2001] ECR I-5107, para 26; Case C-499/99, *Commission v Spain* [2002] ECR I-6031, para 28; Case C-99/02, *Commission v Italy* [2004] ECR I-3353, para 24; Case C-207/05, *Commission v Italy* [2006] I-70*, para 31; Case C-232/05, *Commission v France* [2006] ECR I-71, para 32; Cases C-485/03 to C-490/03, *Commission v Spain* [2006] ECR I-11887, para 53; Case C-331/09, *Commission v Poland* [2011] ECR I-2933, para 50; Case C-354/10, *Commission v Greece* EU:C:2012:109, para 61; Case C-483/10, *Commission v Greece* EU:C:2012:395, para 31; Case C-529/09, *Commission v Spain* EU:C:2013:31, para 95.

[159] Case C-404/00, *Commission v Spain* [2003] ECR I-6695, para 56; Case C-99/02, *Commission v Italy* [2004] ECR I-3353, para 23.

[160] Cases C-485/03 to C-490/03, *Commission v Spain* [2006] ECR I-11887, para 59.

[161] Case C-177/06, *Commission v Spain* [2007] ECR I-7689, paras 49-51.

Infringement proceedings pursuant to Article 258 TFEU If unlawful State aid is introduced in breach of the duty to notify new aid in Article 108(3) TFEU, it is open to the Commission to bring the Member State concerned before the ECJ pursuant to Article 258 TFEU since the infringement of the FEU Treaty is independent of the issue of the compatibility of the aid with the internal market.[162] The Commission may also act in accordance with the procedure under Article 258 TFEU, as an alternative to acting under Article 108(2) TFEU, where a Member State fails to comply with a Commission decision requiring aid to be altered or abolished or requiring unlawful aid to be recovered.[163] In those circumstances, the Commission decision finding the aid incompatible with the internal market will itself have been taken in accordance with the procedures applicable under Article 108(2) TFEU.

Where a measure granting aid is prohibited as being contrary to other provisions of EU law, a breach of that prohibition must be dealt with by means of infringement proceedings under Article 258 TFEU. For example, if the Commission brings infringement proceedings against a Member State alleging practices which constitute a breach of the prohibition on discriminatory taxation contrary to Article 110 TFEU, that procedure does not lose its purpose because the Commission also takes the view that the same practices form part of a system of aids incompatible with the internal market and initiates the procedure provided for in Article 108(2) TFEU.[164] Similarly, regulations on the common organisation of the market in agricultural products may contain provisions prohibiting wholly or partially certain forms of national aids for the production and marketing of the products in question. An infringement of such a prohibition may be dealt with within the specific framework of such an organisation. The procedure in Article 108 TFEU for appraising the compatibility of the aid with the internal market is inapplicable, since it cannot affect the necessity of the Member States to observe the rules on the common organisation of the market.[165]

Interested parties and infringement proceedings Where a Member State refuses to comply with a Commission decision requiring aid to be altered or abolished, any interested Member State may, in the same manner as the Commission itself, refer the matter to the ECJ direct pursuant to Article 108(2) TFEU.[166] Similarly, any Member State is entitled to initiate infringement proceedings against another Member State pursuant to Article 259 TFEU

---

[162] Case 169/82, *Commission v Italy* [1984] ECR 1603, para 11; Case C-35/88, *Commission v Greece* [1990] ECR I-3125, para 34; Case C-61/90, *Commission v Greece* [1992] ECR I-2407, para 25.

[163] Case 70/72, *Commission v Germany* [1973] ECR 813, para 13.

[164] Case 73/79, *Commission v Italy* [1980] ECR 1553, para 10.

[165] Case 72/79, *Commission v Italy* [1980] ECR 1411, para 12.

[166] Article 108(2) TFEU.

where it considers that the latter has failed to fulfil an obligation under the FEU Treaty. In this case, before the Member State may bring its action, it must first bring the matter before the Commission. The Commission is required to deliver a reasoned opinion after each of the Member States has been given the opportunity to submit its own case and its observations on the other party's case both orally and in writing. If the Commission has not delivered an opinion within three months of the date on which the matter was brought before it, the absence of such opinion may not prevent the matter from being brought to the ECJ by the complainant Member State.[167]

Interested parties other than Member States, such as competitors, have no right under the FEU Treaty to commence infringement actions before the ECJ against a Member State for implementing unlawful State aid or for failing to comply with Commission decisions requiring aid to be altered or abolished. Moreover, where a complainant requests the Commission to bring a Member State before the ECJ and the Commission refuses to take such action, the complainant has no standing under Article 263 TFEU to commence proceedings against the Commission.[168] Nor would such an applicant have standing under Article 265 TFEU, since the exercise by the Commission of its discretion to bring proceedings does not entail any actionable failure to act on its part.[169]

Infringement proceedings and unlawful decisions Where a Member State wishes to contest the legality of a decision addressed to it by the Commission finding that aid is incompatible with the internal market, the proper legal remedy is judicial review by the ECJ pursuant to Article 263 TFEU. In view of the fact that the periods within which applications for judicial review must be lodged are intended to safeguard legal certainty by preventing Community measures which involve legal effects from being called into question indefinitely, it is not possible for a Member State, which has allowed the strict two-month time limits in Article 263 TFEU to expire without contesting the legality of the decision addressed to it, to be able to call in question that decision or its applicability by means of Article 277 TFEU when an application is lodged by the Commission at the ECJ, pursuant to Articles 108(2) or 258 TFEU, alleging a failure to comply with that decision.[170] Indeed, except where

---

[167] Article 259 TFEU.

[168] Case T-277/94, *AITEC v Commission* [1996] ECR II-351, para 56; Case T-148/00, *The Panhellenic Union of Cotton Ginners and Exporters v Commission* [2003] ECR II-4415, para 62; Case T-289/03, *BUPA Ltd v Commission* [2008] ECR II-81, para 313.

[169] Case T-277/94, *AITEC v Commission* [1996] ECR II-351, para 68.

[170] Case 156/77, *Commission v Belgium* [1978] ECR 1881, para 21; Case 52/83, *Commission v France* [1983] ECR 3707, para 10. See also Case 130/83, *Commission v Italy* [1984] ECR 2849; Case 93/84, *Commission v France* [1985] ECR 829; Case 52/84, *Commission v Belgium* [1986] ECR 89; Case C-183/91, *Commission v Greece* [1993]

a decision contains serious and manifest defects such that it could be deemed non-existent, a Member State cannot plead the unlawfulness of a decision addressed to it as a defence in an action for a declaration that it has failed to fulfil its obligations arising out of its failure to implement that decision, even if it has commenced judicial review proceedings seeking annulment of the contested decision.[171] A decision is presumed to be lawful so that, despite an action for annulment, it remains binding in all respects on the Member State to which it is addressed.[172] Moreover, Article 278 TFEU provides that actions before the ECJ do not have suspensory effect, although a Member State may apply for the suspension of a Commission decision requiring aid to be abolished, amended or recovered. It follows that, in the absence of any suspension order, a Member State remains bound in the interim by any obligation to recover unlawful aid.[173]

Obligation of Member States to effect recovery A decision ordering recovery will specify the period within which recovery is to be effected by the Member State, which is normally four months. Proceedings brought by the Commission for failure to recover aid will normally specify that recovery has not been effected by that date. It is no defence for a Member State to argue that it has begun proceedings for recovery after the date required by the decision.[174] The Commission also normally seeks a declaration that no notification has been made by the Member State to the Commission of the actions taken to effect such recovery, although it is common practice of the ECJ not to grant such a declaration where it has held that no steps have actually been taken to effect recovery. It is no defence for a Member State to seek to

---

ECR I-3131, para 10; Case C-188/92, *TWD v Germany* [1994] ECR I-833, para 15; Case C-135/93, *Spain v Commission* [1995] ECR I-1651, para 17.

[171] Case C-404/97, *Commission v Portugal* [2000] ECR I-4897, paras 34-36; Case C-261/99, *Commission v France* [2001] ECR I-2537, paras 18-20; Case C-415/03, *Commission v Greece* [2005] ECR I-3875, para 38; Case C-177/06, *Commission v Spain* [2007] ECR I-7689, paras 30-32; Case C-419/06, *Commission v Greece* [2008] ECR I-27*, para 52; Case C-39/06, *Commission v Germany* [2008] ECR I-93*, para 18-20; Case C-353/12, *Commission v Italy* EU:C:2013:651, para 43; Case C-37/14, *Commission v France* EU:C:2015:90, para 77.

[172] Case C-404/97, *Commission v Portugal* [2000] ECR I-4897, para 57; Case C-261/99, *Commission v France* [2001] ECR I-2537, para 26; Case C-177/06, *Commission v Spain* [2007] ECR I-7689, para 36; Case C-63/14, *Commission v France* EU:C:2015:458, para 44..

[173] Case C-261/99, *Commission v France* [2001] ECR I-2537, para 27; Case C-280/05, *Commission v Italy* [2007] ECR I-181*, para 21.

[174] Case C-411/12 *Commission v Italy* EU:C:2013:832, para 35; Case C-353/12, *Commission v Italy* EU:C:2013:651, para 32; Case C-63/14, *Commission v France* EU:C:2015:458, para 45.

rely on problems internal to its legal order to justify not having taken the requisite recovery steps.[175]

Member States are under an obligation pursuant to Article 4(3) TEU to facilitate the achievement of the recovery of unlawful aid and not to take any steps that would jeopardise recovery. In *Commission v France*, where the final amount of the aid to be recovered from France Télécom was to be determined on the basis of discussions between France and the Commission, the ECJ held that France had infringed the duty of cooperation under Article 4(3) TEU. France had failed to provide information requested by the Commission and had raised numerous questions concerning the parameters of the calculations necessary to determine the amount of the aid to be recovered. It had also repeatedly stated that it was technically impossible to identify a reliable and precise methodology for calculating the aid that had been granted and had concluded that there was no sufficiently sound legal basis on which to initiate a recovery procedure without a major risk of litigation.[176] In *Commission v Germany*, concerning aid to be recovered from Deutsche Post, Germany was held to have failed in its recovery obligations by not taking steps to define the market in parcel delivery services that was subject to competition which was necessary to determine the parameters for establishing the extent of recovery.[177]

In *Commission v Greece*, the Commission had ordered recovery of unlawful aid that had been granted to Olympic Airways. Subsequently, Greek legislation provided for the transfer of all the assets of Olympic Airways, free of all debts, to a new company Olympic Airlines. This operation was structured in such a way as to make it impossible, under national law, to recover the debts of the former company Olympic Airways from the new company Olympic Airlines. The ECJ held that the operation created an obstacle to the effective implementation of the Commission's decision and to the recovery of the aid so that the purpose of that decision was seriously compromised. Moreover, the Greek authorities' subsequent decision ordering recovery of the aid from Olympic Airways had no real effect with regard to any actual reimbursement by that company.[178]

Where the Member State seeks to rely on a block exemption or an individual Commission decision as not requiring recovery from individual beneficiaries, it must produce proof, in each individual case, that the requisite conditions have been fulfilled.[179] For instance, in *France v Commission*,

---

[175] Case C-674/13, *Commission v Germany* EU:C:2015:302, para 59.
[176] Case C-441/06, *Commission v France* [2007] ECR I-8887, paras 46-52.
[177] Case C-674/13, *Commission v Germany* EU:C:2015:302, para 60.
[178] Case C-415/03, *Commission v Greece* [2005] ECR I-3875, paras 33-35.
[179] Case C-37/14, *Commission v France* EU:C:2015:90, para 74.

France argued that aid totalling €1.3 million was covered by the applicable *de minimis* rule where the individual beneficiaries received only €34 each.[180]

Obligation to abolish future effects of aid   The Commission may require Member States to abolish aid schemes in so far as they continue to produce effects.   In *Commission v Spain*, concerning unlawful aid granted through the tax regimes applicable in the Basque region, actual receipt of the aid was subject to an administrative decision of the local tax authority, the effects of which could apply to reduce the tax payable for several years.   Accordingly, depending on the aid scheme in question, the administrative decisions granting aid actually adopted were liable to produce or would necessarily produce effects subsequent to the Commission's decisions requiring recovery, failing concrete national measures taken in execution of those decisions.   The ECJ held that Spain had not adopted measures capable of preventing prior decisions to grant aid from continuing to produce effects.   Indeed, even assuming that the appropriate and necessary measure under domestic law to comply with the contested decisions was simply to inform the firms in question that they could henceforth no longer continue to benefit from the tax measures referred to in the contested decisions, the ECJ also found that nor had it been established that the undertakings in receipt of aid were in fact so informed.[181]

Absolute impossibility of complying with decision   The only defence available to a Member State in opposing an infringement action by the Commission is to plead that it is absolutely impossible for it to implement the decision.[182]   A Member State to which a decision has been addressed may, if it encounters unforeseen or unforeseeable difficulties or perceives consequences overlooked by the Commission, submit those problems for consideration by the Commission, together with proposals for suitable amendments.   In such a case, the Commission and the Member State concerned must, in accordance with

---

[180]   Case C-37/14, *Commission v France* EU:C:2015:90, para 72.
[181]   Cases C-485/03 to C-490/03, *Commission v Spain* [2006] ECR I-11887, paras 64-67.
[182]   Case 52/84, *Commission v Belgium* [1986] ECR 89, para 14; Case C-348/93, *Commission v Italy* [1995] ECR I-673, para 16; Case C-280/95, *Commission v Italy* [1998] ECR I-259, para 13; Case C-261/99, *Commission v France* [2001] ECR I-2537, para 23; Case C-378/98, *Commission v Belgium* [2001] ECR I-5107, para 30; Case C-209/00, *Commission v Germany* [2002] ECR I-11695, para 70; Case C-404/00, *Commission v Spain* [2003] ECR I-6695, para 45; Case C-415/03, *Commission v Greece* [2005] ECR I-3875, para 35; Cases C-485/03 to C-490/03, *Commission v Spain* [2006] ECR I-11887, para 72; Case C-441/06, *Commission v France* [2007] ECR I-8887, para 27; Case C-419/06, *Commission v Greece* [2008] ECR I-27*, para 39; Case C-177/06, *Commission v Spain* [2007] ECR I-7689, para 46; Case C-214/07, *Commission v France* [2008] ECR I-8357, para 44; Case C-304/09, *Commission v Italy* [2010] ECR I-13903, para 35; Case C-411/12, *Commission v Italy* EU:C:2013:832, para 36; Case C-527/12, *Commission v Germany* EU:C:2014:2193, para 48; Case C-37/14, *Commission v France* EU:C:2015:90, para 65; Case C-63/14, *Commission v France* EU:C:2015:458, para 48.

Article 4(3) TEU which imposes a duty of genuine cooperation on the Member States and the Community institutions, work together in good faith with a view to overcoming the difficulties whilst fully observing the FEU Treaty provisions.[183] It follows that it is not sufficient for the Member State merely to inform the Commission of the legal and practical difficulties involved in implementing the decision, without taking any step whatsoever to recover the aid from the undertakings in question and without proposing to the Commission any alternative arrangements for implementing the decision which would have enabled the alleged difficulties to be overcome.[184] In particular, a Member State cannot excuse its failure to recover aid merely on the fact that a national court has suspended the execution of individual recovery proceedings.[185]

The mere fact that the measure giving rise to the aid is illegal under national law does not mean that recovery is impossible. In *DHL Aviation v Commission*, DHL gained an economic advantage from the inclusion in an agreement with the public authority owners of Leipzig-Halle airport of certain warranties which were provided for no further consideration. Under German law, since the aid measure was not notified in advance to the Commission under Article 108(3) TFEU, it was illegal. The General Court, which rejected an argument that it was therefore impossible to recover the aid, since it was capable of being quantified as the amount of the foregone consideration, held that the objective of recovering unlawful aid would be seriously compromised if it were possible for recovery to be precluded on the basis that domestic law deemed the measure null and void.[186]

---

[183] Case 52/84, *Commission v Belgium* [1986] ECR 89, para 16; Case 94/87, *Commission v Germany* [1989] ECR 175, para 9; Case C-348/93, *Commission v Italy* [1995] ECR I-673, para 17; Case C-404/87, *Commission v Portugal* [2000] ECR I-4897, para 4; Case C-261/99, *Commission v France* [2001] ECR I-2537, para 24; Case C-378/98, *Commission v Belgium* [2001] ECR I-5107, para 31; Case C-499/99, *Commission v Spain* [2002] ECR I-6031, para 24; Case C-382/99, *Netherlands v Commission* [2002] ECR I-5163, para 92; Case C-415/03, *Commission v Greece* [2005] ECR I-3875, para 42; Case C-441/06, *Commission v France* [2007] ECR I-8887, para 28; Case C-214/07, *Commission v France* [2008] ECR I-8357, para 45; Case C-304/09, *Commission v Italy* [2010] ECR I-13903, para 37; Case C-344/12, *Commission v Italy* EU:C:2013:667, para 50.

[184] Case 94/87, *Commission v Germany* [1989] ECR 175, para 10; Case C-183/91, *Commission v Greece* [1993] ECR I-3131, para 20; Case C-378/98, *Commission v Belgium* [2001] ECR I-5107, para 32; Case C-499/99, *Commission v Spain* [2002] ECR I-6031, para 25; Case C-404/00, *Commission v Spain* [2003] ECR I-6695, para 47; Case C-415/03, *Commission v Greece* [2005] ECR I-3875, para 43; Case C-207/05, *Commission v Italy* [2006] ECR I-70*, para 48; Cases C-485/03 to C-490/03, *Commission v Spain* [2006] ECR I-11887, para 74; Case C-419/06, *Commission v Greece* [2008] ECR I-8887, para 40; Case C-214/07, *Commission v France* [2008] ECR I-8357, para 46; Case C-304/09, *Commission v Italy* [2010] ECR I-13903, para 36.

[185] Case C-547/11, *Commission v Italy* EU:C:2014:1319, para 62.

[186] Case T-452/08, *DHL Aviation SA/NV v Commission* [2010] ECR II-218*, paras 42-43.

In *France v Commission*, it was argued that it was impossible to recover aid that had been granted to SNCM on the ground that social unrest might arise following the announcement of the compulsory liquidation of SNCM, unrest which would undermine public order and cause a break in the territorial continuity between Corsica and the French mainland. This was rejected by the ECJ, however, on the ground that France had provided no evidence to show either that it would be unable to deal with any social unrest or that services between Corsica and the mainland by other routes which enabled the island to be supplied with basic necessities would be impossible.[187]

Article 4(3) TEU also imposes a duty of cooperation on the Commission, although a breach of that duty does not affect the Member State's obligations to effect recovery. In *Commission v Germany*, the German Government contended that, with respect to the implementation of the recovery decision, the Commission had failed to comply with its obligation to cooperate in good faith in cases which presented difficulties. Although it notified an implementation measure to the Commission and, in addition, submitted an implementation proposal which could have replaced the first measure, the Commission had rejected both that measure and that proposal without any explanation. The ECJ held, in that regard, that the only defence available to a Member State in opposing an application by the Commission for a declaration that it has failed to fulfil its obligations was to plead that it was absolutely impossible for it to implement the decision properly. Since Germany had failed to take the measures necessary to recover the aid from the beneficiary, it followed that the alleged failure by the Commission to cooperate in good faith could not affect its failure to comply with its obligations.[188]

Proof of impossibility of complying with recovery decision The burden of proof in establishing that there are unforeseen or unforeseeable difficulties lies on the Member State.[189] In this respect, the Member State concerned must substantiate its defence and cannot rely on a bare statement that it would encounter difficulties in complying with the recovery order.[190] For example, the mere fact that the unlawful aid may need to be recovered from a large number of persons does not necessarily mean that recovery is impossible.[191] Equally, the fact that the Member State finds it necessary to examine the individual situation of each undertaking concerned for the purposes of

---

[187] Case C-63/14, *Commission v France* EU:C:2015:458, para 53.

[188] Case C-209/00, *Commission v Germany* [2002] ECR I-11695, para 72.

[189] Case C-349/93, *Commission v Italy* [1995] ECR I-343, para 16.

[190] Case C-349/93, *Commission v Italy* [1995] ECR I-343, paras 15-16; Case C-214/07, *Commission v France* [2008] ECR I-8357, para 63.

[191] Case C-280/95, *Commission v Italy* [1998] ECR I-259, para 23; Case C-378/98, *Commission v Belgium* [2001] ECR I-5107, para 42; Case C-441/06, *Commission v France* [2007] ECR I-8887, para 42.

recovering unlawful does not justify the failure to implement the decision.[192] In *Commission v Italy*, Italy sought to excuse its failure to recover unlawful aid where a scheme for employment and training aid had been partly allowed and partly declared incompatible with the internal market. It argued that the individual application of the scheme needed to be considered so that particular undertakings could be excluded from the recovery proceedings because of their size, location or type of business, or where they might reasonably be considered able to plead a legitimate expectation. The ECJ held, however, that Italy's failure to take the requisite recovery measures could not be justified on these grounds.[193]

Financial difficulties with which recipients might be confronted by the withdrawal of aid are not to be considered as making it absolutely impossible to implement a recovery decision.[194] Indeed, the fact that, on account of the financial position of the recipient of the aid, the Member State is wholly or partially unable to recover the sum paid does not constitute proof that implementation of the decision is impossible. In such a case, the Commission's objective of abolishing the aid can be attained by proceedings for winding up the company.[195]

Recovery not subject to requirements of national law A Member State may not plead requirements of its national law or other internal circumstances in order to justify its failure to comply with obligations arising out of a decision requiring it to alter, abolish or recover aid which has been found to be incompatible with the internal market.[196] A Member State may not rely, as making it absolutely impossible to implement the Commission's decision, on the obligations to which the competent administrative authority may be subject, under the rules governing the protection of legitimate expectations in national law with regard to the weighing up of the interests involved, concerning the

---

[192] Case C-99/02, *Commission v Italy* [2004] ECR I-3353, para 23; Case C-207/05, *Commission v Italy* [2006] I-70*, para 50; Case C-305/09, *Commission v Italy* [2011] ECR I-3225, para 37; Case C-303/09, *Commission v Italy* [2011] ECR I-102*, para 38; Case C-302/09, *Commission v Italy* [2011] ECR I-146*, para 51; Case C-549/09, *Commission v Italy* [2011] ECR I-155*, para 39; Case C-354/10, *Commission v Greece* EU:C:2012:109, para 73; Case C-243/10, *Commission v Italy* EU:C:2012:182, para 45; Case C-37/14, *Commission v France* EU:C:2015:90, para 69.

[193] Case C-99/02, *Commission v Italy* [2004] ECR I-3353, para 23.

[194] Case 63/87, *Commission v Greece* [1988] ECR 2875, para 14; Case C-404/87, *Commission v Portugal* [2000] ECR I-4897, para 53; Case C-280/05, *Commission v Italy* [2007] ECR I-181*, para 28.

[195] Case 52/84, *Commission v Belgium* [1986] ECR 89, para 14.

[196] Case 52/84, *Commission v Belgium* [1986] ECR 89, para 9; Case C-52/95 *Commission v France* [1995] ECR I-4443, para 38; Case C-265/95 *Commission v France* [1997] ECR I-6959, para 55; Case C-280/95 *Commission v Italy* [1998] ECR I-259, para 16; Case C-69/05, *Commission v Luxembourg* [2006] ECR I-7*, para 10; Case C-441/06, *Commission v France* [2007] ECR I-8887, para 43.

period within which an administrative act granting a benefit may be revoked. All relevant provisions of national law must be applied in such a way that the recovery required by EU law is not rendered practically impossible and the interests of the EU are fully taken into consideration.[197] In *Commission v Germany*, it was argued that a decision requiring recovery of aid should be interpreted as merely a requirement to recover the aid subject to the principles of national law, that being the law applicable to the recovery of the aid, and that the aid could not, in fact, be recovered without a breach of the principle of the protection of legitimate expectations. This submission was rejected outright by the ECJ on the ground that an obligation to recover aid is unconditional and unambiguous and is, therefore, definitive.[198] Accordingly, a Member State may not rely on the legitimate expectations of recipients in order to justify a failure to comply with the obligation to take steps necessary to implement a decision instructing it to recover the aid.[199] Nor may it rely on the principle of legal certainty.[200]

In *Belgium v Commission*, where the recipient of aid was the subject of composition proceedings, it was argued that the decision requiring the immediate recovery of unlawful aid was impossible to implement since this was contrary to the general principles of insolvency law whereby the State could only declare itself as an unsecured creditor of the undertaking and could not demand any privileged position over other creditors. The ECJ merely commented that the contested decision confined itself to ordering recovery of the aid, without prescribing the way in which that was to be done.[201] In *Germany v Commission*, the Bavarian authorities, as required by a decision of the Commission, sought the recovery of unlawful aid in proceedings in the Landgericht. That court ordered a stay of proceedings pursuant to the German civil code, whereby such an order was to be made if the result of the case depended on a legal relationship which was the subject of proceedings in another court, since an action for annulment of the Commission's decision was pending in the General Court. Since no appeal was lodged against that stay of proceedings, the Commission brought infringement proceedings against Germany.[202]

---

[197] Case C-5/89, *Commission v Germany* [1990] ECR I-3437, paras 18-19; Case C-404/87, *Commission v Portugal* [2000] ECR I-4897, para 55; Case C-404/00, *Commission v Spain* [2003] ECR I-6695, para 51.

[198] Case 94/87, *Commission v Germany* [1989] ECR 175, paras 6-8.

[199] Case C-5/89, *Commission v Germany* [1990] ECR I-3437, para 17; Case C-310/99, *Italy v Commission* [2002] ECR I-2289, para 104; Case C-39/06, *Commission v Germany* [2008] ECR I-93*, para 24; Cases T-116/01 & T-118/01, *P&O European Ferries (Vizcaya) SA v Commission* [2003] ECR II-2957, para 202.

[200] Case C-39/94, *SFEI v La Poste* [1996] ECR I-3547, para 73.

[201] Case C-142/87, *Belgium v Commission* [1990] ECR I-959, para 60.

[202] Case C-276/99, *Germany v Commission* [2001] ECR I-8055, para 11.

Interim measures The Commission may seek interim measures, pursuant to Article 279 TFEU, requiring a Member State to suspend or recover aid pending the judgment of the ECJ in infringement proceedings. In order for interim measures to be granted by the ECJ, the Commission must demonstrate the urgency of the matter in order to prevent serious and irreparable harm due to the continuation of the disputed practices from occurring whilst the main proceedings are pending.[203] In *Commission v United Kingdom*, the United Kingdom had unlawfully introduced and maintained in force a system of subsidies to pig farmers despite it being declared incompatible with the internal market by the Commission. On an application by the Commission for interim measures pending a declaration that the United Kingdom had infringed its Treaty obligations, the ECJ held that disregard of the prohibition in Article 108(3) TFEU, which prevents the Member States from putting into effect proposed measures until the Commission has come to a final decision on their compatibility with the Treaty, which is the means of safeguarding the machinery of review laid down in Article 108 TFEU, interferes with the proper operation of that machinery to such an extent as to be capable by itself of giving rise to the application of Article 279 TFEU. The fact that the Commission may have originally tried to remedy the situation without recourse to the ECJ cannot affect the gravity of that interference and thus exclude the application of Article 279 TFEU. Nor can the fact that the ECJ would hear the case in the near future militate against the need to ensure that the dispute between the Commission and the Member State concerned should be conducted with proper regard to the conditions and procedural requirements laid down by the Treaty.[204]

As to the effects on the recipients of the aid, at least where the Commission has made clear its objections to the compatibility of the aid with the internal market, the beneficiaries may be deemed to be aware of the precarious nature of the scheme.[205] Moreover, suspension would not necessarily have irreversible consequences since, if the decision is annulled, the Member State would be entitled to apply the aid measure retroactively.[206] On the other hand, if the aid was continued to be granted on a provisional basis, the effects on competitive relationships in the internal market would be more and more difficult to reverse where the aid was subsequently found to be incompatible with the internal market.[207]

Penalties for failure to comply with ECJ judgments Member States are required, pursuant to Article 260 TFEU, to take the steps necessary to comply

---

[203] Case 171/83R, *Commission v France* [1983] ECR 2621, para 17.

[204] Cases 31/77R & 53/77R, *Commission v United Kingdom* [1977] ECR 921, paras 20-22.

[205] Case 171/83R, *Commission v France* [1983] ECR 2621, para 26.

[206] Cases 31/77R & 53/77R, *Commission v United Kingdom* [1977] ECR 921, para 23.

[207] Case 171/83R, *Commission v France* [1983] ECR 2621, para 26.

with judgments of the ECJ. Failure to comply with the judgment puts the Member State concerned at risk of being brought before the ECJ again by the Commission, at which stage a financial penalty, in the form of a lump sum or periodic penalty payment or both, may be imposed. In exercising its discretion, it is for the ECJ to set the fine so that it is both appropriate to the circumstances and proportionate to the infringement established and the ability to pay of the Member State concerned.[208] The basic criteria which must be taken into account in order to ensure that financial penalties have coercive force and that EU law is applied uniformly and effectively are, in principle, the duration of the infringement, its degree of seriousness, the effect of the Member State's failure to comply on public and private interests and the urgency for the Member State concerned to fulfil its obligations.[209]

This procedure is commenced by the Commission specifying the amount of the lump sum or penalty payment that it considers appropriate in the circumstances,[210] although it is for the ECJ itself to assess, in the light of the circumstances of each case, the financial penalties to be imposed.[211] As with infringement proceedings under Article 258 TFEU, a Member State cannot plead provisions, practices or situations prevailing in its domestic legal order to justify the failure to observe obligations arising under EU law.[212] For instance, it cannot avoid liability by claiming that a regional authority is responsible.[213]

A penalty payment is, in principle, justified only in so far as the failure to comply with an earlier judgment continues up to the time of the ECJ's examination of the facts.[214] Such a penalty must be decided upon according to the degree of persuasion needed in order for the Member State concerned to

---

[208] Case C-278/01 *Commission v Spain* [2003] ECR I-14141, para 41; Case C-610/10, *Commission v Spain* EU:C:2012:781, para 118.

[209] Case C-369/07, *Commission v Greece* [2009] ECR I-5703, para 115; Case C-610/10, *Commission v Spain* EU:C:2012:781, para 144.

[210] The Commission issued a communication in 2005, which was updated in 2010, setting out the parameters on which it would recommend penalty and lump sum payments. These include a coefficient applicable to each Member State, which is regarded as an appropriate means of reflecting the ability to pay of Member States while keeping the variation between Member States within a reasonable range: Case C-369/07, *Commission v Greece* [2009] ECR I-5703, para 123. These guidelines, whilst not being binding on the ECJ, contribute to ensuring that the action brought by the Commission is transparent, foreseeable and consistent with legal certainty: Case C-70/06, *Commission v Portugal* [2008] ECR I-1, para 34; Case C-369/07, *Commission v Greece* [2009] ECR I-5703, para 112; Case C-96/09, *Commission v Italy* [2011] ECR I-11483, para 37.

[211] Case C-304/02, *Commission v France* [2005] ECR I-6263, para 86; Case C-369/07, *Commission v Greece* [2009] ECR I-5703, para 111.

[212] Case C-503/04, *Commission v Germany* [2007] ECR I-6153, para 19; Case C-369/07, *Commission v Greece* [2009] ECR I-5703, para 45.

[213] Case C-184/11, *Commission v Spain* EU:C:2014:316, para 43.

[214] Case C-119/04, *Commission v Italy* [2006] ECR I-6885, para 27; Case C-369/07, *Commission v Greece* [2009] ECR I-5703, para 59.

alter its conduct and bring to the infringement to an end.[215] Thus, for example, in *Commission v Spain*, the ECJ noted that 22 years had elapsed since the date of the recovery decision, thereby justifying a daily fine of €50,000,[216] whereas in *Commission v Greece*, in which a penalty payment of €16,000 per day was ordered for failure to recover fully aid from Olympic Airways, the ECJ noted that the amounts of aid that Greece had failed to prove had been repaid formed a relatively small part of the overall aid that had been granted.[217] In *Commission v Italy*, which concerned unlawful aid for training and work experience contracts, the penalty payment was fixed on a six monthly basis as a proportion of the aid that had not been recovered. With the unrecovered aid amounting to nearly €190 million, the ECJ fixed the penalty payment at €30 million per half-year.[218]

The decision whether to impose a lump sum payment must, in each individual case, depend on all the relevant factors pertaining to both the particular nature of the infringement established and the individual conduct of the Member State. The Court has a wide discretion in deciding whether or not to impose such a sanction.[219] In the *Olympic Airways* case, a lump sum payment of €2 million was ordered. In *Commission v Italy*, the lump sum was fixed at €30 million, taking account, in particular, of the fact that it was twelve years since the recovery decision had been issued. It might have been higher, but for the fact that the ECJ took into account that it accepted that recovery of the aid was made more difficult by the fact that it had been paid under an aid scheme and the Italian authorities had first to identify the recipients of the aid and the amounts received by each of them.[220] In *Commission v Spain*, on the contrary, where the ECJ held that compliance with the recovery obligation should not have met with major difficulties, given that the recipients of the unlawful aid in question were few in number, they were identified by name and the sums to be recovered were specified in the recovery decision, a lump sum fine of €20 million was imposed.[221] In another action against Spain, a lump sum penalty of €30 million was imposed as a dissuasive measure on account of the persistent failure to take steps to comply with a recovery decision.[222]

---

[215] Case C-304/02, *Commission v France* [2005] ECR I-6263, para 91; Case C-369/07, *Commission v Greece* [2009] ECR I-5703, para 113.

[216] Case C-610/10, *Commission v Spain* EU:C:2012:781, paras 122 and 135.

[217] Case C-367/09, *Commission v Greece* [2009] ECR I-5703, para 122.

[218] Case C-96/09, *Commission v Italy* [2011] ECR I-11483, para 67.

[219] Case C-121/07, *Commission v France* [2008] ECR I-9159, paras 62-63; Case C-367/09, *Commission v Greece* [2009] ECR I-5703, para 144.

[220] Case C-96/09, *Commission v Italy* [2011] ECR I-11483, para 96.

[221] Case C-610/10, *Commission v Spain* EU:C:2012:781, paras 145-147.

[222] Case C-184/11, *Commission v Spain* EU:C:2014:316, para 83.

Chapter Eighteen

ENFORCEMENT OF STATE AID LAW
IN NATIONAL COURT PROCEEDINGS

18.1 STATE AID LAW IN NATIONAL COURT PROCEEDINGS

State aid and national court proceedings Implementation of the system for supervision of State aid is a matter, on the one hand, for the Commission and, on the other, for the national courts. In that regard, the national courts and the Commission fulfil distinct but complementary roles, with differing powers and responsibilities.[1] Proceedings concerning State aid may arise in national courts in several contexts. A recipient of aid may have reason to seek a declaration that a measure does not constitute aid and does not need, therefore, to be notified to the Commission or he may seek to challenge an action for recovery by the national authorities following a negative decision by the Commission. Alternatively, a competitor or other interested party may seek a declaration that aid is unlawful. It may argue that the Commission's decision authorising an aid scheme is invalid so that aid should not be granted pursuant to it, or that aid either has not been notified to the Commission or has been implemented without it having been authorised by the Commission or the Council. Such proceedings may also involve an application for suspension or recovery of unlawful aid and, possibly, damages.

In 2006, the Commission commissioned a study on the enforcement of State aid law at national level which was aimed at providing a detailed analysis of private State aid enforcement in the different Member States.[2] Whilst the study found that there was a considerable amount of State aid litigation, it also revealed that a large number of the legal proceedings were not aimed at reducing the anti-competitive effect of the underlying State aid measures. Almost two thirds of the proceedings concerned actions brought by taxpayers who sought relief from the allegedly discriminatory imposition of a tax burden

---

[1] Case C-39/94, *SFEI v La Poste* [1996] ECR I-3547, para 41; Cases C-261/01 & C-262/01, *van Calster v Belgium* [2003] ECR I-12249, para 74; Case C-368/04, *Transalpine Ölleitung in Österreich v Finanzlandesdirektion für Tirol* [2006] ECR I-9957, paras 36-37; Case C-275/10, *Residex Capital IV CV v Gemeente Rotterdam* [2011] ECR I-13043, paras 25-26; Case C-6/12, *P Oy* EU:C:2013:525, para 37; Case C-284/12, *Deutsche Lufthansa AG v Flughafen Frankfurt-Hahn GmbH* EC:C:2013:755, para 27; Case C-69/13, *Mediaset v Ministero dello Sviluppo Economico* EU:C:2014:71, para 19.

[2] http://ec.europa.eu/comm/competition/state_aid/studies_reports/studies_reports.cfm.

or actions brought by beneficiaries to challenge the recovery of unlawful and incompatible State aid. The number of legal challenges aimed at enforcing compliance with the State aid rules was relatively small: actions by competitors against a Member State authority for damages, recovery or injunctive measures based on Article 108(3) TFEU accounted for only 19% of the judgments, whilst actions by competitors directly against beneficiaries accounted for only 6% of the judgments.

References to the ECJ for preliminary ruling National courts may refer questions to the ECJ for a preliminary ruling on interpretation and validity of EU State aid provisions pursuant to Article 267 TFEU. The ECJ does not have jurisdiction to rule upon the compatibility of a national measure with EU law, nor does it have jurisdiction to rule on the compatibility of State aid or of an aid scheme with the internal market. On the other hand, it does have jurisdiction to give the national court full guidance on the interpretation of EU law in order to enable it to determine the issue of compatibility of a national measure with that law for the purposes of deciding the case before it. In the area of State aid, the ECJ has jurisdiction, *inter alia*, to give the national court guidance on interpretation in order to enable it to determine whether a national measure may be classified as State aid under EU law.[3]

The need to provide an interpretation of EU law which will be of use to the national court makes it necessary that the national court define the factual and legislative context of the questions it is asking or, at the very least, explain the factual circumstances on which those questions are based. The national court should set out the precise reasons why it was unsure as to the interpretation of EU law and why it considered it necessary to refer questions for a preliminary ruling. In that connection, it is essential that the referring court provide at the very least some explanation of the reasons for the choice of the EU provisions which it requires to be interpreted and of the link it establishes between those provisions and the national legislation applicable to the dispute in the main proceedings. The information provided in the decision making the reference serves not only to enable the ECJ to give useful answers, but also to enable the governments of the Member States and other interested parties to submit observations.[4] Failure to satisfy these requirements will result in the reference being refused. Moreover, the ECJ will not entertain a reference where the interpretation that is sought of provisions of EU law bear no relation to the

---

[3] Case C-118/08, *Transportes Urbanos y Servicios Generles v Administracion del Estado* [2010] ECR I-635, para 23; Case C-140/09, *Fallimento Traghetti del Mediterraneo SpA v Presidenza del Consiglio dei Ministri* [2010] ECR I-5243, paras 22-24.

[4] Case C-567/07, *Minister van Wonen, Wijken en Integratie v Woningstichting Sint Servatius* [2009] ECR I-9021, paras 50-52; Case C-138/09, *Todaro Nunziatina v Assessorato del Lavoro* [2010 ECR I4561, para 16; Case C-523/12, *Dirextra Alta Formazione srl v Regione Puglia* EU:C:2013:831, para 19.

actual facts or where the problem is hypothetical.[5] Thus, for instance, in *Adiamix*, which concerned an action for recovery of unlawful aid following a negative decision of the Commission, a reference was refused on the ground that the national court had not provided any reasons as to why the issue of validity was necessary in the context of the national litigation.[6] In *Portugal v Banco Privado Português*, the ECJ declined to answer a question on the interpretation of Regulation (EC) No 659/1999, Article 14 in order to assess the compatibility of a particular national insolvency rule, on the ground that there was nothing in the file submitted by the national court to show that the rule in question was applicable to the proceedings.[7]

Cooperation between national courts and the Commission   Whereas Council Regulation (EC) No 659/1999 codifies and reinforces the procedures concerning the Commission's powers of supervision and enforcement of the State aid rules, that regulation does not contain any provision relating to the powers and obligations of national courts, which continue to be governed by the provisions of the EU Treaties as interpreted by the ECJ.[8] The Commission recognises that the principles for the application of State aid law by the national courts are complex and has issued a notice on enforcement of State aid law by national courts in order to clarify the issues involved.[9] In accordance with the duty of cooperation under Article 4(3) TEU, the Commission must assist national courts when they apply State aid law. The Commission is committed to helping national courts where the latter find such assistance necessary for their decision on a pending case.[10] Equally, national courts must take all the necessary measures, whether general or specific, to ensure fulfilment of their obligations under EU law and refrain from those which might jeopardise the attainment of the objectives of the EU Treaties.[11]

---

[5]   Case C-140/09, *Fallimento Traghetti del Mediterraneo SpA v Presidenza del Consiglio dei Ministri* [2010] ECR I-5243, para 29; Case C-181/13, *Acanfora v Equitalia Sud SpA* EU:C:2014:127, paras 16-19; Case C-68/14, *Equitalia Nord SpA v CLR di Camelliti Serafino & C Snc.* EU:C:2015:57, para 26.

[6]   Case C-368/12, *Adiamix v Direction departmentale des finances publiques de l'Orne* EU:C:2013:257, paras 27-32.

[7]   Case C-667/13, *Portugal v Banco Privado Português SA* EU:C:2015:151, paras 37-41.

[8]   Case C-368/04, *Transalpine Ölleitung in Österreich v Finanzlandesdirektion für Tirol* [2006] ECR I-9957, para 35.

[9]   http://ec.europa.eu/competition/state_aid/legislation/sa_law_enforcement_en.pdf.

[10]   Notice on the enforcement of State aid law by national courts, paras 77-78.

[11]   Article 4(3) TEU; Case C-69/13, *Mediaset v Ministero dello Sviluppo Economico* EU:C:2014:71, paras 29; Case C-527/12, *Commission v Germany* EU:C:2014:2193, para 56.

Transmission of information by the Commission National courts may ask the Commission for information in its possession.[12] This can, *inter alia*, include information on whether a procedure regarding a particular aid measure is pending before the Commission, whether a certain aid measure has been duly notified in accordance with Article 108(3) TFEU, whether the Commission has initiated a formal investigation, and whether the Commission has already taken a decision. In the absence of a decision, the national court may ask the Commission to clarify when this is likely to be adopted. In addition, national courts may ask the Commission to transmit documents in its possession. This can include copies of existing Commission decisions to the extent that these decisions are not already published on the Commission's website, factual data, statistics, market studies and economic analysis.[13] As a consequence of the duty of cooperation under Article 4(3) TEU, the Commission must respond as quickly as possible to requests from national courts.[14] The Commission will endeavour to provide the national court with the information requested within one month.[15] Any answer given by the Commission will not be binding on the national court,[16] although, if it so wishes, the national court may, pursuant to Article 267 TFEU, request the ECJ for a preliminary ruling on the definitive interpretation of Article 107(1) TFEU.

In transmitting information to national courts, the Commission needs to uphold the provisions on professional secrecy under Article 339 TFEU which prevents members, officials and other servants of the Commission from disclosing information, including business secrets, which is covered by the obligation of professional secrecy. This does not lead to an absolute prohibition for the Commission to transmit to national courts information covered by professional secrecy. On the contrary, the Commission must provide the national court with whatever information the latter may seek, including information covered by the obligation of professional secrecy. It follows that, where it intends to provide information covered by professional secrecy to a national court, the Commission will remind the court of its obligations under Article 339 TFEU and will ask the national court whether it can and will guarantee the protection of such confidential information and business secrets. Where the national court cannot offer such a guarantee, the Commission will not transmit the information concerned. Where, on the other hand, the national court has offered such a guarantee, the Commission will

---

[12] Council Regulation (EC) No 659/1999, Article 23a(1), (inserted by Council Regulation (EU) No 734/2013).

[13] Notice on the enforcement of State aid law by national courts, para 83.

[14] Case C-39/94, *SFEI v La Poste* [1996] ECR I-3547, para 50.

[15] Notice on the enforcement of State aid law by national courts, para 84.

[16] *Ibid.*, para 93.

transmit the information requested. Information concerning internal decision making will not be disclosed.[17]

Opinions of the Commission concerning State aid rules In the light of its obligations under Article 4(3) TEU and given the important and complex role which national courts play in State aid enforcement, national courts may request the Commission's opinion on relevant issues concerning the application of the State aid rules.[18] The introduction of the Commission's opinion to the national proceeding is subject to the relevant national procedural rules, which have to respect the general principles of EU law. When giving its opinion, the Commission will limit itself to providing the national court with the factual information or the economic or legal clarification sought, without considering the merits of the case pending before the national court. Moreover, the opinion of the Commission does not legally bind the national court. The Commission will endeavour to provide the national court with the requested opinion within four months from the date of the request. Since the Commission's assistance to national courts is part of its duty to defend the public interest, the Commission has no intention to serve the private interests of the parties involved in the case pending before the national court. The Commission will therefore not hear any of the parties involved in the national proceedings about its assistance to the national court.[19]

Commission opinions may, in principle, cover all economic, factual or legal matters which arise in the context of the national proceedings. Possible subject matters for Commission opinions include, *inter alia*: whether a certain measure qualifies as State aid within the meaning of Article 107(1) TFEU and, if so, how the exact aid amount is to be calculated; whether an aid measure meets the requirements of a block exemption regulation so that no individual notification is necessary and the standstill obligation under Article 108(3) TFEU does not apply; whether a certain aid measure falls under a specific aid scheme which has been notified and approved by the Commission or otherwise qualifies as existing aid; whether exceptional circumstances exist which would prevent the national court from ordering full recovery under EU law; assistance as regards the interest calculation and the interest rate to be applied on the recovery of unlawful aid; the legal prerequisites for damages claims under EU law and issues concerning the calculation of the damage incurred. Whilst national courts are not competent to assess the compatibility of State aid with the internal market, which falls within the exclusive competence of the Commission, this does not prevent the national court from requesting procedural information as to whether the Commission is already assessing the

---

[17] *Ibid.*, paras 85-88.
[18] Council Regulation (EC) No 659/1999, Article 23a(1), (inserted by Council Regulation (EU) No 734/2013).
[19] Notice on the enforcement of State aid law by national courts, paras 80, 93-96.

compatibility of a certain aid measure or intends to do so and, if so, when its decision is likely to be adopted.[20]

Commission submissions in national court proceedings Where the coherent application of Article 107(1) TFEU or Article 108 TFEU so requires, the Commission, acting on its own initiative, may submit written observations to the national courts that are responsible for applying the State aid rules. It may also, with the permission of the court, make oral observations. The Commission must, before formally doing so, inform the Member State concerned of its intention to submit observations. For the exclusive purpose of preparing its observations, the Commission may request the national court to transmit documents at the disposal of the court which are necessary for the Commission's assessment of the matter.[21]

Interpretation of Article 107(1) TFEU A national court may have cause to interpret and apply the concept of State aid contained in Article 107(1) TFEU in order to determine, for example, whether aid ought to have been notified.[22] It is by now well established that the notion of State aid as a matter of EU law must be determined objectively.[23] A court may have to make certain factual assessments, such as whether the measure in question may distort competition and affect trade between Member States or whether a measure conforms to the market transaction principle, but this does not grant the court any discretion as regards whether a measure constitutes aid or not. In *Ferring v ACOSS*, for example, the ECJ held that the national court was required to determine whether exemption for wholesale distributors of pharmaceutical products from a sales tax imposed on pharmaceutical laboratories resulted in any real advantage to the distributors who were entrusted with a public service

---

[20] *Ibid.*, paras 90-92.

[21] Council Regulation (EC) No 659/1999, Article 23a(2), (inserted by Council Regulation (EU) No 734/2013).

[22] Case 78/76, *Steinike und Weinlig v Germany* [1977] ECR 595, para 14; Case C-354/90, *FNCEPA v France* [1991] ECR I-5505, para 10; Case C-189/91, *Kirsammer-Hack v Sidal* [1993] ECR I-6185, para 14; Case C-39/94, *SFEI v La Poste* [1996] ECR I-3547, para 49; Case C-390/98, *HJ Banks & Co Ltd. v Coal Authority* [2001] ECR I-6117, para 72; Case C-345/02, *Pearle BV v Hoofdbedrijfschap Ambachten* [2004] ECR I-7139, para 31; Case C-368/04, *Transalpine Ölleitung in Österreich v Finanzlandes-direktion für Tirol* [2006] ECR I-9957, para 39; Case C-119/05, *Ministero dell'Industria, del Commercio e dell'Artigianato v Lucchini SpA* [2007] ECR I-6199, para 50; Case C-6/12, *P Oy*, EU:C:2013:525, para 38; Case C-672/13, *OTP Bank Nyrt v Hungary* EU:C:2015:185, para 31. M. Ross "State aids and national courts: Definitions and other problems - a case of premature emancipation?" (2000) 37 CMLRev 401.

[23] Case C-83/98P, *France v Ladbroke Racing Ltd. and Commission* [2000] I-3271, para 25; Case T-67/94, *Ladbroke Racing v Commission* [1998] ECR II-1, para 52; Case T-613/97, *Ufex v Commission* [2000] ECR I-4055, para 67; Cases T-195/01R & T-207/01R, *Government of Gibraltar v Commission* [2001] ECR II-3915, para 75.

obligation consisting of stocking sufficient supplies for a given geographical area.[24]

The national court should interpret national law in such a way that it is consistent with the requirements of EU law.[25] It should also take care not to adopt a decision which would have the sole effect of extending the circle of recipients of unlawful aid.[26] For example in *Sicilcassa v IRA Construzioni*, the ECJ held that a transitional system maintaining the effects of a State aid scheme that had not been notified to the Commission and which had been declared incompatible with the internal market by a Commission decision, had to be interpreted so far as possible in such a way as to ensure its compatibility with that decision, namely in such a way that it did not authorise the granting of new State aid after the abrogation of the aid scheme censured by the Commission decision.[27]

Assessment of compatibility of aid with the internal market Article 107(1) TFEU provides that State aid is incompatible with the internal market in so far as it distorts or threatens to distort competition and affects trade between Member States. In contrast to Article 101(1) TFEU which prohibits agreements which restrict competition and Article 101(2) TFEU which declares such agreements void, State aid is not declared by Article 107(1) TFEU to be prohibited as such.[28] By contrast, the incompatibility of State aid with the internal market is neither absolute nor unconditional, since the Commission and the Council have wide powers to determine that particular awards of aid or certain categories of aid are compatible with the internal market.[29] Given that assessment of the compatibility of aid measures falls within the exclusive competence of the Commission and the Council,[30] it

---

[24] Case C-53/00, *Ferring SA v ACOSS* [2001] ECR I-9067, para 28. See also, Case C-206/06, *Essent Netwerk Noord BV v Alumimium Delfzijl* BV [2008] ECR I-5497, para 86.

[25] Case C-119/05, *Ministero dell'Industria, del Commercio e dell'Artigianato v Lucchini* [2007] ECR I-6199, para 60.

[26] Case C-368/04, *Transalpine Ölleitung in Österreich v Finanzlandes-direktion für Tirol* [2006] ECR I-9957, para 57; Cases T-81/07 to T-83/07, *KG Holding NV v Commission* [2009] ECR II-2411, para 135.

[27] Case C-297/01, *Sicilcassa SpA v IRA Construzioni SpA* [2003] ECR I-7849, para 44; Case C-110/02, *Commission v Council* [2004] ECR I-6333, para 40.

[28] This may also be contrasted with Article 4(c) CS which prohibited State aid.

[29] Case 78/76, *Steinike und Weinlig v Germany* [1977] ECR 595, para 8; Case C-301/87, *Commission v France* [1990] ECR I-307, para 15; Case C-39/94, *SFEI v La Poste* [1996] ECR I-3547, para 36.

[30] Case 78/76, *Steinike und Weinlig v Germany* [1977] ECR 595, para 9; Case C-354/90, *FNCEPA v France* [1991] ECR I-5505, para 14; Case C-39/94, *SFEI v La Poste* [1996] ECR I-3547, para 42; Case C-295/97, *Piaggio v Ifitalia* [1999] ECR I-3735, para 31; Case C-119/05, *Ministero dell'Industria, del Commercio e dell'Artigianato v Lucchini SpA* [2007] ECR I-6199, para 52; Case C-284/12, *Deutsche Lufthansa AG v Flughafen*

follows that national courts have no jurisdiction to declare aid incompatible with the internal market pursuant to Article 107(1) TFEU or that it is compatible with the internal market pursuant to Article 107(3) TFEU.[31] Furthermore, national courts may not ask the ECJ on a reference under Article 267 TFEU for guidance as to the compatibility with the internal market of a given State aid or aid scheme.[32] On the other hand, national courts are competent to interpret and apply the block exemption regulations. They are not obliged to accept the Commission's interpretation of those regulations, and references may be made pursuant to Article 267 TFEU to the ECJ on such matters. National courts may also, in certain circumstances, have to interpret the Commission's guidelines. The ECJ has held that guidelines should be treated in a manner similar to Commission recommendations. Thus, even if those guidelines are not intended to produce binding effects, the national courts are bound to take them into consideration in order to decide disputes submitted to them, in particular where they cast light on the interpretation of national measures adopted in order to implement them or where they are designed to supplement binding EU provisions.[33]

Different considerations may arise in respect of assessments by national courts of aid under either Article 106(2) TFEU or Article 107(2) TFEU in so far as measures fulfilling the criteria set out in those provisions are *ipso facto* compatible with the internal market. Under Article 107(2) TFEU, certain types of aid are to be considered automatically to be compatible with the internal market. It may be that national courts should be competent to interpret the scope of the categories set out in Article 107(2) TFEU and to assess whether a particular aid or aid scheme falls within its scope. Advocate General Roemer in *Capolonga v Maya* took the view that the definition of permissible aid within the scope of Article 107(2) TFEU gives rise to a considerable margin of discretion which could not be left to national courts but rather ought to be implemented in a uniform manner throughout the European Union.[34] By contrast, Advocate General Tizzano, in *Ferring v ACOSS*, thought that the

---

Frankfurt-Hahn GmbH EU:C:2013:755, para 28; Case C-667/13, *Portugal v Banco Privado Português SA* EU:C:2015:151, para 66; Case T-60/05, *Ufex v Commission* [2007] ECR II-3397, para 106.

[31] Case 74/76, *Iannelli v Meroni* [1977] ECR 557, paras 11-12; Case C-72/92, *Herbert Scharbakte GmbH v Germany* [1993] ECR I-5509, para 19; Case C-451/03, *Servizi Ausiliari Dottori Commercialisti Srl v Calafiori* [2006] ECR I-2941, para 71; Case C-119/05, *Ministero dell'Industria, del Commercio e dell'Artigianato v Lucchini SpA* [2007] ECR I-6199, para 51.

[32] Case C-297/01, *Sicilcassa SpA v IRA Construzioni SpA* [2003] ECR I-7849, para 47; Case C-148/04, *Unicredito Italiano SpA v Agenzia delle Entrate, Ufficio Genova 1* [2005] ECR I-11137, para 42; Case C-237/04, *Enirisorse SpA v Sotocarbo SpA* [2006] ECR I-2843, para 23.

[33] Case C-410/13, *Batlanta UAB v Lietuvos valstybė* EU:C:2014:2134, para 64.

[34] Case 77/72, *Capolonga v Maya* [1973] ECR 611, at pp. 627-630. See also, Case 9/70, *Grad v Finanzamt Traunstein* [1970] ECR 825, at p. 853.

application of Article 106(2) TFEU, concerning payment for services in the public interest, is directly effective so that a national court may determine whether State payment compensates appropriately for the fulfilment of a general interest obligation.[35] This is now subject to the decision of the ECJ in *Altmark*, which lays down the criteria that need to be fulfilled for such compensation to be regarded as escaping the scope of the State aid rules.[36] In the application of these criteria, a national court is competent to determine that payment is a *quid pro quo* for the provision of the service. Where the compensation is not transparent or otherwise fails to comply with the *Altmark* criteria, so that it may involve State aid, it is for the Commission to decide whether it is permissible.[37] Moreover, Article 106(2) TFEU also provides that the derogation from the competition rules must not affect the development of trade to such an extent as would be contrary to the interests of the EU. In circumstances where that proviso is called into consideration, a national court may be an inappropriate forum.

Interim relief suspending aid measures pending ECJ reference Where a national court, in determining whether a measure constitutes aid which has not been notified to the Commission, seeks clarification from the Commission or refers questions to the ECJ for a preliminary ruling pursuant to Article 267 TFEU, and it is likely that some time will elapse before it gives its final judgment, it must decide whether it is necessary to order interim relief such as the suspension of the measures at issue in order to safeguard the interests of the parties.[38] The Commission, in its notice on enforcement of State aid law by national courts, commented that the power of national courts to adopt interim measures can be of central importance to interested parties where fast relief is required.[39] In the Commission's view, where the national judge has reached a reasonable *prima facie* conviction that the measure at stake involves unlawful State aid, the most expedient remedy will, subject to national procedural law, be to order the unlawful aid to be put on a blocked account until the substance of the matter is resolved. In its final judgment, the national court would then either order the funds on the blocked account to be returned to the State aid

---

[35] Case C-53/00, *Ferring SA v ACOSS* [2001] ECR I-9067, *per* Advocate General Tizzano, at para 78.

[36] Case C-280/00, *Altmark Trans v Nahverkehrsgesellschaft Altmark* GmbH [2003] ECR I-7747, para 95.

[37] Case C-126/01, *Ministre de l'économie, des finances et de l'industrie v GEMO SA* [2003] ECR I-13769, *per* Advocate General Jacobs, at paras 119-120.

[38] Case C-39/94, *SFEI v La Poste* [1996] ECR I-3547, para 52; Case C-368/04, *Transalpine Ölleitung in Österreich v Finanzlandesdirektion für Tirol* [2006] ECR I-9957, para 46.

[39] Notice on enforcement of State aid law by national courts, para 57.

granting authority, if the unlawfulness is confirmed, or order the funds to be released to the beneficiary.[40]

In *CELF v SIDE II*, the ECJ held that there is an obligation to adopt safeguard measures only if the conditions justifying such measures are satisfied, namely, that there is no doubt regarding the classification as State aid, that the aid is about to be, or has been, implemented, and that no exceptional circumstances have been found which would make recovery inappropriate. When ruling on the application, the national court may order either the repayment of the aid with interest or, for example, the placement of the funds on a blocked account so that they do not remain at the disposal of the recipient, without prejudice to the payment of interest for the period between the expected implementation of the aid and its placement on that blocked account.[41] By contrast, the standstill obligation set out in Article 108(3) TFEU would not be fulfilled, at that stage, by simply ordering interest to be paid on amounts which remain in the accounts of the undertaking, since it cannot be assumed that an undertaking which has unlawfully received State aid could, were it not for that aid, have obtained an equivalent amount by way of loan from a financial institution under normal market conditions and thus have that amount at its disposal prior to the Commission decision.[42]

Concurrent assessment by national court and Commission Concurrent assessment as to whether a measure constitutes State aid that should be notified may arise in proceedings in a national court and in a Commission investigation. A complainant, in particular, may well couple its complaint to the Commission with an action in the national court seeking an interim injunction preventing the aid from being given effect. This may give rise to concern that the national court and the Commission will come to opposite conclusions. In competition law concerning the enforcement of Articles 101-102 TFEU, it is generally the case that national courts should stay their proceedings where there is a danger of conflicting decisions.[43] No such provision was included in Council Regulation (EC) No 659/1999 as regards State aid procedures. In this respect, it may be noted that the scope of the proceedings in national courts is more restrictive in State aid matters than in other competition law disputes. Given the possible urgency of the proceedings before the national court, it cannot be necessary for it to suspend its proceedings pending a decision by the Commission, particularly given the possible delay in the Commission reaching a final decision.

---

[40] *Ibid.*, para 61.

[41] Case C-1/09, *CELF v SIDE* [2010] ECR I-2099, paras 35-37.

[42] *Ibid.*, para 38.

[43] Council Regulation (EC) No 1/2003, Article 16; Case C-344/98, *Masterfoods v HB Ice Cream* [2000] ECR I-11369, paras 55-57.

Nevertheless, the national court is somewhat circumscribed in its freedom to determine whether a measure constitutes State aid within the scope of Article 107(1) TFEU once the Commission has also started an investigation. In *Deutsche Lufthansa v Flughafen Frankfurt-Hahn*, Lufthansa brought an action in the German courts claiming that the airline fee structure at the publicly-owned Frankfurt-Hahn airport resulted in State aid being granted to Ryanair and seeking recovery of that aid coupled with an order that no further aid be granted.   In addition, following a complaint, the Commission investigated the matter and decided to open a formal investigation procedure, having come to the preliminary conclusion that the fee structures were selective and constituted State aid.   The ECJ held that the scope of the obligation imposed on the national court may vary depending on whether or not the Commission has initiated the formal investigation procedure with regard to the measure at issue in the proceedings before the national court.[44] Where the Commission has not yet initiated the formal examination procedure and has therefore not yet taken a decision as to whether the measures under consideration are capable of constituting State aid, it is for the national courts to verify whether the measure at issue constitutes an aid within the meaning of Article 107(1) TFEU.[45] On the other hand, where the Commission has already taken a decision to open a formal investigation procedure, national courts must refrain from taking decisions which conflict with the Commission's decision, even though the opening decision is provisional.[46]

Interim relief suspending aid measures during concurrent proceedings
The freedom of the national court as regards interim relief may also be constrained once the Commission has decided to open the formal investigation procedure under Article 108(2) TFEU, since such a decision necessarily alters the legal position of the measure under consideration, particularly as regards the pursuit of its implementation. In *Italy v Commission*, the Commission took the view that an aid measure constituted new aid, whereas Italy argued that it was an existing aid. The ECJ held that, whereas, until the adoption of such a decision, the Member State, the beneficiaries and other economic operators may think that the measure is lawful, after its adoption there is at the very least a significant element of doubt as to the legality of the measure which must lead the Member State to suspend it, since the initiation of the formal investigation procedure excludes the possibility of an immediate decision holding the measure compatible with the internal market which would enable it to be lawfully pursued. Such a decision might also be invoked before a national

---

[44] Case C-284/12, *Deutsche Lufthansa AG v Flughafen Frankfurt-Hahn GmbH* EC:C:2013:755, para 33.

[45] *Ibid.*, para 34.

[46] *Ibid.*, para 41.

court called upon to enforce the standstill requirement in Article 108(3) TFEU and that court could impose interim measures.[47]

Even if in its final decision the Commission were to conclude that there were no aid elements, the preventive aim of the State aid control system requires that, following the doubt raised in the decision to initiate the formal examination procedure, implementation of the measure should be deferred until that doubt is resolved by the Commission's final decision.[48] Consequently, the ECJ held in *Deutsche Lufthansa v Flughafen Frankfurt-Hahn* that, where the Commission has initiated the formal examination procedure with regard to a measure which is being implemented, national courts are required to adopt all the necessary measures with a view to drawing the appropriate conclusions from an infringement of the obligation to suspend the implementation of that measure. To that end, national courts may decide to suspend the implementation of the measure in question and order the recovery of payments already made. They may also decide to order provisional measures in order to safeguard both the interests of the parties concerned and the effectiveness of the Commission's decision to initiate the formal examination procedure.[49]

The ECJ also stated that, if national courts were able to hold that a measure does not constitute aid within the meaning of Article 107(1) TFEU and, therefore, not to suspend its implementation, even though the Commission had just stated in its decision to initiate the formal examination procedure that that measure was capable of presenting aid elements, the effectiveness of Article 108(3) TFEU would be frustrated. If the Commission's preliminary assessment is that the measure at issue constitutes aid and that assessment is subsequently confirmed in the Commission's final decision, the national courts would have failed to observe their obligation under Article 108(3) TFEU and Article 3 of Regulation (EC) No 659/1999 to suspend the implementation of any aid proposal until the adoption of the Commission's decision on the compatibility of that proposal with the internal market.[50]

Moreover, an ongoing Commission investigation does not release the national court from its duty to safeguard the rights of individuals in the event of an infringement of the obligation to notify aid in advance.[51] Thus, in *Flughafen Lübeck v Air Berlin*, in relation to aid allegedly granted to Ryanair at Lubeck-Blankensee airport, it was held that the national court may not just stay the proceedings pending the termination of the Commission's formal

---

[47] Case C-400/99, *Italy v Commission* [2001] ECR I-7303, para 59.

[48] Case C-284/12, *Deutsche Lufthansa AG v Flughafen Frankfurt-Hahn GmbH* EC:C:2013:755, para 40.

[49] *Ibid.*, paras 42-43.

[50] *Ibid.*, paras 38-39; Case C-27/13, *Flughafen Lübeck GmbH v Air Berlin plc* EU:C:2014:240, paras 20-27.

[51] Case C-39/94, *SFEI v La Poste* [1996] ECR I-3547, para 44.

investigation, since a decision to stay proceedings would, *de facto*, have the same effect as a decision to refuse the application for safeguard measures, equivalent to no decision on the merits being taken before the Commission's final decision.[52] By contrast, in *Gemeente Nijmegen v Commission*, where suspension was refused of a Commission opening decision concerning aid that had already been granted and was thus no longer in the course of implementation, the General Court held that even where a national court, before which an application of recovery was made, could order recovery of the aid in question, there was no obligation on it to do so at that stage. There was no absolute, unconditional obligation requiring the national court automatically to follow the Commission's provisional assessment, since it could, where it entertained doubts as to whether the measure constituted aid, refer the question to the ECJ.[53]

Res judicata of conflicting decisions of national court If the Commission and the national court come to conflicting determination as regards the status of an aid measure, it is likely that the Commission decision will be given precedence in order to ensure the effectiveness of EU law. For example, where the Commission ultimately decides that aid is unlawful and must be recovered, the recipient will not be able to rely in subsequent recovery decisions on a previous contrary decision of a national court finding that the measure in question did not constitute aid. In *Lucchini*, where aid was awarded to an Italian steel company in breach of the applicable provisions under the ECSC Treaty, the Commission adopted a decision declaring the aid incompatible with the internal market. Nevertheless, the beneficiary of the aid, which had not yet been paid, commenced proceedings in the national court claiming entitlement to the payments under the applicable Italian legislation and the court, without any reference to the Commission's decision, found in favour of the beneficiary. Subsequently, in further proceedings to enforce that payment, Lucchini relied on the principle of *res judicata*, which was recognised under the Italian Civil Code, to prevent the court from invoking the applicability of the Commission's decision. The ECJ, on the basis that the Commission had sole competence to determine the compatibility of the aid with the internal market and that this applied within the national legal order as a result of the primacy of EU law, required the national court to set aside the principle of *res judicata* in so far as it would prevent the recovery of State aid granted in breach of EU law which has been found to be incompatible with the internal market in a decision of the Commission which has become final.[54]

---

[52] Case C-27/13, *Flughafen Lübeck GmbH v Air Berlin plc* EU:C:2014:240, paras 30-32; Notice on enforcement of State aid law by national courts, para 62.

[53] Case T-251/13, *Gemeente Nijmegen v Commission* EU:T:2015:142, para 46.

[54] Case C-119/05, *Ministero dell'Industria, del Commercio e dell'Artigianato v Lucchini SpA* [2007] ECR I-6199, paras 62-63;.

In a subsequent case, however, the ECJ has recognised the importance of the principle of *res judicata* in the context of State aid proceedings and sought to portray the *Lucchini* judgment as concerning a highly specific situation.[55] In *Commission v Slovakia*, a tax liability was partially written off in the course of bankruptcy proceedings that required court approval. Subsequently, the Commission held that the tax write-off had been unduly generous and amounted to State aid. In recovery proceedings in the national court, the issue was raised as to whether the finality of the national court judgment could prevent recovery of the aid. The ECJ refused to rely on disapplying the principle of *res judicata*, holding instead that under Slovak law there were means, such as an extraordinary appeal procedure, which might have been used to challenge the judgment. Accordingly, it had not been shown by Slovakia that it had taken all the measures which it could have employed in order to obtain repayment of the aid.[56]

18.2 DIRECT EFFECT OF EU STATE AID LAW

Direct effect and existing aid The provisions of Article 107(1) TFEU are intended to have effect in the legal systems of the Member States where they have been put in concrete form by acts having general application provided for by Article 109 TFEU or by decisions in particular cases.[57] National courts must, therefore, accept as compatible with the internal market any State aid which has been authorised by the Commission or the Council, whether in a block exemption regulation or by an individual decision pursuant to Council Regulation (EC) No 659/1999, Article 4 or Article 7. Such aid is classified as existing aid. The Commission is required, in cooperation with the Member States, to keep existing systems of aid under constant review pursuant to Article 108(1) TFEU and to set in motion the appropriate procedure for finding that aid may be incompatible with the internal market.[58] This obligation is not, however, directly effective and does not give individuals the right to plead either failure by the State concerned to fulfil any of its obligations or breach of duty on the part of the Commission.[59] Since existing aid must be regarded as lawful as long as the Commission has not found it to be incompatible with the internal market, Article 108(3) TFEU does not give national courts the power

---

[55] Case C-2/08, *Amministrazione dell'Economia e delle Finanze v Fallimento Olimpiclub srl* [2009] ECR I-7501, para 22-25; Case C-507/08, *Commission v Slovakia* [2010] ECR I-13489, paras 59; Case C-529/09, *Commission v Spain* EU:C:2013:31, para 64; Case C-213/13, *Impresa Pizzarotti SpA v Comune di Bari* EU:C:2014:2067, para 61.

[56] Case C-507/08, *Commission v Slovakia* [2010] ECR I-13489, paras 56-64.

[57] Case 77/72, *Capolonga v Maya* [1973] ECR 611, para 6.

[58] Case 78/76, *Steinike und Weinlig v Germany* [1977] ECR 595, para 9; Case C-354/90, *FNCEPA v France* [1991] ECR I-5505, para 9.

[59] Case 6/64, *Costa v ENEL* [1964] ECR 585, at p.596.

to prohibit it.[60]   By contrast, where the Commission opens a formal investigation pursuant to Article 19(2) of Regulation (EC) No 659/1999 and subsequently takes a negative or conditional decision requiring the aid to be altered or abolished, direct effect will attach to that decision.

In *Pigs and Bacon Commission v McCarren*, an argument was raised to the effect that national courts were obliged as a matter of EU law to disapply national measures constituting existing aid where such aid was viewed by the national court as being incompatible, or as no longer being compatible, with the internal market. The argument was essentially on the basis that Article 4(3) TEU imposes on all Member States, and, therefore, on their national courts, a general obligation to ensure the fulfilment of the objectives of the EU Treaties. Accordingly, if a national court suspected that a provision of national law was potentially in conflict with the objectives of Article 107 TFEU, it was under an obligation to refrain from enforcing that law until it had been satisfied that no incompatibility with the internal market existed. That might require the court to stay proceedings before it until the Commission had ruled on the question of compatibility. At the very least, it was argued, Article 107 TFEU must be interpreted in the case of existing aids as according to the national court a discretion to refuse to enforce a national system or measure which is suspected of being incompatible with the internal market until a decision about it is forthcoming from the Commission. Otherwise a national court would be obliged, against its better judgement, to enforce provisions of national law which afterwards turned out to be illegal. Although the ECJ did not deal with this argument, Advocate General Warner dismissed it as being misconceived. He held that an existing aid lawfully introduced remains entirely lawful unless and until the Commission decides to abolish or alter it. Indeed, even then, it remains lawful until the expiry of the period of time prescribed by the Commission for its abolition or alteration. Such a decision of the Commission has no retroactive or declaratory effect. It follows that a national court is under no obligation under EU law, and has no discretion, to refuse to enforce a national law providing for such aid pending a decision of the Commission as to its compatibility with the internal market. It follows likewise that it is inappropriate for that court to refer to the ECJ pursuant to Article 267 TFEU any question as to the compatibility of the aid.[61]

Direct effect and new aid   Article 108(3) TFEU provides for a standstill requirement whereby Member States must notify any plan to grant new aid and must not put its proposed measure into effect until the Commission or the

---

[60]   Case C-262/11, *Kremikovtzi AD v Ministar na Ikonomikata* EU:C:2012:760, para 49; Case C-6/12, *P Oy* EU:C:2013:525, para 41; Case C-690/13, *Trapeza Eurobank Ergasias v ATE* EU:C:2015:235, para 37.

[61]   Case 177/78, *Pigs and Bacon Commission v McCarren* [1979] ECR 2161, *per* Advocate General Warner, at p. 2206.

Council has approved the aid. Direct effect is attributable to the prohibition on implementation of new aid arising from Article 108(3) TFEU, since it is defined with sufficient clarity and precision and does not require further implementing action, thereby establishing procedural criteria which the national court can appraise. The prohibition on implementation of new aid or of alterations to existing aid, therefore, gives rise to subjective rights in favour of individuals which national courts are bound to safeguard.[62] The provisions of Article 107(1) TFEU are also intended to have direct effect where they have been put in concrete form by decisions of the Commission or the Council in particular cases.[63] National courts are bound to enforce the prohibitions contained in conditional and negative decisions pursuant to Council Regulation (EC) No 659/1999, Article 7(4)-(5). They are also bound by decisions pursuant to Article 4(2)-(3) and Article 7(2)-(3) of Regulation (EC) No 659/1999 declaring either that the measure does not constitute State aid or that the aid is compatible with the internal market. Apart from the fact that national courts may not declare decisions void,[64] usually the decision being considered by the national court will be addressed to the Member State in which it is based and is, accordingly, binding on the court pursuant to Article 288 TFEU.

Direct effect and unlawful aid Where aid has been implemented in breach of the notification requirement in Article 108(3) TFEU, it will be regarded as unlawful.[65] The immediate enforceability of the prohibition on implementation referred to in Article 108(3) TFEU extends to all aid which has been implemented without being notified.[66] National courts and the Commission each have a procedural role to play in the enforcement of Article 108(3) TFEU, but these roles are complementary and separate.[67] Although the Commission does not have the power to declare aid incompatible with the internal market solely on the ground that the obligation to notify has not been complied with and without having investigated whether the aid may be permissible pursuant to Article 107(3) TFEU, that has no effect on the obligations of national courts deriving from the direct effect of the standstill requirement in Article 108(3)

---

[62] Case 6/64, *Costa v ENEL* [1964] ECR 585, at p.596; Case 120/73, *Lorenz v Germany* [1973] ECR 1471, para 8; Case C-354/90, *FNCEPA v France* [1991] ECR I-5505, para 11.

[63] Case 77/72, *Capolonga v Maya* [1973] ECR 611, para 6.

[64] Case 314/85, *Foto-Frost v Hza Lübeck-Ost* [1987] ECR 4199, para 20; Case C-119/05, *Ministero dell'Industria, del Commercio e dell'Artigianato v Lucchini SpA* [2007] ECR I-6199, para 53.

[65] Case C-354/90, *FNCEPA v France* [1991] ECR I-5505, para 14; Case C-275/10, *Residex Capital IV CV v Gemeente Rotterdam* [2011] ECR I-13043, para 28.

[66] Case 120/73, *Lorenz v Germany* [1973] ECR 1471, para 8; Case C-354/90, *FNCEPA v France* [1991] ECR I-5505, para 11; Case C-174/02, *Streekgeweest Westelijk Noord-Brabant v Staatsecretaris van Financiën* [2005] ECR I-85, para 15; Case C-284/12, *Deutsche Lufthansa AG v Flughafen Frankfurt-Hahn GmbH* EC:C:2013:755, para 29.

[67] Case C-39/94, *SFEI v La Poste* [1996] ECR I-3547, para 41.

TFEU. It follows that, whereas the Commission must examine the compatibility of the aid with the internal market, even where the Member State has acted in breach of the prohibition on giving effect to the aid,[68] national courts must preserve, until a final decision of the Commission approving the aid, the directly effective right of individuals not to be subject to measures which have not been notified and approved.[69]

Thus, the initiation by the Commission of the preliminary examination procedure or of the formal investigation procedure does not release the national court from its duty to safeguard the rights of individuals in the event of a breach of the requirement to give prior notification.[70] Even where the Commission's final decision approves the aid as compatible with the internal market, that decision is not retroactive and does not have the effect of regularising *ex post facto* the invalid measures, since otherwise the direct effect of the prohibition in Article 108(3) TFEU would be impaired and the interests of individuals would be disregarded. Any other interpretation would have the effect of according a favourable outcome to the non-observance of that provision by the Member State concerned and would deprive it of its effectiveness.[71]

Remedies for infringement of directly effective provisions Regarding the consequences of the direct effect of the prohibition in Article 108(3) TFEU, the ECJ has merely held that, whilst national courts are required to apply it without any possibility of its being excluded by rules of national law of any kind whatsoever, it is for the internal procedure of every Member State to determine the legal procedure leading to this result.[72] This is subject to the requirement that when preserving the interests of individuals, the national courts must take full account of the interests of the European Union.[73] National rules that are incompatible with directly applicable provisions of EU law must be left unapplied.[74] The ECJ has stated that, if the Member State has infringed Article 108(3) TFEU, the national court is required to exclude the application of

---

[68]   Case C-301/87, *France v Commission* [1990] ECR I-307, para 22.

[69]   Case C-354/90, *FNCEPA v France* [1991] ECR I-5505, para 14.

[70]   Case C-39/94, *SFEI v La Poste* [1996] ECR I-3547, para 44; Case C-284/12, *Deutsche Lufthansa AG v Flughafen Frankfurt-Hahn GmbH* EC:C:2013:755, para 32.

[71]   Case C-354/90, *FNCEPA v France* [1991] ECR I-5505, para 16; Cases C-261/01 & C-262/01, *Van Calster v Belgium* [2003] ECR I-12249, para 63; Case C-368/04, *Transalpine Ölleitung in Österreich v Finanzlandesdirektion für Tirol* [2006] ECR I-9957, para 41; Case C-199/06, *CELF v SIDE* [2008] ECR I-469, para 40.

[72]   Case 120/73, *Lorenz v Germany* [1973] ECR 1471, para 9.

[73]   Case C-368/04, *Transalpine Ölleitung in Österreich v Finanzlandesdirektion für Tirol* [2006] ECR I-9957, para 48.

[74]   Case 106/77, *Amministrazione delle Finanze delloe Stato v Simmenthal SpA* [1978] ECR 619, para 21.

national provisions establishing the aid.[75] In most cases, the remedy sought in the national court will be an injunction suspending or revoking the implementation of the contested measure. Nevertheless, the validity of a measure giving effect to aid is affected if national authorities put the measure into effect prior to a final decision from the Commission regarding the compatibility of the measure with the internal market.

In this respect, the national courts are not limited to procedural measures, such as a provisional block on further implementation.[76] Rather, national courts must offer to individuals in a position to rely on such breach the certain prospect that all the necessary inferences and appropriate conclusions will be drawn, in accordance with their national law, as regards the validity of measures giving effect to the aid, the recovery of financial support granted in disregard of that provision as well as interim measures.[77] It follows that, in appropriate circumstances, the national court must order restitution of payments made pursuant to an invalid aid measure by persons who have been required to fund the aid.[78] Actions for damages may also be brought against the Member State, or its authorities, that awarded the unlawful aid. Where the Commission ultimately adopts a positive decision, the national court, notwithstanding the declaration of the compatibility of the aid in question with the internal market, must still adjudicate on the validity of the implementing measures, at least during the interim period prior to approval, and on the recovery of any financial support granted.[79]

---

[75] Case C-690/13, *Trapeza Eurobank Ergasias v ATE* EU:C:2015:235, para 53.

[76] Case C-301/87, *France v Commission* [1990] ECR I-307, *per* Advocate General Jacobs, at para 37.

[77] Case C-354/90, *FNCEPA v France* [1991] ECR I-5505, para 12; Case C-39/94, *SFEI v La Poste* [1996] ECR I-3547, para 40; Case C-143/99, *Adria-Wien Pipeline GmbH v Finanzlandesdirektion für Kärnten* [2001] ECR I-8365, para 27; Case C-390/98, *HJ Banks & Co Ltd. v Coal Authority* [2001] ECR I-6117, para 73; Case C-400/99, *Italy v Commission* [2001] ECR I-7303, para 59; Cases C-261/01 and C-262/01, *Van Calster v Belgium* [2003] ECR-12249, para 64; Cases C-34/01 & C-38/01, *Enirisorse SpA v Ministero delle Finanze* [2003] ECR I-14243, para 42; Case C-174/02, *Streekgeweest Westelijk Noord-Brabant v Staatsecretaris van Financiën* [2005] ECR I-85, para 17; Case C-71/04, *Administración del Estado v Xunta de Galicia* [2005] ECR I-7419, para 49; Cases C-393/04 & C-41/05, *Air Liquide Industries Belgium SA v Ville de Seraing* [2006] ECR I-5293, para 42; Cases C-266/04 to C-270/04, C-276/04 & C-321/04 to C-325/04, *Distribution Casino France v Organic* [2005] ECR I-9481, para 30; Case C-526/04, *Laboratoires Boiron SA v URSSAF* [2006] ECR I-7529, para 29; Case C-368/04 *Transalpine Ölleitung in Österreich v Finanzlandesdirektion für Tirol* [2006] ECR I-9957, para 47; Case C-199/06, *CELF v SIDE* [2008] ECR I-469, para 41; Case C-275/10, *Residex Capital IV CV v Gemeente Rotterdam* [2011] ECR I-13043, para 29; Case C-690/13, *Trapeza Eurobank Ergasias v ATE* EU:C:2015:235, para 52.

[78] Case C-174/02, *Streekgeweest Westelijk Noord-Brabant v Staatsecretaris van Financiën* [2005] ECR I-85, para 19.

[79] Case C-199/06, *CELF v SIDE* [2008] ECR I-469, para 45.

National procedural rules In the absence of EU rules governing the matter, it is for national law to lay down detailed procedural rules governing actions safeguarding rights which individuals derive from the direct effect of EU law, provided that such rules are not less favourable than those governing similar domestic actions and that they do not render practically impossible or excessively difficult the exercise of rights conferred by EU law.[80] As regards the national rules relating to the determination of an individual's standing and legal interest in bringing proceedings, the ECJ has held that EU law requires that such rules must not undermine the right to effective judicial protection when exercising the rights conferred by EU law.[81] Where an undertaking that financed an aid subsequently discovers that the aid is unlawful, it will be bound by national limitation period provisions.[82] In *Q-Beef v Belgium*, where an exporter of animals had paid the levy that was subsequently declared unlawful in the *Van Calster* case,[83] the Belgian five year limitation period precluded his bringing an action for recovery. The ECJ held that this was not incompatible with the requirement of effectiveness, since proceedings might have been commenced within the five year period.[84]

National evidential rules National rules governing the requirement of proof must not affect the scope or effectiveness of EU law.[85] Any requirement of proof which has the effect of making it virtually impossible or excessively difficult to secure the repayment of charges levied contrary to EU law is incompatible with that principle. That is particularly so in the case of presumptions or rules of evidence.[86] In *Laboratoires Boiron v URSSAF*, in order to ensure compliance with the principle of effectiveness, the ECJ held that if the fact of requiring a pharmaceutical laboratory to prove that wholesale distributors were overcompensated, and thus that the tax on direct sales amounted to State aid, was likely to make it impossible or excessively difficult for such evidence to be produced, since *inter alia* that evidence related to data which the laboratory would not have, the national court was required to use all procedures available to it under national law, including that of ordering the

---

[80] Case 33/76, *Rewe-Zentralfinanz eG v Landwirtschaftskammer für das Saarland* [1976] ECR 1989, para 5; Case C-276/01, *Steffenson* [2003] ECR I-3735, para 60; Case C-526/04, *Laboratoires Boiron SA v URSSAF* [2006] ECR I-7529, para 51; Cases C-89/10 & C-96/10, *Q-Beef NV v Belgium* [2011] ECR I-7819, para 32; Case T-273/11, *NRJ Global v Commission* EU:T:2013:239, para 32.

[81] Case C-174/02, *Streekgeweest Westelijk Noord-Brabant v Staatsecretaris van Financiën* [2005] ECR I-85, para 18.

[82] Case T-273/11, *NRJ Global v Commission* EU:T:2013:239, para 35.

[83] Cases C-261/01 & C-262/01, *Van Calster v Belgium* [2003] RCR I-12249.

[84] Cases C-89/10 & C-96/10, *Q-Beef NV v Belgium* [2011] ECR I-7819, para 37.

[85] Case C-212/94, *FMC plc v IBAP* [1996] ECR I-389, para 53.

[86] Case 199/82, *Amministrazione delle Finanze dello Stato v San Giorgio SpA* [1983] ECR I-3595, para 14.

necessary measures of inquiry, in particular the production by one of the parties or a third party of a particular document.[87]

National substantive rules Certain substantive rules of national law governing remedies could affect the effectiveness of directly effective provisions of EU law in the national courts. For instance, a rule of law by virtue of which a sum paid under a mistake of law may be recovered only if it was paid under protest manifestly fails to provide a full and effective protection.[88] Similarly, national rules may not exclude a Member State's liability for loss of profit.[89]

Effect on validity of aid measure Although national courts must draw all the necessary consequences of an infringement of Article 108(3) TFEU with regard to the validity of the acts giving rise to the aid, EU law does not impose any specific consequence that the national courts must necessarily draw with regard to the validity of those acts. In *Residex Capital IV v Gemeente Rotterdam*, which concerned aid granted through a guarantee, the ECJ held that it was for the national court to determine whether cancellation of the guarantee might be a more effective means of restoring the pre-existing competitive situation than other measures. In particular, the ECJ acknowledged that there may be situations in which the cancellation of a contract, in so far as this is liable to lead to the mutual restitution of the services performed by the parties or the disappearance of an advantage for the future, may be better able to achieve the objective of restoring the competitive situation which existed before the aid was granted.[90]

18.3 CHALLENGES TO VALIDITY OF EU STATE AID DECISIONS

Challenge to validity of Commission decisions A national court cannot declare an EU act, including a Commission decision concerning State aid, void.[91] If a national court has reason to doubt the validity of an EU decision authorising aid, it may make a reference to the ECJ pursuant to Article 267 TFEU for a ruling on that issue. Where the Member State to which the decision has been addressed or any other interested party has also commenced proceedings for the annulment of the Commission's decision pursuant to

---

[87] Case C-526/04, *Laboratoires Boiron SA v URSSAF* [2006] ECR I-7529, para 55.
[88] Case C-212/94, *FMC plc v IBAP* [1996] ECR I-389, para 72.
[89] Case C-46 & 48/93, *Brasserie du Pêcheur SA v Germany* [1996] ECR I-1029, para 87.
[90] Case C-275/10, *Residex Capital IV CV v Gemeente Rotterdam* [2011] ECR I-13043, paras 44-48.
[91] Case 314/85, *Foto-Frost v Hza Lübeck-Ost* [1987] ECR 4199, para 20; Case C-119/05, *Ministero dell'Industria, del Commercio e dell'Artigianato v Lucchini SpA* [2007] ECR I-6199, para 53.

Article 263 TFEU, these will be heard in the General Court. In those circumstances, it is normal for one of the two courts to stay its proceedings pending the judgment of the other court.

In *Salt Union v Commission*, the General Court, having dismissed as inadmissible a challenge under Article 263 TFEU to the Commission's refusal to adopt appropriate measures in respect of an existing aid scheme, emphasised that this did not mean that in general undertakings are denied the right to challenge the grant of aid to their competitors. It was open to those undertakings to contest, before the national courts, the decision of national authorities to grant State aid. If the aid formed part of a general aid scheme, undertakings could call in question in those proceedings the validity of the Commission's decision approving the aid scheme.[92] This does not appear to take account of the fact that a decision approving an aid scheme can only be declared unlawful by reference to the circumstances prevailing at the time that it was taken.[93] It is because those circumstances might since have altered which prompts competitors to urge the Commission to propose appropriate measures to amend or abolish them.

***TWD* limitations to challenges on validity** State aid decisions are addressed to the Member State concerned. A decision adopted by an EU institution which has not been challenged by the addressee within the two-month time-limit laid down by Article 263 TFEU becomes definitive as against that person.[94] Furthermore, it is not possible for a recipient of State aid forming the subject-matter of a Commission decision addressed to a Member State, who could undoubtedly have challenged that decision as being directly and individually concerned by it but who allowed the time-limit in Article 263 TFEU to pass, effectively to call in question the lawfulness of that decision before the national courts in an action brought against the measures taken by the national authorities in implementation of that decision. Accordingly, the ECJ will not consider the purported illegality of a Commission decision where the party challenging the decision should have commenced annulment

---

[92]   Case T-330/94, *Salt Union Ltd. v Commission* [1996] ECR II-1475, para 39. See also, Case C-50/00P, *Unión de Pequeños Agricultores v Council* [2002] ECR I-6677, paras 36-44.

[93]   Case 234/84, *Commission v Belgium* [1986] ECR 2263, para 16; Case C-241/94, *France v Commission* [1996] ECR I-4551, para 33; Case C-288/96, *Germany v Commission* [2000] ECR I-8237, para 34; Case T-73/98, *Société Chimique Prayon-Rupel SA v Commission* [2001] ECR II-867, para 49.

[94]   Case C-188/92 *TWD Textilwerke Deggendorf* [1994] ECR I-833, para 13; Case C-241/01, *National Farmers' Union* [2002] ECR I-9079, para 34; Case C-119/05, *Ministero dell'Industria, del Commercio e dell'Artigianato v Lucchini SpA* [2007] ECR I-6199, para 54.

proceedings pursuant to Article 263 TFEU before the General Court but failed to do so.[95]

In *TWD v Germany*, the German Government was ordered by the Commission to recover aid which had been paid unlawfully to TWD. When Germany sought recovery in the national court, TWD argued that the Commission's decision was invalid and a reference was made to the ECJ pursuant to Article 267 TFEU in that respect. The ECJ held, however, that, since no proceedings had been brought for annulment pursuant to Article 263 TFEU despite the fact that TWD, being the recipient of the aid, was clearly directly and individually concerned by the decision, it was not open to TWD to plead the illegality of the decision in the national recovery proceedings. To accept that in such circumstances the person concerned could challenge the implementation of the decision in proceedings before the national court would in effect enable that person to overcome the definitive nature which the decision assumes as against that person once the time limit for bringing an action had expired.[96] By contrast, in *Portugal v Banco Privado Português*, where separate annulment proceedings had been brought against the Commission decision finding aid unlawful, it was open to the national court in enforcement proceedings to refer the question of validity of the decision to the ECJ. The fact that no suspension of the decision had been sought in the annulment proceedings pursuant to Article 278 TFEU was irrelevant.[97]

Limits to the *TWD* restriction Where a claimant has brought an action for annulment under Article 263 TFEU which has been rejected by the General Court as inadmissible on the ground that the applicant lacked a vested legal interest in having the decision annulled, nothing should prevent the applicant from requesting in subsequent national court proceedings that a reference be made pursuant to Article 267 TFEU putting in issue the validity of the decision.[98] The ECJ has commented that *TWD v Germany* concerned a company that had been undoubtedly entitled, and had been informed that it was

---

[95] Case C-188/92, *TWD v Germany* [1994] ECR I-833, para 17; Case C-178/95, *Wiljo NV v Belgium* [1997] ECR I-585, para 21; Case C-310/97P, *Commission v AssiDomän Kraft Products AB* [1999] ECR I-5363, para 60; Case C-390/98, *HJ Banks & Co Ltd. v Coal Authority* [2001] ECR I-6117, para 111; Case C-241/01 *National Farmers' Union* [2002] ECR I-9079, para 35; Cases C-346/03 & C-529/03, *Atzeni v Regione autonoma della Sardegna* [2006] ECR I-1875, para 31; Case C-119/05, *Ministero dell'Industria, del Commercio e dell'Artigianato v Lucchini SpA* [2007] ECR I-6199, para 55; Cases C-71/09P, C-73/09P & C-76/09P, *Comitato Venezia vuole vivere v Commission* [2011] ECR I-4727, para 58.

[96] Case C-188/92, *TWD v Germany* [1994] ECR I-833, para 18.

[97] Case C-667/13, *Portugal v Banco Privado Português SA* EU:C:2015:151, para 31.

[98] Case T-141/03, *Sniace SA v Commission* [2005] ECR II-1197, para 40.

entitled, to bring an action for annulment.[99] Thus, applicants are required to challenge a decision pursuant to Article 263 TFEU to protect their interests only if it has been concluded that such action is admissible beyond any doubt.[100] Other claimants, including competitors or other interested parties, in respect of whom it is not clear beyond doubt that they might have been directly and individually concerned by the Commission's decision and who did not commence annulment proceedings pursuant to Article 263 TFEU, will not be precluded from commencing national court proceedings.[101]

In *Atzeni v Regione autonoma della Sardegna*, the decision in question concerned aid schemes intended for categories of persons defined in a general manner. The ECJ held that since it was not self-evident that an action for annulment could have been brought by the recipients of the aid, they were entitled to challenge the decisions in national proceedings.[102] In *Gruppo ormeggiatori del porto di Venezia v Commission*, the General Court held that, in accordance with the principle of the sound administration of justice, beneficiaries of an aid scheme who had not directly challenged the Commission decision ordering recovery of the aid could not, for that reason, be declared out of time for pleading, as a defence, the unlawfulness of that decision before the national court, if, having regard to the particular circumstances of the case or to the complexity of the criteria which the Commission decision applied to the obligation of recovery, the question of whether those beneficiaries would be required to repay the aid in question, in implementation of the Commission decision, could reasonably have given rise to doubt initially, so that their interest in bringing proceedings against that decision was not obvious.[103] A similar problem of admissibility would arise where a claimant seeks to rely on the fact that the Member State to which the decision was addressed initially commenced annulment proceedings at the ECJ but subsequently withdrew its application for annulment. It might be open to the claimant to argue that it had a legitimate expectation that the Member State would have continued the proceedings or that it should be entitled to rely on the principle of procedural economy to excuse its forbearance from commencing its own annulment proceedings.

---

[99] Case C-241/95, *R v IBAP, ex parte Accrington Beef* [1996] ECR I-6699, paras 15-16; Case C-408/95, *Eurotunnel SA v Seafrance* [1997] ECR I-6315, paras 28-29.

[100] Cases C-71/09P, C-73/09P & C-76/09P, *Comitato Venezia vuole vivere v Commission* [2011] ECR I-4727, para 59.

[101] *Ibid.*, para 58.

[102] Cases C-346/03 & C-529/03, *Atzeni v Regione autonoma della Sardegna* [2006] ECR I-1875, paras 33-34.

[103] Cases T-228/00 etc., *Gruppo ormeggiatori del porto di Venezia Soc. Coop. rl v Commission* [2005] ECR II-787, para 31; Cases T-254/00, T-270/00 & T-277/00, *Hotel Cipriani SpA v Commission* [2008] ECR II-3269, para 90.

Temporal effects of a judgment declaring decision invalid Where an act is declared invalid following a reference to the ECJ, in exceptional circumstances the court may limit the temporal effects of its judgment, excluding from that limit only those undertakings which, prior to the judgment being delivered, brought proceedings or made an equivalent complaint regarding the matter. This is justified on the ground that overriding considerations of legal certainty affecting all the interests involved make it impossible in principle to reopen the question as regards the past.[104] A request by a Member State to limit the effects of a judgment may arise where it involves an aid scheme financed by parafiscal levies which may have to be repaid where the decision approving the scheme is subsequently annulled. Thus, in *Régie Networks v Direction de Contrôle Fiscal Rhône-Alpes Bourgogne*, concerning a French aid scheme for local radio stations financed by a levy on advertising, the ECJ, in limiting the effect of its judgment until the Commission adopted a fresh decision on the matter, took into consideration that the aid scheme had been applicable for five years and that a great deal of aid was paid under the scheme, affecting a large number of operators.[105]

Interim relief suspending EU decisions Where an enforcement action is brought in a national court seeking recovery of unlawful aid pursuant to a Commission decision, the national court may be faced with a challenge to the validity of the decision itself and must consider whether to suspend its enforcement. The ECJ has held that suspension of Commission decisions could be considered by the national court in appropriate circumstances. In *Deufil v Commission*, where an application to the ECJ for interim measures under Article 279 TFEU suspending a Commission decision requiring recovery of unlawfully granted aid was refused, the ECJ noted that the only directly applicable obligation under the decision was that imposed on Germany to recover the aid and that there was no direct obligation to pay on the part of the applicant. Recovery of the aid could not, therefore, be sought immediately. Rather, the applicant could only be made liable to repay the aid by a decision ordering recovery adopted by the German authorities on the basis of national provisions concerning cancellation of unlawful administrative acts. In that regard, the ECJ noted that the applicant would be entitled to institute administrative proceedings under German law for suspension of the operation of such a decision by the German authorities.[106] In *Department of Trade v British Aerospace*, where the United Kingdom authorities sought recovery of

---

[104] Case 43/75, *Defrenne v Sabena* [1976] ECR 455, para 75; Case C-38/90, *Regina v Lomas* [1992] ECR I-1781, para 28; Case C-333/07, *Régie Networks v Direction de Contrôle Fiscal Rhône-Alpes Bourgogne* [2008] ECR I-10807, para 121.

[105] Case C-333/07, *Régie Networks v Direction de Contrôle Fiscal Rhône-Alpes Bourgogne* [2008] ECR I-10807, para 123.

[106] Case 310/85R, *Deufil v Commission* [1986] ECR 537, para 19.

aid which had been held by the Commission to be illegal, the High Court suspended the recovery order on the ground that the Commission's decision was the subject of annulment proceedings in the ECJ pursuant to Article 263 TFEU which, if successful, would result in the claim for recovery being struck out.[107] This decision has been criticised on the ground that the High Court suspended recovery of the aid solely because the matter was the subject of judicial review at the ECJ, without considering the merits of the legality of the Commission's decision.[108]

It follows that the fact that an application for suspension has not been successful before the EU courts does not necessarily prevent suspension being ordered by the national court.[109] Nevertheless, in *Commission v Italy*, where the Italian courts had stayed recovery proceedings on the ground that the Commission decision ordering recovery was the subject of separate judicial review proceedings before the General Court, the ECJ held that it was not open to national courts to suspend recovery decisions other than where the criteria established in the *Zuckerfabrik Suderdithmarschen* case law were satisfied.[110] These require that the validity of the measure be referred to the ECJ, that the matter be urgent in that the interim relief is necessary to avoid serious and irreparable damage being caused to the person seeking the relief, that the national court takes account of the EU interest and that, in its assessment of those issues, the national court complies with any decisions of the EU courts on the lawfulness of the measure, including any applications for interim measures.[111]

18.4 RECOVERY OF UNLAWFUL AID

Recovery of unlawful aid following a Commission decision National courts must protect parties affected by the distortion of competition caused by the

---

[107] *Department of Trade v British Aerospace* [1991] 1 CMLR 165. The Commission's decision was subsequently annulled in Case C-294/90, *British Aerospace v Commission* [1992] ECR I-493.

[108] T. Sharpe, "The role of national courts in relation to Community law of State aids" in I. Harden ed., *State Aid: Community Law and Policy* (Cologne, 1993).

[109] Case T-181/02R, *Neue Erba Lautex v Commission* [2002] ECR II-5081, para 108; Case T-27/13R, *Elan v Commission* EU:T:2013:122, para 24.

[110] Case C-304/09, *Commission v Italy* [2010] ECR I-13903, para 45; Case C-305/09, *Commission v Italy* [2011] ECR I-3225, para 43; Case C-302/09, *Commission v Italy* [2011] ECR I-146*, para 46; Case C-243/10, *Commission v Italy* EU:C:2012:182, para 48; Case C-527/12, *Commission v Germany* EU:C:2014:2193, para 57.

[111] Cases C-143/88 & C-92/89, *Zuckerfabrik Süderdithmarschen AG v Hza Itzehoe* [1991] ECR I-415, para 33; Case C-465/93, *Atlanta Fruchthandelsgesellschaft v Bundesanstalt für Landwirtschaft* [1995] ECR I-3761, para 51.

grant of unlawful aid.[112] Where the Commission has taken a decision ordering the recovery of unlawful aid, the Member State is under an obligation pursuant to Council Regulation (EC) No 659/1999, Article 14(3) to take all steps necessary to recover the aid from the beneficiary without delay and in accordance with the procedures under national law, provided that they allow the immediate and effective execution of the Commission's decision.[113] Where the beneficiary refuses to repay the aid, the Member State should, therefore, commence enforcement proceedings in the national court for the recovery of the debt. If national procedural rules do not enable the enforcement of recovery, the Member State must take steps to put the necessary mechanisms in place.[114] Moreover, a national court is obliged to give full effect to EU law, including Commission decisions ordering recovery of aid, if necessary by refusing to apply any conflicting provision of national law.[115] Any national procedural rule that does not fulfil the conditions laid down in Article 14(3) of Regulation No 659/1999 as regards immediate and effective execution must, therefore, be left unapplied, thereby allowing the national court to have recourse to any other national law measures that are available to it to enforce recovery of the aid.[116] In that regard, review by the national court of the formal legality of an assessment issued for the recovery of unlawful State aid and possible annulment of the assessment on grounds of non-compliance with the requirements of national law must be viewed simply as an expression of the principle of effective judicial protection.[117]

In *Commission v Slovakia*, the Commission contested the fact that the Slovak authorities brought a debt recovery action in the national courts, rather than directly executing the recovery decision, as being in breach of the requirement of immediate and effective recovery. The ECJ, however, confirmed that Member States are free to choose the means of fulfilling the recovery obligation, provided that they do not affect the scope and effectiveness of EU law. The fact that recovery was sought through the initiation of legal proceedings was not therefore in itself a ground for

---

[112] Case C-368/04 *Transalpine Ölleitung in Österreich v Finanzlandesdirektion für Tirol* [2006] ECR I-9957, para 46; Case C-199/06, *CELF v SIDE* [2008] ECR I-469, para 38.

[113] Council Regulation (EC) No 659/1999, Article 14(3).

[114] Case C-214/07, *Commission v France* [2008] ECR I-8357, *per* Advocate General Sharpston, at para 76.

[115] Case 106/77, *Simmenthal* [1978] ECR 629, paras 21-24 Case C-213/89, *Queen v Secretary of State for Transport, ex parte Factortame* [1990] ECR I-2433, paras 19-21; Case C-119/05, *Ministero dell'Industria, del Commercio e dell'Artigianato v Lucchini SpA* [2007] ECR I-6199, para 61.

[116] Case C-232/05, *Commission v France* [2006] ECR I-10071, para 53; Case C-527/12, *Commission v Germany* EU:C:2014:2193, para 55.

[117] Case C-210/09, *Scott SA v Ville d'Orleans* [2010] ECR I-4613, para 25; Case C-527/12, *Commission v Germany* EU:C:2014:2193, para 45.

criticism.[118]   Similarly, in *Commission v Germany*, the ECJ stated that the German authorities were entitled to bring civil court proceedings in order to recover the aid.[119]   In *Commission v Greece*, where Greece argued that recovery of aid granted through the sale of property at an undervalue required a new legislative basis, the ECJ merely stated that Greek law provided for recovery actions where aid had been granted in the form of loans, guarantees or capital, and that new legislation for recovery was unnecessary.[120]

National recovery measures implementing Commission decisions   Where the Member State concerned has pleaded difficulties in implementing the Commission's decision on aid and has resolved those difficulties by cooperating in good faith with the Commission, the implementation measures ultimately adopted by that Member State fall to be assessed by the national court.   This is so even where the Commission has given its approval to the implementation proposed by the Member State concerned.   That approval merely serves to express the Commission's opinion as to whether that implementation is acceptable from an EU point of view, in the light of the difficulties in implementation encountered by that Member State, but it does not in any way affect the responsibility of the Member State concerned as to the identification and method of resolving those difficulties. If there were to be a dispute concerning the recovery of the aid after that approval, in particular with respect to the findings of fact contained in the contested decision or in the light of the precise quantification of the actual advantage to be recovered, it would be for the national court to resolve those remaining difficulties in implementation through its national rules, having regard to the contested decision and, if necessary, having regard to those remaining difficulties, bearing in mind the Commission's approval.[121]

In *Mediaset v Ministero dello Sviluppo Economico*, in a decision ordering recovery of aid granted as part of an aid scheme for digital terrestrial broadcasters offering pay-TV services and cable pay-TV operators, the Commission stated that, because of the special characteristics of the case, a suitable method for assessing the amounts to be recovered would be to determine the amount of additional profits generated as a result of the measure in question. In the context of establishing subsequent recovery measures with the Italian authorities, the Commission sent letters commenting on the proposed methods of calculating the aid to be recovered. In national court proceedings challenging these methods, the ECJ held that, while the recovery decision was binding on the national court, the Commission's letters could not

---

[118] Case C-507/08, *Commission v Slovakia* [2010] ECR I-13489, paras 51-53.
[119] Case C-527/12, *Commission v Germany* EU:C:2014:2193, para 44.
[120] Case C-263/12, *Commission v Greece* EU:C:2013:673, para 37.
[121] Case T-354/99, *Kuwait Petroleum (Nederland) BV v Commission* [2006] ECR II-1475, para 69.

be binding as they did not constitute decisions within the meaning of Article 288 TFEU and were not acts adopted on the basis of Regulation (EC) No 659/1999. Nevertheless, the principle of cooperation in good faith in Article 4(3) TEU required the court to take the letters into account to the extent that the Commission's statement of position was intended to facilitate the recovery of the aid.[122]

Disputes arising in connection with the enforcement of recovery are a matter for the national court alone. Recovery of aid is to be carried out in accordance with the rules and procedures laid down by national law, in so far as those rules and procedures do not have the effect of making the recovery required by EU law practically impossible and do not undermine the principle of equivalence with procedures for deciding similar but purely national disputes.[123] In *Mediaset*, the ECJ confirmed that, taking account of all the information available to it, it could not be excluded that a national court would find that the actual quantification of the aid to be repaid amounts to zero.[124]

Recovery of unlawful aid without a Commission decision In proceedings where a claimant has successfully invoked the direct effect of the prohibition on the implementation of unapproved aid in Article 108(3) TFEU, national courts must order the necessary remedial action and are not limited to measures suspending the aid or preventing further grants of aid. On the contrary, they are required, having decided that any measures already taken are unlawful, to provide all appropriate available remedies, including the repayment of aid already paid.[125] Furthermore, the recovery of aid may entail the adoption of measures to ensure the re-establishment of the pre-existing competitive position, in order to place the relevant parties in the competitive position that would have existed in the absence of the aid having been unlawfully granted and to eliminate any undue competitive advantage gained by the recipient.[126] In addition, damages may be available to a competitor who has suffered as a result of the distortion of competition.

Interest should normally be ordered on the amount repayable, since the recipient has had the benefit of the unlawful aid as equivalent to an interest free loan. Where the Commission has taken a negative decision, Council Regulation (EC) No 659/1999, Article 14(2) requires that interest be included in the amount to be recovered and Commission Regulation (EC) No 794/2004,

---

[122] Case C-69/13, *Mediaset v Ministero dello Sviluppo Economico* EU:C:2014:71, paras 25-32.

[123] Case C-297/01, *Sicilcassa and Others* [2003] ECR I-7849, paras 41-42; Case C-69/13, *Mediaset v Ministero dello Sviluppo Economico* EU:C:2014:71, para 34; Case C-527/12, *Commission v Germany* EU:C:2014:2193, para 41.

[124] Case C-69/13, *Mediaset v Ministero dello Sviluppo Economico* EU:C:2014:71, para 37.

[125] Case C-301/87, *France v Commission* [1990] ECR I-307, *per* Advocate General Jacobs, at p. 339.

[126] Case C-199/06, *CELF v SIDE* [2008] ECR I-469, para 51.

Article 11(2) states that this is to be calculated on a compound basis. In the case where a national court itself orders recovery, based on the infringement of Article 108(3) TFEU, in the absence of EU rules governing interest, it should normally be for national law to determine whether simple or compound interest will apply.[127] The Commission, which takes a different view in its notice on the enforcement of State aid law by national courts, states that national courts should apply their procedural rules consistently with Regulation (EC) No 794/2004, so that interest must be calculated on a compound basis. On the other hand, where national law allows for a stricter calculation of the interest rate, the principle of equivalence requires that that higher rate be applied also to claims based on Article 108(3) TFEU.[128]

Subsequent positive decision approving aid   Where the Commission subsequently adopts a positive decision finding aid that was unlawfully implemented in breach of Article 108(3) TFEU compatible with the common market, the national court must order the measures appropriate effectively to remedy the consequences of the period of unlawfulness. Nevertheless, since the aid is lawful as to the future, the national court is not necessarily required to order full recovery of the previously unlawful aid.[129] Indeed, a beneficiary may even be able to enforce the payment of such aid.[130] Advocate General Jacobs stated in *FNCEPA v France* that in order to ensure that no benefit is obtained from the illegal payment of the aid, if it is necessary in the circumstances to allow an undertaking to retain any aid paid prematurely, such aid being set off against aid payable subsequently under a plan found compatible with the common market, then an adjustment may have to be made to offset any competitive advantage that would accrue to the undertaking concerned by reason of the early payment.[131] In general, this will require interest to be paid in respect of the period during which the aid was unlawful, although it is not inconceivable that other measures may also have to be taken to reinstate the previously existing competitive position. The period in respect of which interest in payable is the entire period from the aid being first paid to the date of the Commission's approval decision. In *CELF v SIDE I*, where previous decisions approving the aid had been annulled, the ECJ held that since those decisions were void the aid granted under them had been unlawful and interest had to be paid accordingly for the whole period of the unlawful aid.[132]

---

[127] Case C-295/07P, *Commission v Départment du Loiret* [2008] ECR I-9363, para 85.

[128] Notice on the enforcement of State aid law by national courts, para 41.

[129] Case C-199/06, *CELF v SIDE* [2008] ECR I-469, para 46; Case C-384/07, *Wienstrom GmbH v Bundesminister für Wirtschaft und Arbeit* [2008] ECR I-10393, para 28.

[130] Case C-384/07, *Wienstrom GmbH v Bundesminister für Wirtschaft und Arbeit* [2008] ECR I-10393, para 32.

[131] Case C-354/90, *FNCEPA v France* [1991] ECR I-5505, *per* Advocate General Jacobs, at p. 5520.

[132] Case C-199/06, *CELF v SIDE* [2008] ECR I-469, para 69.

In *CELF v SIDE I*, the ECJ explained that the standstill provision in Article 108(3) TFEU is based on the preservative purpose of ensuring that an incompatible aid will never be implemented. That purpose is achieved first, provisionally, by means of the prohibition which it lays down, and, later, definitively, by means of the Commission's final decision, which, if negative, precludes for the future the implementation of the notified aid plan. The intention of the prohibition is, therefore, that compatible aid may alone be implemented. In order to achieve that purpose, the implementation of planned aid is to be deferred until the doubt as to its compatibility is resolved by the Commission's final decision. When the Commission adopts a positive decision, it is then apparent that this purpose has not been frustrated by the premature payment of the aid.[133] In that case, competitors of the recipient will have suffered earlier than they would have had to, in competition terms, the effects of compatible aid. The undue advantage will have consisted, first, in the non-payment of the interest which it would have paid on the amount in question of the compatible aid, had it had to borrow that amount on the market pending the Commission's decision, and, second, in the improvement of its competitive position as against the other operators in the market while the unlawfulness lasts.[134] Advocate General Mazák argued that the mere requirement to pay interest on the aid for the period prior to the Commission's approval decision would not constitute an effective sanction and that full recovery of the aid as a matter of EC law was needed.[135] The ECJ held, however, that the remedy to be imposed by the national court is based partly on EU law and, if appropriate, partly on national law. Applying EU law, the court must order the recipient to pay interest in respect of the period of unlawfulness.[136] In addition, within the framework of its domestic law, the national court may, if appropriate, also order the recovery of the unlawful aid, without prejudice to the Member State's right to re-implement it subsequently.[137]

Annulment of subsequent positive decision   The position is further complicated where a positive decision declaring previously unnotified aid compatible with the internal market is itself subsequently annulled and national court proceedings for recovery of the aid are commenced while the Commission reconsiders the compatibility of the measure. In *CELF v SIDE II*, the ECJ reiterated that the national court must make an immediate ruling and

---

[133] *Ibid.*, paras 47-49.

[134] *Ibid.*, paras 50-51.

[135] Case C-199/06, *CELF v SIDE* [2008] ECR I-469, per Advocate General Mazák at paras 32-33.

[136] Case C-199/06, *CELF v SIDE* [2008] ECR I-469, para 52.

[137] Case C-368/04 *Transalpine Ölleitung in Österreich v Finanzlandesdirektion für Tirol* [2006] ECR I-9957, para 56; Case C-199/06, *CELF v SIDE* [2008] ECR I-469, paras 53.

may not stay its proceedings until the Commission has ruled again on the compatibility of the aid. The situation in such proceedings was similar to a situation in which proceedings were brought before the national court on the basis of Article 108(3) TFEU, even though no decision had yet been adopted by the Commission on the compatibility of aid under assessment. The ECJ stressed the national court's obligation not to defer its examination of any application for safeguard measures. A decision to stay proceedings would have the same effect as a decision to refuse the application for safeguard measures in that no decision on the merits of that application would be taken before the Commission's decision. This would amount to maintaining the benefit of aid during the period in which implementation was prohibited, which would be inconsistent with the very purpose of Article 108(3) TFEU and would render that provision ineffective.[138]

Legitimate expectations justifying non-recovery There may be exceptional circumstances in which it would be inappropriate to order repayment of the aid.[139] In particular, EU law does not prevent national law from having regard to such considerations as the protection of legitimate expectations.[140] Accordingly, in national court proceedings for the recovery of unlawful aid, a recipient of illegally granted aid is not precluded from relying on exceptional circumstances, on the basis of which it had legitimately assumed the aid to be lawful, to decline to refund the aid.[141] For example, in *Sicilcassa v IRA Construzionio*, the Commission had taken a decision declaring certain aid that had not been notified incompatible with the internal market, but declined to order recovery on the ground that the Commission's prior classification of the aid scheme as existing aid had engendered a legitimate expectation on the part of the aid recipients. The ECJ held that, in proceedings in the Italian courts in which the issue of recovery of the aid was raised by reason of the fact that it had not been notified, it was for the national court to decide whether any such aid should be recovered or not, taking into account the general principles of its own internal law, including the principle of the protection of legitimate

---

[138] Case C-1/09, *CELF v SIDE* [2010] ECR I-2099, paras 24-33.

[139] Case C-39/94, *SFEI v La Poste* [1996] ECR I-3547, para 70; Case C-199/06, *CELF v SIDE* [2008] ECR I-469, para 42; Case C-275/10, *Residex Capital IV CV v Gemeente Rotterdam* [2011] ECR I-13043, para 35; Case C-672/13, *OTP Bank Nyrt v Hungary* EU:C:2015:185, para 72.

[140] Cases 205-215/82, *Deutsche Milchkontor v Germany* [1983] ECR 2633, para 33; Case 310/85, *Deufil v Commission* [1987] ECR 901, *per* Advocate General Darmon, at p. 919. See, by analogy, Council Regulation (EC) No 659/1999, Articles 14-15; Commission Notice on enforcement of State aid law by national courts, para 32.

[141] Case C-5/89, *Commission v Germany* [1990] ECR I-3437, para 16; Case C-310/99, *Italy v Commission* [2002] ECR I-2289, para 103; Case C-199/06, *CELF v SIDE* [2008] ECR I-469, para 43; Case T-109/01, *Fleuren Compost BV v Commission* [2004] ECR II-127, para 136; Cases T-239/04 & T-323/04, *Italy v Commission* [2007] ECR II-3265, para 155.

expectations, the circumstances of the case and especially the Commission's decision.[142] Nevertheless, the fact that the Commission may have previously declared the aid measure compatible with the internal market, even on three separate occasions as in *CELF v SIDE II*, is not of itself such as to give rise to exceptional circumstances. The ECJ noted that such circumstances arise as part of the normal operation of the judicial system, which grants individuals who believe that they have suffered as a result of the unlawfulness of aid the possibility of bringing proceedings for the annulment of successive decisions which they consider to be the cause of that situation.[143]

The application of a principle, such as the protection of legitimate expectations, requires the various interests involved to be weighed up.[144] In this respect, however, the ECJ has also held that the national law must be applied in such a way that the recovery required by EU law is not rendered practically impossible and that the interests of the European Union are taken fully into consideration.[145] Without prejudice to its right to rely on exceptional circumstances on the basis of which it had legitimately assumed the aid to be lawful, the recipient cannot invoke the principle of legitimate expectations in respect of aid granted pursuant to a decision which has been challenged under Article 263 TFEU within the relevant time limit so long as the court has not delivered a definitive judgment.[146]

National procedural rules preventing recovery National procedural rules must allow for the immediate and effective recovery of unlawful aid. In *Scott v Ville d'Orleans*, proceedings were brought challenging the validity of an assessment issued by the French authorities for recovery of aid on the ground that the assessment had not specified certain particulars required by French law, including the name of the official who signed the assessment. The ECJ acknowledged that such requirements were intended to increase administrative transparency and to afford citizens the opportunity to ascertain that an administrative decision was taken by a competent authority. In that regard, review by the national court of the formal legality of an assessment must be viewed as an expression of the principle of effective judicial protection which is a general principle of EU law.[147] In those proceedings, however, given that the aid had in fact already been repaid, the ECJ held that it would be contrary to the effective application of the recovery decision if the funds were to be

---

[142] Case C-297/01, *Sicilcassa SpA v IRA Construzioni SpA* [2003] ECR I-7849, para 41.

[143] Case C-1/09, *CELF v SIDE* [2010] ECR I-2099, paras 51-54.

[144] Case 94/87, *Commission v Germany* [1989] ECR 175, para 12.

[145] Case C-142/87, *Belgium v Commission* [1990] ECR I-959, para 61; Case C-480/98, *Spain v Commission* [2000] ECR I-8717, para 34.

[146] Case C-169/95, *Spain v Commission* [1997] ECR I-135, para 53; Case C-199/06, *CELF v SIDE* [2008] ECR I-469, paras 64-68; Cases T-116/01 & T-118/01, *P&O European Ferries (Vizcaya) SA v Commission* [2003] ECR II-2957, para 205.

[147] Case C-210/09, *Scott SA v Ville d'Orleans* [2010] ECR I-4613, paras 23-25.

made available again, even provisionally, to the recipient. Such a consequence would be incompatible with the recovery decision. Accordingly, Regulation (EC) No 659/1999, Article 14(3) was to be interpreted as not precluding annulment by the national court of assessments issued in order to recover the unlawful State aid on grounds of there being a procedural defect, where it was possible to rectify that procedural defect under national law, but it did preclude those amounts being paid once again, even provisionally, to the beneficiary of that aid.[148] In *Commission v Italy*, concerning recovery of tax incentives for trade fairs abroad, the Italian authorities sought recovery of the aid by adopting legislation which the Commission regarded as having been taken too late and which proved ineffective. Accordingly, this was not consistent with the requirement for immediate and effective recovery.[149]

Suspension of recovery under national law In *Commission v France*, where the Commission brought proceedings against France for having failed to recover aid granted to Scott in the form of a sale of land at less than market value, the French authorities relied on the fact that its demand for repayment had been challenged in the French courts and that French law provides for automatic suspensory effect attaching to actions brought against demands for payment, so that those demands could not produce any concrete effect in terms of reimbursement of that aid before the competent national court has given its decision. Under Article 14(3) of Council Regulation (EC) No 659/1999, the application of national procedures is subject to the condition that they allow the immediate and effective execution of the Commission's decision. The ECJ emphasised that the application of national procedures should not impede the restoration of effective competition by preventing the immediate and effective execution of the Commission's decision. To achieve this result, Member States should take all necessary measures ensuring the effectiveness of that decision. By providing for the suspensory effect of actions brought against demands for payment issued for the recovery of aid granted, the procedure laid down by French law could not be considered to allow the immediate and effective execution of the decision. On the contrary, it could considerably delay the recovery of the aid. Thus, by failing to have regard to the objectives pursued by the EU rules on State aid, that national procedure prevented the immediate restoration of the previously existing situation and prolonged the unfair competitive advantage resulting from the aid at issue. It followed that the French procedural rule providing for the suspensory effect of actions brought against demands for payment did not fulfil the conditions laid down in Article 14(3) of Regulation No 659/1999 and should therefore have been left unapplied.[150]

---

[148] *Ibid.*, paras 26-33.
[149] Case C-305/09, *Commission v Italy* [2011] ECR I-3225, para 40.
[150] Case C-232/05, *Commission v France* [2006] ECR I-10071, paras 51-53.

18.5 ACTIONS FOR RESTITUTION AND DAMAGES

Illegality of measures giving rise to unlawful aid Member States are in principle required to repay charges that are levied in breach of EU law.[151] Persons who have been affected by a measure giving rise to unlawful aid may be entitled to a declaration that that measure is itself invalid and that any payments made pursuant to it are subject to restitution. This is particularly relevant where the aid has been granted through the tax system. Where unlawful aid is financed out of a charge levied specifically for the purpose, as distinct from out of general taxation, so that the tax is an integral part of the aid measure in that it is hypothecated to the aid, the national court must order that those charges be refunded.[152] Thus, where an aid measure of which the method of financing is an integral part has been implemented in breach of the obligation to notify, national courts must in principle order reimbursement of charges or contributions levied specifically for the purpose of financing that aid.[153] This follows from the fact that the obligation to notify also covers the method of financing the aid, so that the consequences of a failure to comply with Article 108(3) TFEU apply also to that aspect of the aid.[154] Where a person seeks repayment of taxes levied in breach of Article 108(3) TFEU, the question whether he has been affected by the distortion of competition arising from the aid measure is irrelevant to the assessment of his interest in bringing proceedings. The only fact to be taken into consideration is that he is subject to a tax which is an integral part of a measure implemented in breach of the prohibition referred to in that provision.[155]

In *Van Calster*, the ECJ authorised the national court to order the reimbursement of a charge that had been levied on the import or slaughter of animals to finance an aid scheme for the protection of public and animal health that had not been notified in advance to the Commission.[156] In *Enirisorse v*

---

[151] Cases C-192/95 to C-218/95, *Comateb v Directeur Général des Douanes et Droits Indirects* [1997] ECR I-165, para 20; Cases C-261/01 & C-262/01, *Van Calster v Belgium* [2003] ECR-12249, para 53; Case C-174/02, *Streekgeweest Westelijk Noord-Brabant v Staatsecretaris van Financiën* [2005] ECR I-85, para 16.

[152] Cases C-261/01 & C-262/01, *Van Calster v Belgium* [2003] ECR-12249, paras 53-54; Case C-526/04, *Laboratoires Boiron SA v URSSAF* [2006] ECR I-7529, para 43; Case T-473/12, *Aer Lingus Ltd v Commission* EU:T:2015:78, para 67. See also, Case 177/78, *Pigs and Bacon Commission v McCarren* [1979] ECR 2161, *per* Advocate General Warner, at p. 2205; Case C-354/90, *FNCEPA v France* [1991] ECR I-5505, *per* Advocate General Jacobs, at p. 5520.

[153] Cases C-261/01 & C-262/01, *Van Calster v Belgium* [2003] ECR I-12249, paras 53-54.

[154] *Ibid*, para 52.

[155] Case C-174/02, *Streekgeweest Westelijk Noord-Brabant v Staatsecretaris van Financiën* [2005] ECR I-85, para 19; Case C-522/13, *Ministerio de Defensa v Concello de Ferrol* EU:C:2014:2262, para 50.

[156] Cases C-261/01 & C-262/01, *Van Calster v Belgium* [2003] ECR-12249, para 64.

Ministero delle Finanze, which concerned port charges for loading and unloading of goods, the ECJ held that it was not only the allocation of a proportion of the port charges to the undertaking concerned that might constitute State aid but also the collection from users of the proportion corresponding to the sum so allocated and that, if that aid has not been notified, it was for the national court to take all measures necessary to prevent both the allocation of a proportion of the charges to the recipient undertakings and the collection of that proportion of the charges.[157]   In *Laboratoires Boiron v URSSAF*, reimbursement could be claimed of that part of the tax imposed on the direct supply of medicinal products which amounted to overcompensation of wholesale distributors for the public service obligations involved in maintaining a full range of products.[158]

Reimbursement of special taxes that constitute State aid   In *Banks v Coal Authority*, the ECJ held that persons liable to pay an obligatory contribution could not rely on the argument that an exemption enjoyed by other persons constituted State aid in order to avoid payment of that contribution.[159] However, a right to reimbursement will exist in the exceptional case where the tax and the aid measure constitute two inseparable elements of one and the same fiscal measure.[160]   In that event, the tax and the aid are more closely linked than in the case of a parafiscal charge, such that the measure alleged to constitute aid is the tax itself and not some exemption which is separable from that tax.[161]   Accordingly, in *Laboratoires Boiron v URSSAF*, reimbursement of the tax at issue in *Ferring v ACOSS* was claimed before the French courts by a direct supplier of medicinal products, with the ECJ holding that in such a case, those who were subject to the tax could plead that the tax itself was unlawful, for the purposes of applying for reimbursement, on the ground that it amounted to an aid measure.   It followed, in the circumstances, that reimbursement could be claimed of that part of the tax which amounted to overcompensation of wholesale distributors for the public service obligations involved in

---

[157]   Cases C-34/01 to C-38/01, *Enirisorse SpA v Ministero delle Finanze* [2003] ECR I-14243, para 45.

[158]   Case C-526/04, *Laboratoires Boiron SA v URSSAF* [2006] ECR I-7529, para 47.

[159]   Case C-390/98, *HJ Banks & Co Ltd v Coal Authority* [2001] ECR I-6117, para 80; Cases C-430/99 & C-431/99, *Inspecteur van de Belastingdienst Douane v Sea-Land Service Inc.* [2002] ECR I-5235, para 47; Cases C-266/04 to C-270/04, C-276/04 & C-321/04 to C-325/04, *Distribution Casino France v Organic* [2005] ECR I-9481, para 42; Cases C-393/04 & C-41/05, *Air Liquide Industries Belgium SA v Ville de Seraing* [2006] ECR I-5293, para 43; Case C-526/04, *Laboratoires Boiron SA v URSSAF* [2006] ECR I-7529, para 30; Case C-368/04 *Transalpine Ölleitung in Österreich v Finanzlandesdirektion für Tirol* [2006] ECR I-9957, para 49; Case T-533/10; *DTS v Commission* EU:T:2014:629, para 92.

[160]   Case C-526/04, *Laboratoires Boiron SA v URSSAF* [2006] ECR I-7529, para 45.

[161]   Case C-526/04, *Laboratoires Boiron SA v URSSAF* [2006] ECR I-7529, para 39; Case T-473/12, *Aer Lingus Ltd v Commission* EU:T:2015:78, para 67.

maintaining a full range of products.[162] By contrast, in *Distribution Casino France v Organic*, where it was claimed that an exemption for small stores from a tax on retailer outlets constituted aid, the tax itself was not unlawful, so that business which were liable to pay the tax could not rely on the illegality of the exemption in order to avoid payment of the tax or obtain reimbursement.[163]

Aid granted through differential taxation   In cases where a claimant successfully argues that aid has been granted through differential taxation, whereby its competitors have been subject to a lower rate of tax, it should be borne in mind that the primary obligation on the national court is to recover the aid so as to restore the competitive situation prior to the payment of the unlawful aid, rather than to place competitors on an equal footing as such.[164] In *Banks v Coal Authority*, the ECJ held that where there is differential treatment in the application of charges, which does not appear to be justified by the nature or general scheme of the system, it is necessary to determine what is the normal application of the system of charges in relation to the nature or general scheme of that system.[165]   On this basis, the court, where it finds that the lower rate is a derogation from the general scheme, should order those who were charged at that rate to pay an amount to compensate for the reduction in their past liability.   It is not open to the national court, therefore, to order that the claimant also be subject to tax at the lower rate, at least as to past transactions, in order to eliminate the distortion of competition, since that may result merely in State aid also being granted to other operators.[166]   As to the future, the aid element in the differential taxation can be eliminated by the Member State concerned either by lowering the higher rate or by increasing the lower rate.[167]

Damages for infringement of EU law   The principle that the State is liable for damage caused to individuals as a result of breaches of EU law for which it can be held responsible is inherent in the system of the EU Treaties.[168]   Intentional fault or negligence is not a prerequisite to liability.[169]   Rather, with regard to a

---

[162] Case C-526/04, *Laboratoires Boiron SA v URSSAF* [2006] ECR I-7529, para 47.

[163] Cases C-266/04 to C-270/04, C-276/04 & C-321/04 to C-325/04, *Distribution Casino France v Organic* [2005] ECR I-9481, para 44.

[164] Case C-390/98, *HJ Banks & Co Ltd. v Coal Authority* [2001] ECR I-6117, para 75.

[165] *Ibid.*, para 34.

[166] *Ibid.*, para 80; Cases C-266/04 to C-270/04, C-276/04 & C-321/04 to C-325/04, *Distribution Casino France v Organic* [2005] ECR I-9481, para 42; Cases C-393/04 & C-41/05, *Air Liquide Industries Belgium SA v Ville de Seraing* [2006] ECR I-5293, para 43; Case C-526/04, *Laboratoires Boiron SA v URSSAF* [2006] ECR I-7529, para 30.

[167] Case T-473/12, *Aer Lingus Ltd v Commission* EU:T:2015:78, para 60.

[168] Cases C-6 & 9/90, *Francovich v Italy* [1991] ECR I-5357, para 35.

[169] Cases C-46 & 48/93, *Brasserie du Pêcheur SA v Germany* [1996] ECR I-1029, para 80; Cases C-178-179 & 188-190/94, *Dillenkofer v Germany* [1996] ECR I-4845, para 28.

breach of EU law for which a Member State, acting in a field in which it has a wide discretion in taking legislative decisions, can be held responsible, there is a right to compensation when three conditions are met: the rule of law infringed must be intended to confer rights on individuals; the breach must be sufficiently serious; and there must be a direct causal link between the breach of the obligation resting on the Member State and the damage sustained by the injured parties.[170] If the Member State is not required to make any legislative choices and has only reduced, or even no, discretion, the mere infringement of a provision of EU law may be sufficient to establish the existence of a sufficiently serious breach.[171]

Actions for damages against the State The ECJ has recognised that the grant of unlawful aid may cause the Member States to have to make reparation for damage caused by the unlawful nature of the aid.[172] Equally, an action for damages may be commenced against a Member State that fails to comply with a recovery order.[173] Actions for damages against the State in relation to State aid matters may arise in several contexts. An undertaking may sue the national authorities for failure to grant aid under a particular scheme. For example, in *Technische Glaswerke Ilmenau v Commission*, the Commission recognised that the applicant might have had rights against the Land of Thuringia which had allegedly failed to grant investment aid due under a particular scheme, although such rights would presumably arise solely under national law governing the award of the investment aid, rather than as a matter of EC law.[174] In *Nuova Agricast Srl v Ministero delle Attività Produttive*, a claim for damages was made in the Italian courts against the State for failing to ensure in its negotiations with the Commission that the Commission's approval included certain investments in accordance with the principle of equal treatment.[175]

The Commission, in its decisions finding that aid has been granted unlawfully, has no power to award compensation to competitors who may have suffered damage as a result of the aid. Nevertheless, a breach of the

---

[170] Cases C-46 & 48/93, *Brasserie du Pêcheur SA v Germany* [1996] ECR I-1029, para 51; Case C-173/03, *Traghetti del Mediterraneo SpA v Italy* [2006] ECR I-5177, para 45.

[171] Case C-5/94, *The Queen v Ministry of Agriculture, Fisheries and Food, ex parte Hedley Lomas (Ireland) Limited* [1996] ECR I-2553, para 28; Case C-127/95 *Norbrook Laboratories Ltd v MAFF* [1998] ECR I-1531, para 109; Case C-424/97, *Haim v Kassenzahnärztliche Vereinigung Nordrhein* [2000] ECR I-5123, para 38; Case C-278/05, *Robins v Secretary of State for Work and Pensions* [2007] ECR I-1053, para 71.

[172] Case C-199/06, *CELF v SIDE* [2008] ECR I-469, para 55; Case C-334/07P, *Commission v Freistaat Sachsen* [2008] ECR I-9465, para 54.

[173] Notice on the enforcement of State aid law by national courts, para 69.

[174] Case T-198/01, *Technische Glaswerke Ilmenau GmbH v Commission* [2004] ECR II-2717, para 69.

[175] Case C-390/06, *Nuova Agricast Srl v Ministero delle Attività Produttive* [2008] ECR I-2577, para 2.

prohibition in Article 108(3) TFEU on implementation of aid prior to the decision of the Commission or the Council approving it as being compatible with the internal market may well satisfy the criteria for making the State liable in damages to persons who have suffered damage. In *Belgium v Commission*, Advocate General Tesauro thought that an infringement of Article 108(3) TFEU may lead to an action for damages against the State by competitors of the recipient who were damaged by the unlawful grant of aid.[176] Advocate General Jacobs agreed, in *SFEI v La Poste*, that the State may be subject to claims for damages brought in respect of unlawfully paid aid.[177] Certainly, Article 108(3) TFEU is intended to confer rights on individuals and Member States have no discretion not to notify State aid measures.[178] It may not always be evident, however, that a measure constitutes aid which required notification, so that a failure to notify may not necessarily always be regarded as a sufficiently serious breach by the State of its obligations under EU law. One of the factors that a national court may take into account in establishing liability is the clarity and precision of the rule breached.[179]

Damages and distortion of competition A mere breach of Article 108(3) TFEU is not of itself sufficient to confer a right to damages in all cases of unlawful State aid.[180] In *Banks v Coal Authority*, the ECJ, having held that repayment of unlawful aid could not, in the circumstances, be recovered, thought, nevertheless, that this was without prejudice to any action for compensation which competitors might bring, if the conditions were met, for compensation for any damage caused to them by the distortion of competition.[181] Thus, whereas the unlawful action is the infringement of the standstill clause in Article 108(3) TFEU, as Advocate General Jacobs pointed out in *Transalpine Ölleitung in Österreich v Finanzlandesdirektion für Tirol*, an award of damages is not automatically consequent on the infringement of the direct effect of that provision.[182] Damages are required only in so far as there is a distortion of competition which affects the relevant competitors. Distortion of competition is not, however, a cause of action in itself, but must

---

[176] Case 142/87, *Belgium v Commission* [1990] ECR I-959, *per* Advocate General Tesauro, at p. 985.

[177] Case C-39/94, *SFEI v La Poste* [1996] ECR I-3547, at *per* Advocate General Jacobs, at p. 3573.

[178] Notice on the enforcement of State aid law by national courts, para 47.

[179] Cases C-46 & 48/93, *Brasserie du Pêcheur SA v Germany* [1996] ECR I-1029, para 56; Case C-392/93, *The Queen v H.M. Treasury, ex parte British Telecommunications plc* [1996] ECR I-1631, para 42; Case C-283, 291 & 292/94, *Denkavit Internationaal BV v Bundesamt für Finanzen* [1996] ECR I-5063, para 50.

[180] M. Honoré and N. Jensen, "Damages in State aid cases" [2011] EStALQ 265.

[181] Case C-390/98, *HJ Banks & Co Ltd. v Coal Authority* [2001] ECR I-6117, para 80.

[182] Case C-368/04 *Transalpine Ölleitung in Österreich v Finanzlandesdirektion für Tirol* [2006] ECR I-9957, *per* Advocate General Jacobs at para 86.

be proved as a consequence of the State's unlawful action. Advocate General Tesauro, in *Belgium v Commission*, recognised the difficulties in bringing an action for damages where there is uncertainty, especially in a market which is not oligopolistic, in regard to determining the link between the aid granted and the alleged damage.[183]

In its notice on the enforcement of State aid law in national courts, the Commission identifies various elements that may arise for consideration in determining the amount of damages. Where the unlawful aid enabled the beneficiary to win over a contract or a specific business opportunity from the claimant, damages would be available for the revenue which the claimant was likely to generate under this contract. More complicated damage assessments are necessary where the aid merely leads to an overall loss of market share. One possible way for dealing with such cases could be to compare the claimant's actual income situation with the hypothetical income situation had the unlawful aid not been granted. There can also be circumstances where the damage suffered by the claimant exceeds the lost profit. This could, for example, be the case where, as a consequence of the unlawful aid, the claimant is forced out of business.[184] Even where the aid is subsequently declared compatible with the internal market by the Commission, a claim for compensation may be made for damage caused by the premature implementation of the aid.[185]

Claimants other than competitors Persons other than competitors may suffer damage as a result of aid being granted unlawfully, although it seems unlikely that EU law, as opposed to national law, would require any payment of compensation. It was argued, in *Commission v Belgium*, that the recovery of State aid would operate to damage the interests of the creditors of the undertaking if it was forced into liquidation. Advocate General Lenz, in holding that the aid should nevertheless be recovered, thought that, should third parties be harmed by the unlawful conduct of the Member State, their remedy lay in the national courts and reliance on the legal provisions governing the liability of public bodies for unlawful acts.[186] Advocate General Tesauro, in *Belgium v Commission*, even thought that the recipient of aid, payment of which was suspended or cancelled by reason of the infringement of the procedural rules, might be entitled to damages against the State.[187] Such a claim was brought in proceedings in the Italian courts by Atzeni and others

[183] Case C-142/87, *Belgium v Commission* [1990] ECR I-959, *per* Advocate General Tesauro, at p. 986.
[184] Notice on the enforcement of State aid law by national courts, para 49.
[185] Case C-199/06, *CELF v SIDE* [2008] ECR I-469, para 55.
[186] Case 52/84, *Commission v Belgium* [1986] ECR 89, *per* Advocate General Lenz, at p. 99.
[187] Case C-142/87, *Belgium v Commission* [1990] ECR I-959, *per* Advocate General Tesauro, at p. 986.

against the Italian authorities in respect of damage allegedly suffered on the reimbursement of certain unlawful aid, although the ECJ did not comment on this issue.[188] A contrary conclusion was reached by Advocate General Slynn in *Asteris v Greece*, on the ground that such compensation would itself amount to unlawful State aid.[189] In *Départment du Loiret v Commission*, the General Court held that if the central administration of a Member State has not complied with its obligation to notify aid, to the detriment of a regional or local authority or of the beneficiary of the aid, those circumstances constitute a problem internal to the parties, although the General Court gave no indication whether this might give rise to a right to compensation in the national courts.[190]

Actions for damages against the recipient The machinery for reviewing and examining State aid established by Article 108 TFEU and Regulation (EC) No 659/1999 does not impose any specific obligation on the recipient of aid. Rather, the notification requirement and the prohibition on implementing unnotified aid are directed to the Member States.[191] Advocate General Jacobs in *SFEI v La Poste* thought that the remedies available to a competitor, such as recovery orders and damages against a Member State, were capable of providing an effective response to a breach of those provisions.[192] That being so, EU law does not provide a sufficient basis for the recipient to incur liability to any competitor where he has failed to verify that the aid received was duly notified to the Commission. That does not prejudice the possible application of national law concerning non-contractual liability which might provide that the acceptance by an economic operator of unlawful assistance of a nature such as to occasion damage to other economic operators may cause him to incur liability.[193] National law might, for example, provide for an action in damages against a recipient who has induced the authorities of a Member State to grant it aid, knowing that the aid was unlawful and would damages the interests of its competitors. In *Betws Anthracite v DSK*, however, the English High Court held that where a recipient misused aid, and thereby causes a distortion of competition to the detriment of its competitors, there was no cause of action in English or EU law against the recipient.[194]

---

[188] Cases C-346/03 & C-529/03, *Atzeni v Regione autonoma della Sardegna* [2006] ECR I-1875, paras 20 and 22.

[189] Cases 106-120/87, *Asteris v Greece* [1988] ECR 5515, *per* Advocate General Slynn, at p. 5530.

[190] Case T-369/00, *Départment du Loiret v Commission* [2003] ECR II-1789, para 58.

[191] Cases C-278-280/92, *Spain v Commission* [1994] ECR I-4103, para 76.

[192] Case C-39/94, *SFEI v La Poste* [1996] ECR I-3547, *per* Advocate General Jacobs, at p. 3574.

[193] Case C-39/94, *SFEI v La Poste* [1996] ECR I-3547, paras 74-75; Case C-140/09, *Fallimento Traghetti del Mediterraneo SpA v Presidenza del Consiglio dei Ministri* [2010] ECR I-5243, para 20.

[194] *Betws Anthracite Ltd. v DSK Anthrazit Ibbenburen* [2003] EWHC 2403.

Part IV

JUDICIAL REVIEW OF
EU STATE AID DECISIONS

Chapter Nineteen

JUDICIAL REVIEW OF EU DECISIONS: ADMISSIBILITY

19.1 ACTIONS FOR ANNULMENT OF EU DECISIONS

Judicial review of EU decisions Judicial review by the European Court of Justice and the General Court is available under Article 263 TFEU in order to ensure the legality of acts of the Commission and the Council.[1] Acts of these institutions, other than recommendations and opinions, may be annulled on grounds of lack of competence, infringement of an essential procedural requirement, infringement of the EU Treaties or of any rule of law relating to their application, or misuse of powers. In addition, should the Council or the Commission, in infringement of the Treaty, fail to act, an action may be brought pursuant to Article 265 TFEU to have the infringement established. For such an action to be admissible, the institution concerned must first have been called upon to act and have failed to define its position within two months. Actions for judicial review may be commenced by the Member States and by the Council and the Commission, as well as the European Parliament and the European Central Bank when seeking to protect their prerogatives. As regards State aid decisions, which are always addressed to the Member State concerned, other interested parties may bring proceedings where they can show that they are directly and individually concerned by the measure. Time limits of two months apply for the commencement of proceedings under both Article 263 TFEU and Article 265 TFEU. The admissibility of an action must be assessed, as a general rule, with reference to the situation at the time when it is brought.[2] A plea of inadmissibility constitutes a ground involving a question of public policy which may, and even must, be raised of its own motion by the court and consequently may be raised by the defendant at any stage of the proceedings.[3] Occasionally, for reasons of procedural economy where the

---

[1]   See C. Nordberg, "Judicial remedies for private parties under the State aid procedure" (1997) 24 LIEI 35; J. Winter, "The rights of complainants in State aid case: Judicial review of Commission decisions adopted under Article 88 (ex 93) EC" (1999) 36 CMLRev 521; M. Honoré, "The standing of third parties in State aid cases" [2006] EStALQ 269.

[2]   Cases C-71/09P, C-73/09P & C-76/09P, *Comitato Venezia vuole vivere v Commission* [2011] ECR I-4727, para 31.

[3]   Case C-298/00P, *Italy v Commission* [2004] ECR I-4087, para 35; Case C-47/10P, *Austria v Commission* [2011] ECR I-10707, para 97; Case T-27/02, *Kronofrance SA v*

application is to be dismissed on its merits, the court proceeds directly to the substance of the matter without ruling on the admissibility of the action.[4]

Whereas, previously, actions for judicial review brought by the Member States were commenced at the ECJ and actions brought by individuals or other persons were commenced at the General Court, now all judicial review proceedings in State aid cases are commenced at the General Court. An appeal lies to the ECJ on points of law only.[5] Judicial review is limited to establishing the legality of the act or failure to act in question, so that the ECJ or General Court can neither substitute its own view for that of the Commission[6] or order the Commission to declare aid as being compatible with the internal market[7] or order the Commission to define its position without further delay.[8] It is for the institution concerned, pursuant to Article 266 TFEU, to take the measures necessary to comply with the judgment of the court.[9]

Reviewable acts   Generally, a measure may be challenged in judicial review proceedings only where it produces legal effects, which must be ascertained by looking at its substance.[10]   Moreover, if a measure produces legal effects, it must be susceptible to judicial review.[11]   Most decisions taken by the

Commission [2004] ECR II-4177, para 30; Case T-332/06, *Alcoa Trasformazioni Srl v Commission* [2009] ECR II-29*, para 33.

4   Case C-23/00P, *Council* v *Boehringer* [2002] ECR I-1873, para 52; Case T-171/02, *Regione autonoma della Sardegna v Commission* [2005] ECR II-2123, para 155; Cases T-226/09 & T-230/09, *British Telecommunications plc v Commission* EU:T:2013:466, para 32; Case T-533/10, *DTS v Commission* EU:T:2014:629, para 33; Case T-151/11, *Telefónica de España SA v Commission* EU:T:2014:631, para 34; Case T-140/13, *Netherlands Maritime Technology Association v Commission* EU:T:2014:1029, para 117; Case T-58/13, *Club Hotel Loutraki AE v Commission* EU:T:2015:1, para 85.

5   Protocol on the Statute of the ECJ, paras 49-51.

6   Case C-169/95, *Spain v Commission* [1997] ECR I-135, para 34; Case C-288/96, *Germany v Commission* [2000] ECR I-8237, para 26; Cases T-371 & 394/94, *British Airways v Commission* [1998] ECR II-2405, para 79; Cases T-127/99, T-129/99 &T-148/99, *Territorio Histórico de Álava - Diputación Foral de Álava v Commission* [2002] ECR II-1275, para 273.

7   Case T-126/99, *Graphischer Maschinenbau GmbH v Commission* [2002] ECR II-2427, para 17.

8   Case T-395/04, *Air One SpA v Commission* [2006] ECR II-1343, para 24.

9   Whether a measure is susceptible to judicial review under Article 263 TFEU is not determined by whether any such measures under Article 266 TFEU may subsequently need to be taken: Case T-233/04, *Netherlands v Commission* [2008] ECR II-591, para 48.

10   Case 60/81, *IBM v Commission* [1981] ECR 2639, para 9; Cases T-425/04, T-444/04, T-450/04 & T-456/04, *France v Commission* [2010] ECR II-2099, para 119.

11   Case 22/70, *Commission v Council* [1971] ECR 263, para 42; Case C-316/91, *Parliament v Council* [1994] ECR I-625, para 8; Case C-27/04, *Commission v Council* [2004] ECR I-6649, para 44; Case C-521/06P, *Athinaïki Techniki v Commission* [2008] ECR I-5829, para 29; Case C-322/09P, *NDSHT v Commission* [2010] ECR I-11911, para 45; Case T-87/09, *Andersen v Commission* [2009] ECR II-225*, para 50.

Commission pursuant to Council Regulation (EC) No 659/1999 satisfy the criteria for reviewability. Recommendations and opinions are specifically precluded from judicial review under Article 263 TFEU. Moreover, certain decisions, such as decisions that merely confirm previous decisions, will not necessarily be reviewable. In the context of State aid supervision, the Commission may take decisions in the course of its preliminary assessment as well as at the end of the formal investigation. Not all of these decisions will produce legal effects that are susceptible to judicial review. Clearly, decisions following a formal investigation declaring aid compatible or incompatible with the internal market may be challenged. Issues of admissibility arise, however, where the decision in question is taken as an interim step towards the final decision, particularly where it is not certain whether or not the decision in question has affected the applicant's present legal position.[12]

In *Athinaiki Techniki v Commission*, the ECJ held that it is necessary to look to the substance of the contested acts, as well as the intention of those who drafted them, to classify those acts. In that regard, it is in principle those measures which definitively determine the position of the Commission upon the conclusion of an administrative procedure, and which are intended to have legal effects capable of affecting the interests of the complainant, which are open to challenge and not intermediate measures whose purpose is to prepare for the definitive decision, or measures which are mere confirmation of an earlier measure which was not challenged within the prescribed period.[13] Thus, the form in which an act or decision is adopted is in principle irrelevant to the right to challenge such acts or decisions by way of an action for annulment and it is, in principle, irrelevant for the classification of the act in question whether or not it satisfies certain formal requirements, namely, that it is duly named by its author; that it is sufficiently reasoned, and that it mentions the provisions providing the legal basis for it. It is therefore irrelevant that the act may not be described as a decision or that it does not refer to Article 4(2), (3) or (4) of Regulation (EC) No 659/1999. It is also of no importance that the Member State concerned was not notified of it by the Commission, infringing Article 25 of that regulation, as such an error is not capable of altering the substance of that act.[14]

Where a complaint has been made to the Commission, the decision terminating the investigation is addressed to the Member State and it is that decision which must form the subject matter of any subsequent action for

---

[12] Case C-312/90, *Spain v Commission* [1992] ECR I-4117, para 24; Case C-47/91, *Italy v Commission* [1992] ECR I-4145, para 30.

[13] Case C-521/06P, *Athinaïki Techniki v Commission* [2008] ECR I-5829, para 42; Case T-407/09, *Neubrandenburger Wohnungsgesellschaft mbH v Commission* EU:T:2012:1, para 26.

[14] Case C-521/06P, *Athinaïki Techniki v Commission* [2008] ECR I-5829, paras 43-44; Case T-407/09, *Neubrandenburger Wohnungsgesellschaft mbH v Commission* EU:T:2012:1, para 27.

annulment brought by the complainant.[15] A letter sent by the Commission notifying the complainant of that decision is purely informative in nature and does not itself constitute a challengeable decision.[16]

Where a decision has subsequently been withdrawn by the Commission, annulment proceedings become devoid of purpose and will be discontinued.[17]

Regulatory acts not entailing implementing measures Article 263 TFEU also provides that judicial review extends, in the case of natural or legal persons, to a regulatory act which is of direct concern to the applicant and which does not entail implementing measures.[18] The applicant need not show individual concern in such cases. The objective of this provision is to enable natural and legal persons to bring an action against acts of general application which are not legislative acts, which are of direct concern to them and which do not entail implementing measures, therefore avoiding a situation in which such a person would have to break the law in order to have access to justice.[19] In the absence of implementing measures, such persons would be able to obtain a judicial review of the contested act only after having infringed its provisions, by pleading that those provisions are unlawful in proceedings initiated against them before the national courts.[20] The extent to which this applies in State aid cases remains to be seen, in particular whether State aid decisions may be considered as regulatory acts,[21] although a number of issues concerning the notion of implementing measures have been considered by both the ECJ and the General Court.[22]

In *Telefónica v Commission*, the ECJ held that the question whether a regulatory act entails implementing measures should be assessed by reference to the position of the person pleading the right to bring proceedings under

---

[15] Case C-367/95P, *Commission v Sytraval* [1998] CR I-1719, para 45.

[16] Case T-57/13, *Club Hotel Loutraki AE v Commission* EU:T:2014:183, para 25.

[17] Case T-291/02, *González y Díez SA v Commission* [2004] (unreported), para 16; Case T-79/09, *France v Commission* EU:T:2014:73, para 21; Case T-478/11, *France v Commission* EU:T:2014:209, para 16; Case T-575/11, *Inaporc v Commission* EU:T:2014:210, para 16; Case T-18/12, *Interbev v Commission* EU:T:2014:211, para 17; Case T-11/07 RENV, *Frucona Košice as v Commission* EU:T:2014:173, paras 35-39.

[18] Article 263 TFEU, fourth paragraph.

[19] Case T-381/11, *Eurofer v Commission* EU:T:2012:273, para 60; Case T-429/11, *Banco Bilbao Vizcaya Argentaria SA v Commission* EU:T:2013:488, para 53; Case T-430/11, *Telefónica SA v Commission* EU:T:2013: 489, para 53.

[20] Case C-274/12P, *Telefónica SA v Commission* EU:C:2013:852, para 27.

[21] Case C-274/12P, *Telefónica SA v Commission* EU:C:2013:852, para 38; Case T-221/10, *Iberdrola SA v Commission* EU:T:2012:112, para 48; Case T-228/10, *Telefónica SA v Commission* EU:T:2012:140, para 45.

[22] Case C-274/12P, *Telefónica SA v Commission* EU:C:2013:852; Case T-429/11, *Banco Bilbao Vizcaya Argentaria SA v Commission* EU:T:2013:488; Case T-430/11, *Telefónica SA v Commission* EU:T:2013: 489; Case T-400/11, *Altadis SA v Commission* EU:T:2013:490.

Article 263 TFEU. It is therefore irrelevant whether the act in question entails implementing measures with regard to other persons.[23] In order to determine whether the measure being challenged entails implementing measures, reference should be made exclusively to the subject-matter of the action and, where an applicant seeks only the partial annulment of an act, it is solely any implementing measures which that part of the act may entail that must, as the case may be, be taken into consideration.[24] Telefónica's action was concerned solely with challenging the declaration in the Commission's decision that the scheme at issue was partially incompatible with the internal market. Since that provision did not define the specific consequences which that declaration had for each taxpayer, which consequences would be embodied in administrative documents such as a tax notice, such an administrative document would constitute an implementing measure within the meaning of Article 263 TFEU. It followed that measures for giving effect to the decision as to compatibility, including in particular the measure consisting of rejection of an application for grant of the tax advantage at issue, a rejection which Telefónica would also be able to contest before the national courts, are implementing measures in respect of the contested decision.[25] Similarly, in *Stichting Woonpunt v Commission*, concerning commitments accepted in the course of a review of existing State aid to housing associations in the Netherlands, the ECJ held that the measures necessary to implement the commitments meant that the decision, whether or not it could be regarded as a regulatory act, did not constitute a measure not entailing implementing measures.[26] A similar conclusion was arrived at by the General Court in *Dansk Automat Brancheforening v Commission* in relation to a challenge against a Commission decision authorising aid in respect of online gambling in Denmark which would only materialise through measures to be adopted by the Danish authorities.[27]

In so far as this argument has been raised against recovery decisions, the General Court has held that a decision ordering recovery entails implementing national measures.[28] In *Altadis v Commission*, the Commission argued that the

---

[23] Case C-274/12P, *Telefónica SA v Commission* EU:C:2013:852, para 30; Case C-132/12P, *Stichting Woonpunt v Commission* EU:C:2014:100, para 50; Case C-133/12P, *Stichting Woonlinie v Commission* EU:C:2014:105, para 37.

[24] Case C-274/12P, *Telefónica SA v Commission* EU:C:2013:852, para 31; Case C-132/12P, *Stichting Woonpunt v Commission* EU:C:2014:100, para 51; Case C-133/12P, *Stichting Woonlinie v Commission* EU:C:2014:105, para 38.

[25] Case C-274/12P, *Telefónica SA v Commission* EU:C:2013:852, paras 33-36.

[26] Case C-132/12P, *Stichting Woonpunt v Commission* EU:C:2014:100, para 52-54; Case C-133/12P, *Stichting Woonlinie v Commission* EU:C:2014:105, paras 39-41.

[27] Case T-601/11, *Dansk Automat Brancheforening v Commission* EU:T:2014:839, para 59; Case T-615/11, *Royal Scandinavian Casino Århus I/S v Commission* EU:T:2014:838, para 51.

[28] Case T-400/11, *Altadis SA v Commission* EU:T:2013:490, para 48; Case T-221/10, *Iberdrola SA v Commission* EU:T:2012:112, paras 46-48; Case T-228/10, *Telefónica SA v Commission* EU:T:2012:140, paras 44-45.

contested decision was not a regulatory act not entailing implementing measures, invoking several national measures implementing the contested decision, in particular, the abolition of the aid scheme by the Spanish legislature, the recovery by the tax authorities of the aid unlawfully granted under the scheme from the beneficiaries and the agreement or refusal by those authorities to grant the tax advantage at issue. The applicant, by contrast, argued that these national measures were not implementing measures within the meaning of Article 263 TFEU since recovery of the aid was binding on Spain, without the latter having any margin of discretion, and that the recovery measures, including abolition of the scheme, were already determined in the Commission's decision and were merely the legal consequence of that decision. In its judgment, the General Court noted that, since a decision is binding in its entirety only on those to whom it is addressed, the obligation to refuse to grant the advantage of the aid, to annul the tax advantages conferred and to recover any aid paid under that scheme are legal consequences of the decision that are binding on the relevant Member State alone. It followed that, as the Commission's decision did not produce any binding legal effects on the beneficiaries of the scheme, the consequences of the incompatibility of the aid must be individually itemised by a legal act emanating from the competent national authorities, such as a tax notice, which constitutes a measure implementing the decision within the meaning of Article 263 TFEU.[29] It was immaterial in this regard whether the Member State has no discretion in implementing the decision.[30]

Non-existent acts Acts of the EU institutions are presumed to be valid.[31] The gravity of the consequences attaching to a finding that a measure of an EU institution is non-existent means that, for reasons of legal certainty, such a finding must be reserved for quite extreme situations.[32] The ECJ has held that it follows from the legislative and judicial system established by the FEU Treaty that the principle of the rule of law imposes upon all persons subject to EU law the obligation to acknowledge that EU measures are fully effective as long as they have not been declared to be invalid.[33] A decision of the Commission, therefore, remains binding in its entirety upon the Member State to which it is addressed unless the ECJ or the General Court decides to the contrary. It follows that, even if the Member State takes the view that an aid

---

[29] Case T-400/11, *Altadis SA v Commission* EU:T:2013:490, para 46.

[30] *Ibid.*, para 47.

[31] Case 15/85, *Consorzio Cooperative d'Abruzzo v Commission* [1987] ECR 1005, para 10.

[32] Case C-137/92P, *Commission v BASF* [1994] ECR I-2555, para 50; Case C-475/01, *Commission v Greece* [2004] ECR I-8923, para 20; Cases T-494/08 to T-500/08 & T-509/08, *Ryanair Ltd v Commission* [2010] ECR II-5723, para 49; Cases T-50/06 RENV, T-56/06 RENV, T-60/06 RENV, T-62/06 RENV & T-69/06 RENV, *Ireland v Commission* EU:T:2012:134, para 61.

[33] Case 63/87, *Commission v Greece* [1988] ECR 2875, para 10.

measure is compatible with the internal market and that a contrary decision by the Commission is unlawful, that fact cannot permit the Member State to act as if that decision were non-existent in law. In *United Kingdom v Commission*, therefore, the United Kingdom was held not to be entitled refuse to comply with a Commission decision declaring a subsidy for pig producers incompatible with the internal market merely because it had commenced proceedings under Article 263 TFEU.[34]

In *Commission v Belgium*, Advocate General Lenz recognised the concept of a void administrative act. Unlike a merely unlawful administrative act, which must be challenged if it is not to be complied with, such an act need not be contested because, being void, it is without legal effect.[35] Thus, a decision may be void and unenforceable for lack of precision or specificity.[36] It is also arguable that a decision may be automatically void where the Commission or the Council had no competence to adopt it.[37] Nevertheless, in *ASPEC v Commission*, a decision taken by the Commissioner with responsibility for competition policy which should have been taken by the whole Commission acting collegiately was held not to be vitiated by formal defects of such a nature that it could be declared non-existent, although the decision was annulled for infringement of an essential procedural requirement.[38]

Legality of national provisions An action for annulment under Article 263 TFEU is inadmissible if it is based principally on allegations that certain national provisions are unlawful. In *Triveneta Zuccheri v Commission*, the Commission had taken a decision finding incompatible with the internal market aid granted to Italian sugar producers in the form of compensation for reduction of their profit margin when the maximum resale price for sugar in Italy had been reduced. The sugar producers challenged this decision arguing that the national pricing rules were unlawful in the context of the common agricultural policy and that the payments amounted solely to restitution of the damage caused by the Italian rules. They maintained that the contested decision and the Italian provisions governing the pricing system were inextricably linked in such a way that it was impossible to challenge the lawfulness of the decision without at the same time raising the question of the compatibility with EU law of the Italian system for fixing maximum prices. The ECJ held, however, that in order to give a decision on the merits of the case, it would necessarily be required to rule on the question of the

---

[34] Cases 31/77R & 53/77R, *Commission v United Kingdom* [1977] ECR 921, paras 18-19.

[35] Case 52/84, *Commission v Belgium* [1986] ECR 89, *per* Advocate General Lenz at p. 95.

[36] Case 70/72, *Commission v Germany* [1973] ECR 813, para 23; Case 52/83, *Commission v France* [1983] ECR 3707, para 9.

[37] Cases 6 & 11/69, *Commission v France* [1969] ECR 523, para 13; Case 156/77, *Commission v Belgium* [1978] ECR 1881, *per* Advocate General Mayras, at p. 1909.

[38] Case T-435/93, *ASPEC v Commission* [1995] ECR II-1281, para 125; Case T-442/93, *AAC v Commission* [1995] ECR II-1329, para 106.

compatibility of the Italian provisions with EU law. It declared the action inadmissible on the ground that the proper way to consider the legality of national provision was either through Article 258 TFEU proceedings or through national court proceedings with a possible reference under Article 267 TFEU.[39]

Effective judicial protection through national court proceedings The EU courts have sought to justify their restrictive attitude to admissibility under Articles 263 TFEU and Article 265 TFEU on the ground that an alternative means of legal protection is available through national court proceedings.[40] In *Altadis v Commission*, the General Court stated that, since the European Union is a union based on the rule of law in which its institutions are subject to judicial review of the compatibility of their acts with the FEU Treaty and with the general principles of law, which include fundamental rights, individuals are therefore entitled to effective judicial protection of the rights which they derive from the EU legal order. It held that the applicant, whose action for annulment of a decision declaring a tax-based aid scheme incompatible with the internal market was dismissed as inadmissible, was not in any way deprived of effective judicial protection since there was nothing to prevent it from challenging, before the national courts, the measures implementing the contested decision and, in particular, the tax notices refusing to grant it the benefit of the scheme at issue. The national courts would then be able incidentally to review the validity of the decision and, if necessary, refer a question to the ECJ for a preliminary ruling on the assessment of validity under Article 267 TFEU.[41]

19.2 REVIEWABLE ACTS

Measures producing legal effects In the context of State aid, the most common act of the Commission is a decision taken pursuant to Council Regulation (EC) No 659/1999. Although most decisions are now required to be published, a measure does not have to be published to be the object of an action for annulment.[42] A measure may be contested under Article 263 TFEU only if it produces legal effects.[43] In *IBM v Commission*, the ECJ held that a

---

[39]   Case C-347/87, *Triveneta Zuccheri v Commission* [1990] ECR I-1083, paras 15-16.
[40]   Cases C-587/13P & C-588/13P, *Banco Bilbao Vizcaya Argentaria SA v Commission* EU:C:2015:18, para 49.
[41]   Case T-400/11, *Altadis SA v Commission* EU:T:2013:490, para 50.
[42]   Case T-351/02, *Deutsche Bahn AG v Commission* [2006] ECR II-1047, para 59.
[43]   Case 22/70, *Commission v Council* [1971] ECR 263, para 42; Case C-400/99, *Italy v Commission* [2001] ECR I-7303, para 49; Case C-208/99, *Portugal v Commission* [2004] ECR I-9183, para 22; Case T-233/04, *Netherlands v Commission* [2008] ECR I-

measure has such legal effects where it is binding on, and capable of affecting the interests of, the applicant by bringing about a distinct change in his legal position.[44] In *Netherlands v Commission*, where the Netherlands notified to the Commission a measure concerning an emission trading scheme and requested that it take a decision finding that there was no State aid involved, the Commission's finding in the operative part that the measure did in fact constitute aid was subject to judicial review, even though it declared the measure compatible with the internal market pursuant to Article 107(3) TFEU. The General Court considered that the finding that the measure constituted aid enabled the Commission to examine, in the decision, the compatibility of the measure in question with the internal market. It also triggered the application of the procedure for existing State aid schemes laid down by Regulation (EC) No 659/1999 which requires the Member States to submit an annual report on all existing aid schemes. The classification as State aid could also have an impact on overlapping aid as a result of the rules on cumulation of aid laid down *inter alia* in the Commission's guidelines on State aid for environmental protection. It followed that the decision gave rise to binding legal effects and the action by the Netherlands was therefore admissible.[45] This analysis was confirmed on appeal by the ECJ.[46] This approach was followed in *Belgium v Commission*, where the General Court also held irrelevant the fact that Belgium had previously admitted that the measure in question constituted new aid.[47]

A measure that produces no legal effects is not susceptible to judicial review. In *Tramarin v Commission*, the Commission, in the course of a preliminary assessment of a regional aid scheme, had sent a letter to the Italian authorities stating that proposed aid for a particular investment project was not in accordance with the regional aid guidelines and requesting the withdrawal of the proposal. On an application for annulment of that letter, the General Court held that the letter had no legal effect since the Commission had no power, in

---

591, para 37; Cases T-309/04, T-317/04, T-329/04 & T-336/04, *TV2/Danmark A/S v Commission* [2008] ECR II-2935, para 63.

[44] Case 60/81, *IBM v Commission* [1981] ECR 2639, para 9; Case C-521/06 P, *Athinaïki Techniki v Commission* [2008] ECR I-5829, para 29; Case T-64/89, *Automec v Commission* [1990] ECR II-367, para 42; Case T-3/93, *Air France v Commission* [1994] ECR II-121, para 43; Case T-154/94, *Comité des Salines de France v Commission* [1996] ECR II-1377, para 37; Case T-330/94, *Salt Union Ltd. v Commission* [1996] ECR II-1475, para 31; Cases T-273/06 & T-297/06, *ISD Polska v Commission* [2009] ECR II-2185, para 66; Case T-251/13, *Gemeente Nijmegen v Commission* EU:T:2015:142, para 27.

[45] Case T-233/04, *Netherlands v Commission* [2008] ECR I-591, paras 41-42; Cases T-15/12 & T-16/12, *Provincie Groningen v Commission* EU:T:2013:74, para 43.

[46] Case C-279/08P, *Commission v Netherlands* [2011] ECR I-7671, paras 37-42; Case T-347/09, *Germany v Commission* EU:T:2013:418, para 16; Case T-538/11, *Belgium v Commission* EU:T:2015:188, para 49.

[47] Case T-538/11, *Belgium v Commission* EU:T:2015:188, para 54.

the context of its preliminary assessment, to order Italy to withdraw the proposal and Italy was, accordingly, free either to comply with the Commission's suggestion or to leave its original plan unchanged.[48] Similarly, in *Neubrandenburger Wohnungsgesellschaft v Commission*, the General Court held that a letter sent by the Commission pursuant to Regulation (EC) No 659/1999, Article 20(2), which explicitly stated that it did not contain any definitive position of the Commission and inviting the complainant to submit further information, did not constitute a final decision giving rise to legal effects.[49]

A decision may cease to produce legal effects by reason of events subsequent to the commencement of annulment proceedings. For instance, in *Stahlwerk Bous v Commission*, an action for annulment was brought against a decision to open a formal investigation. Subsequently, the Commission closed its investigation with a final decision finding the aid compatible with the internal market. The applicant conceded that the decision to open the formal investigation no longer produced any legal effects as far as it was concerned.[50] Moreover, the General Court held that it was not possible for the applicant, in the course of those proceedings, to amend its application to challenge the final decision instead of the opening decision.[51]

Measure consisting of several distinct parts Where a measure against which an action for annulment has been brought consists of several distinct parts, only those parts of the measure which produce binding legal effects capable of bringing about a significant change in the applicant's legal position may be challenged.[52] In *Italy v Commission*, the Commission, in its decision opening the formal investigation into alleged aid to Tirrenia di Navigazione in respect of public service obligations concerning certain ferry services, took the view that the aid was new aid and urged Italy to suspend the aid, failing which it would issue a suspension injunction. Italy sought the annulment of this decision on the ground that the aid was existing aid rather than new aid and was not subject to suspension. Subsequently, the Commission closed the formal investigation with a decision declaring the aid compatible with the internal market. When Italy continued with its application for annulment of the decision to open the formal investigation, the Commission argued that the action had become devoid of purpose. This contention was rejected by the ECJ

---

[48] Case T-426/04, *Tramarin Snc di Tramarin Andrea e Sergio v Commission* [2005] ECR II-4765, paras 34-35.

[49] Case T-407/09, *Neubrandenburger Wohnungsgesellschaft mbH v Commission* EU:T:2012:1, paras 30-34.

[50] Case T-172/14, *Stahlwerk Bous GmbH v Commission* EU:T:2015:402, para 19.

[51] Case T-172/14, *Stahlwerk Bous GmbH v Commission* EU:T:2015:402, para 23.

[52] Case 60/81, *IBM v Commission* [1981] ECR 2639, para 10; Case T-184/97, *BP Chemicals Ltd v Commission* [2000] ECR II-3145, para 34; Case T-251/13, *Gemeente Nijmegen v Commission* EU:T:2015:142, para 28.

which held that the essential aim of the action was to secure a judgment to the effect that the measures of which the Commission called for suspension should not be suspended pending the decision closing the formal investigation. Since a question of that kind did not fall within the scope of a decision closing proceedings, it was not affected by that decision.[53]

Partial annulment of an EU act is possible only if the elements the annulment of which is sought may be severed from the remainder of the act.[54] In that regard, the requirement of severability is not satisfied in the case where the partial annulment of an act would have the effect of altering its substance.[55] Thus, in *Carbunión v Council*, a challenge against part of Council Decision 2010/787/EU concerning State aid to facilitate the closure of uncompetitive mines was rejected on the ground that the annulment of the parts of the decision sought by the applicant, which allowed only limited short term aid, would have resulted in that decision being effectively replaced by a different decision which would have allowed aid to coal mines to be authorised indefinitely on conditions that were much broader than those envisaged in the original decision.[56]

Statement of reasons Only the operative part of a decision is capable of producing legal effects and, as a consequence, of adversely affecting an applicant's interests. By contrast, the assessments made in the recitals to a decision are not in themselves capable of forming the subject of an application for annulment. They can be subject to judicial review under Article 263 TFEU only to the extent that, as grounds of an act adversely affecting a person's interests, they constitute the essential basis for the operative part of that act[57] or if, at the very least, those grounds are likely to alter the substance of what was

[53] Case C-400/99, *Italy v Commission* [2005] ECR I-3657, para 17.

[54] Case C-29/99, *Commission v Council* [2002] ECR I-11221, para 45; Case C-244/03, *France v Parliament and Council* [2005] ECR I-4021, para 12; Case C-224/12P, *Commission v ING Groep NV* EU:C:2014:213, para 57; Case C-99/14P *Carbunión v Council* EU:C:2014:2446, para 26; Case T-150/11, *Gobierno de Aragón v Council* EU:T:2013:676, para 20; Case T-176/11 *Carbunión v Council* EU:T:2013:686, para 31.

[55] Cases C-68/94 & C-30/95 *France and Others v Commission* [1998] ECR I-1375, para 257; Case C-29/99, *Commission v Council* [2002] ECR I-11221, para 46; Case C-244/03, *France v Parliament and Council* [2005] ECR I-4021, para 13; Case C-99/14P *Carbunión v Council* EU:C:2014:2446, para 26; Case T-150/11, *Gobierno de Aragón v Council* EU:T:2013:676, para 20; Case T-176/11, *Carbunión v Council* EU:T:2013:686, para 31.

[56] Case C-99/14P *Carbunión v Council* EU:C:2014:2446, paras 31-32; Case T-150/11, *Gobierno de Aragón v Council* EU:T:2013:676, paras 25-29; Case T-176/11, *Carbunión v Council* EU:T:2013:686, paras 37-40.

[57] Case C-164/02, *Netherlands v Commission* [2004] ECR I-1177, para 21; Case T-289/03, *BUPA Ltd v Commission* [2008] ECR II-81, para 316; Cases T-81/07 to T-83/07, *KG Holding NV v Commission* [2009] ECR II-2411, para 46.

decided in the operative part.[58] In *Netherlands v Commission*, the statement of reasons which was challenged by the Netherlands in so far as it classified certain measures funding dredging by port authorities as aid did not constitute the essential basis for the operative part of a decision adversely affecting the Netherlands, since the operative part was limited to finding that the measure was compatible with the internal market pursuant to Article 107(3)(c) TFEU. Since the statement of reasons for the decision had no binding legal effect such as to affect the interests of the Netherlands, it could not constitute a legal act open to challenge.[59] Similarly, in *Wheyco v Commission*, an action was brought against a Commission decision that declared fiscal aid granted by Germany to be compatible with the internal market. In the preamble to the decision the Commission stated that aid granted earlier than the date of the decision would be illegal, and the German authorities had made clear that the aid would not be applied retrospectively. Dismissing the action as inadmissible, the General Court held that the decision itself did not affect the legal position of the applicant, which was more concerned with the position taken by the German authorities.[60] In *Provincie Groningen v Commission*, in which certain forestry aid was declared to be compatible with the internal market pursuant to Article 106(2) TFEU, the beneficiaries sought to have the decision annulled on the ground that it implied that they were undertakings for the purposes of Article 107(1) TFEU so that any time they might receive a public subsidy in the future they would be obliged to have it notified as aid. The General Court held that their status as undertakings or as economic operators was mentioned only in the recitals and that the Commission had taken no position on it in the operative part such as would found a basis for an interest to act on the part of the applicants.[61]

Confirmation of previous decision A decision which merely confirms or follows up on a previous decision has no legal effects and is not subject to judicial review.[62] A decision is purely confirmatory of a previous decision when it contains no new elements compared to the earlier decision and has not been preceded by a re-examination of the facts.[63] Thus, in *Pollmeier Massivholz v Commission*, a letter sent to the complainant enclosing a copy of its decision was held not to be subject to judicial review.[64] Equally, in *Comité*

---

[58] Cases T-81/07 to T-83/07, *KG Holding NV v Commission* [2009] ECR II-2411, para 46.
[59] Case C-164/02, *Netherlands v Commission* [2004] ECR I-1177, para 24.
[60] Case T-6/06, *Wheyco GmbH v Commission* [2007] ECR II-72*, para 95.
[61] Cases T-15/12 & T-16/12, *Provincie Groningen v Commission* EU:T:2013:74, para 38.
[62] Case C-480/93P, *Zunis Holding v Commission* [1996] ECR I-1, para 14; Cases T-529/08 to T-531/08, *Territorio Historico de Álava v Commission* [2010] ECR II-53*, para 28.
[63] Case C-521/03P, *Internationaler Hilfsfonds v Commission* EU:C:2004:778, para 47; Cases T-529/08 to T-531/08, *Territorio Historico de Álava v Commission* [2010] ECR II-53*, para 29.
[64] Case T-89/09, *Pollmeier Massivholz GmbH v Commission* EU:T:2015:153, para 36.

des Salines de France v Commission, a letter sent to the applicant enclosing a copy of a previous decision approving a general aid scheme was held not to produce legal effects.[65] Where a complaint has been made and decided upon by the Commission without that decision being challenged in judicial review proceedings, the complainant cannot circumvent the limitation period by requesting the Commission to consider the matter again. In *Irish Cement Ltd v Commission*, a complaint was made to the Commission concerning the grant of investment aid to a cement producer in Northern Ireland. The Commission responded that the aid fell within the relevant regional aid guidelines. No challenge was made against that decision, but several months later the complainant again wrote to the Commission asking it to reconsider its position. The ECJ held that the Commission's refusal to intervene in the award of the aid in response to this second complaint did not constitute a new decision so that the action was inadmissible.[66] In *Otto Wöhr v Commission*, where the Commission had approved aid following a preliminary assessment, a subsequent refusal to agree to open the formal investigation procedure was held not to produce any legal effects, since the earlier decision was definitive.[67]

In assessing the confirmatory character of an act, account should be taken not only of its content in relation to a previous measure but also of the nature of the request to which the act in question is a response. In particular, if the request contains new and substantial facts which leads to a re-examination of the earlier act, the subsequent act may not be regarded as a confirmatory act in so far as it contains a new element compared to the earlier act.[68] Where, however, the Commission merely explains in greater detail the reasoning in the earlier act, the subsequent act will not be regarded as justiciable. For instance, in *Territorio Historico de Álava v Commission*, a letter from the Commission subsequent to the commencement of recovery proceedings which stipulated that interest was payable in line with the Commission's recovery notice was held merely to be confirmatory of the Commission's pre-existing position on the method of calculating interest, even though this was mentioned for the first time in the later act.[69] In *Kronoply v Commission*, a letter sent by a Commission official refusing to re-assess on a more favourable basis aid that had already been declared compatible with the internal market was held not to constitute a decision, but merely a measure of information which was not

---

[65] Case T-154/94, *Comité des Salines de France v Commission* [1996] ECR II-1377, para 48.
[66] Cases 166 & 220/86, *Irish Cement Ltd v Commission* [1988] ECR 6473, para 13.
[67] Case T-222/00, *Otto Wöhr GmbH v Commission* [2001] ECR II-3463, para 40. See also, Case T-148/00, *The Panhellenic Union of Cotton Ginners and Exporters v Commission* [2003] ECR II-4415, para 61.
[68] Case T-308/02, *SGL Carbon v Commission* [2004] ECR II-1363, para 53; Cases T-529/08 to T-531/08, *Territorio Historico de Álava v Commission* [2010] ECR II-53*, para 30.
[69] Cases T-529/08 to T-531/08, *Territorio Historico de Álava v Commission* [2010] ECR II-53*, paras 31-37.

actionable.[70]   In *SP Entertainment Development v Commission*, the Commission had ordered Germany to recover certain aid. Subsequently, the German authorities wrote to the Commission setting out the action they had taken to effect recovery. The applicant sought to challenge the Commission's letter in reply which stated that recovery had not been effected in full and that, in the absence of complete recovery of the unlawful aid, proceedings before the ECJ pursuant to Article 108(2) TFEU would be commenced. The General Court dismissed the action on the ground that the Commission's letter did not produce any independent legal effects.[71]

Even where the Commission, in the subsequent letter, advises that any unlawful aid must be recovered, that will not convert the letter into a decision. In *RapidEye v Commission*, a German regional aid scheme had been approved by the Commission, which had set maximum intensity levels for individual grants under the scheme. Subsequently, the German authorities wrote to the Commission advising that the maximum level might have been exceeded in relation to a particular grant.   In response, the Commission sent a letter confirming that the maximum level of aid that could be granted was that set out in the decision approving the scheme, that any additional aid had to be notified separately as new aid and any overpayment would be subject to recovery. On an action for annulment of the letter, the General Court held that the letter had produced no binding legal effects, despite the fact that the Commission had stated that the overpayment should be recovered.[72] More generally, it held that in the context of the rules governing the Commission's supervisory control *a posteriori* of State aid, there was nothing which required the Commission to adopt a legally binding act each time it is presented with a question from the national authorities. The German authorities had not made a notification of any new aid, but had merely sought clarification on the scope of the decision concerning the scheme.[73]

Earlier decision distinguished   Where a subsequent decision can be distinguished from the earlier decision, its legality may be challenged.   In *France v Commission*, France challenged a Commission decision concerning aid to an undertaking involved in the export of French language books on the ground that Article 106(2) TFEU should have been applied to exempt the aid from the competition rules, even though the Commission decided that the aid was compatible with the internal market on cultural grounds pursuant to Article 107(3)(d) TFEU. Since a previous decision on the same matter had found the aid to be subject to Articles 107 and 108 TFEU, and had been annulled solely

---

[70]   Case T-130/02, *Kronoply GmbH v Commission* [2003] ECR II-4857, para 45.
[71]   Case T-44/05, *SP Entertainment Development GmbH v Commission* [2007] ECR II-19*, para 23.
[72]   Case T-330/09, *RapidEye AG v Commission* [2011] ECR II-26*, paras 52- 53.
[73]   *Ibid.*, paras 28-35.

on procedural grounds for failure of the Commission to institute the formal investigation procedure, the Commission argued that this issue was *res judicata*, so that the latter decision merely confirmed in this respect the earlier finding. The ECJ held, however, that the action was admissible since the Commission retained its discretionary power of assessment in regard to the substance of the measure in its detailed examination, so that the subsequent decision could not be regarded merely as confirming the earlier decision.[74]

In *ARAP v Commission*, the General Court declared admissible a challenge to a Commission decision allowing an individual grant of aid which was made pursuant to an earlier decision approving a general scheme. The individual grants of aid, regarded as existing aid, could only be checked by the Commission in the light of the conditions which it had set out in the earlier decision. In those circumstances, regardless of whether the applicants could have been recognised as having standing to contest the earlier decision, the General Court held that effective judicial protection of their rights was in any event assured only if they had an opportunity to raise an objection alleging the irregularity of that decision in proceedings challenging the Commission decision relating to the individual aid, which alone allows them to determine precisely the extent to which their individual interests are affected.[75]

19.3 REVIEWABLE DECISIONS ON STATE AID

Decision following preliminary investigation In the area of State aid, it is those measures which definitively determine the position of the Commission upon the conclusion of an administrative procedure, and which are intended to have binding legal effects capable of affecting the interests of the complainant, which are open to challenge, and not intermediate measures whose purpose is to prepare the final decision, which do not have those effects.[76] Where new aid or an alteration to existing aid is notified to the Commission, the Commission, within two months, must take a decision that the measure does not constitute aid within Article 107(1) TFEU, or that it is permissible aid which is compatible with the internal market, or that doubts are raised as to its compatibility with the internal market in which case the formal investigation procedure must be instigated.[77] In the past, there was some debate as to whether each of these cases gives rise to an actionable decision, primarily because of the wording of Article 108(3) TFFEU which did not explicitly categorise each of these three types of decision. It might have been assumed

---

[74] Case C-332/98P, *France v Commission* [2000] ECR I-4833, para 21.

[75] Case T-82/96, *ARAP v Commission* [1999] ECR II-1889, para 49.

[76] Case C-521/06P, *Athinaïki Techniki v Commission* [2008] ECR I-5829, para 42; Case T-87/09, *Andersen v Commission* [2009] ECR II-225*, para 51; .

[77] Article 108(3) TFEU; Council Regulation (EC) No 659/1999, Article 4(1).

that this uncertainty is no longer valid in the light of Council Regulation (EC) No 659/1999, Article 4, which specifically states, as recognised by the ECJ in *Athinaïki Techniki v Commission*, that the Commission must definitively establish its position by taking a decision recording its determination following the preliminary investigation.[78] Nevertheless, the General Court has insisted, on the basis that it is the substance of an act which determines whether it is actionable and not its form, that the mere description of an act as a decision, in particular in the case of an decision to open an formal investigation procedure pursuant to Council Regulation (EC) No 659/1999, Article 4(4), is not sufficient.[79]

The ECJ has held that a decision by the Commission not to initiate the formal investigation procedure is actionable since it is definitive.[80] Thus, a decision finding that a measure does not constitute aid and a decision finding that an aid has been granted but that no concerns are raised as to its compatibility with the internal market are both susceptible to judicial review since they are final decisions which bring the investigation procedure to an end. Equally, where a complaint is made to the Commission alleging the grant of a new aid but the Commission takes the view that the aid is in fact an existing aid which does not require notification, the consequential decision refusing to open the formal investigation procedure is also actionable. In *CIRFS v Commission*, a complaint was made to the Commission concerning aid in the synthetic fibres industry. The Commission, taking the view that the aid was covered by an earlier authorisation for regional aid, determined that the aid was existing aid. The ECJ held that the decision had definitive legal effects and could be challenged.[81] Similarly, in *ARAP v Commission*, the General Court held that the fact that an individual grant of aid forming part of a general scheme duly approved by the Commission is regarded as existing aid whose payment has already been authorised does not prevent an applicant from challenging the Commission's decision treating it as such, precisely because the aid might not in fact be covered by the approval decision.[82]

Decision to initiate the formal investigation   A decision, pursuant to Regulation (EC) No 659/1999, Article 4(4), to open the formal investigation procedure is a preparatory step prior to the adoption of the decision at the end of the Commission's investigation.[83] Under Article 108(3) TFEU, reiterated

---

[78] Case C-521/06P, *Athinaïki Techniki v Commission* [2008] ECR I-5829, para 42; Cases C-465/09P – C-470/09P, *Territorio Histórico de Álava – Diputación Foral de Álava v Commission* [2011] ECR I-83*, para 94.

[79] Case T-517/12, *Alro SA v Commission* EU:T:2014:890, para 50.

[80] Case C-313/90, *CIRFS v Commission* [1993] ECR I-1125, para 26.

[81] *Ibid.*, para 27.

[82] Case T-82/96, *ARAP v Commission* [1999] ECR II-1889, para 36; upheld on appeal, Case C-321/99P, *ARAP v Commission* [2002] ECR I-4287, para 62.

[83] Case T-151/11, *Telefónica de España SA v Commission* EU:T:2014:631, para 46.

by Regulation (EC) No 659/1999, Article 3, where a measure is notified to the Commission, Member States are precluded from putting it into effect until the Commission's final decision. The decision to open the formal investigation procedure into new aid merely results in the Commission entering into a fuller investigation of the measure. The ECJ held, in *IBM v Commission*, that, in the case of acts or decisions adopted by a procedure involving several stages, in particular where they are the culmination of an internal procedure, in principle an act is open to review only if it is a measure definitively laying down the position of the Council or the Commission on the conclusion of that procedure, and not a provisional measure intended to pave the way for the final decision. It would be otherwise only if acts or decisions adopted in the course of the preparatory proceedings not only bore such legal characteristics but in addition were themselves the culmination of a special procedure distinct from that intended to permit the Council or Commission to take a decision on the substance of the case.[84] In *Alro v Commission*, which concerned a decision to open a formal investigation into an alleged aid measure which was no longer in the course of implementation, it held the challenge inadmissible on the ground that the decision in question was not a challengeable act. The decision did not produce an immediate, certain and sufficiently binding effect on the Member State concerned and was not intended to have binding legal effects on the applicant since it did not entail any requirement that the measure be suspended or recovered.[85] Equally, in *Alpiq RomIndustries v Commission*, the fact that the applicant put aside reserves in case the final decision required recovery of the alleged aid was held not to be regarded as a legal effect of the decision to open the formal investigation.[86] In *Gemeente Nijmegen v Commission*, which concerned an opening decision into aid that had already been granted, the General Court held that the decision did not entail independent legal effects since the measure could not be suspended given that it had already been implemented in its entirety.[87] Moreover, there was no immediate general obligation arising out of the decision for the Member State to recover the aid.[88] In addition, even if the decision had an effect on the commercial relations of the recipient with third parties arising from the uncertainty as to the legality of the decision, there was no obvious causal link between the legality of the decision and the repercussions on the applicant's legal position. The commercial uncertainty and perceptions of other traders were merely factual consequences and not legal effects of the decision.[89]

---

[84] Case 60/81, *IBM v Commission* [1981] ECR 2639, paras 10-11.

[85] Case T-517/12, *Alro SA v Commission* EU:T:2014:890, paras 35-44; Case T-129/13, *Alpiq RomIndustries srl v Commission* EU:T:2014:895, paras 40-45; Case T-251/13, *Gemeente Nijmegen v Commission* EU:T:2015:142, para 29.

[86] Case T-129/13, *Alpiq RomIndustries srl v Commission* EU:T:2014:895, para 55.

[87] Case T-251/13, *Gemeente Nijmegen v Commission* EU:T:2015:142, para 38.

[88] *Ibid.*, paras 40-43.

[89] *Ibid.*, paras 49-51.

In *Andersen v Commission*, a complaint was made to the Commission concerning public service compensation for a railway service in Denmark. The Commission opened a formal investigation, but stated that it thought that the service in question satisfied the criteria for being considered a public service. The action for annulment was dismissed as inadmissible on the ground that, even though the Commission had not expressed doubts as to the classification of the rail link as a public service, it remained free to change its mind in the final decision. It followed that the decision was provisional in nature and did not produce any independent legal effects.[90]

In *Deutsche Post v Commission*, the Commission had opened a formal investigation into three distinct matters that it felt might constitute unlawful State aid to Deutsche Post. It subsequently closed the formal investigation with a negative decision in respect of only one of those matters, without specifically concluding its investigation into the other matters. Following a complaint, it took a fresh decision which reopened the formal investigation into the other matters. When Deutsche Post sought the annulment of this decision, the Commission argued that the claim was inadmissible on the ground that the previous decision to open the formal investigation was still open in relation to the additional matters, with the consequence that the later decision had no effect on Deutsche Post's legal position. This argument was accepted by the General Court which held that the decision was not susceptible to judicial review.[91] On appeal, the ECJ held that the Commission's negative decision had closed the earlier formal investigation procedure in general, including in relation to the additional matters.[92] It followed that the reopening of the formal investigation was a challengeable act under Article 263 TFEU.[93]

Contentious classification as new aid In *Spain v Commission* and *Italy v Commission*, Advocate General Van Gerven concluded that a decision to initiate the formal investigation procedure could not normally be subject to review in the absence of some specific threat to the immediate interests of the aid recipient.[94] The ECJ took a different view, on the ground that there was a dispute between the Member States and the Commission as to whether the aid measures in question constituted new aid or existing aid. The Commission, being of the view that the aid was new aid, coupled its decisions to open the formal investigation procedure with orders that payment of the aid be suspended. Since such an order could not have been made where the aid was existing aid, the ECJ held that it followed that the decision had legal effects

---

[90]   Case T-87/09, *Andersen v Commission* [2009] ECR II-225*, para 61.
[91]   Case T-421/07, *Deutsche Post AG v Commission* [2011] ECR II-8105, paras 74-78.
[92]   Case C-77/12P, *Deutsche Post AG v Commission* EU:C:2013: 695, paras 56-63.
[93]   *Ibid.*, para 67.
[94]   Case C-312/90, *Spain v Commission* [1992] ECR I-4117 and Case C-47/91, *Italy v Commission* [1992] ECR I-4145, *per* Advocate General Van Gerven, at pp. 4131-35.

and was actionable.[95] Advocate General Van Gerven's view must nevertheless remain valid where there is no dispute that the aid is new aid, in which case the prohibition on putting the measure into effect remains in force until a final decision of the Commission or the Council approving the aid. Where the annulment action is brought by an applicant, such as an alleged recipient of the aid, the mere fact that the Member State did not object to the classification of the measure as new aid is irrelevant in categorising the measure as a challengeable act with regard to the applicant.[96]

Clearly, a decision comprising an injunction to suspend an aid measure pending determination of its compatibility with the internal market produces legal effects.[97] Even if no suspension order is made, however, the ECJ recognised, in a case concerning Italian aid to Tirrenia, that the mere fact that the Commission classifies as new aid a measure which the Member State regards as existing aid has independent legal effects, since such a decision implies that the Commission does not intend to examine the aid and propose appropriate measures in the context of Article 108(1) TFEU. Rather, the decision necessarily alters the legal position of the measure and that of the beneficiaries, particularly as regards the pursuit of its implementation. There is, at the very least, a significant element of doubt as to the legality of the measure which, according to the ECJ, must lead the Member State to suspend the aid. The Commission's decision might also be invoked by competitors before national courts seeking suspension of the aid. Moreover, it might also lead beneficiaries to refuse payments in any event or to hold the necessary sums as provision for possible subsequent repayment. Businesses would also take account, in their relations with those beneficiaries, of the fragile legal and financial position of the latter.[98] The ECJ also noted that such decisions are not simply preparatory steps to the taking of a final decision following the formal investigation procedure. In particular, the success of an action brought against a final decision that the aid was incompatible with the internal market would do nothing to eradicate the irreversible consequences that would result from

---

[95] Case C-312/90, *Spain v Commission* [1992] ECR I-4117, para 24; Case C-47/91, *Italy v Commission* [1992] ECR I-4145, para 30; Case T-246/99, *Tirrenia di Navigazione SpA v Commission* [2007] ECR II-65*, para 43.

[96] Cases T-80/06 & T-182/09, *Budapesti Erőmű Zrt v Commission* EU:T:2012:65, para 40.

[97] Case C-400/99, *Italy v Commission* [2001] ECR I-7303, para 52.

[98] Case C-400/99, *Italy v Commission* [2001] ECR I-7303, paras 57-59; Case C-77/12P, *Deutsche Post AG v Commission* EU:C:2013: 695, para 52; Cases T-195/01R & T-207/01R, *Government of Gibraltar v Commission* [2001] ECR II-3915, para 58; Cases T-195/01 & T-207/01, *Government of Gibraltar v Commission* [2002] ECR II-2309, paras 82-86; Cases T-346/99 to T-348/99, *Diputación Foral de Álava v Commission* [2002] ECR II-4259, para 33; Case T-80/06, *Budapesti Erőmű v Commission* EU:T:2008:65, para 11; Case T-421/07, *Deutsche Post AG v Commission* [2011] ECR II-8105, para 51; Cases T-80/06 & T-182/09, *Budapesti Erőmű Zrt v Commission* EU:T:2012:65, para 38.

suspension of the aid.[99] In *Deutsche Lufthansa v Flughafen Frankfurt-Hahn*, the ECJ acknowledged that, while the assessments carried out in the decision to initiate the formal examination procedure are preliminary in nature, that does not mean that the decision lacks legal effects, in that national courts were bound by the Commission's preliminary assessment.[100]

The same reasoning applies where the Member State argues that the measure in question does not constitute aid at all.[101] In cases involving the introduction of new preferential tax measures in the Basque region, the Commission argued that the actions were inadmissible on the ground that the decision to open the formal investigation was merely a preparatory measure which did not affect the legal position of the applicants. It argued, *inter alia*, that if its decision to initiate the formal investigation procedure were to have definitive legal consequences as to the classification of measures as State aid, then the fact that an action might be brought to challenge that classification would render inadmissible any action against the Commission's final decision on whether or not the measure in question constituted aid, because the later decision would merely be confirmatory of the earlier definitive decision. The General Court noted that the tax measures in question had already been implemented by the Basque authorities which took the view that they did not constitute the grant of any State aid. It followed that the same reasoning applied as above in relation to measures where there was a dispute as to whether they constituted new or existing aid.[102]

Information injunctions Pursuant to Regulation (EC) No 659/1999, Article 10(3), where the Commission has made a request for information from a Member State and either no information or incomplete information is provided by the Member State, the Commission may, by decision, require the information to be provided by issuing an information injunction. In proceedings concerning State aid to Deutsche Post, the Commission issued

---

[99] Case C-312/90, *Spain v Commission* [1992] ECR I-4117, para 23; Case C-47/91, *Italy v Commission* [1992] ECR I-4145, para 29; Case C-400/99, *Italy v Commission* [2001] ECR I-7303, para 63; Case C-77/12P, *Deutsche Post AG v Commission* EU:C:2013: 695, para 53.

[100] Case C-284/12, *Deutsche Lufthansa AG v Flughafen Frankfurt-Hahn GmbH* EU:C:2013:755, para 37.

[101] Cases T-269/99, T-271/99 & T-272/99, *Territorio Histórico de Álava – Diputación Foral de Álava v Commission* [2002] ECR II-4217, para 37; Cases T-346/99, T-347/99 & T-348/99, *Territorio Histórico de Álava – Diputación Foral de Álava v Commission* [2002] ECR II-4259, para 33; Cases T-80/06 & T-182/09, *Budapesti Erőmű Zrt v Commission* EU:T:2012:65, para 37; Case T-461/12, *Hansestadt Lübeck v Commission* EU:T:2014:758, para 27.

[102] Cases T-269/99, T-271/99 & T-272/99, *Territorio Histórico de Álava – Diputación Foral de Álava v Commission* [2002] ECR II-4217, paras 38-41; Cases T-346/99, T-347/99 & T-348/99, *Territorio Histórico de Álava – Diputación Foral de Álava v Commission* [2002] ECR II-4259, paras 34-36.

such an injunction requiring substantial information to be provided to it. Germany resisted the injunction on the ground that it was disproportionate. The General Court held that the action was inadmissible on the ground that it fell between the decision to open the formal investigation procedure and the final decision and was, accordingly, an intermediate measure the aim of which was to prepare for the final decision.[103] On appeal, the ECJ held that the injunction decision itself produced binding legal effects and was therefore an act open to challenge for the purposes of Article 263 TFEU.[104]

On the other hand, any evaluation by the Commission of the information received does not give rise to a separate challengeable decision. In *ThyssenKrupp Acciai Speciali Terni v Commission*, it was argued that the Commission made a radical change in its assessment in the course of the formal investigation procedure after having received further information from the Italian authorities. The General Court confirmed, however, that the formal investigation procedure does not accommodate a definitive ruling on certain aspects of the case before the final decision is adopted.[105]

Decision following formal investigation procedure Following the Commission's formal investigation, a decision must be taken pursuant to Council Regulation (EC) No 659/1999, Article 7. The Commission may decide that the measure does not constitute aid, or take a positive or conditional decision that the aid is compatible with the internal market, or take a negative decision that the aid is incompatible with the internal market and may not be put into effect. The Commission may also take a decision finding that the measure constitutes aid but is exempted by virtue of Article 106(2) TFEU. The final decision adopted by the Commission in order to conclude the formal review procedure provided for in Article 108(2) TFEU constitutes a measure which may be subject to judicial review. Such a decision produces effects which are binding on and capable of affecting the interests of the parties concerned, since it concludes the procedure in question and definitively decides whether the measure under review is compatible with the rules applying to State aid.[106]

---

[103] Case T-570/08, *Deutsche Post AG v Commission* [2010] ECR II-151*, paras 31-32; Case T-571/08, *Germany v Commission* [2010] ECR II-152*, paras 30-31.

[104] Cases C-463/10P & C-475/10P, *Deutsche Post AG v Commission* [2011] ECR I-9639, para 45; Case T-570/08 RENV, *Deutsche Post AG v Commission* EU:T:2013:589, para 33.

[105] Case T-53/08, *Italy v Commission* [2010] ECR II-3187, paras123; Case T-62/08, *ThyssenKrupp Acciai Speciali Terni SpA v Commission* [2010] ECR II-3229, para 175.

[106] Case T-190/00, *Regione Siciliana v Commission* [2003] ECR II-5015, para 45; T-25/04, *González y Díez SA v Commission* [2007] ECR II-3121, para 91.

An applicant may base its action for annulment on arguments even though they had not been raised during the administrative procedure.[107]   In *Regione Siciliana v Commission*, where the applicant argued that the aid should have been classified and examined as existing aid, the Commission argued that the applicant could no longer challenge the final decision in so far it classified the measure as new aid inasmuch as that classification was the result of the decision to initiate the formal review procedure which the applicant did not challenge within the prescribed period and which therefore became definitive. The General Court held, however, that interested parties are always able to contest the final decision which concludes the formal review procedure and must, in that context, be able to challenge the various elements which form the basis for the position definitively adopted by the commission. That right was independent of whether the decision to initiate the formal review procedure gave rise to legal effects which may be the subject matter of an action for annulment. The right to contest a decision to initiate review could not diminish the procedural right to interested parties by preventing them from challenging the final decision and relying on support of their action on defects at any stage of the procedure leading to that decision.[108]

Decision imposing conditions accepted by Member State   A decision pursuant to Article 7(4) of Regulation (EC) No 659/1999 in which conditions are imposed on a Member State may be challenged. In *Commission v Netherlands and ING Groep*, following lengthy negotiations with the Netherlands, the Commission adopted a decision allowing aid to ING subject to certain conditions that the Netherlands had accepted. When both the Netherlands and ING sought the annulment of the decision, the Commission argued that it did not have the power to refuse commitments made by a Member State in conjunction with a notified measure on the ground that they go beyond what is necessary to render State aid compatible with the internal market. The Netherlands and ING stated that, while they did offer the commitments in question, this was because the Commission indicated that it would not give a favourable decision if those minimum compensatory measures were not offered. Dismissing the challenge to admissibility, the ECJ held that the commitments listed in the decision were not the result of merely unilateral proposals by the Netherlands and ING, in relation to which the Commission played no part, but, on the contrary, were imposed by the Commission.[109]

---

[107]   Case T-380/94, *AIUFFASS v Commission* [1996] ECR II-2169, para 64; Case T-16/96, *Cityflyer Express v Commission* [1998] ECR II-757, para 39; Cases T-81/07 to T-83/07, *KG Holding NV v Commission* [2009] ECR II-2411, para 195.

[108]   Case T-190/00, *Regione Siciliana v Commission* [2003] ECR II-5015, paras 46-47; Case T-25/04, *González y Díez SA v Commission* [2007] ECR II-3121, para 92.

[109]   Case C-224/12P, *Commission v Netherlands and ING Groep NV* EU:C:2014:213, paras 75-80, upholding Cases T-29/10 & T-33/10, *Netherlands v Commission* EU:C:2012:98.

Classification as existing aid The Commission's review of existing aid pursuant to Article 108(1) TFEU entails legal effects of a different nature from those applicable to decisions concerning new aid. In *Forum 187 v Commission*, the Commission classified in 1984 and 1987 the tax treatment in Belgium of coordination centres as not constituting State aid. Following a review of this type of taxation after the adoption in 1998 of the Commission's notice on the application of the State aid rules to direct taxation, the Commission took the view that State aid was involved and proposed to Belgium appropriate measures within the meaning of Article 108(1) TFEU. When Belgium failed to accept these measures, the Commission opened a formal investigation procedure. Forum 187, an association representing the interests of companies operating coordination centres, sought the annulment of its decision. The General Court held that the action was inadmissible on the ground that the decision did not produce any legal effect. In that regard, first, unlike decisions initiating the formal examination procedure in regard to measures which have been provisionally classified as new aid, the decision classifying the coordination centres scheme as a scheme of existing aid did not have any independent legal effects deriving from the suspension of measures provided for in Article 108(3) TFEU in regard to new aid. Second, the classification of the scheme as existing aid did not imply that the Commission had decided to revoke its 1984 and 1987 decisions. That classification was provisional in nature, and the Commission could still close the formal examination procedure by a decision finding that, unlike the classification adopted at the outset of that procedure, the measure in question did not constitute aid. Third, any diminution of Belgium's legitimate expectation or that of the applicant's members, merely because it was possible that at the end of the investigation procedure the scheme might be regarded as incompatible existing aid, did not constitute a legal effect bringing about a distinct change in the legal position of the applicant or its members.[110]

Review of existing aid Where the Commission considers that an existing aid scheme is not, or is no longer, compatible with the internal market, it must inform the Member State concerned of its preliminary view.[111] No decision is taken at this stage, and the mere formation of a preliminary view by the Commission would not appear to produce any legal effects. Having given the Member State concerned the opportunity to submit its comments, the Commission may propose any appropriate measures required by the progressive development or the functioning of the internal market.[112] In this respect, the Commission may issue a recommendation proposing amendment or abolition of the aid scheme or the introduction of procedural

---

[110] Case T-276/02, *Forum 187 ASBL v Commission* [2003] ECR II-2075, paras 43-49.
[111] Council Regulation (EC) No 659/1999, Article 17(2).
[112] Article 108(1) TFEU.

requirements.[113]   Judicial review of recommendations is specifically excluded from the jurisdiction of the ECJ and the General Court under Article 263 TFEU, so that a recommendation may not be challenged directly in those courts either by the Member State concerned or by any other interested party.[114]

A decision by the Commission not to issue a recommendation is also not capable of being judicially reviewed, since a refusal to adopt an act is subject to review under Article 263 TFEU only if the act itself may be challenged.[115] In *Salt Union v Commission*, where the Commission refused to accede to a request to propose appropriate measures in respect of an existing aid scheme, the applicant argued that, since Article 108(1) TFEU obliged the Commission to keep existing aid under review, its application sought only to obtain the annulment of an unlawful decision to bring to an end an incomplete mandatory review and that it had an interest in ensuring that the type of review carried out by the Commission was sufficiently extensive to enable it to assess whether action was called for.   The General Court dismissed the application as inadmissible on the ground that appropriate measures, even if they had been proposed, could not produce binding legal effects and could not, therefore, be subject to judicial review.[116]

Measures following review of existing aid   Where it is not disputed that the Commission has correctly decided to deal with a measure as an existing aid, the legal situation does not change until such time as the Commission adopts a final decision.[117]   There is no requirement to suspend or revoke the aid measure pending a final determination by the Commission of the compatibility of the aid with the internal market. The decision to initiate the formal investigation procedure, therefore, cannot be said necessarily to produce legal effects. Where the Commission accepts proposals from the Member State so that it accepts that the measures will be compatible with the internal market as to the future, it will be deemed to have taken a decision having legal effect that may be challenged.[118]   Accordingly, in *Stichting Woonpunt v Commission*, a decision accepting commitments by the Netherlands in relation to amending an existing aid scheme was a challengeable decision, since it was the Commission's decision which rendered the commitments binding.[119]   Where the Member State accepts the Commission's recommendation, it becomes

---

[113] Council Regulation (EC) No 659/1999, Article 18.
[114] Case T-330/94, *Salt Union Ltd. v Commission* [1996] ECR II-1475, para 36.
[115] Cases 97/86, 193/86, 99/86 & 215/86, *Asteris v Commission* [1988] ECR 2181, para 17.
[116] Case T-330/94, *Salt Union Ltd. v Commission* [1996] ECR II-1475, para 36.
[117] Case C-400/99, *Italy v Commission* [2001] ECR I-7303, para 61.
[118] Case T-354/05, *TF1 v Commission* [2009] ECR II-471, para 72.
[119] Case C-132/12P, *Stichting Woonpunt v Commission* EU:C:2014:100, para 72; Case C-133/12P, *Stichting Woonlinie v Commission* EU:C:2014:105, para 59.

bound by its acceptance to implement the proposed measures.[120]   Where it rejects the recommendation, and the Commission still considers that its proposed measures are necessary, it must take a decision pursuant to Regulation (EC) No 659/1999, Article 4(4) to initiate the formal investigation procedure.[121]   If the Commission does not recommend appropriate measures but proceeds unilaterally to amend the rules governing existing aid, without seeking the agreement of the Member States involved, its decision may be challenged.   For example, in *Spain v Commission*, a decision to prolong the motor vehicle framework for a further period of two years was held to produce legal effects since, in the absence of such a decision, the framework would have come to an end.[122]

19.4 REVIEW OF FAILURE TO ACT

Failure to act   Under Article 265 TFEU, an action may be brought against the Commission or the Council by a Member State or by any other EU institution alleging failure to act.   The action is admissible only where the institution concerned is under a duty to act, has first been called upon to act and, within two months, has not defined its position.   Any natural or legal person may commence proceedings before the General Court alleging that an EU institution has failed to address to that person any act other than a recommendation or opinion.   Where a valid complaint has been made to the Commission that is sufficient to require the Commission to open a preliminary assessment, and the Commission has not done so, a failure to respond will constitute a failure to define a position for the purposes of Article 265 TFEU.[123]

Article 265 TFEU cannot be the basis of an action against the adoption of a measure different from that desired or considered necessary by the person concerned.   The fact that the position adopted by the institution has not satisfied the applicant is of no relevance in this respect.[124]   A failure to act comes to an end when the Commission has defined its position.[125]   Where the applicant considers that the Commission has taken a wrong decision, that is a

---

[120]   Council Regulation (EC) No 659/1999, Article 19(1).

[121]   *Ibid.*, Article 19(2).

[122]   Case C-135/93, *Spain v Commission* [1995] ECR I-1651, para 29.

[123]   Case C-615/11P, *Commission v Ryanair Ltd* EU:C:2013:310, para 39; Case T-442/07, *Ryanair Ltd v Commission* [2011] ECR II-333*, para 37.

[124]   Case C-44/00P, *Sodima v Commission* [2000] ECR I-11231, para 83; Case T-361/02, *Deutsche Bahn AG v Commission* [2005] (unreported), para 25; Case T-407/09, *Neubrandenburger Wohnungsgesellschaft mbH v Commission* EU:T:2012:1, para 41.

[125]   Cases T-194/97 & T-83/98, *Branco v Commission* [2000] ECR II-69, para 55; Case T-407/09, *Neubrandenburger Wohnungsgesellschaft mbH v Commission* EU:T:2012:1, para 42.

matter of the legality of the decision and is irrelevant in an action for failure to act.[126] Equally, where the Commission rejects a complaint by giving a clear and explicit reasoning, it is taken to have defined its position so that proceedings cannot be sustained alleging a failure to act.[127] Where the Commission adopts an act after proceedings have been commenced but prior to judgment being given, the proceedings will be treated as being devoid of purpose.[128]

Obligation to act   The situations in which the Commission must take a decision are set out in the provisions of Council Regulation (EC) No 659/1999. For Article 265 TFEU to be applicable, the institution concerned must be under an obligation to act. It is not sufficient that it merely has a power to act within the framework of a discretion.[129] Where proceedings are commenced alleging failure to act in the context of State aid, it is, therefore, incumbent on the applicant to show that its application relates to a specific duty to take a decision, failing which the application must be declared inadmissible.[130] An action for failure to act is directed to the state of affairs at the time when formal notice is given to the institution calling on it to act.[131] Thus, the institution must be under an obligation to act at that time. Premature commencement of proceedings will be dismissed as inadmissible, as happened in *Asklepios Kliniken v Commission*, where a complaint which was made to the Commission was followed up twelve months later by a letter calling on the Commission to act.[132]

Commission must be called upon to act   Where the Commission has not been called upon to act, an action for failure to act will be inadmissible. In *Germany*

---

[126] Case T-26/01, *Fiocchi Munizioni SpA v Commission* [2003] ECR II-3951, para 82; Cases T-297/01 & T-298/01, *SIC v Commission* [2004] ECR 743, para 31.

[127] Case 8/71, *Deutsche Komponistenverband v Commission* [1971] ECR 705, para 2; Cases 166 & 220/86, *Irish Cement Ltd v Commission* [1988] ECR 6473, para 17; Case T-107/96, *Pantochim SA v Commission* [1998] ECR II-311, para 30; Case T-361/02, *Deutsche Bahn AG v Commission* [2005] (unreported), para 20; Case T-351/02, *Deutsche Bahn AG v Commission* [2006] ECR II-1047, para 46.

[128] Case C-145/12P, *Neubrandenburger Wohnungsgesellschaft mbH v Commission* EU:C:2012:724, para 24; Case T-107/96, *Pantochim SA v Commission* [1998] ECR II-311, para 29; Cases T-297/01 & T-298/01, *SIC v Commission* [2004] ECR 743, para 31; Cases T-128/08 & T-241/08, *CBI v Commission* EU:T:2010:175, para 28; Case T-423/07, *Ryanair Ltd v Commission* [2011] ECR II-2397, para 32.

[129] Cases 10 & 18/68, *Eridania v Commission* [1969] ECR 459, *per* Advocate General Roemer, at p. 494.

[130] Cases 166 & 220/86, *Irish Cement v Commission* [1988] ECR 6473, *per* Advocate General Darmon, at p. 6495.

[131] Case T-95/96, *Gestevisión Telecinco SA v Commission* [1998] ECR II-3407, para 71; Case T-395/04, *Air One SpA v Commission* [2006] ECR II-1343, para 60; Case T-167/04, *Asklepios Kliniken GmbH v Commission* [2007] ECR II-2379, para 80.

[132] Case T-167/04, *Asklepios Kliniken GmbH v Commission* [2007] ECR II-2379, para 91.

v Commission, the Commission investigated the grant of aid to the Belgian textile industry. In the context of consultations with the other Member States concerning the compatibility of the aid with the internal market, Germany requested the Commission not to authorise implementation of the plan. The Commission informed Belgium by letter that it did not object to implementation of the aid. Proceedings alleging a failure to act were dismissed on the ground that, although Germany had expressed the opinion that the plan was incompatible with the internal market, it had not expressly called on the Commission to act.[133] In *Ryanair v Commission*, the Commission had been called to investigate alleged State aid to Lufthansa at Munich airport. That being the subject matter of the complaint, the Commission was under no duty to act in relation also to alleged State aid to Star Alliance, which had not formed part of the complaint.[134]

Similarly, in *Fédération Nationale des Producteurs de Vins de Table et Vins de Pays v Commission*, the applicant lodged a complaint with the Commission alleging that certain aid granted by Italy was incompatible with Article 107(1) TFEU and requesting the Commission to decide accordingly under Article 108 TFEU. When the Commission did not reply to this complaint, the applicant brought an action under Article 265 TFEU for failure to act, claiming that the Commission had not dealt with its complaint. The ECJ held that the action was inadmissible since the applicant had not called upon the Commission to address to the applicant any act as required by Article 265 TFEU. Prior to the complaint being received, the Commission had already initiated a formal investigation procedure into the aid and had called for comments from interested parties. The fact that the applicant availed itself of this opportunity during the investigation procedure to submit its comments could not be assimilated to the Commission being called upon to act within the meaning of Article 265 TFEU.[135]

Failure to define a position Article 265 TFEU applies only where the Commission has failed to take a decision or to define a position. In this context, defining a position does not necessarily require that the institution adopt an act that is capable of annulment. An act may constitute a definition of position terminating the failure to act if it is the prerequisite for the next step in a procedure which has, in principle, to culminate in a legal act that itself will be challengeable.[136] Thus, in *SIC v Commission*, where the Commission had sent a letter to the Portuguese authorities on the basis that certain measures were

---

[133] Case 84/82, *Germany v Commission* [1984] ECR 1451, para 23.

[134] Case T-423/07, *Ryanair Ltd v Commission* [2011] ECR II-2397, para 40.

[135] Case 59/79, *Fédération Nationale des Producteurs de Vins de Table et Vins de Pays v Commission* [1979] ECR 2425, para 2.

[136] Case T-105/96, *Pharos v Commission* [1998] ECR II-285, para 43; Cases T-194/97 & T-83/98, *Branco v Commission* [2000] ECR II-69, para 54; Case T-407/09, *Neubrandenburger Wohnungsgesellschaft mbH v Commission* EU:T:2012:1, para 40.

existing aid, the Commission was held to have defined its position on the issue of whether the measures constituted new or existing aid, even though the letter was classifiable as a preparatory act which not challengeable in an annulment action.[137] Similarly, in *Neubrandenburger Wohnungsgesellschaft v Commission*, an alleged failure to consider a complaint came to an end with the issuance of a letter to the complainant pursuant to Regulation (EC) No 659/1999, Article 20(2).[138] On the other hand, a letter from the Commission stating that the questions raised are being examined does not amount to the defining of a position.[139]

A definition of position must relate to the particular complaint. In *Asklepios Kliniken v Commission*, the Commission was called on to act in relation to a complaint concerning compensation paid to German public hospitals in respect of public service obligations. The Commission sought to invoke the subsequent adoption of Decision 2005/842/EC on the application of Article 106(2) TFEU to State aid in the form of compensation in respect of services of general economic interest as an argument that there was no longer any need to act. This was rejected by the General Court on the ground that laying down abstract criteria in a decision of general scope does not by itself constitute a definition of position on a specific complaint. Those criteria do no more than set out the elements which should be taken into account for the purpose of assessing the compatibility with EU law of financing comparable to that criticised by the applicant. Only the actual application of those criteria by the Commission to the situations complained of by the applicant could demonstrate clearly the institution's willingness to act in respect of the applicant's request, and, therefore, constitute a definition of position.[140]

19.5 APPLICANT'S INTEREST IN JUDICIAL REVIEW PROCEEDINGS

Member States and EU institutions Under Article 263 TFEU, actions for annulment may be commenced by the Member States, the Council or the Commission. In proceedings for failure to act, the Member States and the other EU institutions may bring an action to establish that the Council or the Commission has infringed the EU Treaties. Thus, for example, a Member State may challenge a Commission decision refusing to permit it to grant State aid or imposing conditions on the grant of aid, or it may challenge a decision allowing another Member State to grant aid. The Commission may challenge a

---

[137] Cases T-297/01 & T-298/01, *SIC v Commission* [2004] ECR 743, para 53.

[138] Case T-407/09, *Neubrandenburger Wohnungsgesellschaft mbH v Commission* EU:T:2012:1, para 42.

[139] Case 13/83 *Parliament* v *Council* [1985] ECR 1513, para 25; Case T-95/96, *Gestevisión Telecinco SA v Commission*, [1998] ECR II-3407, para 88.

[140] Case T-167/04, *Asklepios Kliniken GmbH v Commission* [2007] ECR II-2379, para 77.

decision of the Council under Article 108(2) TFEU deciding that aid shall be considered compatible with the internal market, alleging, for example, that the decision is not justified by exceptional circumstances.   The European Parliament and the European Central Bank may also bring actions for the purpose of protecting their prerogatives.   Although the European Parliament and the European Central Bank are not involved in the decision-taking process regarding State aid, it is not inconceivable that, for instance, the ECB might take the view that certain aid might impinge on its responsibilities in the field of monetary policy.

Natural or legal persons Article 263 TFEU provides that any natural or legal person may institute proceedings against a decision addressed to another person but which is of direct and individual concern to him.   An action for failure to act under Article 265 TFEU may be brought by a person who claims that an institution has failed to adopt a measure which, if it had been adopted, would have been of direct and individual concern to it.[141]   The possibility for the applicant to seek a remedy in the national courts, whereby, for instance, it could challenge the grant of the aid, is irrelevant in determining the admissibility of the applicant's claim before the General Court.[142]

Decisions in State aid cases under Article 108 TFEU and Council Regulation (EC) No 659/1999 are always addressed to Member States.[143]   In *Sytraval v Commission*, a challenge was brought against a letter informing the complainant that the Commission had decided that the measure complained of did not constitute State aid.   The General Court held that this letter to the complainant was itself a decision, so that it could be challenged by the complainant since it was the addressee.[144]   On appeal, the ECJ held that this approach was incorrect and that decisions adopted by the Commission in the field of State aid must always be addressed to the Member States concerned.

---

[141] Case 15/70, *Chevalley v Commission* [1970] ECR 975, para 6; Case C-68/95, *T. Port GmbH v Bundesanstalt für Landwirtchaft und Ernährung* [1996] ECR I-6065, para 59; Case T-95/96, *Gestevisión Telecinco SA v Commission*, [1998] ECR II-3407, para 58; Case T-17/96, *TF1 v Commission* [1999] ECR II-1757, para 27; Case T-395/04, *Air One v Commission* [2006] ECR II-1343, para 25; Case T-167/04, *Asklepios Kliniken GmbH v Commission* [2007] ECR II-2379, para 45.

[142] Case T-398/94, *Kahn Scheepvaart BV v Commission* [1996] ECR II-477, para 50; Case T-95/96, *Gestevisión Telecinco SA v Commission*, [1998] ECR II-3407, para 68; Case T-86/96, *Arbeitsgemeinschaft Deutscher Luftfahrt-Unternehmen v Commission* [1999] ECR II-179, para 52; Case T-17/96, *TF1 v Commission* [1999] ECR II-1757, para 35; Case T-69/96, *Hamburger Hafen- und Lagerhaus AG v Commission* [2001] ECR II-1037, para 51; Case T-212/00, *Nuove Industrie Molisane v Commission* [2002] ECR II-347, para 48.

[143] Council Regulation (EC) No 659/1999, Article 25.

[144] Case T-95/94, *Sytraval v Commission* [1995] ECR II-2651, para 51. This approach had been adopted previously by the ECJ in Cases 166 & 220/86, *Irish Cement v Commission* [1988] ECR 6473.

Accordingly, where the Commission adopts such a decision and proceeds, in the interests of sound administration, to inform the complainant of its decision, it is the decision addressed to the Member State which must form the subject matter of the action for annulment which the complainant may bring, and not the letter to that complainant informing him of the decision.[145]

Vested legal interest in bringing proceedings Although, in order for an act of the Commission to be the subject of an action for annulment, it must be intended to have legal effects, a Member State or an EU institution need not prove that the act it seeks to challenge produces legal effects with regard to itself.[146] Non-privileged applicants, however, must establish a vested legal interest in bringing the proceedings.[147] Such an interest exists only if the annulment of the measure is of itself capable of affecting the applicant's legal position.[148] The action must be capable, through its outcome, of procuring an advantage to the applicant.[149] Only measures which produce binding legal effects such as to affect the interests of the applicant by bringing about a distinct change in his legal position may be the subject of an action for annulment.[150] The burden of proof in this respect lies on the applicant.[151]

---

[145] Case C-367/95P, *Commission v Sytraval* [1998] ECR I-1719, para 45.

[146] Case C-208/99, *Portugal v Commission* [2001] ECR I-9183, para 22; Cases C-463/10P & C-475/10P, *Deutsche Post AG v Commission* [2011] ECR I-9639, para 36; Case T-233/04, *Netherlands v Commission* [2008] ECR I-591, para 37; Cases T-309/04, T-317/04, T-329/04 & T-336/04, *TV2/Danmark A/S v Commission* [2008] ECR II-2935, para 63; Cases T-415/05, T-416/05 & T-423/05, *Greece v Commission* [2010] ECR II-4749, para 57; Case T-154/10, *France v Commission* EU:T:2012:452, para 37; Case T-425/11, *Greece v Commission* EU:T:2014:768, para 33.

[147] Case T-138/89, *NBV and NVB v Commission* [1992] II-2181, para 33; Case T-212/00, *Nuove Industrie Molisane v Commission* [2002] ECR II-347, para 33; Case T-141/03, *Sniace SA v Commission* [2005] ECR II-1197, para 25; Case T-136/05, *Salvat père & fils v Commission* [2007] ECR II-4063, para 34; Case T-301/01, *Alitalia SpA v Commission* [2008] ECR II-1753, para 35; Cases T-309/04, T-317/04, T-329/04 & T-336/04, *TV2/Danmark A/S v Commission* [2008] ECR II-2935, para 67; Case T-261/11, *European Goldfields Ltd v Commission* EU:T:2012:157, para 17.

[148] Case C-242/00, *Germany v Commission* [2002] ECR I-5603, para 46; Case T-138/89, *Nederlandse Bankiersvereniging v Commission* [1992] ECR II-2181, para 33; Case T-9/98, *Mitteldeutsche Erdoel-Raffinerie GmbH v Commission* [2001] ECR II-3367, para 32; Cases T-239/04 & T-323/04, *Italy v Commission* [2007] ECR II-3265, para 43; Case T-114/09, *Viasat Broadcasting UK Ltd v Commission* EU:T:2012:144, para 22.

[149] Case C-519/07P, *Commission v Koninklijke Friesland Campina NV* [2009] ECR I-8495, para 63; Case T-354/05, *TF1 SA v Commission* [2009] ECR II-471, para 85; Case T-273/11, *NRJ Global v Commission* EU:T:2013:239, para 27; Case T-369/00, *Départment du Loiret v Commission* EU:T:2013:78, para 21; Cases T-15/12 & T-16/12, *Provincie Groningen v Commission* EU:T:2013:74, para 31; Case T-321/13, *Adorisio v Commission* EU:T:2014:175, para 21.

[150] Cases C-68/94 & C-30/95, *France v Commission* [1998] ECR I-1375, para 62; Case C-164/02, *Netherlands v Commission* [2004] ECR I-1177, para 18; Case T-212/00, *Nuove*

Thus, for example, a recipient of aid that is the subject of a recovery decision has an interest in seeking the annulment of the decision.[152] Equally, a challenge to a Commission decision accepting commitments in relation to amendments to existing aid is capable of affecting the legal position of the applicant where, in so far as it concerns the aid scheme, annulment of the decision would have the effect of maintaining previous conditions which were more favourable to the applicant.[153] Interested parties seeking to defend their procedural rights by challenging a decision approving a measure taken at the end of the preliminary assessment have a legal interest in annulling the decision, since such an annulment would require the Commission to initiate the formal investigation procedure, permitting them to present their observations and thus exert an influence on the new decision.[154]

The applicant's legal interest must be determined at the time when the application is lodged.[155] The applicant's legal interest must also continue until the date of the final decision of the court.[156] In this respect, a person's legal interest in bringing proceedings may be established or eliminated by reason of events extraneous to the applicant and to the contested decision.[157] There is no longer any need to adjudicate on the action if the applicant has lost all personal interest in having the contested act annulled on account of an event occurring in the course of the proceedings, the effect of which is that the annulment of

---

Industrie Molisane v Commission [2002] ECR II-347, para 36; T-25/04, *González y Díez SA v Commission* [2007] ECR II-3121, para 89.

[151] Case T-141/03, *Sniace SA v Commission* [2005] ECR II-1197, para 31; Case T-156/10, *CCAE v Commission* EU:T:2014:41, para 28.

[152] Cases C-71/09P, C-73/09P & C-76/09P, *Comitato Venezia vuole vivere v Commission* [2011] ECR I-4727, para 77; Case C-318/09P, *A2A SpA v Commission* [2011] ECR I-207*, paras 69-70; Case C-319/09P, *ACEA SpA v Commisssion* [2011] ECR I-209*, paras 68-69; Case C-320/09P, *A2A SpA v Commission* [2011] ECR II-210*, paras 69-70.

[153] Case C-132/12P, *Stichting Woonpunt v Commission* EU:C:2014:100, para 69; Case C-133/12P, *Stichting Woonlinie v Commission* EU:C:2014:105, para 56

[154] Case T-388/03, *Deutsche Post AG v Commission* [2009] ECR II-199, para 62.

[155] Case T-16/96 *Cityflyer Express* v *Commission* [1998] ECR II-757, para 30; Cases T-228/00 etc., *Gruppo Ormeggiatori del Porto di Venezia Soc. Coop. rl v Commission* [2005] ECR II-787, para 23; Case T-141/03, *Sniace SA v Commission* [2005] ECR II-1197, para 25; Case T-96/07, *Telecom Italia Media SpA v Commission* EU:T:2009:74, para 18; Case T-261/11, *European Goldfields Ltd v Commission* EU:T:2012:157, para 17; Cases T-15/12 & T-16/12, *Provincie Groningen v Commission* EU:T:2013:74, para 30; Case T-570/08 RENV, *Deutsche Post AG v Commission* EU:T:2013:589, para 41; Case T-156/10, *CCAE v Commission* EU:T:2014:41, para 54.

[156] Case C-319/09P, *ACEA SpA v Commisssion* [2-11] ECR I-209*, para 67; Case T-570/08 RENV, *Deutsche Post AG v Commission* EU:T:2013:589, para 41; Case T-11/07 RENV, *Frucona Košice as v Commission* EU:T:2014:1 3, para 35; Case T-321/13, *Adorisio v Commission* EU:T:2014:175, para 20.

[157] Case T-400/11, *Altadis SA v Commission* EU:T:2013:490, para 38; Case T-156/10, *CCAE v Commission* EU:T:2014:41, para 55.

that act is no longer capable, by itself, of having legal consequences to the advantage of the applicant.[158]

The mere fact that an applicant who has already repaid unlawful aid pursuant to a recovery decision has subsequently gone into liquidation does not mean that it no longer has a present interest in seeking annulment of that decision, since, if the decision is annulled, the applicant will be entitled to seek recovery of the repayment, which will then be entered as an asset in its liquidation balance sheet.[159]   In *Deutsche Post v Commission*, the General Court held, in respect of an action to annul an information injunction, that the fact that the Germany authorities had in fact complied with the injunction and given the requested information to the Commission did not preclude the applicant from having an ongoing vested interest in annulling the decision. In particular, the General Court held that the annulment of the decision would have legal consequences in that it would prevent the Commission form repeating such a practice.[160]   It might also form the basis of an action for damages against the Commission.[161]

In *Mitteldeutsche Erdoel-Raffinerie v Commission*, the Commission argued that the applicant's challenge to the validity of a Commission decision prohibiting certain aid was of no legal interest to it since the German Government had already abolished the provisions giving rise to the aid and had made it clear that it had no intention of re-introducing them even if the decision was annulled. The General Court held that the action was admissible, given that it could not be excluded that the applicant might have certain claims under German law, based on the principle of the protection of legitimate expectations, if the decision was found to have been unlawful.[162]   In *Saxonia Edelmetalle v Commission*, the Commission argued that if the application for annulment was successful, the Commission would be required to adopt a new decision which, in the circumstances, would necessarily be less favourable to the applicant. Dismissing this objection, the General Court held that the Commission could not yet be in a position to determine the content of the measure which it would be required to adopt. Since the applicant was required,

---

[158] Cases T-415/05, T-416/05 & T-423/05, *Greece v Commission* [2010] ECR II-4749, para 61; Cases T-494/08 to T-500/08 & T-509/08, *Ryanair Ltd v Commission* [2010] ECR II-5723, para 43.

[159] Cases T-415/05, T-416/05 & T-423/05, *Greece v Commission* [2010] ECR II-4749, para 62.

[160] Case T-570/08 RENV, *Deutsche Post AG v Commission* EU:T:2013:589, para 46,

[161] *Ibid.*, para 47; Cases T-425/04 RENV & T-444/04 RENV, *France v Commission* EU:T:2015:450, para 119.

[162] Case T-9/98, *Mitteldeutsche Erdoel-Raffinerie GmbH v Commission* [2001] ECR II-3367, para 34.

under the contested decision, to repay unlawful aid, it had a legal interest in obtaining the annulment of that act.[163]

In *Operator ARP v Commission*, the applicant's interest in bringing proceedings could not be denied merely by virtue of the fact that the aid in question was repaid by one of the other entities designated in the decision as being jointly and severally liable for the repayment. According to Polish law, entities which have actually repaid unlawful aid may assert a right of action in that regard during a 10-year period. In those circumstances, the applicant should be considered to have retained an interest in the annulment of the decision, since, were its action to be upheld, it would be capable of removing any risk of proceedings against it.[164]

Lack of vested interest in bring proceedings Where the applicant cannot show a vested interest in bringing proceedings, the application for annulment will be declared inadmissible. In *Nuove Industrie Molisane v Commission*, an application to annul a decision restricting the coefficient relating to the competition factor allowed by the Commission in respect of aid for a large Italian regional investment project was dismissed as inadmissible on the ground that the aid notified by the Italian Government was in any event less than that authorised by the Commission in the decision. Annulment of the decision would not, therefore, have led to an increase in the aid.[165] In *NRJ Global v Commission*, a fiscal aid scheme had been declared invalid, allowing recovery of the tax paid to finance the scheme, although the ECJ restricted this to persons who had already commenced recovery proceedings at the time of its judgment, which included the applicant. Subsequently, the Commission adopted a fresh decision approving the aid scheme, whilst declaring the method of financing to be incompatible with the internal market. The applicant sought annulment of that decision on the ground that it prejudiced its ability to recover previously paid tax. The General Court held that the decision could not retroactively affect the applicant's right of recovery, so that it had no vested interest in seeking annulment of the decision.[166]

In *Netherlands v Commission*, the Netherlands notified a measure which funded the dredging of certain estuaries by port authorities and requested the Commission to assess the legality of the measure in the light of Articles 107 and 108 TFEU. The Commission declared the system of aid to be compatible with the internal market under Article 107(3)(c) TFEU. Nevertheless, the Netherlands sought to challenge the decision on the ground that it classified the measure as State aid. The ECJ rejected the claim on the ground that the

---

[163] Case T-111/01R, *Saxonia Edelmetalle GmbH v Commission* [2001] ECR II-2335, para 17; Cases T-239/04 & T-323/04, *Italy v Commission* [2007] ECR II-3265, para 43.

[164] Case T-291/06, *Operator ARP v Commission* [2009] ECR II-2275, para 27.

[165] Case T-212/00, *Nuove Industrie Molisane v Commission* [2002] ECR II-347, para 46.

[166] Case T-273/11, *NRJ Global v Commission* EU:T:2013:239, para 30.

decision did not bring about a distinct change in the legal position of the Netherlands. The decision did not have wider application, in that it did not in the least constitute the adoption of a position as to whether all port authorities are undertakings or whether all of the activities of such authorities are economic in nature. Nor did the decision prejudge the assessment under Article 107(1) TFEU of any other contributions paid to the port authorities.[167] In *Forum 187 v Commission* and *Centre de Coordination Carrefour v Commission*, the applicants challenged a Commission decision which terminated a system of existing aid. Since the Belgian authorities had in any event already terminated their authorisation under the system, which they were not compelled to do, annulment of the decision could not result in the applicants being allowed retroactively a further transitional period.[168]

In *European Goldfields v Commission*, the applicant was the parent company of an undertaking that was the object of a decision ordering recovery of aid. It claimed to have an independent right of action on the basis that its economic activities were affected by the decision. The General Court held that its shareholding interest in the recipient of the aid did not give it a right of action.[169] Moreover, there was no evidence that the recovery decision was capable of threatening its current or future solvency and no action was pending before the national courts concerning the recovery of the aid, whereby the liability of the applicant was in issue.[170] Similarly, in *Post Invest Europe v Commission*, a claim for annulment was brought by the applicant, a 49% shareholder in a company that was held to have received unlawful aid, on the ground that it had a personal interest in bringing proceedings since reimbursement of the aid that had been repaid would restore the value of its shareholding in the recipient and therefore the value of its own capital. The General Court rejected the action as inadmissible on the ground that none of the arguments put forward by the applicant were such as to establish the existence, with regard to it, of a personal interest in bringing proceedings that was separate from that of the recipient.[171] By contrast, in *Westfälisch-Lippischer Sparkassen- und Giroverband v Commission*, a shareholder in a bank that had received restructuring aid on condition that the shareholders sold certain assets was regarded as having an interest separate from the beneficiary as regards the sale obligation, though not as regards other obligations imposed on the beneficiary by the Commission.[172]

---

[167] Case C-164/02, *Netherlands v Commission* [2004] ECR I-1177, paras 20-23.

[168] Case T-94/08, *Centre de Coordination Carrefour v Commission* [2010] ECR II-1015, para 56; Case T-189/08, *Forum 187 ASBL v Commission* [2010] ECR II-1039, para 79.

[169] Case T-261/11, *European Goldfields Ltd v Commission* EU:T:2012:157, para 27.

[170] *Ibid.*, para 28.

[171] Case T-413/12, *Post Invest Europe sàrl v Commission* EU:T:2013:246, paras 24-30.

[172] Case T-457/09, *Westfälisch-Lippischer Sparkassen- und Giroverband v Commission* EU:T:2014:683, paras 112-117.

In *Mory v Commission*, the applicants had been competitors of a recipient of unlawful aid which was required by the Commission to be recovered. Subsequently, the applicants went into liquidation and discontinued trading and the recipient of the aid, having also gone into administration, was sold to an independent third party. Following an application from the French authorities, the Commission decided that the aid need not be recovered from the third party. The application to annul that decision was rejected as inadmissible on the ground that the applicants were no longer trading and were thus not competitors of the third party with any interest in whether the aid should be recovered.[173]   In *Adorisio v Commission*, the applicants were holders of subordinated bonds in a Netherlands bank that had been nationalised in the financial crisis, with the bonds being expropriated.   The Commission's decision, approving the bank's restructuring plan as State aid that was compatible with the internal market, was challenged on the ground that annulment of the decision would result in the bank being declared insolvent, thereby allowing the applicants to obtain partial repayment of their subordinated bonds.   Rejecting the claim as inadmissible, the General Court held that the annulment would not in fact result in the Netherland's expropriation decision being reversed, that being a matter solely for the Netherlands courts.[174]

In any event, an application for annulment which has become without purpose will be declared inadmissible.   For instance, in *Viasat Broadcasting v Commission*, an application for annulment of a Commission decision approving rescue aid was declared to have lost its purpose on the ground that the aid had already in fact been repaid, so that annulment of the decision would neither have affected the position of the recipient nor conferred any benefit on the applicant.[175]   In *CCAE v Commission*, in which the annulment was sought of a decision requiring recovery of unlawful aid in Spain, the applicants were held to have lost all interest in continuing with the proceedings due to the fact that the Spanish authorities had subsequently notified the Commission that no recovery action would be taken as aid actually granted to all beneficiaries fell below the *de minimis* threshold.[176]

Future or uncertain events   A vested legal interest cannot be dependent on a future and uncertain occurrence.   In particular, if the interest which an applicant claims concerns a future legal situation, he must demonstrate that the prejudice to that situation is already certain.[177]   In *Gruppo Ormeggiatori del*

---

[173]   Case T-545/12, *Mory SA v Commission* EU:T:2013:607, para 48.

[174]   Case T-321/13, *Adorisio v Commission* EU:T:2014:175, paras 24-27.

[175]   Case T-114/09, *Viasat Broadcasting UK Ltd v Commission* EU:T:2012:144, para 21.

[176]   Case T-156/10, *CCAE v Commission* EU:T:2014:41, paras 56-57.

[177]   Case T-138/89 *NBV and NVB v Commission* [1992] II-2181, para 33; Cases T-228/00 etc., *Gruppo Ormeggiatori del Porto di Venezia Soc. Coop. rl v Commission* [2005] ECR II-787, para 23; Case T-141/03, *Sniace SA v Commission* [2005] ECR II-1197, para

Porto di Venezia v Commission, an action was brought by a group of companies seeking annulment of a Commission decision ordering Italy to recover aid granted pursuant to legislation allowing relief from social security contributions. The action was declared inadmissible on the ground that the Italian authorities had indicated that they had no intention of including the applicants in the category of undertakings from whom recovery would be sought. The General Court held that, since only a future and uncertain decision by the Commission calling in question the implementing decision taken by the Italian authorities could affect their legal position, the applicants did not have a vested and present interest in the annulment of the decision.[178]

In *Sniace v Commission*, where the Commission had taken a decision finding that a loan granted by a credit institution with the legal status of a private foundation constituted State aid which was nevertheless compatible with the internal market, the General Court dismissed as inadmissible an application by Sniace, the Spanish recipient of the loan. Sniace argued that the classification of the loan, which had not been notified in advance to the Commission, as State aid was likely to affect its legal position, in particular by opening it up to the possibility of proceedings being brought by third parties relying on the initial unlawful character of the aid. The General Court held, however, that Sniace had not shown at all that the risk of legal proceedings was vested and present. Even though the Commission's investigation procedure had been triggered by a complaint, Sniace had not alleged that any proceedings were pending before the Spanish courts and had merely claimed, purely hypothetically, that such actions could be brought.[179] Moreover, the finding by the Commission that the credit institution granting the loan was a public undertaking was not such as to affect Sniace's future relations with that institution.[180]

In *TV2/Danmark v Commission*, although proceedings in the national court had not been commenced at the time the action for annulment was brought, the General Court held that it had been more than sufficiently demonstrated that

---

26; Case T-136/05, *Salvat père & fils v Commission* [2007] ECR II-4063, para 47; Cases T-309/04, T-317/04, T-329/04 & T-336/04, *TV2/Danmark A/S v Commission* [2008] ECR II-2935, para 78; Cases T-443/08 & T-455/08, *Freistaat Sachsen v Commission* [2011] ECR II-1311, paras 58; Case T-94/08, *Centre de Coordination Carrefour v Commission* [2010] ECR II-1015, para 63; Case T-189/08, *Forum 187 ASBL v Commission* [2010] ECR II-1039, para 84; Case T-261/11, *European Goldfields Ltd v Commission* EU:T:2012:157, para 29; Cases T-15/12 & T-16/12, *Provincie Groningen v Commission* EU:T:2013:74, para 53; Case T-156/10, *CCAE v Commission* EU:T:2014:41, para 60..

[178] Cases T-228/00 etc., *Gruppo Ormeggiatori del Porto di Venezia Soc. Coop. rl v Commission* [2005] ECR II-787, para 29; Cases T-254/00, T-270/00 & T-277/00, *Hotel Cipriani SpA v Commission* [2008] ECR II-3269, para 89.

[179] Case T-141/03, *Sniace SA v Commission* [2005] ECR II-1197, paras 27-30. See also, Case T-136/05, *Salvat père & fils v Commission* [2007] ECR II-4063, paras 41-43.

[180] Case T-141/03, *Sniace SA v Commission* [2005] ECR II-1197, para 37.

the risk of legal proceedings at that time was vested and present since, far from remaining hypothetical, that risk had actually materialised shortly thereafter when national proceedings were in fact commenced.[181] Moreover, in *Deutsche Post v Commission*, where the General Court held that the applicant was entitled to seek annulment of an information injunction, it was untroubled by the fact that the possibility of the Commission seeking to re-use the information in other proceedings was future and uncertain.[182]

By contrast, in *CCAE v Commission*, where the Spanish authorities had informed the Commission that all aid granted under a scheme had been below the *de minimis* threshold, the General Court held that any possibility of actions being brought in the national courts by competitors seeking recovery of the aid was dependent on future and uncertain circumstances.[183] In *Freistaat Sachsen v Commission*, the public authorities that had granted aid were unable to show any vested interest in so far as the possibility of national court proceedings was regarded by the General Court as hypothetical and uncertain.[184] In *Alro v Commission*, which concerned a decision to open a formal investigation into an alleged aid measure that was no longer in the course of implementation, it was held that the possibility of recovery proceedings before a national court could not be regarded as being an immediate, certain or sufficiently binding effect of that decision and that, in any event, the national court was under no obligation to order recovery of aid at this stage.[185]

Acts not adversely affecting the applicant A decision which gives a result that is entirely satisfactory to the applicant is not, by definition, capable of adversely affecting it, so that it can have no interest in seeking its annulment.[186] In *Germany v Commission*, Germany had reluctantly agreed to a Commission proposal determining the German regions to be designated under Article 107(3)(c) TFEU whilst reserving its position as regards other regions which it also wished to be included. Proceedings challenging the subsequent Commission decision approving the agreed regions were held to be inadmissible, on the ground that Germany had not been adversely affected by the decision. It remained open to the German authorities to submit a further list of regions for fresh consideration by the Commission as to their compatibility with Article 107(3)(c) TFEU.[187] In *Provincie Groningen v*

---

[181] Cases T-309/04, T-317/04, T-329/04 & T-336/04, *TV2/Danmark A/S v Commission* [2008] ECR II-2935, para 81.

[182] Case T-570/08 RENV, *Deutsche Post AG v Commission* EU:T:2013:589, para 48.

[183] Case T-156/10, *CCAE v Commission* EU:T:2014:41, para 59.

[184] Cases T-443/08 & T-455/08, *Freistaat Sachsen v Commission* [2011] ECR II-1311, para 63.

[185] Case T-517/12, *Alro SA v Commission* EU:T:2014:890, para 55.

[186] Case T-354/05, *TF1 v Commission* [2009] ECR II-471, para 85; Cases T-15/12 & T-16/12, *Provincie Groningen v Commission* EU:T:2013:74, para 31.

[187] Case C-242/00, *Germany v Commission* [2002] ECR I-5603, paras 43-46.

Commission, in which a challenge was brought against a decision declaring a measure, which had been notified by the Netherlands as non-aid, as State aid compatible with the internal market on the basis of Article 106(2) TFEU, the regional authorities which were responsible for paying the aid were held not to have a legal interest in the annulment of the decision by reason of any requirement of having to notify any future amendments to the aid scheme, since that was an obligation arising out of Article 108(3) TFEU which applied only to the Netherlands.[188]   Similarly, in *Stichting Woonpunt v Commission*, the General Court queried the admissibility of an action for annulment by a recipient of aid of a decision finding that the measure in question constituted aid, but which was compatible with the internal market pursuant to Article 106(2) TFEU.[189]   By contrast, in a decision concerning aid to France Télécom in which a measure was classified as aid and declared incompatible with the internal market but was not ordered to be recovered, a subsequent challenge by FT to the classification as aid was held to be admissible on the ground that Bouygues had also challenged the non-recovery order.   FT was held to have a vested interest, since if Bouygues' action was successful, it would, in the absence of annulment of the classification of the measure as aid, require the Commission to order recovery.[190]

In *Kuwait Petroleum v Commission*, which involved a challenge to the Commission's decision finding that aid had been awarded to petrol service stations in the Netherlands border region with Germany, the action was declared inadmissible in so far as it concerned a number of specific service stations in respect of which the Commission had already agreed with the Netherlands authorities that it would not seek repayment of the aid from the applicant.[191]   In *Makro Cash & Carry Nederland v Commission*, the applicant sought the annulment of a Commission decision ordering recovery from petrol stations in the Netherlands of aid in excess of that applicable under the *de minimis* block exemption.   The General Court rejected the application as inadmissible on the ground that the evidence showed that the applicant had only received aid in an amount less than that allowable under the block exemption, so that annulment of the decision would have had no effect on its legal position.[192]   The General Court rejected the application as inadmissible in *Schmitz-Gotha Farhzeugwerke v Commission*, where the applicant claimed that a decision ordering recovery of aid had identified it as being jointly and

---

[188]   Cases T-15/12 & T-16/12, *Provincie Groningen v Commission* EU:T:2013:74, para 46.

[189]   Case T-203/10 RENV, *Stichting Woonpunt v Commission* EU:T:2015:286, para 54; Case T-202/10 RENV, *Stichting Woonlinie v Commission* EU:T:2015:287, para 54.

[190]   Cases T-425/04, T-444/04, T-450/04 & T-456/04, *France v Commission* [2010] ECR II-2099, paras 119-124.

[191]   Case T-354/99, *Kuwait Petroleum (Nederland) BV v Commission* [2006] ECR II-1475, paras 32-35.

[192]   Case T-258/99, *Makro Cash & Carry Nederland v Commission* [2005] ECR II-14*, para 45.

severally liable to repay unlawful aid. The General Court held that the decision had not in fact identified the applicant as being jointly and severally liable so that the decision was not an act adversely affecting the applicant who, accordingly, had no legal interest in seeking its annulment. Furthermore, the General Court pointed out that in any event the finding that the applicant has no legal interest in bringing proceedings was required *a fortiori* because full repayment by the beneficiary before the action was brought had already discharged the obligation to repay the aid, also releasing any possible joint and several debtors from that liability.[193]

19.6 DIRECT AND INDIVIDUAL CONCERN

Direct and individual concern Under Article 263 TFEU, any natural or legal person may institute proceedings against a decision which, although in the form of a decision addressed to another person, is of direct and individual concern to the former. These are two separate and cumulative conditions. Where two or more parties commence an action for annulment in the same application and one party is clearly directly and individually concerned so that the application is admissible on that basis, the EU courts will not consider a plea of inadmissibility against the other party or parties.[194]

An applicant must show that he is concerned by a decision on the date on which the decision is adopted.[195] In *Banco Bilbao Vizcaya Argentaria SA v Commission*, where the Commission had declared a Spanish tax exemption to be incompatible with the internal market but did not require recovery on the basis of protection of the legitimate expectations of the beneficiaries, the applicants argued that they faced the possibility of proceedings against them in the national court by competitors on the basis of the illegality of the aid pursuant to the infringement of Article 108(3) TFEU. The ECJ held, however, that this did not allow them to be regarded as concerned by the recovery obligation in the decision since they were specifically exempted.[196] The General Court has held that the question whether a person is concerned by a decision is to be assessed on the date on which the proceedings for annulment are brought and is determined only by the contested decision. Thus, for instance, a person individually concerned by a decision that declares aid to be

---

[193] Case T-167/01, *Schmitz-Gotha Farhzeugwerke GmbH v Commission* [2003] ECR II-1873, paras 62-63.

[194] Case C-313/90, *CIRFS v Commission* [1993] ECR I-1125, paras 30-32; Cases C-71/09P, C-73/09P & C-76/09P, *Comitato Venezia vuole vivere v Commission* [2011] ECR I-4727, para 37; Case T-452/08, *DHL Aviation SA/NV v Commission* [2010] ECR II-218*, para 27; Cases T-319/12 & T-321/12, *Spain v Commission* EU:T:2014:604, para 28.

[195] Cases C-587/13P & C-588/13P, *Banco Bilbao Vizcaya Argentaria SA v Commission* EU:C:2015:18, para 52.

[196] *Ibid.*, para 56.

incompatible with the internal market and orders its recovery remains individually concerned, even if it subsequently emerges that he will not be required to refund the aid.[197]

The applicant must produce adequate proof that its position is affected by the contested decision. In *CCAE v Commission*, which concerned aid to compensate for a rise in petrol prices, the General Court held that the applicant representative association had failed to demonstrate the individual concern of its members by merely providing a statement confirming that they sold diesel to third parties.[198]

Direct concern For a decision to be considered as being of direct concern to the applicant, two conditions must be satisfied: first, the measure at issue must directly affect its legal situation; secondly, the measure must leave no discretion to its addressees who are entrusted with the task of implementing it, such implementation being purely automatic and resulting from EU rules alone without the application of other intermediate rules.[199]

A direct connection must be established between the decision and the applicant.[200] Where the applicant cannot establish a direct interest in the annulment of the decision, the application will be dismissed as inadmissible. In *ATM v Commission*, for example, an application to quash a decision concerning alleged unlawful aid was refused on the ground that repayment, if it were ordered, would not have any effect on the applicant. ATM, which represented the pension and social welfare interests of employees of a Spanish company, argued that aid had been granted to the company through State measures which reduced the company's social security payments and which had the effect of diminishing the pension entitlements of its members. It was held, however, that, even if the Commission's decision terminating the investigation into the alleged aid was annulled and the aid was ultimately repaid to the Spanish authorities, there was no requirement under the applicable law that any further benefits would accrue to ATM or its members.[201] In *US Steel Košice v Commission*, a Commission decision, which related to the Slovak national allocation plan for greenhouse gas emission allowances in accordance with Directive 2003/87/EC, was challenged *inter*

---

[197] Case T-400/11, *Altadis SA v Commission* EU:T:2013:490, para 39.

[198] Case T-156/10, *CCAE v Commission* EU:T:2014:41, para 48.

[199] Case C-386/96P, *Dreyfus v Commission* [1998] ECR I-2309, paras 43-44; Case T-27/07, *US Steel Košice s.r.o. v Commission* [2007] ECR II-128*, para 55; Case T-289/03, *BUPA v Commission* [2008] ECR II-81, para 81; Case T-375/04, *Scheucher-Fleisch GmbH v Commission* [2009] ECR II-4155, para 36.

[200] Case T-9/98, *Mitteldeutsche Erdoel-Raffinerie GmbH v Commission* [2001] ECR II-3367, para 47.

[201] Case T-178/94, *ATM v Commission* [1997] ECR II-2529, para 60. See also Case T-189/97, *Comité d'Entreprise de la Société Française de Production v Commission* [1998] ECR II-335, paras 46-52.

alia on the ground that the notified allocation plan was rejected because it involved State aid to the applicant. The General Court held, however, that the decision did not in fact call into question the authorisation of that State aid and addressed the field of State aid in a purely provisional and preliminary manner. Such a provisional assessment could not be interpreted as the adoption of a definitive position on the point, so that it followed that the decision, as regards the criterion of direct concern, did not have the effect of placing the applicant in the same position as a recipient of aid which had been declared incompatible with the internal market.[202]

A negative decision declaring aid incompatible with the internal market or requiring aid to be recovered is of direct concern to the recipient, since it is the decision itself, without any intervening discretion of the Member State, which is effective.[203] Equally, where aid has been granted prior to authorisation, a positive decision by the Commission approving the aid as compatible with the internal market is of direct concern to a competitor of the recipient. Since the aid has already been granted, the decision has immediate and direct effect in that it leaves intact all the effects of the contested aid.[204] In the case of positive decisions concerning aid which has been properly notified in advance, a decision allowing aid to be granted normally still requires action by the national authorities to implement the aid. Nevertheless, where a system of aid has already been approved by the national authorities and is merely contingent on Commission approval, the Commission's decision approving the aid is of direct concern to a complainant given that the possibility of the national authority deciding not to grant the aid is purely theoretical since there is no doubt that the national authorities intend to take such action.[205] Where the possibility that such measures would not be taken is not merely hypothetical,

---

[202] Case T-27/07, *US Steel Košice s.r.o. v Commission* [2007] ECR II-128*, paras 67-73.

[203] Cases C-15/98 & C-105/99, *Italy v Commission* [2000] ECR I-8855, para 36; Cases C-182/03 & C-217/03, *Belgium and Forum 187 ASBL v Commission* [2006] ECR I-5479, para 57; Case T-136/05, *Salvat père & fils v Commission* [2007] ECR II-4063, para 75; Case T-348/03, *Koninklijke Friesland Foods NV v Commission* [2007] ECR II-101*, para 94; Case T-445/05, *Associazione Italiana del Risparmio Gestito v Commission* [2009] ECR II-289, para 52; Case T-301/02, *AEM SpA v Commission* [2009] ECR II-1757, para 49..

[204] Case 169/84, *Cofaz v Commission* [1986] ECR 391, para 30; Cases T-447-449/93, *AITEC v Commission* [1995] ECR II-1971, para 41; Case T-149/95, *Ducros v Commission* [1997] ECR II-2031, para 32; Case T-358/02, *Deutsche Post AG v Commission* [2004] ECR II-1565, para 32.

[205] Case T-435/93, *ASPEC v Commission* [1995] ECR II-1281, para 60; Case T-442/93, *AAC v Commission* [1995] ECR II-1329, para 45; Case T-9/98, *Mitteldeutsche Erdoel-Raffinerie GmbH v Commission* [2001] ECR II-3367, para 48; Case T-289/03, *BUPA Ltd v Commission* [2008] ECR II-81, para 81; Case T-375/04, *Scheucher-Fleisch GmbH v Commission* [2009] ECR II-4155, para 36; Case T-57/11, *Castelnou Energía v Commission* EU:T:2014:1021, para 43.

the applicant will not be directly concerned.[206] Similarly, where the Commission has failed to take a decision in respect of aid which has already been granted, a competitor seeking a declaration under Article 265 TFEU for failure to act is entitled to claim that it would have been directly affected by the Commission decision had it been taken.[207]

In *Deutsche Post v Commission*, an information injunction under Regulation (EC) No 659/1999, Article 10(3) was issued by the Commission addressed to Germany ordering it to provide information in the course of an investigation into alleged State aid provided to Deutsche Post. It was held that the decision was of direct concern to Deutsche Post, as beneficiary of the measure in question and holder of the information. Moreover, the definitive and exhaustive content of the information requested was apparent from the injunction itself, without leaving any discretion in that respect to Germany.[208]

Individual concern The ECJ has consistently held to the *Plaumann* doctrine that persons other than those to whom a decision is addressed may claim to be individually concerned by that decision only if it affects them by reason of certain attributes which are peculiar to them or by reason of circumstances in which they are differentiated from all other persons and if by virtue of those factors it distinguishes them individually just as in the case of the person addressed.[209] In order for the decision to be of individual concern, the applicant must establish that it belongs to a closed class, that is to say, a group which can no longer be extended after the decision has been adopted.[210]

---

[206] Case T-238/97, *Comunidad Autónoma de Cantabria v Council* [1998] ECR II-2271, para 53.

[207] Case T-95/96, *Gestevisión Telecinco SA v Commission*, [1998] ECR II-3407, para 61; Case T-17/96, *TF1 v Commission* [1999] ECR II-1757, para 30.

[208] Cases C-463/10P & C-475/10P, *Deutsche Post AG v Commission* [2011] ECR I-9639, paras 68-70.

[209] Case 25/62, *Plaumann v Commission* [1963] ECR 95, at p. 107; Case C-50/00P, *Unión de Pequeños Agricultores v Council* [2002] ECR I-6677, para 36; Case C-298/00P, *Italy v Commission* [2004] ECR I-4087, para 36; Case C-176/06P, *Stadwerke Schwäbisch Hall v Commission* [2007] ECR I-170*, para 19; Cases C-75/05P & C-80/05P, *Germany v Kronofrance* [2008] ECR I-6619, para 36; Case C-487/06P, *British Aggregates Association v Commission* [2008] ECR I-10515, para 26; Cases C-71/09P, C-73/09P & C-76/09P, *Comitato Venezia vuole vivere v Commission* [2011] ECR I-4727, para 51; Case T-266/94, *Skibsværftsforeningen v Commission* [1996] ECR II-1399, para 44; Cases T-132/96 & T-143/96, *Freistaat Sachsen v Commission* [1999] ECR II-3663, para 83; Case T-69/96, *Hamburger Hafen- und Lagerhaus AG v Commission* [2001] ECR II-1037, para 35; Case T-9/98, *Mitteldeutsche Erdoel-Raffinerie GmbH v Commission* [2001] ECR II-3367, para 75; Case T-388/02, *Kronoply GmbH v Commission* [2008] ECR II-305*, para 56.

[210] Case C-152/88, *Sofrimport v Commission* [1990] ECR I-2477, para 11; Joined Cases C-182/03 & C-217/03, *Belgium and Forum 187 v Commission* [2006] ECR I-5479, para 63; Case T-429/11, *Banco Bilbao Vizcaya Argentaria SA v Commission*

Failure to show that the applicant is distinguished individually will result in the action being declared inadmissible. Thus, where the number of economic operators potentially affected by the Commission's decision is indeterminate and capable of expanding after the adoption of the decision, an applicant will not be able to assert individual concern.[211] In *Federmineraria v Commission*, a decision concerning aid for the transportation by rail of bulk ores in Sicily was challenged by a number of producers involved in the extraction of such bulk ore who claimed that they were part of a known and limited category of persons to whom the decision was of concern. They were denied standing on the ground that the decision did not affect their interests alone, but also affected the interests of the railways, whose competitive position compared to other modes of transport was favoured by the aid, other carriers to whom the producers might entrust their goods, as well as their customers who might have been induced to bear some of the transport costs. The decision could not therefore be of individual concern to the applicants since it could not be considered to affect operators whose number or identity was fixed and ascertainable at the time of its adoption.[212] In *Stichting Woonpunt v Commission*, concerning aid to housing associations in the Netherlands, the ECJ held that since the status of housing association was granted through a system of approval by royal decree, their number and identity were precisely determined at the time the decision was adopted, so that they belonged to a closed class allowing them to be individually distinguished.[213]

The fact that a decision requires in a general and abstract manner recovery of aid is not such as to make that decision equivalent to a bundle of individual decisions.[214] By contrast, where the aid scheme is in fact intended to benefit only one undertaking, it will not be regarded as a general measure for the purposes of admissibility.[215] In *Asklepios Kliniken v Commission*, the General Court distinguished the individual award of aid to some 700 public sector hospitals from a general aid scheme, so that a claim for annulment brought by

---

EU:T:2013:488, para 35; Case T-430/11, *Telefónica SA v Commission* EU:T:2013: 489, para 35; Case T-400/11, *Altadis SA v Commission* EU:T:2013:490, para 39.

[211] Case 323/82, *Intermills v Commission* [1984] ECR 3809, para 16; Case T-7/13, *ADEAS v Commission* EU:T:2014:221, paras 39-44; Case T-2/13, *CFE-CGC France Télécom-Orange v Commission* EU:T:2014:226, paras 51-54.

[212] Case C-6/92, *Federmineraria v Commission* [1993] ECR I-6357, paras 14-16.

[213] Case C-132/12P, *Stichting Woonpunt v Commission* EU:C:2014:100, paras 60-62.; Case C-133/12P, *Stichting Woonlinie v Commission* EU:C:2014:105, paras 47-49. These cases overturned the General Court's dismissal of the actions as inadmissible: Case T-202/10, *Stichting Woonpunt v Commission* [2011] ECR II-461*; Case T-203/10, *Stichting Woonlinie v Commission* [2011] ECR II-462*.

[214] Case C-503/07P, *Saint-Gobain Glass Deutschland GmbH v Commission* [2008] ECR I-2217, para 72; Cases T-254/00, T-270/00 & T-277/00, *Hotel Cipriani SpA v Commission* [2008] ECR II-3269, para 73.

[215] Cases T-239/04 & T-323/04, *Italy v Commission* [2007] ECR II-3265, para 42.

competitor of some of those hospitals was admissible.[216] Moreover, where the Commission examines the individual situation of some of the actual beneficiaries of an aid scheme, its decision is an individual decision in relation to those beneficiaries.[217]

Individual concern and general measures In *Van der Kooy v Commission*, the ECJ held that, where the Commission prohibits aid which may apply generally to any person satisfying certain objective conditions, that decision is of concern to those persons solely by virtue of their objective capacity. Such a decision, being a measure of general application covering situations which are determined objectively and entailing legal effects for categories of persons envisaged in a general and abstract manner, cannot be regarded as being of individual concern to those persons.[218] Thus, in *Telefónica v Commission*, concerning the prohibition of a Spanish tax exemption scheme, the ECJ held that the decision was not such that Telefónica could claim to be individually distinguished.[219] Equally, in *Kahn Scheepvaart v Commission*, the General Court held that, where the Commission authorised a generally applicable scheme of aid, a competitor of persons benefiting from subsequent individual grants of the aid could not claim to be individually concerned by the Commission's decision.[220] The General Court, in its decision in *Jégo Quéré v Commission*, attempted to loosen the rigidity of these rules of admissibility by stating that a person should be regarded as individually concerned by a measure of general application which concerned him directly if the measure affected his legal position, in a manner which is both definite and immediate, by restricting his rights or by imposing obligations on him.[221] In *Unión de Pequeños Agricultores v Council*, the ECJ reiterated its longstanding approach

---

[216] Case T-167/04, *Asklepios Kliniken GmbH v Commission* [2007] ECR II-2379, para 56.

[217] Cases T-254/00, T-270/00 & T-277/00, *Hotel Cipriani SpA v Commission* [2008] ECR II-3269, para 73.

[218] Cases 67, 68 & 70/85, *Van der Kooy v Commission* [1988] ECR 219, para 15; Cases C-15/98 & C-105/99, *Italy v Commission* [2000] ECR I-8855, para 33; Case C-298/00P, *Italy v Commission* [2004] ECR I-4087, para 37; Case T-136/05, *Salvat père & fils v Commission* [2007] ECR II-4063, para 67; Cases T-254/00, T-270/00 & T-277/00, *Hotel Cipriani SpA v Commission* [2008] ECR II-3269, para 73; Case T-445/05, *Associazione Italiana del Risparmio Gestito v Commission* [2009] ECR II-289, para 46.

[219] Case C-274/12P, *Telefónica SA v Commission* EU:C:2013:852, para 48; Cases C-587/13P & C-588/13P, *Banco Bilbao Vizcaya Argentaria SA v Commission* EU:C:2015:18, para 43. See also Case T-221/10, *Iberdrola SA v Commission* EU:T:2012:112; Case T-225/10, *Banco Bilbao Vizcaya Argentaria SA v Commission* EU:T:2012:139; Case T-228/10, *Telefónica SA v Commission* EU:T:2012:140; Case T-234/10, *Ebro Foods SA v Commission* EU:T:2012:141; Case T-174/11, *Modelo Continente Hipermercados SA v Commission* EU:T:2012:143; Case T-236/10, *Associación Española de Banca v Commission* EU:T:2012:176.

[220] Case T-398/94, *Kahn Scheepvaart BV v Commission* [1996] ECR II-477, para 41.

[221] Case T-177/01, *Jégo Quéré v Commission* [2002] ECR II-2365, para 51.

and emphasised that the proper forum for challenging measures of general application is the national court, holding that the conditions for admissibility could not be set aside on the basis of arguments concerning the right to effective judicial protection.[222]

Nevertheless, in *Belgium and Forum 187 v Commission*, the ECJ relaxed its stance and held that the fact that the tax measure in question was of general application, in that it applied to the traders concerned in general, did not of itself prevent it being of individual concern to some of them.[223] In that case, the applicants comprised an identifiable closed class by virtue of the fact that they each had an application for renewal of their authorisation as coordination centres pending at the date of the Commission's decision declaring the tax treatment of such centres to constitute State aid.[224] In *British Aggregates Association v Commission*, the ECJ went further, holding that a measure could be of individual concern irrespective of whether the aid measure in question is individual or general in nature, as long as the applicant can otherwise show that it has status in accordance with the *Plaumann* doctrine.[225] Thus, where, for instance, a competitor can show that its competitive position is substantially affected by the aid scheme, the fact that an undefined number of other competitors may allege that they have suffered similar harm does not constitute an obstacle to admissibility.[226]

Interest must be distinct from that of the Member State In order to establish individual concern, an applicant must show that its interest is distinct from that of the Member State concerned.[227] In *DEFI v Commission*, a challenge was brought against a Commission decision concerning an aid scheme for the textile industry in France which had declared the aid incompatible with the internal market. The proceedings were instituted by the French public body charged with implementing the aid scheme. The ECJ upheld the Commission's objection of inadmissibility on the grounds that the

---

[222] Case C-50/00P, *Unión de Pequeños Agricultores v Council* [2002] ECR I-6677, paras 36-44; Case C-263/02P, *Commission v Jégo Quéré* [2004] ECR I-3425, para 36; Case C-379/03P, *Pérez Escolar v Commission* EU:C:2004:580, para 41; Case C-260/05P, *Sniace SA v Commission* [2007] ECR I-10005, para 64; Case C-274/12P, *Telefónica SA v Commission* EU:C:2013:852, para 59; Cases C-587/13P & C-588/13P, *Banco Bilbao Vizcaya Argentaria SA v Commission* EU:C:2015:18, para 48.

[223] Cases C-182/03 & C-217/03, *Belgium and Forum 187 ASBL v Commission* [2006] ECR I-5479, para 58.

[224] Cases C-182/03 & C-217/03, *Belgium and Forum 187 ASBL v Commission* [2006] ECR I-5479, para 63; Case C-519/07P, *Commission v Koninklijke Friesland Campina NV* [2009] ECR I-8495, para 56; Case T-348/03, *Koninklijke Friesland Foods NV v Commission* [2007] ECR II-101*, para 100.

[225] Case C-487/06P, *British Aggregates Association v Commission* [2008] ECR I-10515, para 35.

[226] *Ibid.*, para 56.

[227] Cases T-15/12 & T-16/12, *Provincie Groningen v Commission* EU:T:2013:74, para 57.

applicant did not have an interest distinct from that of France, but was merely a conduit for the State in the allocation of the aid, and that the decision was therefore not of concern to it.[228]   Similar reasoning led the General Court to deny admissibility in actions brought by public authorities in charge of switching television media from analogue to digital transmission[229] and by Dutch provincial authorities against a decision concerning environmental aid.[230]   By contrast, in *Regione Autonoma Friuli Venezia Giulia v Commission*, it was noted that the applicant was an autonomous regional body which had rights and interests of its own. The aid with which the decision was concerned constituted a set of measures taken in the exercise of the legislative and financial autonomy which was invested in it directly under the Italian constitution.[231]   In a case concerning an Italian restructuring aid scheme, the General Court accepted that Italy, in adopting the measure at issue, had sought to prevent a social crisis by facilitating the transfer of employees, whereas for the applicant, which had acquired the employees, the transfer was a commercial choice, made easier by the measure at issue.[232]

Regional and local authorities A regional or local authority is not part of the Member State for the purposes of establishing standing to bring an action for judicial review under Article 263 TFEU.[233] Legal protection will, however, be available to such an authority which is affected by the decision in the same way as the Member State.[234] Where it has legal personality under domestic law, it may bring an action for annulment of a State aid decision under the same conditions as any natural or legal person when it can show that the decision is of direct and individual concern to it.[235] Thus, in *Vlaams Gewest v*

---

[228] Case 282/85, *DEFI v Commission* [1986] ECR 2469, para 16.

[229] Case T-2/08, *Landesanstalt für Medien Nordrhein-Westfalen v Commission* [2009] ECR II-195*, para 43; Case T-24/06, *Medienanstalt Berlin-Brandenburg v Commission* [2009] ECR II-198*, para 55.

[230] Cases T-15/12 & T-16/12, *Provincie Groningen v Commission* EU:T:2013:74, para 45.

[231] Case T-288/97, *Regione Autonoma Friuli Venezia Giulia v Commission* [1999] ECR II-1871, para 34.

[232] Cases T-239/04 & T-323/04, *Italy v Commission* [2007] ECR II-3265, para 41.

[233] Case C-95/97, *Région Wallone v Commission* [1997] ECR I-1787, para 6; Case C-180/97, *Regione Toscana v Commission* [1997] ECR I-5245, para 8; Case T-214/95, *Vlaams Gewest v Commission* [1998] ECR II-717, para 28; Case T-238/97, *Comunidad Autónoma de Cantabria v Council* [1998] ECR II-2271, para 42.

[234] Case 222/83, *Differdange v Commission* [1984] ECR 2889, para 9. In Cases 62 & 72/87, *Exécutif Régional Wallon v Commission* [1988] ECR 1573, admissibility was not raised as an issue and was implicitly accepted by the ECJ.

[235] Case T-214/95, *Vlaams Gewest v Commission* [1998] ECR II-717, para 28; Case T-288/97, *Regione Autonoma Friuli Venezia Giulia v Commission* [1999] ECR II-1871, para 28. Under the ECSC Treaty, the right of action was limited, by Article 33 CS, to undertakings and associations of undertakings, thereby excluding regional and local authorities: Case 222/83, *Differdange v Commission* [1984] ECR 2889, para 8; Case T-70/97, *Région Wallone v Commission* [1997] ECR II-1513, para 22; Case T-77/01,

Commission, the Flemish regional authority was individually concerned by the Commission's decision which had the effect of preventing it from granting aid to the Flemish airline VLM and exercising its powers as it saw fit.[236] In *Regione Autonoma Friuli Venezia Giulia v Commission*, the Commission's decision prevented the applicant from continuing to apply the aid legislation in question, nullified the effects of that legislation and required it to initiate the administrative procedure for the recovery of the aid from the beneficiaries. Even though the decision was addressed to Italy, the national authorities, when communicating it to the applicant, did not act in the exercise of a discretion, so that the applicant was individually concerned.[237] The Free State of Saxony was also individually concerned by a decision addressed to Germany which had similar repercussions.[238] In an application brought by the Government of Gibraltar requesting the annulment of two Commission decisions addressed to the United Kingdom initiating the formal investigation procedure into a system of tax relief for certain companies registered in Gibraltar, the action was declared admissible since Gibraltar, a colony of the United Kingdom, had responsibility for domestic matters, including taxation, and was therefore individually concerned by the decisions.[239] By contrast, in *Westfälisch-Lippischer Sparkassen- und Giroverband v Commission*, a publicly-owned bank, was unable to show that it, rather than the Land which had made State aid available through a guarantee, had granted the aid in question.[240]

Admissibility may be denied where the connection between the decision and the local authority is more indirect. In *Differdange v Commission*, a number of municipalities in Luxembourg challenged a Commission decision addressed to Luxembourg declaring that aid to certain steel undertakings was compatible with the internal market provided specific reductions in capacity were carried out by the recipients. Since the decision did not identify the establishments in which capacity was to be reduced, the Luxembourg authorities and the undertakings concerned were left with a margin of

---

Territorio Histórico de Álava - Diputación Foral de Álava v Commission [2002] ECR II-81, paras 29-30.

[236] Case T-214/95, *Vlaams Gewest v Commission* [1998] ECR II-717, para 29; Case T-457/09, *Westfälisch-Lippischer Sparkassen- und Giroverband v Commission* EU:T:2014:683, para 83 .

[237] Case T-288/97, *Regione Autonoma Friuli Venezia Giulia v Commission* [1999] ECR II-1871, paras 32-33.

[238] Cases T-132/96 & T-143/96, *Freistaat Sachsen v Commission* [1999] ECR II-3663, paras 84-92. See also, Case T-155/96R, *City of Mainz v Commission* [1996] ECR II-1655; Cases T-127/99, T-129/99 &T-148/99, *Territorio Histórico de Álava - Disputación Foral de Álava v Commission* [2002] ECR II-1275, para 50.

[239] Cases T-195/01R & T-207/01R, *Government of Gibraltar v Commission* [2001] ECR II-3915, para 55; Cases T-195/01 & T-207/01, *Government of Gibraltar v Commission* [2002] ECR II-2309, para 53.

[240] Case T-457/09, *Westfälisch-Lippischer Sparkassen- und Giroverband v Commission* EU:T:2014:683, para 109.

discretion with regard to the manner of implementation of the decision and, in particular, with regard to the choice of the factories to be closed. The decision could not, therefore, be regarded as being of direct and individual concern to the municipalities with which the undertakings, by virtue of the location of their factories, were connected.[241]   Similarly, in *Comunidad Autónoma de Cantabria v Council*, the application seeking the annulment of a Council regulation, which limited the amount of State aid which could be granted to Spanish publicly-owned shipyards, was declared inadmissible on the ground that the distinguishing factor pleaded by the applicant was limited to the socio-economic repercussions of the contested act on its territory.

Recipients of aid   A recipient of aid referred to in a negative decision declaring individual aid incompatible with the internal market and requiring it to be discontinued is individually concerned by the decision.[242]   Equally, a potential recipient of individual aid, in respect of whom a plan to award the aid has been the subject of a negative decision by the Commission, has standing to challenge the decision.[243]   Where the recipient of the aid has been taken over by another company which has guaranteed reimbursement of the aid, the latter may also be regarded as individually concerned.[244]   Moreover, a recipient of aid may also be individually concerned by a decision to open a formal investigation into alleged unlawful aid.[245]   Similarly, an alleged recipient of aid is individually concerned by an information injunction issued by the Commission pursuant to Regulation (EC) No 659/199, Article 10(3) demanding information concerning the recipient.[246]

An undertaking cannot, as a general rule, bring an action for the annulment of a Commission decision prohibiting a sectoral aid scheme if it is concerned by that decision solely by virtue of the fact that it belongs to the sector in question and is a potential beneficiary of the scheme. Such a decision is, *vis-à-vis* that undertaking, a measure of general application covering situations which are determined objectively and entails legal effects for a class of persons envisaged in a general and abstract manner.[247]   Recipients of aid under an aid

---

[241] Case 222/83, *Differdange v Commission* [1984] ECR 2889, para 12.

[242] Case 323/82, *Intermills v Commission* [1984] ECR 3809, para 5; Case C-188/92, *TWD v Germany* [1994] ECR I-833, para 14; Cases T-239/04 & T-323/04, *Italy v Commission* [2007] ECR II-3265, para 44; Cases T-80/06 & T-182/09, *Budapesti Erőmű Zrt v Commission* EU:T:2012:65, para 42.

[243] Case 730/79, *Philip Morris v Commission* [1980] ECR 2671, para 5.

[244] Cases T-273/06 & T-297/06, *ISD Polska v Commission* [2009] ECR II-2185, para 45.

[245] Case T-461/12, *Hansestadt Lübeck v Commission* EU:T:2014:758, para 27.

[246] Cases C-463/10P & C-475/10P, *Deutsche Post AG v Commission* [2011] ECR I-9639, para 74.

[247] Cases 67/85, 68/85 & 70/85, *Van de Kooy v Commission* [1988] ECR 219, para 15; Case C-298/00P, *Italy v Commission* [2004] ECR I-4087, para 37; Case T-300/02, *AMGA v Commission* [2009] ECR II-1737, para 47; Case T-301/02, *AEM SpA v Commission* [2009] ECR II-1757, para 43; Case T-309/02, *Acegas-APS SpA v Commission* [2009]

scheme are individually concerned, however, where the aid is ordered to be recovered.[248] In *Italy v Commission*, in proceedings challenging the validity of a Commission decision finding aid for Sardinian shipowners unlawful, Sardegna Lines was held to be individually concerned by the decision by virtue of being an actual beneficiary of individual aid granted under that scheme, the recovery of which had been ordered by the Commission, and also by virtue of being an undertaking in the shipping sector in Sardinia and a potential beneficiary of the aid scheme.[249] Equally, a number of Italian transport companies were entitled to challenge a Commission decision prohibiting an aid for the road haulage sector on the ground that they were potential and actual beneficiaries of the scheme.[250] In *Salvat v Commission*, an action for annulment brought by a recipient of aid under a sectoral scheme was declared admissible since the Commission had ordered recovery of the aid.[251] A recipient of aid may also be able to challenge a negative decision concerning a general aid scheme where it can show that its position is affected not solely by virtue of its objective capacity but also by reason of factors which place it in a position which differentiates it from all other operators.[252] Conditional decisions imposing conditions which a recipient or potential recipient finds objectionable are similarly challengeable.

Accordingly, it is necessary to determine whether the applicant is an actual beneficiary of individual aid granted under the aid scheme, recovery of which has been ordered by the Commission.[253] Where the applicant is merely a potential, as opposed to an actual, beneficiary under an aid scheme, it will not have standing to challenge the decision.[254] Thus, an application for annulment of a Commission decision prohibiting aid granted through a tax exemption was inadmissible on the ground that the applicant had made only losses during the

---

248 ECR II-1809, para 47; Case T-400/11, *Altadis SA v Commission* EU:T:2013:490, para 25.

248 Cases C-71/09P, C-73/09P & C-76/09P, *Comitato Venezia vuole vivere v Commission* [2011] ECR I-4727, para 53; Cases T-254/00, T-270/00 & T-277/00, *Hotel Cipriani SpA v Commission* [2008] ECR II-3269, para 77; Case T-327/09, *Connefroy v Commission* EU:T:2102:155, para 22.

249 Cases C-15/98 & C-105/99, *Italy v Commission* [2000] ECR I-8855, paras 34-35; Case T-445/05, *Associazione Italiana del Risparmio Gestito v Commission* [2009] ECR II-289, para 48; Case T-75/03, *Banco Comercial dos Açores SA v Commission* [2009] ECR II-143*, para 44.

250 Case C-298/00P, *Italy v Commission* [2004] ERCR I-4087, para 39.

251 Case T-136/05, *Salvat père & fils v Commission* [2007] ECR II-4063, para 73.

252 Case T-9/98, *Mitteldeutsche Erdoel-Raffinerie GmbH v Commission* [2001] ECR II-3367, para 79.

253 Cases C-71/09P, C-73/09P & C-76/09P, *Comitato Venezia vuole vivere v Commission* [2011] ECR I-4727, paras 53-56; Case T-221/10, *Iberdrola v Commission* EU:T:2012:112, para 27; Case T-400/11, *Altadis SA v Commission* EU:T:2013:490, para 27.

254 Case T-429/11, *Banco Bilbao Vizcaya Argentaria SA v Commission* EU:T:2013:488, para 36; Case T-430/11, *Telefónica SA v Commission* EU:T:2013: 489, para 36.

period in question and was thus not in fact liable to tax, so that it had not benefitted from the tax exemption in question,[255] whereas applicants that had made profits were entitled to challenge the decision since they were to be required to repay the aid.[256] Similarly, a challenge to decision outlawing an aid scheme whereby aid was granted through low-interest loans was dismissed since the applicant had not actually benefitted from any such loans during the period in question.[257] In *Banco Bilbao Vizcaya Argentaria SA v Commission*, where the Commission decided that a Spanish tax exemption was incompatible with the internal market but did not require recovery due to the legitimate expectation of the beneficiaries, a challenge to the validity of the decision was declared inadmissible on the ground that the applicants were not individually affected by the decision.[258]

Competitors whose market position is substantially affected   An undertaking cannot rely solely on its position as a competitor of the undertaking in receipt of aid in order to challenge a decision of the Commission, but must additionally show that its circumstances distinguish it in a similar way to the recipient.[259] Competitors must generally adduce sufficient

---

[255] Case T-300/02, *AMGA v Commission* [2009] ECR II-1737, para 50, upheld on appeal in Case C-329/09P, *Iride SpA v Commission* [2011] ECR I-212*, paras 37-44; Case T-309/02, *Acegas-APS SpA v Commission* [2009] ECR II-1809, paras 51-54.

[256] Case C-318/09P, *A2A SpA v Commission* [2011] ECR I-207*, paras 55-61; Case C-319/09P, *ACEA SpA v Commisssion* [2-11] ECR I-209*, paras 54-60; Case C-320/09P, *A2A SpA v Commission* [2011] ECR II-210*, paras 57-61; Case T-297/02, *ACEA SpA v Commission* [2009] ECR II-1683, para 48; Case T-301/02, *AEM SpA v Commission* [2009] ECR II-1757, para 48; Case T-189/03, *AEM Brescia SpA v Commission* [2009] ECR II-1831, para 46.

[257] Case T-297/02, *ACEA SpA v Commission* [2009] ECR II-1683, paras 50-51.

[258] Cases C-587/13P & C-588/13P, *Banco Bilbao Vizcaya Argentaria SA v Commission* EU:C:2015:18, para 43-45.

[259] Case C-106/98P, *Comité d'Entreprise de la Société Française de Production v Commission* [2000] ECR I-3271, para 41; Case C-525/04P, *Spain v Lenzing* [2007] ECR I-9947, para 32; Case C-487/06P, *British Aggregates Association v Commission* [2008] ECR I-10515, para 48; Case T-388/03, *Deutsche Post AG v Commission* [2009] II-199, para 48; Case T-375/04, *Scheucher-Fleisch GmbH v Commission* [2009] ECR II-4155, para 57; Case T-481/07, *Deltalinqs v Commission* [2009] ECR II-233*, para 48; Case T-54/07, *Vtesse Networks Ltd v Commission* [2011] ECR II-6*, para 95. Under the ECSC treaty, an undertaking was concerned by a Commission decision permitting benefits to be granted to one or more undertakings in competition with it: cf. Article 33 CS: Cases 172 & 226/83, *Hoogovens Groep v Commission* [1985] ECR 2831, para 15; Cases T-12/99 & T-63/99, *UK Coal plc v Commission* [2001] ECR II-2153, para 52; Case T-344/10, *UPS Europe NV v Commission* EU:T:2012:216, para 48; Case T-206/10, *Vesteda Groep BV v Commission* EU:T:2012:283, para 39; Case T-198/09, *UOP Ltd v Commission* EU:T:2013:105, para 25; Case T-488/11, *Sarc BV v Commission* EU:T:2014:497, para 35; Case T-601/11, *Dansk Automat Brancheforening v Commission* EU:T:2014:839, para 41; Case T-362/10, *Vtesse Networks Ltd v Commission* EU:T:2014:928, para 36.

evidence to show that their competitive position on the market has been substantially affected by the grant of the aid.[260] It is for the applicant to adduce pertinent evidence to show that the Commission's decision may adversely affect its legitimate interests by seriously jeopardising its position on the market.[261] It is not sufficient that the competitor might have lost out on certain commercial opportunities as a result of the aid.[262] Thus, in *Vtesse v Commission*, the applicant's competitive position was not sufficiently affected simply because a substantial contract had been awarded to a competitor.[263] The correct market must be identified and the applicant must be active on that market. In *Mojo Concerts v Commission*, which concerned alleged aid to an operator of an arena in Rotterdam, the applicants failed to establish that they were active either on the market for the exploitation of arenas or the market for the promotion of concerts.[264] In *Sarc v Commission*, the applicant was held not to have shown that its competitive position on the market was significantly affected, in that it failed to provide the main information relating to the structure of the relevant market establishing its competitive position in that market. In particular, it was criticised for not having provided information about the relevant geographic market, its share of that market and the share of its competitors and any shift in market shares since the measure at issue was granted.[265]

In *Lenzing v Commission*, the Commission challenged the admissibility of the applicant's action on the basis that the applicant's market position had improved during the period when the aid had allegedly been granted to its competitor. The General Court found, however, that the recipient of the aid had a share of 9% in a market that was suffering from overcapacity, which was sufficient to show that the applicant's position on the market was substantially

---

[260] Case C-176/06 P, *Stadtwerke Schäbisch Hall GmbH v Commission* [2007] 170*, para 31; Case T-69/96, *Hamburger Hafen- und Lagerhaus AG v Commission* [2001] ECR II-1037, para 48; Case T-315/05, *Adomex International BV v Commission* [2008] ECR II-145*, para 29; Case T-193/06, *TF1 v Commission* [2010] ECR II-4967, para 72; Case T-58/10, *Phoenix-Reisen GmbH v Commission* EU:T:2102:3, para 44; Case T-344/10, *UPS Europe NV v Commission* EU:T:2012:216, para 43; Case T-321/13, *Adorisio v Commission* EU:T:2014:175, para 44.

[261] Case 169/84, *Cofaz v Commission* [1986] ECR 391, para 28; Case C-525/04P, *Spain v Lenzing* [2007] ECR I-9947, para 41; Case T-88/01, *Sniace SA v Commission* [2005] ECR II-1165, para 60; Case T-36/99, *Lenzing v Commission* [2004] ECR I-3597, para 80; Case T-90/09, *Mojo Concerts BV v Commission* EU:T:2012:30, para 33; Case T-182/10 *Aiscat v Commission* EU:T:2013:9, para 60; Case T-362/10, *Vtesse Networks Ltd v Commission* EU:T:2014:928, para 37; Case T-57/11, *Castelnou Energía v Commission* EU:T:2014:1021, para 31.

[262] Case T-201/10, *IVBN v Commission* EU:T:2012:385, paras 38-39.

[263] Case T-362/10, *Vtesse Networks Ltd v Commission* EU:T:2014:928, para 57.

[264] Case T-90/09, *Mojo Concerts BV v Commission* EU:T:2012:30, paras 41 & 49.

[265] Case T-488/11, *Sarc BV v Commission* EU:T:2014:497, para 43.

affected.[266]   The fact that the applicant had good results and increased its production during that period was wholly irrelevant.[267]   On appeal, this approach was confirmed by the ECJ, which held that State aid can have an adverse effect on the competitive situation of an operator in other ways, in particular by causing the loss of an opportunity to make a profit or a less favourable development than would have been the case without the aid. The seriousness of such an effect may vary according to a large number of factors such as, in particular, the structure of the market concerned or the nature of the aid in question.[268]   In *Castelnou Erergía v Commission*, concerning aid to Spanish coal producers, the applicant was able to show that its competitive position was particularly seriously affected in a market suffering from overcapacity.[269]

By contrast, in *UPS Europe v Commission*, the General Court did not accept that UPS had provided sufficient evidence to show that its position on the market for parcel services was significantly affected by alleged aid to Deutsche Post.[270]   In *Smurfit Kappa v Commission*, the applicant was only one of approximately 130 competitors of the recipient of investment aid for a new plant in Brandenburg, such that, although the General Court was satisfied that the competitive relationship between the competitors would be influenced by the aid, it was not established that the applicant would suffer substantial harm to its competitive position in such a way as to distinguish it from its competitors.   Furthermore, the fact that the relevant market might be undergoing structural imbalance characterised by surplus production capacity and that the applicant had been forced to close a large number of its own plants was not capable of distinguishing the applicant individually from other competitors.[271]   Indeed, in *UOP v Commission*, where the Commission found in the decision that the applicant was one of the seven principal competitors of the recipient of aid, the General Court accepted that the applicant had not established, by evidence of a sufficiently probative value, that it was in a distinct situation as compared to other operators in the relevant market.[272]

In *Sniace v Commission*, the General Court rejected an application for annulment as inadmissible on the ground, *inter alia*, that the aid was granted in respect of lyocell which the applicant neither manufactured nor foresaw doing

---

[266] Case T-36/99, *Lenzing AG v Commission* [2004] ECR II-3597, para 85.

[267] *Ibid.*, para 90.

[268] Case C-525/04P, *Spain v Lenzing* [2007] ECR I-9947, para 35; Case C-487/06P, *British Aggregates Association v Commission* [2008] ECR I-10515, para 53; Case T-344/10, *UPS Europe NV v Commission* EU:T:2012:216, para 49; Case T-182/10 *Aiscat v Commission* EU:T:2013:9, para 66; Case T-57/11, *Castelnou Energía v Commission* EU:T:2014:1021, para 31.

[269] Case T-57/11, *Castelnou Energía v Commission* EU:T:2014:1021, paras 32-37.

[270] Case T-344/10, *UPS Europe NV v Commission* EU:T:2012:216, para 61.

[271] Case T-304/08, *Smurfit Kappa Group plc v Commission* EU:T:2012:351, para 57-59.

[272] Case T-198/09, *UOP Ltd v Commission* EU:T:2013:105, paras 35-40.

so in the future, and which the applicant was unable to show was in direct competition with viscose, which it did produce, such as to seriously jeopardise its position on the market.[273] In *Commerciële Jachthavens v Commission*, the applicants alleged that their profitability had been affected by the aid, but they failed to demonstrate this by means of concrete evidence, such as turnover achieved before and after the adoption of the measures at issue. The applicants represented only 6 of approximately 1200 marinas in the Netherlands that might be concerned by the aid. The General Court dismissed the action as inadmissible, stating that each applicant should have set out in what respect aid granted to any individual harbour might prejudice its own activities, for example, by risking loss of custom or reduction in profit margin.[274] Similarly, in a range of cases, the applicants did not provide sufficient evidence to show that their competitive position was substantially affected more than other operators on the market.[275] In *Commission v Aktionsgemeinschaft Recht und Eigentum*, the applicant's members included farmers who could be regarded as direct competitors of the beneficiaries of the aid. The ECJ held, however, that it did not follow that their position on the market could be substantially affected since all farmers in the European Union could be regarded as competitors of the beneficiaries.[276]

The applicant must actually be a competitor of the recipient of the aid. In *Kronofrance v Commission*, the General Court, in addition to declaring the action admissible on the ground that the applicant was a competitor of the recipient, acknowledged that the applicant was also a subsidiary of a company that was in competition with the recipient.[277] On appeal, this latter consideration was implicitly disapproved of by the ECJ.[278] Where a competitor has ceased to be in competition with the aid recipient, it can no longer claim to be directly and individually concerned by the grant of aid. For example, in *Casillo Grani v Commission*, the applicant was declared bankrupt prior to the grant of the aid to its competitor, prompting the General Court to declare the application inadmissible on the ground that the decision to grant aid could not have affected the competitive situation of the applicant.[279]

---

[273] Case T-88/01, *Sniace SA v Commission* [2005] ECR II-1165, paras 61 & 78; upheld on appeal in Case C-260/05P, *Sniace SA v Commission* [2007] ECR I-10005, para 39.

[274] Case T-117/04, *Vereniging Werkgroep Commerciële Jachthavens Zuidelijke Randmeren v Commission* [2006] ECR II-3861, paras 56-60.

[275] Case T-388/02, *Kronoply GmbH v Commission* [2008] ECR II-305*, paras 64-69; Case T-388/03, *Deutsche Post AG v Commission* [2009] II-199, para 51; Case T-54/07, *Vtesse Networks Ltd v Commission* [2011] ECR II-6*, para 98; Case T-615/11, *Royal Scandinavian Casino Århus I/S v Commission* EU:T:2014:838, para 40.

[276] Case C-78/03P, *Commission v Aktionsgemeinschaft Recht und Eigentum eV* [2005] ECR I-10737, para 72.

[277] Case T-27/02, *Kronofance SA v Commission* [2004] ECR II-4177, para 43.

[278] Cases C-75/05P & C-80/05P, *Germany v Kronofrance* [2008] ECR I-6619, para 52.

[279] Case T-443/93, *Casillo Grani v Commission* [1995] ECR II-1375, para 8.

Employees of a recipient of aid cannot establish an interest in bringing proceedings on account of competitive effects, since they do not compete with the recipient.[280] Similarly, a minority shareholder in a recipient is not, by reason of that status, an undertaking whose competitive position is adversely affected by the grant of aid.[281]

Competitor's input as complainant In *Cofaz v Commission*, the ECJ held that where an undertaking makes a complaint which leads to the opening of the investigation procedure under Article 108(2) TFEU, its views are heard during that procedure and the conduct of the procedure is largely determined by its observations, that undertaking will be regarded as directly and individually concerned by the Commission's subsequent decision, provided that its position on the market is significantly affected by the aid.[282] The mere fact that a competitor has played an active role in the administrative procedure is not of itself sufficient to establish individual concern.[283] Nor does the additional fact that it has commenced proceedings for failure to act confer any special status in this regard.[284] In *Ducros v Commission*, in which Ducros had lodged a complaint against aid granted to a competitor and had been the sole undertaking to participate in the administrative procedure, a particular feature of the market in question was that the market shares of the undertakings concerned were difficult to quantify. Moreover, the complaint had been prompted by the fact that Ducros and the recipient of the aid had participated in the same tender procedure for a public-works contract that had been awarded to the recipient but which was of considerable importance to Ducros because it would have represented a significant part of its annual turnover.[285] By contrast, in *Commerciële Jachthavens v Commission*, the General Court held,

---

[280] Case T-178/94, *ATM v Commission* [1997] ECR II-2529, para 63.
[281] Case T-41/01, *Pérez Escolar v Commission* [2003] ECR II-2157, para 46, upheld on appeal in Case C-379/03P, *Pérez Escolar v Commission* EU:C:2004:580, para 27.
[282] Case 169/84, *Cofaz v Commission* [1986] ECR 391, paras 24-25; Case C-78/03P, *Commission v Aktionsgemeinschaft Recht und Eigentum eV* [2005] ECR I-10737, para 37; Case C-176/06P, *Stadtwerke Schäbisch Hall GmbH v Commission* [2007] ECR I-170*, para 30; Case T-11/95, *BP Chemicals Limited v Commission* [1998] ECR II-3235, para 72; Case T-188/95, *Waterleiding Maatschappij Noord-West Brabant NV v Commission* [1998] ECR II-3713, para 62; Case T-69/96, *Hamburger Hafen- und Lagerhaus AG v Commission* [2001] ECR II-1037, para 41; Case T-358/02, *Deutsche Post AG v Commission* [2004] ECR II-1565, para 34; Case T-117/04, *Vereniging Werkgroep Commerciële Jachthavens Zuidelijke Randmeren v Commission* [2006] ECR II-3861, para 52; Case T-601/11, *Dansk Automat Brancheforening v Commission* EU:T:2014:839, para 34.
[283] Case C-260/05P, *Sniace SA v Commission* [2007] ECR I-10005, para 60; Case T-54/07, *Vtesse Networks Ltd v Commission* [2011] ECR II-6*, para 92; Case T-261/11, *European Goldfields Ltd v Commission* EU:T:2012:157, para 26.
[284] Case T-344/10, *UPS Europe NV v Commission* EU:T:2012:216, para 45.
[285] Case T-149/95, *Ducros v Commission* [1997] ECR II-2031, paras 35-39.

as a factor in denying admissibility, that, although the applicant had made the initial complaint to the Commission and on a number of occasions provided supplementary information, it had not sent any additional information since the formal investigation procedure was opened.[286] This decision may be criticised on the ground that the General Court did not explain why for admissibility purposes it is relevant that the applicant's input into the Commission's examination should have to follow the initiation of the formal investigation procedure. The annulment action is taken against the reasoning of the final decision, which may be based on an assessment of all the information acquired by the Commission at any stage in the investigation procedure. Moreover, in *TV2/Danmark v Commission*, the fact that the applicant did not itself take part in the formal investigation procedure was not considered as a bar to admissibility in an action for annulment of the Commission's decision.[287]

Standing cannot be claimed as a complainant competitor where the applicant did not actually complain to the Commission merely because it expresses an interest in the proceedings indirectly. In *BP Chemicals v Commission*, the applicant participated in a working group set up by the United Kingdom Government's Department of Trade and Industry which prepared the United Kingdom's observations to the Commission in respect of a formal investigation procedure into aid which the French authorities proposed to grant in the petrochemical sector. Nevertheless, the General Court held that the mere participation in a working group could not be equated with the exercise of the right to submit comments pursuant to Article 108(2) TFEU. The General Court's reasoning for this conclusion was that the Commission was bound, in the interests of legal certainty and sound administration, to be aware, so far as is possible, of the particular circumstances of every undertaking which considers that it may be injured by the grant of the proposed aid. Since the applicant had not identified itself individually to the Commission, the Commission could not have been aware either of its specific objections or of any role which it had played in the preparation of the United Kingdom's comments.[288]

Competitors showing specific circumstances Even if an undertaking has not played an active role in the administrative procedure before the Commission, it may demonstrate by other means that it is individually concerned, but it must in any case show that the measure approved by the decision is capable of

---

[286] Case T-117/04, *Vereniging Werkgroep Commerciële Jachthavens Zuidelijke Randmeren v Commission* [2006] ECR II-3861, para 55.

[287] Cases T-309/04, T-317/04, T-329/04 & T-336/04, *TV2/Danmark A/S v Commission* [2008] ECR II-2935, para 216.

[288] Case T-11/95, *BP Chemicals Limited v Commission* [1998] ECR II-3235, para 75; Case T-86/96, *Arbeitsgemeinschaft Deutscher Luftfahrt-Unternehmen v Commission* [1999] ECR II-179, para 61.

significantly affecting its position on the market in question.[289] In *Sniace v Commission*, an application for annulment was held by the General Court to be inadmissible, in part because the applicant had played only a minor role in the investigation procedure.[290] On appeal this was criticised as an error of law by the ECJ which held that, whilst the *Cofaz* judgment showed that significant involvement in the procedure was relevant to assessing *locus standi*, such participation was not a necessary condition for the finding that a decision was of individual concern to the applicant, precluding the possibility of the undertaking putting forward other specific circumstances which distinguished it individually in a way similar to the case of the addressee of the decision.[291] In *ASPEC v Commission*, the General Court held that individual concern might be established by an undertaking by reference to specific circumstances distinguishing it individually.[292] Nevertheless, the mere fact that a measure is capable of influencing competitive relationships within the relevant market does not in itself suffice to deem any trader in any competitive relationship with the beneficiary of aid to be individually concerned by it.[293] Rather, the applicant must prove that it is in a distinct competitive position which differentiates it, as regards the aid in question, from any other trader.[294]

In *ASPEC v Commission*, the applicants held a market share of 95% in some of the products for which aid had been granted and, as regards another product, there were only five producers in the EU, with significant overcapacity in the market such that an increase in capacity was capable of directly and seriously affecting the competitive position of the few producers already on the market. The General Court considered that they had established the existence of a set of factors amounting to a situation peculiar to them in regard to the measures in question in relation to any other trader.[295] In *BUPA v Commission*, concerning a risk equalisation scheme on the Irish health insurance market, although in principle this was to apply to all insurers active on the Irish market, in practice BUPA was the only net contributor to the fund. The General Court held that this was sufficient to establish the existence of a set of facts constituting a special situation which distinguished BUPA from any

---

[289] Case C-260/05P, *Sniace SA v Commission* [2007] ECR I-10005, para 60; Case T-358/02, *Deutsche Post AG v Commission* [2004] ECR II-1565, para 36.

[290] Case T-88/01, *Sniace SA v Commission* [2005] ECR II-1165, paras 59 and 79.

[291] Case C-260/05P, *Sniace SA v Commission* [2007] ECR I-10005, paras 57-59.

[292] Case T-435/93, *ASPEC v Commission* [1995] ECR II-1281, para 64; Case T-442/93, *AAC v Commission* [1995] ECR II-1329, para 49; Case T-266/94, *Skibsværftsforenigingen v Commission* [1996] ECR II-1399, para 47.

[293] Cases 10/68 & 18/68, *Eridania v Commission* [1969] ECR 459, para 7; Case T-266/94, *Skibsværftsforeningen v Commission* [1996] ECR II-1399, para 47; Case T-117/04, *Vereniging Werkgroep Commerciële Jachthavens Zuidelijke Randmeren v Commission* [2006] ECR II-3861, para 53.

[294] Case T-11/95, *BP Chemicals Limited v Commission* [1998] ECR II-3235, para 77.

[295] Case T-435/93, *ASPEC v Commission* [1995] ECR II-1281, para 70.

other economic operator.[296]   In *BP Chemicals v Commission*, however, admissibility was not established where the applicant was only the seventh largest out of twenty competitors on the relevant market, accounting for a mere 7% of capacity.[297] Similarly, in *Deutsche Post v Commission*, the applicants did not adduce sufficient evidence to show that their position on the Italian postal market, on which they had an 8% share, had been significantly affected by the grant of State funding to Poste Italiana to cover its operating losses.[298] In *Fachvereinigung Mineralfaserindustrie eV v Commission*, admissibility was denied by the General Court where the amounts of aid represented an extremely weak section of the relevant market.[299]

Representative associations   An association, in its capacity as the representative of a category of businesses, may be an interested party within the meaning of Article 108(2) TFEU.[300] Nevertheless, it is not by that capacity alone that an association may be individually concerned by a measure affecting the general interests of that category.[301] There are three sets of circumstances in which a representative association may claim admissibility in State aid proceedings. First, an association may be individually concerned by a decision where it represents persons who would themselves have been individually concerned by the decision. Secondly, it may rely on special circumstances affording it a particular interest in acting.[302] Thirdly, exceptionally, a legal provision may expressly grant trade associations certain procedural rights.[303]

---

[296] Case T-289/03, *BUPA Ltd v Commission* [2008] ECR II-81, paras 78-79.

[297] Case T-11/95, *BP Chemicals Limited v Commission* [1998] ECR II-3235, para 80.

[298] Case T-358/02, *Deutsche Post AG v Commission* [2004] ECR II-1565, paras 40-44.

[299] Case T-375/03, *Fachvereinigung Mineralfaserindustrie eV v Commission* [2007] ECR II-121*, para 60; Case T-254/05, *Fachvereinigung Mineralfaserindustrie eV v Commission* [2007] ECR II-124*, para 44.

[300] Case T-137/10, *CBI v Commission* EU:T:2012:584, para 62.

[301] Case 60/79, *Fédération Nationale des Producteurs de Vins de Table et Vins de Pays v Commission* [1979] ECR 2429, para 3; Case T-238/97, *Comunidad Autónoma de Cantabria v Council* [1998] ECR II-2271, para 48; Case T-86/96, *Arbeitsgemeinschaft Deutscher Luftfahrt-Unternehmen v Commission* [1999] ECR II-179, para 55. Under the ECSC Treaty, an association, within the meaning of Article 48 CS, made up of undertakings in the steel industry, whose purpose is to represent the common interests of its members, could be concerned within the meaning of Article 33 CS by decisions authorizing the payment of State aid to competing undertakings: Case C-180/88, *Wirtschaftsvereinigung Eisen-und Stahlindustrie v Commission* [1990] ECR I-4413, para 23; Case T-239/94, *EISA v Commission* [1997] ECR II-1839, para 28.

[302] Case T-380/94, *AIUFFASS v Commission* [1996] ECR II-2169, para 50; Case T-86/96, *Arbeitsgemeinschaft Deutscher Luftfahrt-Unternehmen v Commission* [1999] ECR II-179, paras 56-57; Case T-55/99, *CETM v Commission* [2000] ECR II-3207, para 23; Case T-117/04, *Vereniging Werkgroep Commerciële Jachthavens Zuidelijke Randmeren v Commission* [2006] ECR II-3861, para 65; Case T-95/03, *Asociación de Estaciones de Servicio de Madrid v Commission* [2006] ECR II-4739, para 42; Case T-146/03, *Asociación de Estaciones de Servicio de Madrid v Commission* [2006] ECR II-98*, para

Members of representative association individually concerned An action may be admissible on the ground that an association may be individually concerned by a decision where it represents persons who would themselves have been individually concerned by the decision.[304] Where the applicant association cannot prove that its members are in a position to bring an admissible action, the application is inadmissible.[305] In *AITEC v Commission*, the applicant association, in accordance with its statute, was regarded as having substituted itself for some of its members who could themselves have brought an admissible action, without any objection from those members.[306] In *British Aggregates Association v Commission*, members of the association that were subject to a special levy were in direct competition with the producers of materials that were exempt from the levy and which had become competitive as a result of its introduction.[307] Similarly, in *CETM v Commission*, the applicant was held to be protecting the interests of its members which were required to repay illegally granted aid.[308] In *Asociación de Estaciones de Servicio de Madrid v Commission*, the applicant associations represented more than a quarter of all service stations in Spain, including 85% of those in Madrid and 70% of those in Catalonia. The purpose of the alleged aid measure was to facilitate the entry of hypermarkets into the Spanish market for the retail supply of petroleum products in order to promote competition in that market, which was likely substantially to alter the competitive situation on the market to the disadvantage of certain other service station operators, several of whom had suffered a significant drop in sales leading to the closing down of their business. The General Court held that it had been established that the State measure was likely substantially to affect the competitive position of certain

---

42; Case T-445/05, *Associazione Italiana del Risparmio Gestito v Commission* [2009] ECR II-289, para 55; Case T-236/10, *Asociación Española de Banca v Commission* EU:T:2012:176, para 19; Case T-201/10, *IVBN v Commission* EU:T:2012:385, para 32; Case T-182/10 *Aiscat v Commission* EU:T:2013:9, para 48; Case T-156/10, *CCAE v Commission* EU:T:2014:41, para 33; Case T-2/13, *CFE-CGC France Télécom-Orange v Commission* EU:T:2014:226, para 49.

[303] Case T-122/96, *Federolio v Commission* [1997] ECR II-1559, para 61; Case T-559/11, *Sdruženi nájemníků BytyOKD.cz v Commission* EU:T:2013:255, para 29; Case T-7/13, *ADEAS v Commission* EU:T:2014:221, para 32.

[304] Case C-409/96P, *Sveriges Betoldares Centralförening v Commission* [1997] ECR I-7531, para 45; Case C-487/06P, *British Aggregates Association v Commission* [2008] ECR I-10515, para 39; Cases T-447-449/93, *AITEC v Commission* [1995] ECR II-1971, para 62; Cases T-254/00, T-270/00 & T-277/00, *Hotel Cipriani SpA v Commission* [2008] ECR II-3269, para 115; Case T-559/11, *Sdruženi nájemníků BytyOKD.cz v Commission* EU:T:2013:255, para 31.

[305] Case T-69/96, *Hamburger Hafen- und Lagerhaus AG v Commission* [2001] ECR II-1037, para 49; Case T-182/10 *Aiscat v Commission* EU:T:2013:9, para 60.

[306] Cases T-447-449/93, *AITEC v Commission* [1995] ECR II-1971, para 62; Case T-266/94, *Skibsværftsforeningen v Commission* [1996] ECR II-1399, para 50.

[307] Case T-210/02, *British Aggregates Association v Commission* [2006] ECR II-2789, para 58.

[308] Case T-55/99, *CETM v Commission* [2000] ECR II-3207, paras 24-25.

members of the applicants which, therefore, had standing to bring the action for annulment.[309]

By contrast, in *DEFI v Commission*, the ECJ noted that the applicant was not the ultimate beneficiary of the aid but was required to pay the aid to undertakings making certain investments. The aid plan did not determine which undertakings were to receive aid, so that any undertaking wishing to bring an action in that connection was no more concerned by the Commission's decision than all the other traders in the sector in question. Insofar as the applicant's claim was analogous to that of an association set up to represent the collective interests of other traders, it did not have a right of action.[310] In *Landbouwschap v Commission*, where a challenge was made to a Commission decision approving certain aid, the application was declared inadmissible on the ground that the aid benefited only a group of large industrial undertakings with whom neither the applicant not the undertakings which it represented were in competition.[311] In *Aiscat v Commission*, which concerned the award of an Italian motorway concession of some 32 km in length, the applicant represented 23 operators of toll motorways but the relevant market was determined by the General Court to be all 5,500 km of Italian toll motorways, such that the competitive position of the applicant's members could not be regarded as substantially affected.[312] By contrast, in the same case, in relation to a claim concerning an increase in the toll on two competing stretches of motorway, the relevant market was the making available of motorway connections on the competing stretches in return for a toll payment and the respective concessionaires were in competition with one another, such that an increase in tolls could have a sufficient impact on their competitive position.[313] In *Sdruženi nájemníků BytyOKD.cz v Commission*, a tenants' association was not able to establish a right of action as the tenants themselves were not undertakings engaged in any economic activity.[314]

Particular interest of representative association A representative association may rely on special circumstances affording it a particular interest in acting. In *Van der Kooy v Commission*, a public body which acted as a collective representative in negotiating gas supply tariffs was concerned with a decision that the tariff contained an element of State aid since its position as a negotiator was affected and it was obliged, in order to give effect to the

---

[309] Case T-95/03, *Asociación de Estaciones de Servicio de Madrid v Commission* [2006] ECR II-4739, paras 51-55.

[310] Case 282/85, *DEFI v Commission* [1986] ECR 2469, para 18.

[311] Case C-295/92, *Landbouwschap v Commission* [1992] ECR I-5003, para 12.

[312] Case T-182/10 *Aiscat v Commission* EU:T:2013:9, para 68.

[313] *Ibid.*, paras 70-74.

[314] Case T-559/11, *Sdruženi nájemníků BytyOKD.cz v Commission* EU:T:2013:255, para 35.

decision, to renegotiate the tariffs.[315]   Similarly, in *CIRFS v Commission*, standing was granted to an association, the membership of which consisted of the main international manufacturers of synthetic fibres, which had pursued, in the interests of those manufacturers, a number of actions connected with the policy of that sector. In particular, it had negotiated with the Commission in relation to the introduction of the aid discipline which was at the heart of the proceedings and, during the procedure prior to the proceedings, had submitted written observations and kept in close contact with the relevant departments. The position of CIRFS in its capacity as negotiator of the discipline was therefore affected by the decision.[316]

In *Danske Busvognmaend v Commission*, a trade association representing the interests of the majority of Danish bus companies complained to the Commission about aid granted to a competing bus company, as a result of which Denmark notified the aid to the Commission which found it compatible with the internal market. The applicant had standing to bring the challenge in its capacity as a complainant which had influenced the course of the administrative procedure and at least some of its members were in competition with the beneficiary of the aid.[317]   Where a representative association's role does not go beyond the exercise of the procedural rights granted to interested parties under Article 108(2) TFEU, special circumstances will not be established.[318] The General Court rejected claims by Spanish undertakings as being representatives that were individually concerned by virtue of having submitted comments to the Commission in an investigation into Spanish legislation granting a tax exemption.[319] Similarly, in *CCAE v Commission*, an action brought by a Spanish association representing the interests of agricultural cooperatives was declared inadmissible on the ground that the association had made submissions only in the formal investigation procedure.[320]

Works council and trade unions A works council or trade union may have much more difficulty in establishing that its position as a negotiator in wage

---

[315] Cases 67, 68 & 70/85, *Van der Kooy v Commission* [1988] ECR 219, paras 21-23.

[316] Case C-313/90, *CIRFS v Commission* [1993 EC I-1125, paras 29-30.

[317] Case T-157/01, *Danske Busvognmaend v Commission* [2004] ECR II-197, para 40.

[318] Case C-78/03P, *Commission v Aktionsgemeinschaft Recht und Eigentum eV* [2005] ECR I-10737, para 58; Case T-117/04, *Vereniging Werkgroep Commerciële Jacht-havens Zuidelijke Randmeren v Commission* [2006] ECR II-3861, para 73; Case T-375/03, *Fachvereinigung Mineralfaserindustrie eV v Commission* [2007] ECR II-121*, para 55; Case T-254/05, *Fachvereinigung Mineralfaserindustrie eV v Commission* [2007] ECR II-124*, para 39; Case T-292/02, *Conservizi v Commission* [2009] ECR II-1659, para 58; Case T-156/10, *CCAE v Commission* EU:T:2014:41, para 35.

[319] Case T-221/10, *Iberdrola SA v Commission* EU:T:2012:112, para 35; Case T-228/10, *Telefónica SA v Commission* EU:T:2012:140, para 31; Case T-236/10, *Associación Española de Banca v Commission* EU:T:2012:176, paras 43-45.

[320] Case T-156/10, *CCAE v Commission* EU:T:2014:41, paras 36-37.

settlements for employees of an undertaking is such as to make it directly and individually concerned by a decision of the Commission declaring aid to that undertaking incompatible with the internal market. In *Comité d'Entreprise de la Société Française de Production v Commission*, the ECJ held that the status of the works council and trade unions as negotiators with regard to social aspects such as staffing and salary structure within the recipient undertaking did not suffice to distinguish them individually just as in the case of the person to whom the decision was addressed. Whilst social aspects are liable to be taken into account by the Commission as part of its overall assessment which includes a large number of considerations, in the circumstances they constituted only a tenuous link with the actual subject matter of the Commission's decision.[321] Similarly, in *CFE-CGC France Télécom-Orange v Commission*, a trade union, which had not taken any part in negotiations with the Commission as regards an aid scheme, was unable to rely on the fact that it negotiated with France Télécom on behalf of its members in order to claim that it was individually concerned.[322]

In *SID v Commission*, an action for annulment brought by a Danish trade union representing the interests of seafarers employed on board the ordinary Danish shipping register which objected to preferential fiscal treatment for ships on the Danish international shipping register was declared inadmissible. The General Court held that the trade union's position could not have been affected by the aid in question since it could not be said to be in competition with the recipients of the aid, namely the owners of the ships registered on the international shipping register.[323] On appeal, the ECJ stated that it could not be excluded that a trade union may be regarded as concerned within the meaning of Article 108(2) TFEU if it shows that its interests or those of its members might be affected by the granting of aid.[324] It was open to it to show that its interests might be affected by reason of the effect of the measures on its competitive position in relation to other trade unions whose members were employed on board vessels registered in the international shipping register. The trade union, as an organisation representing workers was by definition established to promote the collective interests of its members. It argued that it was an economic operator which negotiated the terms and conditions on which labour was provided to undertakings and that the aid resulting from the fiscal measures at issue affected the ability of its members to compete with non-EU seafarers in seeking employment with shipping companies, the recipients of the

---

[321] Case C-106/98P, *Comité d'Entreprise de la Société Française de Production v Commission* [2000] ECR I-3271, paras 51-53; Case T-189/97, *Comité d'Entreprise de la Société Française de Production v Commission* [1998] ECR II-335, paras 48-52.

[322] Case T-2/13, *CFE-CGC France Télécom-Orange v Commission* EU:T:2014:226, paras 36-42.

[323] Case T-30/03, *Specialarbejderforbundet i Danmark v Commission* [2007] ECR II-34*, para 32.

[324] Case C-319/07P, *3F v Commission* [2009] ECR I-5963, para 33.

aid. Its market position as such was therefore affected as regards its ability to compete in the market for the supply of labour to those companies, and consequently its ability to recruit members. Accordingly, the ECJ accepted that the case concerned the question whether the trade union's competitive position in relation to other trade unions was affected by the granting of the aid. It also emphasised that the rights under EU law on State aid and competition must be balanced, where appropriate, against the objectives pursued by social policy, which include, as is clear from Article 151 TFEU, improved living and working conditions, proper social protection and dialogue between management and labour. This precluded an excessively restrictive interpretation of the concept of market in connection with the question of the status of party concerned within the meaning of Article 108(2) TFEU. [325] Since the trade union had explained how the fiscal measures at issue could affect its position and that of its members in collective negotiations with shipowners whose vessels are registered in the international register, and since the Commission's maritime aid guidelines acknowledged the part played by trade unions in those negotiations, the ECJ concluded that it had shown that its interests and those of its members could be affected by the decision.[326]

Even though the trade union had been one of the negotiators of collective agreements for seafarers on board ships registered in one of the Danish shipping registers and as such played a part in the machinery for passing the aid on to the shipowners, the General Court held that it had not shown that it negotiated either the drafting of the Commission's guidelines on State aid to maritime transport or the adoption of the Danish fiscal measures.[327] On appeal, the ECJ agreed with this assessment, since the trade union, as only one of many in the European Union representing seafarers and only one of the many trade unions operating in Denmark, did not occupy a clearly circumscribed position as negotiator which was intimately linked to the actual subject-matter of the contested decision. It was not directly involved in the adoption by the Danish legislature of the fiscal measures at issue.[328]

Interested parties Interested parties or concerned parties within the meaning of Article 108(2) TFEU are defined in Council Regulation (EC) No 659/1999, Article 1(h) as any Member State and any person, undertaking or association of undertakings whose interests might be affected by the granting of the aid, in particular the beneficiary of the aid, competing undertakings and trade associations.[329] Thus, in order to establish admissibility in an action for

---

[325] Case C-319/07P, *3F v Commission* [2009] ECR I-5963, paras 54- 59.

[326] *Ibid.*, para 104.

[327] Case T-30/03, *Specialarbejderforbundet i Danmark v Commission* [2007] ECR II-34*, para 40.

[328] Case C-319/07P, *3F v Commission* [2009] ECR I-5963, para 92.

[329] Council Regulation (EC) No 659/1999, Article 1(h). The French language version shows that no distinction should be drawn between the phrases interested parties

annulment pursuant to Article 263 TFEU, applicants must show that their legitimate interests have been affected by the grant of the aid.[330] A distinction as regards admissibility of proceedings commenced by interested parties is drawn between applications for annulment where the applicant challenges the merits of a decision and other challenges where the applicant is merely seeking to protect its procedural rights under Article 108(2) TFEU to make comments during a formal investigation procedure.[331]

The mere fact of having made a complaint to the Commission is insufficient to confer on the complainant the status of party concerned within the meaning of Article 108(2) TFEU.[332] Similarly, a person having a purely general or indirect interest with regard to the State measure to which objection is taken is not a party concerned. The General Court has held that recognising that any taxpayer is a party concerned in relation to aid financed through the general tax resources of a Member State would have the effect of depriving the concept of a person individually concerned for the purposes of Article 263 TFEU of all legal significance by transforming that remedy into a sort of *actio popularis*.[333] In *Pérez Escolar v Commission,* the applicant was a minority shareholder in a bank. In rejecting his challenge to the Commission's decision that certain measures adopted by Spain relating to the restructuring of the bank did not constitute State aid, the General Court held that he had not shown any direct causal link as to how his status as a minority shareholder was affected by the alleged aid, so that he had no legitimate interest in challenging the Commission's decision.[334] By contrast, in *Westfälisch-Lippischer Sparkassen- und Giroverband v Commission*, a shareholder was regarded as individually concerned by a decision on restructuring aid which required the shareholders in

---

('*parties intéressés*') in the Regulation and concerned parties ('*les intéressés*') in Article 108(2) TFEU.

[330] Case T-388/02, *Kronoply GmbH v Commission* [2008] ECR II-305*, para 71.

[331] In his opinion in Case C-78/03P, *Commission v Aktionsgemeinschaft Recht und Eigentum eV* [2005] ECR I-10737, at paras 138-142, Advocate General Jacobs criticised this distinction and suggested that a single test of admissibility be established, using a standard which should not be as narrow as the *Plaumann* test. The ECJ did not take up this suggestion.

[332] Case C-319/07P, *3F v Commission* [2009] ECR I-5963, para 94; Case T-398/94, *Kahn Scheepvaart BV v Commission* [1996] ECR II-477, para 42; Case T-41/01, *Pérez Escolar v Commission* [2003] ECR II-2157, para 39; Case T-210/02, *British Aggregates Association v Commission* [2006] ECR II-2789, para 46; Case T-30/03, *Specialarbejderforbundet i Danmark v Commission* [2007] ECR II-34*, para 40; Case T-315/05, *Adomex International BV v Commission* [2008] ECR II-145*, para 30; Case T-304/08, *Smurfit Kappa Group plc v Commission* EU:T:2012:351, para 56.

[333] Case T-188/95, *Waterleiding Maatschappij Noord West Brabant NV v Commission* [1998] ECR II-3713, para, 68; Case T-41/01, *Pérez Escolar v Commission* [2003] ECR II-2157, para 36.

[334] Case T-41/01, *Pérez Escolar v Commission* [2003] ECR II-2157, paras 41-45, upheld on appeal in Case C-379/03P, *Pérez Escolar v Commission* EU:C:2004:580, para 34.

the beneficiary to sell off certain assets.[335] In *SID v Commission*, where the Danish trade union challenged aid granted to shipowners on an international shipping register, the General Court, in rejecting the action as inadmissible, stated that the social aspects of the register, which were themselves of legitimate concern to the trade union, were only indirectly linked to the subject matter of the Commission's decision declaring the aid compatible with the internal market. The trade union could not, therefore, rely on those social aspects to establish that it was individually concerned.[336] This was also overturned on appeal in *3F v Commission* where the ECJ held that it cannot be ruled out that organisations representing the workers of the undertakings benefiting from aid may, as parties concerned, submit observations to the Commission on considerations of a social nature.[337]

Proceedings by interested parties challenging merits   Where the Commission has taken a decision following a formal investigation procedure, interested parties do not generally have standing to bring an action for annulment unless they are competitors whose competitive position is significantly affected or can otherwise prove specific circumstances distinguishing them individually. The mere fact that a person is an interested party within the meaning of Article 108(2) TFEU does not confer on it *locus standi* entitling it to bring an action against such decisions.[338] Even the fact that it might have submitted comments to the Commission in the formal investigation procedure does not suffice to distinguish it individually.[339] Instead, where the Commission has taken a decision following a preliminary investigation to allow aid as compatible with the internal market, an interested party seeking to challenge the merits of the decision must demonstrate that it has a particular status of individual concern under the *Plaumann* doctrine, such as, in particular, that its market position is substantially affected by the aid to which the decision at issue relates.[340]

---

[335] Case T-457/09, *Westfälisch-Lippischer Sparkassen- und Giroverband v Commission* EU:T:2014:683, para 111.

[336] Case T-30/03, *Specialarbejderforbundet i Danmark v Commission* [2007] ECR II-34*, para 36.

[337] Case C-319/07P, *3F v Commission* [2009] ECR I-5963, para 70..

[338] Case T-86/96, *Arbeitsgemeinschaft Deutscher Luftfahrt-Unternehmen v Commission* [1999] ECR II-179, para 47; Case T-266/94, *Skibsværftsforeningen v Commission* [1996] ECR II-1399, para 45.

[339] Case T-86/96, *Arbeitsgemeinschaft Deutscher Luftfahrt-Unternehmen v Commission* [1999] ECR II-179, para 50.

[340] Case C-78/03P, *Commission v Aktionsgemeinschaft Recht und Eigentum eV* [2005] ECR I-10737, para 37; Case C-176/06P, *Stadtwerke Schwäbisch Hall GmbH v Commission* [2007] ECR I-170*, para 29; Cases C-75/05P & C-80/05P, *Germany v Kronofrance* [2008] ECR I-6619, para 40; Case C-487/06P, *British Aggregates Association v Commission* [2008] ECR I-10515, para 30; Case C-287/12P, *Ryanair Ltd v Commission* EU:C:2013:395, para 112; Case T-266/94, *Skibsværftsforeningen v Commission*

Protection of procedural rights under Article 108(2) TFEU Admissibility of actions by interested parties seeking the annulment of decisions not to open the formal investigation procedure is subject to a more liberal approach where the applicant is seeking to protect its procedural rights. Where, without initiating the formal investigation procedure, the Commission decides, on the basis of its preliminary examination, that a measure does not constitute aid or that aid is compatible with the internal market, the ECJ has recognised that the persons intended to benefit from the procedural guarantees inherent in a formal investigation may secure compliance therewith only if they are able to challenge that decision by the Commission. In this instance, the category of persons who may challenge the Commission's decision not to initiate the formal investigation procedure was declared, in *Cook v Commission* and *Matra v Commission*, to be wider than those who would be able to challenge any decision following such an investigation. Accordingly, any parties concerned within the meaning of Article 108(2) TFEU will be considered as individually concerned by the decision not to initiate the formal investigation procedure.[341] Moreover, a person who claims the status of interested party is not also required to show that its position on the market has been substantially affected by the adoption of the decision.[342] The fact that the persons concerned may have had the opportunity to put their case to the Commission during the preliminary assessment procedure under Article 108(3) TFEU does not deprive them of the right to respect for the procedural guarantee expressly conferred on

---

[1996] ECR II-1399, para 47; Case T-395/04, *Air One SpA v Commission* [2006] ECR II-1343, para 33; Case T-95/03, *Asociación de Estaciones de Servicio de Madrid v Commission* [2006] ECR II-4739, para 48; Case T-388/02, *Kronoply GmbH v Commission* [2008] ECR II-305*, para 64; Case T-388/03, *Deutsche Post AG v Commission* [2009] II-199, para 44; Case T-123/09, *Ryanair Ltd v Commission* EU:T:2012:164, para 194.

[341] Case C-198/91, *William Cook plc v Commission* [1993] ECR I-2487, paras 23-26; Case C-225/91, *Matra SA v Commission* [1993] ECR I-3203, paras 17-20; Case C-367/95P, *Commission v Sytraval* [1998] ECR I-1719, para 41; Case C-78/03P, *Commission v Aktionsgemeinschaft Recht und Eigentum eV* [2005] ECR I-10737, para 35; Case C-487/06P, *British Aggregates Association v Commission* [2008] ECR I-10515, para 28; Case C-83/09P, *Commission v Kronoply GmbH* [2011] ECR I-4441, para 48; Case C-47/10P, *Austria v Commission* [2011] ECR I-10707, para 44; Case C-287/12P, *Ryanair Ltd v Commission* EU:C:2013:395, para 55; Case T-11/95, *BP Chemicals Limited v Commission* [1998] ECR II-3235, para 89; Case T-95/96, *Gestevisión Telecinco SA v Commission*, [1998] ECR II-3407, para 64; Cases T-197/97 & T-198/97, *Weyl Beef Products BV v Commission* [2001] ECR II-303, para 50; Case T-69/96, *Hamburger Hafen- und Lagerhaus v Commission* [2001] ECR II-1037, para 37; Cases T-12/99 & T-63/99, *UK Coal plc v Commission* [2001] ECR II-2153, para 198; Case T-114/00, *Aktionsgemeinschaft Recht und Eigentum eV v Commission* [2002] ECR II-5121, para 45; Case T-158/99, *Thermenhotel Stoiser Franz GmbH v Commission* [2004] ECR II-1, para 73; Case T-388/03, *Deutsche Post AG v Commission* [2009] II-199, para 42; Case T-123/09, *Ryanair Ltd v Commission* EU:T:2012:164, para 64.

[342] Cases C-75/05P & C-80/05P, *Germany v Kronofrance* [2008] ECR I-6619, para 44.

them by Article 108(2) TFEU.[343] Furthermore, there is nothing to preclude an application to a decision not to open the formal investigation procedure on the ground that the Commission should have encountered serious difficulties from being based on arguments that might also arise in a challenge on the substantive merits. The use of such arguments does not alter the subject matter of the challenge or the conditions for its admissibility by turning it into a challenge on the merits.[344] On the contrary, the existence of doubts concerning compatibility of the aid is precisely the evidence that must be adduced in order to show that the Commission was required to initiate the formal investigation procedure.[345] The General Court has observed that it is for the applicant to identify those arguments in its pleadings, and that it cannot be for the Court or the Commission to search amongst the various arguments pleaded on the merits in order to ascertain which of them might also be relied on to show a violation of procedural rights.[346] Moreover, where the applicant does not specifically raise the issue of protection of procedural rights, it cannot claim that such an issue is intrinsically linked to its action on the merits.[347] The burden of proving the existence of serious difficulties rests on the applicant.[348]

Potential competitors are treated as parties concerned having standing to bring proceedings to secure their procedural rights under Article 108(2) TFEU.[349] In *Air One v Commission*, where an Italian airline challenged alleged aid granted by the Italian authorities to Ryanair, the General Court found that since the applicant already operated in the Italian market providing scheduled air transport of passengers, it could not be denied the status of party concerned merely on the ground that the routes it operated directly did not

---

[343] Case T-289/03, *BUPA Ltd v Commission* [2008] ECR II-81, para 76.

[344] Case C-319/07P, *3F v Commission* [2009] ECR I-5963, para 31; Case C-83/09P, *Commission v Kronoply GmbH* [2011] ECR I-4441, paras 56-59; Case C-47/10P, *Austria v Commission* [2011] ECR I-10707, para 50; Case C-287/12P, *Ryanair Ltd v Commission* EU:C:2013:395, para 60; Case T-304/08, *Smurfit Kappa Group plc v Commission* EU:T:2012:351, para 52; Case T-325/10, *Iliad v Commission* EU:T:2013:472, para 83.

[345] Case C-83/09P, *Commission v Kronoply GmbH* [2011] ECR I-4441, para 59; Case C-451/10P, *Television Française 1 SA v Commission* [2011] I-85*, para 52; Case C-148/09P, *Belgium v Deutsche Post* [2011] ECR I-8573, para 55; Case C-47/10P, *Austria v Commission* [2011] ECR I-10707, para 50; Case C-287/12P, *Ryanair Ltd v Commission* EU:C:2013:395, para 60; Case T-137/10, *CBI v Commission* EU:T:2012:584, para 65.

[346] Case T-201/10, *IVBN v Commission* EU:T:2012:385, para 56; Case T-362/10, *Vtesse Networks Ltd v Commission* EU:T:2014:928, para 75.

[347] Case T-182/10 *Aiscat v Commission* EU:T:2013:9, para 46.

[348] Case T-36/06, *Bundesverband deutscher Banken v Commission* [2010] ECR II-537, para 127; Case T-512/11, *Ryanair Ltd. v Commission* EU:T:2014:989, para 63; Case T-140/13, *Netherlands Maritime Technology Association v Commission* EU:T:2014:1029, para 46.

[349] Case T-395/04, *Air One SpA v Commission* [2006] ECR II-1343, para 39; Case T-167/04, *Asklepios Kliniken GmbH v Commission* [2007] ECR II-2379, para 45.

coincide exactly with those operated by Ryanair. For the purposes of admissibility, it was sufficient that the applicant was a competitor of Ryanair insofar as those two undertakings operated, directly or indirectly, services providing scheduled air transport of passengers from or to Italian airports and, in particular, regional airports. As far as international routes were concerned, the applicant provided, *inter alia*, services between Rome and Frankfurt, two cities which were also served by Ryanair. With regard to domestic routes, it was clear that whilst, at the material time, Ryanair did not operate routes between Italian cities, the possibility could not be excluded that it could subsequently do so in direct competition with the applicant. In those circumstances, it was possible to conclude that there was a sufficient relationship of competition, for the purposes of admissibility, between the applicant and the recipient of the alleged aid.[350] In *Asklepios Kliniken v Commission*, the applicant managed 39 private hospitals throughout Germany and was therefore considered to have a sufficient competitive relationship with at least some of the 700 German public sector hospitals that it alleged received aid.[351]

Admissibility will be allowed in so far as the applicant can show that there were serious difficulties which should have led the Commission to open the formal investigation procedure.[352] This approach was justified by Advocate General Tesauro on the ground that the only information regarding the aid at the disposal of undertakings which challenge a decision to raise no objections is either that communicated to them by the Commission or that resulting from the bare extract published in the *Official Journal of the European Union*. They could not be required, therefore, to formulate in the application instituting the proceedings precise submissions regarding the size and effect of the aid, such as its impact on the recipient's production costs, shifts in market shares or the effect on trading patterns. In order to have standing, Advocate General Tesauro argued that the applicant only had to establish that it was competing genuinely and not just marginally with the recipient of the aid.[353] The General Court, however, has held that there is no need for interested parties to show any further effect on their competitive position.[354]

---

[350] Case T-395/04, *Air One SpA v Commission* [2006] ECR II-1343, paras 38-40.

[351] Case T-167/04, *Asklepios Kliniken GmbH v Commission* [2007] ECR II-2379, para 51.

[352] Case T-158/99, *Thermenhotel Stoiser Franz GmbH v Commission* [2004] ECR II-1, para 91; Case T-375/03, *Fachvereinigung Mineralfaserindustrie eV v Commission* [2007] ECR II-121*, para 67.

[353] Case C-198/91, *William Cook plc v Commission* [1993] ECR I-2487, *per* Advocate General Tesauro, at p. 2511. This reasoning was questioned by Advocate General Jacobs in his Opinion in Case C-78/03P, *Commission v Aktionsgemeinschaft Recht und Eigentum eV* [2005] ECR I-10737, at para 140.

[354] Case T-188/95, *Waterleiding Maatschappij Noord-West Brabant NV v Commission* [1998] ECR II-3713, para 58.

This only applies where the contested decision finding that aid is compatible with the internal market concerns a grant of individual aid. By contrast, where the contested decision concerns the approval of an aid scheme whose potential beneficiaries are defined only in a general and abstract manner, there cannot be any competing undertakings for the purposes of invoking the procedural guarantees within Article 108(2) TFEU, since there can have been no grant of individual aid in application of that scheme at the time of the adoption of the decision.[355] In *Waterleiding Maatschappij Noord-West Brabant v Commission*, the applicant, a water supply company, challenged the Commission's decision to approve Netherlands legislation granting exemptions from a tax imposed on the consumption of groundwater. The General Court held that the fact that the applicant was charged the full rate of the groundwater tax did not in itself demonstrate that its competitive position on the market was affected by the aid granted in the form of the reduced rate of tax applicable to certain other undertakings.[356] The legislation, however, also granted specific reliefs for undertakings which switched to self-supply to satisfy their water needs. Those undertakings were current or potential customers of the applicant, so that the reliefs directly affected the structure of the market in the supply of water and therefore affected the applicant's competitive position. The proceedings were, accordingly, declared admissible in so far as they concerned those reliefs.[357] Similar reasoning was used by the General Court in *Fachvereinigung Mineralfaser-industrie eV v Commission*.[358]

19.7 LIMITATION PERIODS FOR COMMENCING PROCEEDINGS

Limitation periods for commencing proceedings Time limits for bringing an action for annulment are strictly enforced.[359] Article 263 TFEU provides that actions for annulment must be brought within two months of the publication of the decision or of its notification to the applicant or, in the absence of publication or notification, of the day on which it came to the knowledge of the applicant. Applications brought after that date will be

---

[355] Case T-398/94, *Kahn Scheepvaart BV v Commission* [1996] ECR II-477, para 49; Case C-78/03P, *Commission v Aktionsgemeinschaft Recht und Eigentum eV* [2005] ECR I-10737, *per* Advocate General Jacobs, at para 119.

[356] Case T-188/95, *Waterleiding Maatschappij Noord-West Brabant NV v Commission* [1998] ECR II-3713, para 67.

[357] *Ibid.*, para 81.

[358] Case T-375/03, *Fachvereinigung Mineralfaserindustrie eV v Commission* [2007] ECR II-121*, para 62; Case T-254/05, *Fachvereinigung Mineralfaserindustrie eV v Commission* [2007] ECR II-124*, para 46.

[359] Case T-126/00, *Confindustria v Commission* [2001] ECR I-85, para 21.

declared inadmissible.[360] The criterion of the day on which a measure came to the knowledge of an applicant, as the starting point of the period prescribed for instituting proceedings, is subsidiary to the criteria of publication or notification of the measure.[361] It follows that even where an applicant has or could reasonably have had knowledge of a Commission decision prior to its publication in the *Official Journal of the European Union*, the limitation period runs from the date of publication itself.[362]

Publication in the *Official Journal of the European Union* Publication in the *Official Journal of the European Union* of decisions concerning State aid is governed by the provisions of Council Regulation (EC) No 659/1999, Article 26. The Commission is under an obligation to publish the full text in all languages only in respect of decisions taken following a formal investigation procedure.[363] The Council may also decide to publish the decisions its takes pursuant to Article 108(2) TFEU approving aid in exceptional circumstances.[364] For Commission decisions opening a formal investigation procedure, the Commission must publish the full text in the authentic language of the decision, accompanied by a meaningful summary in other language versions of the *Official Journal*.[365]

---

[360] Case C-67/09P, *Nuova Agricast srl v Commission* [2010] ECR I-9811, para 26; Case C-616/12P, *Ellinika Nafpigeia AE v Commission* EU:C:2013:884, para 32; Case T-466/11, *Ellinika Nafpigeia AE v Commission* EU:T:2012:558, para 26; Case T-205/11, *Germany v Commission* EU:T:2012:704, para 52.

[361] Case C-122/95, *Germany v Council* [1998] ECR I-973, para 35; Case T-14/96, *BAI v Commission* [1999] ECR II-139, para 33; Case T-11/95, *BP Chemicals Limited v Commission* [1998] ECR II-3235, para 47; Case T-110/97, *Kneissl Dachstein Sportartikel AG v Commission* [1999] ECR II-2881, para 41; Case T-123/97, *Salomon SA v Commission* [1999] ECR II-2925, para 42; Case T-296/97, *Alitalia v Commission* [2000] ECR II-3871, para 61; Case T-190/00, *Regione Siciliana v Commission* [2003] ECR II-5015, para 30; Case T-17/02, *Fred Olsen SA v Commission* [2005] ECR II-2031, para 73; Case T-426/04, *Tramarin Snc di Tramarin Anrea e Sergio v Commission* [2005] ECR II-4765, para 48; Case T-144/04, *TF1 v Commission* [2008] ECR II-761, para 19; Case T-388/02, *Kronoply GmbH v Commission* [2008] ECR II-305*, para 29; Case T-354/05, *TF1 v Commission* [2009] ECR II-471, para 33; Cases T-273/06 & T-297/06, *ISD Polska v Commission* [2009] ECR II-2185, para 55.

[362] Case C-122/95, *Germany v Council* [1998] ECR I-973, para 39; Case T-14/96, *BAI v Commission* [1999] ECR II-139, para 36; Case T-110/97, *Kneissl Dachstein Sportartikel AG v Commission* [1999] ECR II-2881, para 43; Case T-123/97, *Salomon SA v Commission* [1999] ECR II-2925, para 44; Case T-296/97, *Alitalia v Commission* [2000] ECR II-3871, para 63; Case T-17/02, *Fred Olsen SA v Commission* [2005] ECR II-2031, para 80; Case T-426/04, *Tramarin Snc di Tramarin Anrea e Sergio v Commission* [2005] ECR II-4765, para 49; Case T-144/04, *TF1 v Commission* [2008] ECR II-761, para 20.

[363] Council Regulation (EC) No 659/1999, Article 26(3). These decisions are published in the L series of the *Official Journal*, whereas all other Commission decisions are published in the C series.

[364] Council Regulation (EC) No 659/1999, Article 26(5).

[365] *Ibid.*, Article 26(2).

Other decisions following a preliminary assessment on new aid, finding that the measure does not constitute the grant of aid or that the aid is compatible with the internal market, as well as recommendations on appropriate measures for existing aid merit only publication of a summary notice which must state that a copy of the decision may be obtained in the authentic language version.[366] Such a notice, the purpose of which is to provide interested third parties with a brief summary of the main facts of the decision, mentions, in essence, the Member State involved, the aid number, its title, objective, legal basis, amount and intensity, the budget allocated to it and its duration. In practice, the publication of a summary notice includes a reference to the Commission's website where the full non-confidential text of the decision is available. The General Court has held that the fact that the Commission gives third parties full access to the text of a decision placed on its website, combined with publication of a summary notice in the *Official Journal* enabling interested parties to identify the decision in question and notifying them of this possibility of access via the internet, must be considered as publication for the purposes of Article 263 TFEU.[367] The fact that access to the text of the decision is not immediate does not invalidate this conclusion.[368] A short notice is only required in two separate circumstances: where aid is deemed to be authorised where the Commission has failed to take a decision within two months following notification; and where the Commission closes a formal investigation procedure following the withdrawal by a Member State of a notification of aid.[369]

Notification to the addressee Notification is made, pursuant to Article 297(3) TFEU, only to the addressee of the decision. Where the applicant is not the addressee of the decision, the ECJ has held that the criterion of notification is thus not applicable to it.[370] Nevertheless, pursuant to Regulation (EC) No 659/1999, Article 20(1), any interested party who has submitted comments to the Commission in a formal investigation procedure and any beneficiary of individual aid must, be sent a copy of the Commission's decision terminating

---

[366] *Ibid.*, Article 26(1).

[367] Case T-17/02, *Fred Olsen SA v Commission* [2005] ECR II-2031, para 80; Case T-321/04, *Air Bourbon SAS v Commission* [2005] ECR I-3469, para 34; Case T-426/04, *Tramarin Snc di Tramarin Anrea e Sergio v Commission* [2005] ECR II-4765, para 53; Case T-375/03, *Fachvereinigung Mineralfaserindustrie eV v Commission* [2007] ECR II-121*, para 74; Case T-327/04, *SNIV v Commission* [2008] ECR II-72*, para 27; Case T-388/02, *Kronoply GmbH v Commission* [2008] ECR II-305*, para 32; Case T-354/05, *TF1 v Commission* [2009] ECR II-471, para 35.

[368] Case T-426/04, *Tramarin Snc di Tramarin Anrea e Sergio v Commission* [2005] ECR II-4765, para 55; Case T-388/02, *Kronoply GmbH v Commission* [2008] ECR II-305*, para 33.

[369] Council Regulation (EC) No 659/1999, Article 26(4).

[370] Case C-309/95, *Commission v Council* [1998] ECR I-655, para 17; Case T-17/02, *Fred Olsen SA v Commission* [2005] ECR II-2031, para 76.

the formal investigation. It is not yet clear that this constitutes notification, as opposed to merely having knowledge, for the purposes of Article 263 TFEU and the General Court has left open the question of whether a decision may be notified to a person other than the addressee.[371]

Knowledge of the decision Failing publication or notification, a party who has knowledge of a decision concerning it should request the whole text from the Commission within a reasonable period. Subject thereto, the period for bringing an action can begin to run only from the moment when the third party concerned acquires precise knowledge of the content of the decision and of the reasons on which it is based in such a way as to enable it to exercise its right of action.[372] In *BAI v Commission*, the Commission argued that this criterion was satisfied by a press release sent to the applicant on the date of the decision repeating the main points of the decision, in particular the reasoning on the basis of which the Commission concluded that the measure in question did not constitute State aid.[373] In *Fred Olsen v Commission*, the General Court held that this criterion was not fulfilled in the case of an e-mail sent to the applicant by the Commission attaching a copy of a non-confidential version of a decision sent to the Spanish authorities but specifically stating that the decision would be published in the *Official Journal* in the near future and that the e-mail did not in any event constitute a formal commitment on the part of the Commission.[374] In *Commission v Council*, which concerned a Council decision addressed to a Member State, a draft of which was disclosed to the Commission and the procedure for the adoption of which was the subject of minutes drawn up by the Commission's secretariat, the Commission was held to have had precise and detailed knowledge of the decision at the latest by the date on which the minutes were drawn up.[375]

---

[371] Case T-11/95, *BP Chemicals Limited v Commission* [1998] ECR II-3235, para 52; Case T-17/02, *Fred Olsen SA v Commission* [2005] ECR II-2031, para 76.

[372] Case 59/84, *Tezi Textiel BV v Commission* [1986] ECR 887, paras 10-11; Case 236/86 *Dillinger Hüttenwerke* v *Commission* [1988] ECR 3761, para 14; Case C-180/88, *Wirtschaftsvereinigung Eisen- und Stahlindustrie v Commission* [1990] ECR I-4413, para 22; Case C-309/95 *Commission* v *Council* [1998] ECR I-655, para 18; Case T-17/02, *Fred Olsen SA v Commission* [2005] ECR II-2031, para 73.

[373] Case T-14/96, *BAI v Commission* [1999] ECR II-139, para 27.

[374] Case T-17/02, *Fred Olsen SA v Commission* [2005] ECR II-2031, para 76; Cases T-273/06 & T-297/06, *ISD Polska v Commission* [2009] ECR II-2185, para 58.

[375] Case C-309/95, *Commission v Council* [1998] ECR I-655, para 22.

Chapter Twenty

JUDICIAL REVIEW OF EU DECISIONS: SUBSTANCE

20.1 GROUNDS OF REVIEW

Grounds of review State aid decisions of the Commission or the Council may be annulled by the ECJ or General Court pursuant to Article 263 TFEU on grounds of lack of competence, infringement of an essential procedural requirement, infringement of the EU Treaties or of any rule of law relating to its application, or misuse of powers. The burden of proof in an action for annulment lies on the applicant challenging the decision.[1] An application for judicial review may be based on any relevant legal argument, and there is nothing, for instance, to prevent an applicant from developing a legal plea which it did not raise, as an interested party, during the formal investigation procedure.[2] Certain fundamental principles, such as the requirement to state adequate reasons or an infringement of essential procedural requirements, are matters of public policy which, even if the applicant fails to raise them, the General Court or ECJ may raise of its own motion, whereas allegations concerning the substantive legality of the decision may be examined by the court only if they are raised by the applicant.[3]

---

[1]   Case T-110/97, *Kneissl Dachstein Sportartikel AG v Commission* [1999] ECR II-2881, para 45; Case T-123/97, *Salomon SA v Commission* [1999] ECR II-2925, para 46

[2]   Case T-110/97, *Kneissl Dachstein Sportartikel AG v Commission* [1999] ECR II-2881, para 102; Case T-123/97, *Salomon SA v Commission* [1999] ECR II-2925, para 55; Case T-274/01, *Valmont Nederland BV v Commission* [2004] ECR II-3145, para 102; Cases T-111/01 & T-133/01, *Saxonia Edelmetalle GmbH v Commission* [2005] ECR II-1579, para 68; Case T-217/02, *Ter Lembeek International NV v Commission* [2006] ECR II-4483, para 84; Case T-442/03, *SIC v Commission* [2008] ECR II-1161, para 141.

[3]   Case C-367/95P, *Sytraval v Commission* [1998] ECR I-1719, para 67; Case C-457/00, *Belgium v Commission* [2003] ECR I-6931, para 102; Case C-295/07P, *Commission v Département du Loiret* [2008] ECR I-9363, para 57; Case C-89/08P, *Commission v Ireland* [2009] ECR I-11245, para 34; Case C-212/12P, *Commission v Ireland* EU:C:2013:812, para 28; Cases T-228/99 & T-233/99, *Westdeutsche Landesbank Girozentrale v Commission* [2003] ECR II-435, para 143. Case T-166/01, *Lucchini SpA v Commission* [2006] ECR II-2875, para 144; Cases T-50/06 etc., *Ireland v Commission* [2007] ECR II-172*, para 46; Cases T-309/04, T-317/04, T-329/04 & T-336/04, *TV2/Danmark A/S v Commission* [2008] ECR II-2935, para 215.

Limits to judicial review It may not be sufficient merely to establish the applicability of any of these infringements. If the breach of the rule concerned is not such as to affect the probity of the underlying decision, the court may refuse to exercise its discretion to annul the decision. For instance, it is an infringement of the right to be heard for the Commission to fail to inform a Member State of information which an interested party has given it in the course of an investigation so as to afford the Member State concerned the opportunity to comment on those observations.[4] For such an infringement of the right to a fair hearing to result in annulment of the decision, it must be established that, had it not been for the irregularity, the outcome of the procedure might have been different.[5] Similarly, a finding that the Commission has made an error of assessment will not result in the decision being annulled if, in the circumstances, the mistake had no influence on the result.[6]

Thus, in *González y Díez SA v Commission*, the fact that the Commission applied rules on State aid in the coal sector based on Regulation (EC) No 1407/2002 rather than Decision 3632/93/ECSC did not have any repercussions on the meaning and content of the Commission's decision, since the applicable substantive rules were identical in both measures.[7] In *Asociación de Estaciones de Servicio de Madrid v Commission*, where the Commission was held to have acted unreasonably in its preliminary investigation by taking 28 months to reach a decision that the contested measure did not constitute State aid, the General Court held that there was nothing in the circumstances apart from the unreasonable length of that period to suggest that the Commission had made a mistake in its conclusions.[8] In *Technische Glaswerke Ilmenau v Commission*, it was alleged that there was an infringement of the obligation in Article 20(1) of Council Regulation (EC) No 659/1999 to send a copy of the Commission's decision to the recipient as an interested party. The General Court held that, even if the obligation had been infringed, this could not affect the legality of the decision, since it was an obligation only to take certain steps after the decision had been adopted whereas the legality of the decision itself

---

[4] Case 234/84, *Belgium v Commission* [1986] ECR 2263, paras 27-29; Case 40/85, *Belgium v Commission* [1986] ECR 2321, paras 28-30; Case 259/85, *France v Commission* [1987] ECR 4393, para 12.

[5] Case 259/85, *France v Commission* [1987] ECR 4393, para 13; Case C-301/87, *France v Commission* [1990] ECR I-307, para 31; Case C-142/87, *Belgium v Commisssion* [1990] ECR I-959, para 48; Case C-288/96, *Germany v Commission* [2000] ECR I-8237, para 99; Case C-404/04P, *Technische Glaswerke Ilmenau GmbH v Commission* [2007] ECR I-1*, para 131; Case T-211/05, *Italy v Commission* [2009] ECR II-2777, para 45.

[6] Case T-126/99, *Graphischer Maschinenbau GmbH v Commission* [2002] ECR II-2427, para 49; Case T-157/01, *Danske Busvognmaend v Commission* [2004] ECR II-197, para 58.

[7] T-25/04, *González y Díez SA v Commission* [2007] ECR II-3121, para 77.

[8] Case T-95/03, *Asociación de Estaciones de Servicio de Madrid v Commission* [2006] ECR II-4739, para 136.

had to be assessed by reference to the facts and legal factors prevailing at the time of its adoption.[9]

It is not generally acceptable for the Commission to seek to remedy a fault in a decision in the course of judicial review proceedings. Thus, in *SIDE v Commission*, where the Commission's decision was held to be unlawful in that it applied the exemption in Article 107(3)(d) TFEU to the period before it came into effect on 1 November 1993, the General Court refused to consider that Article 107(3)(c) TFEU would have been a valid basis for the exemption.[10]

Lack of competence The Council or the Commission can only act where the FEU Treaty or secondary legislation provides the necessary power. Where action is taken which exceeds this power, proceedings for annulment may be brought alleging lack of competence. The Commission, on this basis, has on several occasions challenged the right of the Council to adopt decisions permitting certain aid pursuant to Article 108(2) TFEU after the Commission had already taken decisions declaring the aid incompatible with the internal market.[11] In *Belgium v Commission*, Belgium argued unsuccessfully *inter alia* that the Commission, in adopting Regulation (EC) No 2204/2002 on aid for employment, had exceeded its competence, on the ground that Article 153(3) TFEU reserved to the Council the right to adopt measures concerning financial contributions for the promotion of employment.[12]

Essential procedural requirements Infringement of an essential procedural requirement may lead to annulment of the decision. For example, the obligation to state reasons is an essential procedural requirement, as distinct from the question whether the reasons given are correct.[13] It is not necessary that the procedural requirement in question be for the direct benefit or protection of the applicant. Thus, an applicant in State aid cases bringing an action for annulment as an interested person may invoke an infringement of the right to be heard by the Member State that granted the aid. In *Westdeutsche Landesbank Girozentrale v Commission*, the Commission argued that the applicant could not rely on an alleged infringement of Germany's right to be heard. The General Court held, however, that, having regard to the Member State's central role in the procedure, it must be held that its right to be heard constituted an essential procedural requirement and that failure to comply with

---

[9] Case T-198/01, *Technische Glaswerke Ilmenau GmbH v Commission* [2004] ECR II-2717, para 220.

[10] Case T-348/04, *SIDE v Commission* [2008] ECR II-625, para 69.

[11] Case C-110/02, *Commission v Council* [2004] ECR I-6333, para 47; Case C-399/03, *Commission v Council* [2006] ECR I-5629, para 29; Case C-117/10, *Commission v Council* EU:C:2013:786.

[12] Case C-110/03, *Belgium v Commission* [2005] ECR I-2801, paras 76-81.

[13] Case T-36/06, *Bundesverband Deutscher Banken v Commission* [2010] ECR II-537, para 47.

that requirement entails the nullity of a Commission decision ordering that aid be abolished or altered. Consequently, the beneficiary of the aid, and the local government body which had granted it, had a legitimate interest in pleading such a defect in the Commission's decision where a failure to comply with the Member State's right to be heard may have a bearing on the legality of the contested measure.[14]

Infringement of the EU Treaties Most often, in the context of actions for annulment in State aid cases, the allegation will be that there has been an infringement of some aspect of Articles 107-109 TFEU. Infringement of any other provision of the EU Treaties will equally be susceptible to challenge. Most particularly, in exercising its discretion to allow State aid as being compatible with the internal market, the Commission is required to ensure that Articles 107 and 108 TFEU are applied consistently with other provisions of the FEU Treaty.[15]

Infringement of rule of law relating to application of the EU Treaties Rules of law relating to the application of the EU Treaties include certain provisions of international law, such as international treaties and customary international law, as well as the general principles of EU law that have been recognised by the ECJ and the General Court. General principles include the principles of effectiveness, equality, legal certainty, protection of legitimate expectations, proportionality, protection of property and sound administration.

Misuse of powers Decisions of the Council or the Commission may be challenged as a misuse of powers or abuse of process.[16] A measure may amount to a misuse of power only if it appears, on the basis of objective, relevant and consistent factors, to have been taken with the exclusive purpose, or at any rate the main purpose, of achieving an end other than that stated or of evading a procedure specifically provided for dealing with the circumstances of the case.[17] In *Kronoply v Commission*, it was unsuccessfully argued that the

---

[14] Cases T-228/99 & T-233/99, *Westdeutsche Landesbank Girozentrale v Commission* [2003] ECR II-435, paras 140-142.

[15] Case C-225/91 *Matra* v *Commission* [1993] ECR I-3203, para 42; Case C-110/03, *Belgium v Commission* [2005] ECR I-2801, para 64.

[16] Case C-225/91, *Matra SA v Commission* [1993] ECR I-3203, para 25.

[17] Case C-331/88, *R v MAFF, ex parte Fedesa* [1990] ECR I-4023, para 24; Case C-48/96P *Windpark Groothusen* v *Commission* [1998] ECR I-2873, para 52; Case C-110/97, *Netherlands* v *Council* [2001] ECR I-8763, para 137; Case C-310/99, *Italy* v *Commission* [2002] ECR I-2289, para 47; Cases C-186/02P & C-188/02P, *Ramondin SA v Commission* [2004] ECR I-10653, para 44; Case C-400/99, *Italy v Commission* [2005] ECR I-3657, para 38; Cases T-244 & 486/93, *TWD v Commission* [1995] ECR II-2265, para 61; Case T-57/91, *NALOO v Commission* [1996] ECR II-1019, para 327; Case T-234/95, *Dradenauer Stahlgesellschaft mbH v Commission* [2000] ECR II-2603, para

Commission had misused its powers by not fully examining the criterion of incentive effect in relation to an aid for investment that had already taken place in order to be able to conclude that there was no such effect.[18] In *Italy v Commission*, where the Commission classified a measure in its decision opening the formal investigation as new aid, the ECJ held that a misuse of power could only have been established if it had been shown that the Commission had deliberately classified as new aid measures about whose status as existing aid or as measures not falling within the scope of Article 107 TFEU it could have entertained no doubts, that is to say if it had been shown that the Commission had sought deliberately to bring about within a short period the suspension of measures about whose capability of being implemented legally, at least until closure of the procedure, it could not have entertained any doubts. At the date of adoption of the decision and in the light of the information then available to the Commission, it did not appear to be beyond doubt that the subsidies paid to the Tirrenia group in excess of the net additional costs linked with the provision of services in the general economic interest, covered by the suspension deriving from that decision, constituted either existing aid or measures not incorporating any element of aid.[19]

It was alleged in the Basque tax cases that the Commission's decisions investigating the tax measures as State aid were taken in order to pursue a tax harmonisation objective, that the contested decisions were part of a larger endeavour on the Commission's part to call into question the entire Basque tax system and that the Commission was attempting to achieve tax harmonisation by means of State aid politics instead of taking the proper course laid down by the EC Treaty, that is to say the procedure provided for in Articles 116 TFEU and 117 TFEU. This allegation was rejected as entirely unsubstantiated and based on subjective speculation.[20] Similarly, in the *Olympic Airways* case, the General Court rejected the contention that the Commission's decision requiring

---

193; Cases T-12/99 & T-63/99, *UK Coal plc v Commission* [2001] ECR II-2153, para 158; Case T-158/99, *Thermenhotel Stoiser Franz GmbH v Commission* [2004] ECR II-1, para 164; Case T-17/03, *Schimtz-Gotha Fahrzeugwerke GmbH v Commission* [2006] ECR II-1139, para 81; Case T-68/03, *Olympiaki Aeroporia Ypiresies AE v Commission* [2007] ECR II-2911, para 484; Case T-70/07, *Cantieri Navali Termoli SpA v Commission* [2008] ECR II-250*, para 93; Cases T-267/08 & T-279/08, *Région Nord-Pas-de-Calais v Commission* [2011] ECR II-1999, para 196; Case T-570/08 RENV, *Deutsche Post AG v Commission* EU:T:2013:589, para 142.

18 Case T-162/06, *Kronoply GmbH v Commission* [2009] ECR II-1, paras 114-120.

19 Case C-400/99, *Italy v Commission* [2005] ECR I-3657, paras 39-40.

20 Cases T-92/00 & T-103/00, *Territorio Histórico de Álava - Diputación Foral de Álava v Commission* [2002] ECR II-1385, paras 85-87, upheld on appeal in Cases C-186/02P & C-188/02P, *Ramondin SA v Commission* [2004] ECR I-10653, paras 45-48. Cases T-269/99, T-271/99 & T-272/99, *Territorio Histórico de Álava – Diputación Foral de Álava v Commission* [2002] ECR II-4217, paras 90-93; Cases T-346/99, T-347/99 & T-348/99, *Territorio Histórico de Álava – Diputación Foral de Álava v Commission* [2002] ECR II-4259, paras 86-90.

recovery of restructuring aid involved a particularly rigorous application of the State aid rules for the purpose, in particular, of reducing the number of airlines in Europe.[21] An allegation in *Schmitz-Gotha Fahrzeugwerke v Commission* that the real aim of the Commission in taking a decision rejecting restructuring aid was to sanction an alleged enrichment of the manager of the recipient undertaking was rejected by the General Court on the ground that there was no objective evidence to support it.[22]

20.2 REVIEW OF THE COMMISSION'S ASSESSMENT

Error of assessment State aid control involves the application of the State aid rules to a given factual situation. Where the Commission is found to have committed a sufficient error of assessment, the decision will be annulled.[23] The courts must in principle, having regard both to the specific features of the case before them and to the technical or complex nature of the Commission's assessments, carry out a comprehensive review as to whether a measure falls within the scope of Article 107(1) TFEU.[24] Thus, in *Valmont Nederland v Commission*, where the Commission had decided that State aid was involved in the sale of land by a public authority, basing its decision on a report that had been furnished to it by the Netherlands authorities whilst rejecting another report commissioned by the recipient, the General Court held that it was entitled to review fully whether the Commission had based itself exclusively

---

[21] Case T-68/03, *Olympiaki Aeroporia Ypiresies AE v Commission* [2007] ECR II-2911, para 485.

[22] Case T-17/03, *Schimtz-Gotha Fahrzeugwerke GmbH v Commission* [2006] ECR II-1139, paras 82-84

[23] Case C-169/84, *CDF Chimie AZF v Commission* [1990] ECR I-3083, para 52; Case T-155/98, *SIDE v Commission* [2002] ECR II-1179, paras 71-73; Cases T-227/99 & T-134/00, *Kvaerner Warnow Werft GmbH v Commission* [2002] ECR II-1205, paras 110-112.

[24] Case C-83/98P, *France v Ladbroke Racing Ltd. and Commission* [2000] I-3271, para 25; Case C-487/06P, *British Aggregates Association v Commission* [2008] ECR I-10515, para 111; Case T-67/94, *Ladbroke Racing v Commission* [1998] ECR II-1, para 52; Case T-296/97 *Alitalia v Commission* [2000] ECR II-3871, para 95; Case T-613/97, *Ufex v Commission* [2000] ECR I-4055, para 67; Cases T-195/01R & T-207/01R, *Government of Gibraltar v Commission* [2001] ECR II-3915, para 75; Case T-198/01R, *Technische Glaswerke Ilmenau GmbH v Commission* [2002] ECR II-2153, para 76; Case T-152/99, *Hijos de Andrés Molina SA v Commission* [2002] ECR II-3049, para 159; Case T-98/00, *Linde AG v Commission* [2002] ECR II-3961, para 40; Case T-274/01, *Valmont Nederland BV v Commission* [2004] ECR II-3145, para 37; Case T-366/00 *Scott SA v Commission* [2007] ECR II-797, para 91; Case T-68/03, *Olympiaki Aeroporia Ypiresies AE v Commission* [2007] ECR II-2911, para 284; Case T-196/04, *Ryanair Ltd v Commission* [2008] ECR II-3643, para 40; Cases T-211/04 & T-215/04, *Government of Gibraltar v Commission* [2008] ECR II-3745, para 142; Cases T-226/09 & T-230/09, *British Telecommunications plc v Commission* EU:T:2013:466, para 39.

on a report devoid of any evidential value.[25] In *Scott v Commission*, which
also involved a sale of land at a purportedly advantageous price, the General
Court held that the mere fact that the Commission might have had to resort to
an approximate evaluation, owing to the significant period of time that had
elapsed since the transaction such that it was difficult to determine the precise
value of any aid by reference to the prevailing market value, did not mean that
it had a margin of appreciation with regard to the determination of the amount
to be recovered.[26]

A minor error, caused by a slip of the pen, does not affect the validity of the
decision as long as it has no effect on the content of the decision.[27] Otherwise,
the ECJ and the General Court, when examining the lawfulness of the exercise
of discretion cannot substitute their own assessment of the matter for that of the
Commission.[28] For the most part, these rules are to be determined objectively
and judicial review will lie in order to ensure that they have been complied
with.   In general, the question whether a measure constitutes State aid must be
determined on the basis of objective elements, which must be appraised on the
date on which the Commission takes its decision.[29]

Manifest error of assessment   Insofar as the Commission enjoys a wide
discretion in applying the State aid provisions, the exercise of which involves
complex appraisal of an economic and social nature, the review of legality of
its decisions is restricted, in this respect, to determining whether the
Commission has exceeded the scope of its discretion by a distortion or
manifest error of assessment of the facts.[30]   Such an appraisal may be

---

25   Case T-274/01, *Valmont Nederland BV v Commission* [2004] ECR II-3145, para 43.
26   Case T-366/00 *Scott SA v Commission* [2007] ECR II-797, para 96.
27   Case T-328/09, *Producteurs de légumes de France v Commission* EU:T:2012:498, para
     35.
28   Case C-169/95, *Spain v Commission* [1997] ECR I-135, para 34; Case C-288/96,
     Germany v Commission [2000] ECR I-8237, para 26; Case C-487/06P, *British
     Aggregates Association v Commission* [2008] ECR I-10515, para 141; Case C-290/07P,
     Commission v Scott SA [2010] ECR I-7763, para 66; Case C-73/11P, *Frucona Košice as
     v Commission* EU:C:2013:32, para 89; Cases T-371/94 & 394/94, *British Airways v
     Commission* [1998] ECR II-2405, para 79; Cases T-127/99, T-129/99 & T-148/99,
     Territorio Histórico de Álava - Disputación Foral de Álava v Commission [2002] ECR
     II-1275, para 273; Case T-274/01, *Valmont Nederland BV v Commission* [2004] ECR II-
     3145, para 136; Case T-198/01, *Technische Glaswerke Ilmenau GmbH v Commission*
     [2004] ECR II-2717, para 97; Case T-266/02, *Deutsche Post AG v Commission* [2008]
     ECR II-1233, para 95; Case T-301/01, *Alitalia SpA v Commission* [2008] ECR II-1753,
     para 185.
29   Cases C-182/03 & C-217/03, *Belgium and Forum 187 v Commission* [2006] ECR I-
     5479, para 137; Cases C-341/06P & C-342/06P, *Chronopost v Ufex* [2008] ECR I-4777,
     para 95; Case C-334/07P, *Commission v Freistaat Sachsen* [2008] ECR I-9465, para 50.
30   Case C-225/91, *Matra SA v Commission* [1993] ECR I-3203, para 25; Case C-56/93,
     Belgium v Commission [1996] ECR I-723, para 11; Case C-310/99, *Italy v Commission*
     [2002] ECR I-2289, para 46; Case C-456/00 *France v Commission* [2002] ECR I-11949,

necessary, for example, in determining whether a private investor would have been prepared in similar circumstances to inject capital into a company,[31] or whether a private vendor would have acted in the same way as a public authority;[32] or whether the aid should be deemed compatible with the internal market under Article 107(3) TFEU[33] or whether a service falls within the notion of a service of general economic interest for the purposes of Article 106(2) TFEU.[34] Similarly, any assessment by the Commission in determining whether companies which form part of a group should be regarded as an economic unit or rather as legally and financially independent will involve the exercise of a broad discretion.[35]

To establish a manifest error of assessment, there must be sufficient evidence that the Commission must have made an obvious error of evaluation of the situation.[36] The evidence adduced must be such as to make the factual assessments used in the decision implausible.[37] Nevertheless, whilst the

---

para 41; Cases C-328/99 & C-399/00, *Italy v Commission* [2003] ECR I-4135, para 39; Case C-110/03, *Belgium v Commission* [2005] ECR I-2801, para 68; Case C-66/02 *Italy v Commission* [2005] ECR I-10901, para 135; Case C-88/03, *Portugal v Commission* [2006] ECR I-7115, para 99; Cases T-371/94 & 394/94, *British Airways v Commission* [1998] ECR II-2405, para 293; Case T-35/99, *Keller SpA v Commission* [2002] ECR II-261, para 77; Case T-274/01, *Valmont Nederland BV v Commission* [2004] ECR II-3145, para 37; Cases T-111/01 & T-133/01, *Saxonia Edelmetalle GmbH v Commission* [2005] ECR II-1579, para 91; Case T-266/02, *Deutsche Post AG v Commission* [2008] ECR II-1233, para 90.

[31] Case T-301/01, *Alitalia SpA v Commission* [2008] ECR II-1753, para 185; Case T-196/04, *Ryanair Ltd v Commission* [2008] ECR II-3643, para 41; Case T-1/12, *France v Commission* EU:T:2015:17, para 35.

[32] Cases C-214/12P, C-215/12P & C-223/12P, *Land Burgenland v Commission* EU:C:2013:682, para 77; Case T-511/09, *Niki Luftfahrt GmbH v Commission* EU:T:2015:284, para 124.

[33] Case T-20/03, *Kahla/Thüringen Porzellan GmbH v Commission* [2008] ECR II-2305, para 115.

[34] Case T-17/02, *Fred Olsen SA v Commission* [2005] ECR II-2031, para 216; Case T-289/03, *BUPA Ltd v Commission* [2008] ECR II-81, para 166.

[35] Case C-323/00P, *Dradenauer Stahlgesellschaft mbH v Commission* [2002] ECR II-3919, para 33; Cases T-371/94 & T-394/94, *British Airways v Commission* [1998] ECR II-2405, para 314; Case T-137/02, *Pollmeier Malchow GmbH v Commission* [2004] ECR II-3541, para 51; Case T-89/09, *Pollmeier Massivholz GmbH v Commission* EU:T:2015:153, para 123.

[36] Case C-399/95R, *Germany v Commission* [1996] ECR I-2441, para 63. See, for example, Case C-525/04P, *Spain v Commission* [2007] ECR I-9947, paras 59-61; Cases T-127/99, T-129/99 &T-148/99, *Territorio Histórico de Álava - Diputación Foral de Álava v Commission* [2002] ECR II-1275, paras 63-92; Case T-126/99, *Graphischer Maschinenbau GmbH v Commission* [2002] ECR II-2427, para 88.

[37] Case T-380/94 *AIUFFASS v Commission* [1996] ECR II-2169, para 59; Case T-308/00, *Salzgitter v Commission* [2004] ECR II-1933, para 198; Case T-348/04, *SIDE v Commission* [2008] ECR II-625, para 97; Case T-68/05, *Aker Warnow Werft GmbH v Commission* [2009] ECR II-355, para 42.

Commission has a margin of discretion with regard to economic matters, that does not means that the courts must refrain from reviewing the Commission's interpretation of information of an economic nature. The court must establish not only whether the evidence relied on is factually accurate, reliable and consistent, but also whether that evidence contains all the information which must be taken into account in order to assess a complex situation and whether it is capable of substantiating the conclusions drawn from it.[38] In annulling the Commission's decision on State aid granted to Grupo de Empresas Álvarez,[39] the ECJ held that, given the fact that the Spanish authorities had produced evidence of various attempts to seize property, bank accounts and debts owed in order to cover outstanding liability for tax and social security payments, the Commission could not properly have considered that the Spanish authorities had not acted as a private creditor in seeking to recover the amounts owed.[40]

In *Frucona Košice v Commission*, the ECJ held that, by failing to take account, in its assessment of the private creditor test, of the duration of a bankruptcy procedure as an alternative to immediate partially writing off a debt, the Commission had committed a manifest error of assessment.[41] In *Corsica Ferries v Commission*, the Commission was held to have committed a manifest error of assessment in determining a particular value of assets held in a firm that was seeking restructuring aid when the Commission had at its disposal information to the contrary.[42] In *González y Díez SA v Commission*, the Commission incorrectly assessed the amount of aid that was to be recovered, despite the available evidence.[43] Similarly, in *SIDE v Commission*, the General Court annulled the Commission's decision for overestimating the costs borne by the recipient.[44] In *Aker Warnow Werft v Commission*, the Commission's decision finding that shipbuilding aid had been used to cover contract losses was held to be manifestly erroneous.[45] By contrast, the ECJ rejected Belgium's attempt to annul Commission Regulation (EC) No 2204/2002 on the ground, *inter alia*, that Belgium had failed to produce any

---

[38]   Case C-12/03P, *Commission v Tetra Laval BV* [2005] ECR I-987, para 39; Case C-525/04P, *Spain v Commission* [2007] ECR I-9947, paras 56-57; Case C-290/07P, *Commission v Scott SA* [2010] ECR I-7763, para 64; Case C-47/10P, *Austria v Commission* [2011] ECR I-10707, para 84; Case C-73/11P, *Frucona Košice as v Commission* EU:C:2013:32, para 76; Cases C-214/12P, C-215/12P & C-223/12P, *Land Burgenland v Commission* EU:C:2013:682, para 79; Case T-11/07, *Frucona Košice as v Commission* [2010] ECR II-5453, para 110.

[39]   Commission Decision 2002/935/EC, OJ 2002 L329/1.

[40]   Case C-276/02, *Spain v Commission* [2004] ECR I-8091, paras 35-36.

[41]   Case C-73/11P, *Frucona Košice as v Commission* EU:C:2013:32, para 103.

[42]   Case T-349/03, *Corsica Ferries France SAS v Commission* [2005] ECR II-2197, para 300.

[43]   Case T-25/04, *González y Díez SA v Commission* [2007] ECR II-3121, para 219.

[44]   Case T-348/04, *SIDE v Commission* [2008] ECR II-625, para 136.

[45]   Case T-68/05, *Aker Warnow Werft GmbH v Commission* [2009] ECR II-355, para 69.

evidence to support its claim that the Commission had exceeded its discretion.[46]

Decision on opening formal investigation procedure In determining whether or not to open the formal investigation procedure in respect of new aid, the Commission enjoys a certain margin of discretion in identifying and evaluating the circumstances of the case in order to determine whether or not they present serious difficulties. Whether or not the measure gives rise to serious difficulties in assessing its compatibility is to be determined objectively, comparing the grounds of the decision with the information available to the Commission when it took the decision.[47] In *Prayon-Rupel v Commission*, where the Commission did not open the formal investigation procedure, the General Court held that it followed that judicial review under Article 263 TFEU of the existence of serious difficulties would, by nature, go beyond simple consideration of whether or not the Commission has committed a manifest error of assessment.[48] In challenging a decision to approve aid following a preliminary assessment, it is the applicant who bears the burden of proving the existence of serious difficulties which would have justified the opening of the formal investigation procedure.[49]

A different approach is taken in respect of decisions by the Commission to open the formal investigation procedure. In *Government of Gibraltar v Commission,* the General Court, on an application to suspend the Commission's decision opening the formal investigation procedure, held that the applicant had to show that a manifest error of assessment had occurred.[50] In the Basque tax cases, the General Court explained that the classification of a measure as State aid in a decision to initiate the formal investigation procedure is merely provisional and the very aim of initiating the procedure is to enable

---

[46] Case C-110/03, *Belgium v Commission* [2005] ECR I-2801, paras 64-69.

[47] Case T-49/93, *SIDE v Commission* [1995] ECR II-2501, para 60; Case T-73/98, *Société Chimique Prayon-Rupel SA v Commission* [2001] ECR II-867, paras 45-47; Cases T-195/01R & T-207/01R, *Government of Gibraltar v Commission* [2001] ECR II-3915, para 78; Case T-388/03, *Deutsche Post AG v Commission* [2009] ECR II-199, para 92; Case T-520/09, *TF1 v Commission* EU:T:2012:352, para 50.

[48] Case T-73/98, *Société Chimique Prayon-Rupel SA v Commission* [2001] ECR II-867, para 47; Case T-388/03, *Deutsche Post AG v Commission* [2009] ECR II-199, para 92; Case T-520/09, *TF1 v Commission* EU:T:2012:352, para 50; Case T-359/04, *British Aggregates v Commission* [2010] ECR II-4227, para 56; Case T-137/10, *CBI v Commission* EU:T:2012:584, para 76.

[49] Case T-73/98, *Société Chimique Prayon-Rupel SA v Commission* [2001] ECR II-867, para 49; Case T-388/03, *Deutsche Post AG v Commission* [2009] ECR II-199, para 93; Case T-36/06, *Bundesverband Deutscher Banken v Commission* [2010] ECR II-537, para 127; Case T-520/09, *TF1 v Commission* EU:T:2012:352, para 49; Case T-325/10, *Iliad v Commission* EU:T:2013:472, para 38.

[50] Cases T-195/01R & T-207/01R, *Government of Gibraltar v Commission* [2001] ECR II-3915, para 79.

the Commission to obtain all the views it needs in order to be able to adopt a definitive decision on the point. In order to avoid confusion between the administrative and judicial proceedings, and to preserve the division of powers between the Commission and the court, any review of the legality of a decision to initiate the formal investigation procedure must necessarily be limited. The court must in fact avoid giving a final ruling on questions on which the Commission had merely formed a provisional view.[51] This approach has been confirmed by the ECJ.[52]

Assessment on basis of facts and law when measure was adopted In the context of an application for annulment under Article 263 TFEU, the legality of the contested measure must be assessed on the basis of the elements of fact and of law existing at the time when the measure was adopted.[53] It follows that the legality of a decision concerning State aid must be assessed in the light of the information available to the Commission when the decision was adopted.[54] It is also appropriate to take into consideration information in the

---

[51] Cases T-269/99, T-271/99 & T-272/99, *Territorio Histórico de Álava – Diputación Foral de Álava v Commission* [2002] ECR II-4217, paras 47-49; Cases T-346/99, T-347/99 & T-348/99, *Territorio Histórico de Álava – Diputación Foral de Álava v Commission* [2002] ECR II-4259, paras 43-45.

[52] Case C-194/09P, *Alcoa Trasformazioni srl v Commission* [2011] ECR I-6311, para 61; Case T-332/06, *Alcoa Trasformazioni Srl v Commission* [2009] II-29*, paras 60-62.

[53] Cases 15 & 16/76, *France v Commission* [1979] ECR 321, para 7.

[54] Case C-234/84, *Belgium v Commission* [1986] ECR 2263, para 16; Case C-241/94, *France v Commission* [1996] ECR I-4551, para 33; Case C-288/96, *Germany v Commission* [2000] ECR I-8237, para 34; Case C-382/99, *Netherlands v Commission* [2002] ECR I-5163, para 49; Cases C-74/00P & C-75/00P, *Falck v Commission* [2002] ECR I-7869, para 168; Case C-394/01, *France v Commission* [2002] ECR I-8245, para 34; Case C-197/99P, *Belgium v Commission* [2003] ECR I-8461, para 86; Case C-277/00, *Germany v Commission* [2004] ECR I-3925, para 39; Case C-276/02, *Spain v Commission* [2004] ECR I-8091, para 31; Case C-390/06, *Nuova Agricast Srl v Ministero delle Attività Produttive* [2008] ECR I-2577, para 54; Case C-333/07, *Régie Networks v Direction de Contrôle Fiscal Rhône-Alpes Bourgogne* [2008] ECR I-10807, para 81; Cases T-371/94 & 394/94, *British Airways v Commission* [1998] ECR II-2405, para 81; Case T-296/97, *Alitalia v Commission* [2000] ECR II-3871, para 86; Case T-73/98, *Société Chimique Prayon Rupel SA v Commission* [2001] ECR II-867, para 49; Case T-35/99, *Keller SpA v Commission* [2002] ECR II-261, para 83; Case T-126/99, *Graphischer Maschinenbau GmbH v Commission* [2002] ECR II-2427, para 33; Case T-354/99, *Kuwait Petroleum (Nederland) BV v Commission* [2006] ECR II-1475, para 65; Case T-366/00, *Scott v Commission* [2007] ECR II-797, para 45; Case T-246/99, *Tirrenia di Navizagione SpA v Commission* [2007] ECR II-65*, para 108; Case T-20/03, *Kahla/Thüringen Porzellan GmbH v Commission* [2008] ECR II-2305, para 269; Cases T-254/00, T-270/00 & T-277/00, *Hotel Cipriani SpA v Commission* [2008] ECR II-3269, para 238.

public domain that was without doubt available to the Commission at that time.[55]

A Member State which seeks to be allowed to grant aid has a duty to collaborate with the Commission. In pursuance of that duty, it must in particular provide all the information to enable the Commission to verify that the conditions for the derogations sought are fulfilled. Where the Member State has not fulfilled this duty of cooperation so that the Commission has only a small amount of information at its disposal, the Commission cannot be charged with having erred in its assessment.[56] In *Scott v Commission*, the French authorities submitted a document to the Commission but omitted certain pages, which was not obvious from the pages sent. As a result, the Commission could not be blamed for not having asked the French authorities to submit the missing pages, so that the legality of the decision could not be assessed in light of the content of those pages.[57]

Where an interested party has submitted factual information during the administrative procedure that has not been challenged by the Member State that allegedly granted aid, the Member State cannot for the first time at the judicial stage challenge those observations.[58] Equally, where an applicant has participated in the formal investigation procedure, it may not rely on factual arguments which it has not notified to the Commission and which are unknown to it.[59] This applies also, save in entirely exceptional cases, where the applicant did not participate in the formal investigation procedure, particularly if it was mentioned by name during that procedure as being the beneficiary of the aid.[60] Once the Commission has given the interested parties the opportunity to submit their comments, it cannot be criticised for having failed to take account of any elements of fact which could have been submitted to it during the administrative procedure but which were not, as the Commission is under no obligation to consider, of its own motion and on the basis of prediction, what elements might have been submitted to it.[61]

---

[55] Case T-73/98, *Société Chimique Prayon Rupel SA v Commission* [2001] ECR II-867, para 50.

[56] Case C-364/90, *Italy v Commission* [1993] ECR I-2097, paras 20-22; Case C-382/99, *Netherlands v Commission* [2002] ECR I-5163, para 76.

[57] Case T-366/00, *Scott v Commission* [2007] ECR II-797, para 49.

[58] Case T-139/09, *France v Commission* EU:T:2012:496, para 55.

[59] Cases T-111/01 & T-133/01, *Saxonia Edelmetalle GmbH v Commission* [2005] ECR II-1579, para 68; Case T-217/02, *Ter Lembeek International NV v Commission* [2006] ECR II-4483, para 84; Case T-243/09, *Fedecom v Commission* EU:T:2012:497, para 40.

[60] Cases T-111/01 & T-133/01, *Saxonia Edelmetalle GmbH v Commission* [2005] ECR II-1579, para 69; Case T-217/02, *Ter Lembeek International NV v Commission* [2006] ECR II-4483, para 85.

[61] Case C-367/95P *Commission v Sytraval* [1998] ECR I-1719, para 59; Case T-109/01, *Fleuren Compost BV v Commission* [2004] ECR II-127, para 49; Case T-17/03, *Schimtz-Gotha Fahrzeugwerke GmbH v Commission* [2006] ECR II-1139, para 54.

This approach applies equally where the Commission takes a decision after a preliminary investigation procedure not to raise objections against an aid or an aid scheme, even though interested parties have not been called upon to make comments. In *Nuova Agricast v Ministero delle Attività Produttive*, the ECJ held that if the validity of a decision not to raise objections were to fall to be determined by reference to information which could not have been available to the Commission after the preliminary investigation had been concluded, the Commission would be encouraged systematically to initiate the formal investigation procedure under Article 108(2) TFEU and to give the parties concerned notice to submit their comments, in order to prevent the information which could not be available to it leading to the annulment of its decision to authorise the aid measure or the aid scheme in question. This would undermine the division of the review of State aid into two distinct stages, the second of which is not always required.[62]

20.3 STATEMENT OF REASONS

Adequate statement of reasons Every decision of the Commission must, pursuant to Article 296 TFEU, state the reasons on which it is based. It follows that the operative part of a decision is indissociably linked to the statement of reasons for it.[63] Failure on the part of the Commission to state the reasons adequately will result in the decision being annulled.[64] The obligation to state reasons is an essential procedural requirement that must be distinguished from the question of whether the reasons are correct.[65] Equally, a contradiction in

---

[62] Case C-390/06, *Nuova Agricast Srl v Ministero delle Attività Produttive* [2008] ECR I-2577, para 60.

[63] Case C-355/95P, *TWD v Commission* [1997] ECR I-2549, para 21; Case C-91/01, *Italy v Commission* [2004] ECR I-4355, para 49; Case C-415/03, *Commission v Greece* [2005] ECR I-3875, para 41; Case T-137/02, *Pollmeier Malchow GmbH v Commission* [2004] ECR II-3541, para 60; Case T-93/02, *Confédération Nationale du Crédit Mutuel v Commission* [2005] ECR II-143, para 74; Case T-150/12, *Greece v Commission* EU:T:2014:191, para 31.

[64] Case C-204/97, *Portugal v Commission* [2001] ECR I-3175, paras 50-51; Case T-68/03, *Olympiaki Aeroporia Ypiresies AE v Commission* [2007] ECR II-2911, para 318; Case T-268/06, *Olympiaki Aeroporia Ypiresies AE v Commission* [2008] ECR II-1091, para 87; Cases T-265/04, T-292/04 & T-504/04, *Tirrenia di Navigazione SpA v Commission* [2009] ECR II-21*, para 134.

[65] Case C-367/95P, *Commission v Sytraval* [1998] ECR I-1719, para 67; Case C-17/99, *France v Commission* [2001] ECR I-2481, para 35; Case C-310/99, *Italy v Commission* [2002] ECR I-2289, para 48; Case C-494/06P, *Commission v Italy* [2009] ECR I-3639, para 32; Case T-93/02, *Confédération Nationale du Crédit Mutuel v Commission* [2005] ECR II-143, para 67; Case T-150/12, *Greece v Commission* EU:T:2014:191, para 29; Case T-511/09, *Niki Luftfahrt GmbH v Commission* EU:T:2015:284, para 104; Case T-500/12 *Ryanair Ltd v Commission* EU:T:2015:73, para 34; Case T-473/12, *Aer Lingus Ltd v Commission* EU:T:2015:78, para 33.

the statement of the reasons on which a decision is based affects the validity of the decision if it is established that, as a result of that contradiction, the addressee is not in a position to ascertain, wholly or in part, the real reasons for the decision.[66] The ECJ or General Court must confine itself to checking the legality of the contested act and must not make up for the possible lack of a statement of reasons or complete the Commission's statement of reasons by adding to it or substituting it with elements that do not come from the decision itself.[67] Similarly, since the statement of reasons for a decision must appear in the actual body of the decision, save in exceptional circumstances, explanations given *ex post facto* by the Commission cannot be taken into account. It follows that the decision must be self-sufficient and that the reasons on which it is based may not be stated in written or oral explanations given subsequently when the decision in question is already the subject of judicial review proceedings.[68]

The extent of the requirement to state reasons depends on the circumstances of each case, in particular the content of the act in question, the nature of the reasons given and the needs of the addressees, or of other parties directly and individually concerned by the decision, to be informed and on the context in which it was adopted.[69] In the case of a decision adversely affecting an undertaking, the statement of reasons must be such as to allow the ECJ or General Court to review its legality and to provide the undertakings concerned

---

[66] Case T-65/96, *Kish Glass & Co Ltd. v Commission* [2000] ECR II-1885, para 85; Case T-445/05, *Associazione Italiana del Risparmio Gestito v Commission* [2009] ECR II-289, para 82.

[67] Case T-67/94, *Ladbroke Racing v Commission* [1998] ECR II-1, paras 147-148; Cases T-126/96 & T-127/96, *BFM v Commission* [1998] ECR II-3437, para 81; Case T-349/03, *Corsica Ferries France sas v Commission* [2005] ECR I-2197, para 58; Cases T-309/04, T-317/04, T-329/04 & T-336/04, *TV2/Danmark A/S v Commission* [2008] ECR II-2935, para 182.

[68] Case 195/80, *Michel v Parliament* [1981] ECR 2861, para 22; Cases C-189/02P, etc., *Dansk Rørindustri A/S v Commission* [2005] ECR I-5425, para 463; Case T-16/91, *Rendo v Commission* [1996] ECR II-1827, para 45; Case T-349/03, *Corsica Ferries France v Commission* [2005] ECR II-2197, para 287; Case T-68/03, *Olympiaki Aeroporia Ypiresies AE v Commission* [2007] ECR II-2911, para 254; Case T-25/04, *González y Díez SA v Commission* [2007] ECR II-3121, para 220; Case T-455/05, *Componenta Oyj v Commission* [2008] ECR II-336*, para 121; Cases T-309/04, T-317/04, T-329/04 & T-336/04, *TV2/Danmark A/S v Commission* [2008] ECR II-2935, para 181.

[69] Case 13/72, *Netherlands v Commission* [1973] ECR 27, para 11; Case C-341/06P & C-342/06P, *Chronopost SA v Ufex* [2008] ECR I-4777, para 88; Case C-333/07, *Régie Networks v Direction de Contrôle Fiscal Rhône-Alpes Bourgogne* [2008] ECR I-10807, Case C-150/09P, *Iride SpA v Commission* [2010] ECR I-5*, para 21; Case T-504/93, *Tiercé Ladbroke SA v Commission* [1997] ECR II-923, para 52; Case T-162/06, *Kronoply GmbH v Commission* [2009] ECR II-1, para 26; para 63; Case T-25/07, *Iride SpA v Commission* [2009] ECR II-245, para 68; Case T-308/11, *Eurallumina SpA v Commission* EU:T:2014:894, para 44.

with the information necessary to enable them to ascertain whether or not the decision is well-founded.[70] It must be appropriate to the act in issue and must disclose in a clear and unequivocal fashion the reasoning followed by the Commission, although it is not necessary for the reasoning to go into all the relevant facts and points of law. The reasoning must be assessed with regard not only to its wording but also to its context and to all the legal rules governing the matter in question.[71] If a decision clearly discloses the essential objective pursued by the Commission, it would be excessive to require a specific statement of reasons for each of the technical choices made.[72] Although a decision of the Commission which fits into a well-established line of decisions may be reasoned in a summary manner, for example by a reference to those decisions, if it goes appreciably further than the previous decisions, the Commission must give an account of its reasoning.[73]

---

[70] Cases 296/82 & 318/82, *Netherlands and Leeuwarder Papierwarenfabriek v Commission* [1985] ECR 809, para 19; Cases C-329/93 & C-62 & 63/95, *Germany v Commission* [1996] ECR I-5151, para 31; Case T-318/00, *Freistaat Thüringen v Commission* [2005] ECR II-4179, para 109; Case T-34/02, *Le Levant 001 v Commission* [2005] ECR II-267, para 111.

[71] Case C-56/93, *Belgium v Commission* [1996] ECR I-723, para 86; Case C-122/94, *Commission v Council* [1996] ECR I-881, para 29; Case C-278/95P, *Siemens SA v Commission* [1997] ECR I-2507, para 17; Case C-367/95P, *Commission v Sytraval* [1998] ECR I-1719, para 63; Cases C-15/98 & C-105/99, *Italy v Commission* [2000] ECR I-8855, para 65; Case C-17/99, *France v Commission* [2001] ECR I-2481, para 35; Case C-310/99, *Italy v Commission* [2002] ECR I-2289, para 48; Case C-301/96, *Germany v Commission* [2003] ECR I-9919, para 87; Case C-159/01, *Netherlands v Commission* [2004] ECR I-4461, para 65; Case C-66/02, *Italy v Commission* [2005] ECR I-10901, para 26; Case C-88/03, *Portugal v Commission* [2006] ECR I-7115, para 88; Case C-494/06P, *Commission v Italy* [2009] ECR I-3639, para 47; Cases T-371/94 & T-394/94, *British Airways v Commission* [1998] ECR II-2405, para 94; Case T-318/00, *Freistaat Thüringen v Commission* [2005] ECR II-4179, para 202; Case T-68/03, *Olympiaki Aeroporia Ypiresies AE v Commission* [2007] ECR II-2911, para 80; Cases T-239/04 & T-323/04, *Italy v Commission* [2007] ECR II-3265, para 118; Cases T-309/04, T-317/04, T-329/04 & T-336/04, *TV2/Danmark A/S v Commission* [2008] ECR II-2935, para 178; Case T-308/11, *Eurallumina SpA v Commission* EU:T:2014:894, para 44.

[72] Case C-122/94, *Commission v Council* [1996] ECR I-881, para 29; Case C-341/06P & C-342/06P, *Chronopost SA v Ufex* [2008] ECR I-4777, para 108.

[73] Case 73/74, *Groupement des fabricants de Papiers Peints de Belgique v Commission* [1975] ECR 1491, para 31; Case C-156/98, *Germany v Commisssion* [2000] ECR I-6857, para 105; Case C-301/96, *Germany v Commission* [2003] ECR I-9919, para 92; Case C-295/07P, *Commission v Départment du Loiret* [2008] ECR I-9363, para 44; Case C-150/09P, *Iride SpA v Commission* [2010] ECR I-5*, para 23; Case T-36/06, *Bundesverband Deutscher Banken v Commission* [2010] ECR II-537, para 61; Case T-139/09, *France v Commission* EU:T:2012:496, para 39; Case T-500/12 *Ryanair Ltd v Commission* EU:T:2015:73, para 27; Case T-473/12, *Aer Lingus Ltd v Commission* EU:T:2015:78, para 26.

Correct statement of facts The statement of reasons must contain a correct statement of the facts on which the decision is based. Even if a stated reason contains an incorrect reference of fact, for the decision to be annulled it must be established that, in the absence of that error, the decision would have been different.[74] That defect need not lead to the annulment of the decision if the other stated reasons are capable of establishing that the decision is well founded.[75] Where the Member State has been uncooperative in providing information to the Commission or has omitted certain information, and in the absence of any information to the contrary, the Commission is entitled to give a brief statement of reasons based on the information in its possession.[76] Since the Commission has the power to order a Member State to provide it with information so that an informed decision may be made, it cannot rely on the lack of information in its possession to justify an inadequately reasoned decision if it did not in fact make use of all its powers to cause the Member State to provide it with all the necessary information.[77] Where a decision to open the formal investigation procedure alleges findings of fact that are disputed, it behoves the Commission in its final decision to set out the reasons why it reaches its conclusions.[78]

The Commission must not make unsubstantiated allegations. For example, in *RSV v Commission*, the Commission, which had taken a decision finding certain State aid to a shipbuilding undertaking to be incompatible with the internal market, was unable to produce any documents to confirm its statement that the recipient undertaking's competitors had been prevented for more than two years from bidding for tenders which the recipient had set its sights on with the result that attempts by the EU shipbuilding industry to diversify had been hampered. Advocate General Slynn stated that if the Commission wished to draw an inference that competitors would be deterred from going to the considerable expense of tendering for contracts if they believed that a company such as RSV had its losses underwritten by the State, it must say so and not set out an inference as a statement of fact.[79] In *Germany v Commission*, the

---

[74] Cases T-162/94 & T-165/94, *NTN Corporation v Council* [1995] ECR II-1381, para 115; Case T-162/06, *Kronoply GmbH v Commission* [2009] ECR II-1, para 108.

[75] Cases T-129/95, T-2/96 & T-97/96 *Neue Maxhütte Stahlwerke* v *Commission* [1999] ECR II-17, para 160; Case T-318/00, *Freistaat Thüringen v Commission* [2005] ECR II-4179, para 191.

[76] Case 234/84, *Belgium v Commission* [1986] ECR 2263, para 22; Case 40/85, *Belgium v Commission* [1986] ECR 2321, para 22; Case C-364/90, *Italy v Commission* [1993] ECR I-2097, para 22; Cases T-239/04 & T-323/04, *Italy v Commission* [2007] ECR II-3265, para 124.

[77] Case C-324 & 342/90, *Germany & Pleuger Worthington v Commission* [1994] ECR I-1173, para 29.

[78] Case T-268/06, *Olympiaki Aeroporia Ypiresies AE v Commission* [2008] ECR II-1091, para 82.

[79] Case 223/85, *RSV v Commission* [1987] ECR 4617, *per* Advocate General Slynn at p. 4649.

Commission was criticised for alleging that aid had been granted to a certain undertaking without any supporting evidence or explanation to substantiate that allegation.[80]

Issues raised by interested parties and complainants The decision should set out clearly and unequivocally the reasoning which led the Commission to its conclusions such that interested parties understand the justification for the decision.[81] Since interested parties, including recipients of aid, are not treated as equivalent to the defendant Member State in administrative proceedings concerning State aid, the Commission is not required to state reasons for rejecting propositions made by such persons as exhaustively as would be the case were those arguments to be raised by the Member State.[82] The Commission is not required to address in the statement of reasons all the issues of fact and law raised by the persons concerned, as long as it has taken into account all the circumstances and all the relevant factors of the case.[83] It is sufficient if it sets out the facts and the legal considerations having decisive importance in the context of the decision.[84] Where the party concerned was closely involved in the process whereby the decision came about and is therefore aware of the reasons for which the Commission decided not to uphold its request, the scope of the obligation will be defined by the context thus created by the party's involvement in that process. In such circumstances, the requirements to state reasons are considerably relaxed.[85]

Where a complaint is rejected, the Commission must provide the complainant with an adequate explanation of the reasons for which the facts and points of law put forward in the complaint have failed to prove the

---

[80] Cases C-329/93, C-62/95 & C-63/95, *Germany v Commission* [1996] ECR I-5151, para 56.

[81] Case T-95/03, *Asociación de Estaciones de Servicio de Madrid v Commission* [2006] ECR II-4739, para 113.

[82] Case C-404/04P, *Technische Glaswerke Ilmenau GmbH v Commission* [2007] ECR I-1*, para 31; Case T-198/01, *Technische Glaswerke Ilmenau GmbH v Commission* [2004] ECR II-2717, para 61.

[83] Cases C-329/93 & C-62/95 & 63/95, *Germany v Commission* [1996] ECR I-5151, paras 32; Case C-301/96, *Germany v Commission* [2003] ECR I-9919, para 140.

[84] Case T-459/93, *Siemens v Commission* [1995] ECR II-1675, para 31; Case T-214/95, *Vlaams Gewest v Commission* [1998] ECR II-717, para 63; Case T-16/96, *Cityflyer Express v Commission* [1998] ECR II-757, para 65; Case T-187/99, *Agrana Zucker und Stärke AG v Commission* [2001] ECR II-1587, para 84; Case T-323/99, *INMA v Commission* [2002] ECR II-545, para 98; Cases T-228/99 & T-233/99 *Westdeutsche Landesbank Girozentrale v Commission* [2003] ECR II-435, para 280; Case T-198/01, *Technische Glaswerke Ilmenau GmbH v Commission* [2004] ECR II-2717, para 60; Case T-349/03, *Corsica Ferries France sas v Commission* [2005] ECR II-2197, para 64; Case T-289/03, *BUPA Ltd v Commission* [2008] ECR II-81, para 341; Cases T-102/07 & T-120/07, *Freistaat Sachsen v Commission* [2010] ECR II-585, para 180; Case T-511/09, *Niki Luftfahrt GmbH v Commission* EU:T:2015:284, para 106.

[85] Case T-504/93, *Tiercé Ladbroke SA v Commission* [1997] ECR II-923, para 52; Case T-301/01, *Alitalia SpA v Commission* [2008] ECR II-1753, para 57.

allegations. The Commission is not required, however, to define its position on matters which are manifestly irrelevant or insignificant or plainly of secondary importance.[86] For example, in *Bouygues SA v Commission*, where the Commission rejected a complaint concerning the allocation of licences for third generation mobile phones in France on the ground that the allocation was justified by France's obligations under the relevant telecommunications directive, the General Court held that the Commission was not required to give reasons for rejecting the complainant's plea that the allocation involved a transfer of State resources since this was secondary to the main finding which took precedence.[87]

Criteria establishing State aid The Commission must clearly identify the elements which it considers, or does not consider, constitute aid. The statement of reasons must indicate why each of the conditions for the aid to fall within Article 107(1) TFEU are or, as the case may be, are not satisfied.[88] In particular, the Commission is obliged to set out its reasons where, for the first time, it applies the notion of aid to specific circumstances. For example, in *France v Commission*, the Commission set out the reasons why measures financed by both State contributions and voluntary contributions from professionals in a sector could constitute State aid.[89] Where the Commission finds that one of the cumulative factors defining the notion of aid is absent, it is not required to give reasons in respect of the other factors as well, even if these have been raised by an interested party or a complainant.[90]

---

[86] Case C-367/95P, *Commission v Sytraval* [1998] ECR I-1719, para 64; Case C-487/06P, *British Aggregates Association v Commission* [2008] ECR I-10515, para 173; Cases T-371/94 & T-394/94, *British Airways v Commission*[1998] ECR II-2405, para 106; Cases T-12/99 & T-63/99, *UK Coal plc v Commission* [2001] ECR II-2153, para 197; Case T-475/04, *Bouygues SA v Commission* [2007] ECR II-2097, para 53; Cases T-239/04 & T-323/04, *Italy v Commission* [2007] ECR II-3265, para 119.

[87] Case T-475/04, *Bouygues SA v Commission* [2007] ECR II-2097, para 55.

[88] Case C-88/03, *Portugal v Commission* [2006] ECR I-7115, para 89; Case C-494/06P, *Italy v Commission* [2009] ECR I-3639, para 49; Case T-16/96, *Cityflyer Express v Commission* [1998] ECR II-757, para 66; Cases T-204/97 & 270/97, *EPAC v Commission* [2000] ECR II-2267, para 36; Case T-55/99, *CETM v Commission* [2000] ECR II-3207, para 59; Case T-323/99, *INMA v Commission* [2002] ECR II-545, para 57; Cases T-228/99 & T-233/99 *Westdeutsche Landesbank Girozentrale v Commission* [2003] ECR II-435, para 281; Case T-349/03, *Corsica Ferries France SAS v Commission* [2005] ECR II-2197, para 65; Case T-217/02, *Ter Lembeek International NV v Commission* [2006] ECR II-4483, para 236; Cases T-239/04 & T-323/04, *Italy v Commission* [2007] ECR II-3265, para 119; Case T-455/05, *Componenta Oyj v Commission* [2008] ECR II-336*, para 98; Case T-387/11, *Nitrogénművek Vegyipari Zst v Commission* EU:T:2013:98, para 102; Case T-150/12, *Greece v Commission* EU:T:2014:191, para 103.

[89] Case T-139/09, *France v Commission* EU:T:2012:496, para 41.

[90] Case T-475/04, *Bouygues SA v Commission* [2007] ECR II-2097, para 55.

In *Confédération Nationale du Crédit Mutuel v Commission*, the General Court annulled a Commission decision finding that aid was granted through the method of financing the *Livret Bleu* regulated savings product in France on the ground that the Commission had failed to express clearly its position on the identification of the measures which conferred the aid.[91] In *INMA v Commission*, the General Court criticised the Commission for failing to set out clearly and unequivocally its reasons for refusing to accept an argument that aid was not involved where a public company had acted as a private investor in preferring to cover a subsidiary's losses in order to minimise the costs which it might incur as guarantor and sole shareholder.[92] In *Germany v Commission*, whether aid had been granted in relation to a share purchase in the context of a restructuring operation depended on the valuation of the shareholding. The ECJ annulled the Commission decision which was solely based, without adequate explanation, on the stock market price on the ground that this was too formal, rigid and restrictive in the circumstances. Several other factors should have been considered, such as the synergy effects expected from the merger, which a private investor guided by prospects of profitability in the longer term would have taken into account.[93]

In *Asociación de Estaciones de Servicio de Madrid v Commission*, the Commission's decision was annulled on the ground that it failed to explain why a preferential tax regime did not constitute an advantage within the meaning of Article 107(1) TFEU or, if it did constitute an advantage, why it was justified by the nature of the system.[94] In the *Olympic Airways* case, Olympic Aviation was not required by the Greek authorities to pay VAT on the acquisition of spare parts. The Commission's decision that this constituted State aid was annulled by the General Court on the ground that it had not been shown by the Commission that Olympic Aviation had been granted a real economic advantage. Since the VAT regime was intended to be neutral for business carrying on an economic activity by allowing for the deduction or recovery of input VAT, the Commission had to show that non-payment had conferred a temporary cash-flow advantage.[95] In a follow up case on the transfer of aircraft by Olympic Airways to a successor company, the Commission's decision finding that the sale price contained State aid was annulled on the ground that the Commission had failed to state its reasons to the requisite legal standard as to why, for the purposes of the private operator test, it took into consideration the net book value of the aircraft rather than their

---

[91] Case T-93/02, *Confédération Nationale du Crédit Mutuel v Commission* [2005] ECR II-143, para 118.

[92] Case T-323/99, *INMA v Commission* [2002] ECR II-545, para 100.

[93] Cases C-329/93 & C-62 & 63/95, *Germany v Commission* [1996] ECR I-5151, paras 33-36.

[94] Case T-146/03, *Asociación de Estaciones de Servicio de Madrid v Commission*, [2006] ECR II-98*, paras 80-91 and 116-122.

[95] Case T-68/03, *Olympiaki Aeroporia Ypiresies AE v Commission* [2007] ECR II-2911, paras 362-264.

market value.[96] In *TV2/Danmark v Commission*, the Commission's decision finding that TV2 had built up financial reserves on the basis of over-compensation from State resources for providing a public broadcasting service was annulled on the ground that there was nothing in the decision to prove that this assertion was true. The General Court held that the decision should have included a precise and detailed assessment of the actual legal and economic conditions which governed the setting of the amount of licence fee income payable to TV2.[97]

In *Freistaat Sachsen v Commission*, the Commission's decision finding that loans and guarantees to a firm in difficulty constituted State aid and requiring recovery of the aid, calculated as the difference between the reference interest rate plus 700-1000 basis points and the remuneration against which the participations were provided, was annulled since the Commission had not explained why it had used that method of calculation, creating the impression that the premiums may have been randomly chosen. The Commission should have explained why it resorted to additional premiums and how it chose their amounts by way of an analysis of market practice.[98] In *Frucona Košice v Commission*, concerning a decision declaring a reduction in a tax debt to be inconsistent with the action of a comparable private creditor, the ECJ held that the Commission had failed adequately to explain how the length of the alternative procedure of bankruptcy might have affected that action.[99] Similarly, in *Buczek v Commission*, a case concerning the private creditor test where a hypothetical private creditor would be faced with a choice between, on the one hand, the proceeds from legal proceedings for the recovery of debts and, on the other, the amount it might expect to receive following insolvency proceedings, the Commission's decision finding aid was annulled for failing to state whether it had in its possession analyses comparing the two possible outcomes.[100]

Distortion of competition and effect on trade Reasons must be stated with regard to the requirements that the aid affect trade between Member States and distort or threaten to distort competition. The requirements imposed on the Commission in this respect vary depending on the individual or general nature of the aid measure.[101] In any event, the Commission is required, not to

---

[96] Cases T-415/05, T-416/05 & T-423/05, *Greece v Commission* [2010] ECR II-4749, para 308.

[97] Cases T-309/04, T-317/04, T-329/04 & T-336/04, *TV2/Danmark A/S v Commission* [2008] ECR II-2935, para 201.

[98] Cases T-102/07 & T-120/07, *Freistaat Sachsen v Commission* [2010] ECR II-585, para 218.

[99] Case C-73/11P, *Frucona Košice as v Commission* EU:C:2013:32, para 103.

[100] Case T-1/08, *Buczek Automotive v Commission* [2011] ECR II-2107, para 93.

[101] Cases T-254/00, T-270/00 & T-277/00, *Hotel Cipriani SpA v Commission* [2008] ECR II-3269, para 227.

establish that such aid has a real effect on trade between Member States and that competition is actually being distorted, but only to examine whether that aid is liable to affect such trade and distort competition.[102] Where aid has been unlawfully granted in breach of the requirement of prior notification under Article 108(3) TFEU, in determining that the aid is incompatible with the internal market, the Commission is not required to make an up-to-date assessment of the real effects which the aid has already had on competition and trade between Member States. If the Commission were required to demonstrate the real effect of aid which had already been granted, this would ultimately favour those Member States which grant aid in breach of the notification requirements to the detriment of those who do notify aid in advance.[103] Thus, in *Greece v Commission*, the General Court refuted the suggestion that the Commission was required to show a comparison between the economic situation of the aid beneficiaries and that of competing undertakings.[104] Nevertheless, even if all issues raised by the Member State concerned need not be individually dealt with, the Commission should respond to specific arguments that competition or trade are not affected. For example, in *Italy v Commission*, concerning reductions in excise duty for greenhouse producers, the Commission specifically rejected various arguments in this respect raised by Italy.[105]

Even if in certain cases the very circumstances in which aid is granted are sufficient to show that the aid is capable of affecting trade between Member States and of distorting or threatening to distort competition, the Commission must at least set out those circumstances in the statement of reasons for its

---

[102] Case C-301/87, *France v Commission* [1990] ECR I-307, para 33; Case C-372/97, *Italy v Commission* [2004] ECR I-3679, para 44; Case C-298/00P, *Italy v Commission* [2004] ECR I-4087, para 49; Cases C-442/03P & C-471/03P *P & O European Ferries (Vizcaya) SA v Commission* [2006] ECR I-4845, para 110; Case C-222/04, *Ministero dell'Economia e delle Finanze v Cassa di Risparmio di Firenze SpA* [2006] ECR I-289, para 140; Case C-494/06P, *Commission v Italy* [2009] ECR I-3639, para 49; Case C-667/13, *Portugal v Banco Privado Português SA* EU:C:2015:151, para 46; Cases T-298/97, etc. *Alzetta v Commission* [2000] ECR II-2319, para 76; Case T-171/02, *Regione autonoma della Sardegna v Commission* [2005] ECR II-2123, para 85; Cases T-239/04 & T-323/04, *Italy v Commission* [2007] ECR II-3265, para 127; Case T-150/12, *Greece v Commission* EU:T:2014:191, para 127.

[103] Case C-301/87, *France v Commission* [1991] ECR I-307, para 33; Case C-113/00, *Spain v Commission* [2002] ECR I-7601, para 54; Case C-372/97, *Italy v Commission* [2004] ECR I-3679, para 45; Case T-214/95, *Vlaamse Gewest v Commission* [1998] ECR II-717, para 67; Case T-35/99, *Keller SpA v Commission* [2002] ECR II-261, para 85; Case T-198/01, *Technische Glaswerke Ilmenau GmbH v Commission* [2004] ECR II-2717, para 215; Case T-445/05, *Associazione Italiana del Risparmio Gestito v Commission* [2009] ECR II-289, para 102.

[104] Case T-150/12, *Greece v Commission* EU:T:2014:191, para 110.

[105] Case T-379/09, *Italy v Commission* EU:T:2012:422, paras 26-32.

decision.[106] Mere reference to the criteria set out in Article 107(1) TFEU, without any discussion of the facts and legal considerations taken into account in the assessment, is not sufficient.[107] In *Exécutif Régional Wallon v Commission*, reference by the Commission to the vulnerability of the market for flat glass due to stagnant demand, unused production capacity and steady decline in employment, the use of trade figures showing that 50% of the aid recipient's exports were to other Member States, and reference to three previous decisions declaring aid to the flat glass industry to be incompatible with the internal market was held to constitute sufficient reasoning.[108] Similarly, in *ENI-Lanerossi*, the Commission's findings that the textile industry was suffering from stagnation of demand, depressed prices and overcapacity and that intra-EU trade had recently increased from 19.3% to 29.1%, thus indicating keen competition, were sufficient to show that the aid was likely to affect trade and distort competition.[109] In *Regione autonoma della Sardegna v Commission*, the decision setting out statistical information to show that Italy was the principal vegetable producer in the European Union and that Sardinia constituted an important production area in Italy was sufficiently reasoned as to why trade between Member States was affected.[110] Similarly, in *Portugal v Commission*, the ECJ held that, in relation to regional taxation in the Azores, the Commission's decision logically deduced from the characteristics of the system in question and from the general scope of the reduced rates of tax that the result of that system, since those reductions apply to all economic sectors in the Azores, was that at least some of the undertakings concerned carried on economic activities involving trade between Member States.[111]

---

[106] Cases 296 & 318/82, *Netherlands v Commission* [1985] ECR 809, para 24; Case 57/86, *Greece v Commission* [1988] ECR 2855, para 15; Cases C-329/93 & C-62/95 & 63/95, *Germany v Commission* [1996] ECR I-5151, para 52; Case C-156/98, *Germany v Commission* [2000] ECR I-6857, para 98; Cases C-15/98 & C-105/98, *Italy v Commission* [2000] ECR I-8855, para 66; Case C-334/99, *Germany v Commission* [2003] ECR I-1139, para 59; Case C-457/00, *Belgium v Commission* [2003] ECR I-6931, para 103; Case C-88/03, *Portugal v Commission* [2006] ECR I-7115, para 89; Case C-150/09P, *Iride SpA v Commission* [2010] ECR I-5*, para 22; Case C-494/06P, *Commission v Italy* [2009] ECR I-3639, para 49; Cases T-304/04 & T-316/04, *Italy v Commission*, [2006] ECR II-64*, para 63; Cases T-239/04 & T-323/04, *Italy v Commission* [2007] ECR II-3265, para 126; Case T-1/08, *Buczek Automotive v Commission* [2011] ECR II-2107, para 102; Case T-295/12, *Germany v Commission* EU:T:2014:675, para 163.

[107] Case T-1/08, *Buczek Automotive v Commission* [2011] ECR II-2107, para 105.

[108] Cases 62/87 & 72/87, *Exécutif Régional Wallon v Commission* [1988] ECR 1537, paras 17-18.

[109] Case C-303/88, *Commission v Italy* [1991] ECR I-1433, paras 28-29.

[110] Case T-171/02, *Regione autonoma della Sardegna v Commission* [2005] ECR II-2123, para 76.

[111] Case C-88/03, *Portugal v Commission* [2006] ECR I-7115, para 91; Case C-494/06P, *Commission v Italy* [2009] ECR I-3639, para 50.

The Commission may not limit itself to abstract analysis when considering sectoral aid schemes.[112]   Thus, a decision concerning aid to Sardinian shipowners was annulled in *Italy v Commission* where it was held that a mere statement that aid was selective and restricted to the shipping sector in Sardinia did not amount to a statement of reasons as to why competition had been adversely affected. Moreover, the decision did not provide any information concerning competition between the Sardinian shipping companies and those established in other Member States, particularly in light of the fact that island cabotage in the Mediterranean was excluded from the liberalisation of maritime transport services within Member States until January 1999.[113] In cases concerning aid for the replacement of transport vehicles owned by SMEs in Spain, the Commission observed that the aid was likely to help the beneficiaries compete with large undertakings established in Spain and that the liberalisation of road transport had led to intra-EU competition in the international transport and cabotage sector. Those reasons were held by the ECJ to be sufficient to describe the real or potential effect of the aid on competition and its effect on trade between Member States.[114]

On several occasions, the General Court has criticised the Commission for failing to state specific reasons concerning distortion of competition and effects on trade in relation to individual aid. Where necessary, the Commission must take into account the specific circumstances of the case.[115] In *Le Levant v Commission*, concerning aid granted in respect of the building of a shipping vessel which was intended for operation in Saint-Pierre-et-Miquelon, a French administrative territory in the north Atlantic off the coast of Newfoundland which was one of the overseas countries and territories (OCTs) which are not part of the territory of the EU, the General Court criticised the Commission for failing to explain how the aid was likely to affect trade between Member States.[116] Moreover, there was nothing in the decision explaining how and on what market competition was affected or likely to be affected by the aid.[117] Similarly, in *Commission v Italy and Wam*, where aid was granted to finance a market penetration programme in third countries, the Commission was criticised for failing to specify how competition and trade between Member

---

[112] Cases T-254/00, T-270/00 & T-277/00, *Hotel Cipriani SpA v Commission* [2008] ECR II-3269, para 229.

[113] Cases C-15/98 & C-105/99, *Italy v Commission* [2000] ECR I-8855, paras 67-68.

[114] Case C-351/98, *Spain v Commission* [2002] ECR I-8031, para 58; Case C-409/00, *Spain v Commission* [2003] ECR I-1487, para 75.

[115] Cases C-329/93, C-62/95 & C-63/95, *Germany v Commission* [1996] ECR I-5151, para 53; Case C-494/06P, *Commission v Italy* [2009] ECR I-3639, para 63; Cases T-254/00, T-270/00 & T-277/00, *Hotel Cipriani SpA v Commission* [2008] ECR II-3269, para 228.

[116] Case T-34/02, *Le Levant 001 v Commission* [2005] ECR II-267, para 117.

[117] *Ibid.*, para 123.

States was affected.[118]   This was rectified by a fresh decision which specifically linked the financing of the market penetration programme to effects on exports within the EU.[119]

Applicability of an exemption   The Commission is required to exercise its discretion on whether the aid in question is compatible with the internal market to the full.[120] In relation to the applicability of an exemption, whilst the burden of proving that aid is compatible with the internal market is on the Member State concerned,[121] the statement of reasons must indicate that the Commission considered all the essential elements of fact or law which could have justified the granting of the exemption.[122] Thus, for example, in *Westfälisch-Lippischer Sparkassen- und Giroverband v Commission*, the statement of reasons describing the need to subject the authorisation of a guarantee to conditions set out in a restructuring plan was regarded as adequate where it indicated why the Commission regarded respect of those conditions as necessary for realising the long term viability of the beneficiary.[123] By contrast, a statement of reasons was defective where the Commission stated, in relation to a possible exemption under Article 107(3)(c) TFEU, that the aid would not facilitate the development of certain economic areas and that it would not be in the common interest. No indication was evident in the decision that the Commission had considered the essential fact, which might have caused it to make a different assessment, that the aid in question was accompanied by a restructuring of the recipient undertaking which, by diverting its production to high-quality products, led to a reduction in its production capacity and in its market share.[124] In *Freistaat Thüringen v Commission*, the General Court held that the Commission could not merely state that the waiver of the repayment of a loan constituted aid that was incompatible with the internal market merely because it was granted without any legal basis.[125]

---

[118] Case C-494/06P, *Commission v Italy* [2009] ECR I-3639, para 61; Cases T-304/04 & T-316/04, *Italy v Commission* [2006] ECR II-64*, paras 63-66.

[119] Case C-587/12P, *Italy v Commission* EU:C:2013:721, para 25-32; Case C-560/12P, *Wam Industriale SpA v Commission* EU:C:2013:726, paras 22-24; Case T-257/10, *Italy v Commission* EU:T:2012:504, paras 83-87; Case T-303/10, *Wam Industriale SpA v Commission* EU:T:2012:505, paras 31-53.

[120] Case T-304/08, *Smurfit Kappa Group plc v Commission* EU:T:2012:351, para 90.

[121] Cases T-394/08, T-408/08, T-453/08 & T-454/08, *Regione autonoma della Sardegna v Commission* [2011] ECR II-6255, para 132.

[122] Cases 296 & 318/82, *Netherlands v Commission* [1985] ECR 809, para 25; Case C-364/90, *Italy v Commission* [1993] ECR I-2097, paras 44-45; Cases C-329/93, C-62/95 & C-63/95, *Germany v Commission* [1996] ECR I-5151, para 48; Case T-157/01, *Danske Busvognmaend v Commission* [2004] ECR II-197, para 96.

[123] Case T-457/09, *Westfälisch-Lippischer Sparkassen- und Giroverband v Commission* EU:T:2014:683, para 317.

[124] Cases 296 & 318/82, *Netherlands v Commission* [1985] ECR 809, para 26.

[125] Case T-318/00, *Freistaat Thüringen v Commission* [2005] ECR II-4179, para 128.

The extent of the required reasoning may also be influenced by the fact that the decision was adopted in a context well-known to the applicant.[126] Thus, decisions concerning German aid which included only a brief résumé of the grounds on which the Commission refused to apply the derogation provided for by Article 107(2)(c) TFEU to the facts of the case was upheld on the ground that the decision was adopted in a context well known to the German Government, so that the decision could be reasoned in a summary manner in that regard.[127] In appropriate cases, a failure to specify the precise provision of Article 107(3) TFEU for approving the aid will not lead to the decision's nullity if it is implicit in the reasoning which provision is applicable. Thus, in *Régie Networks v Direction de Contrôle Fiscal Rhône-Alpes Bourgogne*, it was implicit from the statements that the beneficiaries of the aid were local radio stations and the intra-EU trade would not be affected to an extent contrary to the common interest that the Commission was relying on Article 107(3)(c) TFEU, namely aid to facilitate the development of certain economic activities.[128] Where the classification of aid as operating aid rather than investment aid is essential to determine the applicable rules governing whether the aid may be compatible with the internal market, the statement of reasons must explain the Commission's view clearly and unambiguously.[129] In *Alitalia v Commission*, the Commission's decision finding that aid had been granted through a capital injection to the Italian airline was annulled on the ground that the Commission had failed to address specific reasons given by the Italian authorities distinguishing the investment from a similar case concerning public investment in Iberia, the Spanish airline, on which the Commission had relied.[130]

The obligation to state reasons is in principle restricted to the reasons for which a given category of operators is to benefit from a given measure and does not mean that it is necessary to justify the exclusion of all other operators which are not in a comparable situation. Since the number of categories excluded from the benefit of a measure is potentially unlimited, the Commission cannot be under a duty to provide specific reasoning in relation to each of them. None the less, where the beneficiaries of the measure, on the one hand, and other excluded operators, on the other, are in a comparable situation, the Commission is under a duty to explain in what way the difference

---

[126] Case T-17/02, *Fred Olsen SA v Commission* [2005] ECR II-2031, para 97.

[127] Case C-156/98, *Germany v Commission* [2000] ECR I-6857, para 105; Case C-301/96, *Germany v Commission* [2003] ECR I-9919, paras 88-93; Case C-277/00, *Germany v Commission* [2004] ECR I-3925, para 56.

[128] Case C-333/07, *Régie Networks v Direction de Contrôle Fiscal Rhône-Alpes Bourgogne* [2008] ECR I-10807, para 73.

[129] Case C-351/98, *Spain v Commission* [2002] ECR I-8031, para 82; Case C-409/00, *Spain v Commission* [2003] ECR I-1487, para 98.

[130] Case T-296/97, *Alitalia SpA v Commission* [2000] ECR II-3871, para 132.

in treatment thus introduced is objectively justified and to give specific reasons in that regard.[131]

Consistent Commission policy Where the Commission has set out a policy whereby aid can be approved only if certain conditions are satisfied, the statement of reasons need only show that the criteria applied under the policy were not satisfied in the instant case.[132]   As regards, for instance, the compatibility of State aid for restructuring with Article 107(3)(c) TFEU, the obligation to state reasons is complied with when the Commission's decision states the reasons why it considers the aid to be justified having regard to the conditions laid down in the restructuring aid guidelines, in particular the existence of a restructuring plan, satisfactory evidence as to the long-term viability and the proportionality of the aid taking into account the contribution of the beneficiary of it.[133]   Consistency may also be derived from previous individual decisions. Thus, in *Régie Networks v Direction de Contrôle Fiscal Rhône-Alpes Bourgogne*, where the Commission had already adopted two previous positive decisions regarding aid for local radio stations in France, it was entitled to give succinct reasons for approving a further similar scheme.[134]

Change of Commission policy The principle of equal treatment requires that comparable situations must not be treated differently and that different situations must not be treated in the same way unless such treatment is objectively justified.[135] Where the Commission has adopted guidelines that are to apply to given situations, it cannot depart from those guidelines unless it gives adequate reasons justifying, in light of the principles of equal treatment and the protection of legitimate expectations, its departure from its own rules.[136]   Equally, a change in Commission policy must be addressed in the statement of reasons. Where the Commission has assessed a measure in the past in any particular manner, a change of position will be allowed as long as

---

[131] Case C-390/06, *Nuova Agricast Srl v Ministero delle Attività Produttive* [2008] ECR I-2577, paras 81-82.

[132] Case C-261/89 *Italy v Commission* [1991] ECR I-4437, para 20; Cases C-356/90 & C-280-282/99P, *Moccia Irme SpA v Commission* [2001] ECR I-4717, para 90; Case T-109/01, *Fleuren Compost BV v Commission* [2004] ECR II-127, para 125; Case T-318/00, *Freistaat Thüringen v Commission* [2005] ECR II-4179, para 180; Case T-162/06, *Kronoply GmbH v Commission* [2009] ECR II-1, para 30.

[133] Case C-17/99, *France v Commission* [2001] ECR I-2481, para 37; Case T-214/95, *Vlaamse Gewest v Commission* [1998] ECR II-717, para 102; Case T-349/03, *Corsica Ferries France sas v Commission* [2005] ECR II-2197, para 66.

[134] Case C-333/07, *Régie Networks v Direction de Contrôle Fiscal Rhône-Alpes Bourgogne* [2008] ECR I-10807, paras 66-67.

[135] Case C-390/06, *Nuova Agricast srl v Ministero delle Attivita Produttive* [2008] ECR I-2577, para 66.

[136] Cases C-75/05P & C-80/05P, *Germany v Kronofrance* [2008] ECR I-6619, para 60; Case T-304/08, *Smurfit Kappa Group plc v Commission* EU:T:2012:351, para 84.

the Commission sets out the factors which justify it taking that position.[137] By contrast, where the Commission has previously approved measures in similar circumstances as not falling within the scope of Article 107(1) TFEU, a failure to explain why it has come to a contrary conclusion will result in the decision being annulled.[138] In *Ireland, France and Italy v Commission*, where previous Commission decisions concerning an exemption for mineral oils in the production of alumina had stated that the exemptions did not give rise to any distortion of competition, the General Court annulled a subsequent decision refusing to allow an extension of the exemption since no explanation was given as to why there was a difference in the situations. The General Court accepted that the Commission could not be required, as a general rule, to assess, in each case, whether any of the situations making it possible to classify a measure as existing aid applied, and to give exhaustive reasons for its decisions in that regard, in particular where, during the administrative procedure, the parties had not pleaded the applicability of one or more of those specific situations. Given the previous decisions, the General Court held that it was necessary to ascertain whether there were particular circumstances regarding the contested exemptions such as to impose on the Commission the duty to give specific reasons for the non-application of Article 1(b)(v) of Regulation No 659/1999 concerning the evolution of the common market.[139] On appeal, this was overturned by the ECJ which held that the Commission was not under an obligation to set out reasons for the inapplicability of Article 1(b)(v). Since the concept of aid, whether new or existing, corresponds to an objective situation, the Commission is not required to state reasons why it made a different assessment of the regime in question in previous decisions.[140]

Where a decision involves a new and important policy, the Commission must explain why it has adopted that policy. Thus, in *Départment du Loiret v Commission*, where the Commission charged compound interest for the first time in a recovery order, the decision was correctly challenged on the ground that the Commission had failed to explain why it had changed from the previous policy of charging only simple interest.[141] On the other hand, in *Belgium v Commission*, where the Commission found that State aid had been granted through the payment of employees' wages directly from public funds, a claim that the Commission's decision was vitiated for having failed to deal with the arguments raised concerning the risk of creating inconsistencies in European employment policy was rejected as manifestly immaterial.[142]

---

[137] Case C-66/02, *Italy v Commission* [2005] ECR I-10901, para 56; Case T-17/02, *Fred Olsen SA v Commission* [2005] ECR II-2031, para 169.

[138] Case T-34/02, *Le Levant 001 v Commission* [2005] ECR II-267, paras 128-131.

[139] Cases T-50/06 etc., *Ireland v Commission* [2007] ECR II-172*, para 54-56.

[140] Case C-89/08P, *Commission v Ireland* [2009] ECR I-11245, paras 72-76.

[141] Case C-295/07P, *Commission v Départment du Loiret* [2008] ECR I-9363, para 49; Case T-369/00, *Départment du Loiret v Commission* [2007] ECR II-851, para 43.

[142] Case C-5/01 *Belgium v Commission* [2002] ECR I-11991, para 71.

Decision following preliminary assessment A decision at the end of the preliminary assessment in which the Commission decides that there is no aid or that the aid is compatible with the internal market must simply set out the reasons why the Commission takes the view that it is not faced with serious difficulties.[143] On the other hand, a decision to open a formal investigation procedure must be sufficiently reasoned.[144] In *Saxonia Edelmetalle v Commission*, the General Court held that the Commission decision was sufficiently reasoned in relation to a decision concerning alleged misuse of aid that had been previously approved in a restructuring plan involving a group of companies that had been privatised by the Treuhandanstalt in Germany. The Commission had found that the key elements of the restructuring plans, as they had been approved, had not been implemented, that the approval decision no longer covered the aid in question giving several specific examples, including aid intended to cover the undertakings' losses and to finance investment after the failure of the restructuring plans, and that it was possible that significant supplementary aid had been granted to the beneficiaries. It had also expressed doubts as to the compatibility of that aid with the internal market, particularly because some of the aid may have been used for purposes other than the approved restructuring and because the restructuring plans had not been fully implemented. In addition, the Commission had specifically drawn the attention of the German authorities and potential parties concerned to the fact that aid found to have been granted illegally would have to be recovered from the beneficiary.[145] Similarly, in the *Olympic Airways* case, the Commission's decision to open a formal investigation procedure was sufficiently reasoned since it indicated, in particular, that the restructuring plan, on which an earlier decision approving the restructuring aid was based, had not been implemented as planned and that the existence of serious doubts as to the compatibility of Olympic Airway's current economic and financial situation with the operational and financial indicators of the plan at issue justified a re-examination of that decision with regard to the correct implementation of that plan.[146]

---

[143] Case C-225/91, *Matra SA v Commission* [1993] ECR I-3203, para 48; Case C-333/07, *Régie Networks v Direction de Contrôle Fiscal Rhône-Alpes Bourgogne* [2008] ECR I-10807, para 65; Case C-47/10P, *Austria v Commission* [2011] ECR I-10707, para 111; Case T-123/09, *Ryanair Ltd v Commission* EU:T:2012:164, para 182; Case T-89/09, *Pollmeier Massivholz GmbH v Commission* EU:T:2015:153, para 296.

[144] Cases T-111/01 & T-133/01, *Saxonia Edelmetalle GmbH v Commission* [2005] ECR II-1579, para 50.

[145] Cases T-111/01 & T-133/01, *Saxonia Edelmetalle GmbH v Commission* [2005] ECR II-1579, para 52.

[146] Case T-68/03, *Olympiaki Aeroporia Ypiresies AE v Commission* [2007] ECR II-2911, para 83.

Decision following formal investigation procedure   Since the formal investigation procedure enables a more in-depth examination and clarification of questions raised in the opening decision, any difference between the opening decision and the final decision cannot be regarded in itself as constituting a defect rendering the final decision unlawful.[147]   Moreover, the Commission is not under any enhanced obligation to state reasons.[148]

Where the final decision concludes that aid has been put into effect unlawfully, the Commission is not obliged to provide specific reasons in order to justify the exercise of its power to require the Member State to recover the aid, since this follows automatically from the finding that the aid is unlawful.[149]   In other respects, the Commission cannot satisfy the requirement to state reasons merely by stating that its decision is based on information received from the relevant Member State.[150]   If the Commission specifies a particular method for calculating the amount to be recovered, it must state the reasons why that method is appropriate.[151]   Where recovery of aid is required from a person other than the recipient of the aid, such as where assets allegedly benefiting from the aid have been passed on to a third party, the Commission must deal with all relevant issues.   In the *Seleco* decision, where the Commission alleged that assets benefiting from aid had been transferred to a new company the shares in which were subsequently sold, the ECJ annulled the recovery order against the transferee on the ground that the Commission had failed to show why it was irrelevant that the shares in the transferee were bought at a price which seemed to be the market price.[152]

As regards interest charged on recovery, the General Court held in *Département du Loiret v Commission*, where the Commission charged compound interest for the first time and argued that this was necessary to eliminate the advantage received by the recipient, that it was not possible from the reasoning in the decision to determine whether the use of such a rate of interest resulted in a present-day value corresponding to the value that had to be eliminated.[153]   In *Région Nord-Pas-de-Calais v Commission*, the General Court held that the imposition of an increased rate of interest in calculating the

---

[147]   Case T-211/05, *Italy v Commission* [2009] ECR II-2777, para 55.

[148]   Case T-387/11, *Nitrogénművek Vegyipari Zst v Commission* EU:T:2013:98, para 97.

[149]   Cases C-278/92-C-280/92, *Spain v Commission* [1994] ECR I-4103, para 78; Case C-75/97, *Belgium v Commission* [1999] ECR I-3671, para 82; Case C-310/99, *Italy v Commission* [2002] ECR I-2289, para 106; Case C-372/97, *Italy v Commission* [2004] ECR I-3679, para 129; Case C-148/04, *Unicredito Italiano SpA v Agenzia delle Entrate, Ufficio Genova 1* [2005] ECR I-11137, para 99.

[150]   Cases T-111/01 & T-133/01, *Saxonia Edelmetalle GmbH v Commission* [2005] ECR II-1579, para 140; Case T-318/00, *Freistaat Thüringen v Commission* [2005] ECR II-4179, para 155.

[151]   Case T-305/13, *SACE BT SpA v Commission* EU:T:2015:435, para 155.

[152]   Cases C-328/99 & C-399/00, *Italy v Commission* [2003] ECR I-4135, para 85.

[153]   Case T-369/00, *Départment du Loiret v Commission* [2007] ECR II-851, para 52.

market value of a loan to a company in difficulty was adequately reasoned since it included a detailed description of the chosen calculation method.[154]

The statement of reasons must be such that the Member State has the information necessary to enable it to comply with the decision.[155] In *France v Commission*, where the aid was stated to be an interest subsidy of 4.75% related to a loan of FFr 40 million, the requirement to recover the aid was stated to be sufficiently clear since the addressee of the decision was able to determine without too much difficulty the actual amount which was to be recovered.[156] By contrast, where a Member State was required to ensure that the aid granted did not continue to distort competition in the future, the content and scope of that obligation had to be defined in the light of the elements of fact and law which led the Commission to conclude that the aid had such effects. If the Commission adopted this wording precisely in order to allow the Member State some latitude in deciding what measures were to be taken to bring to an end the infringement of EU law which it had established, it was obliged to provide the information necessary to enable the Member State to ascertain what measures might be considered appropriate.[157]

Legal basis for the decision As regards the legal basis for taking a decision, the lack of any reference in the decision to Regulation (EC) No 659/1999 or any of its provisions might constitute a defective statement of reasons only if the Commission had applied provisions of that regulation that did not derive directly from Article 108 TFEU. In *Italy v Commission*, the Commission in its decision formally called on the Italian authorities to submit their comments on the measures referred to in it, pursuant to Article 108(2) TFEU, and, in making that request, provisionally classified that aid as new aid, thereby entailing the suspension of the aid to the extent indicated in the decision. Since no procedure or legal effect of that decision was based on any innovative provision of the procedural regulation, it could not be challenged on the ground of failure to state reasons.[158]

Professional secrecy The Commission is bound to respect the principle of professional secrecy, so that published Commission decisions must not disclose information which a Member State legitimately wishes to keep secret.[159] Nevertheless, the Commission cannot rely on the fact that it has a

---

[154] Cases T-267/08 & T-279/08, *Région Nord-Pas-de-Calais v Commission* [2011] ECR II-1999, para 50.

[155] Case C-404/97, *Commission v Portugal* [2000] ECR I-4897, para 47; Case T-323/99, *INMA v Commission* [2002] ECR II-545, para 58.

[156] Case 102/87, *France v Commission* [1988] ECR 4067, para 33; Case C-480/98, *Spain v Commission* [2000] ECR I-8717, para 25.

[157] Cases 296/82 & 318/82, *Netherlands v Commission* [1985] ECR 809, para 29.

[158] Case C-400/99, *Italy v Commission* [2005] ECR I-3657, para 24.

[159] Article 337 TFEU; Council Regulation (EC) No 659/1999, Article 24.

duty to preserve professional secrecy to such an extent as to deprive of their substance the rules relating to the burden of proof to the detriment of the rights of defence of interested parties. In so far as it wishes to argue confidentiality of information, it is incumbent on the Commission to state the reasons for such confidentiality so that they might be effectively reviewed.[160] In any event, an applicant will not be able to invoke Article 296 TFEU where the Commission's reasoning is clear from the non-confidential version of the decision.[161]

20.4 CONSEQUENCES OF ANNULMENT

Annulment of decisions   Where a decision is annulled under Article 263 TFEU, it is declared void.[162] The principle that acts of the EU institutions are presumed to be lawful means that they produce legal effects until such time as they are withdrawn, annulled in an action for annulment or declared invalid following a reference for a preliminary ruling or a plea of illegality.[163]   A decision of annulment leads to the disappearance retroactively of the contested act with regard to all persons.[164] Partial annulment of an act is possible if the elements the annulment of which is sought may be severed from the remainder of the decision.[165] Accordingly, in *Commission v Département du Loiret*, the ECJ held that the Commission decision finding that aid granted through the sale of land at an undervalue had to be recovered was severable from the issue of whether the present-day value of the aid was to be calculated by applying a simple interest rate or a compound interest rate.[166] Exceptionally, the ECJ or General Court may declare that the effects of an annulled decision should be definitive pursuant to Article 264 TFEU.

Consequences of annulment   The consequences of annulment depend on the reasons for the declaration of annulment, so that annulment does not

---

[160]   Cases 296/82 & 318/82, *Netherlands v Commission* [1985] ECR 809, para 27; Case T-73/98, *Société Chimique Prayon Rupel SA v Commission* [2001] ECR II-867, para 84; Case T-58/13, *Club Hotel Loutraki AE v Commission* EU:T:2015:1, para 72.

[161]   Case T-58/13, *Club Hotel Loutraki AE v Commission* EU:T:2015:1, para 74.

[162]   Article 264 TFEU.

[163]   Case C-475/01 *Commission v Greece* [2004] ECR I-8923, para 18; Case C-199/06, *CELF v SIDE* [2008] ECR I-469, para 60.

[164]   Cases C-442/03P & C-471/03P *P & O European Ferries (Vizcaya) SA v Commission* [2006] ECR I-4845, para 43; Case C-199/06, *CELF v SIDE* [2008] ECR I-469, para 61; Cases T-265/04, T-292/04 & T-504/04, *Tirrenia di Navigazione SpA v Commission* [2009] ECR II-21*, para 159.

[165]   Case C-244/03, *France v Parliament and Council* [2005] ECR I-4021, para 12; Case C-295/07P, *Commission v Département du Loiret* [2008] ECR I-9363, para 105.

[166]   Case C-295/07P, *Commission v Département du Loiret* [2008] ECR I-9363, para 107.

necessarily affect preparatory acts connected to the void act.[167]   In *Spain v Commission*, where an earlier Commission decision concerning aid to Hytasa had been declared void on grounds of insufficient reasoning, a subsequent decision also finding the aid incompatible with the internal market and which was properly reasoned was upheld by the ECJ even though the Commission had not commenced a new investigation into the aid.   The investigation measures which had previously been completed by the Commission had been sufficient to allow for an exhaustive analysis to be made of the compatibility of the aid with the internal market.   Since the initial analysis carried out by the Commission had been incomplete, thus entailing the illegality of that decision, the procedure for replacing that decision was lawfully resumed at that point by means of a fresh analysis of the earlier material, without the need for a whole new investigation procedure.[168]   Similarly, in *Corsica Ferries v Commission*, the General Court, having annulled the Commission decision on the ground that it had under-assessed the value of assets held by the recipient of restructuring aid and had consequently erred in its assessment of the minimum amount of aid that was necessary, held that it was open to the Commission merely to undertake a reappraisal of the extent to which the measure concerned constituted aid and to vary its decision accordingly.[169]

On the other hand, in *France v Commission*, the ECJ held that the Commission was not entitled to regard as *res judicata* those aspects of a previous decision which had not been annulled. The Commission had taken a decision concerning financial assistance for the export of French language books in which it had found that the measure constituted State aid within the meaning of Article 107(1) TFEU which had been granted unlawfully but which was nevertheless compatible with the internal market.   The decision was annulled on the ground that the Commission should have opened the formal investigation procedure because there were doubts as to the compatibility of the aid with the internal market. Subsequently, a fresh decision was taken in which the Commission declared the aid unlawful. When that decision was also challenged, the Commission sought to argue that the earlier decision was *res judicata* in so far as it had held the measure to be State aid, introduced without prior notification and, therefore, unlawful. This submission was rejected by the ECJ which held that, the earlier decision having been annulled, the Commission retained its discretionary powers of assessment in regard to the substance of the measure.[170]

---

[167] Case C-415/96, *Spain v Commission* [1998] ECR I-6993, para 32; Case C-331/88, *R v MAFF, ex parte Fedesa* [1990] ECR I-4023, para 34; Case T-301/01, *Alitalia SpA v Commission* [2008] ECR II-1753, para 100.

[168] Case C-415/96, *Spain v Commission* [1998] ECR I-6993, para 34.

[169] Case T-349/03, *Corsica Ferries France SAS v Commission* [2005] ECR II-2197, para 320.

[170] Case C-332/98, *France v Commission* [2000] ECR I-4833, para 20.

Measures necessary to comply with the judgment It is not for the ECJ or the General Court to issue directions to the institutions concerned as to how they should proceed.[171] Rather, pursuant to Article 266 TFEU, the institution whose act has been declared void or whose failure to act has been declared unlawful must take the measures necessary to comply with the judgment. The time needed to take the necessary measures depends on the nature of the measure concerned and the attendant circumstances.[172] A failure by the institution concerned to take the necessary measures is itself capable of being the subject of an action for failure to act pursuant to Article 265 TFEU.[173] It follows, for example, that, where the Commission has taken a decision wrongfully analysing an aid measure, refusing to open the formal investigation procedure or refusing to order the recovery of aid, it will normally have to take a fresh decision in accordance with the court's judgment.[174] Where, on the other hand, the annulled decision requires the recovery of unlawful aid, that requirement, which is imposed on the Member State concerned, no longer stands. The extent to which recipients of the aid might be entitled to rely on the declaration of nullity in order to restore any right to the aid is most likely a matter for the relevant national law.[175]

Action for damages under Article 340 TFEU An action for damages under Article 340 TFEU may be brought where the Commission has acted unlawfully. In order to establish a right to compensation, the applicant must establish the unlawfulness of the Commission's action or inaction, actual damage and a causal connection between the unlawful act or failure to act and the damage suffered.[176] This applies equally in the case of unlawful State aid decisions. Thus, in *SIC v Commission*, the General Court suggested that an applicant might bring a claim for compensation against the Commission where it had suffered loss arising from the Commission's failure to act within a

---

[171] Case T-67/94, *Ladbroke Racing Ltd. v Commission* [1998] ECR II-1, para 200; Case T-107/96, *Pantochim SA v Commission* [1998] ECR II-311, para 52.

[172] Case 266/82, *Turner v Commission* [1984] ECR 1, para 6; Case T-73/95, *Oliveira SA v Commission* [1997] ECR II-381, para 41; Case T-301/01, *Alitalia SpA v Commission* [2008] ECR II-1753, para 155.

[173] Cases T-297/01 & T-298/01, *SIC v Commission* [2004] ECR 743, para 32.

[174] See, for example, Cases T-297/01 & T-298/01, *SIC v Commission* [2004] ECR 743, paras 47-49.

[175] See, for example, Case T-9/98, *Mitteldeutsche Erdoel-Raffinerie GmbH v Commission* [2002] ECR II-3367, para 37.

[176] Case C-352/98P, *Bergaderm v Commission* [2000] ECR I-5291, para 42; Case T-107/96, *Pantochim v Commission* [1998] ECR II-311, para 48; Case T-230/95, *BAI v Commission* [1999] ECR II-123, para 29; Case T-176/01, *Ferriere Nord SpA v Commission* [2004] ECR II-3931, para 170; Case T-344/04 *Bouychou v Commission* [2007] ECR II-91*, para 33; Case T-360/04, *FG Marine SA v Commission* [2007] ECR II-92*, para 40; Case T-340/11, *Régie Networks v Commission* EU:T:2012:555, para 25.

reasonable time period.[177]   In *AES-Tisza v Commission*, in dismissing an application for interim measures, the General Court held that the applicant had failed to show that the damage allegedly caused by the Commission's decision declaring certain long-term purchasing agreements as aid and ordering recovery was irreparable on the ground that it had failed to show that it would be unable to obtain compensation from the Commission by means of an action under Article 340 TFEU.[178]   In *Idromacchine v Commission, the Commission* was ordered to pay damages for having acted unlawfully by disclosing in a decision certain information that was damaging to Idromacchine's legitimate interests and which should have been protected by virtue of the requirements of professional secrecy.[179]   On the other hand, in *Saxonia Edelmetalle v Commission*, the General Court noted that the Commission could not be held liable for the failure by the Member State concerned to inform the beneficiary of the initiation of the formal investigation procedure, since there was no legal obligation to do so.[180]   Similarly, in *Nuova Agricast v Commission*, a claim against the Commission was dismissed on the ground that it had not been shown in any event that the Commission had acted unlawfully.[181]

The burden of proof as regards the causal connection lies with the applicant.[182]   In *Produits Bertrand v Commission*, the applicant claimed compensation for the damage allegedly suffered by it by reason of the wrongful act or omission on the part of the Commission in failing to initiate proceedings concerning aid granted unlawfully by Italy to manufacturers of pasta. It was contended that the subsidised pasta had been exported to France and that the subsequent depression of market prices in France had caused the applicant to suffer loss of profit. The claim was rejected, since the evidence was not available to substantiate the applicant's claim.[183]   Similarly, in *BAI v Commission*, an action for damages alleged loss caused by delay in the Commission communicating a decision authorising State aid to a competitor which resulted in it being prevented from challenging the legality of the decision as soon as possible and allowed the competitor to establish itself on the market by means of the aid which had been unlawfully received.   The application was rejected by the General Court on the ground that the existence

---

[177] Cases T-297/01 & T-298/01, *SIC v Commission* [2004] ECR 743, para 58.

[178] Case T-468/08R, *AES-Tisza kft v Commission* [2008] ECR II-346*, para 46; Case T-62/02 RENV-R, *Eurallumina SpA v Commission* [2011] ECR II-167*, para 46; Case T-489/11R, *Rousse Industry v Commission* [2011] ECR II-362*, para 12.

[179] Case T-88/09, *Idromacchine srl v Commission* [2011] ECR II-7833, paras 45-50.

[180] Cases T-111/01 & T-133/01, *Saxonia Edelmetalle GmbH v Commission* [2005] ECR II-1579, para 53.

[181] Case T-373/08, *Nuova Agricast srl v Commission* [2011] ECR II-147*, para 91.

[182] Case T-344/04 *Bouychou v Commission* [2007] ECR II-91*, para 40; Case T-360/04, *FG Marine SA v Commission* [2007] ECR II-92*, para 50.

[183] Case 40/75, *Produits Bertrand v Commission* [1976] ECR 1, paras 9-14.

of a causal link between the conduct of the Commission and the damage allegedly suffered was not proven.[184]

There must be a causal connection between the unlawful act and the damage. In *Sniace v Commission*, Sniace, which sought the annulment of a Commission decision finding that a loan that it had been granted constituted State aid, although it was in any event compatible with the internal market, alleged that it had suffered economic loss since the administrative procedure lasted several years and obliged it to engage human, financial and technical resources, both internal and external, which were not as a rule required in the course of the company's usual activities and it has suffered non-material damage flowing from a loss of confidence amongst its associates, shareholders, suppliers and customers caused by the conduct of the administrative procedure. The General Court rejected the claim on the ground that the alleged damage could not be linked to the classification in the decision of the measures as State aid.[185] In *González y Díez SA v Commission*, it was argued that the failure by the Commission to revoke immediately a decision that it knew to be unlawful forced the applicant to bear the costs and disadvantages related to enforcement proceedings.[186]

It is also necessary to ascertain whether the applicant showed reasonable diligence in limiting the extent of the damage which it claims to have suffered.[187] In *FG Marine SA v Commission*, the applicant had held shares in Stardust Marine which was being investigated by the Commission for having received State aid from the Crédit Lyonnais group. In anticipation of the Commission's negative decision, the applicant resold its shareholding back to the group for the same price that it had previously paid. Following the ECJ's judgment overturning the Commission's decision finding that Stardust Marine had benefited from State aid, the applicant sued the Commission for damages representing the difference between the resale price and the current value of the company. The General Court dismissed the claim, holding that the causal connection between the Commission's unlawful decision and the damage had been broken by the applicant's negligent behaviour. At the time when the applicant sold its shares back to the group, the Commission's decision had not taken any legal effect as against the applicant, so that it was not obliged to sell its shares immediately, but could have waited to ascertain the full legal situation in the light of the judgment annulling the decision. Moreover, the applicant had failed to seek interim measures against the effects of the Commission's decision either in national court proceedings or from the

---

[184] Case T-230/95, *BAI v Commission* [1999] ECR II-123, para 34.
[185] Case T-141/03, *Sniace SA v Commission* [2005] ECR II-1197, para 38.
[186] Case T-25/04, *González y Díez SA v Commission* [2007] ECR II-3121, para 82.
[187] Case T-178/98, *Fresh Marine Company AS v Commission* [2000] ECR II-3331, para 121; Case T-344/04 *Bouychou v Commission* [2007] ECR II-91*, para 41; Case T-360/04, *FG Marine SA v Commission* [2007] ECR II-92*, para 51.

General Court. Accordingly, the applicant had not acted with the requisite degree of diligence, so that its losses were not the direct result of the Commission's decision, but rather arose solely from the economic risk that the applicant had freely chosen.[188]

The limitation period for bringing an action for damages is five years.[189] In *Régie Networks v Commission*, a Commission decision in 1997 raising no objections to an aid scheme financed by a French tax imposed on advertising was declared invalid by the ECJ in 2008 on the ground that the method of financing discriminated against imports.[190] In subsequent proceedings before the national courts, the applicants were unable to recover the tax paid before 2001 due to national limitation rules. Accordingly, they commenced proceedings for non-contractual liability against the Commission in respect of the losses of the earlier years, arguing that the limitation period in those proceedings should commence from the date when it became clear that the Commission decision was unlawful. The General Court dismissed the claim on the basis that the limitation period commenced as of the date on which the unlawful act occurred, which was 1997.[191] The fact that the EU courts may have declared an act unlawful has no bearing on the starting point of the limitation period.[192]

20.5 INTERIM RELIEF

Interim measures Actions for annulment under Article 263 TFEU do not have suspensory effect.[193] It is therefore only exceptionally that the court may order suspension of an act that is being contested in annulment proceedings.[194] The ECJ or the General Court may, if it considers that circumstances so require, order, pursuant to Article 278 TFEU, that application of the contested act be suspended. They may also, pursuant to Article 279 TFEU, prescribe any necessary interim measures. Applications for interim measures may equally be made in cases where the Commission has taken a decision concerning illegal

---

[188] Case T-344/04 *Bouychou v Commission* [2007] ECR II-91*, paras 44-64; Case T-360/04, *FG Marine SA v Commission* [2007] ECR II-92*, para 57-77.

[189] Statute of the Court of Justice of the European Union, Article 46.

[190] Case C-333/07, *Régie Networks v Commission* [2008] ECR I-10807.

[191] Case T-340/11, *Régie Networks v Commission* EU:T:2012:555, para 39.

[192] Cases C-89/10 & C-96/10, *Q-Beef NV v Commission* [2011] ECR I-7819, para 47; Case T-340/11, *Régie Networks v Commission* EU:T:2012:555, para 39.

[193] Case 213/85, *Commission v Netherlands* [1988] ECR 281, para 21; Case T-468/08R, *AES-Tisza kft v Commission* [2008] ECR II-346*, para 13.

[194] Case T-62/02 RENV-R, *Eurallumina SpA v Commission* [2011] ECR II-167*, para 17; Case T-812/14R, *BPC Lux 2 srl v Commission* EU:T:2015:119, para 17; Case T-826/14R, *Spain v Commission* EU:T:2015:126, para 12.

aid.[195] Applications made under Article 279 TFEU have included requests for suspension of EU decisions[196] and for an order requiring the Commission to refrain from making public the initiation of the formal investigation procedure.[197] In *Pantochim v Commission*, however, the General Court held that Article 279 TFEU cannot be invoked by an applicant in order to force the Commission to require a Member State provisionally to include the applicant in an aid scheme pending a review of the legality of that scheme pursuant to Article 108(2) TFEU.[198] In *Moccia Irme v Commission*, the ECJ held that an application for suspension of a measure cannot, in principle, be envisaged against a negative decision, since the suspension could not have the effect of changing the applicant's position.[199]

An action for interim measures in an EU court is inadmissible insofar as it might seek suspension of national proceedings for the recovery of unlawful aid, since only national courts can control the validity of national measures enforcing EU acts.[200]

Admissibility of applications for interim measures   Under the Rules of Procedure of the ECJ and the General Court, an application for suspension of an EU measure is admissible only if the applicant is challenging that measure in proceedings before the court. An application for any other interim measure is admissible only if it is put forward by a party to a case before the court and relates to that case.[201] The courts will not place unnecessary fetters on the right of an applicant to seek interim measures. Accordingly, in *Commission v Technische Glaswerke Ilmenau*, where the Commission argued that the applicant should have waited for recovery proceedings to be brought in the national courts and then availed itself of the national legal remedies available to it to challenge that recovery, the ECJ held that considerations of expediency as regards the relative efficiency of the various procedures could not prevent the applicant from seeking interim measures.[202]

Admissibility of the main application should not, in principle, be examined in proceedings relating to the application of interim measures.   Where, however, it is contended that the main application is manifestly inadmissible, it

---

[195]   Cases 67, 68 & 70/85, *Van der Kooy v Commission* [1985] ECR 1315, para 37.
[196]   Case T-111/01R, *Saxonia Edelmetalle GmbH v Commission* [2001] ECR II-2335, para 15.
[197]   Cases T-195/01R & T-207/01R, *Government of Gibraltar v Commission* [2001] ECR II-3915, para 31.
[198]   Case T-107/96R, *Pantochim SA v Commission* [1996] ECR II-1361, para 42; Case T-107/96, *Pantochim SA v Commission* [1998] ECR II-311, para 51.
[199]   Case C-89/97P(R), *Moccia Irme SpA v Commission* [1997] ECR I-2327, para 45.
[200]   Case T-1/14R, *Aluminios Cortizo SA v Commission* EU:T:2014:106, para 8.
[201]   Article 83(1) RP ECJ; Article 104(1) RP General Court.
[202]   Case C-232/02P(R), *Commission v Technische Glaswerke Ilmenau* [2002] ECR I-8977, para 33; Case T-181/02R, *Neue Erba Lautex GmbH v Commission* [2002] ECR II-5081, para 38.

may be necessary to establish the existence of certain factors which would justify the *prima facie* conclusion that the main application is admissible.[203] In *Belgium and Forum 187 v Commission*, the Commission argued that the application for annulment by Forum 187, a representative association, was manifestly inadmissible. The ECJ held that its existing case law concerning such questions of admissibility did not seem sufficiently established to entail the conclusion that the action was manifestly inadmissible in as much as it sought to protect the interests of its members.[204] By contrast, in *SEA v Commission* and *Airport Handling v Commission*, where challenges were made to a decision opening a formal investigation into whether capital injections constituted State aid, the General Court refused interim measures suspending the decision on the ground that the main proceedings were manifestly inadmissible given that it did not produce any legal effects allowing the decision to be classified as an act subject to judicial review pursuant to Article 263 TFEU.[205]

In *Carbunión v Council*, an application for the interim suspension of Council Decision 2010/787/EU on State aid to facilitate the closure of uncompetitive coal mines was refused, the General Court holding that the applicant had not demonstrated that it had a legitimate interest in obtaining such suspension, since the general direct application of the State aid rules in Article 107 TFEU would not place the applicants in a more favourable position as regards aid to cover current production losses.[206] In *Dansk Automat Brancheforening v Commission*, a challenge was brought against a Commission decision approving a system of aid in relation to taxation of online gambling. The General Court held that, in so far as the action was intended to safeguard the general economic interest of the Danish gambling sector, the applicant, a trade association, had no standing to seek interim measures.[207] Moreover, in so far as the applicant sought to invoke the serious and irreparable damage that its members might suffer, it could not rely on

---

[203] Case 221/86R, *Groupe des Droites Européennes v Parliament* [1986] ECR 2969, para 19; Case T-111/01R, *Saxonia Edelmetalle GmbH v Commission* [2001] ECR II-2335, para 16; Case T-674/14R, *SEA v Commission* (Order of 27 November 2014), para 21; Case T-688/14R, *Airport Handling SpA v Commission* (Order of 28 November 2014), para 21.

[204] Cases C-182/03R & C-217/03R, *Belgium and Forum 187 ASBL v Commission* [2003] ECR I-6887, para 107.

[205] Case T-674/14R, *SEA v Commission* (Order of 27 November 2014), para 37; Case T-688/14R, *Airport Handling SpA v Commission* (Order of 28 November 2014), para 38.

[206] Case T-176/11R, *Carbunión v Council* [2011] ECR II-434*, paras 20-21.

[207] Case T-601/11R, *Dansk Automat Brancheforening v Commission* EU:T:2012:66, para 26.

general assertions, but needed to prove such damage in relation to each of its members that might be affected by the measure.[208]

Conditions for award of interim measures Applications made pursuant to Article 278 TFEU or Article 279 TFEU must state the subject matter of the proceedings, the pleas of fact and law establishing a *prima facie* case for the interim measures applied for and the circumstances giving rise to urgency.[209] The urgency of an application for the adoption of interim measures must be assessed in the light of the extent to which an interlocutory order is necessary to avoid serious and irreparable damage to the party seeking the adoption of the interim measure.[210] It is only the applicant's interests that may be taken into consideration, to the exclusion of other factors of a general nature or the interest of third parties.[211] The court will then proceed to exercise its discretion in granting interim measures by balancing the various interests, in particular the EU interest and that of the applicant. These conditions are cumulative.[212] Thus, for example, in *Germany v Commission*, the ECJ held that, even if immediate implementation of the Commission's decision requiring recovery may lead to the winding up of the recipient so as to satisfy the criterion of urgency, suspension would not be ordered where the applicant failed to establish a *prima facie* case against the legality of the decision.[213] Equally, even where a *prima facie* case is clearly made out, it is still necessary to establish grounds of urgency.[214]

Establishment of *prima facie* case The condition relating to a *prima facie* case is satisfied where at least one of the pleas in law put forward by the applicant in support of the main action appears at first sight to be relevant and in any event not unfounded, in that it reveals the existence of a difficult legal issue the solution to which is not immediately obvious and merits fuller

---

[208] Case T-601/11R, *Dansk Automat Brancheforening v Commission* EU:T:2012:66, para 27.

[209] Article 83(2) RP ECJ; Article 104(2) RP General Court.

[210] Case 310/85R, *Deufil v Commission* [1986] ECR 537, para 15; Case T-593/93R, *Gestivisión Telecinco v Commission* [1993] ECR II-1409, para 27; Cases T-195/01R & T-207/01R, *Government of Gibraltar v Commission* [2001] ECR II-3915, para 94.

[211] Case T-812/14R, *BPC Lux 2 srl v Commission* EU:T:2015:119, para 24.

[212] Case C-268/96P(R), *SCK v Commission* [1996] ECR I-4971, para 30; Case T-111/01R, *Saxonia Edelmetalle GmbH v Commission* [2001] ECR II-2335, para 11; Cases T-195/01R & T-207/01R, *Government of Gibraltar v Commission* [2001] ECR II-3915, para 48; Case T-181/02R, *Neue Erba Lautex GmbH v Commission* [2002] ECR II-5081, para 36; Case T-468/08R, *AES-Tisza kft v Commission* [2008] ECR II-346*, para 11; Case T-305/13R, *SACE SpA v Commission* EU:T:2014:595, para 17.

[213] Case C-399/95R, *Germany v Commission* [1996] ECR I-2441, paras 76-80.

[214] Case T-484/10R, *Gas Natural Fenosa SDG v Commission* EU:T:2011:53, para 93; Case T-826/14R, *Spain v Commission* EU:T:2015:126, para 23.

examination.[215] It is not sufficient merely to refer to the application for annulment to show that there is a likelihood that the action will be successful. Rather, a clear, coherent and comprehensible statement of the *prima facie* case for suspension must be set out in the application for interim measures.[216] In *Frucona Košice v Commission*, having dismissed certain of the matters raised by the applicant as confused and incoherent, the General Court stressed that it would be necessary to supplement them with other documents from the main proceedings in order to give them a meaning capable of making out the applicant's *prima facie* case, a task that was not for the court to undertake in place of the applicant.[217]

The court will not necessarily examine the arguments in detail. In *Belgium and Forum 187 v Commission*, the ECJ considered merely that the pleas raised by the applicants seemed reasonable and were impossible to reject at the interim stage.[218] In *SACE v Commission*, the Commission did not, in the interim measures proceedings, challenge the arguments raised by the applicants. Accordingly, the General Court was content to examine relatively cursorily the arguments raised by the applicants and found that these raised complex questions that raised serious doubts as to the legality of the decision.[219] In *Greece v Commission*, which concerned a decision ordering recovery of small compensatory payments granted to Greek farmers during the financial crisis, the General Court recognised that the question in issue, namely, whether, in the exceptional circumstances of the case, the financial impact of the payments was genuinely such as to threaten to distort competition and to affect trade between Member States, had not yet been specifically considered by the courts. A *prima facie* case had therefore been made out that Greece might legitimately plead exceptional circumstances such as to render it excessive to recover the payments at issue.[220] By contrast, in *Stahlwerk Bous v Commission*, the General Court held that, when seeking the suspension of a decision to open a formal investigation, it was necessary for the applicant to show that the serious difficulties invoked by the Commission

---

[215] Case C-39/03P(R), *Commission v Artegodan* [2003] ECR I-4485, para 40; Case C-278/13P(R), *Commission v Pilkington Group* EU:C:2013:558, para 67; Case C-431/14P(R), *Greece v Commission* EU:C:2014:2418, para 20; Case T-52/12R, *Greece v Commission* EU:T:2012:447, para 13; Case T-305/13R, *SACE SpA v Commission* EU:T:2014:595, para 20; Case T-103/14R, *Frucona Košice as v Commission* EU:T:2014:255, para 22.

[216] Case C-278/00R, *Greece v Commission* [2000] ECR I-8787, para 27; Case T-103/14R, *Frucona Košice as v Commission* EU:T:2014:255, para 22.

[217] Case T-103/14R, *Frucona Košice as v Commission* EU:T:2014:255, para 46.

[218] Cases C-182/03R & C-217/03R, *Belgium and Forum 187 ASBL v Commission* [2003] ECR I-6887, paras 116 and 127-128. See also, Case T-520/10R, *Comunidad Autónoma de Galicia v Commission* [2011] ECR II-27*, para 58; Case T-484/10R, *Gas Natural Fenosa SDG v Commission* EU:T:2011:53, para 70.

[219] Case T-305/13R, *SACE SpA v Commission* EU:T:2014:595, paras 29-31.

[220] Case T-52/12R, *Greece v Commission* EU:T:2012:447, paras 29-34.

did not objectively exist and that the legal and factual situation was so clear that the Commission's decision amounted to a misuse of procedure on the part of the Commission.[221]

Where a decision has been challenged unsuccessfully in the General Court and an appeal against that judgment has been commenced in the ECJ, an application for interim measures seeking the suspension of that judgment will be considered as implicitly seeking the suspension of the original decision.[222] It must be noted, however, that arguments that might have been considered *prima facie* sustainable before the General Court in order to seek suspension of the decision pending its final judgment might no longer be so when seeking suspension of the decision before the ECJ. In *Technische Glaswerke Ilmenau v Commission*, following the dismissal of the main action by the General Court, the applicant sought interim suspension of the Commission's decision. The ECJ held that, in assessing the condition relating to the existence of a *prima facie* case, account must be taken of the fact that the decision has already been considered by an EU court, both as to the facts and the law, and that that court had found the action against the decision to be unfounded.[223] Similarly, the application for interim measures accompanying the appeal in *Greece v Commission* was dismissed on the ground that the General Court appeared to have dealt adequately with the various arguments raised.[224] By contrast, where an action for annulment concerns a decision which is similar to a decision that has already been annulled in earlier proceedings, a particularly strong *prima facie* case will be presumed.[225]

Burden of proof of serious and irreparable damage It is for the party who pleads serious and irreparable harm to prove its existence.[226] Owing to the exceptional nature of interim measures, the applicant must produce hard and precise information, supported by detailed documents showing its financial situation and enabling the court to determine the precise effects which would,

[221] Case T-172/14R, *Stahlwerk Bous GmbH v Commission* EU:T:2014:558, para 50.
[222] Case C-431/14P(R), *Greece v Commission* EU:C:2014:2418, para 15.
[223] Case C-404/04P(R), *Technische Glaswerke Ilmenau GmbH v Commission* [2005] ECR I-3539, para 19; Case C-431/14P(R), *Greece v Commission* EU:C:2014:2418, para 24.
[224] Case C-431/14P(R), *Greece v Commission* EU:C:2014:2418, paras 26-47.
[225] Case T-826/14R, *Spain v Commission* EU:T:2015:126, para 21.
[226] Case C-377/98R, *Netherlands v Parliament and Council* [2000] ECR I-6229, para 50; Case C-278/00, *Greece v Commission* [2000] ECR I-8787, para 14; Case C-278/13P(R), *Commission v Pilkington Group* EU:C:2013:558, paras 36-37; Case T-155/96R, *City of Mainz v Commission* [1996] ECR II-1655, para 19; Case T-86/96R, *Arbeitsgemeinschaft Deutscher Luftfahrt-Unternehmen v Commission* [1998] ECR II-641, para 58; Cases T-195/01R & T-207/01R, *Government of Gibraltar v Commission* [2001] ECR II-3915, para 96; Case T-34/02R, *B. v Commission* [2002] ECR II-2803, para 85; Case T-601/11R, *Dansk Automat Brancheforening v Commission* EU:T:2012:66, para 36; Case T-305/13R, *SACE SpA v Commission* EU:T:2014:595, para 41; Case T-103/14R, *Frucona Košice as v Commission* EU:T:2014:255, para 51.

probably, follow if the suspension were not granted.[227] Thus, in *Aluminios Cortizo v Commission*, the application to suspend a recovery decision was rejected on the ground that the evidence consisted solely of statements by the applicant that the Spanish authorities had commenced recovery procedures which were causing enormous losses to the recipients, without showing how this affected their financial viability.[228] Moreover, it is not for the judge hearing the application for interim measures to compensate of his own motion for any lack of evidence.[229] The applicant, therefore, must furnish proof that he cannot await the conclusion of the main action without suffering damage which would entail serious and irreparable consequences.[230] To grant a suspension without requiring such proof would be tantamount to making the action for annulment suspensory in nature.[231] In *Prayon Rupel v Commission*, the General Court stated that the applicant must establish the risk of harm to a sufficient degree of probability.[232] In *ADL v Commission*, it went further, holding that the judge hearing the application must have hard evidence allowing him to determine the precise consequences which the absence of the measures applied for would in all probability entail for each of the undertakings concerned.[233] Damage which is entirely hypothetical and based on the occurrence of future and uncertain events is insufficient.[234]

It follows that, although it is not necessary to require absolute proof that the damage would occur and it is enough for it to be reasonably foreseeable, the applicant is required to prove the facts which are deemed to attest to the

---

[227] Case T-62/02 RENV-R, *Eurallumina SpA v Commission* [2011] ECR II-167*, para 22.

[228] Case T-1/14R, *Aluminios Cortizo SA v Commission* EU:T:2014:106, paras 17-18.

[229] Case T-111/01R, *Saxonia Edelmetalle GmbH v Commission* [2001] ECR II-2335, para 28.

[230] Case 142/87R, *Belgium v Commission* [1987] ECR 2589, para 23; Cases T-231/94R, 232/94R & 234/94R, *Transacciones Marítimas SA v Commission* [1994] ECR II-885, para 41; Case T-73/98R, *Prayon Rupel SA v Commission* [1998] ECR II-2769, para 36; Case T-111/01R, *Saxonia Edelmetalle GmbH v Commission* [2001] ECR II-2335, para 21.

[231] Case C-278/00R, *Greece v Commission* [2000] ECR I-8787, para 19.

[232] Case T-73/98R, *Prayon Rupel SA v Commission* [1998] ECR II-2769, para 38.

[233] Case T-86/96R, *Arbeitsgemeinschaft Deutscher Luftfahrt-Unternehmen v Commission* [1998] ECR II-641, para 64.

[234] Case T-239/94R, *EISA v Commission* [1994] ECR II-703, para 22; Case T-237/99R, *BP Nederland v Commission* [2000] ECR II-3849, para 57; Cases T-195/01R & T-207/01R, *Government of Gibraltar v Commission* [2001] ECR II-3915, para 101; Case T-316/04R, *Wam SpA v Commission* [2004] ECR II-3917, para 31; Case T-455/05R, *Componenta Oyj v Commission* [2006] ECR II-38*, para 39; Case T-468/08R, *AES-Tisza kft v Commission* [2008] ECR II-346*, para 29; Case T-352/08R, *Pannon Hőerőmű Zrt. v Commission* [2009] ECR II-9*, para 28; Case T-520/10R, *Comunidad Autónoma de Galicia v Commission* [2011] ECR II-27*, para 61; Case T-457/09R, *Westfälisch-Lippischer Sparkassen- und Giroverband v Commission* [2011] ECR II-51*, para 45; Case T-52/12R, *Greece v Commission* EU:T:2012:447, para 36; Case T-507/12R, *Slovenia v Commission* EU:T:2013:25, para 14.

probability of serious and irreparable damage.[235]   Where there are several applicants against whom a recovery order is pending, proof of urgency must be established in relation to each individual applicant in order for the measure to be suspended *vis-à-vis* that applicant.[236]   In *Greece v Commission*, Greece alleged that the Commission decision requiring recovery of aid which had been unlawfully paid to agricultural cooperatives would affect hundreds of cooperative organisations and lead to very serious social and commercial upheaval. The ECJ refused to suspend the decision on the ground that Greece had merely made general observations without adducing any specific evidence in support of its claims.   No information whatever had been provided concerning the financial position of the interested parties or of the possible serious impact on the social harmony of the State.[237]

Immediate danger of serious and irreparable damage   An applicant for interim measures must establish the urgency of the action. It must show that there is an immediate danger that it will suffer serious and irreparable damage which could not be made good even if the main action is successful.[238] Equally, it must prove that it cannot wait for the outcome of the main proceedings without suffering serious and irreparable harm.[239] Mere breach of a procedural right, such as a right to take part in a formal investigation procedure, is insufficient to establish serious and irreparable harm.[240] In order to establish urgency, an applicant cannot plead damage to an interest which is not personal to him, such as for example to an aspect of public interest or to the rights of third parties, whether individuals or a State.[241]   In *BPC Lux 2 srl v Commission*, where a challenge was brought against a Commission decision approving bank restructuring aid, the alleged irreversibility of the transaction

---

[235] Case C-335/99P(R), *HFB v Commission* [1999] ECR I-8705, para 67; Case C-377/98R, *Netherlands v Parliament and Council* [2000] ECR I-6229, para 51; Case C-278/00R, *Greece v Commission* [2000] ECR I-8787, para 15; Case T-111/01R, *Saxonia Edelmetalle GmbH v Commission* [2001] ECR II-2335, para 22; Cases T-195/01R & T-207/01R, *Government of Gibraltar v Commission* [2001] ECR II-3915, para 96; Case T-316/04R, *Wam SpA v Commission* [2004] ECR II-3917, para 27; Case T-455/05R, *Componenta Oyj v Commission* [2006] ECR II-38*, para 34; Cases T-234/00R, T-235/00R & T-283/00R, *Fondazione Opera S. Maria della Carità v Commission* [2008] ECR II-113*, para 25; Case T-103/14R, *Frucona Košice as v Commission* EU:T:2014:255, para 52.

[236] Case T-34/02R, *B. v Commission* [2002] ECR II-2803, paras 95-97.

[237] Case C-278/00R, *Greece v Commission* [2000] ECR I-8787, paras 16-18.

[238] Cases C-182/03R & C-217/03R, *Belgium and Forum 187 ASBL v Commission* [2003] ECR I-6887, para 130; Case T-52/12R, *Greece v Commission* EU:T:2012:447, para 36; Case T-826/14R, *Spain v Commission* EU:T:2015:126, para 24.

[239] Case C-278/00R, *Greece v Commission* [2000] ECR I-8787, para 14; Case C-574/13P(R), *France v Commission* EU:C:2014:36, para 19.

[240] Case T-812/14R, *BPC Lux 2 srl v Commission* EU:T:2015:119, para 29.

[241] Case T-316/04R, *Wam SpA v Commission* [2004] ECR II-3917, para 28.

made possible by the decision and the alleged impossibility of recovering the aid from the beneficiary in the event that the decision was annulled could not suffice, irrespective of the applicants' interests, to establish urgency of suspending the decision.[242] In *COLT Telecommunications France v Commission*, an allegation that aid for fibre optic infrastructure would damage the economic landscape was regarded as too general.[243]

Where the damage referred to is of a financial nature, the interim measures sought are, in principle, justified when it is apparent that, without those measures, the party applying for them would find itself in a position that could imperil its financial viability before final judgment is given in the main action or its market share would be substantially affected having regard to, inter alia, the size and turnover of its undertaking and to the characteristics of the group to which it belongs.[244] Whereas recovery of unlawful aid necessarily has a financial effect on recipients which are required to repay the aid, the adverse impact on recipients of the requirement to recover aid imposed on a Member State forms an integral part of any Commission decision requiring recovery and cannot be regarded in itself as constituting serious and irreparable damage.[245] In *Huta Częstochowa v Commission*, the General Court rejected a plea by the applicant that its financial equilibrium would be upset.[246] In *DTS v Commission*, the applicant's claim that it faced a potential loss of market share was dismissed on the ground that this raised issues of a financial nature.[247] Indeed, generally, damage of a financial nature cannot, save in exceptional circumstances, be regarded as irreparable, or even as being reparable only with difficulty, if it can ultimately be the subject of financial compensation.[248]

The danger of serious and irreparable harm must be immediate. Although an applicant against whom recovery of aid is being sought may, if it can establish serious and irreparable harm would be caused to it by enforcement of the recovery order, seek suspension of the recovery decision pursuant to Article 278 TFEU rather than wait until national court proceedings enforcing

---

[242] Case T-812/14R, *BPC Lux 2 srl v Commission* EU:T:2015:119, para 25.

[243] Case T-79/10R, *COLT Telecommunications France v Commission* [2010] ECR II-207*, para 34.

[244] Case C-551/12P(R), *EDF v Commission* EU:C:2013:157, para 54; Case T-103/14R, *Frucona Košice as v Commission* EU:T:2014:255, para 52.

[245] Case C-278/00R, *Greece v Commission* [2000] ECR I-8787, para 21.

[246] Case T-288/06R, *Huta Częstochowa SA v Commission* [2006] ECR II-101*, para 16.

[247] Case T-533/10R, *DTS Distribuidora de Televisión Digital SA v Commission* [2011] ECR II-168*, para 29.

[248] Case C-213/91R, *Abertal v Commission* [1991] ECR I-5109, para 24; Case C-446/10P(R), *Alcoa Trasformazioni srl v Commission* [2011] ECR I-194*, para 54; Case T-111/01R, *Saxonia Edelmetalle GmbH v Commission* [2001] ECR II-2335, para 23; Case T-468/08R, *AES-Tisza kft v Commission* [2008] ECR II-346*, para 35; Case T-352/08R, *Pannon Hőerőmű Zrt. v Commission* [2009] ECR II-9*, para 40; Case T-79/10R, *COLT Telecommunications France v Commission* [2010] ECR II-207*, para 37.

the decision have been commenced against it,[249] where there is no proof that such proceedings are imminent, it will not be able to show that there is any immediate danger of serious and irreparable harm.[250] A Commission decision ordering a Member State to recover the aid in question imposes no legally binding obligation on the recipient. Consequently, it cannot prove a risk of serious, irreparable harm unless and until the national authorities have adopted binding measures to cancel the aid and to recover any aid paid.[251] Thus, in *Pannon Hőerőmű v Commission*, where the decision ordering recovery allowed for a period of ten months during which the precise amount to be recovered would be determined by the Hungarian authorities, the General Court held that, since the action for interim measures had been brought before the end of that period, there was no legal framework in Hungary for the immediate recovery of the aid.[252] By contrast, in *SACE v Commission*, where the Italian courts had refused to suspend recovery proceedings instituted by the Italian authorities, the General Court held that SACE had proved that suspension of the Commission's decision was necessary to prevent serious and irreparable damage.[253]

Inasmuch as the applicant has challenged the legality of the decision under Article 263 TFEU, a national court is not bound by that decision being definitive. In addition, the fact that an application for suspension before the EU courts has been unsuccessful does not prevent the national court from ordering suspension. Thus, the existence of internal avenues of review in the national court permitting the applicant to resist recovery will be regarded as providing a means for the applicant to avoid serious and irreparable damage.[254] More generally, the applicant must show that national law does not allow for any serious and irreparable harm to be avoided.[255] The General Court has

---

[249] Case T-198/01R, *Technische Glaswerke Ilmenau GmbH v Commission* [2002] ECR II-2153, paras 52-54.

[250] Case T-34/02R, *B. v Commission* [2002] ECR II-2803, para 89; Case T-416/05R, *Olympiakes Aerogrammes AE v Commission* [2006] ECR II-45*, para 52; Case T-507/12R, *Slovenia v Commission* EU:T:2013:25, para 21; Case T-27/13R, *Elan v Commission* EU:T:2013:122, para 18.

[251] Case C-574/13P(R), *France v Commission* EU:C:2014:36, para 22.

[252] Case T-352/08R, *Pannon Hőerőmű Zrt. v Commission* [2009] ECR II-9*, para 33.

[253] Case T-305/13R, *SACE SpA v Commission* EU:T:2014:595, paras 47-48.

[254] Case C-446/10P(R), *Alcoa Trasformazioni srl v Commission* [2011] ECR I-194*, para 46; Case T-366/13R, *France v Commission* EU:T:2013:396, para 44; Case T-103/14R, *Frucona Košice as v Commission* EU:T:2014:255, paras 59-60; Case T-826/14R, *Spain v Commission* EU:T:2015:126, para 41.

[255] Case T-181/02R, *Neue Erba Lautex GmbH v Commission* [2002] ECR II-5081, paras 105-109; Case T-440/07R, *Huta Buczek v Commission* [2008] ECR II-39*, para 68; Case T-238/09R, *Sniace SA v Commission* [2009] ECR II-125*, para 27; Case T-489/11R, *Rousse Industry v Commission* [2011] ECR II-362*, para 14; Case T-507/12R, *Slovenia v Commission* EU:T:2013:25, para 22; Case T-27/13R, *Elan v Commission*

stated that this places the EU judge faced with an application of interim measures in a subsidiary position to the national judge, since the latter is better placed to appreciate the legality of national acts and the financial situation of the applicant with regard to national insolvency and liquidation laws.[256]

Threat to existence of the applicant Suspension of a recovery order can be justified if it appears that, without such a measure, the applicant would be placed in a situation likely to endanger its very existence.[257] In *Transacciones Marítimas v Commission*, there was a real risk that the recipient of aid would be placed in liquidation if an order for recovery of aid was immediately enforced. The General Court recognised that this would entail serious personal consequences for the managers and shareholders of those companies and granted an interim order suspending the recovery.[258] By contrast, in *Buczek Automotive v Commission*, the applicant had already voluntarily submitted to an insolvency process, so that it could not rely on a plea of urgency in respect of the enforcement of the recovery order.[259]

In the examination of an undertaking's financial viability, the crucial question when assessing financial circumstances is whether the company which claims it will suffer serious damage has other potential sources of income which might help it to avert that damage.[260] In particular, the assessment of its material circumstance may include consideration of the characteristics of any group to which it is linked, directly or indirectly, through its shareholders and to any resources available to that group.[261] Thus, in

EU:T:2013:122, para 23; Case T-103/14R, *Frucona Košice as v Commission* EU:T:2014:255, para 59.

[256] Case T-366/13R, *France v Commission* EU:T:2013:396, para 45; Case T-27/13R, *Elan v Commission* EU:T:2013:122, para 24; Case T-103/14R, *Frucona Košice as v Commission* EU:T:2014:255, para 60.

[257] Case T-111/01R, *Saxonia Edelmetalle GmbH v Commission* [2001] ECR II-2335, para 24; Case T-198/01R, *Technische Glaswerke Ilmenau GmbH v Commission* [2002] ECR II-2153, para 99; Case T-181/02R, *Neue Erba Lautex GmbH v Commission* [2002] ECR II-5081, para 84; Case T-69/06R, *Aughinish Alumina Ltd v Commission* [2006] ECR II-58*, para 67; Case T-468/08R, *AES-Tisza kft v Commission* [2008] ECR II-346*, para 36.

[258] Cases T-231/94R, 232/94R & 234/94R, *Transacciones Marítimas SA v Commission* [1994] ECR II-885, para 42; upheld, as to the terms imposed, in Case C-12/95P, *Transacciones Marítimas SA v Commission* [1995] ECR I-467.

[259] Case T-1/08R, *Buczek Automotive v Commission* [2008] ECR II-42*, para 37.

[260] Case T-62/02 RENV-R, *Eurallumina SpA v Commission* [2011] ECR II-167*, para 35.

[261] Case C-12/95P, *Transacciones Marítimas SA v Commission* [1995] ECR I-467, para 12; Case C-43/98P(R), *Camar v Commission* [1998] ECR I-1815, para 36; Case C-329/99P(R), *Pfizer Animal Health v Commission* [1999] ECR I-8343, para 67; Case C-232/02P(R), *Commission v Technische Glaswerke Ilmenau* [2002] ECR I-8977, para 56; Case C-446/10P(R), *Alcoa Trasformazioni srl v Commission* [2011] ECR I-194*, para 17; Case C-551/12P(R), *EDF v Commission* EU:C:2013:157, para 54; Case T-181/02R, *Neue Erba Lautex GmbH v Commission* [2002] ECR II-5081, para 92; Case T-69/06R,

Saxonia Edelmetalle v Commission, where the application for interim measures was dismissed, it appeared that the applicant had been acquired by a group of companies that had considerable financial strength enabling it to repay the aid and that neither the applicant nor the group was in financial difficulty.[262] Similarly, in *Alcoa Trasformazioni v Commission*, the applicant specifically admitted that compliance with a recovery order of €137 million did not threaten the existence of the Alcoa group of companies.[263] In *MB Immobilien Verwaltungs v Commission*, the General Court, in refusing interim measures, held that there was no evidence that the owner of the group of companies to which the applicant had belonged did not have sufficient resources to provide loan guarantees to keep the applicant in business.[264] Similarly, in *Aughinish Alumina v Commission*, the General Court rejected the applicant's claim that the group of companies to which it belonged would not support it financially. The group had recently invested substantially in new plant for the applicant and had substantial financial capacity to provide the necessary support.[265] In *Neue Erba Lautex v Commission*, the General Court held that the applicant's financial viability was a main concern of the administrator in bankruptcy of its predecessor who was required to use its assets to pay off its creditors, which would help cover the repayment of the aid.[266]

The unilateral decision of a group not to support one of its subsidiary companies cannot have the result of avoiding the requirement to take into account the financial resources of the group.[267] On the other hand, this taking into consideration of the financial strength of the group to which the applicant belongs is based on the idea that the objective interests of the undertaking concerned are not distinct from those of the persons that control it or are

---

Aughinish Alumina Ltd v Commission [2006] ECR II-58*, para 69; Case T-120/07R, *MB Immobilien Verwaltungs GmbH v Commission* [2007] ECR II-130*, para 36; Case T-440/07R, *Huta Buczek v Commission* [2008] ECR II-39*, para 49; Case T-468/08R, *AES-Tisza kft v Commission* [2008] ECR II-346*, para 37; Case T-352/08R, *Pannon Hőerőmű Zrt. v Commission* [2009] ECR II-9*, para 46; Case T-177/10R, *Alcoa Trasformazioi v Commission* [2010] ECR II-149*, para 49; Case T-62/02 RENV-R, *Eurallumina SpA v Commission* [2011] ECR II-167*, para 29; Case T-209/11R, *MB System v Commission* EU:T:2011:297, paras 29-30; Case T-305/13R, *SACE SpA v Commission* EU:T:2014:595, para 42; Case T-103/14R, *Frucona Košice as v Commission* EU:T:2014:255, paras 52-53; Case T-172/14R, *Stahlwerk Bous GmbH v Commission* EU:T:2014:558, para 20.

[262] Case T-111/01R, *Saxonia Edelmetalle GmbH v Commission* [2001] ECR II-2335, paras 25-27. See also, Case T-155/96R, *City of Mainz v Commission* [1996] ECR II-1655, para 28; Case T-440/07R, *Huta Buczek v Commission* [2008] ECR II-39*, para 71.

[263] Case T-177/10R, *Alcoa Trasformazioi v Commission* [2010] ECR II-149*, para 52.

[264] Case T-120/07R, *MB Immobilien Verwaltungs GmbH v Commission* [2007] ECR II-130*, para 41.

[265] Case T-69/06R, *Aughinish Alumina Ltd v Commission* [2006] ECR II-58*, paras 74-77.

[266] Case T-181/02R, *Neue Erba Lautex GmbH v Commission* [2002] ECR II-5081, paras 99-102.

[267] Case T-172/14R, *Stahlwerk Bous GmbH v Commission* EU:T:2014:558, para 30.

members of the same group. It follows that this will not apply where the applicant can prove that its objective interests are independent from those of its shareholders.[268] The General Court recognised, in *Eurallumina v Commission*, that any presumption in relation to group financial support may be rebutted. Thus, a company belonging to a group is not precluded from demonstrating the seriousness of the potential damage by establishing in particular that its objective interests do not coincide with those of its group or its parent company, that the parent company is not legally entitled to provide it with financial support, or that the group as a whole is financially incapable of coming to its aid.[269]

Applications for suspension by a Member State A Member State may make an application for suspension of a Commission decision seeking recovery of aid from undertakings to which it has granted the aid. In *Belgium and Forum 187 v Commission*, where the Commission failed to allow for adequate transitional measures when it sought the abolition of favourable tax treatment concerning coordination centres that constituted State aid, the ECJ recognised that the almost immediate interruption of the tax regime could have consequences that were serious and largely irreversible and which were not limited to the possible adverse financial consequences for the coordination centres. Rather, by ending a regime which had applied for many years without waiting for an assessment of the merits of the regime designed to succeed it, the decision created a situation of harmful legal uncertainty both for Belgium and for the groups to which the coordination centres concerned belonged. Belgium had a certain interest in being able to supply economic operators with a legal and fiscal environment as far as possible free from uncertainty. Similarly, for certain coordination centres, a legislative vacuum in their specific tax regime, between the expiry of the current regime and the entry into force of any new regime, seemed likely to cause significant problems.[270]

It is not sufficient for a Member State to invoke the prejudice that a single undertaking or a limited number of undertakings may suffer when they, taken individually, do not represent an entire sector of the national economy.[271] Thus, in *Slovenia v Commission*, which concerned an order requiring recovery of €10 million restructuring aid, the General Court refused an application for suspension on the ground that Slovenia had failed to produce any evidence that immediate recovery would cause serious and irreparable damage not only to

---

[268] Case T-103/14R, *Frucona Košice as v Commission* EU:T:2014:255, paras 54-55.

[269] Case T-62/02 RENV-R, *Eurallumina SpA v Commission* [2011] ECR II-167*, para 51; Case T-207/07R, *Eurallumina SpA v Commission* [2011] ECR II-171*, para 54.

[270] Cases C-182/03R & C-217/03R, *Belgium and Forum 187 ASBL v Commission* [2003] ECR I-6887, paras 131-135.

[271] Case T-507/12R, *Slovenia v Commission* EU:T:2013:25, para 15; Case T-366/13R, *France v Commission* EU:T:2013:396, para 25; Case T-826/14R, *Spain v Commission* EU:T:2015:126, para 25.

the recipient of the aid but also to the Slovene national economy or, at least, to an entire economic sector.[272]   In *Spain v Commission*, the General Court refused to suspend a decision concerning a Spanish tax exemption where it was clear that only 94 undertakings were affected which was not such as to show a sufficient effect on any sector of the economy.[273]

Member States are responsible for those interests which are regarded as general interests at national level and may defend them in proceedings for interim measures. They may, in particular, seek the grant of interim measures by asserting that the contested measure could seriously jeopardise performance of their State tasks and public order.[274]   In *Greece v Commission*, a challenge was made to the Commission's decision ordering recovery of €425 million from all the farmers in the country, numbering roughly 800,000, who, with their families, accounted for a third of the population of Greece.   Greece argued that enforcement of the decision could trigger numerous reactions on the part of the agricultural community, which was affected by the financial crisis and by exceptional austerity measures, in particular as strikes had become a common occurrence whilst acute social tensions and confrontations between demonstrators and police were constantly increasing. Moreover, the Greek authorities' attempts to combat tax avoidance would be affected if they had to concentrate efforts on implementing the recovery decision. The General Court accepted that a deterioration of confidence in the public authorities, generalised discontent and a feeling of injustice were features of the prevailing social climate in Greece.   In those circumstances, the risk that immediate recovery of the payments might trigger demonstrations liable to generate violence was neither hypothetical nor uncertain.[275]   By contrast, in proceedings brought by Greece some years previously concerning recovery of aid from dairy cooperatives, reliance upon allegedly very serious social upheaval had been rejected on the ground that no specific supporting evidence had been produced.[276]   Similarly, the General Court refused to grant interim measures suspending a decision requiring recovery of aid granted to Corsican ferry operator SNCM, rejecting the argument that the liquidation of SNCM would result in severe social unrest and have negative consequences for Marseilles and Corsica as a whole.[277]   In *Spain v Commission*, the General Court rejected an argument that unnecessary time and effort would be wasted by the tax authorities in enforcing the decision that was clearly *prima facie* unlawful.[278]

---

[272] Case T-507/12R, *Slovenia v Commission* EU:T:2013:25, paras 16-17.

[273] Case T-826/14R, *Spain v Commission* EU:T:2015:126, para 31.

[274] Case T-52/12R, *Greece v Commission* EU:T:2012:447, para 37; Case T-826/14R, *Spain v Commission* EU:T:2015:126, para 25.

[275] Case T-52/12R, *Greece v Commission* EU:T:2012:447, paras 48-49.

[276] Case C-278/00R, *Greece v Commission* [2000] ECR I-8787, para 18.

[277] Case T-366/13R, *France v Commission* EU:T:2013:396, paras 20-22.

[278] Case T-826/14R, *Spain v Commission* EU:T:2015:126, paras 27-31.

Balancing of European Union interest In deciding whether to grant the interim measures sought, the court must weigh up the risks associated with each possible result. In practical terms, that means examining whether or not the interest of the applicant in obtaining part suspension of the operation of the decision outweighs the interest in its immediate application. When carrying out that examination, the court must determine whether the possible annulment of the decision in the main action would make it possible to reverse the situation that would be brought about by its immediate implementation and, conversely, to what extent suspension would be such as to prevent the objectives pursued by the contested decision in the event of the main application being dismissed.[279] In the context of an application for interim measures seeking the suspension of operation of the obligation imposed by the Commission to repay aid which it has declared to be incompatible with the internal market, the EU interest will normally, if not always, take precedence over the interests of a beneficiary of unlawful aid in avoiding enforcement of the obligation to repay it before judgment is given in the main proceedings.[280] In *Carbunión v Council*, which concerned an unsuccessful application to suspend a new regime for control of State aid in the coal sector, it was held that account had to be taken on the general public interest associated with the implementation of a measure aimed at reintegrating into the EU competition rules, including the State aid rules, an economic sector which for a long time had benefited from a special set of rules.[281] By contrast, in *Technische Glaswerke Ilmenau v Commission*, an application for suspension of a Commission decision was partially successful where it was shown that such effective judicial protection of the applicant was justified by exceptional circumstances.[282]

---

[279] Case C-149/95P(R), *Commission* v *Atlantic Container Line and Others* [1995] ECR I-2165, para 50; Case C-180/96R, *United Kingdom* v *Commission* [1996] ECR I-3903, para 89; Cases C-182/03R & C-217/03R, *Belgium and Forum 187 ASBL v Commission* [2003] ECR I-6887, para 142; Case T-601/11R, *Dansk Automat Brancheforening v Commission* EU:T:2012:66, para 47.

[280] Case T-198/01R, *Technische Glaswerke Ilmenau GmbH v Commission* [2002] ECR II-2153, para 114; Case T-181/02R, *Neue Erba Lautex GmbH v Commission* [2002] ECR II-5081, para 113; Case T-120/07R, *MB Immobilien Verwaltungs GmbH v Commission* [2007] CR II-130*, para 45; Case T-468/08R, *AES-Tisza kft v Commission* [2008] ECR II-346*, para 62; Case T-27/13R, *Elan v Commission* EU:T:2013:122, paras 28-29; Case T-305/13R, *SACE SpA v Commission* EU:T:2014:595, para 50. See also, Case C-232/02P(R), *Commission v Technische Glaswerke Ilmenau* [2002] ECR I-8977, paras 54-61.

[281] Case T-176/11R, *Carbunión v Council* [2011] ECR II-434*, para 37.

[282] Case T-198/01R, *Technische Glaswerke Ilmenau GmbH v Commission* [2002] ECR II-2153, paras 115-120, Case T-378/02R, *Technische Glaswerke Ilmenau GmbH v Commission* [2003] ECR II-2921, para 98.

Where appropriate, the relevant interests of all those affected must be balanced.[283] For example, in determining whether the applicant may suffer serious and irreversible harm, the alleged aid must be viewed in the light of any undesirable effects which the aid has already had and will continue to have on competitors in other Member States.[284] The fact that the recipient of aid does not have a large market share does not preclude there from being an EU interest in the immediate withdrawal of State aid harmful to competition.[285] On the other hand, in *Belgium and Forum 187 v Commission*, the ECJ held that the fact that only a small number of coordination centres were affected by the lack of the transitional measures showed that suspension of the Commission decision would not have a significant economic effect.[286] In *SACE v Commission*, SACE agreed, in order to balance its interest in not having to repay alleged aid with the EU interest in immediate recovery of unlawful aid, that suspension of the amount required by the Commission might be partial. Accordingly, the General Court suspended the Commission's decision in part, leaving the rest to be recovered immediately.[287] In *Gas Natural Fenosa v Commission*, the General Court held that the interests of the Member State in ensuring the continued operation of a service of general economic interest took priority over the interests of the applicant which sought to have the aid declared incompatible with the internal market.[288]

The court's discretion to grant interim measures should not normally be influenced by procedural aspects of the Commission's investigation. In *Neue Erba Lautex v Commission*, the General Court held that the fact that the Commission may not have issued an interim injunction pursuant to Article 11(2) of Council Regulation (EC) No 659/1999 provisionally ordering recovery of the aid in no way prevented it from deciding at the end of the formal investigation procedure that the EU interest justified immediate withdrawal of the aid in question and the immediate restoration of the situation which prevailed prior to payment of that aid.[289] Similarly, the fact that it may have taken a significant period of time for the Commission to reach its conclusion that the aid was incompatible with the internal market does not alter in any way the EU interest in that aid being repaid without delay.[290]

---

[283] Case C-107/99R, *Italy v Commission* [1999] ECR I-4011, para 59; Case C-445/00R, *Austria v Council* [2001] ECR I-1461, para 73; Case T-111/01R, *Saxonia Edelmetalle GmbH v Commission* [2001] ECR II-2335, para 11; Cases T-195/01R & T-207/01R, *Government of Gibraltar v Commission* [2001] ECR II-3915, para 48.

[284] Cases 67, 68 & 70/85, *Van der Kooy v Commission* [1985] ECR 1315, para 45.

[285] Case T-181/02R, *Neue Erba Lautex GmbH v Commission* [2002] ECR II-5081, para 115.

[286] Cases C-182/03R & C-217/03R, *Belgium and Forum 187 ASBL v Commission* [2003] ECR I-6887, para 144.

[287] Case T-305/13R, *SACE SpA v Commission* EU:T:2014:595, paras 52-54.

[288] Case T-484/10R, *Gas Natural Fenosa SDG v Commission* EU:T:2011:53, para 112.

[289] Case T-181/02R, *Neue Erba Lautex GmbH v Commission* [2002] ECR II-5081, para 116.

[290] *Ibid.*, para 117.

INDEX